D0349107

NEW ENCYCLOPEDIA OF
GARDEN PLANTS & FLOWERS

IN ASSOCIATION WITH
READER'S DIGEST

This edition of READER'S DIGEST NEW ENCYCLOPEDIA OF
GARDEN PLANTS AND FLOWERS
was published in 2001 exclusively for WHSmith,
Greenbridge Road, Swindon SN3 3LD.

READER'S DIGEST NEW ENCYCLOPEDIA OF
GARDEN PLANTS & FLOWERS was edited and designed by
The Reader's Digest Association Limited, London.

First edition Copyright © 1997 The Reader's Digest Association Limited,
11 Westferry Circus, Canary Wharf, London E14 4HE.
www.readersdigest.co.uk
We are committed to both the quality of our products and the service
we provide to our customers. We value your comments, so please feel
free to contact us on 08705 113366, or by email at
cust_service@readersdigest.co.uk
If you have any comments about the contents of our books, you
can contact us at gbeditorial@readersdigest.co.uk

Reprinted 2003

Printed in France.
ISBN 0 276 42619 3
460-007-02

Published by The Reader's Digest Association Limited
London • New York • Sydney • Montreal

EDITOR
Justine Scott-Macnab

ART EDITOR
Joanna Walker

EDITORIAL GROUP HEAD
Noel Buchanan

ASSOCIATE ART EDITORS
Julie Busby, Colin Goody, Sue Mims

SENIOR ASSISTANT EDITORS
Kim Davies, Judith Taylor

ASSISTANT EDITORS
Roger Boulanger, Jane Chapman, Celia Coyne, Diane Cross,
Theresa Donaghey, Judy Fovargue, Derek Hall, Liz Hodgson,
Margaret Hotson, Peter Maloney, Diane Mansfield,
Claire Nash, Meg Sanders, Caroline Smith, Helen Spence,
Stella Vayne, Diana Vowles

SENIOR DESIGNERS
Ian Cleaver, Jane McKenna, Rachael Stone

DESIGNERS
Emma Gilbert, Keith Miller, Austin Taylor

ASSISTANT DESIGNERS
Laura Jackson, Evie Loizides, Justin Rickwood, Clare Sadler,
Jonathan Scott, Jessica Watts, Dave Weston,
Miranda Wheaton Rush

RESEARCHERS
Louise Anderson, Sally Bamber, Sarah Courtney,
Geoff Holden, Gwenda Kitchener, Jay Venn, Sarah Wilson

PICTURE RESEARCHER
Rosie Taylor

PROOFREADERS
Roy Butcher, Barry Gage

EDITORIAL ASSISTANTS
David Bruce, Louise Catcheside, Niki Khoroushi,
Lucy Protheroe, Tara St John

READER'S DIGEST GENERAL BOOKS

EDITORIAL DIRECTOR
Cortina Butler

ART DIRECTOR
Nick Clark

EXECUTIVE EDITOR
Julian Browne

PUBLISHING PROJECTS MANAGER
Alastair Holmes

DEVELOPMENT EDITOR
Ruth Binney

PICTURE RESOURCE MANAGER
Martin Smith

STYLE EDITOR
Ron Pankhurst

CONSULTANT EDITORS
Kenneth A. Beckett Barbara Haynes

CONTRIBUTORS

John Amand
Hugh Angus
Bill Ash
Helen L. Baldwin
Richard E. Baldwin
Peter Barnes
Trevor Bath
Kathryn Bradley-Hole
Denis Bradshaw
Ursula Buchan
Stephen Cafferty
Andi Clevely
Dilys Davies
Li De-Zhu
John A. Dyter
John Edgeley
Jack Elliott
Sue Fisher
Eileen Galbally
Jim Gardiner
Michael Gibson
Peter Gregory
Diana Grenfell
Christine Grey-Wilson
Christopher Grey-Wilson
Roger Grounds
John Howells
Alan Hulme
David Hunt
Graham Hutchins
Noel Kingsbury
Colin Lewis
Paul Lewis
Duncan Lowe
David McClintock

Graham Madill
Colin Morgan
John Bramwell Paton
Pauline Pears
Sue Phillips
Christine Skelmersdale
David Small
Anne Stevens
John Sutton
Philip Swindells
Alan Toogood
Timothy Walker
John Edward James White
Peter Wood

**PLANT IDENTIFIER
COMPILER**
Charlie Butterworth

PHOTOGRAPHERS
Jonathan Buckley
Vernon Morgan
Emma Peios
Richard Surman
Pia Tryde
Juliet Wade
Jo Whitworth
Justyn Wilsmore

ILLUSTRATORS
Ian Atkinson
Peter Barrat
Wendy Bramall
Graham Byfield
Gavin Dunn

Will Giles
Mike Grey
Jack Hayward
Roy Knipe
Sandra Pond
Tamara Sternberg
Gill Tomblin

**SPECIALIST
ADVISERS**
Peter Addington
Wendy Akers
James Allison
Sandra Bell
Peter Boyce
Madeleine Broome
David Lawrence Brown
Alan Cook
Anna Corbett
Ruth Davies
Peter Edwards
Barrie Frankland
Jack G. Grint
Peter William Harkness
Chris Lowe
Charles Miller
Steve Nickells
Andrew Norton
Paul Picton
Martin Raymond Puddle
David Pyecraft
Eric V. Rogers
Barbara Segall
Michael Upward
Christine Walkden

The publishers wish to thank the following organisations and
their staff for help in compiling
New Encyclopedia of Garden Plants & Flowers

Capel Manor Horticultural and Environmental Centre, Enfield, Middlesex
Chelsea Physic Garden, London
Sir Harold Hillier Gardens and Arboretum, Ampfield, Hampshire
Henry Doubleday Research Association, Ryton on Dunsmore, Warwickshire
Merrist Wood College, Worplesdon, Surrey
Pershore College, Pershore, Worcestershire
Royal Botanic Gardens, Kew, Surrey
Royal Horticultural Society Gardens, Wisley, Surrey
Royal Horticultural Society Lindley Library, London
Savill Gardens, Windsor, Berkshire

The following people, organisations and companies
also assisted in the making of this book

a

Abbey Dore Court Gardens, Hereford & Worcester • Acton Beauchamp Roses, Acton Beauchamp, Hereford & Worcester • Agar's Nursery, Lymington, Hampshire • Alpine Garden Society • Anglia Alpines & Herbs Ltd, Huntingdon, Cambridgeshire • J.B. Angrave, Hadlow, Kent • Anthony Archer-Wills Ltd, West Chiltington, West Sussex • Apple Court, Lymington, Hampshire • Architectural Plants, Horsham, West Sussex • Arley House, Nr Bewdley, Hereford & Worcester • Arne Herbs, Chew Magna, Avon • Arrow Cottage, Ledgemoor, Hereford & Worcester • Avon Bulbs, South Petherton, Somerset • Axletree Nursery, Rye, East Sussex

b

Barncroft Nurseries, Stoke-on-Trent, Staffordshire • Barnhawk Nursery, Fordingbridge, Hampshire • Batsford Arboretum, Moreton-in-Marsh, Gloucestershire • Bayston Hill Nurseries, Bayley's Garden Centre, Shrewsbury, Shropshire • Beechcroft Nursery, Ewell, Surrey • Beeches Nursery, Saffron Walden, Essex • Beth Chatto Gardens Ltd, Elmstead Market, Colchester, Essex • Rn & R Bewley, Durham • The Birmingham Botanical Gardens • Bodenham Arboretum, Wolverley, Hereford & Worcester • The Botanic Nursery, Nr Melksham, Wiltshire • Bourton House Garden, Bourton-on-the-Hill, Gloucestershire • Bouts Cottage Nurseries, Inkberrow, Hereford & Worcester • Brackenbury Coombe, Gloucestershire • J Bradshaw & Son, Busheyfields Nursery, Herne Bay, Kent • Brandy Mount House, Hampshire • Brian and Heather Hiley Nursery, Wallington, Surrey • Brian Goodey Cacti, Southfield Nurseries, Bourne, Lincolnshire • Bridgemere Nurseries, Nr Nantwich, Cheshire • Broadleigh Gardens, Taunton, Somerset • Brockings Exotics, North Petherwin, Cornwall • Brodick Castle and Country Park, Isle of Arran, Scotland • Mrs P. J. Brown, Westlees Farm, Westcott, Surrey • Burncoose & Southdown Nurseries, Redruth, Cornwall

c

Cambridge University Botanic Garden • Camp Cottage, Highleadon, Nr Newent, Gloucestershire • Cannington College, Nr Bridgwater, Somerset • Caves Folly Nurseries, Hereford & Worcester • Cedarwood Lily Farm, Stoke on Trent, Staffordshire • Chennels Gate, Eardisley, Kington, Hereford & Worcester • Churchills Garden Nursery, Chudleigh, Devon • Churchtown Nurseries • The Citrus Centre, Pulborough, West Sussex • Clifton Nurseries, London • Colgrave Seeds Ltd, West Adderbury, Oxon • Collinwood Nurseries, Macclesfield, Cheshire • Conderton Manor, Tewkesbury, Hereford & Worcester • The Conservatory, Gomshall, Guildford, Surrey • Cotswold Garden Flowers, Evesham, Hereford & Worcester • County Park Nursery, Hornchurch, Essex • Craig House Cacti, Lancashire • J. Craven Garden Creation, Doncaster • Creative Landscapes, Hartlebury, Kidderminster

d

David Austin Roses Ltd, Albrighton, West Midlands • Delamare Street Nurseries, Winsford, Cheshire • D'Arcy & Everest, Huntingdon, Cambridgeshire • Dibley's Nurseries, Ruthin, Clwyd • Dobwalls, Higman Close, Cornwall • Drysdale Garden Exotics, Fordingbridge, Hampshire • Duchy of Cornwall, Lostwithiel, Cornwall • Dyffryn Botanical Garden, Cardiff

e-f

Eastgrove Cottage Garden Nursery, Little Witley, Hereford & Worcester • East Lambrook Manor Garden, Nr South Petherton, Somerset • Edrom Nurseries, Coldingham, Eyemouth, Berwick-on-Tweed • Fibrex Nurseries Ltd, Stratford-upon-Avon, Warwickshire • Fir Tree Farm Nursery, Falmouth, Cornwall • Kaytie Fisher, Ockham, Surrey • Floral Guernsey • Four Seasons, Norwich, Norfolk • Foxgrove Plants, Nr Newbury, Berkshire • Fuchsia Vale Nurseries, Kidderminster, Hereford & Worcester

g

The Gardens of the Rose, St Albans, Hertfordshire • Glebe Cottage Plants, Umberleigh, North Devon • Goldbrook Hostas, Eye, Suffolk • Goscote Nurseries Ltd, Cossington, Leicestershire • Grange Court • Grange Farm Nursery, Malvern, Hereford & Worcester • Great Campston, Llanushangel, Abergavenny • Greenacres Nursery, Bringsty, Bromyard, Hereford & Worcester • Greenholm Nurseries Ltd, Kingston Seymour Clevedon, Avon • Mr G.S. Greenway, Priorswood Clematis, Ware, Hertfordshire • Grove Cottage, Lower Lydbrook, Gloucestershire

h-i

Hadlow College of Agriculture and Horticulture • Hall Farm Nursery, Kinnerley, Shropshire • Hambrooks, Titchfield, Fareham, Hampshire • The Hannays of Bath, Bathwick, Bath, Avon • Hardy Exotics, Penzance, Cornwall • Hardy's Cottage Garden Plants, Whitchurch, Hampshire • Harlow Carr Botanical Gardens, Crag Lane, Harrogate • Hatsford Fuchsias, Aylton, Ledbury, Hereford & Worcester • Heldon Nursery, Uttoxeter, Staffordshire • Ivan Hicks • Hidcote Manor Garden, Hidcote Bartrim, Gloucestershire • Highgates Nursery, Belper, Derbyshire • Mr A. D. Hill, Umberleigh, Devon • The Hillier Garden, Nr Alcester, Warwickshire • Hillview Hardy Plants, Nr Bridgnorth, Shropshire • Hoecroft Plants, Dereham, Norfolk • Holehird, Windermere, Cumbria • Holly Gate Cactus Nursery, Ashington, West Sussex • Hoo House Nursery, Tewkesbury, Gloucestershire • Hopleys Plants Ltd, Much Hadham, Hertfordshire • Hunts Court Garden and Nursery, North Nibley, Gloucestershire • W.E. Th. Ingwerson Ltd, East Grinstead, West Sussex

j-k

Jacques Amand Ltd, Stanmore, Middlesex • Jasmine Cottage Gardens, Clevedon, North Somerset • Jeffs and Southorn • Jekkas Herb Farm, Alveston, Bristol • John Austen & Co, Covent Garden, London • Keepers Nursery, Maidstone, Kent • Kettlesing Nurseries • Kingsfield Conservation Nursery, Chard, Somerset • Kingston Maurward College, Dorchester, Dorset • Knap Hill and Slocock Nurseries, Woking, Surrey • Knoll Gardens, Nr Wimborne, Dorset

l

Lacham College, Lacock, Chippenham, Wiltshire • Langley Boxwood Nursery, Rake, Hampshire • Langthorns Plantery, Dunmow, Essex • Lingen Alpine Nursery, Nr Bucknell, Shropshire • Little Brook Fuchsia, Ash Green, Hampshire • Longstock Park Gardens, Nr Stockbridge, Hampshire • Lower Severalls Herb Nursery, Crewkerne, Somerset • Lydford Alpine Nursery, Okehampton, Devon

m

Macpennys Garden Nurseries, Christchurch, Dorset • Mallet Court Nursery • Malvern Flower Shows, Three Counties Showground, Great Malvern • Marston Exotics, Madley, Herefordshire • Marwood Hill Gardens, Barnstaple, Devon • Maureen Iddon Nursery • The Mead Nursery, Brokerswood, Nr Westbury, Wiltshire • Merriments Gardens, Hurst Green, East Sussex • Merton Nurseries, Shrewsbury, Shropshire • MJM Nursery, Sandiacre, Nottingham

n

Naked Cross Nurseries, Wimborne, Dorset • National Bamboo Collection, Drysdale Garden Exotics, Fordingbridge, Hampshire • Newby Hall Gardens, Ripon, Yorkshire • Nicky's Rock Garden Nursery, Honiton, Devon • Miss Sylvia Norton, Weavers Cottage, Wickham, Cambridge • Notcutts Nurseries

o

Oland Plants, Sawley • Old Court Nurseries, Nr Malvern, Worcestershire • Overcourt Garden Nursery, Sutton St Nicholas, Hereford & Worcester • Owen Bros Nursery, Bevere, Hereford & Worcester • Oxford Botanical Gardens, Oxford

p-q

Pantiles Nurseries Ltd, Chertsey, Surrey • Paradise Centre, Bures, Suffolk • Park Green Nurseries, Suffolk • Patio Clematis, Bransford Garden Plants, Bransford, Hereford & Worcester • Pear Tree Cottage, Stapely, Somerset • Penpregwm Plants, Abergevenny, Gwent • Pentwyn Cottage Garden, Bacton, Hereford & Worcester • Perryhill Nurseries, Hartfield, East Sussex • Peter Beales Roses, Attleborough, Norfolk • Philip Fivey & Sons, Leicester • Picton Garden, Colwall, Hereford & Worcester • Plantasia, Parc Tawe, West Glamorgan, Swansea • The Plant Lovers, Lincolnshire • The Plantsman Nursery, Okehampton, Devon • Plantworld Botanic Gardens, Newton Abbot, Devon • Plaxtol Nurseries, Sevenoaks, Kent • Mr Poulton and Mr Stenlake, St Johns, Hereford & Worcester • Potash Nurseries, Stowmarket, Suffolk • Potterton & Martin, Caistor, Lincolnshire • Preen Manor Church, Nr Church Stretton, Shropshire • The Priory, Tewkesbury, Gloucestershire • Queen Mary's Rose Garden, Regent's Park, London • Queenswood County Park, Hereford & Worcester

r

R.D. Plants, Axminster, Devon • Ravensthorpe Nursery, Ravensthorpe, Northamptonshire • Redwood House • Regent's Park, London • G. Reuthe Ltd, Crown Point Nursery, Nr Sevenoaks, Kent • Rhodes & Rockliffe, Nazeing, Essex • Roundhay Park, Leeds, Yorkshire • Rowden Gardens, Nr Tavistock, Devon • Royal Horticultural Society Chelsea Flower Show • Royal Horticultural Society Hampton Court Palace Flower Show • Royal Horticultural Society Hyde Hall • Royal Horticultural Society Rosemoor • Rumsey Gardens, Waterlooville, Hampshire • Rushfields of Ledbury, Ledbury, Hereford & Worcester

s

Jean Sambrook • Scotts Nurseries (Merriott) Ltd, Merriott, Somerset • Sherborne Garden, Litton, Avon • Shillinglee Nursery, Chiddingfold, Surrey • Snape Cottage, Chaffeymoor, Dorset • Southcombe Nurseries, Southcombe Gardens, Exeter, Devon • Southfield Nurseries, Lincolnshire • Southview Nurseries, Basingstoke, Hampshire • Springfields Gardens, Spalding, Lincolnshire • Springwood Pleione • Starborough Nursery, Edenbridge, Kent • Steven Bailey Ltd, Lymington, Hampshire • Richard Stockwell, Sherwood, Nottinghamshire • Stone House, Wellington, Hereford & Worcester • Stone House Cottage Nurseries, Stone, Nr Kidderminster, Hereford & Worcester • Stourton House & Nutkin Nursery, Ukfield, East Sussex • Strawberry Cottage, Leominster, Hereford & Worcester • Swallow Hayes, Albrighton, Shropshire • Swanland Nurseries, Hull, East Yorkshire • Swansea Botanic Gardens, Clyne Garden, Swansea

t

O.A. Taylor & Sons, Spalding, Lincolnshire • Taylor Service & Supplies, Cheshire • A. & A. Thorp, Theddingworth, Leicestershire • Three Counties Nurseries, Bridport, Dorset • Tin Penny Cottage, Nr Miserden, Stroud, Gloucestershire • Mrs S.M. Tracey, Shaugh Prior, Devon • Treasures of Tenbury Ltd, Burford House Gardens, Tenbury Wells, Hereford & Worcester • Trebah Garden, Falmouth, Cornwall • Trehane Camellia Nursery, Wimborne, Dorset • Tresco Abbey Gardens, Isles of Scilly • Trevi Garden, Hartpury, Gloucestershire • The Tropical Rainforest Nursery, Leeds

u-v

Ulverscroft Grange Nursery, Ulverscroft, Leicestershire • University of Bristol Botanical Garden • University of Exeter • University of Southampton • The Urn Cottage, Avon • Usual & Unusual Plants, Hailsham, East Sussex • Ventnor Botanic Garden, Isle of Wight

w-z

Wakehurst Place Garden, Ardingly, West Sussex • J. Walker's Bulbs, Spalding, Lincolnshire • Mr & Mrs Ward, 53 Ladywood, Eastleigh, Hampshire • Water Meadow Nursery, Cheriton, Hampshire • Waterperry Gardens, Wheatley, Oxfordshire • Webbs Garden Centres, Wychbold, Droitwich, Hereford & Worcester • Westonbirt Arboretum, Tetbury, Gloucestershire • The Wild Flower Centre, Loddon, Norfolk • Wilford Bulb Co. Ltd, East Leake, Leicestershire • Willow Cottage, Ross on Wye, Gloucestershire • Mr & Mrs J.H. Wood, Nr Mayhill, Gloucestershire • Woodfield Brothers, Stratford-upon-Avon, Warwickshire • Woodland Services and Supplies Ltd, Abergavenny, Gwent • Woodpeckers, Bidford-on-Avon, Warwickshire • Woodstock Orchids & Exotics, Milton Keynes • Writtle College, Chelmsford, Essex • Wychwood Waterlily and Carp Farm, Odiham, Hampshire

Contents of this book

Introduction

For more than two decades the Reader's Digest *Encyclopaedia of Garden Plants and Flowers* has been an acknowledged classic among gardening reference books. Now, after countless reprints and revisions, the time has come for a completely new book to meet the demands of a new era of gardening. The *New Encyclopedia of Garden Plants & Flowers* has been designed to preserve and build on the strengths of its predecessor while at the same time reflecting the profound changes that have occurred in gardening practice and the vast number of new plants available to modern gardeners. The consultants, writers, photographers and editors who worked on this book hope that it will prove both a worthy successor to the old encyclopedia and a source of untiring inspiration and delight to the new generation now discovering that fascinating and rewarding enthusiasm – a passion for plants.

HOW TO USE THIS BOOK

If you know the name of a plant – either the common English name or the Latin botanical name – you can turn straight to the main section of the encyclopedia (pp. 10-718) which contains A-Z entries on hundreds of the most important genera, with thousands of synonyms and common names given as cross-references.

But gardeners do not always know the name of the plant they want to grow. To overcome this problem, an easy-to-use Plant Identifier chart has been specially devised for this book – see pp. 750-95. Alternatively, if you are faced with a specific problem such as a damp, shady corner, or a requirement such as autumn colour, the place to start is with Plants for Special Purposes (pp. 796-800).

Gardeners interested in particular types of plants, such as bamboos, ferns or orchids, or in using plants in a certain way, such as in a rock garden or for topiary, will find the 21 special features in the main section of the book helpful. At the back of the book are sections on fruit and vegetable gardening (ornamental varieties appear in the main A-Z section); cultivation, propagation and pruning techniques; and the diagnosis, prevention and treatment of pests and diseases. Finally, a Glossary has been included at the end of the book, which explains technical terms in layman's language.

UNDERSTANDING PLANT NAMES

For the gardener, the naming of a plant begins with its genus – roughly the equivalent of a surname. Each genus belongs to a larger group called a family, and above that to yet larger groupings, but these bear little practical relevance to gardening. Within a genus, plants are closely related and share important characteristics. They may, but need not, also look similar and have similar requirements. Genera are sub-divided into species, and the species name is written after the genus name. Thus the plant *Abutilon vitifolium* belongs to the genus *Abutilon* and is of the species *vitifolium*. Plants of the same species are very similar physically and genetically, and can interbreed. Even so, some wild species show enough variability to require further division into sub-species (ssp.), variety (var.) or forma (f.), the lowest level in plant classification. This nomenclature is international, and is presented with Latin names in italics (for example, *Abutilon vitifolium* var. *album*).

In cultivation, plants are frequently bred to enhance characteristics such as flower size, vigour, height or leaf variegation. This is known as hybridisation and the resulting plants are called cultivars (cultivated varieties) and given a cultivar name after the species name or, if the species is not known, after the genus name. The cultivar name is not italicised but appears in quotation marks (for example, *Abutilon vitifolium* 'Veronica Tennant', *Rosa* 'Masquerade').

Where variability exists among plants with the same parentage, they are described as groups, hybrids, series or selections (for example, *Anemone coronaria* De Caen Group, *Impatiens* New Guinea Hybrids). Hybrids between species of the same genus are indicated by a multiplication sign between the genus and the species name (for example, *Abutilon* × *suntense*). Hybrids bred from different genera take a multiplication sign before the genus name (for example, × *Fatshedera lizei*) while those created by grafting plants of different genera take a plus sign (for example, + *Laburnocytisus*).

NAME CHANGES & SYNONYMS

The nomenclature followed in this book is based on that set out in *The International Code of Botanical Nomenclature* and *The International Code of Nomenclature for Cultivated Plants*. Plant classifications do change, however, as botanists acquire new information. Every attempt has been made to incorporate changes up to the time of going to press. However, many older synonyms and well-known common names have also been listed as cross-references.

PRINCIPLES OF SELECTION

The plants recommended in this encyclopedia have been chosen by experts because they are easy to obtain and able to thrive in most gardens in Britain. Within these broad criteria a very wide range of plants is represented, both in terms of type (such as woody, perennial, annual or bulbous) and in the rewards they offer, whether of beauty, usefulness or reliability. The vast majority are suitable for gardeners of all levels, including complete beginners, but there are also plenty of suggestions for enthusiasts, and to encourage gardeners to branch out and explore the exciting ranges now available from specialist nurseries.

HOW ENTRIES ARE STRUCTURED

The genus entries in this book have been designed for ease of use. Immediately beneath the genus name appear any common names applicable to the whole genus, and the family name. Then follows an overall description of the genus, the variety of plants it contains, and their main rewards and uses in the garden. To avoid repetition, any features common to all the plants

---

Order of plant names used in the encyclopedia

Abutilon	genus name
Flowering maple	common name(s) applying to whole genus
Malvaceae	family name
A. vitifolium	species
A. vitifolium var. *album*	natural variety
A. vitifolium 'Veronica Tennant'	cultivated variety (cultivar)
A. × *suntense*	natural hybrid
A. 'Ashford Red'	cultivated hybrid

described in the entry are generally covered in the introduction. Any particular drawbacks such as toxicity and invasiveness are also mentioned.

Individually recommended plants are then listed alphabetically and described in detail. Where both a species and its varieties are mentioned, only the species receives a full description; the varieties are listed in an indented paragraph immediately after the species and only described in so far as they differ from it. Sometimes, however, varieties are not associated with a species, or the species is not described, in which case they are independently listed and fully described in their own right.

The symbol ♀ indicates that a plant holds the Royal Horticultural Society's Award of Garden Merit. Synonyms and common names that apply to a species or variety appear in brackets immediately after the botanical name. While every care has been taken to ensure that plant descriptions are as precise as possible, these are necessarily based on average specimens growing in average conditions, and a certain amount of variation will inevitably occur.

Hardiness

Plants described as hardy are capable of surviving most British winters out of doors, while half-hardy plants are less reliable and need protection. Plants referred to as tender usually originate from warmer or sub-tropical regions and, while they may flourish outside during summer, will be cut down by the first frost of autumn.

Height and spread

Plant size is a crucial factor in garden planning; spread in particular is useful as an indication of planting distance. The figures given in the book are for average specimens grown in appropriate conditions, and individual plants may vary slightly from the norm. In some cases it has been necessary to give a range rather than a single figure. For trees, interim measurements are given as appropriate – usually at ten, fifteen or twenty years – as well as at full mature size, and shrubs at five years and at maturity. The measurements given for perennials are for well-established plants, generally of about two or three years. For bulbous plants, only a height measurement is given, as the upright habit and brief period above ground make spread largely irrelevant. The height given for houseplants is what is normal for indoor cultivation in Britain, rather than the height that may be achieved in the natural habitat.

Cultivation, propagation, pruning, and pests and diseases

While specific advice appears in every genus entry, the basic techniques of good plant care are explained and illustrated in the reference sections on pp. 801-59.

Because of climatic variations across the British Isles, flowering periods and times for operations such as sowing seed are generally given as seasons rather than months.

For the purposes of this book greenhouses are described as 'cold' (completely unheated, with temperatures likely to drop below freezing in winter), 'cool' (heated to maintain a temperature above 4°C (39°F)) or 'warm' (heated to maintain a temperature above 10°C (50°F)).

ILLUSTRATIONS IN THIS BOOK

The many thousands of photographs in this book have been specially commissioned and selected to help gardeners to choose and plan planting schemes, and to aid in plant identification. While every attempt has been made to show representative specimens, factors such as soil type; a light, shady, protected or exposed site; and natural variation among plant populations, will inevitably affect the colour, size and habit of any individual example.

The small watercolour illustrations that appear in many entries are not intended to be accurate botanical representations, but rather to give a subjective impression of a plant's overall appearance and habit.

HELPING WITH CONSERVATION

Across the world, natural habitats and flora are under threat, and unfortunately gardening practices are not always blameless. However, there are many steps that responsible gardeners can take to ensure that their hobby does not have a detrimental effect. Excellent peat substitutes are now available and should be used whenever possible to preserve threatened peat bogs. Limestone, which was once much used in landscaping and rockeries, is similarly irreplaceable and supports a unique flora. Most rock and alpine plants do just as well without it in carefully prepared raised beds, among artificial 'rocks' or on scree.

Before buying plants, bulbs or seeds, check that they have been raised in cultivation and not taken from the wild, particularly in the case of orchids, bulbs, alpines, palms, cacti and succulents. Many sellers declare the source of their stock; if not, it is wise to ask, both to set your own mind at ease and to raise awareness in the trade.

However tempting, resist the urge to collect plants from the wild when travelling. Although packets of seed are admitted from most countries, with more generous allowances within the European Union, other plant material is subject to many restrictions. These are set out in the *Traveller's guide to bringing plants back from abroad*, published by the Ministry of Agriculture, Fisheries and Food, and available from the Plant Health Division, MAFF, Whitehall Place (East Block), London SW1A 2HH.

Abbreviations and symbols

cv.	cultivar
f.	forma
hort.	hortulanorum ('of gardens') – term indicating a botanically incorrect but widely used name
ssp.	sub-species
spp.	'and its species' – used after a genus name to refer to all species within the genus
syn.	synonym
var.	variety
♀	Award of Garden Merit (AGM) – bestowed by the Royal Horticultural Society on the most rewarding and reliable plants for garden decoration, whether grown in the open or under glass.

Abelia
Caprifoliaceae

Abelia × grandiflora 'Francis Mason'

Abundant small clusters of white, pink or red funnel-shaped flowers are borne by these graceful shrubs or trees. They are deciduous or semi-evergreen and plants generally have slender, arching branches. Most species in cultivation need protection from cold, wind and frost in many areas and grow best against a warm south or west-facing wall. The sepals are 6–15 mm (¼–½ in) long and remain conspicuous and often colourful long after the flowers have fallen. The oval, pointed leaves are 1.5–4 cm (½–1½ in) long. Plants are native to China, Japan, the Himalayas and Mexico.

RECOMMENDED SPECIES AND VARIETIES
A. chinensis Fragrant white flowers, flushed pink outside, are borne in clusters from mid to late summer. Each flower is 1.5 cm (½ in) long and has 5 rose-pink sepals. A compact deciduous shrub with dark green leaves. HEIGHT & SPREAD 80×80 cm (32×32 in) after 5 years, ultimately 1.5 m (5 ft) tall.
A. 'Edward Goucher'♀ Clusters of purplish pink flowers appear from mid to late summer. Each flower is 2 cm (¾ in) long with 2 reddish sepals. This deciduous or

♥ *Abelia 'Edward Goucher'*

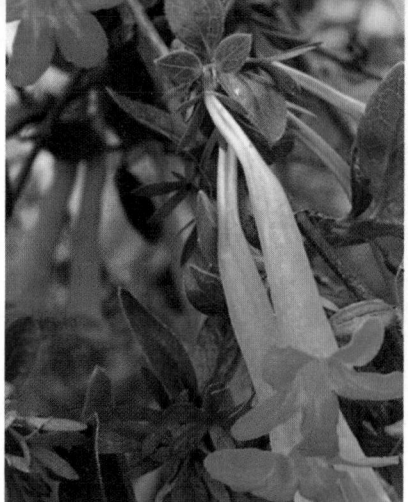

▲ *Abelia floribunda*

semi-evergreen shrub has glossy, slightly toothed leaves, usually tinged bronze when young and bright green by summer. HEIGHT & SPREAD 80×80 cm (32×32 in) after 5 years, ultimately 1.5 m (5 ft) tall.
A. floribunda♀ Bright cherry-red flowers, 5 cm (2 in) long, are borne in drooping clusters in early summer. Each flower has 5 dull, reddish green sepals. This evergreen shrub with glossy, dark green, slightly toothed leaves is only hardy to about -10°C (14°F). HEIGHT & SPREAD 1×1 m (3×3 ft) after 5 years, ultimately 3 m (10 ft) tall.

▲ *Abelia × grandiflora*

A. × grandiflora♀ (syn. *A. rupestris* hort.) Slightly scented white flowers, tinged with pink, appear from mid summer to mid autumn. They are 2 cm (¾ in) long and have 2–5 pinkish sepals. This evergreen shrub has glossy, deep green, slightly toothed leaves. HEIGHT & SPREAD 1×1 m (3×3 ft) after 5 years, ultimately 1.8 m (6 ft) tall.
   The leaves of **'Francis Mason'**♀ have a golden-yellow edge that is brighter on plants grown in a sunny position. It only reaches about 1.5 m (5 ft). **'Goldsport'** (syn. 'Aurea', 'Gold Strike') is the same height and has golden leaves.
A. rupestris hort. see *A. × grandiflora*
A. schumannii Rosy pink outside and white with an orange blotch inside, the

flowers appear from late summer to mid autumn. Each flower is 2.5 cm (1 in) long and has 2 reddish sepals. A deciduous shrub that has slender purple young shoots and glossy bright green leaves. HEIGHT & SPREAD 80×80 cm (32×32 in) after 5 years, ultimately 1.5 m (5 ft) tall.
A. triflora Clusters of fragrant white flowers, tinged pink outside and 2 cm (¾ in) long, appear in early summer. The slender flower tubes flare outwards, spreading to 1.5 cm (½ in) across. Each flower has 5 narrow red sepals. The deciduous leaves are up to 7.5 cm (3 in) long and sometimes have toothed edges. They are dull dark green above and paler and slightly hairy beneath. This large shrub or small spreading tree develops a ridged grey bark with age. HEIGHT & SPREAD 1.5×1 m (5×3 ft) after 5 years, ultimately 5 m (16 ft) tall.
CULTIVATION Plant in any well-drained, moderately fertile soil in full sun. All plants benefit from a sheltered position against a warm south or west-facing wall.
PRUNING None required but cut out any dead wood in spring. Trim or shape plants, if necessary, after flowering.
PROPAGATION Raise plants by taking softwood cuttings in summer.
PESTS AND DISEASES Usually trouble free.

Abies
Silver fir
Pinaceae

Abies koreana

Pyramids of long, graceful branches sweeping horizontally from a silvery grey trunk give these aromatic evergreen conifers their characteristic look. The glossy green, flat needles are between 1.5–7.5 cm (½–3 in) long and usually have two bold grey-green or white stripes on the lower surfaces.

   Many species reach a majestic size at maturity: the rapid-growing *Abies grandis* eventually tops 100 m (330 ft) and *A. nordmanniana,* whose saplings are popular as Christmas trees, reaches 55 m (180 ft). Slow-growing and prostrate varieties are more suited for gardens but these can lack the strong shape of the tall species. The trees grow best in damp climates with cool winters, and prefer moist, acid soil. Most are hardy though some cultivated species need protection from late spring frosts.

   Small male and large female cones are borne on the same tree in spring. The colour of the female cones varies according to variety from red through purple to blue

▲ *Abies balsamea* f. *hudsonia*

and even white or all green. All ripen to a dull brown when frost occurs and disintegrate in autumn winds. Male cones are usually carried in clusters on lower branches while female cones, borne singly and in clusters, are on upper branches. The female cones, 6-20 cm (2½-8 in) long, have scales spiralling around a central spike which is left on the tree after the scales and seeds have blown away. They are mostly cigar to barrel shaped and are held upright on the twigs. Silver firs generally bear cones after 20-25 years with the exception of *A. koreana,* which has blue cones after 5-10 years.

RECOMMENDED SPECIES AND VARIETIES

A. balsamea f. *hudsonia*♀ The dwarf globular bush has short, aromatic glossy green needles. It does not bear cones but white resin-covered buds. The hardy native of the eastern United States is the most lime tolerant of the genus. HEIGHT & SPREAD 80×100 cm (32×40 in) after 20-30 years.

A. b. 'Nana' is very similar to *hudsonia* but slower growing, forming a compact spherical bush. The glossy dark green needles are very densely arranged.

▲ *Abies concolor* 'Compacta'

A. concolor 'Compacta'♀ Stout, short stiff needles are a strong blue on the irregular-shaped dwarf plant. It has round, sticky resinous leaf buds. Cones are seldom produced. Annual growth is only about 3-5 cm (1¼-2 in). HEIGHT & SPREAD 50×75 cm (20×30 in) in 15-20 years.

A. koreana (Korean fir) The low, wide-spreading hardy tree forms a pyramid densely clothed with dark shiny needles that are a bright silver underneath. From an early age, 5-10 years old, it produces deep purplish blue, upright cylindrical cones with green inverted seed bracts in mid autumn, these turn brown as they mature. Rows of pink and green upright female flowers are borne in late spring. HEIGHT & SPREAD 2-3×1.2 m (6½-10×4 ft), but only

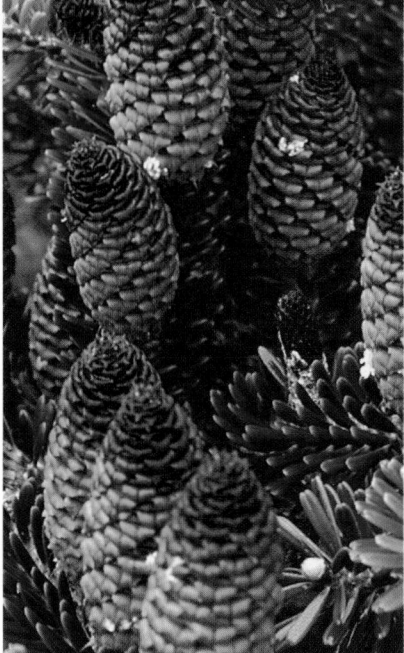

▲ *Abies koreana*

after 30-40 years of very slow growth; ultimately 15 m (50 ft) in favourable conditions.

'Flava' has all the characteristics of the species but grows to just over half its size and the immature cones are pale green ripening to yellowish brown cones with the same inverted bracts. 'Silberlocke', whose cones resemble those of 'Flava', has a silvery appearance because many of the needles display their pale grey underside. It is the smallest of the three, about half the size of the species, with the slowest growth.

A. lasiocarpa 'Arizonica Compacta'♀ The compact cone-shaped tree of deep silvery blue needles brightens up any garden corner that sees little sunshine as it does not tolerate high temperatures. It thrives in cool damp corners and is slow growing, making only 3-4 cm (1¼-1½ in) of growth a year. The cones are small and brown. HEIGHT & SPREAD 60-100×45 cm (24-40×18 in) after about 10 years, 2×1 m (6½×3 ft) when fully grown, after about 30 years.

A. nordmanniana 'Golden Spreader'♀ Light golden yellow needles with a yellowish white underside make a vivid, compact dwarf bush with wide-spreading branches. Cones are rarely produced. Protect the

▼ *Abies koreana* 'Silberlocke'

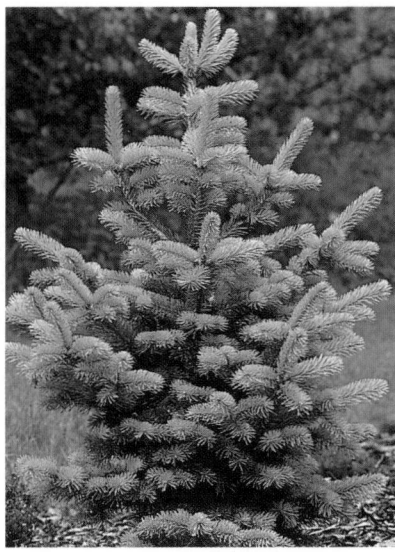

▲ *Abies lasiocarpa* 'Arizonica Compacta'

plant from frosts. Once established, annual growth is about 4-5 cm (1½-2 in). HEIGHT & SPREAD 1×1.5 m (3×5 ft) after 15 years.

A. procera 'Glauca Prostrata' The pale, prostrate plant has bluish white needles. Some plants revert to having a leader which must be removed for the proper ground-hugging, broad shape to develop. HEIGHT & SPREAD 75 cm×7 m (2½×23 ft).

CULTIVATION The plants grow well on most acid soils, including clays, but not on chalky soils. They are intolerant of atmospheric pollution. Late spring frosts can damage plants that receive early morning sun as new growth begins early in the year. The white and golden cultivars also require afternoon shade as strong sunlight can scorch the leaves. Plant in their permanent position when young.

PROPAGATION Grow plants from seed as cuttings will not root. Cultivars are best reproduced by grafting in early autumn.

PRUNING None required unless a length of clear stem is desired; remove any unwanted branches in winter.

PESTS AND DISEASES Aphids called adelgids can damage the plants but the chief threat to them is late spring frosts.

Abutilon

Malvaceae

Abutilon
'Souvenir de Bonn'

Exotic flowers smother these fast-growing, soft-wooded shrubs for long periods. The flowers are generally bell or funnel-shaped, or they may be an open, saucer shape. Usually the flowers are borne singly, but some species produce flowers in small clusters. Colours include yellow, orange, red, pink, apricot, purple-red and white, and some flowers have conspicuous veins. The leaves are generally maple-like. Native to the tropics and subtropics, abutilons are generally short-lived but vary in hardiness. Species grown as small trees may be freestanding, but do best against a warm south or west-facing wall. Some abutilons make excellent conservatory plants. Others are good for summer bedding, providing dots of colour, while others do well in hanging baskets. The average height and spread measurements of the recommended plants are for specimens trained against a wall.

RECOMMENDED SPECIES AND VARIETIES

A. megapotamicum♀ (trailing abutilon) Orange-red and yellow lantern-like flowers make this a distinctive plant. The protective outer parts of the flower (calyxes) are orange-red and about 2.5 cm (1 in) long, while the yellow petals are about 4 cm (1½ in) long. This plant has dark evergreen leaves, 5–10 cm (2–4 in) long, which are ovate, slender and pointed, and a graceful habit. In flower from late spring to autumn, *A. megapotamicum* is fairly hardy but will grow best trained against a warm wall. HEIGHT & SPREAD 2×2 m (6½×6½ ft) after 5 years, ultimately 3 m (10 ft) tall.

'Variegatum' has mottled yellow leaves.

▼ *Abutilon megapotamicum* 'Variegatum'

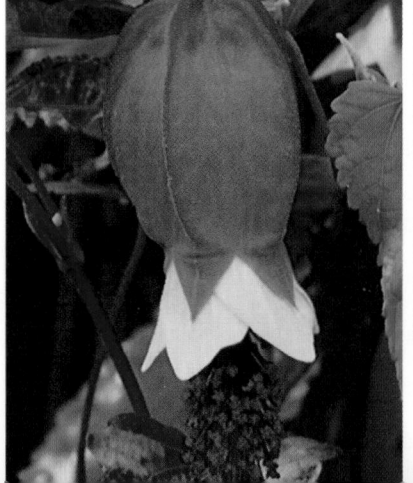

A. × milleri♀ Orange bell-shaped flowers, about 4 cm (1½ in) long, with red veins and crimson stamens are borne continuously from summer through to late autumn. The dark green leaves are up to 10 cm (4 in) long. A tender plant, it can be grown successfully outdoors only in milder areas against a warm wall and is most commonly grown in a greenhouse or a conservatory, where it reaches about 1.8 m (6 ft) tall after 5 years. As a pot plant used as an outdoor annual, it reaches about 1 m (3 ft) tall. HEIGHT & SPREAD 1.8×1.8 m (6×6 ft) after 5 years, ultimately 3 m (10 ft) tall.

▲ *Abutilon* × *suntense*

A. × suntense Bowl-shaped flowers, about 4 cm (1½ in) across, in bright, bluish mauve with paler centres, bloom from late spring to mid summer. The leaves, to 12.5 cm (5 in) in length, are slightly grey, oval, lobed and toothed. This is a very fast-growing plant that particularly benefits from staking or being grown against a sunny wall. HEIGHT & SPREAD 3×1.8 m (10×6 ft) after 5 years, ultimately 4.5×3 m (15×10 ft).

'Jermyns'♀ has dark mauve flowers, while 'Violetta' has deep violet flowers.

A. vitifolium Saucer-shaped, mauve or lavender flowers, up to 7.5 cm (3 in) across, open out flat when mature and are borne from mid spring to mid summer. The grey-green leaves, 10–15 cm (4–6 in) long, are sharply toothed, finely pointed and vine-like. The plant grows best given the protection of a warm wall, especially in cold areas. HEIGHT & SPREAD 1.5×1 m (5×3 ft) after 5 years, ultimately 3 m (10 ft) tall.

The snow white flowers of var. *album* are tinged pink when young. 'Tennant's White'♀ has masses of pure white blooms, while 'Veronica Tennant'♀ has large mauve flowers.

OTHER HYBRIDS

Many hybrids are available, offering a wide selection of flower colours. Most of the plants are half hardy and are best grown in a greenhouse or in a sheltered position against a warm wall. Alternatively, they may be

used as summer bedding. They generally flower from early summer to late autumn outdoors and will flower all year round in a conservatory, with the best display in autumn. The flowers, unless stated otherwise, are open cups 5–7.5 cm (2–3 in) wide. The leaves are up to 12.5 cm (5 in) long. If treated as half-hardy annuals and grown as summer bedding, they will reach a height of 1 m (3 ft) and a spread of 60 cm (2 ft). Unless otherwise stated, plants trained against a wall reach a height and spread of about 1.8 m (6 ft) in 5 years and may ultimately grow to 3 m (10 ft) tall.

▲ *Abutilon* 'Ashford Red'

'Ashford Red'♀ has textured, bell-shaped flowers in salmon red. Appearing from spring to autumn, the flowers contrast with the pale green, evergreen leaves which are almost heart-shaped and serrated. The vigorous 'Boule de Neige' has pure white flowers with orange stamens against dark

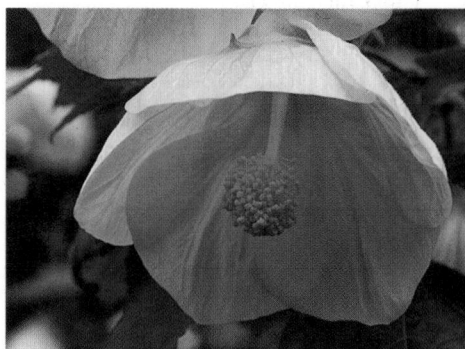

▲ *Abutilon* 'Canary Bird'

green leaves. The primrose yellow, open bells of 'Canary Bird'♀ appear against glossy leaves. This plant can be grown outdoors only in milder areas. The scarlet flowers, mottled yellow leaves and dwarf habit of 'Cannington Carol'♀ make this plant ideal for hanging baskets, where it grows to a height and spread of 45 cm (18 in). 'Cannington Peter'♀ has dark crimson

▼ *Abutilon* 'Cannington Peter'

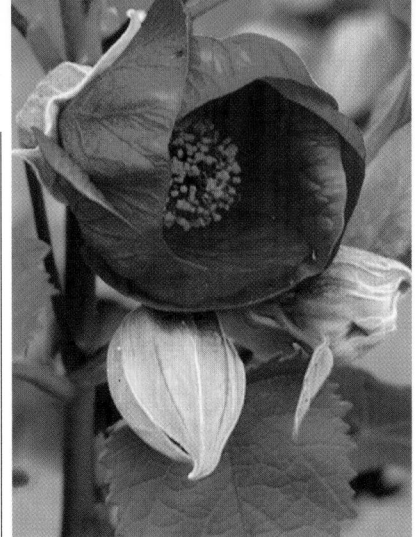

⚠ *Abutilon* 'Nabob'

flowers hanging among yellow mottled leaves. The flowers of **'Kentish Belle'**♀ are apricot coloured with faint red veins and are about 4cm (1½in) long. They hang all summer and autumn from this semi-ever-green, arching shrub which has purple shoots and deep green, deeply lobed leaves with purple veins. It thrives outdoors where it attains a height and spread of 1.2m (4ft). The dark purplish red flowers of **'Nabob'**♀ appear against dark green leaves on this plant, which can be grown outdoors in milder areas. **'Souvenir de Bonn'**♀ has long stalked, closed cups of deep orange-pink flowers with red veins. The leaves are edged with white. An erect plant, it grows to 3.5m (12ft) tall.

CULTIVATION Plant in spring in fertile, well-drained soil, avoiding heavy clays. For the best results outdoors, grow plants in a sheltered position against a warm south or west-facing wall, particularly in northern and eastern areas, in full or part sun. Tie the shoots of wall specimens close to the wall regularly. In winter, protect all species from cold with straw or bracken in all but the mildest areas. Repot greenhouse and con-servatory specimens every spring, or discard plants every two years and replace with new. Water freely during the growing season, keeping the soil just moist for the rest of the year. Feed regularly from mid spring to early autumn.

PROPAGATION Take semi-ripe cuttings in late summer. Plants can be raised from seed but named varieties do not come true. Raise *A. vitifolium* from seed sown in spring, as rooting cuttings can be difficult.

PRUNING Cut out frost-damaged and dead wood in spring, and cut back the previous season's stems by two-thirds of their length. Cut back main stems of greenhouse plants by half and lateral shoots to about 10cm (4in) in early spring. Pinch out the tips of free-standing specimens in the growing season if necessary to encourage bushiness.

PESTS AND DISEASES Usually trouble free but greenhouse plants may need treatment against scale insects, greenhouse whitefly, mealy bugs and red spider mite.

Acacia
Wattle
Leguminosae

Acacia dealbata

The brilliant yellow flowers of these fast-growing, somewhat tender evergreen or semi-evergreen shrubs brighten the garden or conservatory in winter and spring and are often very fragrant. Native to Australia and Africa, acacia can be grown outdoors only in the milder regions of Britain, but if given the protection of a warm south or west-facing wall, plants can rapidly reach a large size. They are also particularly tolerant of drought conditions. In colder and exposed areas plants should be grown in large pots or specially prepared beds in a cool greenhouse or conservatory with plenty of space. Plants grown indoors will flower earlier than out-door specimens.

Looking like a small fluffy pompom, each blossom is actually a tight ball of petal-less flowers. Some acacias have modified leaf stalks, called phyllodes, that look like leaves. Others have bipinnate leaves, leaves made up of several stems which in turn carry many tiny leaflets.

RECOMMENDED SPECIES AND VARIETIES
A. baileyana♀ (Cootamundra wattle) Throughout late winter and spring this graceful, spreading shrub is profusely cov-ered with bright yellow flowers in clusters up to 10cm (4in) long. The often pendu-lous branches carry fern-like bipinnate leaves, up to 5cm (2in) long with 10-20 pairs of narrow leaflets. The leaflets and young shoots are blue-green with a silvery bloom. HEIGHT & SPREAD 3.5×1.5m (12×5ft) after 5 years, ultimately 8m (26ft) tall.

'Purpurea'♀ has deep purple young foliage that creates an effective contrast with the blue green of older foliage.
A. dealbata♀ (mimosa, silver wattle) Clusters up to 15cm (6in) long of scented, fluffy, bright yellow flowers are borne

❦ *Acacia dealbata*

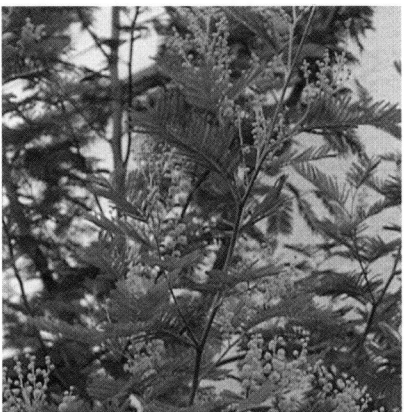

throughout winter and spring, on plants that are grown outdoors usually in mid spring. Of an upright, open habit, these shrubs have bipinnate leaves, up to 12cm (4¾in) long, with 20-40 pairs of feathery, blue-green leaflets. HEIGHT & SPREAD 4×1.8m (13×6ft) after 5 years, ultimately 7.5m (25ft) tall.
A. pravissima (Oven's wattle) The slender, angular branches of this graceful shrub are covered with clusters of rich yellow flowers throughout spring. Covered with a bluish grey bloom, the grey-green phyllodes are up to 2cm (¾in) long. HEIGHT & SPREAD 3×1.8m (10×6ft) after 5 years, ultimately 6m (20ft) tall.
A. retinodes♀ Large, loose flowerheads of pale yellow blossoms are produced freely, on and off, in spring and summer. The narrow, grey-green phyllodes are up to 18cm (7in) long and look like willow leaves. Forming a shrub or small tree, this species is more tolerant of limy soils. HEIGHT & SPREAD 4×2.4m (13×8ft) after 5 years, ultimately 6m (20ft) tall.

⚠ *Acacia retinodes*

CULTIVATION Plant in well-drained, fertile soil that is not too limy, although *A. retinodes* tolerates lime, against a south or west-facing wall. Protect plants in winter with a dry mulch. Where temperatures fre-quently fall below -5°C (23°F), grow under glass in pots or a greenhouse, maintaining a minimum winter temperature of 4°C (39°F). Plant in John Innes No.2 compost. Provide plenty of year-round light and ven-tilation and water moderately in autumn and winter, freely in spring and summer. Repot established specimens every other year in early spring. Feed fortnightly from late spring to late summer.

PROPAGATION Sow seed in mid spring or take heeled semi-ripe cuttings.

PRUNING Remove dead, diseased or cross-ing branches and restrict the size of large specimens by cutting plants back after flow-ering by up to two-thirds of their height.

PESTS AND DISEASES Root mealy bug, red spider mite and tortrix caterpillar can attack the plants.

Acacia, false see *Robinia pseudoacacia*

Acaena
New Zealand bur
Rosaceae

Acaena microphylla

The name of the genus is derived from the Greek *akaina*, 'thorn', and refers to the coloured burs (prickly seed vessels) which are the main attraction of the plants. Most species also have colourful leaves, 6-12 cm (2½-4¾ in) long and divided into 9-15 oval, toothed leaflets. The small greenish white to brown flowers are insignificant and are carried on erect stems above the ground-hugging foliage in late spring and summer. The tight balls of flowers are followed by spherical spiny burs, up to 4 cm (1½ in) across, in late summer and autumn which last throughout winter.

The creeping habit of these hardy evergreens makes them suitable for rock gardens although they can be very invasive. They can also be used to carpet the ground in which small early bulbs have been planted and, as they tolerate being trodden on, may be grown among paving stones.

Plants within this genus are vigorous and do best in well-drained soil and a sunny situation. They are native to the Southern Hemisphere, mostly from New Zealand.

RECOMMENDED SPECIES AND VARIETIES
A. adscendens see *A. magellanica* ssp. *laevigata*
A. **'Blue Haze'** (syn. *A.* 'Pewter') The pale blue foliage sets off the dark red burs. HEIGHT & SPREAD 10×75 cm (4×30 in).
A. buchananii Greenish yellow burs appear above the grey-green leaves in late summer. HEIGHT & SPREAD 2.5×75 cm (1×30 in).
A. caerulea see *A. caesiiglauca*

⚘ *Acaena* 'Blue Haze'

Acaena buchananii ⚘

⚘ *Acaena caesiiglauca*

A. caesiiglauca (syn. *A. caerulea*, *A. microphylla* 'Glauca') The mats of mid blue-green leaflets are covered in reddish brown burs in late summer. HEIGHT & SPREAD 5×75 cm (2×30 in).
A. **'Copper Carpet'** see *A. microphylla* 'Kupferteppich'
A. magellanica ssp. *laevigata* (syn. *A. adscendens*) The grey-green foliage is covered with dark red burs in summer. Native to southern South America. HEIGHT & SPREAD 15×15 cm (6×6 in).

⚘ *Acaena microphylla*

A. microphylla ⚘ The bright crimson burs in late summer look stunning against the loose mats of rosy bronze tinted foliage. HEIGHT & SPREAD 5×15 cm (2×6 in).
'Kupferteppich' (syn. *A.* 'Copper Carpet', *A.* 'Purple Carpet') is a vigorous cultivar with coppery black foliage. Red burs appear in late summer.
A. microphylla 'Glauca' see *A. caesiiglauca*
A. novae-zelandiae A shrubby perennial which produces red burs above bright grey-green leaves. This species is native to New Guinea as well as to New Zealand where it is known as bidgee-widgee and pirri-pirri bur. It is naturalised in sandy places near the coast in the British Isles. HEIGHT & SPREAD 15×90 cm (6×36 in).
A. ovalifolia Yellowish purple flowers in early summer appear above grey-green leaves, followed by white, globular burs. Native to South America and the Falkland Islands. HEIGHT & SPREAD 5×80 cm (2×32 in).
A. **'Pewter'** see *A.* 'Blue Haze'
A. **'Purple Carpet'** see *A. microphylla* 'Kupferteppich'
CULTIVATION Plant in well-drained sandy soil in full sun or partial shade. Most species tolerate poor soil. *A. microphylla* grows well in shade. Most species can be very invasive and smother less vigorous neighbouring plants. Excess growth should be cut back.
PROPAGATION In spring the plants can be increased by replanting self-rooting stolons or by division. Plants may also be raised from seed sown in autumn or early spring.
PESTS AND DISEASES Usually trouble free.

Acalypha
Euphorbiaceae

Of these tropical, evergreen shrubs there are two species in cultivation, one grown for its flowers, the other for its colourful foliage. The plants are very fast-growing and if the right conditions of warmth, humidity and strong light are met they make good indoor plants. The sap of the plants is toxic.
RECOMMENDED SPECIES
A. hispida ⚘ (chenille plant, red-hot cat's tail) Tiny crimson flowers, packed in narrow, pendent spikes up to 40 cm (16 in) long, look like giant, fluffy catkins. The oval leaves are bright green and grow to

⚘ *Acalypha hispida*

12 cm (4¾ in). Flowering is continuous when light levels are high. HEIGHT & SPREAD 1.5 m×75 cm (5×2½ ft) after 5 years.
A. wilkesiana (Jacob's coat, copperleaf) Coppery leaves, up to 12 cm (4¾ in) long, splashed with patches of red-brown are roughly triangular in shape. The flowers are carried in cream-coloured, narrow spikes and are quite inconspicuous. HEIGHT & SPREAD 1.2 m×60 cm (4×2 ft) after 5 years.
CULTIVATION Site in direct sunlight or very good indirect light with a minimum temperature of 15°C (59°F) at night, and 17°C (63°F) in daytime. Keep humidity high and plants moist and well fed in the growing season. Plants survive temperatures as low as 7°C (45°F) in winter, but lose their leaves, and watering must be occasional. Propagate new plants every year or two.

PRUNING Cut down to within 30 cm (12 in) of the base in early spring.

PROPAGATION Take semi-ripe cuttings up to 10 cm (4 in) long. They root easily.

PESTS AND DISEASES Dry air encourages red spider mite and leaf-drop. Mealy bug can also be a problem.

Acanthocalycium see CACTI p. 106

Acantholimon
Prickly heath
Plumbaginaceae

Spikes of long-lasting, delicate flowers are borne from early summer to early autumn on these low-growing, hardy evergreens. The plants form dense cushions of spiny foliage suitable for growing in rock gardens and on dry walls. The five-petalled flowers are about 1 cm (⅜ in) across, the needle-like leaves are up to 3 cm (1¼ in) long. Although plants are tolerant of low temperatures, they do not like excessive winter wet. They require sharp drainage, full sun and prefer limy soil. Plants are native throughout E Mediterranean to central Asia.

RECOMMENDED SPECIES

A. androsaceum see *A. ulicinum*

A. glumaceum White veined purple in bud, the flowers open to reveal bright pink petals. The flower spikes are about 10 cm (4 in) long. The leaves are deep green or grey-green. HEIGHT & SPREAD 15×30 cm (6×12 in).

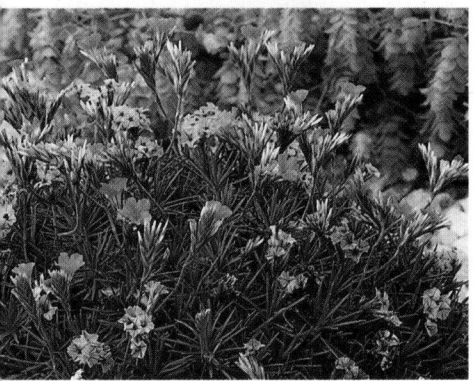

▲ *Acantholimon glumaceum*

A. ulicinum (syn. *A. androsaceum*) Bright pink flowers, white or purple in bud, are held in spikes about 8 cm (3¼ in) long above the dense cushions of blue-grey spines. HEIGHT & SPREAD 25×30 cm (10×12 in).

CULTIVATION Plant during spring in full sun in very well-drained, gritty, limy soil. Protect from winter wet with a cloche or pane of glass. The plants can also be grown in an alpine house.

PROPAGATION Sow ripe seed under glass in winter, although germination is unreliable, or take basal cuttings in summer.

PESTS AND DISEASES Usually trouble free.

Acanthus
Bear's breeches
Acanthaceae

Acanthus spinosus

These hardy perennials are grown for their handsome foliage and summer display of tall spikes of hooded flowers, which vary in colour from white to purple. Acanthus leaves are thought to have been the inspiration for the decoration on Corinthian columns in ancient Greece.

So that their striking basal leaves can be fully appreciated, the plants are often grown at the front of a border. The faded flower spikes may be dried for winter decoration.

RECOMMENDED SPECIES AND VARIETIES

A. balcanicus see *A. hungaricus*

A. hungaricus (syn. *A. balcanicus*, *A. longifolius*) The matt green, deeply lobed leaves are not as attractive as those of *A. mollis* and *A. spinosus*. They reach 60 cm (2 ft) in length and are not spiny. The pinkish white flowers, surrounded by purple bracts, are produced freely in summer. Native to the Balkans. HEIGHT & SPREAD 90×60 cm (3×2 ft).

A. longifolius see *A. hungaricus*

A. mollis Handsome, deeply cut green leaves, which grow to 60 cm (2 ft) long, are topped with spikes of mauve and white flowers in early summer. The leaves carry short, soft spines at the tips. Native to S Europe and NW Africa. HEIGHT & SPREAD 120×90 cm (4×3 ft).

The **Latifolius Group** of cultivars have particularly fine, shiny green leaves, but flowering is not as free as with the species.

A. spinosus ♀ Often considered to be the most striking acanthus because of its large leaves, up to 90 cm (3 ft) long, which are deeply toothed with long spines at their tips.

▼ *Acanthus hungaricus*

▲ *Acanthus mollis*

It is also the hardiest species. The pale mauve and white flowers are freely produced in late summer. Native to S Europe. HEIGHT & SPREAD 120×60 cm (4×2 ft).

The **Spinosissimus Group** of cultivars display more finely divided and spiny leaves but need to be grown in hot, sunny positions to flower well.

CULTIVATION Plants of this genus are not fussy about soil, provided it is well drained. They need a sunny spot to flower well, although they will tolerate some shade. Their long, tough roots make the plants difficult to remove if wrongly positioned.

Plant them in spring and cut back the old flower stems in autumn. In cold areas, cover the crowns with straw for protection through winter as they will not tolerate wet, frozen soil.

PROPAGATION Lift and divide large clumps in spring. In winter use the thick roots as root cuttings – they will soon form new plants when placed in containers in a cold-frame. Plants may also be raised from seed sown under glass in spring.

PESTS AND DISEASES Usually trouble free.

▼ *Acanthus spinosus*

a

Acer
Maple
Aceraceae

Finely cut, attractively coloured foliage, decorative bark and brilliant autumn tints make maples ideal as specimen plants, creating a highlight in the garden. The species listed here are all deciduous and range from large trees over 30 m (100 ft) to small shrubs just 1 m (3 ft) high.

Most grow throughout the temperate regions of the world and so are generally hardy in Britain, although some, particularly *Acer palmatum* and its cultivars, can be damaged by frost when they are small. They grow best in rich, moist but well-drained soil in a shady, sheltered spot.

Maples are easily recognised from their palmate leaves and the red and green winged seeds which appear in summer or autumn. Leaves generally have five rounded or pointed lobes. The Japanese maples, listed under *A. japonicum* and *A. palmatum*, are prized for their delicate appearance and spectacular red or yellow autumn colour. Many of the Japanese cultivars are particularly suitable for small gardens as they are slow-growing.

Ornamental bark gives several species interest in winter. The snake bark group of maples, including *A. capillipes, A. pensylvanicum* and *A. davidii*, has distinctively striped bark, while the new bark of *A. griseum* (the paper bark maple) is a rich cinnamon colour and the young stems of *A. palmatum* 'Sango-kaku' (coral bark maple) are a brilliant coral-red.

Pale yellow or green flower clusters, 2.5-15 cm (1-6 in) long, appear in spring on all maples, sometimes before the leaves, but in general these add little ornamental value.

RECOMMENDED SPECIES AND VARIETIES

A. capillipes♀ (snake bark maple) This densely branched, domed tree has outstanding bark – white stripes run lengthways on a surface that is reddish green when young, aging to a more grey-green colour. Shiny leaves, 12 cm (4¾ in) long, with 3-5 lobes emerge with a reddish tint and turn a strong red or sometimes orange in autumn. The winged seeds are green. Native to Japan. HEIGHT & SPREAD 3×2 m (10×6½ ft) after 20 years, eventually 10 m (33 ft) tall.

A. circinatum♀ (vine maple) The leaves, 12.5 cm (5 in) long, have 7-9 lobes and turn a bright reddish orange in autumn. This large shrub or small tree is upright and densely branched. Clusters of insignificant white flowers with purple sepals are borne in spring, followed by red, winged fruits during summer. Native to N America. HEIGHT & SPREAD 3×1 m (10×3 ft) in 20 years, ultimately 10 m (33 ft) tall.

A. davidii 'George Forrest'♀ This elegant small tree is of open, spreading, pendulous habit. It has striking striated bark and large

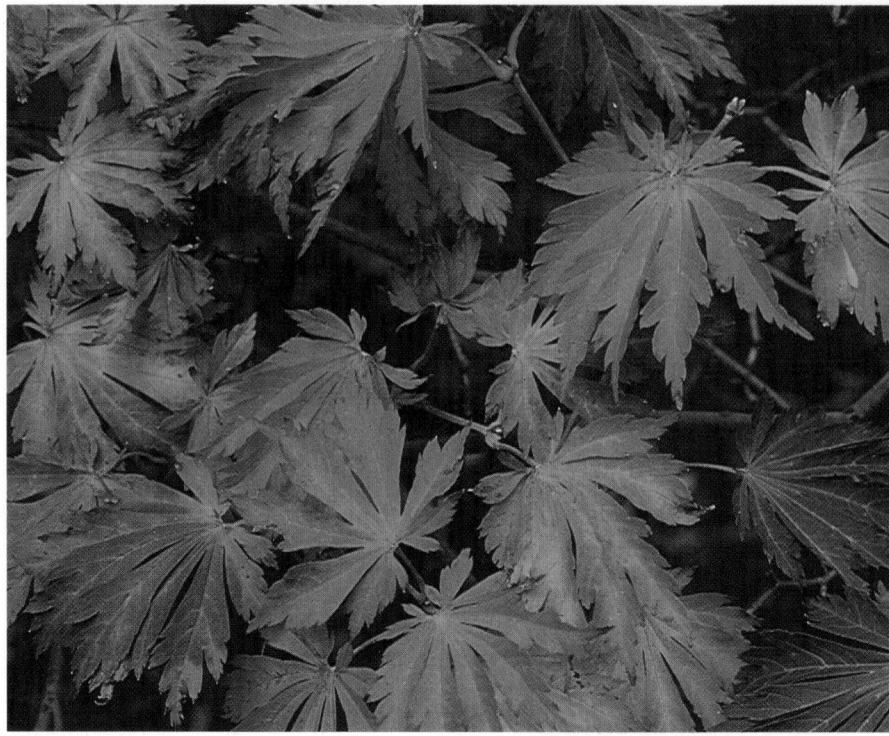

▲ *Acer japonicum* 'Aconitifolium'

rounded leaves, up to 18 cm (7 in) long, with pinkish red stems. In autumn, red, winged seed capsules hang among the reddish gold foliage. Although frost-hardy, this tree requires protection from harsh winds. HEIGHT & SPREAD 4×2 m (13×6½ ft) in 20 years, ultimately 10 m (33 ft) tall.

A. davidii 'Serpentine'♀ The richly coloured bark is purplish red, heavily striped with white on a large erect shrub. The oval leaves, 10 cm (4 in) long, are dark green. Although it is frost-hardy, it requires protection from harsh winds. HEIGHT & SPREAD 5×3 m (16×10 ft) in 20 years, ultimately 6 m (20 ft) tall.

A. griseum♀ (paper bark maple) One of the finest of all maples, this shapely tree has interest at every season and is tolerant of any soil. Its leaves, 10 cm (4 in) long and made up of 3 leaflets, colour a brilliant red in autumn and the cinnamon-coloured bark peels in tattered strips all year round revealing richer colouring beneath. It thrives best in a sheltered position with some shade from full sun. Native to China. HEIGHT & SPREAD 5×2 m (16×6½ ft) after 20 years, ultimately 12 m (40 ft) tall.

A. grosseri var. **hersii**♀ Long, arching branches form an upright tree with a rounded crown. Its smooth green bark has white stripes that are tinged green. The shallowly lobed leaves, 12.5 cm (5 in) long, are a rich orange in autumn. Native to China. HEIGHT & SPREAD 4×2 m (13×6½ ft) after 20 years, ultimately 10 m (33 ft) tall.

A. japonicum (full moon maple, Japanese maple) This slow-growing, multistemmed tree of rounded habit has leaves, 15-20 cm

▲ *Acer griseum*

(6-8 in) long with 7-9 lobes, which give brilliant crimson autumn colour. The winged seeds are red. Native to Japan. HEIGHT & SPREAD 5×3 m (16×10 ft) in 20 years, ultimately 15 m (50 ft) tall.

'Aconitifolium'♀ has deeply cut, soft green leaves which give a lovely feathered appearance and turn a brilliant scarlet suffused with tints of gold and orange in autumn. This tree reaches 3 m (10 ft) high, has a spreading habit and is often as broad as it is tall. 'Aureum' see *A. shirasawanum* 'Aureum'. 'Vitifolium'♀ the soft green, vine-shaped leaves, 5-25 cm (2-10 in) long,

▲ Acer palmatum 'Crimson Queen'

▲ Acer palmatum var. dissectum

Acer japonicum 'Vitifolium'

are flushed with yellow, crimson, gold and red in autumn. Often as broad as it is tall, this spreading tree reaches up to 12 m (40 ft) in height.

A. maximowiczianum (syn. *A. nikoense*) (Nikko maple) This pretty, slow-growing tree has a spreading habit and becomes rather flat-topped in old age. It is particularly lime-tolerant. The leaves, 10 cm (4 in) long, have 3 leaflets and turn rich reddish orange in late autumn. Native to Japan and China. HEIGHT & SPREAD 5×3 m (16×10 ft) after 20 years, ultimately 10 m (33 ft) tall.

A. micranthum ♀ Dainty leaves, up to 7 cm (2¾ in) long, have 5-7 lobes and turn bright reddish orange in autumn. The seed wings are an attractive red throughout summer. This small graceful tree of upright habit prefers a sheltered position. Native to Japan. HEIGHT & SPREAD 3×1 m (10×3 ft) after 20 years, ultimately 7 m (23 ft) tall.

A. negundo (box elder) This rounded spreading tree has pinnate leaves, 10 cm (4 in) long, with up to 9 leaflets and winged green seeds. Native to N America. HEIGHT & SPREAD 6×4 m (20×13 ft) after 20 years, ultimately 15 m (50 ft) tall.

The varieties are prized for their variegation and shoot colour. 'Flamingo' ♀ has 5-7 lobed leaflets edged with white to pink. These colours fade with age but regular pruning each winter produces new leaves. This upright tree reaches 6 m (20 ft). For best results it requires shelter from wind. The young shoots of var. *violaceum* ♀ are blackish purple. This upright tree reaches a height of 12 m (40 ft) and a spread of 9 m (30 ft). It does best in a spot where some shelter is provided.

A. nikoense see *A. maximowiczianum*

A. palmatum (Japanese maple) This rounded multistemmed tree has red and green winged seeds. The delicately formed leaves, 5-12 cm (2-4¾ in) long, have 5-7 lobes and are bright green when they emerge. Autumn colour can be dazzling although variable from plant to plant and

from year to year. Young specimens can be damaged by frosts. Native to E China, Japan and Korea. HEIGHT & SPREAD 4×3 m (13×10 ft) after 20 years, ultimately about 12 m (40 ft) tall.

The huge diversity of this species has allowed for more than 600 varieties to be developed. Their autumn colour is more reliable than that of the species. Most of them are less hardy than the species, and in greater need of shelter. 'Aureum' is a handsome, upright shrub with finely cut small leaves which emerge yellow with a touch of scarlet at the margins. They gradually show less scarlet as the season advances and finally turn golden yellow in autumn. It is fast-growing and reaches a height of 8 m (26 ft). 'Bloodgood' ♀ has foliage that is a very deep purple throughout the season. It is a narrow, upright tree that reaches 5 m (16 ft) in height. The seed capsules have decorative red wings in the autumn. 'Burgundy Lace' ♀ has deeply cut, purple serrated leaves, 8-10 cm (3¼-4 in) across. The colour can fade in dry conditions. This large, rounded shrub reaches a height of 5 m (16 ft). 'Butterfly' ♀ has grey-green leaves, 3-5 cm (1¼-2 in) long, irregularly lobed and with silvery white margins. The upright, densely branched shrub eventually grows to 3 m (10 ft), but so slowly that it is suitable for a small garden. 'Chitoseyama' ♀ is similar in height and slow growth but is spreading

in habit. Its deep purple, 7-lobed, serrated leaves gradually turn a lighter red before turning scarlet in autumn. It will grow to 3 m (10 ft). 'Crimson Queen' ♀ is an outstanding weeping shrub, often wider than it is high and only slowly reaching its ultimate 2 m (6½ ft). The finely cut leaves emerge deep purple, gradually turning reddish purple by the end of summer.

The cascading branches of var. *dissectum* ♀ form a large, spreading dome. Slow-growing, it reaches 4 m (13 ft) at most. The light green, deeply cut and lobed leaves give this shrub a delightful ferny appearance. In autumn its foliage can be brilliant red or yellow. Its cultivar, 'Dissectum Atropurpureum' has deeply cut leaves that are a rich purple, turning crimson in autumn.

'Inaba-shidare' ♀ has dark purple leaves and an open habit. It reaches only 2 m (6½ ft) in height. 'Linearilobum' ♀ gains a delicate look from its bright green, very narrowly lobed leaves. These colour to a warm yellow in autumn. This rounded

Acer palmatum 'Osakazuki'

shrub ultimately reaches 5 m (16 ft) in height. 'Osakazuki' ♀ forms a rounded tree with delicate 7-lobed leaves, up to 12 cm (4¾ in) long, that are a rich green during summer, turning to the most brilliant reds in autumn. It eventually reaches 8 m (26 ft) tall. 'Red Pygmy' ♀ makes a colourful, rounded mound that grows slowly to 2 m (6½ ft). Its narrow-lobed leaves emerge dark red, turning blue-green and eventually golden yellow in autumn. 'Sango-kaku' ♀ (syn. 'Senkaki') (coral bark maple) is a large upright shrub, eventually 7 m (23 ft) tall, whose young twigs of a brilliant coral-red retain their rich colour in winter. The leaves are a fresh green turning soft yellow in autumn and 3-7 cm (1½-2¾ in) long. 'Seiryû' ♀ grows into a wide rounded shrub, eventually 5 m (16 ft) tall, which is one of the very best for autumn colour. Its small delicate leaves are deeply dissected and

▼ Acer palmatum

▼ Acer palmatum 'Chitoseyama'

▼ Acer palmatum 'Sango-kaku'

turn many shades of red, yellow and orange in autumn.

A. pensylvanicum (snake bark maple)♀ White stripes mark the mature green bark while the young shoots are pink striped with white. This hardy tree is rounded with large 3-lobed leaves, up to 20 cm (8 in) long, that turn bright yellow in autumn. Native to eastern N America. HEIGHT & SPREAD 5×3 m (16×10 ft) after 20 years, ultimately 11 m (36 ft) tall.

'Erythrocladum'♀ has even better bark colour, more striking in winter when it is brilliant pinky red. It reaches a height of 5-6 m (16-20 ft).

A. platanoides♀ (Norway maple) This fast-growing, rounded tree tolerates chalky soil. Its shiny green leaves, 8-15 cm (3¼-6 in) long with 3-5 lobes, turn golden yellow in autumn. Bright, small green-yellow flowerheads 5-7.5 cm (2-3 in) across, appear before the leaves in spring. Native to Europe, the species is too tall for most gardens. HEIGHT & SPREAD 8×6 m (26×20 ft) after 20 years, ultimately 30 m (100 ft).

The cultivars are a more suitable size for the average garden. 'Crimson King'♀, which eventually reaches 15 m (50 ft), is one of the best purple-crimson leaved forms but lacks vivid autumn tints. It has pretty yellow flowers in spring. 'Drummondii'♀ reaches 10-12 m (30-40 ft) high and has small green

▲ *Acer platanoides* 'Drummondii'
Acer platanoides 'Schwedleri' ▲

leaves with white edges. 'Schwedleri'♀ is about 20 m (66 ft) tall when mature. The leaves are a lighter purple than 'Crimson King' and its autumn colour is brighter.

A. pseudoplatanus (Scottish maple, sycamore) These trees need to be planted at least 15 m (50 ft) from any building. The leaves are 10-15 cm (4-6 in) long, with 3-5 lobes. There are many plants bred from this native of central Europe that are more suit-

▼ *Acer pseudoplatanus* 'Brilliantissimum'

able with more colourful leaves. HEIGHT & SPREAD 9×6 m (30×20 ft) after 20 years, ultimately 30 m (100 ft).

'Brilliantissimum'♀ has leaves that are pinky yellow when they emerge and which are an outstanding feature in spring. Slow-growing, it rarely exceeds 3 m (10 ft) tall. 'Leopoldii'♀ is a similar size with leaves that emerge pinkish but quickly become green, mottled with white and yellow. The 5-lobed leaves of 'Worley'♀ are a golden yellow when young, becoming pale green in summer. This tree reaches up to 15 m (50 ft) in height.

A. rubrum (red maple) Eye-catching small red flowers appear on the bare branches in spring. The 5-lobed leaves, 10 cm (4 in) long, are silvery grey on the underside, turning a brilliant red-orange in autumn. This rounded, open large tree is native to the USA. HEIGHT & SPREAD 6×4 m (20×13 ft) after 20 years, ultimately 20 m (66 ft) tall.

'October Glory'♀ is smaller, more upright and less hardy, needing protection from strong winds. Autumn colour is a reliable brilliant crimson or dark orange-red. 'Scanlon'♀ has rich autumn colour and a very columnar form, growing to 15 m (50 ft) in height.

▲ *Acer rufinerve*

A. rufinerve (snake bark maple)♀ Distinctive white stripes mark the green bark of this small tree. The 3 or 5-lobed leaves, 12.5 cm (5 in) long, are dark green above, light green beneath, turning bright red-orange in autumn. The tree is upright with slightly ascending branches. Native to Japan. HEIGHT & SPREAD 5×3 m (16×10 ft) after 20 years, ultimately 10 m (33 ft) tall.

A. shirasawanum 'Aureum'♀ (syn. *A. japonicum* 'Aureum') This slow-growing, compact, rounded shrub is excellent for a small garden. It has 7 or 9-lobed, golden yellow leaves, up to 10 cm (4 in) long, often with reddish edges. Winged seeds are red and green. Best grown in partial shade as hot sun can scorch the leaves; this maple also needs a site protected from wind. HEIGHT & SPREAD 3×2 m (10×6½ ft) after 20 years, ultimately 5 m (16 ft) tall.

A. tataricum ssp. *ginnala*♀ (Amur maple) Small, dark green, 3-lobed leaves, 10 cm (4 in) long, turn scarlet in autumn. This rounded shrub becomes large but is slow-growing. HEIGHT & SPREAD 5×3 m (16×10 ft) after 20 years, eventually 10 m (33 ft).

CULTIVATION Plant in autumn or spring in any soil that is moisture retentive yet free-draining. Protect *A. palmatum* and other smaller species by providing shelter from strong winds and spring frosts; they also benefit from overhead shade.

PROPAGATION Maples can be raised from seed but the seedlings are then variable. Sow seed in late autumn in a coldframe. Some species, for example *A. griseum*, rarely produce viable seed and other species need cold stratification. Plants grown from seed are naturally variable so a grafted plant must be purchased if particular features are required. Most cultivars are grafted.

PRUNING None is required except to confine maples to a specific size, or to remove reverted branches on variegated plants.

PESTS AND DISEASES Generally free from pests, though squirrels can damage young trees. Maples are, on the whole, disease-free, but honey fungus is a problem in some areas, particularly if trees are already weakened by poor growing conditions.

Achillea
Milfoil, yarrow
Compositae

Achillea filipendulina 'Gold Plate'

Flowers in a wide range of colours make these hardy herbaceous and evergreen perennials a mainstay of a border for much of the summer and sometimes into autumn. The tiny blooms form flowerheads which are often closely massed into flat-topped clusters, although some are single. Upright leafy stems hold the flowers well above the foliage which, for all except *Achillea ptarmica* and *A. clavennae*, is soft and fern-like. Taller forms make good cut flowers and keep their colour well for dried display.

Smaller species, many with silvery foliage, are excellent rock-garden plants, adding colour at the height of summer when many alpines have finished flowering. These plants attract insects, especially bees and butterflies, into the garden. All are native to Europe and Asia.

RECOMMENDED SPECIES AND VARIETIES
A. ageratifolia♀ White daisy-like flowerheads, 2-3 cm (¾-1¼ in) across, are carried

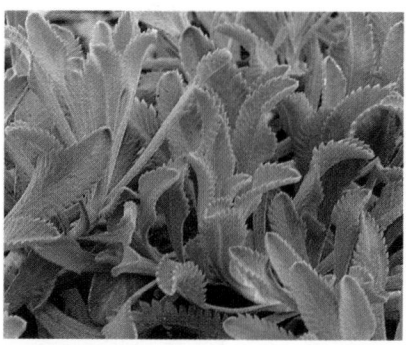

▲ Achillea ageratifolia

singly or in clusters. This evergreen forms whitish grey tufts of narrow, sometimes tapering, neatly toothed leaves, 4 cm (1½ in) long. HEIGHT & SPREAD 20×30 cm (8×12 in).

A. ageratum (sweet nancy) Numerous yellow flowerheads form flat clusters up to 12.5 cm (5 in) wide. The grey-green, oblong, toothed leaves are 5 cm (2 in) long. This is a woody-based plant. HEIGHT & SPREAD 80×60 cm (32×24 in).

'**W.B. Childs**' has white flowers with a yellowish brown, central disk.

A. argentea hort. see *A. clavennae*

A. chrysocoma Sunny yellow flowerheads, 1 cm (⅜ in) across, open in broad clusters. Bright green, narrow leaves, 8 cm (3¼ in) long, form moss-like, spreading mats. A tuft of leaves remains in winter. HEIGHT & SPREAD 30×40 cm (12×16 in).

A. clavennae (syn. *A. argentea* hort.) Daisy-like white flowers, 1.5 cm (½ in) across, are borne in loose clusters. The white, hairy, oval leaves are lobed and up to 8 cm (3¼ in)

▲ Achillea ageratum 'W.B. Childs'

▲ Achillea chrysocoma

long They form mats on prostrate stems. This species dislikes winter wet. HEIGHT & SPREAD 15×25 cm (6×10 in).

A. erba-rotta ssp. *rupestris* The clusters of white, daisy-like flowers are about 1.5 cm (½ in) across. Spatula-like, 3 cm (1¼ in) long leaves have toothed tips. Tufts of leaves remain during winter. HEIGHT & SPREAD 15×20 cm (6×8 in).

A. filipendulina (syn. *A. eupatorium*) Deep gold flowerheads form flat clusters, 12.5 cm (5 in) wide. Mid green leaves, 20 cm (8 in) long, grow in clumps. HEIGHT & SPREAD 1.5×1 m (5×3 ft).

'**Cloth of Gold**' grows to 1 m (3 ft) tall, 60 cm (2 ft) wide, with flowerheads 15 cm (6 in) across. '**Gold Plate**'♀ is a vigorous form, 1.2 m (4 ft) tall and 60 cm (2 ft) wide.

A. grandifolia Creamy white flowers in heads, 6-10 cm (2½-4 in) wide, last into early autumn. Oval greyish leaves up to 12.5 cm (5 in) long form an evergreen clump. HEIGHT & SPREAD 1 m×60 cm (3×2 ft).

A. × *kolbiana* White flowers, about 1.5 cm (½ in) across, form small, lax pompoms or can be solitary. Lobed, mostly basal, 6 cm (2½ in) long, whitish leaves, are narrow, oblong and hairy. A clump-forming hybrid. HEIGHT & SPREAD 25×25 cm (10×10 in).

A. × *lewisii* '**King Edward**'♀ Pale buff yellow flowers appear in clusters, 5 cm (2 in) wide. Softly hairy, grey-green leaves, up to 5 cm (2 in) long, form compact mats. HEIGHT & SPREAD 10×30 cm (4×12 in).

A. millefolium White or pink flowers last into early autumn, borne in dense flat heads up to 12.5 cm (5 in) wide. Green or greyish leaves, each up to 20 cm (8 in) long, form a wide mat. This common weed in lawns is the parent of many colourful varieties and hybrids. HEIGHT & SPREAD 60×60 cm (2×2 ft).

'**Cerise Queen**' is taller, to 1 m (3 ft), and has cerise or light crimson flowers with white centres. '**Lilac Beauty**' (syn. 'Lavender Beauty') has light lilac-mauve flowers with creamy white centres. '**Paprika**' has a mix of orange-red and yellow flowers. '**Sammetriese**' reaches 75 cm (2½ ft) tall and has bright crimson flowerheads. 'Paprika' has greyish green leaves; the other 3 have dark green foliage.

A. ptarmica (sneezewort) Flowers with short white petals and yellowish centres form lax clusters. The upright stems bear narrow,

▲ Achillea 'Huteri'

▲ Achillea tomentosa

dark green leaves, up to 8 cm (3¼ in) long. HEIGHT & SPREAD 75×60 cm (2½×2 ft).

'**Perry's White**' has pure white, rosette-like double flowers. **The Pearl Group** have many button-like flowerheads.

A. tomentosa♀ Numerous yellow flowerheads open in dense, 7.5 cm (3 in) wide clusters. Narrow, greyish or silvery 8 cm (3¼ in) long leaves, form hairy clumps. HEIGHT & SPREAD 30×40 cm (12×16 in).

'**Aurea**' (syn. 'Maynard's Gold') has bright yellow flowerheads.

OTHER HYBRIDS

There are many hybrid varieties available. Unless otherwise stated, they have a height of 60-75 cm (2-2½ ft) and a spread of 45-60 cm (1½-2 ft). Flowerheads are borne in clusters up to 12.5 cm (5 in) across.

'**Apfelblüte**' ('Appleblossom') has light pink flowers and mid green foliage. '**Coronation Gold**'♀ has rich golden flowerheads and grey-green leaves. A basal leaf rosette remains in winter. It reaches a height of 1 m (3 ft). The vigorous '**Fanal**' (syn. 'The Beacon') has darker leaves and rich red flowers. '**Hoffnung**' (syn. 'Great Expectations') bears unusual light yellow flowers and greyish green foliage. '**Huteri**' has white flowers and deep green oblong leaves in tufts that persist through winter. This plant has a height and spread of 30 cm (1 ft). '**Lachsschönheit**' ('Salmon Beauty') has salmon-pink blooms and greyish green leaves. '**Moonshine**'♀ has bright, light yellow flowerheads and grey-green leaves. **Summer Pastels Group** have cream, crimson, light buff yellow, pale purple, pink, salmon and white flowers. '**Taygetea**' has pale yellow blooms and grey-green leaves.

CULTIVATION Plant in early spring in well-drained soil in full sun, although *A. ptarmica* prefers damper conditions. Lift and divide every 3 years, after flowering or in early spring. Support taller types. Low-growing species, those less than 30 cm (1 ft) tall, will thrive in rock-garden pockets in gritty, preferably alkaline, soil. Protect these species from excessive winter wet.

PROPAGATION Sow seed under glass in late winter or early spring. Alternatively, divide in early spring.

PESTS AND DISEASES *A. ptarmica* is liable to powdery mildew in a dry situation.

Achimenes
Gesneriaceae

Achimenes longiflora

The trumpet-like flowers of these tropical houseplants provide a continuous display in summer and well into autumn. With their upright to trailing, wiry stems, they are ideal for hanging containers and, with some support, they can also grow into bushy plants in conventional pots. They die back during winter, coming back to life in late spring.

RECOMMENDED SPECIES AND VARIETIES

A. longiflora Abundant deep purple to mauve flowers appear from early summer to mid autumn. Each flower is up to 5 cm (2 in) long. The dark green, rather downy, oval leaves are reddish underneath and up to 5 cm (2 in) long. HEIGHT & SPREAD 25×45 cm (10×18 in).

'Alba' has white flowers spotted with yellow and faintly lined with purple. The white flowers of 'Ambroise Verschaffelt' are heavily marked with purple. 'Paul Arnold' has leaves strongly tinged with purple and dark purple flowers with a white throat and red dots.

OTHER HYBRIDS

There are many cultivated varieties available. The flowers are about 5 cm (2 in) long, the leaves are up to 7.5 cm (3 in) long and, unless otherwise stated, mid green. They reach 30-60 cm (1-2 ft) in height and spread.

'Admiration' has blue flowers and dark green foliage. 'Cattleya' has light blue blooms. The flowers of 'Charm' are coral-pink with a velvety crimson sheen. 'Little Beauty' has deep pink flowers with a yellow eye. 'Old Rose Pink' has deep pink blooms. 'Peach Blossom' has soft peach-pink flowers. 'Purple King' has deep purple flowers and dark green leaves with a purplish tinge. 'Vivid' has crimson blooms.

▼ *Achimenes* 'Old Rose Pink'

Achimenes longiflora 'Ambroise Verschaffelt' ▲

CULTIVATION Plant rhizomes in spring in a peaty, soil-less compost in hanging baskets or pots; plants grown in an upright pot will need some staking. Grow in a well-lit place out of direct sun and keep at a minimum of 10°C (50°F). Water freely throughout the growing period, administering a liquid houseplant feed every 2-3 weeks once flower buds appear. When flowering has finished, stop watering and allow the plants to die back naturally. The rhizomes can remain in the compost until the spring or be removed and stored in a tray of peat kept in cool but frost-free conditions.

PROPAGATION Divide rhizomes in winter when dormant. Seed for mixed hybrids is often offered that will not come true to any named variety; this can be sown in spring.

PESTS AND DISEASES Greenfly can be a problem on achimenes.

Acidanthera see *Gladiolus*
Acinos see *Clinopodium*
Aconite, winter see *Eranthis*

Aconitum
Monkshood, wolf's bane
Ranunculaceae

Aconitum 'Bressingham spire'

In late summer and autumn the typically blue or purple pyramids of aconitum flowers are a welcome foil to the predominant golds and russets of the border – but the genus does offer a few yellow, white or salmon-pink variants. The hooded flowers are up to 4 cm (1½ in) long and generally in loose spires up to 15 cm (6 in) long. Aconitums are hardy herbaceous perennials that generally form neat clumps about 50 cm (20 in) across and up to 1.2 m (4 ft) high. The stiff stalks are mostly self-supporting, but taller, branching varieties may need to be staked in exposed situations. The dark green, deeply divided, palmate leaves emerge in early spring and are beautiful throughout the growing season. Aconitums provide long-lasting flowers for indoor arrangements. Found throughout the Northern Hemisphere in lightly wooded mountain areas or alpine meadows, the plants are generally tuberous rooted so they tend to be drought resistant but prefer the moister parts of the garden and grow well in partial shade. *Aconitum lycoctonum* is fibrous rooted. All species and all parts of the plant are very poisonous, especially the root.

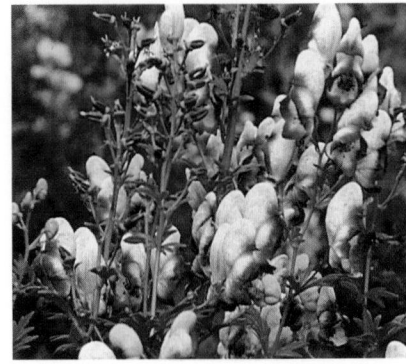

▲ *Aconitum* × *cammarum* 'Bicolor'

RECOMMENDED SPECIES AND VARIETIES

A. × *cammarum* 'Bicolor'♀ Wide-branching stems bear spikes of violet-blue and white flowers arching forward from the stem in mid to late summer. The leaves are a glossy dark green. HEIGHT & SPREAD 1.2 m×50 cm (4 ft×20 in).

A. carmichaelii (syn. *A. fischeri* hort.) Stout flower stalks bear violet-blue flowers in profusion during late summer and early autumn. This species is native to central and W China and N America. HEIGHT & SPREAD 1.5 m×50 cm (5 ft×20 in).

'Arendsii' has very deep blue flowers. The larger, violet-blue flowers of 'Barker's Variety' and the rich lavender-blue flowers of 'Kelmscott'♀ appear in late summer and early autumn on stems up to 1.8 m (6 ft) tall.

A. cilicicum see *Eranthis hyemalis* Cilicica Group

A. fischeri hort. see *A. carmichaelii*

A. hemsleyanum This trailing plant has dark purple-blue to indigo flowers carried in loose racemes from mid to late summer. Plant it where it can scramble over shrubs rather than in a herbaceous border. The dark green leaves are paler on the undersides. Native to central and W China. HEIGHT & SPREAD 2×1 m (6½×3 ft).

A. hyemalis see *Eranthis hyemalis*

A. lycoctonum ssp. *vulparia* (syn. *A. vulparia*) These rather slender, upright plants need staking when the sparse yellowish green flowers appear in late summer above deeply incised leaves. It grows best in shady sites which do not dry out and flourishes at

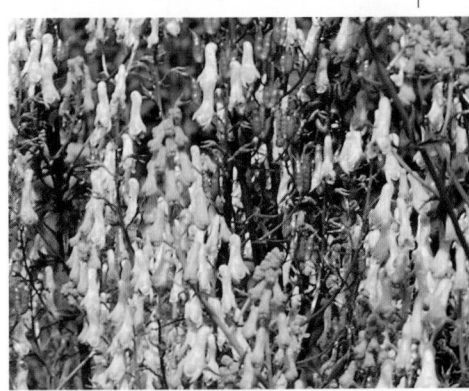

▲ *Aconitum lycoctonum* ssp. *vulparia*

▲ *Aconitum napellus*

the edges of ponds. Native to Europe. HEIGHT & SPREAD 1.5 m×30 cm (5×1 ft).

A. napellus (helmet flower, friar's cap) Deep pinkish violet flowers are borne from early to mid summer and if the spikes are cut back as soon as the flowers fade it is possible to obtain an autumn display. The glossy leaves are deeply divided. This perennial is a British native but is found also throughout Asia and Europe. HEIGHT & SPREAD 1.2 m×30 cm (4×1 ft).

The flowers of ssp. *vulgare* 'Albidum' are white. The blooms of ssp. *v.* 'Carneum' are soft salmon-pink. It does best in northern gardens where the sun does not bleach colour from its flowers.

OTHER HYBRIDS

There are a variety of garden hybrids available, mostly derived from *A. napellus*.

From mid to late summer 'Blue Sceptre' has deep violet-blue flowers with some white on the hoods. It reaches a height of 50 cm (20 in) and a spread of 15 cm (6 in). 'Bressingham Spire'♀ is a slender plant with violet-blue hooded flowers, that reaches 1 m (3 ft) in height and 40 cm (16 in) in spread. 'Ivorine' has pale yellow flowers from late spring onwards on strong stems which form neat bushy clumps, 50 cm (20 in) tall and 30 cm (12 in) wide. 'Newry Blue' has deep blue flowers on upright stems from early to mid summer. It reaches a height of 1 m (3 ft) and a spread of 38 cm (15 in). 'Spark's Variety'♀ has the darkest violet-blue flowers on open branching heads set against paler green leaves. It

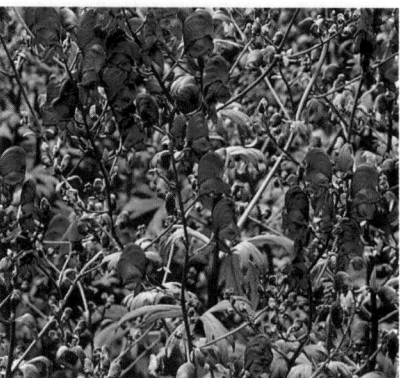

▲ *Aconitum* 'Spark's Variety'

reaches a height of 1.5 m (5 ft) and a spread of 45 cm (1½ ft).

CULTIVATION Plant in rich, cool, moisture-retentive soil, particularly in warmer southern gardens where it prefers semi-shade with a mulch in spring to keep the soil moist. Cut plants down in autumn.

PROPAGATION Divide roots between autumn and spring; take care when handling the poisonous root. Sow seed in early or mid spring.

PESTS AND DISEASES Usually trouble free.

Acorus
Araceae

The decorative foliage of these hardy marginal aquatics makes them striking plants for the edge of a pond or in a bog garden. In autumn, the leaves rarely die back completely, providing welcome interest throughout all but the most severe of winters. Freely growing, rhizomatous perennials, they do not become invasive like many reeds and rushes can. Plants occasionally produce small flower spikes – greenish, horn-like structures, about 5 cm (2 in) long – borne on the leaf blades during summer.

RECOMMENDED SPECIES AND VARIETIES

A. calamus (sweet flag) The bright green sword-like leaves are glossy and prominently ridged. Emitting a rich tangerine fragrance when bruised, the leaves were originally cultivated for strewing across floors. If grown in baskets, plants will achieve only about half the size of unrestricted plants. HEIGHT & SPREAD 1.5 m×60 cm (5×2 ft).

'Variegatus' has cream and green variegated leaves. In early spring, the emerging shoots are heavily flushed with rose-pink which fades slowly as the foliage ages. The plants are no more than 1 m (3 ft) tall.

A. gramineus The narrowly tapering, grass-like leaves are a glossy dark green and mildly fragrant. This species is often planted in miniature water gardens or sink gardens. HEIGHT & SPREAD 30×30 cm (1×1 ft).

'Ogon' has bright greenish yellow

▼ *Acorus gramineus* 'Variegatus'

leaves variegated with cream. 'Pusillus' is a compact green-leaved plant, no more than 8 cm (3¼ in) high. 'Variegatus' has mid green foliage striped creamy yellow.

CULTIVATION Plant in wet soil, directly in the pond or in aquatic planting baskets, choosing a position in full sun or partial shade. *A. calamus* and its cultivar will grow in up to 15 cm (6 in) of water while *A. gramineus* and its cultivars prefer no more than 5 cm (2 in).

PROPAGATION Raise new plants by dividing the rhizomes during spring.

PESTS AND DISEASES Usually trouble free.

Actaea
Baneberry
Ranunculaceae

These are hardy, clump-forming perennials grown for their attractive berries, which are highly poisonous. The berries of *Actaea spicata*, which is often found growing wild in northern Britain, are particularly toxic. The divided and toothed foliage reaches up to 80 cm (32 in) in length and is made up of two to three leaflets, 2.5–10 cm (1–4 in) long. Stems reaching 60 cm–1 m (2–3 ft) are crowned with small, feathery flowers held on flower spikes in summer followed by colourful pea-sized berries throughout the autumn. The plants do well in woodland conditions and may also be grown in borders or beside a pool or stream.

RECOMMENDED SPECIES AND VARIETIES

A. alba♀ (syn. *A. pachypoda*) (doll's eyes, white baneberry) Elegant green foliage accompanies spikes of white, fluffy flowers in early summer. White berries, carried on fleshy red stalks, appear in late summer. Native to eastern N America. HEIGHT & SPREAD 1 m×45 cm (3×1½ ft).

▼ *Actaea alba*

A. erythrocarpa (syn. *A. spicata* var. *rubra*) Creamy white flowers are framed by finely divided leaves. The deep red berries appear in late summer. Native to NE Europe, Siberia and Japan. HEIGHT & SPREAD 75×45 cm (2½×1½ft).

A. pachypoda see *A. alba*

A. rubra♀ (red baneberry) The whitish flowers of this popular species are held above oval, divided, bright green leaves in summer. Shiny red berries follow in early autumn. Native to western N America. HEIGHT & SPREAD 45×30 cm (1½×1 ft).

A. spicata (herb Christopher) White flowers are followed by large black berries in late summer. The deeply toothed oval leaves are mid green. Native to Europe and W Asia. HEIGHT & SPREAD 45×45 cm (1½×1½ ft).

A. spicata var. *rubra* see *A. erythrocarpa*

CULTIVATION Plant in moist soil, well enriched with organic matter, in autumn or spring, preferably in partial shade.

PROPAGATION Lift and divide rhizomes in spring. Sow fresh seed in autumn in a coldframe or greenhouse.

PESTS AND DISEASES Usually trouble free.

Actinidia
Actinidiaceae

Actinidia kolomikta

Admired for their flowers, foliage and fruit, these hardy, deciduous, twining climbers are ideal for clothing walls and pergolas, while the taller varieties can ramble through trees. The fragrant, cup-shaped flowers are usually white and are carried in clusters along the branches among the toothed leaves. Apart from *Actinidia arguta*, the species below carry male and female flowers on separate plants – so to ensure an autumn crop of the gooseberry-like, edible fruit, both sexes must be grown in proximity. For more reliable fruiting, grow in a cool greenhouse. Native to E Asia.

RECOMMENDED SPECIES AND VARIETIES

A. arguta 'Issai' White flowers, 2 cm (¾ in) across, with a pale green tint appear from early to mid summer. The bright, lustrous green, bristly leaves are broadly egg shaped and up to 12.5 cm (5 in) long. The greenish yellow, oblong fruits are edible but insipid. HEIGHT & SPREAD 6×3 m (20×10 ft) after 5 years, ultimately 15 m (50 ft) tall.

A. deliciosa (Chinese gooseberry, kiwi fruit) Creamy white flowers, 4 cm (1½ in) across, are borne from mid to late summer. The heart-shaped leaves, up to 20 cm (8 in) long, are covered with shaggy reddish hairs.

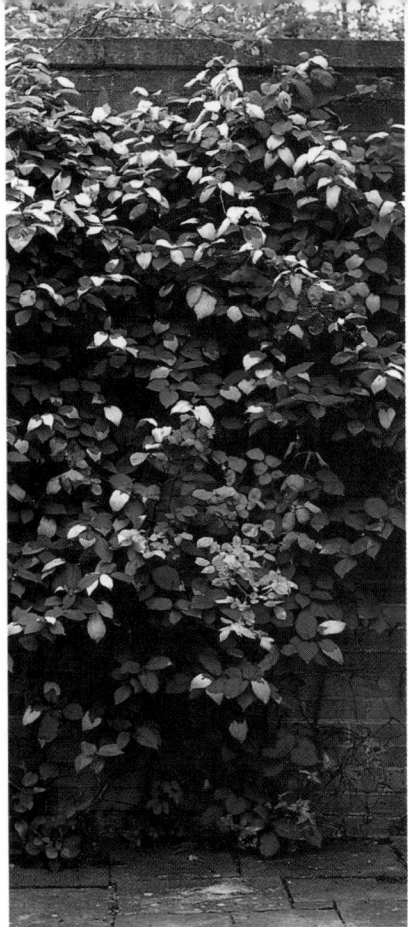

▲ *Actinidia kolomikta*

To encourage flowering and fruiting, pinch young shoots back to about 30 cm (1 ft) in summer. Further shorten the long spurs in winter. After harvesting, allow the fruit to develop in flavour for a month before using. HEIGHT & SPREAD 3×3 m (10×10 ft) after 5 years, ultimately 10 m (33 ft) tall.

'Hayward', a female clone, is one of the most reliable varieties for British gardens. 'Tomuri' is the male counterpart.

A. kolomikta♀ Large, heart-shaped leaves, up to 15 cm (6 in) long, are green at first, then the upper sections of the leaves assume cream and pink variegations. The colour will not show on young plants nor on old plants grown in too much shade. Small white flowers, 1.5 cm (½ in) across, are borne in summer. The small, yellowish fruits are inconspicuous. HEIGHT & SPREAD 2.4×1.5 m (8×5 ft) after 5 years, ultimately 5 m (16 ft) tall.

CULTIVATION Plant in rich loam; avoid badly drained and chalky soils. Plant from mid autumn to early spring in a sunny or partially shaded site. The plants may require some initial training.

PROPAGATION Take semi-ripe cuttings in summer or sow seed of species in autumn.

PRUNING If space is restricted, thin out and cut back growth in late winter.

PESTS AND DISEASES Cats are attracted to some species, particularly *A. kolomikta*, and may damage the stems, occasionally killing the plants. Otherwise trouble free.

Adam's needle see *Yucca filamentosa*

Adenophora
Gland bellflower
Campanulaceae

Tall, slender spikes of blue or violet bell-shaped flowers hanging prettily on tiny stalks, lend a delicate beauty to a mixed herbaceous border in summer. Native to Europe and Asia, these herbaceous perennials are reliably hardy.

RECOMMENDED SPECIES

A. aurita Mauve-blue flowers, up to 4 cm (1½ in) long, are produced in spikes in mid or late summer. The coarse, silvery grey, leaves are up to 10 cm (4 in) long. HEIGHT & SPREAD 1 m×45 cm (3×1½ ft).

A. bulleyana Pale blue pendent blooms, up to 1 cm (⅜ in) long, are produced in branching clusters in late summer. The oval, downy green leaves are up to 7.5 cm (3 in) long. HEIGHT & SPREAD 1.2 m×60 cm (4×2 ft).

A. liliifolia Loose, spreading heads of fragrant blue or whitish blue flowers, each up to 2.5 cm (1 in) long, appear in late summer. The mid green leaves are rounded and tapering and up to 7.5 cm (3 in) long. HEIGHT & SPREAD 45×30 cm (1½×1 ft).

A. nikoensis Off-white flowers tinged with

▲ *Adenophora bulleyana*

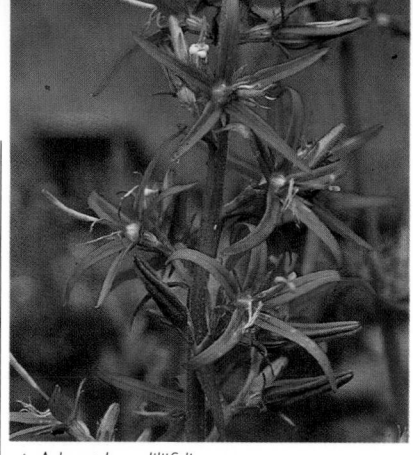

▲ *Adenophora liliifolia*

blue and up to 2.5 cm (1 in) long are borne from mid to late summer. The mid green leaves are up to 10 cm (4 in) long. HEIGHT & SPREAD 45×45 cm (1½×1½ ft).

A. pereskiifolia Mid blue flowers, each 2.5 cm (1 in) long, appear in mid summer. The mid green, oval, toothed leaves, up to 15 cm (6 in) long, are arranged in whorls. HEIGHT & SPREAD 45×30 cm (1½×1 ft).

A. potaninii Bluish lavender flowers, each 2.5 cm (1 in) long, appear in arching sprays in late summer on this rosette-forming, woody-based plant. The mid green, oval or lance-shaped leaves are up to 10 cm (4 in) long. HEIGHT & SPREAD 45×60 cm (1½×2 ft).

A. tashiroi Sparse, pendent, violet blooms are produced on slender stems in late summer. The oval or lance-shaped mid green leaves are up to 7.5 cm (3 in) long. HEIGHT & SPREAD 45×45 cm (1½×1½ ft).

CULTIVATION Plant in moist but free-draining soil in full sun. Do not disturb established plants unnecessarily.

PROPAGATION Sow seed in spring or autumn, or take basal cuttings in spring.

PESTS AND DISEASES Froghoppers and downy mildew can damage plants.

Adiantum see FERNS p.262

Adonis
Pheasant's eye
Ranunculaceae

From late winter to early spring the brightly coloured flowers of hardy herbaceous perennials will enliven any rock garden or border front. The shiny, bowl-shaped flowers are composed of more petals and when

▼ *Adonis amurensis* 'Flore Pleno'

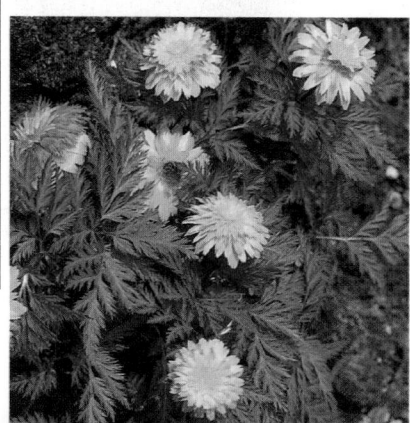

fully open they are similar to daisies. The finely cut leaves are up to 10 cm (4 in) long.

RECOMMENDED SPECIES AND VARIETIES

A. amurensis Golden yellow flowers, up to 4 cm (1½ in) across, appear above ruffs of feathery foliage in late winter and early spring. Native to China and Japan. HEIGHT & SPREAD 30×23 cm (12×9 in).

'Flore Pleno', with double flowers, is more commonly grown than the species. 'Fukujukai' has large, semidouble flowers.

CULTIVATION Plant in moist but well-drained soil. The plants are dormant in late summer and planting should be carried out between high summer and mid autumn. Grow in a sunny or partially shaded spot.

PROPAGATION Sow fresh seed in late summer in trays in a coldframe or unheated greenhouse, although germination may be slow. Alternatively, divide clumps of established plants in early autumn but do not allow the roots to dry out.

PESTS AND DISEASES The flower buds are particularly attractive to slugs.

Aechmea
Bromeliaceae

Bold foliage and showy flowers make these tropical evergreen perennials popular plants for the greenhouse or in the home. All have leaves that are sheathed at the base to form distinctive vase-shaped rosettes out of which rise striking, heavily bracted flower spikes which persist for several weeks. Native to S America.

RECOMMENDED SPECIES AND VARIETIES

A. chantinii♀ At the end of a 25 cm (10 in) stem, the bracted flower spike is crowded with red and white or pale blue tubular flowers. The dull green, toothed leaves are

strap-shaped, up to 30 cm (1 ft) long and 5 cm (2 in) wide with 'blurred' greyish white stripes beneath. HEIGHT & SPREAD 30×30 cm (1×1 ft).

A. fasciata♀ (silver vase plant, urn plant) Dense, conical rose-pink and purple flowerheads are produced at almost any time of the year from the centre of the 'vase' of leaves. The grey-green leaves are up to 45 cm (1½ ft) long and 7.5 cm (3 in) wide. HEIGHT & SPREAD 45×60 cm (1½×2 ft).

A. Foster's Favorite Group♀ (lacquered wine cup) Drooping spikes of 1 cm (⅜ in) long deep blue tubular flowers are produced from among the foliage throughout the summer. These are followed by tear-shaped red fruits up to 1 cm (⅜ in) long. The wine red leaves are strap-shaped, up to 30 cm (1 ft) long and 4 cm (1½ in) wide. HEIGHT & SPREAD 30×60 cm (1½×2 ft).

A. fulgens var. *discolor*♀ During summer a stout flower stem emerges, densely clothed with tiny tubular violet blooms which turn red with age. These flowers are scarcely 1 cm (⅜ in) long, up to 50 being clustered together in a terminal spike. The glossy purple-green leaves are up to 45 cm (1½ ft) long and 5 cm (2 in) wide. HEIGHT & SPREAD 45×60 cm (1½×2 ft).

CULTIVATION Grow at a minimum temperature of 10°C (50°F) in plenty of light, but not in full sun. Plant in containers in a mixture of peat or coir, leaf mould and gritty sand and feed every 3 weeks from late spring to late summer. Water freely into the centre of the vase-shaped rosettes using soft, tepid water whenever possible. The plants benefit from occasional misting. Remove old flower spikes.

PROPAGATION Remove and plant off-sets during spring and early summer.

PESTS AND DISEASES Usually trouble free.

▲ *Aechmea fasciata*

Aechmea fulgens var. *discolor* ▲

Aegopodium
Ground elder
Umbelliferae

Of these invasive hardy perennials only *Aegopodium podagraria* 'Variegatum' is commonly cultivated for dense low ground cover in areas where little else will grow.

RECOMMENDED VARIETY

A. podagraria **'Variegatum'** This vigorous, spreading plant makes decorative ground cover for moist, shady or partially shady sites where it can be kept in control. The lobed leaves, up to 10 cm (4 in) across, are edged and splashed a pale creamy white. White flowers are carried in clusters in early summer. Native to Europe. HEIGHT & SPREAD 15×50 cm (6×20 in) after a year.

▲ *Aegopodium podagraria* 'Variegatum'

CULTIVATION Grow in any moist soil in a shaded position. Dig up and discard any portions that revert to full green leaves.

PROPAGATION Divide the rhizomes in autumn or spring.

PESTS AND DISEASES Usually trouble free.

Aeonium
Crassulaceae

The fleshy leaves of these tender succulents are gathered in neat, symmetrical rosettes. Clusters of tiny star-shaped flowers appear early in the season. Mostly evergreen perennials, these plants are usually grown in a frost-free greenhouse or conservatory. However, in summer they can be planted outdoors as bedding or in containers placed in a warm sunny position, as long as they have gritty free-draining soil or compost.

RECOMMENDED SPECIES AND VARIETIES

A. arboreum♀ At the end of the branching stems of this succulent are leaf rosettes, each up to 15 cm (6 in) across. These are made up of narrow, glossy green leaves, up to 7.5 cm (3 in) long. Tiny yellow flowers, less than 1 cm (⅜ in) across, are produced in a dense oval flowerhead during spring and early summer. They are borne on stems that grow out of the older rosettes which then die back after flowering. HEIGHT & SPREAD 60 cm×1 m (2×3 ft) or more.

▲ *Aeonium arboreum* 'Atropurpureum'

'Atropurpureum'♀ has foliage that is strongly flushed with dark purple-red and maroon. The leaves of **'Schwarzkopf'** are dark maroon and emerald green at the base. Both produce pyramidal clusters of yellow flowers during spring.

A. haworthii♀ (pinwheel) Neat green to blue-green leaf rosettes, up to 10 cm (4 in) across, are borne at the ends of the stems of this bushy plant. The leaves are roughly oval, up to 5 cm (2 in) long, and often have distinctive reddish edges. Spikes of small pale yellow flowers tinged with pink are produced during spring and early summer on stems that rise out of the leaf rosettes. HEIGHT & SPREAD 60×60 cm (2×2 ft).

A. tabuliforme♀ The flat, green leaf rosettes of this succulent hug the ground. The broadly triangular leaves are up to 10 cm (4 in) long. Tiny, pale yellow flowers are produced in loose spikes up to 30 cm (1 ft) tall that emerge from the centre of the leaf rosettes. After flowering, the main rosettes die. HEIGHT & SPREAD 30×45 cm (1×1½ ft).

CULTIVATION Outdoors, plant in an open position in full sun, in very well-drained soil, when all danger of frost has passed. Indoors, plant in pots of gritty compost and grow in a frost-free greenhouse. Feed sparingly during early autumn and early spring with a weak liquid houseplant feed.

PROPAGATION Sow seed under glass during summer. Raise shrubby species by taking cuttings of stems with small rosettes on them in late spring or early summer.

PESTS AND DISEASES Usually trouble free.

Aeschynanthus
Gesneriaceae

Brightly coloured flowers smother these tender, long-stemmed trailing plants throughout the summer and often well into autumn. Individual flowers last for two or three days. Plants of this genus are evergreen perennials that are usually grown in a greenhouse or conservatory, planted in hanging pots to make the most of their tumbling fleshy foliage and hooded, tubular, generally fragrant flowers. They can also be grown as houseplants. All prosper in any well-drained proprietary potting compost.

RECOMMENDED SPECIES AND VARIETIES

A. lobbianus (lipstick plant) (syn. *A. radicans* var. *lobbianus*) Bright red and purple flowers, up to 5 cm (2 in) long, are held in clusters at the ends of the stems. The grey-green fleshy leaves, up to 7 cm (2¾ in) long, are flushed with purple and carried densely on purple stems. If allowed to trail, the stems can reach up to 1 m (3 ft) in length. HEIGHT & SPREAD 15×30 cm (6×12 in).

A. longicaulis♀ (syn. *A. marmoratus*) Orange-red flowers, up to 2 cm (¾ in) long, are held singly in leaf axils and in small clusters at the ends of the stems. Each narrow, pointed, fleshy leaf is up to 7 cm (2¾ in) long. Trailing stems can reach 1 m (3 ft) long. HEIGHT & SPREAD 15×30 cm (6×12 in).

▲ *Aeschynanthus speciosus*

A. speciosus♀ Orange-red flowers, up to 10 cm (4 in) long, are produced in upright clusters at the ends of the stems. The glossy leaves are narrowly oval and about 15 cm (6 in) long. Stems can trail up to 1 m (3 ft) long. HEIGHT & SPREAD 30×60 cm (1×2 ft).

CULTIVATION Plant in pots or hanging baskets in any well-drained proprietary potting compost. Line hanging baskets with traditional sphagnum moss. Keep plants in a greenhouse, conservatory or indoors, choosing a position shaded from full sun. Provide a minimum night-time temperature of 18°C (64°F). Water copiously during summer and feed regularly. Remove faded flowers or yellowing leaves.

PROPAGATION Take tip cuttings from non-flowering shoots in late spring and summer.

PESTS AND DISEASES Usually trouble free.

Aesculus
Horse chestnut, buckeye
Hippocastanaceae

Aesculus indica

Flowering deciduous trees and shrubs with spreading branches and colourful foliage, horse chestnuts grow vigorously and become quickly established, with strong, wide-spreading roots. Some species, such as

Aesculus hippocastanum (common horse chestnut), are far too big for most gardens and are best planted in parks and open spaces. There are smaller trees and shrubs to choose from within the genus, although they are really only suited to large gardens. Lifespan varies from 50-60 years for the more shrubby types to several hundred years for the larger trees.

Trees are generally hardy and mostly have rough flaky bark and thick, sweeping branches. Most have large, and often sticky, leaf buds. The palmate leaves, arranged in opposite pairs, are composed of 5-11 large toothed leaflets up to 25cm (10in) long. The prominent flowers are borne on large, erect, narrowly conical panicles, known as candles, and vary from 15-40cm (6-16in) tall. The fruit ripens in autumn; a leathery capsule that can be smooth, knobbly or spiny and contains up to three large, shiny brown seeds, called conkers, 2-6cm (¾-2½in) wide. The conkers, leaves, flowers and bark of all species are poisonous to humans and to animals. Trees in this genus are native to SE Europe, the Himalayas, E Asia and N America.

RECOMMENDED SPECIES AND VARIETIES

A. × *carnea* 'Briotii'♀ Red flower candles appear in great profusion in late spring and are followed by knobbly round fruit. The dark green leaves turn golden in autumn. HEIGHT & SPREAD 10×6m (33×20ft) after 20 years, ultimately 25m (80ft) tall.

A. indica♀ (Indian horse chestnut) The yellow-green leaves are tinged with bronze or chocolate when they emerge in spring. In autumn, they turn pale yellow to orange. White or pink-flushed flower candles, 30-40cm (12-16in) long, appear in mid summer. The knobbly, pear-shaped fruit contains shiny, almost black conkers. HEIGHT & SPREAD 7×5m (23×16ft) after 20 years, ultimately 20m (66ft) tall.

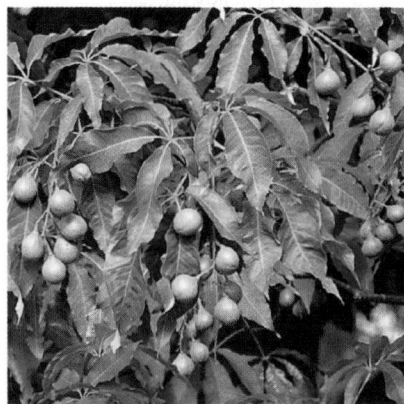

⚘ *Aesculus indica*

'Sydney Pearce'♀ is very free-flowering with even denser flower candles.

A. × *neglecta* 'Erythroblastos'♀ Bright pink as they emerge, the leaves become lighter pink and then pale yellow. They then turn green in early summer followed

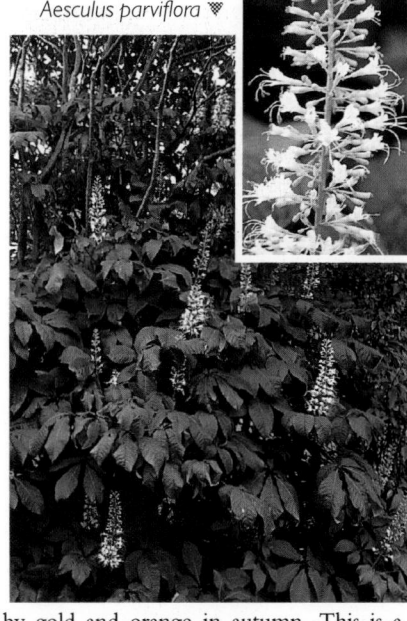

Aesculus parviflora ❦

by gold and orange in autumn. This is a slow-growing tree which rarely flowers – when it does the flowers are yellowish tinged pink – and so rarely produces fruit. HEIGHT & SPREAD 6×4m (20×13ft) after 20 years, ultimately 15m (50ft) tall.

A. parviflora♀ A very free-flowering, vigorous, open shrub that spreads via suckers. Bronzed at first, the mid green leaves often turn a glowing yellow in autumn. White flowers are borne in mid to late summer on candles, 30cm (12in) long, and are followed by smooth, pear-shaped fruit. HEIGHT & SPREAD 2×3m (6½×10ft) after 10 years, ultimately 4m (13ft) tall.

A. pavia♀ (syn. *A. splendens*) Bright red tubular flowers appear in early summer, followed in late summer by smooth, egg-shaped fruit. An attractive medium-sized shrub or small shrubby tree that has non-sticky winter buds and glossy green leaves that turn red in autumn. HEIGHT & SPREAD 2.1×2m (7×6½ft) after 10 years, ultimately 5m (16ft) tall.

A. splendens see *A. pavia*

CULTIVATION Plant in any fertile, well-drained, moist soil. Most species are hardy, except in very exposed conditions, and thrive in sun or semi-shade. *A. indica* and *A.* × *neglecta* 'Erythroblastos' do best in moist, semi-shade or woodland conditions which provide protection from late frosts.

PROPAGATION Raise species and natural varieties by sowing ripe seed in autumn. Hybrids and cultivars are propagated by budding or top-grafting.

PRUNING None normally needed, although older shrubby species may be thinned in late winter by cutting the oldest stems down to about 15cm (6in) from the ground.

PESTS AND DISEASES Occasionally, the leaves brown and wither and ugly eruptions may appear on some tree trunks; neither of these will affect the health of a plant. Scale insects may cause unsightly but harmless

white patches. The genus is moderately susceptible to honey fungus and witches' broom are often seen on older trees.

Aethionema
Stonecress
Cruciferae

Small evergreens or semi-evergreens that thrive in a sunny rock garden or dry-stone wall. Their popularity is partly due to the masses of white or pink flowers carried above compact foliage. The flowers, which are around 1cm (⅜in) across, are made up of four rounded petals. The narrow leaves are 5-15mm (¼-½in) long. All species are hardy and easy to grow provided they are given well-drained soil.

RECOMMENDED SPECIES AND VARIETIES

A. armenum A dwarf, shrubby species with blue-green, lance-shaped leaves. Pale to dark pink flowers appear in profusion in summer. The plants are not long-lived. Native to Armenia and the Caucasus. HEIGHT & SPREAD 15×15cm (6×6in).

A. grandiflorum♀ (syn. *A. pulchellum*) (Persian stonecress) Large pink flowerheads appear above blue-green oblong-shaped leaves from early to mid summer. Native to Iran, Iraq and Turkey. HEIGHT & SPREAD 40×23cm (16×9in).

⚘ *Aethionema grandiflorum*

A. oppositifolium A tufted, cushion-forming species carrying a summer display of lilac-pink flowers above overlapping grey-green oval leaves. Native to the Lebanon, Caucasus and Turkey. HEIGHT & SPREAD 5×10cm (2×4in).

A. pulchellum see *A. grandiflorum*

A. 'Warley Rose'♀ A low-growing plant with profuse dark pink flowers from late spring to mid summer and blue-grey leaves. HEIGHT & SPREAD 15×15cm (6×6in).

CULTIVATION Grow in a sunny position in well-drained, alkaline soil; growth will be more compact in poor soil.

PROPAGATION Sow seed in spring in a coldframe, or take cuttings of semi-ripe shoots in mid summer and root them in gritty soil in a coldframe or under a cloche.

PESTS AND DISEASES Usually trouble free.

Agapanthus
African lily
Liliaceae

Agapanthus africanus

Although the first plants to be introduced to this country from South Africa were tender and had to be kept in a frost-free conservatory over winter, there are now several compact, hardy forms available which can be grown in the open in most districts. All plants produce impressive blooms: the large umbels of tubular to trumpet-shaped flowers, 10-20 cm (4-8 in) across, are held on erect stems which can be up to 1.2 m (4 ft) tall. Flower colours vary from dark to light blue; white flowers are also available.

The leaves are strap-like and arching, up to 70 cm (28 in) long and 5 cm (2 in) wide. The deciduous species have narrower leaves and are more hardy than the evergreens.

Agapanthus thrives in a sunny position and fertile soil. Apart from garden decoration, the long-lived blooms make good cut flowers. Tender species in large containers look elegant on a sunny patio or terrace.

RECOMMENDED SPECIES AND VARIETIES
A. africanus♀ (African lily) As the original agapanthus to be introduced from South Africa, this remains a tender species with evergreen leaves and deep blue flowers in late summer. It is best grown in a large pot or tub that is kept almost dry in a frost-free greenhouse or conservatory over winter. HEIGHT & SPREAD up to 90×46 cm (36×18½ in).

'Albus'♀ has white flowers.
A. campanulatus Deciduous and hardy in most areas, this plant has flattish umbels of

Agapanthus africanus 'Albus'

Agapanthus campanulatus 'Isis'

Agapanthus caulescens

soft blue flowers in late summer above narrow, grey-green arching leaves. HEIGHT & SPREAD up to 120×46 cm (48×18½ in).

The flowers of var. *albidus* are white. 'Isis' has deep blue flowers on stems up to 75 cm (30 in). The light blue flowers of ssp. *patens*♀ (syn. *A. globosus*) are more open.
A. caulescens♀ Similar to *A. africanus*, this species is deciduous and hardier. Blue flowers are borne in late summer. HEIGHT & SPREAD up to 120 × 60 cm (4 × 2 ft).
A. globosus see *A. campanulatus* ssp. *patens*
A. orientalis see *A. praecox* ssp. *orientalis*
A. praecox 'Variegatus'♀ Silvery white striped leaves are the most distinctive feature of this tender, blue-flowered cultivar. HEIGHT & SPREAD 90×60 cm (3×2 ft).
OTHER RECOMMENDED VARIETIES
Many cultivated forms exist where the parent species is unclear. Those recommended below flower in late summer.

'Bressingham White' is a pure white at 1 m (3 ft). The Headbourne Hybrids are a widely available race of hardy types that are also known as Palmer's Hybrids. Plants grow to 1 m (3 ft) tall with flowers in varying shades of blue. 'Lilliput' is a dwarf plant, which reaches 45 cm (18 in) and has dark blue flowers. 'Peter Pan' displays light blue flowers on stems up to 30 cm (1 ft) tall.
CULTIVATION Only the hardy hybrids survive outdoors during winter in most areas. Plant in mid spring in a sunny position in fertile, well-drained soil, with the crowns 5 cm (2 in) below soil level. In cold districts protect the plants in winter with a layer of bark fibre or bracken.

Grow more tender kinds in containers. Keep them in a frost-free conservatory or

greenhouse for winter but stand them in a sunny position during summer. Feed plants in summer with liquid fertiliser.
PROPAGATION Lift and divide the rhizomatous rootstock of well-established plants in mid spring, replanting the divisions as soon as possible so that they do not dry out.

Plants are easily raised from seed sown under glass in spring. Grow the seedlings in small pots and plant in the open when good plants have been established. Seedlings take 2-3 years to flower. Seed collected from hybrid plants will not come true.
PESTS AND DISEASES Usually trouble free but slugs and snails may be a problem in mild, moist weather.

Agapetes
Ericaceae

Agapetes serpens

Agapetes serpens is the most commonly grown species in this genus of tender evergreen scrambling shrubs. Although it can be trained up a wall, it is more appealing when planted in a position where its long shoots bearing boldly coloured flowers are allowed to trail or hang down in graceful arches, such as in an old tree stump or hanging basket. Native to India and Nepal, it survives outside only in the mildest western gardens. Elsewhere it needs to be grown in a frost-free greenhouse or conservatory. The plant requires an acid soil.
RECOMMENDED SPECIES AND VARIETIES
A. serpens♀ Bright red tubular flowers, 2 cm (¾ in) long with v-shaped darker markings, hang in long rows beneath the arching branches from mid winter to mid spring. Green lance-shaped to oblong leaves are up to 2 cm (¾ in) long and sometimes flushed with purple above. HEIGHT & SPREAD 10×50 cm (4×20 in) after 5 years, ultimately 60 cm (2 ft) tall with stems climbing or trailing to 3 m (10 ft).

'Nepal Cream' has ivory flowers.
CULTIVATION Plants need to grow in well-drained, acid, humus-rich soil. In mild western gardens choose a shady, sheltered site, in cooler areas plant in a frost-free greenhouse or conservatory.
PROPAGATION Root semi-ripe cuttings in a peat compost under polythene with bottom heat or layer trailing shoots into pots.
PRUNING None normally required.
PESTS AND DISEASES The roots may be attacked by vine weevil larvae.

Agastache
Giant hyssop
Labiatae

Agastache foeniculum

Numerous spikes carry dense whorls of small flowers on these summer-flowering perennials. The oval, pointed, mid green leaves are serrated and resemble mint. They are aromatic and 3-8 cm (1¼-3¼ in) long. Most species are hardy, although *Agastache mexicana* should be treated as a half-hardy annual in cold areas. Most are native to the United States and Mexico, but *A. rugosa* is native to China and Japan.

RECOMMENDED SPECIES AND VARIETIES

A. anethiodora see *A. foeniculum*

A. anisata see *A. foeniculum*

A. barberi **'Firebird'** This cultivar produces coppery orange flowers in late summer. HEIGHT & SPREAD 60×30 cm (2×1 ft).

A. cana (syn. *A. mexicana* 'Rosea', *Cedronella cana*) Whitish, pink-tinged flowers are borne in mid summer. HEIGHT & SPREAD 60×30 cm (2×1 ft).

A. foeniculum (syn. *A. anethiodora*, *A. anisata*) Spikes of violet-blue flowers are borne on this hardy plant in late summer. HEIGHT & SPREAD 90×30 cm (3×1 ft).

'Alabaster' has white flowers.

A. mexicana (syn. *Cedronella mexicana*), (Mexican giant hyssop) A bushy plant with crimson-pink flower spikes from early summer to early autumn. It needs warm, dry conditions and is not long-lived. Grow as a half-hardy annual in cold areas. HEIGHT & SPREAD 60×30 cm (2×1 ft).

A. mexicana **'Rosea'** see *A. cana*

A. rugosa A hardy species with aniseed-flavoured leaves. The rose-purple flower spikes appear in late summer. HEIGHT & SPREAD 90-120×30 cm (3-4×1 ft) or more.

CULTIVATION Best grown in a warm, sunny position, ideally in front of a south-facing wall, and in fertile soil.

⚘ *Agastache foeniculum*

⚘ *Agastache mexicana*

PROPAGATION Sow seed under glass in spring. Alternatively, divide established clumps in spring. Root cuttings of young shoots in gritty soil during summer.

PESTS AND DISEASES Powdery mildew can be a problem, particularly in hot weather.

Agave
Agavaceae

These succulent tropical perennials are grown for their large, stiff, sword-shaped leaves arranged in rosettes. Flower spikes are rarely produced except on large, old plants. Native to Central and S America.

RECOMMENDED SPECIES AND VARIETIES

A. americana ♀ (century plant) Curvy grey-green leaves, which are both toothed and armed with sharp spines, are arranged in bold rosettes. Leaves are up to 2 m (6½ ft) long. HEIGHT & SPREAD 2×2 m (6½ ×6½ ft).

'Mediopicta' ♀ has grey-green leaves with a central pale yellow stripe.

A. filifera ♀ Greyish green leaves, up to 30 cm (12 in) long, form neat rosettes. HEIGHT & SPREAD 45×60 cm (18×24 in).

CULTIVATION Under glass, grow in a free-draining gritty compost in a sunny position. Plants require a minimum temperature of 7°C (45°F) in winter.

PROPAGATION Sow seed under glass in spring or remove and plant the occasional suckers during spring or summer.

PESTS AND DISEASES Scale and mealy bug may cause problems.

▽ *Agave filifera*

Ageratum
Flossflower
Compositae

Small, powder-puff flowers in blue, lilac, pink or white cluster above the foliage of these half-hardy annuals. They are grown mainly for summer bedding displays, window boxes and containers, where they flower from early summer through to the first severe frosts. Although most are small plants, there are taller-growing varieties suitable for borders or to grow for cut blooms. Compact varieties are sometimes grown as greenhouse pot plants. Plants are native to the Americas.

RECOMMENDED SPECIES AND VARIETIES

A. houstonianum The mainly blue flowers are held in loose clusters of 5-15. The mid green leaves are 9 cm (3½ in) long, ovate, and serrated. HEIGHT & SPREAD 15-30×15-30 cm (6-12×6-12 in).

Flowers of hybrid plants are generally larger than the species. **'Adriatic'** grows to 20 cm (8 in) tall, with mid blue flowers early in the season. **'Bavaria'**, a 25 cm (10 in) bicolour, has blue flowers with white centres. **'Blue Horizon'** ♀ reaches 75 cm (30 in) tall with clusters of purplish blue flowers. **'Blue Mink'** has powder-blue flowers and reaches to 23 cm (9 in). **'Pacific'** ♀ has violet-blue flowers and reaches 20 cm (8 in) tall. **'Pink Powderpuffs'** is a compact plant to 15 cm (6 in) with masses of rose-pink

⚘ *Ageratum houstonianum* 'Pink Powderpuffs'

flowers. **'White Hawaii'** is a compact variety with pure white flowers and a height of 15 cm (6 in).

CULTIVATION Grow in full sun and a sheltered position. Plant outside in late spring or early summer, once there is no danger of frost. Plants will suffer in dry soil and should be watered in dry weather. Deadhead to prolong flowering.

PROPAGATION Sow shop-bought seed under glass at a temperature of 18°C (64°F) in early spring. Prick out the seedlings in boxes or trays and harden off before planting in the open. Sow seed in early autumn for early flowering in a greenhouse.

PESTS AND DISEASES Usually trouble free.

Aglaonema
Chinese evergreen
Araceae

Attractively marbled foliage and the ability to survive in most indoor situations are the main virtues of these evergreen perennials. The leaves, about 20 cm (8 in) long, are oblong to oval and have distinctly pointed tips. As the plant ages it develops a short trunk. The flowers, which are rarely produced, are arum-like with a cream or greenish spathe and creamy green spadix.

Aglaonemas come from the tropical forests of SE Asia, where they grow in poor light at ground level. They are compact, slow growing and relatively shade tolerant, all of which make them valuable houseplants, especially as they do not need quite such high humidity levels as many other tropical plants. Windowsills with indirect sunlight are best, but perhaps aglaonemas are more useful farther back in rooms. There is a good selection of varieties on the market and when several are grouped together they make an attractive display.

RECOMMENDED SPECIES AND VARIETIES
A. commutatum The original species has green leaves with occasional silver splashes. It is best appreciated when grown as a contrast to the more colourful varieties. HEIGHT 50 cm (20 in).

The leaves of var. *maculatum* 'Pseudobracteatum' are a complex pattern of gold, cream and several shades of green radiating out from the centre. The leaves are large, reaching 30 cm (12 in) in length.
A. 'Silver Queen' ♀ This is the most silvery variety that is commonly available, the green on the leaves being restricted to odd streaks against a background of silver-grey. HEIGHT 40 cm (16 in).

▼ *Aglaonema* 'Silver Queen'

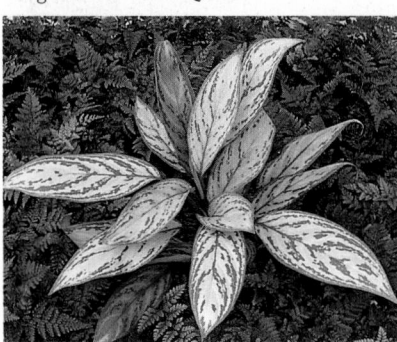

▼ *Aglaonema commutatum* var. *maculatum* 'Pseudobracteatum'

CULTIVATION Pot in early spring in a rich, soil-less, well-drained compost. Plants do best in good but indirect sunlight, although largely green-leaved varieties will grow in poorer light. Do not allow the temperature to fall below 13°C (55°F) for long periods in winter and maintain local humidity by regularly misting plants. Keep compost just moist, and a little drier in winter. Feeding encourages steady growth but need not be generous. Repot in spring, but plants can go several years without repotting.
PROPAGATION Divide plants or take stem cuttings in spring.
PESTS AND DISEASES Red spider mite and mealy bug are the main pests.

Agrostemma
Corn cockle
Caryophyllaceae

The corn cockle used to be a common weed of cornfields, its poisonous seeds ripening with the crop and contaminating rye or wheat flour. Nowadays the corn cockle brings summer colour to cottage gardens, and is often included in wild flower seed mixtures. It is an easy-to-grow hardy annual. The flowers are good for cutting. They also attract bees. Plants may persist through mild winters. Native to the Mediterranean.

RECOMMENDED SPECIES AND VARIETIES
A. coronaria see *Lychnis coronaria*
A. githago Slender graceful stems carry magenta flowers, sometimes white-eyed, delicately veined. The flowers have 5 petals

▲ *Agrostemma githago*

and measure about 7.5 cm (3 in) across. The lance-shaped mid green leaves are as long as 12 cm (4¾ in) long. HEIGHT & SPREAD 60–90×25 cm (2–3 ft×10 in).

'Milas' has deeper purplish red flowers.
CULTIVATION Grow in not too fertile, well-drained soil in full sun. Deadhead to prolong the flowering period.
PROPAGATION Sow seed in autumn or spring where the plants are to flower.
PESTS AND DISEASES Usually trouble free.

Ajuga
Bugle
Labiatae

Ajuga pyramidalis

Because of their creeping habit, these evergreens with colourful leaves and short flower spikes make excellent ground-cover plants. They are hardy perennials, thriving in sun or shade. Only two species (both from Europe) are widely cultivated. Both have rhizomatous roots, but *Ajuga repens* also produces stolons.

RECOMMENDED SPECIES AND VARIETIES
A. pyramidalis (syn. *A. metallica*) (pyramid bugle) The spoon-shaped leaves, up to 11 cm (4¼ in) long, are dark green. The creeping stems form a low carpet, through which small blue flower spikes protrude in spring. HEIGHT & SPREAD 15×45 cm (6×18 in).

'Metallica Crispa' is slightly smaller, reaching a height of 10 cm (4 in). It has dark blue flowers and bronze-tinted leaves that are crinkled at the edges.
A. reptans (common bugle) The glossy, paddle-shaped, dark green leaves are up to 9 cm (3½ in) long. Short blue flower spikes appear in spring to early summer. This species, a mat-forming creeper, puts out stolons carrying plantlets. HEIGHT & SPREAD 12.5×45 cm (5×18 in).

A. reptans has many cultivars. Some are grown for their flowers and others have colourful foliage. Those listed below all reach a height of 10–30 cm (4–12 in).

Cultivars grown for their flowers include the following: 'Alba', with white flowers and dark green leaves; the smaller 'Pink Elf', with pink flowers and dark green leaves; 'Pink Surprise', with deep pink flowers and dark purplish leaves; and 'Purple Torch', with pink flowers and dark green leaves.

Cultivars grown for their colourful foliage include: 'Atropurpurea' ♀ (syn. 'Purpurea'), with dark purple leaves, tinted with bronze; 'Braunherz' ♀, with dark purple shiny leaves; 'Burgundy Glow' ♀,

▼ *Ajuga reptans*

▲ Ajuga reptans 'Burgundy Glow'

▲ Ajuga reptans 'Delight'

with whitish green leaves variegated red; **'Catlin's Giant'**♀ (syn. 'Macrophylla'), a tall cultivar, reaching 30 cm (1 ft), with large bronze-coloured leaves; **'Delight'**, with bronze-coloured leaves marked yellow and pink; **'Jungle Beauty'** (syn. 'Jumbo'), with very large green leaves that turn brownish in winter; **'Multicolor'** (also sold as 'Rainbow' or 'Tricolor'), with dark brownish leaves marked with red, pink and gold; and **'Variegata'** (also sold as 'Argentea'), which has leaves marked with grey-green and cream, and a particularly neat habit of growth.

CULTIVATION Plant in autumn or spring in moisture-retentive soil. Plants will grow in sun or shade. The foliage of *A. reptans* 'Atropurpurea' colours best in a sunny position but *A. r.* 'Variegata' produces more colourful foliage in a shady spot.

PROPAGATION Divide clumps in the spring and, for *A. reptans*, lift the plantlets that form on the stolons.

PESTS AND DISEASES Usually trouble free.

Akebia
Lardizabalaceae

Vigorous, hardy climbing shrubs, akebia are grown for their unusually coloured spring flowers and shapely leaves. Fast-growing, deciduous or semi-evergreen plants, they climb by means of their twining stems and are excellent for growing over old stumps, through bushes or on wires to cover an unsightly wall.

The flowers have no petals but consist of large, slightly fleshy sepals and are borne in drooping flowerheads of both male and female blooms – the female flowers at the base, the male ones at the tip. The light green leaves are composed of 3–5 radiating rounded leaflets. In early autumn, if

▲ Akebia × pentaphylla

pollination has occurred, plants produce purplish sausage-shaped fruit, as long as 12.5 cm (5 in). The ripe fruit split lengthways to reveal black seeds embedded in a sticky, white pulp. The genus is native to China, Japan and Korea.

RECOMMENDED SPECIES
A. × *pentaphylla* The slightly scented blooms have maroon or deep purple female flowers, 3 cm (1¼ in) wide, and pale purple male flowers, up to 1 cm (⅜ in) wide. The deciduous leaves have 3–5 slightly lobed ovate leaflets, up to 10 cm (4 in) long. HEIGHT & SPREAD 4×4 m (13×13 ft) after 5 years, ultimately 10 m (33 ft) tall.
A. quinata Vanilla-scented flowerheads have maroon or deep purple female flowers, 3 cm (1¼ in) wide, and pale purple male flowers, up to 1 cm (⅜ in) wide. The semi-evergreen leaves usually have 5 oval or obovate leaflets, often notched at the tip, which are up to 7.5 cm (3 in) long. HEIGHT & SPREAD 4×4 m (13×13 ft) after 5 years, ultimately 6 m (20 ft) tall.

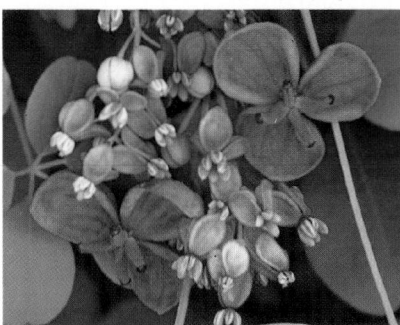

▲ Akebia quinata

A. trifoliata The deep purple, female flowers are 2 cm (¾ in) wide, the paler purple male flowers are 6 mm (¼ in) wide. The leaves are deciduous. They have 3 oval leaflets up to 10 cm (4 in) long, with scalloped or shallowly lobed edges. HEIGHT & SPREAD 4×4 m (13×13 ft) after 5 years, ultimately 10 m (33 ft) tall.
CULTIVATION Plant in a fertile, well-drained soil, in a sunny place. Provide some support for young twining stems. Young specimens will benefit from some protection in winter.
PROPAGATION Sow ripe seed in autumn or spring. Alternatively, take semi-ripe cuttings or layer in autumn.
PRUNING Not necessary but plants can be thinned in winter every 2–3 years.
PESTS AND DISEASES Usually trouble free.

Albizia
Leguminosae

Albizia julibrissin f. rosea

Clusters of fluffy flowerheads cover these deciduous large shrubs or small trees late in the season. Mostly native to tropical or subtropical regions, only one species is reliably hardy in Britain. Quick-growing plants, they need well-drained soil and a sheltered position in full sun to bloom and prosper.

RECOMMENDED SPECIES AND VARIETIES
A. julibrissin (silk tree) White to pink flowers in fluffy clumps no more than 3.5 cm (1⅜ in) across, are freely produced during late summer and into autumn. The handsome ferny leaves are bipinnate; that is, they are leaves made up of several stems which are clothed in tiny oblong leaflets, 1.5 cm (½ in) long. Free-standing specimens have a dome-shaped canopy consisting of many branches. They are best grown against a south or west-facing aspect and adapt easily to being trained on a wall.

▲ Albizia julibrissin f. rosea

HEIGHT & SPREAD 6×6 m (20×20 ft) after 10 years, also its ultimate size.

The flowers of f. *rosea* are a much brighter pink. It is hardier than the species.
CULTIVATION Plant in a sheltered sunny spot in free-draining soil. Dress with a slow-release fertiliser in late spring. Purchase container-grown rather than bare-rooted plants as albizias resent their roots being disturbed. To train plants against a wall, tie in young shoots to wires or other supports.
PROPAGATION Sow seed in small pots under glass during early spring.
PRUNING Prune sparingly in late spring, removing any weak or crossing growths or stems damaged during winter. Cut back protruding branches of wall-trained plants to buds that face sideways.
PESTS AND DISEASES Usually trouble free.

Alcea
Hollyhock
Malvaceae

Alcea rosea

Tall spikes of open, funnel-shaped flowers, keep these old-fashioned cottage garden stalwarts firm favourites. Hollyhocks are hardy perennials but are best treated as biennials since the fungal disease known as rust, tends to spoil any plants allowed to grow for more than two years.

In the wild, hollyhocks grow in hot, sunny places in light, well-drained soil. Give them similar conditions in gardens, but improve the soil with organic matter for best results. They can reach a height of 3m (10ft) and the taller forms require staking as the stems develop.

RECOMMENDED SPECIES AND VARIETIES
A. rosea Long stems of single flowers, 5-10cm (2-4in) across, bloom throughout summer in a wide range of colours, including pink, white, purple, yellow and cream. The leaves, about 20cm (8in) long, are light green, slightly lobed and rough to the touch. The species is sometimes incorrectly called by its former name, *Althaea rosea*. It is native to Turkey. HEIGHT & SPREAD 3m×60cm (10×2ft).

Recommended forms include: **Chater's Double Group**, with fully double flowers in a variety of colours on spikes up to 2.4m (8ft) tall; the **Majorette Group**, containing dwarf forms that grow to 60cm (2ft), with semidouble flowers in pastel shades – usually grown as annuals; **'Nigra'**, which is impressive for its very dark, chocolate-maroon flowers; the **Powder Puff Group**, with fully double flowers in a good range of

▲ *Alcea rosea*

▲ *Alcea rosea* 'Nigra'

colours; and **'Summer Carnival'**, with fully double flowers in various hues, covering most of the stems.

A. rugosa The pale yellow flowers are up to 12cm (4¾in) across. The foliage is coarse and hairy, with deeply lobed leaves growing to 20cm (8in) in length. It will hybridise freely with *A. rosea* to produce some interesting colours. The species is fairly resistant to rust. Native to the Ukraine. HEIGHT & SPREAD 2m×60cm (6½×2ft).

CULTIVATION To grow as biennials, sow seed in summer and plant out in early autumn. Plants in the Majorette Group and 'Summer Carnival' may be treated as half-hardy annuals: sow seed under glass in early spring and plant out when the seedlings are large enough to handle.

PESTS AND DISEASES Rust can be troublesome. To overcome it, raise new plants on a regular basis from clean seed. Cut back stems after flowering and burn them. Remove and burn the first leaves that appear in spring. *A. rugosa* has some resistance to the disease.

Alchemilla
Lady's mantle
Rosaceae

Alchemilla mollis

Plants form low mounds of silky green foliage. Masses of tiny star-shaped yellowish green flowers on short flower stalks make up many-branched inflorescences, held on long stems. These pretty sprays of flowers appear in summer, last for weeks, gradually turning brown, and are much sought after by flower arrangers.

Most alchemillas are hardy perennials and easy to grow in most soils. Taller plants, up to 50cm (20in) high when in flower, are

useful for the front of a border while low-growing species, 10-20cm (4-8in) tall, can be used for ground cover. Dwarf plants, up to 15cm (6in) tall, are more suitable for a rock garden.

RECOMMENDED SPECIES
A. abyssinica (syn. *A. pedata*) The soft green, hairy leaves, up to 4cm (1½in) long, are kidney-shaped overall, with 7 serrated lobes. The plant creeps, with prostrate stems rooting at the leaf nodes. Native to E Africa. HEIGHT & SPREAD 5×60cm (2×24in).
A. alpina (alpine lady's mantle) The rounded, dark green leaves, up to 5cm (2in) wide, have 5-7 serrated lobes. They are smooth on the upper surface, but have silky hairs beneath. The flowers are held in upright clusters. Native to Europe. HEIGHT & SPREAD 15×45cm (6×18in).
A. conjuncta Clumps of relatively thick, star-shaped leaves, made up of 7-9 rounded lobes, are bluish green above with silvery hairs on the underside and up to 15cm (6in) across. A native of E France, the plant is naturalised in parts of northern Britain. HEIGHT & SPREAD 20×30cm (8×12in).

▲ *Alchemilla conjuncta*

▲ *Alchemilla elisabethae*

A. elisabethae This dwarf plant has blue-green, rounded leaves, up to 9cm (3½in) across, with 7 deep lobes. Native to the Caucasus. HEIGHT & SPREAD 15×30cm (6×12in).
A. ellenbeckii One of the smallest-leaved of the genus, this dwarf plant has red creeping stems, bearing soft green leaves, which are no more than 2cm (¾in) across, deeply cut with 5 square, serrated lobes. It likes damp soil but is not reliably hardy. Native to the mountains of E Africa. HEIGHT & SPREAD 5×60cm (2×24in).

A. erythropoda♀ The blue-green, rounded and serrated leaves of the small, hairy plants are slightly lobed and 3–5 cm (1¼–2 in) across. Native throughout the Balkans, Turkey and the Caucasus. HEIGHT & SPREAD 20×30 cm (8×12 in).

A. faeroensis The lobed, kidney-shaped leaves of this low-growing species are about 4 cm (1½ in) across and hairy beneath. As its name suggests, this plant is native to E Iceland and the Faeroe Islands. HEIGHT & SPREAD 15×25 cm (6×10 in).

A. mollis♀ (lady's mantle) The most widely grown species has sprays of fluffy, yellowy green flowers in early summer. The relatively large flowers, 5 mm (¼ in) across, are valued for cutting and suitable for drying. They are held above mounds of softly hairy, almost circular light green leaves with shallow lobes and serrated edges. Native to Turkey and the Caucasus. HEIGHT & SPREAD 50×75 cm (20×30 in).

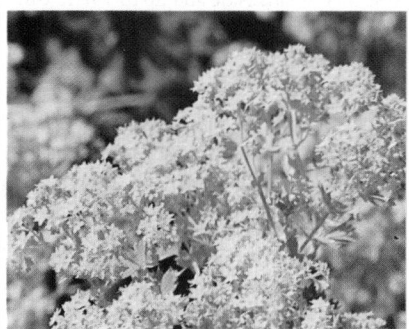

▲ *Alchemilla mollis*

A. pedata see *A. abyssinica*

A. xanthochlora (syn. *A. vulgaris*) The yellowy green, rounded, lobed leaves reach 10 cm (4 in) across. They are smooth above but hairy beneath. A native to NW and central Europe, including Britain. HEIGHT & SPREAD 25–50×50 cm (10–20×20 in).

CULTIVATION Will grow in most soil provided it is not waterlogged. Plant in either autumn or spring in sun or shade.

PROPAGATION Divide established plants in autumn or spring or sow seed in spring. Some species, such as *A. mollis*, seed themselves freely in positions to their liking.

PESTS AND DISEASES Usually trouble free.

Alder see *Alnus*
Alecost see *Tanacetum balsamita*

———

Alisma
Water plantain
Alismataceae

Clouds of small flowers on large, branching sprays above neat clumps of greyish green leaves make water plantain particularly effective in a semi-wild setting. These plants are hardy herbaceous perennials that are easily grown in permanently wet ground or in shallow water at the edge of a pool. Native to temperate regions worldwide, including Britain.

RECOMMENDED SPECIES AND VARIETIES
A. plantago-aquatica Masses of white or pale lilac flowers open in the afternoon from mid to late summer. About 1 cm (⅜ in) across, the flowers have 3 petals that are sometimes tinged with pink or brown. Seedheads follow, about 6 mm (¼ in) wide. The oval leaves, up to 25 cm (10 in) long and held on long upright stalks, form a clump from which the tall flowering stems rise. HEIGHT & SPREAD 75×45 cm (30×18 in).

▲ *Alisma plantago-aquatica*

The flowers of var. *parviflorum* are smaller, measuring 4 mm (⅛ in) across, and the leaves are rounded rather than oval.

CULTIVATION Plant during mid or late spring in full sun in permanently wet soil or in water up to 25 cm (10 in) deep. In small ponds, deadhead flowers to prevent seed setting and the plants becoming invasive, and remove dead leaves in autumn so that rotting matter will not foul the water.

PROPAGATION Sow ripe seed or divide established plants in early spring.

PESTS AND DISEASES Usually trouble free.

Allamanda
Apocynaceae

Allamanda cathartica

Waxy, trumpet-shaped flowers produced freely among glossy, lance-shaped leaves offer a stunning display all summer long. These tropical shrubby or climbing plants are frost tender and are usually grown up into the roof of a conservatory or greenhouse, or twined around a cane or wire framework in large pots. Allamandas require copious amounts of water in summer. The genus is native to tropical N, Central and S America.

RECOMMENDED SPECIES AND VARIETIES
A. blanchetii (syn. *A. violacea*) Rose-purple blossoms, up to 6 cm (2½ in) across, appear in late summer and early autumn. The ever-

▲ *Allamanda schottii*

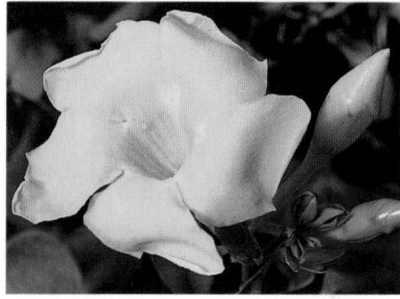

▲ *Allamanda cathartica*

green leaves, up to 12 cm (4¾ in) long, are almost oblong and are arranged in whorls. HEIGHT & SPREAD 3×1 m (10×3 ft).

A. cathartica (golden trumpet) Striking yellow trumpet-like flowers, up to 10 cm (4 in) across, are borne in late summer and early autumn. The evergreen leaves of this strong and fast-growing climbing plant grow up to 15 cm (6 in) long and are arranged in whorls. HEIGHT & SPREAD 6×1 m (20×3 ft).

'Grandiflora' bears larger, more profuse flowers up to 10 cm (4 in) across.

A. schottii (syn. *A. neriifolia*) (bush allamanda) The yellow flowers, up to 6 cm (2½ in) across, each have a distinctive brown marking in the throat. The leaves are evergreen and up to 10 cm (4 in) long. They are produced on erect to clambering stems. Bushier than *A. cathartica*, this plant is excellent for training into the roof of a greenhouse. HEIGHT & SPREAD 6×1 m (20×3 ft).

A. violacea see *A. blanchetii*

CULTIVATION Grow in a greenhouse border or in large pots in any good proprietary potting compost. Tie in the twining stems as they develop. Avoid direct sunlight and water liberally in summer. The plants demand a minimum night temperature of 10°C (50°F).

PROPAGATION Take softwood cuttings in late spring and summer. Tie in the twining stems as they develop.

PRUNING In early spring cut stems back hard to 3 or 4 buds to encourage vigorous new growth.

PESTS AND DISEASES Red spider mite and whitefly can be a problem.

ALLIES IN THE GARDENER'S WORLD

TAKE A CLOSER LOOK AT THE CREATURES IN
YOUR GARDEN – YOU MAY BE SURPRISED TO SEE
JUST HOW MANY ACT ON YOUR BEHALF

Every gardener is familiar with garden pests – the damage they cause is often apparent. Yet many creatures that inhabit flowerbeds, vegetable plots and other areas of the garden are our allies. They feed on pests and so help to keep them under control. These useful creatures come in all shapes and sizes, from tiny mites and insects to frogs and toads, hedgehogs, birds and bats (see guide overleaf).

The numbers of pests and thus their predators fluctuate from season to season and year to year. When conditions favour a particular pest, its

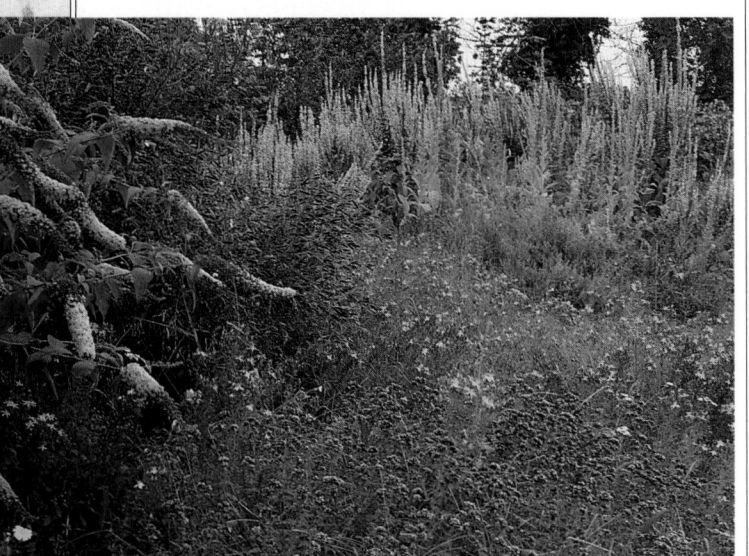

FRUITY FEAST
*Pyracantha berries are
irresistible to birds.*

numbers rise rapidly – and so do those of its predators and parasites. Eventually the pest's level falls dramatically and, with most of their prey consumed, the predators are left without food and subsequently die off. This enables any remaining pests to increase in number again, and so the cycle continues.

To encourage garden allies, all that is needed is the provision of suitable food and shelter, and a minimal use of chemicals, as these may disrupt the natural cycle and destroy many beneficial creatures in addition to the target pests.

PROVIDING FOOD FOR YOUR ALLIES

Many garden allies require food sources other than pests in order to complete their life cycle and to support them when their prey is not present. Having a range of nectar and pollen-rich plants in flower throughout most of the year is an effective way of attracting beneficial insects and keeping them in your garden.

Plants that have simple and open flowers or small flowers which provide easy access to their pollen and nectar are most useful because many predatory insects have short mouthparts and cannot reach into deep flowers.

Plants in the Umbelliferae family are particularly suitable. Their tiny flowers, which are carried in flat umbels, produce large amounts of nectar over short periods of time and are accessible to the smallest of parasitic wasps. For example, the golden flowers of *Foeniculum vulgare* (fennel), which appear in mid summer, attract almost 500 different types of insect.

Members of the Compositae family, such as *Helianthus annuus* (sunflower) which flowers in late summer and early autumn, are also popular with insects. They produce less nectar than umbellifers but over a longer period.

The list on the facing page gives a selection of the range of other plants that attract beneficial insects into the garden.

As so many plants flower over the summer, it is particularly important to provide nectar and pollen in spring and autumn when it is scarce. The catkins of *Corylus* (hazel) and *Salix* (willow) make good early food sources. In addition, most annuals, including *Limnanthes douglasii* (poached-egg flower) and *Phacelia tanacetifolia*, can be sown in autumn, or under glass in late winter for spring flowers. Grow *Solidago* (golden rod) and *Aster novi-belgii* (Michaelmas daisy) to provide an autumn food supply. Alternatively, sow annuals in late spring for a late flowering.

◀ NATURAL BEAUTY *A border filled with nectar-rich flowers is a charming way to support allies.*

▲ FLOWER POWER *Flat umbels of tiny flowers attract hundreds of beneficial insects.*

Do not confine flowering plants to flowerbeds and borders. For maximum effect, grow them among vegetables and fruit bushes, where pest control is often vital.

Include long-living plants, such as trees and shrubs, in the garden. Berry-bearing plants, which include *Cotoneaster* and *Pyracantha* (firethorn), are particularly useful as sources of food for birds.

Plants generally thought of as weeds – including *Achillea millefolium* (yarrow), *Anthriscus*

▼ RELAXED STYLE *Do not be too tidy; dead leaves provide shelter for spiders and beetles.*

sylvestris (cow parsley), *Carduus* and *Cirsium* (thistles) and *Urtica dioica* (stinging nettle) – attract a variety of beneficial creatures so it is worth allowing some to flourish in a corner.

As many as 100 species of insect may visit stinging nettles, for example. They include lacewings, hoverflies, anthocorid bugs, earwigs and a range of parasitic flies and wasps. In spring, nettle aphids are an important food source for the first generations of several species of ladybird, which then move on to feed on blackfly on garden plants. Cut the nettles down in summer to encourage predators to move out into the rest of your garden.

GIVING SHELTER

Provide features and grow plants that offer shelter to your allies. Many of these can be incorporated into even the smallest garden. There is no need to create a specific wildlife area or for a garden to look wild or unkempt.

Encourage birds, bats and hedgehogs by installing nesting and hibernation boxes. The absence of cats will also help to encourage birds. Create a wildlife pond, which will serve as a breeding ground for frogs and toads, a bath for birds and provide drinking facilities for all manner of creatures. See WILDLIFE GARDENS (p.710).

A hedge or woodland area, makes a natural habitat for many beneficial creatures. Give preference to native species when choosing plants as they act as hosts to a more diverse range than imported species. *Fagus sylvatica* (beech), *Prunus spinosa* (blackthorn), *Corylus avellana* (hazel), *Carpinus betulus* (hornbeam), and *Crataegus monogyna* (hawthorn) are particularly good plants for garden allies. Leave the areas along the bottom of hedges undisturbed and let any autumn leaves that collect on the ground remain in place over winter.

Useful predators also make their homes among the plants that grow alongside hedges or underneath trees. For example, ground-cover plants provide protection for many creatures, including frogs, toads and insects. Bark, wood chip or

▲ WILD WOOD *A woodland edge is home to bats, birds and all manner of helpful insects.*

compost mulches also act as safe cover for the smaller predators, such as centipedes, beetles and spiders.

A heap of logs or woody prunings – material that will not go through the compost heap – helps to support many small garden creatures. The insects and fungi that gradually consume the wood will, in their turn, feed other creatures.

Above all, do not be too tidy. Clearing up every corner is a sure way to discourage garden friends. Leave an area of grass in your garden uncut for overwintering insects. Hollow stems and fallen leaves in a herbaceous border are also favourite spots so allow the dead plants to remain in place until spring. However, you will still need to remove any diseased plant matter.

LIVING SOIL

The soil is full of living organisms: some are beneficial but there are pests and diseases too, just as there are above ground. Most of these organisms are microscopic, but despite their size they play an important role in soil and plant health. For example, tiny nematode worms

infect slugs, helping to keep their numbers down. The more diverse and active the soil community, the less likely it is that any particular organism will get out of hand.

The key to creating a healthy community is to build up the soil's structure and fertility. This is achieved by digging in plenty of organic matter in the form of compost, leaf-mould and manure (see p.807).

THE LAST RESORT

Garden allies can never completely eradicate pests and may also fail to keep pest numbers down to the levels the gardener would like. If necessary, use additional methods of pest and disease control, but whenever possible choose those which do not harm wildlife or valuable allies. These include netting and using traps and biological controls (see p.807).

Use pesticides only as a last resort. Young seedlings may need instant attention but most plants can tolerate low levels of infestations until the garden allies arrive to do their work.

If it is essential to spray, limit yourself to treating a specific pest or disease and spray only appropriate plants rather than the whole garden. Choose the least toxic product that is available.

PLANTS FOR BENEFICIAL INSECTS

● *Anaphalis* spp. (pearl everlasting) Erect perennials which bear flat-topped heads of fluffy white flowers in late summer to early autumn.

● *Angelica archangelica* Tall biennial bearing large rounded heads of greenish white flowers from early to late summer.

● *Artemisia* spp. (wormwood) Feathery-leaved perennials producing button-like flowerheads from summer to autumn.

● *Convolvulus tricolor* (annual convolvulus) Bushy annual with deep blue, funnel-shaped flowers from mid to late summer.

● *Echium vulgare* (viper's bugloss) Bushy annual with dense spikes of pink, blue or purple, tubular flowers in summer.

● *Eryngium* spp. Upright perennials bearing spiky thistle-like flowerheads from mid to late summer.

● *Eschscholzia* spp. (California poppy) Erect annuals bearing colourful poppy-like blooms from early to late summer.

● *Iberis* spp. (candytuft) Perennials and annuals with cross-shaped white or purple flowers in spring and summer.

● *Leucanthemum* x *superbum* (shasta daisy) Perennial bearing white-petalled flowers, with yellow centres, in early and mid summer.

● *Limnanthes douglasii* (poached-egg flower) Sprawling annual which bears many saucer-shaped white flowers, with yellow centres, from late spring to late summer.

● *Nemophila menziesii* (baby blue eyes) Spreading annual with saucer-shaped sky-blue flowers, with white centres, from early summer to mid autumn.

● *Phacelia tanacetifolia* Tall annual bearing dense spikes of fragrant blue or mauve flowers in summer.

KNOW YOUR FRIENDS

In the war against pests it pays to know which creatures are your enemies and which are your friends. Many insects look unpleasant but do no damage to your plants at all — they may even be helpful. If in doubt, leave them alone. The following guide will help you to recognise some of the more common garden allies and provide any particular conditions they need to thrive in your garden.

1 Lacewings

Delicate-looking insects with green or brown bodies, large lacy wings and long antennae. The larvae are wingless with distinctive mouthparts and vary in colour. From late spring to mid autumn the adults and larvae feed on aphids, red spider and other mites, scale insects and caterpillars. Flowers provide adults with nectar and pollen.

2 Harvestmen

The eight very long legs of these arachnids make them look like spiders but they do not have a segmented body. Harvestmen are nocturnal hunters of aphids, caterpillars and other insects from spring to autumn. Give them undisturbed areas of vegetation in which to shelter and breed.

3 Earwigs

Dark brown shiny insects with horny pincers. From spring to autumn earwigs feed on aphids, mites and insect eggs, including those of the codling moth. Provide undisturbed sites, such as heaps of leaves and logs, for daytime shelter, breeding and overwintering.

4 Common wasps

Flying insects, with distinctive black and yellow stripes, active from spring to autumn. Wasps devour caterpillars, craneflies and other insect pests. Leave nests undisturbed.

5 Hoverflies

Black-and-gold flies that hover in the air making a high-pitched whine. From late spring to the end of summer the tiny pale green hoverfly larvae consume aphids, small caterpillars and fruit-tree red spider mites.

6 Capsids

Though most of these tiny, winged, beetle-like insects are sap-sucking pests, some are major predators of fruit-tree red spider mites, greenfly, thrips and caterpillars.

7 Spiders

Eight legs and a body divided into two parts characterise these arachnids. Spiders are voracious hunters of flies, woodlice, aphids and other flying insects. They are active from spring to autumn. Provide undisturbed vegetation, stones and logs for shelter and breeding.

8 Ladybirds

Small, rounded, red or yellow beetles with 2-14 black spots. The larvae are segmented and slate-blue with orange or yellow marks. From spring to autumn, adults and larvae feed on aphids, mealy bugs, mites, scale insects, caterpillars and plants affected by some diseases, such as mildew. Hollow stems provide overwintering sites.

9 Red velvet mites

Tiny velvety red mites that feed on aphids, caterpillars and other insects from spring to autumn. Provide undisturbed leaves for overwintering adults.

10 Anthocorid bugs

Small beetle-like insects with chequered bodies and long 'beaks' used to pierce prey. Adults are seen in late spring to early autumn, feeding on aphids, scale insects, midges, capsid bugs, caterpillars and mites.

11 Typhlodromid mites

Tiny narrow-bodied mites seen from spring to autumn. They feed on red spider mites. Adults overwinter under bark and in shrubs.

20 Toads

Small amphibians with dry, warty, greyish brown skin. Toads do not leap like frogs but crawl rather slowly. They eat slugs, snails, caterpillars, woodlice and other insects and, like frogs, require a pond in which to lay their eggs. Toads are active from spring to autumn and hibernate under stones, piles of logs and in other sheltered sites.

19 Birds

Vast quantities of garden pests, including caterpillars, snails, slugs, aphids and leatherjackets, are consumed by birds. One pair of blue tits, for example, needs 15 000 caterpillars to raise a single brood of young. In winter, birds will prey on surviving aphids and codling moths. Nesting sites and boxes, birdbaths and plants that produce edible berries will entice birds into your garden.

18 Bats

Small, night-flying mammals with an appetite for moths, aphids, gnats and other flying insects. One tiny pipistrelle, with a thumb-sized body, can eat 3000 insects in a night. Bats are active from spring to autumn, hibernating in cool caves, tunnels or similar hideaways. Bat boxes and a woodland edge encourage bats; ponds are also an attraction because bats feed on the insects that live and breed in or over them.

17 Slow-worms

Harmless smooth-skinned reptiles often mistaken for snakes. Slow-worms are legless lizards, grey-brown or fawn in colour and up to 25 cm (10 in) long. They can live for 20-30 years, clearing the garden of slugs, caterpillars and other small insects from spring to autumn. They hibernate deep in friable soil on a south-facing bank. Rock gardens, tall grass and other undisturbed sites encourage slow-worms. Do not disturb a compost heap during winter as slow-worms may be hibernating there.

16 Frogs

Smooth, slightly shiny amphibians with brown, green and yellow markings. Frogs move about by hopping or leaping. From spring to autumn they eat slugs, snails, caterpillars, woodlice and other insects. A pond encourages frogs into the garden as this is where they lay their eggs. Dense vegetation will give them cover while piles of stones and other secluded places will be used as hibernation sites. Many hibernate in the mud at the bottom of ponds, so always keep part of a pond clear of ice in winter.

14 Parasitic wasps

These tiny wasps are harmless to people. They lay their eggs in the bodies of host creatures, including aphids, caterpillars and scale insects, which are then killed as the young wasps develop. Active in spring and summer, the wasps need flat-topped, open flowers for nectar and pollen.

15 Hedgehogs

Small, spiny mammals that are rarely seen because they are active at night. From spring to autumn they help to rid the garden of slugs, caterpillars, leatherjackets and other soil-inhabiting pests. Heaps of leaves, uncleared hedge bottoms and other undisturbed areas make good resting sites and will be useful when the hedgehogs need to hibernate. You could also provide a hedgehog box, covered with leaves to camouflage it.

13 Centipedes

Many-legged creatures, about 2.5 cm (1 in) long, with one pair of legs per segment. They feed on slugs, snails and cabbage and carrot rootfly larvae all year round. Mulches, ground-cover plants and piles of logs provide safe cover.

12 Ground and rove beetles

Shiny black beetles, up to 2.5 cm (1 in) long, which are active at night. They prey on slugs, root aphids, vine weevils, New Zealand flatworms and cabbage and carrot rootfly larvae all year round. Give them undisturbed soil for breeding, mulches, leaf litter, ground-cover plants and other shelter. Avoid using slug pellets that contain methiocarb as they poison beetles.

Allium
Onion
Alliaceae

Allium giganteum

There are many highly ornamental allium species, which are grown for their large flowerheads held high on erect stems. They belong to the same genus as onions (*Allium cepa*) and garlic (*A. sativum*), and when their roots or leaves are bruised they give off a strong onion smell. The plants grow from bulbs or rhizomes, with flowers held on leafless stems rising above the leaves. While the larger ornamental species make excellent border plants, others are suited to raised beds or terraces, rock or sink gardens, or containers. Many make good cut flowers and the large, spherical flowerheads of *A. christophii* and several others can be dried for arrangements. Most are hardy in Britain, but a few need a cool greenhouse.

It is vital to give alliums well-drained soil, though species from the Far East must never be allowed to dry out. Most species bloom in early summer, but some have their flowers in spring and autumn.

Allium is a genus of great diversity. Fine grassy leaves give some species a delicate appearance, and fleshy strap-like leaves form sturdy clumps in others. There is even considerable variation within individual species in terms of height – as the list of recommended plants shows.

RECOMMENDED SPECIES AND VARIETIES

A. aflatunense see *A. hollandicum*

A. albopilosum see *A. christophii*

A. atropurpureum Reddish purple starry flowers are produced in handsome heads shaped like shuttlecocks in early to mid summer. An easy-to-grow plant, native to S Europe. HEIGHT 40cm-1m (16in-3ft).

A. bulgaricum see *Nectaroscordum siculum* ssp. *bulgaricum*

A. carinatum ssp. *pulchellum*♀ (syn. *A. cirrhosum*, *A. pulchellum*) (keeled garlic) The flower stems, carrying loose heads of pendent, pinkish purple flowers, emerge from clumps of long narrow leaves in mid summer. The white f. *album* flowers at the same time, and the 2 make fine companions at the front of a border. Native to S Europe. HEIGHT 30-60cm (1-2ft).

A. cepa see onion p. 741

A. cernuum♀ (lady's leek, nodding onion) The loose, drooping flowerheads consist of 30-40 pinkish purple, cup-shaped flowers. They appear from early to mid summer above clumps of narrow leaves. Native to

▲ *Allium karataviense*

▲ *Allium cyaneum*

▲ *Allium cyathophorum* var. *farreri*

N America. HEIGHT 30-70cm (12-28in).

A. christophii♀ (syn. *A. albopilosum*) (star of Persia) Given a sunny, well-drained position, this outstanding plant is easy to establish. Its large spherical flowerheads in early summer are up to 20cm (8in) across, made up of 50 or more star-shaped, silvery lilac flowers. It has hairy, pale green, strap-shaped leaves. Native to Iran and Turkey. HEIGHT 1.2m (4ft).

A. cirrhosum see *A. carinatum*

A. cyaneum♀ This easy-to-grow plant with fine grassy leaves produces brilliant violet-blue, pendent flower clusters in summer. Native to China. HEIGHT 10-30cm (4-12in).

A. cyathophorum var. *farreri* (syn. *A. farreri*) Given peaty well-drained soil that is kept moist in summer, this plant does well. It has grass-like leaves and loose heads of purplish flowers in late summer. Native to NW China. HEIGHT 15-30cm (6-12in).

A. fistulosum see Welsh onion p. 742

A. flavum♀ The yellow flowers of this easily grown species appear in pendent clusters of up to 30 flowers in mid and late summer. Native to S Europe. HEIGHT 30-50cm (12-20in).

The dwarf varieties var. *minus* and var.

nanum, which are useful rock-garden plants, grow to 15cm (6in) in height.

A. giganteum♀ Perhaps the most eye-catching species, this soaring plant has light violet flowers, carried in spherical heads 12cm (4¾in) in diameter on stout stems. They appear in early summer as the blue-green strap-shaped leaves wither, and last well as cut flowers. Native to central Asia and not fully hardy, so in cold areas apply a mulch in winter. HEIGHT 1-2m (3-6½ft).

A. glaucum see *A. senescens*

A. hollandicum♀ (syn *A. aflatunense*) Appearing in spring and early summer, the spectacular hemispherical flowerheads consist of hundreds of pale violet flowers. The heads open on stout stems as the strap-like leaves wither. They are excellent cut flowers and their dried seed heads are used in floral arrangements. HEIGHT 75cm (2½ft).

'Purple Sensation'♀ has very dark purple flowers.

A. kansuense see *A. sikkimense*

A. karataviense♀ Unusually, this species is grown for its broad, handsome leaves rather than its flowers. Each bulb produces 2 prostrate, grey-green leaves with reddish edges. The ball-shaped flowerheads are a dusky pink and appear in late spring or early summer. The plant is suitable for a rock garden or the front of a border. Native to Turkestan. HEIGHT 15-20cm (6-8in).

Allium moly

A. moly (golden garlic) ♀ This well-known species produces clumps of glossy, bright yellow flowers in early to mid summer. Each stem carries up to 40 flowers in loose clusters 4-7 cm (1½-2¾ in) across. It spreads rapidly. Native to S Europe. HEIGHT 10-35 cm (4-14 in).

'Jeannine' ♀ has larger flowerheads, about 9 cm (3½ in) across, and often produces 2 flower stems per bulb.

A. murrayanum see *A. unifolium*

A. neapolitanum (Naples garlic) As one of the earliest species to flower (from early spring), this allium is often grown to cut and enjoy indoors. Each flowerhead is made up of around 40 starry white flowers and is 5-8 cm (2-3¼ in) across. Originating in S Europe and N Africa, it is not fully hardy in Britain, but will succeed outside in a warm spot in southern Britain. It can also be grown as a pot plant in a cool greenhouse. HEIGHT 20-50 cm (8-20 in).

A. oreophilum ♀ (syn. *A. ostrowskianum*) This colourful rock-garden plant bears loose clusters of pink to purple flowers in early and mid summer. Native to Turkestan. HEIGHT 5-10 cm (2-4 in).

▲ *Allium moly*

▲ *Allium moly* 'Jeannine'

'Zwanenburg' ♀ is a particularly striking variety with carmine-pink flowers.

A. ostrowskianum see *A. oreophilum*

A. porrum see leeks p.739

A. pulchellum see *A. carinatum*

A. sativum see garlic p.742

A. schoenoprasum see chives p.331

A. senescens (syn. *A. glaucum, A. spirale*) (German garlic, mountain garlic) This very variable species, useful in a rock garden or at the edge of a path, prefers well-drained soil. Lilac or pinkish purple, cup-shaped flowers are carried in hemispherical clusters up to 5 cm (2 in) across in mid summer to early autumn. HEIGHT 10-50 cm (4-20 in).

Many garden hybrids have developed from the 2 subspecies found in the wild. The European ssp. *montanum* has narrow grass-green leaves and grows to about 45 cm (1½ ft) tall. The Asian ssp. *senescens* has fleshy, green to grey-green leaves, sometimes attractively twisted, and grows from just a few to 60 cm (2 ft) tall. Plants bred to have grey or bluish green leaves are sometimes named *A. glaucum*, and those with twisted leaves *A. spirale*.

A. siculum see *Nectaroscordum siculum*

A. sikkimense (syn. *A. kansuense, A. tibeticum*) This clump-forming bulb has pretty, bell-shaped, blue flowers which hang in small clusters in summer among narrow leaves. Native to the Himalayas. HEIGHT 10-25 cm (4-10 in).

A. sphaerocephalon (round-headed leek) The flowers of this species are good for cutting and loved by bees. The pink to reddish purple, bell-shaped flowers are carried in dense heads in mid to late summer. Plant in tight clumps. Native to Europe, N Africa and W Asia. HEIGHT 50-60 cm (20-24 in).

A. spirale see *A. senescens*

A. tibeticum see *A. sikkimense*

A. triquetrum (three-cornered leek) Easily recognised by its 3-sided stems, this plant is

▼ *Allium sikkimense*

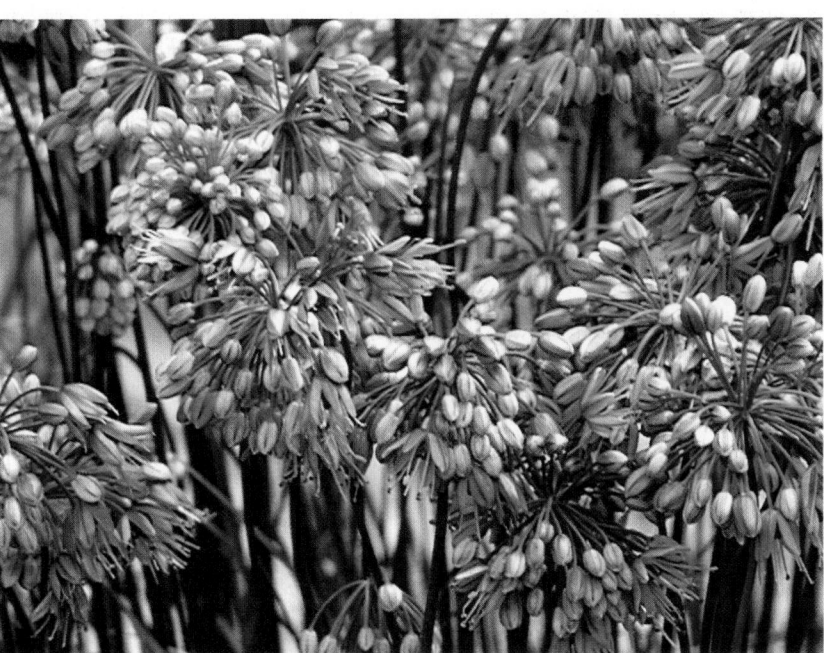

pretty but invasive, and should be planted with caution. The white flowers, from early spring, have green stripes and hang in loose heads. Native to S Europe but naturalised in Britain. HEIGHT 15-30 cm (6-12 in).

A. tuberosum see Chinese chives p.331

A. unifolium (syn. *A. murrayanum*) This plant does well in a hot and sunny position that recreates the conditions of its native habitat in western USA. In early summer it carries domed heads, consisting of up to 30 deep pink, bell-shaped flowers. HEIGHT 20-60 cm (8-24 in).

A. ursinum (ramson, wild garlic) The broad, bright green leaves grow in clumps round stems that bear loose heads of clear white starry flowers in late spring. The species is found throughout Europe and is often regarded as a weed in Britain. However, it is useful for growing in woodland conditions. The leaves give off a strong smell of garlic when crushed. HEIGHT 10-45 cm (4-18 in).

CULTIVATION Grow in fertile well-drained soil and a sunny sheltered position. Plant the bulbs in autumn, covering them to twice their diameter with soil. Leave them undisturbed for several years. Bulbs such as *A. cyaneum* and *A. oreophilum* may also be grown in pots in a cool greenhouse.

PROPAGATION Lift and divide old clumps of bulbs as soon as they have died down after flowering. Most can also be raised from seed sown in pots of gritty soil in late summer. If the old flowerheads are left on the plants, some species seed themselves.

PESTS AND DISEASES The bulbs may be damaged by the larvae of onion flies. Diseases such as white rot, fusarium and rust can also attack the plants. Aphids may be a problem for species grown under glass and can spread viruses.

Almond, ornamental see *Prunus*

Alnus
Alder
Betulaceae

Alnus glutinosa 'Imperialis'

Striking catkins, unusual cones and fine foliage are features of these splendid deciduous trees and shrubs. The bark splits into thick plates with age. Alders are hardy and fast-growing and thrive on poorer soils. They are also able to survive very wet conditions and often found growing by rivers and streams. *Alnus cordata* and *A. glutinosa* reach a height of 18m (60ft) or more.

Both male and female catkins are carried on the same plant and usually appear in clusters of between two and six from late winter to early spring – before the leaves. The male catkins are pendulous and can grow to about 10cm (4in) long; the females are shorter and develop into round, woody cones usually less than 2.5cm (1in) in diameter. The cones ripen in autumn and remain on the tree for several months. Alder is the only deciduous tree to produce a cone-like casing for its seeds. The leaves are alternate, grow up to 10cm (4in) long and often have a serrated edge.

RECOMMENDED SPECIES AND VARIETIES
A. cordata♀ (Italian alder) Heart-shaped finely toothed leaves, dark glossy green above and lighter beneath, are borne on an upright, rather conical tree. The yellow

▲ *Alnus cordata*

catkins grow to 7.5cm (3in) long. The tree grows well in all types of soil. Native to Italy. HEIGHT & SPREAD 8×3m (26×10ft) after 20 years, ultimately 18m (60ft) tall.
A. glutinosa (common alder) This conical tree is ideal for growing in very wet condi-

▲ *Alnus glutinosa* (bark)

tions and is often seen beside streams. The irregularly toothed leaves are generally pear-shaped and tapered at the base. They are dark green above and lighter beneath. The male catkins are dark yellow and can grow to 10cm (4in) long. Native to Britain. HEIGHT & SPREAD 8×3m (26×10ft) after 20 years, ultimately 18m (60ft) tall.

'Imperialis'♀ is a beautiful conical tree with deeply cut leaves that give it a graceful feathery appearance. It is about half the size of the species. 'Laciniata' is similar but has less deeply cut leaves.
A. incana (grey alder) An upright tree with dark green, serrated, oval leaves which are grey-hairy underneath. The yellow-brown catkins are 5-10cm (2-4in) long. Native to Europe and the Caucasus. HEIGHT & SPREAD 6×2m (20×6½ft) after 20 years, ultimately 15m (50ft) tall.
A. rugosa (speckled alder) This small tree of rounded habit has 10cm (4in) long, oval leaves that are dark green above and lighter beneath. The greenish yellow catkins grow to 10cm (4in) long. Native to N America. HEIGHT & SPREAD 2×2m (6½×6½ft) after 5 years, ultimately 5m (16ft) tall.
A. × *spaethii*♀ A fast-growing upright tree with large serrated leaves up to 15cm (6in) long. These are purplish at first, turning dark green above and lighter beneath with age. The catkins can grow to 15cm (6in) long. HEIGHT & SPREAD 7×3m (23×10ft) after 20 years, ultimately 15m (50ft) tall.
CULTIVATION Alders grow in a variety of soils. Most tolerate lime but *A. cordata* and *A. glutinosa* do not do well on shallow soils over chalk. *A. cordata* and *A. incana* prefer drier soil, and *A. glutinosa* tolerates very wet soils.
PROPAGATION Most alders are best grown from seed, but hardwood cuttings can also be successful. Cultivars need to be grafted.
PRUNING None is required.
PESTS AND DISEASES Phytophthora may affect alders on wet ground.

Aloe
Aloeaceae

Aloe variegata

Prominent rosettes of fleshy leaves give these perennial succulents and sub-shrubs an architectural character. The plants are also prized for their dense spikes of tubular flowers. Aloes require a minimum temperature of 7°C (45°F) and are suitable only as house or greenhouse plants.

RECOMMENDED SPECIES AND VARIETIES
A. aristata♀ Dark green, lance-shaped, leaves, 10cm (4in) long and 2cm (¾in) wide, form tight rosettes, up to 20cm (8in) across, which grow in dense clusters. The leaves are sparsely spined and have bands of white spots. Soft white teeth at the margins complete their unusual appearance. Red flowers, up to 4cm (1½in) long, are carried on branched spikes in early summer. HEIGHT & SPREAD 50×20cm (20×8in).
A. variegata (partridge breast aloe) The triangular dark green leaves, up to 15cm (6in) long and 5cm (2in) wide, are banded and blotched with white and form neat angular rosettes. An occasional spike of flesh-pink or dull scarlet flowers is produced in winter. HEIGHT & SPREAD 30×20cm (12×8in).

▲ *Aloe variegata*

CULTIVATION Grow in a very sunny spot in compost made up of equal parts of sharp grit and John Innes No. 3. Water freely in spring and summer, sparingly in winter. Repot annually in spring and feed once or twice in summer with liquid houseplant fertiliser.
PROPAGATION Sow seeds under glass during spring, or divide the clusters of rosettes in spring or summer.
PESTS AND DISEASES Usually trouble free.

Alonsoa
Mask flower
Scrophulariaceae

Pink, orange and red are the predominant colours of the 2cm (¾in) wide flowers of these tropical American perennials, which are often grown as half-hardy annuals. Each flower resembles a tiny asymmetrical dish with a deeply scalloped edge, or possibly a theatrical mask. They are fairly easy summer-flowering bedding plants, though results can be disappointing in cool wet seasons. They may also be grown as conservatory and greenhouse plants. Those described are very free-flowering, much-branched species, which may bloom all summer.

RECOMMENDED SPECIES AND VARIETIES
A. meridionalis This good cut flower has pink, red and white blooms, available mixed and as the varieties **'Pink Beauty'** and **'Salmon Beauty'**. The toothed elongated oval leaves are up to 3.5cm (1⅜in) long. HEIGHT & SPREAD 60×30cm (2×1ft).
A. warscewiczii♀ Scarlet flowers adorn this popular species, which has toothed oval leaves, heart-shaped at the base. HEIGHT & SPREAD 60×30cm (2×1ft).
'Peachy-keen' has pale apricot flowers.

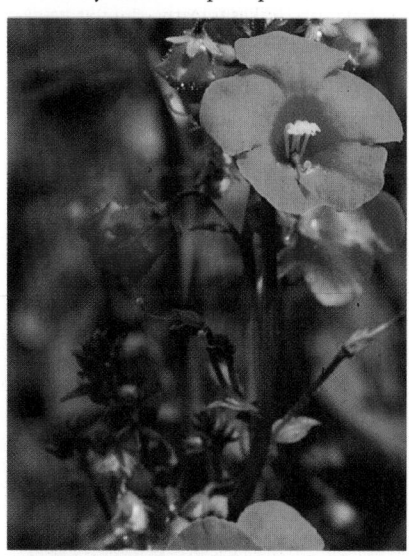
▲ *Alonsoa warscewiczii*

CULTIVATION Sow seed in heat – at least 18°C (64°F) – in early spring. Prick out 5cm (2in) apart, or into 8cm (3in) pots or cell trays. At 5cm (2in) high, pinch out the growing points to encourage branching. Harden off and plant out, 15-25cm (6-10in) apart, in a sunny, sheltered spot.
For greenhouse or conservatory plants, sow in late summer. During winter maintain a minimum temperature of 10°C (50°F). Use a 13cm (5in) diameter final pot and support the flowering stems.
PROPAGATION Sow seed, or take ripewood cuttings in late summer.
PESTS AND DISEASES Aphids may attack.

Aloysia
Verbenaceae

Aloysia triphylla

Handsome aromatic foliage and slender spikes of small tubular flowers characterise aloysias. *Aloysia triphylla*, a half-hardy deciduous shrub or sub-shrub, makes a splendid pot plant for a conservatory. It can also be grown outside in a sunny, sheltered spot. Its dried leaves are used for flavouring and potpourri.

RECOMMENDED SPECIES AND VARIETIES
A. triphylla (syn. *Lippia citriodora*) (lemon verbena) The coarse, lemon-scented leaves, up to 10cm (4in) long, are lance-shaped. Sprays of tiny white or purplish flowers are produced during summer on new terminal growths. Native to Argentina and Chile. HEIGHT & SPREAD 1.5×1.2m (5×4ft) tall.

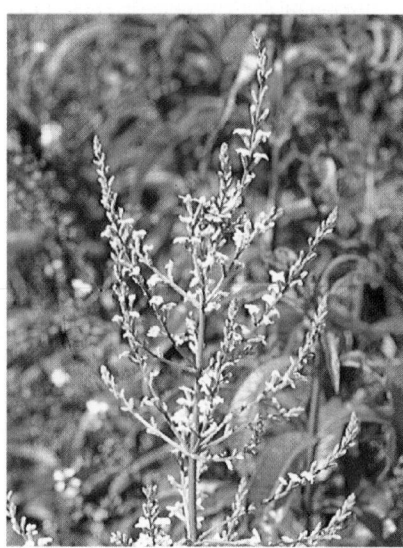
▲ *Aloysia triphylla*

CULTIVATION Grow indoors in large pots in a soil-based compost such as John Innes No. 3. Outside, plant in free-draining soil against a sunny south or west-facing wall. Give a protective mulch of composted bark or well-rotted garden compost in autumn.
PROPAGATION Take softwood cuttings in summer.
PRUNING Indoor plants retain their shrubby habit, but those grown outside usually suffer frost damage and may need to be pruned to the ground each spring.
PESTS AND DISEASES Greenfly can be a problem outside; whitefly and red spider mite may attack the plants under glass.

Alstroemeria
Peruvian lily, lily of the Incas
Alstroemeriaceae

Alstroemeria Ligtu Hybrids

Grown for their attractive, showy flowers, alstroemerias are colourful plants for garden borders and containers. Long-lasting when cut, the flowers are popular with both gardeners and commercial growers and, over the years, many hybrids have been bred to meet an increasing demand for new flower colours and a longer flowering period.

Herbaceous perennials, native to S America, alstroemerias have thick, rather brittle tubers, which spread to form colonies up to 1.2m (4ft) across. They are easily grown in fertile well-drained soil but do not like thin dry soils. The plants recommended below are hardy to -10°C (14°F).

Open, funnel-shaped flowers are borne in loose clusters at the ends of the stems. They are about 5cm (2in) long and have three narrow inner petals and three broader outer ones. The inner petals, two upper and one lower, are usually marked in a contrasting colour. Flower colours include shades of purple, pink, red, orange and yellow. The long stems bear many slightly twisted, lanceolate leaves, 5-10cm (2-4in) long.

RECOMMENDED SPECIES AND VARIETIES
A. aurea (syn. *A. aurantiaca*) Clusters of

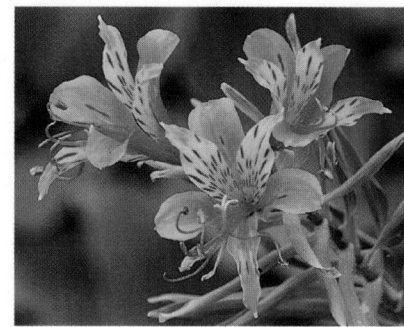
▲ *Alstroemeria aurea* 'Dover Orange'

bright orange flowers, marked with deep red flecks, appear in summer. A vigorous plant, which often spreads to form large patches. HEIGHT 1m (3ft).
'Dover Orange' is slightly taller and has deeper orange flowers.
A. psittacina (syn. *A. pulchella*) Stems, spotted with mauve, bear clusters of flowers from late summer to early autumn. The narrow flowers are green and deep wine-

a

red, spotted and streaked with maroon. HEIGHT 1 m (3 ft).

ALSTROEMERIA HYBRIDS
There are many hybrids that produce a wide range of different coloured flowers. Apart from the Ligtu Hybrids, which flower in early summer, all bloom from mid summer until the first frosts of autumn. Most grow to 1 m (3 ft) high, though there are dwarf hybrids that are excellent for pots. 'Apollo'♀ has ivory-white flowers with a yellow spot and brown flecks on the inner petals. 'Charm'♀ has pale pink blooms with creamy yellow inner petals, flecked with brown. The **Ligtu Hybrids**♀ produce flowers in a wide range of colours, from soft

▲ Alstroemeria 'Apollo'

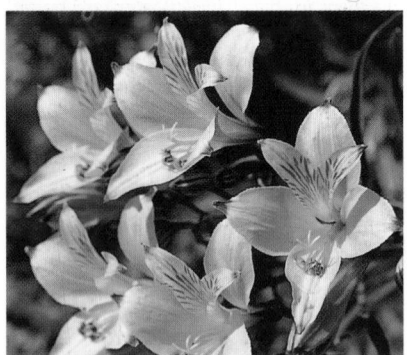
▲ Alstroemeria Ligtu Hybrids

pink to orange and yellow. 'Marina'♀ has dark pink flowers with a lemon-yellow centre and brown flecks. The brick-red petals of 'Mars'♀ have a yellow flash; the inner petals are flecked brownish purple. 'Orange Glory'♀ has deep orange-red flowers with a yellow mark and brown flecks on the inner petals. 'Princess Caroline'♀ has soft apricot-orange flowers with a red blotch on the outer petals and a yellow throat. The flowers of 'Princess Elizabeth'♀ are cream with a pink flush and a yellow throat. This hybrid only reaches 30 cm (1 ft). 'Princess Mira'♀ has rich lilac-pink flowers with a white throat, and grows to 30 cm (1 ft). The flowers of 'Yellow Friendship'♀ have lemon-yellow outer petals and deep yellow inner ones; the upper inner petals are flecked with brown.
CULTIVATION Outside, choose a sunny sheltered position with fertile, well-drained

but moisture-retentive soil. Plant tubers 4-8 cm (1½-3¼ in) deep in early spring. Protect them from bright sun and water regularly until established. In winter, mulch young plants or plants growing in cold areas. Pot-grown alstroemerias are planted from spring to autumn, 3 cm (1¼ in) deep, in 30 cm (12 in) pots of loam-based compost. Overwinter in a light frost-free place, keeping the compost almost dry. Move pots outside once the danger of frost has passed. Deadhead for continuous flowering.
PROPAGATION Divide roots in early autumn or spring, replanting immediately.
PESTS AND DISEASES Young shoots can be damaged by slugs and snails, and swift moth caterpillars may feed on the roots. Red spider mite can be a problem under glass.

Althaea
Malvaceae

Pretty, pink to purple, cup-shaped flowers are carried on tall, erect stems in summer. Althaeas are closely related to the hollyhock, *Alcea rosea*, but have smaller flowers with five notched petals. The round, toothed leaves, up to 6 cm (2½ in) long, are pale green. Hardy plants, althaeas spread to form clumps and are suitable for a sunny spot at the back of a border.
RECOMMENDED SPECIES AND VARIETIES
A. officinalis (marsh mallow) The pale lilac-pink flowers, 3 cm (1¼ in) across, have a central boss of purplish red anthers and are borne singly or in small clusters at the leaf axils. The velvety ovate leaves have 3-5 lobes. A hardy perennial, native to grassy coastal areas or salt marshes in Europe. HEIGHT & SPREAD 2 m × 30 cm (6½ × 1 ft).

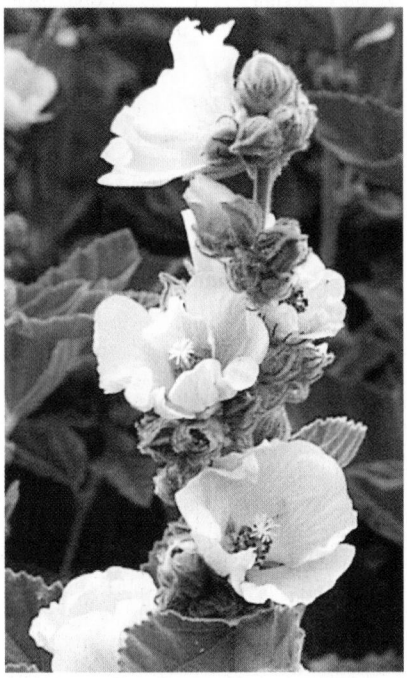
▲ Althaea officinalis

CULTIVATION Grow in any fertile soil in full sun. On windy sites stake taller plants.
PROPAGATION Divide in autumn or spring, or sow seed in open ground in spring and transplant to the final position in autumn.
PESTS AND DISEASES Capsid bugs, caterpillars and, in hot summers, red spider mites may be troublesome.

Aluminium plant see *Pilea cadierei*
Alum root see *Heuchera*

Alyogyne
Malvaceae

Though mostly confined to the greenhouse or conservatory, these hibiscus-like shrubs, with their large, purple hued, satiny flowers, can be moved outside in summer to bring colour to a patio or terrace. Native to Australia, they survive outside in Britain only when planted in a frost-free garden.
RECOMMENDED SPECIES AND VARIETIES
A. hakeifolia (satin hibiscus) Pale lilac or lilac-purple flowers are borne from early summer to mid autumn by this vigorous species. The finely cut, coarse green leaves are up to 7.5 cm (3 in) long. HEIGHT & SPREAD 3 × 1 m (10 × 3 ft) after 5 years and ultimately.
A. huegelii (lilac hibiscus) Saucer-shaped flowers, up to 10 cm (4 in) across, in lilac-purple or red with a darker spotted base, are carried from early summer to mid autumn. The deep green leaves are lobed and up to 8 cm (3¼ in) long. HEIGHT & SPREAD 3 × 1.2 m (10 × 4 ft) after 5 years and ultimately, half this size in smaller containers.
'Santa Cruz' has soft blue flowers tinged with pink, up to 10 cm (4 in) across.

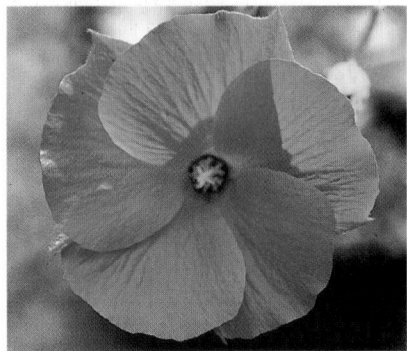
▲ Alyogyne huegelii

CULTIVATION Grow in large pots in a frost-free conservatory or cool greenhouse. Bring outside during the summer and feed regularly. Water sparingly in winter.
PROPAGATION Take softwood cuttings in summer or sow seeds in warmth in spring.
PRUNING Trim off die-back in spring and reduce the main branches by two-thirds.
PESTS AND DISEASES Aphids, whitefly and red spider mites can trouble alyogynes, especially when they are under glass.

Alyssum
Cruciferae

Alyssum montanum

Dense clusters of tiny four-petalled flowers, usually yellow, occasionally white or pink, smother hummocks of grey or silver foliage from late spring to mid summer. Alyssums are hardy plants, but in the garden grow best in a well-drained, sunny position, edging borders, draping down walls or tucked into rock gardens. Most species are native to dry highlands in S Europe and W Asia. The hardy annual bedding plants known as alyssums have been reclassified as *Lobularia maritima*. The perennial once called *Alyssum saxatile* (yellow alyssum) is now *Aurinia saxatilis*. All the species listed below are low-growing evergreen perennials, except *A. spinosum*, which is a semi-deciduous shrub.

RECOMMENDED SPECIES AND VARIETIES
A. cuneifolium Buttercup-yellow flower clusters, 3.5 cm (1⅜ in) across, are borne on a compact plant. The silvery, hairy leaves form dense evergreen rosettes. HEIGHT & SPREAD 15×15 cm (6×6 in).

A dwarf variety is ssp. *pirinicum*.

A. maritimum see *Lobularia maritima*

A. montanum Fragrant, deep yellow flowers are borne in clusters 5 cm (2 in) across. The leaves form dense, whitish rosettes. The plant has a spreading, mat-forming habit. It is easy to grow and often seeds around once established. HEIGHT & SPREAD 15×30 cm (6×12 in).

'Berggold' ('Mountain Gold') is lower growing with golden yellow flowers.

A. saxatile see *Aurinia saxatilis*

A. serpyllifolium This alyssum forms a sprawling mat of grey-green to silvery leaves. The bright yellow flower clusters measure 2.5 cm (1 in) across. HEIGHT & SPREAD 8×30 cm (3¼×12 in).

▼ *Alyssum cuneifolium*

▲ *Alyssum serpyllifolium*

A. spinosum (syn. *Ptilotrichum spinosum*) White to pink-purple flowers are borne in abundant rounded clusters 3.5 cm (1⅜ in) across. Colour varies considerably in plants raised from seed. This semi-deciduous, dense and rather prickly shrub forms rounded hummocks with silvery grey leaves. HEIGHT & SPREAD 60×30 cm (2×1 ft).

'Roseum'♥ has pale to deep pink-purple flowers. It is easy to grow and a reliable performer, especially in a raised bed or a scree, created by mixing coarse gravel or stone chippings with peat and soil.

▲ *Alyssum spinosum* 'Roseum'

A. wulfenianum Pale yellow flowers, in flat clusters up to 2.5 cm (1 in) across, appear in early to late summer above rosettes of silver-green foliage. This species does well in crevices in walls, paths and banks, being a tufted plant with spreading stems. HEIGHT & SPREAD 20×30 cm (8×12 in).

CULTIVATION Plant alyssums from spring to autumn on sunny well-drained sites. They especially like alkaline soils. In wetter areas protect them with a pane of glass or a cloche during winter.

PROPAGATION Take softwood cuttings in late spring or early summer, or sow seed from late summer to winter.

PRUNING Trim back lightly after flowering to encourage bushy growth.

PESTS AND DISEASES Usually trouble free.

Alyssum, sweet see *Lobularia maritima*

▼ *Alyssum wulfenianum*

Amaranthus
Amaranthaceae

Dangling flower tassels and varieties offering brilliantly coloured foliage earn these half-hardy annuals their place in borders and containers.

RECOMMENDED SPECIES AND VARIETIES
A. caudatus (love-lies-bleeding) Long drooping tassels, up to 45 cm (1½ ft) long, of tiny blood-red flowers, hang among pale green leaves in mid and late summer. HEIGHT & SPREAD 60×40 cm (24×16 in).

▲ *Amaranthus caudatus*

The tassels of 'Viridis' are vivid green.

A. cruentus (syn. *A. paniculatus*) 'Foxtail' Upright, deep blood-red flower spikes grow among bronze-red foliage on a plant 60 cm (2 ft) tall. 'Red Cathedral', with scarlet foliage and purple flowers, reaches 1 m (3 ft) or more tall. Both varieties have a spread of 40 cm (16 in).

A. hypochondriacus Deep crimson flowers are carried in densely packed, erect spikes among purple-tinted foliage from mid summer to mid autumn. HEIGHT & SPREAD 1.2 m×50 cm (4 ft×20 in).

'Green Thumb'♥ has green flowers and 'Pygmy Torch'♥ has purple leaves and crimson flowers. They both grow to 60 cm (2 ft) high and 40 cm (16 in) wide.

A. paniculatus see *A. cruentus*

A. tricolor This tender species, grown for its striking foliage, makes a bright summer pot plant in a conservatory. The lower leaves of 'Illumination' are green and chocolate-brown, the upper leaves bright rose-red and yellow. 'Joseph's Coat' has chocolate-brown, yellow and green lower leaves and crimson, scarlet and gold upper leaves. HEIGHT & SPREAD 60×40 cm (2 ft×16 in).

CULTIVATION All, except the more tender *A. tricolor*, are easily grown in any soil. They do best in full sun. *A. tricolor* needs sheltered conditions in full sun. Support taller varieties and plants on exposed sites. Pinch out the growing points of *A. cruentus* while still small, to encourage branching.

PROPAGATION Sow seed in early spring in a heated greenhouse.

PESTS AND DISEASES Aphids can be troublesome to amaranthus.

41

a

Amaryllis
Amaryllidaceae

Large, pink or white, sweetly scented flowers are borne in late summer and early autumn by this not fully hardy, bulbous perennial. It should not be confused with the tender winter-flowering houseplant, native to S America, *Hippeastrum*, which is often mistakenly sold as *Amaryllis*. There is only one species in the genus.

Amaryllis belladonna (belladonna lily, Jersey lily) The trumpet-shaped blooms, 6–10 cm (2½–4 in) long, are borne in clusters of 6 on long purple stems. Dark green, strap-like leaves, 50 cm (20 in) long, appear in autumn after the flowers, and last through winter until the following summer. Native to South Africa, *A. belladonna* grows outdoors in Britain, and is also suitable for container planting, both indoors and out. HEIGHT 60 cm (2 ft).

▲ *Amaryllis belladonna*

'Johannesburg' has pale pink flowers with a lighter centre. 'Kimberley' has deep crimson-pink flowers with a white centre.

CULTIVATION Plant amaryllis bulbs during late summer in mild areas and in spring elsewhere, choosing a sunny position in well-drained, humus-rich soil. The bulbs must receive direct sunlight in summer or they will not flower. Make sure that the top of the bulb is level with the soil surface; over time the bulb pulls itself down, sometimes as deep as 20 cm (8 in). In areas where winter temperatures often fall below -5°C (23°F), plants need the protection of a wall facing south or south-west and a winter mulch. Allow the leaves and flowers to die back before removing them.

PROPAGATION Lift mature plants between early and mid summer, remove large offsets and replant immediately. Plants propagated this way can take up to 3 years to flower. Sow seed when ripe, though plants may take up to 8 years to flower.

PESTS AND DISEASES Slugs, snails, narcissus flies, eelworm, bulb rot and narcissus leaf scorch may damage plants.

Amaryllis see also *Hippeastrum*

Amelanchier
Serviceberry, Snowy mespilus
Rosaceae

Amelanchier canadensis

White spring blossom and spectacular bright red and gold autumn foliage make this an outstanding plant at most times of the year. The star-shaped flowers, no more than 2.5 cm (1 in) in diameter, appear in a profusion of clusters. Most are pure white and are dazzling against the young coppery foliage. The simple, alternate leaves grow to 5 cm (2 in) long and are generally finely toothed. The summer berries are red at first, darkening to black. Most of the ten or so species of these hardy deciduous shrubs or small trees are native to N America.

▲ *Amelanchier 'Ballerina'*

RECOMMENDED SPECIES AND VARIETIES

A. 'Ballerina'♀ This large shrub or small tree of rounded habit bears 6 cm (2½ in) long clusters of white flowers in early spring. The finely toothed leaves are bronze when young and give good red and brown autumn colour. HEIGHT & SPREAD 1×1 m (3×3 ft) after 5 years, finally 3 m (10 ft) tall.

A. canadensis Small white flowers appear

▼ *Amelanchier canadensis*

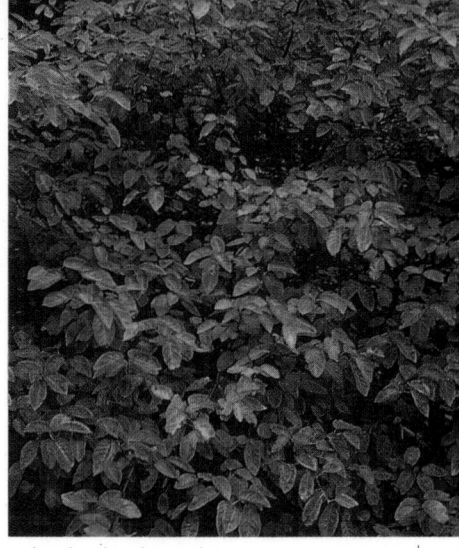

▲ *Amelanchier lamarckii*

in erect clusters, up to 6 cm (2½ in) long, in mid to late spring with the leaves. This erect, often multistemmed large shrub or small tree grows well in damp conditions. HEIGHT & SPREAD 1.2×1 m (4×3 ft) after 5 years, ultimately 7 m (23 ft) tall.

A. laevis Pendulous, 12 cm (4¾ in) long clusters of small white flowers appear in late spring and contrast with the young bronze foliage. The leaves turn dark green with age and give a display of orange and red autumn colour. The purple-black fruits are edible. This often multistemmed tree has a rather upright habit that becomes more spreading in old age. HEIGHT & SPREAD 1.5×1 m (5×3 ft) after 5 years, ultimately 8 m (26 ft) tall.

A. lamarckii♀ Profuse clusters of small white flowers appear in mid to late spring and grow to 7.5 cm (3 in) long. The new, coppery bronze leaves emerge at the same time as the flowers and are covered in silky hairs which are eventually lost. The spectacular autumn colour normally combines brilliant yellows and reds. The plant has a multi-stemmed, rounded habit. HEIGHT & SPREAD 1.5×1.2 m (5×4 ft) after 5 years, ultimately 10 m (33 ft) tall.

CULTIVATION Plant in autumn and spring in any well-drained, moisture-retentive soil. Grow in full sun or partial shade. Amelanchiers prefer lime-free soil.

PROPAGATION This is normally from seed sown in autumn. But if a particular feature is required then grafting needs to be carried out. Layering and division are also success-

ful with the smaller, multistemmed shrubs.
PRUNING The multistemmed species may need thinning out from time to time.
PESTS AND DISEASES Usually trouble free, though fire blight is sometimes a problem.

Amicia
Leguminosae

Ramrod-straight, hollow, downy stems and eye-catching leaves distinguish this tall, semi-tender sub-shrub. Bamboo-like stems carry the leaves horizontally, giving the plants a layered appearance. Formed by four almost rectangular, notched leaflets, the leaves are bright green with prominent, paler midribs. Just beneath the flowers are pale green, almost circular leafy scales (stipules) which are streaked purplish brown with creamy beige edges. *Amicia zygomeris*, from the mountains of Mexico, is the only species generally grown in Britain. It needs a sheltered border or the protection of a wall in a warm, sunny garden.

RECOMMENDED SPECIES
A. zygomeris Yellow pea-like flowers, often flushed purple, appear in short axillary racemes from summer to autumn. The leaflets are about 7 cm (2¾ in) long. The narrow seedpods are jointed and flattened. HEIGHT & SPREAD 1-2 m×1.2 m (3-6½×4 ft).
CULTIVATION Plant in spring in any fertile soil in a warm sunny position. Shelter from wind to avoid damage to the foliage. Protect the roots with a mulch in winter.
PROPAGATION Sow seed in spring or take semi-ripe cuttings in summer.
PESTS AND DISEASES Young plants are attacked by slugs and snails.

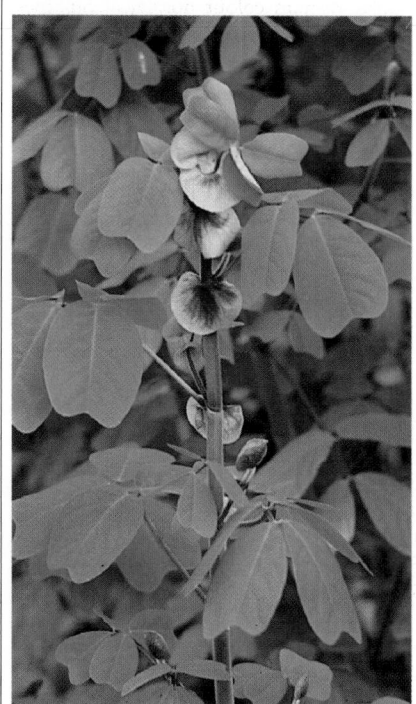
▲ *Amicia zygomeris*

Ammi
Umbelliferae

Frothy sprays of delicate white flowers distinguish these relatively tall, fast-growing, hardy annuals. They are closely related to the common native hedgerow plant known as cow parsley, though the foliage is more finely divided and therefore more appealing. The flowerheads last well when cut, and in arrangements provide a light-textured contrast to bolder, colourful blooms. Native to SW Asia, S Europe and N Africa.

▲ *Ammi majus*

RECOMMENDED SPECIES
A. majus Tiny white flowers are carried in compound umbels, up to 15 cm (6 in) across, on branching, upright stems from mid summer to early autumn. The leaves are mid to bluish green. The lower ones are pinnate with tooth-edged leaflets, the upper ones are still more divided, with a fern-like appearance. HEIGHT & SPREAD up to 1.2 m×40 cm (4 ft×16 in).
A. visnaga This species is very similar to *A. majus*, but has more finely divided foliage. HEIGHT & SPREAD 1.2 m×40 cm (4 ft×16 in).
CULTIVATION Ammis thrive even on poor, dry soils. Full-grown plants need staking against strong winds.
PROPAGATION Sow seed where the plants are to flower in mid to late spring.
PESTS AND DISEASES Aphids are an occasional nuisance.

Amorpha
Leguminosae

These fully hardy, free-flowering shrubs, many-branched and spreading, thrive in an open sunny position. The flowers have the characteristic pea-flower shape, with standard, wings and keel, constructed in this case from a single five-lobed petal. They appear in spiked clusters in summer. The deciduous leaves are pinnate, often fern-like in appearance, and sometimes strongly aromatic. The grey-green leaflets are downy and oval or elliptic in shape.

RECOMMENDED SPECIES
A. canescens (lead plant) This short, erect shrub has oval leaflets, no more than 2.5 cm (1 in) long, in a fern-like arrangement. The leaves are surmounted by terminal, upright, cylindrical heads of small violet flowers with orange anthers from mid to late summer. The flowerheads are as long as 15 cm (6 in). Native to eastern N America. HEIGHT & SPREAD 90×90 cm (3×3 ft) after 5 years and ultimately.
A. fruticosa (false indigo, bastard indigo) The leaflets on the divided foliage are oval and up to 5 cm (2 in) long. Tiny, purplish blue flowers with orange anthers, packed tightly into erect spikes up to 15 cm (6 in) tall, are produced in profusion in summer. A vigorous and fast-growing plant, native to southern USA. HEIGHT & SPREAD 4×3 m (13×10 ft) after 5 years and ultimately.

Amorpha fruticosa

CULTIVATION Grow amorphas in full sun in a very free-draining soil, not too rich in organic matter. Young plants should be pot grown if they are to establish quickly when planted outside in spring. Once established, plants benefit from regular feeding with a general liquid fertiliser in summer.
PROPAGATION Take softwood cuttings in summer or sow seed in a coldframe in autumn or early spring. *A. fruticosa* may also be propagated by removing rooted suckers in autumn.
PRUNING Remove damaged or badly placed branches and shoots in spring, bearing in mind that flowers are borne on the current season's growth.
PESTS AND DISEASES Usually trouble free.

▲ *Amorpha fruticosa*

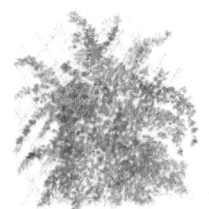

Ampelopsis
Vitaceae

*Ampelopsis glandulosa
var. brevipedunculata*

The handsome foliage of these vigorous, climbing deciduous shrubs provides dense cover for walls, pergolas or tree stumps. The oval leaves are lobed or divided. The plants cling by curling tendrils. Although easily cultivated and frost-hardy, they need plenty of room and a sheltered position.

RECOMMENDED SPECIES AND VARIETIES
A. glandulosa var. *brevipedunculata* (syn. *A. brevipedunculata*) This vigorous climber has dark green foliage. The leaves, up to 15 cm (6 in) long, are divided usually into 3 lobes, sometimes into 5. The small, late-summer clusters of tiny greenish flowers are followed in warm years by deep, greenish blue berries, 6 mm (¼ in) wide. Native to NE Asia. HEIGHT & SPREAD 3×1.8 m (10×6 ft) after 5 years, ultimately 5 m (16 ft) tall.

▲ *Ampelopsis glandulosa* var. *brevipedunculata* 'Elegans'

'Elegans' (syn. 'Tricolor') has smaller leaves, heavily splashed with pink and white. It reaches 3 m (10 ft) if given shelter.
A. henryana see *Parthenocissus henryana*
A. megalophylla Spectacularly large leaves, up to 60 cm (2 ft) long, are divided into 7 or more mid green, ovate leaflets which are whitish beneath. Tiny greenish flowers appear in clusters in late summer, sometimes followed by purple-black berries, 6 mm (¼ in) long. Native to W China. HEIGHT & SPREAD 6×3 m (20×10 ft) after 5 years, ultimately 10 m (33 ft).
A. sempervirens see *Cissus striata*
A. tricuspidata 'Veitchii' see *Parthenocissus tricuspidata* 'Veitchii'
A. veitchii see *Parthenocissus tricuspidata* 'Veitchii'

CULTIVATION Plant in a sheltered position in any garden soil, in sun or partial shade. Provide adequate support while plants become established.
PROPAGATION Take semi-ripe cuttings during summer.
PRUNING None essential, but if the plant outgrows its space cut back in spring.
PESTS AND DISEASES Usually trouble free.

Amsonia
Blue star
Apocynaceae

In early summer, these slow-growing, hardy herbaceous perennials and sub-shrubs carry loose clusters of bright blue flowers. Suitable for the front of a border or in light shade, these plants form compact clumps of upright stems with abundant whorls of pointed, dark green leaves. The flowers are tubular, flaring open to star-shaped blooms with five petals.

RECOMMENDED SPECIES AND VARIETIES
A. ciliata Bright blue flowers, up to 2 cm (¾ in) across, are borne in clusters on slender upright stems. The long, narrow leaves, rolled under at the edges, are up to 5 cm (2 in) long. The least hardy of the species included here, it prefers a warm, sunny, sheltered site. Native to S United States. HEIGHT & SPREAD 1 m×50 cm (3 ft×20 in).
A. orientalis♀ The flowers are mostly blue, occasionally deep violet, and 1.5 cm (½ in) across. The narrow, pointed leaves, hairy along the edges, are up to 5 cm (2 in) long. Native to Greece and Turkey. HEIGHT & SPREAD 1 m×50 cm (3 ft×20 in).
A. tabernaemontana Pale sky-blue flowers, up to 2 cm (¾ in) across, are borne in short clusters. The smooth, dull green leaves are ovate or obovate and up to 6 cm (2½ in) long. This plant does best in a moist, shady position. Native to SE United States. HEIGHT & SPREAD 1 m×50 cm (3 ft×20 in).
The flower clusters of var. *salicifolia* are

▲ *Amsonia tabernaemontana*

looser and smaller, the leaves are narrower and up to 9 cm (3½ in) long.
CULTIVATION Plant in autumn in fertile, moist but well-drained soil, placing in sun or light shade.
PROPAGATION Divide plants or sow seed in spring. Alternatively, take softwood cuttings in mid summer.
PESTS AND DISEASES Usually trouble free.

Anacyclus
Compositae

Forming small clumps of feathery foliage scattered with white daisies on arching stems, anacyclus are at their best in sheltered and sunny positions in rock gardens and raised beds. Native to the mountains of S Spain and N Africa, these plants are hardy if grown in freely draining soil.

RECOMMENDED SPECIES AND VARIETIES
A. pyrethrum (Mount Atlas daisy) This evergreen perennial has loose mats of tightly packed leaf rosettes, formed by ferny, grey-green leaves up to 4 cm (1½ in) long. The petals have a broad purple stripe underneath so that the flowers are purple in bud. They open out to white blooms, up to 5 cm (2 in) across. HEIGHT & SPREAD 7.5×30 cm (3×12 in).
The petals of var. *depressus* are deep crimson beneath and it reaches a height of 5 cm (2 in) and spread of 25 cm (10 in). 'Golden Gnome' has yellow flowerheads.
CULTIVATION Plant during spring in full sun in very well-drained soil. Protect from wet weather in winter with a cloche or a pane of glass. Alternatively, grow in an unheated greenhouse or alpine house. Unless seed is wanted, deadhead regularly to prolong flowering.
PROPAGATION Sow seed in spring or take softwood cuttings in late summer.
PESTS AND DISEASES Aphids sometimes infest foliage, inviting sooty mould. Young plants are attractive to slugs.

▲ *Anacyclus pyrethrum* var. *depressus*

Anagallis
Pimpernel
Primulaceae

The vivid little flowers of this genus come in blues and reds, providing a splash of summer colour. The flowers, with five broad, rounded petals that open wide and flat or remain cupped, are borne singly. These annuals and evergreen perennials are suitable for a wild garden, a rock garden or the front of a border.

RECOMMENDED SPECIES AND VARIETIES

A. arvensis (common pimpernel, scarlet pimpernel) Wide open, scarlet, more rarely pink, flowers about 1cm (⅜in) across are borne in late spring and summer. The close-set pairs or whorls of light green ovate leaves are on sprawling stems that form a loose mat of growth. Because this annual or short-lived perennial seeds itself freely, it is best suited to a wild or informal garden. Native to Europe and W Asia. HEIGHT & SPREAD 10×50cm (4×20in).

The flowers produced by var. *caerulea* are bright blue.

A. monellii (syn. *A. linifolia*) Profuse saucer-shaped flowers in brilliant blue, but occasionally red or pink, bloom from mid to late summer and are up to 1.5cm (½in) across. The pairs or whorls of narrow, pointed leaves are dark, glossy and evergreen. This short-lived perennial is not reliably hardy and should be treated as an annual. Native to SW Europe. HEIGHT & SPREAD 15×40cm (6×16in).

'Sunrise' has flowers of rich scarlet.

A. tenella (bog pimpernel) Bell-shaped pink flowers, up to 1cm (⅜in) across, appear in early to mid summer. The thread-like stems bear pairs of pale green

▲ *Anagallis arvensis var. caerulea*

▲ *Anagallis monellii*

oval to rounded leaves. Fairly hardy, this plant needs damp soil. A prostrate, evergreen perennial, native to W Europe. HEIGHT & SPREAD 4×40cm (1½×16in).

'Studland' has deep pink, sweetly scented flowers.

CULTIVATION Plant *A. arvensis* and *A. monelli* in a sunny spot in gritty, well-drained soil. Grow *A. tenella* in moist soil and divide every 2 years to maintain vigour.

PROPAGATION Sow seed as soon as it is ripe. Take cuttings of *A. monelli* in summer. For *A. tenella,* pull off and pot up rooted shoots.

PESTS AND DISEASES Aphids, especially under glass, and slugs can cause damage.

Ananas
Pineapple
Bromeliaceae

In tropical countries these evergreen perennials are grown for their fruit, but in the cooler climate of Britain they are valued more for their foliage. Rigid, strap-shaped leaves form rosettes out of which rise large, dense oblong heads of tiny tubular flowers, mainly in summer. The flowers are replaced by fleshy, succulent pineapples. All species need warm, humid conditions and make unusual houseplants or greenhouse specimens. Native to Brazil.

RECOMMENDED SPECIES AND VARIETIES

A. bracteatus (red pineapple, wild pineapple) Deep green leaves, up to about 1m (3ft) long and 2.5cm (1in) wide, have sharp red spines along the edges. The flowers are purplish blue to lilac surrounded by bracts. Keep at a minimum of 15°C (59°F). HEIGHT & SPREAD 1×1m (3×3ft).

The cultivar 'Striatus' has variegated

▲ *Ananas comosus*

leaves that are striped with green and cream.

A. comosus (pineapple) Channelled, spiny-edged grey-green leaves, up to about 1m (3ft) long and 5cm (2in) wide, form rosettes. The tiny flowers, which are bluish, green or yellow and sometimes suffused with pink, are enclosed by bracts. Keep at a minimum of 10°C (50°F). HEIGHT & SPREAD 1m×60cm (3×2ft).

The leaves of var. *variegatus* are green and gold.

CULTIVATION Grow in pots of John Innes No. 2 in a greenhouse or on a warm, well-lit windowsill. Keep out of draughts and water sparingly in winter. Feed when the fruit have set. Repot yearly in early spring.

PROPAGATION Remove sideshoots in spring or slice off the tuft of leaves on a healthy fruit and pot on.

PESTS AND DISEASES Red spider mite and mealy bug can be a nuisance.

Anaphalis
Pearly everlasting
Compositae

Small, fluffy, pearly white flowers with yellow stamens glisten in summer on the hardy, easily grown perennials. They are borne in loose flat clusters, 10cm (4in) across. The undersides of the silver-grey, downy, narrow leaves, 6cm (2½in) long, are covered with fine hairs and look like white felt. The blooms often last until early autumn and are excellent for cutting and drying. To dry, cut stems soon after the flowers are fully open and hang upside down in small bunches in a light airy place. Plants are upright and clump-forming, standing up well at the front or middle of a herbaceous border. They are also generous contributors to a white border as both the foliage and flowers provide many months of silvery white colour.

RECOMMENDED SPECIES AND VARIETIES

A. cinnamomea see *A. margaritacea* var. *cinnamomea*

A. margaritacea Bushy clumps of silver-grey foliage form quickly and produce their loose heads of profuse white flowers in late summer and early autumn. This plant is found widely in the Northern Hemisphere, and is more drought tolerant than other

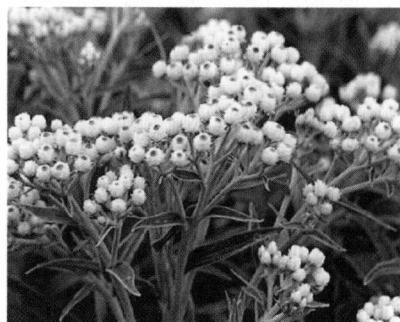

▲ *Anaphalis margaritacea*

a

species. HEIGHT & SPREAD 60×60cm (2×2ft).

Similar in growth and habit is var. *cinnamomea* (syn. *A. cinnamomea*) whose leaves are more densely covered with felt. **'Neuschnee'** ('New Snow') is a more compact variety, with a height and spread of 45cm (1½ft) and long grey-green leaves. The flowerheads of var. *yedonensis*♀ (syn. *A. yedonensis*) are larger. It reaches up to 75cm (2½ft) in height.

A. **nepalensis** var. **monocephala** (syn. *A. nubigena*) These compact little plants are suitable for rock gardens, forming neat clumps of white woolly foliage with cream-white flowers in mid summer. Native to the Himalayas and W China. HEIGHT & SPREAD 15×15cm (6×6in).

A. **nubigena** see *A. nepalensis* var. *monocephala*

A. **triplinervis**♀ This serves as a ground-cover plant during mid summer and autumn, forming dense clumps of grey-green foliage with wide domed clusters of white flowers. Originating from the Himalayas and SW China. HEIGHT & SPREAD 60×60cm (2×2ft).

▲ *Anaphalis triplinervis*

▲ *Anaphalis triplinervis* 'Sommerschnee'

'Sommerschnee' ('Summer Snow') is a more compact variety with a height and spread of 45cm (1½ft).

A. **yedonensis** see *A. margaritacea* var. *yedonensis*

CULTIVATION Plant in a sunny position between autumn and early spring in soil that does not dry out too much in summer but is also free draining.

PROPAGATION Divide in autumn or spring or take basal cuttings in early spring.

PESTS AND DISEASES Usually trouble free.

Anchusa
Alkanet
Boraginaceae

Anchusa azurea 'Loddon Royalist'

Sprays of small, vivid blue flowers, carried on branching stems in early summer, provide a rare depth of colour especially when planted in groups. The foliage is bristly and somewhat coarse. Annuals, biennials and herbaceous perennials are included in the genus; the recommended plants are short-lived, hardy perennials. *Anchusa azurea* does well in the herbaceous border while *A. caespitosa* is more usually found in the rock garden; both are tolerant of drought.

RECOMMENDED SPECIES AND VARIETIES

A. **azurea** Tall spikes of tiny bright blue flowers, up to 2cm (¾in) across, sometimes with a white or yellow eye, are borne above coarse, mid green, lance-shaped leaves from late spring to early summer. Young plants give the best display. Native to Europe, N Africa and W Asia. HEIGHT & SPREAD 1.5m × 60cm (5×2ft).

'Dropmore' has profuse deep blue, purple-tinted flowers. It reaches 1.8m (6ft) tall. **'Feltham Pride'** is shorter at 75cm (2½ft) and has true blue flowers. **'Little John'** has deep blue flowers and reaches 45cm (1½ft) tall. **'Loddon Royalist'**♀

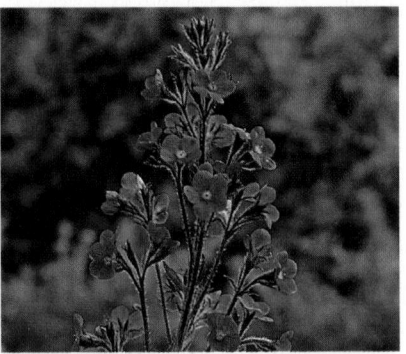

▲ *Anchusa azurea* 'Loddon Royalist'
▼ *Anchusa azurea* 'Opal'

▲ *Anchusa caespitosa*

grows to 1m (3ft) with a profusion of royal blue flowers on a bushy plant. **'Opal'**, at 1m (3ft), has light blue flowers set against dark green leaves.

A. **caespitosa**♀ Deep blue, almost stemless flowers with a white eye are borne in mid summer in clusters above rough-haired rosettes of dark green strap leaves. This dwarf, Mediterranean plant is best suited to a rock garden. Native to Crete. HEIGHT & SPREAD 7.5×23cm (3×9in).

A. **myosotidiflora** see *Brunnera macrophylla*

CULTIVATION Plant in spring or autumn in full sun. *A. azurea* and its cultivars need fertile soil and *A. caespitosa* does best on sharply drained soil; protect it from winter rain with a pane of glass. Taller plants need staking. Cut back after flowering.

PROPAGATION Take root cuttings in late winter. Alternatively, raise *A. caespitosa* from seed sown in spring or from basal cuttings taken in mid summer.

PESTS AND DISEASES Usually trouble free but cucumber mosaic virus can cause mottling on the leaves.

Andromeda
Bog rosemary
Ericaceae

Andromeda polifolia

A heather bed, with its lime-free soil and open position, is particularly suitable for these dwarf shrubs bearing delightful, cluttered, bell-shaped flowers and evergreen foliage. These plants are equally at home in a rock garden, coldframe, alpine house or unheated greenhouse. They are extremely hardy plants, native to acid bogs and tundra in temperate and sub-Arctic regions of the Northern Hemisphere. Of the two species in this genus, *Andromeda polifolia* is the most widely available.

RECOMMENDED SPECIES AND VARIETIES

A. polifolia (marsh andromeda) The rounded bell-shaped flowers, about 6 mm (¼ in) long, are bright pink initially, gradually turning to white. They are borne in loose clusters from late spring to mid summer. The plant forms a low mound with shiny dark green, lanceolate to oval leaves, about 3 cm (1¼ in) long. HEIGHT & SPREAD 25×50 cm (10×20 in).

'**Alba**' bears white flowers. This cultivar forms a compact bush only 15 cm (6 in) tall.

Andromeda polifolia 'Kirigamine' ▲
▲ *Andromeda polifolia* 'Alba'

'**Compacta**'♀ has numerous white flowers and wide glaucous leaves up to 2.5 cm (1 in) long. '**Grandiflora**' has large clusters of pale to mid pink flowers and broad glaucous leaves on a plant just 15 cm (6 in) tall. '**Kirigamine**' can tolerate drier conditions than most varieties and has numerous mid pink flowers among narrow leaves. '**Macrophylla**'♀ has flowers which turn from dark pink to white set off against broad dark green leaves. '**Nana**' reaches just 15 cm (6 in) tall and is ideal for growing in troughs. '**Nikko**' has pale pink flowers on a compact plant with 2 cm (¾ in) long grey-green leaves. '**Shibutsu**' is free-flowering, with dense clusters of shiny pink flowers which gradually turn to white.

CULTIVATION Plant in lime-free, humus-rich soil in partial sun. Protect from strong summer sun.

Andromedas grow well in pots filled with a humus-rich compost in an unheated greenhouse or alpine house. Place under a

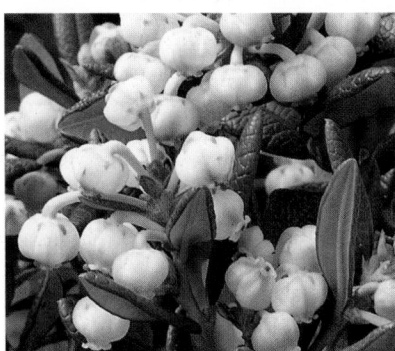

▲ *Andromeda polifolia* 'Macrophylla'

partially shaded coldframe in the summer.

PROPAGATION Sow seed in autumn or early winter, or take greenwood cuttings in summer. Alternatively, lift and divide established plants in autumn.

PRUNING Trim back untidy growth after plants have flowered.

PESTS AND DISEASES Vine weevils can be a problem occasionally.

Androsace
Rock jasmine
Primulaceae

Androsace carnea

Dense cushions or loose mats of evergreen foliage, smothered in pink or white flowers, make these hardy evergreen perennials suitable for growing on rock gardens, in troughs and raised beds or in crevices in walls. They can also be grown in an unheated greenhouse or alpine house. The five-petalled flowers, about 1 cm (⅜ in) across, are borne singly or in clusters and have yellow eyes that turn red or pink after pollination. Most plants are made up of small leaf rosettes, composed of tiny leaves no more than 1.5 cm (½ in) in length. Androsaces need sharp drainage to thrive and do not tolerate excessive winter wet.

RECOMMENDED SPECIES AND VARIETIES

A. carnea Clusters of pink flowers on stalks 6 cm (2½ in) tall, are borne on this hairy plant from mid to late summer. The bright green, grass-like leaves form dense rosettes

▲ *Androsace carnea* ssp. *brigantiaca*

▲ *Androsace cylindrica*

up to 2 cm (¾ in) across. HEIGHT & SPREAD 7.5×20 cm (3×8 in).

'**Alba**' has white flowers; '**Andorra**' is the most reliable cultivar to grow and has deep pink flowers; ssp. *brigantiaca* has larger rosettes and white flowers on stalks up to 15 cm (6 in) long; var. *halleri* see ssp. *rosea*; ssp. *laggeri*♀ has rosettes about 1 cm (⅜ in) across and deep pink flowers; ssp. *rosea*♀ (syn. var. *halleri*) is more vigorous with larger rosettes and larger, more open, pink flowers.

A. cylindrica White and yellow, early summer flowers on stalks 2 cm (¾ in) long, cover deep leaf cushions. Bristly, oblong, grey-green leaves form tiny rosettes, up to 2 cm (¾ in) across. Dead leaf rosettes persist on the plant; the new leaf rosettes grow on top of them, forming dense cylindrical masses. This plant should be grown in an alpine house or unheated greenhouse. HEIGHT & SPREAD 15×15 cm (6×6 in).

A. hirtella The white, spring flowers are borne singly or in pairs on short stems just above the leaf rosettes. Narrow, grey-green leaves covered with white hairs are grouped in tight rosettes, up to 1 cm (⅜ in) across, that form dense cushions. This species needs the protection of an alpine house or unheated greenhouse. HEIGHT & SPREAD 10×10 cm (4×4 in).

A. jacquemontii see *A. villosa* var. *jacquemontii*

▲ *Androsace lanuginosa*

A. lanuginosa♀ Clusters of flowers on stalks up to 10 cm (4 in) long, appear in late summer. Lilac with a greenish yellow eye at first, the flowers gradually turn pale pink with a darker pink eye. The grey-green, oval leaves, up to 2.5 cm (1 in) long, are not grouped in rosettes but form a loose mat, covered in silky hairs. This plant will grow on heavy clay soils provided that grit is added to improve drainage. HEIGHT & SPREAD 10×45 cm (4×18 in).

A. mollis see *A. sarmentosa* var. *yunnanensis*

A. mucronifolia hort. see *A. sempervivoides*

A. primuloides hort. see *A. sarmentosa*

A. primuloides '**Salmon's Variety**' see *A. sarmentosa* 'Salmon's Variety'

A. rotundifolia Clusters of pink, spring flowers surrounded by wide bracts are held on stems 15 cm (6 in) long. The rounded, lobed leaves are up to 6 cm (2½ in) in

Androsace sarmentosa

diameter. They are held on long stalks and form loose rosettes. HEIGHT & SPREAD 20×30cm (8×12in).

A. sarmentosa♀ (syn. *A. primuloides* hort.) Compact clusters of deep pink flowers surrounded by leafy bracts are borne on hairy stems, 4-10cm (1½-4in) long, from summer to autumn. The oval leaves are covered in silvery hairs. In winter, they make dense leaf rosettes about 1cm (⅜in) across; in spring these expand to 3cm (1¼in) across. This mat-forming plant spreads by reddish runners. HEIGHT & SPREAD 10×30cm (4×12in).

▲ Androsace sarmentosa

'Chumbyi' is hairier and forms denser mats than the species. 'Salmon's Variety' has slightly larger flowers. 'Sherriff's' has silvery leaves and pale pink flowers. The leaves of var. *yunnanensis* (syn. *A. mollis*) are very woolly.

A. sempervivoides♀ (syn. *A. mucronifolia* hort.) Clusters of bright pink flowers on stems up to 7.5cm (3in) long appear from late spring to mid summer. Long, smooth, symmetrical deep green leaves make rosettes, up to 2.5cm (1in) across, that form neat mats spread by short red runners. HEIGHT & SPREAD 7.5×30cm (3×12in).

A. villosa var. *jacquemontii* Dense clusters of deep purple flowers on stems up to 4cm (1½in) long, appear in late spring to early summer. The oval leaves are covered in silvery hairs and sometimes have tiny red glands at the tips. The leaf rosettes are dense and 1cm (⅜in) across in winter, becoming looser and 1.5cm (½in) wide in summer. This mat-forming plant spreads by means of reddish runners. HEIGHT & SPREAD 4×30cm (1½×12in).

A. vitaliana see *Vitaliana primuliflora*
CULTIVATION Plant during spring or early summer in well-drained, gritty soil and add a top dressing of gravel. Choose a position in full sun or part shade. Protect plants from excessive winter wet with a pane of glass or cloche. *A. cylindrica* and *A. hirtella* should be grown in an unheated greenhouse or alpine house; the other species can also be grown indoors if wished.

PROPAGATION Sow seed as soon as it ripens or divide plants that spread by runners.

PESTS AND DISEASES Aphids, red spider mite and grey mould may be problems, especially in plants grown under glass.

Anemone
Windflower
Ranunculaceae

Anemone blanda

Whether it's in full sun or partial shade, in the herbaceous border or in light woodland, there is an anemone suitable for almost every garden situation. There are plants to provide flowers from early spring right through to late autumn, be they a delicate white, pink or blue, or a vibrant shade of red, yellow or violet.

Most anemones have deeply divided leaves with toothed edges that form a lush green foil to the delicate flowers. Each leaf usually has three to five main segments which again may be toothed or divided. The leaves generally grow in clumps at the base of the flowering stems and in whorls of three on the stems just below the flowers.

The rootstock of these hardy herbaceous perennials varies considerably. Some have a simple tuber, whereas others have a fibrous rootstock or a thick creeping rhizome.

RECOMMENDED SPECIES AND VARIETIES
EARLY-FLOWERING ANEMONES
These plants begin flowering in spring, early summer and mid summer and can be divided into two groups; those that prefer cool, semi-shaded spots and those that are best for hot, dry positions.

PLANTS FOR COOL, SEMI-SHADED SPOTS
These plants will grow in full sun but prefer dappled shade or shade for part of the day. They can be grown in the border, on the rock garden or in the woodland garden.

A. apennina♀ (blue anemone) Appearing in early spring, the starry flowers are bright blue, occasionally flushed with pink. Each flower is up to 3cm (1¼in) across and has 8-14 narrow oblong petals. The leaves are deep green and sometimes flushed purple. These plants grow from a thick rhizome. HEIGHT & SPREAD 15×30cm (6×12in).

The flowers of var. *albiflora* are white. 'Petrovac' has deep blue flowers and more petals. 'Purpurea' has rose-purple flowers.

A. baldensis (syn. *A. fragifera*) (Mt Baldo anemone) Slightly nodding, cup-shaped white flowers, sometimes flushed pink or purple outside, appear from early to mid summer. Each flower is up to 4cm (1½in) wide, with 8-10 oval petals. This clump-forming species has a fibrous rootstock. HEIGHT & SPREAD 12×30cm (4¾×12in).

A. fragifera see *A. baldensis*

A. × *lesseri* Rose-pink or sometimes yellowish, mauve or white, the upright flowers are borne from late spring to mid summer. The flowers are up to 3cm (1¼in) across and have from 5-8 broadly oval petals. This plant has a fibrous rootstock. HEIGHT & SPREAD 20×20cm (8×8in).

A. × *lipsiensis* Pale, sulphur-yellow, open flowers appear in spring. Each flower is up to 2cm (¾in) across and has 6-8 oval petals. This plant is grown from a rhizome. HEIGHT & SPREAD 15×15cm (6×6in).

A. multifida Cream, white, sometimes red or greenish cup-shaped flowers are seen from late spring through summer and, if the seed heads are removed, often into autumn. Borne in clusters of 1-8 upright flowers, each bloom is up to 2.5cm (1in) across with 5-10 elliptical petals. Grown from fibrous rootstock, this plant often seeds itself. HEIGHT & SPREAD 40×20cm (16×8in).

'Major' has creamy yellow flowers.

A. nemorosa (wood anemone) White, cup-shaped flowers, often flushed pink, purple or, occasionally, blue outside appear in spring. They are up to 4cm (1½in) across, with 6-8, sometimes more, oval petals. This woodland plant grows from a rhizome. HEIGHT & SPREAD 15×30cm (6×12in).

'Alba Plena' has white flowers with a pompom of pale yellow stamens. 'Allenii'♀

▲ Anemone nemorosa 'Allenii'

has lavender flowers with a lilac or pale blue reverse and maroon leaf stalks. 'Blue Beauty' has pale blue flowers and the foliage is often bronze-flushed. 'Bowles Purple' has rich purple flowers. 'Grandiflora' has large, white blooms, up to 5cm (2in) across. The white flowers of 'Leeds Variety'♀ become flushed with pink. 'Lychette' has white flowers. 'Robinsoniana'♀ has lavender flowers, greyish on the outside, and maroon leaf stalks. The white flowers of 'Rosea' turn pink. The flowers of 'Vestal'♀ are white

▲ *Anemone nemorosa* 'Blue Beauty'

and have a pompom of white stamens. **'Viridiflora'** has green flowers.

A. ranunculoides ♀ (yellow wood anemone) Cup-shaped yellow flowers, up to 2 cm (¾ in) across, with 5-7 oval petals are seen throughout spring. This patch-forming plant grows from a rhizome. HEIGHT & SPREAD 15×30 cm (6×12 in).

A. rivularis Blue or white flowers, flushed blue or pink on the outside, are borne in clusters of 3-5 from late spring to mid summer. Each flower is 1.5-3 cm (½-1¼ in) across, with 5-8 oval petals. This clump-forming plant grows from fibrous rootstock. HEIGHT & SPREAD 1 m×45 cm (3×1½ ft).

A. sylvestris (snowdrop windflower) White, slightly nodding, cup-shaped flowers appear in early summer. Each flower, up to 6 cm (2½ in) across, has 5 oval petals. This patch-forming plant grows from a rhizome. HEIGHT & SPREAD 25×40 cm (10×16 in).

PLANTS FOR HOT, DRY POSITIONS

These plants need full sun and dry conditions, particularly during their summer dormancy, and can be planted anywhere in the garden that fulfils these requirements. They are also excellent plants for growing in pots.

A. blanda Starry flowers in blue, purple, pink or white, appear in early to mid spring. The flowers are up to 4 cm (1½ in) wide, with 12-18 narrow, oblong petals. This patch-forming plant grows from a tuber and it can be invasive. It will grow in dry woodland. HEIGHT & SPREAD 20×30 cm (8×12 in).

'Blue Mist' has pale blue flowers; **'Blue Pearl'**, mid blue flowers; **'Charmer'**, deep pink flowers; **'Fairy'**, snow-white flowers; **'Ingramii'** ♀ (syn. 'Atrocaerulea'), dark sky-blue flowers and **'Pink Star'**, mid pink flowers. **'Radar'** ♀ has deep magenta flowers with a white centre. The flowers of var. *rosea* are pale pink. **'Violet Star'** has amethyst flowers, whitish beneath. **'White Splendour'** ♀ has glistening white flowers.

A. coronaria (crown anemone) The scarlet, pink, blue, mauve, white or bicoloured flowers have striking black stamens. Upright and cup-shaped, the flowers appear in spring and early summer. They have 5-8 oval, overlapping petals and measure 3-6 cm (1¼-2½ in) across. They grow from a thick, knobbly tuber and need to be fed regularly throughout the growing season. HEIGHT & SPREAD 60×15 cm (24×6 in).

This species has produced many popular cultivars. The **De Caen Group** has single flowers and includes different coloured varieties; **'Die Braut'** ('The Bride') has white flowers, **'Hollandia'** (syn. 'His Excellency') has large scarlet flowers with a white centre and **'Mister Fokker'** has violet-blue flowers. The **Saint Brigid Group** has semidouble flowers and includes **'The Admiral'** with bright pink flowers, **'Lord Lieutenant'**, with deep blue blooms and **'Mount Everest'**, with white flowers. The **Mona Lisa Group** includes F₁ hybrids, 10 cm (4 in) tall and with flowers up to 8 cm (3¼ in) across; **'Sylphide'** has single mauve flowers.

A. hortensis (syn. *A. stellata*) The pink, mauve or purple, upright starry flowers

▲ *Anemone nemorosa* 'Robinsoniana'

▲ *Anemone blanda* 'Radar'

▲ *Anemone blanda* var. *rosea*

▲ *Anemone nemorosa* 'Vestal'

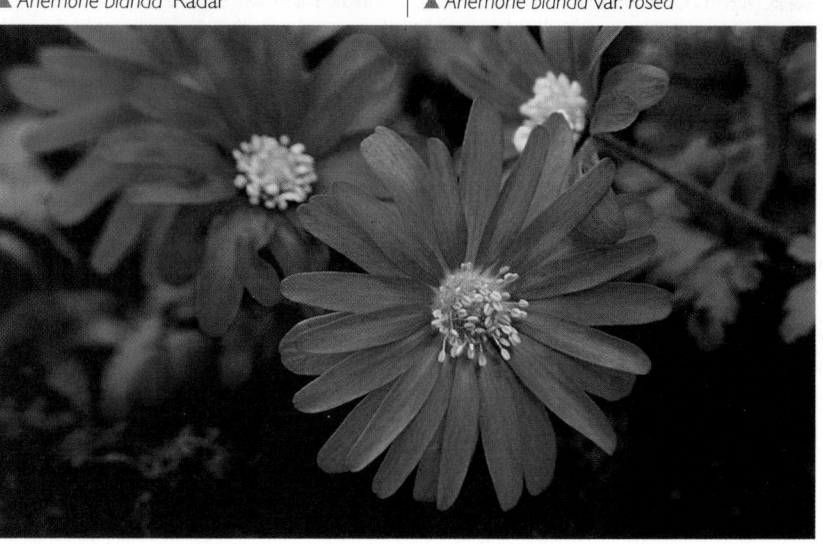

▲ *Anemone blanda* 'Ingramii'

appear from mid to late spring. Each one is up to 4 cm (1½ in) wide and with 12-20 narrow oval petals. Plants grow from a thick tuber. HEIGHT & SPREAD 30×20 cm (12×8 in).

A. pavonina (peacock anemone) The flowers are scarlet, purple, deep blue, pink and, very rarely, white or yellowish with black stamens. The 8-12 oval petals are often white or creamish at the flower's centre. Upright, cupped up to 7.5 cm (3 in) across, and the blooms appear from mid to late spring. The stem leaves are bract-like and undivided. Grown from tubers, this is a patch-forming plant. HEIGHT & SPREAD 30×30 cm (1×1 ft).

A. pulsatilla see *Pulsatilla vulgaris*
A. vernalis see *Pulsatilla vernalis*
A. sulphurea see *Pulsatilla alpina* ssp. *apiifolia*
A. stellata see *A. hortensis*

LATE-FLOWERING ANEMONES
Tall plants with branching stems that flower from late summer to autumn, this group of anemones are particularly suitable for the herbaceous border. They prefer a partially shaded site but will grow in full sun in cooler, wetter regions. All are grown from creeping rhizomes.

A. hupehensis Clusters of white, pale pink or deep pink flowers, often tinged pink or mauve on the reverse, appear from late summer to mid autumn. Upright and cup-shaped, each flower is up to 6 cm (2½ in) in width, with 5-6 petals. HEIGHT & SPREAD 75×45 cm (2½×1½ ft).

'Bowles Pink' has deep purplish pink flowers and reaches up to 1 m (3 ft) in height. 'Hadspen Abundance'♀ has very dark purplish pink flowers.

The flowers of var. *japonica* have up to 20 narrow, clear pink petals. Among its cultivars are 'Bressingham Glow', with semi-double flowers and up to 60 cm (2 ft) in height and 'Prinz Heinrich'♀ ('Prince Henry'), with deep pink flowers.

The flowers of 'Praecox' are more rosy pink than those of the species. 'September Charm'♀ has silvery pink flowers, darker on the outside, and is about 1 m (3 ft) tall.

A. × hybrida (syn. *A. japonica* hort.) White, pink or mauve, shallow cup-shaped flowers appear from late summer to mid autumn. The flowers have 5-6 petals and are up to 6 cm (2½ in) wide. HEIGHT & SPREAD 1.5 m×60 cm (5×2 ft).

'Geante des Blanches'♀ has white semidouble flowers with 15-20 petals. 'Honorine Jobert'♀ has pure white, single flowers. 'Königin Charlotte'♀ ('Queen Charlotte') has semidouble, pale purple flowers with frilly edges. 'Luise Uhink' has white flowers, 4 cm (1½ in) wide with 8-10 petals. 'Margarete' (syn. 'Lady Gilmour') has pale pink, double flowers. 'Monterosa' has double, deep pink flowers. 'Richard Ahrens' has rose-pink flowers up to 7 cm (2¾ in) wide. 'Whirlwind' ('Wirbelwind') has semidouble white flowers with twisted

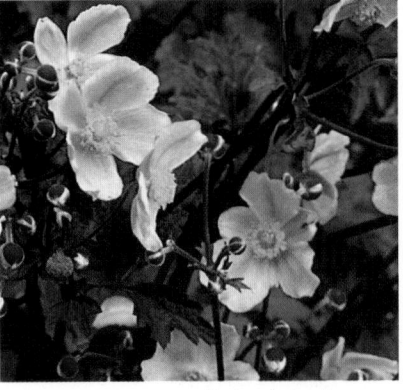

▲ *Anemone tomentosa* 'Robustissima'

petals and reaches a height of 1 m (3 ft).
A. japonica hort. see *A. × hybrida*
A. tomentosa Clusters of up to 12 pale pink flowers appear from late summer to mid autumn. Each flower is up to 7.5 cm (3 in) in width and has 5-6 oval petals. HEIGHT & SPREAD 1 m×40 cm (3 ft×16 in).

'Robustissima' has darker pink flowers.

Anemone tomentosa

CULTIVATION
EARLY-FLOWERING ANEMONES
Plant the anemones grown from rhizomes during autumn in rich, moist but well-drained soil in sun or, preferably, partial shade. They will tolerate dry conditions during their summer dormancy.

Plants that grow from tubers should be planted in autumn in well-drained soil in a sunny position. Do not water during their summer dormancy. Alternatively, lift the tubers when the foliage has died back and store in sand. *A. coronaria* can be brought into flower throughout the year; grow under glass at a minimum of 10°C (50°F) and stagger planting over the year.

Plant the anemones with fibrous rootstock during spring and summer in well-drained soil in sun or semi-shade.

LATE-FLOWERING ANEMONES
Plant during spring or early summer in moist, yet well-drained soil, adding ample organic matter. Choose a position in sun or partial shade. Mulch during the hot, summer months. In cold areas protect the vulnerable crowns from frost damage with dry organic matter. Avoid disturbing plants except for purposes of propagation.

PROPAGATION
EARLY-FLOWERING ANEMONES
Divide plants grown from rhizomes in autumn or shortly after flowering.

Lift tubers and cut into pieces, ensuring

each bit has at least one growing point. Leave the cut surfaces to dry before replanting, or treat with a suitable fungicide.

The plants with fibrous rootstock are best left undisturbed once planted; sow ripe seed in autumn or early winter.

LATE-FLOWERING ANEMONES
Divide plants in spring and replant straight away. Or take root cuttings in summer, choosing only thick healthy pieces.

PESTS AND DISEASES Pests include the eelworm and flea beetles. Slugs, snails and earwigs may also be a problem. Diseases include grey mould – especially on the flowerbuds – powdery and downy mildew, plum rust, anemone smut and cucumber mosaic viruses.

Anemonella
Ranunculaceae

Pretty, anemone-like white flowers nestle among delicate fern-like leaves on this hardy, tuberous perennial, the only species of its genus. This plant is fully frost hardy, but may succumb to excessive winter wet.

Anemonella thalictroides (rue anemone) Fine stems carry 2-5 cup-shaped flowers, up to 2 cm (¾ in) across, from mid spring to early summer. The pale olive green leaves have 5-9 rounded leaflets, each up to 2 cm (¾ in) long. Native to eastern N America. HEIGHT & SPREAD 25×30 cm (10×12 in).

'Flore Pleno' produces double white flowers. 'Rosea' has single pink flowers and 'Rosea Plena' has double pink flowers.

CULTIVATION Plant in rich, moist, but not wet, soil. In wet areas, grow in rich, gritty soil in an unheated greenhouse or conservatory, or grow in a coldframe.

PROPAGATION Sow fresh seed in summer, or divide established plants in autumn.

PESTS AND DISEASES Slugs can be a problem, especially with seedlings.

▼ *Anemonella thalictroides* 'Rosea Plena'

Anemonopsis
Ranunculaceae

This hardy herbaceous perennial, the sole species in the genus, forms large clumps of glossy dark green leaves that surround nodding, lavender-coloured flowers.

Anemonopsis macrophylla Loose clusters of waxy, drooping flowers, about 4 cm (1½ in) across and palest at the centre, are carried on slender, branching stems in mid summer. The 15-30 cm (6-12 in) long leaves have 9 or more rounded, toothed leaflets. The stems are blackish. Native to Japan. HEIGHT & SPREAD 80×80 cm (32×32 in).

CULTIVATION Plant in a moist, lime-free, leafy soil in partial shade – they will scorch badly in a sunny position. They do not thrive in dry conditions and do best in a cool situation.

PROPAGATION Sow seed in late summer, as soon as it ripens. Alternatively, divide established clumps in early spring.

PESTS AND DISEASES Slugs may be a particular problem.

Anethum
Dill
Umbelliferae

Popular for its herbal and medicinal properties, dill is also grown for its attractive feathery foliage with small greenish yellow, cartwheel-like flowers. There is only one species in the genus.

Anethum graveolens Finely divided aromatic fern-like leaflets are carried on this slender, easily grown annual. Tiny yellow blooms form plate-like flowerheads, about 10 cm (4 in) across, in summer. HEIGHT & SPREAD 60×25 cm (24×10 in).

CULTIVATION Plant in full sun in a free-draining, fertile soil.

PROPAGATION Sow seed in open ground between spring and late summer. Dill does

▲ *Anethum graveolens*

not transplant well so seedlings should be thinned to about 10 cm (4 in) apart as soon as they are large enough to handle. A pinch of seed can be sown into a large pot and the seedlings thinned out if a suitable place is not available in the garden.

PESTS AND DISEASES Greenfly may invade the crowded flowerheads.

Angelica
Umbelliferae

Magnificent foliage and domed flowerheads make these biennial and short-lived, hardy, perennial herbs ideal ornamental plants. The flower clusters are borne on rigid and hollow branching stems from early to late summer above large, deeply divided leaves. Native to Europe and central Asia.

RECOMMENDED SPECIES AND VARIETIES

A. archangelica This tall biennial has thick, purple-tinged green stems and pale green, divided leaves, up to 60 cm (2 ft) long. Tiny greenish cream flowers are carried in clusters, 25 cm (10 in) across, from early to late summer. The plant has many culinary uses. HEIGHT & SPREAD 2 m×75 cm (6½×2½ ft).

A. sylvestris This bushy biennial has ridged, purple-tinged green stems and bright green, sharply toothed, divided leaves up to 60 cm (2 ft) long. The small white or pinkish blooms are carried in flat flowerheads, 15 cm (6 in) across, in summer. HEIGHT & SPREAD 2 m×60 cm (6½×2 ft).

CULTIVATION Plant in autumn in any moist, fertile soil in full sun or partial shade. Mulch in spring to conserve soil moisture. Plants need staking in windy positions.

PROPAGATION Sow seed in spring in the open ground. These plants will not flower the year they are sown but in the following year. Alternatively, transplant self-sown seedlings in autumn.

PESTS AND DISEASES Usually trouble free.

Angelica tree, Japanese see *Aralia elata*
Angel's fishing rods see *Dierama*
Angel's trumpet see *Brugmansia arborea*
Angel's wings see *Caladium bicolor*

▲ *Angelica archangelica*

Anigozanthos
Kangaroo paw
Haemodoraceae

Upright flowering stems arise from fans of sword-shaped leaves on these half-hardy perennials. They are usually cultivated under glass, but where there is little or no frost they can be grown outside in a well-drained, sunny spot.

RECOMMENDED SPECIES AND VARIETIES

A. flavidus (yellow kangaroo paw) The 5 cm (2 in) long flowers are mostly yellow, sometimes flushed red and pink. The flowers are downy when they first appear in late spring. The narrow leaves of this bushy plant grow to 60 cm (2 ft) long. HEIGHT & SPREAD 1 m×45 cm (3×1½ ft).

▲ *Anigozanthos flavidus*

A. manglesii♀ Green and red blooms are borne in clusters in late spring on this clump-forming plant. The narrow grey-green leaves, up to 60 cm (2 ft) long, are arranged in dense clumps. HEIGHT & SPREAD 1 m×60 cm (3×2 ft).

CULTIVATION In frost-free areas, plant outdoors in a very sheltered spot in free-draining soil. Elsewhere, grow in large pots of free-draining compost in a sunny position under glass. Pots can be moved outdoors during summer and then overwintered in a frost-free conservatory or greenhouse. Water freely in summer, incorporating a regular liquid feed. Water sparingly in winter. Remove old flowerheads from the base of the plant.

PROPAGATION Divide plants in early spring or sow ripe seed under glass in late summer.

PESTS AND DISEASES Greenfly may attack the plants.

Anise see *Pimpinella anisum*
Anise, Chinese see *Illicium anisatum*
Anise, purple see *Illicium floridanum*

Anomatheca
Iridaceae

The only anomatheca species suitable for planting in a British garden is *A. laxa*. Even then, the trumpet-shaped flowers that lend a delicate beauty to the front of a border or to a rockery can be enjoyed only in mild areas. In colder districts, this bulbous plant from S and E Africa is best kept under glass.

RECOMMENDED SPECIES AND VARIETIES

A. laxa (syn. *A. cruenta*, *Lapeirousia cruenta*) Clusters of pinkish red flowers open on arching wiry stems all summer. The flower tubes, each 2 cm (¾ in) long, flare out into 6-pointed flat-faced blooms,

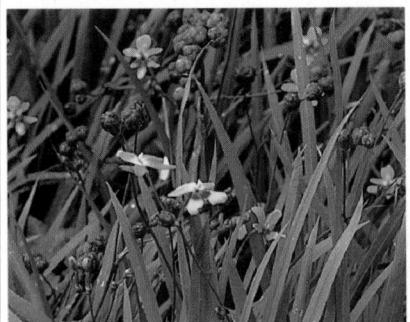

▲ *Anomatheca laxa*

2.5 cm (1 in) across, all facing outwards. The lower 3 petals are marked with a darker colour at the centre of the flower. Egg-shaped seedpods follow the flowers and split to reveal bright red seeds. The sword-shaped basal leaves, up to 10 cm (4 in) long, form an upright fan. HEIGHT 20 cm (8 in).

The flowers of var. *alba* are pure white, 'Joan Evans' has white petals with a bright red blotch in the centre of the flower.

CULTIVATION Plant 4 cm (1½ in) deep in spring in sun. In cold districts lift and store for winter or grow in pots in a greenhouse.

PROPAGATION Divide clumps of corms in autumn. Sow seed in spring in a coldframe or greenhouse. *A. laxa* self-sows freely.

PESTS AND DISEASES Usually trouble free.

Antennaria
Everlasting, pussy toes
Compositae

Antennaria dioica

Small clusters of white to cream, pink or red daisy-like flowers with papery bracts appear above mats of silvery leaves in late spring to early summer. The leaves of the hardy ever-green perennials, native to Europe, Asia and

▲ *Antennaria parvifolia*

N America, are grey or whitish with hairs. They are well suited to path edges and patios and as ground cover for small bulbs, but can become invasive in a rock garden.

RECOMMENDED SPECIES AND VARIETIES

A. aprica see *A. parvifolia*

A. candida see *A. dioica* 'Minima'

A. dioica (syn. *Gnaphalium dioicum*, *Omalotheca dioica*) (catsfoot) Narrow oval leaves, up to 4 cm (1½ in) long, are densely woolly, especially underneath, and form silvery white mats. The flower bracts are white to pink-brown at the tips. HEIGHT & SPREAD 10×60 cm (4×24 in).

'Alex Duguid' has deep reddish pink flowers; 'Minima' (syn. *A. candida*) is a dwarf form; 'Nyewoods Variety' is compact, with deep rose-pink flowers; and 'Rubra' has dark red flowers.

A. microphylla ♀ (syn. *A. rosea*) The 2.5 cm (1 in) long leaves are woolly all over and form a spreading mat. The flowers are pink. HEIGHT & SPREAD 10×60 cm (4×24 in).

A. parvifolia (syn. *A. aprica*) Densely woolly leaves, 2–4 cm (¾–1½ in) long, form silvery grey mats. The brown-spotted flower bracts have white, sometimes pink, tips. HEIGHT & SPREAD 8×30 cm (3¼×12 in).

A. rosea see *A. microphylla*

CULTIVATION Plant from late autumn to spring in well-drained, gritty soil in full sun.

PROPAGATION Sow seed as soon as it is ripe in autumn or early winter. Divide in spring.

PESTS AND DISEASES Usually trouble free.

Anthemis
Compositae

Anthemis punctata ssp. cupaniana

The hardy annuals, herbaceous perennials and dwarf shrubs of this genus are grown for their daisy-like flowers and finely divided, occasionally aromatic, foliage. The perennials described offer the best garden value, with the low-growing *Anthemis punctata* ssp. *cupaniana* suitable for growing in large rock gardens and the others at their best in herbaceous borders. Native to Asia, Europe and N Africa.

RECOMMENDED SPECIES AND VARIETIES

A. nobilis see *Chamaemelum nobile*

A. punctata ssp. *cupaniana* ♀ Long-lasting, yellow-centred flowers, up to 6 cm (2½ in) across, with white 'petals' (ray florets) are carried above a mat of aromatic grey foliage in early summer. This woody-based perennial has finely divided pinnate leaves, up to 12.5 cm (5 in) long, covered in silky white hairs. HEIGHT & SPREAD 30×60 cm (12×24 in).

A. sancti-johannis (St. John's camomile) Daisy-like flowers, 5 cm (2 in) across, with yellow centres and orange 'petals' (ray florets) are carried individually at the ends of leafy stems from early to mid summer on this herbaceous perennial. The mid green feathery leaves are up to 5 cm (2 in) long. HEIGHT & SPREAD 60×60 cm (24×24 in).

A. tinctoria (golden marguerite) Golden yellow flowers, up to 4 cm (1½ in) across, are borne on branching stems from early to late summer. The flowering stems rise above a clump of ferny leaves that are mid green above and grey beneath. HEIGHT & SPREAD 60×60 cm (24×24 in).

'Alba' has white flowers. 'E.C. Buxton' has pale lemon-yellow flowers and reaches 1 m (3 ft) tall. 'Grallach Gold' bears large, vibrant flowers and attains a height and spread of up to 1 m (3 ft), but is not reliably perennial. 'Kelwayi' is similar to 'Grallach

▲ *Anthemis tinctoria* 'Grallach Gold'

Gold', but has more finely divided leaves. 'Wargrave' has very pale yellow flowers.

CULTIVATION Plant in an open, sunny site in well-drained soil in spring. Cut back the stems as soon as flowering is over.

PROPAGATION Divide in autumn or spring every 2 or 3 years. Alternatively, take basal cuttings in spring or late summer.

PESTS AND DISEASES Usually trouble free.

▼ *Anthemis punctata* ssp. *cupaniana*

Anthericum
St Bernard's lily
Anthericaceae

Loose spikes of starry, white flowers rise in summer from the compact tufts of shiny, grass-like leaves of these hardy herbaceous perennials. They are valuable for planting in a herbaceous border, in deep containers or in grass or light woodland. The plants are native to grassy plains and woodlands in Europe, Turkey and Africa.

RECOMMENDED SPECIES AND VARIETIES

A. algeriense see *A. liliago* var. *major*

A. liliago Each white flower on the spike is up to 4 cm (1½ in) across and has 6 pointed petals. At the centre is a cluster of stamens with prominent yellow anthers. The grey-green leaves are up to 40 cm (16 in) long. HEIGHT & SPREAD 1 m×30 cm (3×1 ft).

The flowers of var. *major*♀ (syn. *A. algeriense*) open out slightly flatter than those of the species.

A. ramosum The white flowers with 6 pointed petals and prominent yellow anthers are 1.5 cm (½ in) across and are borne on branched spikes. Up to 40 cm (16 in) long, the leaves are greyish green. HEIGHT & SPREAD 60×30 cm (2×1 ft).

CULTIVATION Plant in spring, in well-drained but moisture-retentive soil, choosing a position in sun or partial shade. Unless seed is wanted, cut back the stems after flowering to encourage foliage growth. Allow the leaves to die back naturally in autumn. Both species are hardy to -10°C (14°F) and *A. liliago* improves in flowering after a cold winter.

PROPAGATION Sow seed or divide plants in spring. Do not divide plants more frequently than every 5 years. Plants raised by division may not flower until the following year; those raised from seed may take 2-3 years to bloom.

PESTS AND DISEASES Usually trouble free.

▼ *Anthericum liliago*

Anthriscus
Umbelliferae

Anthriscus sylvestris 'Ravenswing'

Round, flattened domes of tiny white flowers rise above much divided, fern-like leaves on these easily cultivated, annual, biennial or sometimes perennial plants. *Anthriscus sylvestris*, commonly known as cow parsley or Queen Anne's lace, is a native British hedgerow plant that can be invasive in a garden. Cultivated varieties are grown for their ornamental foliage and flowers suitable for growing in a border, wild garden or among shrubs. Chervil (*A. cerefolium*) is a culinary herb with aniseed-flavoured leaves (see HERBS p.330).

RECOMMENDED SPECIES AND VARIETIES

A. cerefolium (chervil) see HERBS p.330.

A. sylvestris **'Ravenswing'** The finely divided, striking leaves of this biennial, sometimes perennial plant are brownish purple and fern-like, thin-textured and up to 30 cm (12 in) long. Small, 4-petalled creamy white flowers are borne in delicate clusters, up to 6 cm (2½ in) wide, from mid spring to early summer. These ripen into small, oval, green fruits which eventually become light brown. The furrowed stems are hollow and hairy towards the base. Native to Europe, N Asia, N Africa. HEIGHT & SPREAD Up to 1.5 m×60 cm (5×2 ft).

CULTIVATION Best grown in a sunny or part-shaded border.

PROPAGATION Propagate *A. sylvestris* 'Ravenswing' by division.

PESTS AND DISEASES Usually trouble free.

Anthurium
Araceae

This eye-catching plant has exotic sail-like, red, pink or creamy white spathes with a central tail known as a spadix. The glossy leaves are oval or heart-shaped and sometimes strikingly marked. These tropical evergreen perennials, usually grown as greenhouse pot plants or houseplants, are very long-lived, making them one of the most popular pot plants where humidity and a minimum night temperature of 18°C (64°F) can be maintained.

A. andraeanum (tail flower) The leathery heart-shaped spathe, up to 12.5 cm (5 in) long, is bright red with a yellowish white central tail-like spike. The oval or arrow-like glossy green leaves grow up to 20 cm (8 in) long. HEIGHT & SPREAD 60×50 cm (24×20 in).

'Flamingo' has a bright pink spathe.

A. × ferrierense A fleshy, heart-shaped pink spathe, up to 15 cm (6 in) long, with a distinctive ivory-white, tail-like central spadix. The oval or heart-shaped glossy green leaves grow to 40 cm (16 in) long. This scrambling plant can be attached to a moss pole in the centre of the pot. HEIGHT & SPREAD 1 m×45 cm (3×1½ ft).

'Roseum' has a large deep red spathe with a white spadix tipped with yellow.

A. scherzerianum (flamingo flower) Bright red oval spathes, up to 10 cm (4 in) long, have a distinctive twisted, pinkish spadix and are freely produced for much of the year. The erect, lance-shaped leaves, up to 20 cm (8 in) long, are dark green and leathery. This is one of the most widely grown houseplants. HEIGHT & SPREAD 30×30 cm (12×12 in).

CULTIVATION Grow in a free-draining compost with bark chippings or chopped sphagnum moss incorporated. Position away from direct sunlight and maintain a temperature of not less than 18°C (64°F) and humidity, even if this is just localised by regular spraying. Water freely throughout the growing season and administer a general liquid houseplant feed when the plants are flowering. Repot annually but keep the plants quite tight in their pots. Overpotting leads to excess foliage at the expense of the flowers. Clean the foliage regularly.

PROPAGATION Divide in spring or summer.

PESTS AND DISEASES Mealy bugs and scale insects can be a problem.

▲ *Anthurium andraeanum*

Araucaria
Araucariaceae

Araucaria araucana

Stiff, overlapping, scale-like leaves in spirals around sweeping, tiered branches give these conifers their distinctive appearance. Only one tree from this Chilean genus is hardy enough to be grown outdoors in Britain.

RECOMMENDED SPECIES

A. araucana (monkey puzzle, Chile pine) This statuesque evergreen tree is suitable for large gardens only. Individual leaves are oval with a narrowed, pointed end. Cones, up to 15 cm (6 in) across and either cylindrical or rounded, are sometimes produced on upper branches. Male and female cones are usually borne on different trees. The greyish brown trunk is straight and strongly ridged horizontally. HEIGHT & SPREAD 6×3 m (20×10 ft) after 10 years, ultimately 20 m (66 ft) tall.

CULTIVATION Plant in any well-drained soil in any position except full shade. Water well when the tree is young.

PRUNING None is required.

PROPAGATION Sow seed as soon as it is ripe in a propagator or in a greenhouse with a temperature of 20°C (68°F).

PESTS AND DISEASES Usually trouble free.

Arbutus
Strawberry tree
Ericaceae

Arbutus menziesii

Year round beauty is provided by these evergreen trees and shrubs with abundant, glossy, usually ovate leaves and round strawberry-like autumn fruits. Clusters of small, bell-shaped, white or pink flowers are borne in spring or autumn. Native to Europe, Asia Minor and NW America, the recommended plants are fairly hardy once they are established.

RECOMMENDED SPECIES AND VARIETIES

A. × *andrachnoides*♀ Smooth, peeling, cinnamon bark contrasts with the ivory white flowers that hang in dense clusters in late autumn or early spring. Fruiting is not reliable. HEIGHT & SPREAD 5×3.5 m (16×12 ft) after 10-15 years, ultimately 9 m (30 ft) tall.

A. menziesii♀ (madrona) This tree thrives only in acid soil in milder areas. In late spring fragrant white flowers open in large upright clusters among leaves that are whitish underneath. Fruits are red-orange. The bark is cinnamon-coloured. HEIGHT & SPREAD 7.5×5 m (25×16 ft) after 10-15 years, ultimately 10 m (33 ft) tall.

A. unedo♀ (strawberry tree) Clusters of pendulous, small, honey-scented white or pink tinged flowers in late autumn are often accompanied by the previous year's orange-red fruit. This plant is not completely hardy in the coldest gardens. HEIGHT & SPREAD 4.5-6 × 3 m (15-20×10 ft) after 10-15 years, ultimately 10 m (33 ft) tall.

▲ *Arbutus unedo*

The form *rubra*♀ has deep pink flowers.

CULTIVATION Plant in soil with good drainage with shelter from cold winds, especially when trees are young. *A. menziesii* requires acid soil but other plants tolerate limy soil and dry, poor soil. Strawberry trees do best in full sun.

PROPAGATION Sow seed in spring, except for *A. unedo* which should be raised from semi-ripe cuttings taken in mid summer.

PRUNING None is required.

PESTS AND DISEASES Leaf spot tends to occur if overwatered in summer.

Arctostaphylos
Bearberry
Ericaceae

Arctostaphylos uva-ursi

Clusters of tiny urn-shaped flowers followed by roundish fruits hang among the evergreen foliage of these acid-loving plants. The bearberries range from creeping shrubs to small trees, but from more than 50 mainly N American species, only a few are widely grown in Britain. They are chosen mainly for ground cover.

RECOMMENDED SPECIES AND VARIETIES

A. × *media* 'Woods Red' This hybrid has obovate leaves, up to 2.5 cm (1 in) long, which are downy underneath. Clusters of white to pink flowers in mid spring are followed by red fruits. HEIGHT & SPREAD 25 cm×1.5 m (10 in×5 ft) after 5 years, ultimately spreading to 3 m (10 ft).

A. stanfordiana The smooth mahogany-coloured bark is most attractive as are the pale pink flowers in mid winter, which are followed by light red fruits. The ovate to lanceolate leaves are greyish blue, leathery and up to 6 cm (2½ in) long. This is the finest of the upright species although it is the least hardy of all the bearberries and requires a particularly warm and well-drained site if it is to survive the winter. HEIGHT & SPREAD 1 m×60 cm (3×2 ft) after 5 years, ultimately 2 m (6½ ft) tall.

A. uva-ursi (common bearberry) Small white or pink flowers are produced in mid to late spring in drooping clusters above downy, greyish green foliage. They are followed by red berries. The alternate dark

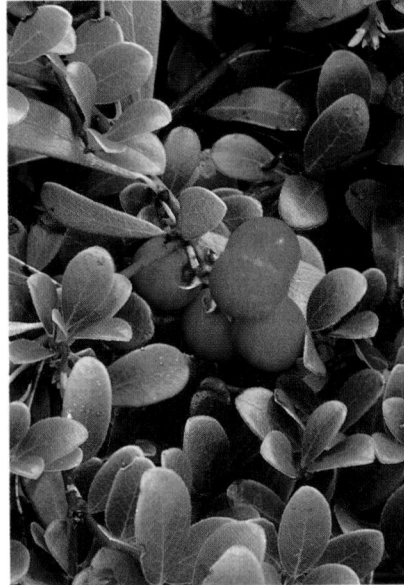

▲ *Arctostaphylos uva-ursi*

green glossy leaves, up to 3 cm (1¼ in) long, are obovate with pointed tips. The plant has a ranging and trailing habit. HEIGHT & SPREAD 20 cm×1.5 m (8 in×5 ft) after 5 years, ultimately spreading to 3 m (10 ft).

'Vancouver Jade' has pink flowers.

CULTIVATION Plant in any acid soil, including poor soil, on a warm dry site. *A. stanfordiana* requires a dry root run.

PROPAGATION Separate natural layers, or peg down shoots to promote layers, in spring. Alternatively take semi-ripe cuttings in summer.

PRUNING None is required, but cut back in spring to limit the spread if necessary.

PESTS AND DISEASES Usually trouble free.

Arctotis
African daisy
Compositae

Arctotis x hybrida

Brightly coloured daisy-like flowers appear from mid summer until early autumn, bringing long-lasting colour to a sunny border. The plants, which are half-hardy annuals and perennials, can also be grown in containers. The flowers generally have lighter coloured petals, properly called ray florets, surrounding darker central discs. They are borne one to a stem, usually leafless, rising from a tuft of coarse oval or lance-shaped leaves, often indented. Flowers tend to close in the afternoon and in dull weather. Native to South Africa.

RECOMMENDED SPECIES AND VARIETIES
A. acaulis Yellow flowers with coppery undersides and purple centres are carried on downy stems. Plants with orange or red flowers are also available. Flowers are up to 7.5 cm (3 in) wide. The plant, an easily grown perennial, has a thick, woody root system from which grow narrow, irregularly lobed, green leaves, up to 20 cm (8 in) long, with white woolly undersides. HEIGHT & SPREAD 25×45 cm (10×18 in).

A. fastuosa (Cape daisy) Flowers are orange, with purple-brown bases and maroon centres, and up to 5 cm (2 in) wide. The hoary leaves, up to 15 cm (6 in), are oblong and indented. This species is an annual. HEIGHT & SPREAD 60×60 cm (2×2 ft).

A. x hybrida Flowers are available in white, cream, yellow, peach, orange, pink or red. Many are attractively zoned with a contrasting colour. As wide as 7.5 cm (3 in), the flowers are borne on stems sometimes as long as 45 cm (18 in). The long, indented, lance-like leaves are felted or silvery and 15-30 cm (6-12 in) long. These strong-growing hybrids are treated as annuals, although they are short-lived perennials. HEIGHT & SPREAD 45×30 cm (18×12 in).

'Apricot' has flowers of a rich orange, while 'Flame' is a brilliant orange-red.

A. venusta (blue-eyed African daisy) Purple-red flowers with blue centres are up to 10 cm (4 in) across. The indented, oval or lance-shaped leaves with grey undersides, are up to 20 cm (8 in) long. This

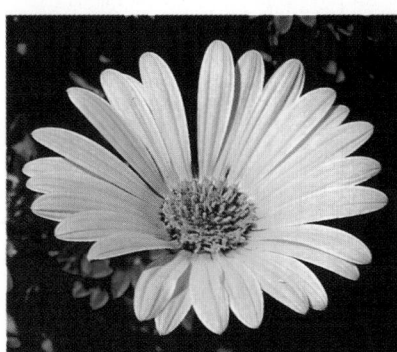
▲ *Arctotis x hybrida* 'Apricot'

perennial that flowers in late summer is usually treated as an annual. HEIGHT & SPREAD 30-60×30-40 cm (12-24×12-16 in).

'Grandis' has a height and spread of 45 cm (18 in), and larger, white to pale yellow flowers.

CULTIVATION Plant in an open, free-draining, sunny position, when all danger of frost has passed. Lift perennials for the winter and store in boxes of peat or a similar growing medium in a cool but frost-free place with good light.

PROPAGATION Sow annuals and perennials in a cool greenhouse or coldframe in spring. Grow on in small pots before planting out once there is no chance of frost. Alternatively, take stem cuttings of perennials at any time in the active growing season.

PESTS AND DISEASES Slugs may be a problem in damp weather.

Arenaria
Sandwort
Caryophyllaceae

Arenaria montana

Spreading mats or tufts with small paired leaves support a mass of white or, rarely, pink flowers in spring or summer in a rock garden or raised bed. The flowers have four to five rounded petals and are held aloft on upright stems.

Most sandworts thrive in a sunny rock garden although *Arenaria balearica* does best on cool damp rocks beside a garden waterfall or pond, while *A. tetraquetra* is best grown in an alpine house or unheated greenhouse, or in an outdoor trough. These perennials, which are native to heathlands, woods and high rocky areas in temperate and Arctic regions of the Northern Hemisphere, come from a genus of some 150 species closely related to chickweeds.

RECOMMENDED SPECIES AND VARIETIES
A. balearica (mossy sandwort) White flowers, up to 1 cm (⅜ in) across, open above the

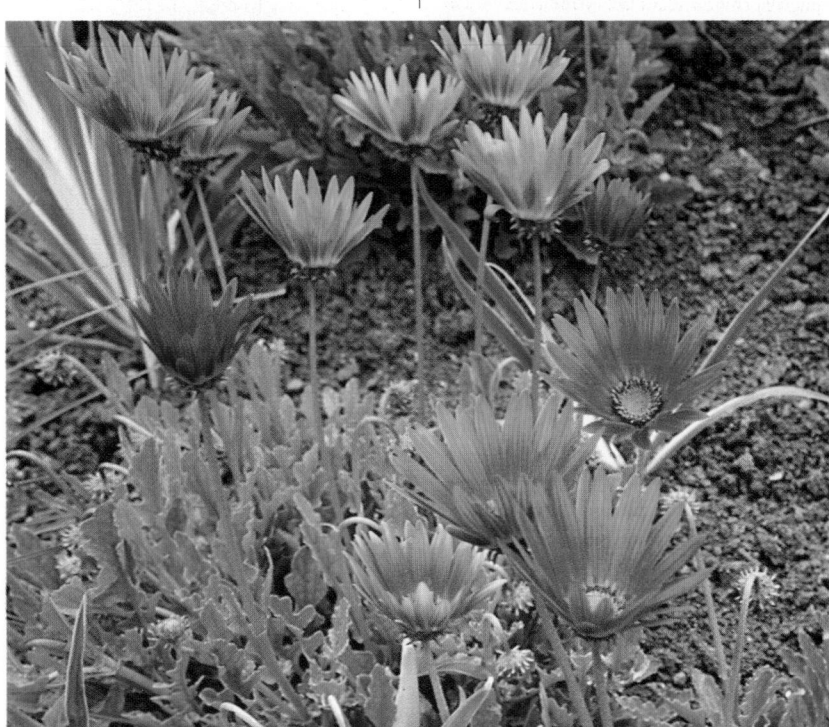
▲ *Arctotis × hybrida* 'Flame'

▲ *Arenaria balearica*

▲ *Arenaria montana*

bright green evergreen foliage in spring and summer, each on its own thread-like stem. The moss-like mats of foliage root down as they spread. The leaves are roundish, about 3 mm (⅛ in) long. HEIGHT & SPREAD 3×50 cm (1¼×20 in).

A. montana♀ Neat white flowers, about 2 cm (¾ in) across, appear on slender stems 10-20 cm (4-8 in) tall in early summer. The plant forms a loose, spreading mat of grey, narrowly oblong, hairy leaves, up to 2 cm (¾ in) long. HEIGHT & SPREAD 10-20×50 cm (4-8×20 in).

A. purpurascens (pink sandwort) This pretty sandwort has small clusters of pink, purplish or whitish flowers, up to 1 cm (⅜ in) across, on stems about 5 cm (2 in) tall in summer. Small rosettes of pointed evergreen leaves, up to 1 cm (⅜ in) long, form a loose, tufted cushion. HEIGHT & SPREAD 10×20 cm (4×8 in).

'Elliott's Variety' is more compact with an abundance of deep lilac-pink flowers.

A. tetraquetra White flowers, up to 1 cm (⅜ in) across, appear one to each very short stem in summer. The plant forms dense cushions of neatly packed, squarish rosettes of tiny evergreen leaves just 4 mm (⅛ in) long. HEIGHT & SPREAD 20×30 cm (8×12 in).

With grey-green foliage, ssp. *amabilis* is an even denser plant.

CULTIVATION Plant in a sunny, well-drained position. *A. purpurascens* grows best in a shady spot. *A. balearica* thrives in a damp, shady situation and must not dry out. This species may spread rampantly in mild, moist districts, but it tends to die off in a hard winter.

PROPAGATION Sow seed in pots in a cold-frame in autumn or early spring. Alternatively, lift and divide *A. balearica* and *A. montana* after flowering. Take semi-ripe cuttings of *A. purpurascens* and *A. tetraquetra* in spring or summer.

PESTS AND DISEASES Usually trouble free.

Argemone
Papaveraceae

Showy poppy-like blooms make these annuals or short-lived perennials popular for an open sunny border, although most have prickly or bristly stems and thistle-like leaves which could be a hazard near a path. Stems exude a yellowish sap if bruised. These rather untidy plants, which flower from mid to late summer, require free-draining soil. They are native to N, S and Central America, Hawaii and the W Indies.

RECOMMENDED SPECIES AND VARIETIES

A. grandiflora White or sometimes yellow flowers, up to 10 cm (4 in) wide, appear among the leafy stems of this perennial which is best treated as an annual. The prickly, lance-like leaves, up to 20 cm (8 in) long, are irregularly lobed and toothed. HEIGHT & SPREAD 75×75 cm (30×30 in).

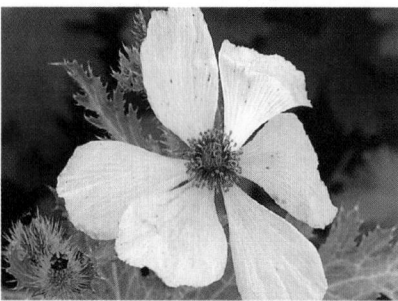

▲ *Argemone grandiflora*

A. mexicana (Devil's fig, Mexican poppy) Papery, fragrant, bright yellow flowers, up to 7.5 cm (3 in) wide, appear among the foliage of this annual. The prickly leaves, up to 20 cm (8 in) long, have a grey waxy sheen and distinctive white markings over the veins. HEIGHT & SPREAD 90×45 cm (3×1½ ft).

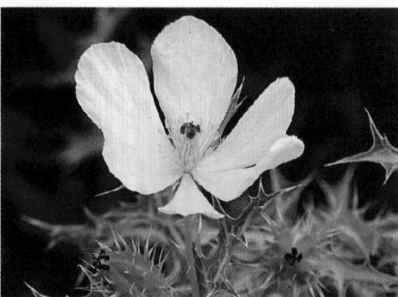

▲ *Argemone mexicana*

CULTIVATION Plant in any gritty, free-draining soil in a sunny position. In exposed areas, grow the plants through thin supporting canes to keep them tidy. Remove dead flowerheads regularly to prolong the flowering season.

PROPAGATION Sow seed in the flowering position in spring. Thin when the seedlings are large enough to handle. They do not always transplant satisfactorily.

PESTS AND DISEASES Usually trouble free.

Argyranthemum
Marguerite, Paris daisy
Compositae

Argyranthemum frutescens

Abundant, daisy-like flowers, framed by attractive feathery foliage, have earned the marguerites a place among bedding plants since Victorian times. In S Europe they are widely grown as garden perennials but in Britain they are not quite hardy enough and must usually be grown afresh from cuttings each year, or overwintered in a frost-free greenhouse or conservatory.

In recent years the fashion for container gardening has boosted their popularity and they are particularly suitable for large patio tubs in sunny positions, flowering from early summer to mid autumn. Argyranthemums can also be trained as standard plants up to 1 m (3 ft) tall. They are useful for adding height to summer bedding schemes.

All the recommended plants have woody stem bases from which soft flowering shoots arise. The single flowers are generally about 5 cm (2 in) wide, made up of central yellow disc florets and radiating white ray florets. Most are native to the Canary Islands.

RECOMMENDED SPECIES AND VARIETIES

A. broussonetii The flowers of this species are larger than most, reaching up to 8 cm (3¼ in) across. The leaves are bright green. HEIGHT & SPREAD 30 cm×1 m (1×3 ft).

▼ *Argyranthemum foeniculaceum*

▼ *Argyranthemum frutescens*

▼ *Argyranthemum* 'Jamaica Primrose'

▼ *Argyranthemum* 'Vancouver'

A. foeniculaceum Blue-green, finely cut foliage is seen on this species. HEIGHT & SPREAD 40 cm×1 m (16 in×3 ft).

'Royal Haze'♀ has blue-grey foliage.

A. frutescens This plant is similar to *A. foeniculaceum*, but has coarser bright green to greyish foliage and smaller flowers. HEIGHT & SPREAD 50 cm×1 m (20 in×3 ft).

A. gracile Especially finely divided greyish green leaves are carried on this upright species. HEIGHT & SPREAD 50 cm×1 m (20 in×3 ft).

'Chelsea Girl'♀ has even more finely divided foliage.

A. maderense♀ Small, 4 cm (1½ in) wide, yellow flowers and blue-grey lobed foliage distinguish this plant. HEIGHT & SPREAD 30 cm×1 m (1×3 ft).

HYBRID VARIETIES

Most of the more widely grown argyranthemums are hybrids with at least two species as parents. They generally grow to 50 cm (20 in) tall and spread to 1 m (3 ft).

'Edelweiss' has semidouble white flowers. 'Jamaica Primrose'♀ is vigorous, with dark green leaves and 6 cm (2½ in) wide, soft-yellow flowers. 'Mary Cheek'♀ is compact with pale pink pompom flowers. 'Mary Wootton' has pink, anemone-centred flowers with long outer florets. 'Peach Cheeks' has pink blooms. 'Petite Pink'♀ has a compact habit, silvery foliage and abundant small pink flowers. 'Powder Puff' is compact with pale pink double flowers with quilled petals. 'Qinta White'♀ (syn. 'Sark') has a slightly sprawling habit and anemone-centred flowers. 'Snowflake' has semidouble flowers. 'Vancouver'♀ is vigorous with deep pink anemone-centred flowers.

CULTIVATION Plant in a well-drained soil in a sunny position once the risk of frost has passed. Plants will survive outdoors in mild areas if covered with 10 cm (4 in) straw. Use a large tub or planter if growing as a container plant. Replace every 2 or 3 years. In a cool greenhouse or conservatory, plants need a winter temperature of about 10°C (50°F) to flower. Remove dead flowerheads to prolong the flowering season.

PROPAGATION Take cuttings in late summer and grow under glass.

PESTS AND DISEASES Aphids, capsid bugs and leaf miners may cause damage. Plants grown under glass may also suffer from red spider mite.

Arisaema
Araceae

Grown for their unusual blooms and glossy leaves, this genus of perennial tubers thrives in shady positions, and the plants do well under deciduous shrubs and trees. Each plant produces a leaf-like hood, called a spathe, in summer just before the true leaves unfurl. The spathe contains a prominent stalk, called a spadix. The tiny, true flowers cluster around its base. Orange-red berries, which are poisonous and can cause skin irritation, appear after the spathe dies.

RECOMMENDED SPECIES AND VARIETIES

A. candidissimum♀ White to greenish white with pale pink stripes at the top and with apple green white stripes at the base, the spathe contains a tapering, green spadix. The rose-scented flowers appear in early

▼ *Arisaema candidissimum*

summer. Each plant has one leaf, made up of 3 broad leaflets, 10-20 cm (4-8 in) long. HEIGHT 30-40 cm (12-16 in).

A. consanguineum The spathe, which is usually white, striped in green, appears in mid to late summer. The leaf, made up of 10-20 slender leaflets, 20-40 cm (8-16 in) long, is held umbrella-like above the barely visible green spathe. HEIGHT 40-100 cm (16-36 in).

A. sikokianum The blackish to purple spathe appears in late spring and early summer. The white club-shaped spadix stands proud of the spathe. There are 2 leaves consisting of a total of 5 leaflets, each 15 cm (6 in) long. This plant is not hardy. HEIGHT 20-40 cm (8-16 in).

A. triphyllum (Jack-in-the-pulpit) A green or purple spathe with green or white stripes appears in late spring or early summer and encloses a green or purple spadix. The 2-3 leaves are made up of 3 leaflets about 8-15 cm (3¼-6 in) long. HEIGHT 20-60 cm (8-24 in).

CULTIVATION Plant tubers in late autumn or early spring in a moisture-retentive, humus-rich, well-drained soil. Protect with a mulch of leaves or bracken when temperatures fall below freezing for long periods.

PROPAGATION Remove offsets from mature plants in late autumn. Alternatively, sow ripe seed in late autumn.

PESTS AND DISEASES Usually trouble free.

Arisarum
Araceae

Unusual flowers peep out from the glossy, arrowhead-shaped foliage of these herbaceous perennials that thrive in woodland conditions. Native to Italy and Spain.

RECOMMENDED SPECIES

A. proboscideum (mouse plant) Sail-like, maroon and white, leaf-like spathes, up to 10 cm (4 in) long, have slender appendages curling outwards in late spring and early summer. At the base, they are wrapped round spikes of tiny petal-less flowers. The glossy leaves, up to 10 cm (4 in) long, half conceal these striking flowers. HEIGHT & SPREAD 15×30 cm (6×12 in).

CULTIVATION Plant in late summer or autumn in fertile, moist soil in partial shade. Mulch with leaf-mould in early spring.

PROPAGATION Divide in late summer or autumn.

PESTS AND DISEASES Usually trouble free.

▼ *Arisarum proboscideum*

Arthropodium
Anthericaceae

Dainty white or pale lilac drooping flowers are profusely borne in loose sprays on these perennial plants that are suitable for moist but well-drained borders or rock gardens. Native to New Guinea, Australia and New Zealand, they are hardy only in the southern counties and need shelter in colder areas. The flowers, borne above tufts of grass-like leaves, have petals that curve back, revealing hairy stamens. They are followed by seed capsules each of which holds a few black seeds.

RECOMMENDED SPECIES AND VARIETIES
A. candidum (grass lily) In mid summer, loose sprays of white flowers each about 1cm (⅜in) across droop from erect stems that hold them well above the leaves. The leaves are 20cm (8in) tall, soft and pale green; they die back in winter. HEIGHT & SPREAD 20×30cm (8×12in).

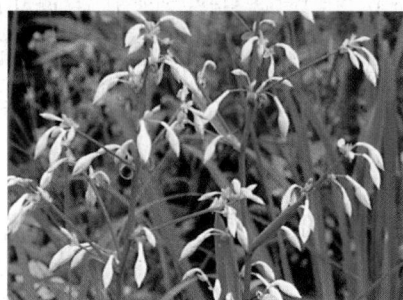

▲ *Arthropodium cirratum*

The leaves of f. *purpureum* are bronze.
A. cirratum (New Zealand rock lily) Broad sprays of numerous drooping flowers, each about 3cm (1¼in) across, are pale lilac in bud, opening to white with yellow and lilac stamens. They bloom in late spring or early summer on slender but stiff stems that hold them above pale green, arching, evergreen leaves about 40cm (16in) long. This plant is suitable for growing outside only where temperatures do not fall below -5°C (23°F). HEIGHT & SPREAD 55×60cm (22×24in).
A. milleflorum (vanilla lily) Pale lilac flowers 1.5cm (½in) across hang in summer from the wiry, erect, branched stems. The flowers are carried well above the stiff, grassy, evergreen leaves about 20cm (8in) tall. HEIGHT & SPREAD 30×30cm (1×1ft).
CULTIVATION Plant in well-drained, fertile soil and keep it moist in summer. *A. candidum* prefers shade but *A. cirratum* thrives in sun or shade. *A milleflorum* does best on sandy or gravelly soil and in full sun. In cold areas grow the plants in containers and move them into a conservatory or greenhouse for winter.
PROPAGATION Raise from seed or divide established plants in late spring. *A. candidum* and *A. milleflorum* often self seed.
PESTS AND DISEASES Usually trouble free.

Arum
Araceae

The glossy, arrowhead-like leaves of the arum provide interest in the garden in late autumn and winter or emerge in spring. Most of these tuberous perennials flower in spring when the leaf-like spathe appears. Enclosed within the spathe is a prominent stalk called a spadix; the tiny petal-less true flowers cluster around its base. Most arums have an unpleasant odour of decay that attracts pollinating insects. The spadix bears bright red berries in late summer, after the leaves and spathe die back. The berries are poisonous if eaten and the plant sap and the juice of the berries can cause skin irritation.

RECOMMENDED SPECIES AND VARIETIES
A. creticum The cream or yellow showy spathe, 5-25cm (2-10in) long, turns back to reveal a yellow or dark purple spadix, sometimes longer than the spathe. This species is sweetly scented. The leaves, 8-25cm (3¼-10in) long, appear in late autumn. A Mediterranean plant for a rock garden. HEIGHT & SPREAD 40×20cm (16×8in).
A. italicum Dark green leaves, marked with white veins and up to 35cm (14in) long, emerge in late autumn or early winter. The greenish yellow spathe, 15-40cm (6-16in) long, encloses a yellow spadix up to half the length of the spathe. A Mediterranean plant for woodland gardens or for a shrub bed. HEIGHT & SPREAD 40×20cm (16×8in).

▲ *Arum italicum* 'Marmoratum'

'Marmoratum'♀ is grown for the pronounced marbling on its leaves.
A. maculatum (cuckoo pint, lords and ladies) A vigorous, spreading British native. Dark green leaves, sometimes spotted black and up to 20cm (8in) long, emerge in spring; so does the spathe, which is greenish white, sometimes edged with purple. Up to 25cm (10in) long, it encloses a purple or yellow spadix, half the length of the spathe. HEIGHT & SPREAD 30×30cm (12×12in).
CULTIVATION Plant tubers in summer, 10cm (4in) deep and 30cm (1ft) apart, in any soil that does not dry out too quickly and in partial shade. Top dress with well-rotted compost in late summer; keep moist in the growing season in winter and spring. Mulch *A. creticum* and *A. italicum* with dry organic matter in severe winters.

▲ *Arum creticum*

PROPAGATION Divide after flowering.
PESTS AND DISEASES Usually trouble free.

Arum, dragon see *Dracunculus vulgaris*
Arum lily see *Zantedeschia*

Aruncus
Goat's beard
Rosaceae

Elegant sprays of light green leaves make lush mounds from which feathery plumes of tiny cream flowers rise in mid summer. Female plants develop small, dull green seed pods that dry well for indoor arrangements. Male plants do not self seed. These hardy perennials thrive in moist soil round a pond.

RECOMMENDED SPECIES AND VARIETIES
A. aethusifolius Creamy white 20cm (8in) plumes of flowers are borne above deeply divided dark green leaves. Native to Korea. HEIGHT & SPREAD 23-30×30cm (9-12×12in).
A. dioicus♀ (syn. *A. plumosus*, *A. sylvestris*, *A. vulgaris*) Graceful, light green leaves, up

▼ *Aruncus dioicus*

to 30cm (12in) long, are enhanced by 20cm (8in) plumes of star-shaped, creamy white flowers, borne on tall stout stems in mid summer. Native to W and C Europe, S Russia and the Caucasus. HEIGHT & SPREAD 1.8×1.2m (6×4ft).

The variety 'Glasnevin' reaches only 1.2m×60cm (4×2ft), as does 'Kneiffii', which has dark, very finely cut, lacy leaves and thinner stems than those of the species.

A. plumosus see *A. dioicus*
A. sylvester see *A. dioicus*
A. vulgaris see *A. dioicus*

CULTIVATION Plant from autumn to early spring in rich, moist soil, ideally in partial shade, spacing the plants 60cm (2ft) apart.
PROPAGATION Lift and divide in autumn every 2 to 3 years.
PESTS AND DISEASES Usually trouble free.

Asarabacca see *Asarum europaeum*

Asarina
Creeping snapdragon
Scrophulariaceae

The trailing stems of this evergreen, short-lived perennial make year-round cover beneath trees, over rocks or down walls. A long flowering period increases its garden value. It is not fully hardy in Britain. There is only one species in the genus.

A. hispanica see *Antirrhinum hispanicum*

▼ *Asarina procumbens*

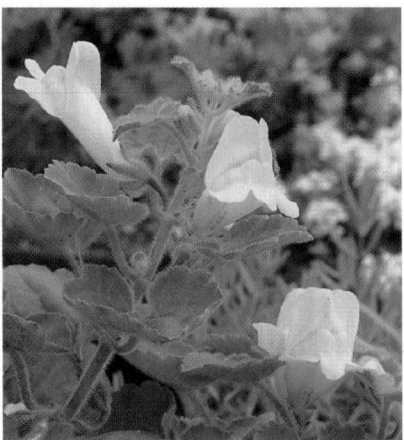

Asarina procumbens (syn. *Antirrhinum asarina, Antirrhinum procumbens, Maurandya asarina*) Snapdragon-like flowers, closed at the mouth by rounded upper and lower lips, are up to 4cm (1½in) long and borne from early summer to early autumn. They are creamy with faint purple veins. A softly hairy plant, sticky to the touch. The greyish green leaves, which grow in pairs along the stems are kidney-shaped and up to 6cm (2½in) wide. Native to the Pyrenees and N Spain. HEIGHT & SPREAD 10×60cm (4×24in).

'Nuria' is a more compact plant, suitable for small rock gardens and troughs.

CULTIVATION Plant in late spring after the last frosts in a well-drained soil, rich in humus, preferably alkaline, in partial shade. The species is hardy to –10°C (14°F); protect plants in winter with a cloche or overhead glass. In colder areas, grow the plants in pots and overwinter them under cover.
PROPAGATION Once established, the plant seeds itself freely each year. Alternatively, take cuttings in late spring or summer.
PESTS AND DISEASES Slugs may attack young plants.

Asarum
Wild ginger
Aristolochiaceae

Asarum europaeum

The glossy, deep green leaves of these low-growing, hardy herbaceous perennials provide luxuriant ground cover and are useful in shade. Curious, often sombre, urn-shaped flowers are held at ground level beneath the leaves. The insignificant, fleshy oval fruits break open and the seeds are dispersed by ants. They are mostly woodland plants in the wild and grow best in moist leafy soil but *Asarum caudatum* and *A. europaeum* are reasonably drought resistant. Plants form spreading evergreen or deciduous mats. Those described are evergreen.

RECOMMENDED SPECIES AND VARIETIES
A. caudatum Red-purple flowers appear below the leaves in spring, each one opening into a hairy urn from a folded bud. The heart-shaped, hairy leaves are up to 15cm (6in) long. Native to western N America. HEIGHT & SPREAD 15×40cm (6×16in).
A. europaeum (asarabacca) This hardy evergreen forms wide patches of shiny, kidney-shaped leaves, up to 12cm (4¾in) wide, usually plain green, sometimes with silver markings. Greeny purple, hairy, urn-shaped flowers appear in early spring. Best grown in deep shade. Native to W Europe. HEIGHT & SPREAD 10×50cm (4×20in).
A. hartwegii (syn. *A. marmoratum*) Purple-brown, hairy flowers appear in spring. The veins of the heart-shaped leaves are marked silver-grey. Native to SW North America. HEIGHT & SPREAD 10×30cm (4×12in).

'Silver Heart' is an especially well-marked leaf form.
CULTIVATION Plant in spring for ground cover in shade or as a specimen in a cool corner of a rock garden.
PROPAGATION Sow seed under glass or outdoors in autumn. Divide in early spring.
PESTS AND DISEASES The leaves are liable to slug and snail damage.

Asclepias
Silkweed, milkweed
Asclepiadaceae

Bright orange and red or pink flowers appear throughout summer or from late summer to autumn on these annuals, herbaceous perennials and shrubs. The fruits carry seeds with tufts of soft white hairs. The tops of the stems contain a milky sap, which can be a skin irritant. Asclepias have deep, fleshy tuberous roots which tend to spread. The plants listed are grown in sunny, protected borders or in a greenhouse or conservatory.

RECOMMENDED SPECIES AND VARIETIES
A. curassavica The flowers, 2cm (¾in) wide, are carried in clusters of 5 to 10. They are usually orange and red but from seed white and yellow forms can appear. The evergreen lance-shaped leaves, 5-15cm (2-6in) long, are carried in pairs on this sub-shrub. Native to Central America. HEIGHT & SPREAD 90×45cm (36×18in).

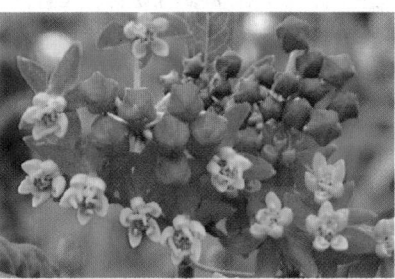

▲ *Asclepias curassavica*

A. incarnata (swamp milkweed) The pink, occasionally white, tubular flowers of this hardy perennial are carried in the leaf axils. The narrow leaves grow up to 15cm (6in) long. Native to NE and SE USA. HEIGHT & SPREAD 1.5m×50cm (5ft×20in).
A. tuberosa The orange and red flowers, 1cm (⅜in) across, are carried in tight clusters from late summer to early autumn. The lance-shaped leaves, 12cm (4¾in) long, spiral round the woody stem of this hardy herbaceous perennial. Native to S and E USA. HEIGHT & SPREAD 90×30cm (3×1ft).
CULTIVATION Grow in ordinary, well-drained soil in full sun. Plant after all danger of frost is over; protect with fleece initially.
PROPAGATION Sow seed under glass in late winter or divide in late spring.
PESTS AND DISEASES Whitefly can infest plants grown under glass.

Ash see *Fraxinus*
Ash, mountain see *Sorbus aucuparia*

▼ *Asclepias tuberosa*

Asparagus
Asparagaceae

Asparagus densiflorus
Sprengeri Group

Fern-like foliage is the main appeal of these diverse perennials, which are native to Africa, Europe and Asia. With the exception of the culinary asparagus, *Asparagus officinalis*, they are evergreen indoor pot plants. *A. officinalis* is a hardy herbaceous perennial, commonly grown outdoors. Small white flowers appear amid the foliage of all species, sometimes followed by red, or more rarely black, berries.

RECOMMENDED SPECIES AND VARIETIES
A. densiflorus 'Myersii'♥ (foxtail fern) Fine foliage in dense feathery spines adorns this half-hardy perennial which is popular for hanging pots or baskets. HEIGHT & SPREAD 90×50cm (36×20in).
   Sprengeri Group♥ (emerald fern) has arching or scrambling wiry green stems densely clothed with bright green needle-like leaves up to 2.5cm (1in) long.
A. officinalis♥ Feathery, fine, green foliage is a feature of this hardy plant, the female forms of which have orange-red berries. Male plants, and all-male varieties, produce the strongest spears for culinary use. HEIGHT & SPREAD 1.2-1.5m×60cm (4-5×2ft).
A. setaceus♥ A flat, fern-like triangular spray is formed by groups of up to 20 bright green needle-like leaflets which clothe the wiry stems of this twining plant. HEIGHT & SPREAD 1-2m×50cm (3-6½ft×20in).
   'Pyramidalis' has a loose pyramidal non-twining habit.
A. verticillatus This prickly, scrambling, much-branched species for the greenhouse has fine green leaves in groups of up to 20. HEIGHT & SPREAD 4×1m (13×3ft).
CULTIVATION Grow indoor species in an open or partially shaded cool situation in a soil-based compost, such as John Innes No.3, which is moist but well drained. Give a liquid houseplant feed regularly in late spring and summer. Indoor species must be kept frost free. Cultivation details for culinary asparagus, *A. officinalis*, are given on p.732.

▼ *Asparagus densiflorus* 'Myersii'

PROPAGATION Sow seed in spring. Divide houseplant species in spring.
PESTS AND DISEASES Asparagus beetle may attack culinary asparagus; red spider mite affects indoor plants.

Asparagus see p.732

Asperula
Woodruff
Rubiaceae

Dainty tubular flowers flaring into four-pointed stars at the mouth bloom generously on these annual, perennial or shrubby plants. Those listed below are lime-tolerant evergreen perennials that flower in spring and early summer. They do well in an unheated greenhouse or conservatory or can be grown in troughs and raised beds, given protection from winter wet. Native mainly to the Mediterranean and SW Asia.
RECOMMENDED SPECIES AND VARIETIES
A. arcadiensis♥ (syn. *A. suberosa* hort.) Small clusters of pink flowers, each flower about 1cm (⅜in) long, cover pale grey-green mats of foliage in early summer. The spreading mats are formed by dense tufts of narrow elliptical, woolly leaves up to 1cm (⅜in) long, which grow in whorls up the stems. HEIGHT & SPREAD 5×30cm (2×12in).

▼ *Asperula arcadiensis*

A. gussonii Dense clusters of red flowers appear in late spring just above a mat of grey-green leaves. Each flower is up to 5mm (¼in) long. The leaves are elliptical and up to 1cm (⅜in) long. HEIGHT & SPREAD 2.5×30cm (1×12in).
A. odorata see *Galium odoratum*
A. sintenisii♥ Pink flowers, up to 1cm (⅜in) long, are held singly or in pairs smothering the dense tufts of foliage. The deep green elliptical to linear leaves are each up to about 1cm (⅜in) long, and pointed. HEIGHT & SPREAD 2×20cm (¾×8in).

▼ *Asperula sintenisii*

A. suberosa hort. see *A. arcadiensis*
CULTIVATION Plant in moist, well-drained soil in a sunny position. Protect from winter wet using overhead glass. Plants grow well on tufa. Otherwise grow in shallow pans in an unheated greenhouse or conservatory.
PROPAGATION Sow seed in winter or early spring or divide in spring or autumn.
PESTS AND DISEASES Occasionally troubled by aphids or slugs. In autumn and winter grey mould may be a problem.

Asphodeline
Jacob's rod
Asphodelaceae

Asphodeline lutea

Spires of yellow, star-like flowers rise in spring and summer above clumps of grassy leaves on these hardy herbaceous perennials. The plants, native to the Mediterranean area, have swollen rhizomatous roots that help them to withstand dry conditions.
RECOMMENDED SPECIES AND VARIETIES
A. liburnica Slender stems carry erect spikes, 20cm (8in) tall, of pale yellow flowers, sometimes striped with green, 3cm (1¼in) across, in early to mid summer. The narrow leaves are grey-green. HEIGHT & SPREAD 60×30cm (2×1ft).
A. lutea (syn. *Asphodelus luteus*) The linear, silver or dark green leaves form a tufted plant. Spikes of numerous, yellow fragrant flowers, each bloom 3cm (1¼in) across, appear from late spring to early summer and are followed by globular green seeds. HEIGHT & SPREAD 1.2m×30cm (4×1ft).
CULTIVATION Plant out in early spring in free-draining soil that is fertile but not over-rich. If planted in autumn young plants may need some protection in a hard winter.
PROPAGATION Raise plants from seed sown when ripe in a coldframe. Grow on in open ground or in pots and plant out 30cm (1ft) apart early in the following spring.
PESTS AND DISEASES Usually trouble free.

Asphodelus
Asphodel
Asphodelaceae

With long, dense spikes of delicate white starry flowers that open in late spring or early summer above upright grassy foliage, these plants are excellent for the herbaceous border or in light shade among trees and shrubs. The plants included here are annuals

▲ *Asphodelus albus*

or herbaceous perennials with rhizomatous roots. Native to the Mediterranean, they need good drainage and some protection in winter where temperatures regularly fall below -5°C (23°F).

RECOMMENDED SPECIES AND VARIETIES

A. albus (white asphodel) The white or pink star-shaped flowers have long, fine prominent stamens. Each flower is about 4cm (1½in) across and has 6 petals, each with a pinkish brown central vein. The flowering stems rise out of dense clumps of narrow, grey-green, ridged leaves, up to 60cm (2ft) long. An herbaceous perennial. HEIGHT & SPREAD 1m×30cm (3×1ft).

▲ *Asphodelus fistulosus*

A. fistulosus (hollow-leaved asphodel) The white or pink flowers are about 2.5cm (1in) wide and have prominent stamens. Each of the 6 petals has a light brown central vein. The stems and narrow mid green leaves, up to 35cm (14in) long, are hollow. This plant is an annual or short-lived perennial. HEIGHT & SPREAD 75×30cm (2½×1ft).

A. luteus see *Asphodeline lutea*

CULTIVATION Plant in early spring in free-draining soil in full sun or semi-shade. Unless seed is wanted, cut back the flowering stems when the blooms are over. Cut back the leaves in winter. Do not over-water or overfeed. Give plants protection during winter in colder areas of Britain.

PROPAGATION Sow seed or divide plants carefully in spring.

PESTS AND DISEASES Usually trouble free.

Aspidistra
Convallariaceae

Leathery, glossy, dark green foliage is the outstanding feature of these handsome evergreen perennials. The leaves are erect and lance-shaped and retain a healthy appearance in quite extreme conditions indoors. In the warmest parts of the country, areas in the south and west, given a moist, sheltered and shady position the plants can be grown outdoors, associating well with ferns.

A. elatior♀ (cast-iron plant) Most commonly grown as a houseplant, this slow-spreading plant has arching, long-stalked, tapering leaves, up to 60cm (24in) long. The leaves rise singly from a stout rhizome and it forms broad clumps. Insignificant urn-shaped flowers that are easily overlooked may be borne in spring or summer on a short stem at soil level. Fruits are dull brown berries in late summer but are rarely seen on a cultivated plant. Native to China. HEIGHT & SPREAD 60×60cm (24×24in).

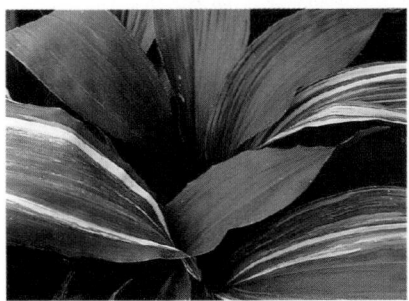

▲ *Aspidistra elatior* 'Variegata'

The leaves of **'Variegata'**♀ are marked lengthways with irregular creamy stripes.

CULTIVATION Strong sunlight can scorch the foliage of an aspidistra though the colour of the variegated plant is more distinct given brighter light. Plant in well-drained, humus-rich soil in a sheltered, shady place not subject to frost.

PROPAGATION Divide established plants in spring.

PESTS AND DISEASES Usually trouble free, but slugs may damage the leaves. Scale insects and mealy bugs may infest pot plants.

Astelia
Asteliaceae

Bold sword-leaved clumps of silvery green are the outstanding plants in this genus, but it also includes small and unobtrusive green plants. These perennials from New Zealand, Tasmania and islands in the South Pacific need moist, acid soil and are not all hardy. In milder areas of Britain they make striking features in open borders, but in exposed gardens and colder areas they are generally best grown in tubs to be put out-

side in summer. The flowers and fruits are rarely seen in gardens, but if female plants are grown with a male nearby to fertilise them, the flower clusters develop into showy yellow, orange or red berries that are edible and sweet.

▲ *Astelia chathamica* 'Silver Spear'

RECOMMENDED SPECIES AND VARIETIES

A. chathamica **'Silver Spear'** Sword-like, evergreen leaves, 2m (6½ft) or more long and up to 10cm (4in) wide on established plants, curve outward. The upper surface is green with a silvery covering that eventually peels off. The underside is felted with white hairs. Sprays of greenish to maroon flowers are followed on fertilised plants by orange berries in summer. Give protection when temperatures drop below -5°C (23°F). HEIGHT & SPREAD 1.5×2.4m (5×8ft).

A. nervosa Silvery evergreen leaves 1m (3ft) and more long, arch stiffly outwards, hiding the flower clusters, which vary from green to dark maroon. The rarely seen summer fruits are orange to red. Tolerates temperatures down to -10°C (14°F). HEIGHT & SPREAD 60cm×1.5m (2×5ft).

CULTIVATION Plant in moist, loamy, acid soil; make sure it stays moist in summer. In cold areas, grow the plants in tubs and over-winter in a conservatory or greenhouse.

PROPAGATION Raise from seed if it is available. Soak seed of *A. nervosa* overnight before sowing in late winter; germination is often very slow. Alternatively, divide a young plant carefully in summer, or lift and divide established clumps in spring.

PESTS AND DISEASES Usually trouble free.

▼ *Astelia nervosa*

Aster

Michaelmas daisy, starwort
Compositae

Aster alpinus

Daisy-like asters bring fresh colour to the garden in late summer and autumn or spring. Violet to lavender, white, pink, red or blue flowers with golden yellow centres are carried singly or in clusters. Asters are mostly herbaceous perennials – a few are annuals or biennials. The asters described are all hardy herbaceous perennials.

Autumn-flowering asters – known as Michaelmas daisies because they flower around Michaelmas, September 29 – make a fine show in a garden border, especially when planted in bold groups of one colour. They are excellent as cut flowers. Lower-growing asters, often spring-flowering, are suitable for rock gardens, raised beds, small borders and containers.

The petals are properly called ray florets and the central disc is made up of disc florets. Leaves are arranged alternately on the stems. All the recommended species and varieties flower between late summer and late autumn, except for *Aster alpinus* and *A. tongolensis* 'Napsbury', which bloom in late spring and early summer. The flowers attract butterflies and bees. Native to Europe, Asia, N America and South Africa.

RECOMMENDED SPECIES AND VARIETIES

A. acris see *A. sedifolius*

A. alpinus♀ (alpine aster) Flowers with violet, white or pink petals bloom from late spring to early summer on a small plant. Erect stems carry solitary flowers 3–5 cm (1¼–2 in) across. Spoon-shaped, grey-green leaves, 5–8 cm (2–3¼ in) long, form rosettes. HEIGHT & SPREAD 25×25 cm (10×10 in).

A. amellus (Italian starwort) Listed cultivars all have large flowers in loose, flat-topped clusters, about 15 cm (6 in) long and 25 cm (10 in) wide, on erect, woody stems. The grey-green leaves, 6 cm (2½ in) long, are oblong to lance-shaped. Mildew resistant.

The following grow 50 cm (20 in) tall and spread to 65 cm (26 in) unless stated otherwise. **'Framfieldii'**♀ is bushy, with violet-purple flowers; **'King George'**♀ has larger, rich violet-blue flowers; **'Nocturne'** produces large, deep lilac flowers and is 70 cm (28 in) tall; **'Pink Zenith'** ('Rosa Erfüllung') is sturdy and has bright pink flowers; the compact **'Veilchenkönigin'**♀ ('Violet Queen') has violet-purple blooms.

A. cordifolius Cultivars thrive in dappled shade as well as in sun. The small flowers are

▲ *Aster amellus* 'King George'

carried in graceful, open sprays about 60 cm (24 in) across. Erect wiry stems bear deep green, heart-shaped to broadly oval leaves, 8 cm (3¼ in) long. Resistant to mildew.

'Elegans', with white, lavender-tinted flowers, emerging in mid autumn, and **'Sweet Lavender'**♀, with pale violet-blue flowers, are both 1.2 m (4 ft) tall, spreading to 75 cm (30 in).

A. divaricatus This species is useful for shaded sites, where dark brown wiry stems, 60 cm (24 in) long, arch to the ground, creating effective cover when massed with white, starry flowers, 2.5 cm (1 in) wide, borne in clusters up to 20 cm (8 in) across. The broad, oval, pointed leaves are light green and up to 10 cm (4 in) long. HEIGHT & SPREAD 30 cm×1 m (1×3 ft).

A. ericoides Cultivars have elegant, spreading sprays, about 70 cm (28 in) long, carrying lots of small flowers. The mid green, narrow leaves are 1–7 cm (⅜–2¾ in) long. This is a very bushy plant. It survives drought better than many other autumn asters. Some resistance to mildew.

Listed plants reach heights and spreads of 1 m (3 ft), except the lavender-blue **'Blue Star'**♀, 80 cm (32 in) tall; **'Golden Spray'**♀ has white flowers; **'Pink Cloud'**♀ has mauve-pink flowers; **'White Heather'** bears upright sprays of white flowers.

A. × *frikartii* All cultivars are exceptionally free flowering and vigorous. Flowers are solitary. The dark green, oblong leaves, rough to the touch, are 8 cm (3¼ in) long on some plants. Resistant to mildew.

▼ *Aster ericoides* 'Golden Spray'

▼ *Aster ericoides* 'Pink Cloud'

'Flora's Delight', with rosy lilac flowers 4 cm (1½ in) across, is a compact plant, with a height and spread of about 45 cm (18 in). **'Wunder von Stäfa'**♀ has lavender-blue flowers up to 7 cm (2¾ in) across, and attains a height and spread of 1 m (3 ft).

A. **'Kylie'**♀ Small, pale rose-pink flowers are carried in elegant sprays 80 cm (32 in) long on tall, woody stems on this vigorous plant. The pale grey-green leaves are lance-shaped and up to 40 cm (16 in) long. Resistant to mildew. HEIGHT & SPREAD 1.4 m×80 cm (4½ ft×32 in).

A. lateriflorus Small, white-petalled flowers, with pale yellow discs that turn purple after the first few days, are produced in profusion within flat-topped clusters borne on the upper side of slender, spreading branches that extend almost at right angles from the main stem. Leaves are lance-shaped, as long as 15 cm (6 in), green often tinted purple, especially colourful in some cultivars. HEIGHT & SPREAD 1×1 m (3×3 ft).

'Coombe Fishacre' has flowers with pink petals encircling rosy purple central discs. **'Horizontalis'**♀, with purple-tinted leaves, is a compact plant that reaches a height of 60 cm (24 in) and spreads to 70 cm (28 in), flowering late, in mid autumn.

A. **'Little Carlow'**♀ Violet-blue flowers, 2.5 cm (1 in) wide, bloom abundantly in broad, branching clusters, 30 cm (12 in) across, on upright stems. The pointed, deep green leaves are about 12 cm (4¾ in) long. Some resistance to mildew. HEIGHT & SPREAD 1.4 m×80 cm (4½ ft×32 in).

A. novae-angliae (New England aster) Cultivars have flowers 3–5 cm (1¼–2 in) wide, appearing in open clusters, up to 18 cm (7 in) across, at the top of stout, woody stems covered with rough, lance-shaped, dull green leaves. Plants require very little staking. Resistant to mildew.

The following are 1 m (3 ft) tall and spread to 80–100 cm (32–40 in), unless stated otherwise. **'Andenken an Alma Pötschke'**♀, vivid cerise; **'Harrington's Pink'**♀, rose-pink, 1.2 m (4 ft) tall; **'Herbstschnee'**, ('Autumn Snow'), white; **'Lye End Beauty'** purple-pink, 1.2 m (4 ft) tall; **'Mrs S.T. Wright'**, rosy mauve, large

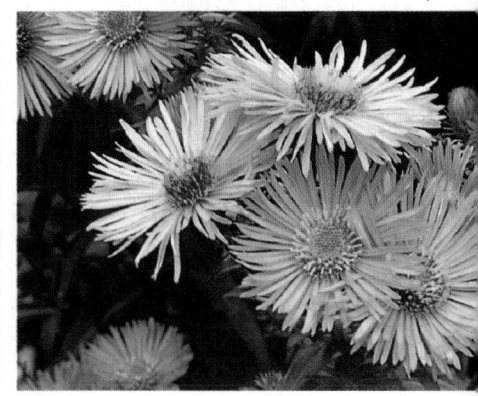

▼ *Aster novae-angliae* 'Mrs S.T. Wright'

▲ *Aster novae-angliae* 'Rosa Sieger'

flowers, 1.2 m (4 ft) tall; **'Purple Dome'**, blue-purple, compact, with a height and spread of 60 cm (24 in); **'Rosa Sieger'**, rose-pink, large flowers; **'Septemberrubin'** ('September Ruby'), red-purple flowers.

A. novi-belgii The selected cultivars bear flowers 3-5 cm (1¼-2 in) across, or more, in branched sprays, often pyramid-shaped, up to 30 cm (12 in) wide, on erect, branched stems. Leaves are narrow, mid to dark green and as long as 10 cm (4 in). Single offsets, taken in early spring and planted singly or in groups, produce the finest flowering stems.

TALL CULTIVARS

Plants listed here attain a height of about 1 m (3 ft) and a spread of 60 cm (2 ft), unless stated otherwise. **'Albanian'** white, double flowers; **'Anita Webb'**, pink flowers; **'Blue Eyes'**, deep lavender-pink, vigorous, 1.4 m

▼ *Aster novi-belgii* 'Albanian'

▼ *Aster novi-belgii* 'Fellowship'

▲ *Aster novi-belgii* 'Helen Ballard'

▲ *Aster novi-belgii* 'Rufus'

(4½ ft) tall; **'Coombe Rosemary'**, heather purple, double flowers; **'Fellowship'**, pale pink-mauve, large double flowers; **'Helen Ballard'**, purple-red, large double flowers; **'Marie Ballard'**, lavender-blue, large double flowers; **'Mistress Quickly'**, violet flowers with prominent yellow discs; **'Patricia Ballard'**, mauve-pink, large double flowers, grows quickly; **'Percy Thrower'**, lavender-blue, large double flowers; **'Rufus'**, purple-red, bushy habit; **'Sheena'**, pink, large double flowers; **'Winston S. Churchill'**, purple-red, bushy habit, 80 cm (32 in) tall.

DWARF CULTIVARS

These dense, bushy plants have short, stout branches, clothed to the ground with leaves. Those listed grow to a height of about 30 cm (12 in), and spread to about 45 cm (18 in), unless stated otherwise. **'Chatterbox'**, pale pink, double flowers; **'Chequers'**, bright violet flowers, 60 cm (24 in) tall; **'Jenny'**, purple-red, large double flowers; **'Kristina'**, white; **'Lady in Blue'**, lavender-blue; **'Remembrance'** lavender-blue, large, 50 cm (20 in) tall.

*A. **'Ochtendgloren'**♀* Pink flowers up to 2.5 cm (1 in) wide are carried profusely in loose sprays, 80 cm (32 in) long, on erect stems. The long, narrow, mid green leaves are up to 10 cm (4 in) long. HEIGHT & SPREAD 1 m×60 cm (3×2 ft).

*A. **'Photograph'**♀* Open sprays, 50 cm (20 in) long, of small lavender-blue flowers are borne on slightly arching stems. Leaves are mid green, pointed and 7 cm (2¾ in)

long. HEIGHT & SPREAD 1 m×60 cm (3×2 ft).

A. pringlei **'Monte Cassino'**♀ Dainty white flowers are carried in 40 cm (16 in) sprays. The stems are wiry and erect, the bright green leaves narrow and up to 10 cm (4 in) long. HEIGHT & SPREAD 75×80 cm (30×32 in).

A. pyrenaeus **'Lutetia'** Large, lilac-blue flowers appear in branched clusters 35 cm (14 in) wide. Leaves are grey-green, pointed and 9 cm (3½ in) long. Resistant to mildew. HEIGHT & SPREAD 50 cm×1.2 m (20 in×4 ft).

A. sedifolius (syn. *A. acris*) Masses of small, starry, lavender-blue flowers are borne in flat-topped clusters, about 25 cm (10 in) across. Each flower has just 8-12 petals. The long, narrow leaves are grey-green and about 2 cm (¾ in) long. Mildew free. HEIGHT & SPREAD 75×80 cm (30×32 in).

A. thomsonii **'Nanus'** Large, lilac-blue flowers are held in numerous clusters, 10-15 cm (4-6 in) across. The grey-green leaves are ovate, toothed, hairy and 4 cm (1½ in) long. Mildew free. HEIGHT & SPREAD 40×55 cm (16×22 in).

A. tongolensis **'Napsbury'** This showy cultivar flowers from late spring to early summer. The large, solitary flowers are bright violet with prominent orange-yellow central discs. Leaves are grey-green, oval, slightly hairy and 5-10 cm (2-4 in) long. HEIGHT & SPREAD 40×20 cm (16×8 in).

A. umbellatus Masses of small flowers, each with 10-15 white petals, are carried in flat-topped clusters 40 cm (16 in) across on a vigorous plant. The light green, pointed, broad leaves are 12 cm (4¾ in) long. Mildew free. HEIGHT & SPREAD 1.5×1 m (5×3 ft).

CULTIVATION Plant in an open, sunny situation, in soil that is alkaline to slightly acid, fertile and retains moisture in spring and summer. *A. alpinus*, cultivars of *A. amellus* and *A.* × *frikartii*, plus *A. pyrenaeus* 'Lutetia' and *A. thomsonii* 'Nanus' require alkaline soils and good to sharp winter drainage. Plant out autumn-flowering asters in mid or late spring and spring-flowering asters in mid autumn or early spring. Many varieties over 60 cm (24 in) tall need staking with twiggy supports.

PROPAGATION Divide plants every 3-5 years, in early spring, to increase numbers and to maintain vigour. Divide cultivars of *A. novi-belgii* annually. Most species can be raised from seed. Sow seed of autumn-flowering asters between early spring and mid summer, and seed of spring-flowering asters in early spring, in a coldframe, to produce plants that flower the following year. Alternatively, take softwood cuttings in mid or late spring. *A. thomsonii* 'Nanus' is best propagated by this method.

PESTS AND DISEASES Spray plants against powdery mildew with a systemic fungicide. Destroy any plants affected by aster wilt.

Aster, China see *Callistephus*
Aster, Stokes' see *Stokesia*

Asteriscus
Compositae

An abundance of deep yellow, daisy-like flowers appears throughout summer on these herbaceous perennials with their soft, silky, greyish green foliage. *A. maritimus*, the only species commonly in cultivation, dislikes cold, wet conditions and requires a sunny sheltered spot in a rock garden or in the crevice of a stone wall. Asteriscus may be grown in containers as an annual and also does well in hanging baskets. Native to the Mediterranean coast and North Africa.

RECOMMENDED SPECIES AND VARIETIES
A. maritimus A dwarf, free-flowering, tufted plant. The deep yellow flowers, 4 cm (1½ in) across, have finely toothed petals. The silky greyish green leaves, 2 cm (¾ in) long, are wider near the tip than at the base. HEIGHT & SPREAD 25×30 cm (10×12 in).

▲ *Asteriscus maritimus*

CULTIVATION Plant in spring in a warm, sunny, sheltered spot in free-draining soil or grow in pots and place in a sunny, sheltered position outdoors or in a cold greenhouse.
PROPAGATION Take semi-ripe cuttings in summer, or sow seed in late winter in a warm greenhouse or frame. Keep young plants under glass for the first winter.
PESTS AND DISEASES Usually trouble free.

Astilbe
Saxifragaceae

Astilbe chinensis var. pumila

Fluffy-plumed astilbes are among the most rewarding summer-flowering hardy perennials when they are established in the rich, moist soil they need. They have handsome, fern-like leaves, up to 23 cm (9 in) long, and during mid to late summer produce spires, 15-20 cm (6-8 in) long, of tiny flowers on stiff stems that never require staking. The flowers are white, shades of pink, lilac or red. When the flowers have finished they leave a tracery of interesting seed heads which are a lovely shade of light brown; these remain intact throughout winter. The height of the different species and varieties ranges from dwarf astilbes of 30 cm (1 ft) to tall specimens of over 1.2 m (4 ft).

Astilbes are happiest in moist conditions near a pond or stream, in sun or half shade. They will never make a vigorous plant if allowed to dry out in summer. Where there is plenty of space in a garden, plant them in groups of three, five or more. They associate well with moisture-loving perennials including suitable shades of candelabra primulas, hostas, *Iris sibirica* and *Trollius*.

Nearly all astilbes sold are crosses from the following species: *A. × arendsii*, *A. chinensis*, *A. japonica*, *A. × rosea*, *A. simplicifolia* and *A. thunbergii*. To simplify the classification of cultivars they are listed in alphabetical order under HYBRIDS at the end of the recommended plants.

RECOMMENDED SPECIES AND VARIETIES
A. chinensis var. *pumila*♀ Narrow 15 cm (6 in) spikes of mauve-pink flowers are produced from mid summer to early autumn above fast-spreading, crowded rosettes of 15 cm (6 in) long leaves. Native to China. HEIGHT & SPREAD 30×40 cm (12×16 in).
A. glaberrima var. *saxatilis*♀ Finely cut, fern-like leaves are delicately edged with red. During mid summer the dwarf plant bears spikes of pink flowers, 10 cm (4 in) tall. Native to China and Japan. HEIGHT & SPREAD 23×23 cm (9×9 in).
A. simplicifolia♀ The rich green leaves are deeply cut and fern-like. Spikes of flowers, 15 cm (6 in) long, are a pretty, pale pink and are produced from mid summer onwards, sometimes still blooming in early autumn. The dwarf plant is excellent for pockets of moist soil at the edge of a small pond as it grows fairly slowly. Native to Japan. HEIGHT & SPREAD 23×23 cm (9×9 in).

HYBRIDS
The great range of named hybrids have ferny foliage and require moist soil at all times, especially when they are in bloom. They flower in mid summer unless otherwise indicated. The spread is generally equal to the height of the plants, which is given below. The list is grouped according to flower colour.

WHITE FLOWERS
'Brautschleier'♀ ('Bridal Veil'), flowers in early summer, 75 cm (30 in); **'Bridal Veil'** see 'Brautschleier'; **'Bumalda'**, dark green foliage, 75 cm (30 in); **'Deutschland'**, large lax spikes of flowers, 60 cm (2 ft); **'Irrlicht'**, deep green foliage, 45 cm (18 in); **'Praecox Alba'**, small bushy plant, 36 cm (14 in); **'Professor van der Wielen'**, 45 cm (18 in); **'Snowdrift'**, 60 cm (2 ft); **'W. E. Gladstone'**, 60 cm (2 ft); **'Weisse Gloria'** ('White Gloria'), creamy white flowers, early summer flowering, 60 cm (2 ft);

▲ *Astilbe chinensis* var. *pumila*

Astilbe 'Deutschland' ▲

'White Gloria' see 'Weisse Gloria'; **'William Buchanan'**, dwarf, compact plant, creamy white flowers, 23 cm (9 in).

PALE PINK FLOWERS
'Drayton Glory' see 'Peach Blossom'; **'Dunkellachs'**, thin spikes of pale salmon flowers, 60 cm (2 ft); **'Europa'**, 60 cm (2 ft); **'Peach Blossom'** ('Drayton Glory'), 60 cm (2 ft); **'Sprite'**♀, deep green foliage, graceful branching spikes of pale pink flowers, 30 cm (1 ft); **'Venus'**, pale salmon-pink, 1 m (3 ft).

MID PINK TO MAUVE FLOWERS
'Amethyst', deep pinky lilac flowers, 1 m (3 ft); **'Bressingham Beauty'**, pink spikes on strong stiff stems, 1 m (3 ft); **'Bronce Elegans'**♀, bronze-tinged foliage, pink flowers, 23 cm (9 in); **'Düsseldorf'**, bright pink, 50 cm (20 in); **'Federsee'**, dark stems, deep rose-pink, 60 cm (2 ft); **'Finale'**, dwarf plant, pink flowers, 40 cm (16 in); **'Granat'**, bright green foliage, dark stem, deep pink flowers, 80 cm (32 in); **'Hyacinth'** see 'Hyazinth'; **'Hyazinth'** ('Hyacinth'), deep mauve-pink flowers, 1 m (3 ft); **'Inshriach Pink'**, dwarf plant, pink, 36 cm (14 in); **'Jo Ophorst'**, upright habit, branched stems, bright lilac pink, late flowering, 75 cm (30 in); **'Ostrich Plume'** see 'Straussenfeder'; **'Perkeo'**♀, dwarf compact plant, deep pink flowers, 23 cm (9 in); **'Purpurlanze'** ('Purple Lance'), mauve-pink flowers, 1 m (3 ft); **'Purple Lance'** see 'Purpurlanze'; **'Rheinland'**♀, compact, bright pink, 50 cm (20 in); **'Straussenfeder'** ('Ostrich Plume'), feathery plumes of salmon-pink, 1 m (3 ft); **'Superba'**♀, tall narrow spikes of mauve-pink flowers, 1 m (3 ft).

▼ *Astilbe* 'Amethyst'

▼ *Astilbe* 'Bressingham Beaut'

▲ *Astilbe* 'Hyazinth'

RED FLOWERS

'Aphrodite', carmine red, 40 cm (16 in); **'Cherry Ripe'** see 'Feuer'; **'Etna'**, deep red, 60 cm (2 ft); **'Fanal'**, light green foliage tinged with red, dark red stems and bright red flowers in early summer, 60 cm (2 ft); **'Feuer'** ('Fire'), deep salmon red, 60 cm (2 ft); **'Fire'** see 'Feuer'; **'Glow'** see 'Glut'; **'Glut'** ('Glow'), bright red flowers mid to late summer, 80 cm (32 in); **'Montgomery'**, bright orange-red, 60 cm (2 ft); **'Red Sentinel'**, dark foliage, deep red, 75 cm (30 in); **'Spartan'**, deep red, 60 cm (2 ft).

CULTIVATION Plant any time from autumn to early spring in rich, moist soil in a sunny or half-shady position. Space dwarf varieties

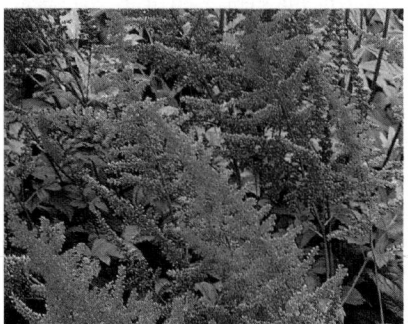

▲ *Astilbe* 'Feuer'

45 cm (18 in) apart and more vigorous varieties 60 cm (2 ft) apart. Apply a thick mulch of well-rotted manure or forest bark around the plants to retain soil moisture; manure also feeds the plants. Ensure that the plants do not dry out during summer.

Lift and divide established plants about every 4 years otherwise they can die in the centre.

Late frosts can scorch new spring leaves and kill the buds; foliage will be replaced but not the flowers. If frost is forecast, protect the plants at night with garden fleece.

PROPAGATION Species can be increased from seed but as germination is sometimes slow, it is easier to divide plants in autumn. Increase cultivars by division only. Seed-raised plants will not come true.

PESTS AND DISEASES Powdery mildew and leaf spot can be troublesome, especially in dry seasons. New foliage is sometimes nibbled by mice, voles and rabbits.

Astilboides
Saxifragaceae

The sole species of astilboides is a stunning hardy perennial foliage plant, prized for its large, round, pale green leaves. It needs a rich, moist soil and a sheltered spot in half-shade. It is native to China.

Astilboides tabularis Measuring up to 1 m (3 ft) across, the leaves are gently scalloped and held umbrella-like, on strong stems, 45 cm (18 in) tall, that support the leaf in the middle. In mid summer, tiny, starry white flowers are carried well above the leaves, arranged in 15 cm (6 in) drooping panicles. HEIGHT & SPREAD 120×90 cm (4×3 ft).

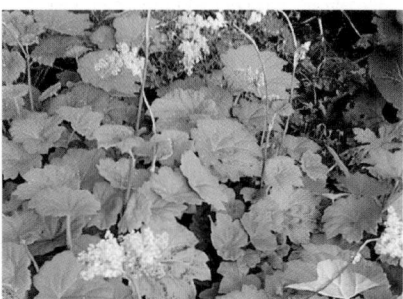

▲ *Astilboides tabularis*

CULTIVATION Plant the rhizomes in spring in rich, damp soil that does not dry out in summer, choosing a sheltered spot in sun or half-shade. New growth may be damaged by late frosts.

PROPAGATION Divide and replant the rhizomes in spring.

PESTS AND DISEASES Usually trouble free.

Astrantia
Umbelliferae

The blooms of these herbaceous perennials are excellent for flower arrangements, both fresh and dried. The mid summer flowers are produced in star-like whorls of papery bracts, each flowerhead consisting of several flowers grouped together on short wiry stalks. All the species are very tolerant as to soil conditions, although they do prefer sun or partial shade. While they are often thought of as woodland plants, it is the richly organic nature of the soil rather than the canopy of shade that they appreciate. They are native to Europe and Asia.

RECOMMENDED SPECIES AND VARIETIES
A. carniolica Each silvery white flower is up to 2.5 cm (1 in) across, carried in clusters

▼ *Astrantia major* ssp. *involucrata* 'Shaggy'

of 3-5 on upright stems. The coarse green leaves are irregularly toothed, with 5-7 roughly oval lobes up to 7.5 cm (3 in) long. HEIGHT & SPREAD 30-45×30 cm (1-1½×1 ft).

The flowers of var. *rubra* are silvery with a strong pink infusion.

A. major (greater masterwort) The handsome crispy flowers, held in groups of 5 or more, are up to 2.5 cm (1 in) across and whitish green and rose. They are borne just above coarse, toothed, mid green leaves, up to 10 cm (4 in) long, with 5-7 oval to lance-shaped lobes. The plant self-seeds easily. HEIGHT & SPREAD 60×45 cm (2×1½ ft).

There is a white-flowered form, var. *alba*, while **'Hadspen Blood'** produces deep crimson blossoms. The flowers of ssp. *involucrata* are larger. Its cultivar **'Shaggy'** is untidy, but with beautiful pinkish white blooms. The flowers of var. *rosea* and var. *rubra* are soft pink-white. **'Ruby Wedding'** has purplish red blooms. **'Sunningdale Variegated'** has bold cream and green leaves and nondescript off-white flowers.

A. maxima Pink flowers up to 2.5 cm (1 in) across bloom on branching stems. Shallowly toothed leaves, up to 10 cm (4 in) long, have 3-5 elliptical to oval lobes. HEIGHT & SPREAD 60×45 cm (2×1½ ft).

A. minor This neat compact plant has white, or occasionally pink-flushed flowers up to 2.5 cm (1 in) across, carried on stout branching stems. The leaves are finely toothed, with 7 lance-shaped lobes. HEIGHT & SPREAD 30×30 cm (1×1 ft).

CULTIVATION Plant from late autumn until spring in soil enriched with organic matter and in sun or semi-shade. Lift and divide every 3-4 years; deadhead after flowering.

PROPAGATION Sow seed in late summer or early spring in a coldframe. Increase named varieties by division in early spring as these do not come true from seed.

PESTS AND DISEASES Usually trouble free.

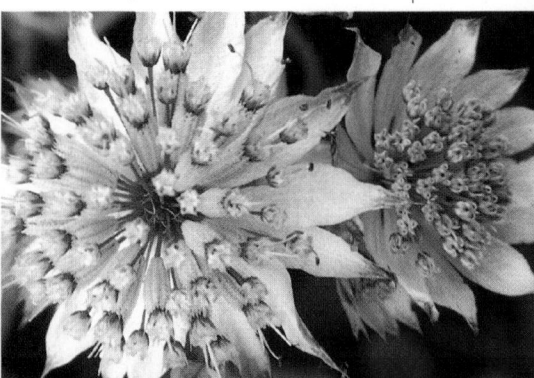

▼ *Astrantia major* var. *rosea*

▼ *Astrantia maxima*

71

a

Astrophytum see CACTI p.106
Athyrium see FERNS p.262

Atriplex
Chenopodiaceae

Grown for its silvery leaves, the shrubby *Atriplex halimus* resists the effects of salt-laden winds so is a valuable screen in seaside gardens. It is native to S Europe but fairly hardy. The half-hardy annual *A. hortensis* var. *rubra* is also salt-tolerant and grown for its decorative foliage. It is edible.

RECOMMENDED SPECIES AND VARIETIES
A. halimus (tree purslane) Silvery grey, 1.5-6 cm (½-2½ in) long, oval leaves cover this loosely branching, semi-evergreen shrub. The insignificant flowers and fruit are rarely seen. HEIGHT & SPREAD 1×1.2 m (3×4 ft) after 5 years, ultimately 2.4 m (8 ft) tall.

▲ *Atriplex hortensis var. rubra*

A. hortensis var. *rubra* (purple orache, red mountain spinach) Fast-growing, upright plants, these annuals can quickly form a temporary hedge. The triangular, deep purple leaves, 15 cm (6 in) long, can be used when young in salads or as a substitute for spinach. Spikes of insignificant flowers appear in summer. HEIGHT & SPREAD 1.2 m×30 cm (4×1 ft).

CULTIVATION Plant *A. halimus* in full sun in well-drained, not too fertile soil from mid autumn to early spring. *A. hortensis* var. *rubra* thrives in moisture-retentive, fertile soil in full sun. Water well during dry spells. Unless seed is required, pinch out the flowers as they appear.

PROPAGATION Raise *A. halimus* from semi-ripe or ripewood cuttings. Sow seed of *A. hortensis* var. *rubra* in the garden from late spring to early summer.

PRUNING To encourage more bushy growth, cut *A. halimus* back hard in spring to within 2 or 3 buds of old wood. Do the same with any loose sprays or frost-damaged shoots.

PESTS AND DISEASES Usually trouble free.

Aubrieta
Cruciferae

Aubrieta deltoidea

Forming low, compact cushions of grey-green foliage smothered in pink, purple or blue flowers throughout spring, these hardy evergreen perennials are ideally suited to rock gardens and for growing on dry sunny walls or in the cracks between paving. Native to dry rocky places in the mountain areas of SE Europe eastwards to the Lebanon and Iran, aubrietias thrive in neutral or limy soils. The colourful, cross-shaped flowers have four petals and are borne in elongating clusters.

RECOMMENDED SPECIES AND VARIETIES
A. deltoidea Violet to red-purple, sometimes white, flowers, each up to 2.5 cm (1 in) across, appear in spring. The grey-green oval leaves, up to 1 cm (⅜ in) long and with toothed edges, are borne on rather straggly stems that form a spreading mat. HEIGHT & SPREAD 15×60 cm (6×24 in).

'Nana Variegata' has leaves with cream markings. The plants of **Variegata Group** have pale blue flowers and leaves variegated with cream.

OTHER VARIETIES
There are many cultivated varieties available, most of which probably originate from *A. deltoidea*. Unless otherwise stated, the varieties included below have flowers up to 3 cm (1¼ in) across, held on stalks about 15 cm (6 in) tall, and toothed, grey-green, oval leaves, up to 1 cm (⅜ in) long, that form dense cushions. The plants, except where stated otherwise, grow to 15 cm (6 in) high and 60 cm (2 ft) wide.
'**Alix Brett**' has double, carmine flowers.
'**April Joy**' has double, dark mauve blooms. The flowers of '**Argenteovariegata**' are purple and single and the leaves have silvery variegation. '**Astolat**' has single, purple blooms; its leaves are variegated. '**Aureovariegata**' has pale lavender-blue, single flowers and golden-green leaves.

▼ *Aubrieta 'Astolat'*

'**Belisha Beacon**' has bright rose-red, single flowers. '**Bob Saunders**' has double, red-purple flowers on stems up to 20 cm (8 in) long. '**Bressingham Pink**' has double, pink flowers. The single flowers of '**Doctor Mules**'♥ are rich violet. '**Greencourt Purple**' has semidouble, dark purple blooms. The single flowers of '**Gurgedyke**'

▲ *Aubrieta 'Gurgedyke'*

are deep purple. '**Mrs Rodewald**' has large, single, deep red blooms. The single flowers of '**Oakington Lavender**' are lavender-blue. '**Purple Cascade**' has single, deep purple flowers. '**Red Carpet**' has single, deep red flowers. '**Red Cascade**' and '**Royal Red**' both have single, red flowers. The single blooms of '**Triumphant**' are almost pure blue. '**Wanda**' has double, light red flowers.

CULTIVATION Plant aubrietias in free-draining, preferably limy, soil in full sun or partial shade. They can be planted in crevices in walls and paving, though they do not tolerate being walked upon. Trim back moderately after flowering to keep plants from becoming too straggly.

PROPAGATION Sow seed in early spring, take semi-ripe cuttings of named cultivars in summer or autumn, or divide plants in late summer and early autumn. Move self-sown seedlings and replant in autumn.

PESTS AND DISEASES Aubrietias can suffer from downy mildew and powdery mildew.

Aucuba
Cornaceae

Aucuba japonica

Glossy, green, leathery leaves give permanent garden value to the sturdy evergreen shrub, aucuba – and in many varieties golden yellow markings light up the foliage. The shrubs are easily grown, thrive in sun or shade, tolerate pollution and are good as background plants as well as more prominent features. They do well in containers, for placing in inhospitable corners or on paved areas. The pale purple flowers, which appear in early spring, are insignificant but quite decorative. Male and female flowers usually appear on different plants, so both sexes should be grown together to produce the vivid red, oval berries, which are borne in clusters and last for several months.

RECOMMENDED SPECIES AND VARIETIES
A. japonica (spotted laurel) Glossy, deep green, oval leaves, sometimes irregularly

▲ *Aucuba japonica* 'Crotonifolia'

finely toothed, grow up to 20 cm (8 in) long and 7.5 cm (3 in) wide. Male and female flowers appear on different plants during mid to late spring, and are followed on fertilised female plants by bright red berries in autumn. The small flowers are in short spikes, held upright. The bushy rounded shrub is frost hardy. Native to Japan. HEIGHT & SPREAD 1.5×1.2 m (5×4 ft) after 5 years, ultimately 3 m (10 ft) tall and wide.

Many of the cultivars are more decorative than the species, and they are generally smaller, reaching 2 m (6½ ft) in height. 'Crotonifolia'♀, a female plant, is one of the brightest variegated forms with large, pale green, glossy leaves blotched with gold. 'Golden King' is a male plant whose leaves have large splashes of gold. It does best in semi-shade. In the female plant f. *longifolia*♀, the narrow lance-shaped leaves, up to 12.5 cm (5 in) long, have a slightly wavy margin and are pale glossy green. 'Nana Rotundifolia' is a small round shrub reaching 1 m (3 ft) tall at best. It is a female selection, which fruits freely when grown near a

▲ *Aucuba japonica* f. *longifolia*

male bush. The small deep green leaves are sharply toothed near the tip. 'Rozannie' is a compact shrub with bisexual flowers, which produces abundant berries without the assistance of another plant. The leaves are glossy dark green and toothed on the margin. 'Salicifolia' is a female selection producing an abundance of bright red berries in autumn if a male aucuba is present. The leaves are narrow and willow-like. The leaves of 'Variegata' (syn. 'Maculata') are densely spotted with gold. They are slightly wider and more toothed than the species. Both male and female plants are available.

CULTIVATION Aucubas grow under a very wide range of situations and conditions and are particularly good for areas of dense shade, though the variegated plants need to be planted in sun for good colour.

PROPAGATION To ensure plants with the characteristics of a particular cultivar, take semi-ripe cuttings in early to mid summer.

PRUNING Not normally required. Some of the variegated cultivars, however, may

▲ *Aucuba japonica* 'Variegata'

revert to plain green; cut out any green shoots as soon as they are noticed.

PESTS AND DISEASES Usually trouble free.

Aurinia
Cruciferae

There can be few more dazzling sights in spring than the brilliant yellow flowers of *Aurinia saxatilis*, long known as *Alyssum saxatile*. A hardy evergreen sub-shrub with soft stems and woody bases, it forms low hummocks smothered with flowers. Plant against a wall or bank, in a rock garden or a border in a sunny sheltered site.

RECOMMENDED SPECIES AND VARIETIES
A. saxatilis♀ (syn. *Alyssum saxatile*) (yellow alyssum, gold dust) Oval, silvery grey leaves, up to 15 cm (6 in) long, are a perfect contrast to the mass of small 4-petalled flowers borne in dense, flat-topped clusters, 12 cm (4¾ in) across, from mid spring to early summer. It is particularly

▼ *Aurinia saxatilis*

BAMBOOS

AIRY FOLIAGE AND UPRIGHT SHAPES

DISTINCTIVE ARCHITECTURAL FORMS AND MASSES OF ORNAMENTAL FOLIAGE GIVE THESE PLANTS GREAT CREATIVE POTENTIAL

Dramatic plants that transform a garden, bamboos make excellent focal points and superb screens. They are essential for Japanese-style gardens and also make unusual container plants. Bamboos are usually hardy but benefit from shelter in cold, exposed or coastal areas. Most do best in full sun but a few tolerate shade.

Some of these evergreens form clumps and make excellent specimens. Others have running rhizomes and need to be confined unless grown in a wild garden or as ground cover. Both running and clumping bamboos make good hedging.

Bamboos belong to the grass family Gramineae. Most reach 1-6 m (3-20 ft) in height when grown in Britain, though there are also some dwarf species. The canes, which are known as culms, are usually hollow and green, but can be brown, black, yellow, pink or purple, or mottled or streaked. They range in diameter from 1 mm-3 cm (1⁄16-1¼ in) and are usually erect; the culms of a few species, such as *Phyllostachys flexuosa*, may grow in a zigzag formation.

Bamboo culms are jointed, and branches, which carry the foliage, grow from the joints, or nodes. Protective sheaths surround new growth which appears in late spring or early summer. The sheaths of most bamboos are dull and short-lived, but in some species they may be an attractive feature and last for a year or more.

The plants bloom at irregular intervals, sometimes more than 100 years. Flowering may last a year or continue for decades. The flowerheads usually emerge in early summer, are brown and grass-like and can give the plant an untidy appearance. At flowering, the bamboo's foliage is reduced or dies, and the culms which have carried the flowers usually die. To encourage new growth, cut out these culms and feed and water the plant.

RECOMMENDED PLANTS

Species that were formerly grouped under the genus *Arundinaria* have been reclassified to some of the genera listed below. Unless otherwise stated, the recommended plants have green culms that are hollow between the nodes. The leaves are narrow, lance-shaped and

◀ ELEGANT GROVE *The slender culms of* Fargesia murieliae *arch gracefully over a stone ornament.*

mid green with paler undersides, and the sheaths are short-lived, and almost colourless.

Chimonobambusa

The ornamental plants in this genus have running rhizomes and vary greatly in appearance.
C. marmorea (syn. *Arundinaria marmorea*) This colourful, slow-growing plant produces mottled brown and white, pink-tipped shoots that mature to thin, bronze-purple culms. Three or five branches grow from each node, carrying 10 cm (4 in) long leaves. The sheaths are marbled purple and brown and last a year. Native to Japan. HEIGHT & SPREAD 2.4×1 m (8×3 ft).
'Variegata' has pink culms and white-striped foliage.
C. quadrangularis (syn. *Arundinaria quadrangularis*) (square bamboo) The distinctive culms are stout and square-shaped with rounded edges. They have prominent nodes from which 3-8 branches grow with 15 cm

▲ *Chimonobambusa quadrangularis*

(6 in) long leaves. The plant may be invasive in mild areas. Native to China. HEIGHT & SPREAD 4×1.8 m (13×6 ft).
C. tumidissinoda (syn. *Quiongzhuea tumidinoda*) The thick culms spread out elegantly and have markedly flared nodes. Between 3 and 8 branches grow from each of the nodes and the leaves reach 15 cm (6 in). Vigorous growth makes this shade-tolerant bamboo unsuitable for a small garden unless confined. Native to China. HEIGHT & SPREAD 3×3.5 m (10×12 ft).

Chusquea

These clump-forming plants have thick, pith-filled culms.
C. culeou♀ Tall, graceful culms have numerous short branches growing from the nodes and

▲ *Chusquea culeou*

8 cm (3¼ in) long leaves. The upper branches may weigh over the tops of the culms. Prominent sheaths are white and papery and last up to a year. Native to S America. HEIGHT & SPREAD 4×1 m (13×3 ft).

The thin culms of f. *tenuis* reach 2.1 m (7 ft) and grow outwards at a wide angle. It has longer leaves than the species.

Fargesia

Vigorous growers, these bamboos form clumps and make particularly elegant specimens.
F. murieliae♀ (syn. *Arundinaria murieliae, Sinarundinaria murieliae, Thamnocalamus spathaceus*) Narrow pale green culms have numerous slender branches growing from the nodes. The leaves are tapered and reach

▲ *Fargesia murieliae*

6 cm (2½ in) in length. Native to China. HEIGHT & SPREAD 3×1 m (10×3 ft).
'Simba' reaches only half the height or less.
F. nitida♀ (syn. *Arundinaria nitida, Sinarundinaria nitida*) Many branches grow from the nodes on the slender and often purple-tinged culms. The leaves are slightly tapered and 8 cm (3¼ in) long. Native to China. HEIGHT & SPREAD 4×1 m (13×3 ft).

× Hibanobambusa

There is only one plant in the genus, which is a hybrid of a *Phyllostachys* and a *Sasa*.
× *H. tranquillans* A single branch grows from each node on the thick culms. Broad leaves reach 15–25 cm (6–10 in)

▲ *× Hibanobambusa tranquillans* 'Shiroshima'

in length. The plant is moderately slow-running but vigorous. It is native to Japan. HEIGHT & SPREAD 3×1 m (10×3 ft).
The leaves of **'Shiroshima'** are striped with pale yellow which slowly turns to white.

Himalayacalamus

These elegant clump formers are native to the Himalayas.
H. *falconeri* (syn. *Arundinaria falconeri*) The thick culms have purple markings round their nodes and spread out at a wide

▲ *Himalayacalamus falconeri* 'Damarapa'

angle when mature. The plant has many branches which carry 6–10 cm (2½–4 in) long leaves.

It is not fully hardy and grows best in mild areas. HEIGHT & SPREAD 5×1.8 m (16×6 ft).
The culms of **'Damarapa'** have purple mottling and pink and yellow streaks.

Indocalamus

Exceptionally long leaves are carried on the single branch that grows from each node. The sheaths persist for up to a year.
I. *latifolius* This short bamboo has thin, downy culms and leaves that grow up to 40 cm (16 in) long and 8 cm (3¼ in) wide. Native to China. HEIGHT & SPREAD 1.5 m×60 cm (5×2 ft).

▲ *Indocalamus tessellatus*

I. *tessellatus* Slender culms are bent down by the weight of the large leaves to create a mound. The leaves reach 60 cm (2 ft) in length and 8 cm (3¼ in) in width, and the sheaths are longer than the internodes. Native to China. HEIGHT & SPREAD 1×1 m (3×3 ft).

Phyllostachys

The distinctive culms are stout and shallowly grooved on alternate sides. A waxy white powder appears beneath the nodes. At each node, there are two branches of unequal size and a third small one which often drops off. Numerous shoots grow from the branches. The leaves are 10 cm (4 in) long, and short-lived sheaths often have striking colouring. The plants, which are native to China, have running rhizomes but usually form clumps in Britain.
P. *aurea* ♀ (fishpole bamboo) Graceful culms become yellow-brown with age. There are

▲ *Phyllostachys aurea*

unusual cup-shaped swellings below the nodes which are especially noticeable at the base of the plant where they are close together and often asymmetrical. The sheaths have light brown streaks and spots. HEIGHT & SPREAD 4×1.5 m (13×5 ft).
'Holochrysa' has all-yellow culms; the leaves of **'Variegata'** are white striped.
P. *aureosulcata* (yellow-groove bamboo) The culms of this very hardy bamboo are yellow-green with dull yellow grooves. They can grow in a zigzag formation low down. The new growth is protected by white-striped sheaths. HEIGHT & SPREAD 4×1.5 m (13×5 ft).
The culms of **'Spectabilis'** are yellow with green grooves.
P. *bambusoides* (giant timber bamboo) Long leaves grow to 20 cm (8 in). The sheaths are heavily marked in brown and there is little or no waxy powder on the culms. HEIGHT & SPREAD 6×1.5 m (20×5 ft).
'Allgold' has all-yellow culms; **'Castillonis'** ♀ has culms which are rich golden yellow with green grooves.
P. *edulis* (giant bamboo) This tall plant has culms that are grey and velvety when young. The thick hairy sheaths have brown

▲ *Phyllostachys edulis*

mottling and the leaves are 7.5 cm (3 in) long. HEIGHT & SPREAD 6×1 m (20×3 ft).
P. *flexuosa* The slender culms of this bamboo can grow in a zigzag pattern low down and may turn almost black before dying. The sheaths have dark brown markings. HEIGHT & SPREAD 4×1.5 m (13×5 ft).

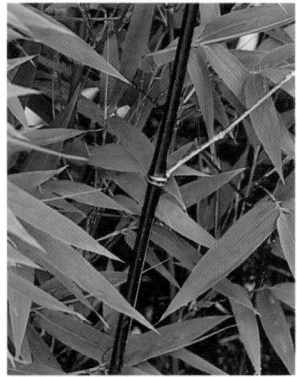

▲ *Phyllostachys nigra*

P. *nigra* ♀ (black bamboo) This attractive bamboo has slender culms which turn shiny black when mature. The tops of the sheaths are bristly. HEIGHT & SPREAD 3×1 m (10×3 ft).

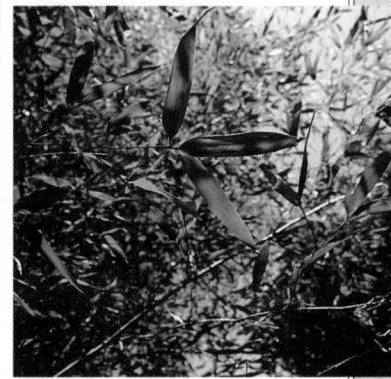

▲ *Phyllostachys nigra* 'Boryana'

'Boryana' has taller, stouter culms that are blotched with brown; the all-green culms of var. *henonis* ♀ are also stouter and the plant has dense foliage. In f. *punctata*, the stout culms have dark brown, sometimes almost black, markings.
P. *sulphurea* (syn. *P. viridis* 'Sulphurea') A curious pigskin-like texture distinguishes the culms of this bamboo. They become yellow with age and some have green stripes of varying widths. The thick sheaths are spotted and blotched with dark brown. HEIGHT & SPREAD 4×1 m (13×3 ft).

'Robert Young' has golden yellow culms, and the culms of var. *viridis* (syn. *P. viridis* 'Mitis') are mid green.

P. viridiglaucescens♀ This vigorous plant is one of the first to produce new shoots in spring. Its rough sheaths are marked with dark brown. HEIGHT & SPREAD 4×1m (13×3ft).

Pleioblastus

The plants in this genus have running rhizomes and sheaths that last for up to a year. They are native to Japan and China.

P. auricomus♀ (syn. *Arundinaria auricoma, A. viridistriata*) The broad leaves are pale green

▲ *Pleioblastus auricomus*

with yellow stripes. Slender, often purple-tinged culms are downy when young and branch almost from the base with 1-2 branches at each node. The leaves are 3.5cm (1½in) wide and 20cm (8in) long and have downy undersides. This plant grows slowly and is an excellent choice for a small garden. Cut the culms to the ground at the end of winter. HEIGHT & SPREAD 1.2m×60cm (4×2ft).

P. chino (syn. *Arundinaria chino*) The leaves are green on both sides, 25cm (10in) long and vary in width. They are carried on the 3 or more branches that grow from each upper node. HEIGHT & SPREAD 3m×75cm (10×2½ft).

The leaves of f. *elegantissimus* have narrow white stripes.

P. gramineus Drooping grass-like leaves reach 28cm (11in) in length and 1cm (⅜in) in width. They are carried on the many

branches that grow from each node. The culms may arch when mature. HEIGHT & SPREAD 4×1.5m (13×5ft).

▲ *Pleioblastus humilis* var. *pumilus*

P. humilis var. *pumilus* (syn. *Arundinaria pumila*) Short culms branch from low down and have 1-3 branches growing from each markedly bristly node. The fresh green leaves are 15cm (6in) long. HEIGHT & SPREAD 1×1m (3×3ft).

P. pygmaeus (syn. *Arundinaria pygmaea*) (dwarf fern-leaved bamboo) Very slender, solid culms have 1-2 branches growing from each node. Pairs of leaves, which are 2-8cm (¾-3¼in) long, are arranged along the branches. The plant spreads to form short thickets and makes good ground cover. It also looks attractive grown in a shallow container. HEIGHT & SPREAD 25×12cm (10×4¾in).

The culms of var. *distichus* (syn. *Arundinaria disticha*) grow to 1m (3ft) and the leaves are longer and broader. It has a vigorous growth pattern.

P. simonii (syn. *Arundinaria simonii*) Very tall, stout culms have 3-7 branches from each

▲ *Pleioblastus simonii* f. *variegatus*

upper node. The leaves are 20cm (8in) long. HEIGHT & SPREAD 5×1m (16×3ft).

Some of the narrow leaves of f. *variegatus* (syn. var. *heterophyllus*) are striped white.

P. variegatus♀ (syn. *Arundinaria variegata, A. fortunei*) White-striped and downy leaves

▲ *Pleioblastus variegatus*

are 20cm (8in) long. One or two branches grow from nodes low down. The plant spreads slowly and is suitable for a small garden. Cut down culms in spring for fresh growth. HEIGHT & SPREAD 1×1.2m (3×4ft).

Pseudosasa

Plants in this genus have rhizomes that can run but usually form clumps in Britain.

P. japonica♀ (syn. *Arundinaria japonica*) A single branch grows

▲ *Pseudosasa japonica*

from each upper node on the tall culms and the rough, dull brown sheaths are long-lived. The leaves are 25cm (10in) long. This bamboo is probably native to China. HEIGHT & SPREAD 4×1m (13×3ft).

Quiongzhuea see *Chimonobambusa*

Sasa

Sasas, which are native to Japan, are tolerant of shade and have running rhizomes. Their culms curve at the base and a single branch grows from each node. The leaves may wither at the edges in winter.

S. japonica see *Pseudosasa japonica*

S. palmata♀ (syn. *Arundinaria palmata*) Large, lustrous, rich green leaves have yellow mid-ribs and look attractive all year round. They grow 40cm (16in)

▲ *Sasa palmata*

long and 9cm (3½in) wide. The branches grow from the upper parts of the mottled brown culms. This rampant bamboo is very hardy. HEIGHT & SPREAD 3×1.5m (10×5ft).

S. tsuboiana This bamboo, which runs very slowly, has low-branching and erect culms. Its leaves reach 20cm (8in) in length. HEIGHT & SPREAD 1m×30cm (3×1ft).

S. veitchii The leaves develop strikingly decorative broad white stripes round their edges in early autumn. The leaves are 20cm (8in) long, have bluntly pointed tips and remain attractive all winter. The culms are purple-tinged. HEIGHT & SPREAD 1.5×1m (5×3ft).

Sasaealla

A single branch grows from each node of the erect culms. These plants have running rhizomes and are native to Japan.

S. masamuneana f. *albostriata* Grown for its attractive foliage, the leaves of this bamboo are 15cm (6in) long and have

▲ *Sasaella masamuneana*
f. *albostriata*

white stripes that become yellow in maturity. HEIGHT & SPREAD 2×1m (6½×3ft).
S. ramosa (syn. *Arundinaria vagans*) This short bamboo branches horizontally from the middle of the culms, which are sometimes purple-tinged. It makes good ground cover in a wild garden but is very invasive. The leaves are 10-15cm (4-6in) long and have downy undersides. They may decay at the edges in winter. HEIGHT & SPREAD 1m×45cm (3×1½ft).

Semiarundinaria

Plants in this genus have running rhizomes but are generally clump-forming in Britain.
S. fastuosa♀ (syn. *Arundinaria fastuosa*) This tall and stately bamboo has thick glossy culms, slightly grooved at the tops. Between 3 and 7 branches grow from each node. The attractive

▲ *Semiarundinaria fastuosa*

sheaths are shiny and wine-coloured inside and the thin leaves are 25cm (10in) long. The plant makes good hedging. Native to Japan. HEIGHT & SPREAD 5m×60cm (16×2ft).

Sinarundinaria anceps see
    Yushania anceps
Sinarundinaria murieliae see
    Fargesia murieliae
Sinarundinaria nitida see
    Fargesia nitida

Shibataea

These bamboos have running rhizomes but tend to form clumps in Britain.
S. kumasasa The culms are slightly grooved and have short branches with 1 or 2 leaves,

▲ *Shibataea kumasasa*

which reach 8cm (3¼in) in length. The leaves are broad and may wither at the tips. The plant grows best in a moist soil. It is native to Japan. HEIGHT & SPREAD 1.5m×30cm (5×1ft).

Thamnocalamus

These clump-forming plants produce numerous branches. Their sheaths last for up to a year and can be very decorative.
T. aristatus see *T. spathiflorus*
T. crassinodus The culms are grey when young and mature to yellowish green. They have prominent nodes and distinctive, white, tapered sheaths. The leaves are small and dainty-looking. This bamboo is native to the Himalayas. HEIGHT & SPREAD 5×1.5m (16×5ft).
    'Kew Beauty' has purple-tinged leafstalks.
T. spathaceus see
    Fargesia murieliae
T. spathiflorus (syn. *Arundinaria spathiflora, T. aristatus*) This elegant, somewhat tender bamboo is best grown in milder areas. It has thin leaves, which are 10cm (4in) long, and tolerates a shady spot. Native to the Himalayas. HEIGHT & SPREAD 4×1m (13×3ft).
T. tessellatus Purple-tinged culms have numerous, rather

▲ *Thamnocalamus tessellatus*

short branches growing from each node, and sheaths that are noticeably white when young. The leaves are 10cm (4in) long. Native to South Africa. HEIGHT & SPREAD 4m×60cm (13×2ft).

Yushania

Plants in this genus form tight clumps but their rhizomes run every few years.
Y. anceps♀ (syn. *Arundinaria anceps, A. jaunsarensis*) The culms arch at their tops and numerous branches grow from the nodes. The leaves are 10cm (4in) long. This bamboo is not

▲ *Yushania anceps*

fully hardy. It is native to the Himalayas. HEIGHT & SPREAD 4×1m (13×3ft).
    'Pitt White' grows to twice the height.

GROWING BAMBOOS

CULTIVATION Most bamboos do well in well-drained soil in a sunny site but a few, including sasas, tolerate a shady spot. Prepare the ground well before

planting in late spring, digging plenty of well-rotted organic matter and a general fertiliser into the soil.
    Contain a species that has running rhizomes by digging a 23cm (9in) deep ditch round the plant and cutting off any rhizomes that appear in the ditch. Alternatively, surround the rhizome with a permanent underground barrier made from tough plastic or corrugated metal 30cm (1ft) deep.
    Water a bamboo during the first summer, until it develops a good root system. Apply a general fertiliser in spring and summer and after flowering.
    Once established, bamboos need little attention. Cut out any old culms in the centre of the plants in spring and remove dead culms after flowering. If bamboos spread beyond desirable limits, use a mattock or sharp spade to chop away any excess growth.
PROPAGATION Sever well-rooted sections of the running rhizomes in spring or early summer. Plant them in well-drained soil or a nursery bed and shelter from wind, then plant out the following summer. Divide large clumps in early spring. Chusqueas have solid rhizomes and culms and cannot easily be propagated.
PESTS AND DISEASES Bamboos are usually trouble free but rabbits, squirrels and deer may eat young shoots.

▶ RISING HIGH *The tall culms of* Phyllostachys sulphurea *create an imposing garden feature.*

b

Begonia
Begoniaceae

Begonia rex

Renowned for their generous displays of bright, colourful flowers – most notably in pink and red – and beautifully marked leaves, begonias thrive in a range of garden situations. Though only one species is hardy enough to be grown as a garden perennial, the genus contains some of the most widely grown bedding plants. There are pendulous varieties which make outstandingly showy plants for hanging baskets and window boxes, while other species and varieties are grown for the rich colours and exotic markings of their lop-sided leaves.

Begonias can thrive in shaded areas of the garden, where many other bedding plants cannot. This is in keeping with their native origins as part of the ground-level flora of tropical forests. Begonias also grow well in shaded conservatories and greenhouses. A few will also thrive in the relatively poor light conditions of the home.

RECOMMENDED SPECIES AND VARIETIES
Begonias can be divided into five groups: cane-stemmed, rhizomatous, semperflorens, shrub-like and tuberous. Plants within each group share similarities in terms of habit and/or cultivation techniques.

CANE-STEMMED BEGONIAS
These large, long-lived evergreens are often grown for many years as permanent features of a greenhouse or conservatory and their ability to withstand a little neglect makes them valuable houseplants. The taller varieties reach over 1m (3ft) in height and require staking, while the low-growing varieties are a good choice for hanging baskets. Height and spread details given below refer to plants grown in large pots.

B. albopicta White flowers appear on a freely branching species in summer. The spearhead-shaped, mid green leaves have white spots. HEIGHT & SPREAD 60×50cm (24×20in). 'Rosea' bears pink flowers.

B. × *corallina* 'Lucerna' This vigorous plant has large, bronze-green leaves with silver spots. It flowers all year round, producing large sprays of small pink blooms. HEIGHT & SPREAD 2m×60cm (6½×2ft).

B. 'Irene Nuss' Pink flowers are borne in large clusters throughout the year. This vigorous plant has large velvety green leaves, serrated and speckled with silver. HEIGHT & SPREAD 1.2m×60cm (4×2ft).

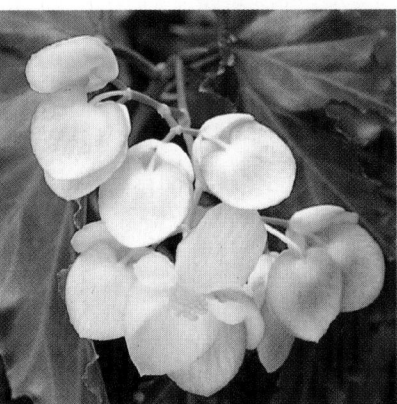

▲ *Begonia* 'Irene Nuss'

B. 'Looking Glass' Pink flowers are borne in early summer among the metallic-silver leaves with green veins and red undersides. HEIGHT & SPREAD 1m×60cm (3×2ft).

B. maculata This robust species bears long, tapered olive-green leaves with large silver spots. The small, pristine white flowers hang in clusters from mid to late summer. HEIGHT & SPREAD 2m×60cm (6½×2ft).

B. 'Orange Rubra' Orange-and-white flowers are freely produced throughout the year by this pendulous plant. The light green, lance-shaped leaves carry silver spots. It is an ideal plant for hanging baskets. HEIGHT & SPREAD 75cm×1m (2½×3ft).

▼ *Begonia* 'Orange Rubra'

RHIZOMATOUS BEGONIAS
These are characterised by a thickened stem – the rhizome – which develops on the surface of the soil, or in some cases just below it. Roots, leaf stalks and flowerheads all arise directly from the rhizome, which may be branched. Most are fine foliage plants.

B. bowerae (eyelash begonia) This dwarf, clump-forming species has oval leaves, up to 4cm (1½in) long. The waxy-looking, bright green leaves have brown stitch-like markings around the margins and are edged with fine, eyelash-like hairs. Delicate pale pink flowers are carried on long stems above the foliage in late winter and spring. This species and its varieties make fine houseplants, given a minimum temperature of 13°C (55°F). HEIGHT & SPREAD 15×25cm (6×10in).

Among the many hybrids are 'Beatrice Haddrell', 'Chantilly Lace', 'Norah Bedson' and 'Red Planet'. The last three reach just 10cm (4in) tall.

B. 'Cleopatra' (maple-leaf begonia) Maple-leaf shaped leaves, about 5cm (2in) across, are green and a rich bronze-brown, with long hairs around the edges. Clusters of small, pale pink flowers are sometimes carried well above the foliage, in spring. HEIGHT & SPREAD 20×25cm (8×10in).

▲ *Begonia* 'Cleopatra'

B. 'Little Brother Montgomery' This upright begonia has large star-shaped leaves, heavily spotted with silver. HEIGHT & SPREAD 75×60cm (2½×2ft).

▲ *Begonia* 'Little Brother Montgomery'

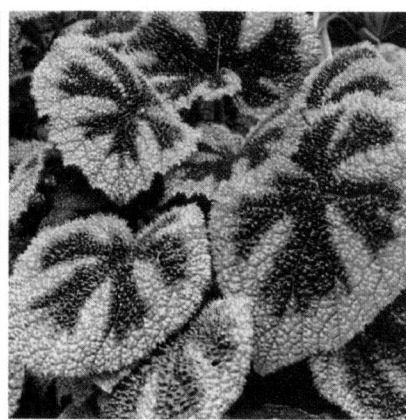

▲ *Begonia masoniana*

B. masoniana♀ (Iron Cross begonia) Each green leaf bears a dark marking resembling the German medal. The plant is very like *B. rex* but slower growing. It requires a winter temperature of at least 13°C (55°F) and is sensitive to overwatering. HEIGHT & SPREAD 60×45 cm (2×1½ ft).

B. rex (king, painted leaf, fan begonia) This is one of the most striking of all ornamental foliage plants. The variously coloured, lop-sidedly heart-shaped leaves attain a width of up to 30 cm (1 ft). The surface is puckered and slightly hairy with a metallic sheen. The plant requires good humidity and a minimum temperature of 13°C (55°F). HEIGHT & SPREAD 40×50 cm (16×20 in).

▲ *Begonia rex* 'Fireworks'

'**Fire Flush**' has olive-green and red leaves. '**Fireworks**' has silver and raspberry-purple leaves. '**Princess of Hanover**' has velvety green leaves with white patches in a spiral pattern. '**Raspberry Swirl**' has red and silver leaves. '**Vesuvius**' has leaves in various shades of red.

B. 'Tiger Paws' Small white flowers are borne in spring. The small leaves have a

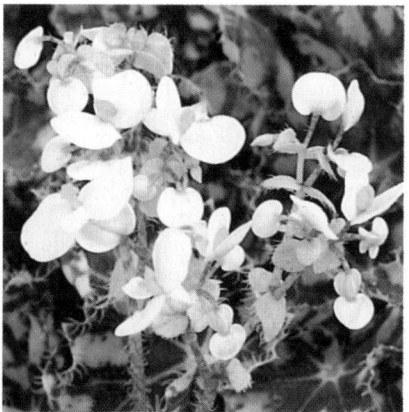

▲ *Begonia* 'Tiger Paws'

characteristic yellow-green and brown pattern. HEIGHT & SPREAD 25×25 cm (10×10 in).

SEMPERFLORENS GROUP

B. semperflorens (syn. *B.* × *carrierei*) (wax begonia) Numerous 3 cm (1¼ in) pink, red, white or bicoloured flowers are borne on

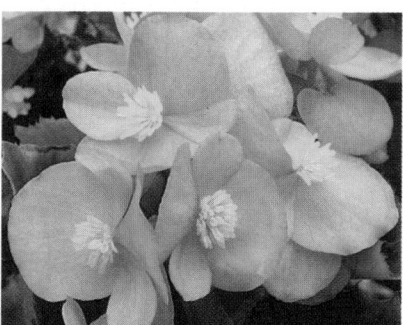

▲ *Begonia semperflorens*

these compact, bushy plants with fibrous roots. These popular bedding plants flower continuously from early summer until the first frosts. The rounded, shiny leaves are either dark green or bronze, contrasting attractively with the flowers. The height varies with the individual varieties and the spread is usually the same as the height.

The **Cocktail Series**, reaching 15 cm (6 in) tall, comprises only bronze-leaved varieties. Both green and bronze-leaved varieties are included in the **Excel, Olympia** and **Organdy Mixed Series**, which all reach 20 cm (8 in) tall.

SHRUB-LIKE BEGONIAS

Like the cane-stemmed begonias, these are also evergreen and long-lived, and best grown in a greenhouse, a conservatory or inside a house. Shrub-like begonias are fibrous rooted and most branch freely, producing basal shoots. Heights vary from 30 cm (1 ft) to 2 m (6½ ft) and their stems often need support.

B. foliosa White pendulous flowers appear along slender, arching stems in spring and autumn. The stems carry small leaves and may grow longer than 1 m (3 ft). This plant looks very attractive in a hanging basket. HEIGHT & SPREAD 30×80 cm (1 ft×2 ft 8 in).

B. fuchsioides♀ Fuchsia-like flowers are borne mainly during winter on freely branching stems with small leaves. Both a red and a pink variety are available. Keep this plant at or above 13°C (55°F). HEIGHT & SPREAD 75×60 cm (2½×2 ft).

B. haageana see *B. scharffii*

B. listada♀ White flowers are carried in autumn and winter against dark green, softly hairy leaves with red undersides. The plant is upright, branching and slow-growing. HEIGHT & SPREAD 30×30 cm (1×1 ft).

B. luxurians (palm leaf begonia) Large palmate leaves with up to 16 leaflets are borne by tall red stems. White flowers appear in winter or spring. HEIGHT & SPREAD 2 m×60 cm (6½×2 ft).

B. metallica♀ White flowers are borne in large clusters in summer and autumn, contrasting attractively with the large, lustrous

▲ *Begonia metallica*

metallic green leaves. It is an easy-to-grow, vigorous and well-branched begonia that is safe at a winter minimum of 7°C (45°F). HEIGHT & SPREAD 1.5 m×50 cm (5 ft×20 in).

B. scharffii (syn. *B. haageana*) (elephant's ear) Pinkish white to pink flowers are produced all year round against heart-shaped leaves. The leaves, up to 25 cm (10 in) long, are bronze-green above and red beneath, and covered in red veins and fine hairs. HEIGHT & SPREAD 1.5 m×75 cm (5×2½ ft).

B. serratipetala Striking serrated leaves distinguish this plant which bears its pink-and-white flowers intermittently throughout the year. It makes a good hanging-basket plant. HEIGHT & SPREAD 60×80 cm (2×2 ft 8 in).

TUBEROUS BEGONIAS

B. grandis ssp. *evansiana* This is the only readily available begonia that is suitable for growing outdoors as a perennial in mild, sheltered regions of Britain. Sprays of pink flowers, each bloom up to 3 cm (1¼ in) across, are carried on fleshy stems above the handsome coppery foliage from late summer to mid autumn. The plants grow from tubers and produce bulbils in the leaf axils from which they can be propagated. HEIGHT & SPREAD 60×30 cm (2×1 ft).

'**Alba**' has white flowers.

B. × hiemalis These semi-tuberous begonias flower freely throughout the year and are widely available wherever pot plants are sold. Only the **Rieger** hybrids are commonly grown. Bushy plants bear single or double flowers up to 5 cm (2 in) across. They remain attractive for up to 3 months in a living room (for much longer in greenhouses) and are quite resistant to powdery mildew. Numerous varieties are grown commercially, but variety names are rarely shown on the labels. The **Charisma** hybrids (in orange and pink) come true from seed. HEIGHT & SPREAD 45×30 cm (1½×1 ft).

Begonia sutherlandii

B. sutherlandii♀ Orange flowers are freely produced throughout summer among pointed, yellowish green leaves. Growth dies down in autumn, when watering should cease. This species has a weeping habit, making it good for hanging baskets. HEIGHT & SPREAD 30×45 cm (1×1½ ft).

▲ *Begonia sutherlandii*
Begonia × tuberhybrida Multiflora Group ▼

B. × tuberhybrida For outdoor garden cultivation as summer bedding plants, begonias in the **Multiflora Group** are usually chosen. These bushy plants attain a size of up to 30×30 cm (1×1 ft), with upright, succulent stems and leaves about 8 cm (3 in) long. The red, pink, orange, yellow or white flowers are 7.5 cm (3 in) across, and may be single, semi-double or double. They are freely produced throughout summer.

The **Non-Stop** hybrids and the **Prima Donna Series** are double-flowered. **'Pin-Up'** has double white flowers with bold pink edges to the petals.

Plants in the **Pendula Group** are very similar to those in the Multiflora Group, except that their stems are longer and thinner, giving plants a trailing habit suitable for hanging baskets and window boxes. These pendulous begonias have double flowers: the **Cascade Series** in orange, pink, red or yellow; **'Illumination'** in pink; **'Panorama Apricot'**; **'Panorama Orange'**; and the **Sensation Series** in a mix of colours.

Some tuberhybrida varieties produce enormous blooms. These are suitable only for growing in greenhouses. The flowers are double in most cases, and reach diameters of up to 25 cm (10 in). Plants are strong and upright, with leaves up to 25 cm (10 in) long. These hybrids reach a height and spread of 75 cm (2½ ft). **'Fairylight'** (white picotee), **'Majesty'** (yellow), **'Nell**

▲ *Begonia × tuberhybrida* 'Nell Gwynne'

Gwynne' (pale orange), **'Roy Hartley'** (pink), **'Sugar Candy'** (pink) and **'Tahiti'** (orange) are among the most worthwhile.

CULTIVATION Begonias do best in neutral soils or compost and most prefer to be sited in partial shade. Whether in beds or in containers, it is worth removing any early flower buds to allow the plant to reach full size as quickly as possible. After the plant has flowered, deadheading improves its appearance and stimulates further flowers.

When growing begonias in a greenhouse, conservatory or home, they do best at 13°C (55°F) or more, although most will tolerate a minimum winter temperature of 10°C (50°F). In summer protect greenhouse plants from full sun. In the home, give the plants a position where they will receive good, indirect light. In a conservatory or greenhouse, maintain a humid

atmosphere by frequent damping down, but do not spray plants directly. Water at the first sign of dryness in summer, but take care not to overwater in winter. Feed once a week in spring and summer.

Repot annually in early spring. For most begonias a 15 cm (6 in) pot is large enough. Tall plants are best kept in clay pots, to give more stability. Special cultivation requirements follow for each of the five groups.

CANE-STEMMED BEGONIAS
Light shading is required during the summer months – a north-facing conservatory gives ideal light conditions. Varieties with dark foliage can tolerate more sun than those with paler leaves. Cut back each spring, to just above the third or fourth leaf joint from the stem base.

RHIZOMATOUS BEGONIAS
These generally need quite high humidity and it is difficult to provide sufficiently humid conditions in a house. Do not place in direct sunlight – extra shading in mid summer improves leaf colouring. They grow best in a bathroom or kitchen.

SEMPERFLORENS GROUP
Plant out bedding plants when there is no risk of frost. They grow equally well in full sun or partial shade.

SHRUB-LIKE BEGONIAS
Houseplants do best in windows facing north or east. Light shading is required in the greenhouse for most varieties, but hairy-leaved varieties, such as *B. listada*, benefit from extra shading when the temperature exceeds 26°C (79°F).

TUBEROUS BEGONIAS
Plant out the perennial *B. grandis* ssp. *evansiana* in spring in a sheltered position, ideally near to a wall with a southerly aspect. A moisture-retentive, peaty soil helps to ensure flowering in dry weather.

Plant out bedding plants when all risk of frost has passed. They need a site which is sheltered from strong winds, and is not exposed to full sun during the middle of the day. The blooms and the foliage can otherwise scorch easily.

Rieger begonias are normally bought as plants in full flower. Repot about every 6 months, avoiding burying the exposed stem bases with fresh compost.

PROPAGATION
CANE-STEMMED BEGONIAS
Take stem cuttings in spring or summer, ensuring there are growth buds in the axils of the lower leaves. Root in a mix of half soilless compost and half coarse sand and keep at temperature of at least 18°C (65°F).

RHIZOMATOUS BEGONIAS
Divide or root pieces of the small rhizomatous types in spring. For larger plants use leaf cuttings.

SEMPERFLORENS GROUP
Sow seed in late winter in a propagator at 20-25°C (68-77°F). Do not cover the seed with compost. Maintain a high humidity. Protect the seedlings from full sunshine and

prick out after about 6 weeks. Begonias are among the more difficult plants to raise from seed. Even gardeners with well-heated greenhouses often resort to buying small young plants in early or mid spring to grow on to planting stage. Harden off before planting out.

SHRUB-LIKE BEGONIAS

Take stem cuttings in spring or summer. Root in a mixture of half soilless compost and either half perlite or half coarse sand and keep at a minimum temperature of 18°C (65°F).

TUBEROUS BEGONIAS

Divide *B. grandis* ssp. *evansiana* or remove and plant bulbils in early spring.

The tubers of the other species and varieties can be started into growth from early spring onwards in a heated greenhouse, or a month later in an unheated one. Harden off and plant out when there is no risk of frost. It is also possible to plant the tubers directly into their flowering positions in late spring. This results in a later start to flowering.

To save tubers for replanting the following year, move plants in autumn to frost-free conditions and allow them to die down and the soil to dry out. Then store tubers for the winter in almost dry sand, soil or soilless compost, in a cool, frost-free place.

Divide Rieger begonias in late spring or early summer, cutting back the older stems to allow young basal growths to form the new plant.

Some varieties of tuberous begonias can be raised from seed. Treatment is as for the Semperflorens Group, though even earlier sowing is advisable.

PESTS AND DISEASES Mealy bug and vine weevil can be troublesome. Most begonias are susceptible to powdery mildew.

Belladonna lily
   see *Amaryllis belladonna*
Bellflower see *Campanula*
Bellflower, gland see *Adenophora*
Bellflower, trailing see *Cyananthus*

Bellis
Daisy
Compositae

Bellis perennis 'Dresden China'

The most common species, *Bellis perennis*, a lawn weed, has given rise to many garden varieties, which make excellent plants for edging borders, carpet bedding or containers. Flowers with white, pink, red, purple

or even blue petals – properly called ray florets – rise from mats or clumps of leaf rosettes. The flower centres, made up of disc florets, are usually yellow. These daisies are hardy perennials, but they are often grown in the garden as biennials, because flower size and quality declines with each flowering. Native to Europe and the Mediterranean.

RECOMMENDED SPECIES AND VARIETIES

B. perennis (common daisy) Flowers have white petals tinged pink encircling a yellow disc and measure up to 2.5 cm (1 in) across. The common daisy looks pretty on a lawn where wild flowers are encouraged. HEIGHT & SPREAD 13×20 cm (5×8 in).

Cultivars have single, semi-double or fully double flowers, up to 5 cm (2 in) wide and sometimes more, with white, pink,

purple or red petals. All but the double forms have yellow centres. The bright green leaves, oblong or spatulate, grow in coarsely formed rosettes. Plants bloom from spring to early autumn. 'Alba Plena' is a double white cultivar. 'Alice' has large, semi-double, pink flowers. 'Aucubifolia' has single white flowers and glossy gold-mottled foliage. 'Dresden China'♀, a miniature pink form, has double flowers with quilled petals. 'Prolifera' (Hen and Chickens) has double flowers, the petals white speckled pink, with smaller secondary flowers below the main bloom. 'Rob Roy'♀ has large, double, crimson flowers.

▼ *Bellis perennis 'Dresden China'*

▲ *Bellis rotundifolia 'Caerulescens'*

▲ *Bellis perennis 'Alice'*

B. rotundifolia White petals flushed purple red surround a pale yellow centre, forming a flower up to 4 cm (1½ in) across. The grey-green leaves are rounded, toothed and shiny, 2.5-9 cm (1-3½ in) long. The flowers appear in spring. This plant needs a very sheltered site in the open garden or, better still, the protection of a coldframe or an unheated greenhouse in winter. HEIGHT & SPREAD 20×20 cm (8×8 in).

'Caerulescens' (syn. *B. perennis* 'Single Blue') is the most widely available form, with petals that are a soft pale blue.

CULTIVATION Grow in a well-drained yet moist soil that is rich with humus, in sun or partial shade. Regular deadheading prolongs flowering and prevents inferior seedlings sowing themselves.

PROPAGATION Divide at least every 2 years, in spring or autumn. This is the only way of propagating sterile cultivars. Sow seed of species in spring or early summer, or immediately after flowering, and plant out in late summer or early autumn.

PESTS AND DISEASES Aphids can get into the centre of the leaf rosettes, distorting and quickly weakening the plant.

Bells of Ireland see *Molucella laevis*
Bellwort see *Uvularia*
Beloperone see *Justicia*

BEDDING PLANTS

DISPLAYS FOR JUST A SEASON

THESE SHORT-LIVED BUT VALUABLE PLANTS
BRING A MASS OF COLOURFUL FLOWERS
AND FOLIAGE TO BEDS AND CONTAINERS

While shrubs, trees and perennials provide the garden with a permanent framework, bedding plants offer temporary colour and interest. Moved into position at the young leafy or early flowering stage, they display their attractive flowers or foliage over several months. Most are at their best in summer but some bloom in spring and a few provide welcome colour during winter.

Many bedding plants are true annuals and die at the end of the season. Others are perennials which are treated as annuals because they produce their best displays in the first year or are not frost-hardy. Bulbs and evergreens can also be used as bedding and planted out for a single season.

There are many hundreds of

SPRING INTEREST
A carpet of polyanthus dispels the winter gloom.

varieties of bedding plants, with blooms in the full spectrum of colours and ranging in shape from the wide saucers of *Cosmos* to the dense spikes of *Salvia*. A few, such as *Canna*, have architectural outlines. Bedding plants vary greatly in size, from neat, low-growing *Lobelia* to the tall *Helianthus* (sunflower).

The tremendous wealth of plants that falls into the loose category of bedding means that there are plants for both formal and informal displays, for subtropical schemes and carpet bedding, and to provide instant interest in mixed borders or newly laid out beds. Bedding plants are also ideal for use in containers, bringing colour to balconies, windowsills, patios and small gardens.

ANNUAL BEDS

Flowerbeds and borders filled with solid blocks of colourful bedding plants are a traditional feature of summer. For the best effect, create informal clumps or drifts by grouping several plants of each species together. Use tall and striking plants, such as *Ricinus communis* (castor-oil plant), *Abutilon* or standard *Fuchsia*, to add height. Alternatively, grow climbing annuals like *Ipomoea* (morning glory) over a freestanding structure, such as a pyramid of canes, or up a trellis fixed to a wall at the back of a border.

Annual beds look attractive with a mixture of strong, bright colours, with toning shades of pastel colours, or with different shades of a single colour. The fewer colours used in a planting scheme, the more contrasts in habit, shape and texture are needed to create interest.

For a striking single-colour display, combine bright yellow-flowered varieties of *Dahlia*, which has an upright growth habit, with spreading *Gazania* (treasure flower) and bushy *Tagetes patula* (French marigold). Alternatively, pair pink-flowered varieties of *Cosmos*, which has bold single daisy-like flowers and feathery foliage, with the large spidery blooms of pink *Cleome* (spider flower).

Use exotic-looking plants to create an unusual sub-tropical scheme. Choose plants which have bold, dramatic shapes and strong colours. For example, *Tithonia rotundifolia* (Mexican sunflower), which has orange blooms, and the red-flowered *Amaranthus caudatus* (love-lies-bleeding) look very effective grouped with the bronze-leaved castor-oil plant.

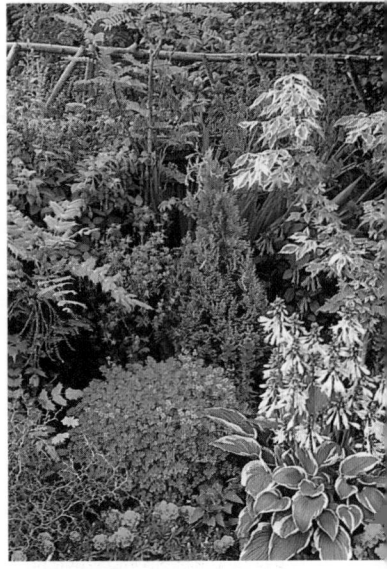

▲ FILLING THE GAPS *Summer blooms enliven the permanent display of a mixed border.*

FORMAL SCHEMES

For a formal flowerbed, plant rows of compact, low-growing plants, such as *Lobelia erinus* or *Lobularia maritima* (sweet alyssum), as edging round geometric rows or blocks of taller bedding. Bushy plants, which include French marigolds and *Pelargonium* (geranium), are suitable for this. Use tall specimens, such as *Cordyline* (cabbage tree), as dot plants at strictly regular intervals.

Low-growing foliage plants, including *Echeveria*, with its

▼ PERFECT FOIL *Silver senecio and variegated pelargoniums contrast with purple heliotrope.*

◄ HOT SUMMER COLOUR
An informal planting in a border creates a riotous mass of flowers.

A YEAR OF PLANTING

Bedding plants can be raised from seed in a warm greenhouse (see p.814) or are widely available as young plants or plugs (very young plants). Plugs should be grown on in a heated greenhouse or on a sunny indoor windowsill before being planted out.

A few of the hardier species, such as *Antirrhinum* (snapdragon) and pansies, can be planted out safely in early spring, as long as they have been hardened off. Plant out other bedding plants in late spring, when all danger of frost is past.

Most bedding plants grow best in well-drained soil in a sunny area of the garden. Remove any debris and weeds from the site, fork over the soil to loosen it and rake in a general fertiliser before planting.

Summer bedding plants flower from early or mid summer until the first frosts. At the end of the growing season, dig up and discard any annuals. Lift half-hardy perennials, such as fuchsias, osteospermums and pelargoniums, cut them back to a few centimetres from their bases and repot them. Keep the containers in a frost-free place throughout the winter. Alternatively, take cuttings in late summer – these will provide better specimens for the next year than plants that have been repotted.

After clearing away summer bedding, dig plenty of organic matter into the soil and plant out winter and spring bedding. Alternatively, wait until spring and plant out container-grown bedding plants that are coming into flower to create instant and colourful displays.

After spring bulbs have flowered, dig them up and replant elsewhere in the garden to allow their foliage to die down out of sight. Replace them with the summer bedding.

geometric rosettes of leaves tinged with grey, blue or green, and *Sempervivum* (houseleek), whose green rosettes are tipped with purple or brown, can be used to form complicated patterns. This kind of scheme, which is known as carpet bedding, is often found in parks and can be effective in the garden too, although it takes large numbers of plants and a considerable time to plant up.

FILLERS AND FOILS

Bedding plants are invaluable for filling spaces in mixed borders where early flowering plants have been cut back, or between new shrubs or perennials which have yet to grow and fill up their allocated spaces.

Use a mass of tall plants, such as stately cleomes and spider flowers, to create informal drifts. Alternatively, use plants which have many small flowers and spreading or bushy habits, such as *Diascia*, *Lobelia* or *Verbena*, to form low carpets. These can look particularly

effective when they are planted beneath tall flowering plants, such as fuchsias.

Foliage bedding plants are excellent foils for flowering plants. For example, the handsome, lobed, silver-grey foliage of *Senecio cineraria* makes it an excellent choice for underplanting roses or as a contrast to the brightly coloured flowers of salvias and French marigolds.

Plants with silvery grey leaves, including *Echeveria elegans*, or attractive green foliage, such as *Bassia scoparia* var. *childsii* 'Evergreen', help to break up clashing colours by introducing a neutral background colour into the display.

Annual grasses, which have linear shapes and elegant seed heads, make striking textural contrasts when grouped informally among flowering plants.

AWKWARD SITES

Although most bedding plants require a well-drained soil and full sun, some tolerate less favourable conditions. In hot,

▲ IN FULL FLOWER *Pendulous fuchsia blooms hang above clumps of pelargonium and senecio, edged with ageratum.*

▼ IDEAL PARTNERS *Blood-red flowers of* Tulipa *'Cassini' rise from a sea of forget-me-nots.*

dry areas, choose drought-tolerant plants, such as *Dorotheanthus* (Livingstone daisy), *Osteospermum* or *Portulaca*. Pelargoniums also thrive in these sites, making cheerful Mediterranean-style displays.

Begonia semperflorens, Fuchsia and *Impatiens* do well in shady sites, particularly when planted after they have started to bloom. *Tropaeolum majus* (nasturtium) actually prefers an impoverished soil; on rich soil it produces large, parasol-like leaves but very few flowers.

WINTER AND SPRING COLOUR

For early winter colour, plant *Brassica oleracea* var. *capitata* (ornamental cabbage), which has mauve or cream frilly leaves. Winter-flowering cultivars of *Viola × wittrockiana* (pansy) bloom until late spring in all but the worst weather and the tolerant winter-flowering heather *Erica × darleyensis* makes excellent bedding in cold or exposed sites.

Use massed plantings of *Erysimum* (wallflower), *Bellis* (daisy) and primrose or polyanthus cultivars of *Primula* to create spring interest. Bulbs also make good bedding and look most effective when they are planted in rows or blocks with other bedding plants. *Tulipa* (tulip) brings height to a carpet of daisies or *Myosotis* (forget-me-not); and *Narcissus* (daffodil) looks attractive in a bed of yellow primroses.

Where possible, match plants to the style of the container. For example, old-fashioned chimney pots are suited to cottage-style plants, such as nasturtiums, while a stately urn is appropriate for a tall specimen, such as *Datura* (thorn apple).

PLANTING DISPLAYS

Containers should be generously filled from the start. Pack in as many plants as possible – the adjacent rootballs of the plants can touch, provided that the container is sufficiently deep to allow at least a few centimetres of compost underneath. A simple display of a single species looks impressive. For

▲ FLORAL FRAME *Summer bedding and a clematis create a colourful setting for a window.*

▼ SITTING PRETTY *The foliage of helichrysum mingles with nicotiana and marigold flowers.*

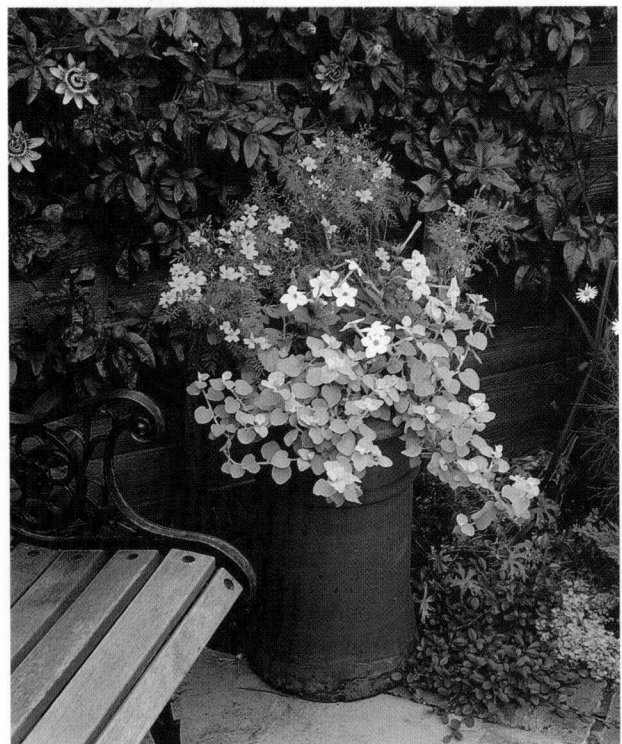

BEDDING PLANTS •FOR CONTAINERS•

Their long seasons make bedding plants ideal for growing in containers and bringing colour and interest to the smallest of areas. Use hanging baskets, troughs and tubs filled with flowers to decorate porches, entranceways and flights of steps; or patios and small town gardens where lack of space demands a concentrated effort. Create a welcoming floral display at the front of the house with several window boxes and hanging baskets.

▶ POT OF PLENTY *Pansies and brassica combine with perennials for a colourful autumn display.*

◀ COLOUR TRAIL *A mass of begonias, pelargoniums and petunias spill from hanging baskets and a window box.*

example, an annual climber, such as *Tropaeolum peregrinum* (canary creeper), makes an effective showing when trained over a trelliswork pergola or a wigwam of canes in a large tub.

Alternatively, create a varied display by grouping several different types of plants. Use an odd number for the strongest effect – three or five different types is sufficient for a medium-sized tub or hanging basket.

Choose plants of contrasting shape, texture and flower size, particularly if the display is based on a single colour, or use plants with small simple flowers, such as petunias, to surround a dominant larger plant, such as fuchsia. Modest-looking plants with scented flowers, such as *Matthiola longipetala* (night-scented stock), mixed in with more spectacular plants add perfume to a show of blooms and enhance the pleasure given, especially when the container is placed by a doorway or garden seat.

Choose trailing plants, such as verbenas and ivy-leaved pelargoniums, to cascade over the edges of window boxes. Team these with compact, upright plants, such as begonias, miniature pelargoniums and many ornamental herbs. Do not use very tall or climbing plants in a window box as they will obscure the window.

▼ BOLD BULBS *A terracotta container complements the spring colour of* Tulipa *'Prinses Irene'.*

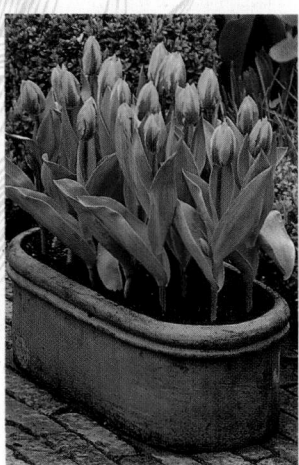

Plant up hanging and wall baskets with compact plants and luxuriant climbers and trailers: climbers, such as *Lathyrus odoratus* (sweet pea), morning glory or *Thunbergia alata* (black-eyed Susan), will twine up the chains of a hanging basket, and trailers, including pendulous begonias, provide cascades of flowers.

Compact bushy plants, such as *Impatiens*, are good for cladding the sides of a wire hanging basket with a dense mass of blooms. Plants which have wiry stems, such as *Scaevola* (fan flower) or *Helichrysum petiolare*, are useful for supporting flowering plants with lax habits.

USING FOLIAGE

Foliage plants can transform the appearance of a container display. Silver-grey *Helichrysum petiolare* and cream or white-striped *Chlorophytum comosum* (spider plant) produce stunning foliage to contrast with the trailing flowers of many petunias, fuchsias and begonias.

Small evergreens provide excellent year-round backdrops to flowering displays. Use dwarf conifers for their crisp, textured foliage, ivies, such as the golden-leaved *Hedera helix* 'Midas Touch', for trails that tumble over the sides of containers, and small evergreen shrubs, such as *Santolina* or *Hebe*, for their green, purple, silver or variegated leaves. Plant up a large container with a permanent display of evergreens, leaving spaces for a few pots to be sunk between them. Use the pots to grow bedding plants for seasonal displays that can be replaced easily.

EARLY INTEREST

Fill containers with a selection of winter and spring bedding plants to introduce colour at colder times of year (see facing page). In hanging baskets try *Gaultheria procumbens* (wintergreen), whose red berries and evergreen foliage look attractive spilling out over the edges.

In the mild microclimates of some city gardens, hardier houseplants, such as *Cyclamen* and *Solanum pseudocapsicum* (Jerusalem cherry), can be moved into the garden to provide early winter colour.

LOOKING AFTER CONTAINERS

For flowers throughout the summer months, plant up containers in late spring – or in mid spring if they can be kept at first in a greenhouse or conservatory to protect them from frosts. For winter and spring flowers, plant up containers in early autumn, after the summer bedding has been cleared away.

Use a peat or soil-based potting compost or a specially formulated hanging-basket or container compost rather than garden soil for containers. Mix slow-release fertiliser and water-retaining gel granules into the compost. Plant up very large containers in place, as they will be too heavy to move once they are filled.

Line a wire hanging basket with moss or a fibrous liner to hold in the compost. To plant up the sides and the base, make holes in the liner with a sharp knife and push the roots of the plants through them. Then fill the container with the potting compost.

Keep containers in a sheltered position, where they receive full sun for at least part of the day. Regular care is necessary to keep displays looking their best. The soil in a pot dries out quickly so water plants frequently. If a hanging basket dries out, soak its base in a bucket of water for at least an hour. Feed flowering plants once or twice a week with a high-potash liquid feed, such as a tomato fertiliser, to encourage continuous flowering. Deadhead plants that have large flowers, such as fuchsias and pelargoniums, once a week.

In winter, keep containers in a very sheltered spot or plants will stop flowering. Water displays when the compost gets dry but prevent waterlogging by raising pots up on either bricks or pot feet (small ceramic angle-pieces).

SEASONS OF BEDDING PLANTS

Cultivated varieties of the following plants provide long-lasting colour.

SPRING

● *Bellis perennis* (daisy) White, pink, purple or red, single or double flowers and rosettes of leaves.

● *Erysimum cheiri* (wallflower) Spikes of fragrant colourful flowers and lance-shaped leaves.

● *Primula* (primrose and polyanthus) Small, flat-faced, colourful flowers and rosettes of leaves.

● *Tulipa* Colourful cup or goblet-shaped flowers and broad lance-shaped leaves.

SUMMER

● *Begonia semperflorens* Bright pink or red flowers and rounded, green or copper-coloured leaves.

● *Cosmos bipinnatus* Large, crimson, pink or white, saucer-shaped blooms and feathery foliage.

● *Fuchsia* Bell-like flowers, often in purples and pinks, and oval pointed leaves.

● *Impatiens walleriana* (busy lizzie) Masses of flat-faced colourful flowers and oval leaves.

● *Lobelia erinus* Small tubular flowers in blue, red or white, and tiny leaves.

● *Pelargonium* (geranium) Clusters of colourful flowers and rounded, sometimes marked, leaves.

● *Petunia* Trumpet-shaped flowers, in many colours, and oval leaves.

● *Ricinus communis* (castor-oil plant) Striking, lobed, bronze to green leaves.

WINTER

● *Brassica oleracea* var. *capitata* (ornamental cabbage) Green outer leaves and striking, red, white or pink inner foliage.

● *Erica* x *darleyensis* (winter-flowering heather) Tiny, white, pink or red, urn-shaped flowers and colourful foliage.

● *Viola* x *wittrockiana* (pansy) Colourful flat-faced flowers, with oval to heart-shaped leaves.

Berberis
Barberry
Berberidaceae

Berberis darwinii

Foliage, flowers and berries give good garden value in these versatile, easily grown shrubs. More than 450 species include evergreen and deciduous plants, from dwarf to large shrubs, for mixed borders, hedging, screening, rock gardens or specimen planting. Evergreen species have glossy dark green foliage and some, such as *Berberis darwinii* and *B. × stenophylla*, have abundant spring flowers and generally blue-black fruits. Deciduous shrubs can have brilliantly coloured autumn foliage and clusters of bright reddish berries which usually persist well into winter. The flowers of deciduous and evergreen species are yellow or orange, globular or cup-shaped, and up to 2 cm (¾ in) across. Flowers are most commonly borne in late spring, in small rounded clusters, or, occasionally, singly. Berberis plants mainly have small leaves 1 to 4 cm (⅜ to 1½ in) long, and spiny tough stems which make impenetrable barrier hedging. The recommended plants are all hardy.

RECOMMENDED SPECIES AND VARIETIES
DECIDUOUS SHRUBS

B. 'Little Favourite' see *B. thunbergii* 'Atropurpurea Nana'.

B. × ottawensis 'Superba'♀ (syn. *B. thunbergii* 'Atropurpurea Superba') The rounded to oval leaves are a rich wine purple on this vigorous shrub that complements or contrasts with many border plants. In spring upright branches, which arch at the top, bear hanging clusters of small, red-tinged yellow flowers; red fruits appear in autumn. HEIGHT & SPREAD 1.5×1.5 m (5×5 ft) after 5 years, 2.4×2.4 m (8×8 ft) after 10 years.

B. 'Rubrostilla'♀ Small pale green leaves with silver undersides colour a brilliant red in autumn. Lax in habit with arching stems,

▼ *Berberis* 'Rubrostilla'

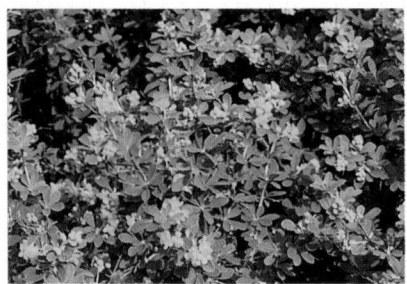

the shrub bears large pale yellow flowers in early summer. Clusters of coral-red berries hang from the branches in autumn. HEIGHT & SPREAD 1.2×1.2 m (4×4 ft) after 5 years, 1.5×1.5 m (5×5 ft) after 10 years.

B. thunbergii♀ In spring, the neat compact shrub is covered in flowers of pale straw colour suffused with red on stiff, reddish brown thorny branches. Its small, broadly oval leaves are pale to mid green above, glaucous beneath. In autumn the small red ovoid berries harmonise with the brilliant red and orange foliage. Native to Japan. HEIGHT & SPREAD 1.5×1.5 m (5×5 ft) after 5 years, 1.8×2.4 m (6×8 ft) after 10 years.

▲ *Berberis thunbergii*

▲ *Berberis thunbergii* 'Atropurpurea Nana'

'Atropurpurea Nana'♀ (syn. 'Crimson Pygmy', 'Little Favourite') is an almost thornless dwarf shrub which, at 60×60 cm (2×2 ft), is suitable for a rock garden. The foliage is rich purple-red. Planted 38 cm (15 in) apart, the shrubs make a colourful low hedge. **'Atropurpurea Superba'** see *B. × ottawensis* 'Superba'. **'Aurea'** slowly makes a rounded bush, 1×1 m (3×3 ft) in 10 years, with stunning yellow leaves that fade to pale green by late summer. Yellow flowers bloom in mid spring; red berries appear in autumn. Plant in a sheltered and slightly shady position; in full sun the young leaves may scorch but the colour is best in good light. **'Bagatelle'**♀, with globular habit and bronze-purple foliage, is compact – 30×30 cm (1×1 ft) in 10 years. **'Crimson Pygmy'** see *B. thunbergii* 'Atropurpurea Nana'. **'Golden Ring'** has reddish purple leaves with a narrow gold margin, and reaches 1.5×1.5 m (5×5 ft) in 10 years. **'Helmond Pillar'** is a stiff erect shrub with large, rounded reddish bronze leaves. It reaches 1.5 m×45 cm (5×1½ ft) after 10 years and makes an excellent hedge when

▲ *Berberis thunbergii* 'Bagatelle'

plants are set 45 cm (1½ ft) apart. **'Red Chief'**♀ is also upright growing to about 1.8×1.5 m (6×5 ft) after 10 years, but with branches arching at the top. The stems are bright red with narrow, wine-red leaves. **'Red Pillar'** is an erect shrub to 1.5 m×45 cm (5×1½ ft) after 10 years. Its reddish purple leaves turn scarlet in autumn. **'Rose Glow'**♀ has young leaves of purple marbled with silver and pink. It grows to 1.5×1.2 m (5×4 ft) after 10 years. **'Silver Beauty'** is a compact, slowly spreading bush to 1.2×1 m (4×3 ft) after 10 years, with white and bluish green variegated leaves, sometimes flushing through pink to crimson late in the season.

B. wilsoniae♀ Clusters of yellow flowers in early summer contrast with the small, lance-shaped, almost evergreen, grey-green leaves. These turn red and orange in autumn when large drooping clusters of berries ripen to orange-red. This low-growing, densely branched shrub is native to W China. HEIGHT & SPREAD 60 cm×1 m (2×3 ft) after 5 years, 1×1.2 m (3×4 ft) after 10 years.

EVERGREEN SHRUBS

B. calliantha♀ Yellow flowers are borne in late spring on this dwarf shrub, followed in

▼ *Berberis wilsoniae*

▼ *Berberis calliantha*

autumn by blue-black berries with a white bloom. Its small holly-like leaves are waxy white beneath. Native to SE China. HEIGHT & SPREAD Up to 60×60cm (2×2ft) after 5 years, 1.5×1.5m (3×3ft) after 10 years.

▲ *Berberis darwinii*

B. darwinii♀ Small, dark green, holly-like leaves provide a rich backdrop for the abundant clusters of crimson-tinted, golden yellow flowers that are borne in mid spring. Blue-purple berries ripen in early autumn. The dense shrubs make a good hedge when planted 60cm (2ft) apart. Native to Chile. HEIGHT & SPREAD 1.5×1.2m (5×4ft) after 5 years, 2×1.5m (6½×5ft) after 10 years.

B. x frikartii 'Amstelveen'♀ This dense, compact shrub has glossy, fresh green leaves with blue-white undersides. Yellow flowers in spring are followed by blue-black berries. HEIGHT & SPREAD 50×50cm (20×20in) in 5 years, 1×1m (3×3ft) in 10 years.

B. gagnepainii var. **lanceifolia** The dense growth of erect stems slowly forms an impenetrable hedge when plants are set 45-60cm (1½-2ft) apart. Clusters of bright yellow flowers in mid spring are followed in early autumn by black berries with a blue bloom. The narrow dark green leaves have a wavy margin. Native to China. HEIGHT & SPREAD 100×75cm (3×2½ft) in 5 years, 1.5×1.2m (5×4ft) after 10 years.

B. glaucocarpa 'Goldilocks'♀ Clusters of yellow flowers in spring, are followed by blackish purple berries. The spiny, holly-like leaves are a glossy dark green. HEIGHT & SPREAD 4×3m (13×10ft) after 10 years.

B. julianae Long sharp spines make the shrubs an excellent barrier hedge when planted 1m (3ft) apart. Narrow dark green leaves are copper-tinted when young. Yellow spring flowers in dense clusters are followed in autumn by black berries with a blue bloom. Native to central China. HEIGHT & SPREAD 1.5×1m (5×3ft) after 5 years, 3×2.4m (10×8ft) after 10 years.

B. x lologensis 'Apricot Queen'♀ Clusters of large orange flowers are massed on the stems in early to mid spring. Oval purple berries follow in autumn. The small holly-like leaves are glossy and dark green. HEIGHT & SPREAD 120×60cm (4×2ft) in 5 years, 2.4×1.2m (8×4ft) in 10 years.

B. x media 'Parkjuweel'♀ (Park Jewel) A

low shrub forming a dense mound of oval, bright green glossy leaves that give good red autumn colour. Yellow flowers appear in late spring. HEIGHT & SPREAD 60×60cm (2×2ft) in 5 years, ultimately 1×1m (3×3ft).

▲ *Berberis* x *media* 'Parkjuweel' (Park Jewel)

B. x stenophylla♀ From mid to late spring scented golden yellow flowers clothe the mass of long, thorny, arching branches on this graceful spreading shrub. Light crops of purple berries follow in autumn. The deep green narrow leaves are blue white beneath. The shrubs make an impenetrable hedge when planted 60cm (2ft) apart. HEIGHT & SPREAD 1.5×1.5m (5×5ft) in 5 years, 2.4×2.4m (8×8ft) in 10 years.

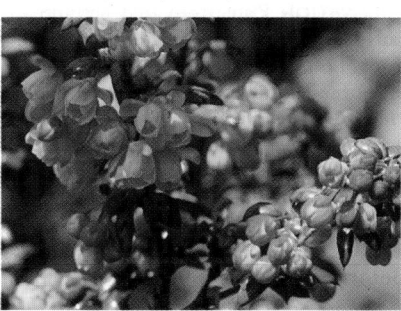

▲ *Berberis* x *stenophylla* 'Corallina Compacta'

'Corallina Compacta'♀ is a slow growing dwarf shrub, reaching only 25×25cm (10×10in) in 10 years, with spiny stems and narrowly oval leaves. Coral buds open to small orange-yellow flowers in late spring.

B. verruculosa♀ The neat, dense, slow-growing shrub has small, shiny, dark green, oval leaves that are white beneath. Golden yellow flowers appear singly or in pairs in early summer. Blue-black berries ripen in autumn. Set plants 60cm (2ft) apart for a compact hedge. Native to China. HEIGHT & SPREAD 75×75cm (2½×2½ft) in 5 years.

CULTIVATION Deciduous shrubs grown for autumn berries and colour are best in sunny positions. Evergreen plants thrive in sun or light shade. Berberis plants grow in a wide range of soils, but avoid waterlogged soil. Plant deciduous shrubs mid autumn to early spring and evergreen shrubs in early to mid autumn or early to mid spring. When planting a hedge cut off the upper quarter of all shoots to promote bushy growth.

PROPAGATION The species come true from seed; most of the cultivars come from cuttings. Take 8-12cm (3¼-4¾in) heeled cuttings in late summer from deciduous shrubs and in early autumn from evergreens. Root in a coldframe; transplant to a nursery bed the following spring; and, when shrubs are two years old, plant in their final positions.

PRUNING No regular pruning is required. Encourage fresh strong growth by cutting back a few of the oldest stems or removing them to ground level each year. Trim straggly shoots to maintain well-shaped plants. Cut deciduous species in late winter, evergreens after flowering. Trim hedges once a year – evergreens after flowering and deciduous hedges in late summer, or late autumn after the berries have fallen. Beware of thorns when pruning.

PESTS AND DISEASES Generally trouble free but honey fungus can kill quickly.

Bergamot see *Monarda*

Bergenia
Elephant's ear, pigsqueak
Saxifragaceae

Bergenia 'Silberlicht'

Grown for their decorative foliage and early spring flowers, these hardy evergreen and semi-evergreen perennials make excellent ground cover and edging plants. The large handsome leaves are rounded or spoon-shaped and sometimes change to shades of red and purple in autumn and winter. Pink, mauve, red or white, the bell-shaped flowers grow in loose clusters among or above the foliage. Thick, crinkly, rhizome-like prostrate stems support flower stalks and leaf rosettes. Although plants are hardy, the early blooms can be damaged by hard frosts.

RECOMMENDED SPECIES AND VARIETIES

B. beesiana see *B. purpurascens*

B. ciliata White flowers, up to 5cm (2in) long, become tinged with rose. The round leaves are dark green, up to 30cm (1ft) long, and covered with short stubbly hairs. HEIGHT & SPREAD 30×45cm (1×1½ft).

B. cordifolia♀ Pink flowers, 2.5cm (1in) long, rise above puckered, leathery round leaves up to 25cm (10in) wide. HEIGHT & SPREAD 45×60cm (1½×2ft).

'Purpurea'♀ has dark purple flowers in spring and intermittently through summer. The leaves are bright purple in winter.

B. crassifolia Dark green, turning reddish

Billardiera
Pittosporaceae

These evergreen, climbing plants are grown for their flowers and colourful fruits. Native to Australia, the plants are half hardy.

RECOMMENDED SPECIES

B. longiflora A freely flowering and fruiting evergreen perennial climber. It is slightly tender, suitable outside only in mild areas where it is best grown in half-shady sheltered situations, away from strong winds. Pale yellow-green, drooping, tubular flowers, 3 cm (1¼ in) long, are borne singly in early summer. In early autumn a showy, dangling display of rounded violet-blue berries is seen. The slender, twining branches are clothed with light green lance-shaped leaves, up to 4 cm (1½ in) long. White or red berried forms are also available. HEIGHT 3 m (10 ft) after 5 years.

▲ *Billardiera longiflora*

CULTIVATION Grow in a cool greenhouse or conservatory, either as a climber or in a hanging basket. Plant in loamy soil and do not allow it to dry out.

PROPAGATION Take semi-ripe cuttings in late summer. To grow from seed, sow seed when ripe in early spring. However, the seed can take a long time to germinate.

PRUNING None is needed, but occasionally cut out old and overcrowded branches.

PESTS AND DISEASES Sometimes attacked by greenfly.

Billbergia
Bromeliaceae

Brightly coloured tubular flowers embraced by a decorative rose-pink bract dangle over handsome rosettes of strap-shaped leaves. The flowers appear anytime between spring and autumn and last for three to four weeks. These tropical evergreen perennials prefer a semi-shaded position in the home or greenhouse, no cooler than 10°C (50°F) at night. Native to Central and S America.

RECOMMENDED SPECIES AND VARIETIES

B. nutans (Queen's tears, friendship plant) Small pale green flowers, edged with violet,

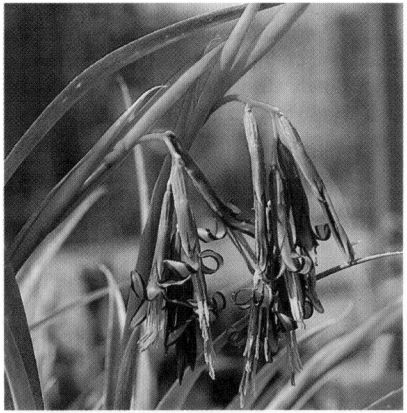

▲ *Billbergia nutans*

are surrounded by slender bracts 2.5 cm (1 in) long and borne on simple arching stems. This suckering houseplant has narrow dull green leaves, up to 45 cm (18 in) long, that are occasionally toothed. HEIGHT & SPREAD 45×30 cm (1½×1 ft).

B. pyramidalis A strong-growing plant, it has erect, pyramidal flower spikes – massed ranks of small red or orange flowers often edged blue with bright rose-pink bracts up to 4 cm (1½ in) long. Lance-shaped green leaves, up to 60 cm (2 ft) long, are flushed purple and have white banding beneath. HEIGHT & SPREAD 60×45 cm (2×1½ ft).

B. × windii♀ (angel's tears) The pendulous flower stem consists of a wiry stalk with terminal bright pink or deep rose bracts. The emerging narrow green flowers, edged red with distinctive blue tips, are up to 7.5 cm (3 in) long. This erect, somewhat tubular-shaped plant has dull green leaves. HEIGHT & SPREAD 45×30 cm (1½×1 ft).

CULTIVATION Grow in pots in a well-lit position away from direct sunlight. The plants should be kept growing tightly in their pots and not overpotted. Do not let the compost dry out and add a liquid houseplant feed to the water in summer. Mist the foliage regularly with clear water. All billbergias thrive in a variety of potting composts, from peat to soil-based. Remove the flowers after they have faded.

PROPAGATION Remove suckering growths in spring and pot individually.

PESTS AND DISEASES Usually trouble free.

Bindweed see *Calystegia hederacea*
Biota see *Thuja*
Birch see *Betula*
Bird of Paradise see *Strelitzia Reginae*
Birthwort see *Aristolochia dematitis*
Bistort see *Persicaria bistorta*
Bitter root see *Lewisia rediviva*
Bittersweet, oriental see *Celastrus orbiculatus*
Blackberry see FRUIT p.729
Black cohosh see *Cimicifuga racemosa*
Black-eyed Susan see *Thunbergia alata*
Black horehound see *Ballota nigra*
Blackthorn see *Prunus spinosa*

Bladder nut see *Staphylea*
Bladder senna see *Colutea arborescens*
Blanket flower see *Gaillarda*
Blazing star see *Liatris*
Blechnum see FERNS p.263
Bleeding heart see *Dicentra spectabilis*
Bleeding heart vine
    see *Clerodendrum Thomsoniae*

Bletilla
Orchidaceae

The complex and intricate blooms produced by members of the orchid family give a tropical air to an outdoor garden. This is one of the terrestrial orchids – a fairly hardy plant from E Asia – whose corm-like pseudobulb survives to bloom year after year if given some winter protection. In colder areas grow the plants in pots indoors and move them outside for the summer, or keep them in a cool greenhouse (see ORCHIDS, p.464).

RECOMMENDED SPECIES

B. striata (syn. *B. hyacinthina*) Each flower has 5 narrow rose-purple petals radiating above a broad lower petal or lip with an outer lobe raised at either side of the centre lobe, crimped at the rim and marked with 5 shallow ribs. The flowers are about 2.5 cm (1 in) across and borne in early summer in sprays of 3-6 at the top of arching stems up to 40 cm (16 in) long. Slender, upright, pointed leaves of mid green are pleated and arch slightly at the tip. HEIGHT 45 cm (18 in).

CULTIVATION Plant in early spring in moist

▲ *Bletilla striata*

but well-drained humus-rich soil, just covering the pseudobulb. Choose a shady or semi-shaded position sheltered from the north and east. In winter protect with a thick mulch of leaf-mould or other protective material such as conifer clippings.

PROPAGATION Divide the clustered pseudobulbs of established plants between autumn and early spring.

PESTS AND DISEASES Slugs may damage young shoots, but generally the plants are trouble free.

Bluebell see *Hyacinthoides*

Bolax
Umbelliferae

Bolax gummifera

Rosettes of tiny overlapping leaves give this hardy, evergreen perennial the appearance of a neat, tight cushion. This is a slow-growing plant, best suited to the corner of a rock garden, a scree or raised bed, a pot or a trough. There is only one species.

Bolax glebaria see *Azorella trifurcata*

B. gummifera Blue-green leaves, thick and tough to the touch, each has 3 deep lobes and measures up to 6mm (¼ in) in length. Greenish white or yellow flowers appear among the leaf rosettes in summer in miniature domed clusters about 2cm (¾ in) across. The purple-brown fruits, 3.5mm (⅛ in) long and clothed in minute star-shaped hairs, are more attractive. The species is native to the Falkland Islands, Patagonia and Tierra del Fuego. In the wild, bolax inhabits scrub, heaths and rocky places. HEIGHT & SPREAD 10×40cm (4×16in). Its ultimate spread, after about 8 years, is about 75cm (2½ft).

CULTIVATION Plant in a moist, humus-rich, well-drained soil, in full sunshine. Grow outdoors or in a coldframe or unheated greenhouse with plenty of ventilation.

PROPAGATION Sow the seeds when ripe in a coldframe, or take semi-ripe cuttings in late summer; alternatively, take offshoots in spring.

PESTS AND DISEASES Usually trouble free.

Boltonia
False camomile
Compositae

Boltonia asteroides

Loose clusters of daisy-like flowers bloom in late summer on these leafy-stemmed herbaceous perennials. They give height and airy blooms to a garden border, and make excellent cut flowers. Hardy and tolerant of light shade, boltonia grows in moist soils in the wild, in E Asia and the USA.

RECOMMENDED SPECIES AND VARIETIES

B. asteroides Flowers have white, sometimes purple, petals with prominent yellow central discs and measure 2cm (¾ in) across. They are borne in clusters at the top of each stem. The glossy, grey-green, narrow and pointed leaves are up to 12cm (4¾ in) long and 2cm (¾ in) wide. HEIGHT & SPREAD 2.1×1.2m (7×4ft).

The slightly larger flowers of var. *latisquama* are a more definite lilac colour and the plant is shorter at 1.8m (6ft). This natural variety is the parent of 'Nana', suitable for smaller gardens at only 1m (3ft) tall. Its flowers are white. 'Snowbank', with snow-white flowers, is nearer the height of the species at 2m (6½ ft).

CULTIVATION Grow in any reasonably fertile soil. Taller species or varieties need staking, preferably with twiggy sticks for the plant to grow through.

PROPAGATION Sow seed in spring. Divide the plant in autumn. Plant basal cuttings in late spring or early summer.

PESTS AND DISEASES Usually trouble free.

Bougainvillea
Nyctaginaceae

Bougainvillea glabra

Remarkable brilliantly coloured bracts decorate these tropical and sub-tropical flowering shrubs and scramblers. The flowers are generally insignificant. Bougainvilleas can be grown in a conservatory or greenhouse usually in large pots on a framework of wire or canes. Where space is available, however, the plants can be grown very successfully in a greenhouse border and trained up into the roof. All enjoy full sun and require a minimum night temperature of 10°C (50°F).

RECOMMENDED SPECIES AND VARIETIES

B. × buttiana A vigorous, scrambling, woody plant with dark green elliptical leaves up to 7.5cm (3in) long. The bright orange or purple papery bracts are about 3cm (1¼in) wide and slightly undulated. HEIGHT & SPREAD 5×1m (16×3ft).

'Golden Glow' has golden yellow bracts with a hint of pink. 'Killie Campbell'♀ bears large bracts with ruffled edges that are copper through to red and magenta.

'Mrs Butt'♀ produces crimson-magenta bracts. 'Scarlet O'Hara' sports orange to

▲ *Bougainvillea glabra*
Bougainvillea 'Mrs Butt' ▲

deep bright red bracts, which shade to orange.

B. glabra♀ (paper flower) A vigorous, scrambling, shrubby plant with elliptical leaves that are 10cm (4in) long and pale green beneath. The white or magenta bracts, up to 3cm (1¼in) wide, persist long after the central tiny blossom has faded. The insignificant white flowers contrast well with the bold mauve to purple bracts. HEIGHT & SPREAD 5m×1m (16×3ft).

'Alexandra' has magenta bracts.

B. 'Poultonii Special'♀ This moderately vigorous scrambling shrubby plant has elliptical leaves up to 7.5cm (3in) long. The striking rich rosy magenta bracts are 3cm (1¼in) wide. HEIGHT & SPREAD 3×1m (10×3ft).

B. 'Raspberry Ice' This bushy, scrambling plant has elliptical leaves that are 7.5cm (3in) long, and creamy variegated with a pink flush. The bracts, up to 3cm (1in) long, are deep pink to red. HEIGHT & SPREAD 3×1m (10×3ft).

CULTIVATION All bougainvilleas thrive in full sun in a free-draining, soil-based compost. They require a night temperature that does not drop below a minimum of 10°C (50°F). For pot culture use John Innes No.3 compost. Water freely during the summer months, but very sparingly in winter. Use a high-nitrogen liquid feed in spring and change to a high-potash one when flowering begins. Bougainvilleas are not self clinging and must be tied to their supports.

PROPAGATION Take semi-ripe cuttings of non-flowering wood in summer, or hardwood cuttings during winter.

PRUNING Cut back the previous season's lateral growths in spring; only spurs up to 3cm (1¼in) long should remain.

PESTS AND DISEASES Greenfly, whitefly, red spider and mealy bug are all common pest problems. Mildew, too, can sometimes cause trouble.

▲ GRACEFUL MAPLE *Slender branches and neat, elegant foliage give an acer bonsai its charm.*

▲ ROCKY CONTRAST *A stone forms the centrepiece to a display of spruce, elm and cotoneaster.*

▲ BONSAI WOODLAND *A group of hornbeams creates the impression of a leafy grove.*

BONSAI
◆
Miniature images of ancient trees

SEASONAL CHANGES ARE CAPTURED IN SPECTACULAR DETAIL BY BONSAI TREES, WHICH ARE STRAIGHTFORWARD TO CREATE

Bonsai bring the pleasure and variety of trees to the smallest of areas. Once the basic techniques have been mastered, it is possible to create images of an ancient oak, a wind-blown mountain pine or a dense forest of beech within a few years.

Given the correct care, a bonsai can outlive a full-sized tree and will weather attractively throughout the years as pruning wounds heal, bark cracks and moss covers the surrounding soil. Pruning is necessary to simplify the branch structure and wire is used to shape branches and create a natural-looking growth pattern. New shoots are pinched out to keep the foliage neat.

Bonsai can be grown from seed or cuttings but most will take many years to develop; if you begin with an established plant, you should have a recognisable tree in four or five years.

Choose a hardy species that regenerates readily after pruning and has naturally small leaves, flowers and berries. *Carpinus* (hornbeam), *Pinus* (pine), *Picea* (spruce), *Juniperus* (juniper) *Ulmus* (elm) and *Crataegus* (hawthorn) are ideal. Look for a plant that is 30-50 cm (12-20 in) in height and has a well-shaped trunk that is flared at the base.

CREATING THE SHAPE

Specialist bonsai tools are available but all you need to begin with are sharp secateurs, wire cutters and a modelling knife. Aluminium wire for shaping can be bought from a garden centre or bonsai nursery. Make sure the wire is strong enough to keep a branch in place but not so heavy that it crushes the bark when it is applied.

Prune away all the branches of a deciduous tree. As new shoots emerge, shape some of

them with wire and remove the others. Do not remove all the branches of an evergreen at once as the plant will die. Instead, shorten them in stages, cutting back to healthy side-shoots in spring and again in summer. Once ample new shoots have appeared close to the trunk, prune the original branches hard and shape the new shoots to form new branches. The branches should be arranged evenly round the trunk with the bottom half of the front of the tree left clear.

Use wire to shape branches into the desired positions (see facing page). Keep the branches of a broad-leaved tree more or less horizontal and shape conifer branches into slightly downward sweeps. Sideshoots also need wiring in the same way. The trunk can be left to grow upright or, if it is supple enough, shaped with wire to lean as if wind-blown or to dip over the rim of the container.

Once they are wired, the branches and sideshoots should be left to grow freely until they have set in position. At this point, remove the wire before it begins to scar the bark. The branches can then be cut to the desired lengths.

Pinch out new growth throughout the growing season to keep foliage neat and bushy (see facing page). Once you are satisfied with the shape of your

•REMOVING A BRANCH•

Prune between autumn and spring, when the tree is dormant, or in mid summer, when the wounds heal rapidly.

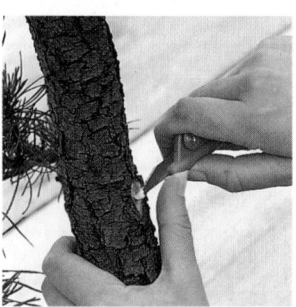

1 To prune, cut the branch as close to the trunk as you can without damaging the bark. Then use a blade to hollow out the wound so it will heal flat.

2 Seal the wound with a non-drying modelling clay, such as Plasticine, mixed with a little olive oil. Bitumen stains the bark and is hard to remove.

▶ SEASONAL SHOW *The resilient hawthorn is most attractive in spring when it produces its blooms.*

bonsai, prune its roots and repot the tree in a shallow bonsai container (see below).

CARING FOR A BONSAI

Repot young trees every year and older trees or pines less often, but before the roots block the drainage holes.

Keep bonsai off the ground, ideally on slatted benches, in dappled shade. Bonsai need shelter from cold winds, severe frost and prolonged periods of rain. Place conifers against a south-facing wall, and broad-leaved trees in a shed or poly-tunnel during winter.

Water bonsai regularly and do not let the soil dry out. Water evaporates quickly from a bonsai's shallow pot, which can also become waterlogged,

so use a compost that is moisture retentive but free draining and well aerated. Equal parts of sifted peat, sterilised loam and grit is a good mix.

When watering, soak the soil well until water runs freely from the container's drainage holes and immerse the pot in water periodically to ensure there are no dry spots.

Feed conifers once in mid winter and all trees from spring to late summer. A general fertiliser suits all except flowering bonsai, which need a tomato or rose fertiliser. Apply feed at half strength twice as often as recommended, to avoid 'burning' the roots. Add a nitrogen-free fertiliser in early autumn to harden growth and toughen the roots before winter.

•PINCHING OUT YOUNG GROWTH•

Finger-pinching encourages the growth of dense twigs and neat, bushy foliage. It also reduces the size of the leaves, which keeps them in proportion with the tree.

Chinese junipers *Juniperus chinensis* produces short, multi-branched shoots with scale-like foliage. To pinch out, grip a fan of shoots between your thumb and forefinger and break off the ends, leaving behind stubs of even length (right). Remove any vigorous shoots individually and continue the process throughout the growing season.

General techniques Remove the tips of young shoots of conifers as they grow. On broad-leaved trees, pinch out the growing tip once the shoot produces two or three leaves (left) or wait until six or seven leaves appear then cut back the shoot to the second leaf.

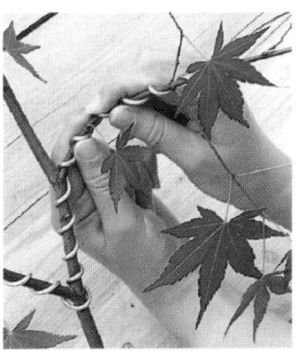

Pines In spring, *Pinus* buds develop into candle-like shoots, covered in needles. Break off half of each candle while the needles are pressed tight (left) or two-thirds when they start to open out. Begin at the bottom of the tree where shoots are weakest and work upwards over a week. Pull out some of the old needles in late summer to give new buds room to develop.

•SHAPING A BRANCH WITH WIRE•

Coil wire round a branch and bend to shape. Leave the wire in place until the branch sets in position. This can take weeks for a young deciduous branch or years for an older conifer.

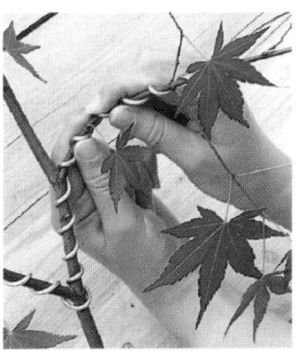

2 Leave the tree to rest in shade for a week, then check it regularly to see if the wire is cutting into the bark. When this happens, remove the wire and, if necessary, replace it coiled in the opposite direction.

1 Anchor the wire by coiling it round the trunk if shaping a branch or by pushing it into the soil if shaping a trunk. Coil the rest of the wire at a 45 degree angle round the branch or trunk and manipulate into position.

▲ NATURAL SHAPE *The branches of this pine tree have been wired to slope downwards.*

•ROOT PRUNING AND REPOTTING•

Pruning roots and repotting is best done in early spring when the roots will heal rapidly. Do not feed for three weeks afterwards and delay wiring or pruning until growth restarts.

2 Cover the drainage holes with mesh and pass wires through the holes to secure the tree. Place a layer of soil in the pot, creating a mound for the tree.

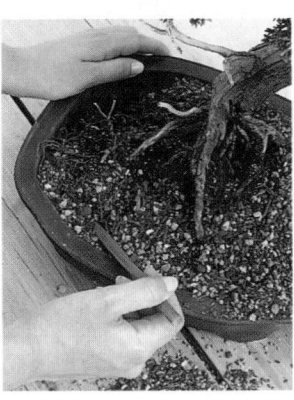

1 Lift the tree from its pot and gently tease out the roots with a stick until they hang loose. Then, cut back all of the thick roots as far as possible and the fine roots by about half.

3 Rotate the tree on the mound to settle it. Pull the wires over the roots. Twist them together and tighten to hold the tree steady. Work soil between the roots with a stick, making sure that there are no spaces. Water well and place the tree in a frost-free site until growth resumes.

Brachyglottis
Compositae

Brachyglottis monroi

Silver-grey foliage and yellow daisy-like flowers in early to mid summer give lasting but unostentatious charm to these evergreen shrubs. The broadly oval leaves have dense white felt beneath and vary from olive to grey-green above. All these New Zealand natives are sun lovers, those listed here are reasonably hardy and tolerant of drought and strong winds.

RECOMMENDED SPECIES AND VARIETIES

B. compacta (syn. *Senecio compactus*) Small wavy-edged leaves clothe the close-set branches. Young branches and stems are densely felted. Flowers are borne in clusters or singly in mid summer. HEIGHT & SPREAD 1×2m (3×6½ft).

▲ *Brachyglottis compacta*

B. monroi♀ (syn. *Senecio monroi*) The small domed shrub bears large dense clusters of flowers in early to mid summer. The scalloped, wavy leaves are heavily felted on the underside. HEIGHT & SPREAD 1×1m (3×3ft).

B. Dunedin Group 'Sunshine'♀ (syn. *Senecio greyi* hort., *S*. 'Sunshine') The leaves are silvery or grey-green above, white felted

▼ *Brachyglottis* Dunedin Group 'Sunshine'

beneath. Flowers are borne in large clusters from mid to late summer. HEIGHT & SPREAD 1×2m (3×6½ft).

CULTIVATION Plant in spring in any well-drained soil in full sun.

PROPAGATION Take semi-ripe cuttings during summer or hardwood cuttings in mid to late autumn.

PRUNING Trim back after flowering to keep within bounds.

PESTS AND DISEASES Usually trouble free.

Brachyscome
Compositae

Grown for their white, blue or purple daisies, the brachyscome species recommended here are a half-hardy annual and an herbaceous perennial. The annual, *Brachyscome iberidifolia*, is suitable for summer bedding or in hanging baskets and other containers. It can also be grown as a winter-flowering indoor plant. The perennial, *B. rigidula*, is good for rock gardens but is only reliably hardy in milder regions. Native to Australasia and New Guinea.

RECOMMENDED SPECIES AND VARIETIES

B. iberidifolia (Swan River daisy) Usually blue, but sometimes violet or white, the abundant, fragrant flowers appear throughout summer. They measure up to 4cm (1½in) across. This bushy plant has pale green, deeply cut leaves, 10cm (4in) long. HEIGHT & SPREAD 30×45cm (12×18in).

▲ *Brachyscome iberidifolia*

Among the single-colour varieties available are **'Blue Star'**, **'Purple Splendour'** and **'White Splendour'**. **'Brachy Blue'** has blue flowers and reaches a height of 15cm (6in) and a spread of 20cm (8in).

B. rigidula Lavender-blue flowers, up to

2.5cm (1in) across, appear throughout summer on 8cm (3¼in) stems. Plants form dense low clumps of numerous leafy stems. The finely divided, dark green glossy leaves are 3cm (1¼in) long. HEIGHT & SPREAD 15×30cm (6×12in).

CULTIVATION Plant in late spring in well-drained soil, choosing a sheltered site in full sun. *B. iberidifolia* benefits from some support. Deadhead regularly.

PROPAGATION Raise *B. iberidifolia* from seed sown in a cool greenhouse in early spring. To grow indoor plants that flower in late winter, sow seed in early autumn, providing a minimum greenhouse temperature of 10°C (50°F). Propagate *B. rigidula* from seed, as for *B. iberidifolia,* or by division or by taking cuttings in spring or late summer.

PESTS AND DISEASES Usually trouble free.

Brassica
Cruciferae

Striking inner leaves that are partly or entirely red, white or pink are the most distinctive feature of these hardy annuals which, although they are the same species as broccoli, brussels sprouts and cauliflower, are unpleasant to eat. The outer leaves are green. The colours develop at night temperatures below 10°C (50°F) so they are at their most interesting in autumn. They thrive in almost any garden situation, including large containers. They have all arisen in cultivation.

RECOMMENDED SPECIES AND VARIETIES

B. oleracea var. **acephala** (ornamental kale) Fringed or deeply serrated foliage is loosely arranged and this plant has no recognisable heart. The varieties listed are F₁ hybrids. HEIGHT & SPREAD 45×45cm (18×18in).

'Nagoya' has heavily fringed red or white younger leaves. **'Peacock'** has white or red inner leaves and white or red veinal areas to outer leaves, all deeply toothed. Both these cultivars are up to 30cm (12in) tall and 30cm (12in) across. **'Feather'** is similar to 'Peacock' but taller, at 35cm (14in).

B. oleracea var. **capitata** (ornamental cabbage group) The fast-growing, uniform F₁ hybrids are more commonly grown. HEIGHT & SPREAD 45×45cm (18×18in).

▼ *Brassica oleracea* var. *capitata* 'Tokyo'

'Northern Lights' and 'Osaka' are up to 50 cm (20 in) across and 25 cm (10 in) tall, with frilled leaf edges. 'Tokyo' has smooth-edged leaves and reaches 25 cm (10 in) tall, with a spread of 30 cm (12 in).

CULTIVATION Plant in late summer or early autumn, in comparatively poor soil.

PROPAGATION Sow seed in a coldframe or unheated greenhouse in early to mid summer. Keep well watered, especially during the first week.

PESTS AND DISEASES Aphids and caterpillars attack plants. Pigeons may damage brassicas in autumn, especially in hard weather.

Brazilian plume see *Justicia carnea*
Bridal wreath see *Francoa*
Briza see GRASSES p. 300
Broccoli see p. 736
Brodiaea see *Triteleia*
Bromeliads see *Aechmea, Ananas, Billbergia, Cryptanthus, Guzmania, Neoregelia, Nidularium, Tillandsia, Vriesea*
Broom see *Cytisus*
Broom, Mt Etna see *Genista aetnensis*
Broom, Spanish see *Spartium*

Browallia
Bush violet
Solanaceae

Star-shaped, tubular flowers adorn these bushy evergreen perennials from early summer to early autumn. These free-flowering, frost-tender plants are grown indoors as pot plants or outdoors as summer bedding or in containers and hanging baskets. They are generally treated as half-hardy annuals and discarded after flowering.

The flowers have five rounded petals and white centres. The slightly sticky, mid green leaves are oval and pointed. Native to tropical S America.

RECOMMENDED SPECIES AND VARIETIES
B. speciosa Violet-blue flowers, about 5 cm (2 in) across, are borne singly on short stalks.

▼ *Browallia speciosa* 'Blue Troll'

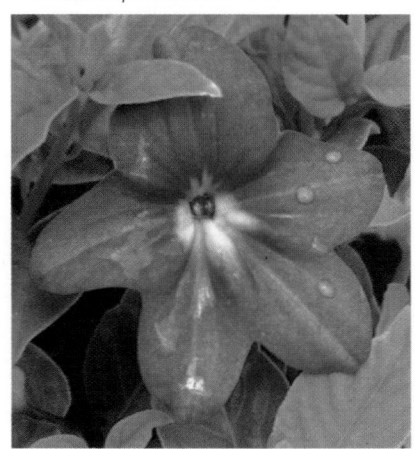

The leaves are up to 9 cm (3½ in) long. HEIGHT & SPREAD 45×45 cm (18×18 in).

'Blue Troll' has clear blue flowers and 'White Troll' has white flowers; both grow to a height and spread of 25 cm (10 in).
B. viscosa This plant has violet-blue flowers 2.5 cm (1 in) across and smaller leaves. HEIGHT & SPREAD 30×20 cm (12×8 in).

'Sapphire' has bright blue flowers.
CULTIVATION Plant outdoors in any soil, preferably moist but not wet, once all risk of frost has passed, choosing a sunny position. Alternatively grow in pots of John Innes No. 2 indoors or in a well-ventilated greenhouse or conservatory, maintaining a minimum winter temperature of 13°C (55°F). Protect plants from direct sun. Pinch out growing points to ensure well-branched, bushy specimens.

PROPAGATION For outdoor plants, sow seed in early spring in a heated greenhouse. For indoor pot plants, sow seed in late winter to produce flowers in late spring and early summer. For flowers in late winter and early spring, sow seed under glass in mid to late summer, maintaining a minimum winter temperature of 13°C (55°F).

PESTS AND DISEASES Usually trouble free.

Bruckenthalia
Spike heath
Ericaceae

Bruckenthalia spiculifolia

This hardy evergreen shrub has a flowering period that falls between the winter-flowering and early summer-flowering heathers, ensuring that a small heather garden has continuity in its display of colour. It is also at home in peaty rock gardens or in pots and other containers. There is only one species in the genus; it is native to acid sub-alpine regions of SE Europe.
Bruckenthalia spiculifolia The neat plant bears short dense spikes, 2 mm (⅛ in) long, of bell-shaped flowers that are generally pink. The flowers are held above dark green whorls of up to 5 needle-like leaves, each up to 5 mm (¼ in) long. The flowers are usually in bloom from early to mid summer. HEIGHT & SPREAD 25×50 cm (10×20 in).

CULTIVATION Plant in lime-free, moist but well-drained soil in full sun.

PROPAGATION Take semi-ripe heeled cuttings in mid summer.

PRUNING Trim lightly after flowering to remove dead flowerheads.

PESTS AND DISEASES Usually trouble free.

▲ *Bruckenthalia spiculifolia*

Brugmansia
Solanaceae

Brugmansia x candida 'Grand Marnier'

The large pendulous flowers of these tender shrubs and small trees are funnel-shaped and often strongly fragrant. They appear in summer and sometimes into autumn. The evergreen leaves, which are coarse and sometimes downy, may be lost in winter. All parts of these plants are poisonous. Native to central and S America, they need a minimum night temperature of 7°C (45°F) and are usually grown as greenhouse or conservatory plants. They can be moved outside in summer to a sheltered sunny position. All the plants recommended below are shrubs which attain their full size in five years. The heights and spreads given are for specimens planted out and either lightly pruned or not pruned at all. Pot-grown plants reach about half these sizes.

RECOMMENDED SPECIES AND VARIETIES
B. arborea (syn. *B. versicolor* hort., *Datura arborea*) (angel's trumpet) Strongly aromatic white flowers up to 20 cm (8 in) long appear from mid summer to autumn. The dull

green, narrowly oval leaves, 20 cm (8 in) long, are coarsely toothed. HEIGHT & SPREAD 4×2 m (13×6½ ft).

B. × candida Fragrant white, pink or yellow flowers up to 30 cm (12 in) long are borne from mid to late summer. Toothed, dull green, elliptic leaves are up to 20 cm (8 in) long. HEIGHT & SPREAD 5×3 m (16×10 ft).

'**Grand Marnier**'♥ has peach-pink flowers. '**Knightii**'♥ (syn. 'Plena') has double white flowers.

B. chlorantha see *B. sanguinea* ssp. *sanguinea* 'Flava'

B. × insignis (syn. *B. suaveolens × versicolor*) Pink to white flowers, up to 40 cm (16 in) long, appear from mid to late summer. Dull green, oval to elliptic leaves are 15 cm (6 in) long. HEIGHT & SPREAD 4×2 m (13×6½ ft).

'**Orange**' bears abundant orange-yellow flowers. There is a **pink** form (syn. *B. sanguinea* 'Rosea', *Datura rosea*) with salmon-pink blooms.

B. rosei see *B. sanguinea* ssp. *sanguinea* 'Flava'

B. sanguinea♥ (syn. *Datura rosei, D. sanguinea*) (red angel's trumpet) Yellow flowers, 25 cm (10 in) long, with a flared mouth that deepens to orange-red appear from mid to late summer. The large, dull green, rounded, lobed leaves are up to 15 cm (6 in) long. HEIGHT & SPREAD 5×4 m (16×13 ft).

▲ *Brugmansia sanguinea*

'**Rosea**' see *B. × insignis* pink. The fragrant flowers of ssp. *sanguinea* '**Flava**' (syn. *B. chlorantha, B. rosei*) bloom all summer. They are up to 15 cm (6 in) long, with a larger flared mouth. The hairless leaves are oval or triangular and sharply toothed. It reaches a height and spread of 2 m (6½ ft).

B. suaveolens♥ (syn. *Datura suaveolens*) Night-scented white flowers, up to 30 cm (12 in) long, widening at the flare, are borne from mid to late summer. The oval or elliptic, dull green leaves are 15 cm (6 in) long. HEIGHT & SPREAD 4×3 m (13×10 ft).

B. suaveolens × versicolor see *B. × insignis*

B. versicolor hort. see *B. arborea*

B. versicolor (syn. *Datura versicolor*) White flowers, sometimes flushed pink or orange with age, up to 40 cm (16 in) long, appear from mid to late summer. Coarse, roughly oval, dull green leaves are 20 cm (8 in) long. HEIGHT & SPREAD 5×3 m (16×10 ft).

CULTIVATION Grow in pots of John Innes No. 3. Place in a warm sunny spot in a greenhouse or conservatory or outside during summer. Water freely in spring and summer; sparingly in winter. Remove faded leaves and spent flowers.

PROPAGATION Sow seed under glass in spring. Take semi-ripe cuttings in summer.

PRUNING Cut back hard to the framework of branches during spring.

PESTS AND DISEASES Greenfly, whitefly and red spider mite attack regularly.

Brunfelsia
Solanaceae

Brunfelsia pauciflora 'Macrantha'

Large saucer-shaped flowers bedeck these tender evergreen shrubs. They make good indoor pot plants if pruned annually and are suitable for a heated greenhouse or conservatory. Natives of tropical America, brunfelsias require a minimum night-time temperature of 13°C (55°F).

RECOMMENDED SPECIES AND VARIETIES

B. americana (lady of the night) Flowers, up to 7.5 cm (3 in) across, appear in summer – often starting white but turning creamy yellow. They are fragrant, especially at night. The leaves are up to 10 cm (4 in) long, oval or elliptical in shape and with distinctive slender, pointed ends. HEIGHT & SPREAD 1.2×1 m (4×3 ft) after 5 years, ultimately 4 m (13 ft) tall.

B. pauciflora♥ (syn. *B. calycina, B. eximia*) (yesterday-today-and-tomorrow) A spreading shrub with clusters of white-eyed flowers, up to 7.5 cm (3 in) across, that start

▲ *Brunfelsia pauciflora*

purple and fade to almost white. They continue most of the year. The oval leaves, up to 7.5 cm (3 in) long, are dark green and glossy. HEIGHT & SPREAD 1×1 m (3×3 ft) after 5 years, ultimately 3 m (10 ft) tall.

'**Macrantha**' has larger flowers.

CULTIVATION Grow in soilless compost indoors or in a heated greenhouse or conservatory. Permit plenty of light, but not direct sun. Repot each spring. Water freely and feed regularly in spring and summer. Water sparingly in winter.

PROPAGATION Take semi-ripe cuttings in late summer of wood that has not flowered.

PRUNING Pinch out the growing points regularly to ensure a shapely bush.

PESTS AND DISEASES Mealy bug, whitefly and greenfly appear regularly.

Brunnera
Boraginaceae

Sprays of small blue or white flowers nestle among handsome coarse leaves in spring. These hardy herbaceous perennials make excellent ground cover. They prosper in most situations except dense shade.

RECOMMENDED SPECIES AND VARIETIES

B. macrophylla♥ (syn. *Anchusa myosotidiflora*) Tiny, star-shaped blue flowers are carried on wiry stems. The mid green leaves, up to 15 cm (6 in) long, are oval or roughly heart-shaped. Native to E Europe. HEIGHT & SPREAD 50×60 cm (20×24 in).

'**Betty Bowring**' has white flowers. '**Dawson's White**' carries white and green variegated foliage and bright blue flowers.

▲ *Brunnera macrophylla* 'Hadspen Cream'

'**Hadspen Cream**'♥ produces blue flowers and light green leaves splashed with cream. '**Langtrees**' has blue flowers and coarse green leaves, spotted silver at the edges.

CULTIVATION Plant in autumn or spring in any ordinary soil in light dappled shade, although brunneras will tolerate sun provided the soil does not dry out. Water well

▼ *Brunnera macrophylla* 'Langtrees'

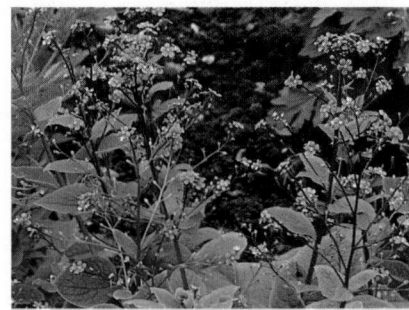

in the first season. Remove faded flower-heads and foliage. Avoid disturbing the roots of the variegated plant, *B. macrophylla* 'Dawson's White', as this can encourage green shoots to appear.

PROPAGATION Divide in autumn or sow seed in a coldframe in spring.
PESTS AND DISEASES Usually trouble free.

Brussels sprouts see p.736
Buckthorn see *Rhamnus*

Buddleja
Buddleiaceae

Buddleja 'Lochinch'

Tiny, profuse nectar-rich flowers, sometimes in globular clusters but mainly in long plumes, provide a long-lasting display in summer. The plumes reach 15-40cm (6-16in) long and range in colour through various shades of mauve, purple, white, orange and red. Some are sweetly scented and all attract butterflies. The often downy leaves taper to a point, and are generally 7.5-20cm (3-8in) long.

These large deciduous or semi-evergreen shrubs are fast-growing. Some are fully hardy, but there are more tender species that need the protection of a south or west-facing wall in mild areas and an unheated greenhouse in harsher climates. All like full sun and well-drained soil. Most species are native to E Asia.

RECOMMENDED SPECIES AND VARIETIES
B. alternifolia♀ Early summer is the best season for the fragrant, purple-lilac flowers which are borne in numerous small, bead-like bunches along the stem. Long, slightly upright young shoots quickly arch out and give the hardy shrub a graceful, rounded shape. The long, narrow leaves are dull green above with whitish down beneath. The fast-growing, deciduous shrub blooms when it is about 3 years old. It makes a fine weeping tree when trained. HEIGHT & SPREAD 2.4×2.4m (8×8ft) after 5 years, ultimately 4m (13ft) tall.
B. asiatica♀ Long, lax, slender spikes of very fragrant white flowers appear from late winter to mid spring. The young stems and the underside of the leaves are densely covered in silvery hairs. This semi-evergreen shrub is not hardy and needs a very sheltered position even in southern Britain. HEIGHT & SPREAD 2×2m (6½×6½ft) after 5 years, ultimately 3m (10ft) tall.
B. crispa The young stems and new leaves

of this upright, deciduous shrub are covered in white hairs which give the pointed, pale grey-green leaves a silvery appearance. The terminal panicles of white-centred, lilac flowers that appear from mid to late summer are quite showy and have a pleasant fragrance. This tender plant needs the protection of a south-facing wall even in the south and a cold greenhouse elsewhere. HEIGHT & SPREAD 2×2m (6½×6½ft) after 5 years, ultimately 3m (10ft) tall.
B. davidii (butterfly bush) Fragrant, pale purple flower spikes are borne from mid summer to early autumn. The pale green leaves, up to 25cm (10in) long, are covered in fine hairs. This vigorous grower needs hard pruning if not to become straggly. Although frost hardy, the young shoots can be cut back by early frosts but without permanent harm being done. HEIGHT & SPREAD 3×3m (10×10ft) after 5 years, ultimately 5m (16ft) tall.

This species is the parent of many fine cultivars which do not usually grow as large, most averaging 2m (6½ft) in height and spread, although they can be kept smaller by pruning. 'Black Knight'♀ has flower plumes of a deep violet. 'Dartmoor'♀ has

▲ *Buddleja davidii* 'Dartmoor'

magenta flowers. 'Empire Blue'♀ is a strong grower with orange-centred violet-blue flowers. The leaves of 'Harlequin' are variegated creamy white, the flowers a deep reddish purple. 'Nanho Blue' has pale blue flowers. The flowers of var. *nanhoensis* 'Alba' are white. It is not a vigorous grower. One of the best red varieties is 'Royal Red'♀ whose deep purple-red flowers are produced in plumes up to 50cm (20in) long. 'White Bouquet' has white flowers with a yellow eye and a pleasant fragrance. The best white variety is 'White Profusion'♀, whose yellow-eyed flowers are produced in abundance.
B. fallowiana Long narrow plumes of richly fragrant, pale lavender-blue flowers are borne in late summer and early autumn. The leaves are dark green above with silvery hairs beneath. The stems are also covered in silvery hairs. The multistemmed, rounded, deciduous shrub is tender and needs the protection of a south-facing wall

▲ *Buddleja davidii* 'White Profusion'

▲ *Buddleja fallowiana* var. *alba*

Buddleja globosa ▲

or a cold greenhouse. HEIGHT & SPREAD 2×2m (6½×6½ft) after 5 years, also the ultimate size.

The flowers of var. *alba*♀ are pure white with an orange eye.
B. globosa♀ (orange ball tree) Globular clusters of small orange-yellow flowers up to 2cm (¾in) across appear in early summer. This rather open semi-evergreen shrub with dark green leaves is large but pruning restricts its size. It is frost hardy but benefits from the protection of a south-facing wall. HEIGHT & SPREAD 2×2m (6½×6½ft) after 5 years, ultimately 5m (16ft) tall.
B. lindleyana Purple-violet flowers are produced in slender, tapering, curved spikes during mid and late summer. The leaves are pale green and slightly hairy. This deciduous shrub needs protection from frost – the ends of the branches are sometimes cut back by winter frost but new spring growth replaces them. HEIGHT & SPREAD 2×2m (6½×6½ft) after 5 years, ultimately 5m (16ft) tall.
B. 'Lochinch'♀ Scented spikes of violet-blue flowers with a deep orange centre are produced in late summer. The young leaves have a covering of grey hairs, which is later lost from the top of the matt green leaves. The deciduous shrub is not frost hardy.

▲ *Buddleja lindleyana*

HEIGHT & SPREAD 2×2m (6½×6½ft) after 5 years, also the ultimate size.

B. 'Pink Delight'♀ Long narrow plumes of pink flowers are borne in late summer. Although frost hardy this deciduous plant may have the ends of the branches cut back by the first frosts, but spring growth replaces them. HEIGHT & SPREAD 2×2m (6½×6½ft) after 5 years, ultimately 4m (13ft) tall.

B. × weyeriana In mid to late summer grey-yellow or orange-yellow flowers open in globular clusters at the end of the branches on the rounded shrub. It is moderately frost hardy. HEIGHT & SPREAD 2×2m (6½×6½ft) after 5 years, ultimately 3m (10ft) tall.

'Golden Glow' makes a larger plant

▼ *Buddleja × weyeriana 'Golden Glow'*

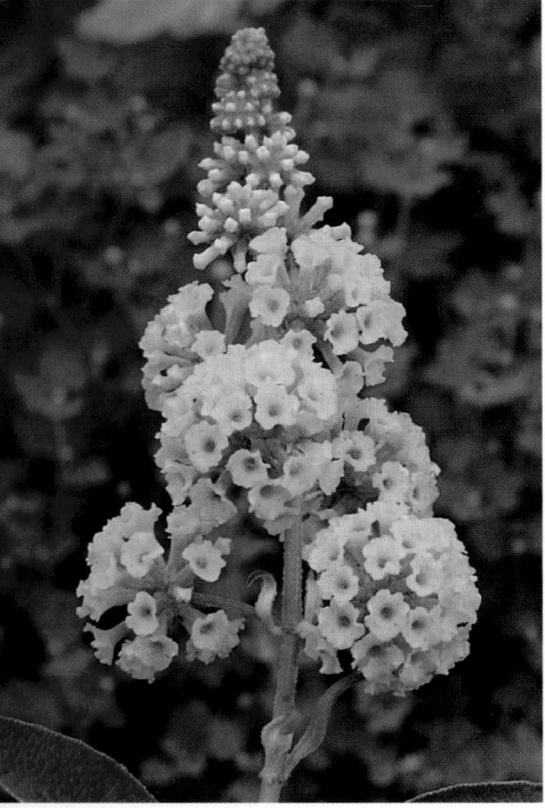

◄ *Buddleja 'Lochinch'*

eventually and has yellow-orange flowers tinged with lilac. **'Sungold'**♀ has deep orange flowers.

CULTIVATION Plant in autumn or spring in any good well-drained garden soil, choosing a position in full sun. Grow less hardy species besides a south-facing wall or in a well-sheltered position. Alternatively, grow in pots of John Innes No.3 and overwinter in an unheated greenhouse or conservatory.

PROPAGATION Take semi-ripe cuttings in mid to late summer or hardwood cuttings from mid autumn to early spring.

PRUNING Prune *B. alternifolia* and *B. globosa* after flowering. Remove a third of the stems of *B. alternifolia*. Cut back the faded flowerheads plus 5-7.5cm (2-3in) of the flowering stems of *B. globosa*. Prune all other species and varieties hard in spring by cutting back all the previous year's growth to within 5-7.5cm (2-3in) of the old wood.

PESTS AND DISEASES Usually trouble free.

Bugbane see *Cimicifuga*
Bugle see *Ajuga*

Bulbocodium

Colchicaceae

Bulbocodium vernum

Starry, funnel-shaped flowers in shades of purple appear from these hardy corms early in the year, growing close to the ground. The leaves emerge with the flowers but only reach their full length after the blooms have finished. The genus consists of just two species, native to alpine meadows in the Pyrenees, Alps and Caucasus. Although fully hardy, plants do not like excessive wet and thrive in sunny rockeries, raised beds and well-drained borders. They also do well in an unheated greenhouse or alpine house.

RECOMMENDED SPECIES

B. vernum Virtually stemless, upright, pinky purple flowers, 4cm (1½in) tall and 2.5-4cm (1-1½in) wide, emerge as early as mid winter in mild regions or in early spring in colder areas. The dark green, arching, grass-like leaves are eventually up to 15cm (6in) long and die back in early or mid summer. HEIGHT 10cm (4in).

CULTIVATION Plant corms during autumn in any well-drained soil, setting them 10cm (4in) deep and 5cm (2in) apart. A sunny site is best but plants tolerate light shade.

PROPAGATION Separate offsets from the corms in summer after the foliage has died

▲ *Bulbocodium vernum*

down. Do this every 3-4 years to maintain vigorous flowering.

PESTS AND DISEASES Usually trouble free.

Buphthalmum

Oxeye
Compositae

Deep yellow, daisy-like flowers, borne on long, slender, upright stems against a mass of loose, dark green foliage appear throughout summer. These hardy herbaceous perennials are most effective in a herbaceous border or a wild garden.

RECOMMENDED SPECIES

B. salicifolium The flowers are solitary and up to 2cm (¾in) across. Both petals and central disc are yellow. The narrow, lance-shaped leaves are about 5cm (2in) long, smooth or slightly hairy. Native to Europe and Asia, where it is found in open wood-

▲ *Buphthalmum salicifolium*

land and the more stony grasslands. HEIGHT & SPREAD 75×45 cm (2½×1½ ft).

B. speciosum see *Telekia speciosa*

CULTIVATION Plant in autumn or spring in full sun or part shade, preferably in poor soil – in fertile soils, plants produce leaves at the expense of flowers and become invasive.

PROPAGATION Divide plants or sow seed in spring or autumn.

PESTS AND DISEASES Usually trouble free.

Burnet see *Sanguisorba*
Burning bush see *Bassia scoparia*
   f. *tricophylla*, *Dictamnus*
Bush violet see *Browallia*
Busy lizzie see *Impatiens walleriana*
Butcher's broom see *Ruscus*

Butomus
Flowering rush
Butomaceae

Grown for its twisted, rush-like leaves and loose clusters of pale pink flowers, this deciduous, hardy perennial aquatic is the only species in the genus. Native to temperate Europe and Asia.

Butomus umbellatus♀ The upright, narrow, twisted leaves, 1.5 m (5 ft) long, have tapering tips. Bronze-green when young, they turn mid green. Each upright stem ends with a loose head, pale pink cup-shaped flower, borne from mid summer to

▲ *Butomus umbellatus*

early autumn. Each 3 cm (1¼ in) wide flower has 6 petals around dark red stamens. The reddish fruit appears in autumn. HEIGHT & SPREAD 1.5 m×1 m (5×3 ft).

CULTIVATION Plant in full sun in any fertile soil in water up to 25 cm (10 in) deep. For strong flowering, divide or replant annually.

PROPAGATION Sow seed in spring in pots standing in 2.5-5 cm (1-2 in) of water. Divide established plants in spring.

PESTS AND DISEASES Aphids can be a problem.

Buttercup see *Ranunculus*
Butterfly bush see *Buddleja davidii*
Butterwort see *Pinguicula*

Buxus
Box
Buxaceae

Buxus sempervirens

Small evergreen leaves, dense growth and tolerance of frequent clipping make box ideal for hedging and topiary. Dwarf parterre hedges are traditionally composed of box. The leaves are 1-3 cm (⅜-1¼ in) long and are opposite, oval and leathery. The flowers are inconspicuous but, in some species, they are scented. In the wild, trees and shrubs usually grow in shady places in woods, but as garden plants they will also tolerate full sun. The deep green glossy foliage contrasts well with bright flowers and gravel paths. Very slow growth and a long lifespan are characteristics of all 70 shrubs and trees in the genus. Most are clipped so that height and spread are rigidly controlled. The smaller plants can be grown in pots and make strong neat features in a formal design.

RECOMMENDED SPECIES AND VARIETIES

B. microphylla A very hardy compact shrub with a dense rounded habit. It has narrow leaves and is widely used for miniature hedges. It may be native to Japan. HEIGHT & SPREAD 40×30 cm (16×12 in) after 5 years, ultimately 1 m (3 ft) tall.

'Compacta' has smaller leaves and grows only 30 cm (12 in) in 30 years.

B. sempervirens♀ (common box) The small, multistemmed tree, a native of Britain, has dark green glossy leaves, broadly oblong with a notch at the apex. It seeds itself freely. It can be clipped as a hedge or free grown. HEIGHT & SPREAD 1.2 m×75 cm (4×2½ ft) after 5 years, ultimately 4 m (13 ft) high.

▲ *Buxus sempervirens*

▲ *Buxus sempervirens* 'Suffruticosa'

▲ *Buxus sempervirens* 'Elegantissima'

'Elegantissima'♀ is a compact bush with variegated cream and green leaves. 'Latifolia Macrophylla'♀ makes a large spreading bush whose small, broadly ovate leaves are dark green and shiny. 'Latifolia Maculata' is a dense compact shrub. Its long leaves are blotched with yellow and are most colourful in full sun. 'Suffruticosa'♀ is a small shrub traditionally used in formal gardens for edging flower-beds. The ovate leaves are a bright shining green. It is very dense and can be clipped hard every year.

CULTIVATION Plant in autumn or spring in any garden soil in full sun or part shade. For hedges, space plants 25-30 cm (10-12 in) tall at intervals of 30-38 cm (12-15 in). Cut back the upper third of leading shoots after planting or in spring to promote bushy growth.

PROPAGATION Take semi-ripe cuttings in summer. These are usually a by-product of clipping back plants.

PRUNING Clip hedges and topiary 2 or 3 times a year.

PESTS AND DISEASES Leaf deformities caused by sucking insects and fungal brown spots may be a minor nuisance.

Cabbage see p.736
Cabbage gum see *Eucalyptus pauciflora*
Cabbage tree see *Cordyline australis*
Cacti see p.106

Caladium
Araceae

Brightly patterned foliage makes these tender herbaceous perennials from tropical S America rewarding greenhouse, conservatory or indoor plants. The insignificant white flowers are normally removed to retain high-quality foliage.

RECOMMENDED SPECIES AND VARIETIES
C. bicolor (syn. *C. × hortulanum*) (angel's wings) The roughly triangular or heart-shaped leaves are mid green, splashed with

▼ *Caladium bicolor*

white, pink or red and may have coloured veins. The leaves are 15–45cm (6–18in) long. HEIGHT & SPREAD 90×75cm (36×30in).
   'Mrs Arno Nehrling' has white leaves with dark green veins and red ribs. 'Pink Beauty' has green leaves with pink marbled centres and prominent red ribs.
C. × hortulanum see *C. bicolor*
C. lindenii The arrow-shaped leaves are 15–45cm (6–18in) long and are dark green with white marked veins. HEIGHT & SPREAD 75×50cm (30×20in).
CULTIVATION Plant tubers in potting compost in early spring and keep indoors or under glass at a minimum of 18°C (64°F)

and high humidity. Place in partial shade but with enough light to maintain leaf colour. Water regularly in the growing season and feed from mid summer to early autumn. Dry plants off in autumn and over-winter tubers at a minimum of 13°C (55°F).
PROPAGATION Separate small tubers before replanting in spring. Large tubers can be divided into sections during spring.
PESTS AND DISEASES Greenfly, whitefly, red spider mite and mealy bug can attack.

Calamagrostis see GRASSES p.300

Calamintha
Calamint
Labiatae

calamintha nepeta

Profuse clusters of tiny flowers, attractive to bees and butterflies, provide a handsome display throughout summer on these aromatic, hardy herbaceous perennials. The two-lipped, tubular flowers are arranged in whorls on loose leafy spikes. The small, toothed mint-like leaves are oval or oblong. *Calamintha cretica* is a good choice for a rock garden and *C. nepeta* is suitable for planting in borders and herb gardens. *C. grandiflora* is best grown along pathways or in dappled shade.

RECOMMENDED SPECIES AND VARIETIES
C. cretica Small white flowers, about 1cm (⅜in) long, are carried from early to late summer. The roundish leaves, up to 1.5cm (½in) long, are covered with greyish hairs. Native to Crete, this woody-based plant forms a low symmetrical dome. HEIGHT & SPREAD 25×25cm (10×10in).
C. grandiflora Pink flowers, up to 4cm

▲ *Calamintha grandiflora* 'Variegata'

▲ *Calamintha nepeta*

(1½in) long, appear from early summer to mid autumn. The deep green, aromatic leaves, up to 8cm (3¼in) long, are rounded. This woody-based plant forms spreading patches. Native to central and S Europe. HEIGHT & SPREAD 40×45cm (16×18in).
   'Variegata' has cream-coloured leaves speckled with green.
C. nepeta (syn. *C. nepetoides*, *Satureja calamintha*) (lesser calamint) White, lilac or mauve flowers, 1.5cm (½in) long, appear on branching stems from mid summer to early autumn. The oval, greyish green leaves, up to 3cm (1¼in) long, are highly aromatic, especially when crushed. This bushy plant self-seeds freely. HEIGHT & SPREAD 50×45cm (20×18in).
   The flowers of ssp. *glandulosa* 'White Cloud' are white and those of ssp. *nepeta* 'Blue Cloud' are bluish mauve.
C. nepetoides see *C. nepeta*
CULTIVATION Plant in spring in well-drained, preferably alkaline soil choosing a position in full sun, although *C. grandiflora* prefers dappled shade.
PROPAGATION Sow seed under glass or divide clumps in spring. Take basal cuttings in late spring to early summer.
PESTS AND DISEASES Usually trouble free.

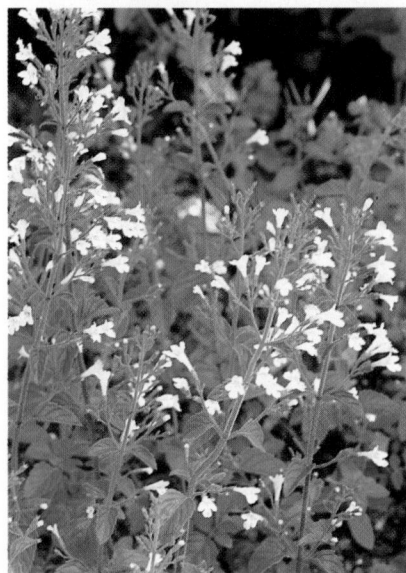

▲ *Calamintha nepeta* ssp. *glandulosa* 'White Cloud'

Calandrinia
Portulacaceae

These low-growing, fleshy-leaved plants are grown for their colourful, silky flowers in early and mid summer. These evergreen perennials are not frost hardy and in colder areas should be treated as half-hardy annuals or grown under glass. They also dislike excessive winter wet. The flowers have up to eight broad petals and a mass of stamens; they open in sunshine or bright light, but close in dull weather. The leaves form flat rosettes. Most species are from S America.

RECOMMENDED SPECIES AND VARIETIES
C. caespitosa Creamy flowers are borne singly on short stems, several flowers growing from the centre of each leaf rosette. Each flower is about 1.5 cm (½ in) across. Leaves are grey-green and narrow, broadest towards the tip, and 5 cm (2 in) long. This highly variable species also includes pink, red and orange-flowering varieties. HEIGHT & SPREAD 10×20 cm (4×8 in).
C. umbellata The cup-shaped flowers, 2 cm (¾ in) across, carried in short-stemmed clusters, are a satiny, rich dark red. Flowers bloom from mid to late summer. Each flower blooms for just 2 days. Leaves are grey-green, hairy, linear and up to 4 cm (1½ in) long. The plant's habit varies from sprawling to compact. It can be grown as a biennial outdoors in the warmer parts of Britain. HEIGHT & SPREAD 15×10 cm (6×4 in).

▼ *Calandrinia umbellata*

CULTIVATION Plant in spring in a light sandy soil, in a sunny, sheltered site. Protect plants from winter wet by covering them with a cloche or pane of glass. Alternatively, grow in pots of John Innes No. 1 in a greenhouse or conservatory with a minimum temperature of 5°C (41°F).
PROPAGATION Sow seed in spring under glass at a minimum of 18°C (64°F).
PESTS AND DISEASES Aphids attack emerging leaves in late winter and early spring.

Calathea
Marantaceae

The intricately marked leaves of these tropical evergreen perennials make them ideal houseplants. Their need for soft light, high temperatures and humidity can, however, limit suitable situations. A shaded, warm conservatory or greenhouse or a warm room that does not receive direct sunlight are probably best. Standing plants on gravel trays will improve humidity. Most calatheas have inconspicuous flowers. Native to rainforest floors in S America.

RECOMMENDED SPECIES AND VARIETIES
C. makoyana (peacock plant, cathedral windows) Light green leaves up to 25 cm (10 in) long with darker oval blotches have closely spaced, fine lines radiating from the midrib. Their purple-tinted underside is often visible because the paddle-shaped leaves are held upright on narrow stems. HEIGHT & SPREAD 60×30 cm (2×1 ft).
C. roseopicta Dark stripes stretch out from the midrib to a cream line just short of the edges of the light green leaves of this compact species. The highly patterned leaves are oval, up to 18 cm (7 in) long and carried on short stalks. They tend to lie horizontally. HEIGHT & SPREAD 25×30 cm (10×12 in).
C. zebrina (zebra plant) Vivid, fresh green leaves, up to 45 cm (18 in) long, have regular dark stripes spreading out from the midrib. Their surfaces have a velvety

▼ *Calathea makoyana*

▼ *Calathea roseopicta*

appearance and the underside, a purple hue. The height and spread given is for plants in a conservatory border; those in pots would probably be smaller. HEIGHT & SPREAD 60×30 cm (2×1 ft).

CULTIVATION Grow in pots of John Innes No. 2 and keep indoors or under glass at a constant temperature of at least 20°C (68°F) and reasonable humidity during the growing season. Maintain a minimum temperature of 13°C (55°F) in winter. Ensure plants are grown in soft light; direct sun is harmful. Feed little and often. Keep compost moist but not wet and somewhat drier in cooler months. Avoid dry air, draughts and sudden temperature changes. Strongly growing plants form good-sized clumps, which may need annual repotting in spring.
PROPAGATION Divide in spring.
PESTS AND DISEASES Red spider mite can be troublesome.

Calceolaria
Slipper flower, slipperwort
Scrophulariaceae

Calceolaria uniflora

Vividly coloured and unusual pouched flowers are borne by these plants from Central and S America. This genus includes biennials and evergreen perennials and subshrubs that vary in hardiness. There are low-growing hardy perennials that are excellent plants for rock gardens or raised beds and troughs. There are also less hardy calceolarias that can be grown as summer bedding plants or in pots indoors or under glass.

RECOMMENDED SPECIES AND VARIETIES
C. biflora (syn. *C. plantaginea*) Small yellow flowers, up to 2 cm (¾ in) long, appear in clusters in summer. The softly hairy, oval leaves, up to 7.5 cm (3 in) long, are borne in neat basal rosettes. A hardy

▼ *Calceolaria biflora*

C

evergreen perennial. HEIGHT & SPREAD 25×20 cm (10×8 in).

C. falklandica Pale yellow flowers, speckled with purple in the throat and up to 1.5 cm (½ in) long, appear in summer. The mid green, oblong, hairy leaves grow to 10 cm (4 in) long. A hardy evergreen perennial. HEIGHT & SPREAD 25×20 cm (10×8 in).

C. **Herbeohybrida Group** Red, orange, yellow or white flowers often with darker spots or blotches and up to 8 cm (3¼ in) long are borne in spring and summer. The oval, mid green, softly hairy leaves are about 10 cm (4 in) long. A tender bushy biennial commonly grown as a pot plant or for summer bedding. HEIGHT & SPREAD 30×25 cm (12×10 in).

Anytime Series bears many 5 cm (2 in) long flowers that bloom at any time of the year just 4 months after sowing. It grows 20 cm (8 in) tall. **'Jewel Cluster'** has early, spotted flowers and grows to 28 cm (11 in).

C. integrifolia♀ (syn. *C. rugosa*) Clusters of rounded, bright yellow flowers, 1.5 cm (½ in) wide, are borne in late summer. The rough, grey-green leaves, up to 10 cm (4 in) long, are lance-shaped. A half-hardy evergreen sub-shrub, usually grown as annual. HEIGHT & SPREAD 1.2 m×60 cm (4×2 ft).

▲ *Calceolaria integrifolia* var. *angustifolia*

The flower clusters of var. *angustifolia*♀ are more elongated. **'Sunshine'**♀ bears dense clusters of bright yellow flowers, up to 2.5 cm (1 in) wide, in mid summer. It reaches a height of 25 cm (10 in).

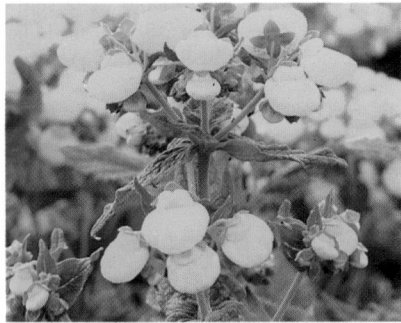

▲ *Calceolaria integrifolia* 'Sunshine'

C. plantaginea see *C. biflora*
C. rugosa see *C. integrifolia*
C. tenella Clusters of bright yellow flowers, 1 cm (⅜ in) across, with a few red marks appearing in summer. This creeping ever-

green perennial has oval, mid green, hairy leaves up to 1 cm (⅜ in) long. Will not withstand prolonged freezing weather. HEIGHT & SPREAD 8×30 cm (3¼×12 in).

C. uniflora The pendent summer flowers, up to 2.5 cm (1 in) long, are yellow with brown mottling and a white band on the large lower pouch. This mat-forming, often short-lived, hardy evergreen perennial has many deep green leaf rosettes made up of elliptical shiny leaves up to 4 cm (1½ in) long. HEIGHT & SPREAD 7.5×20 cm (3×8 in).

CULTIVATION Plant hardy evergreen perennials in a gritty, humus-rich soil and never allow to dry out. They require a bright position but dislike scorching sun. Plant *C. integrifolia* in a sheltered position in full sun; overwinter under glass and bed out in late spring. Grow *C.* Herbeohybrida Group in pots of John Innes No. 2 and keep indoors or in a heated greenhouse or conservatory.

PROPAGATION Sow the seed of hardy evergreen perennials in a coldframe in autumn or early spring or take semi-ripe cuttings in summer. Take softwood cuttings of *C. integrifolia* in late spring or summer. Sow seed of *C. integrifolia* under glass in late winter. Sow seed of *C.* Herbeohybrida Group in gentle heat in spring or late summer; the seed of Anytime Series can be sown at any time except mid summer.

PESTS AND DISEASES Aphids and slugs can be a problem. Grey mould infects old flowers and leaves, especially of the hardy evergreen perennials.

Calendula
Marigold
Compositae

Calendula officinalis

These brightly coloured hardy annuals are easily cultivated, fast growing and long flowering, with blooms that last from late spring to late summer. Flower colours range through yellow, orange and apricot to cream. *Calendula officinalis* and the many varieties developed from it are the only plants of this genus usually grown.

RECOMMENDED SPECIES AND VARIETIES
C. officinalis (pot marigold) Branched stems carry single orange flowers, up to 7 cm (2¾ in) across, among thick aromatic leaves that are lance-shaped and pale green. HEIGHT & SPREAD 60×60 cm (2×2 ft).

The flowers of cultivated varieties are semidouble or double. **Art Shades Mixed** has semidouble flowers and reaches a height of 60 cm (2 ft). The densely branching

▲ *Calendula officinalis*

'Fiesta Gitana'♀ is a dwarf plant usually reaching less than 30 cm (12 in) tall. It is available in orange or yellow or in mixed colours. **Pacific Beauty Mixed** grows to a height of 60 cm (2 ft) and has fully double flowers in lemon and orange shades. **'Radio'** has double flowers with orange rolled petals. **'Touch of Red'** grows to a height of 45 cm (18 in) and is distinguished from other varieties by the red flushing of the oranges, creams and bright yellows contained in the mixture.

▲ *Calendula officinalis* 'Fiesta Gitana'

CULTIVATION Plant in spring in full sun or partial shade in any garden soil, although moist, fertile soil is not desirable since it encourages excessive leaf growth at the expense of flowering. Deadhead regularly.

PROPAGATION Sow seed in mid spring where the plant is to flower. Further sowing in late spring and early summer maintains a succession of flowers. Alternatively, sow seed in an unheated greenhouse from early spring onwards. Harden off and plant out from mid spring.

Calendulas can also be grown as greenhouse pot plants for early flowering. Sow seed in late summer and grow the plants on in 13-18 cm (5-7 in) pots. Given a minimum temperature of 7°C (45°F), they will flower by early spring.

PESTS AND DISEASES Plants are susceptible to powdery mildew and aphids.

Calico bush see *Kalmia latifolia*
Calico flower see *Aristolochia littoralis*
California lilac see *Ceanothus*

Calla
Bog arum
Araceae

Showy flowers and shiny heart-shaped leaves make this plant ideal for the edge of a pond or a bog garden. A hardy creeping perennial, deciduous or semi-evergreen, the plant grows in wet soil or water up to

15 cm (6 in) deep. There is only one species in the genus. Other plants called callas belong to the genus *Zantedeschia*. Native to N Europe and N America.

Calla palustris Each flower has a papery, white spathe, a leaf-like structure, and a spadix, an upright greenish spike that bears the insignificant true flowers and which emerges from the spathe. The spathe is up to 6 cm (2½ in) across and the spadix 2.5 cm (1 in) tall. They appear in late spring to early summer. The spathe has a greenish flush in spring. Red or deep orange poisonous berries are seen on the spadix in autumn. The dark green leaves are up to 8 cm (3¼ in) long. HEIGHT & SPREAD 25×30 cm (10×12 in).

CULTIVATION Plant in spring, at the edge of a pool in a basket filled with heavy, clay-loam soil or aquatic planting compost. Cover the compost with pea gravel. The plant prefers full sun, but will tolerate a little shade. Feed with aquatic fertiliser in spring.

PROPAGATION Divide adult plants every 2-3 years in spring. Take stem cuttings in spring and root in trays of mud. Sow seed in spring, in trays of mud in a coldframe.

PESTS AND DISEASES Usually trouble free.

Callicarpa
Beauty berry
Verbenaceae

Callicarpa bodinieri var. giraldii 'Profusion'

Eye-catching clusters of jewel-like fruit adorn these deciduous shrubs. Found in vivid shades of purple and white, the berries have a pearly lustre and combine with yellow to purple leaves to provide bold autumn colour. The fruit are just 3 mm (⅛ in) across, and appear in early autumn, often lasting well after leaf-fall. They are preceded by tiny, star-shaped flowers. The oval leaves have pointed tips and toothed edges. Plants need a sunny, sheltered position and may not survive outside where winters are prolonged or severe.

RECOMMENDED SPECIES AND VARIETIES

C. bodinieri Clusters of downy, lilac flowers appear in mid summer and are followed by dense clumps of violet fruit. Covered in fine hairs at first, the leaves become smooth and are 5-12 cm (2-4¾ in) long. HEIGHT & SPREAD 2×2 m (6½×6½ ft) after 5 years, ultimately 3 m (10 ft) tall.

The flowers of var. *giraldii* are less downy. **'Profusion'**♀ has pink flowers and bronzed, purple spring leaves that turn green in summer before turning purplish

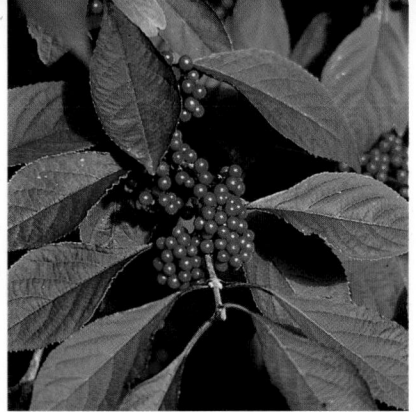

⚘ *Callicarpa bodinieri var. giraldii*

again in autumn. It reaches a height of 2 m (6½ ft) and a spread of 1.2 m (4 ft).

C. japonica **'Leucocarpa'** The white, late-summer flowers are followed by white fruit. The hairless leaves are 7-12 cm (2¾-4¾ in) long. This species is slightly less hardy than *C. bodinieri*. HEIGHT & SPREAD 1.5×1.5 m (5×5 ft) after 5 years (also its ultimate size).

CULTIVATION Plant in autumn or spring in a sunny, sheltered spot in fertile, well-drained loam. Plant in groups to ensure cross-pollination and, therefore, numerous fruit. Mulch plants in late autumn.

PROPAGATION Take semi-ripe heeled cuttings or raise natural varieties from seed.

PRUNING Cut back old and damaged wood and straggly branches in spring, just after new growth commences.

PESTS AND DISEASES Usually trouble free.

Callistemon
Bottlebrush
Myrtaceae

Callistemon citrinus 'splendens'

Minute flowers with long, colourful stamens form bold tufted spikes on these sun-loving, evergreen shrubs or small trees in summer. The cylindrical flowerheads are mostly in shades of yellow and red and measure 5-10 cm (2-4 in) long. The rather leathery leaves, up to 12 cm (4¾ in) long, are narrow and pointed. Of those recommended only *Callistemon salignus* is reasonably hardy and even this needs a sheltered site in colder areas. Others are suitable only for sheltered warm gardens or greenhouses and conservatories. Those grown outside need acid soil. Native to Australia.

RECOMMENDED SPECIES AND VARIETIES

C. citrinus Profuse flower spikes, usually with bright crimson stamens appear in early to mid summer. The grey-green leaves are hairy when young. This shrub is hardy only in mild areas and in a sheltered site. It makes

⚘ *Callistemon citrinus*

an excellent greenhouse or conservatory plant. HEIGHT & SPREAD 2×2 m (6½×6½ ft) after 5 years, ultimately 5 m (16 ft) tall.

'Splendens'♀ has scarlet flowers and grows to a height and spread of 2 m (6½ ft).

C. linearis♀ Red flower spikes appear from late spring to autumn. The linear leaves are dark green. This shrub is hardy only in mild, sheltered gardens. HEIGHT & SPREAD 1.8×1.8 m (6×6 ft) after 5 years, ultimately 3 m (10 ft) tall.

C. salignus♀ The willow-like leaves are reddish while young, becoming grey-green. Pale yellow flower spikes are carried in early summer. This fairly hardy shrub or small tree withstands all but the coldest winters. HEIGHT & SPREAD 3×2 m (10×6½ ft) after 5 years, ultimately 10 m (33 ft).

C. viminalis **'Captain Cook'**♀ A low-growing shrub with spreading to weeping branches. Large red flower spikes are produced abundantly from spring to summer. The leaves are mid green. It is suitable only for frost-free gardens or growing under glass. HEIGHT & SPREAD 1.2×1.2 m (4×4 ft) after 5 years, ultimately 2 m (6½ ft) tall.

CULTIVATION Outdoors, plant in spring in moist but well-drained, preferably acid, soil. Choose a sheltered position in full sun. Alternatively, grow in pots of John Innes No. 2 and keep in a frost-free greenhouse or conservatory in good light.

PROPAGATION Take semi-ripe cuttings in summer or sow seed under glass in early summer and keep the compost moist.

PRUNING None normally required but can be cut back in summer to produce more compact plants.

PESTS AND DISEASES Usually trouble free.

❧ *Callistemon viminalis 'Captain Cook'*

CACTI

Nature's tough survivors

UNUSUAL SHAPES AND OFTEN DAZZLING FLOWERS
MAKE CACTI FASCINATING AND REWARDING PLANTS
TO GROW INDOORS AND IN A GREENHOUSE

With forms that range from tall and statuesque columns to cushions or dangling tentacles, cacti make original sculptural plants for the house, conservatory or greenhouse.

Belonging to the Cactaceae family, cacti are succulents and have fleshy stems. They are distinguished from other succulents by their areoles, the pad-like shoots from which flowers, new growth, wool and spines develop.

Most cacti have spines, which can be straight, curved or hooked, long or short, stout and sharp or hair-like. The central spines emerge from the middle of the areole and are usually stronger and larger than the radial spines, which rise from the outer part.

Although most cacti flower regularly, those that grow very large in the wild are unlikely to bloom when cultivated. The flowers are generally unstalked and funnel-shaped and may be any colour but blue. They are usually unscented but some of those that bloom at night emit a powerful scent to attract pollinating bats and moths. Small fleshy fruits develop after flowering; these appear on only a few cultivated species.

Cacti are native to the Americas, except for *Rhipsalis baccifera*, a species mainly from Sri Lanka and humid parts of Africa. None of the recommended plants are hardy. There are two distinct types of cacti: desert cacti and rain-forest cacti.

RECOMMENDED PLANTS

DESERT CACTI

Most cacti are desert plants and cope with extreme heat and drought by storing moisture in fleshy stems, roots or leaves. The stems are often globular or columnar and usually have vertical ribs, which enable the cactus to expand as it gains moisture and contract as it dries. The areoles may be mounted along the ribs, on conical or pyramidal protrusions, called tubercles, or over the surface of the stems.

Acanthocalycium

Closely related to *Echinopsis*, these plants are distinguished by the sharp scales that grow on the flower tubes.
A. spiniflorum (syn. *Echinopsis spiniflora*) This globular or cylindrical yellow-green cactus

▲ DESERT GARDEN Echinopsis *and* Echinocactus *make a fine display with other succulents.*

has sharp ribs and yellow or brown spines with dark tips. After 3-5 years, mauve, pink or

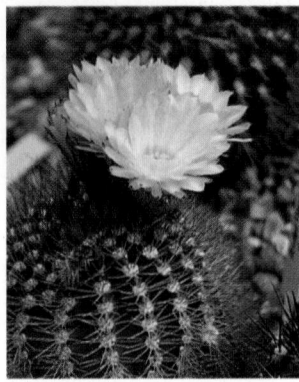

▲ *Acanthocalycium spiniflorum*

white trumpet-shaped flowers, 4-5 cm (1½-2 in) across, appear in summer. HEIGHT & SPREAD 10×8 cm (4×3¼ in) in 5 years.

Aporocactus

Plants in this genus can be epiphytic, an unusual form for desert cacti.
A. flagelliformis The slender, bright green, pendulous stems are ribbed and covered with short yellow-brown spines. In spring, pink trumpet-shaped flowers, which are 5-8 cm (2-3¼ in) long, appear along the

▲ *Aporocactus flagelliformis*

stems. They are followed by small red berries. The plant suits a hanging basket but its fast-growing stems may need cutting back regularly. HEIGHT & SPREAD 70×40 cm (28×16 in) after 5 years.

Astrophytum

The globular bodies of plants in this genus are divided by a small number of ribs into wide segments, rather like an orange.

The cacti are slow-growing and become elongated with age.
A. myriostigma♀ (bishop's cap) The grey-green body of this cacti is covered with small woolly scales and has no spines. After 4 years, funnel-shaped bright yellow flowers are borne

▲ *Astrophytum myriostigma*

in spring and summer. They are 5 cm (2 in) across and grow close to the centre of the plant. HEIGHT & SPREAD 6×6 cm (2½×2½ in) after 5 years.

Cephalocereus

Tall, and slow-growing, these columnar plants are hairy and rarely branch.
C. senilis (old man cactus) Long white hairs grow in tangles from the areoles, obscuring the ribs and spines. In cultivation, the plant is unlikely to bear flowers. To encourage a shaggy look, position the cactus in a window or greenhouse where it receives plenty of sunshine. To keep the hair white, clean occasionally with a warm detergent solution, using a soft

▼ *Cephalocereus senilis*

brush, and rinse with water. Keep the potting mixture covered to avoid soaking it with water. HEIGHT & SPREAD 10×5 cm (4×2 in) after 5 years.

Echinocactus

The spherical to shortly columnar plants of this genus have prominent ribs and attractive spines. Their crowns, sparsely covered in wool, bear rings of yellow or pink flowers when the plants are mature.
E. grusonii (golden barrel, mother-in-law's seat) The barrel-shaped, mid green body of this slow-growing cactus has

▲ *Echinocactus grusonii*

sharp ribs covered in distinctive golden spines. After 30 years, the diameter of the plant reaches 38 cm (15 in) and it produces small, golden, cup-shaped flowers in summer. HEIGHT & SPREAD 12×10 cm (4¾×4 in) after 5 years.

Echinopsis

After 3 years, these ribbed, globular to columnar plants, commonly known as sea-urchin cacti, produce beautiful flowers of various colours.
E. chamaecereus (peanut cactus) Branching readily, the plant forms a cluster of small,

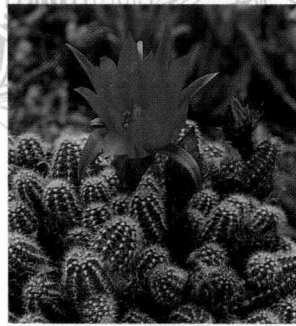
▲ *Echinopsis chamaecereus*

slender, spreading stems that are pale green and have short white spines. During late spring and early summer, scarlet funnel-shaped flowers, 3 cm (1¼ in) long, appear along the sides of the stems. HEIGHT & SPREAD 10×20 cm (4×8 in) after 5 years.
E. oxygona Globular at first, this cactus becomes elongated with age and can form clusters.

▲ *Echinopsis oxygona*

Dark brown spines cover the mid green body. After 3-4 years, fragrant, pink, trumpet-shaped flowers, 17-25 cm (6¾×10 in) long, appear on the crown in summer. Opening at dusk, they wilt the next afternoon. To promote flowering, remove the offsets in the plant's early years. HEIGHT & SPREAD 10×8 cm (4×3¼ in) after 5 years.
E. spiniflora see
Acanthocalycium spiniflorum

Espostoa

After 10 years, these cacti produce beards, called pseudocephalia. The beard grows on one side of the upper part of the ribbed columnar stem.

▲ *Espostoa lanata*

E. lanata (Peruvian old man cactus) Fine, radial spines clothe this cactus in a white wool, through which long red-tipped

central spines protrude. At 10 years or more, plants may form side branches low down on the main stem. HEIGHT & SPREAD 10×5 cm (4×2 in) after 5 years.

Ferocactus

Commonly known as barrel cacti, plants in this genus have dramatic, curved spines and rounded shapes.
F. latispinus (crow's claw) Straw-coloured radial spines surround red central spines, the lowest of which is broad and fiercely hooked. The round or

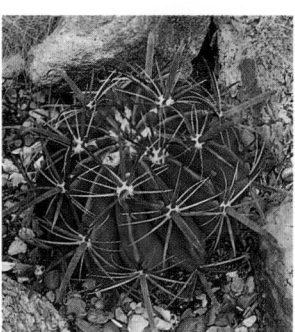
▲ *Ferocactus latispinus*

barrel-shaped, grey-green body has prominent ribs. After 10-15 years, white, pink or purple, funnel-shaped flowers, 3 cm (1¼ in) long, appear close to the centre of the crown in spring or autumn. HEIGHT & SPREAD 5×10 cm (2×4 in) after 5 years.

Mammillaria

Plants of this genus, which is the largest in the cactus family, are known as pincushion cacti. They are mainly small, often clump-forming and flower reliably, producing small, funnel-shaped blooms. The areoles are mounted on tubercles.
M. bocasana♀ (snowball cactus) The blue-green globular body of this small, clump-forming cactus is covered in fine, white, radial spines which are clustered in groups on each tubercle. The central spines are red-brown and hooked at their tips. The flowers, which are 1.5 cm (½ in) long, are borne in a ring in late spring and summer. The petals are yellow to white, with a pink or brownish stripe running down the centre. They are followed by long red berries. HEIGHT & SPREAD 6×6 cm (2½×2½ in) in 5 years.

▲ *Mammillaria bombycina*

M. bombycina♀ The cylindrical green body of this clustering plant is swathed in fine, white down, through which yellow, red or brown hooked spines protrude. When the cactus is 4-5 years old, light carmine to pink flowers, up to 1.5 cm (½ in) in length, appear in a ring round the crown during late spring and summer. It has red or pink berries. HEIGHT & SPREAD 10×10 cm (4×4 in) in 5 years.
M. plumosa♀ This species forms a low cushion covered in fine and feathery, white radial spines. Off-white flowers, up to 1.5 cm (½ in) in length, are borne from mid autumn to

▲ *Mammillaria plumosa*

early spring, as long as the temperature remains above 5°C (41°F). If the temperature falls below this, the flowers will open in spring. HEIGHT & SPREAD 10×10 cm (4×4 in).
M. zeilmanniana♀ After 1 or 2 years, many pink to carmine blooms, which are up to 2 cm (¾ in) long, are borne in spring. This globular or oval, dark green plant may form clusters. White and frequently hair-like radial spines surround the

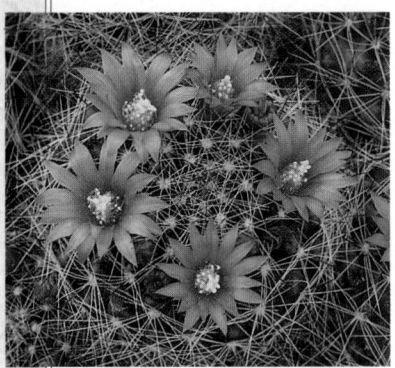

▲ *Mammillaria zeilmanniana*

stouter, brownish, hooked central spines. HEIGHT & SPREAD 10×17 cm (4×6¾ in) in 5 years.

Notocactus see *Parodia*

Opuntia

Plants in this large genus usually have jointed stems, comprising cylindrical or flattened pads. Areoles are scattered over the stem surfaces and have fine barbed bristles, called glochids. Most species also have spines.

O. basilaris The grey-green stems have egg-shaped to round segments, 10-20 cm (4-8 in) long. They may appear velvety and are often red around the areoles. The glochids are reddish-brown. Purple to red, bowl-shaped flowers, which are 5-8 cm (2-3¼ in) wide, appear from late spring to early autumn. HEIGHT & SPREAD 30×30 cm (12×12 in) in 5 years.

▲ *Opuntia basilaris*

O. cylindrica The bright green columnar stem has diamond-shaped tubercles, and yellow spines and glochids. The plant, which rarely flowers, will form branches if the top of a stem is cut off. Small cylindrical leaves appear briefly on the stem ends. HEIGHT & SPREAD 30×20 cm (12×8 in) in 5 years.

O. microdasys (teddy-bear cactus, bunny's ears) Velvety, pale yellow glochids, which are particularly fine and sharp, grow from the closely spaced

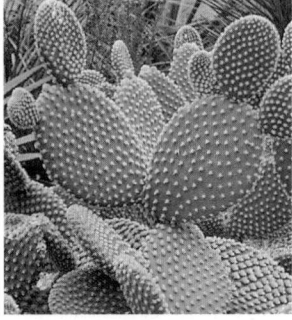

▲ *Opuntia microdasys*

areoles. Mid green pads are 8-15 cm (3¼-6 in) long and round to oval in outline. The pale yellow, bowl-shaped flowers are produced rarely. They are 4-5 cm (1½-2 in) wide and appear in spring and summer. HEIGHT & SPREAD 40×30 cm (16×12 in) in 5 years.

Parodia

These low-growing, ribbed or tuberculate cacti have dense spines and many flower readily.

▲ *Parodia haselbergii*

P. haselbergii (syn. *Notocactus haselbergii*) This grey-green globular cactus has clusters of glossy white spines. In spring and summer, orange-red, funnel-shaped blooms, which are 1-1.5 cm (⅜-½ in) long, appear on the bristly crown. HEIGHT & SPREAD 6×6 cm (2½×2½ in) after 5 years.

P. leninghausii (syn. *Notocactus leninghausii*) (golden ball cactus, Goldfinger) The crown of this short pale green columnar plant slopes towards the sun. The bristly spines are golden yellow

▲ *Parodia leninghausii*

and up to 4 cm (1½ in) long. After 5-10 years, bright yellow, funnel-shaped flowers, which are up to 3 cm (1¼ in) long, are produced from the centre of the crown during the summer. HEIGHT & SPREAD 12×8 cm (4¾×3¼ in) in 5 years.

P. mammulosa (syn. *Notocactus mammulosus*) The dark green globular body of this fast-growing cactus is often flat on top with a woolly crown. The radial spines are creamy white and the longer central spines are brown to grey. The yellow, funnel-shaped flowers, 4-6 cm (1½-2½ in) across, have eye-catching red stigmas and appear during spring and summer. HEIGHT & SPREAD 8×8 cm (3¼×3¼ in) in 5 years.

Rebutia

Cacti of this genus are usually the first to flower in spring.

▲ *Rebutia minuscula*

R. minuscula Orange or red, funnel-shaped blooms, 3 cm (1¼ in) long, are borne in spring and early summer. They grow from the lower parts of globular dark green, tuberculate stems, which form clusters. Short white radials surround brown-tipped central spines, 5 mm (¼ in) long. HEIGHT & SPREAD 4×4 cm (1½×1½ in) in 5 years.

GROWING DESERT CACTI

CULTIVATION Desert cacti need plenty of sunlight and some heat in winter. A well-ventilated cool greenhouse is an ideal site, but they can also be grown indoors on windowsills. If the light is one-sided, turn the cacti regularly to prevent distorted growth.

Use a good, well-drained compost, such as John Innes No. 2. During growth, water plants generously, barely allowing the surface of the compost to dry out between waterings. Use rainwater if possible, or cooled boiled water, as hard tapwater can prevent nutrient uptake. Apply a cactus feed with every second watering. In early autumn, water less frequently until by mid autumn the compost is dry.

Allow cacti to become dormant by overwintering them in a cool greenhouse, an enclosed porch or unheated spare room, leaving them unwatered. If the temperature is above 10°C (50°F) they should be watered very sparingly. In spring, mist dormant plants and start light watering a week later.

Repot cacti in spring, at least every two years. Wear thick gloves or fold newspaper round the body to protect your hands from the spines. Sprinkle a layer of fine pea gravel or granite chippings on the top of the compost to help to distribute water evenly. Water plants lightly after potting.

PROPAGATION Take cuttings of branching or segmented cacti by removing a branch or segment at the joint with a sharp knife. On non-branching or columnar cacti, cut a section at least 5 cm (2 in) long cleanly from the top of the plant. Although this will spoil the plant's appearance, new shoots eventually sprout from the scar and may in turn be taken as cuttings. To propagate clustering cacti, such as *Echinopsis* and *Mammillaria*, cut off the offsets with a sharp knife.

Leave the fresh cuttings in a warm, dry place until the wounds harden. Then stand the cuttings upright in small pots, half-filled with compost and covered with a thin layer of fine grit. Top the pots up to the rim with grit. Large cuttings may need staking.

Offsets of some cacti, including *Echinopsis oxygona*, produce roots while still attached to the parent. These offsets are easily detached and the wounds tend to dry quickly.

All cacti can be propagated from seed. Fill pots that are at least 5 cm (2 in) in diameter with finely sieved John Innes seed compost. Scatter the seeds on top of the compost and stand the pot in water until the surface of the compost appears moist. Add a fungicide to the water to reduce the risk of damping-off. Then sprinkle a thin layer of fine grit over the compost. Place the pot in a propagator or cover it with a clear plastic bag and leave it in light shade, maintaining a temperature between 19°C (66°F) and 25°C (77°F) until the seeds germinate, usually within 2–3 weeks.

One year after germination, remove the pot from the propagator or plastic bag and place it in a bright position, such as a windowsill or greenhouse, but out of direct sunlight. Prick out seedlings when they become crowded, handling them carefully to avoid damage to roots.

PESTS AND DISEASES Desert cacti are prone to fungal diseases and rots caused by excessive watering, humidity or poorly drained compost. Prevention by good culture is important as these diseases are difficult to eradicate. If plants are affected, apply a systemic fungicide.

Mealy bugs may be a problem. Counter attacks by brushing adult insects with surgical spirit, using a small paint brush, or apply a systemic insecticide. Root mealy bugs and red spider mites can also affect cacti.

RAIN-FOREST CACTI

Most rain-forest cacti are epiphytes, living in pockets of leaf-mould in hollows of trees and other large plants. Their stems are designed to help the plant to absorb the maximum amount of light. They are jointed with flattened segments or are long, trailing growths that are flattened or cylindrical. The areoles are sited in notches along the edges of the stems and are naked or have small bristles.

Some of the largest of all cactus flowers are produced by rain-forest cacti, some of which bloom in mid winter. They are good plants for hanging baskets.

Disocactus

Plants of this genus are known as orchid cacti because of their large, showy flowers. Their mid green main stems are cylindrical and the side stems are flattened.
D. nelsonii♀ This freely branching plant has pendent, slightly toothed side stems.

▲ *Disocactus nelsonii*

Its purple-pink, funnel-shaped flowers appear in spring and early summer. HEIGHT & SPREAD 60×30 cm (2×1 ft) in 5 years.

There are many disocactus hybrids, which are similar in appearance to *D. nelsonii*. 'Fortuna' has salmon-pink flowers; those of 'Ignescens' are fiery red; 'J.T.Barber' has pale orange blooms; and 'Reward' flowers have yellow-white inner petals and deeper yellow outer petals.

Epiphyllum

These cacti have luxuriant flowers, and flattened, leaf-like stems with a trailing habit. Spines are almost non-existent.

▲ *Epiphyllum anguliger*

E. anguliger (fishbone cactus) Scented, white or cream funnel-shaped flowers, which are 15 cm (6 in) long, are borne in late spring and summer on flattened, deeply notched, mid green stems. HEIGHT & SPREAD 70×45 cm (28×18 in)

Rhipsalis

The pendulous stems of these cacti can be rounded, thin and interlacing; rounded and segmented; or flat and strap-like.
R. pilocarpa Slender, rounded, segmented stems are dark green, tinged with purple and clothed in fine white spines. When the stems reach between 12 cm (4¾ in) and 15 cm (6 in) in length, they branch profusely. Small, pink-white or cream-coloured flowers are borne near the stem tips between autumn

▲ *Rhipsalis pilocarpa*

and spring. The bright red fruits are covered in pale bristles. HEIGHT & SPREAD 20×20 cm (8×8 in) after 5 years.

Schlumbergera

These reliably flowering, spineless cacti provide bright flushes of pink, red or orange flowers in winter, hence their common name of Christmas cacti. The mid to deep green stems are composed of short, leaf-like segments, which are up to 4 cm (1½ in) long and 3 cm (1¼ in) wide. The ruffled, trumpet-shaped flowers last for up to a week or more. Most cultivated schlumbergeras are hybrids or cultivars. The cacti grow to 15 cm (6 in) in 5 years.

'Firecracker' has bright red flowers; 'Gold Charm' has pale orange blooms that are tinged maroon; and those of 'Lilac Beauty' are pale lilac with deeper petal tips and edges.

▲ *Schlumbergera* 'Lilac Beauty'

GROWING RAIN-FOREST CACTI

CULTIVATION Rain-forest cacti are best grown in a warm greenhouse but can also be grown on a sunny indoor windowsill. They require a well-aerated and moisture-retentive compost – an ericaceous compost is best. They need high humidity. Mist them daily, preferably with rainwater to avoid spotting the stems and damp down the floor of a warm greenhouse. In summer the plants benefit from being moved outside to a sheltered position in filtered sunlight. Water epiphytic cacti all year round, but allow the compost to dry out between waterings. In autumn, bring the plants back into the house and position them away from direct sunlight in a minimum temperature of 12°C (54°F). Water sparingly until mid winter to ensure flower buds develop.
PROPAGATION Rain-forest cacti are propagated by seed. Some, including all the recommended plants, can also be propagated from cuttings taken from segments or branches. (See facing page.)
PESTS AND DISEASES Mealy bugs are the main pest.

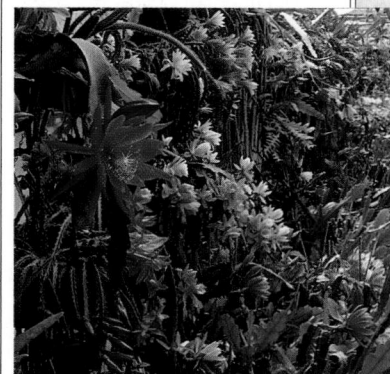

▲ JUNGLE FLOWERS *Epiphytic* Disocactus *hybrids produce a profusion of magnificent blooms.*

C

Callistephus
China aster
Compositae

Daisy-like flowers in bright colours, long-lasting when cut, have established this annual as a favourite. The single species flowers from late summer to early autumn, later than many other bedding plants. For cut flowers, grow taller varieties, in a mixed border. Smaller varieties make good bedding or container plants. Native to China.

Callistephus chinensis The varieties of this almost hardy annual have replaced the species in general cultivation. The species has single flowers, white to violet, with yellow centres. The flowers, very freely produced, are borne singly on branching, leafy stems. The leaves, arranged alternately on the stems, are dark green, oval, toothed, slightly hairy and up to 8 cm (3¼ in) long. HEIGHT & SPREAD 80×40 cm (32×16 in).

The listed varieties are in mixed colours and double-flowered, unless stated otherwise. Varieties sold as seed of mixed colours usually include the colours blue, purple, lavender, pink, red, cream and white. Flowers are 4–12 cm (1½–4¾ in) wide.

TALLER VARIETIES
'Andrella' has single flowers and reaches a height of 75 cm (30 in). 'Duchess', with large chrysanthemum-like flowers, the petals curving inwards, and 'Ostrich Plume', with long, feathery petals that curve backwards, are both 60 cm (24 in) tall. 'Matsumoto' with many tightly formed flowers, grows to a height of 75 cm (30 in).

SHORTER VARIETIES
Plants 40–45 cm (16–18 in) tall, spreading to 30 cm (12 in), are primarily valuable as garden plants, but still have stems long enough for cut flowers. 'All Change Blue' has dark blue flowers and 'All Change Red' has red flowers, both with white tips to the petals. The cultivar 'Pompon Mixed' has button-like flowers.

DWARF VARIETIES
Choose these cultivars – which grow to no more than 40 cm (16 in) tall and spread to about 30 cm (12 in) – for beds, containers or the front of a border. 'Dwarf Comet' is an upright plant, up to 20 cm (8 in) tall, which blooms a few weeks earlier than other cultivars. 'Lilliput' has button-like pompon flowers and grows to 30–40 cm (12–16 in) tall. 'Milady', to 30 cm (12 in) tall, bears flowers with incurving petals. 'Pinocchio',

▼ *Callistephus chinensis* 'Dwarf Comet'

▲ *Callistephus chinensis* 'Milady'

up to 20 cm (8 in) tall, has a compact, round habit. 'Teisa Stars' has quilled petals and an ultimate height of 25 cm (10 in).

CULTIVATION Plant in reasonably fertile soil in a sheltered, sunny spot, as soon as all risk of hard frosts has passed. Deadhead regularly to maintain the production of new flowers. Support taller varieties.

PROPAGATION Sow seed in early spring at 10°C (50°F), hardening the plants off before planting out.

PESTS AND DISEASES Aphids attack young plants. The soil-borne disease callistephus wilt is a problem. Do not replant China asters on soil known to be infected for at least 8 years, except for resistant varieties such as *C. chinensis* 'Ostrich Plume'.

Calluna
Heather, Scots heather, ling
Ericaceae

Calluna vulgaris
'Foxii Nana'

Their hardy, evergreen nature and ability to provide colour throughout the year have made the many varieties of *Calluna vulgaris*, the only species in the genus, important garden plants. They are particularly useful for gardens with acid soil, where they can be grown as specimen plants, as ground cover or, if small enough, in a rock garden. They can be difficult to establish in areas prone to drought, however, and will not tolerate limy soil.

Calluna vulgaris Varieties vary a great deal in habit of growth, ranging from prostrate plants only 5 cm (2 in) high to erect plants that grow as tall as 65 cm (26 in).

The tiny leaves, about 3 mm (⅛ in) long, are linear, slightly fleshy and closely overlapping. They range in colour from bright to dark green to grey, and are sometimes gold or red. The white to crimson flowers are usually held in crowded flower spikes up to 30 cm (12 in) long. Each flower

is normally single with 4 oblong petals, 3 mm (⅛ in) long, concealed by 4 slightly larger, coloured sepals. There are some varieties with double flowers and some where the buds colour as in a normal plant but never open; these 2 kinds tend to flower late in the season.

Heather is widely distributed across W Europe, from Norway and Iceland to S Spain and Morocco. It has also become naturalised in E Canada, from seed contained in packing material used by early settlers. Varieties native to northern regions of Europe flower in Britain from early to late summer, while those from more southerly areas of Europe flower in Britain from late summer to late autumn.

RECOMMENDED VARIETIES
C. vulgaris has hundreds of named varieties. Those listed below are divided into 3 groups – low-growing, medium and tall. Unless stated otherwise, they are upright plants with dark green foliage and single mauve or lavender flowers that bloom between late summer and mid autumn. The heights and spreads given here are for 5 to 7-year-old plants that have been regularly trimmed after flowering.

LOW-GROWING VARIETIES
Unless stated otherwise, low-growing varieties grow to 15–25 cm (6–10 in) tall, with a spread of 30–50 cm (12–20 in).

▲ *Calluna vulgaris* 'County Wicklow'

'County Wicklow'♀ has large double shell-pink flowers and mid green foliage with a compact, semi-prostrate habit. 'Cuprea', with distinctive copper-coloured foliage in summer, turns a warm bronze in winter. It spreads only to 25 cm (10 in).

Calluna vulgaris
'Dark Beauty'

'Dark Beauty' is a neat and compact plant, producing semidouble blood-red flowers turning purple-red with age. 'Darkness'♀ is compact with masses of crimson flowers. 'Dark Star'♀ bears bright, semidouble crimson flowers. 'Drum-ra' produces white flowers in profusion and has light green foliage. **'Foxii Nana'**, with a poor show of flowers, is grown for its bright green dwarf 'pin-cushion' habit, making it very suitable for growing in troughs.

'Inshriach Bronze' has acid yellow foliage in spring, which turns a rich gold in summer and to bronze in winter. **'J.H. Hamilton'**♀ produces double deep pink flowers and its dwarf habit to just 10 cm (4 in) tall with a spread of 25 cm (10 in) makes it suitable for troughs. **'Jan Dekker'** has downy grey foliage and a semi-prostrate habit. **'Jimmy Dyce'**♀ bears double lilac-pink flowers from early to late autumn. It has a semi-prostrate habit. **'John F. Letts'** is a very low-growing form, to just 10 cm (4 in) tall with a spread of 25 cm (10 in). It has gold foliage in summer, which turns bronze in autumn and then red and orange in winter.

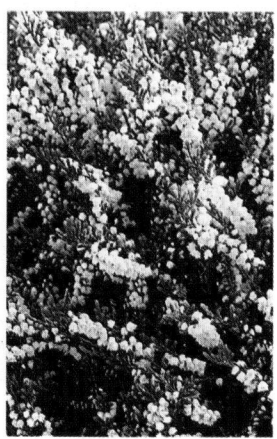

▲ *Calluna vulgaris* 'Inshriach Bronze'
Calluna vulgaris 'Kinlochruel' ▲

Kinlochruel'♀ carries pure white double flowers against bright green foliage which bronzes in winter. **'Mrs Pat'** produces pink new growth which persists for most of the year. **'Mullion'**♀, with lilac-pink flowers, is spreading and suitable for troughs. **'Multicolor'** has copper foliage frequently flecked with brilliant shades of orange and red for most of the year. Its dwarf habit to just 10 cm (4 in) tall with a spread of 25 cm (10 in) makes it ideal for troughs. **'Nana Compacta'** has bright green foliage forming a neat 'pincushion'.

'Radnor'♀ produces a neat hummock of double shell-pink flowers. **'Red Carpet'** is chiefly grown for its intense orange and red winter foliage which turns gold in summer. It has a semi-prostrate habit. **'Robert Chapman'**♀ spreads to 65 cm (26 in) and has gold foliage in summer, orange in autumn and red in winter and spring. **'Roland Haagen'**♀ is chiefly grown for its compact habit and golden yellow foliage which turns bright orange in winter.

'Sir John Charrington'♀ has deep lilac-pink flowers set against gold foliage which deepens to red in winter. **'Sister Anne'**♀ has grey-green summer foliage that

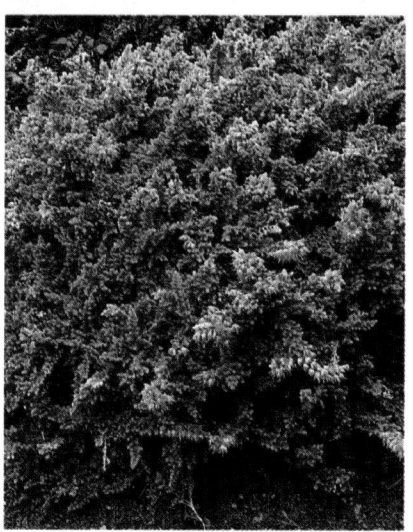

▲ *Calluna vulgaris* 'Sister Anne'

▲ *Calluna vulgaris* 'Sunset'

▲ *Calluna vulgaris* 'White Lawn'

turns a dull bronze in winter. It is just 10 cm (4 in) tall with a spread of 25 cm (10 in), making it suitable for troughs. **'Sunset'**♀ bears lilac-pink flowers against gold foliage that deepens to red in autumn and winter. It has a spreading habit. **'White Lawn'**♀, with its prostrate trailing habit, is ideal for rockeries and troughs. It has white flowers amid clear green foliage. It grows to just 5 cm (2 in) high. **'Winter Chocolate'** is broad and low with golden foliage whose pink summer tips turn bronze in winter. The new spring growth is salmon-pink.

MEDIUM-SIZED VARIETIES
Unless stated otherwise, medium-sized varieties reach 30-35 cm (12-14 in) tall with a spread of 40-50 cm (16-20 in).

'Alexandra' produces long spikes of magenta bud flowers from late summer to early winter; they are suitable for fresh or dried flower arrangements. **'Beoley Gold'**♀ has yellow foliage throughout the year and produces white flowers. **'Blazeaway'** spreads to 60 cm (24 in) and has gold foliage in summer which turns orange then fiery red in winter. **'Boskoop'** has rich gold foliage in summer turning orange with red tints in winter. **'Flamingo'** is chiefly grown for its pinkish red new growth in spring.

'Gold Haze'♀ has white flowers and pale yellow foliage throughout the year. **'H.E. Beale'** bears long spikes of double shell-pink flowers suitable for cutting. **'Hammondii Aureifolia'** produces white flowers against foliage that is light green tipped with yellow in spring and early summer. **'Joy Vanstone'**♀ has straw-coloured foliage in summer, which turns orange in winter.

'Kerstin' has downy, deep lilac-grey foliage in winter, colourfully tipped pale yellow and red in spring. **'Marleen'** carries white buds with purple tips which do not open but persist late into the season. **'Orange Queen'**♀ has orange winter foliage that turns gold in summer. **'Peter Sparkes'** spreads to 55 cm (22 in); it has long spikes of double rose-pink flowers, good as cut flowers, late in the season.

'Schurig's Sensation', with long spikes of dark pink double flowers, spreads to 55 cm (22 in). **'Serlei Aurea'**♀ bears white flowers on dense greenish yellow foliage tipped yellow in summer and autumn. **'Spring Cream'**♀ bears white flowers on mid green foliage, which has cream tips in spring, and makes a neat compact plant. **'Tib'**♀ has double mauve-pink flowers, from mid summer to mid autumn, but is a rather straggly plant. **'Underwoodii'**♀ produces lilac-pink buds, creating a late display of colour which turns silvery white and lasts well into winter. It spreads to 55 cm (22 in).

TALL VARIETIES
Unless stated otherwise, tall varieties reach 40-50 cm (16-20 in) tall with a spread of 50-70 cm (20-28 in).

'Allegro'♀ has ruby flowers, and is vigorous but neat. **'Annemarie'**♀ bears outstanding double rose-pink flowers which are valued for cutting. **'Anthony Davis'**♀ produces long spikes of white flowers, suitable for cutting, against green-grey foliage. **'Battle of Arnhem'**♀ reaches 65 cm (26 in) tall. It has gunmetal-coloured buds opening to lilac-pink flowers composed of many bracts. It flowers from early to mid winter.

'Elsie Purnell'♀ carries long spikes of double lavender flowers, valuable for cutting, with grey-green foliage spreading to 75 cm (30 in). **'Finale'**♀ bears its amethyst

Camellia
Chinese or Japanese rose
Theaceae

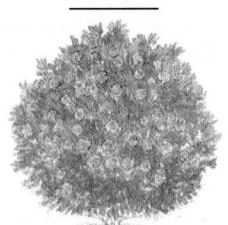

Camellia japonica 'Tricolor'

Conspicuous flowers and handsome evergreen foliage have made this genus of ornamental shrubs and trees deservedly popular. Native to India, China and Japan, there are over 200 species of camellia (about 45 in cultivation) and a staggering 20 000 different types have been grown and described over the years.

The abundant cup or bowl-shaped flowers range from 2.5-20 cm (1-8 in) across and are carried singly or in small bunches of 2-3. Each flower has 5-12 large, brightly coloured petals that are often fused together at the base. They may be white, pink, red or multicoloured and occasionally yellow. Numerous bright yellow stamens form a bold central mass and are sometimes petal-like. Some camellias with small flowers have a strong, sweet fragrance, which is missing in the large, showy varieties.

The mid to dark green, glossy leaves are narrow to broadly oval, almost stalkless and slightly toothed around the edges. They are arranged alternately on the shoots. The fruit, absent in many of the cultivated varieties, consists of a large round woody capsule, splitting from the top when ripe to reveal 5 chambers, each with one large oil-rich seed. Japanese ladies use this oil to dress their hair.

Because of their considerable differences in habit, hardiness, flower size, colour and form, flowering season (between late autumn and early summer) and ease of culture, there are suitable plants for many different garden situations throughout Britain. Most are suitable for borders and beds and there are camellias that make good hedging plants or are suitable for growing against walls. Some camellias make fine specimen plants for containers on patios and terraces, and the more tender varieties can be grown in a conservatory or unheated greenhouse.

When describing the flowers, the following categories are followed: 'single' denotes a flower with a single row of petals and a conspicuous centre of yellow stamens; 'semidouble' describes a flower with two or more rows of petals and a centre of yellow stamens; 'double' refers to a flower with numerous irregular rows of petals and virtually no stamens; 'formal double' describes a flower with numerous overlapping petals symmetrically arranged in spirals or tiers, and no stamens; 'anemone-like' denotes a flower with one or more rows of petals and a centre of petal-like and normal stamens; and 'peony-like' describes a flower with a rounded mass of petals, petal-like stamens and normal stamens.

All the heights and spreads given below are for 5-8-year-old plants. Camellias reach maturity at this age and thereafter growth is very slow.

RECOMMENDED SPECIES AND VARIETIES
C. 'Cornish Snow'♀ Dainty, single white flowers, up to 7 cm (2¾ in) across, appear from early to late spring on this vigorous, spreading shrub. The young foliage is attractively bronzed. HEIGHT & SPREAD 2.4×2 m (8×6½ ft).

▲ *Camellia* 'Cornish Snow'

C. 'Freedom Bell' Bright red, hose-in-hose, semidouble flowers, up to 10 cm (4 in) across, are produced from late winter to late spring. This plant has a dense, twiggy, upright growth. HEIGHT & SPREAD 3×2 m (10×6½ ft).

▲ *Camellia* 'Freedom Bell'

C. japonica Single red flowers, 5-10 cm (2-4 in) across, appear between late winter and early summer, depending on the variety. This compact shrub to small tree has broad oval glossy leaves, with pointed tips and shallowly toothed edges. The majority of cultivated varieties come from this species, a few of them scented, and it is by far the most popular camellia grown. It is also one of the hardiest of the evergreen shrubs, except in very exposed, windy conditions. HEIGHT & SPREAD 3-8×2-4 m (10-26×6½-13 ft).

The following cultivars are all vigorous, with compact, upright growth, unless stated otherwise.

'Adolphe Audusson'♀ bears large, deep red, semidouble flowers from mid to late spring. It is one of the most reliable cultivars. 'Akashigata'♀ (syn. 'Lady Clare') is a spreading, pendulous shrub, ideal for growing against a wall. Large, peach-pink, semidouble flowers are carried from early to late spring. 'Alba Plena' bears white, formal double flowers from early to mid spring. It is a slow-growing variety. 'Alba Simplex'

▲ *Camellia japonica* 'Alba Simplex'

has large single white flowers from mid to late spring on a bushy, medium-sized shrub. 'Alexander Hunter'♀ carries flattish, deep crimson, single flowers from early to late spring. 'Althaeiflora' bears large, dark red, peony-like flowers from early to mid spring. It has very dark green leaves. 'Anemoniflora' bears dark crimson, semidouble to anemone-like flowers in mid spring. 'Apollo' is one of the hardiest of the *C. japonica* cultivars and will tolerate windier conditions than most of the others. The deep rose-pink, semidouble flowers are

▼ *Camellia japonica* 'Alexander Hunter'

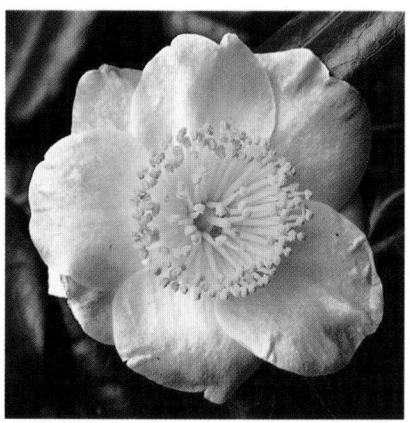

▲ *Camellia japonica* 'Apple Blossom'

occasionally marbled with white and appear in mid spring. The plant has a spreading habit, bearing leaves with characteristically twisted tips. **'Apple Blossom'**♀ (syn. 'Joy Sander') is a medium-sized, bushy shrub, bearing pale blush-pink, semidouble flowers from early to mid spring. **'Arajishi'** has large, narrow, coarsely toothed leaves. Large, blood-red, peony-like flowers with irregular wavy petals are produced from early to mid spring.

'Ballet Dancer'♀ bears cream (shading to coral-pink at the edges), peony-like flowers from early to late spring. **'Berenice Boddy'**♀ is a particularly hardy variety, tolerating windier conditions than most. It starts off with an upright habit, later becoming spreading, bearing light pink, semidouble flowers from early to mid spring. **'Betty Sheffield'** bears large, white, semidouble to loose peony-like flowers in mid spring. The petals are striped and blotched with red and pink. **'Betty Sheffield Supreme'** bears irregular double flowers in mid spring. The blooms are basically white with the petals edged in several shades of pink. **'Blood of China'** carries deep salmon-red, semidouble to peony-like, scented flowers from mid to late spring. **'Bob Hope'**♀ has large, dark red, semidouble to peony-like flowers from mid to late spring. It has dark green glossy leaves. The flower is the deepest red known in camellias and the plant is ideal for growing in containers. **'Bob's Tinsie'**♀ bears small, brilliant-red, anemone-like flowers in mid spring. **'Brushfield's Yellow'** bears

▼ *Camellia japonica* 'Bob's Tinsie'

creamy white (pale primrose in centre), anemone-like flowers from mid to late spring. **'C.M. Hovey'**♀ bears carmine, formal double flowers from early to late spring. **'C.M. Wilson'** is a slowly spreading variety with large, light pink, anemone-like flowers from early to mid spring. **'Carter's Sunburst'**♀ bears large, pale pink (marked with deeper pink flecks and stripes), semidouble to peony-like, scented flowers in mid spring. **'Chandleri Elegans'** see

▲ *Camellia japonica* 'Coquettii'

'Elegans'. **'Coquettii'**♀ (syn. 'Glen 40') is a slow-growing plant and carries bright red, semi to formal double flowers from mid to late spring.

'Debutante' carries light pink, peony-like flowers from early to mid spring. **'Dewatairin'** (syn. 'Hatsuzakura') bears large, light rose-pink, single flowers, with a mass of petal-like stamens in the centre, from mid to late spring. **'Doctor Tinsley'**♀ bears very pale pink (shading to deep pink at the edges), semidouble flowers in mid spring. It tolerates windier conditions than most of the other varieties. **'Donckelaeri'**

▲ *Camellia japonica* 'Drama Girl'

see 'Masayoshi'. **'Drama Girl'**♀ has an open, pendulous habit with large, deep rose-pink, semidouble flowers appearing from mid to late spring. **'Elegans'**♀ (syn. 'Chandleri Elegans') has a slowly spreading habit with large, deep rose-pink (often with white variegations) anemone-like flowers from early to mid spring.

'Glen 40' see 'Coquettii'. **'Gloire de Nantes'**♀ has large, bright rose-pink, flat to saucer-shaped, semidouble flowers from late winter to late spring. **'Grand Prix'**♀ develops a more open habit with age. Large, brilliant-red, flat semidouble flowers with irregular petals are borne from mid to late spring. **'Grand Slam'**♀ has deep green foliage and develops a more open habit with age. The large, semidouble to anemone-like, scented flowers are an unusually deep red for camellias, borne from mid to late spring. **'Guilio Nuccio'**♀ produces large, deep rose-pink, semidouble flowers with wavy petals in mid spring. It develops a spreading habit with age.

'Hagoromo'♀ (syn. 'Magnoliiflora') has cup-shaped, hose-in-hose, semidouble, blush-pink flowers in mid spring. **'Hakurakuten'**♀ bears large, white, semidouble to peony-like flowers with fluted petals from early to mid spring. **'Hatsuzakura'** see 'Dewatairin'. **'Hawaii'** is a slow-growing plant with pale pink, shading to a white edge, peony-like flowers from early to mid spring. **'Imbricata'** (syn. 'Imbricata Rubra') bears light red, formal double flowers from mid to late spring on a medium-sized plant. **'Joseph Pfingstl'** has an open habit and dark red, semidouble to peony-like flowers from early to mid spring. **'Joy Sander'** see 'Apple Blossom'. **'Jupiter'**♀ bears saucer-shaped, bright red, single to semidouble flowers in mid spring. The flowers are sometimes blotched with white. It is one of the best varieties for general planting and hardy in most areas. **'Konronkoku'**♀ (syn. 'Kouron-jura') carries an abundance of very dark red, semidouble to formal double flowers from early to late spring on a medium-sized plant. It is one of the darkest red camellias. **'Kramer's Supreme'** produces large, bright red, peony-like, scented flowers in mid spring. It is best grown under glass.

'Lady Clare' see 'Akashigata'. **'Lady de Saumarez'**♀ carries bright red, semidouble flowers blotched with white in mid spring. **'Lady Vansittart'** is slow-growing with unusual holly-like, twisted foliage. Saucer-shaped, white (flushed rose-pink), semidouble flowers appear from mid to late spring. **'Lady Vansittart Pink'** is a deep pink version of 'Lady Vansittart'. **'Lavinia Maggi'**♀ has an open habit and bears large, white to pale pink (with broad rose-cerise stripes), formal double flowers from early to late spring. **'Magnoliiflora'** see 'Hagoromo'. **'Margaret Davis Picotee'** bears white

▼ *Camellia japonica* 'Lady Vansittart Pink'

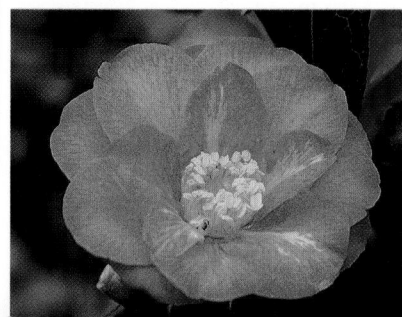

115

peony-like to double flowers with a narrow red border around the edges of the petals. 'Margherita Coleoni' bears dark red, double to formal double flowers from mid to late spring. 'Mars'♀ has an open, spreading habit with large, crimson, semidouble flowers from mid to late spring. Occasionally the flowers have white variegations. 'Masayoshi'♀ (syn. 'Donckelaeri') is a slow-growing, bushy, pendulous plant with large, saucer-shaped, red (often marbled white), semidouble flowers from early to late spring. 'Mathotiana Alba'♀ bears large, white (sometimes with pink spots), formal double flowers from mid to late spring. 'Mathotiana Rosea' produces large, clear pink, formal double flowers from mid to late spring. 'Mercury'♀ bears large, deep soft crimson (with slightly darker veins), semidouble flowers from early to late spring. 'Midnight' carries dark red, semidouble to anemone-like flowers (with ruffled petals) in mid spring. 'Mikenjaku' (syn. 'Nagasaki') is a slow-growing camellia with blotched red and white, semidouble flowers from mid to late spring. 'Miss Charleston'♀ produces large, deep red, semidouble flowers that appear from mid to late spring. 'Mrs D.W. Davis'♀ carries large, pendulous, cup-shaped flowers in mid spring. The semidouble blooms are blush-pink. The plant requires shelter from cold winds and frost or can be grown under glass.

'Nagasaki' see 'Mikenjaku'. 'Nobilissima' bears white (with yellow shading), peony-like flowers from late winter to mid spring. 'Nuccio's Gem'♀ produces white, formal double flowers from early to mid spring. 'Nuccio's Jewel'♀ is slow-growing with white (flushed with pale pink), peony-like flowers from mid to late spring. It is an ideal choice for containers and tubs.

▲ *Camellia japonica* 'Preston Rose'

'Preston Rose' has an open habit with salmon-pink, peony-like flowers from mid to late spring. 'R.L. Wheeler'♀ has large, rose-pink, semidouble to anemone-like flowers in mid spring. It has large, dark green leaves. 'Rubescens Major'♀ bears large, carmine-red (with darker veins),

semidouble to double flowers from early to mid spring. It has broad leaves. 'Scentsation'♀ bears silvery pink, peony-like, scented flowers in mid spring. 'Silver Anniversary' has white, semidouble flowers from early to mid spring. The petals are an irregular size and shape. 'Souvenir de Bahuaud-Litou'♀ bears large, light pink, formal double flowers from mid to late spring. 'Spencer's Pink'♀ has a low, spreading habit with large, light-pink, single flowers from early to mid spring.

▲ *Camellia japonica* 'Spencer's Pink'

'The Czar' bears large crimson semidouble flowers in mid spring. 'Tiffany' bears very large peony-like flowers from mid to late spring. The blooms are pale pink, deepening around the edges. The plant becomes spreading with age and is best grown under glass. 'Tomorrow' has an open, slightly pendulous habit with large, rose-red, semidouble to peony-like flowers from early to mid spring. It is best grown under glass. 'Tricolor'♀ is one of the oldest cultivars. It is a dense, spreading plant bearing medium-sized white (streaked with carmine), semidouble flowers in mid spring. 'Yours Truly' bears pale pink, semidouble flowers from mid to late spring. The petals have darker veining, and are streaked with deep pink and bordered with white. The plant is bushy with glossy dark green, holly-like leaves.

C. reticulata This is the most spectacular camellia of all, producing an abundance of 15-20 cm (6-8 in) wide blooms in vivid pinks and reds from late winter to mid spring. But it is also the most tender of the cultivated forms, only suitable for growing in a conservatory or unheated greenhouse, except in warmer sheltered gardens of

Camellia reticulata 'Captain Rawes'

southern Britain, where its open, spreading habit makes it ideal for training up walls and pergolas. The conspicuous net-like veining of the thick, narrow leaves gave rise to the name 'reticulata'. HEIGHT & SPREAD 3-4.5×2.4-3.5 m (10-15×8-12 ft).

'Arch of Triumph'♀ is a vigorous, upright plant bearing large, deep rose-pink, peony-like flowers with an orange sheen from late winter to early spring. 'Captain Rawes'♀ has a fairly open habit with large, carmine, semidouble flowers with irregular petals from early to late spring. 'Doctor Clifford Parks'♀ bears large, flame-red, semidouble to loose peony-like flowers with wavy petals from early to late spring. It is hardier than most of the other *C. reticulata* cultivars and will survive outside farther north. 'Forty-Niner'♀ has a dense, bushy growth with large, red, peony-like flowers from late winter to early spring. It is also fairly hardy, allowing it to be grown outdoors farther north than most of the other *C. reticulata* cultivars.

'Inspiration'♀ is another hardy hybrid with upright growth and light pink, semidouble, saucer-shaped flowers from early to late spring. 'Lasca Beauty'♀ has an upright open habit, bearing large, soft pink, semidouble flowers with thick petals from early to late spring. The vigorous 'Leonard Messel'♀ has an upright, slightly open habit and bears smaller than average, apricot-pink semidouble flowers with darker veining from early to late spring. 'Mandalay Queen'♀ has an open, upright habit with large, deep rose, semidouble to peony-like flowers with fluted petals from early to mid spring.

'Salutation' is a medium-sized, open shrub with small, soft pink, semidouble flowers from late winter to mid spring. 'Satan's Robe'♀ has wide, spreading growth, slender, arching shoots and large, brilliant-red, semidouble flowers from early to late spring. It is similar in hardiness to *C. japonicum* cultivars. 'Show Girl' is a vigorous, upright, open shrub bearing large, pale pink, semidouble to peony-like flowers with irregular petals from late winter to mid spring.

C. sasanqua (mountain tea flower) Small, 2.5-5 cm (1-2 in) wide, white to rose-pink single flowers are produced freely from late autumn to late winter by this hardy, spreading shrub. The flowers have a sweet fragrance and the narrow oval leaves are dark green. HEIGHT & SPREAD 2.4-4×2-3 m (8-13×6½-10 ft).

'Crimson King'♀ bears deep mahogany-red single flowers with twisted petals. It has a low, spreading habit. 'Hugh Evans' has a vigorous, tall habit with arching branches bearing rose-pink single flowers. It is ideal for growing on walls. 'Jean May' has a dense, bushy growth making it suitable for hedging. The flowers are shell-pink, semidouble to double and up to 10 cm

▲ *Camellia sasanqua* 'Narumigata'

(4in) across. **'Narumigata'**♀ has a vigorous, upright growth with white pink-tinted, cup-shaped, single flowers up to 10cm (4in) across. It is best planted in a sheltered sunny spot against a wall.

C. sinensis (tea plant) Bushy shrub with long, narrow, wavy leaves and 2–3cm (¾–1¼in) waxy white, single, bell-shaped flowers from late autumn to mid winter. It is half hardy and can only be grown outside in the mildest parts of south-west. Britain. Elsewhere, grow it in an unheated conservatory or greenhouse. HEIGHT & SPREAD 2–3×1.5–2m (6½–10×5–6½ft).

'Spring Festival'♀ bears dainty, pink, semidouble to double flowers up to 7.5cm (3in) across from early to late spring. It has a narrow, upright habit and its small leaves are bronzed when young. It makes an excellent specimen tree in a small garden, but needs a sunny, sheltered position.

Camellia x williamsii 'Donation'

C. × williamsii These are the most easily grown and reliable for planting outdoors in Britain. They mostly form tall, dense shrubs with narrow oval leaves. The white to deep red flowers are 10–12cm (4–5in) across, mainly single or semidouble. HEIGHT & SPREAD 2–3×1.2–2m (6½–10×4–6½ft).

▼ *Camellia × williamsii* 'Anticipation'

▲ *Camellia × williamsii* 'Bow Bells'

'Anticipation'♀ is ideal for containers and small gardens. The deep rose-pink, peony-like flowers are produced from early to late spring. **'Ballet Queen'** bears an abundance of salmon-pink, peony-like blooms from early to late spring. **'Black Lace'** has a slow, fairly open growth with deep red, formal double flowers from early to late spring. **'Bow Bells'** bears mid pink, hose-in-hose, semidouble flowers from late winter to late spring. **'Bowen Bryant'**♀ has an upright, but open habit with rose-pink, bowl-shaped, semidouble flowers from early to late spring. **'Brigadoon'**♀ displays a small, dense upright habit with rose-pink, semidouble flowers from late winter to late spring.

'China Clay'♀ has an open habit bearing white, semidouble flowers from early to late spring. **'Citation'** is upright, bearing silvery blush-pink, semidouble flowers with irregular petals from early to mid spring. **'Cornish Spring'**♀ is a compact, bushy shrub, ideal for containers, with vivid pink, single to semidouble flowers, 5cm (2in) across, from early to late spring.

'Daintiness'♀ has an open habit with salmon-pink, semidouble flowers from mid

▼ *Camellia × williamsii* 'Daintiness'

▼ *Camellia × williamsii* 'Debbie'

▲ *Camellia × williamsii* 'Donation'

to late spring. **'Debbie'**♀ has an upright growth with deep clear pink, semidouble to peony-like flowers from late winter to late spring. **'Donation'**♀ is upright with mid pink, semidouble flowers from late winter to early summer. It is one of the most versatile, robust and beautiful of the camellias. **'E.G. Waterhouse'** has a narrow, upright

▲ *Camellia × williamsii* 'E.G. Waterhouse'

habit bearing light pink, formal double flowers from early to late spring. **'E.T.R. Carlyon'**♀ is upright with white, semidouble flowers from early to late spring. **'Elegant Beauty'** has an open habit with long, arching shoots and bronze foliage. It is ideal for training on walls. The deep rose-pink, anemone to peony-like flowers are freely produced from early to late spring. **'Elsie Jury'**♀ has a spreading habit and clear deep pink flowers, shaded with pale pink. The anemone to peony-like flowers appear from early to late spring.

'Francis Hanger' is small and upright with wavy-edged leaves and pure white, single flowers from early to late spring. **'Galaxie'**♀ is upright, bearing pink flowers with darker pink stripes and a rose-bud

▲ *Camellia × williamsii* 'Galaxie'

▲ *Camellia* × *williamsii* 'George Blandford'

▲ *Camellia* × *williamsii* 'Glenn's Orbit'

centre from early to late spring. The bowl-shaped blooms are semidouble to formal double with the petals rolling slightly inward. **'George Blandford'**♀ has a spreading habit with carmine, semidouble to anemone-like flowers from early to mid spring. **'Glenn's Orbit'**♀ has an upright habit with pink semidouble to loose peony-like flowers from early to mid spring. **'Golden Spangles'** has an upright, slightly open habit and dark green leaves with a pale yellow central band. The 7.5 cm (3 in) wide, deep rose-pink, hose-in-hose, semidouble flowers are seen from early to late spring.

'Hiraethlyn'♀ is upright with 7.5 cm (3 in) wide, very pale pink, funnel-shaped, hose-in-hose, semidouble flowers from early to late spring. **'Innovation'** is a very hardy, medium-spreading bush with wine-red, peony-like flowers from late winter to late spring. **'J.C. Williams'**♀ has a spreading, arching habit, bearing pale blush-pink, single flowers from late winter to late spring. **'Joan Trehane'**♀ has an upright, slightly open habit with clear rose-pink, formal double flowers from early to late spring. **'Julia Hamiter'**♀ has a medium-spreading habit with white, peony-like flowers tinged with pink, from early to late spring. **'Jury's Yellow'** forms a dense, upright, cone-shaped bush bearing creamy

▲ *Camellia* × *williamsii* 'Mary Christian'

white, anemone-like flowers with wavy petals from early to late spring.

'Mary Christian'♀ has an upright habit bearing 7.5 cm (3 in) wide, clear deep pink single flowers from early to late spring. **'Mary Phoebe Taylor'** has an upright, slightly open habit with light rose-pink, semidouble to loose peony-like flowers from early to late spring. **'Muskoka'**♀ is upright with mid pink (veined with deeper

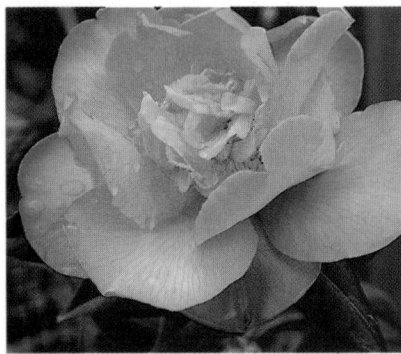

▲ *Camellia* × *williamsii* 'Muskoka'

pink), semidouble flowers from early to late spring.

'Rose Parade'♀ forms a dense, upright shrub with deep rose-pink, formal double flowers from early to late spring. **'Saint Ewe'**♀ has a dense, upright habit with very glossy dark green leaves which contrast with its bright rose-pink flowers. The bell-shaped, single flowers are very freely produced from late winter to late spring. **'Tristrem Carlyon'** has an upright habit and rose-pink, peony-like flowers from early to late spring.

'Water Lily'♀ has an upright habit bearing lavender flowers flushed with bright pink. The formal double blooms have incurving petals and are seen from early to late spring. **'Wilber Foss'** has a dense, upright habit with brilliant pinkish red, peony-like flowers that appear from late winter to late spring.

CULTIVATION Plant between early spring and late summer in any reasonably well-drained, lime-free soil, in light shade or in a sheltered spot with a south-western to northern aspect. To protect the flowers from frost-thaw damage, position the plants

away from full early morning sun and drying winds. *C. reticulata* and other early-flowering camellias are best grown in containers in a conservatory or unheated greenhouse, except in the mildest areas. They can be moved outside when the weather warms up.

Enrich non-peaty soils with leaf-mould or peaty compost. Feed annually in late spring or early summer with a general fertiliser, but do not apply fertiliser between late summer and early spring. Apply a mulch on planting and replenish when necessary. This helps to stop the plants drying out – especially important when they are flowering or coming into bud. Spray the foliage during prolonged dry spells.

PROPAGATION Cultivated varieties, except those of *C. reticulata,* are best propagated by inter-nodal or leaf-bud cuttings, taken in summer. Alternatively, use hardwood cuttings taken in mid autumn to early spring.

Propagate *C. reticulata* cultivars by layering in early autumn. The layers will be strong and well-rooted enough to separate after 18 months. Cleft or wedge grafting on *C. reticulata* rootstock is also used for these cultivated varieties. Natural species and forms are usually propagated by seed.

PRUNING Little pruning is needed other than cutting back straggly shoots, or to prevent plants encroaching on paths, lawns or other plants. Regular annual pruning and deadheading immediately after flowering are more advantageous than infrequent heavy pruning.

PESTS AND DISEASES Aphids may infest young shoots and scale insects suck sap from the undersides of leaves, especially under glass where mealy bugs often attack shoots

▼ *Camellia* × *williamsii* 'Rose Parade'

and buds, producing conspicuous tufts of white wool. Aphids and scale insects produce 'honeydew' which encourages sooty mould fungus. Bud drop occurs if soil conditions are too dry or if rapid thawing occurs after frost. The latter also damages camellia flowers. Where spring frosts occur, this damage can be avoided by providing light overhead shade or by siting the plants in south-west to north-facing positions. The leaves will turn yellow and die if the soil is alkaline or has too little humus.

Camomile see *Chamaemelum nobile*

Campanula
Bellflower, harebell
Campanulaceae

Bell or star-shaped flowers, usually in shades of blue, lavender, purple or white, characterise this group of summer-flowering plants. The flowers may be narrow or broad, pendent, half-nodding or upright. The genus includes large and imposing herbaceous perennials as well as small alpine species. Some are monocarpic, that is they take two or more years to reach flowering size then flower profusely and die. *Campanula portenschlagiana* and *C. poscharskyana* are good plants for rock crevices and gaps in paving and walls. Some high-alpine species, such as *C. cashmeriana* and *C. raineri,* perform best in troughs or raised beds where they can be shielded from winter wet, or in pots in an alpine house. *C. isophylla, C. carpatica* and *C. pyramidalis* all make fine pot plants for the conservatory or cool greenhouse. There are more than 300 species in the genus.

RECOMMENDED SPECIES AND VARIETIES

C. alliariifolia Erect spikes carry a series of pendent white or creamy white bells, 4 cm (1½ in) long, throughout summer. A clump-forming perennial, it has mounds of softly hairy, heart-shaped leaves. Native to Turkey and the Caucasus. HEIGHT & SPREAD 70×50 cm (28×20 in).

▼ *Campanula alliariifolia*

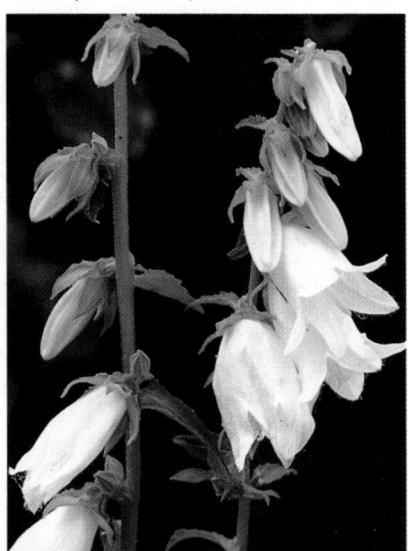

C. barbata (bearded bellflower) Hanging flowers, each up to 3 cm (1¼ in) long, range in colour from white to lavender-blue and are conspicuously bearded inside. They are borne on one-sided spikes during summer. This short-lived evergreen perennial or biennial forms a cluster of rosettes with grey-green, lance to oval-shaped leaves. Native to the Alps. HEIGHT & SPREAD 25×12.5 cm (10×5 in).

C. betulifolia♀ Loose clusters of white or pale pink broad bells, 3 cm (1¼ in) long, are borne on spreading stems. The plant forms a loose tuft of deep green, diamond to wedge-shaped leaves. Native to Turkey. HEIGHT & SPREAD 5×30 cm (2×12 in).

▲ *Campanula* 'Birch Hybrid'

C. **'Birch Hybrid'**♀ Deep violet or purple-blue open bells are borne in profusion throughout summer on this evergreen perennial. The plant forms dense mats of small, deep green, ivy-shaped leaves. HEIGHT & SPREAD 15×60 cm (6×24 in).

C. **'Burghaltii'**♀ (syn. *C.* × *burghaltii*) Upright to arching, leafy spikes of pale lavender hanging bells, 5 cm (2 in) long, appear in early and mid summer. A slightly spreading perennial with mid green, oval to lance-shaped leaves. The stems may need some support. HEIGHT & SPREAD 60×40 cm (24×16 in).

C. carpatica♀ Large upright blue, violet-purple or white bells, 3 cm (1¼ in) across, appear in mid to late summer. A clump or hummock-forming herbaceous perennial with smooth, rounded to oval leaves. A good pot plant, it can seed prolifically in a rock garden. Native to the Carpathians. HEIGHT & SPREAD 15×40 cm (6×16 in).

The flowers of f. *alba* are white. **'Blaeu Clips'** ('Blue Clips') has sky-blue flowers. The broader, saucer-shaped flowers of **'Blue Moonlight'** are grey-blue. **'Bressingham White'** has extra large, pure white flowers. **'Chewton Joy'** has pale blue flowers with a deeper blue rim. The pure white flowers of **'Weisse Clips'** ('White Clips') come true from seed.

Pale lavender flowers are often borne singly on each stem on var. *turbinata* (syn. 'Turbinata') which is not more than 10 cm (4 in) tall. **'Hannah'** has pure white, widespreading, bell-shaped flowers. The flowers of **'Isabel'** are wide-spreading bells of deep violet-blue. **'Karl Foerster'** has saucer-

shaped flowers of deep sky-blue. The flowers of **'Wheatley Violet'** are a deep violet.

C. cashmeriana A mass of delicate, pale to bright blue nodding bells, 2 cm (¾ in) long, appear amid grey oval leaves in summer and early autumn on this short-lived perennial. This evergreen plant is best grown in a cool

Campanula cochleariifolia

greenhouse as it does not tolerate winter wet. Native to W Himalayas. HEIGHT & SPREAD 15×30 cm (6×12 in).

C. cochleariifolia♀ (*C. pusilla*) Masses of small hanging or half-nodding pale blue or lavender bells, up to 1.5 cm (½ in) long, are borne in early to mid summer. This mat-forming herbaceous perennial bears numer-

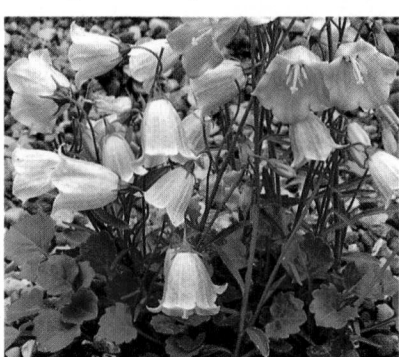

▲ *Campanula cochleariifolia*

ous small, oval to rounded, bright glossy green leaves. Native to Europe. HEIGHT & SPREAD 10×60 cm (4×24 in) or more.

The flowers of var. *alba* are white. **'Cambridge Blue'** has pale blue flowers. The double flowers of **'Elizabeth Oliver'**

▼ *Campanula cochleariifolia* 'Elizabeth Oliver'

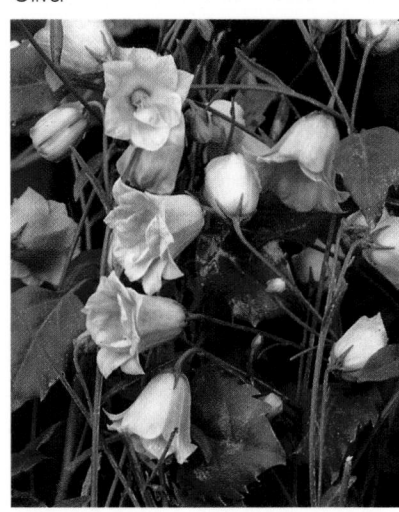

are a very pale blue. **'Flore Pleno'** has rather small double flowers in pale blue. **'Tubby'** has china-blue rounded bells.

C. 'E.K. Toogood' Bright blue, star-shaped flowers with a paler eye, up to 3 cm (1¼ in) across, appear throughout summer.

▲ *Campanula* 'E.K. Toogood'
Campanula fenestrellata ▲

This compact, clump-forming perennial has heart-shaped leaves. HEIGHT & SPREAD 70×50 cm (28×20 in).

C. fenestrellata (syn. *C. garganica* var. *fenestrellata*) Upright, star-shaped, mid blue flowers, 2.5 cm (1 in) across, appear throughout summer on this compact alpine. An evergreen perennial with rounded to heart-shaped leaves. Native to the Balkans. HEIGHT & SPREAD 3×20 cm (1¼×8 in).

C. formanekiana♀ Large white or bluish lilac bells, up to 6 cm (2½ in) long, are borne on this monocarpic perennial. Initially, plants form a large rosette of oval, grey, downy leaves. Native to the Balkans. HEIGHT & SPREAD 30×30 cm (12×12 in).

C. garganica♀ Starry, pale lavender flowers, 2 cm (¾ in) across, are borne in leafy spires during summer. A more or less evergreen perennial forming clumps of bright green, rounded to heart-shaped leaves. The plant flowers best in full sun and thrives in wall crevices. Native to Italy and W Greece. HEIGHT & SPREAD 5×30 cm (2×12 in).

'Dickson's Gold' has pale lavender flowers with yellow-flushed leaves.

C. glomerata Tight clusters of upright violet or purple flowers, 4 cm (1½ in) long, are borne in summer at the ends of leafy stems. This vigorous rhizomatous perennial, with deep green, lance to heart-shaped leaves, can be invasive. Native to Europe. HEIGHT & SPREAD 45×80 cm (18×32 in).

The flowers of var. *acaulis* are violet or blue on 15 cm (6 in) tall stems. The flowers of var. *alba* are white. **'Purple Pixie'** has small, deep violet-blue flowers. The flowers of **'Schneekrone'** ('Crown of Snow') are

▼ *Campanula glomerata* var. *acaulis*

▲ *Campanula glomerata* 'Superba'

white on a plant up to 30 cm (12 in) tall. **'Superba'**♀ grows to 75 cm (30 in) tall, with clusters of deep purple flowers.

C. × haylodgensis 'Plena' A good rock-garden plant with bowl-shaped, double

▲ *Campanula × haylodgensis* 'Plena'

lavender-blue flowers in early to mid summer. The carpet-forming perennial has a mass of small, bright green, heart-shaped leaves. HEIGHT & SPREAD 5×20 cm (2×8 in).

'Warley White' has double white flowers and denser growth.

C. incurva Large, pale violet-blue bells, up to 5 cm (2 in) long, are borne in profusion in summer on this biennial or monocarpic evergreen perennial. Plants form large, softly hairy rosettes of heart-shaped, yellowish green leaves. Native to E Greece. HEIGHT & SPREAD 30×50 cm (12×20 in).

C. isophylla♀ (Italian bellflower) Masses of star-shaped, pale mauve-blue flowers, 2.5 cm (1 in) across, are borne throughout

Campanula isophylla

summer on short stalks. Trailing stems, 20-30 cm (8-12 in) long, are densely covered with small, light green, heart-shaped leaves. The plant is not reliably hardy and is best grown indoors or in a greenhouse. HEIGHT & SPREAD 30×50 cm (12×20 in).

'Alba'♀ has pure white flowers.

C. 'Joe Elliott'♀ Mid lavender-blue, funnel-shaped flowers, 3 cm (1¼ in) long, appear 2-3 to a stem throughout summer. The perennial plant forms mounds of small, heart-shaped, grey-green leaves. It dislikes

winter wet and grows best in troughs or a cool greenhouse. HEIGHT & SPREAD 7.5×12.5 cm (3×5 in).

C. lactiflora Broad panicles of numerous, small upright bells, 2 cm (¾ in) long, in blue, milky blue or occasionally pink or white, are held on stiff leafy stems in summer and early autumn. This clump-forming herbaceous perennial has deep green, oval to oblong leaves. Native to the Caucasus. HEIGHT & SPREAD 120×70 cm (48×28 in).

C. l. white♀ has white flowers. **'Loddon Anna'**♀, up to 90 cm (36 in) tall, has soft lilac-pink flowers. **'Pouffe'** has mid blue flowers on stems up to 60 cm (24 in) tall. **'Prichard's Variety'**♀ has violet-blue flowers and grows to 1.5 m (5 ft)

▲ *Campanula lactiflora* 'Prichard's Variety'

tall so usually needs staking. **'White Pouffe'** has white flowers on stems up to 60 cm (24 in) tall.

C. latifolia (giant bellflower) Large, upright blue or lavender flowers, up to 5 cm (2 in) long, are borne in leafy spikes on stiff stems in mid summer. A clump-forming perennial with heart-shaped deep glossy green leaves. Native to Europe and Kashmir. HEIGHT & SPREAD 100×60 cm (40×24 in).

'Brantwood' has deep violet-blue flowers and oval leaves. The larger flowers of var. *macrantha* are violet-blue. The flowers of var. *macrantha alba* are white.

C. latiloba Deep blue, cup-shaped bellflowers appear in summer on upright stems. A more or less evergreen perennial with lance-shaped leaves. Native to Siberia. HEIGHT & SPREAD 90×50 cm (36×20 in).

alba♀ has white flowers. **'Hidcote Amethyst'**♀ has amethyst-blue flowers. **'Highcliffe Variety'**♀ has violet-blue flowers. **'Percy Piper'**♀ has lavender flowers.

▼ *Campanula latiloba* 'Percy Piper'

C. medium (Canterbury bells) Imposing erect panicles of large blue, purple, mauve, pink or white bell-shaped flowers, 5 cm (2 in) long, are borne on thick stiff stems in late spring and early summer. This biennial has large basal rosettes of lance-shaped, fresh green leaves. Native to S Europe. HEIGHT & SPREAD 80×36 cm (32×14 in).

Various strains are offered as seed including tall and dwarf double-flowered types and the **cup & saucer** kinds with the calyx broad and saucer-shaped.

C. muralis see *C. portenschlagiana*

C. persicifolia Large, open, blue to violet-blue cup-shaped flowers, up to 5 cm (2 in)

Campanula persicifolia

long, are borne on loose slender wand-like spikes. This evergreen perennial has deep green, narrow, lance-shaped leaves. Native to Europe, W Asia and N Africa. HEIGHT & SPREAD 100×50 cm (40×20 in).

The flowers of *alba* are white, as are the semidouble flowers of 'Alba Coronata'. **'Boule de Neige'** has large double white flowers. **'Fleur de Neige'**♀ has snowy white flowers. **'Pride of Exmouth'** has powder-blue flowers. **'Telham Beauty'** (syn. 'Maxima') has very large, pale blue flowers. **'White Queen'** has white flowers.

▲ *Campanula persicifolia* 'Boule de Neige'

Other kinds are listed as **cup & saucer white**♀, **double blue** (syn. 'Caerulea Flore Pleno'), **double white** (syn. 'Alba Flore Pleno') and var. **planiflora**.

C. portenschlagiana♀ (syn. *C. muralis*) Deep lavender-blue open bellflowers, up to 2 cm (¾ in) long, appear in summer in loose clusters on leafy stems. An evergreen spreading perennial that forms dense mats of deep green, heart-shaped to oval leaves. It is a good plant for rock and wall crevices. Native to S Europe. HEIGHT & SPREAD 15×50 cm (6×20 in).

'Resholdt's Variety' carries vivid deep blue flowers.

C. poscharskyana Starry violet-blue flowers, 2 cm (¾ in) long, appear in summer and early autumn in spreading clusters. This often rampant, spreading evergreen perennial has rounded, pale green leaves. It is a good plant for banks and old walls or the wild garden. Native to the Balkans. HEIGHT & SPREAD 10-15×60 cm (4-6×24 in).

'E.H. Frost' has milky-white flowers, **'Lisduggan'** has lavender-pink flowers and **'Stella'** has vivid violet-blue flowers.

C. pulla Dainty, solitary, deep violet bells, 2 cm (¾ in) long, appear in mid summer above a mat of oval to rounded leaves. This

▲ *Campanula pulla*

spreading perennial is an excellent rock-garden plant. Native to the NE Alps. HEIGHT & SPREAD 7.5×30 cm (3×12 in).

C. punctata Loose spires of rosy purple pendent bells, 5 cm (2 in) long and speckled inside with dark purple, appear in mid to late summer. This spreading semi-evergreen rhizomatous perennial has long-stalked oval to heart-shaped leaves. Native to Japan. HEIGHT & SPREAD 40×50 cm (16×20 in).

The creamy white flowers of f. *albiflora* (syn. 'Alba') are speckled with reddish purple inside. **'Rubriflora'** has creamy pink flowers flushed and speckled crimson-red.

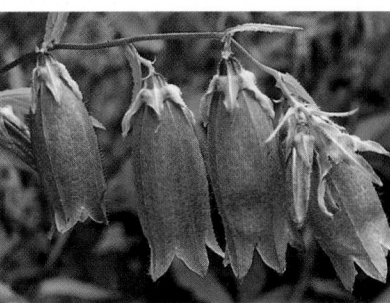

▲ *Campanula punctata* 'Rubriflora'

C. pusilla see *C. cochleariifolia*

C. pyramidalis (chimney bellflower) Long narrow spires of star-shaped, blue, white, or bicoloured flowers, 4 cm (1½ in) across, appear from mid summer to early autumn on thick stems. This upright biennial or short-lived perennial has heart-shaped, deep green and rather glossy leaves. It can be

grown in the open garden or in pots in a conservatory. Native to SE Europe. HEIGHT & SPREAD 70×50 cm (28×20 in).

The flowers of *alba* are white.

C. raineri♀ Solitary, upright broad bells of mid blue or lavender-blue flowers, 3 cm (1¼ in) across, are borne in summer on this perennial with grey-green oval leaves. This makes an excellent plant for an alpine house or a trough outside where it requires protection from winter wet. Native to SE Alps. HEIGHT & SPREAD 70×50 cm (28×20 in).

C. rapunculoides (creeping bellflower) Long leafy spikes of pendent, violet-blue flowers, 2-3 cm (¾-1¼ in) long, appear in summer. This rhizomatous perennial is a vigorous spreader and can be invasive. The long-stalked, deep green basal leaves are oblong or heart-shaped. Native to Europe. HEIGHT & SPREAD 75×75 cm (30×30 in).

C. rotundifolia (harebell) Several dainty, pendent blue bells, 2 cm (¾ in) long, appear in summer and early autumn on sparse, wiry stems. This rhizomatous perennial carries narrow stem leaves and contrasting rounded to heart-shaped basal leaves. It can be invasive. The plant is excellent for naturalising in grass. Native to the Northern Hemisphere. HEIGHT & SPREAD 45×45 cm (18×18 in).

'Olympica' has deep blue flowers on plants up to 25 cm (10 in) tall.

C. rupestris Narrow, upright lilac-blue flowers, 1.5-2 cm (½-¾ in) long, are carried above a rosette of soft hairy leaves. HEIGHT & SPREAD 15×40 cm (6×16 in).

C. takesimana Arching sprays of large, white bells, 5-6 cm (2-2½ in) long, are flushed with lilac and spotted maroon inside. They appear in summer on this spreading rhizomatous perennial with bright green, heart-shaped leaves mainly arranged in basal rosettes. Native to Japan and Korea. HEIGHT & SPREAD 60×50 cm (24×20 in).

C. thyrsoides (yellow bellflower) Soft yellow tubular bells, each 2 cm (¾ in) long

▼ *Campanula thyrsoides*

121

C

and arranged in dense crowded spikes, appear in summer. This biennial or mono-carpic perennial initially has a rosette of rather pale green leaves. Native to the Alps and the Balkans. HEIGHT & SPREAD 25–40×20cm (10–16×8in).

C. trachelium Long violet-blue or purple upright bells, up to 5cm (2in) long, are borne in mid summer on long leafy spikes. This herbaceous perennial carries oval, pointed leaves. Native to Europe and Siberia. HEIGHT & SPREAD 80×40cm (32×16in).

The flowers of var. *alba* are white, as are the double flowers of 'Alba Flore Pleno'. 'Bernice' produces violet-purple double flowers and 'Puck' has violet flowers.

C. zoysii Narrow lavender-blue crimped bells, up to 2cm (¾in) long, are borne in early to mid summer. This tufted perennial produces tiny glossy green leaves. The plant is best grown in an alpine house or trough as it tends to be susceptible to slug damage and winter wet. HEIGHT & SPREAD 5×10cm (2×4in).

CULTIVATION Campanulas are generally fairly easy to grow. Most require a fertile, moist yet well-drained soil and an open sunny position. However, some species – including *C. alliariifolia*, *C. glomerata*, *C. persicifolia*, *C. poscharskyana*, *C. rapunculoides* and *C. trachelium* – flower well in semi-shade. The taller plants need staking.

Many of the smaller campanulas are excellent for a rock garden, although some rhizomatous species, particularly *C. cochleariifolia* and *C. glomerata,* can be invasive. Lift and replant on a regular basis every 3-4 years. Some alpine species need protection from excessive winter wet – for example *C. betulifolia*, *C. cashmeriana* and *C. zoysii* – and need a grittier compost than the others.

PROPAGATION Divide the parent plants of perennial species after flowering or in autumn; those with long underground runners can be lifted around the margins and suitable rooted pieces removed, while the tighter clump formers will need to be lifted entirely and divided as stated. Remove cuttings of basal shoots and place in a propagating frame in spring or early summer.

Sow seed in autumn or late winter in pots in a coldframe.

Sow monocarpic species in spring, pricking out plants into individual pots. When the leaf-rosettes are large enough, generally by late summer, place young plants into their flowering positions.

Propagate alpine species from small summer cuttings or from offsets which may or may not be pre-rooted.

PESTS AND DISEASES Slugs and snails may prove a nuisance. Most species are also prone to rust infection.

Campion see *Silene*
Campion, rose see *Lychnis coronaria*

Campsis
Bignoniaceae

Campsis radicans

Vigorous woody climbers, these deciduous plants bloom from late summer to early autumn. The trumpet-shaped flowers, in shades of yellow, orange and red, are 5-7.5cm (2-3in) long. The tough stems are covered in dark green, pinnate leaves, with oval, toothed leaflets. Slender woody pods up to 12.5cm (5in) long may appear in late autumn. The plants cling to supports by aerial roots and are excellent for growing against a wall, although they do need plenty of space. They are fully hardy if planted in a sheltered, sunny position.

RECOMMENDED SPECIES AND VARIETIES
C. grandiflora Borne in drooping clusters of 6-12 blooms, each flower has a deep orange tapering tube, opening out to 5, spreading crimson lobes. The leaves have 7-9, smooth leaflets, each up to 6cm (2½in) long. HEIGHT & SPREAD 2×1m (6½×3ft) after 5 years, ultimately 6m (20ft) tall.

C. radicans (trumpet vine) The orange to red flowers are borne in clusters of 4-12 blossoms. The leaves have 7-11 leaflets, each 2-10cm (¾-4in) long, with fine hairs underneath. The brown pods may be produced in abundance after a hot summer. HEIGHT & SPREAD 2×1m (6½×3ft) after 5 years, ultimately 10m (33ft) tall.

The flowers of f. *flava*♀ (syn. 'Yellow Trumpet') are a rich, clear yellow.

▲ *Campsis × tagliabuana* 'Madame Galen'

C. × tagliabuana 'Madame Galen'♀ Flowers with yellow to orange tubes and 5 spreading, crimson to scarlet lobes are borne in large loose clusters of 6-12 blooms. The leaves have 7-11 leaflets, slightly hairy

beneath and 8cm (3¼in) long. HEIGHT & SPREAD 2.4×1m (8×3ft) after 5 years, ultimately 10m (33ft) tall.

CULTIVATION Plant from late autumn to mid spring in any fertile, well-drained but moisture-retentive soil. Choose a sheltered sunny position, preferably with the protection of a wall. Tie plants to supports, especially young specimens of *C. grandiflora*.

PROPAGATION Take semi-ripe cuttings or layer long branches in winter.

PRUNING In late winter, prune back to within 2-4 buds.

PESTS AND DISEASES Powdery mildew, leaf spot and scale insects can be a problem.

Candytuft see *Iberis*

Canna
Cannaceae

The brilliant flowers and bold ornamental foliage of cannas always draw the eye in a garden display. Their exotic flowers appear in mid summer and last until the first frosts. These rhizomatous perennials are native to tropical regions of the Americas and are only half-hardy in Britain. As summer bedding plants, they give height in mixed borders and make a feature in a large container.

Most cannas are hybrids with trumpet-shaped blooms up to 15cm (6in) across held in abundance at the top of erect stems. The broadly ovate leaves, up to 60cm (24in) long, spiral up the stem.

RECOMMENDED SPECIES AND VARIETIES
C. edulis see *C. indica*
C. indica (Indian shot, arrowroot) The flowers are red, often spotted or edged with pink or yellow. The green leaves are up to 50cm (20in) long. HEIGHT 2m (6½ft).
C. × generalis (canna lily) This group of hybrids contains many interesting and varied plants. 'Black Knight', with rich red flowers and brown leaves, grows to 60cm (24in). Taller varieties reaching 80cm (32in) include 'Lucifer' with scarlet flowers edged in golden yellow and green leaves;

▼ *Canna indica*

▲ *Canna × generalis* 'Rosemond Coles'

▲ *Canna × generalis* 'Wyoming'

'**Rosemond Coles**' with tomato-red flowers edged in canary-yellow above green leaves; and '**Wyoming**' with frilly, tangerine petals, darker at the edges and blotched with purple, above brown leaves.

CULTIVATION In late winter or early spring plant the rhizomes in a sandy peat mixture in pots and keep in a frost-free greenhouse until planting in a sunny spot outdoors when there is no danger of frosts. Lift the plants in late autumn, trim the rhizomes of dead growth and store in slightly moist peat in a frost-free conservatory or greenhouse.

PROPAGATION Divide the rhizomes before potting up in spring.

PESTS AND DISEASES Usually trouble free.

Canterbury bells
see *Campanula medium*
Caper spurge see *Euphorbia lathyris*

Caragana
Pea tree
Leguminosae

Caragana arborescens 'Lorbergii'

With their small sweet-pea shaped flowers and delicate foliage, it is surprising that so few of these deciduous shrubs and small trees are to be found in British gardens. They are hardy and have decorative appeal with a good show of flowers, normally yellow, in early summer followed by dangling seedpods.

Most of the 80 species are native to central Asia and adapted to hot, dry summers and cold, dry winters. The mild, damp climate of Britain may mean a sparser show of leaves and flowers. The alternate leaves are pinnate and the terminal leaflet is often replaced by a sharp spine.

RECOMMENDED SPECIES AND VARIETIES
C. **arborescens** Yellow flowers, 1.5 cm (½ in) long, appear in a profusion of slightly drooping clusters during late spring and ripen to narrow cylindrical pods about 5 cm

▲ *Caragana arborescens* 'Walker'

(2 in) long. The light green pinnate leaves, up to 7.5 cm (3 in) long, have 4–6 pairs of small leaflets, with a spine at the tip. The plant's rather upright habit becomes rounded with age. It grows in any soil and will survive the bleakest British winter. HEIGHT & SPREAD 1×1 m (3×3 ft) after 5 years, ultimately 5 m (16 ft) tall.

▼ *Caragena arborescens* 'Pendula'

'**Lorbergii**'♀ has narrower, more feathery leaflets than the species and smaller flowers. It reaches an ultimate height of 3 m (10 ft). '**Pendula**' has a weeping habit and makes a small shrub, ultimately no more than 1.5 m (5 ft) tall. '**Walker**' has the weeping habit of 'Pendula' with the feathery foliage of 'Lorbergii'.

CULTIVATION Plant in full sun. The plants will tolerate most soils, doing best in a well-drained position.

PROPAGATION Sow seed in spring. Grafted plants are required for a specific feature.

PRUNING None required except to remove dead wood in spring.

PESTS AND DISEASES Usually trouble free.

C

Cardamine
Cruciferae

Cardamine pratensis 'Flore Pleno'

Clusters of four-petalled flowers appear on erect stems in spring on these tuft or mat-forming hardy perennials. The genus includes some common weeds, but the plants listed are appropriate for a spring border combined with bulbs, a woodland garden or for a corner of a rock garden.

RECOMMENDED SPECIES AND VARIETIES
C. asarifolia see *Pachyphragma macrophyllum*
C. digitata see *C. pentaphyllos*
C. enneaphyllos Nodding clusters of flowers, each 1 cm (⅜ in) across, are pale yellow or cream. The leaves have 3, occasionally 4–5, toothed and pointed leaflets. Native to SE Europe. HEIGHT & SPREAD 20×30 cm (8×12 in).
C. heptaphylla White, pink or purplish flowers, 2 cm (¾ in) across, appear from spring to early summer. The leaves have 5–11 elliptical, toothed leaflets. Native to central and W Europe. HEIGHT & SPREAD 40×50 cm (16×20 in).
C. pentaphyllos (syn. *C. digitata*) The pale purple or white flowers are 2 cm (¾ in)

▼ *Cardamine pentaphyllos*

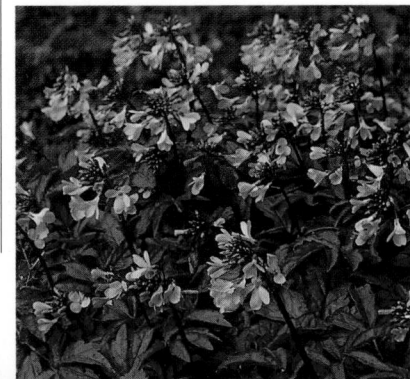

across. The leaves have 3-5 toothed leaflets. Native to mountain woods and rocky places in the Pyrenees and the Alps. HEIGHT & SPREAD 30×30 cm (12×12 in).

C. pratensis (cuckoo flower, lady's smock) The lilac to white flowers are 1.5 cm (½ in)

▲ *Cardamine pratensis*

across. The pinnate, rosette-forming leaves have up to 15 elliptical to rounded leaflets. Native to Europe, E Asia and N America. HEIGHT & SPREAD 50×30 m (20×12 in).

'Edith' has double flowers that are pink in bud, fading to white. 'Flore Pleno'♀ carries double pink to lilac flowers. 'William' produces deep lilac flowers.

C. trifolia The white or pink flowers are 1 cm (⅜ in) across. The plant forms low hummocks or mats of small trifoliate leaves that are purplish below. It thrives in moist, shady places and nooks among rocks. Native to central and S Europe. HEIGHT & SPREAD 10×40 cm (4×16 in).

CULTIVATION Grow cardamines in partial shade in a moist, humus-rich soil. *C. pratensis* requires full sun.

PROPAGATION Divide established plants after flowering or in early autumn. Sow seed when ripe in early to mid summer before the seedpods explode open.

PESTS AND DISEASES Aphids and caterpillars attack the plants; slugs and snails can damage the seedlings.

Cardiocrinum
Liliaceae

Towering above the border, the large fragrant flower trumpets of these hardy, bulbous perennials make a dramatic display in summer. Cardiocrinum bulbs die after flowering but not before producing the bulblets and seed which can be used to replace the parent bulbs. These will take a few years to develop into flowering plants and so gardeners can guarantee flowers every year by planting mature bulbs for a few consecutive seasons. Native to woodland in the Himalayas, China and Japan.

RECOMMENDED SPECIES AND VARIETIES
C. giganteum♀ Richly scented white trumpets, tinged with green outside and striped with maroon inside, appear in mid to late

▲ *Cardiocrinum giganteum*

summer. There are up to 25 flowers, each about 20 cm (8 in) long, on the long stems. Dark green, heart-shaped leaves, some 30 cm (12 in) across, form a rosette at the base of the plant. Smaller leaves spiral up the stems. HEIGHT & SPREAD 1.8×1 m (6×3 ft).

The white flowers of var. *yunnanense* have red markings and the leaves are bronzed when young. The flower stems reach 2.1 m (7 ft).

CULTIVATION Plant bulbs in early autumn over several successive years, setting each with its tip level with the soil's surface. Grow in moist, but well-drained, very fertile soil in partial shade. Protect new growth with dry mulch in winter.

PROPAGATION In autumn, when the leaves have browned, dig up plants and remove the bulblets that have formed around the parent bulb; replant immediately. Plants raised this way will take some 3-5 years to flower. Alternatively, sow seed as soon as it ripens. The seed germinates readily but plants will take up to 7 years to flower.

PESTS AND DISEASES Aphids, botrytis and basal rot may be a problem. Slugs, mice and voles will eat the bulbs.

Carex see GRASSES p. 302
Cardoon see *Cynara cardunculus*

Carlina
Carline thistle
Compositae

These eye-catching, thistle-like plants bear round flowerheads encircled by conspicuous coloured bracts, above rosettes of spiny-toothed leaves. Low-growing, carlinas are suitable for sunny banks, raised beds and larger rock gardens, and make attractive dried flowers. The flowerheads open out in dry weather and close up when it is damp. The plants listed are perennial and fully hardy. Native to S and E Europe.

RECOMMENDED SPECIES AND VARIETIES
C. acanthifolia Purple-brown flowerheads, 15 cm (6 in) wide and surrounded by pale yellow radiating bracts, appear on this stemless herbaceous perennial in summer, after 3 or 4 years. The broad, coarse leaves, up to 30 cm (12 in) long, are grey-green above, white-felted below, and very dissected and spiny. HEIGHT & SPREAD 15×60 cm (6×24 in).

C. acaulis From mid summer to early autumn this stemless or short-stemmed plant bears off-white or pale brown flowerheads 5-10 cm (2-4 in) across, with papery white or pink bracts. The spiny grey-green leaves grow up to 30 cm (12 in) long. Plants can live for 10 years. HEIGHT & SPREAD 20×40 cm (8×16 in).

ssp. *simplex* (syn. ssp. *caulescens*) has stems 30-60 cm (12-24 in) long, each with up to 6 flowerheads.

▲ *Carlina acaulis*

CULTIVATION Plant in any well-drained soil in a warm, sunny place.

PROPAGATION Sow seed in winter or early spring, under glass. Prick out seedlings the moment they are large enough to handle.

PESTS AND DISEASES Seeds are often parasitised by grubs.

Carnation see *Dianthus caryophyllus*

Carpenteria
Hydrangeaceae

Carpenteria californica

The single species in this genus produces a fine display of yellow-centred white flowers in summer. This evergreen shrub, native to California, does best against a sunny wall. After a cold spell it may look a little shabby, but soon regains its bushy appearance.

Carpenteria californica♀ The fragrant flowers, up to 6 cm (2½ in) across, have 5 rounded, often overlapping petals and a central boss of bright yellow stamens. These blooms are carried in clusters at the shoot tips from early to mid summer, and con-

▲ *Carpenteria californica*

▲ *Carpinus betulus*

▲ *Carya ovata*

tinue to appear more sporadically until early autumn. The lanceolate leaves, carried in pairs along the branches and growing up to 11 cm (4¼ in) long, are glossy dark green above and whitish beneath. HEIGHT & SPREAD 1×1 m (3×3 ft) after 5 years, ultimately 3 m (10 ft) tall.

'Ladhams' Variety' is more free-flowering with flowers up to 8 cm (3¼ in) across.

CULTIVATION Choose a compact, bushy specimen with pale young shoots and plant in a sheltered, sunny position, preferably against a wall facing south or west. Any garden soil will do as long as it is well-drained but not too dry.

PROPAGATION Layer in winter or take softwood cuttings in summer.

PRUNING In late winter prune lightly for compactness and to remove winter damage and spent old wood.

PESTS AND DISEASES Usually trouble free.

Carpinus
Hornbeam
Corylaceae

Carpinus betulus 'Fastigiata'

These hardy deciduous trees make graceful specimen plants and common hornbeam is a good hedging plant. Male and female flowers appear as green catkins hanging on the same tree in spring; the female catkins ripen in autumn to clusters of small winged seeds and make a decorative feature among the golden autumn foliage. The oval to ovate leaves, up to 7.5 cm (3 in) long, have a finely serrated edge.

RECOMMENDED SPECIES AND VARIETIES
C. betulus♀ (common hornbeam) The dark green leaves of this medium to large tree have fine teeth and give a good display of yellow in autumn. The tree has a conical,

upright habit when young, but becomes more rounded with age. The grey bark, although smooth, has an undulating surface. Seeds hang in tassels up to 15 cm (6 in) long in early autumn. It withstands severe clipping and the dense leaves stay on the shoots through winter. Native to Europe and Asia Minor. HEIGHT & SPREAD 6×3 m (20×10 ft) after 20 years, ultimately 20 m (66 ft) or more tall.

'Fastigiata'♀ (syn. 'Pyramidalis') has an erect conical habit and a broad base.

▲ *Carpinus betulus 'Fastigiata'*

CULTIVATION Plant in any soil, including clay, from mid autumn to early spring. Plant hedging plants 38–50 cm (15–20 in) apart and do not let them dry out.

PROPAGATION Species are easily grown from seed but cultivars must be grafted.

PRUNING Prune to keep in shape. Clip hedges in mid summer.

PESTS AND DISEASES Usually trouble free.

Carrot see p.736

Carya
Hickory
Juglandaceae

These fast-growing deciduous specimen trees reach a great height and may live for over 100 years. They have slender, upright grey trunks with rounded to conical crowns. The pinnate leaves, up to 36 cm (14 in) long, produce reliable bright yellow autumn colour. Male and female flowers appear in spring on the same tree. Males are greenish yellow and catkin-like on second-year shoots, and females, on the new growth, are inconspicuous, erect, greenish spikes. The autumn nuts are seldom fertile

or edible in Britain. The wide-spreading roots need considerable space.

RECOMMENDED SPECIES AND VARIETIES
C. ovata♀ (shagbark hickory) The trunk of this narrow and upright tree has a flaky grey bark after about 20 years. The dark green leaves have 5 leaflets and change to rich yellow in autumn. Native to eastern USA. HEIGHT & SPREAD 8×5 m (26×16 ft) in 15–20 years, ultimately 20 m (66 ft) tall.

C. tomentosa (big-bud hickory) This round-headed tree has downy shoots with big, velvety winter leaf buds. The slightly aromatic dark green leaves, usually with 7 leaflets, turn a brilliant golden yellow in autumn. Native to USA. HEIGHT & SPREAD 8×6 m (26×20 ft) in 15–20 years, ultimately 18 m (60 ft) tall.

CULTIVATION Hickory trees prefer deep, moist, slightly acid soils.

PROPAGATION Raise from imported seed sown in spring after winter chilling. Plant out young seedlings as soon as possible.

PRUNING If necessary for shaping, prune in summer to avoid sap bleeding in spring.

PESTS AND DISEASES Usually trouble free.

Caryopteris
Verbenaceae

Caryopteris x clandonensis 'Heavenly Blue'

Compact clusters of tiny blue flowers make a stunning display on these deciduous shrubs late in the season. Covered in masses of aromatic leaves, they can look good with silvery leaved plants. The tubular flowers, 6 mm (¼ in) long, have prominent stamens and are held in clusters on the current season's growth. The pointed oval leaves are a dull green and often white or grey beneath. Native to E Asia.

RECOMMENDED SPECIES AND VARIETIES
C. x clandonensis Bright blue or violet-

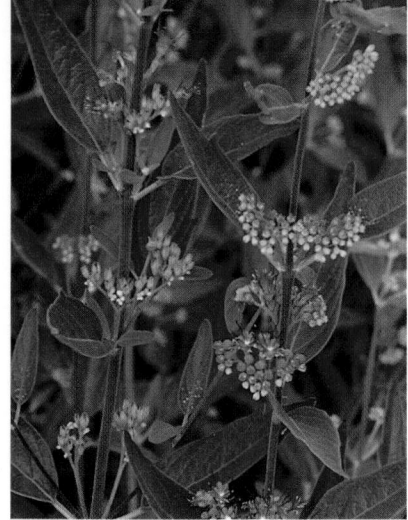

▲ *Caryopteris* × *clandonensis* 'Heavenly Blue'

blue flowers appear in late summer and early autumn on this small, bushy shrub. The leaves, up to 5 cm (2 in) long, have impressed vein markings above and may have sparsely toothed edges. HEIGHT & SPREAD 60×100 cm (2×3 ft) after 5 years, ultimately 1 m (3 ft) tall.

'Arthur Simmonds' is 60 cm (2 ft) tall and more compact. **'Ferndown'** has deep violet-blue flowers from late summer to mid autumn. The more upright **'Heavenly Blue'**♀ has bright blue flowers. **'Kew Blue'** has deep blue flowers. **'Worcester Gold'**, 75 cm (2½ ft) tall, has golden yellow leaves.

▲ *Caryopteris* × *clandonensis* 'Worcester Gold'

C. incana (syn. *C. mastacanthus*) Violet-blue flowers appear in early and mid autumn. Up to 8 cm (3¼ in) long, the leaves may have coarsely toothed edges. The young shoots and flower stalks are covered in fine grey hairs. HEIGHT & SPREAD 70×100 cm (28×40 in) after 5 years, ultimately 1.5 m (5 ft) tall.
C. mastacanthus see *C. incana*
CULTIVATION Plant in autumn or spring in any well-drained soil, including chalk, in a sunny spot. *C. incana* may need the protection of a wall in positions where temperatures regularly fall below -5°C (23°F).
PROPAGATION Raise plants from semi-ripe or greenwood cuttings.
PRUNING In spring, cut the previous year's growth back hard to young healthy buds and cut weak stems down to ground level.
PESTS AND DISEASES Usually trouble free.

Cassia see *Senna*

Cassinia
Cottonwood
Compositae

Cassinia 'Ward silver'

Evergreen foliage and clusters of tiny flowers in summer are the chief virtues of these shrubs. The green, yellow or white ovate leaves grow to 1 cm (⅜ in) long. The species listed here, native to New Zealand, are hardy in all but the coldest of gardens. *Cassinia leptophylla* ssp. *fulvida*, the hardiest, is a suitable hedging plant for coastal gardens.
RECOMMENDED SPECIES AND VARIETIES
C. leptophylla The narrow, oblong leaves are yellowish or silver felted beneath on this shrub with slender, felted branches. The dense clusters of 100 or more white flowers are 2.5-5 cm (1-2 in) wide. HEIGHT & SPREAD 1×1 m (3×3 ft) after 5 years, ultimately up to 1.8 m (6 ft) tall.

The branchlets of ssp. *fulvida* (golden cottonwood) are covered with a golden felt. The young leaves are green above, yellow felted beneath and are sticky with a honey-like smell. In ssp. *vauvilliersii* the felted branches are greenish white.
C. **'Ward Silver'** The branches of this dense bush are white felted and the leaves are silver-grey. The dense clusters of about 100 white flowers are up to 6 cm (2½ in) across. HEIGHT & SPREAD 1×1 m (3×3 ft) after 5 years, ultimately 1.8 m (6 ft) tall.
CULTIVATION Grow in a well-drained soil in an open sunny position.
PROPAGATION Take cuttings from young branchlets at any time of the year.
PRUNING Prune to maintain a good shape.
PESTS AND DISEASES Usually trouble free.

▲ *Cassinia leptophylla* ssp. *fulvida*

Cassiope
Ericaceae

Pretty bell or goblet-shaped white flowers hang singly on delicate stalks in spring and early summer. The wiry stems of these tough, mat-forming evergreen shrubs are covered in overlapping, scale-like green or grey leaves up to 5 mm (¼ in) long. Each flower, up to 1 cm (⅜ in) long, has a pink or red calyx. Cassiopes are slow-growing and will reach their ultimate size in about five to eight years. Native to alpine areas and tundra of the Northern Hemisphere, cassiopes thrive in cool, moist, acid conditions.
RECOMMENDED SPECIES AND VARIETIES
C. **'Badenoch'** A profusion of white flowers are borne on slender, many-branched stems in mid spring. HEIGHT & SPREAD 15×30 cm (6×12 in).
C. **'Edinburgh'**♀ Slender, dark green stems carry many pure white flowers. The green calyxes are edged red. The plant will tolerate warm, dry conditions. HEIGHT & SPREAD 30×40 cm (12×16 in).
C. **lycopodioides**♀ The flowers of this prostrate, wiry shrub are white or cream. The stems are covered in dark green, scaly leaves and form a dense, interwoven mat. HEIGHT & SPREAD 10×30 cm (4×12 in).

'Beatrice Lilley' has abundant white flowers and is shorter and more compact.
C. **'Medusa'** Profuse white flowers on slender, wiry stalks are borne on this much-branched plant. HEIGHT & SPREAD 20×40 cm (8×16 in).

▲ *Cassiope* 'Edinburgh'

▲ *Cassiope lycopodioides*

C

C. mertensiana The white or pink flowers have a red or green calyx. The dark green leaves are pressed close to the stem. The spreading branches of this clump-forming plant are upright at the tips. HEIGHT & SPREAD 25×50cm (10×20in).

ssp. *gracilis* is free-flowering with white flowers and rather hairy leaves.

C. 'Muirhead'♀ Profuse, nodding white flowers are carried on pinkish stalks. The leaves are grey-green. HEIGHT & SPREAD 15×30cm (6×12in).

C. 'Randle Cooke'♀ A profusion of white flowers are borne on the strong, branched stems of this vigorous, easy-to-grow plant. HEIGHT & SPREAD 15×30cm (6×12in).

CULTIVATION Cassiopes thrive in a moist, well-drained acid soil that is rich in humus. They do best in an open cool position away from hot sun, but with good light. They make excellent pan plants for a cool, airy greenhouse or shaded coldframe.

PROPAGATION Take semi-ripe cuttings in late summer or early autumn. Alternatively, layer in spring.

PRUNING Remove any brown or straggly bits in early spring.

PESTS AND DISEASES Vine weevils occasionally attack the plants. Glasshouse specimens may be susceptible to red spider mite.

Castanea
Fagaceae

Castanea sativa

An old sweet chestnut tree in a garden provides a bold landscape feature, and it might even bear edible nuts. However, a castanea tree will take up a great deal of space and could shed branches from time to time. Chestnuts live from 100 to 1000 years. They do not mix well with other plants and can cast a heavy shadow. In the British Isles, *Castanea sativa* is the most widely grown of the 12 species of deciduous trees and shrubs. All have ridged bark, toothed leaves and bear catkins in summer. Newly planted

▼ *Castanea sativa*

trees may take a few years to establish, but then annual growth in excess of 30cm (1ft) may be expected for 50-100 years, though growth is faster in southern Britain.

RECOMMENDED SPECIES AND VARIETIES
C. sativa (sweet chestnut)♀ The huge rounded crown consists of tough, glossy, narrowly oval leaves that are 18cm (7in) long and have coarsely toothed edges. Lax, greenish white scented catkins, 15cm (6in) long, appear in mid summer. Male flowers are spaced along the upper part of the catkin, female flowers are spaced along the lower part and develop into red-brown nuts in bristly husks. The broad trunk becomes ridged, often spirally, when mature. The large, shade-tolerant tree, originally native to S Europe, Asia Minor and N Africa, has been naturalised in Britain for many centuries. HEIGHT & SPREAD 9×5m (30×16ft) in 15-20 years, ultimately 30m (100ft) tall.

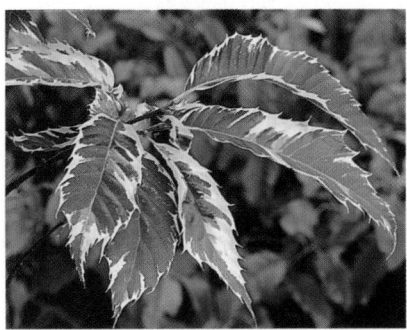

▲ *Castanea sativa* 'Albomarginata'

The smaller cream variegated forms, **'Albomarginata'** and **'Variegata'**, need full light to develop strong leaf colouring.

CULTIVATION Grow in light, well-drained acid soils. The trees are intolerant of lime.

PROPAGATION Easy to grow from seed and seedlings. Young plants transplant well.

PRUNING None is required.

PESTS AND DISEASES Usually trouble free.

Castor-oil plant see *Ricinus*

Catalpa
Bignoniaceae

Catalpa bignonioides

Unmistakable huge leaves and a shapely rounded head make a catalpa an eye-catching specimen tree. There are spectacular late-summer flowers too, but only on

mature trees, often after 25 years or more. Catalpas, although hardy, grow best in warm situations and away from strong winds. They tolerate harsh city conditions. There are about 12 species in the genus.

RECOMMENDED SPECIES AND VARIETIES
C. bignonioides♀ (Indian bean tree) The ornamental, rich green, aromatic leaves are heart-shaped and opposite, and do not appear until early summer on this broad-headed, spreading tree from N America. The leaves grow up to 30cm (12in) long and 20cm (8in) wide. They weigh down the branches so cultivated trees often have to be pollarded, pruned or braced to prevent the branches from snapping. Panicles

▲ *Catalpa bignonioides*

of upright, white, frilly, foxglove-like flowers with yellow and purple markings appear in mid to late summer on mature trees. These are followed by bunches of drooping, thin, green bean pods that are 36cm (14in) long. The pods blacken but remain on the tree throughout winter. HEIGHT & SPREAD 10×8m (33×26ft) after 25 years, ultimately 15m (50ft) tall.

'Aurea'♀ is a velvety, pale yellow-leaved form. It is slightly more tender than the species and does not grow so fast or so large, ultimately reaching up to 10m (33ft) tall.

C. × erubescens **'Purpurea'**♀ The new leaves that emerge in early summer are almost black, changing to dark green as they mature. The tree can grow as broad as it is tall. HEIGHT & SPREAD 4.5×3m (15×10ft) after 20 years in sheltered conditions, ultimately 15m (50ft) tall.

CULTIVATION Catalpas tolerate every kind of soil, even heavy clay, but prefer one that is deep, fertile and moisture-retentive. They do best in hot sunshine and full light. Protect young plants from late frosts.

PROPAGATION Grow from seed sown outside in autumn or take semi-ripe softwood cuttings in mid summer.

PRUNING None required unless the weight of the leaves is cracking branches.

PESTS AND DISEASES Usually trouble free.

C

Catananche
Cupid's dart
Compositae

Dark-eyed, blue or white flowerheads are held on wiry stems in summer (and can be dried for winter decoration). With their narrow, greyish leaves, the catananches are best sited among other grey-foliaged plants at the front or middle of a border. Of the five species of annuals and perennials in the genus, only the hardy perennial, *Catananche caerulea*, is generally grown.

RECOMMENDED SPECIES AND VARIETIES
C. caerulea Shiny, purplish blue flowerheads, about 4 cm (1½ in) across, are made up of strap-shaped ray florets with serrated

▲ *Catananche caerulea* 'Alba'

▲ *Catananche caerulea*

edges. The surrounding papery bracts each have a central silver stripe. The toothed, linear greyish leaves grow to 30 cm (1 ft) long. On heavier clays the plant may be short-lived. Native to SW Europe. HEIGHT & SPREAD 1 m × 45 cm (3 × 1½ ft).

'Alba' has white flowers. 'Major'♀ has deep lavender-blue flowers.
CULTIVATION Plant in spring or autumn in well-drained soil in full sun. Cut the stems back after flowering.
PROPAGATION Divide or take root cuttings in winter. Seed sown in a warm greenhouse in early spring usually produces plants flowering in a range of shades that summer.
PESTS AND DISEASES Usually trouble free.

Catchfly see *Lychnis*, *Silene*

Catharanthus
Apocynaceae

Catharanthus roseus

With their brightly coloured flowers carried above soft green oval leaves for most of the year, these bushy plants look attractive in a well-lit window, conservatory or greenhouse. Keep them at a temperature of at least 7°C (45°F).
RECOMMENDED SPECIES AND VARIETIES
C. roseus♀ (Madagascar periwinkle) Rosepink to red flowers, with mauve throats, up to 4 cm (1½ in) wide, put on a good show from spring until autumn, with a few blooms in winter. Each flower is made up of 5 broadly triangular, satiny petals. The soft, glossy evergreen leaves are up to 5 cm (2 in) long, with prominent midribs. Although a perennial, the plant is often treated as an annual, because young plants look and grow better. Growth can be controlled by pinching back vigorous shoots. Native to tropical and sub-tropical Madagascar. HEIGHT & SPREAD 60 × 45 cm (2 × 1½ ft).

The **Ocellatus Group** produces flowers that are red, pink, white or a mixture of these colours. This group includes the

▼ *Catharanthus roseus*

▲ *Catharanthus roseus* Ocellatus Group

Bright Eyes series and other coloured forms. Some colour selections are shorter-growing than the species.
CULTIVATION Use a soil-based compost such as John Innes No. 2. Keep soil damp by watering regularly in summer; less so in winter. Prune straggly growth in spring.
PROPAGATION Sow seed in a propagator in spring, or raise from softwood cuttings.
PESTS AND DISEASES Greenfly, whitefly and mealy bug can be troublesome.

Cathcartia
Papaveraceae

Nodding, pale yellow poppy-like flowers appear in summer over the clumps of leaf rosettes. These hardy perennials thrive in dappled shade and are an excellent choice for a woodland garden.
RECOMMENDED SPECIES
C. villosa (syn. *Meconopsis villosa*) (woodland poppy) Branched stems carry the 5 cm (2 in) wide flowers made up of 4 rounded, slightly overlapping petals. Rosettes are formed from bristly, oval to round leaves, about 12 cm (4¾ in) long, with 3-5 deep lobes. Smooth, cylindrical seed capsules, about 8 cm (3¼ in) long, follow the flowers. HEIGHT & SPREAD 60 × 30 cm (2 × 1 ft).
CULTIVATION Plant in spring or summer in moist but well-drained, humus-rich, slightly acid to neutral soil in a cool, partially shaded site. Protect from excessive winter wet.
PROPAGATION Sow seed in early spring or divide after flowering or in early spring.
PESTS AND DISEASES Crown rot can kill plants in waterlogged soils and seedlings are prone to damping-off disease.

Catmint see *Nepeta cataria*
Cattleya see ORCHIDS p. 465
Cauliflower see p. 737

Cautleya
Zingiberaceae

Brightly coloured flowers carried in erect spikes and large, glossy lance-shaped leaves are the main features of these exotic-looking plants, which make a distinctive addition to herbaceous and mixed borders. Upright in habit with luxuriant foliage and fleshy stems, these medium-sized herbaceous perennials grow from creeping rhizomes. Plants will tolerate a touch of frost, but must be grown in a free-draining, sheltered position. Native to the Himalayas.

RECOMMENDED SPECIES AND VARIETIES
C. spicata (syn. *C. spicata* 'Robusta') Light orange or soft yellow flowers partly enclosed by maroon-red bracts are borne in large spikes, up to 25 cm (10 in) long and 7.5 cm (3 in) across, during late summer and early autumn. The glossy green leaves are up to 30 cm (12 in) long and 7.5 cm (3 in) wide. HEIGHT & SPREAD 60 cm×1 m (2×3 ft).

CULTIVATION Plant in spring, in a sunny, sheltered corner of the garden, in fertile free-draining soil. Moisture is essential but do not allow the soil to become waterlogged. Scatter a balanced, slow-release fertiliser around the plants in early spring, but do not feed in summer as this may promote soft growth that will not survive winter. Remove faded flowers.

PROPAGATION Divide and replant the rhizomes or sow seed under glass in spring.

PESTS AND DISEASES Usually trouble free.

▼ *Cautleya spicata*

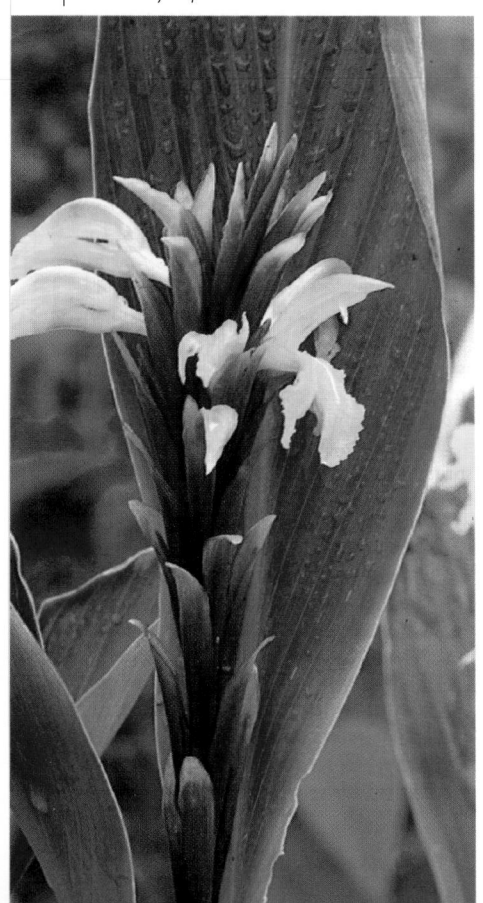

Ceanothus
California lilac
Rhamnaceae

Ceanothus impressus

These sun-loving shrubs are unrivalled for their dense and often showy clusters of blue flowers, ranging in colour from powder blue to deep indigo. Rose-pink and white flowers are also available. In most species the blooms appear in late spring, but some varieties flower through late summer and early autumn. The individual flowers are quite small but they are grouped together in clusters 5–12.5 cm (2–5 in) long.

The genus includes both deciduous and evergreen species. Generally smooth and even glossy, the leaves of most ceanothus are dark green in colour, 2–5 cm (¾–2 in) long and oval, egg-shaped or oblong.

Plants range in habit from ground-coverers to small trees; *Ceanothus prostratus* grows to only 7.5 cm (3 in) in height, while *C. arboreus* 'Trewithen Blue' can reach up to 6 m (20 ft). Most are grown as freestanding shrubs, although some varieties can easily be trained against walls by tying branches to supports. Generally fast growing, most ceanothus species flower abundantly in their second season, particularly if planted in full sun. They are not, however, long-lived in cultivation and it is rare to find specimens more than 20 years old.

Hardiness varies, although healthy plants can survive limited periods of –15°C (5°F). They are ideal for gardens in coastal regions. Native to Central and N America.

RECOMMENDED SPECIES AND VARIETIES
C. arboreus 'Trewithen Blue' ♀ Large conical clusters of deep blue flowers are seen during mid to late spring. The mid green leaves have fine, soft grey hairs beneath and can grow up to 8 cm (3¼ in) long. A round-headed evergreen shrub or small tree, this plant benefits from being trained against a wall. HEIGHT & SPREAD 3.5×3.5 m (12×12 ft) after 5 years, ultimately 6 m (20 ft) tall.
C. 'Autumnal Blue' ♀ This late-flowering variety produces loose clusters of powder-blue flowers in late summer and autumn. An evergreen shrub with large, glossy, mid green leaves, it is one of the hardiest and one of the best for wall-training. HEIGHT & SPREAD 1.5×1.5 m (5×5 ft) after 5 years, ultimately 2.1 m (7 ft) tall.
C. 'Blue Mound' ♀ Dense, rounded clusters of bright blue flowers are seen in late spring and early summer on this thick,

▲ *Ceanothus* 'Blue Mound'

clump-forming evergreen shrub. HEIGHT & SPREAD 1.5×1.8 m (5×6 ft) after 5 years, ultimately 2.1 m (7 ft) tall.
C. 'Burkwoodii' ♀ Lavender-blue flowers are borne in clusters from mid summer to early autumn. One of the hardier evergreens, this dense shrub has glossy serrated leaves that are grey and hairy beneath. HEIGHT & SPREAD 1.5×1.5 m (5×5 ft) after 5 years, ultimately 2.1 m (7 ft) tall.
C. 'Cascade' ♀ This evergreen variety has arching stems that make it suitable for training against a wall, where it can reach a height and spread of 3.5 m (12 ft). Clusters of powder-blue flowers appear in late spring. HEIGHT & SPREAD 1.8×1.8 m (6×6 ft) after 5 years, ultimately 5 m (16 ft) tall.

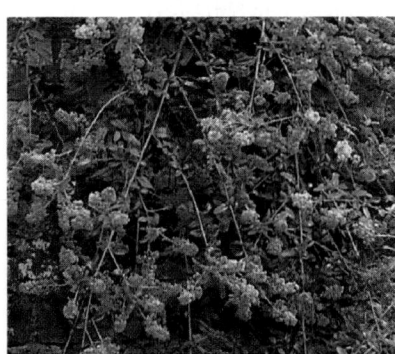

▲ *Ceanothus* 'Cascade'

C. 'Concha' Reliably producing an abundance of flowers, this evergreen shrub has a compact habit and narrow glossy leaves. Reddish in bud, the indigo flowers put on a dazzling display in late spring. HEIGHT & SPREAD 1.8×1.8 m (6×6 ft) after 5 years, ultimately 2.4 m (8 ft) tall.
C. 'Dark Star' resembles *C.* 'Concha', differing only in its darker flowers and tiny leaves, just 1 cm (⅜ in) in length. It also has a more spreading habit. HEIGHT & SPREAD 1.8×2.4 m (6×8 ft) after 5 years, ultimately 2.4 m (8 ft) tall.
C. 'Delight' ♀ Abundant clusters of rich blue flowers appear in late spring. A large, thick evergreen shrub with glossy, light green leaves, this is a good choice for training against a wall. HEIGHT & SPREAD 3×3 m (10×10 ft) after 5 years and ultimately.

C

Celmisia
Compositae

Handsome leaves and white daisy flower-heads, each with a yellow centre, make a striking display. The flowerheads are borne mainly in summer, with a few in late spring. The genus includes evergreen perennials and small shrubs which thrive in rock gardens or raised beds. Larger varieties are valuable in winter for their architectural foliage which may be hairy. The plants listed are hardy but dislike intense cold and need shelter from icy winds.

RECOMMENDED SPECIES AND VARIETIES

C. argentea Dense silvery cushions are formed by tiny narrow leaves, up to 1.5 cm (½ in) long. This perennial bears stemless 3 cm (1¼ in) flowerheads in mid summer. HEIGHT & SPREAD 10×25 cm (4×10 in).

▲ *Celmisia argentea*

C. bellidioides Flowerheads appear in profusion in early summer, about 2 cm (¾ in) across on short stalks. This reliable perennial has 1 cm (⅜ in) long, dark green shiny leaves which form an attractive mat. HEIGHT & SPREAD 5×60 cm (2×24 in).

C. ramulosa Sticky 4 cm (1½ in) stalks carry this small shrub's 2.5 cm (1 in) wide solitary flowerheads in mid summer. The pleated leaves have a white woolly underside and are about 1 cm (⅜ in) long. HEIGHT & SPREAD 20×20 cm (8×8 in).

The dark grey leaves of var. *tuberculata* are covered in silvery knobs.

C. semicordata Erect sword-like leaves up to 40 cm (16 in) long reveal a satiny, silvery underside, making this an eye-catching perennial. It is clump-forming and flowers in early to mid summer with heads about 6 cm (2½ in) across. HEIGHT & SPREAD 40×40 cm (16×16 in).

CULTIVATION Grow in a moist but well-drained soil in a sunny position. Never let it dry out. In too rich a soil plants are more likely to rot or be killed by frost.

PROPAGATION Take greenwood cuttings and keep well watered and well aired until rooted. Seed is fertile only if more than one plant of the same species is grown. Sow it in late summer, as soon as it is ripe.

PESTS AND DISEASES Aphids may attack.

Celosia
Cockscomb, Prince of Wales' feather
Amaranthaceae

Celosia argentea
var. plumosa

Tiny brightly coloured flowers borne in feathery plumes from mid summer to early autumn characterise these tropical plants. Only varieties of the annual species *Celosia argentea* are cultivated in Britain. Some can be grown outdoors as exotic summer bedding, given a warm, sheltered position, while others need to be grown as pot plants in a warm greenhouse or conservatory.

RECOMMENDED VARIETIES

C. argentea Feathery plumes of whitish flowers are seen on this rarely cultivated species. Its varieties are much more garden worthy. HEIGHT & SPREAD 60×30 cm (2×1 ft).

▲ *Celosia argentea*

The crested flowerheads of var. *cristata* look like velvety cockscombs. The pointed leaves are narrow, oval to lance-shaped, and up to 15 cm (6 in) long. This variety should be grown under glass and reaches a height and spread of 30×25 cm (12×10 in).

'Coral Garden' and 'Jewel Box' are

▼ *Celosia argentea* var. *plumosa* 'Century' (rose)

▲ *Celosia argentea* var. *plumosa* 'Century' (yellow)

dwarf plants available in a mixture of orange, pink, purple, red and yellow.

The feathery flowerheads of var. *plumosa* are not usually long-lasting. This plant can be grown outdoors in summer, but only in a warm, sheltered site. It reaches a height and spread of 45×30 cm (1½×1 ft).

'Century', at 50-70 cm (20-28 in), is suitable as a cut flower, both fresh and dried. 'Kimono' is a dwarf strain at 20 cm (8 in) tall. Both 'Century' and 'Kimono' are available in a mixture of purple, pink, orange, red and yellow. 'New Look' has dark red foliage and deep red plumes and reaches 40 cm (16 in) high.

The tall, slender var. *spicata* has plumed flowerheads, like large, coloured ears of wheat, that are suitable as cut flowers. It can be grown as a half-hardy annual outdoors in warm, sheltered spots, reaching a height and spread of 1 m×25 cm (3 ft×10 in).

The flowerheads of 'Flamingo Feather' are deep pink at the top, fading to a paler

▼ *C. argentea* var. *spicata* 'Flamingo Feather'

colour at the base, and are freely produced over a long period.

CULTIVATION Plant outdoors when all risk of frost has passed, in fertile, moisture-retentive soil, choosing a sheltered site in full sun. Pinch out the growing points of *C. argentea* var. *spicata* when the plants are 10 cm (4 in) tall to promote branching.

Alternatively, grow var. *cristata* and var. *plumosa* in pots in the greenhouse. No artificial heating is needed after mid spring. Grow in good light, but shade from direct midday sun. Feed weekly and water generously, maintaining a humid atmosphere.

PROPAGATION Sow seed in a greenhouse in early spring, providing a minimum temperature of 15°C (59°F).

PESTS AND DISEASES Red spider mite can be troublesome under glass. Leaf-spotting and root rot may also occur.

Celtis
Nettle tree, hackberry
Ulmaceae

Celtis australis

Rough-textured, nettle-shaped leaves clothe the broad dome of these deciduous trees which prefers limy soil and warm weather. In some species the foliage may turn yellow in autumn. The small purplish black or red berries that follow the tiny greenish flowers are edible, but they are seldom profuse in Britain. The genus is native to S Europe, SE Asia and N America and the trees tend to be slow-growing in Britain. The American species, such as *Celtis occidentalis*, grow and fruit best.

RECOMMENDED SPECIES

C. australis (European nettle tree) The bark of this round-headed tree is smooth and grey. The leaves are up to 15 cm (6 in) long and 7 cm (2¾ in) wide. They have a rough, dark green upper surface and are greyish beneath. HEIGHT & SPREAD 4×2 m (13×6½ ft) after 10 years, ultimately 12 m (40 ft) tall.

C. occidentalis (hackberry) A broad crown develops above a trunk covered with rough, warty, grey bark. The leaves are slightly smaller than those of *C. australis*. HEIGHT & SPREAD 4×2 m (13×6½ ft) after 10 years, ultimately 18 m (60 ft) tall.

CULTIVATION The trees grow in most soils, but do best in limy conditions. Give them a sunny site. Mature trees tolerate dryness.

PROPAGATION Sow seed in spring.

PRUNING Seldom necessary.

PESTS AND DISEASES Usually trouble free.

Centaurea
Knapweed, cornflower
Compositae

Centaurea montana

Bright summer flowers that attract bees and butterflies into the garden are a valued feature of these popular annuals and perennials. The large flowerheads, some of which are good for drying, have neatly overlapping bracts and a central, thistle-like boss of florets, surrounded by colourful, spreading, rather spidery, ray florets. Stiff upright stems make the larger perennials bold plants for beds and borders. They do well on poor soils, particularly chalky sites in full sun, and survive anywhere with good drainage.

The familiar and colourful annual *Centaurea cyanus* is an important feature of annual wild-flower meadows, mixing well with poppies and corn marigolds. It makes a fine cut flower and its cultivars come in a good range of colours, including blue, pink and red. The genus is native to Europe, W and central Asia and N Africa. All are hardy in Britain except *C. cineraria*.

RECOMMENDED SPECIES AND VARIETIES

C. bella Pink to pale purple flowerheads, up to 4 cm (1½ in) across, appear on this low mound-forming herbaceous perennial from late spring to mid summer. Silvery grey leaves, basically lyre-shaped but with lobes, are 12 cm (4¾ in) long, white with woolly hairs beneath. The plant is sometimes found in nursery catalogues under *C. simplicicaulis*. HEIGHT & SPREAD 40×40 cm (16×16 in).

▲ *Centaurea bella*

C. cineraria♀ (syn. *C. gymnocarpa*) White-felted foliage makes this evergreen perennial useful as a dot or edging plant. The leaves are up to 20 cm (8 in) long and deeply divided with lyre-shaped lobes. Purple flowers, up to 3 cm (1¼ in) across with dark brown pointed bracts beneath, open in small clusters during mid summer but are secondary to the foliage. This plant dislikes

winter wet and is not reliably hardy below -15°C (5°F) in most regions, so is often grown each year from seed. HEIGHT & SPREAD 1 m×45 cm (3×1½ ft).

C. cyanus (cornflower) Blue, pink, purple, red or white flowers 2.5-5 cm (1-2 in) across appear on these annual plants in branching sprays from early summer to early autumn. The narrow, tapering leaves are grey-green and up to 15 cm (6 in) long. HEIGHT & SPREAD up to 1 m×30 cm (3×1 ft).

'**Blue Diadem**' is a tall variety, 60 cm-1 m (2-3 ft) high, with large, deep blue flowers 7.5 cm (3 in) across. Compact forms to 30 cm (1 ft) tall are suited to bedding and growing in pots. They include '**Dwarf Rose Gem**' with rose-red flowers, '**Jubilee Gem**' with blue flowers, and '**Polka Dot**' available in mixed colours.

C. dealbata Bright pink flowers, about 6 cm (2½ in) across, are freely borne from mid to late summer, nestling among the upper leaves on stiff erect stems. This clump-forming herbaceous perennial has finely cut, light green leaves up to 45 cm (18 in) long, grey with woolly hairs beneath. HEIGHT & SPREAD up to 1 m×60 cm (3×2 ft).

'**Steenbergii**' has carmine-lilac flowers and is just 60 cm (2 ft) tall.

C. gymnocarpa see *C. cineraria*♀

C. hypoleuca Bright pink flowers, 4 cm (1½ in) across, are freely borne in mid summer by this upright herbaceous perennial. Finely cut mid green leaves have a white underside with woolly hairs and are 25 cm (10 in) long, basically lyre-shaped but with up to 9 lobes. HEIGHT & SPREAD 60×45 cm (2×1½ ft).

'**John Coutts**' has deep rose flowers up to 7.5 cm (3 in) wide, and is more spreading than the species; to 60 cm (2 ft).

C. macrocephala Large yellow flowers, about 5 cm (2 in) across and surrounded by papery, silvery brown bracts, distinguish this vigorous, clump-forming herbaceous perennial. Narrowly oval mid green leaves are 30 cm (12 in) long and 6 cm (2½ in) wide. The flowers, which appear in mid summer, dry well for display. HEIGHT & SPREAD 1 m×60 cm (3×2 ft).

C. montana (mountain or perennial cornflower) Purple to violet-blue flowers, up to 7.5 cm (3 in) across, appear in profusion during late spring and early summer on this vigorous spreading, herbaceous to partly

▼ *Centaurea montana*

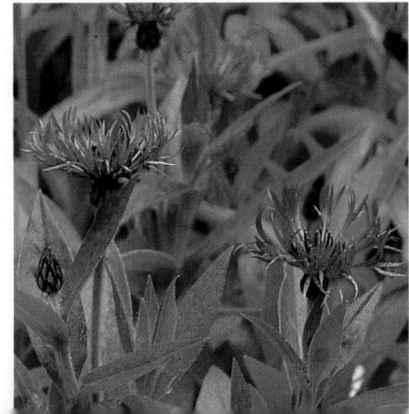

C

evergreen perennial. This popular old cottage garden flower is patch-forming with a dense mass of roots that produce a number of stems carrying one or more flowers. The grey-green leaves, up to 18 cm (7 in) long, are narrow to elliptical and tapering. The undersides of the leaves are woolly. HEIGHT & SPREAD 50×60 cm (20×24 in).

▲ *Centaurea montana* 'Alba'

▲ *Centaurea montana* 'Carnea'

'Alba' has white flowers and paler leaves than the species. 'Carnea' (syn. 'Rosea') bears bright pink flowers. 'Parham' has deep amethyst blooms.
C. ruthenica This imposing herbaceous perennial has solitary sulphur-yellow flowers, about 5 cm (2 in) across, borne in mid summer on stiffly erect stems. The deep green, dissected leaves are oblong and hairless, up to 25 cm (10 in) long at the base of the plant and shorter on the stems. The base of the plant gradually becomes woody as it matures. HEIGHT & SPREAD 1.5 m×80 cm (60×32 in).
C. simplicicaulis Numerous rose-pink flowers, up to 5 cm (2 in) across, appear from late spring to mid summer on this

▼ *Centaurea simplicicaulis*

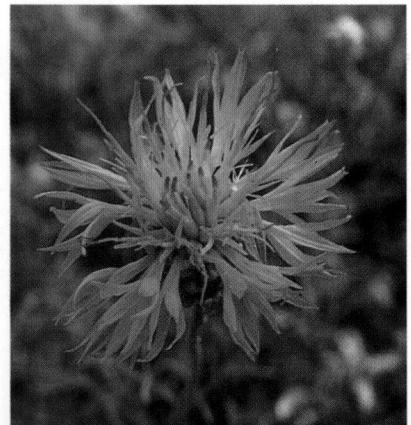

mound-forming herbaceous perennial with stiff erect stems. Lobed, oblong to lyre-shaped leaves are deep green above and grey with hairs beneath. HEIGHT & SPREAD 40×40 cm (16×16 in).
C. triumfettii Blue or lilac flowers, up to 7.5 cm (3 in) across with paler or whitish centres, are produced in early and mid summer. This fairly robust, partly evergreen perennial has short rhizomes and grey-green oblong to elliptical leaves covered at first in whitish cobweb-like hairs. HEIGHT & SPREAD up to 70×50 cm (28×20 in).

White flowers distinguish ssp. *cana* which has woolly leaves and flower bracts and grows up to 20 cm (8 in) tall; 'Rosea' bears rose-pink flowers. The flowers of ssp. *stricta* are blue and the plant grows up to 50 cm (20 in) tall.
CULTIVATION Plant perennials from autumn to spring in any free-draining soil in a sunny spot. *C. montana* tolerates a range of conditions, from moist to dryish sites in sun or semi-shade. Stake taller plants.
PROPAGATION Divide when replanting after flowering or in early spring. Sow seed of perennials in pots in a coldframe in late winter or early spring and plant out as soon as large enough. Examine home-grown seed carefully for maggots. Take cuttings of *C. cineraria* in mid summer, root under glass and plant out in spring. Sow seed of annuals in their flowering position in spring.
PESTS AND DISEASES Powdery mildew may attack foliage and stems of many species, especially in mid to late summer.

Centradenia
Melastomataceae

Centradenia inaequilateralis 'Cascade'

Grown mainly as indoor pot plants or in a greenhouse, these tropical evergreen plants provide beautiful year-round foliage and winter floral colour. They need a minimum temperature of 13°C (55°F) to thrive.
RECOMMENDED SPECIES AND VARIETIES
C. inaequilateralis (syn. *C. rosea*) Small, pink, 4-petalled flowers in clusters about 10 cm (4 in) across, appear at the ends of the branches during winter. The soft, oval to lance-shaped leaves are up to 10 cm (4 in) long. Mid green in colour, they are strongly suffused with red. This species forms a small sub-shrub. Native to Mexico. HEIGHT & SPREAD 30×30 cm (1×1 ft).

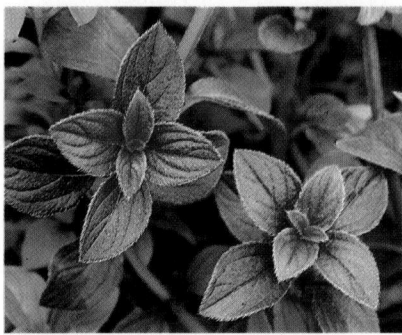

▲ *Centradenia inaequilateralis* 'Cascade'

'Cascade' has a pendulous habit and is ideal for a permanent hanging basket.
C. rosea see *C. inaequilateralis*
CULTIVATION Grow in pots or hanging baskets in good-quality, general-purpose compost. Choose a lightly shaded position in a warm greenhouse or indoors. Repot annually in spring. Feed plants freely and water well in summer; feed and water more moderately in winter.
PROPAGATION Sow seed in spring or summer or take softwood cuttings in summer.
PRUNING Pinch out the tips of young plants to promote a bushy habit and cut back old plants each spring to ensure a leafy, well-clothed plant.
PESTS AND DISEASES Whitefly, red spider mite and mealy bug may attack the plants.

Centranthus
Valerianaceae

The long flowering season, from early summer to early autumn, is a valued feature of these annuals and hardy perennials.
RECOMMENDED SPECIES AND VARIETIES
C. ruber (red valerian) Panicles of 6 mm (¼ in) crimson to pale red, star-shaped flowers are borne above grey-green fleshy oval leaves, up to 10 cm (4 in) long. Native to Europe and the Mediterranean, this species is an easily grown, striking perennial for a sunny dry spot on chalk, where it forms an erect, bushy, compact plant. On richer soils it tends to be more lax and possibly not so long-lived. Its nectar attracts butterflies and hawkmoths into the garden. HEIGHT & SPREAD 60×60 cm (2×2 ft) or more.

▼ *Centranthus ruber*

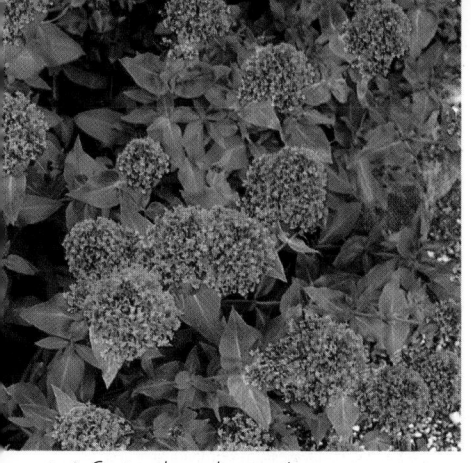

▲ *Centranthus ruber coccineus*

White flowers are seen on ***albus***, while ***coccineus*** has deep red flowers.

CULTIVATION Grow *C. ruber* in the herbaceous border, on dry slopes or in crevices in walls. It does best in poor, particularly chalky soil. In a herbaceous border replant it every 3 or 4 years as it becomes leggy in rich soil, but elsewhere it can be left. Trimming after the first flowering helps to preserve the shape and encourage a second crop of new leaves and flowers.

PROPAGATION Divide or sow seed in spring. The young seedlings should be grown in pots so that the taproot is not damaged in transplanting. In suitable conditions the plant self-seeds.

PESTS AND DISEASES Usually trouble free.

Cephalaria
Giant scabious
Dipsacaceae

Dense, rounded heads of numerous small tubular flowers, resembling pin cushions, appear above the dark green foliage in early summer. The flowers, in buttery-yellow, ivory or white, are long-lasting.

The two hardy perennials listed below make imposing plants in a large border or woodland garden. They need plenty of room to develop and are therefore not suitable for a small garden. The genus contains annuals and perennials – all widely distributed through Europe, Asia and N Africa.

RECOMMENDED SPECIES
C. alpina The yellow flowerheads, 3 cm (1¼ in) across, are carried at the top of thin, hairy stems. The basal leaves are up to 10 cm

▼ *Cephalaria gigantea*

(4 in) long made up of 9–15 paired leaflets. Each leaflet is 3 cm (1¼ in) long, oval with pointed tips and slightly toothed edges. The stem leaves are smaller. HEIGHT & SPREAD 1.2×1 m (4×3 ft).

C. gigantea (syn. *C. tatarica*) Ridged stems carry the ivory to pale yellow flowerheads, up to 5 cm (2 in) across. The 40 cm (16 in) long basal leaves are composed of up to 15 leaflets, each up to 10 cm (4 in) long with coarsely toothed edges. The stem leaves are smaller. HEIGHT & SPREAD 1.8×1.2 m (6×4 ft).

C. tatarica see *C. gigantea*

CULTIVATION Plant in autumn or spring in any soil in full sun. In sheltered gardens the plants can be grown without staking.

PROPAGATION Sow seed in autumn in open ground or divide in spring.

PESTS AND DISEASES Usually trouble free.

Cephalocereus see CACTI p. 106

Cephalotaxus
Plum yew
Cephalotaxaceae

Cephalotaxus harringtonia 'Fastigiata'

Glossy, dark green leaves, straight-sided and very narrow, are lined up in rows on either side of the shoots, luxuriantly clothing these slow-growing evergreen conifers. The plants make handsome, spreading specimens, or can be clipped into a hedge, while *Cephalotaxus fortunei* 'Prostrate Spreader' is useful as ground cover. Native to E Asia and the Himalayas, the species listed below are generally hardy and do best in a shaded part of the garden with cool, moist soil.

Tiny cream flowers open in early spring, or sometimes in late winter, along the underside of the shoot at the base of each leaf on male trees, and on females at the tips of shoots before the flush of new growth. The brown cones borne on female trees (if fertilised by a nearby male) resemble olives or small plums.

RECOMMENDED SPECIES AND VARIETIES
C. fortunei The tree forms a shapely, low umbrella of growth and tolerates constant shade. The soft leaves grow to 10 cm (4 in) long and curve down at the tip. New spring growth suffers damage from late spring frosts. HEIGHT & SPREAD 1×2 m (3×6½ ft) after 10 years, ultimately 10 m (33 ft) tall.

'Prostrate Spreader' is very similar to the species, but much lower and more

spreading, always being wider than it is tall. It reaches 1×5 m (3×16 ft) in 30 years and makes an excellent ground-cover plant for dark, damp positions. Its bark is reddish brown and flaking.

C. harringtonia Dark, shiny leaves, 5 cm (2 in) long with 2 faint silvery, parallel bands underneath, are aligned in rows. The plant is rounded and shrubby with flaky brown bark. HEIGHT & SPREAD 1×1 m (3×3 ft) after 10 years, ultimately 6 m (20 ft) tall.

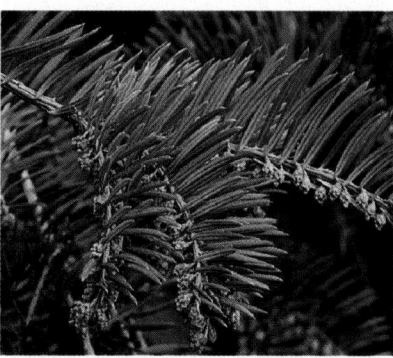

▲ *Cephalotaxus harringtonia* var. *drupacea*

▲ *Cephalotaxus harringtonia* 'Fastigiata'

The smaller var. ***drupacea*** has shorter needles than the species. **'Fastigiata'** has a nearly columnar habit, with steeply upright branches. The needles are spirally arranged rather than ranked.

CULTIVATION Although acid soils suit cephalotaxus plants best, they are among the few conifers that also do well in chalky soils. They thrive in cool, damp sites, including heavy clay, and revel in shade whether dappled or deep.

PROPAGATION Take semi-ripe or hardwood cuttings from terminal shoots; side-shoot cuttings do not produce leaders.

PRUNING None is necessary except for removing any badly shaped branches in mid to late spring. New shoots may appear at wounds exposed to light – a response that makes the plants (except for 'Prostrate Spreader') suitable for clipping as a hedge.

PESTS AND DISEASES Usually trouble free.

Cerastium
Mouse-ear chickweed
Caryophyllaceae

Mounds of attractive grey-green or white foliage are decorated in summer with small white flowers with five deeply notched petals and ten yellowish stamens. There are at least 60 species around the world – hardy annuals and herbaceous perennials. All but a few are too invasive and weedy for the garden. Those that are cultivated are suitable for rock gardens or raised beds or for covering banks or walls.

RECOMMENDED SPECIES AND VARIETIES
C. alpinum (alpine chickweed) Compact and mat-forming, this hardy evergreen perennial is covered with soft greyish hairs. The grey-green leaves are oval and 1 cm (⅜ in) long. White flowers 1.5 cm (½ in) across are borne singly or in loose clusters of up to 5 flowers on short stalks. Flowers appear in late spring and early summer. Some leaves wither in cold winters. Grow in a sunny niche in a rock garden or in a gap between paving. Native to grassy and rocky uplands across Europe. HEIGHT & SPREAD 10×30 cm (4×12 in).

White hairs cover var. *lanatum*. Protect it from damp winter conditions.

▲ *Cerastium tomentosum*

C. tomentosum (snow-in-summer) This popular plant, a hardy evergreen perennial, forms a greyish white spreading mat made up of narrow white-felted leaves, 2 cm (¾ in) long. A profusion of starry white flowers, 2 cm (¾ in) across, are borne in lax clusters throughout summer. This is a very vigorous plant, providing effective cover for banks, walls and dry path edges. It is too invasive for a rock garden or raised bed. Native to the Apennines and Sicily. HEIGHT & SPREAD 20 cm×1 m (8 in×3 ft).

Var. *columnae* is a more compact form.
CULTIVATION Plant in gritty, well-drained soil in a sunny site, in spring or early summer. Protect *C. alpinum* in winter with a pane of glass. Grow *C. alpinum* var. *lanatum* in pans in an unheated greenhouse.
PROPAGATION Divide plants in spring or late summer. Sow seed when ripe or in spring in a coldframe.
PESTS AND DISEASES Usually trouble free.

Ceratostigma
Plumbaginaceae

Ceratostigma willmottianum

Bright blue flowers and fine reddish bronze autumn foliage provide a wonderful display on these low-growing shrubs. Rounded, five-lobed flowers, borne in clusters, last from summer into autumn and make an impact at the front of a border or in a rock garden. The shrubs may be deciduous or evergreen and have small oval to obovate leaves. Ceratostigmas, native to China and the Himalayas, are not fully hardy and are treated as herbaceous perennials and cut back to ground level in winter in cold areas.

RECOMMENDED SPECIES AND VARIETIES
C. griffithii The deep blue flowers, up to 1 cm (⅜ in) across, appear from late summer to mid autumn, but can be rather sparse. The dull green leaves, 3 cm (1¼ in) long, turn bright red in autumn. The multi-stemmed, evergreen shrub has a rounded habit. HEIGHT & SPREAD 80×80 cm (32×32 in).

▲ *Ceratostigma griffithii*

C. plumbaginoides (syn. *C. larpentae*) The brilliant blue flowers, about 1.5 cm (½ in) across, are borne on this plant from early to mid autumn. The deep green, deciduous leaves, up to 4 cm (1½ in) long, produce rich red tints in autumn. The plant is multi-stemmed and spreading. HEIGHT & SPREAD 40×50 cm (16×20 in).
C. willmottianum (Chinese plumbago) Rich blue flowers, 1.5 cm (½ in) across, are carried in profusion from mid summer to mid autumn on this slender, multistemmed, deciduous shrub with a rounded habit. The light green leaves, up to 5 cm (2 in) long, are hairy on both sides and tinted red in autumn. HEIGHT & SPREAD 60×60 cm (2×2 ft).
CULTIVATION Grow in a dry, well-drained soil in full sun. The plant requires protection and does best against a south-facing wall.

PROPAGATION Take semi-ripe cuttings in mid to late summer. Divide in winter.
PRUNING Cut back to ground level any shoots that have been killed by frost.
PESTS AND DISEASES Usually trouble free.

Cercidiphyllum
Cercidiphyllaceae

Cercidiphyllum japonicum

The foliage of this upright, sometimes multistemmed, tree, the sole species of its genus, takes on subtle autumn colours – pale yellows, purple and pink – that light up the garden. It is frost-hardy in all situations and is native to Japan and China.
Cercidiphyllum japonicum (Katsura tree) The deciduous leaves are a rounded heart shape, 5 cm (2 in) across. New spring leaves are often a glowing bronze colour, then become bluish green above and bluish green-white beneath. There are separate male and female trees; both bear small, insignificant red flowers on bare branches in mid spring. Female flowers develop into bunches of small pods, up to 1 cm (⅜ in) long, containing seeds which are fertile only if a male tree grows nearby.

An autumn bonus is the smell of caramel or candyfloss that the tree gives off and that often carries 70 m (75 yd). HEIGHT & SPREAD 6×3 m (20×10 ft) after 20 years, ultimately more than 20 m (66 ft) tall.

The leaves of var. *magnificum* are larger and turn a golden yellow in autumn. It is a rarer and smaller tree reaching 10 m (33 ft) eventually. The leaf size and colour of f. *pendulum* is as the species but the tree has long pendulous branches.
CULTIVATION The trees do best on a fairly deep, rich, moist soil. In times of little rain they sometimes shed their leaves before the autumn display of colour. Plant trees from late autumn to early spring; container-

▼ *Cercidiphyllum japonicum pendulum*

grown trees can be planted out at any time.
PROPAGATION Readily propagated from seed or hardwood cuttings.
PRUNING None required other than to remove dead branches.
PESTS AND DISEASES Usually trouble free.

Cercis
Leguminosae

Cercis siliquastrum

Clusters of small pinkish purple flowers cover the bare branches of these small, spreading deciduous trees in late spring. They remain on the tree for two to three weeks as the foliage unfolds. The distinctive, broad alternate leaves, 5-15 cm (2-6 in) long, are paper-thin, bright green and shaped like a rounded heart. If conditions are favourable, they turn a warm yellow colour in autumn. The fruits contain a line of hard-coated seeds in flat, green pods. Plants are slow-growing in Britain. They need a sheltered, sunny position.

RECOMMENDED SPECIES AND VARIETIES
C. canadensis 'Forest Pansy'♀ The tree or large shrub has distinctive bronze, reddish purple foliage all season. It does not reliably flower in Britain. HEIGHT & SPREAD 4.5 × 3 m (15 × 10 ft) after 15-20 years, ultimately 12 m (40 ft) high. Native to southern USA.

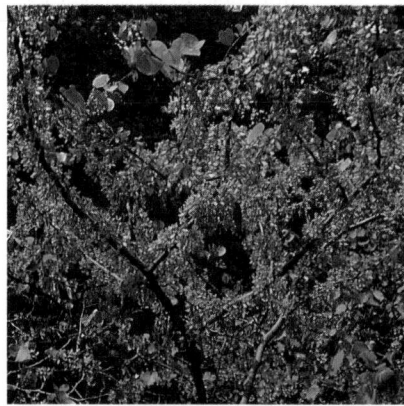

▲ *Cercis siliquastrum*

C. siliquastrum (Judas tree)♀ A spectacular display of rose-purple flowers is borne in late spring on the rounded tree. The plant grows best in hot, dry stony places and is most suited to southern Britain. The pods become rosy coloured in late summer. Native to SE Europe and W Asia. HEIGHT & SPREAD 6 × 3.5 m (20 × 12 ft) in 15-20 years, ultimately 10 m (33 ft) tall and can be equally as wide.

The flowers of f. *albida* are white; the leaves are pale green.
CULTIVATION Trees do well on both acid and lime-rich soils. They prefer dry conditions and good drainage and do not thrive in heavy, wet soils. Shelter from late frosts.
PROPAGATION Sow seed under glass in early spring. Plant into the permanent growing position when 2 years old as these trees do not transplant well. Trees take 5-6 years to bear flowers.
PRUNING None necessary, but trees can be cut back hard in winter or pruned lightly after flowering to keep them small.
PESTS AND DISEASES Coral spot can be a problem. Canker occurs in wild stands of *C. canadensis* in N America, and cultivated specimens could possibly be affected.

Ceropegia
Asclepiadaceae

A fine trailing habit makes this versatile succulent an ideal houseplant. It can be grown in troughs to tumble down as a 'living curtain' and makes a good companion for other succulents and desert plants, like cacti. The recommended species originates in dry regions of E South Africa. Simple cultivation makes it easy for children to grow.

RECOMMENDED SPECIES AND VARIETIES
C. linearis ssp. *woodii*♀ (rosary vine, string of hearts) Curious flowers produced in late summer are up to 2.5 cm (1 in) long and curve upwards, resembling pink pipes. Small potato-like tubers produce long thin stems with, at intervals, heart-shaped leaves up to 2 cm (¾ in) long, attractively marked with shades of grey. These tubers allow easy

▲ *Ceropegia linearis ssp. woodii*

propagation of the plant. It spreads to the width of the container. HEIGHT 2 m (6½ ft).
CULTIVATION Grow where the plant will receive several hours of direct sunlight a day to encourage the leaves to colour, although it tolerates poor light. High temperatures are not necessary; it survives cold conditions, to freezing point if kept dry. Water sparingly, letting the compost dry out first. In winter, water very occasionally; not at all if temperatures fall below 7°C (45°F). Feed little and often if growth is desired. Repot annually only if large plants are wanted. Cut the plant back if it trails too far or is untidy.

PROPAGATION Take cuttings or detach tubers from the stems in spring and pot them up into a very gritty compost. Put additional grit, sharp sand or perlite around the base of the cutting or tuber to prevent rotting. Water sparingly until plants start active growth, which may not happen for several months.
PESTS AND DISEASES Plants may suffer from infestations of mealy bug.

Cestrum
Solanaceae

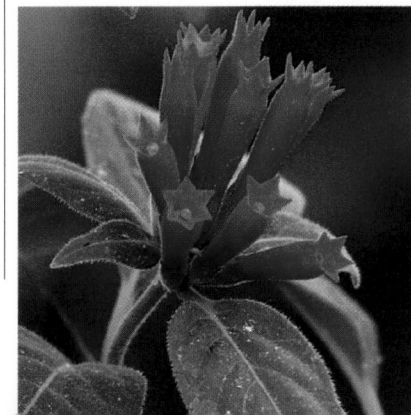

Cestrum parqui

Clusters of small, tubular flowers in shades of red, yellow and purple appear in late spring and summer on these tender evergreen or deciduous shrubs. They can be grown outdoors in mild areas, given a warm sheltered position, but elsewhere they require a conservatory or unheated greenhouse. The plants originate in S America. All parts may be poisonous if eaten.

RECOMMENDED SPECIES AND VARIETIES
C. elegans♀ (syn. *C. purpureum*) An upright evergreen shrub with slender, arching branches that bear clusters of reddish purple flowers throughout summer. The narrow, pitcher-shaped flowers are 2.5 cm (1 in) long. The downy, slender pointed leaves are a dull green and up to 12.5 cm (5 in) long. Shiny, deep purple berries, 2 cm (¾ in) long may form in late summer and autumn. HEIGHT & SPREAD 1.2 × 1 m (4 × 3 ft) after 5 years, ultimately 3 m (10 ft) tall.
C. 'Newellii'♀ Clusters of red, pitcher-shaped flowers, each 2.5 cm (1 in) long, are borne from late spring to mid summer on this evergreen shrub. The narrow, oval, dull green leaves are up to 15 cm (6 in) long. HEIGHT & SPREAD 1.2 × 1 m (4 × 3 ft) after 5 years, ultimately 3 m (10 ft) tall.
C. parqui♀ Large drooping clusters of night-scented flowers appear from mid summer to early autumn on this deciduous

▼ *Cestrum 'Newellii'*

▲ *Cestrum parqui*

shrub. Greenish yellow and tubular, the flowers are 2 cm (¾ in) long with spreading, pointed lobes. The bright green willow-like leaves are up to 12.5 cm (5 in) long. Purplish brown to black fruits, 1 cm (⅜ in) long, are rare. HEIGHT & SPREAD 1.2×1 m (4×3 ft) after 5 years, ultimately 2.4 m (8 ft) tall.

C. purpureum see *C. elegans*

CULTIVATION Outdoors, plant in well-drained, preferably rich, loamy soil against a sheltered, south or west-facing wall. Under glass, plant in well-drained potting compost and place in a sunny or partially shaded spot.

PROPAGATION Raise plants from seed or semi-ripe cuttings.

PRUNING Not necessary but plants can be cut back in early spring to restrict size.

PESTS AND DISEASES Usually trouble free.

Chaenomeles

Flowering quince, japonica
Rosaceae

chaenomeles japonica

Early spring flowers bloom on the bare branches of these easily grown, hardy deciduous shrubs. The bowl-shaped flowers, up to 5 cm (2 in) across, are borne singly or in clusters. Usually five petalled, there are shades of pink, red, orange and white. Flowers are often followed in autumn by large – up to 7.5 cm (3 in) long – fragrant, yellow-green fruits. The dense branches are thorny. Flowering quinces do well trained against a sunny wall; they may also be grown in a border and used for low ornamental hedging. The three species in the genus are native to China and Japan.

RECOMMENDED SPECIES AND VARIETIES

C. japonica Clusters of flowers are mostly red with prominent golden anthers but colour on different plants can vary. For reliability of colour, cultivars of *C. × superba* are more commonly grown. Flowers are followed by apple-shaped fruits, up to 4 cm (1½ in) across. The rounded, oval leaves are toothed and up to 5 cm (2 in) long. The low-growing, spreading shrub has a rounded habit. HEIGHT & SPREAD 60 cm×1 m

(2×3 ft) after 5 years, ultimately 1 m (3 ft) high and twice as broad.

C. speciosa Clusters of flowers on the multistemmed shrub appear in profusion in early spring and can be a range of colours but are predominantly red with attractive pale to bright yellow anthers. The inconsistency in flower colour makes the range of cultivars a more reliable buy. Fragrant fruits, up to 6 cm (2½ in) across, follow the flowers. These are green speckled with white and tend to be apple- or pear-shaped. The oval, glossy green leaves reach 7.5 cm (3 in) long. HEIGHT & SPREAD 1×1.2 m (3×4 ft) after 5 years, ultimately 3×5 m (10×16 ft).

'**Geisha Girl**' ♀ is a smaller, low-growing plant with double, deep apricot-coloured flowers. '**Moerloosei**' ('Apple Blossom')

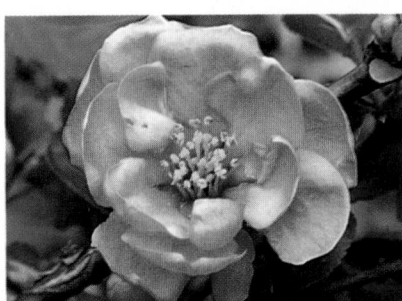

▲ *Chaenomeles speciosa* 'Geisha Girl'

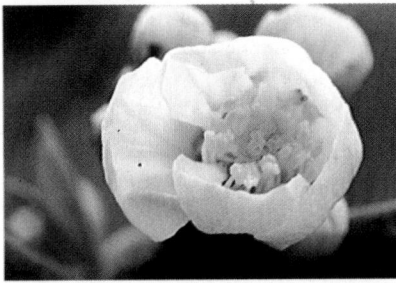

▲ *Chaenomeles speciosa* 'Nivalis'

bears a profusion of white flowers with tinges of pink. '**Nivalis**' reaches 2×3 m (6½×10 ft) and has large pure white flowers. '**Rosea Plena**' has a semidouble pink to coral pink flower. The fruits are more ovate in shape and are quite often ribbed. '**Rubra Grandiflora**' has large crimson flowers and is of a low spreading habit, rarely more than 1 m (3 ft) high. The low-growing '**Simonii**' normally reaches no more than 1 m (3 ft) in height but spreads much wider. It has blood red, semidouble flowers produced in profusion. The large single white flowers of '**Snow**' are rather sparsely produced.

C. × superba It is best to select a named cultivar if a particular colour is required. The flowers of the dense, rounded shrub appear in early spring through to early summer and most have decorative yellow anthers. The apple-shaped fruits ripen in autumn. Leaves are up to 5 cm (2 in) long and are rather rounded with small teeth. HEIGHT & SPREAD 1×1.2 m (3×4 ft) after 5 years, ultimately 1.5 m (5 ft) tall and about twice as wide.

▲ *Chaenomeles speciosa* 'Simonii'

'**Crimson and Gold**' ♀ is a handsome shrub with deep crimson flowers with a mass of golden anthers. '**Jet Trail**' has pure white flowers borne in profusion. The abundant flowers of '**Knap Hill Scarlet**' ♀ are long lasting and are a bright orange-

▲ *Chaenomeles × superba* 'Crimson and Gold'

scarlet. '**Nicoline**' ♀ has scarlet red flowers. '**Pink Lady**' ♀ is dark pink in bud opening to rose pink. The flowers of '**Rowallane**' ♀ are a bright crimson.

CULTIVATION Chaenomeles are adaptable shrubs and grow under a wide range of conditions but they grow best in well-drained soil and flower better in full sun. Plant them from late autumn to early spring.

PROPAGATION Grow from seed but if a particular flower colour is needed a specific cultivar is required and a grafted plant must be purchased.

PRUNING None normally required unless it is to thin out the often numerous branches or to keep a plant to a certain size. Train plants grown against a wall by cutting back the previous season's growth to two or three buds after flowering.

PESTS AND DISEASES Usually trouble free.

Chaenorhinum

Scrophulariaceae

A mass of small, snapdragon-like flowers are produced throughout summer in shades of lilac, violet, blue and yellow by these sun-loving hardy annuals and perennials, suited to raised beds and rock gardens.

RECOMMENDED SPECIES AND VARIETIES

C. glareosum Violet and yellow flowers, about 8 mm (⅜ in) long, are borne in showy spikes by this handsome perennial which has arching stems and spreads to form tufts. Its light blue-green roundish leaves are up to 1.5 cm (½ in) long. Native to S Spain. HEIGHT & SPREAD 15×35 cm (6×14 in).

C. origanifolium (syn. *Linaria origanifolia*) Lilac-blue flowers 1–2 cm (⅜–¾ in) long with darker stripes and a pale yellow or

▲ *Chaenorhinum origanifolium*

white patch on the lip appear in late spring and all summer. This tufted perennial has lax stems up to 35 cm (14 in) long and 1-2 cm (⅜-¾ in) long oval leaves. Some forms spread, while others are more upright. Native to the Pyrenees. HEIGHT & SPREAD 10-20×25-30 cm (4-8×10-12 in).

CULTIVATION Grow in a sunny open site in gritty, well-drained, preferably limy, soil.

PROPAGATION Sow seed in pots in a cold-frame during autumn and winter.

PESTS AND DISEASES Usually trouble free.

Chaerophyllum
Hairy chervil
Umbelliferae

Fern-like foliage sets off the billowing, flattish lilac-pink or white flowerheads of the annuals, biennials and perennials in this genus to perfection. Brighten a late spring border with the hardy herbaceous perennial described; do not confuse it with chervil, the culinary herb, *Anthriscus cerefolium* (see HERBS, p.330), and do not use for cooking.

RECOMMENDED SPECIES AND VARIETIES
C. hirsutum 'Roseum' Numerous tiny lilac-pink flowers grouped in small rosettes are borne in rounded clusters 7.5-12.5 cm (3-4 in) across on erect, branching stems. Each cluster carries as many as 30 rosettes. The broadly incised, dark green leaves, 15×15 cm (6×6 in), are arranged alternately on 25-30 cm (9-12 in) long stalks. Both leaves and stalks are covered with soft hairs. Clusters of flattened, ovoid seeds follow the flowers. Native to Europe. HEIGHT & SPREAD 30-60×30-60 cm (1-2×1-2 ft).

CULTIVATION Plant in dampish ground, wooded areas, or the usual garden soils, in

▼ *Chaerophyllum hirsutum* 'Roseum'

spring or autumn. Position in sun or partial shade. Split clumps every 2-3 years.

PROPAGATION Divide in spring or autumn. Sow seed as soon as it ripens.

PESTS AND DISEASES Slugs and snails attack young plants.

Chamaecyparis
False cypress
Cupressaceae

Chamaecyparis lawsoniana 'Lutea'

Exceptionally varied evergreen conifers – dwarf, tall, round, shrubby, conical and columnar – make up this genus. Foliage colour ranges through green, blue, grey and golden; often the coldest winters bring out the best colour. The scale-like, overlapping leaves form flattened sprays that are held in pairs on either side of the shoots.

The trees are planted in groups for screening and formal schemes, and individually for accent plants in borders, rock gardens, patios and tubs. Growth rates vary with conditions but many of the numerous varieties are too large for most gardens and cannot be kept small by pruning. The plants are hardy but easily damaged by any weight of snow. These natives of eastern N America, Japan and Taiwan prefer acid, clay soils but do well on most fertile garden soils.

RECOMMENDED SPECIES AND VARIETIES
C. lawsoniana (Lawson cypress) This narrow, conical tree gains up to 60 cm (2 ft) of height a year and is far too large for most gardens. There is a great choice of varieties that make more suitable garden plants; all have the drooping leading shoots characteristic of the species. Tiny red male flowers open in spring at the new branchlet tips; blue female flowers appear on the same tree, borne on the previous year's growth tips and sideshoots. The female flowers mature into globular cones almost 1 cm (⅜ in) across. HEIGHT & SPREAD 6×2.4 m (20×8 ft) after 10 years, ultimately 50 m (165 ft) tall.

The recommended varieties are grouped below as broad, narrow and dwarf.

BROAD VARIETIES
'Albospica' has green foliage sprays splashed with creamy white, giving it a speckled appearance. It makes very slow growth, reaching only about 1.5 m×75 cm (5×2½ ft) after 10 years. 'Alumigold' is compact, upright and slow growing, reaching only 2 m×50 cm (6½ ft×20 in) in 10 years; it has yellow, soft-textured new

▲ *Chamaecyparis lawsoniana* 'Golden Wonder'

spring foliage that matures to blue-green on the ascending branches. 'Erecta Viridis' ('Erecta') forms a flame-shaped silhouette, ultimately growing to about 25×6 m (80×20 ft), and has bright green sprays of foliage held upright on erect branches. 'Golden Wonder' bears bright golden foliage all year round, particularly if sited in the sun. It is fast growing, reaching 20×4 m (66×13 ft) or more in just 30 years. 'Green Hedger'♥ is an erect grower with dense, fresh green foliage. If unchecked, it becomes a towering 25×4 m (80×13 ft), but it can be controlled to form a dense hedge with regular clipping in spring and autumn. 'Nana Albospica' is a short and slow grower that reaches only 2×1.5 m (6½×5 ft) after 40 years. The dark blue-green foliage is flecked with creamy white.

NARROW VARIETIES
'Ellwoodii'♥ has dense sprays of grey-green leaves on a bushy, multistemmed tree 10 m (33 ft) high. In winter the foliage turns steel

▼ *Chamaecyparis lawsoniana* 'Ellwoodii'

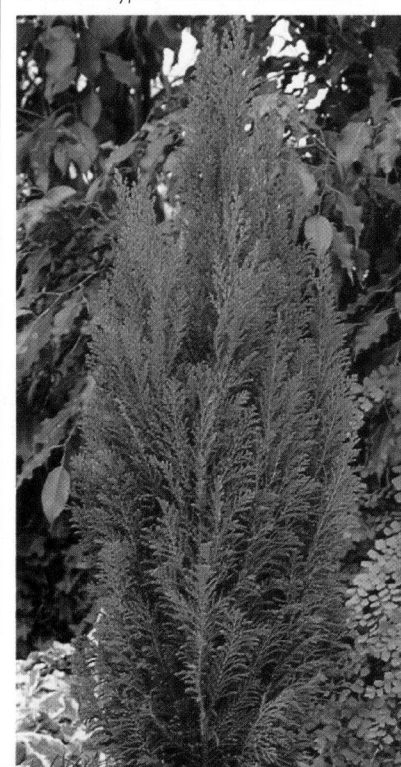

blue. **'Ellwood's Gold'**♀ has dense, yellowish green foliage tipped with gold all year round. It has a compact habit and grows slowly to about 5m (16ft). **'Fletcheri'**♀ is a dense, upright grower suitable for planting in a row to make a screen up to 6m (20ft) high. The feathery sprays of foliage are greyish green. **'Grayswood Pillar'**♀ develops quickly to 9×1m (30×3ft). Its steeply ascending branches bear dense, grey foliage. **'Kilmacurragh'**♀ has short, steeply upright branches bearing dense sprays of dark, grey-green foliage. It reaches about 25×2m (80×6½ft) in 40 years. **'Lane'**♀ makes a golden column about 6×1.5m (20×5ft) high. It is clothed right to its base with drooping, feathery sprays of foliage. **'Lutea'**♀ reaches 25×3m (80×10ft) and has luxuriant, feathery golden foliage. **'Pelt's Blue'**♀ is 4×2m (13×6½ft) with silvery blue foliage. **'Pembury Blue'**♀, with striking silver-blue, dense foliage, grows to 4×1.2m (13×4ft) in 10 years and eventually to twice this size. It needs a warm spot.

▲ *Chamaecyparis lawsoniana* 'Aurea Densa'

▲ *Chamaecyparis obtusa* 'Kosteri'

▲ *Chamaecyparis lawsoniana* 'Pembury Blue'

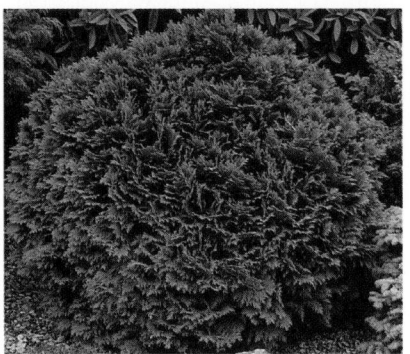

▲ *Chamaecyparis lawsoniana* 'Minima Glauca'

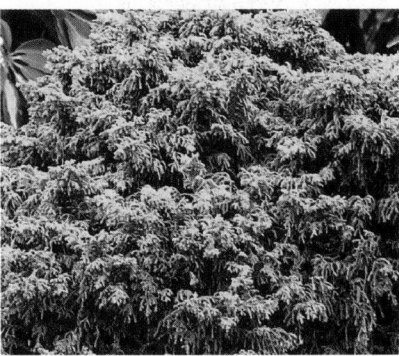

▲ *Chamaecyparis obtusa* 'Tetragona Aurea'

'Wisselii'♀ is particularly striking in spring when all its branch tips are laden with tiny, red male flowers. Sprays of dark green leaves are packed on the branches of a tree that reaches 10×2m (33×6½ft) in 40 years.
DWARF VARIETIES
'Aurea Densa'♀ develops into a rounded, conical shape with dense, overlapping sprays of golden foliage all year round. It grows only 1cm (⅜in) a year, eventually reaching 2m×75cm (6½ft×30in). **'Chilworth Silver'**♀ produces dense, blue-grey, needle-like foliage on upright branches. It grows slowly to 3×1.5m (10×5ft), broadening towards the top. **'Forsteckensis'** forms a globular bush only 1.5×2m (5×6½ft) after 60 years. The foliage, so close-packed that it resembles moss, appears grey-blue from a distance but greener close up. **'Gimbornii'**♀ makes a neat globe of dense, bluish green foliage, tipped with mauve in winter. It barely reaches 2×1.8m (6½×6ft) after 40 years. **'Lutea Nana'**♀ is slow-growing with quite openly arranged golden foliage. It reaches 2×2m (6½×6½ft) after 60 years. **'Minima Aurea'**♀ makes a compact egg shape whose foliage sprays are golden on the upper surface and bright

yellow underneath. The extremely hardy plant reaches just 80cm (32in) after 40 years. **'Minima Glauca'**♀ forms a 2m (6½ft) globe with sea-green foliage in short vertical sprays. **'Pygmaea Argentea'**♀ slowly develops into a rounded bush whose erect branches bear dark, bluish green foliage tipped with silvery white. Strong sunlight scorches this plant. Because it grows to only about 2m×75cm (6½×2½ft), it is suitable for a tub or planter.
C. obtusa (Hinoki cypress) This tall, fast-growing species forms a dense cone with a wide spread at the base. The shiny, deep green, scale-like leaves are borne in flattened sprays and have bright, white 'x' marks on the underside. Small orange male and pale brown female flowers occur on the same tree in clusters at the shoot tips in spring, males on the new leading tips and females on the previous year's shoots and sideshoots. Round, scaly cones ripen from green to brown and grow to 1.5cm (½in) across. HEIGHT & SPREAD 5.5×2.4m (18×8ft) after 10 years, ultimately 30m (100ft) tall.

The varieties listed are smaller than the species and more suitable for gardens.

'Crippsii'♀ reaches approximately 10×3m (33×10ft). The new foliage each year is bright golden yellow, fading rather in its second year, and the inner foliage is green. **'Kosteri'**♀ grows extremely slowly into a densely packed, conical bush about 1.2m (4ft) high. The flattened, dense, moss-like sprays of foliage are bright green. **'Nana'**♀ grows very slowly, taking 40 years to make a neat dome only 75×100cm (30×40in). Tight, rounded sprays of foliage are held in dense tiers and are a very dark, almost black, green. This is an extremely hardy plant. **'Nana Aurea'**♀ has the same shape as 'Nana' but is slightly taller and has more loosely arranged, golden foliage. **'Nana Gracilis'**♀ is more conical in shape and eventually reaches about 2m (6½ft) after some 40 years. Its flat fans of foliage are held erect and are dark, glossy green. **'Tetragona Aurea'**♀ is sparsely branched when young but becomes a bushy, upright plant 5×2.4m (16×8ft) after 50 years. Its dense foliage, in compact sprays, is a strong yellow and needs full sun to bring out the best colour.
C. pisifera (Sawara cypress) The broadly conical tree reaches a majestic height. Its ferny foliage sprays are held at a slight angle

to the shoots and consist of pointed, over-lapping scale-like leaves that are bright green with a conspicuous white line on the underside. Male and female flowers are almost identical but the females are a paler brown. The cones look like peas. The varieties listed are smaller than the species and include plants to suit most gardens. HEIGHT & SPREAD 6×2.4m (20×8ft) after 10 years, ultimately 35m (115ft) tall.

'Boulevard'♀ is 6×3m (20×10ft) after 40 years and a dense grower. Upturned needles, borne on ascending branches, are steel-blue with white stripes on the under-side. 'Filifera Aurea'♀, although an untidy plant, makes a 2.4m (8ft) cascade of golden foliage, spreading to 4.5m (15ft) at ground level after 30 years. The foliage scorches in full sun, but the very similar 'Sungold' raised from this plant is resistant to scorch-ing. 'Golden Mop' reaches only 45×30cm (18×12in), and is a small, densely clothed form of 'Filifera Nana'. The foliage is a richer gold and does not scorch in bright sun. 'Nana Aureovariegata' is also a slow-grower; it forms a tight cushion only 60cm×1.2m (2×4ft) in 40 years. Golden-tinged foliage is held in tightly packed sprays shaped like cockleshells. Splashes of gold variegation occur on some plants. 'Plumosa Compressa' produces yellow, green, grey and blue foliage on the same plant. It can scorch to a dull brown in sun and winter winds and become unsightly. If sheltered and healthy, it reaches 1×1.5m (3×5ft) after 40 years. 'Snow' is a compact, dense-leaved dome with blue-grey foliage flecked white at the tips. It needs protection

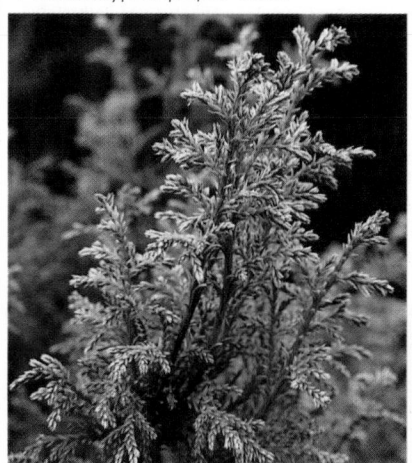

▼ *Chamaecyparis pisifera* 'Snow'

from strong sun and easterly winds, often doing best in a well-placed container since it reaches only 2×2m (6½×6½ft) in 20 years. 'Sungold' see 'Filifera Aurea' above. *C. thyoides* 'Andelyensis'♀ Tiny, abun-dant, red male flowers clothe this tree in spring, followed by pea-size cones. The plant forms a dark bluish green column. HEIGHT & SPREAD 1.2m×75cm (4×2½ft) after 10 years, ultimately 10m (33ft) tall.

'Andelyensis Nana'♀ is a dwarf form of 'Andelyensis' and reaches 1×1.5m (3×5ft). 'Ericoides'♀ has soft-textured, sea-green foliage that turns a striking purplish brown in cold weather. It is conical and grows to about 1.5m×80cm (5ft×32in) in 60 years. 'Rubicon' is upright and its dense foliage is blue-green when new, turning deep plum-purple in winter. It reaches 2×1m (6½×3ft).
CULTIVATION Plant in fertile soil. Acid soils give the best results. Feed plants often.
PROPAGATION Take heeled softwood or hardwood cuttings in spring or autumn; those taken in autumn need bottom heat.
PRUNING None required, except to remove any diseased branches. To raise the canopy, clear the trunk of all branches to the desired height. Make any cuts in spring or autumn.
PESTS AND DISEASES Phytophthora, honey fungus, root rot and butt rot may affect plants. Aphids may be troublesome.

Chamaedorea
Palmae

These palms originate in the shade of Central and S American rain forests and are excellent houseplants for poorly lit rooms. Most types are slow-growing and compact.
RECOMMENDED SPECIES
C. elegans♀ (parlour palm) This neat plant usually grows as a small clump of stems, with the leaves arching attractively away from them. On mature plants the fresh green leaves are around 50-60cm (20-24in) long, less on young plants, with leaflets just over 1cm (⅜in) wide spreading out from a

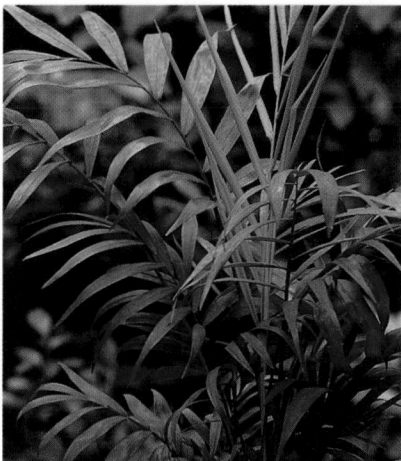

▼ *Chamaedorea elegans*

central midrib. Older specimens flower occasionally, producing pale yellow stems with almost berry-like orange blooms. HEIGHT & SPREAD 100×50cm (40×20in), usually only after many years.
CULTIVATION Grow in soft, indirect light for best results, although they tolerate quite poor light, especially in winter. Avoid long periods of direct sun. Humidity is preferred, but dry air at room temperature is accept-

able. Very dry air, particularly at high tem-peratures, can cause dry brown leaf tips. In winter, plants require slightly dry compost and a minimum of 5°C (41°F). A tempera-ture of up to 25°C (77°F), frequent water-ing and weekly feeding are required during the growing season. Repot every other year if strong growth is desired.
PROPAGATION At home, possible only with seed from a specialist dealer. Sow absolutely fresh seed immediately at 25°C (77°F).
PESTS AND DISEASES Red spider mite.

Chamaemelum
Compositae

The strongly aromatic herb, *Chamaemelum nobile*, or camomile, is the most commonly grown species of this genus. This hardy evergreen perennial forms a dense mat of feathery leaves, sprinkled with white and yellow flowers during summer. It is the flowers which are dried and used to make camomile tea. This is an ideal plant for an open sunny spot on a rock garden or in paving. The foliage smells particularly strong if crushed or stepped upon and *C. nobile* 'Treneague' can be grown into a lush, low-maintenance lawn.

RECOMMENDED SPECIES AND VARIETIES
C. nobile (syn. *Anthemis nobilis*) (camomile) Daisy-like white flowers with yellow centres cover this plant; each flower is 1cm (⅜in) across. The bright green, aro-matic leaves are very finely divided and up to 5cm (2in) long. Native to W Europe. HEIGHT & SPREAD 25×45cm (10×18in).

▼ *Chamaemelum nobile* 'Flore Pleno'

'Flore Pleno' has double flowers and reaches up to 15cm (6in) high and 30cm (12in) across. 'Treneague' is a non-flower-ing variety that can be used to make a camomile lawn. Its height is up to 12.5cm (5in), spreading to 30cm (12in) across.
CULTIVATION Plant during autumn or spring in very free-draining soil, choosing a warm sunny spot. If drying the flowers, cut them at their peak. Otherwise, unless seed is

required, deadhead plants once flowering is over. Clip the foliage often to ensure compact bushy growth. To make a camomile lawn, plant groups of *C. nobile* 'Treneague', placing plants 10 cm (4 in) apart. Clip or mow regularly in summer.

PROPAGATION Divide established plants in spring or sow seed of the species in summer or early autumn. Take cuttings of *C. nobile* 'Treneague' in late spring or late summer.

PESTS AND DISEASES Usually trouble free.

Chamaerops
European fan palm
Palmae

This modest palm tree is popular as a pot plant in a conservatory or greenhouse, or as a summer focal plant in elaborate bedding schemes. It is native to the Mediterranean and there is only one species. It should be kept frost-free throughout winter.

Chamaerops humilis ♀ Broad green fans of lance-shaped leaflets 45 cm (18 in) long and as much as 60 cm (24 in) wide, are carried on prickly stalks up to 90 cm (36 in) long. They usually resemble a crown of leaves emerging almost from ground level and only rarely, in ideal conditions, form a proper trunk. Bunches of greenish yellow flowers are occasionally produced. The plant achieves full height after about 10 years. HEIGHT & SPREAD 4×1 m (13×3 ft).

CULTIVATION Grow in a conservatory or greenhouse, in John Innes No. 2 potting compost and water well. Liquid feed regularly during spring and summer. Stand the plant outside in a sunny spot in summer. Cut fading leaves off at the base and remove flowers as they appear or as soon as they finish. Keep frost-free in winter, at no less than 7°C (45°F), and reduce watering to a minimum. For summer bedding, plunge the whole pot into the ground. Lift in early autumn and put under glass for winter.

PROPAGATION Sow seed in a heated propagator in spring. Remove suckers in spring and summer and insert in compost.

▼ *Chamaerops humilis*

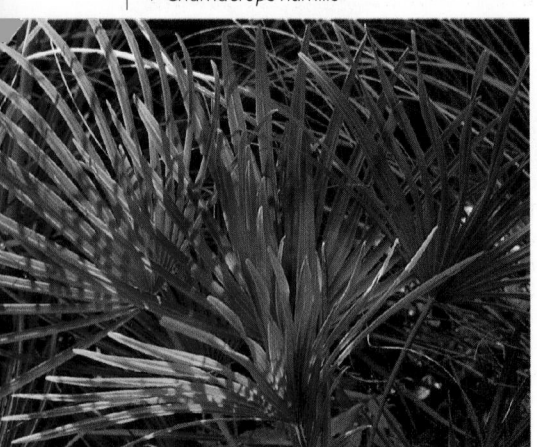

PESTS AND DISEASES Glasshouse red spider mite, scale insects, mealy bug and root mealy bug can attack plants.

Chamomile
    see *Chamaemelum nobile*
Chaste tree see *Vitex agnus-castus*
Cheiranthus see *Erysimum*

Chelidonium
Greater celandine
Papaveraceae

The single species in the genus is a cheerful yellow spring and summer-flowering perennial. Chelidonium takes its name from the Greek for a swallow, *chelidon*, as it is supposed to start flowering when these birds arrive, and to wither as they leave. It is not related to the lesser celandine. This erect branching plant with leafy stems is hardy, easy to grow in any soil that is not waterlogged and freely self-seeding, making it excellent for a wild-flower garden.

C. japonicum see *Hylomecon japonicum*
Chelidonium majus The short-lived flowers are up to 2.5 cm (1 in) wide, made up of 4 rounded, deep yellow, well-spaced petals and are borne in loose clusters. They open

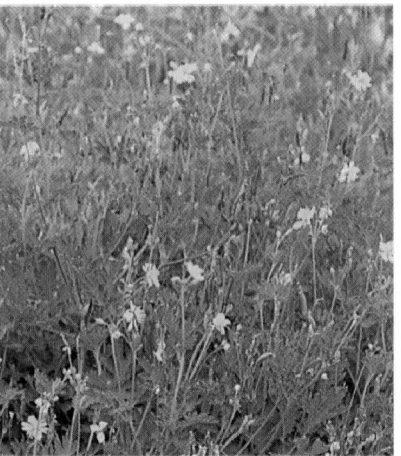
▲ *Chelidonium majus*
▼ *Chelidonium majus* 'Flore Pleno'

in late spring and early summer and are followed by erect narrow seed capsules, up to 5 cm (2 in) long, enclosing black seeds. The fresh green leaves, 10-15 cm (4-6 in) long, are composed of 5-7 oblong, toothed leaflets, whitish beneath with bright orange sap. Native to Britain and much of Europe, N Africa and Asia. HEIGHT & SPREAD 60×30 cm (2×1 ft).

'**Flore Pleno**' has longer-lasting double flowers.

CULTIVATION Plant in any soil that is not waterlogged, in sun or shade.

PROPAGATION Sow seed in the flowering position in spring or when ripe.

PESTS AND DISEASES Usually trouble free.

Chelone
Turtle head
Scrophulariaceae

When other border plants are beginning to succumb to end-of-season raggedness, the new white or pink flowers of these hardy herbaceous perennials are most welcome. They appear at the end of tall, sturdy, leafy stems from late summer to mid autumn. The curiously shaped flowers, up to 3.5 cm (1⅜ in) long, resemble the head of a turtle or tortoise with its mouth open. The interior of the flower is bearded. Chelones spread by underground runners and need plenty of room to expand. A patch of chelones makes good ground cover and suppresses weeds. Natives of marshy places in N America, chelones are at home in waterlogged soils but will also do well on better drained ground.

RECOMMENDED SPECIES AND VARIETIES
C. glabra (syn. *C. obliqua* var. *alba*) (balmony) The flowers are white flushed with pale or deep pink; the beard is white. The mid green leaves are almost stalkless, broadly or narrowly lance-shaped, with toothed edges, up to 7.5 cm (3 in) long. HEIGHT & SPREAD 75×100 cm (30×40 in).
C. lyonii The flowers are pink with a yellow beard. The oval, stalked mid green

▼ *Chelone obliqua*

leaves grow up to 15 cm (6 in) long. HEIGHT & SPREAD 70×100 cm (28×40 in).

C. obliqua The flowers are deep rose-purple with a yellow beard. The stems, maroon-tinged in early growth, are thickly clad with oval or narrow pointed, mid green leaves, to 12 cm (4¾ in) long, on short stalks. The margins are sharply toothed and the veins well marked. Globular seed heads, 1 cm (⅜ in) across, are closely pressed to the stem to form an interesting spike in mid autumn. HEIGHT & SPREAD 1×1 m (3×3 ft).

C. obliqua var. *alba* see *C. glabra*

CULTIVATION Plant at any time of year in any garden soil, in sun or part shade. Divide chelones occasionally to maintain vigour and to prevent them choking other plants.

PROPAGATION Divide roots in spring or after flowering, or sow seeds in spring.

PESTS AND DISEASES Usually trouble free.

Cherry, bladder see *Physalis alkekengi*
Cherry, Cornelian see *Cornus mas*
Cherry, edible see p. 724
Cherry, Jerusalem
    see *Solanum pseudocapsicum*
Cherry, ornamental see *Prunus*
Cherry, winter
    see *Solanum pseudocapsicum*
Cherry laurel see *Prunus laurocerasus*
Cherry pie
    see *Heliotropium arborescens*
Chervil see *Anthriscus cerefolium*
Chervil (culinary herb) see HERBS, p. 330
Chestnut, golden
    see *Chrysolepis chrysophylla*
Chestnut, horse see *Aesculus*
Chestnut, sweet see *Castanea sativa*

Chiastophyllum
Lamb's tail
Crassulaceae

This genus contains only one species, native to the steep, rocky woodlands of the Caucasus. It is a hardy and reliable alpine, suitable for growing in a rock garden or in the crevices of a stone wall and looks very attractive cascading over rocky ledges. A horizontal planting in a wall or ledge also ensures that its roots are well drained.

Chiastophyllum oppositifolium♀ (syn. *C. simplicifolium*) Tiny bright yellow bell-shaped flowers are carried in arching sprays

▼ *Chiastophyllum oppositifolium*

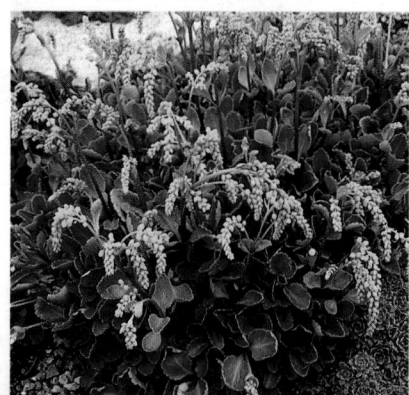

from late spring to early summer. The flower sprays stand well above the creeping foliage, with the drooping tips appearing like golden chains or, indeed, lambs' tails. It is an evergreen, and is grown as much for its fleshy leaves as for its flowers. The bright green oval and toothed leaves, 5 cm (2 in) long, may redden with age. A loose clump of leaf rosettes is formed as the plant spreads. HEIGHT & SPREAD 14×30 cm (5½×12 in).

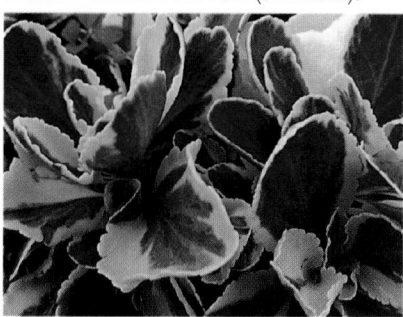

▲ *Chiastophyllum oppositifolium* 'Jim's Pride'

'Jim's Pride' (also known as 'Frosted Jade') has cream-variegated foliage and brighter yellow flowers.

CULTIVATION Plant in most soils in a well-drained position in sun or partial shade. The plant does best if its roots are in the shade and its branches are in the sun.

PROPAGATION Take cuttings or divide well-established plants after flowering.

PESTS AND DISEASES Usually trouble free.

Chimonanthus
Winter sweet
Calycanthaceae

Chimonanthus praecox

Lemon yellow flowers with a delightful spicy fragrance are the glory of this moderately sized, hardy Chinese shrub. It is compact and bushy in habit. Chimonanthus is best mixed with summer-flowering plants – climbers make good companions – because it is not spectacular itself in summer. The shrub also benefits from the shelter provided by neighbouring plants. The flowers are borne on willowy stems before the leaves appear, and superficially resemble pale forsythia. It can take five to six years for plants to flower. There are three species in the genus, only one of which is suitable for cultivation in the British Isles.

RECOMMENDED SPECIES AND VARIETIES

C. praecox Waxy, bell-shaped yellow flowers, 2.5 cm (1 in) across, open in mid winter. They have narrow forward-pointing petals,

▲ *Chimonanthus praecox*

▲ *Chimonanthus praecox*

purple at the centre. The glossy, deciduous, lanceolate leaves, 5-12.5 cm (2-5 in) long, are mid green and willow-like. HEIGHT & SPREAD 1.5×1 m (5×3 ft) in 5 years, ultimately 3×2 m (10×6½ ft).

'Grandiflorus' has showier, larger, deeper yellow flowers, 2.5 cm (1 in) wide, with purplish red centres that sometimes extend as thin lines up the petals. 'Luteus' has clear yellow flowers that appear a little later in the season than those of the species, usually in early spring. Both cultivars are less strongly scented than the species.

CULTIVATION Well-drained, lime-rich soil and a sunny, sheltered position are best. Protect from north and east winds.

PROPAGATION Layering in mid summer is the most reliable way of raising plants. Sow seed under glass in late winter.

PRUNING Cut out weak or overcrowded stems after flowering.

PESTS AND DISEASES Usually trouble free.

Chimonobambusa see BAMBOOS, p. 76
Chinese lantern see *Physalis*

Chionanthus
Fringe tree
Oleaceae

Chionanthus virginicus

Abundant white flowers with unusual, thin narrow petals, produce a decorative show throughout summer on these deciduous trees and shrubs. The leaves are often covered with down when young and turn yellowish in autumn. Small plum-like fruits are occasionally produced after the flowers. The species listed here are both hardy. Native to Asia and eastern USA.

RECOMMENDED SPECIES AND VARIETIES

C. retusus A large shrub with light green leaves about 10 cm (4 in) long with downy white undersides. Erect sprays of snow white flowers, up to 10 cm (4 in) long, appear in mid summer. Dark purple oval fruits may follow in autumn. HEIGHT & SPREAD 2×1 m (6½×3 ft) after 5 years, ultimately 4 m (13 ft) tall.

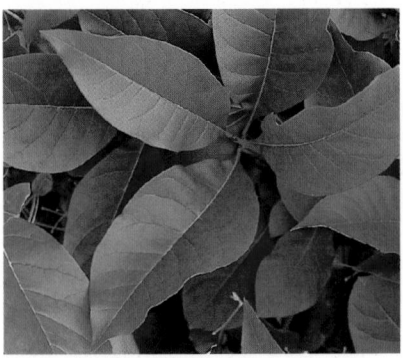

▲ *Chionanthus virginicus*

C. virginicus An attractive large bush or small tree with glossy green leaves, up to 20 cm (8 in) long, that turn yellow in autumn. Drooping sprays of slender, fragrant white flowers, 10 cm (4 in) long, are borne in early summer. Dark blue, egg-shaped single fruits, up to 1 cm (⅜ in) long, sometimes appear in autumn. HEIGHT & SPREAD 3×2 m (10×6½ ft) after 5 years, ultimately 5 m (16 ft) tall.

CULTIVATION Plant during autumn or spring in a free-draining, rich moist soil in a hot, sunny position. Do not allow to dry out at any time.

PROPAGATION Sow seed in autumn in a coldframe.

PRUNING Prune in spring to maintain a good shape. Remove any weak, crossing or damaged shoots at the same time.

PESTS AND DISEASES Usually trouble free.

Chionodoxa
Hyacinthaceae

Chionodoxa sardensis

Starry blue, occasionally pink or white flowers emerge just before the glossy, grass-like foliage appears. These hardy, early spring-flowering bulbs are suitable for a rock garden, the front of a border or for naturalising among shrubs where they will self-seed easily.

RECOMMENDED SPECIES AND VARIETIES

C. forbesii (glory of the snow) This freely spreading dwarf bulb has green grassy leaves up to 25 cm (10 in) long. Deep blue flowers with a white centre are borne in groups of between 4 and 12 on a leafless flower stem. Each blossom is 1 cm (⅜ in) across. HEIGHT & SPREAD 25×10 cm (10×4 in).

'Pink Giant' has soft pink flowers with a

▲ *Chionodoxa forbesii* 'Pink Giant'
Chionodoxa luciliae ▼

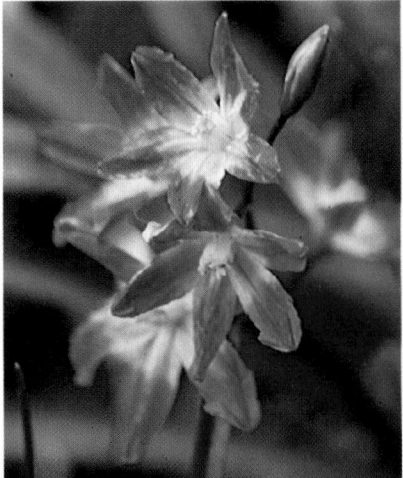

white centre. **Siehei Group** has deep blue to lilac-blue flowers with white centres.

C. gigantea see *C. lucilliae*
Gigantea Group

C. luciliae A free-flowering dwarf bulb with a pair of broad grass-like basal leaves up to 10 cm (4 in) long. The leafless stem produces 1-3 upward-facing blue flowers, each 1 cm (⅜ in) across, with white centres. HEIGHT & SPREAD 10×8 cm (4×3¼ in).

Gigantea Group (syn. *C. gigantea*) has blue to violet-blue flowers.

▲ *Chionodoxa sardensis*

C. sardensis The leafless flower stems carry 5-10 flat, outward-facing or pendent, deep blue flowers up to 2 cm (¾ in) across. These dwarf bulbous plants bear a pair of narrow, lance-shaped, semi-erect basal leaves up to 20 cm (8 in) long. HEIGHT & SPREAD 20×8 cm (8×3¼ in).

CULTIVATION Plant in autumn in a moist, free-draining soil in sun or partial shade.

PROPAGATION Sow seed as soon as it is ripe in a coldframe or greenhouse. Lift and divide bulbs after the foliage has faded and plant immediately.

PESTS AND DISEASES Usually trouble free.

Chionohebe
Scrophulariaceae

A plant for the alpine enthusiast, chionohebe grows into a cushion or mat of tiny overlapping green leaves. Plants are usually grown in pans in a well-ventilated, unheated greenhouse. Outside, they are best grown with other alpine plants in a rock garden or raised or scree bed. Chionohebe is a hardy, slow-growing, evergreen subshrub. Small white or purple flowers appear in spring. Stemless and with five petals, they are borne singly, rather than in clusters, unlike hebe and parahebe. Native to the mountains of Australia and New Zealand.

RECOMMENDED SPECIES AND VARIETIES

C. pulvinaris (syn. *Pygmaea pulvinaris*)

▼ *Chionohebe pulvinaris*

(snow hebe) This plant has a dense cushion-like habit. The greyish green, hairy leaves, about 3mm (⅛in) long, are arranged in small rosettes. White flowers, 4mm (⅛in) across, appear from mid to late spring. HEIGHT & SPREAD 4×15cm (1½×6in).

CULTIVATION Plant at any time of year in gritty, well-drained soil. Position plants where they will get plenty of light, whether in a greenhouse or the garden. Water all year round.

PROPAGATION Divide plants after flowering or in summer.

PESTS AND DISEASES Downy mildew may affect plants forced on under glass.

Chives (culinary herb)
see HERBS p.331

Chlorophytum
Spider plant
Anthericaceae

This popular, easy-to-grow houseplant has distinctive arching, lance-shaped leaves arising from a dense crown. These tropical and sub-tropical evergreen perennials are frost-tender and require a minimum temperature of 5°C (41°F), but given the right conditions they can be used for summer bedding. Tiny plantlets hang from long, slender stems, mainly in spring and summer. The lily-like blooms are insignificant.

RECOMMENDED SPECIES AND VARIETIES
C. comosum Narrow green leaves, up to 45cm (1½ft) long, are arranged in a strong tufted rosette and are often striped with white. HEIGHT & SPREAD 60cm×1m (2×3ft).

'Variegatum'♀ has leaves with white or cream edges. 'Vittatum'♀ carries curved leaves with a bold white central stripe.

CULTIVATION Grow indoors in any good potting compost. Feed regularly in spring

▲ *Chlorophytum comosum* 'Variegatum'

▲ *Chlorophytum comosum* 'Vittatum'

and summer with a liquid houseplant feed. Remove flower stems as they appear, unless plantlets are to be encouraged. Plants tolerate most light levels but should not be placed in direct sunlight. Outdoors, position in a sunny spot in well-drained soil.

PROPAGATION Remove and pot the plantlets in spring and summer. Divide plants in spring or summer.

PESTS AND DISEASES Usually trouble free.

Choisya
Rutaceae

Choisya 'Aztec Pearl'

Profuse clusters of sweetly scented white flowers are set against the glossy evergreen foliage of this shrub. The opposite leaves are composed of three, occasionally two or four, bright green, slender leaflets that are highly aromatic when crushed. The small starry flowers usually have five petals. Native to Mexico and SW United States, this neat, rounded bush is frost resistant.

RECOMMENDED SPECIES AND VARIETIES
C. 'Aztec Pearl'♀ The small white flowers are flushed pink when in bud and have a pleasant almond scent when they open in mid summer. There are 3-5 flowers, each 2.5cm (1in) across, in each cluster. The leaves grow to 10cm (4in) long. HEIGHT & SPREAD 60×60cm (2×2ft) after 5 years, ultimately 2m (6½ft) tall.

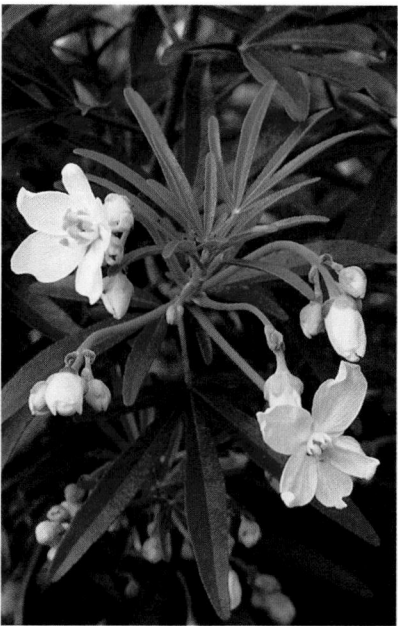
▲ *Choisya* 'Aztec Pearl'

C. ternata♀ (Mexican orange blossom) Abundant small, citrus-scented white flowers, each 1.5-2.5cm (½-1in) across, are produced in clusters of up to 6 from mid spring onwards. The leaves grow to 10cm (4in) long. HEIGHT & SPREAD 1×1m (3×3ft) after 5 years, ultimately 3m (10ft) tall.

▲ *Choisya ternata* 'Sundance'

'Sundance'♀ has bright yellow foliage that fades as the season progresses and which is at its most striking in full sun. It reaches an ultimate height of 1.8m (6ft). It is also more susceptible to frost damage.

CULTIVATION Plant in spring in any well-drained soil in a sunny, sheltered position. In northern gardens they usually require the protection of a south or west-facing wall.

PROPAGATION Raise from softwood or semi-ripe cuttings.

PRUNING None is required.
PESTS AND DISEASES Usually trouble free.

Christmas tree see *Picea abies*
Chrysanthemum For plants known by the common name, chrysanthemum, see *Dendranthema*. For other plants until recently excluded from the genus *Dendranthema* see *Argyranthemum*, *Leucanthemopsis*, *Leucanthemum* and *Tanacetum*

Chrysogonum
Golden star, green-and-gold
Compositae

The yellow daisy-like blooms, long flowering period and the neat size and habit of this semi-evergreen perennial make it an attractive plant for the front of a border. These plants make good ground cover in sun or shade but they require winter protection in very cold gardens. There is only one species in the genus.
Chrysogonum virginianum Each flower has 5 broad, yellow petals up to 3cm (1¼ in) long, surrounding a small, yellow, central

▲ *Chrysogonum virginianum*

disc, with leafy bracts. They bloom from late spring to early autumn. The hairy, bright green, oval, scalloped leaves are up to 7cm (2¾ in) long. Stems are also hairy. Native to eastern N America. HEIGHT & SPREAD 20×30cm (8×12in).
CULTIVATION Plant in spring or autumn in moist but well-drained, humus-rich soil that is not too limy. Choose a position in sun or partial shade.
PROPAGATION Divide plants in spring or sow seed under glass when fresh.
PESTS AND DISEASES Usually trouble free.

Chrysolepis
Fagaceae

Chrysolepis chrysophylla

These half-hardy, shrubby evergreen trees have lustrous deep green leaves that are densely covered underneath with fine, golden yellow hairs. Creamy white, fragrant catkins appear in mid summer and are sometimes followed in autumn by spiky fruit, similar to sweet chestnuts. Slow-growing, these are good trees for small gardens. Native to California and Nevada, these trees will grow only in the milder areas of Britain and should be sheltered from icy winds, especially when young.
RECOMMENDED SPECIES
C. chrysophylla (golden chestnut) The

▲ *Chrysolepsis chrysophylla*

slender pointed leaves are 5–14cm (2–5½ in) long. Held in rigid clusters, the catkins are 4cm (1½ in) long and consist of male and female flowers. Fruits appear in Britain, but when seen they have green, spiny husks that contain 1–3, chestnut-brown, edible nuts. The rough, grey bark is hard and deeply ridged. When shoots are young they are covered with brownish green felt. HEIGHT & SPREAD 3.5×3m (12×10ft) after 15 years, ultimately 10m (33ft) tall.
CULTIVATION Plant in spring in a sheltered site in fertile, well-drained soil that is not too limy. Pinch out the tips of shoots in spring to encourage bushy growth. Do not transplant established specimens.
PROPAGATION Sow seed under glass in late winter, keeping seedlings in the shade.
PRUNING Thin in spring by cutting back branches to the stem or a main branch.
PESTS AND DISEASES Usually trouble free.

Chusquea see BAMBOOS p.76

Cicerbita
Sow thistle
Compositae

Cicerbita plumieri

Tall panicles of blue thistle-like flower-heads appear on these hardy herbaceous perennials in mid summer. These robust plants are best used in a wild or woodland garden and are not really suitable for a herbaceous border. The genus is related to the lettuce, and this is evident in the plants' rosettes of basal leaves.
RECOMMENDED SPECIES
C. plumieri (syn. *Lactuca plumieri*) Pale blue flowers appear in branched spikes on smooth, stout stems in mid summer. Each flower is up to 2cm (¾ in) across. The lobed leaves are up to 25cm (10in) long and 12cm (4¾ in) wide with a large, rounded terminal lobe. Native to mountainous regions of S Europe. HEIGHT & SPREAD 1.5m×50cm (5ft×20in).
CULTIVATION Plant in autumn or spring in a moist but well-drained, humus-rich, acid-to-neutral soil in partial shade. Staking may be necessary. Remove seed heads before they open to stop plants becoming invasive.
PROPAGATION Sow seed in trays in spring.
PESTS AND DISEASES Usually trouble free.

Cider gum see *Eucalyptus gunnii*

Cimicifuga
Bugbane, rattletop
Ranunculaceae

Cimicifuga simplex
'Elstead'

Long spires of tiny white flowers on tall stems rise above compact clumps of fresh green, deeply divided leaves that often change colour in autumn. These tall, hardy herbaceous perennials are excellent plants for the back of the border. Most grow best on damper soils with some shade to protect the leaves from being scorched by the sun. The individual flowers are star-shaped, 1 cm (⅜ in) across and have an unusual, slightly unpleasant smell. Both flowers and leaves are good for cutting.

RECOMMENDED SPECIES AND VARIETIES
C. japonica Tall, leafless stems carry a mass of white flowers in late summer. The glossy leaves have up to 3–9 oval, lobed leaflets, about 10 cm (4 in) long. This species needs a more protected position. HEIGHT & SPREAD 1.5 m × 30 cm (5 × 1 ft).
C. racemosa♀ (black cohosh, black snake-

▼ *Cimicifuga racemosa*

root) Long spikes of white flowers appear throughout summer. The delicate leaves have oval, deeply toothed leaflets, up to 10 cm (4 in) long. HEIGHT & SPREAD 2.1 m × 50 cm (7 ft × 20 in).
C. ramosa see *C. simplex* 'Pritchard's Giant'
C. simplex Mainly unbranched, drooping flower spikes of pure white starry flowers appear in late summer. The glossy leaves have about 20 deeply divided leaflets, up to 8 cm (3¼ in) long. HEIGHT & SPREAD 1.2 m × 60 cm (4 × 2 ft).

Plants in the **Atropurpurea Group** have purple leaves but the colour can vary considerably. **'Elstead'**♀ has purplish stems

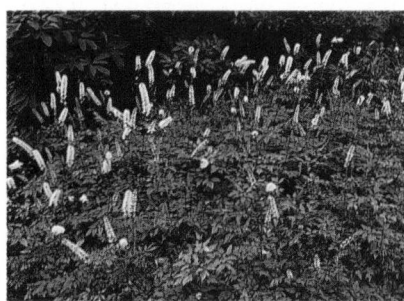

▲ *Cimicifuga simplex* 'Elstead'

with brown buds opening to creamy white flowers. **'Prichard's Giant'** (syn. *C. ramosa*) is a taller plant at 1.5 m (5 ft). **'White Pearl'** has pure white flowers, pale green leaves and pale lime-green seed heads.
CULTIVATION Plant from autumn to spring in moist soil in partial shade. Plants may need some staking. Unless seed is required, deadhead the flowers. Cut back plants to ground level in late autumn or early winter.
PROPAGATION Raise plants from ripe seed sown in autumn or by division from autumn to spring; divide plants no more than every 5 years.
PESTS AND DISEASES Usually trouble free.

Cineraria see *Pericallis × hybrida*
Cinquefoil see *Potentilla*

Cirsium
Compositae

Striking pincushion-like flowerheads are carried on erect stems in summer. As with most thistles the hairy, deeply lobed leaves have bristly margins. Some of the 200 species of biennials and herbaceous perennials are pernicious weeds best left to grow in the wild, but the two hardy species listed here can make colourful additions to the herbaceous border.
RECOMMENDED SPECIES AND VARIETIES
C. japonicum The rose-pink to lilac flowerheads, up to 5 cm (2 in) across, are borne singly or in clusters. The shiny dark green leaves of this short-lived herbaceous peren-

▲ *Cirsium japonicum* 'Rose Beauty'

nial are 30 cm (12 in) long. Native to Japan. HEIGHT & SPREAD 1.5 m × 50 cm (5 ft × 20 in).
'Pink Beauty' has soft pink flowers. **'Rose Beauty'** has deep carmine flowers. **'Snow Beauty'** and **'White Victory'** both have white flowers.
C. rivulare **'Atropurpureum'** The deep crimson flowerheads, carried singly or in clusters, are 3 cm (1¼ in) across. The shiny dark green leaves of this herbaceous perennial grow up to 45 cm (1½ ft) long. HEIGHT & SPREAD 1.2 m × 60 cm (4 × 2 ft).
CULTIVATION Plant in autumn or spring in full sun in any soil. *C. japonicum* will also do well in moister spots. Deadhead before the seed is dispersed.
PROPAGATION Sow seed of the species under glass in spring. Divide cultivars in autumn or spring.
PESTS AND DISEASES Usually trouble free.

▲ *Cirsium rivulare* 'Atropurpureum'

C

Cissus
Vitaceae

Cissus antarctica

Too tender to grow reliably outside, these evergreen, woody-stemmed climbers make fine houseplants with decorative foliage. Most have tendrils and are easy to train over a lightweight cane framework. The tiny summer flowers are greenish and insignificant. Height and spread details given below are the natural height of the plants after about five years. However, growth is usually restricted by pinching back the young shoots to whatever size is required. Native to Africa, S America, Asia and Australasia.

RECOMMENDED SPECIES AND VARIETIES

C. antarctica♀ (kangaroo vine) Glossy, leathery green, oval, pointed leaves densely clothe the woody stems of this vine. The leaves have serrated edges and are up to 10 cm (4 in) long and 5 cm (2 in) wide. HEIGHT & SPREAD 5×1 m (16×3 ft).

▲ *Cissus antarctica*

C. discolor (rex begonia vine) Deep velvety green leaves with prominent silver bands cover the slender woody stems of this climber. The oval, pointed leaves are up to 15 cm (6 in) long and 5 cm (2 in) wide and deep plum, purple or maroon underneath. HEIGHT & SPREAD 3 m×60 cm (10×2 ft).

C. rhombifolia♀ (grape ivy) Coarsely toothed, glossy green leaves cover this moderately vigorous climber. Each leaf is divided into 3 leaflets each up to 8 cm (3¼ in) long and 5 cm (2 in) wide. HEIGHT & SPREAD 3×1 m (10×3 ft).

The widely available **'Ellen Danica'**♀ has a more vigorous, bushier growth and slightly larger, rich green glossy leaves.

C. striata (syn. *Ampelopsis sempervirens*) (ivy of Paraguay, miniature grape ivy) This vigorous woody-stemmed climber bears dull green leaves that are 8 cm (3¼ in) long and across, made up of 3-5 serrated oval

▲ *Cissus rhombifolia*

leaflets. Small, glossy black fruits appear in late summer, after the insignificant flowers. The plant is reasonably hardy outdoors if grown on a warm, sheltered wall. HEIGHT & SPREAD 10×1 m (33×3 ft).

CULTIVATION Position in good light but not full sun. Feed in spring and summer. Most species require a minimum temperature of 7°C (45°F), except *C. discolor* which must be kept above 18°C (64°F). Provide the plants with a framework support and regularly pinch young shoots back to keep them in the desired shape.

PROPAGATION Take semi-ripe stem cuttings in summer.

PESTS AND DISEASES Scale insects and mealy bugs can be troublesome.

Cistus
Sun rose
Cistaceae

Cistus × aguilarii

Evergreen hardy and half-hardy shrubs, native to the Mediterranean and the Iberian peninsula, that are excellent for sunny positions in light, poor soil, particularly in coastal areas. Showy, saucer-shaped papery flowers, 2.5-10 cm (1-4 in) across, are borne in early to mid summer. Leaves are oval or lance-shaped and 2.5-10 cm (1-4 in) long.

RECOMMENDED SPECIES AND VARIETIES

The ultimate size of the plants given below is attained within 5 years.

C. × *aguilarii* The yellow-centred small white flowers of this hardy shrub are profusely borne. The large leaves are bright green. HEIGHT & SPREAD 1×1.5 m (3×5 ft).

The flowers of **'Maculatus'** have a ring of crimson blotches around yellow centres.

C. algarvensis see *Halimium ocymoides*

C. × *corbariensis* see *C.* × *hybridus*

C. crispus Large, purple-red to cerise flowers are borne on this hardy rounded shrub with small, hoary, grey-green leaves. HEIGHT & SPREAD 60×60 cm (2×2 ft).

▲ *Cistus × hybridus*

C. × *cyprius*♀ Large white flowers with carmine basal spots are produced in crowded clusters by this hardy vigorous hybrid. The large, bright green leaves emit a strong aroma. HEIGHT & SPREAD 2×2 m (6½×6½ ft).

C. × *dansereaui* This small hardy shrub bears large white flowers with crimson basal spots and has large dull green leaves. HEIGHT & SPREAD 60×75 cm (2×2½ ft).

'Decumbens'♀ has white flowers and a more spreading habit, to 45 cm (1½ ft) high.

C. **'Elma'**♀ A hardy hybrid of sturdy, bushy habit, this shrub has large, glossy, deep green leaves and large, pure white flowers. HEIGHT & SPREAD 2×2 m (6½×6½ ft).

C. × *florentinus* The medium-sized white flowers have yellow basal spots. Small dull green leaves of this multi-branched, compact, hardy shrub are often downy when young. HEIGHT & SPREAD 1×1 m (3×3 ft).

C. formosus see *Halimium lasianthum*

C. **'Grayswood Pink'** A low-growing hardy shrub with medium-sized pale pink flowers and small grey-green leaves. HEIGHT & SPREAD 60×60 cm (2×2 ft).

C. × *hybridus*♀ (syn. *C.* × *corbariensis*) The white flowers of this dense, hardy shrub have yellow basal spots and are heavily infused with red in bud. Coarse, wrinkled, small leaves are dark green above and paler beneath. HEIGHT & SPREAD 1×1 m (3×3 ft).

C. ingwerseniana see × *Halimiocistus* 'Ingerwersenii'

C. ladanifer♀ (gum cistus) Large white flowers with maroon markings around the yellow stamens are borne on an upright, half-hardy shrub with large dark green leaves. HEIGHT & SPREAD 2.4×1 m (8×3 ft).

The **Palhinhae Group**♀ includes very hardy, low-growing compact plants, rarely

▼ *Cistus ladanifer*

C

exceeding 1m (3ft) in height and spread. The large flowers are pure white.

C. lasianthus see *Halimium lasianthum*

C. laurifolius♀ A hardy, upright plant bearing large white flowers with yellow basal spots. The leaves are dark glaucous green. HEIGHT & SPREAD 1.5×1.5m (5×5ft).

C. × loretii Small white flowers with crimson basal blotches are borne on an upright, dwarf, hardy shrub with medium leaves that are dark green above and greyish beneath. HEIGHT & SPREAD 1×1m (3×3ft).

C. 'Merrist Wood Cream' see × *Halimiocistus wintonensis* 'Merrist Wood Cream'

C. × obtusifolius A small, rounded, hardy shrub bearing small white flowers with a yellow basal mark and small grey-green leaves. HEIGHT & SPREAD 60×60cm (2×2ft).

▲ *Cistus* 'Peggy Sammons'

C. 'Peggy Sammons'♀ Pale pink blossoms on downy stems adorn a bushy, hardy shrub with small grey-green downy leaves. HEIGHT & SPREAD 1×1m (3×3ft).

C. × pulverulentus♀ A half-hardy shrub with medium-sized, purple-pink to cerise-rose flowers and sage green leaves with grey down. HEIGHT & SPREAD 60×60cm (2×2ft).

'Sunset' and 'Warley Rose' have vivid magenta and cerise flowers respectively.

C. × purpureus♀ Medium-sized pink flowers with dark red basal spots are borne on a bushy half-hardy shrub. Small leaves are grey-green. HEIGHT & SPREAD 1×1m (3×3ft).

C. ocymoides see *Halimium ocymoides*

C. sahucii see × *Halimiocistus sahucii*

C. salviifolius Medium-sized white flowers with yellow basal spots are borne on this spreading half-hardy shrub. The small, oval,

▼ *Cistus* × *pulverulentus* 'Sunset'

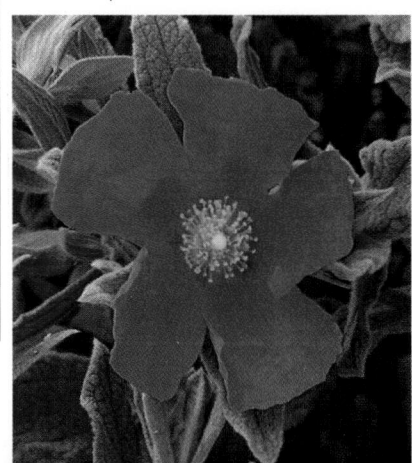

grey-green leaves have a rough, wrinkled surface. HEIGHT & SPREAD 60cm×1m (2×3ft).

C. 'Silver Pink' A hardy and widely planted hybrid with pale, silvery pink medium-sized flowers and leaves, pale green above and greyish beneath. HEIGHT & SPREAD 60×60cm (2×2ft).

C. × skanbergii♀ Pale pink flowers are set off by small green leaves on this hardy shrub. HEIGHT & SPREAD 1×1m (3×3ft).

C. wintonensis see × *Halimiocistus wintonensis*

CULTIVATION Plant in spring in a sunny, well-drained spot. Deadhead regularly.

PROPAGATION Take softwood cuttings in summer or sow seed of the species in spring.

PRUNING Prune out all dead or damaged stems in spring.

PESTS AND DISEASES Aphids can be a problem.

Citron see *Citrus medica*

Citrus

Rutaceae

Citrus aurantium

With their lustrous dark foliage and waxy white flowers these tender evergreen shrubs and trees, native to E Asia, are handsome conservatory plants. This group includes all the popular citrus fruits – orange, lemon, lime and grapefruit. Plants need a minimum winter temperature of 5-10°C (41-50°F). The fragrant flowers have five oblong petals that curve outwards and prominent stamens; these generally appear in summer in a cool conservatory, but in ideal conditions flowers are produced at intervals throughout much of the year. The height and spread of plants given below are for planted out specimens. Plants in large pots will reach only half these sizes.

RECOMMENDED SPECIES AND VARIETIES

C. aurantiifolia (lime) Glossy oval leaves, 8cm (3¼in) long, are carried on spiny branches. The waxy white flowers are followed by green fruits 3-6cm (1¼-2½in) across. HEIGHT & SPREAD 5×2m (16×6½ft).

'Tahiti' bears large seedless fruits.

C. aurantium (Seville orange, bitter orange) This tree with a rounded crown has spiny branches and oval leaves up to 10cm (4in) long. The fragrant, waxy, white flowers are followed by bright orange spherical fruits 8cm (3¼in) across. HEIGHT & SPREAD 10×3m (33×10ft).

▲ *Citrus aurantiifolia* 'Tahiti'

The heavily scented flowers of the dwarf tree 'Bouquet de Fleurs' are used in perfume. It grows to 3m (10ft) high and 1.5m (5ft) wide. 'Seville' has slightly larger flowers and has the best fruit for preserves.

C. limon (lemon) A small tree with glossy oval leaves up to 8cm (3¼in) long. The flowers are white with a purplish tinge and the oval yellow fruits are 5-10cm (2-4in) long. HEIGHT & SPREAD 5×2m (16×6½ft).

'Garey's Eureka' (syn. 'Quatre Saisons') has a continuous flowering and fruiting cycle. 'Variegata' produces striking green and cream variegated glossy foliage. The fruits eventually ripen to clear yellow.

▲ *Citrus limon* 'Variegata'

C. maxima (shaddock) A vigorous tree with a rounded crown. White fragrant flowers are followed by round yellow fruits up to 15cm (6in) across. The oval or elliptical glossy leaves are up to 10cm (4in) long. HEIGHT & SPREAD 5×3m (16×10ft).

C. medica (citron) A shrubby tree with branches that may be flushed purple when young. White flowers with a pink blush are followed by fragrant, oval, yellow fruits, up to 20cm (8in) long. Dark green leaves are oval or elliptical and up to 15cm (6in) long. HEIGHT & SPREAD 3×2m (10×6½ft).

'Ethrog' has lemon-sized fragrant fruits.

C. × meyeri 'Meyer' (Meyer's lemon) A small tree with oval glossy leaves up to 8cm (3¼in) long. The white flowers are waxy and the oval yellow fruits are 8cm (3¼in) wide. This is the hardiest lemon and the best to grow indoors for good-quality fruit. HEIGHT & SPREAD 3×1.5m (10×5ft).

▲ *Citrus × paradisi* 'Golden Special'

C. × paradisi (grapefruit) A large tree with a rounded crown and dense foliage of dark green oval leaves 8 cm (3¼ in) long. The waxy white flowers are followed by large, yellow, globular fruits up to 15 cm (6 in) across. HEIGHT & SPREAD 5×3 m (16×10 ft).

'Golden Special' is a commercial variety and the fruits have white flesh.

C. reticulata (mandarin, clementine, satsuma, tangerine) A shrub or small tree with spiny branches and glossy, oval, dark green leaves up to 8 cm (3¼ in) long. Waxy white flowers are followed by yellow-orange to orange-red globular fruits 8 cm (3¼ in) across. HEIGHT & SPREAD 4×2 m (13×6½ ft).

'Clementine' has bright orange-red fruits and a more upright bushy habit. 'Satsuma' is a compact shrub, up to 3 m (10 ft) tall, with a rather pendulous habit and bright orange fruits. 'Variegata' has cream and green variegated foliage.

C. sinensis (sweet orange) A tree with spiny branches bearing glossy oval leaves 8 cm (3¼ in) long. The waxy white flowers are fragrant and the orange or yellow fruits, up to 10 cm (4 in) across, are oval or globe-shaped. HEIGHT & SPREAD 10×4 m (33×13 ft).

'Valencia' has bright orange fruits, up to 10 cm (4 in) across, with thinner skins. 'Valencia Late' is the same as 'Valencia', but retains its crop much longer. 'Washington Navel' is a virtually seedless orange with fruits up to 10 cm (4 in) across.

C. × tangelo 'Seminole' (tangelo) A hybrid between a grapefruit and a mandarin with leaves up to 8 cm (3¼ in) long. Waxy white

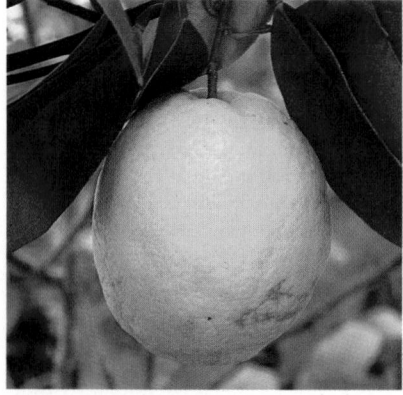

▲ *Citrus sinensis* 'Washington Navel'

flowers are followed by yellow or reddish orange fruit up to 12.5 cm (5 in) across. HEIGHT & SPREAD 5×2 m (16×6½ ft).

CULTIVATION Grow as conservatory plants, and stand pots outside in a sunny place in summer. Rapid changes in light or temperature can result in defoliation. Water freely in spring and summer, sparingly in winter.

PROPAGATION Sow pips from fruits in a propagator, but resulting plants are variable. Most modern varieties are grafted on to a citrus rootstock, but for an amateur semi-ripe cuttings in summer is the best method.

PRUNING During spring prune out any weak wood or any wood that has died back over winter. Shorten long lateral shoots by at least a third.

PESTS AND DISEASES Scale insects and mealy bugs may infest the plants.

Clarkia
Onagraceae

Clarkia unguiculata

Free-flowering, easily grown hardy annuals with spikes or clusters of flowers from mid summer to early autumn. They are erect bushy plants with branched stems and green to grey-green leaves, usually lance-shaped. Native to N America.

Varieties bred from specific species are listed separately in catalogues as godetia, but are now included in clarkia.

RECOMMENDED SPECIES AND VARIETIES

C. bottae Cup-shaped flowers, 3 cm (1¼ in) across, have 4 lavender-blue petals, each with a white base, and are borne in loose spikes. A slender-stemmed plant with 4 cm (1½ in) long narrow leaves. HEIGHT & SPREAD 25×40 cm (10×16 in).

'Pink Joy' has pink flowers.

C. elegans see *C. unguiculata*

C. pulchella Leafy spikes of 4-petalled, cup-shaped lilac flowers are borne near the end of slender stems on this graceful plant. Narrow pointed leaves are 6 cm (2½ in) long. HEIGHT & SPREAD 40×20 cm (16×8 in).

'Filigree' has pink, purple and white semidouble or double flowers. 'Lace Mixed' bears pink, purple and white semi-double flowers. 'Snowflake' has double white flowers.

C. unguiculata (syn. *C. elegans*) Tall plants with upright stems that become long spikes bearing cup-shaped, 4 cm (1½ in) wide, pink, mauve or red 4-petalled flowers. Short-stalked leaves are up to 6 cm (2½ in) long. HEIGHT & SPREAD 120×40 cm (48×16 in).

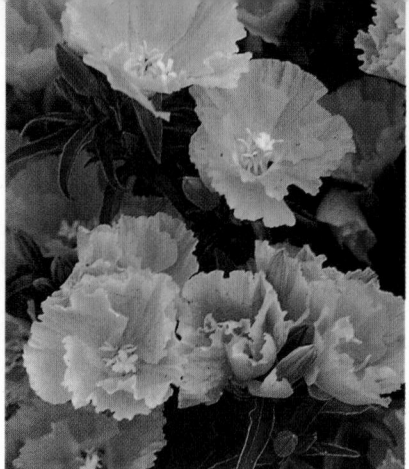

▲ *Clarkia* 'Salmon Princess'

'Apple Blossom' is pink, 1-1.2 m (3-4 ft) tall, 'Asterix' is a dwarf mixture to 30 cm (12 in) tall with a 25 cm (10 in) spread, 'Love Affair' is a colour mixture to 60-75 cm (24-30 in) high with a spread of 30 cm (12 in). All bear double flowers.

Godetia varieties produce their showy, funnel-shaped flowers, up to 10 cm (4 in) across, in clusters at the ends of stems. They range from white to pink, orange and red.

The following have mixed-colour single flowers with 4 petals unless otherwise described, and a spread up to 30 cm (12 in). 'Azalea-Flowered' is 40-50 cm (16-20 in) tall with white to pink semidouble flowers. 'Bonita Mixed' is 25 cm (10 in) tall. 'Cherie' reaches 40-50 cm (16-20 in) with pink double blooms, 'F₁ Grace Mixed' is 75 cm (30 in) tall and especially suitable for cutting. 'Salmon Princess' is 30 cm (12 in) high with pink flowers, 'F₁ Satin Mixed' is 30 cm (12 in) tall, 'Sybil Sherwood' reaches 35 cm (14 in) high and has salmon-pink flowers with a white edge.

CULTIVATION Grow in light shade in any soil. When 7-10 cm (2¾-4 in) high, pinch out growing tips to enhance bushiness.

PROPAGATION Sow seed where required in mid spring. Thin out in stages when they begin to crowd each other, to 25 cm (10 in). For early cut flowers, sow where required in early autumn and cover with cloches, or sow in individual pots under glass in early spring. For spring-flowering pot plants in heated greenhouses, sow in early autumn.

PESTS AND DISEASES Aphids may cause problems.

Clary see *Salvia sclarea* var. *turkestanica*

▼ *Clarkia unguiculata*

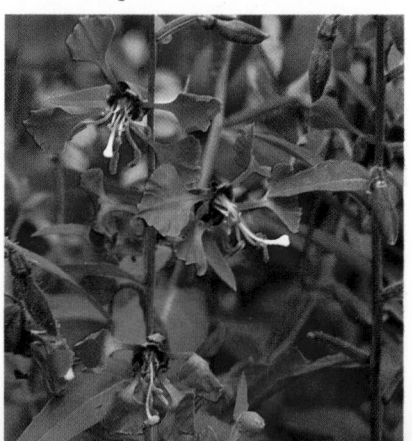

Clematis

Virgin's bower
Ranunculaceae

With its beauty of form, subtleties of
colouring and generous display,
clematis is widely revered as the queen of
climbers. There are plants flowering in
every season, even winter. So with careful
selection, it is possible to enjoy the
delightful blooms of clematis all year round

Twisting through trees or scrambling
over hedges, clematis brightens up drab
greenery with sumptuous colour. Trelliswork, arbours and walls are fitting locations,
and the use of these versatile climbers is limited only by your imagination.

The genus consists of a large number of
woody climbing and scrambling plants as
well as a few herbaceous perennials. Most
plants are deciduous, though there is a small
evergreen group.

Most clematis blooms are single, some
are double and a few are multiple like a
peony. Flowers usually open out flat or
saucer-like, but there are also stars, single
and double bells, lanterns and tulip-shaped
blooms. The largest blooms reach 25 cm
(10 in) in diameter, the smallest less than
1 cm (⅜ in). In general the larger the flowers, the smaller the number produced.

Some flowers are heavily scented – all of
them in the 10 small-flowered groups, with
the exception of the early large-flowered
'Fair Rosamond'. When the flowers have

1 'Duchess of Albany'
2 'Comtesse de
  Bouchaud'
3 'Etoile Rose'
4 'Andromeda'
5 'Minuet'
6 'Royal Velours'
7 'Multi Blue'
8 'Warszawska Nike'
9 'Bill Mackenzie'
10 'Purpurea Plena
   Elegans'
11 'Madame Julia
   Correvon'

INDEX OF SPECIES AND VARIETIES

The species and varieties of clematis can be divided into 12 groups which loosely follow the order of flowering:

(1) The Evergreen Group
(2) The Alpina Group
(3) The Macropetala Group
(4) The Montana Group
(5) The Rockery Group
(6) The Early Large-flowered Group
(7) The Late Large-flowered Group
(8) The Herbaceous Group
(9) The Viticella Group
(10) The Texensis Group
(11) The Orientalis Group
(12) The Late Species Group

A list of plants covered follows in alphabetical order with the relevant group number in brackets.

faded, many clematis go on to create a dramatic effect with their large, fluffy seed heads. Especially fine heads are displayed by plants in the macropetala, orientalis and late species groups.

Though it is not apparent at first glance, clematis flowers do not have petals. Instead, the sepals take on the appearance of petals and are known as 'tepals'. Their colour varies from white through pinks, mauves and purples to dark red, and fades as the flower ages. The stamens are often conspicuous in colour also, while the alpina and macropetala groups have the added interest of colourful petal-like 'staminodes' (infertile stamens situated between the fertile stamens and the tepals). Yellow flowers are found mainly in the orientalis group.

Most clematis climb by twisting the stalks (petioles) of their leaves round a support, but the herbaceous and texensis groups clamber and scramble. The leaves of the large-flowered clematis are usually ternate (made up of 3 leaflets) and opposite (2 leaves face one another at each node along the stem). In the 10 small-flowered groups the leaves may be made up of 5–9 leaflets. Leaf colour varies from dark or grey-green to bright green, but most clematis plants have mid green leaves.

There is an enormous variation in the height of clematis: the shortest species, *C. marmoraria*, is just 4 cm (1½ in) tall, while plants in the montana group can soar to 12 m (40 ft) or more. The measurements given below refer to mature plants.

Clematis plants grow in any soil as long as there is no extreme of acidity or alkalinity and they are given plenty of water. Most are hardy throughout Britain, although a few imported varieties need the shelter of a conservatory. All the climbing species and varieties benefit from a sheltered position as strong winds can tear the petioles away from their supports.

▲ *Clematis armandii*

C

(1) THE EVERGREEN GROUP

These plants provide welcome colour and scent throughout the winter months (and into early summer with the blooms of *C. forsteri*). Because they have been introduced from countries warmer than Britain, they need to be planted in the shelter of a wall facing south or south-west.

C. armandii Clusters of creamy white, vanilla-scented flowers appear in early spring. They are bell-shaped at first and then open almost flat to 4 cm (1½ in) across, displaying 4-7 tepals and yellow stamens. The plant has large, leathery, ternate leaves, up to 15 cm (6 in) long. It can be rather large, but is an exceptional and most desirable plant when there is room for it. HEIGHT & SPREAD 9×4.5 m (30×15 ft).

'Apple Blossom' has pale pink flowers and bronze-tinted young leaves. 'Snowdrift' bears pure white flowers that open out before the new leaves which carry an attractive coppery tint.

C. cirrhosa♀ Citrus-scented, yellow-white hanging bells, 4 cm (1½ in) across, can be seen from early winter to spring. The 4 tepals may be freckled inside with red, contrasting with the cream anthers held on green filaments. The fern-like foliage sometimes turns bronze in winter. HEIGHT & SPREAD 6×2 m (20×6½ ft).

'Freckles'♀ is heavily speckled with red-purple inside. 'Wisley Cream' has cream flowers and a few faint red markings.

C. forrestii see *C. napaulensis*

C. napaulensis (syn. *C. forrestii*) Light green leaves surround clusters of creamy yellow bell flowers which are rather sparsely produced. Each flower is 2.5 cm (1 in) long, made up of 4 tepals and protruding purple stamens. For most of the year this plant appears to be lifeless but its flowers bring an instant revival in a conservatory or on a sheltered warm wall in early winter. HEIGHT & SPREAD 7×3 m (23×10 ft).

New Zealand species

All New Zealand species have separate male and female plants with the male plants having slightly larger blooms. The leaves are ternate unless stated otherwise. For dwarf New Zealand species see the Rockery Group (p.154).

C. forsteri Lemon-scented, pale greenish yellow flowers appear among a mass of tangled, scrambling stems in early summer. The star-like blooms are about 2 cm (¾ in) across, made up of 5-8 tepals, with golden stamens. The pale green leaves are made up of 3 lobed leaflets up to 5 cm (2 in) long. HEIGHT & SPREAD 3.5×2.4 m (12×8 ft).

C. indivisa see *C. paniculata*

C. paniculata (syn. *C. indivisa*) Pure white flowers with yellow stamens appear in clusters in late spring. Each flower has 6-8 tepals and reaches up to 8 cm (3¼ in) across. The large ovate leaves are leathery. HEIGHT & SPREAD 4.5×1.5 m (15×5 ft).

(2) THE ALPINA GROUP

The alpinas are more robust than Group 1 and provide a display of dainty colourful flowers from mid to late spring, even on a north-facing wall. The parent species, *C. alpina*, originated in the mountains of Europe and Asia, and as a result all its descendants are hardy and will grow happily in poor soil.

The pendent blooms are single and bell-shaped, 4-5 cm (1½-2 in) long, made up of 4 tepals which taper to a point; in some varieties the flowers open flat to about 5 cm (2 in) across as they mature. Inside the flowers are petal-like infertile stamens, known as staminodes, which are usually a different colour from the main bloom. The stamens themselves cannot be seen. The flowers are followed by pretty, fluffy seed heads.

The soft green leaves are up to 15 cm (6 in) long and 7.5 cm (3 in) wide, made up of 9 ovate to lance-shaped leaflets. The alpinas are climbers, reaching a height of 1.8-2.7 m (6-9 ft) and a spread of 1.5 m (5 ft).

'Columbine' has elegant flowers made up of pale lavender tepals and creamy white staminodes. 'Frances Rivis'♀ bears flowers up to 6 cm (2½ in) long, made up of rich blue tepals and white staminodes lightly suffused with violet. 'Frankie' has mauve-blue tepals and cream staminodes. 'Jacqueline Du Pré' has rosy mauve tepals and pink staminodes. 'Pamela Jackman' has purple-blue tepals and white staminodes. 'Rosy Pagoda' has red tepals edged with white and creamy white staminodes. 'Ruby' has purple-pink tepals and cream staminodes tinged with red. Creamy white, semi-double flowers are produced by ssp. *sibirica* 'White Moth'. 'White Columbine'♀ has cream tepals and white staminodes. 'Willy' flowers earlier than most, displaying its pale pink tepals, which darken to the base, and cream staminodes in early spring.

(3) THE MACROPETALA GROUP

These plants bloom in mid to late spring, coming into flower just after the alpinas so the two flowering periods overlap. They are similar to the alpinas in many respects, but have larger staminodes which are sometimes longer than the 4 tepals so that they protrude from the bell-shaped bloom and make it look double. The flowers are up to 10 cm (4 in) across and are followed by seed heads that are among the best of all clematis.

The light green leaves are up to 10 cm (4 in) long and 5 cm (2 in) wide, made up of 9 toothed ovate to lance-shaped leaflets. The plants are medium sized and hardy enough to grow on north-facing walls. They climb up to 2.4×2.4 m (8×8 ft).

C. macropetala The parent species is as showy as any in the group. The tepals are dark violet-blue and the staminodes are the same colour flecked with white.

'Blue Lagoon' see 'Maidwell Hall'. 'Jan Lindmark' has mauve tepals and twisted pale purple staminodes. 'Maidwell Hall'♀ (syn. 'Blue Lagoon') has dark mauve tepals and staminodes. 'Markham's Pink'♀ has dark pinky mauve tepals and pink staminodes. 'Rosy O' Grady' has rosy lilac tepals and pink staminodes. 'Snowbird' has white tepals and staminodes tinged with green.

(4) THE MONTANA GROUP

Late spring sees the giants of the clematis world, the montanas, open their abundant, showy blooms. The vigorous, easy-to-grow montanas have some disadvantages, however. They flower for only 3-4 weeks and in a hard winter the leafless twigs are an unappealing sight, although the brief show of glorious colour is worth waiting for. A hard frost may damage or even destroy the flower buds, though not usually the plants.

The parent species, *C. montana*, is native to the mountains of India and China.

▲ *Clematis montana* 'Elizabeth'

Clematis montana

The flowers, many of them scented, vary from 5-9 cm (2-3½ in) across, unless stated otherwise, and consist of 4 tepals. The leaves are ternate and up to 25 cm (10 in) long. Sometimes the foliage is bronzed – notably that of 'Elizabeth', 'Freda', 'Odorata' and 'Tetrarose'. The most vigorous varieties can climb to 9 m (30 ft) and beyond with a spread of 3 m (10 ft) or more.
C. montana (syn. *C. montana alba*) A profusion of short-lived white blooms, up to 4 cm (1½ in) across with cream stamens, are produced by this, the parent species.

'**Broughton Star**' is free-flowering with deep pink double blooms and golden stamens. The inner tepals are a stronger colour than the outer ones, making an unusual two-tone flower. '**Continuity**' bears pink flowers with yellow stamens, held on long stalks. '**Elizabeth**'♀ bears pale pink blooms with yellow stamens and a strong vanilla

▼ *Clematis montana* 'Mayleen'

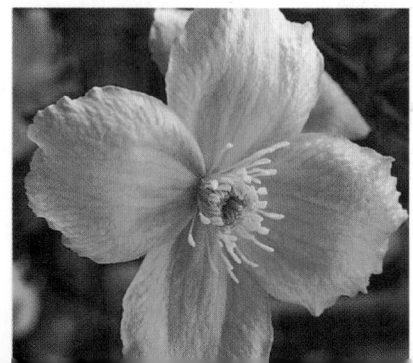

fragrance. '**Freda**'♀ displays its cherry-pink flowers against fine coppery foliage. The blooms, only 4 cm (1½ in) across, have deeper pink on the margins and golden stamens. The plant is less vigorous than most montanas and suitable for a small garden.

The vigorous f. *grandiflora*♀ produces an abundance of large, unscented, white blooms with yellow stamens. '**Marjorie**' bears a smattering of semidouble, creamy pink flowers with salmon-pink stamens. '**Mayleen**' has richly scented pinky mauve blooms, 5 cm (2 in) across, with a prominent

▲ *Clematis montana* 'Tetrarose'

boss of golden stamens. '**Odorata**' produces its creamy pink, heavily scented flowers with yellow stamens in early summer. '**Picton's Variety**' is not vigorous, making it suitable for a small garden. The pink blooms with cream stamens have a spicy fragrance. '**Pink Perfection**' produces a profusion of pale pink flowers with cream stamens. Usually, though not always, a vigorous plant, var. *rubens*♀ has pale violet-pink flowers with yellow stamens. The blooms are scented.

'**Tetrarose**'♀ produces deep pink short-lived blooms with straw-coloured stamens

and a spicy scent. It is not a large plant, making it suitable for a small garden. The vigorous var. *wilsonii* bears white flowers with prominent yellow stamens and a chocolate fragrance. The flowers appear a month later than most montanas.

(5) THE ROCKERY GROUP
Most plants within the rockery group are in flower from mid spring to mid summer. There are two sub-sections: New Zealand and American. The plants are short, from about ankle height to 60 cm (2 ft). Ideally suited to rockeries, these plants also grow well in an alpine house.

New Zealand species
The dwarf New Zealand species bear male and female flowers on separate plants. Larger New Zealand species are found in the Evergreen Group (p. 152).
C. marmoraria♀ It may take 3 or 4 years before this, the smallest clematis, flowers, but when it does you will know it has been worth the wait. In spring its cushion of evergreen parsley-like leaves are covered in creamy white, green-tinged blooms shaped like upright buttercups. The blooms have 5-8 tepals and are about 2 cm (¾ in) across. They give way to spectacular downy yellow-tinged seedheads. Protect from winter wet. In very cold areas the plant is best grown in pots which are put into the ground for the flowering period and moved to a conservatory or porch in the winter. It thrives in an alpine house. HEIGHT & SPREAD 6×25 cm (2½×10 in).
C. × cartmanii '**Joe**' At flowering, in mid spring, this plant is covered with pure white or creamy white male flowers, often tinged with green. The saucer-shaped flowers are up to 4 cm (1½ in) across made up of 4 tepals, borne on trailing growth with evergreen, leathery, finely divided leaves. HEIGHT & SPREAD 30×60 cm (1×2 ft).

The female equivalent, '**Joanna**', has smaller flowers with a boss of green carpels.
American species
C. addisonii Although it is a slow grower, this species is admired for its attractive hanging bells, just 2.5 cm (1 in) long. The flowers are reddish purple on the outside and cream on the inside. The plant has wide, heart-shaped leaves. HEIGHT & SPREAD 30×30 cm (1×1 ft).

(6) THE EARLY LARGE-FLOWERED GROUP
As their name suggests, these plants produce the largest blooms. They all give a spectacular show from late spring to mid summer, often followed by another display in late summer or early autumn. Plants that have double flowers usually produce these in the first flush, with single blooms appearing in the second flush.

The flowers come in a wide range of colours, including whites, pinks, reds, purples, blues and a few yellows. Some have a broad central stripe down each tepal. Blooms vary in size from 10-25 cm (4-10 in) across and can be single, semidouble,

▲ *Clematis* 'Bees' Jubilee'

▲ *Clematis florida* 'Sieboldii'

▲ *Clematis* 'Général Sikorski'

double or multitepalled. The leaves are opposite on the stem and invariably ternate.

Plants in this group are the most susceptible to wilt of all clematis and require special care. A few cultivars have been bred to have some (though not complete) resistance to wilt, including 'Barbara Jackman', 'Doctor Ruppel', 'Lasurstern' and 'Nelly Moser'.

The young growths need to be fanned out and tied in carefully as they are very brittle. The ultimate spread of plants in this group is highly dependent on the gardener's fanning out and can vary from 50 cm to 1.8 m (1½–6 ft). The height varies from 1.5–5 m (5–16 ft). The following varieties are medium sized unless stated otherwise.

▲ *Clematis* 'Elsa Späth'

'Arctic Queen' has fine double white flowers in its first flowering and, unusually, also in its second flush. The flowers have 6–7 tiers of tepals and cream stamens. 'Asao' bears flowers composed of 6–7 large rosy-carmine tepals with a white stripe and brown stamens. 'Barbara Dibley' has flowers made up of 8 deep red tepals with wavy edges and a central red stripe. The stamens are dark red. The vigorous 'Barbara Jackman' bears flowers composed of 8 deep purple tepals with a broad crimson stripe and cream stamens. 'Beauty of Worcester' produces large double flowers in the first

flush followed by a late flush of single blooms. They have deep blue tepals, 6 on the single blooms, and white stamens. 'Bees' Jubilee'♀ has mauve-pink tepals with broad carmine stripes and maroon stamens. The flowers are larger than those of 'Nelly Moser'. 'Belle of Woking' bears large multitepalled silvery mauve flowers with yellow stamens. 'Countess of Lovelace' produces large double lilac-blue flowers with pale cream stamens. 'Daniel Deronda'♀ has multitepalled violet-blue flowers with cream stamens, followed by a second flush of single flowers. 'Dawn' carries flowers made up of 8 pinky white tepals edged in pinky violet and carmine stamens. The compact plant is just 1.5 m (5 ft) tall. 'Doctor Ruppel'♀ bears flowers composed of 8 bright red tepals with a brilliant carmine stripe and golden stamens. The plant is reliably profuse with its flowers and makes vigorous growth. 'Elsa Späth'♀ bears flowers with 6–8 lavender tepals and reddish purple stamens on a reliably vigorous plant. 'Fair Rosamond' has flowers made up of 8 white tepals tinged with violet, and purple stamens. It is violet-scented, the only large-flowered clematis with pronounced perfume. 'Fireworks'♀ produces large light purple blooms with a broad maroon stripe on the 6–8 tepals. Dark red stamens open to reveal white filaments.

C. florida 'Alba Plena' has striking, long-lasting flowers, up to 10 cm (4 in) across with 6 creamy white tepals and a boss of greenish white staminodes that open to make the flower appear double. It requires winter protection by a sheltered wall. *C. florida* 'Bicolour' (see *C. f.* 'Sieboldii'). *C. florida* 'Sieboldii' has the same features as *C. f.* 'Alba Plena', except that the staminodes are maroon-purple.

'Général Sikorski'♀ has blooms with 6 mid blue wavy edged tepals and golden stamens. The plant is vigorous. 'Gillian Blades'♀ produces a flower of delicate beauty with 8 pure white tepals, suffused with purple at the wavy edges, and golden stamens. 'H.F. Young'♀ has blooms composed of 8 Wedgwood blue tepals with creamy white stamens. It is one of the best blues and makes vigorous growth. 'Haku-ôkan' carries a first flush of large, semi-double violet flowers with white stamens and a second flush of single blooms with 7–8 tepals. The vigorous 'Henryi'♀ has flowers composed of 6–8 creamy white tepals with brown stamens. 'Horn of Plenty'♀ bears flowers made up of 8 rosy purple tepals and purple stamens. 'Jackmanii Alba' has a first flush of semidouble flowers with white tepals and brown stamens and a second crop of single blooms with 5–6 tepals. 'Jackmanii Rubra' has flowers with velvety crimson tepals and cream stamens. Semidouble flowers are borne first, followed by a later flush of single blooms with 4–6 tepals. 'John Warren' has flowers with 6–8 rich cerise-pink pointed tepals and brown stamens on a low-growing plant. 'Kakio' (syn. 'Pink Champagne') has rather small, deep pink flowers. Each of the 8 tepals bears a white stripe. 'Kathleen Dunford' bears large rosy purple flowers with yellow stamens. The blooms are semidouble in the first flowering and single with 8 tepals in the later flush. 'Kathleen Wheeler' has flowers with 6–8 large plum-mauve tepals and yellow stamens. 'Lady Caroline Nevill' produces large lavender-blue flowers made up of 8 tepals and beige stamens. 'Lady Northcliffe' has flowers with 6 deep purple-blue tepals and white stamens. 'Lasurstern'♀ is outstanding for its generous display of single blooms and its later second crop. The flowers are a rich

▼ *Clematis* 'Fireworks'

▼ *Clematis* 'Gillian Blades'

▼ *Clematis* 'Horn of Plenty'

▼ *Clematis* 'Henryi'

C

mauve-blue with 7-8 wavy edged tepals and white stamens. The vigorous 'Lawsoniana' carries massive blooms with 6-8 lavender-blue, rosy tinged tepals and beige stamens. 'Liberation' has magenta flowers. Each of the 8 tepals carries a deeper magenta stripe and the stamens are golden. 'Lincoln Star' has large pink flowers made up of 8 tepals, each with a bright pink central stripe. Its growth is moderate. 'Lord Nevill'♀ has large deep blue flowers composed of 6-8 tepals and dark maroon stamens. 'Louise Rowe' is unusual in that it sometimes carries single, semidouble and double flowers at the same time. The white tepals have a violet tinge and the stamens are golden. The plant flowers in early summer and again in early autumn. It is not vigorous and is susceptible to wilt, but is

▼ Clematis 'Marie Boisselot'

Clematis 'Silver Moon' ▼

▲ Clematis 'Mrs N. Thompson'

Clematis 'Proteus' ▲

worth growing for the mixed blooms. 'Madame Le Coultre' see C. 'Marie Boisselot'. 'Marie Boisselot'♀ has flowers with 6-8 pure white tepals and pale yellow stamens. It is tall and one of the best white clematis, continuously flowering from mid spring to early autumn. 'Maureen' bears large velvety purple flowers with 6 tepals and creamy stamens. 'Miss Bateman'♀ produces dramatic white blooms of 6-8 tepals with a conspicuous boss of brownish red stamens. The first flowers are sometimes attractively tinged with green. A second crop is produced in early autumn. 'Moonlight' has flowers with 8 pale creamy yellow tepals and creamy yellow stamens on a short plant reaching only 1.8 m (6 ft). It flowers in late spring and early autumn. 'Mrs Cholmondeley'♀ bears large blooms

with 6-8 lavender-blue tepals and brown stamens on a tall plant. It has a rather gappy flower, but it is valued for its reliability and continuous flowering from late spring to early autumn. 'Mrs N. Thompson' has flowers composed of 4-6 deep violet-blue tepals with a vivid scarlet stripe and deep red stamens. The plant is a weak grower, reaching a maximum of 1.5 m (5 ft) and suits a small garden. 'Multi Blue' has blooms with numerous tepals in varying shades of blue-purple with blue tips. The flower opens up layer by layer – about a layer a day. 'Nelly Moser'♀ produces blooms made up of 8 pale mauve-pink tepals striped with carmine and maroon stamens. The colours last longer when the plant is grown in semi-shade. There are two crops of flowers. 'Niobe'♀ has blooms with 6 velvety ruby-red tepals and golden stamens. The flowers appear almost black when they first open. The plant is vigorous and flowers continuously from mid spring to early autumn. 'Norfolk Lady' has delicate pearly white blooms made up of 6-8 tepals and yellow stamens.

Clematis 'Nelly Moser'

C. patens An attractive curiosity, this is one of the original parents of many of the large-flowered clematis. It bears flowers with 8 mauve tepals and purple-red stamens. 'Pink Champagne' see C. 'Kakio'. 'Proteus' bears flowers with many rose-lilac tepals and yellow stamens in a peony-like flower. 'Richard Pennell'♀ has flowers with 8 rosy purple tepals and golden stamens. It is a reliable flowerer from late spring to early autumn. 'Royalty'♀ has blooms with rich purple-mauve tepals and yellow stamens. It is moderately vigorous. 'Sealand Gem' bears flowers with 6 or 7 pale lavender-blue tepals carrying a carmine stripe and mauve stamens. 'Silver Moon'♀ has large blooms composed of 6-8 lilac tepals and yellow stamens. The vigorous 'Snow Queen' has flowers made up of 6 white tepals with wavy violet edges and deep burgundy stamens. 'Sylvia Denny' bears flowers with white tepals and yellow stamens – semidouble at first and single in the second flush.

'The President'♀ produces blooms with 8 deep purple tepals and reddish purple stamens. The plant is vigorous and flowers continuously from early summer to early autumn. 'Veronica's Choice' has lavender wavy-edged tepals and yellow sta-

▲ Clematis 'Sealand Gem'

mens. It is moderately vigorous, producing double blooms in the first flush followed by single flowers. 'Vyvyan Pennell' is one of the most beautiful of the genus. The flowers are a kaleidoscope of blue, violet and purple in peony-like blooms, multitepalled in the first flush and single (shown) with 6-8 tepals in the second. Unfortunately, the plant is particularly susceptible to wilt.

'Wada's Primrose' has flowers with 8 soft primrose tepals and creamy yellow stamens. Early flowers are sometimes tinged with green. It is a low-growing variety. 'W.E. Gladstone' produces the largest flowers of the group with 6 or 7 lilac-blue tepals and purple stamens. It often dies right back in winter only to reappear in spring with a profuse show of blooms. 'Will Goodwin'♀ has large lavender-blue flowers composed of 6-10 tepals and yellow stamens. 'William Kennett' has large flowers with 8 deep lavender-blue wavy-edged tepals and purple stamens. It is a vigorous plant, flowering continuously from early summer to early autumn.

(7) THE LATE LARGE-FLOWERED GROUP
These strong-growing clematis varieties flower from late summer to early autumn. The flowers are usually 6-15 cm (2½-6 in) across, either flat or saucer shaped, there are no double or yellow flowers and they are not scented. The leaves are usually ternate but this sometimes extends to 5 leaflets.

Many of the plants, which are often known as the jackmanii group, have C. viticella in their parentage and benefit from its resistance to wilt. They may suffer from mildew but this is easily cured.

The spread, 1-2.4 m (3-8 ft), depends on the available support and careful training of the stems. The height ranges from 1.8-6 m (6-20 ft). Smaller plants do well in a tub or a pot if given support. The following varieties are medium sized unless stated otherwise.

▼ Clematis 'The President'

▲ *Clematis* 'Gipsy Queen'

▲ *Clematis* 'Warszawska Nike'

'Allanah' bears large flowers, up to 20 cm (8 in) across, with 8 bright red tepals and dark brown stamens. It thrives in a sunny spot. 'Andromeda' bears white flowers with a pink stripe along each tepal. 'Cardinal Wyszynski' see *C.* 'Kardynal Wyszynski'. 'Comtesse de Bouchaud'♀ is one of the finest varieties and is easy to grow. The freely produced satiny pink blooms have 6 tepals and yellow stamens. 'Gipsy Queen'♀ has flowers composed of 6 bluish purple tepals with dark, reddish purple stamens. This very vigorous plant is often misnamed 'Jackmanii' or 'Jackmanii Superba' but can be distinguished by its stamen colour. 'Hagley Hybrid' is probably the most reliable of all the large-flowered clematis in terms of habit and disease resistance. The freely produced flowers have 6 or 7 shell-pink tepals and brown stamens. 'Jackmanii Superba' has flowers with 4–6 velvety deep purple tepals and green stamens. 'John Huxtable' bears large

▼ *Clematis* 'Vyvyan Pennell'

Clematis 'Hagley Hybrid' ▼

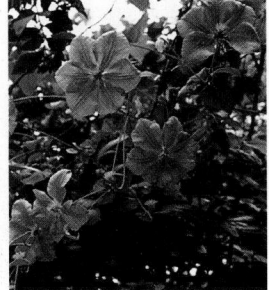

▲ *Clematis* 'John Huxtable'

Clematis 'Perle d'Azur' ▲

flowers with 6 pure white tepals and creamy yellow stamens. 'John Paul II' (also sold as 'Jan Pawel II') produces 6-tepalled large white flowers with pink shading and brown stamens. 'Kardynal Wyszynski' has large flowers with crimson tepals and brown stamens. 'Lilacina Floribunda' bears large blooms with 6–8 rich purple tepals and dark brown stamens. 'Madame Baron Veillard' flowers from mid to late autumn. It is a tall plant bearing abundant blooms with 6 rosy

▲ *Clematis* 'Rouge Cardinal'

pink tepals and white stamens. It needs a sunny position. 'Madame Edouard André'♀ has flowers with 6 wine-red tepals and cream stamens. The flowers are borne

▲ *Clematis* 'Star of India'

from early summer to early autumn on a short plant, reaching only 2.1 m (7 ft). 'Perle d'Azur'♀ is prized for its profuse and vivid flowers. The large flowers that appear from early summer to early autumn are made up of 5 or 6 deep violet tepals and pale green stamens. 'Pink Fantasy', only 1.8 m (6 ft) tall, produces large pinky violet flowers. Each of the 6 tepals has a brown stripe and the stamens are purple. The low-growing 'Rouge Cardinal' carries flowers with 4–6 velvety purple-red tepals and magenta stamens from early summer to early autumn. 'Star of India'♀ has large velvety flowers composed of 6 plummy red tepals with a distinct red stripe, surrounding yellow stamens. This free-flowering plant is vigorous and among the tallest of the group.

'Twilight' has slightly iridescent flowers, up to 15 cm (6 in) across, with 6 mauve tepals and yellow stamens. It is moderately vigorous and flowers from mid summer to

mid autumn. 'Victoria' is an often neglected yet worthwhile clematis. It is very reliable and is a good choice for a cold climate, where it remains vigorous and free flowering. Its flowers have 4–6 rosy-purple tepals and yellow-green stamens and appear from early summer to early autumn on a fairly tall plant. 'Warszawska Nike' (also sold as 'Warsaw Nike') has large rich purple flowers, up to 25 cm (10 in) across, with 6 tepals and yellow stamens.

(8) THE HERBACEOUS GROUP

From early summer into, or through, autumn is the flowering time for this group. The plants do not use petioles for climbing, but scramble instead. The stems die down in winter and so do not need pruning; just clear away any dead matter.

The plants are divided into two subsections: the tidy integrifolias and the larger, coarser heracleifolias.

Integrifolias

The cultivars in this section have been developed from *C. integrifolia*. The nodding bell-like flowers are up to 5 cm (2 in) long and borne singly or in loose clusters. The stems carry pairs of lance-shaped leaves, up to 10 cm (4 in) long. The plants scramble over low shrubs in a border, or make a clump about 1 m (3 ft) high and 3 m (10 ft) across if given artificial support.

'Alba' has scented white flowers. 'Arabella' has large blue-purple flowers on a plant that scrambles up to 1.8 m (6 ft). It blooms in early summer to mid autumn. *C.* x *durandii*♀ is long-flowering species, from early summer to mid autumn, with indigo-blue flowers. The firm stems of the flowers make them excellent for cutting. The plant

▼ *Clematis* x *durandii*

Clematis integrifolia

can clamber up to 1.8 m (6 ft). **'Olgae'** has mid blue, scented blooms. **'Pangbourne Pink'** has reddish pink flowers. **'Pastel Blue'** has light blue, scented flowers. **'Pastel Pink'** has light pink flowers. **'Petit Faucon'** has deep indigo flowers with unusual twisting tepals. **'Rosea'**♀ has deep pink scented flowers. **'Tapestry'** has mauvy red blooms.

Heracleifolias

Most of the plants in this section are developments from *C. heracleifolia*. The small scented blooms are held in dense clusters. Slightly downy ternate leaves, up to 15 cm (6 in) long, almost hide the flowers. The plants grow to 1 m (3 ft) tall, but can scramble up to 3 m (10 ft) over nearby shrubs.

'Campanile' has mid blue flowers. **'Côte d'Azur'** has pale blue flowers. Indigo-blue flowers are carried by var. *davidiana*. Pale blue flowers are seen on var. *davidiana* **'Wyevale'**♀. **'Edward Prichard'** is not as robust as the others but its deep blue flowers are strongly perfumed.

C. x *jouiniana* **'Praecox'**♀ is the finest scrambling clematis and since it can extend over a large area it is useful for ground cover. White flowers with violet margins are produced in profusion, obscuring the coarse leaves. **'Mrs Robert Brydon'** has blue-and-white unscented flowers and is

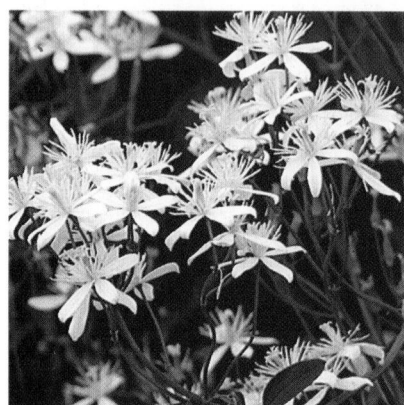

▲ *Clematis recta* 'Purpurea'

vigorous. *C. recta* **'Purpurea'** is a bushy plant, bearing scented clusters of many small, starry white flowers. The dark, pinnate leaves are purplish bronze when young. It reaches a height of 1.2 m (4 ft), spreading widely as a bush.

(9) THE VITICELLA GROUP

Masses of medium-sized flowers appear from mid summer to mid autumn on these vigorous climbers. They are all hardy and

▲ *Clematis* 'Abundance'

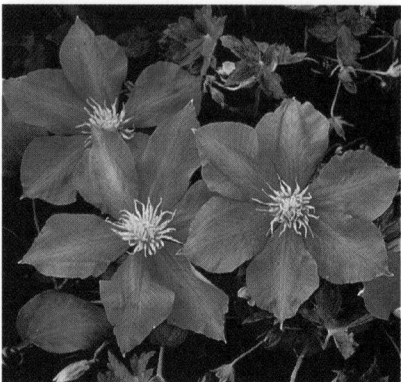

▲ *Clematis* 'Ascotiensis'

disease resistant, offering a trouble-free alternative to the large-flowered clematis. The flowers are in a wide range of colours but not yellow. They are often saucer shaped, though some open as bells at first. The flowers are up to 6 cm (2½ in) across and have 4 tepals.

The plants reach 6 m (20 ft) in height with a spread of up to 3 m (10 ft), depending on the support and training given. Only *C. viticella*, *C.* 'Betty Corning' and *C.* x *triternata* 'Rubromarginata' are scented. Most have leaves of 3-9 leaflets. They are excellent among shrubs, roses and small trees.

C. viticella The parent species from S Europe has small, deep purple nodding bells with green stamens.

'Abundance' has vivid pink-red flowers

▼ *Clematis* 'Ernest Markham'

▲ *Clematis* 'Little Nell'

▲ *Clematis* 'Madame Grangé'

with creamy green stamens. **'Alba Luxurians'**♀ produces green-tipped creamy white blooms with creamy green stamens. It is unusual because the leaves and tepals merge. **'Ascotiensis'**♀ bears azure-blue flowers up to 12 cm (4¾ in) across with creamy green stamens in late summer. **'Betty Corning'** bears its scented pale lavender-blue bells over a long period. **'Blue Belle'** is very vigorous with tepals more mauve than blue and yellow stamens. *C. campaniflora* has small nodding white bells tinged with violet. *C.* x *eriostemon* **'Hendersonii'** makes a shrub-like plant to 3 m (10 ft) tall, with broad, bell-shaped deep blue flowers with yellow stamens. **'Ernest Markham'**♀ has large red blooms, up to 15 cm (6 in) across, with beige stamens.

▲ *Clematis* 'Margaret Hunt'

▲ *Clematis* 'Prince Charles'

'Etoile Violette'♀ has large purple blooms with creamy yellow stamens.

'Huldine' bears large flowers, about 10 cm (4 in) across, with 6 silvery white tepals and greenish white stamens. 'Kermesina' has deep wine-red flowers and red-brown stamens. 'Lady Betty Balfour' blooms in early to mid autumn. The flowers are up to 12.5 cm (5 in) across with violet-blue tepals and yellow stamens. 'Little Nell' has creamy white flowers edged with violet and green stamens. 'Madame Grangé'♀ produces crimson-violet blooms, up to 12.5 cm (5 in) across, with broad red stripes on the tepals and off-white stamens. 'Madame Julia Correvon'♀ has wine-red flowers with golden stamens. 'Margaret Hunt' carries its mauve-pink flowers with brown stamens from early summer to mid autumn. 'Margot Koster' has mauve-pink flowers with white stamens. 'Minuet'♀ has white flowers edged with pinky mauve. The stamens are green. 'Mrs Spencer Castle' bears mauve-pink, semidouble flowers up to 12.5 cm (5 in) across. 'Pagoda' has wide purple-and-white bells with yellow-green stamens. 'Polish Spirit'♀ bears rich purple-blue flowers with rosy purple stamens. 'Prince Charles' produces an abundance of

▲ *Clematis* 'Ville de Lyon'

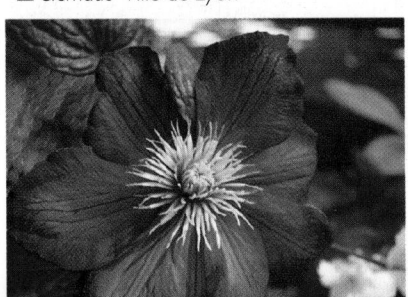

light violet flowers with green stamens. 'Purpurea Plena Elegans'♀ has violet-purple double blooms. 'Royal Velours'♀ bears reddish purple blooms with reddish stamens. The flowers have a velvety sheen. 'Rubra' (see 'Kermesina'). *C.* × *triternata* 'Rubromarginata'♀ produces masses of heavily scented, tiny white star-shaped flowers edged in red with pale yellow stamens. 'Venosa Violacea' bears large white flowers veined and edged with purple. 'Ville de Lyon' blooms in late summer producing carmine flowers with darker edges and creamy stamens. 'Voluceau' has red flowers, up to 14 cm (5½ in) across, with

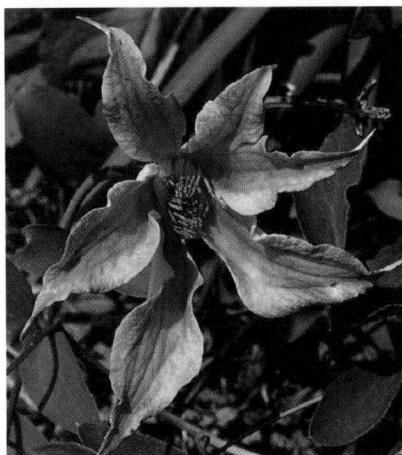

▲ *Clematis* 'Duchess of Albany'

▲ *Clematis* 'Gravetye Beauty'

yellow stamens and blooms from early summer to early autumn.

(10) THE TEXENSIS GROUP
This group flowers from mid summer to mid autumn and contains plants with tulip-shaped blooms of different shades up to 6 cm (2½ in) long. The plants make a bush up to 1.8 m (6 ft) tall and about 1 m (3 ft) wide. The small leaves are glaucous and made up of 5-9 leaflets. Plants within the texensis group have weak petioles for climbing and thus scramble and clamber over shrubs or artificial supports.

'Duchess of Albany'♀ has clear pink flowers with broad, rose-pink stripes and cream stamens. 'Etoile Rose' bears hanging tubular flowers of vivid cherry-purple edged in silver with greeny yellow stamens. 'Gravetye Beauty' produces rich ruby-red flowers with red stamens. 'Ladybird

Johnson' has dusky red flowers with cream stamens. The flowers of 'Sir Trevor Lawrence' are crimson inside with cream-coloured stamens. On the outside they are a satiny cream-and-red mixture. 'The Princess Of Wales' is vivid pink with creamy yellow stamens.

(11) THE ORIENTALIS GROUP
The plants in this group of yellow clematis flower in late summer and early autumn. All have yellow, hanging lanterns or bells up to 7.5 cm (3 in) across. The plants have fine foliage, many have spectacular seed heads, and they are easy to grow. They are hardy throughout Britain, reaching about 3.5 m (12 ft) tall with a spread of up to 1.8 m (6 ft).

'Bill Mackenzie'♀ has large open bells with beige stamens, borne from mid summer to late autumn. It often bears flowers and seed heads together. 'Helios' is a shorter plant than most in this group, reaching only 1.2 m (4 ft), which makes it suitable for a small garden. It starts flowering early – in late spring – and continues until mid summer. The large pale yellow flowers are produced in profusion.
C. tangutica Characterised by 5 cm (2 in) lantern-shaped, lemon-yellow flowers, this plant also has attractive, large seed heads. HEIGHT & SPREAD 4.5×1.8 m (15×6 ft)

Reliable varieties include 'Aureolin'♀, 'Burford', 'Corry', 'Gravetye' and 'Lambton Park'.
C. tibetana ssp. *vernayi* LS&E 13342 (also known as 'Ludlow & Sherrif') This plant is generally known as 'orange peel' clematis because of the thick, yellow tepals that make up the flowers. The blooms are downward-facing open bowls which can be seen in mid autumn. They have slaty purple stamens. HEIGHT & SPREAD 3.5×1.8 m (12×6 ft).

Related plants
Several species resemble the orientalis group in their flowers and flowering time.
C. aethusifolia has pale primrose bell-shaped flowers and lacy foliage. It can be shy to flower, but when it does so it is from late summer to mid autumn. HEIGHT & SPREAD 1.8×1.2 m (6×4 ft).
C. akebioides has glaucous leaves and dark yellowish green bell-shaped flowers. HEIGHT & SPREAD 1.2×1.2 m (4×4 ft).
C. ladakhiana has ferny foliage that tends to hide the yellow star-shaped flowers that appear in late summer. HEIGHT & SPREAD 1.8×1.2 m (6×4 ft).
C. rehderiana♀ is a giant of a plant, reaching 6 m (20 ft) tall. In late summer it is covered with clusters of small straw-yellow tubular flowers with recurving tips and a strong cowslip scent. HEIGHT & SPREAD 6×1.8 m (20×6 ft).
C. serratifolia bears pale yellow, star-shaped flowers with purple stamens for a few weeks in late summer. The leaves are sharply toothed. HEIGHT & SPREAD 2.4×1.2 m (8×4 ft).

(12) THE LATE SPECIES GROUP
The plants within this group flower in late summer and autumn. Most are outstanding for their generous displays of blooms while some are also highly fragrant. As sunlight is limited in autumn the plants benefit from being positioned in the sunniest places.

C. fargesii The flowers have 6 white tepals with greenish white stamens. With no pruning, the plant can start flowering in early summer and goes on to late autumn. With pruning, it starts flowering in mid summer. HEIGHT & SPREAD 7.5×3 m (25×10 ft).

C. flammula A cloud of tiny star-shaped white flowers covers the plant. The 1 cm (⅜ in) wide blooms are held in clusters, have white stamens and a strong, sweet scent. HEIGHT & SPREAD 6×3 m (20×10 ft).

CULTIVATION Spring planting is best because the plants are ready to make growth as the soil warms. Ten groups – all but the two large-flowered groups – are planted just like any other shrubs. The large-flowered clematis, especially the early large-flowered group, need special treatment due to their susceptibility to wilt: work a general-purpose fertiliser into the planting area and set the plants with the junction of roots and

make a great deal of growth in the course of the year. Work manure and compost into the soil around established plants each year in spring, and in autumn apply bone meal at the rate of 100 g per m² (3 oz per sq yd).

The large-flowered clematis have extra feeding requirements. In spring add a handful of artificial fertiliser rich in potash plus additional liquid fertiliser rich in potash once a week during the growing period. Then in mid summer give the plants another handful of fertiliser rich in potash.

The ideal position for a clematis is against a south-facing wall sheltered from strong winds. However, many clematis do well enough in less than ideal surroundings, even on a north-facing wall. They can be used in a number of ways. Walls provide excellent support as do fences, trellises, screens, poles, pyramids, tripods, umbrellas and arches. When using physical structures make sure that you supply wires, struts or netting for the clematis to cling on to. Some gardeners prefer natural supports, such as shrubs, small trees and climbing roses.

Clematis are unlikely to need winter protection apart from an extra mulch in a very cold winter and a layer of garden fleece for tender plants.

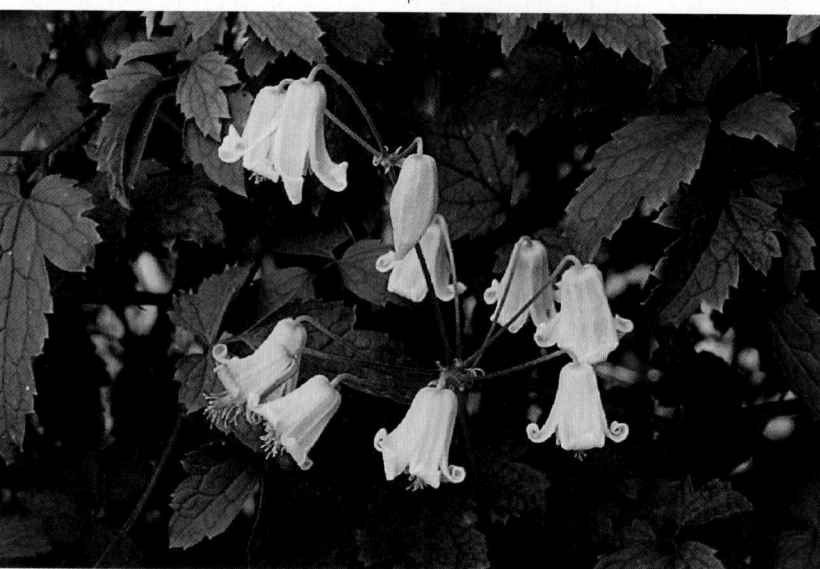

▲ *Clematis rehderiana*

shoots 10 cm (4 in) below the soil surface. They then make several shoots under the ground – if a shoot is killed by wilt another will replace it. In the first year after planting prune all plants hard to within 23 cm (9 in) of the ground to promote the production of several strong shoots.

Soil can be alkaline or acid as long as it is not extreme. It is more important to provide plenty of water – a minimum of 4 litres (7 pints) a week for one plant, with 4 times as much needed in hot weather. A mulch spread around the base of the plant helps to retain moisture. Clematis plants like a rich soil and a rich feeding programme as they

PROPAGATION Layering is the best method for producing a small number of plants. Lift and divide herbaceous plants in winter. Raise from stem cuttings if a large number of plants is required.

Only seed of the species will come true unless they have been hybridised.

PRUNING The earlier a clematis flowers, the less pruning it needs. This is because the flowers are borne on growth made during the previous year, and if this is cut off the next crop of flowers, goes with it. The later a clematis flowers, the more pruning it needs. This is because the flowers are on new growth made in spring. Cutting back

hard in winter encourages a lot of growth and thus a lot of flowers later in the year. If you do not know which group a plant belongs to, let it grow for a year and it will become apparent.

The first five groups of clematis – the evergreen, alpina, macropetala, montana and rockery groups – do not need pruning. If the plant has extended outside its allotted space cut it back when flowering ends to just below its allotted space. New growth that year will just fill the space given to it.

Just one group, the early large-flowered group, needs light pruning. In late winter or early spring examine each stem from the **top** down until you reach an outpointing healthy pair of buds. Prune off the growth above them. Fan out the remaining stems.

Five groups need severe pruning – the late large-flowered, herbaceous, viticella, texensis and late species. In late winter or early spring examine each stem from the **bottom** up until you find a strong pair of outward pointing buds. Cut above the buds. No harm will come to the plant even if the cut is virtually at ground level. If the plants look untidy in autumn you can do a preliminary pruning down to about 1 m (3 ft). Tie the shoots together and then complete the pruning in early spring.

In the orientalis group there is a choice; light pruning promotes early blooming and severe pruning stimulates more and larger flowers, but later.

In all pruning take care not to cut into strong woody stems. Rather, prune the green stems above them. When a plant has been neglected and has become a tangled mass, cut below the mass avoiding the brown woody stems.

PESTS AND DISEASES Clematis plants are remarkably healthy apart from clematis wilt (or 'stem rot'), a serious fungal disease that causes the stems to rot. Wilt strikes before a plant has developed thick brown stems, which are resistant to it. The greatest danger is in the first 2 years. Plants are particularly susceptible in humid conditions at a temperature of about 23°C (73°F), or if their stems are damaged. Plants in the early large-flowered group are the most vulnerable, late large-flowered clematis are less so. The other groups are free of wilt.

Remove any infected stems from below the wilting leaves and burn them. Wilt does not necessarily kill the plant; the roots are alive, so keep watering and fertilising the plant to bring on new growth. Water a fungicide into the ground around large-flowered plants once a month from mid spring until early autumn.

Powdery mildew affects the late large-flowered clematis and the texensis group. As soon as the mildew appears apply systemic fungicides and in the case of the texensis group an appropriate fungicide should be routinely employed once a week when the plants are in flower.

Cleome
Spider flower
Capparaceae

Although always attracting interest wherever it is grown, this free-flowering, half-hardy annual of exotic appearance remains an unusual plant in British gardens. Owners of small gardens may find its size discouraging, as it usually reaches about 1.2m (4ft) in height. It does, however, have a long flowering period and its blooms last well in water when cut. Cleomes can also be grown in pots or other containers as large summer-flowering greenhouse plants.

RECOMMENDED SPECIES AND VARIETIES
C. hassleriana (syn *C. spinosa* hort.) Dense clusters of white, pink, violet or purple scented flowers are borne at the end of each stem from early summer to early autumn. Each flower has 4 narrow petals, up to 3cm (1¼in) long, and long protruding stamens and styles which give the flowers a spidery appearance. The long-stalked, palmate leaves have spines at the base of their stalks. The narrow pointed leaflets are up to 12cm (4¾in) long. Native to S America. HEIGHT & SPREAD 1.2m×45cm (4×1½ft).

▲ *Cleome hassleriana*

'**Cherry Queen**' has cherry-pink flowers. The seed mixture '**Colour Fountain**' offers pink, violet, purple and white flowers. '**Helen Campbell**' produces white flowers, '**Pink Queen**' has pink blooms and '**Violet Queen**' produces violet flowers.
C. spinosa hort. see *C. hassleriana*
CULTIVATION Plant in sandy soil after the risk of frost has passed, choosing a position in full sun. Alternatively, grow in 15cm (6in) pots of multipurpose compost and

keep in a greenhouse, in a brightly lit position, shaded from the midday sun. No artificial heating is required after mid spring. Deadhead plants to prolong flowering.
PROPAGATION Sow seed in a heated greenhouse in early spring. Pot on seedlings into 9cm (3½in) pots and harden off before planting out.
PESTS AND DISEASES Aphids may damage young plants.

Clerodendrum
Verbenaceae

Clerodendrum bungei

Showy, fragrant flower clusters of these shrubs and climbers provide late summer and early autumn interest. Most of the 400 species are not hardy in Britain, but given a sheltered position, *Clerodendrum bungei* and *C. trichotomum* survive outdoors. *C. splendens* and *C. thomsoniae* can be grown in tubs in heated conservatories or greenhouses and moved outside in summer.

RECOMMENDED SPECIES AND VARIETIES
C bungei♀ Deep pink, highly scented flowers bloom in large clusters, 10cm (4in) across. The heart-shaped, mid green leaves grow to 20cm (8in) long and emit an unpleasant smell. This multistemmed, suckering shrub may die back to ground level in a severe winter, but will grow again from the base in spring. Native to China. HEIGHT & SPREAD 80×80cm (2ft8in × 2ft8in) after 5 years, ultimately 1.8m (6ft) tall.
C. splendens♀ Scarlet flowers are carried in clusters 12.5cm (5in) across on this evergreen climber. The dark green ovate leaves grow to 12.5cm (5in) long. The plant is tender and requires the protection of a heated conservatory or greenhouse. Native

▼ *Clerodendrum bungei*

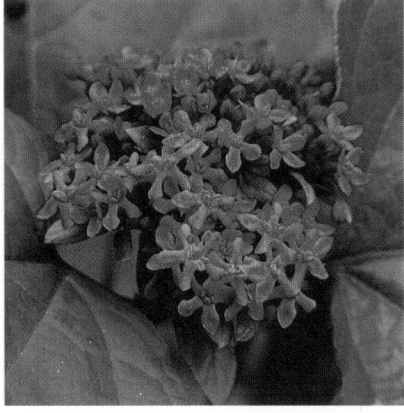

to Sierra Leone. HEIGHT & SPREAD Up to 2×2m (6½×6½ft) after 5 years, ultimately 3m (10ft) tall.
C. thomsoniae♀ Each flower in the hanging clusters, 10cm (4in) across, has a bell-shaped pure white calyx and crimson petals. The ovate leaves grow to 17cm (6¾in) long. This tender evergreen climber needs the protection of a heated conservatory or greenhouse. Native to W Africa. HEIGHT & SPREAD Up to 2×2m (6½×6½ft) after 5 years, ultimately 4m (13ft) tall.
C. trichotomum Small, fragrant white flowers are held in drooping clusters up to 15cm (6in) across. Bright blue berries enclosed in lobed, reddish calyxes follow the flowers and eventually turn black. The leaves, up to 20cm (8in) long, have an unpleasant smell. This rounded deciduous shrub is one of the

▲ *Clerodendrum trichotomum*

hardiest species. Native to Japan and China. HEIGHT & SPREAD 1×1m (3×3ft) after 5 years, ultimately 6m (20ft) tall.

The very similar var. *fargesii*♀ has slightly paler berries and calyxes. The leaves are sometimes red when they emerge, developing a purple hue.
CULTIVATION Plant in a well-drained, humus-rich soil in a sunny, sheltered position. *C. splendens* and *C. thomsoniae* need a minimum temperature of 15°C (59°F).
PROPAGATION Sow seed in spring, take root cuttings in early winter or separate suckers from the parent plant in spring and pot up or replant immediately.
PRUNING Not normally required, but remove any dead wood in early spring.
PESTS AND DISEASES Usually trouble free.

▼ *Clerodendrum trichotomum* var. *fargesii*

CLIMBERS

Versatile plants for vertical sites

A MANTLE OF FLOWERS OR LUXURIANT
FOLIAGE BRIGHTENS UP DULL WALLS AND ADDS
BEAUTY TO MANY OTHER GARDEN STRUCTURES

Practical and ornamental, climbing plants bring a pleasurable extra dimension to gardens, clothing walls, arches, pergolas, screens and even trees and shrubs with their flowers and foliage. They can be used to conceal unattractive features, provide privacy and help to integrate house and garden.

Many climbers produce spectacular blooms, including *Clematis* and *Rosa*. Others are grown for their attractive foliage, such as *Parthenocissus*

SCENT LADEN
The delicate flowers of honeysuckle will fill the air with sweet fragrance.

quinquefolia (Virginia creeper), or for their colourful fruits, such as *Celastrus orbiculatus*.

Some climbing plants will cling unaided to a support: *Hedera* (ivy) uses aerial roots and *Parthenocissus* has sucker pads. However, most ascend by tendrils, like *Lathyrus*, by curling leafstalks, like *Clematis*, by twining stems, like *Lonicera* (honeysuckle), or by hooked thorns, like roses. All these plants will climb unaided through the branches of trees or

shrubs but need training on wires or up a trellis if grown against a wall (see p.809). Although they are not true climbers, some shrubs, including *Ceanothus* (California lilac) and *Jasminum nudiflorum* (winter jasmine), can also be trained against a support.

The extensive range of climbers means there is a choice of plants for most garden situations. *Passiflora* (passion flower) and *Trachelospermum* require a sunny and sheltered site but *Jasminum officinale* (summer jasmine) and *Clematis montana* thrive in shady or sunny areas. Ivy or *Hydrangea anomala* ssp. *petiolaris* (climbing hydrangea) are tough enough to cope with an exposed, shady position.

WALLS AND FENCES

Climbing plants relieve the starkness of bare brickwork or fencing. They look particularly effective when their flowers or foliage contrast with the background. For example, golden or variegated foliage stands out against red-brick walls and dark fences. Try the golden-leaved hop, *Humulus lupulus* 'Aureus', or an ivy with white or cream-splashed foliage, such as *Hedera colchica* 'Dentata Variegata'. Alternatively, choose plants with pale blooms, such as the white-flowered *Clematis* 'Jackmanii Alba' or *C. montana*.

A light-coloured wall or fence makes an effective background for richly coloured blooms, such as the wine-red flowers of *C.* 'Madame Julia Correvon' or the vivid purple of *C.* 'Etoile Violette'. Dark green ivy or the striking *Actinidia kolomikta*, which has pink, cream and green leaves, also look attractive here.

As the soil by a wall is often poorer than elsewhere in the garden and receives less rain, it needs careful preparation before planting (see p.809).

VERTICAL FEATURES

Freestanding structures, such as pergolas or arches, are attractive focal points. They make excellent supports for climbing plants. *Aristolochia macrophylla*,

◀ IN UNION *A combination of climbing rose and clematis makes a stunning display.*

▲ WALL HANGING *Green ivy complements the warm autumn tones of parthenocissus foliage.*

Parthenocissus henryana, *Vitis* (grapevine) or *Wisteria* are all good choices. On a smaller scale, an arbour or gazebo makes a secluded retreat, and an archway or short pergola enhances a path or entranceway. *Humulus* (hop) and other foliage plants grown over them provide leafy shade and some climbers, including *Lonicera caprifolium*, have the added appeal of scent.

A freestanding tripod or obelisk creates height in a border, and is a suitable support for less vigorous climbers, such as the clematis 'H.F. Young', which has Wedgwood blue

▼ SHADED SPOT *Climbing hydrangea brings floral interest to inhospitable and sunless sites.*

flowers, or the small-leaved ivy *Hedera helix* 'Glacier', with its variegated, grey-green leaves.

CLIMBING PARTNERS

Grow two climbers together to create an impressive display. Combine plants that bloom at the same time but have flowers of contrasting colours or shapes. The violet flowers of *Clematis* 'Perle d'Azur' look attractive with the pale pink climbing rose 'New Dawn', for example.

Alternatively, grow climbers that have different flowering times, to create a longer season of interest. Plant early flowering *Lonicera periclymenum* 'Belgica' with the later flowering 'Serotina' or with *C. florida* which bears large creamy white flowers in late summer and early autumn.

A flowering climber, such as *C. alpina* 'Pamela Jackman', looks good against a backdrop of leaves provided by a foliage plant, such as the gold-splashed *Hedera helix* 'Oro di Bogliasco'.

Trees and shrubs make natural supports for less vigorous climbers. Do not use a rampant plant, such as *C. montana* or *Fallopia baldschuanica* (Russian vine), which may overpower and strangle its host. Choose flower colours that contrast with the supporting plant's foliage. For example, pale-flowered *Lathyrus latifolius* 'White Pearl' looks attractive when grown through dark-leaved shrubs, such as *Garrya elliptica*, *Pyracantha* (firethorn) or *Ceanothus*, and bright *Tropaeolum speciosum* combines well with an evergreen hedge, shrub or dark green conifer.

To partner large shrubs or small trees, choose climbers that die back to the ground in

▶ ADDED CHEER Fast-growing Thunbergia alata softens stark lines at the corner of a house.

autumn, such as *Lathyrus latifolius* (perennial pea), or that can be hard pruned annually, such as *Humulus lupulus* 'Aureus' and *Clematis viticella*. Annual climbers are suitable choices for growing through other plants as they die off in autumn, so there is no danger of them taking over.

FAST COVER

A climber can be trained up a trellis to screen a dustbin, compost heap or unsightly area. Ivies, including *Hedera helix* 'Buttercup' which has bright yellow foliage, are particularly useful as they provide year-round cover and thrive in almost any site.

For quick or temporary cover, use an annual climber which grows rapidly. The morning glory *Ipomoea tricolor* 'Heavenly Blue', which has large saucer-shaped blue flowers, and *Thunbergia alata* (black-eyed Susan), which has vivid orange-yellow flowers with black centres, provide effective and colourful cover and are easily raised from seed.

▼ FOCAL POINT The cascading flowers of Clematis montana var. rubens make a floral frame.

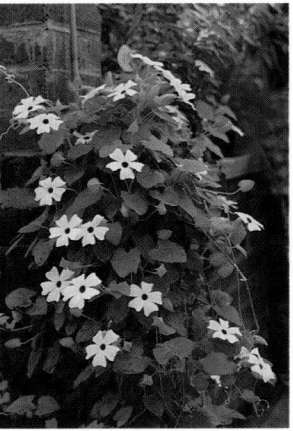

Some perennials can be treated as annuals because they grow quickly and flower well in the first year. They include the purple bell vine *Rhodochiton atrosanguineus*, which has dark purple tubular blooms.

SMALL GARDENS

In small gardens or on patios, choose climbers with compact habits. These can be grown in containers and used to lend height to a group of pot plants. Support the climber with a tripod of bamboo canes, secured with wire mesh, or buy a ready-made support.

Many large-flowered clematis, including 'Arctic Queen' with its ice-white flowers and 'Fireworks', which has red-striped blue flowers, make excellent pot plants, as do many of the annual climbers.

Miniature climbing roses, which reach up to 1.8m (6ft) in height, are valuable plants to train against walls and trellises or over tripods in confined areas. *Rosa* Laura Ford has rich yellow flowers and Warm Welcome has bright orange blooms.

FRAGRANT FLOWERS

For an effect that is more than purely visual, plant climbers that have fragrant blooms. 'Gloire de Dijon', which has yellow flowers, and 'Climbing Etoile de Hollande', with its crimson-red blooms, are magnificently scented climbing roses. Wisteria, summer jasmine and the honeysuckles *Lonicera periclymenum* 'Graham Thomas', 'Belgica' and 'Serotina' also have sweet fragrances. Plant scented climbers near garden seats or round windows for maximum effect.

CLIMBERS FOR SUN AND SHADE

FULL SUN

• *Actinidia kolomikta* Heart-shaped green leaves with pink and cream tips; small white, cup-shaped flowers in early summer.

• *Passiflora caerulea* Pink or purple-flushed, white flowers in late summer and autumn.

• *Rosa* 'Gloire de Dijon' Buff-yellow double or quartered fragrant flowers from summer to autumn.

• *Vitis* 'Brant' Green leaves turning red in autumn, and clusters of black fruit.

• *Wisteria floribunda* 'Alba' Trails of small white fragrant flowers in late spring and early summer.

PARTIAL SHADE

• *Aristolochia macrophylla* Green flowers, marbled with purple, yellow and brown, in summer.

• *Celastrus orbiculatus* Yellow fruits, which have scarlet-coated seeds, and yellow leaves in autumn.

• *Lathyrus latifolius* Purple pea flowers from early summer to early autumn.

• *Lonicera periclymenum* 'Belgica' Fragrant, pink and red tubular flowers in mid summer, followed by orange to red berries.

• *Parthenocissus henryana* Large, dark green leaves, marked silver white, turning red in autumn.

SHADE

• *Clematis* 'Nelly Moser' Large, open mauve-pink flowers, striped with carmine, in early summer.

• *Hedera helix* 'Glacier' Green and silvery grey evergreen leaves with narrow white margins.

• *Hydrangea anomala* ssp. *petiolaris* Large, flat, cream and white lace-cap flowers in early and mid summer.

• *Jasminum nudiflorum* Small, yellow, tubular flowers from late winter to early spring.

• *Lonicera* × *tellmanniana* Large clusters of red-flushed yellow flowers in late spring and early summer.

Clethra
Clethraceae

⚘ *Clianthus puniceus* 'Albus'

Clethra alnifolia

Beautiful spires of small, white or pink-tinged flowers, often fragrant, appear from mid summer to mid autumn on these shrubs and trees. Since evergreen species are generally suitable for only the mildest of British gardens, the plants recommended below are deciduous and need acid soil.

RECOMMENDED SPECIES AND VARIETIES
C. alnifolia (sweet pepper bush) White fragrant flowers are held erect in spires up to 15 cm (6 in) long from late summer to mid autumn. The toothed obovate leaves on upright shoots are 10 cm (4 in) long. They are downy when young and turn yellow in autumn. Native to eastern N America. HEIGHT & SPREAD 1 m×60 cm (3×2 ft) after 5 years, ultimately up to 4 m (13 ft) tall.

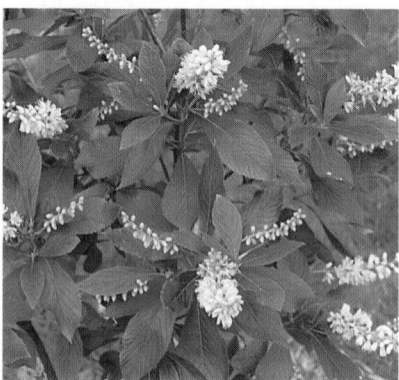

⚘ *Clethra alnifolia*

'Paniculata'♥ has arching branches and larger flowers than the species. **'Pink Spire'** and **'Rosea'** have pink-tinged flowers.
C. barbinervis♥ Fragrant white flowers, in spires up to 15 cm (6 in) long, appear from early summer to early autumn. The sharply toothed obovate leaves, 5-15 cm (2-6 in) long, provide red and yellow autumn colour. The flaking bark is grey-green with fawn patches. In colder, inland gardens this large bushy shrub needs a sheltered site. Native to Japan. HEIGHT & SPREAD 1 m×50 cm (36×20 in) after 5 years, ultimately up to 10 m (33 ft) tall.
C. delavayi♥ From mid to late summer pink buds open into a profusion of scented yellow-tinged white flowers held in spikes up to 15 cm (6 in) long. The deep green, toothed leaves grow up to 15 cm (6 in) long. This upright shrub or small tree requires a

sheltered site except in very mild districts. Native to W China. HEIGHT & SPREAD 1.2 m×30 cm (4×1 ft) after 5 years, ultimately up to 10 m (33 ft) tall.

CULTIVATION Grow in an acid, humus-rich soil in a lightly shaded, moist but well-drained site sheltered from the wind.
PROPAGATION Sow seed in spring or take greenwood cuttings in early summer. Low arching branches can be layered. *C. alnifolia* produces suckers which can be removed from the parent plant.
PRUNING Not necessary, but cut back hard any straggly plants in winter or early spring.
PESTS AND DISEASES Usually trouble free.

Clianthus
Leguminosae

Clianthus puniceus

Only *Clianthus puniceus* is commonly grown, mainly for its crimson flowers, grouped in graceful pendent clusters, and its attractive, trailing foliage. This evergreen shrub is best suited to a cold greenhouse or conservatory, although it will grow outdoors in a warm garden trained against a wall facing south or west. The plant will tolerate temperatures as low as -5°C (23°F).

RECOMMENDED SPECIES AND VARIETIES
C. puniceus♥ (parrot's bill, kaka beak, lobster claw) Pendulous clusters of up to 20 flowers appear in spring and early summer. Each beak-like flower is about 6 cm (2½ in) long. The mid green leaves are up to 10 cm (4 in) long and pinnate, made up of 20-30 narrow leaflets about 2 cm (¾ in) long. The shrub is open branched, the stems forming a fan. When grown unsupported, it tends to spread sideways rather than upwards; when trained against a wall, the drooping flowers are seen more easily. Native to New Zealand. HEIGHT & SPREAD 1.2×1.2 m (4×4 ft) after 5 years, ultimately 3.5 m (12 ft) tall.

'Albus'♥ bears white flowers, subtly tinged with green.

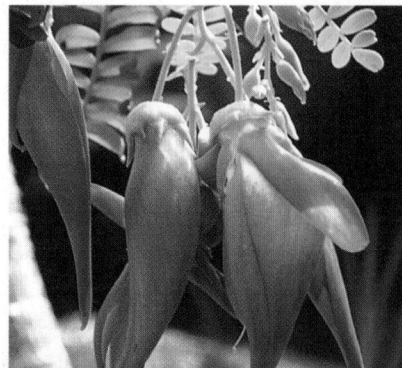

⚘ *Clianthus puniceus*

CULTIVATION Plant in well-drained soil in full sun or light shade. Young plants can grow fast and might flower at one year old.
PROPAGATION Sow seed under glass in early spring. Colour forms usually come true. Take semi-ripe cuttings from young, woody growth and root in summer, growing on in well-drained soil.
PRUNING Cut back after flowering to promote bushiness.
PESTS AND DISEASES Red spider mite, slugs and snails cause problems.

Clinopodium
Labiatae

These attractive plants are grown for their long display of small flowers in summer. Excellent for attracting bees and butterflies, they make useful, easy-to-grow plants for a rock garden or the front of a flower border. Plants of the genus are hardy or half-hardy annuals or perennials. They resemble thyme or mint in appearance, but are not used in the kitchen. The two-lipped flowers are borne in crowded whorls at intervals along the stems. The mid green, oval leaves, carried in pairs, are aromatic when crushed. Native to Europe and W Asia.

RECOMMENDED SPECIES AND VARIETIES
C. acinos (syn. *Acinos arvensis*) (basil thyme) Violet flowers with white markings appear in mid and late summer. Each flower is about 1 cm (⅜ in) long. This tufted plant

⚘ *Clinopodium vulgare*

has evergreen leaves, rather fleshy, up to 1.5 cm (½ in) long, on erect, hairy stems. Although hardy, the plant is short-lived, lasting 2-3 years, but will often self-seed. HEIGHT & SPREAD 30×20 cm (12×8 in).

C. vulgare (syn. *Calamintha vulgaris*) (wild basil) Pinkish purple flowers, 2 cm (¾ in) long, bloom from mid summer to early autumn. This softly hairy, hardy herbaceous perennial, has erect, mostly unbranched stems and leaves up to 6 cm (2½ in) long. HEIGHT & SPREAD 50×30 cm (20×12 in).

CULTIVATION Plant out in late winter or early spring in a light, well-drained soil, choosing a warm, sunny site.

PROPAGATION Sow seed in autumn or early spring in pots in a coldframe. *C. vulgare* can be divided after flowering or in early spring.

PESTS AND DISEASES Usually trouble free.

Clintonia
Convallariaceae

Starry flowers with six white, yellowish green or dull red petals are borne on erect stems, either singly or in clusters. Slender, creeping rhizomes form rosettes of mid to light green, slightly fleshy, oblong or elliptic leaves. These small woodland perennials are native to N America and Asia and require a neutral or acid soil in a shady position. Flowers in late spring or summer are followed in late summer or early autumn by fleshy black or bluish berries. The species listed below are hardy.

RECOMMENDED SPECIES AND VARIETIES
C. andrewsiana Clusters of bell-shaped, deep reddish purple flowers open in early summer at the end of a slender stem and often in one or two clusters along it. The flower stem rises out of a rosette of oval or tongue-shaped leaves up to 25 cm (10 in) long. Each flower has narrow 1.5 cm (½ in) long petals and a slender hairy stalk. The deep blue-black berries that come after the flowers are about 1 cm (⅜ in) across. Native to south-western regions of the USA. HEIGHT & SPREAD 50×30 cm (20×12 in).

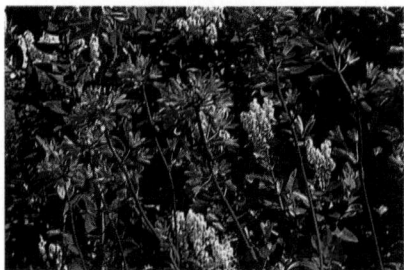

⚘ *Clintonia andrewsiana*

C. borealis A single stem ends with a cluster of nodding greenish yellow flowers with narrow petals 2 cm (¾ in) long. Vigorous plants may have a second and third flower cluster below the first. Clumps of ovate or

tongue-shaped light green leaves, up to 20 cm (8 in) long with slightly hairy margins, are thrown up by the underground stems. Deep blue berries are seen after the flowers. Native to eastern N America. HEIGHT & SPREAD 30×25 cm (12×10 in).

CULTIVATION Plant in spring in moist but well-drained, lime-free soil rich in leaf-mould. Mulch annually with leaf-mould.

PROPAGATION Sow seed in autumn in a coldframe or carefully lift and divide established plants in early spring.

PESTS AND DISEASES Usually trouble free but may need protection from slugs.

Clivia
Amaryllidaceae

With their brightly coloured, trumpet-shaped flowers and gracefully arching long, fleshy leaves, these tender evergreen perennials make striking pot plants. Native to the sunny eastern coasts of South Africa, they must be grown under cover in Britain and will thrive in a warm greenhouse, conservatory or a well-lit window in the home.

RECOMMENDED SPECIES AND VARIETIES
C. miniata♀ Bold scarlet or deep orange trumpets with bright yellow throats appear in late winter or early spring. Up to 20 of the 5 cm (2 in) long flowers are carried at the top of a strong, erect stem. The leathery, strap-like leaves are dark green, and grow to 60 cm (2 ft) long and 5 cm (2 in) wide, splaying out from around the base of the flower stem. Small orange fruits may be produced. HEIGHT & SPREAD 75×60 cm (2½×2 ft).

There are several **Miniata** hybrids available producing flowers in a range of colours from red through to yellow.

CULTIVATION Grow in pots of John Innes No. 3 compost in a sunny spot with a minimum temperature of 10°C (50°F). Water freely in spring and summer and sparingly in winter although the plants must be kept moist as this is when they flower. Feed

❦ *Clivia miniata*

every 3 weeks in spring and summer. Wait until the plants are bursting from their pots and then move only one size up.

PROPAGATION Divide after flowering and plant crowns singly in 13 cm (5 in) pots. Sow seed in spring and raise in a propagator.

PESTS AND DISEASES Mealy bugs are a nuisance, but generally free of diseases.

Clover see *Trifolium*

Cobaea
Cup-and-saucer vine
Polemoniaceae

Large, bell-shaped flowers are carried from mid summer to the first frosts on this climber. *Cobaea scandens* is the only species grown in Britain. It is a perennial which is almost always grown as a half-hardy annual. A rapid grower, it is ideal for covering a sunny trellis or a wall. It can also be grown in containers in a conservatory.

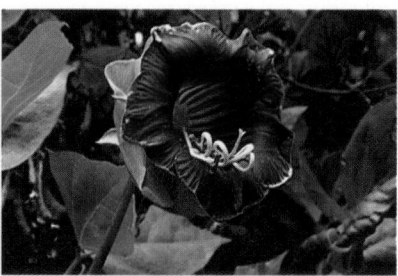

⚘ *Cobaea scandens*

RECOMMENDED SPECIES AND VARIETIES
C. scandens♀ Scented flowers, up to 7.5 cm (3 in) long, are borne singly on long stems. The flowers are greenish cream as they open but change to violet and finally to purple. Plants grown in the open flower from mid summer to mid autumn. The grey-green leaves are divided into 3 pairs of oval leaflets, the end leaflet being replaced by a tendril. In greenhouse conditions the plant can produce stems up to 8 m (26 ft) in length in its first year. Native to Mexico. HEIGHT & SPREAD 3×1.5 m (10×5 ft) when grown outdoors.

The flowers of *alba*♀ are white.

CULTIVATION Plant in a sheltered, sunny spot, allowing 60 cm (2 ft) between plants. Use support wires or netting to train them against a wall. Indoors, grow in a large pot of soil-based compost. Water and feed regularly through the summer months.

PROPAGATION Sow large seeds individually in pots in a warm greenhouse in early spring. Plant out after the risk of frost has passed. Softwood cuttings can be taken.

PESTS AND DISEASES Aphids and red spider mites may be troublesome.

Cobnut see *Corylus avellana*
Cockscomb see *Celosia*

C

165

C

Codiaeum
Euphorbiaceae

Codiaeum variegatum var. pictum

This ornamental foliage plant with brightly coloured leathery leaves is widely grown as a pot plant for the home or heated greenhouse. The flowers are small and insignificant. *Codiaeum* is a tropical evergreen shrub native to Malaysia and the Pacific Islands, and is therefore tender in Britain.

RECOMMENDED SPECIES AND VARIETIES

C. variegatum Oval or lobed leathery leaves, up to 15 cm (6 in) long, are variegated with gold, green, red, pink or orange. The white flowers have no decorative merit. HEIGHT & SPREAD 2×1.5 m (6½×5 ft).

The species is never grown and it is var. *pictum* that is usually offered to gardeners. It is similar to the species, but the leaves have more pronounced veining and stronger colours. 'Mrs Iceton' has black-green oval leaves heavily overlaid with red and pink. The young leaves carry a splash of cream. 'Reidii' has large, broadly oval deep red leaves with prominent black veins, overlaid with green and gold.

CULTIVATION Grow in John Innes No. 3 compost out of full sunlight. Ensure a minimum temperature of 13°C (55°F). Variable light levels and temperature results in leaf drop. Water freely in spring and summer, sparingly in winter. Apply tomato feed in summer to enhance leaf colour.

PROPAGATION Take stem cuttings in spring and summer.

PRUNING Cut back leggy plants in spring.

PESTS AND DISEASES Scale insects and mealy bugs are a regular nuisance.

Codonopsis
Campanulaceae

Codonopsis ovata

Brilliant colours and fascinating forms characterise these twining, erect or sprawling herbaceous perennials which bloom in summer or autumn. Most flowers are bell-shaped while some resemble open saucers.

These tuberous-rooted hardy plants are native to the Himalayas and Japan and thrive in a sunny rock garden. A raised bed is particularly suitable, allowing the inner flower detail to be appreciated. Wasps adore the blooms, undeterred by the unpleasant musky smell that is a feature of many, as it is of some foliage. Plants are best chosen in flower as species are often confused.

RECOMMENDED SPECIES AND VARIETIES

C. clematidea Startling orange markings adorn the insides of distinctive blue-grey hanging bells up to 2.5 cm (1 in) long. Lax stems make this early-summer flowering plant rather untidy. Its oval grey-green

⚘ *Codonopsis clematidea*

leaves are up to 3 cm (1¼ in) long. HEIGHT & SPREAD 60×40 cm (24×16 in).

C. forrestii This robust twining climber has deep lavender-blue saucer-shaped flowers up to 9 cm (3½ in) across from late summer to early autumn. The bright mid green leaves are narrow-oval or lance-shaped and up to 10 cm (4 in) long. HEIGHT & SPREAD 3×1 m (10×3 ft).

C. grey-wilsonii (syn. C. nepalensis hort.) Blue saucer-shaped flowers, about 4 cm (1½ in) across with a red central ring, are carried from late summer to early autumn.

Thin, twining stems carry this vigorous plant up supports and over nearby shrubs. Its plain mid green leaves are up to 7 cm (2¾ in) long and range from oval to lance-shaped and toothed. HEIGHT & SPREAD 1.5 m×50 cm (5 ft×20 in).

'Himal Snow' (syn. 'Alba') has pure white flowers and pale green leaves.

C. meleagris Grey-blue to pale jade, bell-shaped flowers about 3 cm (1¼ in) long with striking dark veins appear at the end of erect stems in mid summer, usually singly. The deep green elliptical leaves are up to 8 cm (3¼ in) long and grow mostly at the base of the stems in a lax rosette. HEIGHT & SPREAD 40×15 cm (16×6 in).

C. nepalensis hort. see *C. grey-wilsonii*

C. ovata Solitary pale blue flared bells, 2 cm (¾ in) long with purple veins and orange markings inside, are borne on slender stems during early summer. This neat erect plant has grey-green oval hairy leaves, up to 2 cm (¾ in) long, near the base of the stems. HEIGHT & SPREAD 40×20 cm (16×8 in).

⚘ *Codonopsis ovata*

C. tangshen Hanging yellowy green bell-shaped flowers, up to 6 cm (2½ in) long with purple flecks and an orange ring inside, appear on this rampant, twining species from mid summer to early autumn. The almost hairless deep grey-green rounded leaves are up to 5 cm (2 in) long. HEIGHT & SPREAD 2×1 m (6½×3 ft).

C. vinciflora Mauve-blue, saucer-shaped flowers, up to 4.5 cm (1¾ in) across, bloom from mid summer to early autumn. This sprawling or climbing plant has delicate, twining, thread-like stems and 2 cm (¾ in)

⚘ *Codonopsis tangshen*

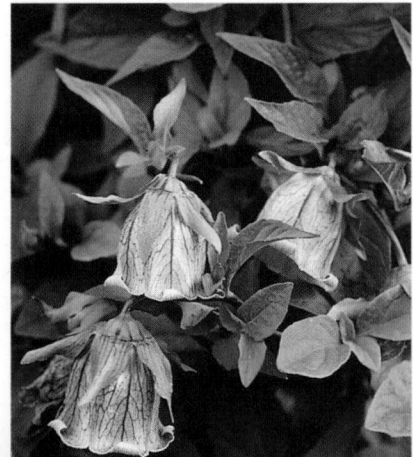

⚘ *Codiaeum variegatum* var. *pictum*

long mid green, neatly toothed, oval leaves. This species needs sheltered, moist conditions. HEIGHT & SPREAD 40×40 cm (16×16 in).

CULTIVATION Grow in a cool, moist humus-rich soil in dappled shade, except *C. clematidea* and *C. ovata* which need full sun.

PROPAGATION Sow seed thinly in pots in a coldframe in autumn or winter. Leave for a year then pot on the tubers. With *C. forrestii*, *C. grey-wilsonii* and *C. vinciflora*, separate small tubers in late winter.

PESTS AND DISEASES Vulnerable to slugs, aphids indoors and out, and red spider mite under glass. Systemic pesticides often cause yellowing of the foliage.

Coelogyne see ORCHIDS p. 464

Colchicum
Autumn crocus, meadow saffron
Colchicaceae

Colchicum speciosum 'Album'

Upright, goblet-shaped flowers are produced from corms mainly in autumn, mostly before the leaves appear. Although the flowers are reminiscent of those of the crocus, colchicums are more closely related to lilies. Plants range in size from large hardy species that make excellent, trouble-free garden plants to tiny alpines. Despite their friendly common name of meadow saffron, however, all colchicums contain the poisonous alkaloid colchicene.

Flowers of the recommended plants are in shades of lilac-pink or white and may be attractively chequered with a darker shade. Some species produce several flowers from the corm, others produce a single bloom. The flowers rise directly from the corm as the flower stalk is a tubular extension of the petals. The plants with weaker tubes need careful placing to give them shelter and support, as do those with very large leaves, which can swamp smaller plants in spring and make mowing a problem when naturalised in grass. There are varieties suitable for growing in grass, planting under shrubs and growing in rock gardens.

The broad ovate to lance-shaped leaves are in general taller than the flowers. Most colchicum leaves appear after flowering and gradually elongate through the spring. They die back in summer for a dormant period.

Colchicums are native to Europe, the Mediterranean, N India and W China. Not all of the 45 species are available but there are plenty of cultivars to choose from. The plants do best in a fertile yet free-draining soil in sun or partial shade. All plants listed are hardy unless stated otherwise.

RECOMMENDED SPECIES AND VARIETIES

C. agrippinum♀ The numerous small pale lilac flowers, produced in early autumn, have pointed petals and are heavily chequered with deep purple. The leaves, with wavy margins, up to 15 cm (6 in) tall, appear after the flowers and are among the smallest in the species so are not too intrusive. Easily grown, this species increases freely in the garden, preferring a well-drained, sunny situation. HEIGHT 10 cm (4 in).

⚘ *Colchicum agrippinum*

C. autumnale (meadow saffron) Up to 6 small lilac flowers are produced in succession in early autumn. The lance-shaped leaves, up to 30 cm (12 in) high, appear later in the year. HEIGHT 15 cm (6 in).

The flowers of *album* are white.

C. bivonae (syn. *C. bowlesianum*) The bold flowers of this autumn-flowering corm are chequered with rosy purple. Each corm produces up to 6 flowers up to 8 cm (3¼ in) long. HEIGHT 20 cm (8 in).

C. bowlesianum see *C. bivonae*

C. byzantinum♀ (syn. *C. autumnale* var. *major*) One of the easiest to grow of the smaller-flowered colchicums, this corm bears up to 20 rounded, lilac-pink blooms from late summer to early autumn. The tips of the petals are deep purple. The pleated

⚘ *Colchicum byzantinum*

leaves appear in spring and are up to 30 cm (12 in) high. No seed is set by this species. HEIGHT 15 cm (6 in).

C. speciosum♀ This robust, vigorous corm produces 1-3 showy flowers in autumn, varying in colour from pale to deep rose-pink (most have a white throat). Erect, glossy leaves, 25 cm (10 in) long, develop after flowering. HEIGHT 23 cm (9 in).

'Album'♀ bears large white flowers.

⚘ *Colchicum speciosum 'Album'*

GARDEN CULTIVARS

Most cultivars produce a succession of large showy flowers on tall tubes. 'Autumn Queen'♀ (syn. 'Queen Astrid') reaches 20 cm (8 in) and has rounded, mid lilac-pink flowers that are lightly chequered. 'Lilac Wonder' bears lilac flowers with narrow segments and faint white lines. The plant grows to 20 cm (8 in) high. 'The Giant' bears a succession of rather tall, lightly chequered pale lilac flowers with white bases. One of the easiest corms to grow, it reaches 23 cm (9 in) and increases rapidly. The large, fully double flowers of 'Waterlily' are rosy purple. Growing to 15 cm (6 in) tall, they tend to collapse and should be planted near other small plants to provide support.

CULTIVATION The large colchicums are easily grown in any well-drained fertile soil that does not become too dry in summer as the leaves must be allowed to mature. An ideal situation is in semi-shade, among shrubs. The most vigorous can be grown in grass but they will not increase as well. Plant in small clumps 10 cm (4 in) deep in late summer or early autumn.

PROPAGATION Remove offsets when plants are dormant in mid summer. Sow seed of species in late summer as soon as the seed is ripe. Keep seed trays outside in shade and do not allow them to dry out. Seedlings can take up to 6 years to reach flowering size.

PESTS AND DISEASES Prone to attack by slugs which can destroy entire colonies.

Coleus see *Solenostemon*

Colletia
Rhamnaceae

Colletia hystrix

The spiny deciduous shrubs within this genus, a member of the buckthorn family, resemble cacti. Colletia produces very few, inconspicuous leaves; instead the fleshy stem divides into rigid, upright branches, covered with deep green, thick, pointed spines. Profuse little bell-shaped flowers, sometimes scented, nestle among the spines in late summer.

Even in winter the plants add architectural interest to a garden. They are moderately hardy natives of southern regions of S America, suited to open borders in milder areas of Britain. In colder areas they must be grown in a sheltered corner.

RECOMMENDED SPECIES AND VARIETIES
C. armata see *C. hystrix*
C. hystrix (syn. *C. armata*) Abundant and richly fragrant tiny white flowers bloom in late summer and early autumn on this spreading shrub. The plant does best when planted in a position where it is given a little protection from the cold by nearby plants. HEIGHT & SPREAD 60×60 cm (2×2 ft) after 5 years, ultimately 2.4 m (8 ft) tall.

⚠ *Colletia hystrix*

⚠ *Colletia hystrix* (in bloom)

The flower buds of **'Rosea'** are flushed pink before opening.
CULTIVATION Plant in well-drained soil in an open, sunny position. The plants tolerate poor soils well.
PROPAGATION Take semi-ripe heel cuttings in mid summer and give them some bottom heat while rooting.
PRUNING None required.
PESTS AND DISEASES Usually trouble free.

Collinsia
Scrophulariaceae

Collinsia heterophylla

Loose clusters of showy bicoloured flowers provide a long-lasting summer display. These easy-to-grow hardy annuals thrive in partly shaded areas and are suitable for bedding, borders and woodland gardens. Collinsias can also be grown as spring and summer-flowering pot plants in an alpine house or unheated greenhouse and make good cut flowers. Only *Collinsia heterophylla* is widely grown in Britain.
RECOMMENDED SPECIES AND VARIETIES
C. heterophylla (syn. *C. bicolor*) Slender stems carry the bicoloured flowers, about 2.5 cm (1 in) long, that have a white upper lip and a rose-purple lower one. These are

freely produced throughout summer. The lance-shaped, mid green leaves are about 8 cm (3¼ in) long. Native to California. HEIGHT & SPREAD 50×20 cm (20×8 in).

The flowers of **'Blushing Rose'** are white and shell pink.
CULTIVATION Grow in moisture-retentive soil in the shade of trees or shrubs. Some support is required unless the plants are in an informal situation where their stems can be left to sprawl. Water in prolonged dry weather. Collinsias self-seed readily.
PROPAGATION Sow seed where it is to flower in early to mid spring, or in autumn for an earlier flowering the following summer. For raising a batch of greenhouse pot plants, sow seed in early autumn, overwinter at 5°C (41°F) and pot up the seedlings in spring in 13 cm (5 in) pots.
PESTS AND DISEASES Usually trouble free.

Colobanthus
Caryophyllaceae

Colobanthus canaliculatus

Masses of tiny bright green leaves clothe these tufted or cushion-forming evergreen perennials. In early summer small greenish flowers appear in tight clusters. The flowers are rather unspectacular and these plants are grown more for their attractive symmetrical cushion-forming habit. They are best grown in a sunny spot in a raised bed, trough or rock garden and will thrive in an alpine house or unheated greenhouse.

The genus is native to Australasia and the Pacific side of S America. Of the 20 species in the genus, *Colobanthus canaliculatus* is the most widely grown.
RECOMMENDED SPECIES
C. canaliculatus Dense, symmetrical cushions are formed of tiny pointed leaves, each up to 4 mm (⅛ in) long. The cushions become covered in clusters of small, greenish flowers in early summer. HEIGHT & SPREAD 3×15 cm (1¼×6 in).
CULTIVATION Plant in gritty, well-drained soil in a sunny position, or in moist, free-draining compost in an alpine house or unheated greenhouse.
PROPAGATION Sow seed into pots in a coldframe when they ripen or in spring and plant out when large enough to handle. Otherwise take short, leafy cuttings in spring or late summer.
PESTS AND DISEASES Usually trouble free.

Columbine see *Aquilegia*

Columnea
Gesneriaceae

Columnea microphylla

Hanging baskets and planters burst into life when these eye-catching evergreen perennials come into bloom. Hooded tubular flowers, often in vivid shades of red, are carried in profusion along trailing stems crowded with velvety dark green leaves. Since these plants are adapted to the tropical regions of Central and S America and the West Indies, they must be grown indoors or in a warm greenhouse in Britain.

RECOMMENDED SPECIES AND VARIETIES
C. × *banksii* Scarlet flowers, up to 7.5 cm (3 in) long, are freely produced throughout winter and spring. The fleshy, dull green, oval leaves, up to 2.5 cm (1 in) long, cover the stems which trail to 1 m (3 ft).

▲ *Columnea* × *banksii*

C. 'Chanticleer'♀ Pale orange flowers, about 4 cm (1½ in) long, appear intermittently throughout the year on this bushy, easy-to-grow plant. The stems bear light green leaves and are quite short, growing upwards before trailing to 30 cm (1 ft).
C. gloriosa (goldfish plant) Scarlet flowers, up to 7.5 cm (3 in) long with yellow throats, appear from autumn to spring. The dull green, oval leaves are 2.5 cm (1 in) long and covered with reddish hairs. The plant trails to 1 m (3 ft).
    'Purpurea' has leaves with a deep purple cast and red flowers.
C. hirta♀ Orange-scarlet flowers, up to 7.5 cm (3 in) long, are produced freely during spring. The irregularly oval, dull green leaves, up to 5 cm (2 in) long, clothe the stems that trail to 60 cm (2 ft).
C. microphylla Scarlet flowers, up to 7.5 cm (3 in) long, are produced during winter and

▲ *Columnea schiedeana*

▲ *Columnea* 'Stavanger'

spring. The rounded dull green leaves, 1 cm (⅜ in) long and covered in brownish hairs, clothe the stems which trail to 60 cm (2 ft).
C. schiedeana Marbled yellow-brown and red flowers, 5 cm (2 in) long, are produced during summer on this scrambling perennial with hairy, purple stems. The lance-shaped leaves, up to 10 cm (4 in) long, lightly cover the stems which trail to 1 m (3 ft).
C. 'Stavanger'♀ (Norse fire plant) This reliable variety bears scarlet flowers, up to 7.5 cm (3 in) long, on and off throughout the year. The stems trail to 60 cm (2 ft) and are lined with tiny dark green glossy leaves.
CULTIVATION Grow in bright but indirect sunlight in a warm, humid atmosphere kept above 15°C (59°F). Water freely during spring and summer but sparingly in autumn and winter. Feed during the summer. Pinch back shoots to maintain a bushy plant.
PROPAGATION Take softwood cuttings after flowering and grow in a propagator.
PESTS AND DISEASES Aphids and mealy bugs may attack the plants.

Colutea
Leguminosae

Colutea arborescens

Clusters of small sweetpea-like flowers appear from early summer to mid autumn and are followed by bladder-like pods enclosing poisonous seeds. The leaves of

these fast-growing, hardy deciduous shrubs have many leaflets. Native to S Europe, NW Africa and SW China.

RECOMMENDED SPECIES AND VARIETIES
C. arborescens (bladder senna) Yellow flowers, 2 cm (¾ in) wide, are carried in clusters from early summer onwards. The decorative 7.5 cm (3 in) pods are flushed red. The pinnate leaves have 9-13 small

▲ *Colutea arborescens*

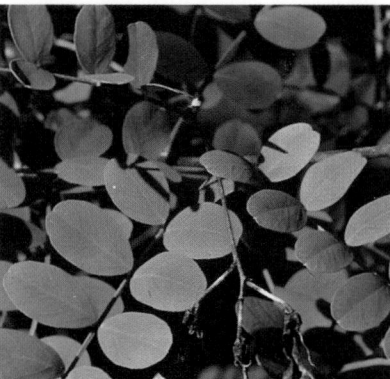

▲ *Colutea* × *media*

leaflets and grow to about 12.5 cm (5 in) long. Pruning may be required to keep the plant in good shape. HEIGHT & SPREAD 1.2 × 1.2 m (4×4 ft) after 5 years, ultimately 4 m (13 ft) tall.
C. × *media* The coppery flowers are 1.5 cm (½ in) across and are followed by red-tinged seedpods up to 7.5 cm (3 in) long. The greyish pinnate leaves grow to 12.5 cm (5 in) long and have 11-13 leaflets. HEIGHT & SPREAD 1.2×1.2 m (4×4 ft) after 5 years, ultimately 4 m (13 ft) tall.
    'Copper Beauty' has bright orange flowers and blue-green leaves.
CULTIVATION Plant in any well-drained soil in full sun. Coluteas will thrive even in poor soils and do not like too much shade.
PROPAGATION Sow seed in early to mid spring. Alternatively take semi-ripe cuttings in mid summer.
PRUNING Hard prune in early spring to give plants a better shape or to keep them under control.
PESTS AND DISEASES Usually trouble free.

Comfrey see *Symphytum*

Cordyline
Cabbage tree
Agavaceae

These palm-like trees, grown for their ever-green architectural form, are attractive plants for gardens where winters are mild. Elsewhere they can be grown in large tubs and containers in a cool greenhouse or conservatory and brought into the garden for summer bedding displays. *Cordyline fruticosa* is a popular houseplant. Native to India, the Pacific Islands and New Zealand.

RECOMMENDED SPECIES AND VARIETIES
C. australis (cabbage tree) The erect rough grey-brown trunk usually grows several feet tall before it branches. Each upright branch culminates in a spiky mass of stiff, sword-like, green leaves that often reach 1 m (3 ft) in length, but are only 6 cm (2½ in) wide. The leaves arch outwards with age. Large dense plumes of starry, white, sweet-scented flowers are produced in summer, followed by small, round, greenish-white berries in autumn. HEIGHT & SPREAD 2.4×2 m (8×6½ ft) after 10 years, ultimately 5 m (16 ft) tall.

Trees with purple or bronze leaves are collectively known as the **Purpurea Group**. **'Pink Stripe'** has leaves with purplish edges and a rich pink central stripe. **'Sundance'** has dark green leaves, sunset-red at the base and with a pinkish midrib. **'Torbay Red'** has plum-red leaves.

There are also a few variegated varieties, such as **'Albertii'** with cream edges to the mid green leaves and a pinkish purple midrib, and **'Torbay Dazzler'** which has bright green leaves with white stripes and creamy yellow edges.

C. fruticosa (goodluck plant, Ti plant) (syn. *Cordyline terminus*) In Britain this species is grown as a houseplant. The broadly lance-shaped leaves, 30–50 cm (12–20 in) long and 6–15 cm (2½–6 in) wide, sprout sideways from an upright trunk. Glossy reddish young growth matures to shiny dark green. In many varieties both young and mature leaves have a coloured banding or edging. Older plants occasionally branch. Plants

▼ *Cordyline australis*

▲ *Cordyline australis* 'Albertii'

raised indoors rarely flower. When they do, they produce white blooms in long dense clusters followed by red berries. HEIGHT & SPREAD 1 m×40 cm (3 ft×16 in).

The leaves of **'Kiwi'** are streaked with pink, cream and green. **'Red Edge'** has green leaves with red streaks and margins.
C. indivisa Broad sword-shaped leaves form a large tuft at the top of a stout trunk. Leaves are 1 m (3 ft) or more long and up to 15 cm (6 in) wide, drooping only as they age. Greenish white flowers in dense clusters, in summer, are followed by dark blue berries. HEIGHT & SPREAD 2×2 m (6½×6½ ft) after 10 years and ultimately.

CULTIVATION Plant in a moist, rich soil. *C. indivisa*, best grown in shade, will not tolerate a dry atmosphere. For overwintering in cold areas tie leaves together to protect the crowns and wrap trunks in fleece or straw.

Grow the houseplant *C. fruticosa* in a pot of free-draining, medium-fertility compost and site in bright, indirect light. Maintain a minimum temperature of 15°C (59°F). Water freely and feed weekly in summer, water sparingly in winter.

PROPAGATION Sow seed in early spring. Take cuttings of young branches in spring or summer. Seed is best for *C. australis*.

PESTS AND DISEASES Usually trouble free. Red spider mite and mealy bug may be troublesome indoors.

Coreopsis
Tickseed
Compositae

Coreopsis verticillata
'Grandiflora'

Bright yellow and, occasionally, red or pink blooms are borne on the fine, wiry, upright stems of these hardy annuals and herbaceous perennials. They form compact plants with bright green foliage that produce masses of single or double flowers in summer. These plants are particularly suitable for a herbaceous border. The taller species provide excellent cut flowers.

RECOMMENDED SPECIES AND VARIETIES
The listed plants are all perennials. Most of them are fast growing but they can be short-lived and it is therefore advisable to raise new plants each year to replace any losses. They all bloom throughout summer, unless stated otherwise.
C. auriculata Single yellow flowers with ragged-edged petals are borne in early summer on this low, bushy plant. The oval or narrow, pointed leaves are light green and often lobed; they measure up to 12 cm (4¾ in) long. HEIGHT & SPREAD 50×45 cm (20×18 in).

'Schnittgold' ('Cutting Gold') has vivid golden petals. **'Superba'** has bright yellow petals, blotched with purple at the base.
C. grandiflora This perennial, often grown as an annual, bears single yellow flowers, 6 cm (2½ in) across, with ragged-edged petals. The bright green leaves are strap-shaped, about 10 cm (4 in) long and often divided. They form a compact clump at the base of the plant. HEIGHT & SPREAD 60×45 cm (2×1½ ft).

▲ *Coreopsis grandiflora* 'Early Sunrise'

▲ *Coreopsis grandiflora* 'Mayfield Giant'
▼ *Coreopsis rosea* 'American Dream'

▲ *Coreopsis verticillata* 'Zagreb'

'Early Sunrise' has golden semidouble flowers. **'Mayfield Giant'** has bright yellow single flowers. **'Sunray'** has deep yellow double flowers.

C. lanceolata The bright yellow single flowers are up to 6cm (2½in) across and have ragged-edged petals. Bright green leaves, up to 15cm (6in) long, form a clump at the plant base. Trim back flowering stems occasionally in summer to strengthen the plant. HEIGHT & SPREAD 55×40cm (22×16in).

'Goldfinck' bears golden, single flowers and reaches a height of 25cm (10in). **'Sonnenkind'** ('Baby Sun') produces gold single flowers and grows to 40cm (16in) tall. **'Sunburst'**, taller at 75cm (2½ft), has yellow double flowers.

C. rosea The single flowers are deep to light pink, occasionally white, up to 2.5cm (1in) wide, with ragged edges to the petals. Leaves are up to 5cm (2in) long, sometimes with 2-3 lobes. This is a compact plant for a border front. It spreads by runners. HEIGHT & SPREAD 30-60×30-45cm (12-24×12-18in).

'American Dream' has rosy pink, starry, single flowers.

C. verticillata When in bloom, this bushy plant is covered with starry, yellow, single flowers, up to 6cm (2½in) across. The finely divided, fern-like, bright green leaves are about 6cm (2½in) long. HEIGHT & SPREAD 60×45cm (2×1½ft).

'Golden Shower' has yellow flowers. The golden flowers of **'Grandiflora'**♀ are 8cm (3¼in) across. **'Moonbeam'**, with pale lemon-yellow blooms, is less robust than the other cultivars. **'Zagreb'** has golden yellow flowers.

CULTIVATION Plant in late spring in fertile, well-drained garden soil, choosing a position in full sun. Overfeeding will encourage leaf growth at the expense of the flowers. Stake tall plants. Cut shoots of perennials down to soil level in late autumn.

PROPAGATION Raise annuals from seed sown under glass in early spring. Propagate perennials by division in spring or by taking stem cuttings in summer.

PESTS AND DISEASES Usually trouble free.

Coriander (culinary herb)
see HERBS p.331
Corn cockle see *Agrostemma*
Cornflower see *Centaurea*

Cornus
Cornel, dogwood
Cornaceae

Cornus kousa var. chinensis

The dogwoods, mainly deciduous small trees or shrubs, are grown for their show of flowers, their brilliant winter stem colour or their foliage. Summer-blooming species have small, button-like clusters of insignificant green-yellow flowers surrounded by larger, petal-like bracts, which may be white, creamy white, pink or red. Many summer-flowering shrubs produce strawberry-like fruits in autumn, while others produce black, red or blue-white berries.

Stem colour, at its most vibrant in winter, ranges from coral-pink to dark red and purple to yellow-green. Some of the best dogwoods combine attractive flaking bark and good autumn leaf colour. Some plants have variegated foliage. All the plants listed below have opposite leaves, except *Cornus alternifolia* and *C. controversa*. In general leaves are oval with a tapered point and not more than 12.5cm (5in) long, often with a slightly curled appearance.

Dogwoods are on the whole fairly hardy. The genus is native to northern temperate zones throughout the world.

RECOMMENDED SPECIES AND VARIETIES
C. alba (red-barked dogwood) This hardy shrub, with crimson-red stems, is best grown as a multistemmed plant. It is a vigorous plant, spreading by suckers. The ovate leaves are dark green above and glaucous beneath, turning crimson and purple in autumn. Flattened clusters of small yellow-white flowers in early summer are followed by pale blue-white berries. HEIGHT & SPREAD Up to 2×2m (6½×6½ft) after 2 years, when pruned regularly; ultimately 3m (10ft) tall, if left unpruned.

'Aurea', with pale yellow leaves, rarely grows more than 2m (6½ft) tall. **'Sibirica'**♀ ('Westonbirt') has brilliant coral-pink to crimson stems. It is less vigorous than the species, rarely growing taller than 1.5m (5ft). **'Sibirica Variegata'** has green and

▼ *Cornus alba* 'Aurea'

▲ *Cornus alba* 'Sibirica Variegata'

creamy white leaves, carried on deep red stems. **'Spaethii'**♀ has oval leaves with golden yellow margins, deep red stems in winter and round black berries in autumn.

C. alternifolia A hardy tall shrub to small tree of spreading habit with branches gracefully arranged in horizontal tiers. The alternate, pointed, oval leaves are dark green above, bluish beneath. Clusters of small white flowers borne from late spring to early summer are followed by black berries. HEIGHT & SPREAD 2×1.2m (6½×4ft) after 5 years, ultimately up to 8×3m (26×10ft).

'Argentea'♀ has small bright green leaves variegated with white and grows to 6m (20ft) tall. Place in a sheltered spot.

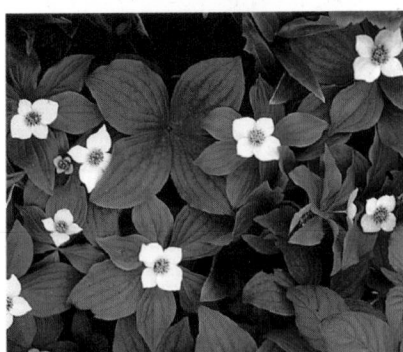

▲ *Cornus canadensis*

C. canadensis♀ This hardy, creeping herbaceous perennial spreads by underground shoots to form a low carpet. A good ground-cover plant, it does best on an acid soil, in partial shade. Clusters of tiny greenish red flowers, each surrounded by 4 large white bracts, appear in early summer. Bright red fruits follow. Shiny mid green oval leaves change to deep red in autumn. HEIGHT & SPREAD 15×60cm (6×24in).

C. controversa (table dogwood) This is a hardy, medium-sized tree of upright habit

▼ *Cornus controversa*

C

species in winter or early spring in a cold-frame. Prick out into pots when large enough to handle and plant out in permanent positions in mid summer. Sow seeds of *C. rubra* in the flowering site in early autumn or early to mid spring. Divide older plants in mid spring.

PESTS AND DISEASES Usually trouble free.

Cress, violet see *Ionopsidium*

Crinodendron
Lantern tree
Elaeocarpaceae

Crinodendron hookerianum

Grown for their dark, shiny foliage and lantern-like flowers, this genus consists of two species of small evergreen trees or large shrubs.

The plants prefer cool root conditions and benefit from the shade of lower growing shrubs. Both species prefer a sheltered site because the leaves scorch if exposed to full sun and cold winds. They do best in the milder south and west, although *Crinodendron hookerianum* can survive temperatures as low as -10°C (14°F) given a sheltered position. *C. patagua* is more tender and can be grown outdoors only in mild areas: it should be grown in a cool conservatory elsewhere. *C. hookerianum* can also be grown as a conservatory plant if so wished. Growing crinodendron in containers will effectively restrict their size.

▼ *Crinodendron hookerianum*

RECOMMENDED SPECIES AND VARIETIES

C. hookerianum♀ (syn. *Tricuspidaria lanceolata*) (Chilean lantern tree) This vigorous plant forms a small, dense, bushy tree or large shrub. Many long-stalked buds appear in spring but it is not until late spring and early summer the following year that they flower. Then the buds swell until the flowers resemble partly opened tulips hanging upside down from the branches. The waxy crimson flowers, about 3 cm (1¼ in) long, are borne from the base of the leaves on downy, reddish stalks up to 7.5 cm (3 in) long. The leathery, narrowly elliptic leaves are up to 12 cm (4¾ in) long with coarsely toothed margins and downy stalks. This species looks good planted among low-growing ericaceous shrubs such as azaleas and gaultherias. HEIGHT & SPREAD 3-4×2 m (10-13×6½ ft) after 10 years, ultimately 9 m (30 ft) tall.

C. patagua (syn. *Tricuspidaria dependens*) Similar in size and habit to *C. hookerianum*, this plant has broader, more finely toothed leaves. Its buds also apppear in autumn. They open to fragrant white flowers in mid to late summer. The flowers are more open and bell-like than those of *C. hookerianum*, and the tips of the petals turn outwards, giving the flowers a fringed appearance. HEIGHT & SPREAD 3×2 m (10×6½ ft) after 10 years, ultimately 10 m (33 ft) tall.

CULTIVATION Plant at any time – although mid to late spring is probably best – in fertile, moist, well-drained soil that is free of lime. Choose a position with partial shade.

PROPAGATION Take semi-ripe heel cuttings or sow seed in autumn.

PRUNING No pruning is necessary, but dead or damaged stems can be removed at any time of year.

PESTS AND DISEASES Usually trouble free.

Crinum
Amaryllidaceae

Glorious trumpet blooms bring a touch of the exotic to the garden in late summer. These are hardy and half-hardy bulbous plants. Flowers have six satiny petals and six prominent stamens. They are borne on tall, erect stalks above a shock of long, narrow, glossy leaves that generally only partially die back in winter. In the garden, plants are best grown at the base of a warm wall. They can be grown in a cool, frost-free greenhouse or conservatory, but not in the house. In summer, move plants outdoors, or keep them under glass that is shaded.

RECOMMENDED SPECIES AND VARIETIES

C. × powellii♀ Large, fragrant, funnel-shaped pink flowers are produced during late summer and early autumn on a strong leafless stem. Several plants together look particularly stunning. Each plant has 3-4 stems and as many as 10 flowers grouped together on each stem. The flowers are up to 15 cm (6 in) long and almost as wide at the flared opening. The bright green strap-shaped leaves are as long as 60 cm (2 ft). Plants will tolerate temperatures as low as -5°C (23°F). HEIGHT & SPREAD 90×60 cm (3×2 ft).

'Album' has pure white flowers.

▲ *Crinum × powellii* 'Album'

CULTIVATION Plant bulbs in spring, in a sheltered, sunny position in free-draining but moisture-retaining soil. In severe winters, cover the bulbs with horticultural fleece or straw to protect their exposed necks. In summer, water freely and apply tomato feed every 3 weeks. Remove faded blossoms.

PROPAGATION Divide clumps of bulbs in spring. Sow seed in spring, ideally in a propagator if one is available.

PESTS AND DISEASES Usually trouble free.

Crocosmia
Montbretia
Iridaceae

Crocosmia 'Lucifer'

With striking yellow, orange or red flowers and abundant bright green, sword-like foliage, crocosmias create a splash of colour from late summer to early autumn. They grow quickly and soon form large clumps that are ideal among shrubs. There are seven species in this genus of perennial corms and many hybrid cultivars. They all have slightly hooded, funnel-shaped flowers with prominent stamens carried above the leaves on tall, arching stems. Each flower has six petals, a yellow throat and some also have darker marks at the base of each petal.

Native to South Africa, crocosmias prefer a rich, moist but well-drained soil in sun or light shade. Although drought tolerant, they benefit from generous watering in hot, dry periods. The well-known montbretia, *Crocosmia × crocosmiiflora,* can be invasive and has become naturalised in mild and wet regions in Britain. Although crocosmias are hardy they do not like long periods of hard frost and a winter mulch is advisable in cold areas. The large-flowered cultivars are less hardy than the smaller-flowered varieties.

RECOMMENDED SPECIES AND VARIETIES

C. × crocosmiiflora (syn. *Montbretia crocosmiiflora*) Small orange or orange-red flowers are borne in short spikes amid broad, grass-like leaves with a papery texture. HEIGHT 1 m (3 ft).

C. masoniorum♀ Orange flowers are carried along the top of arching stems above large, ribbed leaves. HEIGHT 1 m (3 ft).

C. paniculata (syn. *Antholyza coccinea, A. paniculata, Curtonus paniculatus*) Curved orange-red flowers alternate along the branched reddish brown stems giving a zig-zag appearance. Wide, ribbed leaves and tall, flowering stems make this an ideal architectural plant. HEIGHT 1.2 m (4 ft).

C. rosea see *Tritonia disticha* ssp. *rubrolucens*

OTHER VARIETIES

There are many cultivars available with flowers in a wide range of reds, oranges and yellows. They vary in height from 45 cm (1½ ft) to 1 m (3 ft). Small flowered varieties produce a large number of slender blooms, 3–4 cm (1¼–1½ in) across. These plants are very vigorous and increase rapidly. Cultivars with large flowers bear a succession of broad-petalled, wide-open blooms, 6–8 cm (2½–3¼ in) across. Individually, they are very showy but they are less vigorous, less hardy and slower to increase than the small-flowered cultivars.

'**Canary Bird**' has small, golden yellow flowers with unmarked petals. '**Carmin Brilliant**' has small pinkish red flowers on dark stems. '**Citronella**' has small, pale lemon-yellow blooms. '**Emberglow**' has

▲ *Crocosmia* 'Canary Bird'

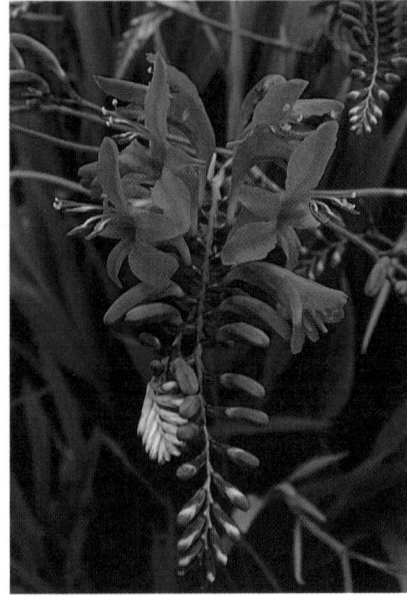
▲ *Crocosmia* 'Lucifer'

small, nodding, dark red flowers on deep reddish brown stems. It is one of the earliest to flower. The large, clear orange flowers of '**Emily McKenzie**' have prominent mahogany-red marks in the throat.

'**Jackanapes**' has small flowers with alternating yellow and dark orange petals. '**James Coey**' has small, deep orange-red flowers. '**Lady Hamilton**' has small yellow flowers with a pale apricot ring inside. The large flowers of '**Lucifer**'♀ are flame red: this plant is 1.1 m (3½ ft) in height. '**Norwich Canary**' has small golden yellow flowers. '**Queen of Spain**' has large orange-red flowers with a yellow centre and contrasting maroon mark at the base of each petal. The flowers of '**Severn Sunrise**' are pinkish orange. '**Solfaterre**'♀ has small apricot-yellow flowers and bronze-green, grass-like foliage. '**Spitfire**' has small, fiery orange flowers. '**Star of the East**' has large, clear orange flowers.

CULTIVATION Plant in moist but well-drained soil, choosing a site in sun or part shade. Put pot-grown crocosmias in during autumn or spring or plant dormant corms in late winter. Plant them 7.5–10 cm (3–4 in)

▼ *Crocosmia* 'Severn Sunrise'

▲ *Crocosmia* 'Spitfire'

▲ *Crocosmia* 'Jakanapes'

deep and 10–15 cm (4–6 in) apart, in clumps. Remove flowerheads when faded but let the leaves die naturally. Cover plants with a mulch in winter. Divide overcrowded clumps every 3–4 years but do not separate individual strings of corms.

PROPAGATION Divide plants in spring before growth starts. This can be done every 2–3 years for cultivars, every 4–5 years for the species. Alternatively, sow the ripe seed of species under glass: seedlings take 2 or more years to flower.

PESTS AND DISEASES Red spider mite may be troublesome in hot summers.

Crocus, autumn see *Colchicum*

Dendranthema
Chrysanthemum
Compositae

Many years ago most of the plants commonly known as garden chrysanthemums were transferred into the genus *Dendranthema*. The new name was accepted by most British horticulturalists but not by many in other countries – which led to some confusion. At the end of the 20th century these plants were restored to their original genus and are once again known as chrysanthemums. However, for practical reasons, some still appear in this book as dendranthemas.

This section includes many of the plants now reclassified under *Chrysanthemum*, the name by which they were previously commonly known. The flowerheads come in a wide range of shapes, sizes and colours. There are chrysanthemums to bring colour to the border late in the season and varieties – both for outdoors and for the greenhouse – whose showy blooms are superb as cut flowers. There are also chrysanthemums suitable for growing in pots as houseplants.

Chrysanthemums are herbaceous perennials, mostly half-hardy, and their blooms are composed of many tiny individual florets. The flowers are classified according to type (see panel, p. 209).

The size and number of flowers a chrysanthemum produces can be controlled by cultivation techniques. They can be grown to have either a large individual bloom at the end of each stem, or sprays of smaller flowers on each stem. Florists' varieties in particular are treated this way.

All chrysanthemums have dark green leaves, up to 15 cm (6 in) long, that are lobed and often deeply toothed.

RECOMMENDED SPECIES AND VARIETIES
The genus can be divided into three groups: (1) Garden varieties – hardy plants that can be grown outdoors throughout Britain. (2) Florists' varieties – plants cultivated for cut flowers or for shows, mostly grown in a greenhouse. (3) Pot plants.

The name of a variety often indicates its flower colour. Where this is not the case, the colour has been given in brackets.

GARDEN VARIETIES
Many chrysanthemums are hardy enough to survive permanently in the open in British gardens with minimal protection against winter weather. They flower in late summer and early autumn. Unlike the florists' varieties, these plants still look attractive when not in flower.

Garden (or Cushion) chrysanthemums These densely branched, mound-forming plants reach about 45 cm (1½ ft) in height and 30 cm (1 ft) in spread.

Varieties include '**Barbara**' (pink, pompon), '**Bravo**'♀ (red, intermediate), '**Debonair**'♀ (lavender, intermediate), '**Holly**'♀ (yellow, pompon), '**Nicole**' (white, pompon), '**Robin**' (orange-bronze, pompon) and '**Sunny Linda**' (yellow, intermediate).

Korean Hybrids Flowering freely from late summer until the first hard frosts, these hybrids have a multi-branched habit, reaching 75 cm (2½ ft) in height and 45 cm (1½ ft) in spread.

Good varieties include '**Brightness**' (red, semidouble), '**Raquel**' (pink, single), '**Ruby Mound**' (red, double) and '**Starlet**' (bronze, double).

Rubellum Hybrids These plants have a multibranched habit and reach a height of 1 m (3 ft) and a spread of 45 cm (1½ ft).

Good varieties include: '**Clara Curtis**' (pink, single), '**Duchess of Edinburgh**' (red, single), '**Emperor of China**' (syn. '**Cottage Pink**') (rose-pink,

1 *D.* 'Raquel'
2 *D.* 'Bronze Margaret'
3 *D.* 'Mary Stoker'
4 *D.* 'Duchess of Edinburgh'
5 *D.* 'Ruby Mound'
6 *D.* 'Mei-kyo'
7 *D.* 'Starlet'
8 *D. yezoense*

▲ *Dendranthema* 'Debonair'

▲ *Dendranthema* 'Max Riley'

d

▲ *Dendranthema* 'Clara Curtis'

▲ *Dendranthema* 'Crimson Yvonne Arnaud'

double), **'Innocence'** (very pale pink, single), **'Mary Stoker'** (yellow, single) and **'Paul Boissier'** (bronze, double).

D. weyrichii This mat-forming species flowers freely in late summer and early autumn, producing white or pink single flowers up to 4 cm (1½ in) across. It makes a useful plant for the rock garden. HEIGHT & SPREAD 20×25 cm (8×10 in).

D. yezoense ♀ (syn. *Chrysanthemum arcticum*) Masses of white, single flowers appear in mid autumn against the dark green foliage. The flowers are up to 5 cm (2 in) wide. This is a good plant for ground cover and does best in full sun. HEIGHT & SPREAD 30×45 cm (1×1½ ft).

'Roseum' has pink flowers.

FLORISTS' VARIETIES

Chrysanthemums are among the longest lasting of all cut flowers and a dozen plants could provide as many as a hundred large blooms from late summer to the New Year.

▲ *Dendranthema weyrichii*

They are popular plants to grow for exhibition and gardeners can use cultivation methods to develop the flowers to a particular standard. The florists' varieties can be subdivided into 2 further groups: early-flowering outdoor varieties and late-flowering indoor varieties.

CHRYSANTHEMUM/DENDRANTHEMA FLOWER FORMS

Within the three main groups of chrysanthemum – garden varieties, florists' varieties and pot plants – plants are further divided into different classifications according to their flower type.
These nine different flower forms are best demonstrated by the illustrations opposite.

Single   Incurved   Intermediate   Reflexed

Anemone-centred   Pompon   Spoon petalled   Quill petalled   Spider form

209

d

Dendranthema 'Wendy'

Early-flowering outdoor varieties

These flower outdoors in late summer and early autumn, with most varieties continuing to bloom until the first frosts. Unfortunately, with very few exceptions, they are not reliably hardy and cannot safely be left outdoors over winter. They should be brought into an unheated or cool greenhouse in mid autumn. Even those plants hardy enough to survive the winter will not flower as well if treated as herbaceous perennials by being grown outdoors all year round. Although excellent for cut flowers, they have long, leggy stems and are not ideal garden plants. The following varieties have a height of about 1 m (3 ft) and a spread of about 30 cm (1 ft). The letter S after a variety name means that the plant is normally grown as a spray.

Among those varieties with incurved blooms are: 'Gazelle' (white), 'Max Riley'♀ (yellow) and 'Winnie Bramley' (yellow). Among those with reflexed blooms are: 'Crimson Yvonne Arnaud' (red), 'Dorridge Beauty' (red), 'Gambit' (purple), 'George Griffiths'♀ (red) and 'Pearl Celebration' (pink). The following varieties have intermediate blooms: 'Allouise'♀ (pink), 'Anna Marie'♀ (white), 'Bronze Margaret'♀S, 'Fleet Margaret'♀S (syn. 'Orange Margaret') (orange), 'Gingernut' (bronze), 'Heide'♀S (white), 'Orange Allouise', 'Pink Margaret'♀S, 'Red Margaret'S, 'Red Wendy'♀S, 'Salmon Allouise', 'Wendy'♀S (bronze), 'White Allouise'♀, 'White Margaret'♀S, 'Yellow Gingernut', 'Yellow Heide'♀S and 'Yellow Margaret'♀S. Single-flowered varieties include: 'Enbee Wedding'♀S (pink), 'Pennine Jade'♀S (bronze), 'Pennine Soldier'♀S (red), 'Red Enbee Wedding'♀S, 'White Enbee Wedding'♀S and 'Yellow Enbee Wedding'♀S. 'Pennine Marie'S (pink) has anemone-centred flowers. The pompon-flowered varieties include: 'Anastasia'S (pink), 'Bronze Elegance'S and 'Mei-kyo'S (pink). These last 3 are hardy.

▲ *Dendranthema 'Wendy'*

▲ *Dendranthema 'Yellow Heide'*

▲ *Dendranthema 'Enbee Wedding'*

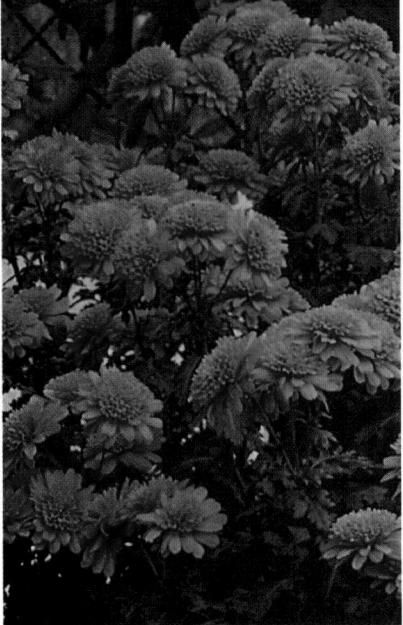

▲ *Dendranthema 'Mei-kyo'*

Late-flowering indoor varieties

These chrysanthemums flower under glass between mid autumn and early winter. They are usually grown in the open in large pots during the summer and moved into a greenhouse in early autumn. These late-flowering varieties are also classified according to time of flowering – those that flower in mid autumn and those that flower in late autumn and early winter. They are about 1.2 m (4 ft) tall, with a spread of about 45 cm (1½ ft) and their blooms are up to 20 cm (8 in) across – even larger if grown by exhibitors' techniques.

The following varieties bloom in mid autumn. Among those with reflexed blooms are: 'Bronze John Wingfield', 'Cream West Bromwich', 'John Wingfield' (white), 'Pink John Wingfield', 'Riley's Dynasty' (pink), 'West Bromwich' (white) and 'Yellow John Wingfield'. These have intermediate blooms: 'Bronze Fairway', 'Bronze Pauline White', 'Cream Pauline White', 'Pauline White' (pink) and 'Pink Fairway'.

The following bloom in late autumn and early winter. Among those with incurved blooms are: 'Cream John Hughes', 'John Hughes' (white), 'Polar Gem' (white) and 'Yellow John Hughes'. With reflexed flowers are: 'Bryan Kirk' (purple), 'Dorridge King' (crimson), 'Red Shoesmith Salmon', 'Roblaze'S (red) and 'Shoesmith Salmon'♀ (pink). Among those with intermediate blooms are: 'Balcombe Perfection' (bronze), 'Bronze Mayford Perfection'♀, 'Fred Shoesmith' (white), 'Gold Foil' (yellow), 'Green Satin', 'Ivy Garland' (cream), 'Mayford Perfection'♀ (pink), 'Red Balcombe Perfection', 'Red Mayford Perfection', 'Yellow Balcombe Perfection', 'Yellow Fred Shoesmith', 'Yellow Ivy Garland' and 'Yellow Mayford Perfection'♀. Among those with single flowers are: 'Galaxy'♀S (bronze), 'My Love' (pink), 'Purple Nu Rosemary'♀S, 'Rynoon' (pink), 'Salmon Nu Rosemary'♀S, 'White Nu Rosemary'S and 'Yellow Galaxy'♀S. 'Long Island Beauty'♀S has white, anemone-centred flowers and 'White Spider'S has white, spider flowers.

POT PLANTS

Nearly all chrysanthemums sold as pot plants have been treated with height-reducing chemicals which are not available to amateur gardeners. However, there are varieties that the amateur can cultivate as pot plants. Garden (Cushion) chrysanthemums can be grown in this way – see varieties section above and the cultivation section below. They will flower in summer and early autumn either indoors in a greenhouse, or outdoors.

Charm chrysanthemums

Spectacular pot plants that flower from mid autumn to early winter, each plant producing hundreds of scented blooms in the full range of chrysanthemum colours. HEIGHT & SPREAD 60 cm × 1 m (2 × 3 ft).

'Bullfinch' has red flowers, 'Morning Star' has yellow blooms.

CULTIVATION

GARDEN VARIETIES

Plant in late spring or when all risk of hard frost has passed, in any fertile, well-drained garden soil, choosing a position in full sun. Provide taller plants with some support. Two weeks after planting, snap off or pinch out the end 1.5 cm (½ in) of the stem tips to

▲ *Dendranthema* 'Cream John Hughes'

▲ *Dendranthema* 'Dorridge King'

Dendranthema 'Morning Star'

▲ *Dendranthema* 'Green Satin'

▲ *Dendranthema* 'Salmon Nu Rosemary'

▲ *Dendranthema* 'Morning Star'

encourage branching. This is referred to as 'stopping'. For Garden (Cushion) chrysanthemums, continue to stop the resulting lateral and side shoots when they reach 10 cm (4 in) in length, until mid summer.

When the first hard frosts kill the flowers, cut stems back to about 10 cm (4 in). Protect plants with a 10 cm (4 in) layer of mulch in winter. In wet soils, lift plants after cutting back and transfer them to a coldframe or unheated greenhouse for winter. Thin out shoots of each clump in spring to encourage stronger stems and a better appearance.

FLORISTS' VARIETIES
Early-flowering outdoor varieties Plant rooted cuttings 13 cm (5¼ in) apart in potting compost in a 10 cm (4 in) deep box. Move the box to a coldframe in mid spring

▲ *Dendranthema* 'Roblaze'

and harden the cuttings off. Plant out in late spring, once the risk of any late hard frost has passed, in any fertile, well-drained soil, choosing a position in full sun, and water in thoroughly.

Support the plants with canes at least 1.2 m (4 ft) long, tying stems loosely to the supports. Alternatively, enclose plants within 13-15 cm (5¼-6 in) mesh netting, stretched around 4 corner posts. Pinch out, or 'stop', the growing points a week after planting. For the largest flowers, reduce the number of lateral shoots to a maximum of 3 per plant. To control the size and number of flowers, disbud plants as soon as the buds appear. To ensure large individual blooms, carefully remove all buds except the one at the very end of each sideshoot. For sprays, reverse the procedure and remove the bud at the end of the sideshoot, retaining all the other buds.

Top dress with fertiliser in mid summer and water it in thoroughly. Water plants frequently in dry weather. After they have flowered, cut the stems back to a height of 20 cm (8 in). Lift the plants and overwinter them in an unheated or cool greenhouse in

pots or trays of multipurpose compost.
Late-flowering indoor varieties Cultivation for these varieties depends on when cuttings were rooted. For exhibition blooms treat plants as follows. Pot cuttings rooted by mid spring into 8 cm (3 in) or 9 cm (3½ in) pots. Transfer to 13 cm (5 in) pots 3-4 weeks later. Alternatively, set rooted cuttings 13 cm (5¼ in) apart in a 10 cm (4 in) deep layer of compost in a box. In mid spring, move plants to a coldframe and harden off. Pot cuttings rooted in late spring into 8 cm (3 in) or 9 cm (3½ in) pots; do not transfer these into 13 cm (5 in) pots.

Transfer cuttings into their final pots, 25 cm (10 in) across, in late spring or early summer. Cuttings rooted by late spring can be planted 2 to a pot. Put pots outside in late spring or early summer. Insert a stout, 1.2 m (4 ft) cane into each pot and tie stems loosely. To ensure that plants do not fall over in high winds, tie tops of canes to a horizontal wire, strung between posts. Water during summer. Feed weekly with a general-purpose fertiliser from early summer until the buds begin to open.

In mid spring, when plants are 20-25 cm (8-10 in) tall, pinch out the growing point of plants raised from cuttings taken in mid or late winter. As lateral shoots develop, remove all but 3 of them. Pinch out the growing points of these in early summer. Remove all but 3 of the sideshoots that develop from each of these shoots, so that plants have up to 9 shoots each.

Stop plants raised from cuttings taken in early or mid spring about 10 days after the final potting; allow up to 9 shoots per plant to grow. Plants grown from cuttings taken in late spring and grown 2 per pot, should be stopped and up to 5 of the resulting sideshoots retained per plant. Chrysanthemums grown for exhibition should have fewer sideshoots per plant; consult specialist publications for more detailed guidance.

Two alternative methods of growing are less time-consuming and troublesome but are also less likely to produce blooms of prize-winning quality. Start with rooted cuttings taken in early spring. Four weeks after rooting, pinch out the growing points; the lateral shoots that then develop are taken as cuttings for both of these methods.

In the first method, take cuttings in early summer and, when rooted, plant 3 in a 25 cm (10 in) pot. Stop the growing points 2 weeks after potting and allow just 3 of the lateral shoots that develop to grow on. Do not stop the growing points of these shoots.

The second and easier method is to take the cuttings in mid summer and, when rooted, plant them straight into prepared soil in the greenhouse 20 cm (8 in) apart. Stop the growing point 2 weeks later, and retain just 2 evenly matched lateral shoots on each plant. Again, do not stop the growing points of these lateral shoots.

Disbud all late-flowering indoor varieties in the same way as given for early-flowering outdoor varieties. Do this when flower buds appear in the late summer.

Move plants back into a well-ventilated greenhouse in early autumn, before the first frosts. Maintain a minimum temperature of 4°C (39°F) for plants that flower in mid autumn and a minimum temperature of 8°C (46°F) for those that flower in late autumn and early winter. Ventilate when the temperature reaches 20°C (68°F), or less in dull weather. Never close ventilators completely once flower buds begin to open.

After flowering, keep the best plants to produce cuttings for the following season. Cut back the main stems to 20 cm (8 in) above their base and overwinter, in their pots, in a cool greenhouse.

POT PLANTS

Once cuttings of Charm chrysanthemums have rooted, pot on in the same way as late-flowering indoor florists' varieties. Final pot size should be 20-25 cm (8-10 in) across.

Move pots outdoors in early summer. Pinch or 'stop' each plant once it reaches 15 cm (6 in) high. Put plants in a well-ventilated, cool greenhouse in early autumn, before risk of night frosts. After flowering, discard plants or keep them to produce cuttings in late winter. Cut back stems to 20 cm (8 in) and keep in a frost-free greenhouse.

Garden (Cushion) chrysanthemums can be used to produce pot plants that flower in summer. When cuttings have rooted, pot up one cutting in a 13 cm (5 in) pot or 3 in an 18 cm (7 in) pot. Stop plants 2 weeks after potting. Keep them in a well-ventilated, cold greenhouse or a sheltered site outdoors and feed the plants weekly.

PROPAGATION All chrysanthemums can be propagated by cuttings taken from the stool – the cluster of shoots that arise from the rootstock at the base of a plant. Take cuttings 5-6 cm (2-2½ in) long. (The time of year cuttings are taken depends on the type of chrysanthemum – see below.) Dip the bottom 1 cm (½ in) of the cutting in rooting hormone powder and insert in pots containing a mixture of half peat and half sand. Water in very thoroughly and provide a bottom temperature of at least 15°C (59°F). Prevent cuttings drying out by placing them in a propagating case or by covering with polythene until they have rooted; this will take up to 3 weeks.

GARDEN VARIETIES

Take cuttings in spring, preferably early spring, and when rooted harden off and plant out in late spring. Alternatively, sow seed in late winter in a heated greenhouse, providing a bottom temperature of 16-20°C (61-68°F) to ensure germination. Prick out into boxes with at least 5 cm (2 in) depth of compost, planting seedlings 8 cm (3¼ in) apart. Once seedlings reach at least 5 cm (2 in) in height, harden off and plant out in late spring. It is also possible to lift and divide plants every 2-3 years, as new

growth starts in spring. Replant vigorous shoots from the edge of the old clump and discard the congested central portion.

FLORISTS' VARIETIES

Take cuttings of early-flowering outdoor varieties in early or mid spring. Take cuttings of late-flowering indoor varieties from mid winter to mid summer, according to the method of growing to be adopted.

POT PLANTS

Take cuttings from Charm chrysanthemums in late winter or early spring, or sow seed in late winter in a heated greenhouse. Take cuttings of Garden chrysanthemums from mid spring to early summer.

Cuttings can be taken from shop-bought pot plants once flowering is over – the new plants will no longer be dwarf and will flower in mid or late autumn in a frost-proof greenhouse. Take cuttings from the shoots that arise from the base of the plant.

PESTS AND DISEASES Capsid bugs, red spider mites and thrips can harm both flowers and foliage. Aphids and chrysanthemum leaf miners may seriously damage leaves. Chrysanthemum eelworms can seriously affect growth by destroying leaf tissue. Chrysanthemum stool miners damage roots and stems. Western flower thrips can transmit the virus disease, tomato spotted wilt. White rust, grey mould and chrysanthemum virus diseases can also be a problem.

Dendrobium see ORCHIDS p.466
Deschampsia see GRASSES p.300

Desfontainia
Desfontainiaceae

Desfontainia spinosa

Bright tubular flowers contrast with glossy, holly-like leaves on these evergreen shrubs whose native habitat is damp cool regions in the mountains of S America. The waxy single flowers, borne in mid to late summer, are pendulous and tubular.

RECOMMENDED SPECIES AND VARIETIES

D. spinosa♀ Yellow-tipped scarlet blooms, up to 4 cm (1½ in) long and very narrow hang from the shoots in profusion, making a dazzling sight in mid to late summer. The small evergreen shrub is slow growing. As it is not frost-hardy, it needs the protection of a south-facing wall. Small leaves, to 4 cm (1½ in) long, are dark green with spiny edges. Native to S America. HEIGHT & SPREAD 1 m×50 cm (3 ft×20 in) after 5 years, ultimately 1.5 m (5 ft) tall and nearly as broad.

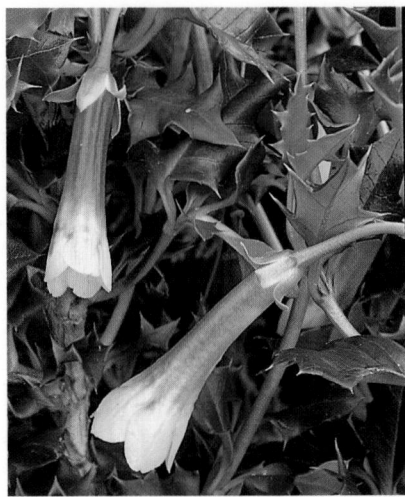

▲ *Desfontainia spinosa*

'Harold Comber' has flowers, up to 5 cm (2 in), which are vermilion-red.

CULTIVATION Plant in late spring. *D. spinosa* needs a cool, lime-free soil, dappled shade, moist air and a sheltered position even in mild areas.

PROPAGATION Take basal cuttings in mid autumn, overwinter in a coldframe and pot up in spring when rooted.

PRUNING Seldom required except to keep the shrub shapely.

PESTS AND DISEASES Usually trouble free.

Deutzia
Hydrangeaceae

Deutzia × elegantissima 'Rosealind'

These free-flowering, easily grown deciduous shrubs bear white, pink or purple flowers from late spring to early summer, when the long stems are studded with clusters of five-petalled, star-shaped or cupped flowers, 1.5-2.5 cm (½-1 in) wide. Opposite leaves are fairly narrow, 5-10 cm (2-4 in) long, and mid green to grey. The plants have an upright, somtimes arching, habit. Almost all are fully hardy, but young growth may be damaged by late frost. Native to the Himalayas, China, Japan and Central America.

RECOMMENDED SPECIES AND VARIETIES

D. compacta 'Lavender Time' Sweet-smelling, cup-shaped lilac flowers, later pale lavender, are held in heads 7.5 cm (3 in) wide. HEIGHT & SPREAD 1.2×1.2 m (4×4 ft) after 5 years, ultimately 1.5 m (5 ft) tall.

D. crenata 'Flore Pleno' see *D. scabra* 'Plena'

A dwarf, compact shrub, var. *nakaiana* 'Nikko' has small white flowers. Leaves are narrow, pointed and up to 6cm (2½in) long. HEIGHT & SPREAD 80×80cm (32×32in) after 5 years, ultimately 1m (3ft) tall.

D. × elegantissima Scented, pink star-shaped flowers in clusters 6cm (2½in) wide, cover the arching branches of this upright, bushy plant. Matt green leaves are lance-shaped. HEIGHT & SPREAD 1×1m (3×3ft) after 5 years, ultimately 1.5m (5ft) tall.

▲ *Deutzia × elegantissima* 'Rosealind'

'Rosealind'♀ is an erect branched bush with deep carmine flowers in upright heads.

D. gracilis A multitude of pure white star-shaped flowers is held in erect heads 7.5cm (3in) tall. Leaves are lance-shaped, toothed and pointed at the end. Protect from late frosts. HEIGHT & SPREAD 1×1m (3×3ft) after 5 years, ultimately 1.2m (4ft) tall.

D. × hybrida A group of free-flowering, bushy shrubs. The star-shaped flowers grow in clusters, 5-7.5cm (2-3in) across, and the leaves are pale to mid green and lance-shaped. HEIGHT & SPREAD 1.2×1m (4×3ft) after 5 years, ultimately 1.8m (6ft) tall.

'Magicien' has mauve-pink petals edged in white. 'Mont Rose'♀ is vigorous and erect with arching stems, deep pink flowers with golden anthers, and dark green, toothed leaves. 'Rosea Plena' has dense heads of pink double flowers that turn white.

D. × kalmiiflora Graceful, arching branches carry clusters of 5-12 flowers, white inside and deep rose on the reverse, 2.5cm (1in) across. Leaves are mid to deep green. HEIGHT & SPREAD 1×1m (3×3ft) after 5 years, ultimately 1.5m (5ft) tall.

D. × magnifica White double flowers appear in broad, erect heads 7.5cm (3in) tall. An elegant, arching shrub with narrow, oval leaves. HEIGHT & SPREAD 1.8×1.5m (6×5ft) after 5 years, ultimately 2.4m (8ft) tall.

D. ningpoensis Starry white flowers with yellow anthers are arranged in pyramidal heads, 10cm (4in) long, on lateral branches. The habit is pendulous. Leaves are willow-like. HEIGHT & SPREAD 1×1m (3×3ft) after 5 years, ultimately 1.8m (6ft) tall.

D. pulchra Pink-tinged, white cupped flowers appear in drooping sprays. Dark leathery leaves last into winter when the bark peels. The plant is less hardy than most. HEIGHT & SPREAD 1.5×1.2m (5×4ft) after 5 years, ultimately 2.4m (8ft) tall.

D. × rosea Open bell-shaped, soft rose-pink flowers grow in rounded clusters, 5-7.5cm (2-3in) wide, amid oval leaves on this compact plant with arching branches. HEIGHT & SPREAD 75×75cm (30×30in) after 5 years, ultimately 1m (3ft) tall.

'Carminea'♀ has petals with outer surfaces deep pink and spreads to 90cm (3ft) or so after 5 years, ultimately to 1.2m (4ft).

▲ *Deutzia × rosea*

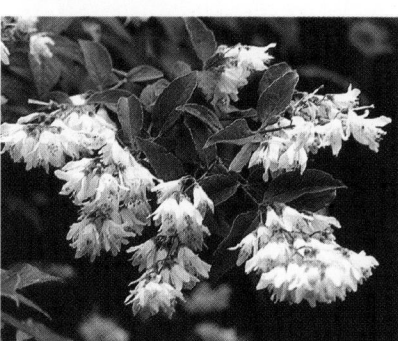

▲ *Deutzia scabra*

D. scabra Cup-shaped white flowers, sometimes flushed pink, appear in erect, branched clusters up to 15cm (6in) high. The brown bark peels in winter. HEIGHT & SPREAD 1.5×1.2m (5×4ft) after 5 years, ultimately 3×1.8m (10×6ft).

'Candidissima' has large clusters of double white flowers and grows ultimately to 3.5m (12ft). 'Plena' (syn. *D. crenata* 'Flore Pleno') has double flowers suffused with rose-purple on the outside. 'Pride of Rochester' has pink tinted double flowers.

CULTIVATION Plant bare-rooted shrubs in well-drained garden soil, between mid autumn and early spring; at any time for container-grown plants. Position in full sun or partial shade, avoiding open positions with northerly aspects. Mulch in spring.

PROPAGATION Take semi-ripe cuttings in late summer or take hardwood cuttings in autumn.

PRUNING Encourage new stems by cutting back old flowering stems to a strong new shoot low down on the stem. Prune once flowering is over, in mid summer.

PESTS AND DISEASES Usually trouble free, but snails can eat new shoots.

Dianella
Flax lily
Phormiaceae

Clumps of sword-like evergreen leaves give constant garden value to these rhizomatous perennials. Erect sprays of small, nodding flowers are borne on long stems in summer. Flowers have six tepals, usually turned back to reveal erect yellow stamens. After flowering, generally shiny berries appear. Native to S America, Asia, Australia and New Zealand, flax lilies are reasonably hardy in southern Britain, but elsewhere need a cold greenhouse or conservatory.

RECOMMENDED SPECIES AND VARIETIES

D. nigra Greenish white flowers, in sprays 30cm (12in) wide and up to 1.2m (4ft) long, rise out of tufts of grassy leaves 50cm (20in) long. The 6mm (¼in) wide flowers are followed by shiny violet-blue or sometimes greyish berries. HEIGHT 50cm (20in).

D. tasmanica Violet-blue flowers 1.5cm (½in) long appear in early to mid summer, followed by violet-blue berries. Flower sprays are branched to 8cm (3¼in) wide. Greyish leaves are 60cm (2ft) or more long and 2cm (¾in) wide. HEIGHT 1m (3ft).

'Variegata' has white-striped leaves.

CULTIVATION Plant in well-drained soil and half shade in spring or summer.

PROPAGATION Lift and divide rhizomes in spring or summer, or sow seed in pots in late summer and keep in an unheated greenhouse. Germination may take 2 years.

PESTS AND DISEASES Usually trouble free.

▲ *Dianella tasmanica* 'Variegata'

213

d

Dianthus

Carnations, pinks
Caryophyllaceae

Few flowers are more evocative of the simple charm of the cottage garden than pinks. Their close relative, the carnation, is a symbol of elegance. Both have a delightful and distinctive perfume

The beautiful clove-scented flowers of carnations, pinks and sweet williams vary widely in size, from five-petalled singles, just 1.5 cm (½ in) across, to doubles with up to 60 petals, about 10 cm (4 in) across. The petals, which emerge from a tubular five-toothed calyx, may be smooth-edged, as in most border carnations, or slightly toothed or deeply fringed, as in many pinks and perpetual-flowering carnations. The main colour groups are: selfs, bicolours, laced pinks, fancies and picotees (see diagram opposite).

The evergreen leaves of carnations and pinks are smooth and linear or lance-shaped, usually with pointed tips. The stalks have swollen nodes, from which the leaves grow in opposite pairs. Most are glaucous blue-grey to grey-green, associating well with many colour schemes in the garden and brightening up the dull days of winter. The leaves of sweet williams are usually matt green.

Perennial border carnations, pinks and dianthus species are fully hardy. They prefer neutral or slightly alkaline soil and an open sunny situation, not overshadowed by trees or taller-growing plants. They are tolerant of salt-laden winds and smoke-polluted air.

The more tender perpetual-flowering carnations may be grown in pots outdoors in summer, but require greenhouse protection with a minimum temperature of 7°C (45°F) if they are to bloom in winter.

RECOMMENDED SPECIES AND VARIETIES
The plants are divided into:
    Dianthus species and varieties
    Alpine hybrids
    Garden pinks
    Border carnations
    Annual carnations
    Perpetual-flowering carnations

DIANTHUS FLOWER-COLOUR GROUPS

The flowers of carnations and pinks are broadly divided into five colour groups. Selfs are of a single uniform colour. Bicolours have an outer zone of one colour and a central eye or zone of another. Laced pinks are of white or pink ground with a contrasting central zone which extends to form an edging round each petal. Fancies have contrasting irregular markings of another colour. Picotees have an edging of contrasting colour round each petal.

| Self | Bicolour | Laced | Fancy | Picotee |

DIANTHUS SPECIES AND VARIETIES

These hardy perennials, with single flowers, are suitable for growing in rock gardens or at the front of herbaceous borders.

D. alpinus♀ (Alpine pink) Solitary rose-pink to crimson flowers, up to 4 cm (1½ in) across and speckled with tiny white spots,

Dianthus alpinus

appear in early and mid summer. This perennial forms a close mat of deep green, blunt-tipped foliage. The plant thrives in a humus-rich, gritty compost in a rock garden or trough. Native to the E Alps. HEIGHT & SPREAD 5×20 cm (2×8 in).

'Joan's Blood'♀ has rich crimson blooms.
D. anatolicus Small white flowers, 6 mm (¼ in) across, appear in mid summer on tall slender stems well above a dense hummock

of narrow, pointed, deep green leaves. The plant dislikes excessive winter wet. Native to Turkey and Iran. HEIGHT & SPREAD 20-30×20-40 cm (8-12×8-16 in).

D. arenarius The fragrant white flowers, 2 cm (¾ in) across and carried in sprays, have deeply cut petals that are often stained with purple at the base. This sub-shrub forms lax hummocks of grassy, dark green leaves. Native to parts of central, N and E Europe. HEIGHT & SPREAD 30×50 cm (12×20 in).

D. armeria♀ (Deptford pink) Tall, wiry stems carry clusters of small, bright cerise-pink flowers, about 1.5 cm (½ in) across, in summer. This biennial or short-lived, tuft-forming perennial, with narrow, lance-shaped, deep green leaves, is suitable for rock gardens and the front of sunny borders or banks. Native to S Europe and W Asia. HEIGHT & SPREAD 30×45 cm (12×18 in).

D. × arvernensis♀ (syn. *D.* 'Arvernensis') Rich pink flowers, up to 3 cm (1¼ in) across, appear in summer on rather short stems. A good rock garden plant, this mat-forming perennial has grey-green linear leaves. A hybrid found naturally in France. HEIGHT & SPREAD 15×30 cm (6×12 in).

'Albus' bears white flowers.
D. barbatus (sweet william) This garden plant, although a short-lived perennial, is usually grown as a biennial. Small, occasionally double, flowers form densely packed, sweetly scented flat clusters up to 12.5 cm (5 in) across. The flowers are white, pink or red, selfs or bicolours. The leaves

1 *D.* 'Marg's Choice'
2 *D.* 'Dunkirk Spirit'
3 *D.* 'Fragrant Ann'
4 *D.* 'Betty Norton'
5 *D.* 'Devon Maid'
6 *D.* 'Monica Wyatt'
7 *D.* 'Joe Vernon'
8 *D.* 'Audrey Robinson'
9 *D.* 'Crompton Princess'
10 *D.* 'Joanne's Highlight'
11 *D.* 'Joanne'
12 *D.* 'Whitesmith'
13 *D.* 'Salamanca'
14 *D. barbatus*
15 *D.* 'Doris'
16 *D.* 'Kesteven Kirkstead'
17 *D.* 'Clara's Lass'
18 *D.* 'Becky Robinson'
19 *D.* 'Peter Wood'
20 *D.* 'Ann Franklin'

▼ *Dianthus arenarius*

▲ *Dianthus barbatus*

d

are matt green. Native to E Europe. HEIGHT & SPREAD 30-60×20-25 cm (12-24×8-10 in).

'**Auricula-eyed**'♀ has flowers of various colours with white central eyes and edging. **Nigrescens Group**♀ has deep crimson-maroon flowers.

D. caesius see *D. gratianopolitanus*

D. callizonus Solitary pink or carmine flowers, about 3 cm (1¼ in) across and with a central zone of darker dots, appear in summer. A flattish, mat-forming perennial with linear, deep green and rather glossy leaves, suitable for a rock garden or raised bed. Native to the Carpathians. HEIGHT & SPREAD 10-15×15-25 cm (4-6×6-10 in).

▲ *Dianthus callizonus*

D. carthusianorum (Carthusian pink) Tall wiry stems bear a tight cluster of deep pink to purple or red flowers in summer. The flowers, about 2 cm (¾ in) across, have contrasting purple-brown calyxes and bracts. A lax tufted perennial with long, grass-like, rather bright green leaves, this rock or wild garden plant naturalises in dry grassy places. Native to central and S Europe. HEIGHT & SPREAD 20-50×10-30 cm (8-20×4-12 in).

D. caryophyllus (carnation, clove-pink, gilliflower) The single, pinkish purple flowers, up to 4 cm (1½ in) across, are scented and borne in mid summer. The leaves are grey-green. Native to W and S France. HEIGHT & SPREAD 60×45 cm (2×1½ ft).

D. chinensis (syn. *D. sinensis*) (Indian pink) The individual flowers may be single or double, selfs or bicolours. They have fringed petals and grow to 4 cm (1½ in) across. In shades of red, pink and white, they bloom from early summer until the first frosts. The leaves are pale to mid green. The species has a number of cultivars, annuals and short-lived perennials which make attractive patio container plants if deadheaded regularly. Native to E Asia. HEIGHT & SPREAD 15-20×15 cm (6-8×6 in).

'**Baby Doll**' comes in shades of red, rose, white and some bicolours. '**Magic Charms**' are coral, pink and crimson selfs. '**Snowfire**' has pure white flowers with scarlet centres. '**Raspberry Parfait**' has deep pink flowers with large crimson eyes and dark green leaves. '**Strawberry Parfait**' has light rose-pink flowers with scarlet eyes and dark green leaves.

D. deltoides♀ (maiden pink) Cerise-pink flowers, about 1.5 cm (½ in) across, appear in lax clusters in summer on this spreading, mat-forming perennial. It has narrow lance-shaped, deep green leaves and is suitable for rock gardens and the front of dry sunny borders or banks. Native to Britain. HEIGHT & SPREAD 15×30 cm (6×12 in).

'**Albus**' has white flowers. '**Brilliant**' has bright carmine flowers. '**Leuchtfunk**' ('Flashing Light') has brilliant cerise flowers. '**Microchip**' is an annual with pink to red flowers.

D. erinaceus (hedgehog pink) Solitary, purplish pink flowers, about 1.5 cm (½ in) across, appear in mid to late summer. This dense, hummock-forming perennial has stiff, pointed, grey-green leaves. The plant is excellent for a raised bed or a rock garden in a warm, sunny position, but dislikes too much winter wet. Native to Turkey. HEIGHT & SPREAD 20×50 cm (8×20 in).

D. freynii The solitary pink flowers, about 1.5 cm (½ in) across, are borne in early to mid summer on this grey-green, tufted perennial with stiff, very narrow leaves. Native to the Balkans. HEIGHT & SPREAD 5-10×10-15 cm (2-4×4-6 in).

D. glacialis (glacier pink) Solitary pale to deep pink flowers, up to 1.5 cm (½ in) across, are borne on short stems in early and mid summer. A tufted to hummock-forming perennial with linear, deep green leaves. Native to E Alps and Carpathians. HEIGHT & SPREAD 5-10×10-20 cm (2-4×4-8 in).

D. gratianopolitanus♀ (syn. *D. caesius*) (Cheddar pink) Intensely fragrant, solitary, pale pink flowers, up to 3 cm (1¼ in) across, appear on long slender stems in summer. The lax tufted or mat-forming perennial has

▲ *Dianthus deltoides* 'Brilliant'

▲ *Dianthus chinensis* 'Raspberry Parfait'

narrow grey-green leaves and is an excellent rock garden plant. Native to Britain. HEIGHT & SPREAD 15×30 cm (6×12 in).

'**Flore Pleno**' has semidouble flowers.

D. haematocalyx The solitary deep pink flowers, up to 3 cm (1¼ in) across and slightly spotted, have a beige reverse and a red calyx. This cushion-forming plant, with grey or blue-green, narrow, sharply pointed leaves, makes a good rock garden or trough plant. Native to the central Balkans. HEIGHT & SPREAD 10-20×10-20 cm (4-8×4-8 in).

D. knappii Sulphur-yellow flowers, 1.5 cm (½ in) across, are borne in clustered heads in summer on this tufted, rather lax perennial. The narrow lance-shaped leaves are pale grey-green. Native to the Balkans. HEIGHT & SPREAD 30-40×10-20 cm (12-16×4-8 in).

D. microlepis Small, solitary, pink to purple flowers, up to 1.5 cm (½ in) across, appear in early to mid summer. Each petal is toothed on the margin, not fringed as in most other pinks. Forming a dense cushion of silvery grey or grey-green leaves, it is best suited to a trough in lime-free soil. Native to Bulgaria. HEIGHT & SPREAD 5×15 cm (2×6 in).

D. myrtinervius Bright pink flowers with darker spotting or markings in the centre appear in summer. They are rather rounded, almost stemless and up to 1.5 cm (½ in) across. Forming low, moss-like cush-

▲ *Dianthus erinaceus*

216

ions of tiny bright green leaves, this perennial requires full sun and a gritty soil to flower well, and tends to be rather short-lived. Native to mountains of N Greece. HEIGHT & SPREAD 5×20 cm (2×8 in).

D. pavonius♀ (syn. *D. neglectus*) (three-veined pink) The rather flat flowers, borne singly or in clusters, are pale to deep purplish pink or pink, with a contrasting buff reverse. They appear in early to mid summer and grow to 2.5 cm (1 in) across. The neat, cushion-forming plant with spiky grey-green leaves makes a good rock garden or trough plant. Native to the Alps. HEIGHT & SPREAD 5-10×20 cm (2-4×8 in).

D. petraeus Solitary, pale pink flowers, about 1 cm (⅜ in) across, appear in mid to late summer on short leafless stems. A cushion-forming or matted perennial with stiff, sharply pointed, green or grey-green leaves, the plant is suitable for a rock garden or a raised bed. Native to the Balkans. HEIGHT & SPREAD 10-15×15-25 cm (4-6×6-10 in).

White flowers are borne by ssp. **noeanus**.

D. plumarius (common pink) Intensely fragrant solitary flowers, about 3 cm (1¼ in) across, appear in summer and vary in colour from white to bright pink. This lax hum-

Dianthus plumarius

mock to mat-forming perennial with narrow, pointed, grey-green leaves is ideal for a rock garden or for dry sunny places. Native to central Europe. HEIGHT & SPREAD 30-40×30-40 cm (12-16×12-16 in).

D. sinensis see *D. chinensis*

D. squarrosus Fragrant, pure white, deeply fringed flowers, about 1.5 cm (½ in) across, appear in summer. This mat or hummock-forming perennial with sharply pointed, grey-green leaves is good for a rock garden or trough. Native to Ukraine and Kazakhstan. HEIGHT & SPREAD 20×20 cm (8×8 in).

D. subacaulis (short pink) Solitary carmine-pink flowers, rarely more than 1.5 cm (½ in) across, appear in summer on this mat-forming perennial suitable for a raised bed or a trough. The tufted, blunt-tipped leaves are deep green. Native to SW Europe. HEIGHT & SPREAD 10-15×10-15 cm (4-6×4-6 in).

D. superbus Beautifully fragrant, deeply fringed pale pink to purple flowers, up to 5 cm (2 in) across, with darker veins, appear in mid to late summer. A rather sprawling perennial with broadly linear, pale to mid green leaves. Native to Europe. HEIGHT & SPREAD 15-20×20-30 cm (6-8×8-12 in).

ALPINE HYBRIDS

Most of the species hybridise easily, producing numerous cultivated varieties suitable for a rock garden, raised bed, trough or alpine house. The plants form tufted or bushy clumps of narrow grey or grey-green foliage and most have fragrant flowers up to 3 cm (1¼ in) across, with fringed or serrated petals and stems 7.5-15 cm (3-6 in) high.

'**Betty Norton**' rose with a maroon centre; single. '**Dewdrop**' white with a yellowish green edge; single. '**Dubarry**' rose-lilac flowers with a crimson centre; double.

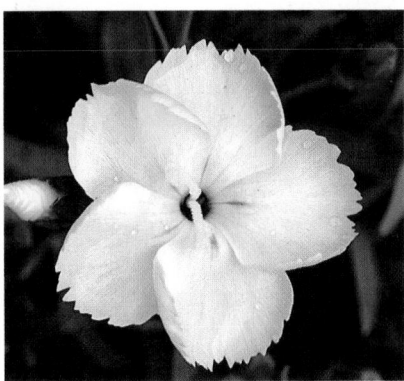

▲ *Dianthus* 'Dewdrop'

'**Fanal**' reddish purple flowers with a deeper crimson centre; single. '**Fusilier**' rose-red, zoned crimson; single. '**Hidcote**' rose-red; single. '**Highland Fraser**' pale pink laced and zoned maroon; single. '**Inshriach Dazzler**'♀ carmine pink with buff reverse on the petals; single. '**La Bourboule**'♀ solitary pink flowers; single. '**La Bourboule Albus**' white; single. '**Lemsii**' pink flushed with purple; single to semidouble. '**Little Jock**' mauve-pink with a crimson eye; semidouble. '**Mars**'

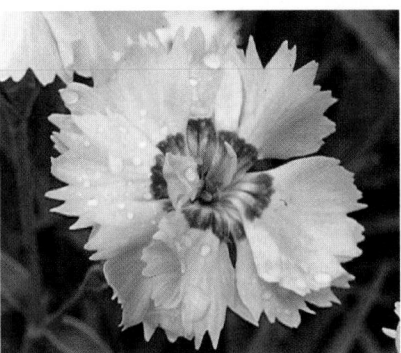

▲ *Dianthus* 'Little Jock'

bright crimson; semidouble. '**Nyewood's Cream**' cream or ivory-white flowers, 1.5 cm (½ in) across, with smooth-edged petals; single. '**Oakington**' solitary, rich purple-pink flowers; semidouble or double. '**Pike's Pink**'♀ pale pink with a cerise eye; double. '**Pink Jewel**' light purple, semidouble flowers 1.5 cm (½ in) across; stems 5-10 cm (2-4 in). '**Prince Charming**' pink flowers that are paler in the centre; single. '**Waithman's Beauty**' ruby splashed pink with clock-face markings; single. '**Whatfield Gem**' pink flowers laced maroon; double. '**Whatfield Joy**' lilac-pink with a darker eye and petals that are smooth-edged; single. '**Whatfield Magenta**' magenta; single. '**Whatfield Wisp**' very pale pink; single. '**Whitehills**'♀ pink with a central crimson zone; single.

GARDEN PINKS

Old-fashioned and modern pinks are hybrids derived from cross-breeding various species. The leaves, stems and nodes of the pink are identical to those of the carnation, but on a smaller scale. The flowers, 4-6 cm (1½-2½ in) across and single, semidouble or double, have fringed or deeply serrated, occasionally smooth, petal edges. The main colour groups are selfs, bicolours, laced pinks and fancies. Most are scented, some with a heavy clove scent. The plants may be low-spreading or bushy. HEIGHT & SPREAD 25-38×23-30 cm (10-15×9-12 in).

Old-fashioned pinks

This group includes older varieties – some claimed to date from the 17th century – and newer ones having the same low-spreading or bushy habit of growth. All have one flush of bloom for 2 or 3 weeks in early summer and, except where stated, all the pinks listed have double flowers.

'**Allspice**' magenta, edged and lightly splashed white; single. '**Brympton Red**' deep rose with a darker zone and edging; single. '**Dad's Favourite**' white ground laced ruby-red. '**Inchmery**' pale pink self. '**Mrs Sinkins**' white, splits its calyx. '**Musgrave's Pink**' (syn. 'Charles Musgrave') white with pale green eye; single. '**Sam Barlow**' white, zoned deep maroon-purple. '**Sops-in-Wine**' white, zoned deep crimson-purple.

▲ *Dianthus* 'Inchmery'

▲ *Dianthus* 'Mrs Sinkins'

Modern pinks

Old-fashioned pinks were crossed with perpetual-flowering carnations, and resulted in the hybrid group known as *D. × allwoodii*, from which most modern pinks derive. These are more vigorous than old-fashioned pinks, producing many more blooms. Flowering is mainly in early to mid summer, and all have double flowers unless otherwise stated. Young plants should have their growing tips pinched out in spring to promote bushy growth.

'Becky Robinson'♀ rose-pink, laced with ruby-red. 'Claret Joy'♀ crimson. 'Cranmere Pool'♀ creamy white with a magenta centre. 'Devon Cream' pale yellow with light magenta flecks. 'Devon Dove'♀ white with a green eye. 'Devon General'♀ deep red. 'Devon Glow'♀ magenta. 'Devon Maid'♀ white with a magenta eye. 'Devon Wizard'♀ cyclamen-purple with a ruby-red centre. 'Diane'♀ salmon-pink. 'Doris'♀ salmon-pink with a scarlet eye. 'Gran's Favourite'♀ white with cerise-pink lacing. 'Haytor White'♀ white. 'Houndspool Cheryl'♀ light crimson. 'Houndspool Ruby'♀ rose-pink with a reddish centre. 'Joy'♀ salmon-pink. 'Kesteven Kirkstead'♀ white with a red-

▲ *Dianthus* 'Becky Robinson'
Dianthus 'Devon Cream' ▲

▲ *Dianthus* 'Cranmere Pool'
Dianthus 'Diane' ▲

▲ *Dianthus* 'Claret Joy'

▲ *Dianthus* 'Gran's Favourite'
Dianthus 'Haytor White' ▲

purple eye; single. 'Laced Monarch' pink laced with maroon-purple. 'Lincolnshire Poacher'♀ lavender-pink with a maroon eye; single. 'Marg's Choice'♀ light salmon-pink. 'Monica Wyatt'♀ cyclamen-pink with a magenta eye. 'Old Mother Hubbard'♀ pink flecked with deeper pink. 'Strawberries and Cream' creamy white, splashed with two shades of pink. 'Valda Wyatt'♀ lavender-pink with a deeper centre. 'Widecombe Fair'♀ pastel pink.

BORDER CARNATIONS

Border carnations have evolved through 4 centuries of selective breeding from *D. caryophyllus*. These hardy perennial plants have grey-green or grey-blue leaves and double flowers that are 6-8 cm (2½-3¼ in) across with smooth-edged petals. They can be selfs, fancies or picotees. They flower only once in the season – in mid to late summer in the south, starting and finishing a little later in the north. Each stem can bear 5 or more flowers. HEIGHT & SPREAD 50-80×45 cm (20-32×18 in).

'Angelo' yellow, edged and marked deep purple. 'Bryony Lisa'♀ white, edged and marked rosy-carmine. 'Catherine Glover' bright yellow, edged and barred scarlet. 'Chris Crew'♀ deep apricot, edged red. 'Eileen O'Connor'♀ golden apricot. 'Flanders'♀ deep scarlet. 'Golden Cross'♀ yellow. 'Hannah Louise'♀ yellow, heavily edged scarlet. 'Hazel Ruth'♀ white, boldly striped blood-red. 'Howard Hitchcock'♀ yellow, edged and evenly striped rosy red.

▲ *Dianthus* 'Devon Dove'

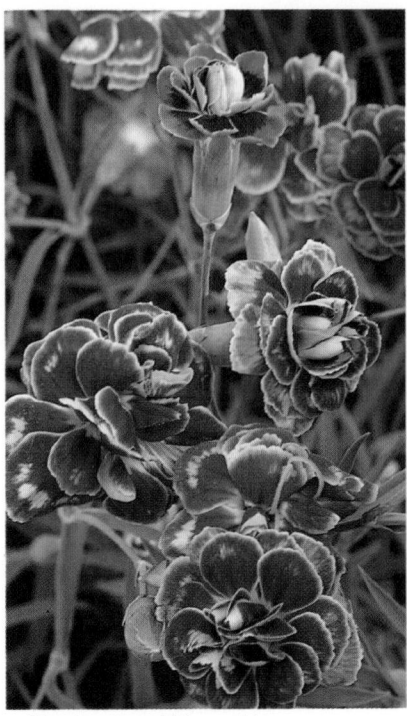

▲ *Dianthus* 'Laced Monarch'

'Irene Della-Torré'♀ white, evenly marked fuchsia-pink, with a scent of cloves. 'Lavender Clove' lavender, clove-scented. 'Merlin Clove' white, heavily edged and striped purple, clove-scented. 'Peter Wood'♀ light pink, flaked bright red. 'Portsdown Clove' shell-pink, clove-scented. 'Sandra Neal'♀ apricot with broad flakes of deep pink. 'Uncle Teddy'♀ white, edged and boldly striped purple. 'Whitesmith'♀ white, sweetly scented.

ANNUAL CARNATIONS

These half-hardy perennials, evolved from *D. caryophyllus,* have double flowers 5 cm (2 in) across. Usually grown from seed as annuals, occasionally as biennials, they flower from mid summer until the first frosts, and are excellent bedding plants. Sometimes sold as border carnations, they should not be confused with the hardy border carnations previously described.

Floristan Series, usually grown as biennials, produce flowers in most carnation self colours, some with picotee markings. They grow to a height of 75 cm (30 in). **Knight Series,** 30 cm (12 in) tall with flowers in a range of colours – orange picotees, rose, crimson, scarlet and white self colours or a mixture of these. **Lillipot Series** are dwarf bushy plants 23 cm (9 in) tall, with double flowers, mostly selfs but some bicolours.

PERPETUAL-FLOWERING CARNATIONS

These carnations, grown under glass for cutting, have double flowers up to 10 cm (4 in) across. They are available as selfs, fancies and picotees. Given a temperature of 10°C (50°F), they bloom all year round. At 7°C (45°F) they still provide a fair number of winter flowers, and at 5°C (41°F) a few blooms may be produced. Plants grown in a cold greenhouse will often survive a few degrees of frost, but growth will be checked and slow to start in spring.

'Ann Franklin' pale yellow, edged and flecked maroon. 'Audrey Robinson' white, heavily edged and marked deep purple. 'Clara' yellow, edged and flecked red; scented. 'Clara's Lass' white, edged and ticked red; scented. 'Cream Sue' cream. 'Crompton Princess' pure white. 'Dunkirk Spirit' orange-apricot, lightly flecked red. 'Fragrant Ann'♀ white, heavily clove-scented. 'Jacqueline Ann'♀ white, flecked rose-pink; scented. 'Joanne' cerise-pink; scented. 'Joanne's Highlight' light pink. 'Joe Vernon' deep purple. 'Raggio di Sole' orange-apricot, marked deeper orange. 'Ron's Joanne' light cerise with light pink markings. 'Salamanca' bright yellow. 'Scarlet Joanne' scarlet, scented. 'Valencia' bronze-yellow.

Malmaison carnations

These old-fashioned carnations, widely grown in Victorian and Edwardian times, produce large, self-coloured blooms with a heavy clove scent. The flowers, up to 12.5 cm (5 in) across, have so many petals that the calyxes invariably split. They are cultivated and propagated in the same way as perpetual-flowering carnations.

'Duchess of Westminster' bright rose-pink. 'Princess of Wales' rose-pink. 'Souvenir de la Malmaison' ('Old Blush') blush-pink flowers. 'Tayside Red' brick-red. 'Thora' pale blush.

CULTIVATION

SPECIES AND ALPINE HYBRIDS Most of the alpine species and their hybrids thrive in full sun in a well-drained rock garden or raised bed in alkaline soil, though most tolerate neutral to slightly acid conditions. The smaller and tighter cushion-forming species are also excellent for troughs or for growing in pots in an alpine house. *D. glacialis* and *D. microlepis* prefer acid soil. *D. callizonus* and *D. glacialis* require a dry atmosphere but also plenty of moisture at the roots, which can be provided by digging a lot of organic matter into the soil. *D. deltoides* and its cultivars tolerate partial shade, but will not flower as profusely.

GARDEN PINKS AND BORDER CARNATIONS Plant out in early to mid autumn. Incorporate well-rotted manure or garden compost into the ground and rake in bonemeal or blood, fish and bone before planting. Do not bury the lower leaves when planting, and after frosty weather check that plants have not been lifted out of the ground. In very exposed areas plants may be overwintered in a coldframe in 8 cm (3 in) pots, and planted out in early spring.

Pinks generally do not require staking, but border carnations should be supported when they start to spindle in late spring.

Border carnations are disbudded to secure larger flowers. With first-year plants remove the small bud below the crown bud; second-year plants may have some of the smaller axillary buds removed as well; and a plant in its third season should be allowed only 2 or 3 flowers a stem.

Pinks are never disbudded, but regular removal of dead flowers from modern pinks and the application of a balanced fertiliser in mid summer encourages further flowering. In their second and third season, carnations and pinks benefit from the application of a balanced fertiliser in spring.

After 3 years, plants become rather lanky and woody, and are best replaced with fresh young plants.

ANNUAL CARNATIONS Before planting, prepare soil as for cultivation of garden pinks and border carnations. Regular deadheading encourages a longer flowering period. Do not disbud.

PERPETUAL-FLOWERING CARNATIONS Plants require full light and plenty of ventilation, and the greenhouse should ideally have glass down to ground level. Move rooted cuttings into 6 cm (2½ in) pots in late winter or early spring, in John Innes No. 1 compost or a soil-less equivalent.

When 8 or 9 pairs of leaves have developed, stop the plant by snapping out the growing tip cleanly at a joint, leaving 5 or 6 joints or pairs of leaves. Sideshoots will then grow from every leaf axil. Before the plant becomes potbound pot on into a 15 cm (6 in) pot, using either John Innes No. 2 compost or a soil-less equivalent, and support with a 1 m (3 ft) cane and rings. Stopping for a second time – when each sideshoot has developed 8 or 9 pairs of leaves – will result in many more side growths, all of which will eventually flower. However, it is more usual to stop only half of the shoots, leaving the remainder to bloom in summer and autumn. These flowers are followed in winter by flowers from the stopped growths. Do not stop all the shoots at once, and all stopping should cease by mid summer. As well as stopping, perpetual-flowering carnations also need disbudding. All sidebuds are removed to leave only the top, or crown, bud on each stem. This disbudding should be a gradual process as removing all the buds at once would result in split calyxes.

Do not allow the plants to dry out, but avoid overwatering. Apply shading to the glass in early summer, and in hot weather damp down the greenhouse path and the area around the pots.

Feed plants grown in soil-less compost 6 weeks after repotting, but for soil-grown plants this is not necessary until the first flower buds develop. Apply a balanced liquid fertiliser every 7-10 days during summer and autumn. In winter, give a monthly feed only when a temperature of 7°C (45°F) is maintained.

In their second year, plants are repotted into 20-23 cm (8-9 in) pots, and supported with a 1.2 m (4 ft) cane. At the end of the second year, plants are best discarded and replaced with fresh young stock.

PROPAGATION

SPECIES AND ALPINE HYBRIDS Take cuttings of non-flowering shoots of species and hybrids in summer. Pot them on as soon as they have rooted adequately, generally after 4-6 weeks. Sow seed of the species in autumn or early winter in pots in a coldframe. Some of the tufted types can be divided in spring or straight after flowering.

Sow seed of sweet williams under glass in late winter or early spring at a temperature of 13°C (55°F). Prick out seedlings and plant in late spring to flower during summer. Alternatively, sow seed in open ground in mid spring and transplant to the flowering site in mid autumn, where the plants will bloom early the following year.

GARDEN PINKS AND BORDER CARNATIONS Layer border carnations in mid summer in the following manner. Strip non-flowering sideshoots of all but the top 5 or 6 pairs of leaves. Insert a sharp-pointed penknife through the middle of the stem immediately below the node or joint with the lowest leaves, and cut downwards through the next joint bringing the blade out just below it. The cut should form a tongue that is held open and pegged down with a wire hoop into a fresh mixture of soil, peat and sand. If the plants are kept just damp, new roots should form in about 6 weeks. Sever the layer from the parent plant and replant elsewhere.

For garden pinks, take cuttings of non-flowering sideshoots in early summer.

ANNUAL CARNATIONS Sow under glass from mid winter to early spring, and either plant out in late spring or grow on as container plants. Floristan Series is raised from seed sown from mid spring to mid summer, and planted out in autumn to flower the following summer.

PERPETUAL-FLOWERING CARNATIONS Take close-jointed, non-flowering shoots, with about 6 pairs of leaves, and cut just below the lowest joint, removing the bottom pair of leaves. Dip the base of the cutting in hormone rooting powder and insert into sharp sand with a bottom heat of 18-24°C (64-75°F). Rooting should take place in about 3 weeks.

PESTS AND DISEASES
Root aphids and other types of aphid can infest most pinks and introduce harmful viruses into plants. Carnation fly maggots and tortrix caterpillars feed on leaves and stems. Thrips infest flowers under glass and outdoors, and red spider mites attack greenhouse carnations.

Carnation stem-rot occurs on some plants under glass after the stems have been cut. Basal rot of cuttings is caused by the same fungus. Rust attacks the leaves and stems and leaf spot can be a problem. Fusarium and verticillium wilt can attack perpetual-flowering carnations under glass.

Diascia
Scrophulariaceae

Diascia integerrima

A profusion of shell-like, two-spurred flowers in shades of pink are borne throughout the summer on these South African perennials and annuals. They form compact clumps of matted sprawling growth or more extensive upright plants with loose spikes of flowers, each flower up to 2 cm (¾ in) across. The leaves are often heart shaped and up to 3.5 cm (1¼ in) long.

The first flush of bloom is in early summer and if the plant is trimmed back new shoots with a second flush of bloom appear later in the season. The plants are not reliably hardy but are easily propagated by division, cuttings and seed, and young plants are more free-flowering. Although they grow best in a sunny position they do not flourish in soil that dries out. Suitable for the front of a border and the rock garden, they also do well in containers. The recommended plants are all perennials.

RECOMMENDED SPECIES AND VARIETIES

D. anastrepta Tangled stems rise from the crown of the plant carrying rich pink flowers in long, lax sprays. The ovate leaves are dark green. It needs a moist site to grow well. HEIGHT & SPREAD 30×50 cm (12×20 in).
D. barberae A dense mass of slender stems bears sprays of deep rose-pink flowers over a long period in summer. The glossy leaves are ovate and dark green. HEIGHT & SPREAD 30×40 cm (12×16 in).
D. cordata A mat-forming plant with sprawling spikes bearing clusters of bright pink flowers. The small rounded leaves are deep green. HEIGHT & SPREAD 30×50 cm (12×20 in).
D. fetcaniensis A very free-flowering plant with a mass of rosy pink flowers from late

▼ *Diascia cordata*

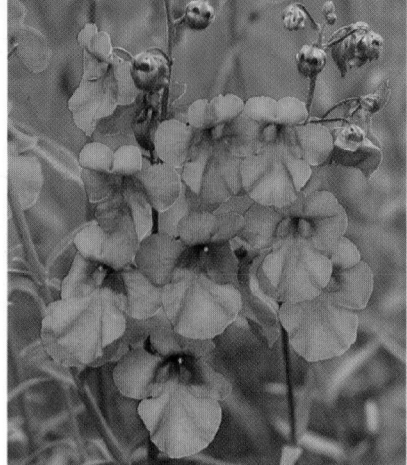

▲ *Diascia integerrima*

spring onwards. An upright bushy plant, it has deep green leaves. HEIGHT & SPREAD 25×40 cm (10×16 in).
D. integerrima♀ A good border plant with slender erect spikes of rose-pink flowers and narrow lance-shaped leaves. HEIGHT & SPREAD 40×40 cm (16×16 in).
D. lilacina A mat-forming plant with solitary lilac-pink flowers, usually in the axils of the pale green leaves, in early summer. HEIGHT & SPREAD 20×40 cm (8×16 in).
D. rigescens♀ A bushy plant with strong stems carrying long spikes of profuse, dusky crimson-pink flowers from late spring until early autumn. The leaves are pale green ageing to a reddy brown. HEIGHT & SPREAD 50×40 cm (20×16 in).
D. stachyoides A mat-forming plant with stems bearing deep rose-pink flowers in the axils of the round leaf-like bracts. It does not always flower regularly. HEIGHT & SPREAD 40×40 cm (16×16 in).
D. vigilis♀ The plant spreads over a wide area so space plants 50 cm (20 in) apart. It is usually regarded as the hardiest species. The flowers are a soft clear pink. HEIGHT & SPREAD 50×50 cm (20×20 in).

GARDEN VARIETIES
These plants are usually up to 45 cm (18 in) high with a spread of 40 cm (16 in) or more.
SALMON-APRICOT SHADES
'Blackthorn Apricot'♀, 'Hopley's Apricot'♀, 'Joyce's Choice'♀, 'Lady Valerie'♀ and 'Salmon Supreme'.
PINK SHADES
'Elizabeth'♀, 'Fisher's Flora'♀, 'Frilly'♀, 'Ruby Field'♀ and 'Rupert Lambert'♀.
PURPLY PINK SHADES
'Lilac Belle'♀, 'Lilac Mist'♀ and 'Twinkle'♀.

▼ *Diascia* 'Hopley's Apricot'

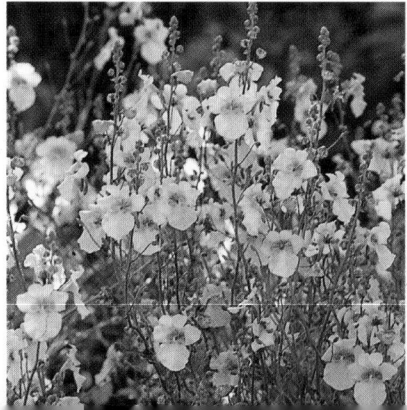

DARK PINK SHADES
'Dark Eyes'♀ and 'Hector's Hardy'♀.
CULTIVATION Plant in late spring in any fertile soil. Trimming off old flowerheads as they fade will encourage a further flush of late-season flowers.
PROPAGATION Sow seed in late winter under glass. Semi-ripe cuttings of cultivars taken from actively growing plants in summer or early autumn root readily under glass. Pot on the resulting plants and keep frost-free until spring planting. Established plants can also be divided in spring.
PESTS AND DISEASES Usually trouble free.

Dicentra
Bleeding hearts
Papaveraceae

Dicentra formosa

Heart-shaped flowers dangle like rows of lockets below the arching stems of these hardy herbaceous perennials. The blooms range from red, purple and deep pink to white or yellow and are borne from early spring to early summer with some species flowering intermittently throughout the summer. The recommended plants form compact clumps, 25-30 cm (10-12 in) across, of finely divided, often glaucous leaves, apart from *Dicentra scandens* which is a climber. In general, they do best in bright semi-shade and moist soils. They also flourish in a woodland setting and are best planted where they are protected from cold spring winds as the early shoots and flowers are rather delicate and easily frost-damaged.

RECOMMENDED SPECIES AND VARIETIES
D. cucullaria (Dutchman's breeches) A woodland plant bearing yellow-tipped, cream white flowers in spring; pink varieties are also known. Blue-green leaves, roughly triangular in outline, are composed of up to 23 segments. Native to N America. HEIGHT & SPREAD 25×25 cm (10×10 in).
D. formosa The plant bears pendent flowers from late spring to early summer, coloured variously from rose-purple to yellow to white. The fern-like, basal leaves are glaucous beneath and often so on the upper surfaces. Native to western N America. HEIGHT & SPREAD 50×50 cm (20×20 in).
D. macrantha The long pale yellow flowers dangle from the stems in late spring. This plant is suitable for cooler conditions in the garden if it is shielded from cold winds. Native to China. HEIGHT & SPREAD 45×25-30 cm (18×10-12 in).

D. scandens (syn. *D. thalictrifolia*) The divided leaves of this climber have the end leaflet modified into a tendril which allows the plant to cling to shrubs or to training wires. Yellow or white flowers have flared tips coloured pink or purple and are borne from late summer to early autumn. Native to SE Asia. HEIGHT Up to 4m (13ft).

D. spectabilis♀ (Dutchman's breeches, bleeding heart) The most widely grown of the species, this plant makes a compact clump of fern-like leaves with a mass of arching stems on which the graceful flowers are borne from early spring to early summer. Each flower is a rich rose red with white protruding inner petals. Even though native to shady woodland in China, Korea and Siberia, it needs protection from cold winds and late spring frosts. HEIGHT & SPREAD 60×45cm (24×18in).

'Alba'♀ is a beautiful form with pure white flowers.

D. thalictrifolia see *D. scandens*

GARDEN VARIETIES

These plants flower in late spring and early summer and spread 15-20cm (6-8in).

'Adrian Bloom' is a large-flowered deep red, 30cm (12in) high. 'Bacchanal' has soft crimson-red flowers on arching stems 30cm (12in) high. 'Bountiful'♀, 30cm (12in) high, has glaucous leaves and deep rosy red flowers. 'Langtrees'♀, 30cm (12in) high, is a pale pink with glaucous blue leaves and can be a rampant grower on light soils in shady sites. 'Luxuriant'♀, 30cm (12in) high, has mounds of fresh green, fern-like foliage and large bright pink flowers. 'Pearl

▲ *Dicentra spectabilis* 'Alba'

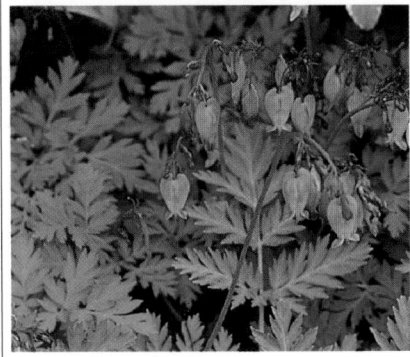

▲ *Dicentra* 'Bountiful'

Drops' has glaucous leaves and dangling pink-tinged white flowers on stems about 30cm (12in) high. 'Snowflakes' has white flowers amid finely cut fresh green foliage and grows up to 25cm (10in) high. 'Spring Morning', 30cm (12in) high, has palest pink flowers. 'Stuart Boothman'♀, 25cm (10in) high, has finely cut, steel blue leaves with dusty pink flowers through summer.

CULTIVATION The plants grow best in a humus-rich moist soil, in sheltered sunny places or in dappled shade.

PROPAGATION Established plants can grow for many years without replanting but when clumps need dividing do this from autumn to late winter, taking care not to damage the central crown. Replant in well-drained soil to which plenty of well-rotted compost has been added. Sow seed in early spring and plant seedlings out in autumn; on heavy soils leave the new plants in pots until early spring. Alternatively, for brittle rooted species such as *D. spectabilis*, take root cuttings, 10cm (4in) long, from established plants. Root in early spring in peat and sand compost in a coldframe.

PESTS AND DISEASES Slugs and snails can be troublesome in spring.

Dicksonia see FERNS p.263

Dictamnus
Burning bush, dittany
Rutaceae

Dictamnus albus

The common name of this plant derives from the volatile lemon-scented oil given off by its flowers, which has been known to ignite spontaneously on still, dry summer evenings. People with sensitive skin can suffer a rash from the oil. There is only one species in the genus, a long-lived herbaceous perennial found throughout SW Europe and across into Asia. It is hardy in Britain and makes a good plant for a sunny border, thriving in alkaline soil.

Dictamnus albus♀ Impressive spikes of white star-shaped flowers are produced in early summer on a bushy plant. The flowers, which are sometimes streaked and spotted with purple, are 3cm (1¼in) across with protruding stamens. The star-shaped seed capsules that come after the flowers are valued by flower arrangers. Dark green leathery leaves, up to 7.5cm (3in) long, consist of 9-11 leaflets. HEIGHT & SPREAD 60×25cm (24×10in).

The plant var. *purpureus* (syn. *D. fraxinella*) is as the species but the flowers are pale mauve-pink, streaked with purple.

D. fraxinella see *D. albus* var. *purpureus*

CULTIVATION Plant in well-drained fertile soil – preferably alkaline – in a sunny or partially shaded site. Avoid moving plants, particularly the large ones, once they have become established.

PROPAGATION Sow seed in late summer into open ground and transplant the seedlings into their final positions as soon as they are large enough to handle, either that autumn or the following spring. It may be several years before these plants flower.

PESTS AND DISEASES Usually trouble free.

d

▲ *Dictamnus albus*

▲ *Dictamnus albus* var. *purpureus*

221

Dieffenbachia
Dumb cane
Araceae

Very large, oval or broadly lance-shaped green leaves, often splashed with cream or white, are the main feature of these evergreen perennials. The leathery leaves grow alternately from an upright, fleshy, cane-like stem as tall as 2 m (6½ ft). Greenish cream to white flowers, 2.5 cm (1 in) long, bloom intermittently, and not at all when the plant is raised indoors. Dieffenbachias are usually grown as houseplants in Britain, in a temperature of at least 15°C (59°F). The sap is poisonous and a skin irritant. Plants are native to tropical Central and S America. The leaves of recommended plants are up to 25 cm (10 in) long and 10 cm (4 in) wide, unless stated otherwise.

RECOMMENDED SPECIES AND VARIETIES
D. x *bausei* Yellowish green leaves have several large green blotches and a number of prominent small white spots. HEIGHT & SPREAD 90×90 cm (36×36 in).

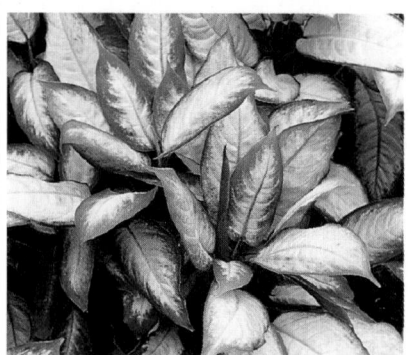
▲ *Dieffenbachia* 'Camille'

D. **'Camille'** Striking greenish cream leaves are edged with green. HEIGHT & SPREAD 80×60 cm (32×24 in).
D. maculata The leaves, as long as 45 cm (18 in) and 10 cm (4 in) wide, are mid green heavily spotted with white. HEIGHT & SPREAD 90×75 cm (36×30 in).
　'Roehrsii' has yellowish green leaves faintly spotted white, with green midribs and margins.
D. oerstedi The velvety, dark green leaves are often slightly asymmetrical. HEIGHT & SPREAD 1 m×60 cm (3×2 ft).
　On **'Variegata'**, the midribs form a bold cream line down the centre of each leaf.
D. seguine Glossy, dark green leaves, often with tiny white spots, grow to 45 cm (18 in) long and 15 cm (6 in) wide. HEIGHT & SPREAD 1 m×60 cm (3×2 ft).
　'Amoena' has dark green leaves with creamy white markings along the veins. This plant grows to 1.5 m (5 ft) or more and spreads to 75 cm (30 in). **'Exotica'** is a slow-growing, relatively small variety, with leaves to 25 cm (10 in) long, dark green splashed greenish white. The plant reaches a height of 45 cm (18 in) and spreads to 50 cm (20 in). **'Rudolph Rhoers'** has creamy green leaves that develop darker green spots, edges and veins as they age. The leaves on **'Tropic Snow'** are a creamy green with paler markings towards the centre, green midribs and darker edges.

CULTIVATION Grow in a warm well-lit room out of direct sunlight and draughts. Use John Innes No. 3 compost and keep constantly damp. Twice a week, syringe the foliage with clean tepid water. Remove any faded leaves immediately.
PROPAGATION Take stem cuttings or air layer in summer. Place pieces of leafless stem horizontally in trays of good rooting medium during spring or summer.
PESTS AND DISEASES Mealy bug and vine weevil are sometimes a nuisance.

Dierama
Angel's fishing rods
Iridaceae

With their arching stems of pendent, bell-like summer flowers and long, sword-like leaves these perennials are ideal for a damp, sunny spot beside a pool or arching across a path. The evergreen, clump-forming plants grow from corms. Recommended species are native to South Africa.

RECOMMENDED SPECIES AND VARIETIES
D. dracomontanum (syn. *D. pumilum*) The nodding pink or purplish, bell or funnel-shaped flowers, 2.5 cm (1 in) long, are borne in mid to late summer. A hardy plant with slender mid green leaves up to 45 cm (18 in) tall. HEIGHT & SPREAD 75×30 cm (30×12 in).
D. pendulum (syn. *D. ensifolium*) Arching sprays of deep pinkish purple, funnel-shaped flowers, up to 2.5 cm (1 in) long, are carried in profusion on tall wiry stems in late summer. These elegant and hardy plants have narrow strap-like leaves that can grow up to 1.5 m (5 ft) in length. HEIGHT & SPREAD 1.5 m×20 cm (5 ft×8 in).
　var. *pumilum* see *D. dracomontanum*

▼ *Dierama dracomontanum*

▲ *Dierama pulcherrimum*

D. pulcherrimum Wiry stems carry graceful, arching sprays of deep pink, funnel-shaped flowers up to 5 cm (2 in) long. A hardy, upright plant with broad grass-like leaves up to 1.5 m (5 ft) long. Native to South Africa. HEIGHT & SPREAD 1.5 m×30 cm (5×1 ft).
CULTIVATION Grow in a richly organic but free-draining soil in a very sunny spot. The plants dislike disturbance so divide the clumps only when there is a noticeable deterioration in flower quality and quantity – usually only after many years. Plant corms in mid autumn or mid spring. Remove old flower stems and faded foliage.
PROPAGATION Divide and replant corms in spring. Sow seed in a coldframe in spring.
PESTS AND DISEASES Thrips are the only persistent problem.

Diervilla
Bush honeysuckle
Caprifoliaceae

Diervilla sessilifolia

Clusters of small yellow flowers are borne on the new season's growth of these easily grown, summer-flowering small shrubs. They are deciduous, multistemmed and of rounded habit. The individual flowers, only 1.5 cm (½ in) long, are tubular and grow from the base of the leaves. The leaves, up to 18 cm (7 in) long, are opposite on the stem. Natives of N America, all diervillas are frost-hardy.

▲ *Diervilla sessilifolia*

▲ *Diervilla × splendens*

RECOMMENDED SPECIES

D. sessilifolia Flower clusters, up to 7.5 cm (3 in) across, appear in early summer and last through to late summer. HEIGHT & SPREAD 80×80 cm (32×32 in) after 5 years, ultimately 1.2 m (4 ft) tall.

D. × splendens Flower clusters in mid summer last through to early autumn. HEIGHT & SPREAD 80×80 cm (32×32 in) after 5 years, ultimately 1.2 m (4 ft) tall.

CULTIVATION Plant in any well-drained soil in full sun or partial shade.

PROPAGATION Take semi-ripe cuttings from mid to late summer, or sow seed in a coldframe in autumn or winter.

PRUNING None usually necessary except to shape plants or to remove dead wood. Prune before growth begins in spring.

PESTS AND DISEASES Usually trouble free.

Digitalis
Foxglove
Scrophulariaceae

Digitalis purpurea

Tall spires of colourful, tubular flowers are borne in summer above glossy or downy foliage. These biennial and perennial border plants, ranging in height from 45 cm (1½ ft) to 2 m (6½ ft), enjoy moist, humus-rich soil and benefit from a little shade. The mainly lance-shaped leaves grow as a basal rosette or clump with smaller leaves growing up the stem. Most foxgloves carry their flowers on one side of the stem. Some perennial species deteriorate after their first flowering and are best treated as biennials. *Digitalis purpurea* and *D. lutea* spread freely by self-seeding. All parts of the plant are poisonous. Native throughout Europe to central Asia.

RECOMMENDED SPECIES AND VARIETIES

D. ambigua see *D. grandiflora*

D. Apricot hybrids see *D. purpurea* 'Sutton's Apricot'

D. ciliata Small, cream tubular flowers are borne on the stout stem of this perennial. Very hairy leaves grow to 15 cm (6 in) long. HEIGHT & SPREAD 60×45 cm (2×1½ ft).

D. davisiana Sparse, pale yellow blooms, 2.5 cm (1 in) long, with distinctive orange veining, are borne in summer. This perennial has smooth, narrow, dark green leaves to 12 cm (4¾ in) long. HEIGHT & SPREAD 75×30 cm (2½×1 ft).

D. dubia Purplish flowers with darker internal spotting, up to 5 cm (2 in) long, are sparsely produced in summer on a short flower stem. The coarse, matt green leaves of this short-lived and half-hardy perennial grow to 20 cm (8 in) and lie in flat rosettes. HEIGHT & SPREAD 45×30 cm (1½×1 ft).

D. eriostachya see *D. lutea*

D. ferruginea (rusty foxglove) Pale orange-brown to off-white flowers, each 3.5 cm (1½ in) long, are borne in summer on tall spikes above rosettes of soft, downy, broad leaves up to 25 cm (10 in) long. A perennial that behaves as a biennial in the garden. HEIGHT & SPREAD 1.2 m×60 cm (4×2 ft).

▼ *Digitalis ferruginea*

D. grandiflora ♀ (syn. *D. ambigua, D. orientalis*) (large yellow foxglove) Stout, upright flower spikes are clothed in mid to late summer with pale yellow flowers with brown veins inside, like pendent tubular bells, each flower up to 5 cm (2 in) long. Finely toothed, mid green leaves are lance-shaped while basal leaves are oval. Leaves are up to 25 cm (10 in) long. This is a perennial plant that is best treated as a biennial. HEIGHT & SPREAD 1 m×45 cm (3×1½ ft).

The flowers of 'Temple Bells' are slightly larger.

D. heywoodii see *D. purpurea* ssp. *heywoodii*

D. kishinskyi see *D. parviflora*.

D. laevigata Small pendent flowers are produced in summer on stiff, upright stems. Each bloom is no more than 3 cm (1¼ in) long and brownish white with internal brown-purple veining and a distinctive white lip. This perennial produces rosettes of dark green, smooth, slightly toothed leaves up to 25 cm (10 in) long. HEIGHT & SPREAD 1 m×60 cm (3×2 ft).

D. lanata ♀ (syn. *D. lamarckii* hort.) (Grecian foxglove) The off-white to pale caramel-coloured flowers, 2.5 cm (1 in) long, are marked with brown veining and appear from mid to late summer. The narrow, grey-green, downy leaves grow to 20 cm (8 in). A short-lived perennial usually treated as an biennial. HEIGHT & SPREAD 75×45 cm (2½×1½ ft).

D. lutea (syn. *D. eriostachya*) (straw foxglove) From mid to late summer the dark green, smooth flower spike is densely covered with pale yellow, pendent flowers, up to 2.5 cm (1 in) long. The glossy, dark green leaves of this reliably perennial foxglove are up to 25 cm (10 in) long. HEIGHT & SPREAD 60-90 cm×45 cm (2-3×1½ ft).

D. × mertonensis ♀ The pendent flowers are crushed strawberry pink and up to 5 cm (2 in) long. Flowers are borne from mid to late summer above neat rosettes of greyish green, soft, downy leaves that are broad lance-shaped and grow to 25 cm (10 in) long. This is a perennial hybrid which is best treated as a biennial. HEIGHT & SPREAD 75×45 cm (2½×1½ ft).

D. obscura (willow-leaved foxglove) A shrubby half-hardy perennial with yellow flowers marked red inside, up to 4 cm (1½ in) long, from mid to late summer. The narrow, shiny, dark green leaves grow to 10 cm (4 in) long. Protect the plant from cold and winter wet. HEIGHT & SPREAD 60×60 cm (2×2 ft).

D. orientalis see *D. grandiflora*

D. parviflora (syn. *D. kishinskyi*) The tiny, reddish brown and white flowers, up to 1.25 cm (½ in) long, are densely borne all round the flowering stem of this plant in summer. The mid green leaves grow up to 10 cm (4 in) long and have slightly toothed edges. Though reasonably reliable as a perennial, the plant is best replaced after 3-4 years. HEIGHT & SPREAD 60×45 cm (2×1½ ft).

d

223

d

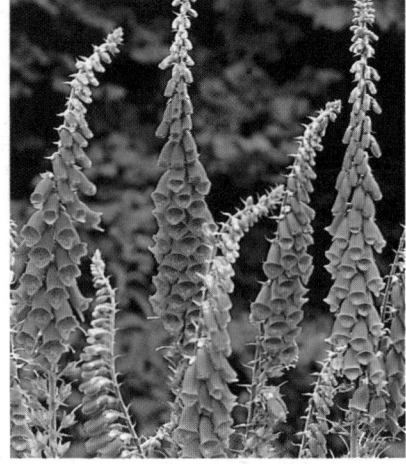

▲ *Digitalis purpurea*

D. purpurea (common foxglove) In summer this biennial species bears flowers up to 5 cm (2 in) long, ranging in colour from pink to purple with deep purple internal spotting. The soft, greyish green, oval or lance-shaped leaves grow up to 25 cm (10 in) long in neat basal clumps. This foxglove is an extremely variable species both in stature and in behaviour. HEIGHT & SPREAD 1.5 m×60 cm (5×2 ft).

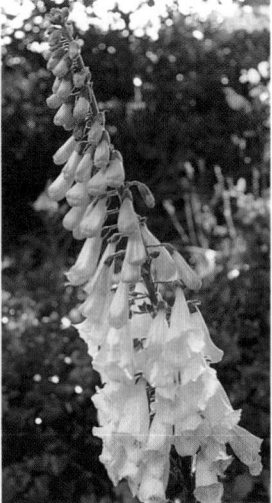

▲ *Digitalis purpurea* Excelsior Group
Digitalis purpurea f. *albiflora* ▲

The flowers of f. *albiflora*♀ are white. It reaches a height of 1-1.5 m (3-5 ft). **Excelsior Group**♀ bears flowers in a wide range of pastel colours, from creamy white to purple-pink, all with purple internal spotting. They are borne more evenly round the stem than in the common species. Plants reach a height of 2 m (6½ ft) or more. **Foxy Group** has red, pink, cream and white flowers, all heavily spotted with maroon. Plants reach a height of 75 cm (2½ ft). **Giant Spotted Group** has red, pink, cream and white flowers, all heavily spotted with maroon. The foliage of ssp. *heywoodii* is silvery grey and the flowers are white to

pale purple. It reaches a height of 1 m (3 ft). **'The Shirley'**♀ in Gloxinioides Group bears funnel-shaped flowers, up to 5 cm (2 in) long and 5 cm (2 in) wide at the opening, in colours ranging from white through cream and pink to purple, all heavily spotted with maroon. **'Sutton's Apricot'** has apricot-coloured flowers and comes true from seed. It reaches a height of 2 m (6½ ft). **D. viridiflora** A perennial with small, green-yellow flowers, up to 1 cm (⅜ in) long, with prominent greenish veins on a slender spike in summer. Lance-shaped, plain green leaves grow up to 15 cm (6 in) long. HEIGHT & SPREAD 60×30 cm (2×1 ft).

CULTIVATION Plant in sun or partial shade in humus-rich, moist but free-draining soil.
PROPAGATION Sow seed from spring until late summer either in a frame or in the open ground. Divide the dependable perennial species in early spring.
PESTS AND DISEASES Usually trouble free.

Dill see *Anethum graveolens*
Dill (culinary herb) see HERBS p. 331

Dimorphotheca
Star of the veldt, Cape marigold
Compositae

These colourful South African daisies are among the easiest and most free-flowering of half-hardy annuals for a well-drained soil. A sunny site is best as the flowers close up in shade and in dull weather. They are fairly drought-tolerant and thrive on rockeries and at the foot of south-facing walls, where they make a quick temporary ground cover. Both species readily available make rather spreading plants with the abundant flowers displayed well above dark green, aromatic, narrow leaves. Leaves are deeply toothed and up to 10 cm (4 in) long.

RECOMMENDED SPECIES AND VARIETIES
D. aurantiaca see *D. sinuata*
D. ecklonis see *Osteospermum ecklonis*
D. pluvialis 'Glistening White' The scented white flowers, borne from mid summer to early autumn, are about 5 cm (2 in) across with a dark brownish purple central disc. The slight violet tinge of the flower arises from the purple underside of the petals. HEIGHT & SPREAD 25-40×15-30 cm (10-16×6-12 in).
D. sinuata (syn. *D. aurantiaca*) The most widely grown species has unscented flowers up to 8 cm (3¼ in) across from mid summer to early autumn. They have a dark golden-brown central disc and are generally available in a mixed colour range, dominated by salmon, orange and pink but also including some whites and creams. HEIGHT & SPREAD 30×30 cm (12×12 in).

'Salmon Queen' is a mixture of apricot and salmon shades. **'Tetra Pole Star'** has white flowers with a purple eye.

▲ *Dimorphotheca pluvialis* 'Glistening White'

CULTIVATION Plant in late spring after the risk of frost has passed in well-drained, preferably sandy, soil, in a sunny spot. Deadhead regularly to prolong flowering. Alternatively, grow in pots and keep in a greenhouse or conservatory at a minimum temperature of 7°C (45°F). Choose a sunny position and water sparingly.
PROPAGATION Sow seed in mid or late spring where the plants are to grow. For earlier flowers, sow the seed in a heated greenhouse in early spring and plant out seedlings in late spring.
PESTS AND DISEASES Grey mould may affect flowers in prolonged wet weather.

Dionysia
Primulaceae

Dionysia aretioides

A multitude of pink, violet or yellow, five-petalled primrose-like flowers cover these compact, cushion-forming alpines in late winter and spring. The cushions of foliage can be loose or dense and are made up of a mass of small leaf-rosettes with the dead leaves of previous years clothing the stems below.

Dionysias are native to the mountains of the Middle East, growing on shaded or partially shaded cliffs, and require the shelter of an alpine house in the relatively cold, damp climate of Britain.

RECOMMENDED SPECIES AND VARIETIES
D. aretioides Solitary yellow flowers cover the hummocks of grey-green leaves from late winter to spring, although some flowers may appear in autumn. The flowers are 1 cm (⅜ in) across. The oblong leaves, up to 1.5 cm (½ in) long, are hairy with their

toothed edges rolled under. HEIGHT & SPREAD 20×50 cm (8×20 in).

'Paul Furse' has large flowers, up to 1.5 cm (½ in) across, with rather rounded petals. 'Phyllis Carter' has an abundance of flowers with narrower petals.

▲ *Dionysia aretioides 'Paul Furse'*

▲ *Dionysia involucrata*

D. curviflora Solitary pink flowers with yellow eyes clothe the dense, greyish cushions of foliage from late winter to spring. Each flower is 6mm (¼ in) across. The tiny leaves are up to 6mm (¼ in) long. HEIGHT & SPREAD 8×40 cm (3¼×16 in).

D. involucrata Violet-purple flower clusters cover the sticky, deep green cushions of foliage in spring. The clusters are composed generally of 2–3 tightly packed tiers of flowers up to 5 cm (2 in) long. Each bloom is about 1 cm (⅜ in) across, with a white eye that gradually turns deep crimson-purple. The leaves are 1 cm (⅜ in) wide, and toothed in the upper half. HEIGHT & SPREAD 15×20 cm (6×8 in).

CULTIVATION Plants of this species must be grown in an alpine house. Plant them in well-drained gritty compost with a layer of grit around the collar of the plant. Water with care always making sure that the cushions of foliage are not left with water lying on them. Water sparingly in winter, and more frequently in summer.

PROPAGATION Sow seed in pots when ripe or in winter.

PESTS AND DISEASES Aphids can be a problem in spring. The fungal disease botrytis can infect the cushions.

Diospyros
Persimmon
Ebenaceae

Diospyros kaki

Colourful autumn foliage is the chief garden value of these trees or large shrubs, though dainty flowers and glossy leaves give interest in summer. On mature plants there may be the bonus of fruits, if male and female plants are grown. Fruits are edible and juicy but full of seeds. Most species in the genus are tropical plants, the two deciduous Asiatic species listed below are most suitable for British gardens and eventually produce fruits, given the right conditions.

RECOMMENDED SPECIES

D. kaki (persimmon) Small yellowish white, bell-shaped flowers appear in mid summer. Male trees carry flowers in clusters while females carry single blooms. Glossy leaves are 15 cm (6 in) long and turn orange, red and purple in autumn, when the fruits are borne. Fruits are orange when ripe, round and 7.5 cm (3 in) in diameter. The greyish brown bark is scaly and furrowed beneath a rounded dome of foliage. HEIGHT & SPREAD 6×4 m (20×13 ft) after 20 years, ultimately 12 m (40 ft) tall.

D. lotus (date plum) The tiny flowers in mid summer are like translucent pale pink porcelain bells carried in clusters (males) or singly (females). Small brown fruits are 3 cm (1¼ in) across. The dark brown bark beneath the rounded crown becomes fissured with age. The tree shape and its growth rate are variable. HEIGHT & SPREAD 5×3 m (16×10 ft) after 20 years, ultimately 20 m (66 ft) tall.

CULTIVATION Plant in a sheltered sunny position when the soil is warm. If fruit is desired, male and female plants need to be grown together. The recommended species grow best on dry fertile sites among other trees to give them shelter.

▼ *Diospyros kaki*

PROPAGATION Sow seed in spring. Alternatively take semi-ripe cuttings in summer or layer in winter. When grown from a seedling, it is 20 years before the tree flowers and its sex can be determined. The waiting time is reduced if the tree is grown from a cutting or a graft (as often sold in garden nurseries).

PRUNING Not usually necessary.

PESTS AND DISEASES Usually trouble free.

Dipelta
Caprifoliaceae

Dipelta floribunda

Small, fragrant flowers are borne in profusion from late spring to early summer on the tall, deciduous shrubs. This genus has only four species, all of them native to China.

RECOMMENDED SPECIES

D. floribunda Fragrant, pinky white flowers, 3 cm (1¼ in) long, with orange markings in the throat are produced in clusters of up to 6. The bark is creamy and flaking.

▲ *Dipelta floribunda*

Oval leaves, up to 10 cm (4 in) long, are light green and hairy. The shrub is fully hardy. HEIGHT & SPREAD 1.5 m (5 ft) tall after 5 years, ultimately 5×2 m (16×6½ ft).

D. ventricosa Pale to deep pink flowers with an orange throat, up to 2.5 cm (1 in) long, are borne in groups on this multi-stemmed shrub. Narrow, pointed, light green leaves are up to 12.5 cm (5 in) long. Grow in a sheltered position as the plant is only moderately frost-hardy. HEIGHT & SPREAD 100×60 cm (3×2 ft) after 5 years, ultimately up to 2 m (6½ ft) tall.

Eccremocarpus
Chilean glory vine
Bignoniaceae

Brightly coloured flowers adorn these half-hardy, fast-growing climbers. Their leaf tendrils cling to walls, fences, trellis or other plants with ease, making them ideal for climbing through hedges or up trees. Only in the mildest areas will plants survive the winter unscathed. Frost destroys most or all of the stem system, but regrowth occurs in spring, both from below ground and from surviving seed. Easily grown from seed and climbing up to 3 m (10 ft) in their first year, eccremocarpus are often treated as half-hardy annuals. They may also be grown in pots under glass.

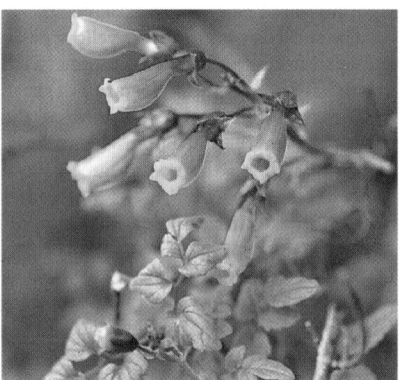

▲ *Eccremocarpus scaber*

RECOMMENDED SPECIES AND VARIETIES
E. scaber♀ Orange, tubular flowers appear in clusters, about 12.5 cm (5 in) long, in summer and early autumn. The dark green, often toothed leaves are bipinnate with a branched tendril at the tip of each stalk. HEIGHT & SPREAD 3×1 m (10×3 ft).

    Anglia Hybrids, **'Fireworks'** and **Tresco Hybrids** provide flowers in a mixture of cream, yellow, red, pink and mauve.
CULTIVATION Plant in spring in a sunny, sheltered spot on light, well-drained soil. Mulch plants in autumn. Alternatively, grow in pots of general-purpose or potting compost in a cool greenhouse or conservatory, choosing a position in full sun.
PROPAGATION Sow seed in early spring, transplant self-sown seedlings in spring or take softwood cuttings in early summer.
PESTS AND DISEASES Usually trouble free.

Echeveria
Crassulaceae

Echeveria derenbergii

Rosettes of fleshy leaves, often grey and brightly coloured at the tips, and cup-shaped or tubular waxy blooms distinguish these popular houseplants. The rosettes are sometimes held on short stems and the flower stalks are often pendent. These tender perennial succulents can be used in summer bedding. Native to Central and S America. The heights given below are the height of leaf rosettes rather than the height of the plant during flowering.

RECOMMENDED SPECIES AND VARIETIES
E. derenbergii♀ Handsome rosettes of small grey-white leaves, up to 2.5 cm (1 in) long, form a clump. In spring a flower stem, up to 7.5 cm (3 in) tall, rises out of the leaf rosettes, bearing small, cup-shaped, yellow-and-red or orange blossoms. HEIGHT & SPREAD 5×30 cm (2×12 in).

▲ *Echeveria derenbergii*

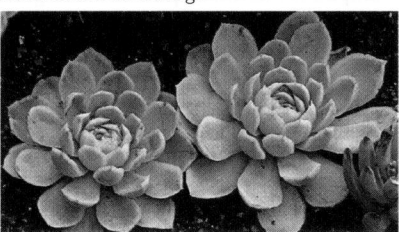

▲ *Echeveria elegans*

E. elegans♀ (Mexican snowball) Small alabaster white rosettes with greenish edges, and up to 2.5 cm (1 in) long, form dense rosettes. If grown in full sun, the foliage often takes on a pinkish tinge. Pink tubular flowers, each tipped with orange-yellow and up to 1.5 cm (½ in) long, are produced on stems up to 15 cm (6 in) high during spring and summer. HEIGHT & SPREAD 15×30 cm (6×12 in).

E. gibbiflora Pointed greyish leaves, 20 cm (8 in) long and 5 cm (2 in) wide and more, form rosettes at the end of short stems. The leaves are tinged with purple and have distinctive wavy margins. In autumn this shrubby succulent produces a large flowering stem which may be as much as 1 m (3 ft) tall. The stem is greatly branched and bears greyish green waxy tubular blossoms strongly flushed with red. HEIGHT & SPREAD 30×25 cm (12×10 in).

    The leaves of var. *carunculata* are covered with blister-like growths, while the leaves of var. *metallica*♀ have a bronzy sheen and fine red edges.
E. harmsii♀ Upright, branching stems, up to 30 cm (12 in) long, terminate in 10 cm (4 in) wide rosettes of short, narrow, spear-shaped, pale green leaves. The leaves have

▲ *Echeveria harmsii*

red tips and edges and are covered in fine hairs. Cup-shaped red flowers have orange-tipped petals that are yellow on the inside. Up to 3 cm (1¼ in) long, they are produced on stems up to 20 cm (8 in) high in summer. HEIGHT & SPREAD 25×30 cm (10×12 in).
E. secunda Short stems terminate in rosettes of fleshy, light greyish green leaves that are reddish at the tips. The individual leaves are up to 5 cm (2 in) long and 2.5 cm (1 in) wide. Cup-shaped blooms, with petals that are red outside and yellow on the inside, are held in groups of 5 or more on flowering stems up to 30 cm (12 in) tall. HEIGHT & SPREAD 4×30 cm (1½×12 in).

    Often seen in gardens, var. *glauca* has a much bluer colour to the foliage.
E. setosa♀ (Mexican firecracker) Small green hairy leaves, convex on both sides and no more than 2.5 cm (1 in) long, form tight stemless rosettes. In summer tubular red flowers with yellow tips and interiors are freely produced on stems up to 25 cm (10 in) high. This is one of the few echeverias that benefit from a little light shade. HEIGHT & SPREAD 4×25 cm (1½×10 in).

CULTIVATION Plant outdoors in free-draining soil in a sunny position. Bring indoors before the first frosts and pot individually for overwintering. Keep houseplants tightly potted in gritty cactus compost or John Innes No. 1 compost mixed with up to a quarter by volume of sharp sand or grit.
PROPAGATION Separate offsets and pot in-

dividually during spring or summer. Alternatively, sow seed under glass during spring or take stem or leaf cuttings in summer.

PESTS AND DISEASES Mealy bug can be a nuisance under glass.

Echinacea
Coneflower
Compositae

Large daisy-like flowers, in purple, rose-pink or white, make a striking display in a late summer herbaceous border. The flowers are up to 15 cm (6 in) across, composed of petals (strictly speaking, ray florets) radiating from a cone-shaped centre. Each flower is held on a tall stem which also carries alternate, lance-shaped, mid green leaves, up to 20 cm (8 in) long. The flowers can continue to appear for over two months and last well when cut. They are often used in dried arrangements. Native to eastern USA, these rhizomatous perennials are completely hardy in Britain.

RECOMMENDED SPECIES AND VARIETIES

E. pallida The flowers are made up of drooping, pale purple petals around a purple-brown cone. HEIGHT & SPREAD 1 m×45 cm (3×1½ ft).

E. purpurea (syn. *Rudbeckia echinacea* var. *purpurea*, *R. purpurea*) The flowers have white to purple petals and an orange-brown centre. Because of variation that can occur in seed-raised plants it is more usual to grow one of the cultivars. HEIGHT & SPREAD 1.5 m×50 cm (5 ft×20 in).

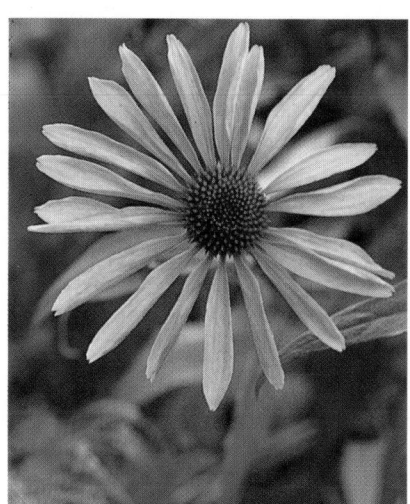

▲ *Echinacea purpurea* 'Magnus'

'**Magnus**' has deep purple petals around a deep orange boss. '**White Lustre**' is a warm white with a green-flushed cone and '**White Swan**' is a pale greenish white with a golden central cone. Both of the white varieties are only 75 cm (2½ ft) tall.

CULTIVATION Plant in any fertile soil in full sun. Deadhead to prolong flowering.

PROPAGATION Divide from autumn to

spring or take root cuttings in early spring and root in peat and sand mixture in a cold-frame to plant out later in the year. Sow seed in early spring under glass or outside in late spring. The resulting plants can be set out in the border during autumn.

PESTS AND DISEASES Usually trouble free.

Echinocactus see CACTI p. 107

Echinops
Globe thistle
Compositae

Echinops bannaticus 'Taplow Blue'

Globular flower clusters are borne from mid summer to early autumn on these stately, erect plants. The flowerheads, up to 4 cm (1½ in) across, are mostly blue or white and carried on stout stems. Thistle-like, spiky leaves, are divided, greyish to deep green and up to 20 cm (8 in) long. The flowerheads can be cut before they open fully and dried. These plants tolerate poor soil and drought and grow best in warm sunny spots. This large genus consists of hardy herbaceous perennials, biennials and annuals and is native to Europe, Asia and Africa.

RECOMMENDED SPECIES AND VARIETIES

E. albus see *E.* 'Nivalis'

E. bannaticus Grey-blue flowerheads are carried on branching stems amid the dark green slender leaves. HEIGHT & SPREAD 1.2 m×38 cm (4 ft×15 in).

'**Blue Globe**' has rounder flowerheads and grows to a height of 1 m (3 ft). '**Taplow Blue**'♀ is a tall plant, at a height of 1.5 m

▼ *Echinops* 'Nivalis'

(5 ft), with powder-blue flowers.

E. '**Nivalis**' (syn. *E. albus*) Greyish white globular flowerheads are carried on grey stems on this hybrid with greyer leaves. HEIGHT & SPREAD 1.2 m×50 cm (4 ft×20 in).

E. ritro♀ The dark steel blue flowerheads of this compact plant colour well in the early stages of growth. HEIGHT & SPREAD 75×30 cm (2½×1 ft).

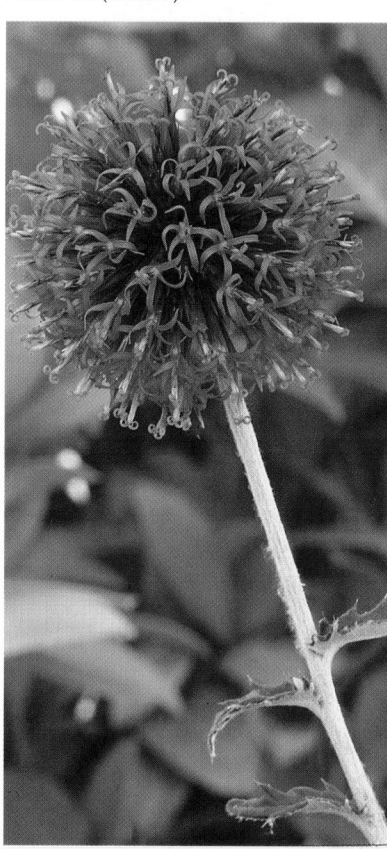

▲ *Echinops ritro* 'Veitch's Blue'

The flowers of ssp. *ruthenicus* are a bright blue. It has dark green shiny leaves that are covered on the underside with a white sheen. This subspecies reaches a height of 1 m (3 ft) and a spread of 50 cm (20 in). '**Veitch's Blue**' produces flowers that are a deeper shade of blue.

E. sphaerocephalus This plant forms a grand clump when allowed to develop to its full majesty. It is larger in all its parts than the others listed here. Flowerheads are 6 cm (2½ in) across and greyish white. HEIGHT & SPREAD 2.1×1 m (7×3 ft).

CULTIVATION Plant at any time from autumn to spring in any well-drained soil, choosing a site in full sun.

PROPAGATION Divide established plants in spring or autumn or take root cuttings in late autumn and root in a coldframe over winter. Seeds of species only can be sown in spring outdoors and grown on for planting out in the autumn.

PESTS AND DISEASES Usually trouble free.

Echinopsis see CACTI p. 107

Echium
Boraginaceae

Echium plantagineum

Upward-facing, bell-shaped flowers in blue, pink, purple or white add colour to a mixed herbaceous border from early to late summer. The flowers, carried in large impressive spikes, also entice bees and butterflies into the garden.

The oblong or lance-shaped leaves, up to 15 cm (6 in) long and 2 cm (¾ in) wide, are usually hairy and can cause an allergic reaction in some people. The genus contains a mix of annuals, biennials and short-lived perennials native to Europe, the Canary Islands, Africa and W Asia, most doing best in a frost-free garden. In colder regions grow the perennials in a cool greenhouse.

RECOMMENDED SPECIES AND VARIETIES
E. candicans (syn. *E. fastuosum*) (pride of Madeira) Blue or white funnel-shaped flowers with protruding pink stamens open from pink buds. This perennial has a woody base and whitish hairy lance-shaped leaves. HEIGHT & SPREAD 2.4×1.5 m (8×5 ft).
E. fastuosum see *E. candicans*
E. lycopsis see *E. plantagineum*
E. pininana (syn. *E. pinnifolium*) This half-hardy, short-lived, perennial bears lance-shaped deep green hairy leaves. After about 3 years it bears rose or mauve tubular flowers, held in spikes on side stems. It dies after flowering. HEIGHT & SPREAD 4×1 m (13×3 ft).

▼ *Echium pininana*

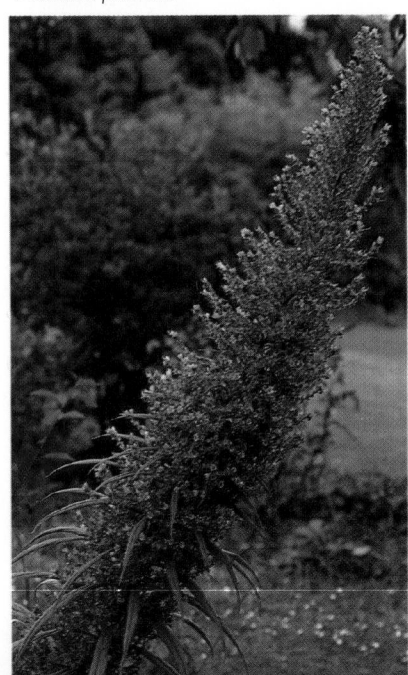

E. pinnifolium see *E. pininana*
E. plantagineum (syn. *E. lycopsis*) (purple viper's bugloss) The bell-shaped flowers of this annual or biennial undergo a change in colour from blue to red over the summer. The mid green basal leaves are lance-shaped, up to 15 cm (6 in) long. HEIGHT & SPREAD 60×25 cm (24×10 in).
E. vulgare (viper's bugloss) Spikes of 1 cm (⅜ in) long, tubular flowers come in white and shades of pink, blue or purple on this erect bushy plant. The mid green hairy leaves are oblong to lance-shaped. It is a long-flowering annual or biennial. HEIGHT & SPREAD 60×30 cm (2×1 ft).

The cultivars reach only 30 cm (1 ft) tall. **'Blue Bedder'** has blue flowers and the **Dwarf Hybrids** are a mixture of colours.
CULTIVATION Plant during spring in any fertile soil in full sun.
PROPAGATION Sow the annuals where they are to flower in spring, or under glass in late winter. Raise the perennials from seed sown in a heated propagator in late winter and planted out in late spring after the danger of frost is over. Take softwood cuttings of perennials in summer.
PESTS AND DISEASES Whitefly can be troublesome, especially in a greenhouse.

Edelweiss see *Leontopodium*
Edelweiss, New Zealand see *Leucogenes leontopodium*

Edraianthus
Campanulaceae

Edraianthus pumilio

These low-growing, cushion or mat-forming herbaceous perennials, grown for their bright, bell-shaped flowers and neat habit, make first-class plants for troughs and raised beds or rock gardens. The summer flowers, borne singly or in clusters, generally nestle on short stems amid the grass-like foliage. Plants are hardy but susceptible to winter wet. Native chiefly to the mountains of central and S Europe.
RECOMMENDED SPECIES AND VARIETIES
E. graminifolius♀ Blue to deep violet flowers, up to 3 cm (1¼ in) long, appear in terminal clusters on slender, wiry, stems in mid and late summer. This is a tufted plant with linear, deep green leaves up to 15 cm (6 in) long. HEIGHT & SPREAD 15×15 cm (6×6 in).
E. pumilio♀ (syn. *Wahlenbergia pumilio*) Deep lavender or violet-blue flowers, about 2 cm (¾ in) long, appear from early to mid summer. They are carried singly on short, leafy, upright stalks. The deep green linear

▲ *Edraianthus graminifolius*

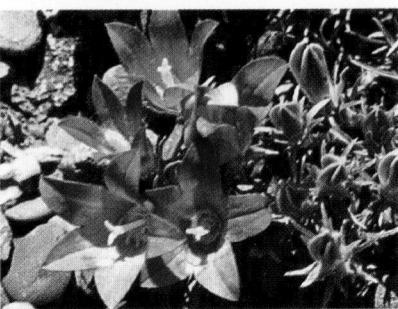

▲ *Edraianthus pumilio*

leaves are not more than 2 cm (¾ in) long. This plant forms a dense tuft or low hummock. HEIGHT & SPREAD 5×15 cm (2×6 in).
E. serpyllifolius (syn. *Wahlenbergia serpyllifolia*) Dark violet flowers, about 2 cm (¾ in) long, bloom in mid summer. The semi-evergreen leaves are narrow, spoon-shaped and up to 3 cm (1¼ in) long on a tufted plant. HEIGHT & SPREAD 5×25 cm (2×10 in).
CULTIVATION Plant in spring or early summer in gritty well-drained soil, choosing a site in full sun. Avoid excessive wet around the collar of the plant during winter – protect plants in wet areas by covering them with a sheet of glass, or a cloche. Alternatively, grow in pots of well-drained gritty compost in an unheated greenhouse or alpine house.
PROPAGATION Sow seed in autumn or early spring in a coldframe, although seed sown fresh gives the best results.
PESTS AND DISEASES Slugs may attack the crown of plants, especially when new growth appears in spring.

Eichhornia
Pontederiaceae

Eichhornia crassipes

Spikes of orchid-like blossoms and interesting buoyant foliage are the distinguishing features of these tropical floating aquatic plants. *Eichhornia crassipes* can be grown in outdoor pools in summer, but should be taken indoors before the first frosts.

RECOMMENDED SPECIES AND VARIETIES

E. crassipes (water hyacinth) This free-floating perennial has glossy bright green leaves with inflated stalks. The oval to rounded leaves, up to 15 cm (6 in) long and 10 cm (4 in) across, are arranged in neat rosettes. The blue to lilac flowers, up to 3 cm (1¼ in) across, are flat with a prominent yellow eye and are carried in erect spikes in summer. Purple-green roots, about 25 cm (10 in) long, hang down in the water. This tender evergreen or semi-evergreen produces plants from runners and can soon form an extensive floating group. Native to S America. HEIGHT & SPREAD 20×30 cm (8×12 in).

'Major', the most commonly grown selection, is a little larger.

CULTIVATION Float in a sunny spot when all danger of frost has passed. Eichhornia, as a free-floating plant, obtains its nourishment directly from the water. Remove dead flower spikes. Take plants indoors before the first frosts and place in a pan of very wet mud and keep in a light, frost-free greenhouse at around 15°C (59°F).

PROPAGATION Detach young plants from runners for overwintering.

PESTS AND DISEASES Usually trouble free.

Elaeagnus
Elaeagnaceae

Elaeagnus pungens
'Maculata'

Attractive glossy foliage is the chief value of these easily grown, hardy evergreen and deciduous trees and shrubs. The leaves are usually pointed, up to 7.5 cm (3 in) long, and can be bright green, silvery or variegated with gold. Small, fragrant, bell-shaped flowers, less than 1.5 cm (½ in) across, are produced in profusion in the leaf axils and may be followed by ornamental, sometimes colourful berries. The stems can be spiny. The plants tolerate wind and the evergreens are useful for hedging and windbreaks in coastal gardens. Elaeagnus are not exacting plants in their soil requirements though they do not grow as well on thin chalk. The plants recommended below are native to S Europe and Asia.

RECOMMENDED SPECIES AND VARIETIES

E. angustifolia♀ Narrow deciduous leaves, up to 7.5 cm (3 in) long, are pale green above and silvery beneath. Small, fragrant, yellow-green flowers are produced in profusion from early summer onwards followed by small silvery orange fruits in autumn. The shoots of this rounded,

Elaeagnus angustifolia

spreading tree can be quite spiny. HEIGHT & SPREAD 3×3 m (10×10 ft) after 10 years, ultimately 9 m (30 ft) tall.

E. angustifolia Caspica Group see *E.* 'Quicksilver'

E. × ebbingei The semi-evergreen leaves are a glossy dark green above and silver beneath. Small, very fragrant flowers are produced from mid autumn through till spring. Fruits appear in autumn and they are orange speckled with silver. The young, gingery brown shoots are also speckled with silver scales. This vigorous shrub is fast-growing once established and is an excellent shelter plant, even in coastal regions. It can be pruned if necessary. HEIGHT & SPREAD 1×1 m (3×3 ft) after 5 years, ultimately 3 m (10 ft) tall.

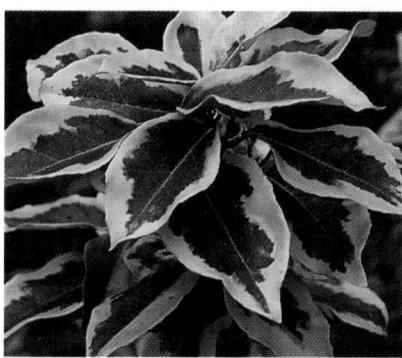

▲ *Elaeagnus × ebbingei* 'Gilt Edge'

'Gilt Edge'♀ has a striking yellow-gold margin to the leaf. 'Limelight' has a golden yellow blotch of variable size in the leaf centre. This cultivar frequently reverts to plain green and any reversion must be pruned out.

E. parvifolia♀ Arching branches are covered in deciduous silvery leaves that become glossy bright green as the season progresses. Small, fragrant, cream-white flowers appear in spring and are followed in autumn by red fruits. A large rounded shrub. HEIGHT & SPREAD 1×1 m (3×3 ft) in 5 years, ultimately 3 m (10 ft) tall.

E. pungens The dark green, upper surface of the leaves has silver scales while the underside is more of a dull silver. The margins have a crinkled edge. Clusters of small, fragrant, white flowers appear during mid and late autumn. A large evergreen shrub. HEIGHT & SPREAD 1.5×1.2 m (5×4 ft) after 5 years, ultimately 4.5 m (15 ft) tall.

The narrow leaves of 'Frederici' are a pale creamy yellow with a green margin. It

▲ *Elaeagnus pungens* 'Frederici'

▲ *Elaeagnus pungens* 'Goldrim'

is slower growing than the species and eventually makes a medium-sized shrub to 3 m (10 ft) tall. 'Goldrim' has glossy dark green leaves with attractive gold margins. It makes a large shrub of similar size to the species. The glossy green leaves of 'Maculata'♀ have a decorative central gold blotch though it is prone to revert. It is a rounded, spreading shrub to 3 m (10 ft) tall.

E. 'Quicksilver'♀ (syn. *E. angustifolia* Caspica Group) Striking, silvery, narrow leaves, at their best when young, clothe this deciduous small tree or large shrub. HEIGHT & SPREAD 1×1 m (3×3 ft) after 5 years, ultimately 3 m (10 ft) tall.

CULTIVATION Plant deciduous species from mid autumn to early winter, evergreen species in mid spring or early autumn. Grow in any fertile well-drained soil, except shallow chalk. Deciduous species need to be grown in full sun, evergreen species will tolerate partial shade.

PROPAGATION Sow seed under glass in autumn. Take greenwood cuttings or semi-ripe cuttings of deciduous species and semi-ripe cuttings of evergreens. Alternatively, remove rooted suckers in autumn.

PRUNING Not normally required, except to control the shape or size by pruning after flowering. Remove shoots on variegated plants that revert to green.

PESTS AND DISEASES Usually trouble free.

e

Embothrium
Proteaceae

Embothrium coccineum

Fiery red flowers set alight these shrubs and small trees in summer. The plants, natives of S America, are not fully hardy and need lime-free soil in a sheltered sunny position if they are to succeed in Britain. But where they do thrive, they draw every eye when the clusters of spidery blooms emerge to stand out against the evergreen leaves. Only one species and its cultivars is available for British gardens.

RECOMMENDED SPECIES AND VARIETIES

E. coccineum (Chilean fire bush) Brilliant scarlet, tubular flowers, very narrow and 5 cm (2 in) long, appear in tight clusters from late spring to early summer. The leathery, dark green, oblong leaves are up to 12 cm (4¾ in) long on a rounded head of slender branches. This plant is suitable for growing outdoors in only the milder parts of Britain. HEIGHT & SPREAD 1.2×1 m (4×3 ft) after 5 years, ultimately 9 m (30 ft) tall.

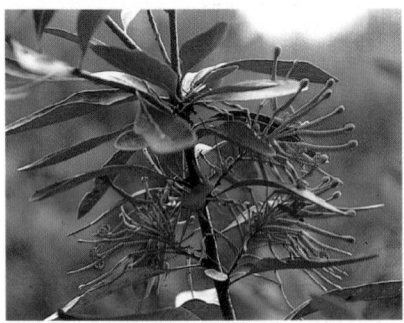

▲ *Embothrium coccineum*

Plants in the **Lanceolatum Group** are hardier than the species and form more slender plants. Among them, **'Inca Flame'** displays fine orange-red flowers and **'Norquinco Form'**♀ bears profuse flowers that are distinctly more orange in colour, but it is semi-evergreen.

CULTIVATION Plant in a sunny position against a south or south-west facing wall or in woodland, in moist but well-drained, lime-free soil. Provide some protection from frost.

PROPAGATION Raise from seed, separate suckers from the parent plant or take semi-ripe cuttings.

PRUNING None is necessary except for removing any dead wood or frost-damaged shoots after flowering.

PESTS AND DISEASES Usually trouble free.

Enkianthus
Ericaceae

Enkianthus campanulatus

Flaming shades of red and yellow mark the autumn foliage of these shrubs and small trees. Dainty cup or bell-shaped flowers, borne in drooping clusters during late spring and early summer, are also a feature. Native to E Asia, they require acid or neutral soil. They make a good specimen plant or can be massed in a woodland garden. All except *Enkianthus chinensis* are hardy. Those listed are deciduous.

RECOMMENDED SPECIES AND VARIETIES

E. campanulatus♀ Pale cream to pink or red cup-shaped flowers, each about 1 cm (⅜ in) long, often with deeper-coloured veins, are borne in abundant clusters of up to 15. The dull green oval leaves are about 5 cm (2 in) long. This shrub is the hardiest species. It spreads less in a shaded site. HEIGHT & SPREAD 2.4×1.2 m (8×4 ft) in 10 years, ultimately 5 m (16 ft) tall.

The flowers of f. *albiflorus* are white or greenish white and those of var. *palibinii* smaller and a deep red.

E. cernuus f. *rubens*♀ Rich red, fringed flowers, each 6 mm (¼ in) long, are borne in nodding clusters of 10-12. This shrub has roundish leaves 2.5 cm (1 in) long. HEIGHT & SPREAD 1 m×60 cm (3×2 ft) in 5 years, ultimately 3 m (10 ft).

E. chinensis Some of the largest flower-heads of the genus adorn this shrub but, unfortunately, it is less hardy than the other species. Bell-shaped cream blooms, 1 cm (⅜ in) long, with thin pink stripes, are borne in hanging clusters of 12-24 during late spring and early summer. The oblong leaves

▼ *Enkianthus cernuus* f. *rubens*

▲ *Enkianthus perulatus*

are up to 7.5 cm (3 in) long. HEIGHT & SPREAD 1.5×1 m (5×3 ft) after 5 years, ultimately 3.5 m (12 ft) tall.

E. perulatus♀ Groups of 3-10, white pitcher-shaped flowers, about 1 cm (⅜ in) long, are carried on the slender, drooping stalks of this compact shrub. The 2.5-5 cm (1-2 in) long, fine-pointed, narrowly oval leaves are exceptionally blazing in autumn. HEIGHT & SPREAD 60×40 cm (2 ft×16 in) after 5 years, ultimately 1.8 m (6 ft) tall.

CULTIVATION Plant in autumn or early spring in acid to neutral soil, enriched with leaf-mould. Choose a site in sun or part shade and sheltered from wind.

PROPAGATION Sow seed under glass in late winter or early spring or take semi-ripe heeled cuttings in summer.

PRUNING Not normally required but older, straggly specimens can be cut back hard if necessary in spring.

PESTS AND DISEASES Usually trouble free.

Eomecon
Snow poppy, dawn poppy
Papaveraceae

The single species of this genus is a vigorously spreading herbaceous perennial, most valued for its attractive foliage, which makes an interesting carpet under large, established shrubs. The flowers are only sparsely produced for a brief period in early summer. The plant is not completely hardy in colder districts and may be short lived.

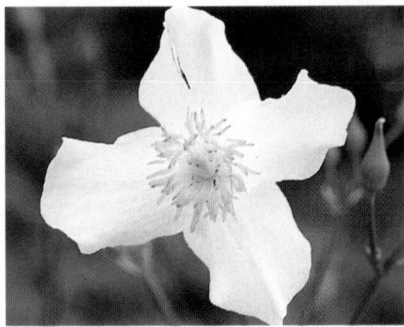

▲ *Eomecon chionantha*

Eomecon chionantha The scalloped, heart-shaped, pale to mid green leaves, up to 10 cm (4 in) across, are borne on fleshy beige-green stalks. The erect, branching stems bear loose clusters of pure white flowers up to 4 cm (1½ in) across, composed of 4 oval petals and a mass of deep yellow stamens. Native to E China. HEIGHT & SPREAD 45×60 cm (1½×2 ft).

CULTIVATION Plant in spring or summer in acid, humus-rich soil, preferably in full sun, although partial shade is tolerated.
PROPAGATION Lift and divide established plants in spring or summer.
PESTS AND DISEASES Usually trouble free.

Epilobium
Willowherb
Onagraceae

Epilobium glabellum

The willowherbs include tall herbaceous perennials as well as several smaller alpine species, some of them evergreen. All have four-petalled flowers and slender seedpods, which burst to release many fluffy seeds.
RECOMMENDED SPECIES AND VARIETIES
E. angustifolium (rosebay willowherb) Tapered spikes of deep rose-pink flowers are borne on erect leafy stems from mid to late summer. This robust, strongly rhizomatous herbaceous perennial is aggressively invasive and best confined to a wild garden. HEIGHT & SPREAD 1.5×1 m (5×3 ft).

'**Album**' has pure white flowers and is less rampant than the species.
E. californicum hort. see *Zauschneria californica*
E. canum see *Zauschneria californica* ssp. *cana*

▲ *Epilobium dodonaei*

E. dodonaei Spikes of deep rose-purple flowers appear in mid to late summer on this hardy herbaceous perennial. The slender, erect stems are densely clothed in narrow leaves. HEIGHT & SPREAD 80×60 cm (32×24 in).

E. fleischeri Abundant purple-pink flowers appear from mid to late summer. A spreading, hardy herbaceous perennial. HEIGHT & SPREAD 30×30 cm (1×1 ft).
E. glabellum Small, white to pale rose-violet flowers appear in short, leafy, erect spikes from late spring to early autumn, on this low-growing, hardy evergreen perennial alpine. The leaves are deep glossy green, often flushed red. An excellent plant for a cool and moist place in a rock garden. HEIGHT & SPREAD 20×40 cm (8×16 in).

'**Sulphureum**' has yellow blooms.
E. microphyllum see *Zauschneria californica* ssp. *cana*
E. obcordatum Rose-purple flowers arise in clusters in late summer on this low-growing, evergreen alpine. Slender stems bear grey-green leaves. It requires a moist, sheltered site and will not withstand prolonged frost. HEIGHT & SPREAD 7.5×30 cm (3×12 in).
E. villosum see *Zauschneria californica* ssp. *mexicana*
CULTIVATION Plant in full sun in soil of average fertility; in rich soils they tend to become vigorous and too leafy. The alpine species tolerate partial shade.
PROPAGATION Sow ripe seed in a cold-frame. Divide plants after flowering or in the early spring. Take softwood cuttings of alpines in summer.
PESTS AND DISEASES Usually trouble free.

Epimedium
Berberidaceae

Epimedium x youngianum 'Niveum'

The various epimediums available are valued for their fine foliage. In spring, the fresh green of the emerging leaves is often tinted with shades of copper, pink or red. The leaves become a deeper green during summer, and many turn to yellow, red or bronze in autumn. Airy sprays of dainty flowers bloom through spring, varying in colour from deep coral-red through orange and yellow to pure white.

Epimediums are clump-forming, herbaceous and evergreen perennials. Many species and varieties retain their leaves throughout winter. Most epimediums are fully hardy, including all the plants recommended below. Larger, more vigorous plants make splendid ground cover, especially in dappled shade, in a border or woodland garden. Grow smaller plants in a rock garden or in pots in an unheated, well-ventilated greenhouse.

The leaves are generally divided into leaflets, often with sharply serrated edges. The pendulous flowers, usually about 1.5 cm (½ in) across, are mostly star-shaped and often spurred. They are borne in lax sprays, that are simple or branched, on wiry stems above or among the leaves. Native to Europe and Asia.
RECOMMENDED SPECIES AND VARIETIES
E. alpinum (barrenwort) Glossy, oval, angled leaves, up to 12.5 cm (5 in) long, with 5-9 leaflets, are bronze when young and bronze or red in autumn. The flowers are yellow with red spurs. This herbaceous plant often has a carpeting growth habit. HEIGHT & SPREAD 25×30 cm (10×12 in).
E. x cantabrigiense This evergreen plant has a clump-forming to carpeting habit of growth. The leaves have oval to heart-shaped, pointed leaflets up to 15 cm (6 in) long, 7-17 to a leaf. They are bronze or tipped with red in spring. The flowers are dull red and pale yellow. HEIGHT & SPREAD 50×60 cm (20×24 in).
E. diphyllum Each leathery, deep green leaf has 2 heart-shaped leaflets, 2-5 cm (¾-2 in) long, flushed purple when young. White flowers, 1 cm (⅜ in) across, are borne in mid and late spring on this herbaceous perennial. HEIGHT & SPREAD 25×30 cm (10×12 in).
E. grandiflorum♀ (syn. *E. macranthum*) A herbaceous plant with narrow, oval, apple-green leaflets, up to 12.5 cm (5 in) long, generally 9 to a leaf, that flush bronze in spring, and again in autumn. Long-spurred flowers, up to 4 cm (1½ in) across, white, pink, violet or rose-red, bloom in spring and early summer. HEIGHT & SPREAD 25×30 cm (10×12 in).

'**Nanum**'♀ has pale purple flowers on a plant not more than 20 cm (8 in) tall. '**Rose Queen**'♀ has deep pink flowers that contrast well with dark, copper-tinged young

▲ *Epimedium grandiflorum 'Rose Queen'*

leaves. '**White Queen**'♀ has bronze-tinged young leaves and pure white flowers.
E. macranthum see *E. grandiflorum*
E. x perralchicum♀ The leaflets are rounded to oval and up to 10 cm (4 in) long on this tufted evergreen plant. There are 9, sometimes 3, leaflets to a leaf. They start off red or bronze in spring, before turning green. The flowers are yellow, with short spurs. HEIGHT & SPREAD 40×30 cm (16×12 in).

Erica

Heath, heather
Ericaceae

Erica cinerea
'Pink Ice'

Year-round displays in sparkling white and every shade of pink are easily created with heaths and heathers in any garden that has acid soil and plenty of light. For alkaline soil the choice is more limited but there are enough lime-tolerant varieties to contribute to the garden in every season – especially all forms of *Erica carnea* and *E.* × *darleyenis*.

Traditionally, heaths and heathers are grown in their own heather bed, but they work equally well in a mixed border and some are useful ground-cover plants, crowding out weeds. The more compact varieties flourish in large pots and tubs – which also give the opportunity to grow acid-loving species in a limy garden.

Heaths and heathers are evergreen shrubs with narrow, folded leaves in various greens and golds, and tubular flowers. The genus contains over 750 diverse species with a wide distribution in the wild, from the temperate conditions of western Europe to the dry, hot climate of South Africa; it has naturalised in Australia.

More than 700 species are from the more southerly regions and suitable only for conservatories or greenhouses in Britain. The European species, however, are hardy in Britain, but they can be difficult to establish in areas prone to drought. The sizes given are for five to seven-year-old plants that have been regularly clipped back following flowering.

RECOMMENDED SPECIES AND VARIETIES

E. arborea (tree heath) Tall, upright branches are covered with whorls of 3 or 4 bright green needles, smooth above and grooved beneath. The 3 mm (⅛ in) bell-shaped flowers, borne in clusters near the ends of the branches in early to late spring, are greyish white and honey scented.

The species is native to S Europe and N Africa and can vary in hardiness, but in general, only hardy strains are sold in Britain. Heavy snow may break the branches, but new growth will come from the root stock. It is not as tolerant of lime as commonly supposed and is best grown in acid soil. Trim young plants to shape in the early years to avoid untidy growth. HEIGHT & SPREAD 6×3 m (20×10 ft).

The following cultivars are all hardy. 'Albert's Gold'♀ has golden foliage with a few white flowers. It reaches 1.8 m (6 ft) tall and spreads to 80 cm (32 in). The variety *alpina*♀, with the same height and spread, produces white flowers in dense cylindrical clusters. 'Estrella Gold'♀ bears white flowers in profusion on compact, lime-green foliage, tipped bright yellow in spring and summer. It grows to 120 cm (4 ft) with a spread of 75 cm (2½ ft).

E. australis♀ (Spanish heath) Showy purplish pink tubular flowers, 8 mm (⅜ in) long, are produced from mid spring to early summer on a tall, open plant. Its dark green, linear leaves, grooved underneath, are in whorls of 4. The plant is hardy but does not tolerate lime and is prone to damage by wind or snow. It requires acid soil conditions. Prune young plants heavily after flowering to avoid straggly growth. Native to W Spain and Portugal. HEIGHT & SPREAD 1.8×1 m (6×3 ft).

'Mr. Robert'♀ produces masses of white flowers. It is 1.8 m (6 ft) tall and 90 cm (3 ft) wide. 'Riverslea'♀ has the same spread, but is only 1.2 m (4 ft) tall. It has lilac-pink flowers.

E. carnea (syn. *E. herbacea*) (alpine heath, winter heath) This hardy, lime-tolerant species flowers in late spring or early summer, bearing urn-shaped, usually pink, 6 mm (¼ in) flowers. The mid to dark green linear leaves are held in whorls of 4.

It forms a low maintenance ground-cover plant, in sun or light shade, needing only an occasional trim round the edges immediately after flowering. Native to the alpine regions of Europe. HEIGHT & SPREAD 15×40 cm (6×16 in).

Unless stated otherwise, the listed cultivars have mid to dark green foliage with a neat compact habit, 15×45 cm (6×18 in). The mauve-pink flowers last for 6 to 8 weeks and open between mid winter and mid spring; plants in milder areas can be as much as 2 months earlier than those in colder spots.

'Adrienne Duncan'♀ has bronze-tinged foliage and a long flowering period. 'Ann Sparkes'♀ has distinctive old gold foliage with bright bronze tips in spring. The flowers open rose-pink, darkening to mauve-pink. It is less spreading than most cultivars – to 25 cm (10 in). 'Challenger'♀

▼ *Erica carnea* 'Challenger'

▲ *Erica carnea* 'Foxhollow Fairy'

▲ *Erica carnea* 'Golden Starlet'

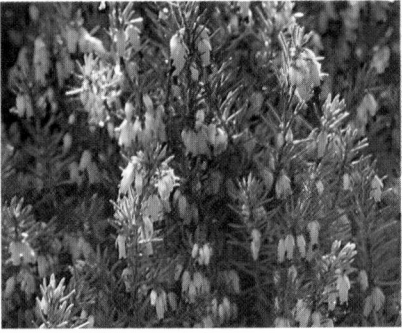

▲ *Erica carnea* 'Loughrigg'

bears striking magenta flowers. 'Foxhollow'♀ has yellow foliage tipped bronze which deepens to reddish orange in very cold weather. 'Foxhollow Fairy', with a trailing habit, produces pale shell-pink flowers which deepen with age. It reaches 20 cm (8 in) in height. 'Golden Starlet'♀ bears white flowers against lime-green foliage which turns a glowing yellow in summer. 'Ice Princess' is perhaps the best white-flowering *E. carnea*, holding its flowers in semi-erect spikes on compact bright green foliage. 'Loughrigg'♀ is a vigorous cultivar with flowers that open pink and deepen through rose-pink to mauve-pink during the season. 'Myretoun Ruby'♀, whose flowers deepen to crimson as the season progresses, is one of the best red forms. 'Nathalie' has the deepest flower colour of all – a glowing deep crimson. 'Pink Spangles'♀, whose shell-pink flowers deepen with age, has a vigorous, trailing habit. It spreads to 30 cm (1 ft). 'Praecox Rubra'♀ is one of the earliest to flower. 'R.B. Cooke'♀ is covered with pink flowers which age to mauve. 'Springwood White'♀ has a vigorous trailing habit and masses of white flowers among bright green foliage. It spreads to 60 cm (2 ft). 'Sunshine

▲ *Erica carnea* 'Praecox Rubra'

Rambler'♀ is grown mainly for its bright yellow foliage which is tinged with red in winter. **'Vivellii'**♀ has a bronze hue to the foliage and the flowers darken to magenta during the season. **'Westwood Yellow'**♀ has a more upright habit than other yellow-leaved cultivars and shell-pink flowers.

E. ciliaris (Dorset heath) Long spikes of flowers, usually lilac-pink, bloom from mid summer to mid autumn on an erect, open shrub. The flowers – the largest of any European species – are 1 cm (⅜ in) long, tubular and sharply contracted at the mouth. The ovate leaves are grey-green or dark green above, white beneath and borne in whorls of 3. Severe winters can damage the plants, so leave the dead flowers on during the winter to provide protection and trim them off by mid spring. Native to W Spain, Portugal, NW France and southern Britain. HEIGHT & SPREAD 36×45 cm (14×18 in).

The cultivars typically reach 25 × 45 cm (10×18 in). **'Corfe Castle'**♀ has rose-pink flowers and mid green foliage. **'David McClintock'**♀ produces bicolour flowers,

▼ *Erica carnea* 'Westwood Yellow'

white at the base, pink at the mouth, set against grey-green leaves. **'Mrs C.H. Gill'**♀ has crimson flowers and dark green foliage. **'Stoborough'**♀ has white flowers and bright green foliage.

E. cinerea (bell heather) White, pink or purple bell-shaped flowers, 6 mm (¼ in) long, are borne in profusion from early summer to early autumn. The leaves are usually bottle green, linear and strongly curled under along the edges. This much underrated species is hardy throughout Britain but does not tolerate lime. HEIGHT & SPREAD 30×50 cm (12×20 in).

There is a multitude of cultivars available. Those listed have dark green foliage and erect growth to 25 × 50 cm (10 × 20 in), unless stated otherwise.

'Alba Minor'♀, with white flowers and mid green foliage, makes a good ground-cover plant and is compact enough for growing in tubs. **'C.D. Eason'**♀ displays bright magenta flowers and makes a good ground-cover plant. **'C.G. Best'**♀ is larger than most, reaching 30 cm (1 ft) tall with a spread of 70 cm (2 ft 4 in). It produces a graceful display of rose-pink flowers. **'Cevennes'**♀ has similar dimensions to 'C.G. Best'. It bears abundant mauve flowers against mid green foliage.

'Cindy'♀, with a semi-prostrate habit, carries its purple flowers from early summer to late autumn. **'Eden Valley'**♀ has lavender flowers shading to white at their base and mid green foliage. **'Fiddler's Gold'**♀, with yellow-gold foliage deepening to red in winter, has lilac-pink flowers and a semi-prostrate habit. **'Golden Hue'**♀ has amethyst flowers and pale yellow foliage tipped with orange in winter. It grows to 35 cm (14 in) tall and 70 cm (28 in) wide. **'Hookstone White'**♀ has similar dimensions to 'Golden Hue'. It produces long spikes of white flowers among mid green foliage. **'P.S. Patrick'**♀ bears long spikes of purple flowers. **'Pentreath'**♀ makes a neat carpet of beetroot-coloured flowers. Its height is 20 cm (8 in) and its spread is 30 cm (12 in). **'Pink Ice'**♀ has clear, rose-pink flowers and a dwarf habit, growing to just

▼ *Erica cinerea* 'Stephen Davis'

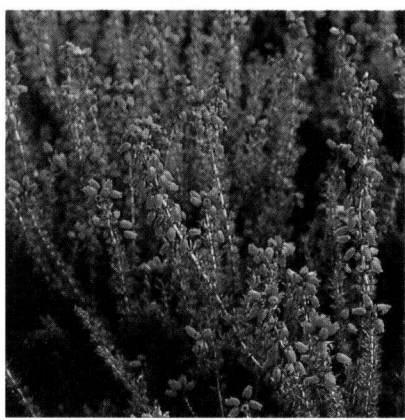

15 cm (6 in) tall with a spread of 35 cm (14 in). **'Stephen Davis'**♀, with a neat erect dwarf habit, produces masses of glowing magenta flowers. **'Velvet Night'**♀ has deep purple flowers. **'Windlebrooke'**♀ has a few mauve flowers and is chiefly grown for its foliage, which is golden in summer, turning orange-red in winter. It has a prostrate habit, 15 cm (6 in) in height and spreading to 45 cm (1½ ft).

E. × *darleyensis* This bushy, hardy plant is one of the easiest heathers to grow and is suitable for all soils. It has needle-like leaves and pink urn-shaped flowers, 5 mm (¼ in) long, usually between mid winter and mid spring; it can start flowering as early as mid autumn in mild conditions. It is particularly effective at smothering weeds. HEIGHT & SPREAD 45×60 cm (1½×2 ft).

Unless stated otherwise, the cultivars listed have pink flowers, mid-green leaves and upright growth to 45×60 cm (1½×2 ft).

'Arthur Johnson'♀ produces 20 cm (8 in) long spikes of slightly scented flowers on foliage which is tipped cream in spring. It grows to 60 cm (2 ft) and has a spread of 75 cm (2½ ft). **'Furzey'**♀ bears lilac-pink flowers deepening to mauve-pink during the season. The leaves are tipped with pink in spring. **'Ghost Hills'**♀ has light green foliage which is tipped cream in spring. **'J.W. Porter'**♀ bears mauve-pink flowers against dark green foliage which is tipped red and cream in spring.

'Jack H. Brummage' has mauve-pink flowers; its foliage is yellow-orange throughout the year. **'Kramer's Rote'** (also sold as **'Kramer's Red'**)♀ has vivid magenta flowers, bronze-green foliage and a spreading habit. **'White Perfection'**♀ has white flowers and bright green foliage.

E. erigena (syn. *E. hibernica*, *E. mediterranea*) (Irish heath) Deep lilac, urn-shaped blooms, 5 mm (¼ in) long, are honey-scented and much loved by bees. They are borne between mid spring and early winter among linear leaves on an upright plant. The plant is hardy and can be grown in most soils. It is suitable for informal hedging but the brittle stems will break under heavy snow. Native to western Ireland and northern Spain. HEIGHT & SPREAD 2.4 m×60 cm (8×2 ft).

'Golden Lady'♀ produces sparse white

▼ *Erica erigena* 'Golden Lady'

Erinus
Scrophulariaceae

Erinus alpinus

A spring and summer display of numerous dainty, bright flowers characterises this delightful small plant. The species most commonly grown is a hardy evergreen – though shortlived – perennial. It flourishes on very little soil, such as on a rock garden or in wall crevices, and will do well in sun or partial shade. It self-sows freely.

RECOMMENDED SPECIES AND VARIETIES
E. alpinus♀ (fairy foxglove) Small pink or purple 5-petalled flowers, up to 1 cm (⅜ in) across, are borne in spikes from late spring to mid summer, appearing intermittently into autumn – especially if old spikes are deadheaded. The deep green leaves are mostly arranged in basal rosettes, and the tufted plant mounds with age. Native to the mountains of central and S Europe. HEIGHT & SPREAD 6×12.5 cm (2½×5 in).

The flowers of var. *albus* are pure white. 'Dr Hähnle' has deep pink flowers. 'Mrs Charles Boyle'♀ has soft pale pink flowers.

▲ *Erinus alpinus*

Erinus alpinus var. *albus* ▼

CULTIVATION Plant in autumn or early spring in any well-drained soil in sun or partial shade. Encourage a second flowering by deadheading, unless seed is required.
PROPAGATION Sow seed under glass in autumn or early spring.
PESTS AND DISEASES Usually trouble free.

Eriobotrya
Rosaceae

Eriobotrya japonica

Large ornamental shrubs or small trees, eriobotryas are grown for their handsome evergreen leaves. In their native habitat, they bear fragrant, creamy white flowers and delicious edible fruit but neither is produced freely in Britain. Carried in upright, branched clusters, the open flowers have five petals and measure up to 2 cm (¾ in) across. The soft orange fruits have velvety skins and contain a few large chestnut-brown seeds; *Eriobotrya japonica* produces the fruit called loquat. Native to the Himalayas and much of E Asia, eriobotryas are fairly hardy, grown against a warm wall.

RECOMMENDED SPECIES AND VARIETIES
E. deflexa The leathery, oblong leaves are up to 25 cm (10 in) long and have strongly impressed veins and toothed edges. Young leaves are sometimes bronze-coloured, becoming mid green above and lighter green beneath. The flowers appear from late spring to mid summer. The sharp but sweet orange oval fruits, about 2.5 cm (1 in) long, may be seen in late autumn, but rarely. HEIGHT & SPREAD 1.5×1 m (5×3 ft) after 5 years, ultimately 9 m (30 ft) tall.
E. japonica♀ (loquat, Japanese medlar) The glossy, dark green, corrugated leaves are covered underneath with rust brown hairs. Oblong or pointed, with sharply toothed edges they measure up to 30 cm (1 ft) long. The flowers have rust-brown stalks and appear intermittently from late autumn to

▼ *Eriobotrya japonica*

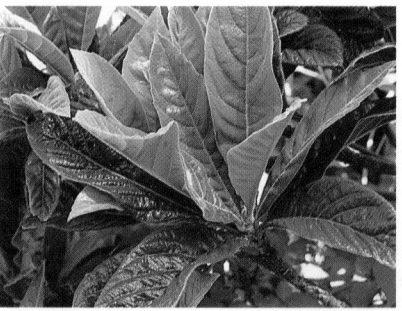

mid spring, being produced in any abundance only after hot summers. When fruit does appear, it ripens in spring and may, therefore, be damaged by late frosts. Rounded or egg-shaped and orange-yellow with a soft downy skin, the juicy fruits have a tart flavour and are up to 4 cm (1½ in) long. HEIGHT & SPREAD 1.5×1 m (5×3 ft) after 5 years, ultimately 8 m (26 ft) tall.
CULTIVATION Plant during early autumn in any fertile, well-drained soil in a sunny, sheltered position, preferably against a south or west-facing wall.
PROPAGATION Sow seed in spring or summer.
PRUNING Not required, although plants can be shaped by cutting back in winter.
PESTS AND DISEASES Usually trouble free.

Eriogonum
Wild buckwheat
Polygonaceae

Rounded clusters of small, cup-shaped flowers adorn these evergreen perennials or sub-shrubs in summer. The plants have a neat habit which fits them perfectly for display in a rock garden or alpine house. Warmly tinted fruits often follow the flowers. Well-drained soil and a position in the sun are vital. The genus is native to mountains of N America.

RECOMMENDED SPECIES AND VARIETIES
E. umbellatum (sulphur flower) Tiny yellow flowers in dense, long-stalked clusters – up to 7.5 cm (3 in) across – appear in mid summer on this matted perennial. The flowers are soon followed by coppery fruits. The elliptical 2 cm (¾ in) leaves are deep

▲ *Eriogonum umbellatum*
Eriogonum umbellatum var. *torreyanum* ▼

green with white hairy undersides. HEIGHT & SPREAD 30×40cm (12×16in).

The flowers of var. *torreyanum* are bright yellow; the deep green leaves are hairless on the undersides.

CULTIVATION Plant in a sunny site in spring in well-drained yet moisture-retentive soil.

PROPAGATION Sow seed when ripe in autumn or early spring in pots and place in a coldframe. Alternatively, take semi-ripe cuttings in mid to late summer.

PESTS AND DISEASES Usually trouble free.

Eriophyllum
Compositae

Eriophyllum lanatum

Showy yellow summer flowerheads embellish the only plant in the genus to be grown in Britain. Because both the centres and surrounding ray florets are yellow, the flowers stand out boldly at the front of a mixed border. Distinctive silvery white foliage adds to the effect. The smaller variety makes more impact in a rock garden. This hardy perennial plant requires well-drained soil and full sun to thrive. The genus is native to N America.

RECOMMENDED SPECIES AND VARIETY

E. lanatum (woolly sunflower) Masses of bright yellow flowerheads, up to 5cm (2in) across, bloom from early to mid summer. Woolly grey or silvery leaves, up to 7.5cm (3in) long, offset them. This clump-forming to spreading hardy perennial is herbaceous or semi-evergreen. HEIGHT & SPREAD 30×40cm (12×16in).

'Nanum' reaches just 20cm (8in) tall.

CULTIVATION Plant in early spring or early autumn in well-drained soil and in full sun.

PROPAGATION Divide plants after flowering or in early spring as growth commences.

PESTS AND DISEASES Slugs or birds may attack young shoots in spring.

▼ *Eriophyllum lanatum*

Erodium
Stork's bill
Geraniaceae

Erodium reichardii

A long summer show of cheerful cup-shaped flowers earns the stork's bills a place in the garden. The fruits that follow the flowers are like long, pointed beaks – giving rise to the common name. The genus mostly contains evergreen or semi-evergreen perennials, although there are some sub-shrubs and annuals. Many of the perennials are neat enough for the rock garden – the smaller ones particularly suited to raised beds, troughs or paving – and these are described below. Native to Europe, W and central Asia, they are generally hardy.

RECOMMENDED SPECIES AND VARIETIES

E. castellanum Rose-pink flowers, 2.5cm (1in) across with darker veins on the 3 upper petals, appear throughout summer. This compact, stemless species bears dissected grey-green leaves up to 15cm (6in) long with alternate large and small lobes. HEIGHT & SPREAD 20×30cm (8×12in).

E. chamaedryoides see *E. reichardii*

E. chrysanthum Pale sulphur-yellow flowers, 2cm (¾in) across, are borne in small

▲ *Erodium chrysanthum*

sprays from late spring to early summer and occasionally later. This mound-forming plant has neatly dissected, silvery grey silky leaves, up to 15cm (6in) long. HEIGHT & SPREAD 20×30cm (8×12in).

E. corsicum Small pink flowers, 2cm (¾in) across, with dark veins are held singly or in small clusters from late spring to early summer. Small, downy, grey-green oval leaves, just 1.5cm (½in) long with crumpled edges, crowd the branches. This compact, mound-forming plant suffers from excess wet but is excellent for a trough, if protected in winter. It thrives in an alpine house. HEIGHT & SPREAD 7.5×20cm (3×8in).

E. foetidum see *E. petraeum*

E. glandulosum♀ (syn. *E. macradenum, E.*

▲ *Erodium glandulosum*

petraeum ssp. *glandulosum*) Pale lilac flowers, 2.5cm (1in) across, have violet-purple blotches on the 2 upper petals. They are borne in small clusters in summer. The leaves of this aromatic plant are deeply divided, grey-green and up to 15cm (6in) long. HEIGHT & SPREAD 20×20cm (8×8in).

E. guttatum Pale pink flowers are borne in small clusters during the summer. The flowers are 2.5cm (1in) across with deep-pink veins and a deep-pink blotch on the two upper petals. This woody-based, clump-former bears numerous heart-shaped leaves, neatly toothed along the edges and up to 2.5cm (1in) long. HEIGHT & SPREAD 15×20cm (6×8in).

E. x *kolbianum* 'Natasha' Pale rose-pink flowers, 2cm (¾in) across, appear in small clusters during the summer on this small plant. The silvery grey leaves are finely dissected, giving the foliage a ferny appearance. HEIGHT & SPREAD 15×15cm (6×6in).

E. macradenum see *E. glandulosum*

E. manescaui Pinkish purple flowers, 3cm (1¼in) across, with darker blotches on the 2 upper petals, appear intermittently from late spring until early autumn. The plant forms mounds of dissected, ferny, blue-green leaves, each up to 30cm (1ft) long. HEIGHT & SPREAD 40×60cm (16in×2ft).

E. petraeum (syn. *E. foetidum*) Small pink flowers, 2cm (¾in) across with red veins, appear throughout the summer. This compact mound-former has softly hairy, grey-green, deeply cut leaves up to 10cm (4in) long. HEIGHT & SPREAD 20×20cm (8×8in).

For ssp. *glandulosum* see *E. glandulosum*.

'Roseum' has rose-pink flowers with darker veins.

E. reichardii (syn. *E. chamaedryoides*) (alpine geranium) Small, solitary white

▲ Erodium petraeum

▲ Erodium reichardii

flowers, 1 cm (⅜ in) across with shell-pink veins, appear throughout the summer. The deep green, heart-shaped leaves have finely toothed edges and are 1.5 cm (½ in) long. This mound-forming perennial suits raised beds and troughs; it dislikes excessive winter wet. HEIGHT & SPREAD 5×20 cm (2×8 in).

E. rupestre Plain white flowers, 1.5 cm (½ in) across, are borne in small clusters in summer. This species bears silvery grey dissected leaves, up to 7.5 cm (3 in) long. HEIGHT & SPREAD 10×20 cm (4×8 in).

▲ Erodium trifolium

E. trifolium Pink flowers are borne in loose sprays in late spring and early summer. The 2.5 cm (1 in) blooms have brown blotches on the two upper petals. Grey-green, 3-lobed leaves, about 5 cm (2 in) long, cover the stems of this short-lived evergreen, which often self-sows in the garden. HEIGHT & SPREAD 35×35 cm (14×14 in).

E. × variabile Small white to bright pink flowers, 1.5 cm (½ in) across, appear during the summer and early autumn. This is a cushion to mound-forming plant bearing deep green to grey-green, oval leaves with scalloped edges, up to 2.5 cm (1 in) long. HEIGHT & SPREAD 20×40 cm (8×16 in).

'Album' has pure white flowers.

'Bishop's Form' has brighter pink flowers and a looser habit. 'Flore Pleno' bears double pink flowers, like tiny rosettes, with darker veins. 'Roseum'♀ has pink flowers with crimson veins.

CULTIVATION Plant in spring, choosing a well-drained, sunny site and preferably a neutral-to-alkaline soil.

PROPAGATION Sow seed in autumn or early spring in pots in a coldframe. The species tend to hybridise in the garden so that seedlings cannot be guaranteed to be pure if two or more species or cultivars are grown side by side. An alternative is to take basal cuttings of leafy shoots from late spring through the summer.

E. glandulosum, E. × kolbianum 'Natasha', E. rupestre and E. trifolium can be divided carefully in autumn or early spring, ensuring that each portion has an ample amount of root attached.

PESTS AND DISEASES Grey rot may infect the crown of cushion-forming plants if they become too wet in winter outdoors. Overhead protection, such as a cloche or pane of glass, may help to prevent this.

Eryngium
Eryngo
Umbelliferae

Eryngium bourgatii
'Oxford Blue'

The bold flowerheads of these majestic plants give interest and add stature to the flower border during summer. The thistle-like flowerheads – which attract butterflies and bees – are adorned by more spectacular, often spiny bracts, which, like the upper stems, are usually highly coloured. Most of the eryngiums listed here are perennial, half of them are evergreen and only two are not fully hardy. They all flower from mid to late summer and make excellent dried flowers for decorative winter arrangements.

▼ Eryngium × giganteum

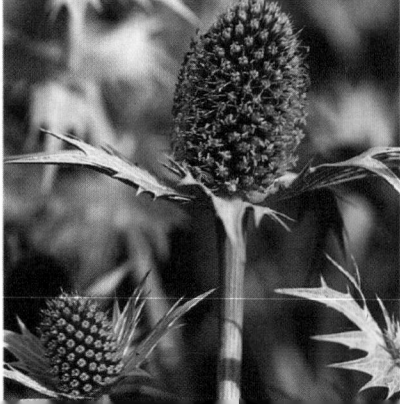

RECOMMENDED SPECIES AND VARIETIES

E. agavifolium This clump-forming, half-hardy, evergreen perennial produces greenish white flowerheads, up to 5 cm (2 in) across. The deep green, stiff, sword-shaped leaves have sharp saw-toothed margins, and mostly grow in basal rosettes. HEIGHT & SPREAD 1.5 m×75 cm (5×2½ ft).

E. alpinum♀ (Alpine eryngo) Purplish blue, teasel-like flowerheads, to 5 cm (2 in) long, are surrounded by similarly coloured, feathery bracts. This clump-forming, hardy herbaceous perennial, has glossy, deep green basal leaves which are heart-shaped with a toothed margin. HEIGHT & SPREAD 1 m×70 cm (3 ft×2 ft 4 in).

'Blue Star' has deep blue flowerheads and bracts.

E. amethystinum Small blue flowerheads, 2 cm (¾ in) across, are surrounded by spiky darker blue bracts. This evergreen hardy perennial has very spiny, dissected basal leaves. HEIGHT & SPREAD 60×60 cm (2×2 ft).

E. bourgatii Rounded flowerheads, 2.5 cm (1 in) across, which change from steely blue and green to lilac-blue, are borne on similarly coloured stems. The deeply cut, grey-green basal leaves of this hardy herbaceous perennial bear striking silver veining. HEIGHT & SPREAD 60×50 cm (24×20 in).

'Oxford Blue'♀ has flowerheads of dark silvery blue.

E. × giganteum♀ (Miss Willmott's ghost) This stiff, robust and statuesque biennial has blue flowerheads, 4 cm (1½ in) long, surrounded by handsome, broad, silvery spiny bracts. The basal leaves are oval and deep

▼ Eryngium bourgatii

green. It spreads itself freely by seed. HEIGHT & SPREAD 1.2 m×75 cm (4×2½ ft).

E. maritimum (sea holly) Small pale blue flowerheads, 2.5 cm (1 in) across, are surrounded by spiny blue-grey bracts on short stiff stems. This tufted, short-lived, evergreen perennial has spiny, leathery, blue-grey basal leaves. Ideal for the rock garden. HEIGHT & SPREAD 50×50 cm (20×20 in).

E. x *oliverianum*♀ Upright stems of lavender-blue flowerheads, about 4 cm (1½ in) long, are surrounded by narrow, spreading, spiny bracts. This hardy herbaceous perennial has mid green oval basal leaves with saw-tooth margins. HEIGHT & SPREAD 1 m×60 cm (3×2 ft).

E. pandanifolium Clusters of small, rounded, purplish flowerheads, to 1 cm (⅜ in) across, are carried on tall, stiff stems. This robust, half-hardy perennial has basal tufts of very long, strap-like, mid green leaves with soft, spiny margins. HEIGHT & SPREAD 2.4×1.2 m (8×4 ft).

E. planum Numerous, small, deep blue flowerheads, 1.5 cm (½ in) across, are surrounded by similarly coloured, spreading, spine-tipped bracts. This partly evergreen hardy perennial has dark green, leathery basal leaves which contrast with the blue-flushed, spiny upper stem leaves. HEIGHT & SPREAD 75×40 cm (2 ft 6 in×1 ft 4 in).

E. x *tripartitum*♀ Airy sprays of small blue flowerheads, 1 cm (⅜ in) long, are surrounded by spreading, spine-tipped bracts. This partly evergreen hardy perennial has wiry stems and basal rosettes of deep grey-green, coarsely toothed leaves. HEIGHT & SPREAD 1 m×50 cm (3 ft×1 ft 8 in).

E. variifolium The branched clusters of small silver-blue flowerheads, up to 2 cm (¾ in) across, have narrow, spreading, silvery white or silvery blue spine-tipped bracts. This evergreen hardy perennial has rosettes of oval, jagged-toothed, deep green basal leaves, marbled with white which contrast with the spiny divided stem leaves. HEIGHT & SPREAD 50×25 cm (20×10 in).

E. x *zabelii* This hybrid bears deep purple-blue flowerheads, up to 2.5 cm (1 in) long, surrounded by rigid, spine-toothed bracts of silvery blue. A hardy herbaceous perennial, it has rounded, three-part basal leaves with spine-toothed margins. HEIGHT & SPREAD 50×30 cm (20×12 in).

'Violetta' has larger violet-blue flowerheads and grows to 75 cm (2½ ft) tall.

CULTIVATION Plant eryngiums on a sunny well-drained site in most garden soils.

PROPAGATION Sow seed in autumn or winter in pots in a coldframe. Alternatively, take root cuttings of perennial species in winter or carefully divide plants in early spring.

PESTS AND DISEASES Crown rot may affect plants in colder and wetter regions. To help to prevent this, particularly in rock gardens, clear the plants of dead leaves and give some protection from winter wet.

Erysimum
Wallflower
Cruciferae

Erysimum cheiri 'Harpur Crewe'

The common wallflower, *Erysimum cheiri*, has long been associated with cottage gardens, admired for its early, fragrant blooms. It is often used in spring bedding schemes, mixing effectively with bulbs, especially tulips. If the plants are cut back they will continue to flower intermittently through the summer.

Most wallflowers can be used at the front of a border for colour in spring and early summer, while *E. helveticum*, *E. hieraciifolium* and *E. pulchellum* make freely flowering rock-garden plants. The plants described below have four-petalled flowers, which are generally about 2 cm (¾ in) across and borne in spikes. Native across the Northern Hemisphere, particularly Europe and Asia. Many of the species were formerly included in the genus *Cheiranthus*.

RECOMMENDED SPECIES AND VARIETIES

E. x *allionii* (hort.) see *E. hieraciifolium*

E. 'Bowles Mauve'♀ Spikes of deep mauve flowers are borne by this evergreen perennial with a bushy habit. It is hardy to -15°C (5°F). The stiff, branched stems carry dark grey-green, narrow to lance-shaped leaves. HEIGHT & SPREAD 75×60 cm (2½×2 ft).

E. 'Bredon'♀ Dense spikes of bright, rich yellow flowers are carried by this partly evergreen bushy perennial. The stems are rather crowded with dark green, narrowly elliptical leaves with a bluish tint. HEIGHT & SPREAD 45×45 cm (1½×1½ ft).

E. 'Butterscotch' Spikes of toffee-yellow flowers are carried by this low-growing perennial which has mid green oval leaves. HEIGHT & SPREAD 25×25 cm (10×10 in).

▼ *Erysimum 'Butterscotch'*

E. capitatum Flowers, varying in colour from yellow to orange-brown and maroon-purple, are borne in clusters. This biennial has erect, somewhat branched stems and deep green, lance-shaped, toothed leaves. HEIGHT & SPREAD 45×25 cm (18×10 in).

E. cheiri (common wallflower) Spikes of large, intensely fragrant flowers are produced in a wide range of colours, particularly yellow, cream, orange, bronze and red. This bushy evergreen is hardy with mid to deep green lanceolate leaves. It is often grown as a biennial for bedding purposes. HEIGHT & SPREAD Seed merchants sell different strains: tall, up to 60×45 cm (2×1½ ft); intermediate, up to 45×30 cm (1½×1 ft); and dwarf, up to 20×20 cm (8×8 in).

'Harpur Crewe' has double yellow flowers, opening in succession from late spring to mid summer. It grows up to 45 cm (1½ ft) tall.

E. 'Chelsea Jacket'♀ Large, rich magenta, scented flowers are borne by this compact evergreen perennial. The lanceolate leaves are deep green. HEIGHT & SPREAD 1 m×50 cm (3 ft×20 in).

E. 'Constant Cheer'♀ Spikes of violet-mauve flowers flushed with amber are borne by this rather upright evergreen perennial. It also bears deep green lanceolate leaves. HEIGHT & SPREAD 60×40 cm (24×16 in).

▲ *Erysimum helveticum*

E. helveticum (syn. *E. pumilum*) Fragrant bright yellow flowers appear in broad clusters from late spring to mid summer. This clump-forming, partly evergreen perennial bears deep green or grey-green, crowded narrow-lanceolate leaves. HEIGHT & SPREAD 15×20 cm (6×8 in).

E. hieraciifolium♀ (syn. *E.* x *allionii* [hort.]) (Siberian wallflower) Orange flowers with hairs on the reverse of the petals are carried by this compact, bushy perennial. The deep green leaves are oblong to lance-shaped, and often wavy and toothed. HEIGHT & SPREAD 1 m×50 cm (36×20 in).

E. 'Moonlight' Pale yellow flowers are borne in spikes from late spring to mid summer and occasionally later. This mat-forming, evergreen perennial has mid green, narrow oval leaves. HEIGHT & SPREAD 10×30 cm (4×12 in).

E. pulchellum Golden-yellow flowers are borne in spikes from early to mid summer. This tufted evergreen perennial has rather dense lance-shaped to oblong, mid to deep green leaves which are coarsely toothed. HEIGHT & SPREAD 40×30 cm (1 ft 4 in × 1 ft).

E. pumilum see *E. helveticum*

E. 'Wenlock Beauty'♀ Spikes of somewhat fragrant yellow flowers, attractively flushed with bronze, are carried by this bushy evergreen perennial. The elliptical to lance-shaped leaves are deep green. HEIGHT & SPREAD 25×25 cm (10×10 in).

CULTIVATION Erysimums will grow in any well-drained soil in sunny but sheltered positions. Rich or moist soil leads to reduced flowering. Plant bedding types in late summer or early autumn; plant out perennials in spring. Trim after flowering to encourage further blooms. As the plants are short-lived, regular propagation is advisable.

PROPAGATION Take 6 cm (2½ in) semi-ripe cuttings with a heel of the perennial species and cultivars in summer, overwinter under glass and plant out the following spring. Seed of the species may be sown in spring under glass and then treated as cuttings. Seed of *E. cheiri* is best sown in early summer and the seedlings planted in their flowering positions in autumn.

PESTS AND DISEASES Cabbage root fly, flea beetles, slugs, snails and caterpillars attack the plants. Various leaf and stem spots and rots, and root rots affect erysimums, as does infection from turnip mosaic virus.

Erythrina
Coral tree
Leguminosae

Spectacular brilliant red flowers characterise this genus of deciduous or semi-evergreen perennials, shrubs and trees. The leaves are composed of three broad leaflets and the branches of some species are spiny. Of the 100 species, only one may be grown in Britain and then only in milder areas.

RECOMMENDED SPECIES

E. crista-galli Scarlet beak-like flowers, up to 5 cm (2 in) long, are borne in late summer and autumn in long spikes. The oval, leathery, sea-green leaflets, up to 12 cm (4¾ in) long, have a spiny stalk. This deciduous shrub will grow outdoors in sheltered spots in mild areas. In harsh winters, stems that have not been pruned may be killed back to ground level but new shoots will emerge the following year. This plant can also be grown in a container under glass. Native to S America. HEIGHT & SPREAD 1×1 m (3×3 ft) after 5 years, ultimately 3 m (10 ft) tall.

CULTIVATION Plant in spring in a fertile, well-drained soil in full sun, ideally against a

▲ *Erythrina crista-galli*

south or west-facing wall. In winter, protect the rootstock with a dry mulch. Alternatively, grow in a container of well-drained potting compost, such as John Innes No 2, and place in a cool greenhouse or conservatory. Plants can be moved outside after the danger of frost has passed. When the leaves fall, keep the compost almost dry.

PROPAGATION Take semi-ripe cuttings in summer or sow seed under glass in early spring.

PRUNING Cut plants growing outdoors to ground level in late autumn, and cut back those under glass every second year.

PESTS AND DISEASES Plants grown under glass are susceptible to red spider mite.

Erythronium
Dog's tooth violet
Liliaceae

Erythronium revolutum

Grown for their pendent blossoms and attractively mottled foliage, these tuberous perennials are a delight to behold in spring. The flowers, with their prominent stamens and reflexed petals, nod gracefully at the top of smooth slender stems rising above the oval to lance-shaped leaves. All species are hardy and benefit from a little shade, doing best in the dappled sunlight of a woodland environment. Native to northern USA, except *Erythronium dens-canis*, which comes from Europe and Asia.

RECOMMENDED SPECIES AND VARIETIES

E. americanum (trout lily) Shy to flower, when solitary bright yellow flowers, 4 cm (1½ in) wide, are carried at the top of beige stems up to 20 cm (8 in) high. The semi-erect green leaves are mottled with brown and up to 15 cm (6 in) long and 4 cm (1½ in) wide. HEIGHT & SPREAD 20×20 cm (8×8 in).

E. californicum♀ In spring pinkish brown buds open into creamy white flowers with a yellow eye. Up to three 5 cm (2 in) wide

blooms are carried on each purple stem. Lance-shaped leaves, 15 cm (6 in) long and 6 cm (2½ in) wide, are mid green mottled white. HEIGHT & SPREAD 30×30 cm (1×1 ft).

'White Beauty'♀, a vigorous plant, has white starry flowers, up to 6 cm (2½ in) across, and more heavily marbled leaves than those of the species.

E. 'Citronella' up to 3 lemon-yellow flowers hang together in a loose spike. The semi-erect leaves, heavily mottled with brown, are 10 cm (4 in) long and 5 cm (2 in) wide. HEIGHT & SPREAD 25×20 cm (10×8 in).

E. dens-canis♀ (dog's tooth violet) Solitary starry flowers, 4 cm (1½ in) wide, with swept-back petals in pink, purple or white are carried on 20 cm (8 in) stems. The leaves of this free-flowering species are mottled brown, 15 cm (6 in) long and 5 cm (2 in) wide. HEIGHT & SPREAD 20×15 cm (8×6 in).

E. japonicum Purple funnel-shaped flowers, 3.5 cm (1⅜ in) across, are borne singly, in spring, on dark green stems with a purplish flush. The lance-shaped leaves are up to 15 cm (6 in) long and dark green mottled purple. HEIGHT & SPREAD 15×15 cm (6×6 in).

E. 'Pagoda'♀ Up to 10 pale yellow blossoms, 6 cm (2½ in) wide, are carried on stems up to 25 cm (10 in) high. At the base of the stems this robust, vigorous plant bears glossy green leaves up to 15 cm (6 in) long and 5 cm (2 in) wide, mottled with brown. HEIGHT & SPREAD 25×20 cm (10×8 in).

▲ *Erythronium californicum*

▲ *Erythronium dens-canis*

Erythronium revolutum ▲

E. revolutum♀ A loose spike of up to 4 pink 7.5 cm (3 in) wide blossoms rises out of the attractive, brown-dappled foliage. The semi-erect, wavy edged green leaves are up to 20 cm (8 in) long and 5 cm (2 in) wide. HEIGHT & SPREAD 25×20 cm (10×8 in).

E. tuolumnense♀ Heads of up to 10 bright yellow flowers, 5 cm (2 in) across, are borne on green stems. This quickly spreading plant bears pairs of semi-erect glossy green leaves up to 15 cm (6 in) long and 5 cm (2 in) wide. HEIGHT & SPREAD 30×20 cm (12×8 in).

CULTIVATION Erythroniums prefer cool conditions. Plant in a richly organic, moist soil in partial shade in autumn, and ensure that the tubers are not baked by the sun during the dormant period in summer.

PROPAGATION Divide the tubers in late summer or early autumn. Replant immediately so that the tubers do not dry out.

PESTS AND DISEASES Usually trouble free.

Escallonia
Escalloniaceae

Escallonia
'C.F. Ball'

Brilliant pink or red flower clusters are set off magnificently by the dark, glossy leaves of this shrub. Escallonias give year-round interest to the garden, with flowers in bloom from early summer to early autumn and gleaming, deep green leaves through winter. These mostly evergreen shrubs and small trees grow well in southern and western Britain, including western Scotland, particularly by the sea, where they withstand salt-laden sea breezes and are much used for hedging and as windbreaks. Elsewhere, most species do best if they have a sheltered position, such as against a wall. Cultivars tend to be hardy, but sometimes lose leaves in periods of prolonged frost.

The small flowers have five rounded petals and are generally cup or bell-shaped. They measure up to 1.5 cm (½ in) across and are borne in clusters 5 to 10 cm (2 to 4 in) long. The flowers appear in abundance in early summer, and then bloom intermittently until early autumn. The leaves, arranged alternately on the stem, are up to 5 cm (2 in) long and fairly narrow, often oval. Plants have a rounded habit, with stems upright or arching downwards. The genus is native to South America.

The varieties listed below are evergreen, with glossy dark green leaves that have finely serrated edges. They are all frost-hardy, except for *E.* 'Iveyi', which is only moderately so.

RECOMMENDED SPECIES AND VARIETIES

E. **'Apple Blossom'**♀ Flowers are cup-shaped and pink or white or a combination of the two. This shrub grows into a good hedge, with pruning. HEIGHT & SPREAD 1×1 m (3×3 ft) after 5 years, ultimate height 1.5 m (5 ft).

E. **'C.F. Ball'** Crimson flowers, tubular in shape, appear from late spring to late summer. This vigorous plant is particularly suited to gardens close to the seashore. The leaves are fragrant when crushed. HEIGHT & SPREAD 1.5×1.5 m (5×5 ft) after 5 years, ultimately 3 m (10 ft) tall.

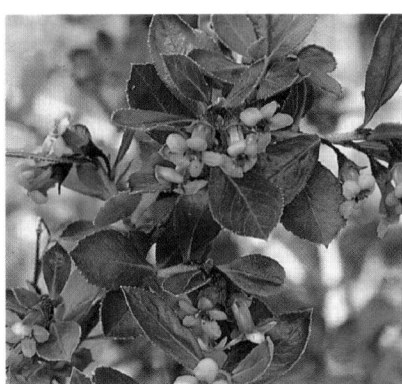

▲ *Escallonia* 'C.F. Ball'

E. **'Donard Beauty'** Decorative pinkish red flowers first appear in early spring. HEIGHT & SPREAD 1×1 m (3×3 ft) after 5 years, ultimately 1.8 m (6 ft) tall.

E. **'Donard Brilliance'** Flowers are carmine red with golden anthers. HEIGHT & SPREAD 1×1 m (3×3 ft) after 5 years, ultimately 1.8 m (6 ft) tall.

E. **'Donard Radiance'**♀ Flowers are deep pink. HEIGHT & SPREAD 1×1 m (3×3 ft) after 5 years, ultimately 1.8 m (6 ft) tall.

E. **'Donard Seedling'** A vigorous plant whose white flowers are tinged with pink, and about 2 cm (¾ in) across. HEIGHT & SPREAD 1.2×1.2 m (4×4 ft) after 5 years, ultimately 3 m (10 ft) tall.

E. **'Edinensis'**♀ A compact shrub with pale pink flowers that are a deeper pink when in bud. HEIGHT & SPREAD 1.2×1.2 m (4×4 ft) after 5 years, ultimately 2.4 m (8 ft) tall.

E. **'Gwendolyn Anley'** This is a fine, spreading shrub. The pale pink flowers can be as much as 2 cm (¾ in) across. HEIGHT & SPREAD 60 cm×1 m (2×3 ft) after 5 years, ultimately 1×2 m (3×6½ ft).

▼ *Escallonia* 'Edinensis'

▲ *Escallonia* 'Iveyi'

E. **'Iveyi'**♀ White flowers grow in branched clusters up to 10 cm (4 in) long, in mid and late summer. The flowers are pale pink in bud. They are slightly fragrant, as are the leaves when crushed. This fine plant is a strong grower, but only moderately frost-hardy and so is best grown against a wall. HEIGHT & SPREAD 1.5×1.5 m (5×5 ft) after 5 years, ultimately 2.7 m (9 ft) tall.

E. **'Langleyensis'**♀ Rose-pink flowers cover the arching branches. The leaves grow to only 2.5 cm (1 in) long. HEIGHT & SPREAD 1.2×1.2 m (4×4 ft) after 5 years, ultimately 2.4 m (8 ft).

E. **'Peach Blossom'**♀ Flowers are a pale pink. HEIGHT & SPREAD 1.2×1.2 m (4×4 ft) after 5 years, ultimately 2.4 m (8 ft).

E. **'Pride of Donard'**♀ The bright red flowers on this outstanding plant, some as wide as 2 cm (¾ in), are among the largest borne by any escallonia. HEIGHT & SPREAD 1.2×1.2 m (4×4 ft) after 5 years, ultimately 2 m (6½ ft) tall.

E. **'Red Elf'** The flowers are a deep crimson. HEIGHT & SPREAD 1.5×1.5 m (5×5 ft) after 5 years, ultimately 2 m (6½ ft) tall.

▼ *Escallonia* 'Peach Blossom'

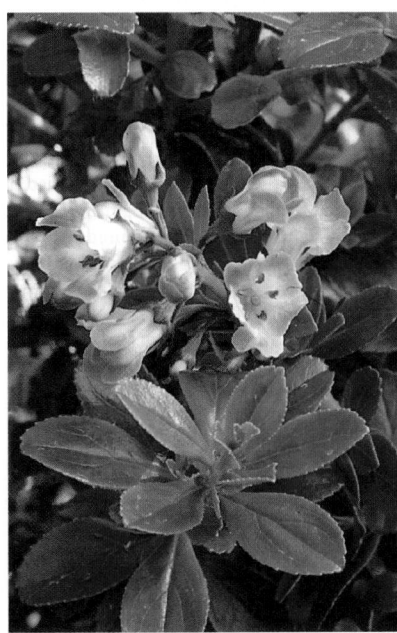

Eucomis
Pineapple flower, pineapple lily
Hyacinthaceae

Numerous small, starry flowers appear in late summer, packed densely around a thick stem and topped with a tuft of leafy bracts to form a flowerhead in the shape of a pineapple – hence the common name. On fading the flowers form long-lasting seed-pods. Dark green strap-shaped leaves come up straight from the bulb to form a rosette around the erect flower stem.

The plants are native to South Africa and suit a sunny border, but in most areas the bulbs need to be brought indoors over winter. They can be grown in pots for the patio in summer and greenhouse in winter.

RECOMMENDED SPECIES AND VARIETIES

E. autumnalis (syn. *E. undulata*) A sturdy flower stalk carries up to 45 whitish green flowers in a compact flowerhead, up to 15 cm (6 in) long. The dark green lanceolate leaves have wavy edges and up to 45 cm (18 in) long. HEIGHT 40 cm (16 in).

E. bicolor Oblong, bright green leaves with purple edges fan out from a thick purple-flecked stem with up to 40 tightly packed, greenish, purple-tinged flowers in a 25 cm (10 in) long head. HEIGHT 50 cm (20 in).

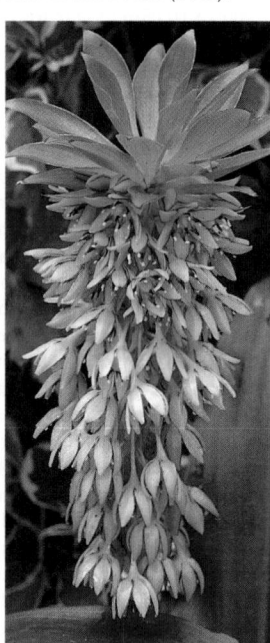

▲ *Eucomis comosa*   *Eucomis bicolor* ▲

E. comosa (syn. *E. punctata*) A stately spike of up to 30 flowers rises out of a basal rosette of strap-shaped, purple-spotted leaves up to 50 cm (20 in) long. The flowers vary in colour from white to shades of pink, each centred by a violet-purple ovary and carried on a purple-spotted stem. HEIGHT 60 cm (2 ft).

E. punctata see *E. comosa*
E. undulata see *E. autumnalis*

CULTIVATION Plant in early spring, setting the bulbs 10 cm (4 in) deep and 25 cm (10 in) apart. Choose a sunny, well-drained spot in a rich soil. In all but the mildest, southern-most regions of Britain, lift and store the bulbs indoors through winter.

PROPAGATION Divide clumps in autumn or spring. Alternatively, sow seed in trays in spring and autumn. Seed-raised plants produce flowers after 5-6 years.

PESTS AND DISEASES Usually trouble free.

Eucryphia
Eucryphiaceae

Eucryphia x nymansensis 'Nymansay'

Abundant white flowers are borne in late summer on these large shrubs or small trees. The flowers, sometimes scented, are usually four-petalled, up to 6 cm (2½ in) across, and cupped round an array of numerous golden tipped stamens which gives them a feathery appearance. Flowers are generally produced on trees 10-15 years old. All the plants are evergreen in their native Australia and S America but some shed most of their leaves in colder climates. The leaves, less than 7.5 cm (3 in) long, generally have a ser-rated or wavy edge and are variable, mostly divided into three or more leaflets. Most shrubs are not fully hardy in cold northern areas of Britain. They grow best in the south and west and even there need a shel-tered site. With the exception of *Eucryphia x nymansensis* and, to a lesser degree, *E. cordifolia* they do not tolerate lime.

RECOMMENDED SPECIES AND VARIETIES

E. cordifolia x lucida Only warm southern gardens suit this small, evergreen tree. The leaves are glossy dark green above and glau-cous beneath. Large, scented white flowers, up to 6 cm (2½ in) across, with numerous stamens appear in late summer. HEIGHT & SPREAD 2 m×75 cm (6½×2½ ft) after 10 years, ultimately 8 m (26 ft) tall.

E. glutinosa♀ Masses of large, unscented white flowers cover this large, spreading shrub or small tree in mid to late summer. The dark green shiny leaves have 3 or 5 leaflets and they take on a rich orange-red autumn colour. Semi-evergreen in milder regions, this species is usually deciduous in most of the country. Though not truly frost-hardy it is one of the hardiest eucryphias. It does not tolerate lime and is a slow-growing plant. HEIGHT & SPREAD 1.5×1 m (5×3 ft) after 5 years, ultimately 6×2 m (20×6½ ft).

E. x intermedia This small evergreen tree flowers profusely, bearing numerous yellow-centred white flowers in late summer to early autumn. The leaves are sometimes divided into 3 leaflets. This species will withstand some frost. HEIGHT & SPREAD 5×2 m (16×6½ ft) after 20 years, ulti-mately 6 m (20 ft) tall.

'Rostrevor'♀ is a very free-flowering, fast-growing variety.

E. lucida Fragrant white flowers, slightly smaller than in other species, appear in pro-fusion from early to mid summer on this slender evergreen tree. The glossy dark green leaves are slightly glaucous beneath. This species is moderately frost-hardy. HEIGHT & SPREAD 2 m×75 cm (6½×2½ ft) after 10 years, ultimately 6 m (20 ft) tall.

E. milliganii This slow-growing, upright, evergreen tree bears its small white flowers, 2 cm (¾ in) wide, in mid summer. It blooms

▲ *Eucryphia x intermedia*

from a very early age – between 7-10 years old. The leaves are shiny dark green above and blue-green beneath. It will stand some degree of frost but is not perfectly hardy. HEIGHT & SPREAD 2 m×60 cm (6½×2 ft) after 10 years, ultimately 6×2 m (20×6½ ft).

E. x nymansensis This small columnar tree is the most frost-hardy and the most tolerant of limy soils. Masses of white flowers are produced, singly or in clusters, in mid to late summer. The evergreen leaves are pin-nate, divided into 3 or 5 leaflets, or undi-vided. HEIGHT & SPREAD 5×1.8 m (16×6 ft) after 20 years, ultimately 12 m (40 ft) tall.

The white flowers of the fast-growing 'Nymansay'♀ are large, as much as 6 cm (2½ in) across, and are generally more numerous than the species.

▼ *Eucryphia x nymansensis* 'Nymansay'

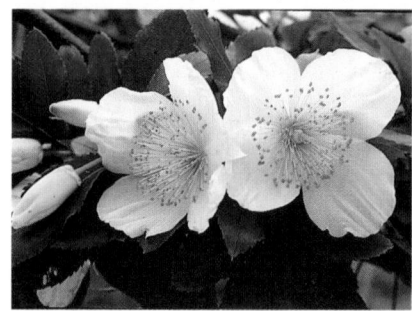

CULTIVATION Plant in late spring after the threat of frosts has passed. Most species do best in an acid soil. All must have protection from cold spring winds and from winter frosts. They grow best in warm, moist climates. A favourable site promotes vigorous growth and as the plants get larger they become less susceptible to wind and frost damage. They do best with their roots in cool soil that is moist.

PROPAGATION Plants are easy to raise from seed, from semi-ripe cuttings taken in late summer or by layering. Those grown from seed do not always come true.

PRUNING None is required.

PESTS AND DISEASES Usually trouble free.

Euonymus
Spindle trees
Celastraceae

Euonymus alatus

Both deciduous and evergreen shrubs and trees belong to this genus. The deciduous species, grown for their eye-catching, yellow to deep scarlet autumn leaves and distinctive lobed fruit, are valued as border plants and freestanding specimens. The evergreen species provide dense, year-round foliage often marked with white, yellow or pink and are grown as climbers, for ground cover and as hedging plants that can be clipped into shape.

The leaves are mostly oval, 2.5-7.5 cm (1-3 in) long, and have serrated edges. Insignificant white, brown or greenish flowers appear in late spring and early summer. The red or pink, lobed or winged fruit, about 1 cm (⅜ in) across, become noticeable in early autumn. They often split to reveal bright orange seeds. All parts of the plants are harmful if eaten.

Most of the species are native to woods and scrubland throughout Europe and Asia. They grow well in any soil and are especially useful on chalky ground. Most species are hardy, although some evergreens are suitable only for milder, sheltered areas.

RECOMMENDED SPECIES AND VARIETIES

E. alatus♀ (winged spindle tree) In mid autumn the deciduous leaves turn a fiery red. The reddish purple, 4-lobed fruits open partially and often look lopsided because some of the 4 orange seeds may fail to develop. Four distinct corky wings run intermittently along the stems of this densely branched, spreading shrub. HEIGHT & SPREAD 1.2×1.5 m (4×5 ft) after 5 years, ultimately 2.4 m (8 ft) tall.

'**Compactus**'♀ (syn. 'Cliodentatus') is a

▲ *Euonymus alatus*

dense plant, reaching only 1 m (3 ft) tall and is often used for low hedging.

E. europaeus '**Red Cascade**'♀ Long slender leaves turn bright red or purple in early autumn. At the same time abundant clusters of ripe, reddish pink, 4-lobed fruit, about 2 cm (¾ in) wide, open to reveal the white and orange seeds. This deciduous bushy shrub or small tree has green angular stems. HEIGHT & SPREAD 2×1.2 m (6½×4 ft) after 5 years, ultimately 5 m (16 ft) tall.

▲ *Euonymus europaeus* 'Red Cascade'

E. fortunei This hardy evergreen shrub and its many cultivated varieties provide ground cover plants, hedging and climbers. The pink fruit are rarely produced in Britain. HEIGHT & SPREAD 3×2 m (10×6½ ft) after 5 years (also its ultimate size).

The leaves of '**Emerald Gaiety**'♀ have a narrow, creamy white edge that turn bronze in the winter. This shrub reaches a height of 1 m (3 ft) and a spread of 1.5 m (5 ft). The leaves of the climber '**Emerald 'n' Gold**'♀ have bright green centres and wide, irregular, golden yellow edges that become tinged with pink in winter. '**Golden Prince**' (syn. 'Gold Tip') has yellow-tinged leaves and its branches are golden yellow at the tip. Unlike the other *E. fortunei* cultivars with yellow leaf mark-

▼ *Euonymus fortunei* 'Emerald Gaiety'

 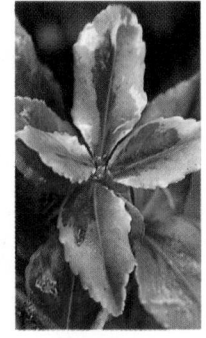

▲ *Euonymus fortunei* 'Emerald 'n' Gold'
Euonymus fortunei 'Golden Prince' ▲

ings, this plant retains its yellow colouring when grown in full sun. '**Harlequin**' has mottled white and green leaves in spring that become whiter in summer and then suffused with pink in winter. A low-growing, mounded shrub, it reaches a height and spread of 1 m (3 ft). '**Kewensis**' is only 5 cm (2 in) high with tiny leaves, 6 mm (¼ in) long. Spreading to form small hummocks or creeping over stones, it is good for rock gar-

▲ *Euonymus fortunei* 'Harlequin'
Euonymus fortunei 'Sunspot' ▲

dens. '**Minimus**' is similar in habit but more vigorous and with larger 1.5 cm (½ in) mid green leaves. '**Sheridan Gold**' makes an erect, compact shrub up to 50 cm (20 in) in height. The young leaves are tinged yellow at first, turning green later. '**Silver Queen**'♀ has leaves with broad white edges that are tinted rose in winter. The deep green leaves of '**Sunspot**' (syn. 'Gold Spot') have a long, golden spot at the centre and are tinged red beneath in winter. '**Variegatus**' (syn. 'Gracilis', 'Silver Gem') has grey-green leaves with white edges, although the leaves tend to revert to grey-green as the plant ages. It is more tolerant of shade and a coastal climate.

E. hamiltonianus ssp. *sieboldianus*♀ (syn. *E. h.* ssp. *hians*, *E. h.* ssp. *yedoensis*, *E. yedoensis*) This upright deciduous shrub or small tree has large leaves, 12 cm (4¾ in) long, that change to pastel shades of yellow and pink in autumn. The abundant 4-lobed, claw-like fruit ripen in early autumn when a few may open slightly to reveal the orange-red seeds. The fruit persist on the tree long after leaf fall. HEIGHT & SPREAD

(4 in) across, appear from late winter to mid spring. The yellowy green bracts may fade to orange during summer. This low-growing plant has prostrate biennial stems – flowers are borne on the previous season's shoots. The thick, obovate, blue-grey leaves, about 3 cm (1¼ in) long, are arranged on the stems in spirals. HEIGHT & SPREAD 15×60 cm (6×24 in).

E. nicaeensis Clusters of flowers appear in late spring; they are 6 cm (2½ in) wide at first but have doubled in size by mid summer. Blue-green leaves, up to 5 cm (2 in) long, are borne on stems that are often tinted red. The plants form hemispherical clumps. HEIGHT & SPREAD 60 cm×1 m (2×3 ft).

E. pithyusa Clusters of flowers, about 10 cm (4 in) across, appear from late spring to early summer. The narrow, pointed blue-green leaves, 1.5 cm (½ in) long, are densely packed. This low, branching species makes a good rock-garden plant. HEIGHT & SPREAD 30 cm×1 m (1×3 ft).

E. rigida (syn. E. biglandulosa) Flower clusters appear in early spring on the previous season's shoots. They turn red in summer. The blue-green leaves are up to 5 cm (2 in) long. This plant has prostrate stems that do not like to lie across wet soil. It needs a sunny position and regular feeding if it is to flower every year. HEIGHT & SPREAD 60 cm×1.2 m (2×4 ft).

E. robbiae see E. amygdaloides var. robbiae
E. seguieriana ssp. niciciana Clear yellow flowerheads, up to 14 cm (5½ in) across, appear in late summer. The grey-green leaves are about 3 cm (1¼ in) long. This plant forms a loose clump. HEIGHT & SPREAD 60 cm×60 cm (2×2 ft).

▲ Euphorbia characias ssp. wulfenii

E. veneta see E. characias ssp. wulfenii
E. wulfenii see E. characias ssp. wulfenii
HERBACEOUS PERENNIALS
E. cornigera (syn. E. longifolia hort.) Borne on red-tinged stems, the dark green leaves, 7.5 cm (3 in) long, have a cream stripe down the middle. The flower clusters, 10 cm (4 in) across, appear in mid summer. HEIGHT & SPREAD 30 cm×75 cm (1×2½ ft).

E. cyparissias Profuse flower clusters, 8 cm (3¼ in) across, appear in mid spring. The bracts turn orange in summer. The light green, needle-like leaves are up to 4 cm (1½ in) long and turn clear yellow in

autumn. This low-growing plant tolerates some shade and is good as ground cover. However, it can be invasive. HEIGHT & SPREAD 40 cm×1.2 m (16 in×4 ft).

E. donii (syn. E. longifolia) The dark green leaves, 13 cm (5¼ in) long, have a distinct white stripe down the centre and a faint pink edge. The stems are sometimes reddish. Lime-green flowers are produced from mid to late summer. This clump-forming plant prefers a sunny site on moist but well-drained soil. HEIGHT & SPREAD 30 cm×1 m (1×3 ft).

E. dulcis 'Chameleon' This plant flowers in mid spring and has dark purple leaves and bracts. The oblanceolate leaves are up to 7 cm (2¾ in) long. This plant will do well in sun and shade. If cut down to ground level after flowering and fed and watered it will produce a second flush of foliage. HEIGHT & SPREAD 60×60 cm (2×2 ft).

▲ Euphorbia dulcis 'Chameleon'

E. epithymoides see E. polychroma
E. griffithii Orange or bright red flower clusters, 10 cm (4 in) across, appear in late spring. The emerging leaves are flushed with red before fading to dark green. They are 11 cm (4¼ in) long. This species prefers a semi-shady, moist site and is a good plant for the bog garden. HEIGHT & SPREAD 75×75 cm (2½×2½ ft).

▲ Euphorbia griffithii

'Dixter'♀ has deep orange flowerheads and reaches a height of 45 cm (1½ ft).
'Fireglow' bears bright red flower clusters.
E. longifolia see E. donii
E. longifolia hort. see E. cornigera
E. oblongata Bright yellow flowerheads appear in late spring. The narrow pointed dark green leaves, 6 cm (2½ in) long, have a

cream stripe down the middle. This clump-forming plant has warty seed capsules. It can be cut down in mid summer to stimulate new growth later in the year. This is a good plant for the dry garden. HEIGHT & SPREAD 30×60 cm (1×2 ft).

E. palustris♀ Clusters of flowers, up to 12.5 cm (5 in) across, with bright yellow glands appear from late spring to early summer. The 10 cm (4 in) long leaves may become tinged with orange in autumn. Plants form leafy clumps that will require some support. This plant prefers shady, moist sites but will still grow in dry, sunny places. HEIGHT & SPREAD 1×1 m (3×3 ft).

E. polychroma♀ (syn. E. epithymoides) Clusters of flowers with bright yellow bracts appear in mid spring. The dark green, pointed, oval leaves are up to 6 cm (2½ in) long and in some plants become tinged with shades of red and purple in autumn. This plant forms a dome that requires some support. HEIGHT & SPREAD 60×60 cm (2×2 ft).

The young shoots and leaves of **'Candy'** (syn. 'Purpurea') are tinged with purple during the spring.

E. schillingii♀ The dark green leaves, up to 10 cm (4 in) long, have a distinct white stripe down the centre. The flowers appear during late summer and the bracts retain their yellow colour well into autumn. These plants form a neat clump and prefer a moist soil in full sun. HEIGHT & SPREAD 60×75 cm (2×2½ ft).

E. sikkimensis Bright pink shoots first appear in late winter but do not grow until the temperature rises in spring. The bright green leaves, up to 12.5 cm (5 in) long, retain some of this pink along their edges and midribs. The flowers appear in early summer. This plant forms a dense, spreading clump and prefers moist soil. HEIGHT & SPREAD 1×1 m (3×3 ft).

E. villosa Flowering in early summer, this plant has mid green leaves up to 7.5 cm (3 in) long, which may be tinged bright red and orange in autumn. It forms a large clump that needs some support. HEIGHT & SPREAD 1×1.2 m (3×4 ft).

E. wallichii Yellow flower clusters, up to 10 cm (4 in) across, appear in early summer. The dark green leaves, up to 8 cm (3¼ in) long, have a white stripe down their centres. The stout stems form a clump which may need some support. HEIGHT & SPREAD 60 cm×1 m (2×3 ft).

ANNUALS AND BIENNIALS
E. lathyris (caper spurge, molewort) This biennial blooms in its second year, producing huge flowerheads, up to 1 m (3 ft) across. The bracts and leaves are deep blue-green, mottled with white veins. The leaves are in opposite pairs, held at right angles to the stem. On a sunny day, the capsules may explode, scattering the seeds widely. HEIGHT & SPREAD 60 cm×1.8 m (2×6 ft).

E. marginata This half-hardy annual has variegated leaves and bracts with bright

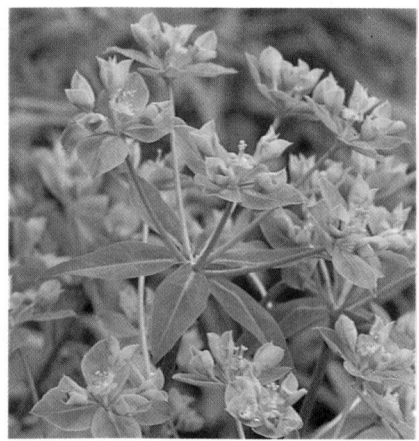

▲ *Euphorbia lathyris*

white edges. The leaves are narrow and pointed and measure up to 7 cm (2¾ in) long. An upright, branching plant. HEIGHT & SPREAD 60 cm × 1.2 m (2 × 4 ft).

GREENHOUSE PLANTS

E. fulgens Bright scarlet flowers, up to 1.5 cm (½ in) across, are borne in clusters at the end of the slender, arching stems, usually in winter. The fresh green, elliptical leaves are up to 10 cm (4 in) long. HEIGHT & SPREAD 1 m × 75 cm (3 × 2½ ft).

E. milii♀ (crown of thorns) This sprawling succulent shrub has very thorny hexagonal stems. The bright green, obovate leaves, about 3 cm (1¼ in) long, sometimes drop off in winter but new ones appear in spring. Clusters of flowers with bright red bracts appear throughout the year. HEIGHT & SPREAD 1 m × 60 cm (3 × 2 ft).

'Splendens' (syn. *E. splendens*) is a larger plant with leaves up to 6 cm (2½ in) long.

E. obesa This ball-shaped succulent bears a circle of small yellow flowers at the top of a dark green, spherical, ridged stem in summer. The stem is often marked with a light green, chequered pattern. Male and female flowers are produced on separate plants. HEIGHT & SPREAD 5 × 5 cm (2 × 2 in).

E. pulcherrima (poinsettia) This popular houseplant has large blood-red, pink or cream bracts, that look like brightly coloured leaves, at the top of upright stems. They surround a cluster of very small yellow flowers and appear when light levels fall to less than 12 hours each day. The true leaves are dark green, oval and sometimes shallowly lobed. Plants are usually discarded when the leaves and bracts have fallen. HEIGHT & SPREAD 75 × 45 cm (2½ × 1½ ft).

E. splendens see *E. milii* 'Splendens'

CULTIVATION Plant outdoor species during spring, in any fertile soil. Unless otherwise specified above, most euphorbias prefer well-drained soil in full sun. *E. myrsinites*, *E. × martinii*, *E. nicaeensis*, *E. rigida* and *E. characias* and its sub species and varieties, all produce biennial stems from a woody crown. This means that plants have 2 types of shoot; the previous season's shoots, on which the flowers are borne, and the current season's growth. Cut back the flowering shoots to ground level in late summer or autumn so that the current season's shoots can flower the following year.

Plant *E. obesa* in a freely draining compost with added grit or sharp sand. Plant the remaining greenhouse species in pots of loam-based compost with added organic matter. Place in a position in direct light but shade from the midday sun during the hottest months. Provide a minimum temperature of 15°C (59°F). Water moderately from spring to autumn and sparingly in winter, ensuring that the compost is dry before each watering. Keep the compost of *E. obesa* completely dry in winter. Mist *E. pulcherrima* frequently during the growing season. Repot *E. fulgens* and *E. milii* regularly in spring.

PROPAGATION Divide the herbaceous species in spring or autumn. *E. polychroma*, *E. palustris*, *E. villosa* and *E. wallichii* have a thick woody stem below the crown; to divide these species, lift the whole crown and cut cleanly in half with a knife, dusting the cut surfaces with a suitable fungicide. Alternatively, sow seed of all species, except most of the greenhouse plants, in spring in a coldframe. Raise *E. obesa* by sowing fresh seed under glass. The evergreen perennials and greenhouse species can be propagated by softwood cuttings taken in late spring or early summer. The young plants should be overwintered in a coldframe.

PESTS AND DISEASES Usually trouble free, although *E. amygdaloides* and *E. × martinii* may suffer from powdery mildew. Plants grown under glass can have problems with mealy bug and whitefly.

Euryops
Compositae

Euryops acraeus

Large, generally yellow or orange, daisy-like flowerheads contrast delightfully with the grey or silvery foliage of these handsome evergreen shrubs. They are bold bushes for formal bedding schemes, or tubs and conservatories where they will flower through much of the summer. They are native to South Africa and only one species, *Euryops acraeus*, is hardy. It makes an unusual small shrub for a sheltered corner of a rock garden. The other species listed require a minimum of 5°C (41°F) and are best grown in a cool greenhouse. Outside, they need a warm sheltered site in free-draining soil. All are vigorous and reach their full size within five years.

RECOMMENDED SPECIES AND VARIETIES

E. acraeus♀ (syn. *E. evansii* hort.) Numerous small, lemon-yellow flowerheads, 2–3 cm (¾–1¼ in) across and borne in a cluster or singly, are produced on this distinguished shrub from late spring to early summer. This species is silvery white, densely branched and hardy to -15°C (5°F). The plant, which sometimes has a suckering habit, has rather leathery and fleshy linear leaves with a 3-toothed tip. HEIGHT & SPREAD 60 × 50 cm (24 × 20 in).

▲ *Euryops acraeus*

E. chrysanthemoides Solitary or clustered yellow flowerheads, each up to 5.5 cm (2¼ in) across, appear on this plant throughout the summer. The deeply lobed, oval grey-green leaves are up to 10 cm (4 in) long and have narrow, tapering to egg-shaped pointed segments. HEIGHT & SPREAD 1.8 × 1.5 m (6 × 5 ft).

E. evansii hort. see *E. acraeus*

E. pectinatus♀ Yellow flowerheads 5–6 cm (2–2½ in) across are carried often singly,

257

easiest species to grow and increases by numerous small bulbils. HEIGHT 30 cm (1 ft).

F. arabica see *F. persica*

F. camschatcensis (black sarana) The large flowers are almost black (occasionally yellowish green), carried in clusters of up to 5, making a striking display against the glossy pale green leaves in early summer. The leaves are up to 5 cm (2 in). This woodland plant thrives in moist conditions, increasing by bulbils. HEIGHT 30 cm (1 ft).

F. imperialis (crown imperial) The regal flowerheads, at the top of tall, stout stems, consist of a ring of large bell-shaped flowers, typically bright orange, crowned by a conspicuous tuft of leaf-like bracts (resembling a pineapple top). Most people find the scent unpleasant. Glossy pale green leaves are carried in numerous whorls on the lower half of the stems. This is the largest of the fritil-

▲ *Fritillaria imperialis* 'Maxima Lutea'

▲ *Fritillaria imperialis* 'Rubra'

laries and grows best in rich, heavy loams. HEIGHT 1.5 m (5 ft).

'Aurora' has bright reddish orange flowers. 'Maxima Lutea'♀ is a robust variety with large lemon-yellow flowers. 'Rubra' has the deepest orange-red flowers.

F. involucrata Large pale green blooms, sometimes covered with a faint to dark red chequering, are borne singly. Slender lanceolate leaves are scattered up the stem and

▼ *Fritillaria meleagris*

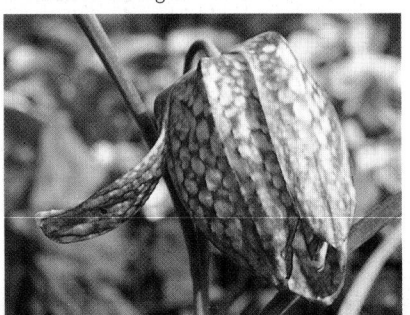

held in a group of 3 above each flower. The plant is slow to increase in the garden. HEIGHT 30 cm (12 in).

F. meleagris♀ (snake's head fritillary) Each slender stem carries 1 (rarely 2) pendent bells, typically pinkish purple, heavily chequered with dark purple, though the flower colour is variable. The narrow lanceolate leaves are grey-green. HEIGHT 25 cm (10 in).

Two pure white varieties are available: ssp. *alba*♀ and 'Aphrodite', the latter often a little larger and with a greenish tinge. These are easy to grow in a border or in grass, in sun or partial shade; they spread by bulb increase and by self-sowing.

F. messanensis The large flowers, generally up to 3 to a stem, are reddish brown with green towards the centre of each petal and a variable amount of darker mottling. The narrow leaves are usually glaucous and scat-

▲ *Fritillaria michailovskyi*

tered up the stem with a cluster of 2-3 above the flowers. The plant increases slowly but is easily raised from seed. Its persistence makes it a good species for the garden. HEIGHT 25 cm (10 in).

F. michailovskyi♀ The striking two-tone flowers are dark purplish brown with deep yellow towards their tips. Short stems carry 1-3 of these blooms and broadly lanceolate, glaucous leaves. This plant needs well-drained soil in full sun. HEIGHT 15 cm (6 in).

F. pallidiflora♀ Flowering later than most (in early summer), this plant produces large, cream-coloured, square-shouldered bells. Each stem bears 1-4 flowers and broad oval bluish green leaves about 4 cm (1½ in) wide. The plant has an unpleasant odour. Since it is a woodland species, give it rich soil in semi-shade. It is easily raised from seed.

▼ *Fritillaria persica*

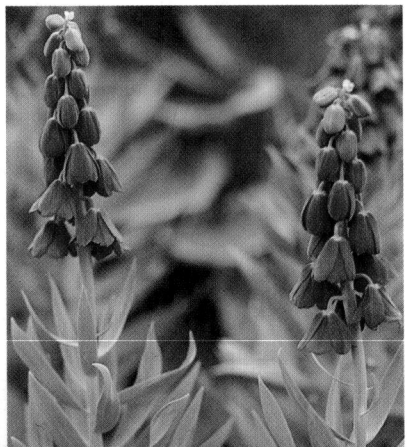

HEIGHT 45 cm (1½ ft).

F. persica (syn. *F. arabica*) Abundant whorls of narrow, highly glaucous leaves anchor tall spires of up to 20 blackish purple, though sometimes greenish, conical flowers. The flowers are 2 cm (¾ in) long, held on long flower stalks. The plant flowers best after a hot summer the previous year. HEIGHT 1 m (3 ft).

'Adiyaman' is a robust variety with many very dark flowers to a stem.

F. pontica The flowers are large, solitary pale green bells. They have no chequering but usually have some reddish brown along the petal edges. Broadly lanceolate bluish leaves are scattered up the stem and held in a group of 3 around the flowers. The plant is best grown from seed, since bulb increase is slow. HEIGHT 30 cm (1 ft).

F. pyrenaica♀ One of the easiest fritillaries to grow, in grass or a border, in full sun or light shade, this plant bears single large bells that vary in colour, but which are green within and mostly dark chocolate-brown outside, usually with some darker mottling. The blue-green leaves are narrow. The plant increases slowly by bulb splitting and by self-sowing. HEIGHT 30 cm (1 ft).

F. uva-vulpis Chocolate-brown, narrow bells with yellow tips are borne 1-3 together on a slender plant with glossy, lanceolate leaves. It is very easy to grow and increases freely from bulbils in well-drained soil in the garden or in an unheated greenhouse. HEIGHT 25 cm (10 in).

F. verticillata Loose spikes of up to 6 creamy, nodding, broad bells appear in early summer. The glossy grey-green tendril-like leaves are carried in whorls up the stem. The plant is easily grown in sun or partial shade, but it takes a year or two to flower freely and increase. HEIGHT 45 cm (1½ ft).

CULTIVATION Plant most species in very well-drained soil in an open sunny spot. Alternatively, grow in well-drained gritty compost in pots or a bulb frame. *F. persica* and *F. michailovskyi* benefit from being kept almost dry from the time the leaves die down until early autumn and in wet areas are best grown in pots. Grow the woodland species in partial shade in moist soil.

PROPAGATION Some species increase rapidly by forming small bulbils around the parent bulb. These can be left on the plants or removed and treated like young bulbs when lifting and dividing in autumn.

Seed is the best method of propagation, producing flowering plants in 3-5 years. Sow seed in autumn and keep the pots cold until germination in spring, or occasionally the following spring. Keep the seedlings well watered (except when dormant) for 2 years, and then separate and repot annually until they reach adult size and are large enough to plant in permanent positions.

PESTS AND DISEASES Slugs may be a problem outdoors and grey mould may affect plants under glass.

Fuchsia

Ladies' eardrops
Onagraceae

———

Abundant, jewel-like blooms hang
from the branches of these deciduous
shrubs for many months. These
exquisite flowers have justly earned
fuchsias a place among the most
popular plants for both
garden and greenhouse

Hanging flowers, often in shades of the
most vivid pink and purple, grace these
free-flowering deciduous shrubs from early
summer to mid autumn, when grown
outdoors. This long flowering period
and the ease of care and great versatility of fuchsias have long made
them favourites.

Flower colour ranges from the gaudy to
pure white, with most possible shades and
combinations in between. The pendulous blooms are formed by a tube
that opens out into four spreading
waxy sepals. Emerging from the sepals
are four overlapping petals, forming a bell,
that are often a contrasting colour to the
sepals. Flowers can be single, double, or semidouble. All have prominent stamens, usually
eight, very rarely four, which can also be
highly coloured, often complementing the
most flamboyant part of the flower. If
grown in a conservatory or greenhouse,
fuchsias can flower for eight months of the
year. Usually inconspicuous, small purple
berries are produced from mid summer
onwards.

Fuchsias differ widely in hardiness and

1 *F.* Nellie Nuttal
2 *F. × bacillaris*
3 *F. procumbens*
4 *F.* Madam
  Cornelissen
5 *F.* Heidi Ann
6 *F.* Tennessee Waltz
7 *F.* Garden News
8 *F.* Mary
9 *F.* Coralle
10 *F.* Abb Farges
11 *F.* Billy Green
12 *F.* Mrs Popple
13 *F.* Margaret Brown

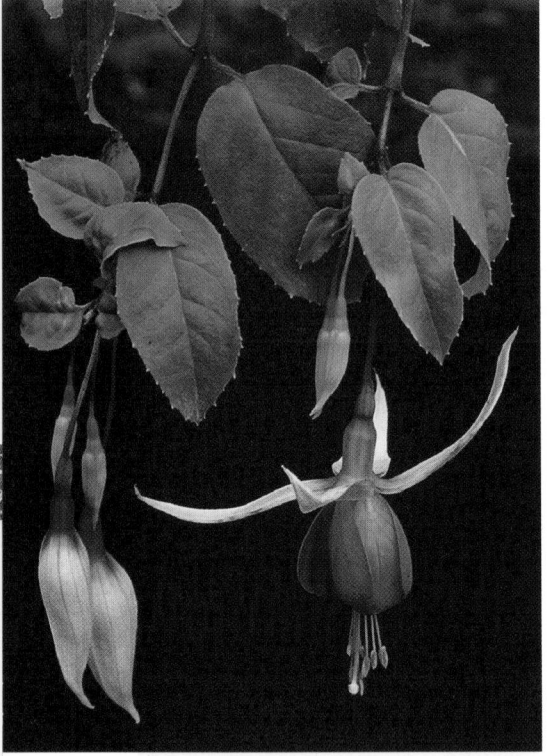

▲ *Fuchsia* 'Cascade'

▼ *Fuchsia* 'Mantilla'

▲ *Fuchsia* 'Red Spider'

▲ *Fuchsia* 'Trumpeter'

flowered unless otherwise indicated. The mid green leaves are oval, pointed and up to 7 cm (2¾ in) long. They reach a height of 10-20 cm (4-8 in) and a spread of 30-40 cm (12-16 in).

'Cascade' is very free-flowering with long flowers. The white sepals are flushed pink and backward-curving; the petals are a rich crimson. 'Florabelle' has small but abundant red and purple semidouble flowers and comes true from seed. 'Golden Marinka'♀ has red sepals, deep red petals and variegated green and gold foliage, streaked with red.

'Mantilla' see Triphylla hybrids below. 'Pink Galore' is very free-flowering and has double blooms with pink sepals and pale rose-pink petals. 'Pink Marshmallow' is easy to grow with very large double flowers. The white sepals are pinkish underneath with a green hue to the tips; the white petals have a hint of light pink and pale pink veins. 'Red Spider' has freely produced long flowers with intense crimson sepals and red petals. 'Trumpeter' see Triphylla hybrids below.

Triphylla hybrids

The triphyllas differ from other hybrid varieties in that the flowers have very short sepals and very long tubes, formed by the bottom of the petals fusing, and the flowers are borne in clusters rather than singly. They are sometimes called clustered fuchsias. Those plants included here have single-colour flowers. The pointed, oval leaves are up to 7 cm (2¾ in) long and arise from the stems in threes. There are upright bushy varieties that reach 30-60 cm (1-2 ft) in height and 30-45 cm (1-1½ ft) in spread. There are also trailing varieties that reach 10-20 cm (4-8 in) tall with a spread of 30-40 cm (12-16 in).

'Billy Green'♀ is very free-flowering with deep pink flowers, olive-green leaves and a vigorous upright habit. 'Coralle'♀ has abundant orange flowers, blue-green leaves and is for use only as a bush plant. 'Gartenmeister Bonstedt'♀ is free-flowering with deep orange flowers, bronze-red leaves and an upright habit. 'Mantilla' has crimson flowers with a purple hue pro-

duced very freely, bronze-green narrow leaves and a vigorous, cascading habit. 'Mary'♀ has scarlet flowers, bronze-purple narrow leaves and an upright habit. 'Thalia'♀ bears orange-red flowers, red to bronze leaves. It has a vigorous, upright habit and is very free-flowering. This is the most widely grown Triphylla hybrid. 'Trumpeter' has freely borne candyfloss-pink flowers, blue-green leaves and a bushy, trailing habit.

Encliandra hybrids

This group is the least often seen, and plants can be purchased only from specialist fuchsia nurseries. They have abundant, very small flowers and a fern-like appearance. Most have a spreading habit which is well adapted to their use in hanging baskets and near the edge of tubs and patio containers.

'Fuksie Foetsie', which has pale pink flowers, is the most widely available.

CULTIVATION

HARDY FUCHSIAS

Plant outdoors from mid spring onwards in any soil, choosing a site in full sun or partial shade. Water new plants to establish them. Apply a protective mulch in autumn around the base of each plant, using bark chips, bracken or straw. Cut all top growth back in autumn to about 30 cm (1 ft) above the ground. This helps to prevent strong winds rocking the roots in wet soil during winter and causing damage. Apply a general-purpose fertiliser in late winter. In spring, when shoot buds appear, cut each branch back hard, leaving 1 or 2 buds to grow from the base of the branch.

▲ *Fuchsia* 'Gartenmeister Bonstedt'

▲ *Fuchsia* 'Mary'

▲ *Fuchsia* 'Coachman'

▲ *Fuchsia* 'Garden News'

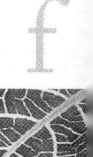

HALF-HARDY FUCHSIAS

If growing as half-hardy fuchsias outdoors as summer bedding, plant them out in any soil after all risk of hard late frosts has passed. Choose a position in full sun or partial shade. Water during dry weather. Apply a potash-rich fertiliser in mid summer and water this in thoroughly.

Fuchsias can also be grown outdoors in pots or hanging baskets containing multi-purpose compost. Containers should be at least 30 cm (1 ft) in diameter. Water pot-grown plants frequently and give a weekly potash-rich liquid feed.

Fork up plants from their beds or remove them from their containers in autumn and move to a cool, dry frost-free environment. This can be either a greenhouse or conservatory with enough heating for frost protection, or a shed or garage. Water just often enough to prevent the roots drying out. In late winter or early spring, restart the plants into growth by watering them and putting them into a greenhouse with a minimum temperature of 5°C (41°F), or placing them on a sunny windowsill. Once the growth of new shoots begins, cut back the previous season's leafless woody shoots to within 1 or 2 buds.

If growing fuchsias indoors, plant at anytime and maintain a minimum temperature of 7°C (45°F) to ensure that plants retain their foliage. In spring and summer, provide shade to protect plants from the full force of the sun, water freely and give regular liquid food. Remove dying flowers to promote the production of more blooms and to improve the plants' appearance. Water much less frequently once growth slows or ceases after summer, but never let the compost dry out.

Avoid a dry atmosphere, which can cause dropping flower buds and leaf-fall. Fuchsias appreciate higher humidity than is normally found in living rooms or even kitchens. To create a more humid microclimate, grow them among plenty of other plants, stand pots on a tray of gravel that is kept permanently wet, plunge the pots in moist peat in a windowsill plant trough, or syringe with a fine spray. *F.* 'Golden Marinka' needs good light conditions.

PROPAGATION Take softwood cuttings any time from late winter to mid autumn. Cuttings taken in late spring or summer are very easily rooted in an unheated greenhouse or on a sunny windowsill. Bottom heat may be needed to ensure rooting at other times.

Maintain high humidity round the cuttings until roots begin to form. Use a propagator, or insert 3 very short lengths of cane round the rim of the pots in which the cuttings are to be rooted and put a polythene bag over the top.

PESTS AND DISEASES Fuchsias are vulnerable to red spider mite and greenfly, rust and bud-drop, although the latter are usually short-lived. Whitefly and grey mould are problems in a greenhouse.

Fuchsia, Australian see *Correa*
Fuchsia, Cape see *Phygelius capensis*
Furze see *Ulex europaeus*

STANDARD FUCHSIAS

A standard fuchsia makes an impressive individual specimen or centrepiece in a large container. It is also traditionally used as a 'dot' plant in large beds. With a single woody stem anything up to 1.2 m (4 ft) tall, the naturally pendent flowers are raised and so are seen to their best advantage.

They are expensive, but gardeners with a greenhouse in which a minimum winter temperature of 10°C (50°F) can be maintained, can produce their own. They are usually saved over winter.

Erect bushy fuchsias are used to make standards. The following varieties are particularly good: *F.* 'Checkerboard', *F.* 'Coachman', *F.* 'Garden News', *F.* 'Royal Velvet', *F.* 'Snowcap', *F.* 'Swingtime' and *F.* 'Tennessee Waltz'.

The process of forming a standard is best carried out entirely in a greenhouse, and takes around a year before the well-grown young standard is ready for planting out in the garden or large container. It will require a final position reasonably sheltered from wind.

Take cuttings in late spring or early summer. The taller the stem required, the earlier cuttings should be taken. Insert in a mixture of half sand, half peat or peat-based compost and water thoroughly. Maintain high humidity until the roots form, either by placing the cuttings in a propagator or by putting 3 short canes round the rim of the pot in which the cuttings are to be rooted and placing a polythene bag over them.

Once rooted, after about 3 weeks, put each cutting into a 9 cm (3½ in) pot and insert a thin cane, 50 cm (20 in) long. Tie the shoot to the cane but do not pinch out the growing point. The ties should be about 8 cm (3¼ in) apart.

When the cutting reaches the top of the cane, pot on into a 13 cm (5 in) pot, and insert a cane at least 1.2 m (4 ft) tall. Canes can be longer but they must be at least 30 cm (1 ft) taller than the intended height of the stem. Continue to support the stem by tying it to the new cane. Remove any sideshoots that develop, but let the leaves remain.

When the stem reaches the height required, pinch out the growing point. Vigorous sideshoots usually develop from the 3 uppermost leaf joints. Remove any sideshoots which develop below these. Pinch out the growing point of each of the retained sideshoots just beyond their second pair of leaves.

As the resulting shoots grow, pinch these out too, just beyond the third pair of leaves. Continue in this manner until a good round head is achieved.

Gaillardia
Blanket flower
Compositae

▲ *Gaillardia 'Kobold'*

Gaillardia 'Dazzler'

Fiery red or yellow daisies bring colour to the garden through summer and into early autumn. Large flowers, about 8-12.5 cm (3¼-5 in) wide, and straight stems make these excellent plants for cutting. They are most commonly available in hybrid form, as hardy, short-lived herbaceous perennials, living three to five years if the soil is not too damp and poorly drained. Annuals are also available. Native to N and S America.

RECOMMENDED SPECIES AND VARIETIES
G. x grandiflora Yellow petals (properly called ray florets) encircle a central red disc (made up of disc florets). The soft, hairy, grey-green leaves are lance-shaped, alternate and up to 15 cm (6 in) long. The whole plant is sticky and aromatic. HEIGHT & SPREAD 60-90×45 cm (2-3×1½ ft).

'Burgunder' has deep wine-red petals with a dark red centre. **'Dazzler'**♀ has orange-red petals with yellow tips. An annual, it reaches 60 cm (2 ft) tall. **'Kobold'**, with red and gold petals and a red centre, is a dwarf, growing only 25 cm (10 in) high.

▼ *Gaillardia 'Dazzler'*

CULTIVATION Plants grow best in a sunny position, in light, well-drained soil. Plant out in spring. Taller plants need twiggy supports. Deadhead fading flowers.

PROPAGATION Sow seeds of perennial species in a row in open ground in spring, then transfer them to their final position in early autumn or the following spring. Divide named cultivars in spring. Take root cuttings in winter and grow on in a coldframe before planting in spring. For annuals, sow seed either in the flowering site in late spring, or under glass in winter at 16°C (61°F). Prick out in boxes, harden off and plant out in late spring.

PESTS AND DISEASES Downy mildew may attack the underside of leaves, causing them to turn yellow.

Galanthus
Snowdrop
Amaryllidaceae

Galanthus nivalis

The common snowdrop, *Galanthus nivalis*, is one of the most widely grown winter-flowering bulbs and it naturalises readily in grass. Most snowdrops flower early in the year, though there are some that flower in autumn. With few exceptions they are very hardy bulbs, being native throughout Europe and into Turkey and Iran.

All snowdrops have hanging flowers, about 6-20 mm (¼-¾ in) long at maturity, with six unequal petals. The longer, outer petals are usually plain white, whereas the shorter, inner ones form a cup with each petal carrying distinctive green markings. The plants normally have two narrow basal leaves, usually 2 cm (¾ in) wide and 15-30 cm (6-12 in) long. The leaves are short at flowering time, extending considerably afterwards.

RECOMMENDED SPECIES AND VARIETIES
G. allenii Almond-scented flowers appear in mid winter and carry a single green mark on each inner petal. The matt green leaves are relatively broad, up to 2.5 cm (1 in) wide. HEIGHT 12 cm (4¾ in).
G. 'Arnott's Seedling' see *G.* 'S. Arnott'

G. 'Atkinsii'♀ A vigorous plant that flowers in mid winter, with flowers up to 4 cm (1½ in) long. One outer petal is sometimes deformed so that it is twisted and longer than the others. Inner petals each carry a single green mark. The leaves have a silver central stripe. HEIGHT 25 cm (10 in).
G. caucasicus♀ The rounded flowers carry a single green mark on each inner petal. This variable species can bloom in late autumn or winter. It has 2.5 cm (1 in) wide grey leaves. HEIGHT 15 cm (6 in).

▲ *Galanthus caucasicus*

G. elwesii♀ The very variable flowers, borne in mid to late winter, have an elongated appearance, to 3 cm (1¼ in), and display 2 green marks on the inner petals. The plant has broad, 3 cm (1¼ in) wide, grey-green leaves, up to 30 cm (12 in) long. It grows best in a dry, limy soil and can be difficult to establish in some gardens. HEIGHT 10-20 cm (4-8 in).
G. gracilis (syn. *G. graecus*) A delicate-looking snowdrop with grey-green leaves, 6 mm (¼ in) wide and 5-15 cm (2-6 in) long, in some forms spirally twisted. The flowers appear in late winter with each inner petal carrying a pair of green marks. It prefers a dry situation. HEIGHT 10 cm (4 in).
G. ikariae ssp. **ikariae**♀ The 2.5 cm (1 in) long, claw-shaped flowers carry a single large green mark on each inner petal. HEIGHT Variable up to 15 cm (6 in).

The **Latifolius Group** has broad green

▼ *Galanthus ikariae ssp. ikariae*

leaves and the flowers have a V-shaped mark on each inner petal.

G. 'Lady Beatrix Stanley' Double flowers are borne by this snowdrop early in the year. HEIGHT 12 cm (4¾ in).

G. 'Magnet'♀ The large flowers, 3 cm (1¼ in) long, of this vigorous variety appear to float on the exceptionally long flower stalks. HEIGHT 23 cm (9 in).

G. 'Merlin' The distinctive flowers have inner petals that are almost entirely green. HEIGHT 20 cm (8 in).

G. *nivalis*♀ (common snowdrop) The inner petals of the 1.5-2.5 cm (½-1 in) long flowers each have a single green mark. Grey-green leaves are up to 1 cm (⅜ in) wide and up to 20 cm (8 in) long. The plant can be naturalised in light grass. HEIGHT Variable, from 7.5-20 cm (3-8 in).

▲ *Galanthus nivalis*

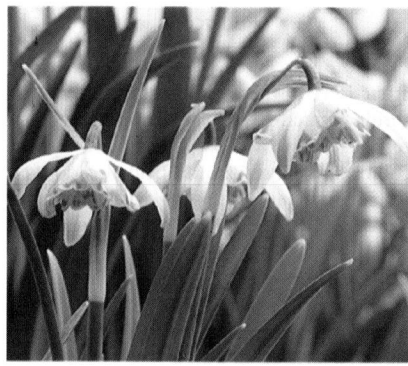

▲ *Galanthus nivalis* 'Pusey Green Tip'

'Flore Pleno'♀ is a vigorous plant with fully double flowers. **'Lady Elphinstone'** has double flowers which in some soils have yellow rather than green markings. **'Pusey Green Tip'** is a double form with green marks on the tips of the outer petals rather than the inner ones. **'Sandersii'** (syn. 'Lutescens') is slow to increase and has small flowers with yellow ovaries and inner markings. **'Scharlockii'** is a delicate plant with small flowers and light green marks on the outer petals. **'Viridapicis'** is a robust snowdrop with bold green marks on the outer petals.

G. 'Ophelia' The double flowers of this tall, imposing snowdrop are up to 3 cm (1¼ in) long. The inner petals each carry a single green mark. HEIGHT 20 cm (8 in).

G. *plicatus*♀' The flowers are 1.5-3 cm (½-1¼ in) long and each inner petal has a single green mark. Leaves are dull green with a grey-green central stripe and margins folded back. The species seeds freely in some gardens. HEIGHT 20 cm (8 in).

ssp. *byzantinus*♀ has 2 green markings on each inner petal; **'Warham'** has broad leaves and large flowers bearing a large U-shaped green mark on each inner petal.

G. *reginae-olgae* An autumn-flowering species very similar to *G. nivalis* but with a silvery central stripe on its narrow leaves. The leaves may be absent or only just showing when the plant is flowering. It requires a dry, sunny position. HEIGHT 10 cm (4 in).

G. 'S. Arnott'♀ (syn. 'Sam Arnott', 'Arnott's Seedling') This robust variety grows well and multiplies rapidly. It has large, well rounded, almond-scented flowers in late winter and 3 cm (1¼ in) wide leaves. HEIGHT 23 cm (9 in).

G. 'Straffan' Waxy flowers are borne in late winter, often 2 from one bulb. HEIGHT 18 cm (7 in).

CULTIVATION Apart from the exceptions given under individual entries, snowdrops are easily grown in a well-drained, humus-rich soil where there is plenty of moisture available when they are growing. They prefer dappled shade during summer when dormant and can be grown under deciduous trees and shrubs. Plant in small groups.

PROPAGATION Plant the bulbs 10 cm (4 in) deep in early autumn if freshly dug bulbs are available, or after flowering. Divide and replant clumps after flowering, making sure that the bulbs do not dry out. Water well after transplanting.

To increase cultivars remove offsets after flowering and replant immediately. Some species increase naturally by seeding if conditions suit them.

PESTS AND DISEASES Stem eelworm, large narcissus fly, grey mould and various rots attack snowdrops.

Galax
Wandflower
Diapensiaceae

The only species in the genus is a hardy, slowly spreading, evergreen perennial useful for year-round ground cover in shady situations and lime-free soil. Native to mountain woods of eastern N America.

Galax urceolata (syn. *G. aphylla*) Erect, wiry stems bear slender spikes, up to 25 cm (10 in) tall, carrying many tiny creamy white flowers from late spring to early summer above a dense mat of foliage. The long-stalked, shiny, rounded to heart-shaped leaves are up to 12.5 cm (5 in) wide. They are tinted with bronze or purple in winter. The plant withstands considerable frosts without damage to its foliage. HEIGHT & SPREAD 30-60 cm × 1 m (1-2 × 3 ft).

CULTIVATION Plant in a shaded or partially shaded position in a cool, humus-rich, acid or neutral soil.

PROPAGATION Divide in spring. Sow seed in spring, although it is rarely available.

PESTS AND DISEASES Usually trouble free.

Galega
Goat's rue, French lilac
Leguminosae

Graceful spikes of small pea-shaped flowers adorn this tall, hardy herbaceous perennial in summer. Position at the back of a large border, or in a wild or herb garden. Plants are floppy, and can be grown through open shrubs rather than being staked. White, blue or violet flowers are carried in loose spikes about 15 cm (6 in) long on erect stems, each flower being up to 1.5 cm (½ in) across. The plentiful foliage is made up of soft green leaves, on short stalks, divided into four to eight pairs of oppositely arranged, oval to oblong leaflets, each leaflet about 5 cm (2 in) long and 1.5 cm (½ in) wide. Native to S Europe, Asia Minor and E Africa.

RECOMMENDED SPECIES AND VARIETIES
G. × *hartlandii* 'Alba'♀ Pure white flowers are borne in summer on this erect, clump-forming plant with dark green divided leaves. HEIGHT & SPREAD 1.5 × 1 m (5 × 3 ft).

G. *officinalis* (syn. *G. bicolor*) Flowers vary in colour from white to purple, occasionally blue, and appear in mid and late summer. HEIGHT & SPREAD 1.5 × 1 m (5 × 3 ft).

The flowers of **'Alba'** are pure white.

▼ *Galega* × *hartlandii* 'Alba'

▼ *Galega officinalis*

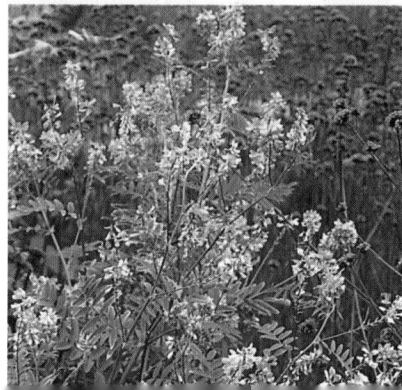

pink flowers. **'Variegatum'** produces pink flowers and makes a splendid foliage plant with grey-green leaves that have strong cream markings.

G. procurrens Subdued purple flowers with a dark eye are carried from mid summer to autumn. The long, prostrate, flowering stems root at the nodes to form new plants which repeat the process. It can be diverted by training it up or through small shrubs. The toothed leaves have 5 large divisions. Native to the Himalayas. HEIGHT & SPREAD 15 cm×1 m (6×36 in).

G. × riversleaianum 'Russell Prichard'♀ has neat mats of small, greyish green leaves with bright rosy magenta flowers from mid summer onwards. HEIGHT & SPREAD 23×45 cm (9×18 in).

'Mavis Simpson' also makes neat mats with soft pink flowers, flecked with white.

G. 'Salome' A trailing plant whose rounded flowers in summer are pale violet-purple with dark centres and veining. Young leaves are blotched with yellow. HEIGHT & SPREAD 30 cm×1 m (12×36 in).

G. wallichianum Mauve-blue, star-shaped flowers, borne from late summer into autumn, have very striking black stamens, stigma and veining. The leaves are mottled. Native to the Himalayas. HEIGHT & SPREAD 25 cm×1 m (10×36 in).

'Buxton's Variety'♀ (syn. 'Buxton's Blue') The round, cupped flowers of clear blue have a white zone at the centre and are often at their best at the end of the season when the leaves take on autumn colour. It is best grown in cool semi-shade.

LOW-GROWING PLANTS WITH COMPACT GROWTH UP TO 30 CM (1 FT)

G. × cantabrigiense 'Cambridge' Small, bright pink flowers bloom in abundance from late spring into summer on this compact, mat-forming plant. The small, neat, aromatic leaves are usually evergreen. HEIGHT & SPREAD 25×30 cm (10×12 in).

The flowers of **'Biokovo'** are white tinged with pink.

G. cinereum Round, pale pink flowers with darker veins bloom from late spring to early summer above dainty tufts of grey-green, deeply divided leaves. Grows best in well-drained soil in sun. HEIGHT & SPREAD 15×23 cm (6×9 in).

'Ballerina'♀ The pale purplish pink flowers of this small alpine geranium have dark brown centres and feathered veins and bloom from early to late summer. Small,

▼ *Geranium cinereum 'Ballerina'*

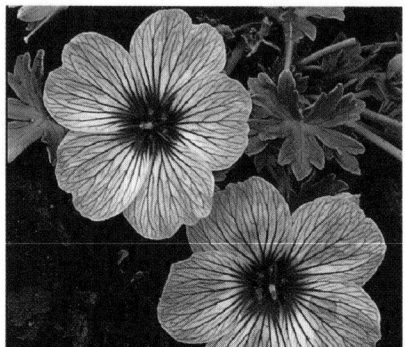

grey-green leaves form mats. The small but showy rockery plant var. *subcaulescens*♀ carries crimson-magenta flowers with a black eye in early summer. The leaves are scalloped and grey-green. **'Splendens'**♀ has round, bright magenta-pink flowers with a small white area at the base of the petals and a dark centre.

G. dalmaticum♀ An alpine species best grown in a raised or scree bed that has clear rose-pink flowers all summer. The small, shiny green, red-edged leaves take on autumn colour before dying back. HEIGHT & SPREAD 10×25 cm (4×10 in).

'Album' has pure white flowers.

G. farreri♀ A dwarf alpine plant with pale pink flowers borne in late spring to early summer and small, delicately cut leaves. Native to W China. HEIGHT & SPREAD 12.5×10 cm (5×4 in).

G. malviflorum Eye-catching flowers in mid to late spring are clear violet-blue with strongly marked veins. The plant dies back after flowering. Finely cut leaves appear in autumn, persisting through the winter. A hot dry site is essential for a good show of flowers. Native to Spain and N Africa. HEIGHT & SPREAD 30×25 cm (12×10 in).

G. nodosum Small, light purplish pink flowers bloom through summer to autumn. The leaves are shiny green. It is a good shade plant. Native to central Europe. HEIGHT & SPREAD 30×40 cm (12×16 in).

G. pylzowianum Deep pink flowers bloom in early summer among plain green finely cut leaves which last through winter. Too invasive for the rockery, it is best in poor soil in paving or beside a path. Native to China. HEIGHT & SPREAD 10×20 cm (4×8 in).

G. renardii♀ A low, clump-forming alpine with rounded, grey-green leaves, scalloped in appearance with a soft texture. Off-white flowers with violet veins bloom in mid summer. Best grown in well-drained soil in a sunny spot. Native to the Caucasus. HEIGHT & SPREAD 30×25 cm (12×10 in).

Geranium sanguineum

G. sanguineum (bloody cranesbill) Round, bright purple flowers bloom in late spring to late summer on this low-growing alpine. Deeply divided leaves form solid mats of dark green, which colour well in autumn. HEIGHT & SPREAD 25×40 cm (10×16 in).

▼ *Geranium renardii*

▲ *Geranium sanguineum*

'Album'♀ has pure white, star-shaped flowers. The large, bright magenta-pink flowers of **'Cedric Morris'** are crumpled-looking. **'Glenluce'** has large, soft pink flowers. **'Shepherd's Warning'**♀ is a good wall plant with clear shocking-pink flowers. The flowers of var. *striatum*♀ (syn. var. *lancastriense*) are palest pink with crimson centres and veining.

Geranium sanguineum 'Glenluce' ▼
▼ *Geranium sanguineum* 'Album'

▲ *Geranium sanguineum* var. *striatum*
Geranium sessiliflorum ssp.
novae-zelandiae 'Nigricans' ▲

G. sessiliflorum ssp. *novae-zelandiae* **'Nigricans'** A very small, mat-forming plant which requires careful placing to show off the miniature clumps of small, very dark brown to bottle-green leaves with minute white flowers almost obscured among them. The plant is native to New Zealand.

▼ *Geranium sanguineum* 'Shepherd's Warning'

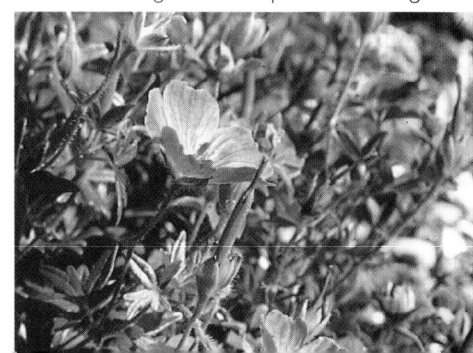

HEIGHT & SPREAD 10×12.5 cm (4×5 in).
'Porter's Pass' has dark red leaves.

G. traversii var. *elegans* Small, mid to pale pink flowers with paler edges are borne in early summer to early autumn above rounded greyish green leaves. Native to the Chatham Islands, this alpine-type plant is not entirely hardy in Britain. It does best in sun in well-drained soil. HEIGHT & SPREAD 15–20×20 cm (6–8×8 in).

CULTIVATION Geraniums adapt to any type of soil, even chalk. Larger varieties tolerate shade, and often prefer it. True alpines or alpine types require a sunny, well-drained position. Cut back larger, clump-forming plants after flowering, to prevent overseeding and to produce new growth.

PROPAGATION Division is easy with most of the medium-sized, clump-forming plants, usually at the end of summer, but also in spring. Most species come true from seed, but not hybrids and named cultivars, which should be propagated by division. Species which form thick roots, such as *G. pratense* and *G. sanguineum,* can be propagated by root division and root cuttings.

Take softwood cuttings of new growth early in the year for alpines such as *G. cinereum* which make plants too small for easy division. Root cuttings may also be taken in late autumn.

PESTS AND DISEASES Rabbits may feast on young leaves. Vine weevil may attack plants with thick rootstocks. *G. pratense* is susceptible to mildew in hot dry weather.

Geranium see also *Pelargonium*

Gerbera
Barbeton daisy
Compositae

Valued for their brightly coloured daisy-like flowers, these half-hardy and tender perennials are mostly grown indoors in Britain, although they may survive outdoors in mild, sheltered areas of the south and west.

Flowers are available in a wide range of colours, including yellow, orange, cream, pink, crimson and purple. The lance-shaped, hairy, mid green leaves are prominently lobed and arranged in rosettes. They will flower for much of the year, if well cared for, and keep some leaves all year round. Gerberas make excellent, long-lasting cut flowers.

RECOMMENDED SPECIES
G. jamesonii Numerous solitary yellow, orange or bright red flowers, 7.5–13 cm (3–5 in) across, are borne from late spring to late summer. Single and double-flowered hybrids and varieties are available. The plant forms an upright clump with leaves, generally evergreen, up to 40 cm (16 in) long. Native to South Africa. HEIGHT & SPREAD 60×45 cm (24×18 in).

▲ *Gerbera jamesonii*

CULTIVATION Grow in deep pots or a permanent position in a border, in a bright, well-lit, frost-free greenhouse or conservatory. Plant in spring, preferably in a richly organic, but free-draining soil. It can be up to 2 years before seed-raised specimens flower freely, although occasional blossoms appear in the first year. Feed plants liberally with a liquid houseplant fertiliser when they are in flower. Water well in spring and summer, sparingly in autumn and winter. Remove faded flowerheads and leaves.

Outdoors, grow in ordinary, well-drained garden soil, in a sunny, sheltered position at the foot of a wall. Cut faded flower stems down to ground level.

PROPAGATION Sow seed under glasss or divide established plants into single crowns in early spring.

PESTS AND DISEASES Red spider mites, mealy bugs and vine weevils may all be troublesome.

Germander see *Teucrium*

Geum
Avens
Rosaceae

Geum chiloense 'Dolly North'

Vibrant globular or cup-shaped blooms in shades of white, yellow, red and orange add impact to the front of a herbaceous border or a large rock garden. The flowers are produced throughout summer, and can be single, semidouble or double. These hardy evergreen or deciduous perennials are best-

▼ *Geum chiloense 'Fire Opal'*

suited to soil that is moist but well-drained.
RECOMMENDED SPECIES AND VARIETIES
G. chiloense Bright, single scarlet flowers, up to 5 cm (2 in) across, are carried in erect, laxly branched clusters in summer. This clump-forming plant has rather woolly, 3-lobed leaves. The stem leaves are smaller and more deeply cut or toothed than the basal ones. Native to Chile. HEIGHT & SPREAD 80×50 cm (32×20 in).

'Dolly North' grows to 50 cm (20 in) tall and bears single yellow flowers flushed orange. 'Fire Opal'♀ grows to 75 cm (30 in) tall and has semidouble orange flowers, flushed scarlet, on purple stems. 'Georgenberg' is a compact plant, 25 cm

▲ *Geum chiloense 'Mrs J. Bradshaw'*

(10 in) tall, with single orange flowers flushed gold. 'Lady Stratheden'♀ grows to 60 cm (24 in) tall and carries bright yellow semidouble flowers with green stamens. 'Mrs J. Bradshaw'♀ is 60 cm (24 in) tall and has bright brick-red flowers that are semi-double and rounded. 'Mrs J. Bradshaw Improved' has flowers twice the size.

G. coccineum Bright red single flowers, up to 4 cm (1½ in) across, are borne in erect, lax clusters in summer and early autumn. The

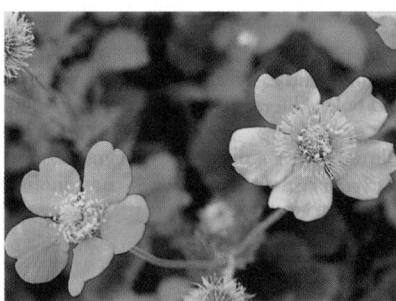

▲ *Geum coccineum 'Borisii'*

deep green, kidney-shaped basal leaves have 5–7 toothed segments and are rather hairy. Native to the Balkans. HEIGHT & SPREAD 45×40 cm (18×16 in).

'Borisii', up to 30 cm (12 in) tall, is compact and has single orange-red flowers with prominent yellow stamens. 'Coppertone' is an early-flowering plant that grows up to 25 cm (10 in) tall and bears single apricot

Haberlea
Gesneriaceae

Haberlea rhodopensis

This shade-loving, hardy herbaceous rock plant can bring interest to cool corners of a rock garden or to north-facing crevices but will also thrive in troughs. Open clusters of funnel-shaped, two-lipped flowers, ranging from violet-blue to white, appear on short stems above foliage rosettes in late spring and summer. The dust-like seeds are held in narrow seed capsules. There is one species of this drought-resistant genus which is native to the Balkans.

Haberlea rhodopensis♀ Violet-blue flowers, up to 2.5 cm (1 in) long, have white throats. The scallop-edged, grey-green leaves are up to 8 cm (3¼ in) long and hairy on both surfaces. HEIGHT & SPREAD 12×40 cm (4¾×16 in).

Smooth hairless leaves distinguish var. *ferdinandi-coburgii* (syn. *H. ferdinandi-coburgii*) which has larger flowers and leaves than the species.

▼ *Haberlea rhodopensis* 'Virginalis'

'Virginalis' bears white flowers with a yellowish throat.

CULTIVATION Plant in early autumn or early spring in fertile, moist but well-drained soil enriched with leaf-mould on a site where rain will not fill the leaf rosettes. Transplant with care once the plant is established.

PROPAGATION Take leaf cuttings in summer or divide mature plants in spring or immediately after flowering. Pot in moist, humus-rich compost and place in a shady coldframe until established. Sow seed in a propagating frame immediately it is ripe or in autumn. Prick out the seedlings when large enough to handle and keep in a humid environment for about a year, then move them to a shaded cool greenhouse or frame. It takes 3-4 years to flower from seed.

PESTS AND DISEASES Slugs may attack young plants and aphids occasionally harm developing flowers.

Hackberry see *Celtis occidentalis*

Hacquetia
Umbelliferae

Thriving in moist shady borders or shaded parts of a rock garden, this low-growing woodland plant looks especially good set against dark-leaved plants. It is easy to grow and, once established, will often self-seed around the garden. Although hacquetia tolerates sun, it dislikes dry, light soils and hot, dry conditions. This hardy herbaceous perennial, native to central Europe, has just one species.

▲ *Hacquetia epipactis*

Hacquetia epipactis♀ (syn. *Dondia epipactis*) Small clusters, 1 cm (⅜ in) across, of tiny yellow flowers appear from early to late spring, surrounded by conspicuous ruffs of brighter, glossy, leaf-like bracts. These gradually change colour over the months, turning from yellow to apple green. The flowers are followed by clumps of bright green, 3-lobed leaves. HEIGHT & SPREAD 6×20 cm (2½×8 in).

CULTIVATION Plant in early spring or autumn in any moisture-retentive soil in dappled or partial shade.

PROPAGATION Sow seed in pots during autumn or winter and overwinter outdoors or in a coldframe. Alternatively, divide the plants after flowering.

PESTS AND DISEASES Usually trouble free.

Haemanthus
Amaryllidaceae

Exotic flowerheads in white, pink or red grace these tender evergreen or deciduous bulbous plants in early summer and early winter. The flowerheads have a conspicuous central boss of stamens surrounded by petal-like bracts. Clusters of white oval berries follow.

Native to S Africa, the plants should be grown in a heated greenhouse or conservatory or, in the case of *Haemanthus coccineus*, as a houseplant.

RECOMMENDED SPECIES AND VARIETIES
H. albiflos Yellow-tipped white stamens and white bracts give the flowerhead the appearance of a shaving brush. The head, up to 3 cm (1¼ in) wide, is carried on a leafless stem above leathery, evergreen leaves, which are oblong or elliptical, up to 40 cm (16 in) long. HEIGHT 35 cm (14 in).

▲ *Haemanthus coccineus*

H. coccineus (blood lily) Red stamens with yellow tips are packed into 6 cm (2½ in) wide flowerheads, enclosed by red bracts. The robust green stems are spotted red. Two or three strap-shaped leaves, up to 60 cm (2 ft) long, appear after flowering. HEIGHT 35 cm (14 in).

CULTIVATION Plant one to a pot in a gritty, humus-rich, well-drained compost in spring. Use a pot twice as wide as the bulb and keep the top of the bulb level with, or just above, the soil surface. Stand in a well-lit position with a minimum temperature of 10°C (50°F). Water copiously and feed regularly during the growing season but keep them dry at other times.

PROPAGATION Separate and replant bulbs in late spring. Sow seed immediately it ripens.

PESTS AND DISEASES Mealy bug may cause problems.

Hakonechloa see GRASSES p. 301

Halesia

Styracaceae

Halesia monticola

In late spring, the bare branches of these large deciduous shrubs or small trees are covered in clusters of nodding, white, bell-shaped flowers. The blooms are up to 2.5 cm (1 in) across and appear in profusion once the plant is about ten years old. Unusual egg-shaped fruit with four wings, about 5 cm (2 in) long, appear in autumn. The oval or oblong leaves, up to 16 cm (6¼ in) long, are sometimes hairy. Native to SE USA, halesia is hardy but does not tolerate limy soils.

The chief difference between the recommended plants is their size.

RECOMMENDED SPECIES AND VARIETIES
H. carolina see *H. tetraptera*
H. monticola (mountain snowdrop tree) Upright when young, this plant spreads with age. HEIGHT & SPREAD 3.5×2.4 m (12×8 ft) after 20 years, ultimately 9 m (30 ft) tall.

The flowers of var. *vestita*♀, up to 4 cm (1½ in) across, are slightly larger than the species and are sometimes flushed pink. The leaves are more hairy.
H. parviflora see *H. tetraptera*
H. tetraptera (syn. *H. carolina*, *H. parviflora*) (snowdrop tree) This is a large

▼ *Halesia monticola*

▼ *Halesia tetraptera*

shrubby species with wide-spreading branches. HEIGHT & SPREAD 1×1 m (3×3 ft) after 5 years, ultimately 3 m (10 ft) tall.
CULTIVATION Plant from late autumn to early spring in moist but well-drained, lime-free soil, in either full sun or partial shade.
PROPAGATION Sow seed in early or mid spring or layer in spring.
PRUNING Not usually necessary.
PESTS AND DISEASES Usually trouble free.

× Halimiocistus

Cistaceae

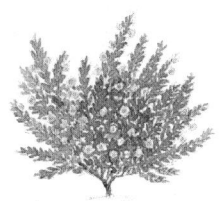

× *Halimiocistus wintonensis* 'Merrist Wood Cream'

From early to mid summer, saucer-shaped papery blossoms cover these evergreen shrubs, which are hardy in all but the coldest winters. All the recommended species are dwarf shrubs, reaching their mature size within five years. They are good plants for poor, dry soils.

RECOMMENDED SPECIES AND VARIETIES
× *H.* 'Ingwersenii' (syn. *Cistus ingwerseniana*) This easy-to-grow spreading shrub bears pure white flowers, up to 2.5 cm (1 in) across. The slender, downy shoots bear narrow dark green, downy leaves. HEIGHT & SPREAD 45 cm × 1 m (1½×3 ft).
× *H. revolii* hort. see × *H. sahucii*
× *H. sahucii*♀ (syn. × *H. revolii* hort., *Cistus sahucii*) Pure white flowers, up to 4 cm (1½ in) across, are borne on this spreading shrub. Flowering sometimes continues into autumn. The plant has narrow, rather downy, dark green leaves. HEIGHT & SPREAD 45 cm × 1 m (1½×3 ft).
× *H. wintonensis*♀ (syn. *Cistus wintonensis*, *Halimium wintonense*) This compact shrub produces flowers up to 5 cm (2 in) across. The flowers are white with a yellow centre and bands of crimson-maroon markings at the base of the petals. The leaves are grey-green. HEIGHT & SPREAD 60×90 cm (2×3 ft).

'Merrist Wood Cream'♀ (syn. *Cistus* 'Merrist Wood Cream') has flowers in shades of deep cream to soft yellow with dark maroon centres.
CULTIVATION Plant in spring in a sunny, sheltered spot in any well-drained soil, preferably light and gritty. Apply a slow-release general fertiliser in spring.
PRUNING Trim to shape in late spring and remove any shoots that have died back.
PROPAGATION Take semi-ripe cuttings during summer and root in a coldframe.
PESTS AND DISEASES Usually trouble free.

Halimium

Cistaceae

Showy, saucer-shaped flowers, about 4 or 5 cm (1½ or 2 in) wide, appear on these dwarf evergreen shrubs in early and mid summer. The small leaves are green or grey-green. Halimiums reach full size after five years and are good plants for coastal gardens. They may be injured by severe frost.

RECOMMENDED SPECIES AND VARIETIES
H. commutatum (syn. *H. libanotis*) Yellow flowers appear on this semi-upright plant. HEIGHT & SPREAD 60×60 cm (2×2 ft).
H. lasianthum♀ (syn. *H. formosum*, *Cistus formosus*, *C. lasianthus*) Golden flowers with crimson blotches cover this spreading shrub. HEIGHT & SPREAD 1×1.5 m (3×5 ft).

The flowers of f. *concolor* are yellow. The blooms of ssp. *formosum* have crimson spots on a yellow background. 'Sandling' has yellow petals blotched with maroon.
H. libanotis see *H. commutatum*
H. ocymoides♀ (syn. *Cistus algarvensis*, *C. ocymoides*) The golden yellow flowers of this dense upright shrub have black or brown spots at the base of the petals. HEIGHT & SPREAD 60×90 cm (2×3 ft).

▲ *Halimium ocymoides*

H. 'Susan'♀ Abundant bright yellow flowers are borne on this dense spreading shrub. HEIGHT & SPREAD 45×60 cm (1½×2 ft).
H. umbellatum (syn. *Helianthemum umbellatum*) Red buds open to white flowers on this upright plant. HEIGHT & SPREAD 45×60 cm (1½×2 ft).
H. wintonense see × *Halimiocistus wintonensis*
CULTIVATION Plant in spring in any well-drained soil in a sunny sheltered position. Apply a slow-release fertiliser in mid spring.
PRUNING Trim dead shoots in spring.
PROPAGATION Take semi-ripe cuttings in summer and root in a coldframe.
PESTS AND DISEASES Usually trouble free.

▼ *Halimium umbellatum*

309

Hamamelis
Witch hazel
Hamamelidaceae

The distinctive spidery flowers of the witch hazels, in glowing shades of yellow, red and orange, bring colour to the garden when it is badly needed from early winter to late spring. The flowers are usually about 3 cm (1¼ in) across, made up of strap-shaped crinkly petals about 1.5 cm (½ in) long. Appearing in clusters on leafless branches, these unusual flowers survive the harshest frosts. Most have at least a slight fragrance.

The witch hazels are also worth growing for their colourful autumn foliage in fiery hues. The shallow-toothed, hairy leaves are usually egg-shaped to almost circular, up to 10 cm (4 in) long and nearly as broad.

Although they are slow-growing, these multistemmed, medium-to-large deciduous shrubs often become as broad as they are tall. They deserve to be given an ample amount of space and prominence in the garden, doing best in a shady spot. Native to eastern N America and Asia.

RECOMMENDED SPECIES AND VARIETIES
H. × intermedia The flowers appear on bare branches from mid to late winter. The plant is rather variable and is rarely grown, being superseded by its many cultivars. HEIGHT & SPREAD 1×1 m (3×3 ft) after 5 years, ultimately 4 m (13 ft) tall.

The following cultivars are reliable in terms of flower colour and tend to make slightly smaller plants than the parent. **'Arnold Promise'**♀ has numerous bright yellow flowers and yellow autumn foliage. **'Diane'**♀ is the best red-flowering variety. The leaves turn bright red in the autumn. **'Jelena'**♀ has yellow flowers tinted with a coppery red, giving them an orange appearance. The leaves in autumn are a burning display of reds, oranges and scarlets. **'Pallida'**♀ see *H. mollis* 'Pallida'. **'Ruby Glow'** has coppery red flowers and reddish autumn foliage (although 'Diane'♀ is a better red variety with more flowers).
H. japonica (Japanese witch hazel) The crinkled yellow flowers appear in mid or

▼ *Hamamelis × intermedia* 'Jelena'

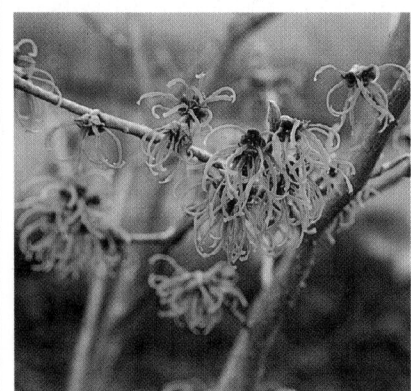

late winter. The leaves are oval. HEIGHT & SPREAD 1×1 m (3×3 ft) after 5 years, ultimately 3 m (10 ft) tall.

The flowers of **'Zuccariniana'** are a paler yellow than the parent species. They are produced later than normal, usually around early spring. The plant is vigorous, reaching 1.2×1.2 m (4×4 ft) in 5 years, ultimately 4 m (13 ft) or more tall and often nearly as broad. The oval leaves turn yellow in the autumn.
H. mollis♀ (Chinese witch hazel) This plant is probably the finest of all the species. The clusters of small golden yellow flowers appear in profusion during mid winter. They have quite a strong, sweet scent. The roundish leaves, up to 12.5 cm (5 in) long and nearly as broad, turn pure yellow in the autumn. HEIGHT & SPREAD 1.2×1.2 m (4×4 ft) after 5 years, ultimately 4 m (13 ft) tall.
'Pallida'♀ (syn. *H. × intermedia* 'Pallida') produces an abundance of strongly scented, pale sulphur-yellow flowers in mid winter. The leaves turn a deep yellow in autumn.
H. vernalis **'Sandra'**♀ The pale yellow flowers appear from mid winter to early spring. The leaves when they emerge are

▲ *Hamamelis vernalis* 'Sandra'

tinted a purplish plum colour but this is lost from the upper surface as the season progresses. They give an attractive display of oranges, purples and reds in the autumn. HEIGHT & SPREAD 80×80 cm (2 ft 8 in×2 ft 8 in) after 5 years, ultimately 2 m (6½ ft) tall.
CULTIVATION Plant in neutral to acid soil that is free draining.
PROPAGATION Sow the hard shiny black seeds in early to mid spring. They may take two years to germinate. Grafting will be necessary if a particular feature is required, although layering can be successful.
PRUNING Not normally required except to remove dead wood in autumn and winter.
PESTS AND DISEASES Usually trouble free.

Harebell see *Campanula rotundifolia*
Hawk's-beard see *Crepis*
Hawkweed see *Hieracium*
Hawthorn see *Crataegus monogyna*
Hazel see *Corylus*
Heartsease see *Viola tricolor*
Heath see *Erica*
Heather see *Calluna*, *Erica*

Hebe
Shrubby veronica
Scrophulariaceae

Hebe 'Midsummer Beauty'

Versatile evergreen shrubs, hebes are popular for their fine blooms and neat foliage. They range considerably in habit, from low-growing, ground-cover plants to taller shrubs for mixed borders, shrubberies or low hedges. Small individual blooms in white and shades of purple, red and blue are grouped together in showy flowerheads.

Leaves vary in shape and size; mostly they are oval, oblong or obovate, often pointed at the tip. Some hebes have tiny overlapping leaves, pressed closely against the stems so that plants look like cypress – these are known as whipcord hebes.

Hebes are tolerant of salt-laden wind, and so are ideal for seaside gardens, but they vary in hardiness. Some are half hardy and in cooler regions they are grown in pots in a cool greenhouse or conservatory, or treated as bedding plants and planted outside in summer – hebes can be happily transplanted. Others are moderately hardy and tolerate short periods at temperatures as low as –10°C (14°F), while the rest are fully hardy. Hebes grow on most soils, even chalk, as long as it is not too wet and not too dry – although the whipcord species tolerate drought. All the species and hybrids included here are native to New Zealand.

RECOMMENDED SPECIES AND VARIETIES
Hebes reach mature size within a few years. Unless otherwise indicated, the heights and spreads given below are the ultimate size of the plants, attained within 5 years.
H. albicans♀ White flowers in dense racemes, up to 6 cm (2½ in) long, appear in mid summer. The thick, grey-green leaves are up to 3 cm (1¼ in) long. This species is hardy. HEIGHT & SPREAD 60 cm×1.5 m (2×5 ft) after 5 years, ultimately 1 m (3 ft) tall.

▲ *Hebe albicans*

H. **'Alicia Amherst'**♥ (syn. *H.* 'Royal Purple', *H.* 'Veitchii') Racemes, up to 15 cm (6 in) long, of rich violet-blue flowers appear in abundance during late summer and autumn. The glossy, dark green leaves are about 9 cm (3½ in) long. This erect shrub is one of the least hardy hebes. HEIGHT & SPREAD 1×1.2 m (3×4 ft).

H. × *andersonii* **'Variegata'** (syn. *H.* × *andersonii* 'Argenteovariegata') The narrow leaves, about 10 cm (4 in) long, are pale greyish green with darker green markings and white to cream edges. Lilac flower spikes up to 12 cm (4¾ in) long are borne abundantly from mid summer to late autumn. A fairly hardy erect to bushy shrub. HEIGHT & SPREAD 2×1.5 m (6½×5 ft).

H. **'Autumn Glory'** Violet flowers in 5 cm (2 in) long racemes are freely produced from

▲ *Hebe* 'Autumn Glory'

mid summer to late autumn. The mid-green leaves are 5 cm (2 in) long and have reddish edges. This bushy shrub is hardy. HEIGHT & SPREAD 60×75 cm (2×2½ ft).

H. **'Baby Marie'** In late spring or early summer the very pale lilac blooms are carried in showy flowerheads, 3 cm (1¼ in) long. The mid green leaves are about 1 cm (⅜ in) long. This compact shrub is moderately hardy. HEIGHT & SPREAD 40×40 cm (16×16 in).

H. **'Blue Clouds'**♥ Bluish mauve flowers, in spikes up to 10 cm (4 in) long, appear from early summer to early winter. Green in summer, the 4 cm (1½ in) long leaves turn purple in winter. A hardy, bushy shrub. HEIGHT & SPREAD 1×1.2 m (3×4 ft).

H. **'buchananii'**♥ White flowers in racemes up to 2 cm (¾ in) long, appear in late spring and early summer. The thick, slightly concave, greyish green leaves are about 6 mm (¼ in) long. This dense, small shrub is hardy. HEIGHT & SPREAD 30×30 cm (1×1 ft).

'Minor' (syn. 'Nana') is a tiny hebe, up to 4 cm (1½ in) tall, that seldom flowers.

H. **'Caledonia'** (syn. *H.* 'E.B. Anderson', *H.* 'Knightshayes') Violet flower spikes, about 6 cm (2½ in) long, are produced in abundance from mid summer to late autumn. The long, pointed leaves have purplish red edges and midribs and measure up

to 3 cm (1¼ in) long. This erect shrub is hardy. HEIGHT & SPREAD 60×60 cm (2×2 ft).

H. cupressoides This whipcord hebe has grey-green leaves and branches that generally emit a resinous scent. Pale lilac-blue

Hebe cupressoides

flower spikes, up to 2.5 cm (1 in) long, appear in early summer. A hardy species. HEIGHT & SPREAD 1.5×2 m (5×6½ ft) after 5 years, ultimately 1.8 m (6 ft) tall.

▲ *Hebe cupressoides* 'Boughton Dome'

'Boughton Dome'♥ forms a dense grey-green dome about 60 cm (2 ft) high and 1 m (3 ft) wide. It rarely flowers.

H. **'E.B. Anderson'** see *H.* 'Caledonia'

H. **'Emerald Green'**♥ (syn. *H.* 'Green Globe') This compact, rounded, hardy bush has bright green, 3 mm (⅛ in) long leaves and bright green stems. Flowers are rare, but if seen are white and appear in summer. HEIGHT & SPREAD 35×50 cm (14×20 in).

H. **'Eveline'** (syn. *H.* 'Gauntlettii') Showy spikes, 8 cm (3¼ in) long, of pink flowers appear from late summer to late autumn. The mid-green leaves are 6-10 cm (2½-4 in) long. A moderately hardy, bushy shrub. HEIGHT & SPREAD 1×1 m (3×3 ft).

H. × *franciscana* Large white, lilac, violet or magenta flowers in broad clusters up to 6 cm (2½ in) long appear from early summer to mid autumn. The thick, light green leaves are 3-7 cm (1¼-2¾ in) long. These bushy shrubs are half hardy. HEIGHT & SPREAD 1.5×1.5 m (5×5 ft).

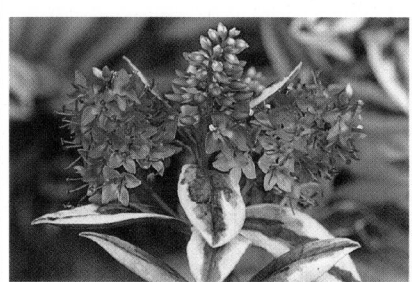

▲ *Hebe* × *franciscana* 'Variegata'

'Blue Gem'♥ has lilac or deep violet flowers. **'Variegata'**♥ has shiny, dark green leaves shaded pale green with a broad, irregular creamy yellow edge. The pretty lilac flowers are on display from mid summer to mid autumn.

H. **'Gauntlettii'** see *H.* 'Eveline'

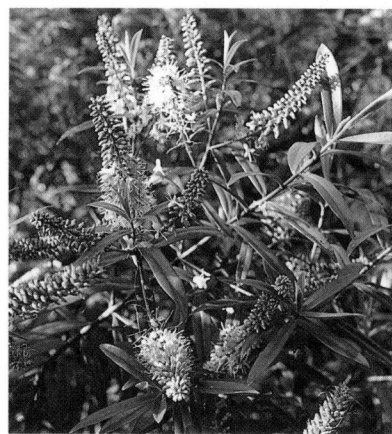

▲ *Hebe* 'Great Orme'

H. **'Great Orme'**♥ The narrow, pointed leaves are up to 9 cm (3½ in) long. Clear pink flowers that gradually turn white are borne in abundant spikes up to 10 cm (4 in) long from mid summer to late autumn. This erect shrub is moderately hardy. HEIGHT & SPREAD 1.5×1 m (5×3 ft).

H. **'Green Globe'** see *H.* 'Emerald Green'

H. **'hulkeana'**♥ Large sprays, up to 40 cm (16 in) long, of delicate white, blue or lilac flowers appear from mid to late spring. The shiny leaves, 3-10 cm (1¼-4 in) long, have toothed edges that are often red. This hardy shrub of loose habit is susceptible to downy mildew and so requires an open, sunny site. HEIGHT & SPREAD 60×60 cm (2×2 ft).

H. **'James Stirling'** see *H. ochracea* 'James Stirling'

H. **'Knightshayes'** see *H.* 'Caledonia'

H. **'La Séduisante'**♥ Large, purplish crimson racemes, up to 10 cm (4 in) long, appear from mid summer to late autumn. Stems and leaf buds are purplish red. The leaves

▼ *Hebe* 'La Séduisante'

h

313

are 8 cm (3¼ in) long and tinged with purple. A small, moderately hardy, bushy shrub. HEIGHT & SPREAD 60×60 cm (2×2 ft).

H. macrantha♀ Large, pure white flowers, up to 3 cm (1¼ in) across, are borne in short racemes of about 10 flowers in early summer. The thick leaves, up to 2 cm (¾ in) long, have toothed edges. A moderately hardy upright shrub which tends to become leggy. HEIGHT & SPREAD 60×60 cm (2×2 ft).

Hebe macrantha

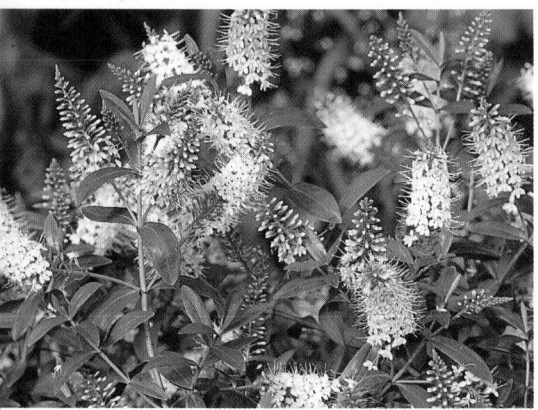

H. 'Midsummer Beauty'♀ Pale violet flowers appear in spikes up to 30 cm (1 ft) long from mid summer to late autumn. The 10 cm (4 in) long leaves are purplish when young. A moderately hardy, bushy to erect shrub. HEIGHT & SPREAD 1.5×1 m (5×3 ft).

H. 'Mrs Winder'♀ (syn. *H.* 'Waikiki') Flower spikes, up to 10 cm (4 in) long, of violet-blue blooms are sparsely produced in autumn. The leaves are up to 4 cm (1½ in) long with reddish purple edges and midrib; younger leaves turn dark purple in winter. The young branches are also dark purple. A compact, hardy shrub. HEIGHT & SPREAD 1×1 m (3×3 ft).

▲ *Hebe* 'Nicola's Blush'

H. 'Nicola's Blush' Pink flowers, fading to white, in broad clusters up to 8 cm (3¼ in) long are very freely produced from late spring to mid summer and again in autumn, often continuing through into mid winter. The leaves are tinged with purple and about 3 cm (1¼ in) long. A hardy, bushy shrub. HEIGHT & SPREAD 75×75 cm (2½×2½ ft).

H. ochracea This whipcord species has ochre, scale-like leaves and branches. Small white flower spikes, up to 2 cm (¾ in) long, appear in late spring and early summer. A slow-growing, hardy shrub. HEIGHT & SPREAD 60×45 cm (2×1½ ft) after 5 years, ultimately 1 m (3 ft) tall.

▲ *Hebe ochracea* 'James Stirling'

'James Stirling'♀ is a compact, spreading form reaching about 40 cm (16 in) tall and spreading to 60 cm (2 ft).

H. odora 'New Zealand Gold' Small, rigid bright green leaves, about 1.5 cm (1½ in) long, are closely set on the upright branches. White flowers, in 3 cm (1¼ in) long spikes, appear in early to mid summer. A hardy, strong growing, erect shrub. HEIGHT & SPREAD 1×1 m (3×3 ft).

H. parviflora var. **angustifolia**♀ Small white flowers in dense clusters, 7 cm (2¾ in) long, appear from late summer to early autumn. Light green, linear leaves, about 3 cm (1¼ in) long, are borne on the erect, slender, brown branchlets of this hardy shrub. HEIGHT & SPREAD 1×1 m (3×3 ft).

H. 'Pewter Dome'♀ White flowers, in broad clusters up to 4 cm (1½ in) long, appear from mid to late summer. The grey-green leaves are 2 cm (¾ in) long. A hardy rounded bush. HEIGHT & SPREAD 60×60 cm (2×2 ft) after 5 years, finally 1 m (3 ft) tall.

H. pimeleoides 'Quicksilver'♀ Violet-blue flowers, in spikes up to 4 cm (1½ in) long, appear in mid and late summer. Stiff, silver-

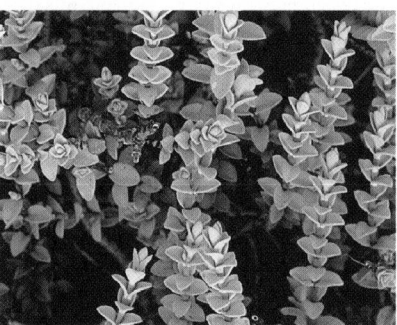

▲ *Hebe pimeleoides* 'Quicksilver'

grey leaves, up to about 1 cm (⅜ in) long, are borne on wiry dark branches. An open, sprawling, hardy shrub. HEIGHT & SPREAD 60 cm×1 m (2×3 ft).

H. pinguifolia 'Pagei'♀ White flower spikes, 3 cm (1¼ in) long, appear in mid and late spring. The thick greyish leaves are about 1 cm (⅜ in) long. A hardy, prostrate shrub that is an excellent ground cover plant. HEIGHT & SPREAD 20×60 cm (8 in×2 ft).

H. pinguifolia 'Sutherlandii' Abundant white flower spikes, 3 cm (1¼ in) long, are produced in late spring and early summer.

The thick, grey-green, concave leaves are up to 1.5 cm (½ in) long. A hardy bushy shrub, upright at first but spreading later. HEIGHT & SPREAD 45×60 cm (1½×2 ft).

H. 'Purple Tips' see *H. speciosa* 'Tricolor'

H. rakaiensis♀ Short clusters of white flowers are produced in summer. The slightly glossy leaves are about 2 cm (¾ in) long. A hardy, spreading, fairly dense, bushy shrub. HEIGHT & SPREAD 60 cm×1 m (2×3 ft).

H. recurva♀ Slender white flower spikes, 4 cm (1½ in) long, appear in late summer. The narrow pointed leaves, 4 cm (1½ in) long, are grey-green. A hardy spreading shrub. HEIGHT & SPREAD 60×75 cm (2×2½ ft).

▲ *Hebe rakaiensis*

▲ *Hebe* 'Red Edge'

H. 'Red Edge'♀ Pale violet-blue flower spikes, up to 3 cm (1¼ in) long, appear in summer. The grey-green leaves, about 2 cm (¾ in) long, have red edges. Leaf buds and young leaves become pinkish in winter. This hardy hebe forms a neat rounded bush. HEIGHT & SPREAD 60×60 cm (2×2 ft).

H. 'Royal Purple' see *H.* 'Alicia Amherst'

H. 'Simon Delaux'♀ Showy crimson flower spikes, up to 10 cm (4 in) long, appear from mid summer to early autumn and sometimes until late autumn. The thick shiny leaves, up to 10 cm (4 in) long, are purplish in bud. A half-hardy, upright shrub. HEIGHT & SPREAD 1 m×60 cm (3×2 ft) after 5 years, ultimately 1.5 m (5 ft) tall.

H. 'Spender's Seedling'♀ Slender, white flower spikes, up to 10 cm (4 in) long, are seen in profusion from mid summer to early autumn. The mid to dark green linear leaves are about 6 cm (2½ in) long. A hardy shrub with erect branches. HEIGHT & SPREAD 1 m×60 cm (3×2 ft).

▲ *Hebe topiaria*

H. topiaria White flower spikes up to 3 cm (1¼ in) long appear from early to mid summer. The thick, grey-green leaves, about 1 cm (⅜ in) long, are slightly concave. A neat, slow-growing, hardy shrub that forms a dense dome. HEIGHT & SPREAD 45×75 m (1½×2½ ft) after 5 years, ultimately 1 m (3 ft) tall.

H. **'Veitchii'** see *H.* 'Alicia Amherst'

H. vernicosa White flower spikes, up to 5 cm (2 in) long, bloom from mid spring to early summer. The glossy, bright green leaves are about 1.5 cm (½ in) long. A low-growing, spreading hardy hebe. HEIGHT & SPREAD 30×45 m (1×1½ ft) after 5 years, ultimately 60 cm (2 ft) tall.

H. **'Waikiki'** see *H.* 'Mrs Winder'

H. **'Wingletye'** Lilac-blue flowers in clusters 5 cm (2 in) long, appear all summer. The grey-green leaves are about 1 cm (⅜ in)

▼ *Hebe* 'Youngii'

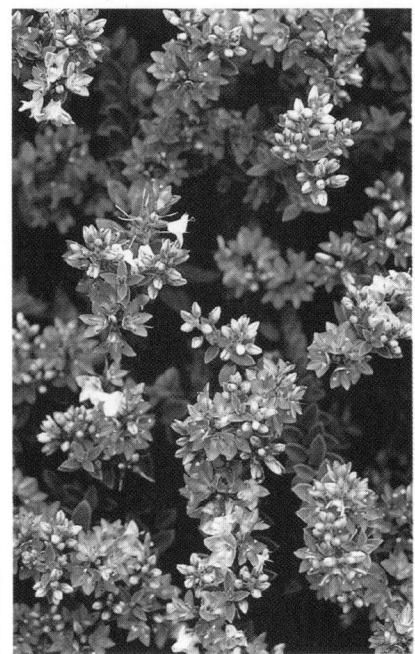

long. A low-growing, hardy shrub. HEIGHT & SPREAD 20 cm×1 m (8 in×3 ft).

H. **'Youngii'** (syn. *H.* 'Carl Teschner') Loose violet-blue flower clusters, fading to white and about 3.5 cm (1⅜ in) long, appear in summer. Shiny, red-edged leaves, about 1 cm (⅜ in) long, are borne on near-black branches. A moderately hardy hebe. HEIGHT & SPREAD 20×60 cm (8 in×2 ft).

CULTIVATION Plant hebes during autumn or spring in any well-drained soil, choosing a site in full sun.

PROPAGATION Raise plants from semi-ripe cuttings in late summer.

PRUNING Not usually necessary, but if plants become leggy or too large cut back some branches hard in spring. Cut back the remaining old growth, the following year.

PESTS AND DISEASES Downy mildew, particularly in damp autumn weather, and leaf spot can be problems.

Hedera
Ivy
Araliaceae

Hedera hibernica

The evergreen foliage of these hardy self-clinging climbers makes a splendid sight growing against walls, fences and pergolas. Some varieties can also be encouraged to grow as ground-cover plants, and are especially useful in shady places. Ivies are popular houseplants and can be grown trailing or scrambling from pots. All have insignificant yellowish green clusters of flowers when mature and often produce black, cream, red, orange or yellow fruits.

RECOMMENDED SPECIES AND VARIETIES

H. algeriensis (syn. *H. canariensis* hort.) (Algerian ivy) The mid to dark green leaves, up to 15 cm (6 in) long, have 3–5 lobes when young, but become more heart-shaped as they mature. They often have reddish hairs on the undersides and leaf stalks. The plant is not reliably evergreen and may lose its foliage in very cold winters. Commonly grown as a houseplant. HEIGHT & SPREAD 6×5 m (20×16 ft) after 5 years.

'Gloire de Marengo'♀ has light green leaves that are heavily variegated with yellow and cream. **'Marginomaculata'**♀ produces leaves with dark and pale green irregular zones with or without cream or white margins. **'Ravensholst'**♀, often used for ground cover, has glossy green leaves.

H. canariensis hort. see *H. algeriensis*

▲ *Hedera algeriensis* 'Marginomaculata'

H. colchica♀ (Persian ivy) A vigorous plant with lobed oval, elliptical or heart-shaped leaves up to 20 cm (8 in) long. The dark green foliage is thick and leathery and emits a strong smell of celery if bruised. The undersides of the young leaves are covered with reddish down. HEIGHT & SPREAD 10×5 m (33×16 ft) after 5 years.

'Dentata'♀ has slightly larger soft green leaves with occasional teeth along the mar-

▲ *Hedera colchica* 'Dentata Variegata'

gins. **'Dentata Variegata'**♀ (syn. 'Dentata Aurea') is a striking plant with bright green leaves shaded with grey. The leaf margins are creamy yellow when young, turning

Hedera colchica
'Dentata Variegata'

creamy white with age. **'Sulphur Heart'**♀ (syn. 'Paddy's Pride') bears foliage that is boldly splashed with yellow and pale green. Some leaves are almost entirely yellow.

H. helix (common ivy) The dark to mid-green leaves, up to 15 cm (6 in) long, have 3–5 lobes. This is one of the most adaptable garden plants, widely used as a climber or for ground cover outdoors. The variegated varieties are suitable for pot culture. HEIGHT & SPREAD 10×5 m (33×16 ft) after 5 years.

'Adam' has small light green leaves, no more than 5 cm (2 in) long, with silvery margins. It is slightly less hardy than most varieties and loses its foliage during severe

h

winters, but rapidly recovers. It grows to 1.2 m (4 ft) tall. **'Angularis Aurea'**♀ has glossy, light green leaves, up to 7.5 cm (3 in) long, with strong yellow variegation. It is not suitable for ground cover. Grows to 4 m (13 ft) tall. **'Atropurpurea'**♀ has leaves, up to 7.5 cm (3 in) long, entire or with 2 small lobes, that are dark purple-green in winter with bright green veins. Grows to 4 m (13 ft) tall. In full sun, **'Buttercup'**♀ has bright yellow leaves about 4 cm (1½ in) long. Grows to 2 m (6½ ft) tall.

'Caecilia' has creamy yellow and green leaves up to 5 cm (2 in) long. Grows to 1.2 m (4 ft) tall. **'Cavendishii'**♀ produces mid-green, 3-lobed leaves, up to 7.5 cm (3 in) long, mottled with grey and with creamy white margins. Grows to 1.2 m (4 ft) tall. **'Chicago'** has mid-green leaves, up to 3 cm (1¼ in) long, with paler veins. Grows to 3 m (10 ft) tall. **'Congesta'**♀ is a slow-growing, stiff, upright plant with small, dark green, arrow-shaped leaves up to 2.5 cm (1 in) long. Although non-climbing it benefits from being grown near a wall, fence or large stone in a rock garden. Grows to 1 m (3 ft) tall. **'Conglomerata'** (clustered ivy) is a hummock-forming plant, ideal for a rock garden. Its stiff upright stems bear dark green wavy leaves up to 2.5 cm (1 in) long. Grows to 1 m (3 ft) tall. **'Dragon Claw'** has grey-green, wavy-edged leaves up to 7.5 cm (3 in) long. Best used as a ground-cover plant. Grows to 2 m (6½ ft). **'Duckfoot'**, an excellent ground-cover plant, has pea-green, 3-lobed leaves up to 2 cm (¾ in) long. Grows to 1 m (3 ft).

'Erecta'♀ is slow-growing with stiff erect branches and 3-lobed, arrow-shaped leaves up to 2.5 cm (1 in) long. Grows to 1 m (3 ft) tall. **'Eva'**♀ is a small-leafed variety with grey-green and cream leaves. The leaves may fall in severe winters. Grows to 1.2 m (4 ft) tall. **'Glacier'**♀ has silvery grey and green leaves, about 4 cm (1½ in) long, with narrow white margins. Grows to 3 m (10 ft) tall. **'Goldchild'**♀, a popular house-plant, has young bright green leaves, up to 7.5 cm (3 in) long, with a pale green centre and a broad golden yellow margin. As they mature the leaves become blue-green and grey-green with creamy yellow margins. Grows to 1.2 m (4 ft) tall. **'Goldheart'** see

▼ *Hedera helix* 'Eva'

▲ *Hedera helix* 'Glacier'

'Oro di Bogliasco'. **'Goldstern'** produces lime-green lobed leaves up to 5 cm (2 in) long with a dark green central splash. Grows to 1.2 m (4 ft) tall. **'Green Ripple'** has mid-green leaves up to 7.5 cm (3 in) long with prominent veins and wavy,

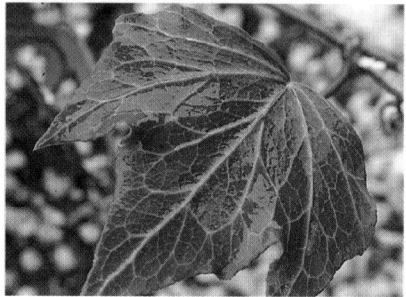

▲ *Hedera helix* 'Green Ripple'

undulating margins. A scrambling plant rather than a climber and excellent for ground cover. Grows to 1.2 m (4 ft) tall. **'Harald'** displays green and grey-green, 5-lobed leaves, up to 5 cm (2 in) long, with creamy white margins. Grows to 1.2 m (4 ft) tall. *H. helix* ssp. *hibernica* see *H. hibernica*. **'Ivalace'**♀, a very good ground-cover plant, has 5-lobed, wavy, glossy green leaves up to 7.5 cm (3 in) long. Grows to 1.2 m (4 ft) tall. **'Jubilee'** is a bushy plant with grey-green and white variegated leaves up to 4 cm (1½ in) long. Grows to 1 m (3 ft) tall. **'Kolibri'**♀ carries mid green leaves, up to 5 cm (2 in) long, that are heavily speckled and variegated white. Grows to 1 m (3 ft) tall. **'Königers Auslese'** has arrow-like mid green leaves up to 7.5 cm (3 in) long. Grows to 1.5 m (5 ft) tall. **'Little Diamond'**♀, a very bushy plant, has roughly diamond-shaped silvery and grey variegated leaves up to 5 cm (2 in) long. It eventually reaches a height of about 60 cm (2 ft).

'Manda's Crested'♀ bears wavy-edged mid-green leaves, up to 7.5 cm (3 in) long, that turn coppery in autumn. Grows to 2 m (6½ ft) tall. **'Melanie'** has mid-green crinkled leaves with a reddish tinge. Grows to 2 m (6½ ft) tall. **'Midas Touch'**♀ is a very slow-growing golden variety with heart-shaped leaves up to 5 cm (2 in) long. Grows to 1 m (3 ft) tall. **'Minor Marmorata'** has small 5-lobed leaves, rarely more than 4 cm (1½ in) long, that are dark green with grey and white spotting and blotching. In cold weather the foliage is often tinged pink. Grows to 2 m (6½ ft) tall. Grows to 1 m (3 ft) tall. **'Oro di Bogliasco'** (syn. 'Goldheart')

carries green leaves up to 5 cm (2 in) long with yellow patches. Grows to 1.2 m (4 ft) tall. **'Parsley Crested'** has light green leaves, up to 7.5 cm (3 in) long, that are crimped and crested at the margins. Not suitable for ground cover. Grows to 2 m (6½ ft) tall. **'Pedata'**♀ (bird's foot ivy) carries deeply lobed grey-green leaves, up to 5 cm (2 in) long, with a longer central lobe. Grows to 4 m (13 ft) tall.

'Sagittifolia' bears deeply cut dark green leaves up to 5 cm (2 in) long. Grows to 1.2 m (4 ft) tall. **'Sagittifolia Variegata'** has deeply cut creamy white and green variegated leaves up to 4 cm (1½ in) long. Grows to 1 m (3 ft) tall. **'Shamrock'**♀ is popularly used for ground cover and has dark green leaves up to 2.5 cm (1 in) long borne on short-jointed stems. Grows to 60 cm (2 ft) tall. **'Spetchley'**, a miniature ivy, has tiny, dark green, arrow-shaped leaves up to 2.5 cm (1 in) long and is suitable

▲ *Hedera helix* 'Sagittifolia Variegata'

▲ *Hedera helix* 'Spetchley'

for a rock garden. Grows to 30 cm (1 ft) tall. **'Très Coupé'** has broadly arrow-shaped deep green leaves that are deeply cut and up to 4 cm (1½ in) long. Grows to 1 m (3 ft) tall. **'Tricolor'** produces roughly triangular, greyish green leaves, about 5 cm (2 in) long, that have pale grey-green or creamy veins and are edged with white and pink in winter. It makes a handsome climber, reaching up to 2 m (6½ ft) tall. **'Triton'** is a sprawling ground-cover plant with deeply cut dark green leaves up to 7.5 cm (3 in) long. Grows to 45 cm (1½ ft) tall.
H. hibernica♀ (syn. *H. helix* ssp. *hibernica*) (Atlantic ivy, Irish ivy) A vigorous climbing ivy that is good for ground cover. The mid-green leaves, up to 15 cm (6 in) long, are roughly heart-shaped. HEIGHT & SPREAD 7×5 m (23×16 ft).

'Anne Marie' has golden cream and bright green leaves up to 12.5cm (5in) long. Grows to 5m (16ft) tall. 'Deltoidea' (shield ivy) is a compact plant with broadly heart-shaped, dark green leaves, up to 10cm (4in) long, which turn purplish in winter. Eventually grows to 5m (16ft) tall.

CULTIVATION Plant ivy from early autumn to early spring in heavy, humus-rich soil, or indoors in pots in John Innes No.3 compost. Ivies tolerate shade, but this often pales the colours of variegated varieties, as does excessively rich compost or soil. Indoors, position away from direct sunlight.

PROPAGATION Cuttings taken in spring and summer root easily in a coldframe.

PRUNING Trim to keep under control. Undertake any major pruning in spring.

PESTS AND DISEASES Indoors ivy is susceptible to mealy bugs and red spider mite.

Hedychium
Ginger lily, garland flower
Zingiberaceae

Tender or half-hardy herbaceous perennials with exotic fragrant flowers, hedychiums are generally grown as large pot plants in Britain. They can be kept under glass all year round or overwintered in a greenhouse and moved to a sunny spot outside in summer. They can also be treated like annuals and planted out as part of tropical bedding schemes. However, in sheltered gardens in milder areas *Hedychium coccineum*, *H. densiflorum* and *H. gardnerianum* will survive outdoors all year round if planted against a sunny wall.

Hedychiums have erect, cane-like stems that bear dense spikes of tubular flowers. These appear in late summer or autumn on plants grown outdoors and between spring and autumn on indoor specimens. The tapering pointed leaves are mid green and carried in two alternate ranks.

RECOMMENDED SPECIES AND VARIETIES

H. coccineum♀ (red ginger lily) Bright scarlet flowers about 5cm (2in) long are held in 25cm (10in) long spikes. The leaves are 50cm (20in) long. When planted outdoors, this species reaches up to 2m (6½ft) in height. Native to the Himalayas. HEIGHT & SPREAD 2×1m (6½×3ft) or more.

'Tara'♀ has orange flowers with protruding orange styles.

H. coronarium (garland flower, butterfly ginger lily) White flowers, 8cm (3¼in) long, are carried in spikes 30cm (1ft) long. The leaves, which are often downy underneath, grow to 60cm (2ft) long. Native to India. HEIGHT & SPREAD 2.4×1m (8×3ft).

H. densiflorum Orange or coral-red flowers, up to 8cm (3¼in) long, are borne on 20cm (8in) long spikes. The leaves are 35cm (14in) long. Outdoors, it may reach 2.4m (8ft) high. Native to the Himalayas. HEIGHT & SPREAD 3×1m (10×3ft) or more.

'Assam Orange' has vivid orange blooms.

H. gardnerianum (Kahili ginger) The flowers, 5cm (2in) long, are pale yellow with bright red protruding stamens. They are carried in spikes up to 35cm (14in) long. The leaves are 40cm (16in) long. In hot summers, specimens planted outdoors may reach the same height as those grown under glass. Native to the Himalayas. HEIGHT & SPREAD 1.5×1m (5×3ft).

▲ *Hedychium spicatum*

H. spicatum White flowers with orange bases and reddish stamens, up to 8cm (3¼in) long, are held in spikes up to 20cm (8in) long. The leaves are 60cm (24in) long. Native to the Himalayas. HEIGHT & SPREAD 1.5m×60cm (5×2ft).

CULTIVATION Plant in pots of fertile, soil-based compost in late winter in a warm greenhouse in full sun. Once established, water well. *H. coccineum*, *H. densiflorum*, *H. gardnerianum* and *H. spicatum* can be moved to a cool greenhouse.

H. coronarium will grow in a cool greenhouse, but does much better in a warm one. All species can be moved outside once the danger of frost has passed and returned to the greenhouse in autumn.

Alternatively, plant established specimens of *H. coccineum*, *H. densiflorum*, *H. gardnerianum* and *H. spicatum* outdoors in late spring in moist, but well-drained soil against a south or west-facing wall, and in as much light as possible. Keep covered with mulch and well watered. Mulch again in autumn to protect plants over winter.

PROPAGATION Divide plants in spring and pot on to grow to flowering size.

PESTS AND DISEASES Usually trouble free.

Hedyotis see *Houstonia*

Hedysarum
Leguminosae

These hardy, deciduous perennials and shrubs are grown for their slender spikes of long-lasting, richly coloured sweetpea-like flowers and attractive leaves. Both plants recommended below are easy to grow in a mixed border in full sun. The shrub, *Hedysarum multijugum*, will also do well in sandy soil on a sunny bank.

RECOMMENDED SPECIES

H. coronarium (French honeysuckle) Intensely fragrant, bright purple to red flowers, 2cm (¾in) long, are carried on elegant spikes all summer by these shrubby perennials. The leaves are composed of 7-15 opposite-growing pairs of mid green, elliptical to oval leaflets up to 3cm (1¼in) long. HEIGHT & SPREAD 1×1m (3×3ft).

H. multijugum Erect spikes of vivid magenta flowers, each 2cm (¾in) long, are borne from early summer to early autumn by these deciduous shrubs. Zig-zag branchlets carry sea-green leaves with up to 20 pairs of oval to oblong leaflets 1.5cm (½in) long. HEIGHT & SPREAD 1×1m (3×3ft) after 5 years, ultimately 1.5m (5ft) tall.

CULTIVATION Plant in full sun in fertile, well-drained soil, preferably in spring. Once established the plants should not be disturbed. *H. coronarium* may be planted in late summer, then cut back to just above ground level in late autumn.

PROPAGATION Sow seed of both species outdoors when ripe or in spring or take semi-ripe cuttings of both species in mid summer. Layer long shoots of *H. multijugum* in early autumn and sever from the parent plant one year later.

PRUNING In mid spring thin out any old and weak wood of *H. multijugum* and shorten straggly shoots of the previous year.

PESTS AND DISEASES Usually trouble free.

▼ *Hedysarum coronarium*

h

Helenium
Sneezeweed
Compositae

Helenium autumnale

From late summer into autumn the daisy-like blooms of helenium bring yellow, orange and bronze hues to a sunny herbaceous border. The flowers, with their silky, fringed petals and central velvety boss of brown or yellow, smother the branching stems of the hardy perennials listed below.

Native to N America, heleniums earned their common name of sneezeweed after being used by early American colonists to make snuff. They are hardy throughout Britain but do not do well in very dry soils.

RECOMMENDED SPECIES AND VARIETIES
H. autumnale Clusters of yellow flowers, up to 5 cm (2 in) across, are borne freely from late summer to mid autumn. This species has winged stems and mid green lance-shaped leaves up to 15 cm (6 in) long. HEIGHT & SPREAD 1.5 m×45 cm (5×1½ ft).
H. bigelovii Orange-yellow flowers, up to 6 cm (2½ in) across with a brownish yellow central disc, are borne from mid to late summer. The lance-shaped, shiny leaves are up to 25 cm (10 in) long. HEIGHT & SPREAD 60×45 cm (2×1½ ft).
H. hoopesii Yellow or orange flowers, up to 8 cm (3¼ in) across, open in early summer. The lance-shaped basal leaves, up to 30 cm (1 ft) long, form a rosette. HEIGHT & SPREAD 1 m×45 cm (3×1½ ft).

GARDEN HYBRIDS
Many hybrid heleniums are available to gardeners – all crosses between *H. autumnale*, *H. bigelovii* and other species, though they are usually listed under their hybrid names.

▲ *Helenium* 'Golden Youth'

▲ *Helenium* 'Bruno'

Unless stated otherwise the following types produce 5 cm (2 in) diameter flowers from late summer to mid autumn and grow to 1 m (3 ft) tall with a spread of 30 cm (1 ft).

'Bruno' is up to 1.2 m (4 ft) tall and has crimson-mahogany flowers. 'Butterpat' has rich yellow flowers. 'Chipperfield Orange' has orange flowers. 'Coppelia' bears rich orange and copper red flowers. 'Crimson Beauty' has soft mahogany-red flowers from early summer onwards. 'Golden Youth' ('Goldene Jugend') has pure yellow flowers from early to mid summer. 'Moerheim Beauty' is a sturdy plant, bearing bronze to crimson flowers from mid summer. 'Pumilum Magnificum' has pale yellow flowers. 'Red and Gold' ('Rotgold') grows to 1.2 m (4 ft) tall and has two-tone flowers in brick-red and yellow. 'The Bishop' has clear yellow flowers in late summer. 'Waldtraut' reaches 1.2 m (4 ft) tall and has large orange-brown flowers. 'Wyndley' grows to a height of 75 cm (30 in) and has yellow and copper flowers from early to late summer.
CULTIVATION Plant in any fertile soil that is not too dry. Support the taller varieties. Remove stem tips immediately after the first flowering of early varieties to encourage a second flush.
PROPAGATION Lift and divide clumps every 2–3 years when dormant. Otherwise take basal cuttings in spring.
PESTS AND DISEASES Slugs may attack the stems, leaves and flowers, and tortrix moth caterpillars may eat the leaves. The plants may suffer from viral diseases and leaf spot.

Helianthemum
Rock rose
Cistaceae

Helianthemum nummularium

These bright, sun-loving evergreen shrubs or sub-shrubs produce a succession of colourful flowers from late spring through the summer months. Rock roses thrive in warm, sunny sites and make excellent rock garden plants, but they are equally useful for lining path edges or for the margin of ter-

races. These low, often spreading plants are also important elements of a Mediterranean garden where they combine well with plants such as cistus. Some of the more vibrant cultivars need to be placed with care, especially in a rock garden, as they can clash and detract from other plants. However, a sunny, gritty bed devoted to a selection of carefully contrasting rock roses can make an interesting feature.

The flowers, borne in one-sided clusters, are available in a range of clear, bright colours including pinks, reds, rusts and yellows, as well as white and more pastel shades. The four or five thin, rather crumpled petals surround a central mass of stamens. The small oval leaves are arranged in pairs, and often have the untoothed margin folded neatly under.
RECOMMENDED SPECIES AND VARIETIES
H. lunulatum Yellow flowers, about 1.5 cm (½ in) across, are borne in early to mid summer. Each petal has a neat crescent-shaped orange mark towards the base. The lance-shaped leaves, up to 1 cm (⅜ in) long, are grey-green. This small, partly deciduous sub-shrub has a rather upright habit, spreading more with age. Native to dry rocky places in the Maritime Alps. HEIGHT & SPREAD 25×30 cm (10×12 in).
H. nummularium (common rock rose) The yellow, pink or white flowers grow up to 2 cm (¾ in) across and are borne in one-sided clusters of up to 12 during the summer. Plants form low, rather dense flattish or domed sub-shrubs, often mat-forming, with oval to lance-shaped green or grey-green leaves, up to 5 cm (2 in) long. This variable plant is native to many parts of Europe, including Britain. HEIGHT & SPREAD 50×60 cm (20×24 in).

ssp. *glabrum* has orange-yellow flowers.
RECOMMENDED HYBRIDS
The colourful rock roses most commonly seen in gardens are hybrids. Plants vary in habit, but most are low-spreading sub-shrubs, 20–40 cm (8–16 in) tall, that form a dense, interlaced hummock or mat. The flowers are single and the leaves are mid green unless otherwise stated.

'Amy Baring'♀ has deep yellow flowers with orange centres and grey-green leaves. 'Annabel' has soft pink double flowers. 'Beech Park Red' carries crimson-pink flowers and grey-green leaves. 'Ben Afflick' produces deep orange buff-flushed flowers with an orange centre. 'Ben Dearg' has vivid orange-red flowers. 'Ben Fhada' carries golden flowers with an orange centre and grey-green leaves. 'Ben Heckla' displays bronzy gold flowers. 'Ben Hope' has carmine-red flowers with an orange centre and pale grey-green leaves. 'Ben Ledi' produces deep bright rose flowers and dark green leaves. 'Ben More' carries bright orange flowers with a deeper centre and deep green leaves. 'Ben Nevis' has rich yellow flowers with a crimson-bronze

h

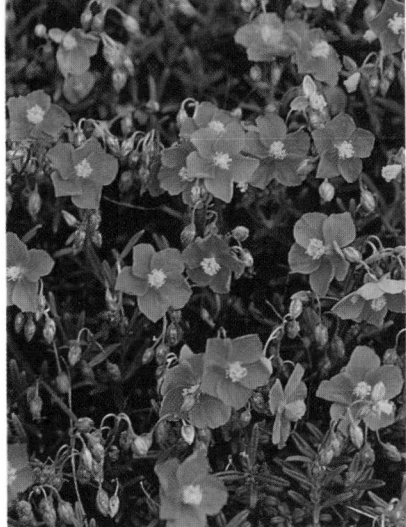

▲ *Helianthemum* 'Ben More'

centre and deep green leaves. **'Boughton Double Primrose'** carries double primrose-yellow flowers and dark green leaves.

'Cerise Queen' produces intense cerise-red double flowers and dark green leaves. **'Chocolate Blotch'** has buff and chocolate flowers. **'Double Cream'** has double cream flowers. **'Fire Dragon'**♀ has bright orange-scarlet flowers and grey-green leaves. **'Georgeham'** bears pink and yellow flowers. **'Golden Queen'** has bright yellow flowers and deep green leaves. **'Henfield Brilliant'**♀ has brick-red flowers

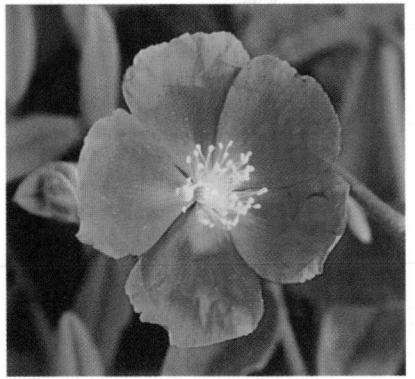

▲ *Helianthemum* 'Henfield Brilliant'

and grey-green leaves. **'Jubilee'**♀ has double primrose-yellow flowers. **'Mrs C.W. Earle'**♀ bears double red flowers with dark green leaves. **'Old Gold'** has soft rich yellow flowers.

'Praecox' produces lemon-yellow flowers and silvery grey leaves. It flowers earlier

▼ *Helianthemum* 'Mrs C.W. Earle'

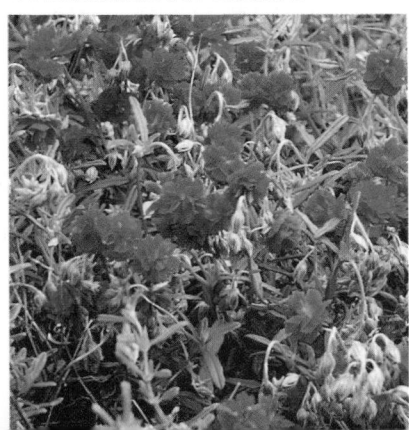

than most of the other cultivars. **'Raspberry Ripple'** bears rich reddish pink flowers edged with white and dark green leaves. **'Red Orient'** see 'Supreme'. **'Rhodanthe Carneum'**♀ carries carmine-pink flowers with an orange centre and silvery grey foliage. **'Rose of Leeswood'** has

▲ *Helianthemum* 'Rhodanthe Carneum'

double pink flowers and deep green leaves. **'Salmon Queen'** displays bright salmon-pink flowers. **'Sudbury Gem'** produces deep pink flowers with a bright red centre and grey-green leaves. **'Supreme'** (syn. 'Red Orient') carries dark red flowers and grey-green leaves. **'The Bride'**♀ bears cream flowers with a bright yellow centre and silvery grey leaves. **'Wisley Primrose'**♀ produces primrose-yellow

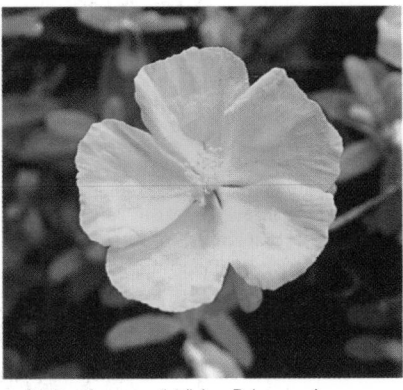

▲ *Helianthemum* 'Wisley Primrose'

flowers and pale grey-green leaves. **'Wisley White'** displays pure white flowers with yellow stamens and grey leaves.

CULTIVATION Plant in any well-drained soil in a warm, sunny position. On heavy soils add sharp grit to assist drainage. Although fully hardy, rock roses may need protection from cold, desiccating winds.

PROPAGATION Sow seed of the species in pots in autumn or winter and overwinter in a coldframe. Prick out seedlings as soon as they are large enough to handle. Raise selected forms and hybrids from semi-ripe cuttings in mid summer.

PRUNING Trim lightly to moderately in early spring or immediately after flowering to keep in shape.

PESTS AND DISEASES Usually trouble free.

Helianthus
Sunflower
Compositae

Helianthus annuus

With their large, brilliant yellow daisy flowers on strong, leafy stems, sunflowers are unmistakable. They are well known as being easy to grow and hardy, but the larger varieties are considered by some to be rather too obtrusive. Indeed, these varieties may look out of place in a small garden, but when there is room for them they make a bold and impressive display clumped together at the back of a border. There are also much smaller-flowered and shorter varieties available which can be used elsewhere, even in window boxes.

All species flower from late summer to early autumn, except *Helianthus salicifolius* which commences flowering in early autumn. The flowers attract bees, and the large edible seeds that follow encourage finches into the garden. The genus includes *H. tuberosus*, the Jerusalem artichoke, grown for its knobbly edible tubers.

RECOMMENDED SPECIES AND VARIETIES
H. annuus (common sunflower) A solitary flower, up to 30 cm (1 ft) across and usually with a brown or purple centre, stands at the top of this annual's stout stem. The stem also bears heart-shaped leaves 20-40 cm (8-16 in) long. HEIGHT & SPREAD 2.4 m × 60 cm (8 × 2 ft).

'Tall Single' (also known as 'Giant Single' or 'Russian Giant') is single stemmed and very widely grown. It is the classic sunflower of childhood memory.

Shorter, branching varieties are listed below, all bearing flowers up to 15 cm (6 in) across. They spread to about 50 cm (20 in).

'Moonwalker' has pale yellow flowers and reaches a height of up to 1.5 m (5 ft).

▼ *Helianthus* 'Moonwalker'

h

▲ *Helianthus annuus* 'Velvet Queen'

'**Music Box Mixed**' is a dwarf variety, reaching about 60 cm (2 ft) tall. It has cream, yellow and red flowers. '**Pacino**', up to 60 cm (2 ft) tall, has single golden yellow flowers. '**Prado Red**' and '**Prado Yellow**' have red and deep yellow flowers respectively, and grow to 1.5 m (5 ft) tall. The flowers produce little pollen, making them useful for cutting.

'**Sunburst**' grows to 1.2 m (4 ft) tall and bears 10 cm (4 in) flowers in a mixture of colours from pale yellow to maroon. Some of them have two-toned 'petals' (ray florets) – red at the base and yellow beyond, for example. '**Teddy Bear**' has fully double yellow flowers and grows up to 60 cm (2 ft) tall. '**Velvet Queen**' grows up to 1.5 m (5 ft) tall and bears deep velvety red flowers.

H. atrorubens (dark-eyed sunflower) The orange-yellow flowers grow up to 9 cm (3½ in) across and have maroon centres. The leaves of this rather invasive perennial are oval to lance-shaped. They grow to a

▼ *Helianthus atrorubens* 'Gullick's Variety'

length of 30 cm (1 ft) long and are crowded towards the stem bases. HEIGHT & SPREAD 2 m × 60 cm (6½ × 2 ft).

The vigorous '**Gullick's Variety**' has smaller flowers. '**Monarch**'♀ has golden semi-double flowers up to 15 cm (6 in) across with quilled petals.

H. × multiflorus Golden yellow flowers, up to 12.5 cm (5 in) across, are borne on this bushy, rapidly spreading perennial. The leaves are lance-shaped to broadly oval and up to 20 cm (8 in) long. HEIGHT & SPREAD 1.5 m × 75 cm (5 ft × 30 in).

'**Capenoch Star**'♀ has lemon-yellow flowers. '**Loddon Gold**'♀ has golden yellow double flowers.

H. salicifolius (willow-leaved sunflower) Loose clusters of golden yellow flowers, 7.5 cm (3 in) across, appear in early autumn. The stout, branching stems are smooth, bearing numerous drooping, shiny, narrow leaves, about 20 cm (8 in) long. This perennial species is valued for its foliage. HEIGHT & SPREAD 2.4 m × 60 cm (8 × 2 ft).

'**Lemon Queen**' is smaller, reaching a height of 1.5 m (5 ft).

CULTIVATION Plant in any soil, but preferably a clay loam. Despite their name, sunflowers do well in partial shade as well as full sun. Bear in mind that the flowerheads will turn to the sun. In a windy site, all but the shortest varieties require support.

Plant perennials in early spring. Yearly lifting and replanting of *H. atrorubens* and *H. multiflorus* helps to curtail their spread.

Sow *H. annuus* and its varieties straight into their flowering positions and thin out the seedlings when large enough to handle.

PROPAGATION Sow seed of *H. annuus* and varieties in mid spring. Divide perennials in early spring, though late autumn is also satisfactory if the soil is not too wet.

PESTS AND DISEASES Aphids and powdery mildew can be a problem, and slugs are a danger to young seedlings.

Helichrysum
Compositae

Helichrysum italicum

Daisy-like flowers, whose 'petals' are, in fact, dry, papery bracts, are the common feature of helichrysums. In some species these are cut and dried as 'everlasting flowers'. Many plants, though, are more prized for their silvery grey foliage. Only one species included here is an annual – *Helichrysum bracteatum* – whose cultivars have everlasting flowers of many colours. The rest are mostly low-growing, evergreen perennials or sub-shrubs, and all are fully hardy, except *H. arwae*. The perennials *H. italicum*, *H. petiolare* and *H. splendidum* reach a height of 45 cm (1½ ft) tall or above and are grown chiefly for their foliage effect. All helichrysums require free-draining soil and full sun, and the smaller plants demand dry winter conditions.

RECOMMENDED SPECIES AND VARIETIES

H. angustifolium see *H. italicum*

H. arwae This dense, evergreen sub-shrub forms a compact mat of prostrate stems clothed with narrow, 1 cm (⅜ in) long leaves, covered with silky, white hairs. White flowers, 2 cm (¾ in) across and flushed with crimson on the back, appear in summer. Native to the Yemen. HEIGHT & SPREAD 5 × 30 cm (2 × 12 in).

H. bellidioides In late spring and summer, brilliant white flowers, 2-3 cm (¾-1¼ in) across, rise on 8 cm (3¼ in) stalks above a dense carpet of short oval or rounded leaves, which are dark green above, silvery white beneath. This evergreen sub-shrub is native to New Zealand. HEIGHT & SPREAD 10 × 30 cm (4 × 12 in).

H. bracteatum (syn. *Bracteantha bracteatum*) (strawflower) This annual or short-lived deciduous perennial bears solitary, lemon-yellow to golden flowers on upright, branching, slightly bristly stems. The plant is native to Australia. HEIGHT & SPREAD 30 cm-1.5 m × 20-40 cm (1-5 ft × 8-16 in).

From this species we get the brightly coloured everlasting strawflowers, much used in dried arrangements. The blooms, 5-7.5 cm (2-3 in) across, are borne from mid summer to mid autumn. There are short varieties for the front of a border or containers, taller varieties for mid border. The double flowers of '**Bright Bikini Mixed**'♀ come in 8 colours ('**Hot Bikini**'♀ is a striking scarlet and gold). These reach a height of 30 cm (12 in). '**Dargan Hill Monarch**'

▲ *Helianthus* × 'Loddon Gold'

h

▲ *Helichrysum frigidum*

▲ *Helichrysum orientale*

h

half-hardy, evergreen sub-shrub, grown mainly for its foliage effect in borders and containers, makes a mound of silver-grey trailing stems. The woolly, grey, broadly oval leaves are 4 cm (1½ in) across. Creamy white flowers appear from mid summer to late autumn, carried in loose terminal clusters up to 5 cm (2 in) across. Native to South Africa. HEIGHT & SPREAD 50 cm × 1 m (20 in × 3 ft).

'Limelight' has lime-green leaves. 'Variegatum'♀ has leaves variegated cream and grey-green.

H. plicatum In mid summer shiny, round, bright yellow flowers are held in branched clusters up to 6 cm (2½ in) across, above the foliage of this hardy evergreen perennial. The narrow, oblong, green leaves are 4 cm (1½ in) long and have woolly hairs on the edges. Native to the Balkans. HEIGHT & SPREAD 45 × 30 cm (1½ × 1 ft).

H. rosmarinifolium see *Ozothamnus rosmarinifolius*

H. selago see *Ozothamnus selago*

H. sessilioides (syn. *H. sessile*) In late summer, solitary, yellow-centred white flowers, sometimes tinged with red and 1 cm (⅜ in) across, spangle mats of small, oval, dark green leaves covered with white, silky hairs. This creeping evergreen sub-shrub is native to South Africa. HEIGHT & SPREAD 5 × 30 cm (2 × 12 in).

H. 'Schwefellicht' ('Sulphur Light') Masses of small, fluffy, sulphur-yellow flowers are borne throughout the summer in clusters, 5 cm (2 in) across. The lance-shaped leaves of this hardy herbaceous perennial are silver-grey, woolly and 4 cm (1½ in) long. The flowers can be dried for winter arrangements. HEIGHT & SPREAD 60 × 30 cm (2 × 1 ft).

H. splendidum♀ This bushy, evergreen sub-shrub, grown mainly for its foliage, has woolly, white shoots clothed in grey, oblong leaves, 6 cm (2½ in) long. Rounded clusters, 4 cm (1½ in) across and composed of a mass of tiny, yellow flowers, appear in mid summer. Native to South Africa. The plant is fairly hardy. HEIGHT & SPREAD 1.2 × 1.2 m (4 × 4 ft).

CULTIVATION Plant helichrysums in spring in any free-draining soil in full sun. Grow the smaller alpine species in an alpine house or protect them from excessive winter wet on the foliage; they are also well suited to cultivation in troughs. The larger sub-shrubs should have frost-damaged growth cut back hard in spring.

PROPAGATION Divide herbaceous perennials in spring. Take semi-ripe cuttings of sub-shrubs and alpines in summer and grow on in a coldframe until the following spring. Sow seed of the annual varieties outside in mid spring, or in gentle heat in early spring for planting out in late spring.

PESTS AND DISEASES Usually trouble free.

Helictotrichon see GRASSES p. 301

---

has golden yellow, single flowers. It grows to 1 m (3 ft) in height, and is hardier, surviving the winter on sheltered sites. **Drakkar Pastel Mixed** has flowers in pale shades of salmon, pink and yellow. It grows to a height of 1 m (3 ft). **Dwarf Spangle Mixed** grows to 30 cm (1 ft) tall and bears double flowers in a wide range of colours.

H. coralloides see *Ozothamnus corralloides*

H. frigidum This evergreen sub-shrub forms a close mat of slender stems, densely covered with white hairs. The narrow, silvery leaves are about 5 mm (¼ in) long. White daisies about 1.5 cm (½ in) across appear singly at the tips of the branches in summer. Native to Corsica and Sardinia. HEIGHT & SPREAD 10 × 20 cm (4 × 8 in).

H. italicum♀ (syn. *H. angustifolium*) (curry plant) This hardy, evergreen sub-shrub from S Europe is admired for its mass of narrow, aromatic grey leaves, 3 cm (1¼ in) long. Clusters 8 cm (3¼ in) across carry

▼ *Helichrysum italicum*

numerous small, mustard-yellow flowers on erect white stems in mid summer. HEIGHT & SPREAD 60 cm × 1 m (2 × 3 ft).

H. ledifolium see *Ozothamnus ledifolius*

H. milfordiae♀ This evergreen perennial forms a low mat of closely packed silvery rosettes with oval leaves, 1.5 cm (½ in) long. Short-stalked, white flowers, 2.5 cm (1 in) across, open from crimson buds in early summer and retain this colour on the undersides. Native to South Africa. HEIGHT & SPREAD 10 × 20 cm (4 × 8 in).

H. orientale Large, branched clusters of round, bright lemon-yellow flowers, 1 cm (⅜ in) wide, are borne at the ends of the stems of this loosely branched, hardy evergreen sub-shrub. The stems and narrow tongue-shaped leaves, up to 6 cm (2½ in) long, are covered with dense, white, woolly hairs. Native to Greece. HEIGHT & SPREAD 30 × 30 cm (1 × 1 ft).

H. petiolare♀ (syn. *H. petiolatum*) This

▼ *Helichrysum petiolare* 'Variegatum'

Heliophila
Cruciferae

Heliophila coronopifolia

The half-hardy annuals, perennials and sub-shrubs of this genus are characterised by dainty, cross-shaped, four-petalled flowers. A sunny border is brightened by the only species that is commonly grown.

RECOMMENDED SPECIES
H. coronopifolia (syn. *H. longifolia*) Papery blue flowers, up to 1 cm (⅜ in) across, with white or yellowish centres, appear in clusters in mid to late summer on this showy annual. They are followed in autumn by narrow green pod-like fruits. Lance-shaped smooth green leaves grow up to 15 cm (6 in) long. Native to southern Africa. HEIGHT & SPREAD 25×30 cm (10×12 in).

CULTIVATION Plant in an open sunny position in a free-draining soil once the danger of frost has passed.

PROPAGATION Sow seed under glass in mid spring, or where plants are to flower in late spring.

PESTS AND DISEASES Usually trouble free.

Heliopsis
Compositae

Only one species of this genus of hardy and half-hardy annuals and perennials is commonly grown. *Heliopsis helianthoides* has showy flowers that stand out in a border from mid summer to early autumn.

RECOMMENDED SPECIES AND VARIETIES
H. helianthoides Upright yellow, daisy-like flowers, up to 7.5 cm (3 in) across, rise above coarse, spear-shaped green leaves, each up to 15 cm (6 in) long. The plant is a free-flowering, hardy herbaceous perennial, native to N America. HEIGHT & SPREAD 1.5×1 m (5×3 ft).

'Hohlspiegel' has semidouble, orange-yellow flowers and dark green leaves. It reaches a height of 1.2 m (4 ft) and a spread of 60 cm (2 ft). The flowers of var. *scabra* are less numerous and the leaves are coarser than those of the species. Its cultivar, 'Goldgrünherz', has semidouble flowers with lime-green centres. It reaches a height of 1 m (3 ft). 'Sommersonne' ('Summer Sun') has single yellow flowers, up to 10 cm (4 in) across, on a compact plant no more than 1 m (3 ft) high.

▲ *Heliopsis helianthoides* 'Hohlspiegel'

▲ *Heliopsis helianthoides* var. *scabra* 'Sommersonne'

CULTIVATION Plant between late autumn and spring in a sunny position in well-drained, medium to heavy, loamy soil. Deadhead regularly and provide plants with some support.

PROPAGATION Divide dormant crowns between late autumn and early spring.

PESTS AND DISEASES Usually trouble free.

Heliotrope see *Heliotropium*

Heliotropium
Heliotrope
Boraginaceae

Heliotropium arborescens 'Marine'

Dense heads of blue, purple or white, sometimes richly fragrant, flowers throughout summer are complemented by wrinkled leaves. The half-hardy annuals, evergreen shrubs and sub-shrubs in this genus bring height and drama to bedding schemes and flourish in outdoor containers and in conservatories. Native to tropical areas the plants described are hardy to 2°C (36°F).

RECOMMENDED SPECIES AND VARIETIES
H. arborescens (cherry pie) Sweet-smelling dense heads of tiny tubular violet, purple or white flowers adorn this evergreen shrub all summer. The leathery oval or elliptical green leaves are up to 10 cm (4 in) long and 5 cm (2 in) wide. The plant may be kept compact by light pruning in spring. If raised annually it will reach about 45 cm (18 in). HEIGHT & SPREAD 2 m×90 cm (6½×3 ft).

'Chatsworth'♀ is strong-growing and suitable for training as a standard. Highly scented purple flowers are borne in dense clusters among mid to dark green leaves.

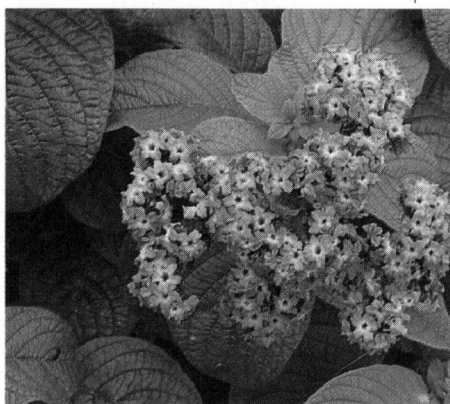

▲ *Heliotropium arborescens* 'Gatton Park'

'Gatton Park' has sweetly scented pale blue flowers and crinkled mid green leaves. It reaches 60 cm (24 in) in height and spread. 'Marine' has large clusters, up to 10 cm (4 in) across, of richly fragrant, deep purple flowers. Very wrinkled dark green leaves add to its character. This compact and bushy plant reaches 45 cm (18 in) in height and spread. 'Dwarf Marine' reaches just 30 cm (12 in). 'P. K. Lowther' bears fragrant pale to lavender blue flowers in dense clusters and has a height of 60 cm (24 in) and a

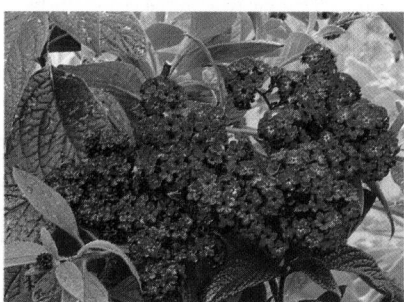

▲ *Heliotropium arborescens* 'Princess Marina'

spread of 45 cm (18 in). 'Princess Marina'♀ has clusters of sweetly scented rich purple flowers offset by violet-green crinkly foliage. Its height is 60 cm (24 in) and spread 45 cm (18 in). 'White Lady' has silvery mauve, sweetly scented flowers that are

▲ *Heliotropium arborescens* 'White Lady'

pink in bud, ageing to white, and mid green foliage. It grows to 60 cm (24 in) with a spread of 45 cm (18 in).

CULTIVATION For conservatory decoration, plant in pots in spring, using John Innes No. 3 soil-based compost. Plants will grow in full sun but require plenty of ventilation. Outdoors, plant after the danger of frost has passed. Lift plants grown outside before any danger of frost, pot and keep in a light but cool frost-free place over winter. Tip-prune plants in early spring and cut back any that are leggy.

PROPAGATION Sow seed of the species and 'Marine' in heat in a greenhouse in early spring. Take softwood cuttings of other recommended cultivars in summer.

PESTS AND DISEASES Greenfly and whitefly may infest plants grown indoors and overwintered plants in early spring.

Helipterum
Strawflower
Compositae

Charming flowers with a straw-like texture that create a decorative display in herbaceous borders and bedding schemes. They also make excellent dried flowers and can be grown in pots under glass. Strawflowers thrive in full sun in poor, dry soils. The flowers close in shade, in dull weather and at night so they should be positioned away from shadows cast by buildings or larger plants. The two species of the genus are annuals and native to Australia.

RECOMMENDED SPECIES AND VARIETIES
H. humboldtianum (syn. *Pteropogon humboldtianum*) Small golden yellow flowers are borne in tight, flat-topped clusters, about 8 cm (3¼ in) across, from mid to late summer. The flowers dry very well, but turn green. The linear leaves, about 3 cm (1¼ in) long, are hairy and appear almost white. This small, neat plant makes a fine addition to the front of a bed or along a path edge. HEIGHT & SPREAD 40×20 cm (16×8 in).
H. roseum (syn. *Acrolinium roseum*) The semidouble, daisy-like flowers, 5 cm (2 in)

▲ *Helipterum roseum*

across, are borne in mid to late summer and are various shades of pink or white, all with a yellow central disc. The petals are papery in texture. The narrow, pointed grey-green leaves are smooth and about 4 cm (1½ in) long. HEIGHT & SPREAD 45×25 cm (18×10 in).

'Goliath' has cerise flowers offset by a dark amber central disc. The flowers dry very well.

CULTIVATION Grow on fast-draining, poor, dry soil in a sunny, open position. On moisture-retentive soil with a good nutrient supply, leaf growth will be favoured and flowering reduced. Cut *H. humboldtianum* for drying when all flowers on the cluster have opened; cut *H. roseum* before the flowers are fully expanded. Hang the flowers upside down to dry in bunches in a cool, airy place.

PROPAGATION Sow seed in the flowering site in mid spring. Alternatively, start in a greenhouse as a half-hardy annual, with young plants grown in small pots or a cell tray so that root disturbance is kept to a minimum. Plant out when the risk of hard, late frosts has passed.

PESTS AND DISEASES Aphids may be troublesome.

Hellebore, stinking
see *Helleborus foetidus*
Helleborine see *Epipactis*

Helleborus
Hellebore
Ranunculaceae

These hardy evergreen and deciduous perennials bring colour and interest to the garden from mid winter to late spring. The cup or saucer-shaped flowers borne on strong, upright stems, come in white and various unusual shades of green and purple. The divided leaves have three to seven or

more oval or lance-shaped leaflets, 10-20 cm (4-8 in) long. Hellebores grow well in shade or semi-shade, provided the soil is moist, and are native to Europe and Asia.

RECOMMENDED SPECIES AND VARIETIES
H. argutifolius♀ (syn. *H. corsicus*) Apple-green, cup-shaped flowers, up to 4 cm (1½ in) across, are borne in terminal clusters on thick, cane-like stems. The flowers last from mid winter well into spring. The dark evergreen leaves are slightly prickly. HEIGHT & SPREAD 1m×60 cm (3×2 ft).

▲ *Helleborus argutifolius*

H. cyclophyllus Scented, yellow-green, cup-shaped flowers, 5-7.5 cm (2-3 in) across, with prominent yellowish stamens appear in spring. The deeply divided dark green leaves are up to 20 cm (8 in) long. HEIGHT & SPREAD 45×45 cm (1½×1½ ft).
H. foetidus♀ (stinking hellebore) Nodding, green cup-shaped flowers, flushed or edged with purple and up to 2.5 cm (1in) across, are borne in clusters from late winter to early spring. The leaves are dark green or grey-green. This evergreen, almost shrubby perennial has an unpleasant scent and can cause skin irritation. HEIGHT & SPREAD 75×60 cm (2½×2 ft).

Plants sold under the name **Wester Flisk Group** have stems, leaf and flower stalks suffused with red.
H. lividus♀ Clusters of cup-shaped yellow-green flowers, tinged with purple and up to 5 cm (2 in) across, appear in late winter. The mid green leaves are marbled with pale green and have purplish undersides. A half-hardy evergreen perennial requiring a warm sheltered site in the garden. HEIGHT & SPREAD 45×45 cm (1½×1½ ft).
H. niger♀ (Christmas rose) This evergreen perennial bears saucer-shaped, nodding flowers on short stout stems in mid winter. Up to 7.5 cm (3 in) across, the flowers have white petals, which may turn pinkish with age, and protruding golden stamens. The leaves have 7 to 9 dark green leaflets. HEIGHT & SPREAD 30×45 cm (1×1½ ft).

'Potter's Wheel' has larger flowers, up to 10 cm (4 in) across, with a greenish

h

▲ *Hemerocallis* 'Helle Berlinerin'

12.5 cm (5 in) across, with orange-yellow throats. HEIGHT 70 cm (28 in).

'**Hyperion**' The narrow, tapered lily-shaped lemon-yellow flowers, 10 cm (4 in) across, are very fragrant and occasionally double. HEIGHT 90 cm (36 in).

'**Joan Senior**' This evergreen has an abundance of lightly ruffled, near-white flowers, 15 cm (6 in) across, with yellowish green throats. HEIGHT 63 cm (25 in).

'**Judah**' Deep gold, bronze-edged rounded flowers, 15 cm (6 in) across, with yellow throats. HEIGHT 75 cm (30 in).

'**Kindly Light**' Spider-shaped with slender, bright yellow flowers, 22 cm (8¾ in) across, and a faint salmon-pink eyezone on cool evenings. Evergreen. HEIGHT 68 cm (27 in).

H. lilioasphodelus♀ (syn. *H. flava*) Fragrant semi-evergreen with tapered lily-shaped lemon-yellow flowers 9 cm (3½ in) across. HEIGHT 1 m (3 ft).

'**Little Gypsy Vagabond**' Evergreen with round, flat, light yellow flowers, 9 cm (3½ in) across, bold black-purple eyezone and green throat. HEIGHT 45 cm (18 in).

'**Little Wine Cup**' Trumpet-shaped wine-red flowers, 5 cm (2 in) across, with tiny chartreuse throats. HEIGHT 50 cm (20 in).

▼ *Hemerocallis* 'Luxury Lace'

'**Luxury Lace**' Frilly, star-shaped pinkish lavender flowers, 10 cm (4 in) across, with green throats. HEIGHT 80 cm (32 in).

'**Marion Vaughn**'♀ Very fragrant, tapered lily-shaped, pale lemon-yellow flowers, 10 cm (4 in) across. HEIGHT 84 cm (33 in).

'**Millie Schlumpf**' Round, ruffled, pure pale pink flowers, 12.5 cm (5 in) across, with a light green throat. HEIGHT 50 cm (20 in).

'**Mini Pearl**' Round, ruffled, blush-pink flowers, 7.5 cm (3 in) across, with a green-lemon throat. HEIGHT 40 cm (16 in).

'**Moonlight Mist**' Evergreen with pale ivory to cream-pink round and ruffled flowers, 7.5 cm (3 in) across, with chartreuse throats. HEIGHT 45 cm (18 in).

'**Night Raider**' Fragrant, round, very dark red flowers, 14 cm (5½ in) across, with small green throats. HEIGHT 70 cm (28 in).

'**Nova**'♀ Fragrant, star-shaped, satiny lemon-yellow flowers, 14 cm (5½ in) across, with green throats. HEIGHT 60 cm (24 in).

'**Olive Bailey Langdon**' This evergreen has rounded, rich violet-purple flowers, 12.5 cm (5 in) across, with yellow-green throats. HEIGHT 70 cm (28 in).

'**Pandora's Box**' Evergreen with fragrant pale cream flowers, 7.5 cm (3 in) across, with a vivid burgundy eyezone and a green throat. HEIGHT 48 cm (19 in).

'**Pardon Me**' Fragrant, round, cranberry-red flowers, 7.5 cm (3 in) across, with chartreuse throats. HEIGHT 45 cm (18 in).

▲ *Hemerocallis* 'Pandora's Box'

▲ *Hemerocallis* 'Pardon Me'

'**Pink Damask**'♀ Star-shaped, buff-tinged rose-pink flowers, 12.5 cm (5 in) across, with yellow throats and distinctive cream-pink midribs. HEIGHT 95 cm (38 in).

'**Prairie Blue Eyes**' This semi-evergreen has trumpet-shaped lavender flowers, 12 cm (4¾ in) across, with a chartreuse throat and a near-blue eyezone. HEIGHT 70 cm (28 in).

'**Purple Rain**' Evergreen with round, ruffled grape-purple flowers, 7.5 cm (3 in) across, with a prominent deep purple to near black eyezone. HEIGHT 38 cm (15 in).

'**Real Wind**' Round salmon-peach flowers, 16.5 cm (6½ in) across. A rose pink eyezone and a gold throat. HEIGHT 65 cm (26 in).

'**Sammy Russell**' Trumpet-shaped dark red flowers 10 cm (4 in) across. HEIGHT 70 cm (28 in).

'**Siloam Fairy Tale**' Round, ruffled, frosted pale pink flowers, 7.5 cm (3 in) across. Deep orchid-pink eyezone. HEIGHT 45 cm (18 in).

'**Siloam Little Girl**' Round, ruffled shrimp-pink flowers, 9 cm (3½ in) across. with a rose-red eyezone and green-gold throat. HEIGHT 45 cm (18 in).

'**Siloam Tiny Mite**' Round, golden-yellow flowers, 6 cm (2½ in) across, with a gold throat and maroon eyezone. HEIGHT 50 cm (20 in).

'**Siloam Virginia Henson**' Round, ruffled, pink-tinted cream flowers, 10 cm (4 in) across, with a ruby-red eyezone and green throat. HEIGHT 45 cm (18 in).

'**Stafford**' Scarlet, tapered lily-shaped flowers, 10 cm (4 in) across, with green-yellow throats. HEIGHT 70 cm (28 in).

'**Stella de Oro**'♀ Fragrant bell-shaped, brassy yellow flowers 7 cm (2¾ in) across. HEIGHT 28 cm (11 in).

▲ *Hemerocallis* 'Summer Wine'

'**Summer Wine**' Trumpet-shaped, light wine-red flowers, 14 cm (5½ in) across, with a chartreuse throat. HEIGHT 60 cm (24 in).

'**Tonia Gay**' Evergreen with round, ruffled, baby-pink flowers, 14 cm (5½ in) across, with green throats. HEIGHT 40 cm (16 in).

'**Varsity**' Trumpet-shaped, ivory flowers,

10 cm (4 in) across, with a maroon eyezone and a green throat. HEIGHT 75 cm (30 in).

'Whichford' ♀ Trumpet-shaped, fragrant, delicate lemon flowers, 10 cm (4 in) across, with green throats. HEIGHT 70 cm (28 in).

CULTIVATION Grow in fertile, moisture-retentive soil in full sun. Generally, adequate flowering cannot be expected if grown in dry conditions or in shade, but red and purple-flowered varieties can be intolerant of heavy rainfall and very hot sun. Plant the more tender evergreen varieties in spring rather than in autumn. Divide every 3 or 4 years to maintain vigour.

PROPAGATION Divide in late summer or early spring.

PESTS AND DISEASES Usually trouble free. Foliage is sometimes disfigured by rust and flower buds may be infected by gall midge. Slugs and snails damage young foliage in late winter and early spring. Crown rot can be a problem in hot and humid situations.

Hemlock see *Tsuga*
Hemp agrimony
  see *Eupatorium cannabinum*

Hepatica
Ranunculaceae

Bright pink, blue or white flowers add a splash of colour to the garden from late winter to early spring. These hardy herbaceous or evergreen perennials are ideal for semi-shaded positions but dislike exposed dry or windy sites. They are fully hardy but take a while to establish and do not like to be disturbed. They make good plants for a woodland garden or for a semi-shaded trough and can also be grown in pots in an unheated greenhouse or conservatory. Each flower has six to ten oval petals with a small ruff of three bracts immediately underneath. The leaves, which are 4-12.5 cm (1½-5 in) across, form a lax basal rosette and last all summer, long after the flowers have faded. They are long-stalked with three lobes and are often attractively mottled or marbled.

RECOMMENDED SPECIES AND VARIETIES
H. acutiloba Lavender-blue, occasionally pink or white, flowers up to 2 cm (¾ in) across appear in late winter and spring. The deep green evergreen leaves have distinctively pointed lobes. Native to calcareous woodland in eastern N America. HEIGHT & SPREAD 15-25×15-25 cm (6-10×6-10 in).
H. americana Bluish lavender flowers up to 2.5 cm (1 in) across appear in spring. The evergreen leaves have broad, blunt, rounded lobes. Native to dry acid woodlands of eastern N America. HEIGHT & SPREAD 10-15×10-15 cm (4-6×4-6 in).
H. angulosa see *H. transsilvanica*
H. × media **'Ballardii'** ♀ Masses of vivid, rich blue, semidouble flowers, 3 cm (1¼ in) across, appear in early spring. Soft green,

scalloped leaves are semi-evergreen. HEIGHT & SPREAD 10×20 cm (4×8 in).
H. nobilis ♀ (syn. *H. triloba*) Blue, purple, pink or white, 2 cm (¾ in) across, are borne in late winter and early spring. Double-flowered forms are occasionally seen. The kidney-shaped evergreen leaves are sometimes marbled with pale or dark green or grey and are often purple beneath. Native to mountains of continental Europe. HEIGHT & SPREAD 7.5×15 cm (3×6 in).

▲ *Hepatica nobilis*

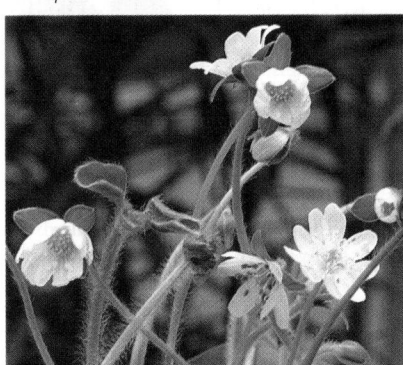
▲ *Hepatica nobilis* var. *japonica*

Selected forms are listed as **blue** (blue shades), **pink** (pink shades) and **white** (pure white); the flowers of var. *japonica* are usually white, sometimes with a hint of pink, and the leaves have more pointed lobes.

▲ *Hepatica transsilvanica*

H. transsilvanica ♀ (syn. *H. angulosa*) Pink, purple or lavender-blue flowers, 3 cm (1¼ in) across, appear in spring on this robust and reliably long-lived herbaceous species. The large mid green leaves, which occasionally have 5 lobes, are markedly round-toothed. Native to mountain woods in Romania. HEIGHT & SPREAD 10×20 cm (4×8 in).
H. triloba see *H. nobilis*
CULTIVATION Plant in early spring or

autumn in moist, humus-rich soil in partial shade and sheltered from the wind. Those grown in pots should be plunged in a sandy medium to keep roots cool during summer.
PROPAGATION Sow seed when ripe in pots in a cool, partially shaded coldframe. Prick out seedlings in autumn or the following spring and pot individually. Divide in late spring or early autumn, taking care not to damage the roots.
PESTS AND DISEASES Vine weevil and aphids can attack those in pots.

Heracleum
Umbelliferae

The giant hogweed *Heracleum mantegazzianum* is a massive, architectural plant that looks spectacular in an informal or wild garden. However, all parts of the plant are poisonous and contact with the skin can cause severe irritation and even permanent scarring, and it is not recommended for areas where children are unsupervised. The plant self-seeds easily, especially on moist ground, and it is considered a widespread nuisance in parts of the country.

RECOMMENDED SPECIES
Heracleum mantegazzianum (giant hogweed) Branched stems carry flat heads, each about 30 cm (1 ft) wide, of white or pink-tinged flowers in mid summer, followed by massive seed heads. The stout stems of this biennial or hardy short-lived perennial are ridged and purple-blotched. The pinnate, lobed leaves are about 3 m (10 ft) long. HEIGHT & SPREAD 3×2.8 m (10×9 ft).

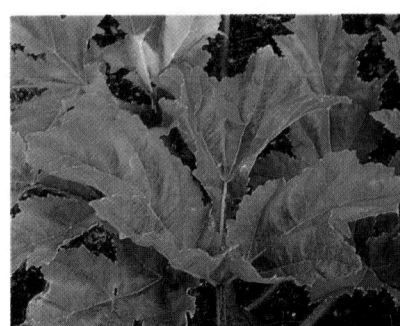
▲ *Heracleum mantegazzianum*

CULTIVATION Plant in spring or autumn in any soil in woodland conditions. Staking is only necessary in windy locations. Remove seed heads to prevent the plant spreading. It is an offence to cause it to grow in the wild, by seeding over a boundary, for example.
PROPAGATION Sow seed in spring in nursery rows and transplant when the seedlings are about 15 cm (6 in) tall, or sow in the final position on well-cultivated open ground.
PESTS AND DISEASES Usually trouble free.

Herb Christopher see *Actaea spicata*
Herb Paris see *Paris*
Herbs see p. 330

Marjoram
Origanum spp.
Labiatae

The small, oval, slightly downy leaves are aromatic and have a sweet, fresh, spicy flavour. Use them fresh or dried in pizzas, pasta dishes or meat and tomato dishes and sauces.

Common marjoram or **oregano** (*O. vulgare*) This tall hardy perennial has apple-green leaves and small rose-purple blooms during summer. HEIGHT & SPREAD 30 cm × 1 m (1×3 ft).

French or **pot marjoram** (*O. onites*) This dwarf shrub is hardy and produces a year-round supply of bright green leaves when grown indoors. It produces mauve to white flowers in summer. HEIGHT & SPREAD 60×60 cm (2×2 ft).

Sweet marjoram (*O. majorana*) The grey-green leaves of this half-hardy perennial have the finest flavour. Best grown as an annual, the plant produces clusters of small white flowers during summer. HEIGHT & SPREAD 60×30 cm (2×1 ft).

CULTIVATION Plant marjoram in any ordinary, well-drained soil in full sun. In autumn cut back common marjoram to keep the plant neat.

PROPAGATION Sow seed under glass in autumn or spring. Take softwood cuttings in late spring or divide in early spring.

PESTS AND DISEASES Marjoram is usually trouble free.

Mint
Mentha spp.
Labiatae

The common mint (*M. spicata*) is the most widely grown of the culinary mints. All have clean, fresh flavours and can be dried or frozen. Mint leaves make good garnishes for vegetables, fruit salads and summer drinks. They are also used to make mint sauce or jelly. These invasive hardy perennials have long growing seasons and bear small purple flowers in summer.

Apple mint (*M. suaveolens*) The rounded, hairy, grey-green leaves have a strong fragrance and aroma, and are particularly good in mint sauce. HEIGHT & SPREAD 1×1.2 m (3×4 ft).

Bowles' mint (*M. × villosa* var. *alopecuroides*) The large and rounded leaves are light green and downy. HEIGHT & SPREAD 1×1.2 m (3×4 ft).

Common mint, garden mint or **spearmint** (*M. spicata*) This robust mint has mauve stems and dark green, pointed leaves with a strong flavour. HEIGHT & SPREAD 1×1.2 m (3×4 ft).

Peppermint (*M. × piperita*) This compact mint has dark green, lance-shaped, pungent leaves. The stems are reddish. HEIGHT & SPREAD 50 cm × 1 m (20×36 in).

CULTIVATION Mint thrives in any ordinary, moist soil, in sun or partial shade. Grow it in a container sunk to the rim to confine the roots. Cut the stems back in summer to promote new leaf growth.

PROPAGATION Sow seed outdoors or take root cuttings in spring; divide plants at any time.

PESTS AND DISEASES Mint rust and mildew may affect plants.

Parsley
Petroselinum crispum
Umbelliferae

The dark green, intricately cut or densely curled leaves of parsley have a clean, refreshing and mildly spicy flavour. Use the fresh leaves in salads, as a garnish or in bouquet garni, and either fresh or dried in herb butter, soups, sauces, egg and fish dishes. The plant is a hardy biennial. Its tiny yellow flowers appear in the summer of the plant's second year. However, because the leaves have a better flavour in the first year, the plant is often grown as an annual. HEIGHT & SPREAD 30×20 cm (12×8 in).

French parsley (var. *neapolitanum*) This tall upright variety of parsley has flattened, dark green leaves which have a more pronounced flavour.

CULTIVATION Plant in moist, fertile soil, in sun or partial shade. Protect plants with cloches during winter.

PROPAGATION Sow seed outdoors in spring and summer for a year-round supply. To aid germination, soak the seeds overnight in warm water before sowing or sow in a seed tray at 21°C (70°F). Alternatively, leave the plant to self-seed.

PESTS AND DISEASES Aphids, slugs, leaf miner and virus diseases may affect plants.

Rosemary
Rosmarinus officinalis
Labiatae

The needle-shaped leaves of this hardy or half-hardy evergreen shrub are mid to dark green with pale silvery undersides. They are strongly aromatic and can be dried. Add sprigs or chopped leaves sparingly to lamb, pork or oily fish. The plant bears clusters of small, pale mauve-blue flowers from spring to late summer. HEIGHT & SPREAD 1.2×1 m (4×3 ft).

CULTIVATION Grow in well-drained soil in a sheltered, sunny position. Cut back straggling or frost-damaged stems in spring. Bring plants grown in containers indoors or under glass for protection in winter.

PROPAGATION Sow seed under glass in spring or take semi-ripe cuttings in mid to late summer.

PESTS AND DISEASES Rosemary is usually trouble free.

Sage
Salvia officinalis
Labiatae

This hardy evergreen shrub has rough, grey-green, oval leaves which have a strong aroma and a slightly bitter taste. Use them fresh or dried to complement rich meats and cheese, or in tomato-based sauces and stuffings. The dried leaves have a stronger flavour than fresh so use them sparingly. Purple-blue flower spikes appear in early to

mid summer. HEIGHT & SPREAD 60 cm × 1 m (2×3 ft).

CULTIVATION Grow in well-drained soil in full sun. Trim in spring and after flowering.

PROPAGATION Sow seed under glass in early spring or outdoors in mid to late spring. Alternatively, layer a long branch by pegging to the soil surface or take semi-ripe cuttings in early autumn. Renew plants every 3 or 4 years.

PESTS AND DISEASES Capsid bugs and powdery mildew may attack the leaves.

Savory
Satureja spp.
Labiatae

Strongly aromatic leaves have a peppery, slightly bitter flavour. Use them in salads or fresh, dried or frozen in bean dishes.

Summer savory (*S. hortensis*) The narrow, dark green leaves of this bushy annual have a slightly spicy flavour, which is especially pronounced before flowering. Tiny lilac blooms are borne from mid summer to early autumn. HEIGHT & SPREAD 45×30 cm (1½×1 ft).

Winter savory (*S. montana*) This hardy evergreen has grey-green leaves which have a coarser flavour than those of summer savory. Small pale rose flowers are borne from mid summer to mid autumn. Winter savory usually gives a year-round supply of leaves although some may drop after hard frosts. HEIGHT & SPREAD 45×30 cm (1½×1 ft).

CULTIVATION Grow in well-drained soil in full sun. Prune winter savory in spring and replace plants every 2 or 3 years.

PROPAGATION Sow summer savory outdoors in either spring or autumn. Sow winter savory under glass in spring or take semi-ripe cuttings in summer.

PESTS AND DISEASES Savory is usually trouble free.

Sorrel
Rumex spp.
Polygonaceae

The leaves of these hardy perennials have an acidic sourness, which counters the richness of meats. Use them fresh, dried or frozen. Sorrel leaves are good as flavourings for soups, added to salads or cooked like spinach.

Buckler-leaf or **French sorrel** (*R. scutatus*). The greyish green, triangular leaves have a mild lemony flavour. Small, reddish green flowers are borne in mid summer. HEIGHT & SPREAD 15×60 cm (6×24 in).

Common sorrel (*R. acetosa*) Spear-shaped leaves are fleshy and mid green. The plant produces spikes of tiny reddish flowers from early to mid summer. HEIGHT & SPREAD 60×30 cm (2×1 ft).

CULTIVATION Grow in well-drained, fertile soil, in full sun or partial shade.

PROPAGATION Sow seed outdoors in spring, or divide plants in spring or early autumn.

PESTS AND DISEASES Leaf-eating insects and slugs may affect plants.

Sweet cicely
Myrrhis odorata
Umbelliferae

The fragrant fern-like leaves of this perennial have a sweet aniseed taste. Use them fresh or dried in omelettes and salad dressings, or with stewed fruit. Cut back some of the clusters of tiny white flowers, which appear in early summer, to prolong leaf harvest. Leave some flowers to produce their sweet, nutty-flavoured seeds. Add these, green or ripe, to fruit salads or pies and ice cream. Lift roots in autumn and use in salads or as a vegetable. HEIGHT & SPREAD 1 m×60 cm (3×2 ft).

CULTIVATION Grow in any moist soil, in sun or light shade.

PROPAGATION Sow seed outside in early to mid spring, leave to self-seed or divide in autumn.

PESTS AND DISEASES Mildew can be troublesome.

Tarragon
Artemisia spp.
Compositae

The needle-shaped leaves of this perennial herb have a peppery-anise flavour. Use them fresh or dried in béarnaise sauce or vinegar and as flavourings in fish, chicken and vegetable dishes.

French tarragon (*A. dracunculus*) This tarragon is the best for culinary purposes. Its dark green foliage has a warm aroma and subtle taste. French tarragon is not fully hardy and needs protection from winter wet. Small yellow flowers appear in late summer. HEIGHT & SPREAD 1 m×45 cm (3×1½ ft).

Russian tarragon (*A. dracunculoides*) The leaves have a slightly bitter and less distinctive flavour

than French tarragon and are narrower and paler. The plant is fully hardy and vigorous. It can be grown from seed. HEIGHT & SPREAD 1.2 m×45 cm (4×1½ ft).

CULTIVATION Tarragon grows best in a sunny, sheltered position in very well-drained soil. Cut back French tarragon in autumn and lay a mulch over the base to protect it from frost or grow it in a pot and bring indoors for winter use.

PROPAGATION Divide French tarragon in spring or take softwood cuttings in late spring to early summer. Replace plants every 2-3 years. Sow Russian tarragon outdoors in spring.

PESTS AND DISEASES Rust may be a problem for both French and Russian tarragon.

Thyme
Thymus spp.
Labiatae

The dark green, aromatic leaves have a pungent flavour. Use fresh sprigs in bouquet garni and fresh or dried leaves or sprigs in stuffings, sauces, stocks, stews or marinades. These dwarf hardy evergreen shrubs have upright habits and produce small mauve or pink flowers in early summer.

Broad-leaved thyme (*T. pulegioides*) The leaves are large and rounded and are strongly flavoured. HEIGHT & SPREAD 8×30 cm (3×12 in).

Common thyme (*T. vulgaris*) Small leaves are oval and pointed. They have a slightly peppery flavour. HEIGHT & SPREAD 15×30 cm (6×12 in).

Lemon thyme (*T. × citriodorus*) The leaves are larger than those of common thyme and have a strong lemon scent. HEIGHT & SPREAD 15×15 cm (6×6 in).

CULTIVATION Grow in well-drained soil, in full sun. Trim regularly in the growing season to encourage new growth. Renew plants every 2-3 years.

PROPAGATION Sow seed under glass in early or mid spring or divide at this time. Layer in summer or take semi-ripe cuttings in early summer.

PESTS AND DISEASES Thyme is usually trouble free.

▼ POTTED DISPLAY *Their compact habits and long seasons make many herbs ideal plants for growing in a container garden.*

h

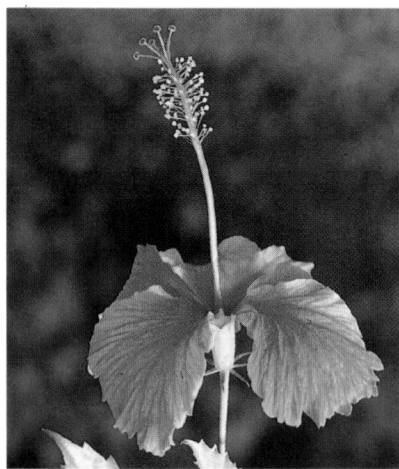

▲ *Hibiscus rosa-sinensis*

container and brought indoors before frosts occur. HEIGHT & SPREAD 2.4×2.4m (8×8ft).

'Cooperi', with scarlet flowers and leaves variegated red, pink and white, grows as tall as 1.5m (5ft). 'La France' has pink flowers. The vigorous 'Lemon Chiffon' has lemon-yellow flowers. 'Weekend' produces rich orange flowers.
H. schizopetalus♀ (Japanese lantern) Grow this evergreen shrub indoors. Pendent pink flowers, 6cm (2½in) across, with fringed, reflexed petals and a conspicuous central stamen column 8cm (3¼in) long, are borne in summer on long stalks. The plant has a spreading habit and can be trained as a climber. The leaves are ovate and toothed. HEIGHT & SPREAD 3×1.8m (10×6ft).

Hibiscus syriacus

H. syriacus A hardy deciduous shrub with an upright habit. Lilac-bue flowers, 8cm (3¼in) across, are freely produced in late summer and early autumn. The leaves are lobed. HEIGHT & SPREAD 2.4×1.8m (8×6ft).

'Diana' has white flowers and petals with crinkled edges. 'Hamabo'♀ bears pink flowers with a crimson eye and reaches a height and spread of 1.5m (5ft). 'Meehanii' carries magenta flowers with a crimson eye and has variegated foliage. 'Oiseau Bleu'♀ ('Blue Bird') has lilac-blue flowers with a deep red eye. 'Pink Giant'♀ bears pink flowers and grows to a height of

▼ *Hibiscus syriacus*

▲ *Hibiscus syriacus* 'Diana'

3m (10ft), spreading to 1.8m (6ft). 'Red Heart'♀ produces white flowers with conspicuous red centres. 'Woodbridge'♀ has large rich pink flowers with dark centres.

▲ *Hibiscus syriacus* 'Pink Giant'

▲ *Hibiscus syriacus* 'Red Heart'

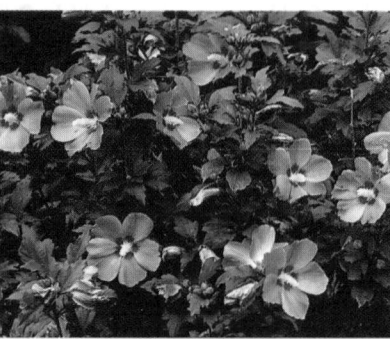

▲ *Hibiscus syriacus* 'Woodbridge'

H. trionum (flower-of-an-hour) This erect plant, grown as an annual, is hardy enough to be sown in the open to flower the same season. Many short-lived flowers, 5cm (2in) across, creamy white or pale yellow with purple centres, are produced in late summer and early autumn. The leaves are deeply divided and coarsely toothed. HEIGHT & SPREAD 60×30cm (24×12in).

'Sunny Day' is a dwarf, with lemon-yellow flowers with dark purple centres.

CULTIVATION H. acetosella, H. manihot and H. moscheutos, although perennials, are usually treated like other frost-tender bedding plants. They need a sunny, sheltered position and well-drained soil. Plant out young plants after the risk of frost has passed. H. trionum is hardy and does best in full sun.

H. rosa-sinensis is generally grown in large pots in a greenhouse or conservatory, with full exposure to sun. When still small the plant will thrive on a sunny windowsill. Keep plants quite dry in winter, in a minimum temperature of 7°C (45°F). In spring, cut plants back hard. Water liberally in summer. Treat H. schizopetalus similarly, but keep plants in a temperature of at least 10°C (50°F) in winter.

The shrub H. syriacus, although hardy, requires a sunny, sheltered situation. In cold areas, plant near a south-facing wall. Plant container-grown specimens in early spring in a well-drained soil; in lighter soils incorporate organic matter before planting. Deadheading, where practicable, will prolong the flowering display of all species.

PROPAGATION Sow seed of H. acetosella 'Coppertone', H. manihot and H. moscheutos under glass in winter. From sowings in mid to late spring, plants may be grown in pots in their first season and over-wintered in a cool greenhouse in at least 5°C (41°F); they will then do very well outdoors in their second season. Sow seed of H. trionum where it is to flower in mid spring; it does not transplant well.

Take semi-ripe cuttings of perennial species. Bottom heat is needed to ensure successful rooting. H. syriacus cultivars will also come from semi-ripe cuttings in late summer, but are slow.

PESTS AND DISEASES Aphids may infest all species. Plants that are grown under glass are susceptible to whitefly, mealy bugs and fungal root rot.

Hieracium
Hawkweed
Compositae

These hardy herbaceous or evergreen perennials bear rosettes of leaves, generally silvery grey, to 15cm (6in) long, and yellow flowers. The flowers – strictly 'flowerheads' made up of ray and disc florets – are borne all summer through. Remove the fluffy seed-heads that follow, or the plants will become weeds. The listed species are attractive to insects and so are good for a wild-flower garden. *Hieracium lanatum* and H. villosum are also suitable for a rock garden, but H. maculatum self-seeds too freely. The featured species are all native to Europe.

RECOMMENDED SPECIES
H. lanatum Mounds of downy grey elliptical leaves retain their beauty into winter. Flowers are small, about 2.5cm (1in) wide. HEIGHT & SPREAD 30×45cm (12×18in).

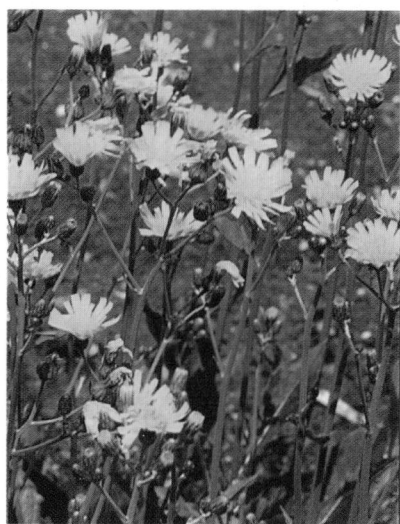

▲ *Hieracium maculatum*

H. maculatum The flowers, about 2.5 cm (1 in) across, are borne in lax clusters, in late spring and summer. The oblong, sharply toothed, evergreen leaves, up to 10 cm (4 in) long, are deep green blotched with purple. HEIGHT & SPREAD 40×30 cm (16×12 in).

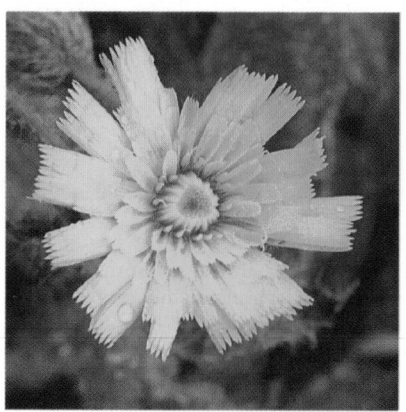

▲ *Hieracium villosum*

H. villosum There are 2-4 sulphur-yellow flowers, about 5 cm (2 in) across, on each downy stem. The woolly, silvery white, oblong leaves are borne in rosettes at the base of the plant – generally several rosettes are grouped together, occasionally there is a single large rosette. This is an evergreen plant. HEIGHT & SPREAD 30×20 cm (12×8 in).

CULTIVATION *H. lanatum* and *H. villosum* thrive in well-drained gritty soil, in a sunny spot. In wet areas, protect leaves during winter by placing a pane of glass or a cloche overhead. *H. maculatum* will thrive in most garden soils and often self-sows freely.

PROPAGATION Sow seed in pots, in winter, and prick out seedlings as soon as they are large enough to handle. Plant out in early to mid summer in the garden.

PESTS AND DISEASES Powdery mildew may appear on the foliage late in the season.

Himalayacalamus see BAMBOOS p.77

Hippeastrum
Amaryllis
Amaryllidaceae

Large funnel-shaped flowers are carried on strong, leafless hollow stems above at least four mid to deep green strap-shaped leaves, about 60 cm (24 in) long. These are among the boldest flowering greenhouse or pot plants. Modern hybrids produce up to six blooms, 20-25 cm (8-10 in) across, each with six petals. They bloom between early autumn and early winter, if heat treated to induce early bud formation, or from mid winter to mid or late spring, if untreated.

These tropical or sub-tropical bulbs are native to S America and not hardy. They are sold before Christmas as 'Amaryllis' for flowering indoors in spring. However, the true *Amaryllis*, which is similar in appearance, is hardier and can be grown outdoors.

RECOMMENDED SPECIES AND VARIETIES
H. papillo (butterfly amaryllis) Pale green flowers streaked and stained dark red appear in spring. This is one of the few species produced commercially. Feed all year round to maintain growth. HEIGHT 60 cm (24 in).

Among the hybrids, of uncertain parentage, are **'Apple Blossom'**, white flushed

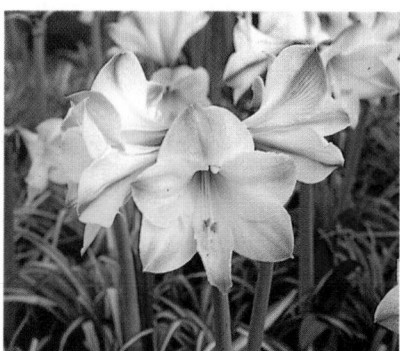

▲ *Hippeastrum* 'Apple Blossom'

and speckled pink; **'Bestseller'**♀, deep cerise, short-stemmed; **'Orange Sovereign'**♀, pure orange; **'Star of Holland'**, scarlet with a white throat and **'White Dazzler'**, white.

CULTIVATION Buy bulbs, up to 15 cm (6 in) wide, from early autumn to early spring for growing in a greenhouse or indoors. Plant at once in a pot 5 cm (2 in) wider than the bulb, half in and half out of an equal mix of well-rotted manure, coarse sand and John Innes compost. Water sparingly, increasing as growth begins. Feed with a liquid fertiliser every 7-10 days. Flowers appear 1-3 months after planting, depending how warm plants are kept. Planting at intervals ensures a succession of blooms, if the temperature is constant, although the later they are planted, the quicker they grow. Remove the flower stem immediately after flowering and keep the plant in a greenhouse. Stop watering in early autumn and let the foliage die down. In mid to late

autumn cut back the old foliage and leave the bulb dormant. Top dress before growth begins and, once it has started, begin watering again. Maintain 12°C (54°F) minimum.

PROPAGATION Sow seed as soon as it is ripe, in summer, in a sand and John Innes mix. Keep a minimum temperature of 16°C (61°F) and transplant into a 10 cm (4 in) pot when the seedlings reach 10-13 cm (4-5¼ in) high, which takes 9-18 months. Water the seedlings all year to sustain growth until mature. Repot annually in autumn, taking care not to damage the roots. When repotting large bulbs, remove offsets and pot on.

PESTS AND DISEASES Mealy bug, red spider mite, thrips and tomato spotted wilt virus can all be problems.

Hippocrepis
Leguminosae

Bright yellow heads of small, sweet-pea shaped flowers add colour to a sunny rock garden or border, generally from late spring into summer. The flowers are followed by curious curved, segmented pods. There are annuals, perennials and shrubs, all hardy, varying in habit from prostrate to upright. Native to Europe, N Africa and W Asia.

RECOMMENDED SPECIES
H. comosa (syn. *Coronilla comosa*) (horseshoe vetch) Whorls of 4–10 flowers are carried on erect stems above a spreading, leafy mat. The mid green leaves are made up of oblong leaflets. Pods are reddish brown and 2.5 cm (1 in) long. This prostrate perennial may overwhelm smaller, less vigorous plants. HEIGHT & SPREAD 10×60 cm (4×24 in).
H. emerus (syn. *Coronilla emerus*) (scorpion senna) Small clusters of fragrant flowers, yellow marked with brown, appear in early and mid summer on slender stalks. Leaves, to 6 cm (2½ in) long, are divided into small, rounded, bright green leaflets, on a robust deciduous shrub. Brown pods as long as 10 cm (4 in) resemble scorpions' tails. HEIGHT & SPREAD 80 cm×1 m (32×36 in) after 5 years, ultimately 2.4 m (8 ft) tall.

CULTIVATION Plant in early spring, in full sun in any well-drained soil. Plants are especially happy on chalk soils.

PROPAGATION Sow seed in early spring. Take softwood cuttings from *H. comosa* at some point during summer.

PRUNING Not normally necessary.

PESTS AND DISEASES Usually trouble free.

▼ *Hippocrepis comosa*

h

Hippophaë
Elaeagnaceae

Bright berries and silvery or sage-green foliage are the principal features of these hardy deciduous shrubs. There are three species, the most commonly grown being *Hippophaë rhamnoides*.

RECOMMENDED SPECIES

H. rhamnoides♀ (sea buckthorn) Tough, salt-tolerant, linear leaves, grey-green above and silver haired below, cover the great tan-

▲ *Hippophaë rhamnoides*

gles of sharp spiny branches. Thick clusters of golden orange berries are borne in autumn and winter. Plants form an impenetrable screen, making excellent windbreaks in exposed areas, both on the coast and inland. There are inconspicuous yellow-green flowers in early spring. Grow a male sea buckthorn with several female shrubs, to allow for pollination by wind. Native to Europe, including coastal areas of Britain, and temperate Asia. HEIGHT & SPREAD 1.8×3m (6×10ft) after 5 years, ultimately 4m (13ft) tall, spread indefinite.

CULTIVATION Grow in any ordinary, well-drained garden soil.

PROPAGATION Easy to raise from seed, or dig up and transplant root suckers in winter.

PRUNING Trim in mid or late summer.

PESTS AND DISEASES Usually trouble free.

Hoheria
Lacebark, ribbon wood
Malvaceae

Masses of delicate white flowers cover small, graceful trees, hardy in southern Britain, in mid to late summer. Trees first flower at about five years old. The five-petalled flowers, up to 4cm (1½in) across, resemble cherry blossom. The smooth bark easily peels off in long strips, revealing several inner layers of lacy fibres. Species may be evergreen or deciduous. The alternate leaves vary in shape according to the tree's age. They are normally smaller and more deeply lobed and toothed on young plants, though adult trees often carry 'juvenile' leaves. Native to New Zealand.

RECOMMENDED SPECIES AND VARIETIES

H. angustifolia This evergreen tree, slender and sparsely leaved, has mid green lance-shaped leaves, to 5cm (2in) long. Young branchlets are often tangled and drooping. HEIGHT & SPREAD 2×1m (6½×3ft) after 10 years, ultimately 8m (26ft) tall.

H. glabrata♀ (mountain ribbonwood) An open, deciduous tree, closely resembling *H. lyallii*. The leaves are much less hairy, with scalloped edges and drip tips.

▲ *Hoheria glabrata*

H. 'Glory of Amlwch'♀ Larger flowers are borne by an untidy tree with pale green, saw-edged leaves, 9cm (3½in) long, that remain through mild winters. HEIGHT & SPREAD 2×2m (6½×6½ft) after 10 years, ultimately 6m (20ft) tall.

H. lyallii♀ This deciduous tree has distinctive white hairy leaves up to 10cm (4in) long and 5cm (2in) wide in various shapes, often toothed. HEIGHT & SPREAD 4×4m (13×13ft) after 10 years, ultimately 6m (20ft) tall.

H. sexstylosa♀ Rich green leaves, acutely toothed, about 10cm (4in) long and 3cm (1¼in) wide, clothe an upright evergreen tree. HEIGHT & SPREAD 4×3m (13×10ft) after 10 years, ultimately 6m (20ft) tall.

CULTIVATION Plant in a well-drained soil in a site that is sheltered from cold winds. All hoherias thrive on chalk.

PROPAGATION Sow seed in spring or take semi-ripe heel cuttings in early autumn.

PRUNING Tidy and thin out in spring.

PESTS AND DISEASES Usually trouble free.

Holcus see GRASSES p.301
Holly see *Ilex*
Hollyhock see *Alcea*

▼ *Hoheria sexstylosa*

Holodiscus
Rosaceae

Feathery plumes of small creamy white flowers tumble down this large deciduous shrub from mid to late summer. This is a graceful spreading plant, particularly suited to a bank, where its arching habit can be fully enjoyed. Native to N and S America.

RECOMMENDED SPECIES

H. discolor (ocean spray) Tiny rounded flowers, white, cream and light brown, are borne in large branched clusters, up to 30cm (12in) long, which hang at the end of long strong shoots. The dark green leaves, with undersides covered in grey hairs, have 4 or 8 lobes and are sharply toothed. The leaves are as long as 9cm (3½in) and sometimes almost as wide. HEIGHT & SPREAD 1.5×1.2m. (5×4ft) after 5 years, ultimately 3.5×3m (12×10ft).

▲ *Holodiscus discolor*

CULTIVATION Grow in sun or shade in any soil. Do not let plants dry out.

PROPAGATION Take semi-ripe cuttings, or sow seed in early or mid spring.

PRUNING Not normally required. Thin out stems, if necessary, in spring.

PESTS AND DISEASES Usually trouble free.

Honesty see *Lunaria*
Honeysuckle see *Lonicera*
Honeysuckle, French
    see *Hedysarum coronarium*
Hop, common see *Humulus lupulus*
Hop tree see *Ptelea trifoliata*
Hordeum see GRASSES p.301

Horminum
Dragonmouth
Labiatae

Dense one-sided spikes of richly coloured flowers rise from lustrous leaf rosettes in summer on this hardy evergreen perennial, native to the Alps and Pyrenees. There is only one species in the genus. The plant is best grown in a rock garden, sandwiched between two rocks, or in a crack in a wall.

Horminum pyrenaicum Nodding, violet-blue, funnel-shaped flowers, about 2cm

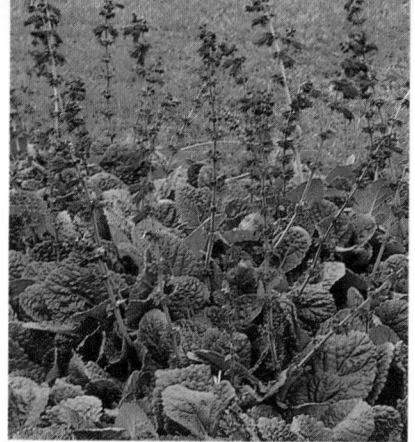

▲ *Horminum pyrenaicum*

(¾ in) long, borne on short stalks, appear in early and mid summer, occasionally later. The deep green, stalked leaves, about 7.5 cm (3 in) long, rounded or oval, are shiny, crinkled and leathery. HEIGHT & SPREAD 25×40 cm (10×16 in).

CULTIVATION Grow plants in moist, well-drained soil, in sun or partial shade. They dislike acid soil.

PROPAGATION Sow seed in pots in winter in a coldframe and prick out seedlings when they are large enough to handle. Divide in early spring or immediately after flowering. They will often self-sow.

PESTS AND DISEASES Usually trouble free.

Hornbeam see *Carpinus*
Hornbeam, hop see *Ostrya*
Horseradish (culinary herb)
see HERBS p. 331

Hosta
Plantain lily
Hostaceae

Hosta fortunei var. albopicta

Most hostas are grown for the architectural qualities of their sumptuous foliage. The sculptured leaves vary from lance-shaped to almost round, and from a few inches to more than a foot long. Leaf colour varies through cool blue-greens, silver-blues, darkest greens and yellow to variegations of gold and cream in splashes and outlined margins. Often richly textured with prominent veins, the leaves can be heavily corrugated and puckered and matt or glossy. They provide interest from spring to first frosts, dying down in late autumn.

Trumpet or bell-shaped flowers, in shades of purple, mauve and white, bloom in summer, usually well above the mound of leaves. They are borne on stems that are bare or have leaf-like bracts.

Hardy and adaptable perennials, hostas provide excellent ground cover and several varieties have a creeping root system that fills a big area, making them attractive and useful plants for mass planting. Once established, they can be left undisturbed for years. Most are suitable for shady borders and woodland gardens and many are ideally suited to container growing. Deeply cupped varieties collect debris from trees in their leaves and are best planted in shade from buildings. Dwarf and miniature varieties are excellent in shaded rock gardens.

All hostas require a moist soil and grow best in light to full shade, unless stated otherwise. They all need to be sheltered from wind, as otherwise their leaves can split or scorch at the edges. Natives of Japan, China and Korea, the genus has 25 or more species and over 1500 registered cultivars.

RECOMMENDED SPECIES AND VARIETIES
The hostas listed below are divided into 3 groups:
(1) Very large to large
(2) Large to medium
(3) Medium to small

VERY LARGE TO LARGE HOSTAS
H. **'Big Daddy'** The rounded, cupped leaves are intensely blue and heavily furrowed and puckered. Pale lavender to nearly white flowers bloom from early to mid summer. It is quite slow to establish. HEIGHT & SPREAD 60×90 cm (24×36 in).
H. **'Blue Angel'**♀ Smooth, arching, blue-grey leaves are nearly heart-shaped and pointed with gently wavy edges. The plant has a lush, tropical appearance. Flowers, from mid to late summer, are near white. HEIGHT & SPREAD 1×1.2 m (3×4 ft).
H. fluctuans **'Sagae'** (syn. *H. fluctuans* 'Variegated'♀) Soft sage-green leaves with bold cream to yellow margins are held horizontally on upright leaf stalks. Broadly wedge-shaped and gracefully pointed, they emerge twisted but become gently wavy. Flowers from early to mid summer are pale lavender suffused with purple. Slow to establish, the plant eventually forms a huge clump. HEIGHT & SPREAD 1×1.2 m (3×4 ft).
H. **'Frances Williams'**♀ A handsome plant with thick, puckered, heart-shaped leaves that are deep blue-green with wide, irregular cream to yellow margins. The pale lavender to near white flowers are borne in dense heads from early to mid summer. Best grown in full shade, as the leaf edges may scorch. HEIGHT & SPREAD 60 cm×1 m (2×3 ft).
H. montana **'Aureomarginata'** Upright and arching, oval to heart-shaped leaves have broad golden yellow margins. This is usually the first hosta to emerge in spring, but the plant is prone to frost damage. If damaged leaves are removed, the next flush

▼ *Hosta montana* 'Aureomarginata'

may escape the frosts. Flowers from early to mid summer are near-white suffused with lavender. The plant grows best in full shade. HEIGHT & SPREAD 75 cm×1 m (2½×3 ft).
H. nigrescens The ashy grey-green leaves are puckered and cupped. Oval to almost heart-shaped, they are carried on long leaf stems. The flowers are pale lavender to nearly white, from mid to late summer. HEIGHT & SPREAD 65×70 cm (26×28 in).
H. sieboldiana The large, thick, heart-shaped to almost round leaves are very puckered and bluish grey-green. The flowers, from early to mid summer, are pale lavender to nearly white on stems about the same height as the leaf mound. HEIGHT & SPREAD 60 cm×1 m (2×3 ft).
'Elegans'♀ is a superb variety with intense blue-green leaves.

▲ *Hosta sieboldiana* 'Elegans'

H. **'Sum and Substance'**♀ The slightly heart-shaped leaves, satiny yellowish green to golden yellow, are very thick and puckered when mature. Flowers are pale lavender to nearly white, from mid summer to early autumn. Leaves assume a better colour in full sun. Requires plenty of moisture. HEIGHT & SPREAD 75 cm×1.5 m (2½×5 ft).
H. **'Zounds'** Heart-shaped leaves, puckered and somewhat twisted, satiny yellow-green to rich yellow-gold, sometimes with green streaks, hold their colour even in the shade. Pale lavender to nearly white flowers are borne from early to mid summer. HEIGHT & SPREAD 40×75 cm (16×30 in).

LARGE TO MEDIUM HOSTAS
H. **'August Moon'** The oval to heart-shaped leaves, slightly puckered, are pale

▼ *Hosta* 'Zounds'

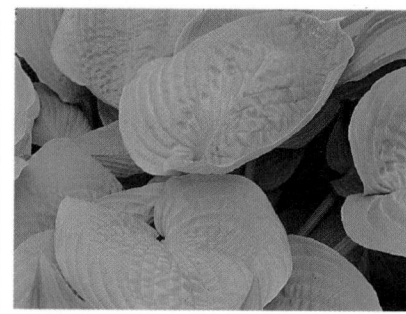

green at first, becoming soft yellow. Pale lavender to near white flowers bloom from mid to late summer. This is a vigorous plant that is easy to grow. It colours better in sun than in shade. HEIGHT & SPREAD 75×75 cm (30×30 in).

H. fortunei var. *albopicta*♥ In spring the heart-shaped leaves are a soft yellow streaked with green, with dark green margins. The leaves fade to a faintly variegated green by flowering time. Blooms are lavender, from early to mid summer. HEIGHT & SPREAD 60 cm×1 m (2×3 ft).

▲ *Hosta fortunei* var. *albopicta*

The leaves of var. *aureomarginata*♥ have an irregular yellow to cream margin and the grey-green leaves of var. *hyacinthina*♥ have a faint pencil-line margin.

H. 'Francee'♥ One of the best of the white-margined hostas. The flat, narrowly heart-shaped leaves are dark olive-green, with a narrow, irregular, white margin. The lavender flowers bloom from mid to late

▲ *Hosta fortunei* var. *aureomarginata*
Hosta fortunei var. *hyacinthina* ▼

▲ *Hosta* 'Francee'

summer. The plant increases rapidly. It is best grown in light shade. HEIGHT & SPREAD 60 cm×1 m (2×3 ft).

H. 'Patriot' is similar, but with much wider margins to the leaves.

H. 'Gold Standard'♥ The oval to heart-shaped leaves are first dark green with yellow-green margins, then golden yellow, fading to beige, with a deep green margin. In too much sun leaves turn white and can burn; in too little sun they remain green. Lavender flowers are borne from mid to late summer. Adequate moisture is essential. HEIGHT & SPREAD 50 cm×1 m (20 in×3 ft).

H. 'Invincible' Thick, glossy, olive-green leaves are wedge-shaped tapering to a long point and very wavy. Many lightly fragrant, lavender to near white flowers are borne from late summer to early autumn. Best grown in light shade to sun. Less attractive to slugs and snails than many other hostas. HEIGHT & SPREAD 40 cm ×1 m (16 in×3 ft).

H. lancifolia♥ The shiny mid green leaves are oval to lance-shaped with a pointed tip and slightly wavy margins. Intense purple-violet flowers are borne from late summer to early autumn. The plant provides useful ground cover. If left undisturbed it forms large colonies. The flowers can be attacked by blackfly. It flourishes in light shade. HEIGHT & SPREAD 30×60 cm (1×2 ft).

H. 'Midas Touch' The cupped and deeply puckered heart-shaped leaves are a rich golden yellow with a bronze-metallic caste. Pale lavender to near white flowers bloom from mid to late summer. Leaves colour best in direct sunlight. HEIGHT & SPREAD 30×75 cm (12×30 in).

H. 'Patriot' see *H.* 'Francee'

H. 'Paul's Glory' The puckered, heart-shaped leaves are first bright yellow, then creamy white, with an irregular, broad blue-green margin. Flowers are pale lavender to near white, from early to mid summer. Grows best in light shade or some sun. HEIGHT & SPREAD 45×65 cm (18×26 in).

H. plantaginea Glossy light to mid green leaves are heart-shaped with deeply impressed veins and lightly wavy edges. The plant rarely flowers. Large, fragrant, white blooms are sometimes produced in late summer and early autumn in warm sheltered areas. Best grown in a large tub, against a south-facing wall or in a conservatory. HEIGHT & SPREAD 45 cm×1 m (1½×3 ft).

'Grandiflora' (syn *H. p.* var. *japonica*) has laxer and longer leaves and flowers with longer tubes.

H. 'Royal Standard'♥ Narrowly heart-shaped, glossy, light green leaves become puckered when mature. Fragrant white flowers bloom from mid summer to early autumn. The plant does best in sun. HEIGHT & SPREAD 45 cm×1 m (1½×3 ft).

▲ *Hosta* 'Royal Standard'

H. 'Shade Fanfare'♥ Heart-shaped leaves are a soft sage green, irregularly margined with cream. Lavender flowers are borne from early to mid summer. HEIGHT & SPREAD 40×60 cm (16×24 in).

H. 'So Sweet'♥ The glossy, deep green, oval leaves, somewhat puckered, with wide creamy white margins, carried on very long stems, form an upright clump. Lightly fragrant white flowers open from mauve buds in mid and late summer. The plant flowers best in more sun than most hostas require. HEIGHT & SPREAD 35×60 cm (14×24 in).

H. 'Thomas Hogg' see *H. undulata* var. *albomarginata*

H. undulata var. *undulata*♥ Twisted leaves, broadly oval to lance shaped, are creamy white with irregular green margins. Lavender flowers appear from early to mid summer. The plant is best grown in full shade because leaves may scorch in the sun. It is prone to damage from pests. HEIGHT & SPREAD 35×45 cm (14×18 in).

▼ *Hosta undulata* var. *undulata*

H. undulata var. *albomarginata* (syn. 'Thomas Hogg') has larger, less wavy edged, matt green leaves with irregular white margins. *H. undulata* var. *univittata*♥ has a larger, flatter, matt green leaf with a narrow, white, central variegation.

H. ventricosa♥ One of the best green-leaved hostas. Glossy, heart-shaped, spinach green leaves have rippled margins and widely spaced veins. Rich bluish purple flowers are borne from mid summer to early

▲ *Hosta ventricosa*

▲ *Hosta 'Halcyon'*

autumn. Best grown in shade as the leaves are somewhat thin and scorch at the edges. HEIGHT & SPREAD 50 cm × 1 m (20 in × 3 ft).

MEDIUM TO SMALL HOSTAS

H. albomarginata see *H. sieboldii* 'Paxton's Original'

H. 'Blue Moon' The blue-grey leaves are rounded to heart-shaped, cupped and puckered. Many pale lavender-grey to white flowers, in early and mid summer. Slow to increase, the plant does best in dappled shade. HEIGHT & SPREAD 20×25 cm (8×10 in).

H. 'Blue Wedgwood' Wedge-shaped blue-green leaves have wavy margins and taper to a point. The flowers are pale lavender to white, in early and mid summer. HEIGHT & SPREAD 25×60 cm (10×24 in).

H. 'Gold Edger' The thick, heart-shaped leaves are at first greenish yellow, then a rich soft yellow. Many pale lavender to near white flowers bloom in early and mid summer. Plants increase rapidly, making good ground cover. Best in light shade to sun. HEIGHT & SPREAD 30×70 cm (12×28 in).

H. 'Golden Prayers' Leaves are deep yellow, oval to heart-shaped and upright. Thick in texture, they become puckered when mature. The flowers are palest lavender to near white, in early and mid summer. The plant is best in light shade. HEIGHT & SPREAD 30×50 cm (12×20 in).

H. 'Golden Tiara'♥ A neat, compact plant that increases rapidly. The oval to heart-shaped, matt green leaves are irregularly

▲ *Hosta* 'Golden Tiara'

margined with creamy yellow. Showy, deep lavender flowers striped with purple bloom from mid to late summer. HEIGHT & SPREAD 36×60 cm (14×24 in).

H. 'Hadspen Blue' The thick, heart-shaped leaves, an intense grey-blue, form neat, dense mounds. Lavender flowers bloom in early and mid summer. The plant grows best in dappled shade. HEIGHT & SPREAD 25×45 cm (10×18 in).

H. 'Halcyon'♥ The smooth, heart-shaped

leaves are silver-blue. Flowers are greyish lavender to near white, in early and mid summer. Best in dappled shade. HEIGHT & SPREAD 50 cm × 1 m (20 in × 3 ft).

H. 'June' is similar, but with yellow leaves with striking, irregular blue-green margins.

H. 'Devon Green' is again similar, with glossy mid green leaves.

H. 'Lemon Lime' Bright greenish yellow leaves are lance-shaped with wavy edges. The flowers, lavender striped with purple, are borne from mid to late summer. Good for a shaded rock garden or peat bed. HEIGHT & SPREAD 10×45 cm (4×18 in).

H. 'Love Pat'♥ see *H. tokudama*

H. sieboldii 'Paxton's Original' (syn. *H. albomarginata*) Narrowish leaves are a dull dark green, edged with white. Lavender flowers with dark purple stripes are borne from mid to late summer. The plant needs a damp situation. It tolerates more sun than many other hostas. It spreads slowly into extensive clumps. HEIGHT & SPREAD 20×25 cm (8×10 in).

H. s. var. *alba* has mid green leaves and white flowers.

H. tokudama The thick, rounded, strongly cupped, deeply puckered leaves are greyish dark blue. Flowers are palest lavender to nearly white, from early to mid summer. This beautiful hosta is slow to increase. HEIGHT & SPREAD 30×60 cm (1×2 ft).

The superb variety *H.* 'Love Pat'♥ is larger and more vigorous.

H. venusta♥ The satiny green leaves are variable on shape, but usually oval to heart-shaped. Flowers are a deep lavender. HEIGHT & SPREAD 8×10 cm (3¼×4 in).

H. 'Wide Brim'♥ The heart-shaped, slightly cupped and puckered leaves are a satiny rich, mid green with a wide irregular cream margin. The flowers are pale lavender to nearly white. This plant increases rapidly. It grows best in light shade. HEIGHT & SPREAD 60 cm × 1 m (2×3 ft).

CULTIVATION Plant hostas in spring or autumn. They thrive best in rich, friable loam just the acid side of neutral. Although they grow well in alkaline soils, they seldom flourish on shallow, chalky soils, which cause leaves to assume a yellowish tinge. Large hostas will grow well on heavy clay soils rich in plant nutrients, but can be slower to become established. They will grow more quickly if, before planting, the soil is lightened by working in copious and equal quantities of coarse grit and garden compost or well-rotted manure. Mulch regularly in autumn and keep well watered.

Smaller and dwarf hostas need a more friable mixture of peat and garden compost, regularly mulched with leaf-mould and coarse grit. Feed all hostas with a balanced plant food in spring and early summer.

PROPAGATION Divide clumps in late summer or early spring. Hostas are easily grown from seed but do not usually come true, other than *H. ventricosa*.

PESTS AND DISEASES Slugs and snails can do considerable damage especially when new shoots first appear above the ground, and again 2 weeks later as leaves unfurl. For container-grown hostas vine weevil larvae can be a problem – renew soil annually. In addition, virus damage can affect hostas, and leaf spot is occasionally a problem.

Hottonia
Primulaceae

Whorls of pale mauve or white flowers up to 2.5 cm (1 in) wide distinguish these submerged or floating aquatic perennials. They are hardy, easily grown herbaceous plants for a sunny pond or slowly running stream. The finely segmented light green leaves, up to 10 cm (4 in) long, are mostly under water. The flowers, borne in early and mid summer, are carried well above the surface. Tiny, rounded, light green fruit pods containing numerous seeds appear in late summer. Native to Europe, W Asia and eastern N America.

RECOMMENDED SPECIES

H. palustris (water violet) Flowers are pale mauve or lilac. Each has a short tube and 5 spreading lobes, which are notched at the tips. Both free-floating and rooted stems bear feathery submerged leaves. HEIGHT & SPREAD 15-25 cm (6-10 in) above water, spread indefinite.

CULTIVATION Plant in spring, in an aquatic plant basket containing a fertile soil-based compost, in 15 cm (6 in) of water, near the edge of a pond or stream, in full sun.

PROPAGATION Take greenwood cuttings in early summer. Established plants may naturalise by self-sown seeds.

PESTS AND DISEASES Usually trouble free.

Hound's tongue see *Cynoglossum*
Houseleek see *Sempervivum*

▼ *Hottonia palustris*

h

HOUSE PLANTS

CREATING AN INDOOR GARDEN

BRING THE OUTSIDE WORLD INTO THE HOME
AND TRANSFORM INTERIORS WITH LIVING
DISPLAYS OF COLOUR AND FORM

Ranging from tiny cacti to tall stately palms, houseplants offer the gardener a vast array of shapes, textures, colours and markings to enjoy. Exotic foliage, showy flowers and colourful ornamental fruits combine to create a diverse indoor garden that provides interest throughout the year.

Choose species that will tolerate the conditions in different areas of your home. Many houseplants prefer a site in bright indirect light but some, such as *Tolmiea menziesii* (pickaback plant) thrive in cool and shady rooms. A few, including

BRILLIANT RED *Bright poinsettias are at their best in deepest winter.*

tough succulents, will flourish in brightly lit, warm areas. Only very dark sites are unsuitable for all houseplants.

As well as bringing a living dimension to a room, indoor plants can add charm and elegance and help to set the room's style. A shapely palm, such as a *Howea*, for example, is ideally suited to a formal setting; a spiky-leaved *Dracaena* or *Yucca* sets off an interior that is starkly architectural; while a row of *Pelargonium* (geranium) cultivars in containers looks bright and cheerful on the windowsill of a country cottage.

◀ LUXURIANT FRUITS
Jerusalem cherry adds colour to a grouping of lush foliage plants.

RICH FOLIAGE

Houseplants that have attractive foliage create long-lived displays that look good all year round. The range of leaf shapes is huge, from the large, luxuriant, deeply cut foliage of *Monstera deliciosa* (Swiss cheese plant) to the sharp-edged geometric leaves of *Sansevieria trifasciata* (mother-in-law's tongue). There are plants with delicately divided fronds, such as *Adiantum* (maidenhair fern), and with palmate leaves, such as *Schefflera elegantissima* (false aralia). There are also rounded shapes, such as the leaves of *Maranta*, or arrow shapes, such as the leaves of *Syngonium podophyllum* (goosefoot plant).

Leaf texture is varied, from the smooth, glossy shininess of *Philodendron* to the intricate, rippled surfaces of the leaves of some species of *Begonia* and *Pilea*. Interest is also provided by variations in shades of green, such as the dark green of *Aspidistra elatior* (cast-iron plant) and the fresh green of *Chamaedorea elegans* (parlour palm), and by richly coloured markings in purples, reds, greens and yellows, such as those of *Solenostemon* (coleus). Other houseplants, including the weeping fig *Ficus benjamina* 'Starlight', display variegated leaves which are marked with silver, gold or cream.

BRIGHT COLOUR

If given the correct conditions, some houseplants will flower regularly and make colourful shows. *Saintpaulia* (African violet) and *Streptocarpus* (Cape primrose) are among the best for length of flowering season. When kept in a warm and well-lit room, *Pelargonium* also provides blooms throughout much of the year.

Schlumbergera (Christmas cactus) flowers reliably and provides a welcome splash of colour in winter. Exotic plants, such as *Anthurium scherzerianum* (flamingo flower) with its large, waxy red flowers, *Phalaenopsis amabilis* (moth orchid) and the scented climber

▲ STRIKING FOLIAGE *The bold, glossy leaves of a variegated schefflera gleam in sunlight.*

Stephanotis floribunda, will produce flowers as long as their needs for warmth, humidity and good indirect light are met.

Some flowering plants can be treated as temporary residents, brought into the house for a display of blooms and removed after flowering. Short-lived flowering plants, such as

▼ LONG-LASTING DISPLAY
Cape primroses provide colourful blooms over several months.

Exacum affine (Persian violet) and *Primula*, are a source of instant colour. Other plants for temporary displays include *Cyclamen*, *Pericallis* and *Euphorbia pulcherrima* (poinsettia), with its brilliant red, pink or cream bracts.

Bright colour is also contributed by plants with ornamental fruits. Chilli peppers and *Solanum pseudocapsicum* (Jerusalem cherry), which has orange-red berries that last through much of autumn and winter, make good houseplants.

SHAPELY FORMS

Houseplants vary dramatically in their size and form. Tall erect plants may have a tree-like appearance, for example *Ficus elastica* 'Robusta' (rubber plant) or false aralia with its attractive whorls of glossy leaves. Tall houseplants can be displayed anywhere with suitable conditions where there is room, and are useful for areas with high ceilings, such as halls.

Plants may be upright, for example columnar cacti, form rosettes like the succulent *Echeveria* or be spreading or bushy like *Pilea*. Bushy species look particularly effective when

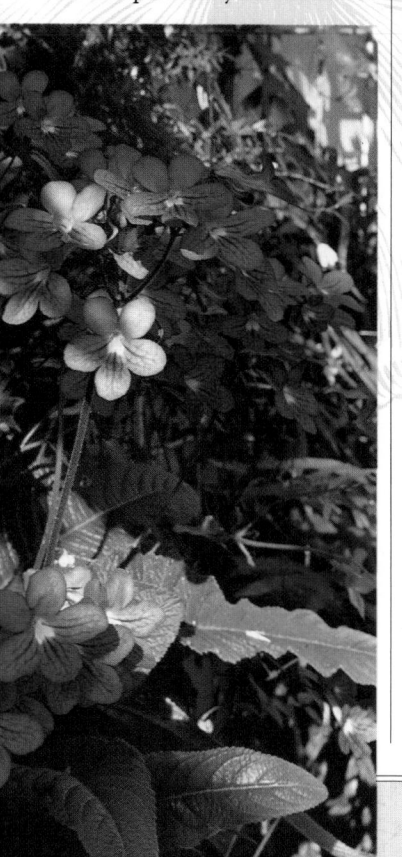

displayed in fireplaces, or on side tables and plant stands. Low-growing plants which have spreading habits, such as *Begonia*, are useful for windowsills or shelves, where there is little vertical space.

Some houseplants have a climbing or trailing habit, such as *Cissus rhombifolia* (grape ivy), *Hedera helix* (ivy) and *Philodendron scandens* (sweetheart plant). Grow a climber up a moss pole or train it up wires or a wall-mounted trellis. A trailing plant looks particularly attractive when its leaves and stems are left to cascade from a hanging basket, a container placed on a high shelf or a pot that has been fixed to a wall.

STRIKING DISPLAYS

Tall houseplants can make good focal points when they are displayed as specimens. A *Howea*, or other large palm, set singly in a high-ceilinged room makes a graceful feature, for example, while a large climber trained up a moss pole in a stairwell commands attention.

Most indoor plants, however, are best displayed in a group, where they create a slightly humid microclimate. Place tall plants with more compact ones for a balanced display. Use climbers as backdrops and upright plants as

centrepieces. Create interest and variety by combining houseplants that have differently shaped, coloured or textured leaves.

Plants which have plain green leaves provide simple contrasts to the strong colour of *Codiaeum* foliage, and accentuate the decorative patterns of *Maranta* leaves. Similarly, the corrugated foliage of some *Peperomia* is highlighted when set against the smooth-surfaced leaves of the peace lily *Spathiphyllum wallisii*. A plant with large, striking foliage, such as the Swiss cheese plant or a big-leaf philodendron, go well with delicate-looking plants, such as *Mimosa pudica* (sensitive plant) which has light green divided leaves.

Flowering plants look good among foliage plants, whose leaves provide an attractive backdrop. The feathery maidenhair fern and *Asparagus setaceus*, for example, combine well with cyclamen in winter, bulbs in spring and pelargoniums in summer. Another colourful combination is the variegated spider plant *Chlorophytum comosum* 'Vittatum' and the dark-leaved *Begonia* 'Cleopatra'. Add Cape primroses to provide extra colour from mid spring right through to early autumn.

LIGHT CONDITIONS

Many houseplants grow best in bright filtered light. Site them on a sunny windowsill and screen the window with a translucent curtain, or place plants a short way back from the window. Houseplants also grow well in areas that receive direct light for only part of the day.

Positioned in a site with too little light, many houseplants produce weak growth and their leaves turn paler. In excess light, foliage becomes scorched. As plants grow towards the light, they benefit from regular turning to prevent lopsided growth.

In very sunny areas in front of south-facing windows, display shrubby flowering conservatory plants, such as *Abutilon*, *Bougainvillea* and *Hibiscus*. The plants will thrive here provided that they have enough space.

In poorly lit areas, use houseplants that are shade tolerant, such as *Aglaonema* (Chinese evergreen), *Ficus deltoidea* var. *diversifolia* (mistletoe fig) and × *Fatshedera lizei*. Even shade-tolerant plants may deteriorate if light levels are very low. Rotate them every few weeks, moving the plants to an area with better light so that they produce healthy growth.

Many other houseplants, especially flowering ones, will benefit from being moved to positions where they can get as much sunlight as possible during the winter months.

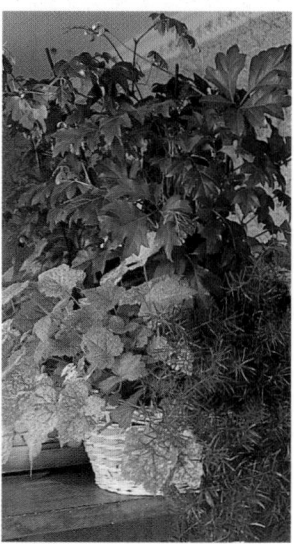

▲ LEAFY VARIATION *Differing shapes and textures of foliage make an eye-catching show.*

TEMPERATURE ZONES

Houseplants need higher temperatures during the day and throughout the growing season than at night and in winter. Many houseplants grow well in centrally heated rooms, in a daytime temperature range of 18-23°C (64-73°F) and a minimum night-time temperature of 13°C (55°F).

Hardy plants, such as ivy and *Fatsia japonica*, thrive in unheated rooms. Provided there is sufficient light and a minimum temperature of 10°C (50°F), *Citrus*, *Bougainvillea* and other half-hardy shrubs that enjoy cool, airy conditions will also do well here.

In rooms that are kept very warm – at temperatures of 23°C (74°F) or above – dry air may cause damage, including brown leaf edges. To combat this, use a humidifier to create a moist atmosphere or group plants on trays of wet gravel. This is particularly important for those that have delicate leaves, such as *Calathea*. Misting the plants also increases humidity and is of particular benefit to those that absorb water through their foliage, such as the bromeliad *Tillandsia*, or through their aerial roots, such as the epiphytic orchids.

Most houseplants react badly to extreme fluctuations in temperature. Do not site them in areas where this is likely to

◀ FOLIAGE FRAME *A weeping fig at a doorway guides the eye towards the garden beyond.*

soil, which will tend to cling if it is moist. Alternatively, lift up the pot to check its weight – it will feel lighter when the soil is dry than when it is wet.

When watering during the growing season, flood the soil until water leaks out of the drainage holes in the bottom of the pot, then drain thoroughly. Water a delicate plant by standing the container in a saucer of water, to avoid splashing and marking the foliage.

During winter, reduce the watering to encourage plants to rest while light levels are low. Drought-tolerant plants, such as *Crassula*, *Aloe* and other succulents, should be kept unwatered in a cool room. If the room is warm, water these plants very sparingly to prevent shrivelling.

Tap water is suitable for many houseplants, but check the individual requirements. Lime haters, such as orchids, and bromeliads, should be watered with rainwater.

FEEDING AND POTTING

A plant growing in a container has a limited supply of nutrients and will cease growth almost entirely when these are exhausted. Feeding and occasional repotting are essential to maintain healthy growth.

Slow-release pellets or sticks save effort as only one application a year is needed. Alternatively, use a general-purpose fertiliser during the growing season; flowering plants benefit from a high-potash feed, such as a tomato fertiliser, which stimulates flowering.

Apply feed at half strength to slow-growing plants, such as succulents and bromeliads. Do not feed plants when growth has slowed or ceased in winter.

If a plant begins to look starved, with little new growth and yellowing leaves, and its soil dries out quickly, it probably needs repotting. When it is tipped from its pot, the plant will reveal a mass of roots round its soil ball.

Young plants benefit from repotting each spring. Move those growing in pots less than 10cm (4in) wide into pots that

occur – above a radiator or near a badly fitted window or door, for example. A plant on a windowsill that is curtained off from the warmth of the room may also suffer damage on a cold night.

WATERING AMOUNTS

Both overwatering and underwatering plants causes poor growth as well as making the plant more vulnerable to pests and diseases.

Except for moisture-lovers, such as *Spathiphyllum*, most houseplants should be watered once the surface 2.5cm (1in) of compost has dried out. Use your finger or a stick to test the

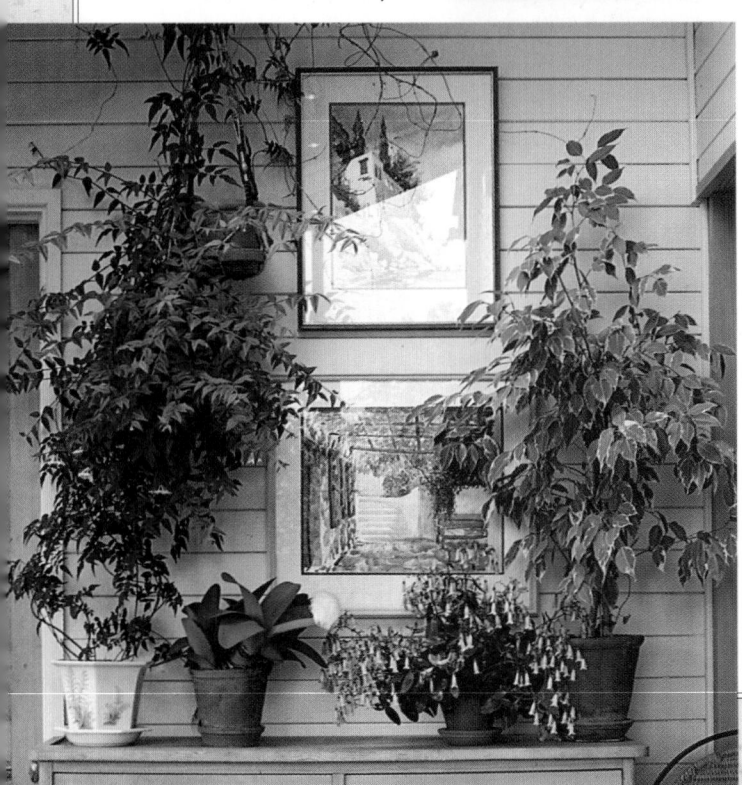

◀ NATURAL HARMONY *A simple grouping of plants is enhanced by the timber setting.*

▲ SHAPELY LEAVES *A Swiss cheese plant and parlour palm bring elegance to a living room.*

are 2-4cm (¾-1½in) wider. Repot plants growing in larger containers into pots 4-6cm (1½-2½in) wider.

Use a compost that is specifically designed for houseplants, preferably a soil-based compost like John Innes No. 2 or No. 3. This provides better stability than a soil-less mixture. Add one part perlite or grit to ten parts compost for plants that are moisture-sensitive, such as African violets and peperomias. For succulents, add one part grit to three parts compost.

Slow-growing species and mature specimens do not need annual repotting; very fast-growing species are also best repotted less frequently or they will soon become too large for their space. Top dress these

plants by removing the top layer of compost, to a depth of around 2-5cm (¾-2in) depending on pot size, and replacing it with fresh compost.

TRAINING AND PRUNING

Tie tall plants to a cane to keep them straight and upright. Climbers also need some support. Slower-growing species that have thick shoots, such as philodendrons, are best trained up a trellis. Lighter, faster-growing plants, including *Cissus*, climb easily up a network of wires.

Many houseplants can be pruned in spring, at the beginning of active growth. This keeps the plants manageable, encourages strong new growth and promotes branching. Pinch out growing tips on fast-growing plants to encourage dense and bushy growth.

PREVENTING PROBLEMS

Meeting the individual needs of houseplants will help to prevent disease. In addition, keep plants free of dust and dirt. Wipe smooth-surfaced leaves with a damp cloth and brush hairy or textured leaves gently with an old toothbrush. If pests or diseases occur, act quickly to prevent spreading. (See PESTS AND DISEASES p. 823.)

▼ SCRAMBLING STEMS *Syngonium podophyllum tumbles over a side table.*

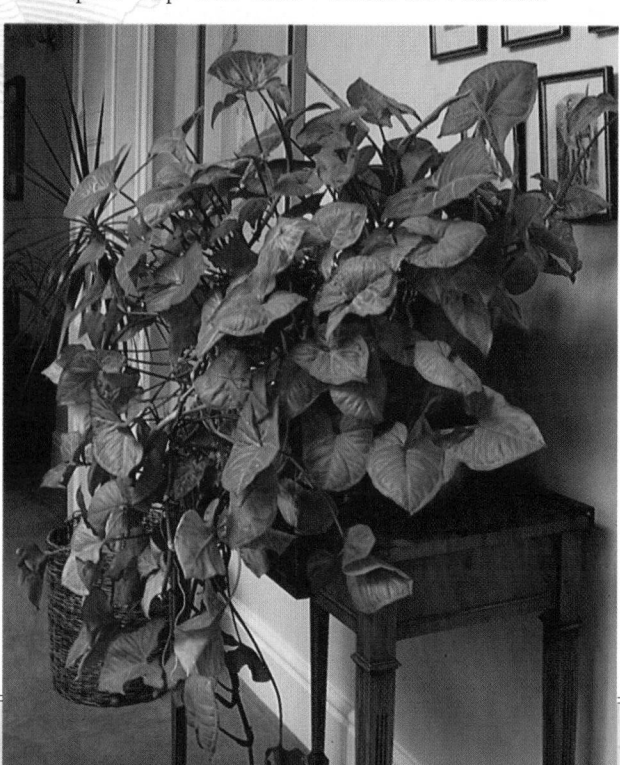

HOUSEPLANTS FOR FLOWERS AND YEAR-ROUND INTEREST

PLANTS FOR FLOWERS

• *Cyclamen persicum* (florist's cyclamen) Scented colourful flowers from winter to spring, above green or grey-green, sometimes patterned, heart-shaped leaves.

• *Phalaenopsis amabilis* (moth orchid) Slender spikes of white moth-like flowers all winter and leathery, oblong, mid green leaves.

• *Saintpaulia* hybrids (African violet) Colourful starry flowers through most of the year above rosettes of rounded, dark or bright green, velvet-textured foliage.

• *Schlumbergera* hybrids (Christmas cactus) Pink, red or orange, trumpet-shaped flowers in winter and fleshy, flattened green stems.

• *Streptocarpus* hybrids (Cape primrose) Clusters of white, pink or purple flowers from spring to autumn and wrinkled, strap-like, mid to dark green leaves.

PLANTS FOR FOLIAGE

• *Aglaonema* 'Silver Queen' Silvery grey, pointed, oval leaves with green streaks.

• *Begonia bowerae* (eyelash plant) Bright green, oval leaves with black stitch-like markings and very small pink flowers on stems from late winter to spring.

• *Maranta leuconeura* var. *kerchoveana* (rabbit's foot) Greyish green, oval leaves patterned with purple-brown or olive-green markings.

• *Nephrolepis exaltata* 'Bostoniensis' (Boston fern) Rich green, feathery fronds with an arching habit.

• *Pelargonium crispum* (lemon geranium) Mid green, lobed leaves with a strong lemon scent and pale pink flower clusters in summer.

TOLERANT PLANTS

• *Asparagus setaceus* Fern-like foliage with bright green, needle-like leaflets. Tolerates low temperatures and poor light.

• *Aspidistra elatior* (cast-iron plant) Dark green, leathery, arching leaves. Tolerates poor light levels.

• *Chlorophytum comosum* 'Vittatum' White-striped, lance-shaped arching leaves. Tolerates cool temperatures and poor light.

• x *Fatshedera lizei* Large and glossy, dark green, deeply lobed leaves and clusters of small greenish white flowers in late summer. Tolerates cool temperatures and poor light.

• *Ficus elastica* 'Robusta' (rubber plant) Large, leathery, glossy green, oval leaves. Tolerates poor light.

SPECIMEN PLANTS

• *Chamaedorea elegans* (parlour palm) Light green divided leaves which arch from a short woody trunk.

• *Ctenanthe oppenheimiana* Silver-grey, paddle-shaped leaves with dark green stripes on purplish stems.

• *Dracaena marginata* 'Tricolor' Green, red and cream-striped, narrow, strap-like leaves above a slender woody trunk.

• *Ficus benjamina* (weeping fig) Leathery, glossy, dark green, oval leaves held on weeping branches.

• *Schefflera elegantissima* (false aralia) Glossy, bronze, evenly toothed, narrow leaves on slender stalks.

• *Yucca aloifolia* (Spanish bayonet) Dark green, rigid, sword-shaped leaves with finely toothed edges, crowning a woody stem.

TRAILERS AND CLIMBERS

• *Cissus rhombifolia* (grape ivy) Climber with coarsely toothed, dark green, diamond-shaped leaves.

• *Ficus pumila* (creeping fig) Climber or trailer with small, heart-shaped to oval, bright green leaves and red-flushed orange fruits in late summer.

• *Philodendron scandens* (sweetheart plant) Climber with large, glossy, rich green, heart-shaped leaves.

• *Tradescantia fluminensis* 'Quicksilver' (inch plant) Trailer with pointed oval leaves, striped green and silver, and clusters of white flowers in summer.

h

Houstonia
Bluet
Rubiaceae

Solitary white, blue or blue-violet flowers sprinkle these low-growing hardy perennials throughout the summer. The dainty four-petalled flowers are held on thread-like stems just above spreading evergreen mats of small shining leaves, ideal for a rock garden. Native to eastern N America.

RECOMMENDED SPECIES AND VARIETIES
H. michauxii (syn. *H. caerulea* hort., *Hedyotis michauxii*) Star-shaped clear blue flowers, 1 cm (⅜ in) across, appear from late spring to early autumn, on a carpet of 1 cm (⅜ in) long, oval bright green leaves. HEIGHT & SPREAD 7.5×40 cm (3×16 in).

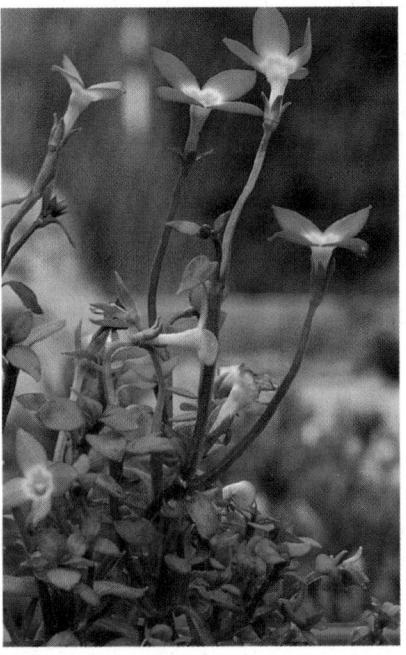

▲ *Houstonia michauxii*

The flowers of var. *alba* are white. **'Fred Mullard'** has deep blue flowers and a dense mat of foliage.

CULTIVATION Plant in spring in a shaded or semi-shaded moist site, ideally lime-free, such as a leafy woodland area or cool corner of a rock garden.

PROPAGATION Divide in spring and replant at once; keep moist until established.

PESTS AND DISEASES Slugs may attack very young plants.

Houttuynia
Saururaceae

Evergreen heart-shaped leaves borne on erect stems, flowers that bloom from early to mid summer, a neat habit and tolerance of different soils make this hardy herbaceous perennial a distinctive ground-cover plant. It flourishes in moist soil, where it may become invasive, but also grows on pond margins or in dry soil. Replant frequently if it outgrows its allotted space, re-using only a small portion of the plant. Some forms have brightly coloured foliage. A delicate citrus fragrance is emitted when the leaves are crushed. The genus consists of a single species, which is native to E Asia.

▲ *Houttuynia cordata*

Houttuynia cordata The flowerhead is a short spike, about 2.5 cm (1 in) long, carried on a leafy stem, 50 cm (20 in) tall. The flowers themselves are inconspicuous – the pure white bracts more striking. The heart-shaped bluish green leaves, up to 9 cm (3½ in) long, have rust-coloured margins. HEIGHT & SPREAD 45×45 cm (1½×1½ ft).

▲ *Houttuynia cordata* 'Chameleon'

'Chameleon' has decorative leaves marked with vivid red, dark green and cream. **'Flore Pleno'** bears crowded flower spikes consisting of numerous petal-like bracts decreasing in size upwards. The leaves are marked red and cream. **Variegata Group** has leaves patterned red and cream.

CULTIVATION Plant in moist soil in autumn in sun or partial shade.

PROPAGATION Divide plants in autumn and plant pieces of underground stem, each with a growing point or developed shoot.

PESTS AND DISEASES Usually trouble free.

Howea
Kentia palm, sentry palm
Palmae

These statuesque and elegant palms from Lord Howe Island in the S Pacific are among the best for indoor cultivation. Growing from a single stem, the leaves are up to 40 cm (16 in) long and divided to the midrib, each dark green leaflet being around 2.5 cm (1 in) wide. In a greenhouse or conservatory they grow well with the other Edwardian favourites, chamaedorea palms and aspidistras, and also group successfully with other, more modern foliage exotics, such as monsteras and philodendrons. Tolerating a wide range of light levels and dry air, they make excellent large houseplants. There are two species.

RECOMMENDED SPECIES
H. belmoreana The leaves initially grow upright but then arch gracefully outwards, a habit shared by the leaflets. HEIGHT & SPREAD 2×2 m (6½×6½ ft) after 5 years, ultimately 2.5 m (8 ft) tall.

▲ *Howea forsteriana* (Kentia palm)

H. forsteriana ♀ (Kentia palm) The leaves of this faster-growing species tend to grow horizontally. The leaflets grow straight at first, then droop. HEIGHT & SPREAD 2×2 m (6½×6½ ft) after 5 years, ultimately 2.5 m (8 ft) tall.

CULTIVATION Pot Kentia palms in soil-based compost or a compost containing grit, to counterbalance the top-heaviness of the plants. They prefer a well-lit position and a temperature that does not fall below 10°C (50°F). In summer, keep slightly moist and feed regularly; allow to dry out between waterings in winter.

PROPAGATION Germinate fresh seed at 25°C (77°F). The seedlings grow slowly.

PRUNING Not normally required.

PESTS AND DISEASES Usually trouble free.

Hoya
Wax flower
Asclepiadaceae

Attractive foliage and waxy flowers make hoyas rewarding indoor plants. Most are climbers, and can be trained round wire hoops or up trelliswork. They do best in good light, and make flamboyant plants in a conservatory, where they are also more likely to produce clusters of star-shaped, 1 cm (⅜ in) wide flowers. Native to SE Asia.

RECOMMENDED SPECIES

H. australis (wax flower) Admired for its fresh green leaves on climbing stems, this plant also bears fragrant white flowers with reddish spots in late summer. The glossy leaves are up to 8 cm (3¼ in) long and rounded with a sharp tip. HEIGHT 3 m (10 ft).

H. carnosa♀ (wax plant) Fleshy mid green oval leaves, up to 8 cm (3¼ in) long, have

▲ *Hoya carnosa*

pointed tips. The fragrant flowers are borne in late summer and vary in colour from white to pale pink, with red spots in the centre. HEIGHT 3 m (10 ft).

H. lanceolata ssp. *bella*♀ (miniature wax plant) Much smaller than most hoyas, this plant has a trailing habit, to about 40 cm (16 in). The mid green leaves are up to 3 cm (1¼ in) long, oval to lance-shaped with a distinctive dark midrib. The branches begin with an upright habit and then start to trail. The fragrant flowers are white with a red centre and appear in late summer. It is ideal for hanging baskets. HEIGHT 30 cm (1 ft).

CULTIVATION Hoyas need moderate sunlight and can survive temperatures of 7°C (45°F) but ideally keep above 13°C (55°F). Water when the top of the compost is beginning to dry out, allowing more pronounced drying in winter. Keep slightly pot bound for a good show of flowers and feed regularly. Use neutral or slightly acid compost mixed with grit or perlite.

PROPAGATION Take cuttings in spring or summer or use layering in late spring.

PRUNING Tidy up older plants in spring or after flowering. Leave old flower stalks as new bunches often grow from them.

PESTS AND DISEASES Mealy bug (rarely).

Humulus
Hop
Cannabaceae

Bold, large-lobed leaves and decorative flowers (hops) on the female plant in autumn earn these herbaceous perennial climbers a place in the garden. Rapid, freely twining growth makes them useful as temporary screening plants for a wall or wire-netting fence. Bright summer foliage can adorn an arch or arbour, or enliven dull hedging. Each plant bears either male or female flowers from mid to late summer.

▲ *Humulus lupulus*

Humulus lupulus 'Aureus' ▼

RECOMMENDED SPECIES AND VARIETIES

H. lupulus (common hop) On female plants aromatic bracts hide pale green, drooping cone-like flower clusters, 2 cm (¾ in) long. The bracts enlarge to form 5 cm (2 in) long pale green fruits. On the males, tiny yellow flowers grow in clusters up to 10 cm (4 in) long. HEIGHT 3-6 m (10-20 ft). 'Aureus'♀ has golden leaves.

CULTIVATION Plant in fertile, well-drained soil. 'Aureus' needs full sun to colour well.

PROPAGATION Propagate by greenwood cuttings in early summer.

PESTS AND DISEASES Usually trouble free.

Hyacinth, grape see *Muscari armeniacum*
Hyacinth, summer see *Galtonia candicans*
Hyacinth, tassel see *Muscari comosum*
Hyacinth, water see *Eichornia crassipes*

Hyacinthoides
Bluebell
Hyacinthaceae

Carpets of intense blue spreading through light woodland are one of the delights of the British countryside in late spring. And, on some soils, bluebells are just as eager to carpet a garden; they are easy to grow and spread vigorously, but can be invasive. Bell-shaped violet-blue, white or pink flowers are borne in loose spikes in late spring. An oval seed pod containing several black seeds follows. These hardy bulbous perennials have slightly fleshy green leaves. Massing bluebells beneath trees intensifies the vivid colour of the flowers, and a border is transformed by bluebells growing beneath deciduous shrubs. The sweetly scented native British bluebell, *Hyacinthoides non-scripta* is especially suitable for a wild-flower garden. *H. hispanica*, with larger flowers, but unscented, is common in British gardens and the two species hybridise readily.

RECOMMENDED SPECIES

H. hispanica (syn. *Scilla campanulata*) (Spanish bluebell) Wide bells, about 2 cm (¾ in) long, hang round an erect stem in a conical cluster. There are from 12-20 flowers on a stem. The most common colour is violet-blue, lightening towards the tips, but flowers are sometimes pink or white. Arching, narrow bright green leaves, up to 30 cm (12 in) long, are produced by fleshy white bulbs. Native to S Europe and N Africa, *H. hispanica* seeds readily and spreads easily. HEIGHT 40 cm (16 in).

▲ *Hyacinthoides hispanica*

H. non-scripta (syn. *Scilla non-scripta, S. nutans*) (bluebell) Rich violet-blue, fragrant narrow bells, up to 2 cm (¾ in) long and curving out markedly at the tips, hang at the arched top of an upright stem, in a loose one-sided spike of up to 16 flowers. White flowers are sometimes seen. The narrow green glossy leaves grow from white bulbs. Bluebells are native to western Europe.

347

▲ *Hydrangea macrophylla* 'Quadricolor'

▲ *Hydrangea paniculata* 'Grandiflora'

leaves of sea-green, greenish white and yellow. The lacecap heads, up to 20 cm (8 in) across, are mauve-pink to white and appear in late summer. It may grow to 2.4 m (8 ft) tall. **'Veitchii'**♀ has pure white flowerheads, up to 20 cm (8 in) across, which turn crimson-pink in autumn. Its broad leaves grow up to 20 cm (8 in) long. It is a very lime-tolerant hydrangea, growing to a height of 1.8 m (6 ft) and spreading to 2.4 m (8 ft). **'White Wave'**♀ bears flattened flowerheads, 15 cm (6 in) across, in late summer and early autumn. The bluish or pinkish fertile flowers are surrounded by pearl-white ray florets with a toothed edge. Grows to 1.5 m (5 ft).

H. paniculata Conical, creamy white flowerheads, 15–20 cm (6–8 in) long, made up of both fertile and sterile flowers are borne in late summer and early autumn. The leaves, up to 15 cm (6 in) long, often appear in threes. HEIGHT & SPREAD 1.8×1.5 m (6×5 ft) after 5 years, ultimately 2.4 m (8 ft) tall.

'Brussels Lace' has yellowish beige fertile flowers with off-white, pink-spotted, very small ray florets, producing the effect of openwork lace. Flowering from mid summer until the frosts, it reaches a height of 1.8 m (6 ft). **'Everest'** has large flowerheads of densely packed, creamy white ray florets, which turn pink with age. A splendid hydrangea with handsome deep green foliage. **'Grandiflora'**♀ bears conical heads, up to 30 cm (12 in) long and 10 cm (4 in) wide at the base, from late summer to early autumn. The flowers, densely packed sterile florets, turn from white to purplish pink. The plant has dark green tapering leaves and may grow to 3 m (10 ft) tall and half as wide. **'Kyushu'**♀ is a fine white variety, freely flowering from late summer to mid

autumn. The flowerheads are liberally sprinkled with ray florets. Of upright habit, it may grow to an ultimate height of 2.4 m (8 ft), twice as tall as wide. **'Pink Diamond'** has conical heads up to 30 cm (1 ft) long and 20 cm (8 in) at the base. The white fertile flowers, which are tinged pink before the buds open, turn bright pink in full sun. The sterile flowers, up to 4 cm (1½ in) wide, open white with a pink centre but rapidly turn all pink. Ultimately 1.8 m (6 ft) tall. **'Praecox'**♀, flowering in early and mid summer, produces abundant, rounded as well as conical, pure white heads, with fertile flowers at the centre or top and sterile flowers on the outside or below. Will grow to 1.8 m (6 ft). **'Tardiva'** bears large conical flowerheads covered with small white ray florets from late summer to mid autumn. Of upright habit, it may grow to an ultimate height of 2.4 m (8 ft), twice as tall as wide. **'Unique'**♀ has conical flowerheads, up to 38 cm (15 in) long, of densely packed sterile florets about 5 cm (2 in) across. Appearing from mid summer to mid autumn, the flowers turn from white to purplish pink. The shrub may reach a height of 4 m (13 ft).

H. petiolaris see *H. anomala* ssp. *petiolaris*

H. **'Preziosa'**♀ Mop-heads, up to 15 cm (6 in) wide, of glistening, salmon-pink, sterile flowers, which turn warm red, are borne in mid summer and early autumn. The young leaves and stems are reddish brown on rather slender woody parts. HEIGHT & SPREAD 1 m×75 cm (3×2½ ft) after 5 years, ultimately 1.5 m (5 ft) tall.

H. quercifolia♀ Conical flowerheads 10–30 cm (4–12 in) long are borne in late summer and mid autumn. The creamy white sterile and fertile flowers turn purplish or orange-pink with age. The dark green, strongly lobed leaves, wrinkled and tough in texture, grow to 20 cm (8 in) in length and change colour in autumn, turning vivid shades of orange, crimson and purple. HEIGHT & SPREAD 1.8×1.5 m (6×5 ft)

after 5 years, ultimately 4 m (13 ft) tall.

'Snow Flake' (syn. 'Flore Pleno') has double ray florets which give an unusual appearance to its conical heads; it may reach 3 m (10 ft) tall. **'Snow Queen'** bears erect, conical flowerheads, in mid summer and early autumn, of numerous greenish white fertile florets, which soon tinge with pink.

H. sargentiana see *H. aspera* ssp. *sargentiana*

H. serrata This species bears flattened lacecap heads of blue or white fertile flowers circled by pink, bluish or white ray florets, turning a deeper colour in autumn. HEIGHT & SPREAD 60×60 cm (2×2 ft) after 5 years, ultimately 1 m (3 ft) tall.

'Bluebird'♀ flowers from early summer to mid autumn. The flowerheads, 15–20 cm (6–8 in) across, have mid blue fertile flowers at the centre, surrounded by light blue ray florets. The flowers are reddish purple on chalk soil and deep blue on acid soil. The narrow pointed leaves are about 5 cm (2 in) long and turn coppery red in the autumn. It reaches a final height of 1.2 m (4 ft). **'Diadem'** has small dome-shaped flowerheads, 10 cm (4 in) across. The scented flowers are vivid blue or pink (redder in full sun), and appear from early summer onwards, rather sparsely at first but with a copious second flush of blooms in early autumn. The flowerheads are borne on side-shoots up the stems. The foliage is purple on plants grown in an open position. Reaches an ultimate height of 1 m (3 ft).

▲ *Hydrangea serrata* 'Grayswood'

'Grayswood'♀ has well-spaced heads, 15 cm (6 in) across, composed of layers of ray florets, which change from white to orange-pink to translucent burgundy-red. They appear early summer to mid autumn. It has lance-shaped leaves up to 10 cm (4 in) long and reaches an ultimate height of 2 m (6½ ft). **'Miranda'**, a dense bush growing to a height of 75 cm (2½ ft), has pale blue or pink lacecap flowerheads, 10 cm (4 in) across. Leaves have a clearly defined network of veins and give good autumn colour. Reddish fertile flowers, surrounded by a lower layer of white outer florets and an upper layer of rose-pink, form the 15 cm (6 in) flowerheads of **'Rosalba'**♀. Light green leaves grow to 15 cm (6 in) long, and the plant to a final height of 1.2 m (4 ft).

H. serratifolia (syn. *H. integerrima*) This evergreen hydrangea of creeping or climbing habit has off-white flowerheads up to 15 cm (6 in) across, usually made entirely of fertile flowers and appearing mid to late summer. The oval leaves, 5-15 cm (2-6 in) long, are light to mid green when young, dark green and leathery when older. HEIGHT & SPREAD 1.8×1.5 m (6×5 ft) after 5 years, ultimately 3 m (10 ft) tall on walls or 4.5 m (15 ft) growing up a tree.

H. villosa see *H. aspera* Villosa Group

CULTIVATION Plant in moisture-retentive soil, which has had well-rotted manure or compost dug in. Some hydrangeas thrive in full sun but most prefer partial shade, so choose a sheltered site against a wall, under high trees or in the lee of, but away from, a hedge. Avoid east-facing sites as tender young growths are damaged by late spring frost. In early spring feed established plants with a balanced fertiliser and apply a 10 cm (4 in) thick mulch.

The blue varieties of *H. macrophylla* are blue only on acid soil. On neutral or slightly alkaline soil, apply an annual dressing of well-decayed compost or manure in the spring; during the growing season apply aluminium sulphate to induce blueing, and sequestrene to combat chlorosis. Pink or red varieties of *H. macrophylla* may be less clear or turn shades of blue on acid soil: apply a 75 g per m² (2 oz per sq yd) dressing of ground limestone annually in winter to preserve the pink colouring.

PROPAGATION Take semi-ripe cuttings of shrubby hydrangeas in late summer and of the climbers in early summer.

PRUNING Leave the faded flowerheads of hydrangeas on as protection against frost until spring. Then cut back weak, old or diseased shoots to the lowest bud. Shorten remaining stems to a strong bud. If extra large flowers are wanted on *H. arborescens* and *H. paniculata*, species that flower on the new season's wood, prune the previous season's growth in late winter or early spring to 2 or 3 pairs of buds. Otherwise, to produce larger shrubs with smaller flowers – often the preferred option – shorten the previous year's flowering shoots by half to two-thirds in late winter or early spring. *H. aspera* and its cultivars need minimal pruning in spring, but be sure to cut out weak or diseased wood. Prune climbers only to keep them close to the wall, not at all if grown on trees. With all species, cut out old, exhausted stems at ground level.

PESTS AND DISEASES. Aphids may attack foliage. Very alkaline soils cause chlorosis.

Hylomecon
Papaveraceae

This woodland poppy is grown for its early display of rich yellow flowers and carpet-like habit. A hardy herbaceous perennial, it is valued for its tolerance of shade. It mixes well with many other woodland species, flowering at the same time as trilliums and wood anemones (*Anemone nemorosa*). It

also shows to advantage in a larger rock garden. It is a single species genus.

Hylomecon japonica Yellow poppy-like flowers appear in spring and early summer. Each flower, up to 5 cm (2 in) across, has 4 petals and a dense cluster of yellow stamens. A vigorous, spreading mat of leaves lasts through summer, dying away in autumn. Each leaf, up to 25 cm (10 in) long, divides into 5-7 toothed, oval leaflets. Native to the forests of Japan, NE China and Korea. HEIGHT & SPREAD 30×40 cm (12×16 in).

▲ *Hylomecon japonica*

CULTIVATION Plant in humus-rich, fairly moist soil in full or partial shade.

PROPAGATION Divide plants in autumn or early spring. Water newly planted portions well until they have become established. Hylomecon is easily grown from seed, sown in autumn or winter in pots in a cold frame, or in the open in spring.

PESTS AND DISEASES Slugs attack young plants, otherwise generally trouble free.

Hymenocallis
Spider lily
Amaryllidaceae

Spectacular, funnel-shaped flowers, usually white or yellow, are borne by these tender bulbous plants. Native to the tropical regions of the Americas, they require a minimum temperature of 15°C (59°F), so are only suitable for growing under glass or as houseplants.

RECOMMENDED SPECIES AND VARIETIES

H. × festalis White, heavily fragrant flowers, up to 15 cm (6 in) across, are produced in mid and late summer. The flower is a long, flared trumpet, surrounded at the base by 6 narrow petals. As many as 6 are carried at the end of a strong, single stem. The leaves, up to 45 cm (18 in) long, are narrow, dark green and strap-like. HEIGHT 60 cm (2 ft).

H. 'Sulphur Queen' Fragrant, sulphurous

▲ *Hymenocallis × festalis*

yellow flowers with greenish veins, up to 20 cm (8 in) across, formed of a frilly-edged trumpet with 6 large petals, are borne from mid to late summer. Between 2 and 5 flowers are carried on the stem. The strap-like, semi-erect, dark green leaves grow to 30 cm (1 ft) long. HEIGHT 60 cm (2 ft).

CULTIVATION Plant the bulbs in John Innes No. 3 potting compost in early spring – one bulb per 10 cm (4 in) pot or 3 bulbs per 25 cm (10 in) pot – with the tip of the bulb just showing. Water sparingly until the young shoots appear, and then freely. Use a houseplant feed when the flower buds appear. Cease watering when the leaves start to wither in autumn. Dry off the bulbs and store in a cool, frost-free place.

PROPAGATION Remove any offsets when repotting.

PESTS AND DISEASES Greenfly can be troublesome.

Hypericum
Saint John's wort
Guttiferae

Hypericum androsaemum

Sparkling yellow flowers, with prominent golden stamens and often borne in abundance, characterise these shrubs, sub-shrubs and herbaceous perennials. The leaves of some hypericums turn an attractive rusty pink in autumn. Some of the low-growing species are ideal as ground cover.

h

Iris

Iridaceae

Named for the Greek goddess of the rainbow, iris flowers combine an exquisite architectural flower form with a huge range of rich and delicate colours and their beauty has been celebrated since earliest times

Irises are prized for the beauty of their flower form and the richness and diversity of their colour range. They comprise a very large genus consisting of some 300 species varying from tiny rockery flowers to giant water irises. There are varieties suitable for many different areas of the garden, in particular alongside ponds, in borders and in rockery beds. The flowering season varies from mid winter to mid summer and with careful selection it is possible to have irises in bloom for nine months of the year. Given the right conditions irises are generally easy to grow and long-lasting, requiring only periodic division.

The typical iris has flower parts in groups of three. The three inner petals, or 'standards', normally stand up while the three outer petals, or 'falls', tend to droop. Within the flower structure are three style branches which can be highly ornamental.

•RHIZOMATOUS IRISES•

Irises that grow from fleshy, creeping stems, or rhizomes, are classified into three groups: bearded irises have a central line of hairs on the falls, beardless irises have no hairs on the falls while those known as crested irises have a fleshy crest on the falls.

BEARDED IRISES

All bearded irises prefer a neutral or slightly alkaline soil. There are two distinct groups, the Arillate Group and the Eupogon Group. The Arillate Group are so called because each seed has attached to it a fleshy outgrowth, or aril. They are very difficult to grow and greenhouse or cloche cultivation is necessary. The Eupogon Group do not have arillate seeds, and provide the most impressive irises of the spring and early

INDEX OF SPECIES AND VARIETIES

Irises can be either rhizomatous or bulbous. Rhizomatous irises are divided into three groups: bearded, beardless and crested. The bearded irises may be miniature dwarf bearded (MDB), standard dwarf bearded (SDB), intermediate bearded (IB), border bearded (BB), miniature tall bearded (MTB) or tall bearded (TB). The beardless irises are sub-divided into Californicae, Hexagonae, Laevigatae, Sibiricae, Spuriae or Miscellaneous.

Bulbous irises are divided into three groups: Reticulata, Juno and Xiphium. A list of plants covered in this book follows in alphabetical order with the relevant divisions in parentheses.

◀ *Iris 'Curlew'*

summer garden. All are hardy and easy to grow given sunshine and good drainage.

The sword-shaped leaves grow in fans from the tip of the rhizome. Most are grey-green. The flowering stems rise from the centre of the fan of leaves and once flowering is over the leaves generally die back.

The flowering season of bearded irises tends to be related to height, with shorter plants flowering earlier than taller ones. Bearded irises are classified into six groups, depending on height and flowering time.

Miniature dwarf bearded (MDB)
The flowers, borne from mid to late spring, are usually 5-7.5 cm (2-3 in) across. These irises are less than 20 cm (8 in) tall. All plants are hardy but most prefer a well-drained sunny position in a rock garden or well-ventilated, unheated greenhouse.

I. attica Yellow flowers are tinged with green on this plant which is not reliably hardy in cold wet winters. Native to Greece and Turkey. HEIGHT 5-10 cm (2-4 in).

I. lutescens (syn. *I. chamaeiris*) Flowers, up to 10 cm (4 in) wide, are white, purple or yellow. Native to SE France and NW Italy. HEIGHT 15-25 cm (6-10 in).

I. pumila The first bearded iris to flower in mid spring, the flowers are up to 7.5 cm

▲ *Iris attica*

(3 in) across with downward-curving falls, in shades of purple, white, yellow or yellow with brown tints. Most forms are stemless, with the flower itself giving height. The plant is best grown in a well-ventilated, unheated greenhouse or a rockery. Native to SE Europe. HEIGHT up to 10 cm (4 in).

Standard dwarf bearded (SDB)
These irises flower in late spring and are 20-38 cm (8-15 in) high. The flowers are up

latifolia (Bulbous/Xiphium)
'Lavender Royal' (Beardless/Californicae)
'Limeheart' (Beardless/Sibiricae)
lutescens (Bearded/MDB)
magnifica (Bulbous/Juno)
'Mary Frances' (Bearded/TB)
'Maui Moonlight' (Bearded/IB)
'Melon Honey' (Bearded/SDB)
milesii (Crested)
'Miss Carla' (Bearded/IB)
'Mystique' (Bearded/TB)
'Natascha' (Bulbous/Reticulata)
'No-name' (Beardless/Californicae)
'Orange Dawn' (Bearded/TB)
orientalis (Beardless/Spuriae)
'Orville Fay' (Beardless/Sibiricae)
pallida (Bearded/TB)
pallida 'Argentea Variegata' (Bearded/TB)
pallida 'Aurea Variegata' (Bearded/TB)
pallida ssp. *cengialtii* (Bearded/MTB)
pallida ssp. *pallida* (Bearded/TB)
'Paradise' (Bearded/TB)
'Paradise Bird' (Bearded/TB)
'Pascoe' (Bearded/TB)
'Pauline' (Bulbous/Reticulata)
'Professor Blaauw' (Bulbous/Xiphium)
pseudacorus (Beardless/Laevigatae)
pseudacorus 'Variegata' (Beardless/Laevigatae)
pumila (Bearded/MDB)
'Rare Edition' (Bearded/IB)
'Raspberry Blush' (Bearded/IB)
reticulata (Bulbous/Reticulata)
'Roman Emperor' (Bearded/TB)

'Ruffled Velvet' (Beardless/Sibiricae)
sanguinea (Beardless/Sibiricae)
'Sarah Taylor' (Bearded/SDB)
setosa (Beardless/Miscellaneous)
'Shelford Giant' (Beardless/Spuriae)
'Shirley Pope' (Beardless/Sibiricae)
sibirica (Beardless/Sibiricae)
'Silver Edge' (Beardless/Sibiricae)
'Snowy Owl' (Bearded/TB)
'Soft Blue' (Beardless/Sibiricae)
'Song of Norway' (Bearded/TB)
spuria (Beardless/Spuriae)
'Stepping Out' (Bearded/TB)
'Sun Dappled' (Bearded/TB)
'Superstition' (Bearded/TB)
'Tangerine Sunrise' (Bearded/TB)
tectorum (Crested)
'Titan's Glory' (Bearded/TB)
unguicularis (Beardless/Miscellaneous)
unguicularis 'Alba' (Beardless/Miscellaneous)
unguicularis 'Mary Barnard' (Beardless/Miscellaneous)
unguicularis 'Walter Butt' (Beardless/Miscellaneous)
'Vanity' (Bearded/TB)
versicolor (Beardless/Laevigatae)
virginica (Beardless/Laevigatae)
'Warleggan' (Bearded/TB)
'Wedgwood' (Bulbous/Xiphium)
'White Excelsior' (Bulbous/Xiphium)
'White Swirl' (Beardless/Sibiricae)
winogradowii (Bulbous/Reticulata)
'Wisley White' (Beardless/Sibiricae)
xiphium (Bulbous/Xiphium)

'Jane Philips' (Bearded/TB)
japonica (Crested)
japonica 'Ledger's Variety' (Crested)
'Jeremy Brian' (Bearded/SDB)
'Joyce' (Bulbous/Reticulata)
'Joyce Terry' (Bearded/TB)
'Katharine Hodgkin' (Bulbous/Reticulata)
'Kent Pride' (Bearded/TB)
'Kentucky Bluegrass' (Bearded/SDB)
kerneriana (Beardless/Spuriae)
laevigata (Beardless/Laevigatae)
laevigata 'Alba' (Beardless/Laevigatae)

Kalmiopsis
Ericaceae

Kalmiopsis leachiana

Purple-tinged, rose-pink, bell-shaped flowers feature on this dwarf evergreen shrub which usually forms a neat, compact mound. It requires acid soil and is suited to a rock garden, or to growing in a container in an alpine house. The genus is native to western N America and is hardy, but it is difficult to grow well, seldom being long-lived. There is only one species.

***Kalmiopsis leachiana*♀** Flowers, 2 cm (¾ in) across, open in 2.5-5 cm (1-2 in) long clusters of 6-9 blooms over a long period throughout spring and into early summer. The numerous bright green leaves, which have a sticky underside, are pointed, oval, sometimes broader towards the tip, and up to 2 cm (¾ in) long. HEIGHT & SPREAD 30×30 cm (1×1 ft) after 5 years, ultimately 30×60-90 cm (1×2-3 ft).

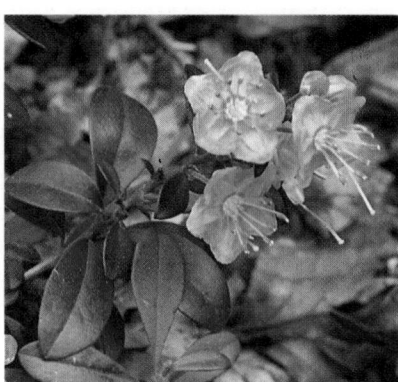

▲ *Kalmiopsis leachiana*

Low-growing, compact **'Umpqua'** is sometimes sold as **'Le Piniec'** after its discoverer; the reliable and free-flowering **'Glendoick'** is more vigorous and easier to please.

CULTIVATION Grow in well-drained acid soil. Choose a sunny site in cool areas, otherwise semi-shade. Keep the roots fairly cool and do not let them dry out in summer.

PROPAGATION Root semi-ripe cuttings in peat, or a peat and grit/perlite mixture.

PRUNING None is required.

PESTS AND DISEASES An as-yet-unknown fungal disease attacks. Treat with a general fungicide.

Kangaroo paw see *Anigozanthos*
Kangaroo vine see *Cissus antarctica*
Katsura tree see *Cercidiphyllum japonica*
Kentia see *Howea*

Kerria
Rosaceae

Kerria japonica 'Picta'

Slender, arching stems carry abundant yellow flowers in spring on this easily grown, deciduous shrub. Suitable for sun or part shade and tolerant of most soils, it can be grown either freestanding or against a wall. A member of the rose family with five-petalled flowers, kerria is native to central and western China, and Japan. It is a genus of a single species.

Kerria japonica An abundance of small, solitary, yellow flowers, like single roses, up to 5 cm (2 in) across, are borne during mid to late spring on this dense, suckering shrub. Narrow oval leaves, up to 7.5 cm (3 in) long, are a dull green with finely toothed margins and the whole leaf has a ridged appearance. The green stems in winter are a bonus. It is frost-hardy. HEIGHT & SPREAD 1×1 m (3×3 ft) after 5 years, ultimately 1.8 m (6 ft) tall.

'Golden Guinea'♀ is a single-flowering variety with larger flowers than the species. The main garden value of **'Picta'** (syn. 'Variegata') is its creamy white variegated foliage as it does not flower prolifically. It tends to be a lower-growing, more spreading plant, reaching a height and spread of 60 cm (2 ft) in 5 years, and rarely growing to more than 1.2 m (4 ft) high and eventually wider than it is tall. **'Pleniflora'♀** is the

▲ *Kerria japonica 'Picta'*

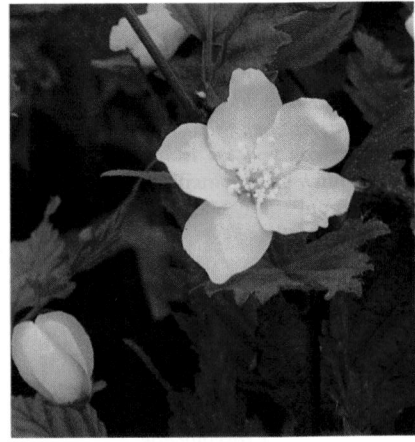

▲ *Kerria japonica 'Golden Guinea'*

most common form grown in gardens with a profusion of double golden yellow flowers in mid or late spring. A more vigorous plant than the species, it has a more upright habit growing to a height of 1.2 m (4 ft) and spreading to 1 m (3 ft) in 5 years, and eventually to 3 m (10 ft) tall. **'Variegata'** see 'Picta'.

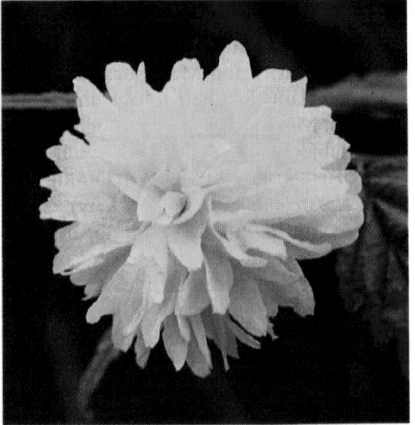

▲ *Kerria japonica 'Pleniflora'*

CULTIVATION Kerria grows in all soils but does best in a well-drained soil. Plant in the spring or autumn in a sunny or semi-shaded position but avoid a site that is very open and exposed. In cold areas, protect kerrias by siting plants against walls or fences; the variegated forms do best on a south or west-facing wall.

PROPAGATION This plant is easily raised from semi-ripe cuttings taken in early to mid summer and can also be layered in autumn to be dug up when rooted after 1 or 2 years. Alternatively, plants composed of many stems may be divided and replanted in autumn or spring.

PRUNING None is normally required but may be needed to maintain a particular size. If the plant becomes old and woody, prune older stems from the base. Any pruning should be done after flowering.

PESTS AND DISEASES Usually trouble free.

Kingcup see *Caltha palustris*

Kirengeshoma
Hydrangeaceae

For late-summer flowers in moist shady places kirengeshoma, which is native to Japan and Korea, makes an elegant feature plant. Tall groups of dark, arching, leafy stems are slowly formed, bent by the weight of loose sprays of creamy yellow, shuttlecock flowers that are the epitome of Oriental grace. The large, maple-like leaves are clear, bright green. This perennial, which prefers acid soil, is hardy to -20°C (-4°F) and deserves a choice place in cool dappled shade recalling the mountain woods of its homeland.

RECOMMENDED SPECIES AND VARIETIES
K. palmata♥ A prominent calyx and 5 fleshy, 3 cm (1¼ in) petals hang on branching, dark brown stems from terminal leaves. Stout rhizomes produce erect stems carrying hand-shaped leaves, 12-20 cm (4¾-8 in) long, with 7-10 shallow, toothed lobes. HEIGHT & SPREAD 1.2×1m (4×3ft).

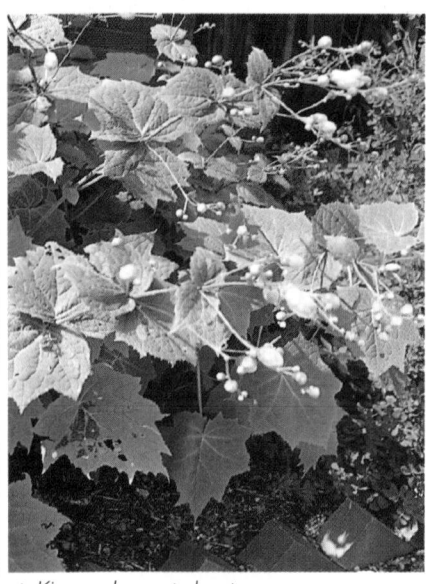
▲ *Kirengeshoma palmata*

Koreana Group are more erect and taller, reaching 1.8 m (6 ft). Paler, upright flowers, 4 cm (1½ in) long, open more widely, and the leaves are slightly egg-shaped.
CULTIVATION Plant in spring or autumn. Although the plant prefers acid soil, it will grow well in any soil provided that it is moist and humus-rich. Choose a site in partial shade. Give ample summer water and mulch well: plants will quickly flag if allowed to become dry in sunshine.
PROPAGATION Divide in spring or autumn when stems die down. Sow seed in spring.
PESTS AND DISEASES Slugs may attack young plants.

Kiwi fruit see *Actinidia deliciosa*
Knapweed see *Centaurea*

Knautia
Dipsacaceae

Knautia macedonica

Flowers packed with prominent stamens and resembling small pincushions, dance on the loose, wiry, thin stems of these hardy perennials in summer and early autumn. Their exuberant habit is especially suited to the informality of cottage and wild-flower gardens. The plants thrive towards the front of a sunny, well-drained border. Plants flowering heavily may exhaust themselves in two or three years.

RECOMMENDED SPECIES AND VARIETIES
K. arvensis (field scabious) Bluish violet pincushion-like flowers, up to 4 cm (1½ in) across, are carried on tall, loose, hairy stems above a base of toothed or tapering pale green, hairy leaves, up to 10 cm (4 in) long, from mid summer to early autumn. Deeply cut leaves grow up the hairy stems. The plant is native to Europe. HEIGHT & SPREAD 80×60 cm (32×24 in).
K. macedonica Crimson, occasionally lilac, pincushion-like flowers, 5 cm (2 in) across, are made up of many small flowers, with an outer basal ring of the most mature. They grow on curving, branched stems, up to 50 cm (20 in) tall, from mid to late summer. The first leaves are basal and wither away before flowering time. The pinnate leaves, about 10 cm (4 in) long, are mid green and have an oval lobe at the top. The plant is native to the Balkans. HEIGHT & SPREAD 50×45 cm (20×18 in).

The flowers of the pink form have a pretty, deep rose hue.
CULTIVATION Plant in spring in any well-drained soil in a sunny site. Plants flourish in chalky or limy soil.
PROPAGATION Sow seeds in spring or take cuttings with a basal heel.
PESTS AND DISEASES Plants rot in wet soils; otherwise trouble free.

Kniphofia
Red-hot poker, torch lily
Asphodelaceae

Tall spikes of flowers in glowing shades of red, orange and yellow do indeed resemble red-hot pokers. Numerous pendent, tubular flowers, up to 4 cm (1½ in) long, are densely packed together to form a tapering head at the top of a strong stem which rises out of a clump of grass-like leaves.

Kniphofia 'Royal Standard'

There are about 70 species of herbaceous perennials in this genus, mostly native to eastern and southern Africa. Though many of the species are unreliably hardy in all but the mildest of British gardens, their survival in cold regions can be helped by siting the plants in a warm spot and using a protective mulch in winter. Most of the garden varieties will grow well in all but the coldest gardens. The roots are rhizomatous but generally do not spread so much as to become a nuisance.

The plants can be used to colour a herbaceous border and, since there is a wide choice of hybrids on the market, careful selection ensures a display of yellow, orange and red flowers throughout the summer.

▼ *Kniphofia caulescens*

Lilium

Lily

Liliaceae

With their exquisite blooms, lilies command a position of honour in mixed borders, woodland gardens and in containers. The flowers, often fragrant and available in a wide palette of colours, are also excellent for cutting

The strikingly beautiful and often richly scented flowers of lilies appear from early summer to early autumn. The flowers of these hardy, occasionally half-hardy, bulbous perennials come in all colours except blue, and many species and cultivars have flowers splashed or spotted with a different colour. In addition, the conspicuous, pollen-bearing anthers of the flowers are frequently of a contrasting colour. Lilies range in height from 30 cm (1 ft) to 2 m (6½ ft). Many lilies are well suited to growing in pots and containers, either outside or under glass.

The flowers of lilies, ranging in size from 5 cm (2 in) to 25 cm (10 in) across, are produced towards the top of the stem, either singly, or in flowerheads that may carry up to 50 blooms, according to species. The shape of the flowers is determined by the degree to which the six petals (correctly speaking tepals) spread out and bend back (or recurve). The appearance of the flowers is also affected by the stalks. These vary greatly in length and may be straight or curved, and this, together with the angle at which the flower grows from the stalk, determines whether the flowers are upward, outward or downward-facing. The upward-facing flowers are cup or star-shaped with spreading petals, which may be straight or recurved at the tips. Outward-facing flowers are either bowl-shaped, with spreading petals that recurve about halfway along their length, or trumpet or funnel-shaped, with petals that overlap for most of their length and recurve at the tips. Downward-facing, or pendulous, flowers may be either bell-shaped, with petals that are not widely spreading and either straight or gently recurved, or of the Turk's-cap type with petals that recurve tightly.

The leaves of lilies are mostly stalkless, varying in length from 5 cm (2 in) to 15 cm (6 in), and in shape from very narrow to broadly oval. They are borne on the stem in two main ways: either scattered up and around the stem (densely or sparsely), or in whorls, like the spokes of a wheel, at intervals up the stem.

Most lilies enjoy partial shade and a cool, deep root run in a humus-rich, well-drained, fertile soil. In many species and cultivars, the stem, put out by the bulb, itself makes roots. Such 'stem-rooting' lilies need to be planted deeply, so it is important to know in advance if the lily you are planting is of this type.

RECOMMENDED SPECIES AND VARIETIES

African Queen Group Large yellow or orange fragrant, trumpet-shaped flowers, up

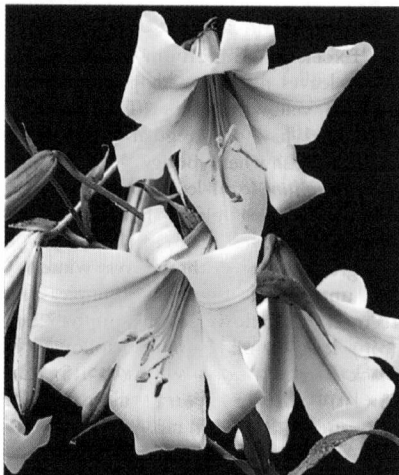

▲ *Lilium* African Queen Group

to 15 cm (6 in) long and as much across, are carried in pyramidal heads in mid to late summer. HEIGHT 1.5 m (5 ft).

L. auratum (golden-rayed lily) The magnificent, outward-facing, bowl-shaped flow-

Lilium auratum

ers, up to 25 cm (10 in) across, are white with prominent golden bands down the centre of each petal. The inside of the flower is heavily sprinkled with maroon or brown spots. A highly fragrant lily, up to 10 blooms are carried on the single stem in late summer. *L. auratum* is stem-rooting and is often grown as a container plant in a conservatory. HEIGHT 1.5 m (5 ft).

The flowers of var. *platyphyllum* ♀ (syn. 'Gold Band') have fewer spots and the plant has slightly broader lance-shaped leaves.

L. Bellingham Hybrids ♀ Turk's-cap lilies in a wide range of both pastel and warm colours, from soft pink to orange, appear from early to mid summer. The individual flowers, most with internal spotting, grow to 15 cm (6 in) across and are borne in groups of up to 15 on a stem. They increase freely. HEIGHT 2 m (6½ ft).

L. **'Black Dragon'** ♀ Outward-facing, scented, trumpet-shaped flowers with dark purplish red exteriors and white interiors are produced from mid to late summer.

▲ *Lilium* Bellingham Hybrids

Lilium canadense

L. candidum♀ (Madonna lily) This is the typical white-flowered lily of the cottage garden, bearing between 5 and 20 outward-facing, broadly funnel-shaped, fragrant blooms, up to 7.5 cm (3 in) long, in early to mid summer. Plant bulbs in late summer in order to establish a root system and a rosette of foliage before winter. HEIGHT 1.5 m (5 ft).

L. 'Casa Blanca'♀ This heavily scented hybrid bears outward-facing, waxy, widely bowl-shaped white flowers up to 25 cm (10 in) across, with conspicuous, orange-brown pollen on the anthers, in mid to late summer. It is a popular pot plant. HEIGHT 1.2 m (4 ft).

L. chalcedonicum♀ (scarlet Turk's-cap lily) Nodding red or reddish orange Turk's-cap flowers, slightly scented and up to 7.5 cm (3 in) long and 12.5 cm (5 in) across are produced in mid summer. Up to 12 blooms are carried on strong stems. Stem-rooting. HEIGHT 90 cm (3 ft).

Several blooms, usually 4 or 5, are produced on a stem, each one up to 15 cm (6 in) long and 10 cm (4 in) across. HEIGHT 1.5 m (5 ft).

L. 'Bright Star' The flattish, outward-facing flowers are white with orange internal streaking and distinctly recurved tepals. As many as 8 blooms, up to 15 cm (6 in) across, are produced on the single stem in mid to late summer. HEIGHT 1.5 m (5 ft).

L. bulbiferum var. **croceum**♀ This attractive short-growing lily produces up to 5 upward-facing, bright orange, bowl-shaped flowers, 7.5 cm (3 in) long and 10 cm (4 in) across, in early to mid summer. Stem-rooting. HEIGHT 90 cm (3 ft).

L. canadense (Canada lily) As many as 12 pendulous, yellow or orange-red, bell-shaped flowers, up to 10 cm (4 in) across and with distinctive recurved tips to the petals, are borne on very long stalks in late summer. This is a beautiful lily for dappled shade, but it must have plenty of moisture and is also a lime-hater. Stem-rooting. HEIGHT 1.5 m (5 ft).

▲ *Lilium candidum*

▲ *Lilium* Citronella Group

L. Citronella Group Up to 30 pendulous, lemon-yellow, Turk's-cap flowers, 7.5 cm (3 in) across, with small, faint black spots are carried in mid summer. HEIGHT 1.5 m (5 ft).

L. 'Connecticut King' As many as 15 bright yellow, upward-facing, star-like flowers, 15 cm (6 in) across, are produced in terminal groups on very leafy stems in early summer. A vigorous variety well suited to the open garden and containers. HEIGHT 90 cm (3 ft).

▲ *Lilium* 'Connecticut King'

▲ *Lilium* 'Côte d'Azur'

L. 'Côte d'Azur' The bowl-shaped, upward-facing blooms of this hybrid are deep rose-pink with darker spotted throats and up to 10 cm (4 in) across. The flowers are produced in terminal groups from early to mid summer. An excellent variety for container cultivation. HEIGHT 60 cm (2 ft).

L. × dalhansonii 'Marhan' (syn. *L.* Marhan) This hybrid has orange-yellow, thick-petalled, Turk's-cap flowers, mostly

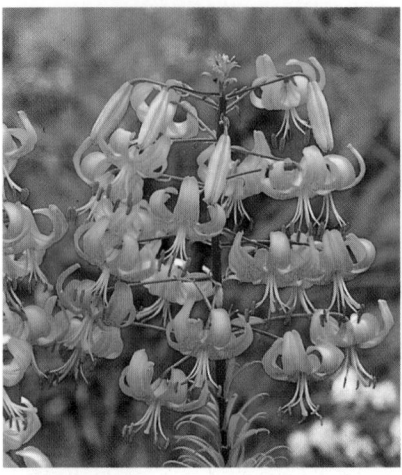

▲ *Lilium davidii*

spotted internally with reddish brown. As many as 13 flowers, 7.5 cm (3 in) across, are borne in extended groups up the slender stems in early summer. A lily of strong constitution which naturalises freely. Stem-rooting. HEIGHT 1.5 m (5 ft).

L. davidii This Turk's-cap lily bears up to 20 pendulous, red or orange flowers with conspicuous, dark internal spots in mid to late summer. The petals are recurved and up to 7.5 cm (3 in) long. Stem-rooting. HEIGHT 90 cm (3 ft).

Lilium 'Enchantment'

L. 'Enchantment' Up to 12 bright orange-red, upward-facing, star-shaped flowers, 10 cm (4 in) across and with black-spotted throats, are produced in large terminal groups on strong stems in early and mid summer. The most popular modern hybrid, widely used for general garden decoration, naturalising, pot and container cultivation, as well as cutting. HEIGHT 90 cm (3 ft).

L. 'Fire King' Widely trumpet-shaped, bright orange-red flowers with purple spots, outward-facing and up to 10 cm (4 in) across, are borne in terminal groups in mid to late summer. Excellent variety for container growing. HEIGHT 90 cm (3 ft).

L. formosanum From 3–5 large, outward-facing, trumpet-shaped, fragrant white flowers, up to 15 cm (6 in) long and often flushed on the exterior with crimson-purple, are borne in late summer. This is a tender lily for growing in a conservatory or a greenhouse and, unlike most other lilies, is commonly raised from seed, flowering just 9 months after sowing. Stem-rooting. HEIGHT 1.5 m (5 ft).

The variety *pricei* is much shorter, rarely growing more than 60 cm (2 ft) tall, making it ideal for pot culture.

L. 'Green Dragon' The large, outward-facing, trumpet-shaped flowers of this hybrid have a deep purplish brown and green exterior and a pure white interior. As many as 8 blooms, up to 15 cm (6 in) long and 10 cm (4 in) across, are borne in terminal heads on strong flower stems in mid to late summer. HEIGHT 1.2 m (4 ft).

L. hansonii The 12.5 cm (5 in) wide flowers of this scented, Turk's-cap lily are orange-yellow with thick petals. Each bulb produces up to 12 blooms in mid summer. The leaves are dark green, up to 20 cm (8 in) long and borne in distinctive whorls. Stem-rooting. HEIGHT 1.2 m (4 ft).

L. henryi Between 20 and 50 nodding, Turk's-cap flowers are borne in late summer on a vigorous stem. The blooms are bright orange, conspicuously spotted with black. Up to 10 cm (4 in) across, they have distinctive warty growths (papillae) at the base of each petal. Preferring an alkaline soil, this plant is ideal for naturalising among shrubs or in grass. Stem-rooting. HEIGHT 3 m (10 ft).

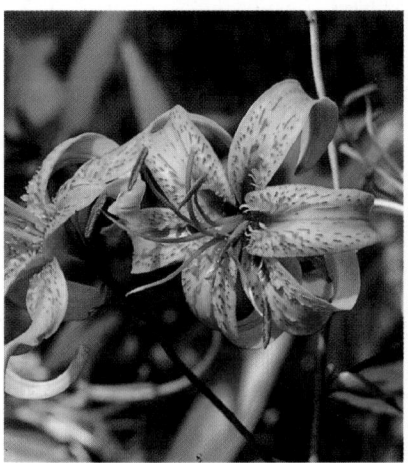

▲ *Lilium henryi*

L. 'Karen North' The Turk's-cap flowers of this hybrid are orange-pink, spotted with deep pink inside. They grow to 10 cm (4 in) across, and 8 or more appear in groups along the upper part of the flower stem in mid to late summer. HEIGHT 1.2 m (4 ft).

L. lancifolium (syn. *L. tigrinum*) (tiger lily) The flowers of this Turk's-cap lily are bright orange spotted with purple. They grow to 10 cm (4 in) across and are borne in late summer and early autumn in spires of up to 40. This stem-rooting lily often carries tiny, black bulbils in the leaf axils. Stem-rooting. HEIGHT 90 cm (3 ft).

The flowers of var. *flaviflorum* are yellow.

L. 'Limelight' Large, trumpet-shaped, soft greenish yellow fragrant flowers, up to 15 cm (6 in) long and 10 cm (4 in) across, are borne in terminal heads on a strong flower

1

▲ *Lilium longiflorum*

▲ *Lilium* 'Mont Blanc'

▲ *Lilium nepalense*

▲ *Lilium* Pink Perfection Group

▲ *Lilium pyrenaicum*

stem in mid to late summer. The individual flowers, although outward-facing, tend to be a little pendent. HEIGHT 1.2m (4ft).

L. longiflorum♀ (Easter lily) Between 1 and 6 large, fragrant, pure white trumpet-shaped flowers, up to 20cm (8in) long, are produced by this half-hardy lily in mid to late summer. Widely grown for cut flowers, it is an excellent lily for containers. Stem-rooting. HEIGHT 90cm (3ft).

L. mackliniae♀ (Manipur lily) Up to 6 bell-shaped, slightly pendent, rose-pink to purple-pink flowers, 7.5cm (3in) across, are borne in early summer. The small, oval or lance-shaped leaves, up to 5cm (2in) in length, are scattered around the lower stem but grow in whorls beneath the flowerhead. Stem-rooting. HEIGHT 45cm (1½ft).

L. 'Marhan' see *L.* × *dalhansonii* 'Marhan'

L. martagon (martagon lily, Turk's cap lily) The scented, waxy flowers of this species are 7.5cm (3in) across, mauve-pink and darkly spotted. Up to 50 are produced on a stem clothed with whorls of dark green lance-shaped leaves, growing to 15cm (6in) long. This is one of the easiest lilies to naturalise in grass and is very tolerant of lime. Stem-rooting. HEIGHT 1.2m (4ft).

Pure white, unspotted flowers are borne by var. *album*♀, while var. *cattaniae*♀ has unspotted, maroon flowers.

L. monadelphum♀ (syn. *L. szovitsianum*) The fragrant, yellow, Turk's-cap flowers are usually strongly marked on the inside with dark red or purple spots. The blooms are up to 15cm (6in) across and the individual recurved petals as long as 10cm (4in). As many as 20 flowers per stem are produced in mid summer. This is a good all-round garden lily, which, if left undisturbed, spreads freely. Stem-rooting. HEIGHT 1.2m (4ft).

L. 'Mont Blanc' Creamy white, upward-facing, star-shaped flowers, up to 15cm (6in) across, are produced in terminal groups from early to mid summer. A popular variety for both border decoration and pot cultivation. HEIGHT 60cm (2ft).

L. 'Mrs R.O. Backhouse'♀ Tawny gold, purple-spotted, Turk's-cap flowers, 10cm (4in) across with thick waxy petals, are borne on slender stems from early to mid summer. An excellent lily for naturalising among shrubs in the open border or in grass. HEIGHT 1.5m (5ft).

L. nepalense Pendulous, bell-shaped flowers with recurved, greenish yellow and purple petals, up to 15cm (6in) long, appear in late summer. It needs a sheltered position and should not be allowed to become too wet. Stem-rooting. HEIGHT 1m (3ft).

L. pardalinum var. *giganteum*♀ (panther lily) As many as 30 often scented Turk's-cap flowers, with recurved densely spotted crimson and yellow petals up to 10cm (4in) long, are borne in mid summer. An excellent lily for a damp, semi-shady position. HEIGHT 3m (10ft).

L. Pink Perfection Group♀ The beautiful, highly scented flowers are trumpet-shaped and rich fuchsia-pink, growing to 15cm (6in) long and 10cm (4in) across. Up to 15 drooping blooms are produced in mid to late summer. Ideal for containers and borders. Stem-rooting. HEIGHT 1.2m (4ft).

L. pumilum♀ (syn. *L. tenuifolium*) This short-growing, Turk's-cap lily has slightly scented, bright red flowers, spotted with black. Between 5 and 20 blooms, just 5cm (2in) across, are produced in mid summer. It requires a well-drained position in full sun. Stem-rooting. HEIGHT 30cm (1ft).

L. pyrenaicum♀ (yellow Turk's-cap lily) Bright yellow, purple-spotted, Turk's-cap flowers appear in early summer. Up to 12 blooms, 10cm (4in) across, are produced on the stem. The flowers are strangely malodorous. This stem-rooting lily is easy to grow and naturalises freely in moist soil. HEIGHT 1.2m (4ft).

L. regale♀ (regal lily) Huge, heavily fragrant and outward-facing funnel-shaped

▼ *Lilium regale*

▲ *Lilium regale* Album Group

blooms, up to 15 cm (6 in) long and 12.5 cm (5 in) across, appear in mid and late summer. As many as 20 are produced on a single stem. The petals have pinkish purple exteriors but are white inside and have a distinctive yellow base. Magnificent in the garden border or in large pots in the conservatory. Stem-rooting. HEIGHT 1.2 m (4 ft).

Album Group has almost pure white flowers with an occasional blush of pink on the outside of the petals.

L. **'Rosemary North'**♀ This graceful lily has slightly fragrant, rich orange flowers, sometimes with darker spots. The Turk's-cap blooms, appearing from mid to late summer, grow to 10 cm (4 in) across and are borne on slender stems in a terminal group of up to 12. HEIGHT 90 cm (3 ft).

L. speciosum♀ This very distinctive, late summer and early autumn-flowering lily has open, richly scented Turk's-cap flowers of waxy, satiny texture up to 10 cm (4 in) across. The petals are white or pink, spotted with pink or crimson. Up to 4 flowers are carried on a stem. This stem-rooting lily is not fully hardy and makes a popular conservatory plant. HEIGHT 1.2 m (4 ft).

Pure white flowers with a faint, greenish band in the centre of each petal are borne on purple stems by var. *album*, while var. *rubrum* has purple or brownish stems and blooms suffused and spotted with carmine.

L. **'Star Gazer'** Open, funnel to star-shaped blooms of rich carmine spotted with crimson are produced in late summer. The upward-facing, richly fragrant flowers are up to 12.5 cm (5 in) across and produced in a cluster of 5–8. HEIGHT 90 cm (3 ft).

L. **'Sterling Star'** Open, upward-facing star-shaped white flowers, up to 12.5 cm (5 in) across, with tiny brown spots on the inside of the petals, are produced in groups of 5–8 in early and mid summer. Excellent for growing in the open ground as well as in pots. HEIGHT 1.2 m (4 ft).

L. superbum♀ (swamp lily) An elegant stem carries up to 40 nodding, Turk's-cap flowers in late summer and early autumn. The blooms, growing to 10 cm (4 in) across, are orange flushed with red and have maroon internal spotting. It revels in moist, acid soil. Stem-rooting. HEIGHT 2 m (6½ ft).

L. szovitsianum see *L. monadelphum*

L. tenuifolium see *L. pumilum*

L. × *testaceum*♀ (Nankeen lily) This Turk's-cap lily produces 6 to 12 fragrant, light orange to brownish yellow flowers, 10 cm (4 in) across and often spotted with red on the inside, in early to mid summer. The narrow, lance-shaped dark green leaves, up to 7.5 cm (3 in) long, tend to be curved and twisted. Grow this lily in a sunny spot with shelter from cold winds. HEIGHT 1.2 m (4 ft).

L. tigrinum see *L. lancifolium*

CULTIVATION

BEDS AND BORDERS

Plant lily bulbs as soon as purchased in well-drained, humus-rich soil at any time from late autumn to early spring. The majority grow best in shade or partial shade, although a number of the Turk's-cap types are quite happy naturalised in the open. Plant stem-rooting lilies at a depth of 15–20 cm (6–8 in). *L. candidum* and *L.* × *testaceum* should be covered by a depth of soil no more than the height of the bulb. Cover the others by a depth of soil twice the height of the bulb. Apply a mulch of well-rotted garden compost or leaf-mould after planting. Scatter slug pellets near the plants in early spring, at the same time making preparations for staking any varieties that require support. Wire ring supports are the easiest to use and the least obtrusive. Remove the faded flowers, but leave as much foliage as possible in order to build up the bulbs for the following year. Each spring apply slow-release fertiliser and mulch. Lift and replant every 3 years to maintain vigour.

POTS AND CONTAINERS

Plant 2 or 3 bulbs in a 25 cm (10 in) pot in John Innes No. 2 compost with a good layer of crocks at the base of the pot. Plant the stem-rooting varieties low down in the container with at least 7.5 cm (3 in) of compost beneath them, gradually filling it as the shoots of the bulbs extend. Plant the others at a depth three times their own height, except *L. candidum* and *L.* × *testaceum*, which should be planted at a depth twice their height. Water freely during the growing period, and give a high-potash liquid feed once a month. Store the bulbs over winter in their pots, or place them in boxes of damp peat in a cool, dry place. Repot every autumn.

PROPAGATION Lift and separate clumps of bulbs in autumn or spring. Remove the outer scales of bulbs in autumn or spring and plant them in trays of moist compost, placed upright with the tip just visible. Some varieties produce bulbils in the leaf axils, where the leaves join the stems. Plant these miniature bulbs as soon as they ripen in late summer or autumn, or store them in damp peat in a cool place for planting in spring. Seed of species may be sown in deep trays or pots in a coldframe in spring. Most lilies take 3–6 years to flower from seed. The exceptions to this are *L. formosanum* and *L. longiflorum,* which may flower 9 months after sowing

PESTS AND DISEASES Aphids are a constant nuisance and spread virus diseases. Slugs, lily beetles, grey mould, basal rot and lily disease (leaf blight) are common problems.

Lily see *Lilium*
Lily, African see *Agapanthus*
Lily, arum see *Zantedeschia aethiopica*
Lily, belladonna see *Amaryllis belladonna*
Lily, corn see *Ixia*
Lily, day see *Hemerocallis*
Lily, flax see *Phormium*
Lily, foxtail see *Eremurus*
Lily, ginger see *Hedychium*
Lily, glory see *Gloriosa*
Lily, kaffir see *Schizostylis*
Lily, Lent see *Narcissus pseudonarcissus*
Lily, May see *Maianthemum*
Lily, Peruvian see *Alstroemeria*
Lily, pineapple see *Eucomis*
Lily, plantain see *Hosta*
Lily, St Bernard's see *Anthericum*
Lily, St Bruno's see *Paradisea liliastrum*
Lily, toad see *Tricyrtis*
Lily, trout see *Erythronium americanum*
Lily, water see *Nymphaea*
Lily-of-the-valley
    see *Convallaria majalis*
Lily-of-the-valley bush
    see *Pieris japonica*
Lily tree see *Ophiopogon*
Lime see *Citrus aurantiifolia*
Lime tree see *Tilia*

Limnanthes
Meadow foam
Limnanthaceae

This fast-growing annual with its buttercup-like flowers makes a cheerful display from late spring to late summer. The profuse blooms look best at the front of a border or in large pockets on a rock garden. Limnanthes seeds easily and often colonises gravel paths and driveways.

RECOMMENDED SPECIES

L. douglasii♀ (poached egg flower) Saucer-shaped flowers with deep golden yellow centres and conspicuous white petal tips give this plant its popular name. Borne on sprawling stems, the flowers, which are up to 3 cm (1¼ in) across, are lightly scented and irresistible to bees. The rather succulent leaves are yellow-green, smooth and shiny with slender segments. The plant's natural habitat is moist grassland and open woods in W America. HEIGHT & SPREAD 15×20 cm (6×8 in).

CULTIVATION Grow on any moist soil, except poorly drained.

1

▲ *Limnanthes douglasii*

PROPAGATION Sow seed in autumn or early spring where the plants are required to flower. Transplant self-sown seedlings that appear the following year.
PESTS AND DISEASES Usually trouble free.

Limonium
Sea lavender, statice
Plumbaginaceae

Limonium platyphyllum

Tiny, funnel-shaped flowers carried for the most part in spreading clusters provide a pleasing contrast with the bolder growth and flowers of other border plants. Smaller species do well in a sunny position in a rock garden. The flowers are in bloom from mid or late summer to early autumn. They are often grown for cutting or drying. *L. dumosum* and *L. sinuatum* make particularly good dried flowers. This genus was known in the past as *Statice*.

All the species commonly grown in Britain are herbaceous perennials. The plants described below are all hardy except *L. sinuatum*, which is grown as a half-hardy annual. The listed species, once again with the exception of *L. sinuatum,* have dark green, often leathery, spoon-shaped leaves arranged in basal rosettes – one rosette in the first year of the plant's life, subsequently more – and leafless flower stems.
RECOMMENDED SPECIES AND VARIETIES
L. bellidifolium Blue to pinkish blue trumpet-shaped flowers are prolifically borne in short, loose sprays on delicate, many-branched stems in late summer and early autumn. The deep green leathery leaves are about 5 cm (2 in) long and clumped at the base of the plant. This is a good plant for a rock garden. It requires especially well-drained soil. Native to Europe. HEIGHT & SPREAD 20×10 cm (8×4 in).

▲ *Limonium bellidifolium*

L. cosyrense Short, upright clusters of mauve flowers bloom from mid summer onwards. The leaves are about 2.5 cm (1 in) long. This small plant is sometimes grown in pots in a conservatory or greenhouse. Native to SE Europe. HEIGHT & SPREAD 10×10 cm (4×4 in).
L. dumosum (syn. *Goniolimon tataricum*) Red and white flowers are produced in spreading clusters from mid summer to early autumn. The leaves are fleshy and leathery, and up to 15 cm (6 in) long. Native to SE Europe. HEIGHT & SPREAD 30×30 cm (12×12 in).
L. platyphyllum (syn. *L. latifolium*) Masses of tiny pale lavender-blue flowers are carried on wiry stems in diffuse clusters up to 25 cm (10 in) long in mid and late summer and early autumn. The leaves are downy, wavy-edged and few in number, but may grow as long as 60 cm (24 in). Native to SE Europe. HEIGHT & SPREAD 60×45 cm (24×18 in).

The flowers of '**Violetta**' are a darker violet colour.

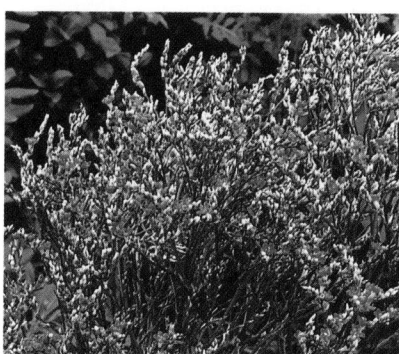
▲ *Limonium platyphyllum* 'Violetta'

L. sinuatum This is a perennial usually treated as a half-hardy annual. It produces blue, pink, red, white or yellow flowers from mid summer to early autumn. Seed is available in single colours and in mixtures. The branched stems, upright and winged, carry flowers in clusters about 10 cm (4 in) long. Leaves clothe the stems as well as forming basal rosettes. They are deep green, lance-shaped with deeply lobed and waved margins, hairy and up to 10 cm (4 in) long. Native to the Mediterranean region. HEIGHT & SPREAD 45×30 cm (18×12 in).
L. suworowii see *Psylliostachys suworowii*
CULTIVATION Plant out in spring, in full sun, in any well-drained soil. Apply lime if the soil is acid. *L. dumosum* and *L. platyphyllum* both do well on naturally dry soils. Deadhead to maintain the display of flowers. Cut out the stems of perennials that have finished flowering.
PROPAGATION Sow seed of species raised as half-hardy annuals in early spring, in a warm greenhouse. A minimum temperature of 15°C (59°F) is needed for swift germination, but subsequently 10°C (50°F) is warm enough. Plant out when all risk of frost has passed. It is possible to sow seed out of doors later on in mid spring, where the plants are to grow, but flowering will not then begin until late summer.

Sow seed of perennials in late spring, or take root cuttings in late winter.
PESTS AND DISEASES Fungal root rot can cause losses in wet soil.

Linanthus
Mountain phlox
Polemoniaceae

Clusters of funnel-shaped flowers and finely divided foliage are the main features of the two linanthus species described below, both of them erect, hardy annuals. They flower from mid summer to early autumn. These species will appeal to gardeners who like to include some unfamiliar plants among better-known ones in mixed beds and borders. They also make unusual pot plants for cool greenhouses or conservatories, where they flower in spring. The flowers are 2-3 cm (¾-1¼ in) wide, with 5 broad spreading lobes. The genus, which includes hardy herbaceous perennials as well as annuals, is mostly native to western N America. It is closely related to gilia.
RECOMMENDED SPECIES AND VARIETIES
L. grandiflorus Lilac or pink flowers, about 3 cm (1¼ in) across, are borne in dense heads. The leaves have 5-11 linear lobes, each up to 3 cm (1¼ in) long. HEIGHT &

▲ *Linanthus grandiflorus*

SPREAD up to 50×20 cm (20×8 in).

L. liniflorus This plant has branched clusters of slender-stalked, lavender-blue flowers, about 2 cm (¾ in) wide. Leaves divide into 3-9 needle-like segments, up to 1.5 cm (½ in) long. HEIGHT & SPREAD up to 50×20 cm (20×8 in).

CULTIVATION Choose a site fully exposed to sun, with light, well-drained soil. The only attention normally needed is weeding and deadheading.

PROPAGATION Sow seed in mid spring, where the plants are to be grown. Once well-established, thin seedlings to 15 cm (6 in) apart.

For pot plants kept in a cool greenhouse or conservatory, sow seed in early autumn in 13 cm (5 in) pots. Thin young plants to 4 per pot in mid autumn. During winter, only water enough to prevent wilting. Provide support with short brushwood in late winter.

PESTS AND DISEASES Usually trouble free.

Linaria
Toadflax
Scrophulariaceae

Linaria alpina

With their clusters or spikes of flowers in a wide range of colours, toadflaxes are popular plants for borders and rock gardens. Among this genus of annuals, biennials and herbaceous perennials are plants that flower over long periods, often from mid summer into autumn. The perennial species tend to be short-lived but they often self-seed.

The flowers are spurred with two lips, often with distinctive markings on the lower lip. The narrow often fleshy leaves are paired or in small whorls along the stem. Native to the northern temperate zone, most species are hardy, but *Linaria genistifolia* ssp. *dalmatica* and *L. triornithophora* will not withstand long periods below freezing.

RECOMMENDED SPECIES AND VARIETIES

L. alpina (alpine toadflax) Purple or violet flowers, about 2 cm (¾ in) long, with yellow or orange markings at the mouth are borne in dense clusters in late spring and summer. The blue or grey-green, lance-like leaves are up to 1 cm (⅜ in) long. A clump-forming alpine, evergreen perennial or biennial. HEIGHT & SPREAD 10×25 cm (4×10 in).

'Purpurea' has deeper purple flowers. The flowers of 'Rosea' are rose-pink.

L. genistifolia ssp. *dalmatica* Spikes of lemon or canary-yellow flowers, with orange at the mouth and about 2-4 cm (¾-1½ in) long, are carried from mid summer to early autumn by this statuesque

▲ *Linaria alpina*

▲ *Linaria alpina* 'Rosea'

semi-evergreen perennial. The upright stems have upward-pointing, lance-like, mid green glossy leaves, up to 12.5 cm (5 in) long. HEIGHT & SPREAD 1 m×60 cm (3×2 ft).

L. maroccana Violet-purple flowers, up to 1.5 cm (½ in) long, with yellow or orange in the throat are borne on spikes during the summer. The narrow leaves are up to 4 cm (1½ in) long. A slender, upright annual. HEIGHT & SPREAD 30×15 cm (12×6 in).

'Carminea' has rose-carmine flowers. The flowers of **Excelsior Hybrids** vary from white to yellow and from pink to red. **'Fairy Bride'** has white flowers and **'Fairy Bridesmaid'** has lemon-yellow flowers. **'Ruby King'** has deep blood-red blooms.

L. purpurea (purple toadflax) Violet flowers, up to 1.5 cm (½ in) long, appear in long slender spikes throughout the summer and early autumn on this graceful semi-evergreen perennial. The narrow mid to grey-green leaves are 6 cm (2½ in) long. HEIGHT & SPREAD 1 m×60 cm (3×2 ft).

'Canon Went' has pink flowers with orange in the mouth and grey-green leaves. 'Springside White' (syn. 'Alba') has white flowers and grey-green leaves.

L. triornithophora Purple and yellow flowers, up to 5 cm (2 in) long, are borne in summer. This short-lived, upright semi-evergreen perennial has grey-green, oval or lance-like leaves, 2.5-7 cm (1-2¾ in) long. HEIGHT & SPREAD 1 m×50 cm (3 ft×20 in).

L. vulgaris (common toadflax) Bright yellow flowers, up to 3 cm (1¼ in) long, in

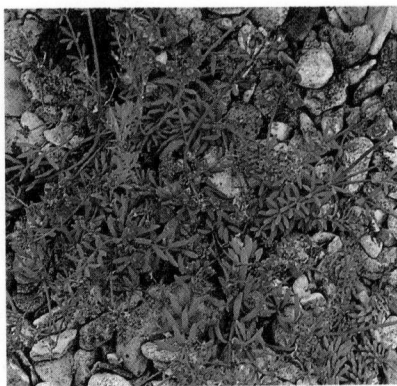

▲ *Linaria alpina* 'Purpurea'

short or long spikes, are produced from mid summer to mid autumn by this invasive herbaceous perennial. Upright stems, often branched near the base, are crowded with elliptical pale to grey-green leaves 2.5-6 cm (1-2½ in) long. HEIGHT & SPREAD 30-45×60 cm (1-1½×2 ft).

CULTIVATION Plant in spring in well-drained soil in an open, sunny position. *L. alpina* prefers gritty soil in a raised bed or in a pocket in a rock garden.

PROPAGATION Sow the seed of annual species in spring, thinly where the plants are to flower. Sow the seed of perennial species in winter or early spring in a coldframe. Alternatively, divide perennials in spring or take softwood cuttings in spring or early summer. Move self-sown seedlings to new positions in late winter or early spring.

PESTS AND DISEASES Usually trouble free.

Lindera
Lauraceae

Lindera obtusiloba

Golden autumn foliage illuminates the lindera plants that are grown in British gardens. Some 80 species of hardy deciduous and evergreen trees and shrubs make up this genus of the laurel family. The few linderas that are readily available in Britain prefer lime-free soil. They are deciduous with unobtrusive tight clusters of small, late spring flowers. On female plants grown close to a male to fertilise them, the flowers are followed in summer by red berries up to 1 cm (⅜ in) long. Leaves, generally less than 10 cm (4 in) long and half as wide, are alternate on the shoots.

RECOMMENDED SPECIES AND VARIETIES

L. benzoin (spice bush) Bright green oval leaves about 10 cm (4 in) long and gently pointed at the top release a pleasant aroma when crushed. They cover a large rounded

▲ *Lindera obtusiloba*

▲ *Lindera benzoin*

▲ *Lindheimera texana*

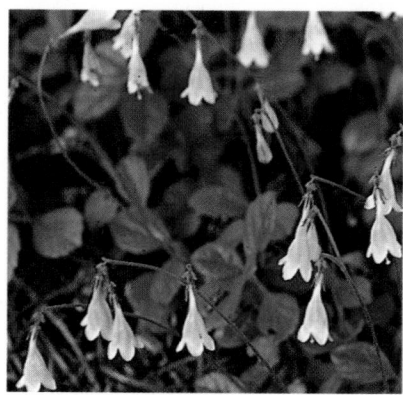

▲ *Linnaea borealis*

shrub with vibrant yellow in autumn. Native to E United States. HEIGHT & SPREAD 80×80cm (32×32in) after 5 years, ultimately 3.5m (12ft) tall.

L. obtusiloba♀ Bright green leaves clothe this small tree in summer and turn butter-yellow in autumn. Tiny bright yellow flowers, covered in fine, silky hairs, appear in clusters in late spring before the leaves emerge. Growing up to 12cm (4¾in) long, the leaves are heart-shaped at the base and usually rounded at the tip, but often plants also carry a few 3-lobed leaves. Native to China, Korea and Japan. HEIGHT & SPREAD 1.2×1m (4×3ft) after 5 years, ultimately 8m (26ft) tall.

CULTIVATION Linderas do best in lime-free soil with some shade from the sun.

PROPAGATION Buy young plants or seed. There is no fertile seed to collect from a single plant in a garden and cuttings are difficult to root.

PRUNING None is required.

PESTS AND DISEASES Usually trouble free.

Lindheimera
Star daisy
Compositae

Yellow flowers bloom from mid summer to mid autumn on this free-flowering hardy annual from Texas, USA. Grow in a mixed bed or border, in a sunny situation. There is only one species in the genus.

Lindheimera texana The flowers, about 2.5cm (1in) across, are produced in loose, branched clusters. Each flower has 5, occa-

sionally 4, broad, petal-like ray florets and a green and yellow centre. Pale green, pointed oval leaves up to 4cm (1in) long grow from the reddish, branched stems. Both stems and leaves are hairy. The plant has an erect habit of growth. Flowers do not last well in water. HEIGHT & SPREAD 60×30cm (24×12in).

CULTIVATION The plant, although hardy, needs full exposure to the sun. Then it will thrive on any well-drained soil. On heavy clay soils it would do best in a raised bed. When it has reached a height of about 10cm (4in), pinch out the growing point to encourage a branching habit of growth. Deadhead regularly.

PROPAGATION Sow seed outdoors in mid spring. Alternatively, sow seed under glass in early spring and plant out in late spring, for an earlier start to flowering.

PESTS AND DISEASES Usually trouble free.

Ling see *Calluna*

Linnaea
Twin-flower
Caprifoliaceae

Linnaea borealis

Pink or white flowers like tiny pendent bells nod above the evergreen carpet of this creeping sub-shrub. This woodland plant forms a loose mat of glossy foliage and makes excellent ground cover for a peat bed or rock garden, or under trees. Native to

cool moist forests and tundra, twin-flowers dislike hot, dry conditions, especially when young, and may be difficult to establish. They do best in acid or neutral soil and dappled shade.

RECOMMENDED SPECIES AND VARIETIES

L. borealis Fragrant, pale pink or white flowers, patterned deep rose inside, and about 8mm (⅜in) long, appear in pairs on slender stems from early to mid summer. The creeping mats have small, oval, deep green leaves and spread by runners. HEIGHT & SPREAD 5×60cm (2in×2ft).

The flowers of var. *americana* are a deep rose pink. They are slightly longer and more tubular.

CULTIVATION Plant during spring in cool, moist, humus-rich acid or neutral soil. Water well, especially in warm, dry weather.

PROPAGATION Tease rooted runners away from the parent plant in spring and plant in a shaded coldframe. Once established, plant out in autumn or early spring. Alternatively, take semi-ripe cuttings from late summer to early autumn.

PESTS AND DISEASES Usually trouble free.

Linum
Flax
Linaceae

Linum flavum 'Compactum'

Brightly coloured cup or saucer-shaped flowers are carried on delicate leafy stems. Individual flowers are short-lived and may stay closed in dull or wet weather, but new ones quickly take their place, giving many weeks of colour. The leaves are usually narrow and rarely more than 3 cm (1¼ in) long. Linum may be annuals, biennials, perennials, or short-lived dwarf shrubs. They are popular in borders, and the smaller plants are ideal for a rock garden. Although fully hardy, some of the rock plants dislike prolonged freezing weather or excessive winter wet. Most flaxes prefer an alkaline soil, but will grow in any soil.

RECOMMENDED SPECIES AND VARIETIES

L. arboreum♀ (shrubby flax) Bright yellow flowers, up to 3 cm (1¼ in) wide, appear in early summer. This compact evergreen shrub, which thrives in a rock garden, has crowded, dark bluish green, elliptical to spoon-shaped leaves. HEIGHT & SPREAD 30×30 cm (12×12 in).

L. flavum (golden flax, yellow flax) Bright yellow flowers, up to 4 cm (1½ in) across, appear from mid summer. This bushy, evergreen perennial has elliptical, deep green leaves. HEIGHT & SPREAD 25×25 cm (10×10 in).

'Compactum', a dwarf plant about 15 cm (6 in) high with pale yellow flowers, is ideal in a trough but dislikes winter wet. 'Gemmell's Hybrid'♀ has rich yellow flowers, 3 cm (1¼ in) wide, in early to mid summer above domes of oval grey-green leaves. It does well in a trough or raised bed. HEIGHT & SPREAD 15×20 cm (6×8 in).

L. monogynum White flowers, 2.5 cm (1 in) wide, appear from early to mid summer on

▲ *Linum flavum* 'Gemmell's Hybrid'

▲ *Linum monogynum*

this short-lived perennial with linear to lance-shaped pointed leaves. HEIGHT & SPREAD 60×40 cm (24×16 in).

L. narbonense (beautiful flax) Pale to deep azure blue flowers, about 3 cm (1¼ in) wide, appear from late spring to mid summer. This herbaceous or semi-evergreen perennial has grey-green, narrow to lance-shaped leaves. It often seeds itself around the garden. HEIGHT & SPREAD 50×30 cm (20×12 in).

'Heavenly Blue'♀ has a profusion of vivid blue flowers.

L. perenne (syn. *L. sibiricum*) (perennial flax) Masses of pale blue flowers, each up to 2.5 cm (1 in) wide, appear throughout summer and early autumn. This herbaceous perennial has grass-like, deep green leaves. HEIGHT & SPREAD 40×25 cm (16×10 in).

White flowers grace f. *album* (syn. *L. perenne* 'Alba'), while 'Blau Saphir' ('Blue Sapphire') has deep, sapphire-blue flowers.

L. sibiricum see *L. perenne*

L. suffruticosum ssp. *salsoloides* The pearly white flowers, flushed and veined in pink with deep violet-pink centres, are about 3 cm (1¼ in) wide. They appear in early to

▲ *Linum narbonense* 'Heavenly Blue'

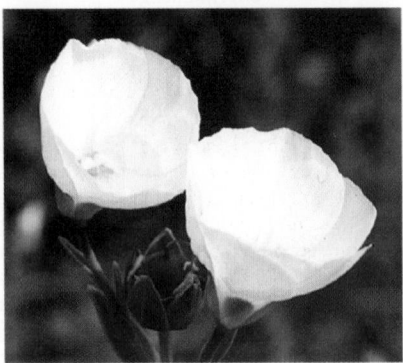

▲ *Linum perenne* f. *album*

---

mid summer. This semi-evergreen perennial has numerous short, linear, grey-green leaves. HEIGHT & SPREAD 20×15 cm (8×6 in).

'Nanum' is a semi-prostrate dwarf plant that is ideal for a raised bed or trough.

CULTIVATION Plant in spring or early summer in any well-drained soil in an open sunny position.

PROPAGATION Sow the seeds of perennials under glass in autumn or late winter, or take cuttings from mid to late summer. Sow the seed of annuals thinly in their growing position in spring.

PESTS AND DISEASES Aphids may infest the young shoots and flower buds.

Lippia see *Aloysia*

Liquidambar
Hamamelidaceae

Liquidambar styraciflua

A kaleidoscope of colour transforms these deciduous trees in autumn. The leaves are purple-hued in spring, but in autumn the colours range from pale yellow to dark crimson. The leaves have pointed lobes with serrated edges. Inconspicuous green or yellow flowers are followed by oval fruits.

RECOMMENDED SPECIES AND VARIETIES

L. formosana This tree, with leaves about 12.5 cm (5 in) wide, becomes roughly conical. Not always frost tolerant, it usually does well in southern Britain. HEIGHT & SPREAD 5×2.4 m (16×8 ft) after 20 years, ultimately 10 m (33 ft) tall.

▼ *Liquidambar styraciflua*

L. styraciflua (sweet gum) One of the best trees for autumn colour, this frost-hardy species has leaves up to 15 cm (6 in) across. HEIGHT & SPREAD 6×4 m (20×13 ft) after 20 years, ultimately 20 m (66 ft) tall.

'**Lane Roberts**'♀ has rich crimson leaves in autumn, while the leaves of '**Worplesdon**'♀ turn bright yellow and orange.

CULTIVATION For the best show of colour, plant in an acid soil in a sheltered position protected from frost. Even mature trees can be killed by prolonged frost.

PROPAGATION Grow the species from seed. Raise cultivars by grafting.

PRUNING None is necessary.

PESTS AND DISEASES Usually trouble free.

Liriodendron
Tulip tree
Magnoliaceae

Liriodendron tulipifera

Curious 'squared off' leaves, which turn a soft yellow in autumn, and remarkable flowers distinguish this monumental deciduous tree. Tulip-like, pale green flowers appear in early to mid summer on trees that are over 15 years old. The flowers mature to cone-shaped fruits which disperse winged seeds in autumn. These trees have a graceful, upswept branch system and need a lot of space. They are also hungry feeders and grow rapidly in deep, fertile soil. There are two species, one native to N America and one to China. They are similar to one another, but the Chinese tulip tree is smaller with slightly smaller flowers.

RECOMMENDED SPECIES AND VARIETIES

L. chinensis (Chinese tulip tree) The pale greenish flowers measure 6 cm (2½ in) across. HEIGHT & SPREAD 7×5 m (23×16 ft) after 20 years, ultimately 22 m (72 ft) tall.

L. tulipifera (tulip tree)♀ This N American tree can grow into a huge specimen – trunks have been recorded at over 2.4 m (8 ft) across, and the crown spread may exceed 20 m (66 ft). The yellowish green cup-shaped flowers, 7.5 cm (3 in) across, have orange markings and prominent stamens. The bark is silvery grey and smooth for 20 years before an intricate lattice of vertical ridges develops, adding interesting textures to its great size. HEIGHT & SPREAD 10×6 m (33×20 ft) in 15-20 years, up to 35 m (115 ft) tall on rich moist sites.

'**Aureomarginatum**' is a slower growing form with variagated yellowish green leaf margins, while '**Fastigiatum**' is columnar.

▲ *Liriodendron tulipifera*

▲ *Liriodendron tulipifera*

▲ *Liriodendron tulipifera* 'Aureomarginatum'

Both trees are smaller than the species, reaching 22×12 m (72×40 ft) and 24×8 m (79×26 ft) respectively.

CULTIVATION For best results, plant in fertile, well-drained, warm soil.

PROPAGATION Plant pot-grown specimens in early autumn or late spring. Growing seed is not usually worth the trouble but if doing so, use only imported seed. Cultivars must be grown from grafts.

PRUNING None usually necessary, but essential cutting or training is best done after flowering.

PESTS AND DISEASES Usually trouble free if planted on a good, fertile, sheltered site.

Liriope
Liliaceae

Upright spikes of dense lavender, mauve or white flowers appear on these evergreen hardy perennials from late summer to late autumn. Glossy, strap-like or grass-like leaves are usually attractively coloured, while the small flowers are bell-like or tubular. The plants, which form clumps, are fairly drought tolerant and make valuable ground cover. The genus is native to China, Taiwan, Vietnam and Japan.

RECOMMENDED SPECIES AND VARIETIES

L. exiliflora '**Ariaka-janshige**' Strongly variegated leaves, up to 45 cm (18 in) long, in white and gold are produced in heavy clumps. The bell-like flowers are mauve. HEIGHT & SPREAD 20×30 cm (8×12 in).

L. muscari♀ Dense clusters of small, dark mauve, bell-like flowers appear densely clustered on stiff spikes in late summer to late autumn. The dark green leaves, up to 45 cm (18 in) long, are strap-like. HEIGHT & SPREAD 30×45 cm (12×18 in).

'**Gold-banded**' has arching leaves edged with gold. It is a very compact plant, up to 35 cm (14 in) tall and spreading to about 30 cm (12 in). '**Majestic**' has handsome green foliage with stems of rich violet flowers. '**Monroe White**' is similar but has spikes of pure white flowers. '**Variegata**' has green leaves striped with gold at the margins. It spreads only about 30 cm (12 in).

L. spicata Small, bell-like flowers in pale mauve to white are carried in dense spikes in late summer. The grassy dark green leaves are glossy and up to 30 cm (12 in) long. HEIGHT & SPREAD 45×30 cm (18×12 in).

▲ *Liriope muscari* 'Majestic'

▲ *Liriope spicata* 'Alba'

'**Alba**' has small, tubular, white flowers amid narrow, grass-like, dark green leaves. It grows about 20 cm (8 in) tall and about 25 cm (10 in) wide.

CULTIVATION Grow liriope in any good well-drained soil, ideally with plenty of well-rotted organic matter incorporated into it. Choose a warm site in full sun if possible. Plant in spring, ideally using pot-grown plants. Remove faded blossoms and old leaves regularly when new foliage appears.

PROPAGATION Lift, divide and replant established crowns in spring.

PESTS AND DISEASES Usually trouble free, but slugs may damage young growth.

Lithodora
Boraginaceae

Lithodora diffusa 'Heavenly Blue'

Masses of tubular or funnel-shaped flowers decorate these small, long-flowering, evergreen shrubs or sub-shrubs. The plants, which form low, bristly mats, are good as specimen plants, or in a rock garden or raised bed. They can also be grown in patio containers. Although hardy, lithodora can be damaged by strong, cold wind. Different species have different soil requirements, but they all favour a well-drained soil.

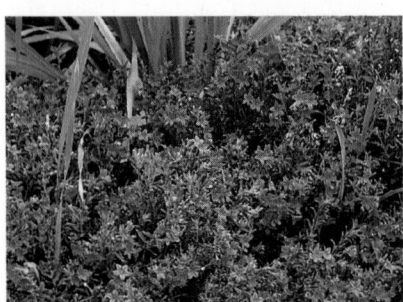

▲ *Lithodora diffusa*

RECOMMENDED SPECIES AND VARIETIES

L. diffusa (syn. *Lithospermum diffusum*, *Lithospermum prostratum*) Bright blue flowers, each up to 2 cm (¾ in) long, appear in clusters at the shoot tips in early summer. This sub-shrub creates an intricately branched mat of rather crowded, bristly, narrow, elliptical leaves. It prefers moist but well-drained, acid soil, otherwise the flowers become more purple than blue and the leaves become more yellow than deep green. The plant is native to woodlands and coastal sands of SW Europe. HEIGHT & SPREAD 30×50 cm (12×20 in).

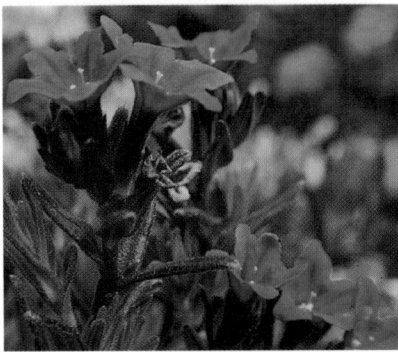

▲ *Lithodora diffusa* 'Grace Ward'

'**Alba**' has white flowers. '**Grace Ward**'♀ has deep blue flowers. '**Heavenly Blue**'♀ aptly describes the azure flowers of this plant with a trailing habit.

L. oleifolia♀ (syn. *Lithospermum oleifolium*) Pale pink flowers that age to blue, about 1 cm (⅜ in) long, appear in curved clusters in early and mid summer, occasionally later. The oblong-oval leaves are grey-green with silky hairs underneath. This plant, which comes from rocky parts of the eastern Pyrenees, prefers alkaline soil and forms a neat hummock. HEIGHT & SPREAD 20×80 cm (8×32 in).

L. zahnii (syn. *Lithospermum zahnii*) Azure flowers, about 1 cm (⅜ in) long, appear from late spring to mid summer. There are many branches with rather upright growth. The bristly greyish green leaves are roughly linear. Originally from the cliffs of southern Greece, this sub-shrub prefers an alkaline soil. It is usually grown in a greenhouse. HEIGHT & SPREAD 30×30 cm (1×1 ft).

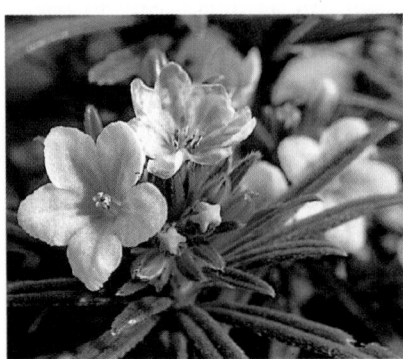

▲ *Lithodora zahnii*

CULTIVATION Plant in spring or early summer in a sheltered, sunny position. Avoid disturbing the roots once the plant is established.

PROPAGATION Sow seed under glass in winter or early spring, or take semi-ripe cuttings in late summer and keep them in a frostproof frame during winter. Plant out the following spring or early summer.

PESTS AND DISEASES Usually trouble free, although red spider mite can cause problems under glass in hot, dry weather.

Lithops
(Living stone, pebble plant)
Aizoaceae

These curious perennial succulents are desert plants from southern Africa. Two swollen elliptical leaves are separated by a narrow slit from which a solitary flower, 4–5 cm (1½–2 in) across, emerges in late summer or early autumn. The upper surfaces of the leaves are opaque or semi-translucent, and are usually marked and coloured rather like a pebble.

RECOMMENDED SPECIES

L. erniana (syn. *L. karasmontana* ssp. *eberlanzii*) A dense network of red-brown lines and spots covers this grey plant with a deeply fissured surface. The white flower opens in early autumn. HEIGHT & SPREAD 3×3 cm (1¼×1¼ in).

L. hookeri see *L. turbiniformis*

L. karasmontana ssp. *eberlanzii* see *L. erniana*

L. lesliei The plants are grey-green to pale brown. Their flat to convex upper surface is olive-green with beige marbling. The yellow flower opens in autumn. HEIGHT & SPREAD 3×5 cm (1¼×2 in).

▲ *Lithops lesliei*

L. salicola Convex, olive-green to grey upper surfaces are irregularly edged with reddish beige. The rest of the plant is greyish green. The white flower appears in late summer or early autumn. HEIGHT & SPREAD 5×3 cm (2×1¼ in).

L. turbiniformis (syn. *L. hookeri*) The flat upper surfaces are rich brown with many darker brown fissures. The yellow flower appears in early autumn. HEIGHT & SPREAD 3×4 cm (1¼×1½ in).

CULTIVATION Plant in an equal mixture of compost and grit or sharp sand in late spring. Place in good light and water lightly at first. Increase watering until late summer, then stop all together until mid spring. Keep at a minimum of 5°C (41°F).

PROPAGATION Surface-sow seeds on a compost such as John Innes No. 2 in mid spring. Maintain a temperature of 21°C (70°F). Alternatively, divide clumps in early summer, leave them to dry for 3-4 days then pot them separately.

PESTS AND DISEASES Mealy bugs and root mealy bugs may be troublesome.

Lithospermum see *Lithodora*
Living stone see *Lithops*

Lobelia

Campanulaceae

Lobelia × speciosa 'Queen Victoria'

Valued for their small flowers in glowing colours, borne profusely over several months, lobelias are available in a wide range of heights and habits of growth, fitting them for a variety of uses in the garden. The genus includes annuals, herbaceous perennials and sub-shrubs. Plants may be hardy, half-hardy or tender. Annuals and those perennials that are grown as half-hardy annuals are often used in containers, especially hanging baskets, as well as for edging and summer bedding plants. The hardy perennials make fine border plants and also do well along the edges of pools and streams. They are among the most dramatic of all herbaceous garden plants – many of them having dark foliage and red flowers. The flowers are tubular and have five lobes with the lower three lobes much larger than the two upper ones and flattening into a characteristic fan-like 'lip'. Some lobelias are poisonous.

RECOMMENDED SPECIES AND VARIETIES

L. cardinalis♀ (cardinal flower) Scarlet flowers, up to 5 cm (2 in) across, are borne in long spikes from mid summer until autumn on this hardy, clump-forming perennial plant. Narrow, toothed, mid green leaves, up to 10 cm (4 in) long, form rosettes at the base of the stems. Both leaves and stems are heavily tinged in purple-bronze. The plant tends to be short-lived, lasting 2-3 years. Native to N America. HEIGHT & SPREAD 1 m × 25 cm (36 × 10 in).

L. erinus (edging and trailing lobelia) Violet-blue and white flowers, each 5 mm (¼ in) across, appear in profusion from late spring until the first autumn frosts. Numerous slender, sprawling branches carry flowers about 10 weeks after sowing. Although a short-lived perennial, *L. erinus* and its varieties are almost all treated as half-hardy annuals. The light green leaves, up to 2 cm (¾ in) long, are ovate at the base of the plant, longer and narrower on the stems. Native to South Africa. HEIGHT & SPREAD 15 × 15 cm (6 × 6 in).

Compact varieties make neat domes suitable for edging borders and for containers. 'Crystal Palace' has deep blue flowers and dark bronze-green leaves. 'Mrs Clibran' produces dark blue flowers, each with a conspicuous white eye. 'Cambridge Blue' carries light blue flowers. 'Kathleen Mallard',

Lobelia erinus 'Cambridge Blue'

bearing blue double flowers, does not come true from seed, so must be propagated from cuttings. The flowers of 'Rosamund' are deep cherry-red with white eyes. 'White Lady' has white flowers, while 'Riviera Lilac' has lilac-blue flowers, and those of 'Riviera Blue Splash' are pale blue, marked darker blue.

Varieties with a trailing habit, spreading to 30 cm (12 in) or more, are ideal for hanging baskets and other containers. They include the 'Cascade', 'Fountain' and 'Regatta' series, which are available in single and mixed colours, including white, blue, lilac, mauve and purple-red. The cultivar 'Sapphire' has deep blue flowers with white eyes.

L. × gerardii Pinkish violet to purple flowers, marked with white, up to 5 cm (2 in) across, form dense spikes from mid summer to early autumn. The leaves are dark green, ovate and 4 cm (1½ in) long. The plant is quite hardy but in colder areas it might not survive winter without a protective mulch. HEIGHT & SPREAD 1 m × 25 cm (36 × 10 in).

'Vedrariensis' has dark violet flowers and dark green leaves tinged with red.

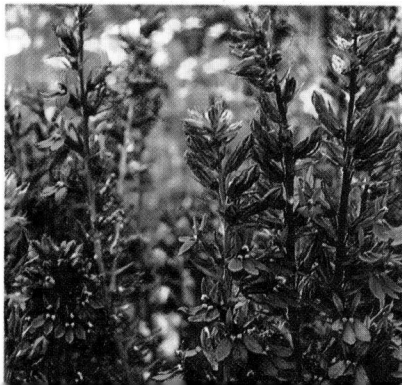

▼ *Lobelia × gerardii 'Vedrariensis'*

▲ *Lobelia × gerardii 'Tania'*

'Tania' has crimson-purple flowers.

L. laxiflora (syn. *L. cavanillesii*) A branching sub-shrub, hardy only in milder areas, the plant has pendulous red-and-yellow flowers, 4 cm (1½ in) long, in late summer and early autumn. Leaves are narrow, dark green and up to 8 cm (3¼ in) long. Native to Arizona, Mexico and Colombia. HEIGHT & SPREAD 60 × 30 cm (24 × 12 in).

▲ *Lobelia laxiflora*

The narrower-leaved var. *angustifolia* is more commonly grown.

L. linnaeoides Each white and purple flower is about 1 cm (⅜ in) across on this perennial which flowers in short spikes from early to mid summer. It has widely spread, slender, prostrate stems. The rounded dark green leaves, up to 1 cm (⅜ in) long, have toothed margins. Native to New Zealand, this moisture-loving plant is for a rock garden in milder areas or an unheated greenhouse. HEIGHT & SPREAD 5 × 20 cm (2 × 8 in).

L. siphilitica (blue cardinal flower) Spikes up to 60 cm (24 in) long of blue flowers, 2.5 cm (1 in) wide, appear from mid summer to early autumn. Leaves are light green, lance-shaped and up to 10 cm (4 in) long. This hardy perennial can be short-lived, unless divided every other year. Native to E United States. HEIGHT & SPREAD 60×30 cm (24×12 in).

There is a white variety, 'Alba'.

L. × speciosa This herbaceous perennial has red or violet flowers, 3 cm (1¼ in) wide, in loose spikes from late summer to mid autumn. Leaves are oblong to ovate and about 10 cm (4 in) long. HEIGHT & SPREAD 90×50 cm (36×20 in).

Most varieties are fully hardy. Those listed below grow to a height of 90 cm (36 in) unless stated otherwise. None can be grown from seed except 'Queen Victoria' and 'Pink Flamingo'.

'Cherry Ripe' has cerise-scarlet flowers with leaves often tinged reddish bronze. 'Dark Crusader', with red flowers and copper tinted leaves, reaches an ultimate height of 75 cm (30 in). 'Eulalia Berridge' bears bright raspberry-coloured flowers. 'Pink Flamingo' has rosy-pink flowers and grows to 120 cm (48 in) high. 'Queen Victoria'♀ has red flowers with dark red foliage. 'Russian Princess' has purple flowers and dark leaves. It grows up to 75 cm (30 in) tall.

The 'Compliment' and 'Fan' series of F₁ hybrids come true from seed. Both are available in a range of colours. Plants of the 'Compliment' series grow to 75 cm (30 in) tall and have unbranched stems. Plants belonging to the 'Fan' series branch at the base and reach a height of 60 cm (24 in). Particularly notable are L. 'Compliment Scarlet'♀ and L. 'Fan Deep Red'.

L. tenuior Erect slender stems carry an abundance of bright blue flowers, 2.5 cm (1 in) across, in loose clusters from mid summer to mid autumn. Leaves are ovate, light green and up to 3 cm (1¼ in) long.

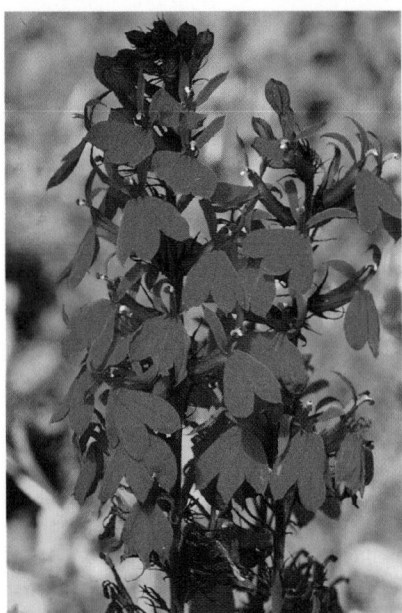

▲ *Lobelia* 'Compliment Scarlet'

This plant resembles *L. erinus* in habit and is also a tender perennial generally treated as a half-hardy annual when grown in the garden. It is also grown as a pot plant. Native to W Australia. HEIGHT & SPREAD 30×25 cm (12×10 in).

The cultivar 'Blue Wings' has cobalt-blue flowers.

L. tupa This large clump-forming perennial has brick-red flowers, 5 cm (2 in) wide, in spikes that bloom from late summer to mid autumn. Pale green, lance-shaped, downy leaves, 15–30 cm (6–12 in) long, grow on the stout stems. The plant particularly suits a waterside site. Native to Chile, *L. tupa* is hardy, except in severe winters. HEIGHT & SPREAD 1.8 m×1 m (6×3 ft).

L. valida Sky-blue flowers with white centres are freely produced from early summer to mid autumn on a bushy plant of upright habit with fleshy, branched stems and dark green leaves. This is a tender perennial, ordinarily treated as a half-hardy annual. Native to South Africa. HEIGHT & SPREAD 1 m×75 cm (3 ft×30 in).

CULTIVATION Plant in a rich, moisture-retaining but well-drained soil in full sun or partial shade, with some shelter from wind. Water generously in summer. Protect half-hardy plants, and those treated as half-hardy, from frost with a dry mulch.

BEDDING AND CONTAINER PLANTS
L. erinus, *L. tenuior* and *L. valida* are usually treated as half-hardy summer bedding plants. Plant out in spring when the risk of hard frosts has passed. They will tolerate slight frosts if properly hardened off before planting out. Position plants in containers out of full sun. Water to keep soil moist – especially those in containers. Feed container-grown plants with a low-nitrogen liquid fertiliser. Cut back straggly growth and older stems that no longer produce many flowers.

L. erinus and *L. tenuior* also make fine pot plants for a cool greenhouse or conservatory. They cannot be kept in a house for any length of time because there is not enough light. Water sparingly in winter.

HERBACEOUS PERENNIALS
Planting is best done in mid spring. Mulch after planting and every spring to reduce loss of moisture from the soil surface. Apply a top dressing of a general-purpose fertiliser to established plants. Support tall plants, such as *L. tupa*.

Cut down stems to ground level after they have been destroyed by frost and apply a thick mulch to protect the plants from frost damage. Bracken or leaves held in place by netting are ideal. If a plant is unlikely to survive the winter, lift it after the first frost and overwinter it in a deep box inside a coldframe.

PROPAGATION
BEDDING AND CONTAINER PLANTS
Sow seed uncovered on the compost surface in late winter if a minimum tempera-

ture of 13°C (55°F) can be maintained after germination. If this minimum temperature cannot be guaranteed, sow later. Prick out the seedlings in groups of 5 or so. Sow seed of *L. erinus* and *L. tenuior* in late winter for summer flowering, or in late summer for flowering in spring. Treat plants as half-hardy annuals.

HERBACEOUS PERENNIALS
Divide in spring and, if possible, grow on the divided shoots in pots in a coldframe for about a month before planting out. Alternatively, sow seed in summer for spring flowers or sow seed in late winter for summer flowers. If possible, keep the young plants in a cool or unheated greenhouse during winter.

PESTS AND DISEASES Slugs can be a menace and leaf spot may affect some plants. In wet winters on soil with poor drainage, plants may be lost because of crown rot.

Lobster claw see *Clianthus*

Lobularia
Cruciferae

Masses of colourful summer flowers earn this group of southern European hardy annuals and perennials its place in gardens. The plant most widely cultivated is the easy-to-grow annual, *Lobularia maritima*.

RECOMMENDED SPECIES AND VARIETIES
L. maritima (sweet alyssum) (syn. *Alyssum maritimum*) Tiny, white, 4-petalled flowers in dense fragrant clusters, up to 5 cm (2 in) across, are borne in profusion throughout summer. The short, multi-branched stems are thickly clothed with greyish green, lance-shaped leaves, up to 1.5 cm (½ in) long. This annual or short-lived perennial is widely used in summer bedding schemes, often as edging. HEIGHT & SPREAD 10×20 cm (4×8 in).

The profuse variety 'Carpet of Snow' has pure white flowers. 'Golf Rose' has deep pink flowers, while those of 'Little Dorrit' are white. 'Oriental Night' bears rich purple flowers. 'Violet Queen' has

▼ *Lobularia maritima* 'Carpet of Snow'

▲ *Lobularia maritima* 'Oriental Night'

violet flowers, while the flowers of **'Wonderland'** are deep purplish pink.

CULTIVATION Plant in late spring in well-drained soil in a sunny situation. Do not incorporate organic material into the soil before planting because it encourages soft growth that can be susceptible to powdery mildew. Keep well watered and treat with a high-potash fertiliser, such as liquid tomato feed, when flowering has started. Remove faded blossoms and dead or withered leaves regularly.

PROPAGATION Sow seed in late winter or early spring in boxes or trays in a greenhouse or coldframe.

PESTS AND DISEASES Flea beetles may attack, especially when plants are young.

London pride see *Saxifrage* × *urbium*

Lonicera
Honeysuckle
Caprifoliaceae

Lonicera periclymenum 'serotina'

Wafts of intensely sweet perfume and distinctive, delicate-looking flowers help to secure honeysuckle a special place in British gardens. Not all the blooms are fragrant, but careful selection from the 180 or so species can guarantee a succession of flowers throughout the year. Honeysuckles have tubular or bell-shaped flowers, up to 5 cm (2 in) long, with five lobes. In many plants the upper four lobes are fused, with the lower lobe curving back to reveal the stamens. The leaves, usually 3–10 cm (1¼–4 in) long, can be oval, or oblong to lance-shaped, or round. The fleshy berries, which

are not poisonous, are ball or egg-shaped. They attract birds, hedgehogs and other wildlife, while the flowers are a good source of nectar for bees and moths – hence lonicera's common name.

Native to most of the Northern Hemisphere, lonicera offers deciduous, evergreen and semi-evergreen plants. All the recommended species and varieties are hardy. They prefer moist, but well-drained, loam-rich soil but will grow in most soil. Some prefer sun, others shade. However, plants on hot, dry sites are more vulnerable to aphids.

RECOMMENDED SPECIES AND VARIETIES
Honeysuckles are either bushy shrubs or woody climbers and the recommended plants are listed separately here.

SHRUBS
These honeysuckles are ideal for mixed and shrub borders. They include the richly scented, winter-flowering *Lonicera fragrantissima* and *L.* × *purpusii*. A low-growing plant, such as *L. pileata,* makes good ground cover, while *L. nitida* is suitable for formal hedges. These are some of the hardiest shrubs, and *L. maackii* tolerates especially severe conditions. Nonetheless, all shrub honeysuckles flower most freely in the sun. The flowers, 1.5–4 cm (½–1½ in) long, are borne in pairs where the leaves join the stem.

L. chaetocarpa Nodding, slightly scented, primrose-yellow flowers appear from late spring to early summer on this upright, deciduous plant. The long flowers, clasped in bracts, give way to bright red berries in mid summer. The leaves are bristly. HEIGHT & SPREAD 1.2×1.2 m (4×4 ft) after 5 years, ultimately 2.4 m (8 ft) tall.

L. fragrantissima The powerful fragrance of the creamy yellow blooms fills the air throughout winter. Dull red berries follow in spring. The leathery leaves are semi-evergreen in exposed positions and fully evergreen if the plant is sheltered from cold winds. HEIGHT & SPREAD 1.5×1.5 m (5×5 ft) after 5 years, ultimately 2.7 m (9 ft) tall.

L. involucrata (twinberry, Californian honeysuckle) Small, yellow or red-tinged flowers surrounded by heart-shaped bracts

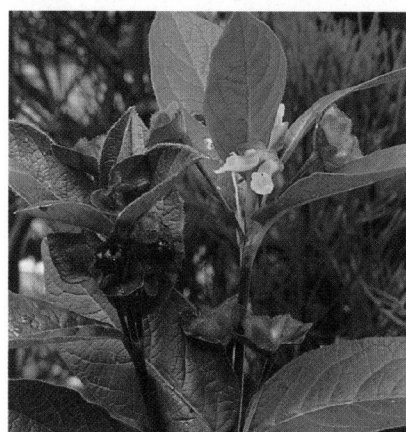

▲ *Lonicera involucrata*

appear on this robust, deciduous plant in spring and are followed by shiny, black berries. The narrow, slightly hairy leaves are about 12.5 cm (5 in) long. HEIGHT & SPREAD 1.2×1.2 m (4×4 ft) after 5 years, ultimately 2.4 m (8 ft) tall.

Deep orange-yellow flowers held by purple-tinged, heart-shaped bracts distinguish var. *ledebourii* which is slightly larger than *L. involucrata.*

L. korolkowii This graceful, deciduous shrub has pale rose-coloured blooms in late spring and early summer, followed by red berries. The young hollow twigs and the leaves are downy. HEIGHT & SPREAD 1.5×1.5 m (5×5 ft) after 5 years, ultimately 3 m (10 ft) tall.

L. maackii Fragrant white flowers turn yellow before fading on this vigorous, deciduous plant. In bloom from late spring to mid summer, the flowers give way to dark red or black berries. The leaf stems are purple with dense hairs. Although very hardy, this plant prefers rich soil and a sunny position. HEIGHT & SPREAD 3×3 m (10×10 ft) after 5 years, ultimately 4.5 m (15 ft) tall.

White blooms distinguish f. *podocarpa* which is slightly smaller than *L. maackii.*

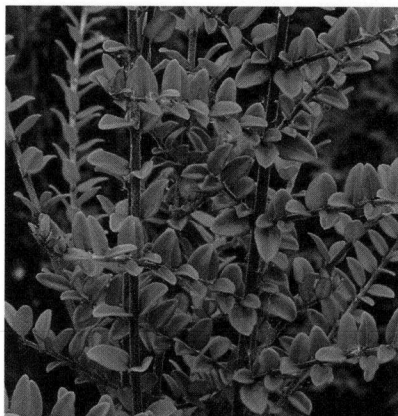

▲ *Lonicera nitida*

L. nitida (box-leaved honeysuckle) With its small, dark green shiny leaves and rounded habit, this fast-growing, dense evergreen makes excellent formal hedging. Provided that it is not pruned into a hedge, creamy white fragrant flowers in spring are followed by shiny, transparent blue-purple berries. HEIGHT & SPREAD 1.5×1.8 m (5×6 ft) after 5 years, ultimately 2.4 m (8 ft) tall.

'Baggesen's Gold'♀ is grown for its dense, nodding branches of small, golden

Lonicera nitida 'Baggesen's Gold'

▲ *Lonicera pileata*

leaves that turn sulphur-green in winter. *L. pileata* Ideal for ground cover, underplanting and rockeries, this evergreen or semi-evergreen shrub has a low, neat, spreading habit and tolerates partial shade. Yellowish white flowers in late spring are followed by transparent amethyst coloured berries. The young twigs are purple and covered with soft hairs, while the leaves are dark and shiny with prominent mid veins. HEIGHT & SPREAD 1×1.5 m (3×5 ft) after 5 years, ultimately 1.5 m (5 ft) tall.

'Moss Green' is a compact cultivar with bright green leaves.

L. × purpusii♀ Cream-coloured flowers, heavy with perfume, appear on the bare twigs of this semi-evergreen from late winter to mid spring. This honeysuckle has dense branches, bristly leaves and red berries. HEIGHT & SPREAD 1.5×1.5 m (5×5 ft) after 5 years, ultimately 3 m (10 ft) tall.

'Winter Beauty'♀ is an exceptionally fragrant winter-flowering plant with creamy white flowers.

L. rupicola var. *syringantha* This graceful, deciduous shrub has lilac-pink sweetly scented flowers in spring and early summer and small grey-green leaves. HEIGHT & SPREAD 1×1 m (3×3 ft) after 5 years, ultimately 1.8 m (6 ft) tall.

▲ *Lonicera rupicola* var. *syringantha*

L. standishii Fragrant creamy white flowers, sometimes tinted pale pink, appear in winter and early spring followed by red, heart-shaped berries. This deciduous or semi-evergreen plant is very hardy. HEIGHT & SPREAD 1.8×1.8 m (6×6 ft) after 5 years, ultimately 2.4 m (8 ft) tall.

L. tatarica This easy-to-grow deciduous plant thrives untamed. Hardy and drought-tolerant, it has white to pinkish flowers in late spring and early summer followed by scarlet or orange berries. HEIGHT & SPREAD 2×2 m (6½×6½ ft) after 5 years, ultimately 3 m (10 ft) tall.

'Arnold's Red' is a vigorous plant with very deep red fragrant flowers and blue tinted leaves. 'Hack's Red' has rose-pink flowers.

L. × xylosteum (fly honeysuckle) This deciduous plant, naturalised in some parts of Britain, has yellowish white flowers, often tinted red, in summer. The berries are red, occasionally yellow. HEIGHT & SPREAD 1.5×1.5 m (5×5 ft) after 5 years, ultimately 3 m (10 ft) tall.

CLIMBERS

These plants, which climb by twining their stems around supports, may be trained over formal arches or left to scramble up trees, through bushes or over garden eyesores, such as a featureless wall. Evergreen species, such as *Lonicera henryi*, make excellent screens supported by trellis. The flowers, 4–5 cm (1½–2 in) long, are borne either in pairs, or in whorls of six, in a cluster or a spike. Some plants have perfoliate leaves. This means that two opposite leaves fuse around the stem, like a small ruff under the blooms. Most climbers prefer their roots in shade and their shoots in the sun.

L. × americana hort. see *L. × italica*

L. × americana♀ Fragrant pink and cream blooms appear from mid summer to mid autumn shielded by oblong-elliptic perfoliate leaves. This evergreen needs a sheltered position in either sun or shade. HEIGHT & SPREAD 1.2×1.2 m (4×4 ft) after 5 years, ultimately 3 m (10 ft) tall.

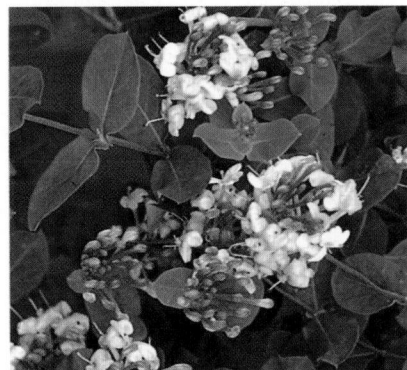

▲ *Lonicera × americana*

L. × brownii 'Dropmore Scarlet' (scarlet trumpet honeysuckle) Spikes of showy, orange-scarlet flowers perch above round, perfoliate leaves from early summer to early autumn, sometimes followed by orange-red berries. The elliptical lower leaves are slightly downy. This very hardy, deciduous hybrid needs part shade to reduce attack by aphids. HEIGHT & SPREAD 1.5×1.5 m (5×5 ft) after 5 years, ultimately 3.5 m (12 ft) tall.

▲ *Lonicera × brownii* 'Dropmore Scarlet'

L. caprifolium♀ (early cream honeysuckle, perfoliate honeysuckle) Cup-like, greyish green leaves cradle the cream-flushed, pink flowers of this vigorous deciduous plant. Whorls of heavily scented flowers open from mid to late spring and are followed by clusters of bright orange-red berries. HEIGHT & SPREAD 1.8×1.8 m (6×6 ft) after 5 years, ultimately 4 m (13 ft) tall.

'Anna Fletcher' has lemon-yellow flowers.

L. etrusca This vigorous deciduous or semi-evergreen climber has creamy yellow fragrant flowers, often tinted red, from early summer to early autumn. Red berries follow. The upper leaves are perfoliate. HEIGHT & SPREAD 1.5×1 m (5×3 ft) after 5 years, ultimately 2.4 m (8 ft) tall.

'Donald Waterer' has striking red and cream fragrant flowers in mid summer followed by abundant red berries in autumn. This upright deciduous plant with red stems prefers a sunny position, and can be grown in a container. 'Michael Rosse' has soft grey-green leaves that complement the slender, mid summer, cream flowers. In bloom at the same time, 'Superba' has large trusses of fragrant yellow flowers flushed with pink emerging from a collar of grey-green, perfoliate, upper leaves. Red berries appear in autumn. This vigorous semi-evergreen, which prefers full sun, grows to about 3.5 m (12 ft) tall.

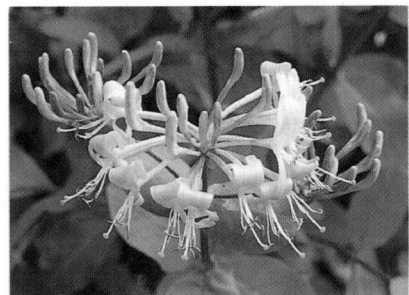

▲ *Lonicera etrusca* 'Superba'

1

L. giraldii Conspicuous yellow stamens decorate the red flowers of this evergreen with hairy leaves and stems. Clusters of early summer flowers give way to small blue-black berries. This hardy plant needs shelter from the wind in a position that is not too wet in winter. HEIGHT & SPREAD 1.2×1.2m (4×4ft) after 5 years, ultimately 3m (10ft) tall.

L. × heckrottii This compact, free-flowering, deciduous hybrid has a shrub-like habit and can be grown in a container in part shade. Long spikes of fragrant pink and orange flowers appear above perfoliate leaves from early to late summer. HEIGHT & SPREAD 1.5×1.2m (5×4ft) after 5 years, ultimately 1.8m (6ft) tall.

'Goldflame' has rounded clusters of fragrant deep pink and yellow flowers.

L. henryi This vigorous evergreen with hairy shoots and dark green leaves has small yellow-orange flowers flushed pink in early and mid summer. Blue-black berries appear in autumn. HEIGHT & SPREAD 2.4×2.4m (8×8ft) after 5 years, ultimately 5m (16ft) tall.

L. × italica (syn. *L. × americana* hort.) Exceptionally fragrant flowers smother this vigorous deciduous plant from late spring to mid summer. Maroon in bud, the blooms open to reveal pink and yellow petals. The young stems are purple with obovate leaves. The late-summer berries are orange-red. HEIGHT & SPREAD 2×2m (6½×6½ft) after 5 years, ultimately 4m (13ft) tall.

L. japonica This evergreen or semi-evergreen plant is very vigorous and can become invasive. The fragrant white flowers appear from early summer to early autumn, ageing to yellow. Black berries follow. HEIGHT & SPREAD 2.4×2.4m (8×8ft) after 5 years, ultimately 4.5m (15ft) tall.

'Aureoreticulata' has leaves with yellow and green veins. Best in part shade, this prostrate semi-evergreen has insignificant, but fragrant white flowers, and can be used as ground cover. Fast-growing 'Halliana' is a semi-evergreen suitable for pergolas and screens in sun or shade. Heavily scented white and yellow flowers are borne from mid summer to early autumn. The young

▲ *Lonicera × italica*

▲ *Lonicera periclymenum* 'Belgica'

▲ *Lonicera periclymenum* 'Graham Thomas'

leaves are hairy. 'Hall's Prolific', also a fast-growing semi-evergreen, flowers profusely.

Crimson and white fragrant flowers and purple-tinted leaves distinguish var. *repens*, a vigorous semi-evergreen.

L. periclymenum (woodbine) Scrambling vigorously, this deciduous plant, which is native to Britain, Europe and W Asia, has sweetly scented creamy white flowers with purple to yellow undersides from early summer to early autumn. HEIGHT & SPREAD 1.8×1.8m (6×6ft) after 5 years, ultimately 3.5m (12ft) tall.

'Belgica' (early Dutch woodbine) has dense heads of heavily scented pink-and-red flowers in mid summer. Large bunches of orange berries in late summer turn red in autumn. This plant benefits from part shade. The vigorous 'Graham Thomas'♀, originally a native wild plant, has profuse, fragrant, cream-white flowers from mid summer to early autumn. The berries are orange-red. This plant ultimately grows to 4m (13ft) tall. 'Serotina'♀ (late Dutch honeysuckle) has abundant richly scented, purple, red and white flowers from mid

▼ *Lonicera japonica* 'Halliana' (flowers)

▼ *Lonicera japonica* 'Halliana'

▼ *Lonicera periclymenum* 'Serotina'

▲ *Lonicera sempervirens*

▲ *Lonicera sempervirens* f. *sulphurea*

▲ *Lonicera similis* var. *delavayi*

summer to early autumn. Bronze-tinted leaves complement the purple-red autumn berries. This plant prefers partial shade.

L. sempervirens♀ (trumpet honeysuckle) Flowering from spring to early autumn, this semi-evergreen has spikes of scarlet blooms emphasised by perfoliate leaves. Large clusters of scarlet berries appear from late summer. This plant needs partial shade to reduce attack by aphids. HEIGHT & SPREAD 1.5×1.5 m (5×5 ft) after 5 years, ultimately 3 m (10 ft) tall.

The more vigorous f. *sulphurea* has bright yellow flowers and yellow berries that turn red. It needs a sheltered position.

L. similis var. *delavayi* A vigorous evergreen that excels on pergolas and archways, this plant has pairs of large, fragrant, white-

and-yellow flowers, about 7 cm (2¾ in) long, in mid summer. The leaves are slightly hairy and the small berries are black. HEIGHT & SPREAD 2.4×2.4 m (8×8 ft) after 5 years, ultimately 4.5 m (15 ft) tall.

L. × tellmanniana♀ Bold displays of red-flushed, coppery yellow flowers perch in large clusters above oval, perfoliate leaves in late spring and early summer on this deciduous plant. HEIGHT & SPREAD 1.5×1.5 m (5×5 ft) after 5 years, ultimately 3.5 m (12 ft) tall.

L. tragophylla♀ Bright golden flowerheads appear in early summer on this vigorous, deciduous climber with slightly hairy, bronze-tinted young leaves. Not always easy to grow, but dramatic when established, this plant needs a moist shady position. HEIGHT & SPREAD 1.8×1.5 m (6×5 ft) after 5 years, ultimately 5 m (16 ft) tall.

CULTIVATION Plant in a shallow hole in moist, but well-drained, humus-rich soil if possible, although honeysuckles will grow in any soil. For shrubs, plant deciduous species and varieties in their dormant season, ideally in a sunny position for profuse flowering. Plant evergreen shrubs in spring. Plant bare-rooted plants of *L. nitida* from late autumn to early spring about 30 cm (1 ft) apart.

For climbers, plant pot-grown species and varieties at any time, bearing in mind that it is easier to establish deciduous climbers between autumn and spring in dry areas and in spring elsewhere. For evergreen climbers, try to plant in spring. If possible, position climbers with their roots in shade and their shoots in the sun. Water and feed in the growing season.

PROPAGATION For shrubs, take semi-ripe cuttings in late summer and plant in sandy compost in a coldframe, or take hardwood cuttings in early to mid autumn. Plant out the following spring. Alternatively, layer the outer shoots. Sow seed in autumn or spring.

For climbers, take ripewood cuttings of evergreens and *L. caprifolium*, *L. periclymenum*, *L. japonica* and their varieties and cultivars in late autumn and plant them in a coldframe. For plants that take some time to root, such as *L. × americana*, *L. etrusca*, *L. giraldii*, *L. sempervirens* and *L. tragophylla*, take softwood cuttings in spring or early summer and grow in a propagator.

PRUNING For evergreen and deciduous shrubs, thin and cut back after flowering. Cut back hedging plants by half their height in their first spring and again in summer to encourage bushiness. In subsequent years cut back by about a half until the hedge reaches the desired size.

For climbers, pruning is not necessary. However, cut back any straggly plants to encourage new growth, and prune vigorous plants to control their size. Autumn is the best time to do this in mild areas and spring is best in cold areas. Cut out any old or diseased wood in winter and encourage new

growth by reducing the main stems by a about a third.

PESTS AND DISEASES Aphids can make flowering shoots unsightly. Leaf spot can affect *L. caprifolium* and mildew can be a problem for *L. japonica* 'Aureoreticulata'.

Loosestrife, purple
see *Lythrum salicaria*
Loosestrife, yellow
see *Lysimachia vulgaris*
Loquat see *Eriobotrya japonica*
Lords and ladies see *Arum maculatum*

Lotus
Leguminosae

Lotus plants are best grown where their long stems can trail and show off the fine silvery foliage and spectacular flowers.

RECOMMENDED SPECIES AND VARIETIES
L. berthelotii♀ (parrot's beak) This tender sub-shrub makes a good choice for a container or hanging basket in a sunny, sheltered spot in the garden provided it is overwintered under glass. It has trailing mats of semi-evergreen, silvery leaves and bears a mass of brilliant red and yellow, curved, beak-like flowers, up to 4 cm (1½ in) long, throughout summer. Each leaf, up to 2 cm (¾ in) long, is divided into 5 narrow segments. Native to the Canary Isles. HEIGHT & SPREAD 20 cm×1 m (8 in×3 ft).

▲ *Lotus berthelotii*

CULTIVATION Plant in early spring in a well-drained soil in a position in full sun. Alternatively, grow in containers of well-drained, soil-based compost in a frost-free greenhouse or conservatory. Plants can be brought outside once the danger of frost has passed.

PROPAGATION Take softwood cuttings in early summer.

PESTS AND DISEASES Usually trouble free.

Lovage (culinary herb) see HERBS p. 331
Love-in-a-mist see *Nigella damascena*
Love-lies-bleeding
see *Amaranthus caudatus*
Lungwort see *Pulmonaria*

Luma
Myrtaceae

These shrubs or small trees are grown for their glossy evergreen leaves and mottled bark. Lumas are not completely hardy and in Britain will thrive outdoors only in warm coastal regions, or in the shelter of a warm wall in mild inland areas.

RECOMMENDED SPECIES

L. apiculata♀ (syn. *Myrtus apiculata, M. luma*) This small, rounded, often many-stemmed tree is grown mainly for its cinnamon-coloured bark, which peels off after 5 years leaving light, dark and golden brown patches. White flowers, up to 2.5 cm (1 in) across, are followed in early autumn by red berries that turn black. The dark green oval leaves are about 2.5 cm (1 in) long. Native to Chile. HEIGHT & SPREAD 2.4×1.2 m (8×4 ft) after 10 years, ultimately 6 m (20 ft) tall.

▲ *Luma apiculata*

CULTIVATION In mild areas, plant outdoors in spring, in a well-drained soil in full sun. Alternatively, grow in a cool greenhouse in pots of multipurpose compost; move outside once the danger of frost has passed and return to the greenhouse before the first frosts return. Feed established pot plants with a weak liquid feed every fortnight from late spring to early summer. Water liberally during spring and summer but keep the compost just moist in winter.
PROPAGATION Sow seed under glass in spring or take semi-ripe cuttings in summer.
PRUNING Not normally required but, if wished, trim plants into shape in spring.
PESTS AND DISEASES Usually trouble free.

Lunaria
Honesty
Cruciferae

Purple or white flowers that bloom in late spring and early summer are followed by rounded, flat, silvery seedpods. Each flower has four petals and is up to 2 cm (¾ in) across. The seedpods are often used dried in flower arrangements: cut in late summer to avoid damage by autumn weather. These biennials or herbaceous perennials are hardy natives of central and southern Europe.

RECOMMENDED SPECIES AND VARIETIES

L. annua (syn. *L. biennis*) Clusters of purple or white flowers are borne on stiff upright stems. The translucent oval seedpods are 3-7.5 cm (1¼-3 in) long. Heart-shaped leaves, up to 15 cm (6 in) long, usually have coarsely toothed edges. A biennial plant, this will do well in dry shade. HEIGHT & SPREAD 1 m×60 cm (3×2 ft).

'**Alba Variegata**' has white flowers and leaves edged in creamy white; var. *albiflora*♀ also has white flowers.
L. biennis see *L. annua*
L. rediviva This short-lived perennial bears fragrant, pale purple flowers in branching clusters up to 30 cm (12 in) across. The pointed oval seedpods are 5-8 cm (2-3¼ in) long. Deep green oval leaves with toothed edges are up to 12.5 cm (5 in) long. HEIGHT & SPREAD 1 m×60 cm (3×2 ft).

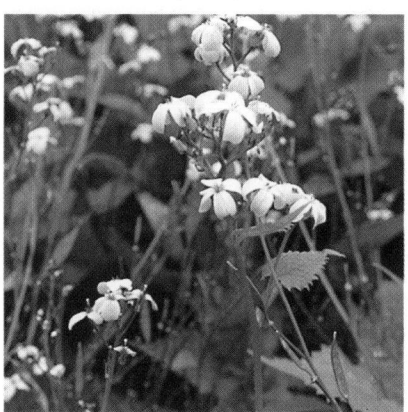

▲ *Lunaria rediviva*

CULTIVATION Plant in autumn or spring in a partly shaded site. *L. annua* needs a light soil and *L. rediviva* does best in moist soil.
PROPAGATION Sow seed where the plants are to grow – sow *L. annua* in late spring or early summer and *L. rediviva* in spring. Divide *L. rediviva* in autumn or spring.
PESTS AND DISEASES White blister may attack leaves; roots are liable to club root.

Lupinus
Leguminosae

The imposing flower spikes of lupins provide some of the brightest colours to be seen in an early-summer garden. Though few of the 250 species of annuals, herbaceous perennials and shrubs are commonly cultivated in Britain, extensive breeding has produced many garden hybrids to choose from. The sweet-pea-shaped flowers (with horizontal keel and reflexed standard) come in yellows, oranges, reds and blues – something for every colour scheme. Sometimes scented, lupins are valued for cutting.

Lupinus arboreus

Unless otherwise stated, all the lupins described below are hardy, and all have palmate leaves. The shrubby species are good for the wild garden; the herbaceous perennials suit more formal borders. The annuals with their smaller and more open flower spikes achieve maximum impact when planted in clumps. All lupins can be harmful if eaten.

RECOMMENDED SPECIES AND VARIETIES

L. arboreus♀ This fast-growing evergreen shrub has a sprawling habit, bearing its small spikes of pale yellow, scented flowers (sometimes suffused with white or purple) above pale green foliage from early to late summer. The leaves are about 5 cm (2 in) long and hairy underneath. The plant grows well in coastal areas and is useful for gardens exposed to sea breezes where it will shelter less wind-tolerant subjects. The seed is set freely which can cause the plant to spread over a wider area than desired – but makes it ideal for naturalising on a sunny bank with a light sandy soil where nothing much else will survive. The shrub is short-lived, lasting less than 5 years – and best replaced sooner. HEIGHT & SPREAD 2.4×2 m (8×6½ ft).

The flowers of '**Golden Spire**' are a deeper yellow. The plant is not completely hardy, except in mild, coastal areas.
L. chamissonis This shrubby evergreen ground-hugging perennial is formed of a mass of silvery grey leaves from which the flowers rise in late summer. The spikes carry

▼ *Lupinus chamissonis*

blue and white flowers, blotched yellow at the base. HEIGHT & SPREAD 1×1.5m (3×5ft).

L. hartwegii This hairy annual bears pale blue flowers from mid summer to early autumn. It is the largest annual species commonly cultivated. HEIGHT & SPREAD 1m×50cm (3ft×20in).

'Sunrise' has blue and gold flowers.

L. luteus Bright yellow, highly fragrant flowers bloom from early to late summer. Like *L. hartwegii*, this is a hairy annual with 5cm (2in) long leaves. HEIGHT & SPREAD 60×30cm (2×1ft).

L. nanus The most widely grown annual bears blue flowers mid summer to early autumn. Its leaves are about 4cm (1½in) long. HEIGHT & SPREAD 40×20cm (16×8in).

'Pixie Delight' has a mixture of blue, pink, white and bicoloured flowers.

GARDEN HYBRIDS

These herbaceous perennials are generally up to 1m (3ft) tall with a spread of 45cm (18in). The divided leaves are up to 20cm (8in) long. They flower in early summer, some producing bicoloured blooms where the keel is one colour (noted first) and the standard another. All the varieties below, except the Band of Nobles Series and Gallery Series, and the 'Lulu' mixture must be propagated by cuttings to come true.

Band of Nobles Series ♀ (a range of colours, including yellow, pink, red, blue and violet); **'Chandelier'** (soft yellow); **'Deborah Woodfield'** ♀ (cream pink); **'Esmerelder'** ♀ (lilac); **'Helen Sharman'** ♀ (orange and yellow); **'Kayleigh Ann Savage'** ♀ (dusky pink flushed with cream). **'My Castle'** (red); **'Noble Maiden'** (creamy white); **'Olive Tolley'** ♀ (pale rose); **'Pope John Paul'** ♀ (white); **'Royal Wedding'** ♀ (white). **'The Chatelaine'** (pink and white); **'The Governor'** (deep blue and white); **'The Page'** (carmine red). The **Gallery Series** and the **'Lulu'** mixture

▼ *Lupinus* 'Kayleigh Ann Savage'

have been bred to meet the demand for perennial lupins which can be raised successfully from seed. These strains will flower in the first season from sowing. Shorter than most hybrids, to 45cm (18in) tall, both have a wide colour range.

CULTIVATION Grow lupins in sun or partial shade in neutral or slightly acid light sandy soil. Rich soils encourage soft growth. Plant out rooted cuttings of perennial species in spring. Taller lupins may need staking. Sow annuals in their final flowering position in early spring. In mild areas sow seed in early autumn for an earlier show. Deadhead plants to prolong flowering and prevent self-seeding.

PROPAGATION Take basal cuttings of the garden hybrids early to mid spring, ideally with a small piece of rootstock attached. For other perennial species, and for extra early flowering of annuals, sow seed in early spring in a coldframe, prick out into 10cm (4in) pots when large enough to handle and plant out in early summer. Soak seed for 24 hours in water before sowing to soften hard coats and accelerate germination.

PESTS AND DISEASES Aphids are troublesome. Powdery mildew infects leaves, as do viruses and fungal leaf spot. The stems can rot, especially if the soil is too rich.

Luzula see GRASSES p.303

Lychnis
Catchfly
Caryophyllaceae

Lychnis alpina

With their bright summer flowers, often vivid pink or red and attractive to butterflies, catchflies give a splash of colour to borders and are suitable for cutting. The smaller kinds are useful for rock gardens or raised beds and *Lychnis flos-cuculi* is a pretty plant for moist places such as pool margins. Many species possess sticky nodes which trap, but do not digest, small insects. All the plants listed are herbaceous perennials.

RECOMMENDED SPECIES AND VARIETIES

L. alpina (syn. *L. viscaria* var. *alpina*) (Alpine catchfly) Rose-purple flowers, about 1cm (⅜in) across with neatly notched petals, are borne in head-like clusters from late spring to summer. The dark green linear to spoon-shaped leaves are mostly crowded at the base of the plant. This small, tufted perennial is short-lived,

but will readily self-seed. HEIGHT & SPREAD 15×10cm (6×4in).

'Alba' has white flowers; 'Rosea', pink.

L. × arkwrightii Scarlet flowers up to 4cm (1½in) across appear in summer. The plant, hardy to about –20°C (–4°F), is especially useful for its dark red-flushed foliage. HEIGHT & SPREAD 40×20cm (16×8in).

'Vesuvius' has vivid scarlet flowers 5cm (2in) across.

▲ *Lychnis × arkwrightii* 'Vesuvius'

L. chalcedonica ♀ An old cottage-garden favourite, the scarlet flowers, 3cm (1¼in) across, with cleft petals, bloom in clusters in early to mid summer. The pale green lance-shaped to oval leaves are paired along stiff stems. It dislikes very dry situations. HEIGHT & SPREAD 1m×40cm (36×16in).

Lychnis chalcedonica

The flowers of var. *albiflora* are white; 'Flore Pleno' has double red blooms; and those of 'Rosea' are pink.

L. coronaria (dusty miller, rose campion) Bold reddish purple flowers, up to 3cm (1¼in) across, bloom in branched clusters throughout summer. Handsome grey-felted ovate to lance-shaped leaves are arranged in pairs up the erect stems. HEIGHT & SPREAD 60×45cm (2×1½ft).

'Abbotswood Rose' see *L. × walkeri* 'Abbotswood Rose'. **Alba Group** ♀ has white flowers. The large white flowers of 'Angel's Blush' are flushed with pink. **Atrosanguinea Group** has deep pink flowers and pale grey foliage. **Oculata Group** has white flowers with a bright pink eye.

L. flos-cuculi (ragged robin) The bright pink flowers, up to 4cm (1½in) across and with deeply cut narrow-lobed petals, appear in laxly branched clusters in summer and early autumn. This rather delicate, spreading perennial has pairs of pointed deep green leaves. Native to Europe and Siberia. HEIGHT & SPREAD 60×40cm (2ft×16in).

'Alba Plena' has double white flowers while var. *albiflora* has white flowers. 'Nana', a dwarf plant only 15 cm (6 in) tall and most suitable for a rock garden has deep pink flowers.

L. flos-jovis Bold purple to pink or white flowers, up to 2 cm (¾ in) across, are borne in dense clusters in summer on the erect stems of this tufted, downy plant. HEIGHT & SPREAD 45×45 cm (18×18 in).

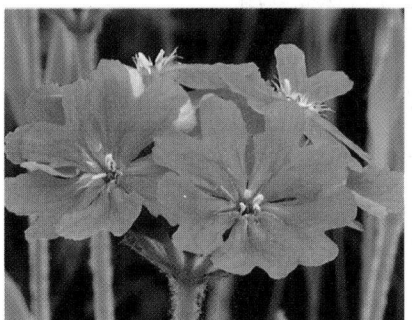

▲ *Lychnis flos-jovis* 'Hort's Variety'

'Hort's Variety' carries dense heads of rose-pink flowers. 'Nana' (syn. 'Minor') has red flowers and reaches only 25 cm (10 in).

L. × haageana Scarlet or orange-red flowers, about 5 cm (2 in) across, are carried in clusters of just a few flowers in summer. Oval mid green leaves may be flushed purple. A short-lived perennial, hardy to -20°C (-4°F), it flowers readily in the first year from seed and can be grown as an annual. HEIGHT & SPREAD 45×30 cm (18×12 in).

'Grandiflora' produces red flowers up to 7 cm (2¾ in) across. 'Salmonea' has salmon-pink flowers.

L. viscaria (sticky catchfly) Clusters of reddish purple flowers, 2 cm (¾ in) across, with purple-flushed calyxes, bloom in summer. The stiff stems of this tufted plant are very sticky at the upper nodes, and carry elliptical dark green leaves. HEIGHT & SPREAD 45×30 cm (18×12 in).

The flowers of var. *alba* are white; var. *alpina* see *L. alpina*. 'Plena' has purplish

▼ *Lychnis viscaria*

▲ *Lychnis viscaria* 'Splendens Plena'

pink double flowers and 'Splendens Plena'♀ has bright magenta double blooms.

L. × walkeri 'Abbotswood Rose'♀ (syn. *L. coronaria* 'Abbotswood Rose') A tufted perennial with grey-green downy leaves and clusters of rose-pink flowers in summer. HEIGHT & SPREAD 40×30 cm (16×12 in).

L. yunnanensis White to pale pink flowers, up to 2 cm (¾ in) across, with cleft petals, bloom in lax clusters from late spring to summer. A useful rock garden species, this hairy perennial has slender stems and narrow, oval, bright green leaves. HEIGHT & SPREAD 20×15 cm (8×6 in).

CULTIVATION All plants are hardy to at least -25°C (-13°F) unless otherwise stated. Apart from *L. flos-cuculi* which needs moist ground, catchflies thrive in most well-drained garden soils in sun or partial shade. The smaller alpines like a gritty compost in full sun. *L. × arkwrightii* and *L. × haageana* can be grown as annuals, flowering readily within the year when sown in late winter or early spring. *L. coronaria*, *L. flos-jovis* and *L. viscaria* will all self-sow in the garden. Young plants can easily be moved.

PROPAGATION Sow seed in autumn or early spring in pots in a coldframe, pricking out seedlings as soon as they are large enough to handle. These will generally flower in their second season. The white-flowered cultivars cross readily so plant away from the coloured forms.

PESTS AND DISEASES Slugs and snails may eat the young shoots as they emerge in spring. The grey-felted leaves of some species, especially of *L. coronaria*, may be shredded by birds in winter. The foliage is sometimes susceptible to attacks of powdery mildew, with *L. coronaria* being the most vulnerable, especially in late summer.

▼ *Lychnis × haageana*

Lysichiton
Skunk cabbage, bog arum
Araceae

Massive, gleaming leaves make these hardy herbaceous perennials impressive features beside a garden pond or in boggy areas. Even more spectacular are the giant yellow or white spathes – leaf-like, open-ended tubes – that appear in spring. Inside the spathe is the spadix, a stiffly erect spike that carries the insignificant flowers. Lysichitons can be very slow to establish themselves and usually do not flower until they are four to six years of age, so it is best to buy plants at least two or three years old. They have stout rhizomes that develop large deep root systems to anchor the heavy plants.

RECOMMENDED SPECIES

L. americanus♀ (yellow skunk cabbage) The oblong, ribbed leaves are 30 cm-1.2 m (1-4 ft) long and 30 cm (1 ft) wide. Bright green at first, they darken a little with age. The yellow spathe, about 30 cm (1 ft) long, sheaths a green spadix that turns yellow. Native to the west coast of N America. HEIGHT & SPREAD 1.2×1.5 m (4×5 ft).

L. camtschatcensis♀ (white skunk cabbage) A white spathe, about 30 cm (1 ft) long, encloses a pale green spadix bearing sweetly scented flowers. The oblong, strongly ribbed leaves are up to 1.2 m (4 ft) long and 30 cm (1 ft) wide. Native to coastal regions of NE Asia. HEIGHT & SPREAD 1×1 m (3×3 ft).

CULTIVATION Plant in spring or autumn in deep, humus-rich, wet or boggy soils, choosing a site in full sun or partial shade.

PROPAGATION Divide the thick clumps or sow seed in spring. Move and replant self-seeded plants in spring.

PESTS AND DISEASES Usually trouble free.

▼ *Lysichiton americanus*

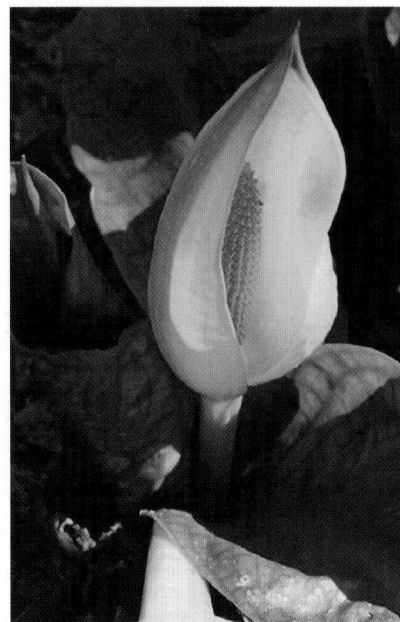

Lysimachia
Loosestrife
Primulaceae

Lysimachia punctata

Tall plants with elegant floral spires and also creeping, ground-cover specimens are included in this varied genus of hardy perennials. They prefer moist soil, whether in a border or at the water's edge, although they will grow in any fertile soil.

Lysimachias are native to N America, Europe and Asia. Of the recommended plants, *Lysimachia nummularia* is evergreen, while the others die down in winter.

RECOMMENDED SPECIES AND VARIETIES
L. ciliata Yellow star-shaped flowers, about 2.5 cm (1 in) wide, each on its own stem, nod from mid to late summer above this graceful plant's 15 cm (6 in) ovate leaves. HEIGHT & SPREAD 1.2 m×45 cm (4×1½ ft).
L. clethroides♀ (gooseneck loosestrife) Small white flowers, up to 1 cm (⅜ in) wide, grow as dense arched spikes in late summer, resembling the necks of geese. The oval to lance-shaped leaves are 13 cm (5¼ in) long. HEIGHT & SPREAD 1 m×60 cm (3×2 ft).

▼ *Lysimachia ephemerum*

▲ *Lysimachia nummularia*

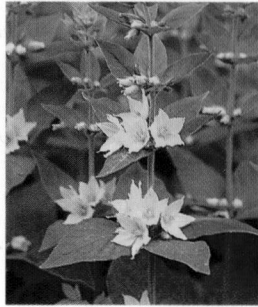

▲ *Lysimachia punctata*

L. ephemerum Pearly white flowers, 1 cm (⅜ in) wide, grow in arched spikes from mid to late summer complemented by grey-green leaves, up to 15 cm (6 in) long. HEIGHT & SPREAD 1 m×60 cm (3×2 ft).
L. henryi Trailing stems carry heads of small yellow flowers from mid to late summer and 6 cm (2½ in) long oval to lance-shaped leaves. HEIGHT & SPREAD 15×45 cm (6×18 in).
L. nummularia (creeping Jenny, money-wort) Tiny black glands dot the shiny yellow cup-shaped flowers – 2 cm (¾ in) across – in early summer. This low-growing, vigorous, evergreen creeper has bright green, oval to round leaves, 2 cm (¾ in) long. HEIGHT & SPREAD 2.5 cm×1 m (1×36 in).
'**Aurea**'♀ makes an attractive carpet of golden leaves.
L. punctata (dotted loosestrife) Thriving near water, this plant also does well in broad swathes in a wild garden where its rampant habit is unlikely to cause problems. Clusters of upright spikes with bright yellow cup-shaped flowers, 1.5 cm (½ in) across, appear in summer. The leaves, 7 cm (2¾ in) long, are carried in pairs or whorls, and are elliptic and pointed with hairy edges. HEIGHT & SPREAD 1 m×60 cm (3×2 ft).
L. thyrsiflora (tufted loosestrife) Tuft-like, open clusters of yellow flowers, 5 mm (¼ in) wide, appear from late spring to early summer from the middle leaf axils. Leaves are lance-shaped and up to 10 cm (3½ in) long. HEIGHT & SPREAD 60×60 cm (2×2 ft).
L. vulgaris (yellow loosestrife) Loose spikes of star-shaped, pale yellow flowers appear in mid summer. The oval to lance-shaped leaves, up to 9 cm (3½ in) long, are opposite or in whorls. This plant spreads by runners. HEIGHT & SPREAD 1×1 m (3×3 ft).
CULTIVATION Plant from autumn to spring in any fertile, preferably moisture-retaining soil. Mulch dry soils thoroughly in late winter or early spring. On open sites, support tall plants with stakes. Divide and replant yearly or every other year to control the spread of plants at water margins.
PROPAGATION Sow seed when ripe, or in early spring in a coldframe. Plant out in autumn. Divide plants from autumn to spring. Take stem cuttings from *L. nummularia* in spring.
PESTS AND DISEASES Usually trouble free.

Lythrum
Loosestrife
Lythraceae

Slender wands of flowers in shades of purplish pink appear in mid summer on these upright, hardy perennials that thrive on boggy ground. The small, tubular-based flowers, up to 2 cm (¾ in) wide, have four to eight petals. They open on tapering spikes on square stems. The leaves, up to 10 cm (4 in) long, are lance-shaped and carried in opposite pairs. They sometimes turn yellow

in autumn. Although lythrums flourish at water margins, they grow elsewhere on rich, moisture-retentive soils. Native to Europe, Asia and N America.
RECOMMENDED SPECIES AND VARIETIES
L. salicaria (purple loosestrife) Suited to boggy ground, reddish purple flowers distinguish this species. It often has branched stems, each bearing 3 or 4 flower spikes. HEIGHT & SPREAD 1.2 m×45 cm (4×1½ ft).

Lythrum salicaria

'**Feuerkerze**'♀ ('Firecandle') has rose-pink flowers, while the flowers of '**Robert**' are bright pink and '**The Beacon**' has intense, rose-pink flowers.
L. virgatum Deep purple-red flowers are borne in pairs or clusters on leafy spikes. HEIGHT & SPREAD 1 m×45 cm (3×1½ ft).
'**Rosy Gem**' has pink-flushed, purple flowers while '**The Rocket**' has bright, rose-pink flowers.
CULTIVATION Plant from autumn to spring ideally in moisture-retentive soil. Remove the flowerheads after flowering to prevent the spread of self-sown seed.
PROPAGATION Sow seed for the species in spring. Divide overcrowded clumps of the cultivars in autumn or spring. Alternatively, take softwood cuttings in spring and plant out later in the year.
PESTS AND DISEASES Usually trouble free.

▲ *Lythrum salicaria* 'Feuerkerze'
Lythrum salicaria 'Robert' ▲
▼ *Lythrum salicaria*

Macleaya
Plume poppy
Papaveraceae

Rising majestically above most other plants, macleaya's feathery flower plumes and shiny decorative leaves make it an ideal choice for a bold display at the back of a border. The small flowers appear in frothy panicles up to 60 cm (2 ft) long in mid summer. The grey-green rounded or heart-shaped leaves, 20 cm (8 in) wide, have serrated lobes with

▼ *Macleaya cordata* 'Flamingo'

▼ *Macleaya cordata*

white downy undersides. Although these hardy herbaceous perennials grow to about 2 m (6½ ft), they rarely need to be staked. Native to China, they like full sun but will tolerate shade. The plants may take two years to establish, but, unless controlled, can then become invasive, spreading by rhizomes. Low-growing plants allow macleaya to be seen in its full splendour; plant *Macleaya microcarpa* 'Kelway's Coral Plume' with phloxes for colour and height contrast.

RECOMMENDED SPECIES AND VARIETIES
M. cordata♀ (plume poppy, tree celandine) Numerous, creamy white flowers form large plumes on this compact plant. HEIGHT & SPREAD 2 m×60 cm (6½×2 ft).

'**Flamingo**' has buff-pink flowers.
M. microcarpa Creamy white buds open as fluffy white flowers. If dead flowers are not removed, papery capsules appear, each containing one orange seed. Can be invasive. HEIGHT & SPREAD 2 m×60 cm (6½×2 ft).

'**Kelway's Coral Plume**'♀ has deep, coral-pink flowers in late summer.
CULTIVATION Plant autumn to spring in deep, moist, well-drained soil. In autumn, control *M. microcarpa* by removing any runners that have grown beyond the clump.
PROPAGATION Divide in spring, or take basal root cuttings and plant out in autumn.
PESTS AND DISEASES Usually trouble free.

Maclura
Moraceae

Orange-like but inedible fruit make these deciduous N American trees curiosities in any garden. They bear either male or female flowers, so both types need to be planted to ensure that fruit is produced. Alternatively, buy a female with a male branch grafted on to it. The trees are hardy to -10°C (14°F) and will flourish in any soil. There is only one species in the genus.

▲ *Maclura pomifera*

Maclura pomifera (Osage orange, bow wood) Insignificant yellow-green flowers appear in summer and are followed by orange-yellow globe-like fruit up to 14 cm (5½ in) across, consisting of numerous seeds in a rubbery pulp. The trees have vicious 2 cm (¾ in) long thorns and russet-brown fissured bark. Mid green leaves, 10 cm (4 in) long, taper to a point at both ends and have wavy edges. They turn yellow in autumn. HEIGHT & SPREAD 10×5 m (33×16 ft) after 20 years, ultimately growing to 16 m (52 ft) tall.
CULTIVATION Plant in late spring in any garden soil, choosing a position in full sun.
PROPAGATION Sow under glass in early spring and plant out late spring the next year; or take semi-ripe cuttings in summer.
PRUNING Trim to tidy up in late winter.
PESTS AND DISEASES Usually trouble free.

Magnolia
Magnoliaceae

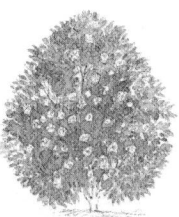

Magnolia grandiflora

Among the first plants to bloom in spring are the elegant magnolias, whose abundant, large and often deliciously scented flowers frequently open before the leaves, making a dramatic show against the bare branches. Ranging in colour from white, through pink to purple, the flowers vary in form from upright and vase-shaped to open and star-like. Instead of having an outer layer of sepals and an inner layer of petals, magnolia flowers have just one layer of petal-like structures called tepals. The leaves, usually 7.5-28 cm (3-11 in) long, are oval to obovate. Some magnolias produce attractive pinky brown cones with bright red seeds.

Varying from compact shrubs to large trees, these densely branched deciduous and evergreen plants are grown as freestanding specimens and trained as wall shrubs. They are hardy, although cold winds and late frosts can be damaging to early-flowering plants. When buying a magnolia, pick one no more than five years old and, since some varieties can take many years to bloom, it may be worth choosing a plant of about this age, especially if flowers are not evident at time of purchase. There are both slow and fast-growing magnolias but all are long-lived and produce more and more flowers as they get older.

RECOMMENDED SPECIES AND VARIETIES

M. **'Charles Raffill'** ♀ Rose-pink in bud, the cup-and-saucer-shaped flowers are carmine-pink outside and white stained pink inside. The blooms, up to 25 cm (10 in) across, appear on leafless branches in early to mid spring. This fast-growing, pyramidal deciduous tree flowers at 7-10 years old. HEIGHT & SPREAD 6×4 m (20×13 ft) after 10 years, ultimately 18 m (60 ft) tall.

M. **denudata** ♀ (syn. *M. heptapeta*) (yulan, lily tree) Lemon-scented, white blooms, tinged pink at the base, appear before the leaves in early to mid-spring. They open to cup-shaped and 15 cm (6 in) across. This broad-spreading deciduous shrub or small tree flowers when 3-5 years old. HEIGHT & SPREAD 3×3 m (10×10 ft) after 10 years, ultimately 4.5 m (15 ft) tall.

M. **'Elizabeth'** ♀ Pale primrose-yellow, slightly scented, vase-shaped flowers, 10 cm (4 in) long, appear on bare branches in mid spring. Copper-coloured on unfurling, the foliage emerges in late spring with the last flowers. A broad-spreading deciduous shrub or small tree that flowers when 2-3 years old. HEIGHT & SPREAD 4.5×3 m (15×10 ft) after 10 years, ultimately 9 m (30 ft) tall.

M. **'Galaxy'** ♀ Rose-pink flowers appear before the leaves in mid to late spring. They open to cup-shaped and 20 cm (8 in) across. A free-flowering deciduous, conical tree that flowers when 3-4 years old. HEIGHT & SPREAD 6×2.4 m (20×8 ft) after 10 years, ultimately 15 m (50 ft) tall.

M. **'George Henry Kern'** Pink, vase-shaped flowers, paler on the inside and 7.5 cm (3 in) across, appear in mid to late spring and sometimes into early summer. A free-flowering, deciduous shrub with small leaves, this shrub flowers when 2-3 years old. HEIGHT & SPREAD 1.2×1.5 m (4×5 ft) after 10 years, ultimately 2.4 m (8 ft) tall.

M. **grandiflora** (southern magnolia, bull bay) This evergreen can be trained against a wall or grown as a freestanding, rounded or pyramidal shrub or tree. The intensely fragrant, white or creamy white, cup-shaped flowers, up to 25 cm (10 in) across, appear from mid summer to mid autumn. The glossy green leaves sometimes have reddish-brown hairs underneath when young. Plants flower when 5-7 years old if raised vegetatively but after 30 years if grown from seed. HEIGHT & SPREAD 3×3 m (10×10 ft) after 10 years, ultimately 15 m (50 ft) tall.

'Exmouth' ♀ has rich cream-coloured, heavily scented flowers. **'Samuel Sommer'** has large blooms, up to 30 cm (12 in) across.

M. **'Heaven Scent'** ♀ Deep pink outside and paler within, vase-shaped flowers 12.5 cm (5 in) long appear in profusion on bare stems in mid to late spring. An upright, deciduous tree that flowers after 5 years. HEIGHT & SPREAD 5.5×3.5 m (18×12 ft) after 10 years, ultimately 13.5 m (45 ft) tall.

M. **heptapeta** see *M. denudata*

M. **'Iolanthe'** ♀ Abundant, clear pink cup-and-saucer-shaped flowers, creamy white inside, appear on bare branches in early to mid spring. Measuring 25 cm (10 in) across, they are held sideways. A broad-spreading deciduous shrub or small tree that flowers when 5 years old. HEIGHT & SPREAD 3.5×3.5 m (12×12 ft) after 10 years, ultimately 12 m (40 ft) tall.

M. **'Jane'** ♀ Upright dark pink buds, 10 cm (4 in) long, open to cup-shaped, fragrant flowers, deep pink outside and very pale pink within. They appear before the leaves in mid to late spring. A rounded to upright,

▲ *Magnolia* 'Heaven Scent'

▲ *Magnolia denudata*

▲ *Magnolia* 'Galaxy'

▲ *Magnolia grandiflora*

▲ *Magnolia* 'Iolanthe'

▲ *Magnolia* 'Jane'

deciduous shrub that will flower in its first year. HEIGHT & SPREAD 2.1×1.5m (7×5ft) after 10 years, ultimately 4.5m (15ft) tall.

M. x *kewensis* **'Wada's Memory'**♀ Profuse white, slightly fragrant flowers are borne on bare branches in mid spring. The tepals droop to one side until the flowers measure about 18cm (7in) across. The leaves are mahogany red on unfurling. A conical, deciduous tree that is free-flowering from 5 years old. HEIGHT & SPREAD 3×1.8m (10×6ft) in 10 years, ultimately 10m (33ft) tall.

M. kobus White flowers appear in early spring before the leaves. Measuring 10cm (4in) in length, they are vase-shaped at first

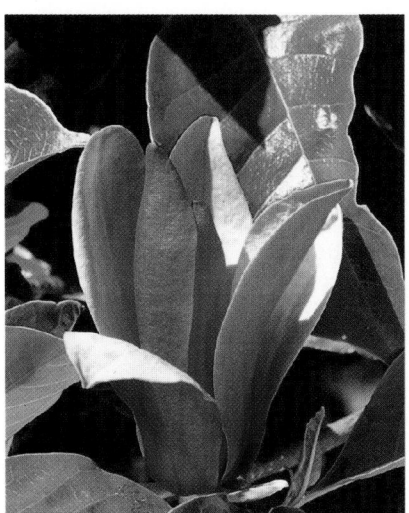

▲ *Magnolia liliiflora* 'Nigra'

before splaying open. A deciduous, many-branched shrub or medium-sized, pyramidal tree. It flowers after 10 years if raised from seed and 5 years if raised vegetatively. HEIGHT & SPREAD 2.4×1.8m (8×6ft) after 10 years, ultimately 9m (30ft) tall.

M. *liliiflora* **'Nigra'**♀ (syn. *M.* x *soulangeana* 'Nigra') Tulip-shaped slightly scented, deep purple flowers, 12.5cm (5in) long, are white stained purple within. They appear in mid or late spring with the unfurling leaves and continue into early summer. A dense, slow-growing deciduous shrub that first flowers at 5-10 years old. HEIGHT & SPREAD 1.5×1.5m (5×5ft) after 10 years, ultimately 3m (10ft) tall.

M. x *loebneri* **'Leonard Messel'**♀ Deep pink tepals, paler within, open out to star-like blooms, 12.5cm (5in) across. They are slightly scented and borne profusely in mid-spring before the leaves appear. Plants first flower when 5 years old. This many-branched, deciduous plant is the most frost hardy of shrubby magnolias. HEIGHT & SPREAD 2.4×1.8m (8×6ft) after 10 years, ultimately 4.5m (15ft) tall.

M. x *loebneri* **'Merrill'**♀ Pure white, slightly scented flowers open to 15cm (6in) across and are seen during mid spring, before the leaves appear. Pyramidal at first, then broad-spreading, this small deciduous tree flowers when 5 years old. HEIGHT & SPREAD 4.5×3m (15×10ft) after 10 years, ultimately 12m (40ft) tall.

M. **'Pinkie'**♀ Dark pink buds opening to pale pink flowers, 18cm (7in) across, appear with the new leaves in mid to late spring. This spreading deciduous shrub flowers when 5 years old. HEIGHT & SPREAD 2.4×2.4m (8×8ft) after 10 years, ultimately 4.5m (15ft) tall.

M. salicifolia♀ Pure white, slightly fragrant flowers, opening to 12.5cm (5in) across, appear in mid spring before the leaves. The narrow, willow-like leaves are downy beneath and, like the bark and wood, have a lemony aniseed smell when crushed. A

▲ *Magnolia salicifolia*

▲ *Magnolia* x *loebneri* 'Leonard Messel'

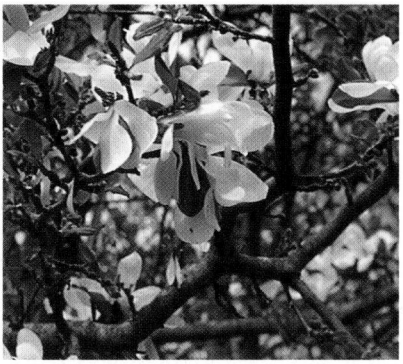

▲ *Magnolia* x *loebneri* 'Merrill'

deciduous, upright shrub or pyramidal tree that first flowers when 5 years old. HEIGHT & SPREAD 4.5×3m (15×10ft) in 10 years, ultimately 15m (50ft) tall.

M. sargentiana var. *robusta* Cup-shaped, rose-pink flowers, 30cm (12in) across, are seen in early and mid spring on leafless stems. A wide-spreading deciduous tree that flowers after 10 years when raised vegetatively, but 30 years if raised from seed. HEIGHT & SPREAD 4×3.5m (13×12ft) after 10 years, ultimately 21.5m (70ft) tall.

M. **'Sayonara'**♀ White, scented, vase-shaped flowers appear in mid spring before the leaves and open to a cup-and-saucer shape, 15-20cm (6-8in) across. This deciduous plant flowers after 5 years and forms a broad-spreading shrub or tree. HEIGHT & SPREAD 4.5×3.5m (15×12ft) after 10 years, ultimately 9m (30ft) tall.

M. sieboldii♀ Intensely fragrant, pure white flowers with distinctive magenta stamens are seen in late spring and early summer and again in late summer and early autumn. The nodding saucer-shaped flowers are 10cm (4in) across and first appear on this broad-spreading deciduous shrub when it's 5 years old, if raised vegetatively, and 10 years old, when grown from seed. HEIGHT & SPREAD 2.4×2.4m (8×8ft) after 10 years, ultimately 6m (20ft) tall.

The pendent flowers of ssp. *sinensis*♀ are lemon-scented and up to 12.5cm (5in) across. The underside of its leaves bear a silvery down. Plants reach a height and spread of 3m (10ft) after 10 years.

Magnolia x soulangeana

M. x soulangeana Goblet to tulip-shaped flowers, up to 10cm (4in) long, appear in mid spring before the leaves, with a second flush sometimes in late summer. They vary in colour from white to intense pink outside and from white to white tinged pink inside. This deciduous, broad-spreading shrub or tree first flowers at 5 years old. HEIGHT & SPREAD 4.5×3m (15×10ft) after 10 years, ultimately 9m (30ft) tall.

'Brozzonii'♀ has large, white flowers, flushed pink at the base, which splay open to 25cm (10in) across and appear in late spring. The goblet-shaped flowers of **'Lennei'**♀, pinky purple outside and white within, appear in mid to late spring. **'Nigra'** see *M. liliiflora* 'Nigra'. **'Picture'** has white tulip-shaped flowers heavily stained with purple outside, 15cm (6in) tall and seen in mid to late spring. **'Rustica Rubra'**♀ (syn. 'Rubra') has goblet-shaped, reddish purple flowers in mid to late spring that open to 20cm (8in) across. **'San Jose'** has deep pink flowers, white inside, that are 10-15cm (4-6in) long and seen in early to mid spring. **M. stellata**♀ (star magnolia) Slightly fragrant, star-like white flowers, sometimes faintly flushed with pink, bloom in profusion in early to mid spring before the leaves. Made up of many ribbon-like tepals, the

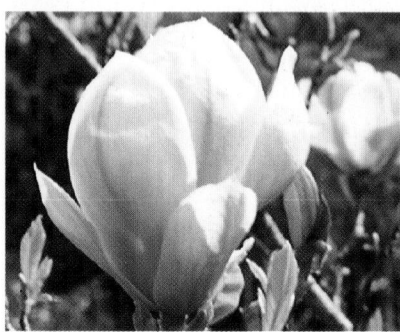

▲ *Magnolia x soulangeana* 'Rustica Rubra'

▲ *Magnolia stellata*

flowers open to 7.5-10cm (3-4in) across. A slow-growing, dense, deciduous shrub good for small gardens or growing in a tub. It will flower in its first season. HEIGHT & SPREAD 1.2×1.5m (4×5ft) after 10 years, ultimately 3.5m (12ft) tall.

'Royal Star' has pink-tinged buds, opening to white flowers. **'Waterlily'**♀ has ivory white flowers, 10cm (4in) across.

Magnolia stellata

▲ *Magnolia stellata* 'Waterlily'

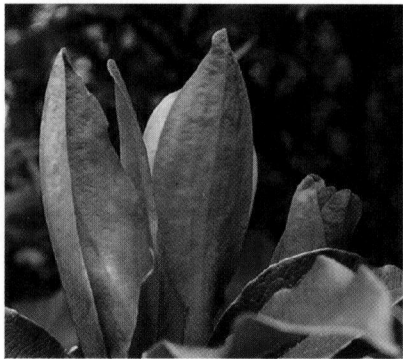

▲ *Magnolia* 'Susan'

M. 'Susan'♀ Deep pink, vase-shaped, fragrant flowers open out to 10-15cm (4-6in) across, revealing a paler pink inside. This upright, deciduous shrub flowers in profusion during mid to late spring, before the leaves appear. Plants bloom in their first year. HEIGHT & SPREAD 2.1×1.5m (7×5ft) after 10 years, ultimately 4.5m (15ft) tall.

M. wilsonii♀ Cup-shaped, highly fragrant, pendulous, white flowers, 10cm (4in) across, with red stamens appear with the foliage in late spring and early summer. This many-branched deciduous shrub has leaves with cinnamon-brown hairs underneath. Plants flower at 5 years old if raised vegetatively, at 5-10 years when grown from seed HEIGHT & SPREAD 3×3m (10×10ft) after 10 years, ultimately 6m (20ft) tall.

CULTIVATION Plant in autumn and spring in any humus-rich, moist but well-drained soil, except chalky. Buy a pot-grown plant and place in its permanent site to avoid any need for transplantation that might damage the tender fleshy roots. Most deciduous species and the evergreen, *M. grandiflora*, tolerate some sun but all, and in particular, *M. sieboldii*, *M. s.* ssp. *sinensis* and *M. wilsonii*, benefit from light shade. Shelter from cold winds. Shake snow from the branches of evergreens or its weight might break the leaves. Mulch plants with organic matter in drought conditions. It is better not to underplant magnolias since hoeing or forking around the base might damage the roots. Suppress weeds with bark chips.

PROPAGATION Sow ripe seed in spring although plants raised this way may take about 30 years to flower. Take greenwood cuttings of deciduous varieties and semi-ripe cuttings of evergreens. Layer plants that produce strong shoots, close to the ground.

PRUNING Cut back untidy plants and remove dead wood in late summer or after flowering for deciduous species and in spring for evergreens. Hard prune only mature specimens; do this in spring. If training *M. grandiflora* against a wall, spur prune to within 30-45cm (12-18in) of the framework in spring.

PESTS AND DISEASES Usually trouble free but sooty mould and bacterial leaf spot affect *M. grandiflora*.

Mahonia
Berberidaceae

Mahonia x media
'Charity'

Clusters of yellow flowers and glossy evergreen foliage help to brighten any winter or spring garden. These architectural shrubs make fine specimen plants, with some of the smaller species being useful as ground cover if left to spread. The tiny globular or bell-shaped flowers are often sweetly scented and are followed by small grape-like berries. The alternate pinnate leaves have a spiny edge. All mahonias are hardy, with the exception of *M. lomariifolia* which will only grow in milder regions. Native to Asia, Japan and Central and N America.

RECOMMENDED SPECIES AND VARIETIES
M. aquifolium (Oregon grape) The glossy dark green leaves, up to 30cm (1ft) long with 5 to 9 leaflets, are purplish in winter. Golden yellow flowers in dense clusters up to 7.5cm (3in) long, appear as early as late winter, but the main flowering period is in mid to late spring. This rounded, spreading

▲ *Mahonia aquifolium*

▲ *Mahonia aquifolium* 'Apollo'

▲ *Mahonia* × *media* 'Buckland'

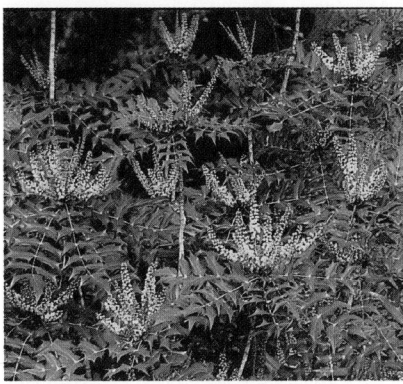

▲ *Mahonia* × *media* 'Charity'

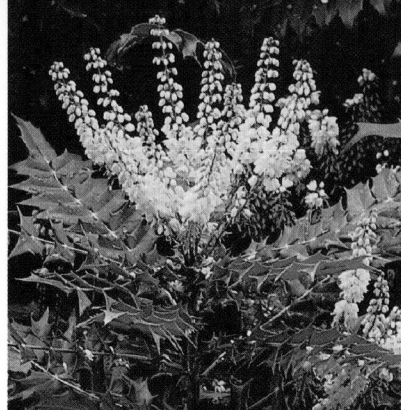

▲ *Mahonia* × *media* 'Winter Sun'

shrub will grow in shade and full sun. Native to western N America. HEIGHT & SPREAD 1 m×60 cm (3×2 ft) after 5 years, ultimately 1.8 m (6 ft) tall.

'Apollo'♀ is a vigorous, low-growing plant with flower clusters up to 10 cm (4 in) long. The leaves have a reddish stem. 'Atropurpurea' has reddish purple leaves in winter. 'Smaragd' has bronze young leaves and flower clusters up to 10 cm (4 in) long.

M. bealei see *M. japonica* Bealei Group

M. japonica♀ The glossy dark green leaves of this upright shrub grow to 40 cm (16 in) long and have 13 to 19 leathery leaflets, each with a coarsely spined margin. The fragrant lemon-yellow flowers are carried in pendulous clusters, up to 20 cm (8 in) long, from mid winter to early spring. Native to China. HEIGHT & SPREAD 1.5×1 m (5×3 ft) after 5 years, ultimately 3 m (10 ft) tall.

▲ *Mahonia japonica*

Bealei Group (syn. *M. bealei*) has shorter, more upright flower clusters and the leaflets sometimes overlap.

M. lomariifolia♀ Thick leathery leaves, up to 60 cm (2 ft) long, have 19 to 40 leaflets. Bright yellow, slightly fragrant flowers, in dense erect clusters up to 25 cm (10 in) long, appear in winter. This upright shrub is not fully hardy and will only survive in the mildest areas. Native to Burma and China. HEIGHT & SPREAD 1.2 m×30 cm (4×1 ft) after 5 years, ultimately 4 m (13 ft) tall.

M. × *media* An upright shrub with deep green leathery leaves about 60 cm (2 ft) long and varying numbers of leaflets. The yellow flowers are produced in clusters up to 25 cm (10 in) long and are at their best in winter. HEIGHT & SPREAD 1 m×30 cm (3×1 ft) after 5

years, ultimately 3 m (10 ft) tall.

'Buckland'♀ has leaves sometimes tinged red in autumn and winter. The yellow flower clusters are long and spreading. 'Charity'♀ has fragrant yellow flowers in erect clusters, at their best in late autumn to mid winter. 'Lionel Fortescue'♀ has bright yellow, slightly fragrant flowers in upright clusters. 'Underway'♀ is more compact with bright yellow flowers in upright clusters. 'Winter Sun'♀ has fragrant yellow flowers in dense, erect clusters.

M. nervosa Leathery, deep green leaves, 38 cm (15 in) long, with 11 to 15 leaflets, often turn red in winter. Erect yellow flower clusters, 20 cm (8 in) long, appear in spring. Native to western N America. HEIGHT & SPREAD 40 cm×1 m (16 in×3 ft) after 5 years, also the ultimate size.

M. pinnata A spreading shrub with leaves up to 12 cm (4¾ in) long, that are bronze when young, turning bright green. They have 5 to 9, generally overlapping, leaflets. The bright yellow flowers, borne in clusters

up to 10 cm (4 in) long, appear from early to mid spring. The plant is only moderately frost hardy and will grow only in a sheltered position. Native to southern N America. HEIGHT & SPREAD 60×30 cm (2×1 ft) after 5 years, ultimately 1 m (3 ft) tall.

M. repens The dull green leaves are 20 cm (8 in) long with 3 to 7 leaflets. Golden yellow flowers open in mid to late spring in dense clusters, up to 7.5 cm (3 in) long, that appear on the end of the previous years' growth. A low-spreading, suckering shrub, native to western N America. HEIGHT & SPREAD 40 cm×1 m (16 in×3 ft) after 5 years, also the ultimate size.

M. × *wagneri* 'Pinnacle'♀ The bright green leaves of this upright shrub are bronze at first. Dense clusters of bright yellow flowers, up to 10 cm (4 in) long, appear in late spring. HEIGHT & SPREAD 1 m×60 cm (3×2 ft) after 5 years, ultimately 1.8 m (6 ft) tall.

M. × *wagneri* 'Undulata'♀ The dark green leaves, up to 20 cm (8 in) long, have wavy edges and are bronze at first. Yellow flowers are carried in dense clusters about 10 cm (4 in) long in spring. A vigorous, erect shrub. HEIGHT & SPREAD 1 m×60 cm (3×2 ft) after 5 years, ultimately 1.8 m (6 ft) tall.

CULTIVATION Mahonias thrive under a wide range of conditions but, as a general rule, plant *M.* × *wagneri* and species native to the Americas (and their cultivars) in drier soils in a sunny position. Plant *M.* × *media* and Asian species and their cultivars in a shady part of the garden. *M. nervosa* does not grow well in chalk soils.

PROPAGATION Sow seed in early to mid spring or take semi-ripe cuttings in early to mid summer. Any suckers can be dug up and replanted, immediately.

PRUNING Not normally required, but suckers may need to be cut or pulled out in late autumn to early spring.

PESTS AND DISEASES Usually trouble free.

Maianthemum
May lily
Convallariaceae

This herbaceous perennial has white flower spikes and glossy green kidney to heart-shaped leaves. Bright red, rounded berries about 6 mm (¼ in) across appear in summer. This ground-cover plant is suited to a shady

423

▲ *Maianthemum bifolium* var. *kamtschaticum*

spot and can be invasive. Native to W Europe, Asia and N America, it is hardy.

RECOMMENDED SPECIES AND VARIETIES
M. bifolium Cream, star-shaped, 4-petalled flowers about 3 mm (⅛ in) across appear from mid to late spring. The leaves, up to 7.5 cm (3 in) long, have wavy edges. HEIGHT & SPREAD 20 cm×1 m (8 in×3 ft).

The leaves of var. **kamtschaticum** (syn. *M. dilatatum*) are up to 20 cm (8 in) long. It can reach 35 cm (14 in) in height.
M. dilatatum see *M. bifolium* var. *kamtschaticum*

CULTIVATION Plant in moist but well-drained humus-rich soil in dappled shade. Protect from bright sunshine and droughts.
PROPAGATION Divide in early spring or summer. Sow seed under glass in winter. Young plants are slow to establish.
PESTS AND DISEASES Slugs and snails may attack foliage, especially when it is young.

Maidenhair tree see *Ginkgo biloba*

Malcolmia
Cruciferae

Malcolmia maritima

Drifts of pastel flowers grace cottage gardens and informal borders in summer. The plants are very fast growing, usually flowering four weeks after sowing and with successive sowings the flowering season can be extended throughout summer. They self-seed readily in undisturbed soil.

RECOMMENDED SPECIES
M. maritima (Virginian stock) Sweetly scented flowers, about 2 cm (¾ in) across, in red, lilac, rose or white, are carried in loose clusters on slender, branching stems. This hardy annual from the Mediterranean is low-growing, bearing elliptic grey-green leaves, up to 4 cm (1½ in) long. HEIGHT & SPREAD 20×36 cm (8×14 in).
CULTIVATION Plant in preferably neutral-

to-alkaline, well-drained soil in a sunny position.
PROPAGATION Sow seed in situ successively throughout spring. Sow in the autumn for flowers the following spring.
PESTS AND DISEASES Usually trouble free.

Mallow see *Malva*
Mallow tree see *Lavatera*

Malope
Malvaceae

The easily grown and free-flowering hardy annual, *Malope trifida,* is the only member of this genus usually cultivated. An attractive addition to a sunny border, it is a stout-stemmed, upright plant. The showy trumpet-shaped flowers are produced over a long period and are suitable for cutting.

RECOMMENDED SPECIES AND VARIETIES
M. trifida Rose-purple, darker veined flowers are freely produced on long stalks from mid summer to mid autumn. Each

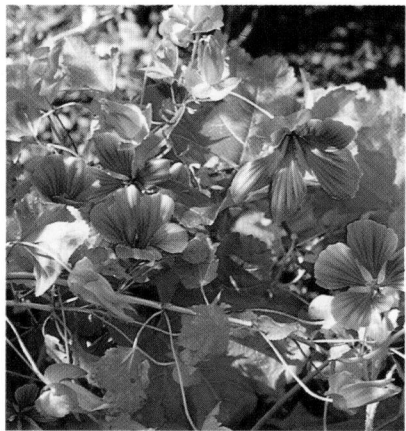

▲ *Malope trifida*

flower has 5 petals and flares open to 8 cm (3¼ in) across. The bright green leaves have 3 or 5 pointed lobes. HEIGHT & SPREAD 1 m×30 cm (3×1 ft).

'Pink Queen' has shell-pink flowers with centres and veins of a deeper shade. 'Vulcan' has brilliant red flowers with an almost metallic sheen. 'White Queen' has white silky-looking flowers. Seed of mixed colours is also available and will produce pink, purple, red and white flowers.
CULTIVATION Plant in late spring in full sun in any ordinary garden soil. Deadhead regularly to prolong the flower display.
PROPAGATION Sow clusters of seed 30 cm (1 ft) apart in mid spring where the plants are to grow. Once the seedlings are established, thin out to leave just one in each position. Alternatively, for earlier flowering, sow seed in early spring in a greenhouse or a coldframe and hardened off.
PESTS AND DISEASES Aphids and hollyhock rust may attack plants.

Malus
Crab apple
Rosaceae

Malus hupehensis

Clouds of spring blossom, colourful fruits and autumn colour make crab apples worthy of garden space. They are hardy, deciduous trees that are easily grown and being generally small are not difficult to place in an average garden. The bowl-shaped flowers with golden stamens are five-petalled and borne in clusters; some are fragrant. Flower colour ranges from white through pink and deep red. The apple-like fruits, 2.5–5 cm (1–2 in) long, ripen in early autumn and can be yellow, red or green flushed with red or purple. All fruits are attractive to birds. The leaves are generally small, less than 7.5 cm (3 in) long and about half as wide. The genus includes the culinary apple; the plants recommended below are all ornamental trees.

RECOMMENDED SPECIES AND VARIETIES
M. 'American Beauty' Deep red, double flowers, to 4 cm (1½ in) across, are borne in spring on this vigorous upright tree. The leaves emerge bronze red but become more bronze green. Fruit is rather sparsely produced. HEIGHT & SPREAD 1.5×1 m (5×3 ft) after 5 years, ultimately 7 m (23 ft) tall.
M. coronaria var. **dasycalyx 'Charlottae'** A small upright tree whose large, 3-lobed leaves, up to 10 cm (4 in) long, give a rich red display of colour in the autumn. The light pink, semi-double flowers, to 4 cm (1½ in) across, are very prolific in late spring and have a good fragrance. Fruit is yellowish green. HEIGHT & SPREAD 1.5×1 m (5×3 ft)

▼ *Malus* 'Evereste'

after 5 years, ultimately 6m (20ft) tall.

M. **'Evereste'**♀ A profusion of large flowers, 5 cm (2 in) across, are pink in bud but open to white. Autumn fruits, to 2.5 cm (1 in) across, are an attractive orange or red. This is a small conical tree. Its dark green leaves are sometimes lobed. HEIGHT & SPREAD 1.5×1m (5×3ft) after 5 years, ultimately 6m (20ft) tall.

M. floribunda♀ (Japanese crab) One of the most prolific flowering crab apples, the branches are covered in crimson buds in mid spring that open to white or pale pink flowers. Once the flowers are over they are followed by small yellow fruits. The leaves are fresh green. A small tree, in maturity it has a rounded crown often as broad as it is tall. Native to Japan. HEIGHT & SPREAD 1.5×1.2m (5×4ft) after 5 years, ultimately 7m (23ft) tall.

M. **'Golden Hornet'** see *M.* × *zumi* 'Golden Hornet'

M. × *hartwigii* **'Katherine'**♀ Large flowers, up to 5 cm (2 in) across, are deep pink in bud and open to semi-double pink flowers which gradually fade to pure white. The fruits although not conspicuous are red flushed with yellow. It is a small upright tree with a spreading crown. HEIGHT & SPREAD 1m×60cm (3×2ft) after 5 years, ultimately 4m (13ft) tall.

M. **'Hillieri'** see *M. schiedeckeri* 'Hillieri'

▲ *Malus* × *hartwigii* 'Katherine'
Malus hupehensis ▲

M. hupehensis♀ In late spring, every branch of this spreading tree is covered in a profusion of slightly scented, pure white flowers, to 4cm (1½in) across. These give way to hundreds of fruits, 1.5 cm (½ in) across, that ripen in early to mid autumn to a beautiful translucent red. As an added bonus the bright green leaves give a good display of autumn colour making this a truly multiseasonal plant. Native to W China. HEIGHT & SPREAD 1.5×1m (5×3ft) after 5 years, ultimately 10m (33ft) tall.

'Rosea' has rosy pink flowers.

M. **'John Downie'**♀ A small tree grown for its outstanding fruit colour of bright orange and red which makes a striking sight in autumn when the branches are laden. The fruits, 2.5 cm (1 in) across, are slightly longer than they are broad and can be made into a jelly. The late spring flowers are white. HEIGHT & SPREAD 1.5×1m (5×3ft) after 5 years, ultimately 6m (20ft) tall.

▲ *Malus* 'John Downie'

▲ *Malus* × *moerlandsii* 'Liset'

M. × *moerlandsii* **'Liset'** Late spring flowers are dark crimson in bud and emerge rose-red, followed by deep crimson fruits. The small rounded tree has new leaves that are purplish when they emerge but turn shiny deep green as they age. HEIGHT & SPREAD 1.2×1m (4×3ft) after 5 years, ultimately 4m (13ft) tall.

Another selection from this hybrid is **'Profusion'**. It is very similar to 'Liset' in size and foliage but holds the purple colour for longer. The fragrant flowers are more prolific and a carmine red. These are followed by deep red fruits, up to 1.5 cm (½ in) across, on long stalks.

M. × *purpurea* The leaves of this small spreading tree or large shrub are purplish green as are the new shoots. These become green as the season progresses. The mid spring flowers are dark purple at first but fade quickly and are followed by purple-red fruits. HEIGHT & SPREAD 1.2×1m (4×3ft) after 5 years, ultimately 4m (13ft) tall.

'Eleyi' is similar but has darker foliage

▲ *Malus* × *moerlandsii* 'Profusion'

▲ *Malus* × *purpurea*

▲ *Malus* × *purpurea* 'Eleyi'
Malus × *purpurea* 'Neville Copeman' ▲

Malus × purpurea

and flowers which hold their colour better. The fruits persist well into late autumn. **'Lemoinei'** is also similar and makes a fine small erect tree with slightly double, more reddish flowers. The leaves of **'Neville Copeman'**♀ are more green in colour with just a hint of purple. This colour is kept well throughout the year. The flowers are light purple and are followed by clusters of striking orange red fruits.

M. × *robusta* A small, upright tree with white or pinkish flowers in mid or late spring. Red fruits generally follow in autumn but the colour can vary, so if a particular fruit colour is required it is best to choose one of the varieties. HEIGHT & SPREAD 1.5×1m (5×3ft) after 5 years, ultimately 6m (20ft) tall.

'Red Sentinel'♀ is grown for its outstanding display of autumn fruits that are up to 2.5 cm (1 in) across and are a deep glossy red in colour. The fruits are produced in great numbers and stay on the tree throughout most of the winter. The flowers, borne in mid to late spring, are white. **'Red Siberian'**♀ is another good selection for fruit colour and quantity. The cherry-like fruits are bright red flushed with yellow and also stay on the tree well into winter.

▲ *Malus* × *robusta*

▲ *Malus* × *robusta* 'Yellow Siberian'
Malus × *robusta* 'Red Sentinel' ▲

'Yellow Siberian'♀ is similar to 'Red Siberian' but has yellow fruits.

M. 'Royal Beauty'♀ This is a small tree of weeping habit and rounded appearance. The leaves and stems are a reddish purple at first but most of this is lost as the season progresses. Deep red-purple flowers give way to dark red fruits in autumn. HEIGHT & SPREAD 1 m×60 cm (3×2 ft) after 5 years, ultimately 3 m (10 ft) tall.

M. 'Royalty' The leaves of this small upright tree emerge dark purple and lighten as the season progresses, giving a good display of red colour in autumn. Large purple-carmine flowers are followed in autumn by small, dark red fruits. HEIGHT & SPREAD 1.2 m×60 cm (4×2 ft) after 5 years, ultimately 4 m (13 ft) tall.

M. sargentii see *M. toringo* ssp. *sargentii*

M. × schiedeckeri 'Hillieri' Semidouble flowers, borne in late spring, are deep pink or crimson in bud but open to light pink. These are followed in autumn by yellow fruits flushed with red. A medium-sized rounded shrub or sometimes a small tree. HEIGHT & SPREAD 1 m×60 cm (3×2 ft) after 5 years, ultimately 3 m (10 ft) tall.

Decorative, cherry-sized red fruits are the main reason for choosing **'Red Jade'**. White flowers emerge from pink buds in late spring. A variable plant, it makes a small tree or medium-sized shrub and has long, slender, weeping branches.

M. toringo ssp. **sargentii** (syn. *M. sargentii*) Profuse pure white flowers in spring give way to abundant bright red autumn fruits. The leaves are often 3-lobed on this rounded, medium-sized shrub. Native to Japan. HEIGHT & SPREAD 1 m×60 cm (3×2 ft) after 5 years, ultimately 2 m (6½ ft) tall.

M. toringoides Slightly fragrant, creamy white flowers open in late spring and give way to pear-shaped, red-yellow fruits in autumn, among red-yellow autumn foliage. The decorative fruits stay on the tree well into winter. An upright tree when young, it becomes more spreading in old age with large, lobed leaves up to 9 cm (3½ in) long and 5 cm (2 in) wide. Native to W China. HEIGHT & SPREAD 1.2 m×60 cm (4×2 ft) after 5 years, ultimately 9 m (30 ft) tall.

M. transitoria♀ A very good tree for yellow and red autumn colour with small, narrowly lobed leaves. The white flowers give way to light yellow fruits in the autumn. An upright tree, it becomes spreading with age. Native to NW China. HEIGHT

▲ *Malus* 'Royalty'

▲ *Malus* × *schiedeckeri* 'Red Jade'

▲ *Malus transitoria*

& SPREAD 1.2 m×60 cm (4×2 ft) after 5 years, ultimately 7 m (23 ft) tall.

M. trilobata The large lobed leaves, up to 10 cm (4 in) long, give a rich display of reds in autumn. Clusters of 6 to 8 white flowers open in late spring on this upright tree. The small fruits in autumn are yellow-ochre. Native to the S Mediterranean. HEIGHT & SPREAD 1.5×1 m (5×3 ft) after 5 years, ultimately 12 m (40 ft) tall.

▲ *Malus trilobata*

M. tschonoskii♀ One of the most outstanding crab apples for autumn colour. The large leaves, up to 12.5 cm (5 in) long, have a silvery appearance when they emerge that is lost as the season progresses. In autumn they give a brilliant display, turning a mixture of reds, oranges, purples and yellows. A small upright tree, it becomes more spreading

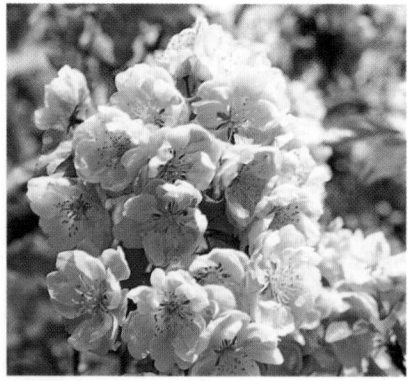

▲ *Malus* 'Van Eseltine'

with age. White flowers flushed with pink give way to yellow-green fruits tinged with purple. Native to Japan. HEIGHT & SPREAD 1.5×1 m (5×3 ft) after 5 years, ultimately 12 m (40 ft) tall.

M. 'Van Eseltine' Large double flowers, up to 5 cm (2 in) across, are borne prolifically on this small, columnar tree. The flowers emerge pink on opening from darker buds and give way to yellow fruits sometimes with a red flush on one side. It is a good plant for a small space. HEIGHT & SPREAD 1.2 m×60 cm (4×2 ft) after 5 years, ultimately 4 m (13 ft) tall.

M. 'Winter Gold' Flowers that are pink in bud open out to become white. In autumn, the flowers are followed by yellow fruits which persist on this malus well into early winter. This plant can form a medium-sized shrub or a small tree. HEIGHT & SPREAD 1 m×60 cm (3×2 ft) after 5 years, ultimately 3 m (10 ft) tall.

M. 'Wisley' Slightly scented, large flowers, to 5 cm (2 in) across, are a rich deep pink in colour. Large, purple-red fruits follow in autumn. The young leaves of the small tree emerge a good bronze red which becomes dark green as the season progresses. HEIGHT

▲ *Malus* 'Wisley'

& SPREAD 1.2 m×60 cm (4×2 ft) after 5 years, ultimately 4 m (13 ft) tall.

M. yunnanensis 'Veitch's Scarlet' White flowers open in late spring from pink buds and give way to large fruits, up to 5 cm (2 in) across. These are scarlet in colour sometimes turning to crimson on one side. The plant can be a large shrub or small tree. HEIGHT & SPREAD 1 m×60 cm (3×2 ft) after 5 years, ultimately 4 m (13 ft) tall.

M. x zumi 'Golden Hornet'♀ A small tree offering an outstanding display of yellow autumn fruits. Produced in abundance, they are a clear bright yellow and persist on the

Malus x zumi 'Golden Hornet'

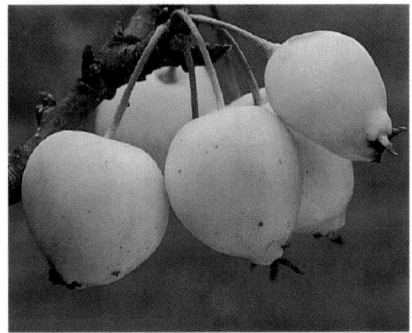

▲ *Malus × zumi* 'Golden Hornet'

tree into the new year. The flowers are white. HEIGHT & SPREAD 1.2 m×1 m (4×3 ft) after 5 years, ultimately 4 m (13 ft) tall.

CULTIVATION Plant in any reasonably good soil which is not too wet. Choose a site preferably in full sun, although they will tolerate some shade.

PROPAGATION Species will grow readily from seed but it can take up to 10 years for plants to flower. Cultivated varieties can be raised by budding or grafting, therefore it is probably advisable to buy a healthy young tree from a reputable supplier.

PRUNING Remove dead wood in winter when plants are dormant.

PESTS AND DISEASES Malus are susceptible to a large number of diseases but on the whole are trouble free. Honey fungus and fireblight can be a particular problem.

Malva
Mallow
Malvaceaea

Malva moschata var. alba

Leafy spires of pink or white flowers appear throughout summer on these upright plants that can flourish on even the poorest soil if they are in full sun. The flowers are bowl or saucer-shaped and about 5 cm (2 in) wide. The palmate, lobed leaves, 10 cm (4 in), are often hairy. The recommended species, which are herbaceous perennials and biennials, are native to Britain and Europe and sometimes grow on waste land alongside roads. They are excellent for a wild or informal garden as well as looking good in a border. However, they tend to be short lived on heavy, damp soil where they do not flower profusely.

RECOMMENDED SPECIES AND VARIETIES

M. alcea var. **fastigiata** (cut leaved mallow) Saucer-shaped, bright pink flowers are car-

ried where the leaves join the stem. This herbaceous perennial has pale green leaves and a narrow habit. HEIGHT & SPREAD 1.5 m×50 cm (5 ft×20 in).

M. moschata (musk mallow) A musk-like fragrance escapes from the flowers of this herbaceous perennial. The pink and white flowers are saucer-shaped and the pale green leaves are kidney-shaped. HEIGHT & SPREAD 1.5 m×50 cm (5 ft×20 in).

The flowers of var. **alba**♀ are white with a strong, musky perfume; var. **rosea** has purple-tinted, rose-coloured flowers.

M. sylvestris (common mallow, tall mallow) Clusters of pale pink, saucer-shaped flowers complement the toothed leaves of this biennial. HEIGHT & SPREAD 1.2 m×50 cm (4 ft×20 in).

▲ *Malva moschata*   *Malva sylvestris* 'Primley Blue' ▲

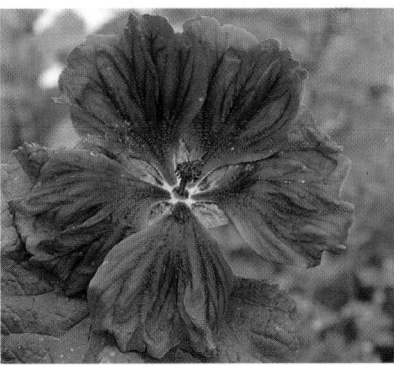

▲ *Malva sylvestris* 'Mauritiana'

'Mauritiana' has magenta, deeply veined, flowers throughout summer to the first frosts. **'Primley Blue'** has veined flowers of delicate blue and grows up to 20 cm (8 in) high, while the flowers of **'Zebrina'** are glistening white with purple veins.

CULTIVATION Plant in autumn or spring on an open, sunny site on any well-drained soil. On exposed sites support young plants with pea sticks.

PROPAGATION Sow the seed of species under glass in early spring and plant out in autumn. Take basal stem cuttings from cultivars in spring and plant out in summer.

PESTS AND DISEASES Rust can be a problem with these plants.

Malvastrum
False mallow
Malvaceae

Saucer-shaped flowers are produced in strong terminal spires during summer and early autumn. The coarse, dull green leaves are heart-shaped or lobed. The recommended species, native to S America, benefits from an open, free-draining position.

RECOMMENDED SPECIES
M. lateritium Saucer-shaped, peach-coloured petals with a yellow base and a rose pink zone, 2.5-4cm (1-1½in) across. A sprawling late summer and early autumn flowering plant which is good for ground cover. The coarse lobed leaves are dull green and up to 8cm (3¼in) long. HEIGHT & SPREAD 30×60cm (1×2ft).

▲ *Malvastrum lateritium*

CULTIVATION Grow in borders in an open position. Plant in spring and trim any untidy stems as necessary during summer. Water freely in very dry weather and apply a slow-release general fertiliser in spring.
PROPAGATION Sow seeds of the species under glass in spring. Root softwood cuttings in a coldframe during summer.
PESTS AND DISEASES Usually trouble free.

Mammilaria see CACTI p.107

Mandevilla
Apocynaceae

Mandevilla
splendens

These evergreen climbers from S America are grown for their showy flowers, some of which are fragrant. They do well in a conservatory or well-lit position indoors. Train

▲ *Mandevilla splendens* 'Rosacea'

plants in conservatories up trelliswork, or around a circular support or up a miniature trellis in the house.

RECOMMENDED VARIETY
M. splendens 'Rosacea' Clusters of pink trumpet-shaped flowers are borne in late summer. The 5 ruffled petals open to make a 10cm (4in) wide bloom, deepening in colour towards the throat. The oval leaves, glossy green with a tinge of bronze, are up to 20cm (8in) long. HEIGHT 3m (10ft).
CULTIVATION Place in good light with several hours of direct sunlight a day. Keep above 15°C (59°F) during active growth; a winter minimum of 7°C (45°F) is acceptable. Reasonable humidity is needed. Keep the compost moist during summer, but water more sparingly in winter, with minimal watering if the temperature falls below 10°C (50°F). Only repot if you want a large plant, otherwise keep in a 10cm (4cm) pot and top-dress in spring or feed once a week.
PROPAGATION Take semi-ripe cuttings in early summer.
PRUNING Prune the plant whenever it gets too big. Wear gloves, or wash hands well afterwards, as the white sap that oozes from cut stems may irritate the skin.
PESTS AND DISEASES Mealy bug can be a problem and aphids can damage young growth.

Manettia
Firecracker vine
Rubiaceae

The twining stems of these evergreen climbers from tropical regions of S America carry small but vivid flowers in spring and summer. They will twist around a trellis or wire loop and do best in a conservatory or well-lit position in the home.

RECOMMENDED SPECIES
M. luteorubra (syn. *M. inflata*) (firecracker

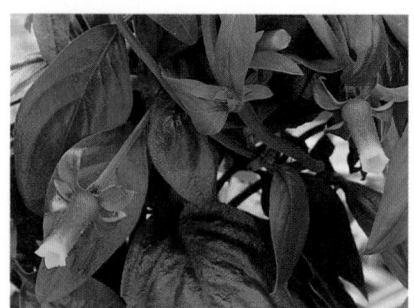

▲ *Manettia luteorubra*

vine) Bright orange-scarlet tubular flowers with bright yellow tips appear on and off throughout spring and summer. Each bloom is 2cm (¾in) long. The bright green leaves are broadly oval. HEIGHT 3m (10ft).
CULTIVATION Place in good light, with direct sun for several hours a day. Keep at a minimum temperature of 10°C (50°F) in winter and provide with reasonable humidity at all times. Keep compost slightly moist during the growing season, and allow it to dry out between waterings in winter. Feed once a week in the growing season. If the plant outgrows its pot, repot in spring.
PROPAGATION Take semi-ripe cuttings in early summer.
PRUNING Hard pruning in spring may restore old, unattractively leggy plants.
PESTS AND DISEASES Whitefly can be troublesome.

Maple see *Acer*

Maranta
Marantaceae

Admired for their patterned foliage, these evergreen perennials provide eye-catching colour for a shady corner of the house. The insignificant flowers, produced in summer, may be removed as they detract from the foliage. Native to forest floors in tropical regions of Central and S America, marantas do best in humid conditions away from direct sunlight at a minimum temperature of 13°C (55°F). They are suitable for growing in a terrarium or bottle garden.

RECOMMENDED SPECIES AND VARIETIES
M. bicolor This plant's oval to oblong leaves are pale green, spotted with brown along a paler central zone, purple beneath, and up to 25cm (10in) long and 10cm (4in) wide. HEIGHT & SPREAD 30×30cm (1×1ft).
M. leuconeura (prayer plant) Dark green oblong to oval leaves, up to 15cm (6in) long and 7.5cm (3in) wide, may have grey or maroon veins with red or purple zoning on the upper surface and grey-green or maroon beneath. The species is not widely grown, though its colourful varieties are popular. HEIGHT & SPREAD 30×30cm (1×1ft).
The leaves of var. *erythroneura* (herringbone plant, also sold as *M. tricolor*) have

▲ *Maranta leuconeura* var. *kerchoveana*

bright red veins which contrast with the dark velvety green background and pale green zoning along the midrib. The grey-green leaves of var. *kerchoveana*♀ (rabbit's foot) have purple-brown or olive-green blotches like a rabbit's tracks on either side of the midrib. The blackish green foliage of var. *massangeana* has silvery central midrib zoning and prominent silver veins.

CULTIVATION Grow out of direct sunlight in one of the standard potting composts. Mist leaves often and feed regularly during the summer months. Keep out of draughts.

PROPAGATION Divide every 2 or 3 years in spring or summer, and keep humidity high. Alternatively, take stem cuttings in summer.

PESTS AND DISEASES Greenfly can be a nuisance.

Marguerite see *Argyranthemum*
Marguerite, blue see *Felicia amelloides*
Marguerite, golden
   see *Anthemis tinctoria*
Marigold, African see *Tagetes*
Marigold, French see *Tagetes*
Marigold, marsh see *Caltha palustris*
Marigold, pot see *Calendula*
Marigold, sun see *Dimorphotheca*
Marjoram see HERBS p. 332
Marjoram see *Origanum*
Marrow see p. 740

Marrubium
Labiatae

Showy or aromatic foliage makes the hardy perennial plants in this genus valuable in a planting scheme. The small tubular-lipped flowers that appear for much of the summer are unremarkable and often removed to retain the quality of the foliage, which provides a decorative backdrop in a summer flower border. The plants are native to temperate Eurasia and N America.

RECOMMENDED SPECIES AND VARIETIES
M. cylleneum Downy, grey-green, oval to rounded leaves, up to 5 cm (2 in) long, with shallowly toothed margins cover this plant. Yellow flowers open from leafy spikes, 25 cm (10 in) long, borne on tall hairy stems. HEIGHT & SPREAD 45×45 cm (1½×1½ ft).
M. incanum The grey-green, downy, oval leaves, up to 5 cm (2 in) long, have distinctly lobed or toothed margins. Tall, hairy white stems carry leafy spikes, 25 cm (10 in) long, dotted with white flowers. HEIGHT & SPREAD 45×60 cm (1½×2 ft).
M. vulgare (white horehound) Strongly scented rounded or oval leaves, up to 4 cm (1½ in) long, are further distinguished by scalloped and crimped edges. The white flowers open from leafy spikes, 25 cm (10 in) long, at the top of tall, downy white stems. HEIGHT & SPREAD 45×60 cm (1½×2 ft).

CULTIVATION Plant in spring in well-drained soil in a sunny position.

PROPAGATION In spring, divide established crowns or sow seeds in a coldframe.

PESTS AND DISEASES Usually trouble free.

Marshmallow see *Althaea officinalis*
Marvel of Peru see *Mirabilis jalapa*
Masdevallia see ORCHIDS p. 466
Mask flower see *Alonsoa*

Matricaria
Mayweed
Compositae

White daisies with a yellow conical, button-like, centre are produced by these pleasantly aromatic annual plants. They have a filigree of finely dissected bright green leaves, with slender pointed segments. Despite often being considered weeds they are useful in the herb garden. The recommended species has a similar fragrance and medicinal uses to the true camomile, *Chamaemelum nobile*. It is also used in preparations to condition and lighten the hair. The genus is native to Europe and central Asia.

RECOMMENDED SPECIES
M. chamomilla see *M. recutita*
M. parthenium see *Tanacetum parthenium*
M. recutita (syn. *M. chamomilla*) (false or wild camomile, scented mayweed) Flowers about 2.5 cm (1 in) across, appear in branched clusters from late spring to late summer. In Britain this hardy plant is a common weed of meadows and is suited to a wild garden where it mixes well with other arable annuals such as cornflowers and poppies. It often colonises disturbed soil. HEIGHT & SPREAD 50×30 cm (20×12 in).

▲ *Matricaria recutita*

CULTIVATION Grow in any well-drained soil, in full or partial sun, sowing seed where it is to flower. Deadhead to prolong flowering.

PROPAGATION Sow seed, which is usually produced in abundance, during spring or summer. The plants usually self-sow in the garden.

PESTS AND DISEASES Occasionally infested with aphids.

Matteuccia see FERNS p. 264

Matthiola
Stock
Cruciferae

Matthiola incana

Grown for their fragrance and their spikes of spring and summer blooms in soft pastel shades, these plants flourish in sun or partial shade outdoors or as flowering pot plants in a cool greenhouse. While the shorter-stemmed types are good for bedding, those with longer stems are suitable as cut flowers. Stocks can be annuals, biennials or herbaceous perennials and are either hardy or half-hardy.

RECOMMENDED SPECIES AND VARIETIES
M. bicornis see *M. longipetala*
M. incana This species is usually biennial, but annual forms and the original herbaceous perennial are available. Single or double flowers are borne, in shades of crimson, lavender, lilac, mauve, pink, violet and white. The narrow, grey-green leaves are hairy and up to 15 cm (6 in) long. HEIGHT & SPREAD 75×45 cm (2½×1½ ft).

There are many cultivars and hybrids of *M. incana*. The annuals are half-hardy and have double or single blooms in the same range of colours as the species which appear in early or mid summer. The plants of 'Beauty of Nice' are branched and grow to 60 cm (2 ft) tall, spreading to 40 cm (16 in). **Column stocks** are unbranched, and each

▼ *Matthiola* Column stocks var. 'Giant Excelsior'

▲ *Matthiola* Ten Week stocks var. 'Cinderella'

plant produces one large flower spike, 25 cm (10 in) long. The variety **'Giant Excelsior'** reaches a height of 75 cm (2½ ft) and a spread of 30 cm (1 ft). **Ten Week stocks** are branching plants which may flower in as few as 10 weeks after their seed is sown in a greenhouse. They grow to a height of 45 cm (1½ ft) and a spread of 30 cm (1 ft). **'Cinderella'** is a dwarf variety, reaching a height of 25 cm (10 in) and a spread of 10 cm (4 in). **Trisomic Seven Week stocks** are even faster growing. These plants attain a height of 45 cm (1½ ft) and a spread of 30 cm (1 ft).

The biennial forms of *M. incana* are upright bushy plants which are not quite fully hardy. They produce a mixture of single and double flowers in the same range of colours as the species, blooming in late spring and early summer. **Brompton stocks** grow to a height of 50 cm (20 in) and a spread of 30 cm (1 ft). **East Lothian stocks** reach a height and spread of 30 cm (1 ft).

The herbaceous perennials are sold as seed or as plants under the name **White perennial form**. White, 4-petalled, single flowers, each about 5 cm (2 in) across, are borne in spikes 15-23 cm (6-9 in) long from late spring to mid summer. This hardy plant forms a branching, shrubby clump with a stout, woody basal stem. Its height is 50 cm (20 in) and its spread 30 cm (1 ft).

M. longipetala (syn. *M. bicornis*) (night-scented stock) The single lilac flowers, in spikes 20 cm (8 in) long, appear in mid and late summer. They stay closed during the day but open in the evening, when their strong scent is evident. The narrow, grey-green leaves are hairy and up to 8 cm (3¼ in) long; the lower leaves are lobed. This hardy annual has a branching habit. HEIGHT & SPREAD 30×25 cm (1 ft×10 in).

CULTIVATION Plant in fairly rich, moist soil in either full sun or partial shade. Improve sandy soil with compost or leaf-mould. Provide some support for taller varieties.

PROPAGATION Sow the seed of the annual stocks in a greenhouse in early spring and plant out the seedlings in late spring. Alternatively, sow seed outdoors in late spring, and where the plants are to grow.

Annual stocks of the Ten Week and Column types can be selected for double flowers. As soon as the seedlings have emerged, move them to an environment, indoors or outdoors, where the temperature does not exceed 8°C (46°F). After a week or so, the first leaves of some seedlings become noticeably paler than others – these will grow into double-flowered plants. Prick these out and grow on in a cool greenhouse; discard the dark green seedlings.

To select Trisomic Seven Week stocks for double flowers, prick out all seedlings. Once they have about 4 leaves, almost half the seedlings will be noticeably weaker in growth than the rest: discard these.

As a pot plant for late winter and very early spring flowering, sow the seed of 'Beauty of Nice' in early or mid summer in a cool greenhouse and grow on in boxes of general-purpose potting compost. In mid autumn move the young plants to pots 13-15 cm (5-6 in) in diameter.

Sow the seed of biennials and perennials in early or mid summer in an outdoor seedbed, or sow very thinly in a tray in a greenhouse. When the seedlings are large enough to handle, plant them 10 cm (4 in) apart, in 10 cm (4 in) deep boxes, filled with general-purpose potting compost. Plant out in early autumn if the climate is mild and the soil is well drained. Elsewhere, over-winter seedlings in a coldframe or cool greenhouse and plant out in mid spring the following year.

PESTS AND DISEASES Aphids, downy mildew and club root disease may be problems.

Maytenus
Celastraceae

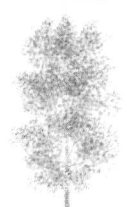

Maytenus boaria

Most of these deciduous and evergreen trees and shrubs are sub-tropical or tropical and are too tender to be grown in British gardens. However, *Maytenus boaria*, with its graceful, weeping habit and handsome foliage, is reasonably hardy and easy to grow in this country.

This large genus, of over 200 species, is native to North or South America and the West Indies.

RECOMMENDED SPECIES
M. boaria This elegant frost-hardy tree has a conical habit when young, becoming

more rounded with age. The narrow evergreen leaves, up to 5 cm (2 in) long, are dark glossy green with a few very fine teeth. The drooping branches are slender and give the tree a weeping appearance. The very small yellow-green flowers appear in early spring and are of no real beauty, but the tree sometimes produces red fruit. Native to Chile. HEIGHT & SPREAD 1.2 m×60 cm (4×2 ft) after 5 years, ultimately 10 m (33 ft) tall.

CULTIVATION Hardy in milder areas and undemanding, *M. boaria* can be grown in any well-drained soil.

PROPAGATION Take semi-ripe cuttings in summer, or sow seed in early to mid spring.

PRUNING None is necessary.

PESTS AND DISEASES Usually trouble free.

Mazus
Scrophulariaceae

The foliage of these creeping perennials is scattered with charming two-lipped flowers in late spring and summer. These low, mat-forming plants are useful for pockets in the rock garden, for gaps in paving or for naturalising in moist gravel.

RECOMMENDED SPECIES AND VARIETY

M. radicans Solitary white flowers with pink or purple in the throat are 2 cm (¾ in) long and appear throughout summer. The robust, creeping stems root down at intervals and carry pairs of small deep green or brownish green elliptical leaves that usually have darker, stitch-like markings around the edge. Native to damp places in New Zealand. HEIGHT & SPREAD 5×50 cm (2×20 in).

M. reptans The two-lipped flowers, up to 2 cm (¾ in) long, are pale to deep purple-

▲ *Mazus reptans*

blue and appear from late spring throughout the summer. The lower lips are neatly spotted with yellow or reddish yellow. A vigorous creeping plant, its prostrate stems root down at intervals and bear small mid to deep green leaves that are narrow and slightly toothed. Native to moist mountain grassland in the Himalayas and W China. HEIGHT & SPREAD 5×50 cm (2×20 in).

'Albus' has white flowers.

CULTIVATION Grow plants in any moist soil in sun or partial shade. Plant out in spring or early summer and ensure that the plants receive adequate watering until they are well established. Avoid exposure to drying winds that will scorch the foliage.

PROPAGATION Remove rooted pieces from the parent plant and grow in a shaded cold-frame until established.

PESTS AND DISEASES Usually trouble free.

Mazzard see *Prunus avium*
Meadowsweet see *Filipendula ulmaria*

Meconopsis
Papaveraceae

Meconopsis cambrica

A member of the poppy family, this genus of hardy perennials includes plants to suit every gardener's palette – from white, yellow, red, pink and purple flowered species, to those whose blooms are various beautiful shades of blue.

Meconopsis flowers usually have between four and nine petals surrounding a central boss of many stamens. All meconopsis prefer cool conditions and, particularly in warmer regions, need some shade. They tend to do best in the cooler climates of the north and west where they can be grown in sunnier positions. Shelter is advisable to prevent winds from damaging the flowers and flattening taller species.

Some meconopsis excel in north-facing herbaceous borders; others thrive in informal areas of a woodland garden; while the smaller species are at home in a rock garden or in humus-rich soils provided they have a moist, cool root run and are in good light, but out of direct sun.

With the exception of the Welsh poppy, *Meconopsis cambrica*, the genus is native to the Himalayas and W China. Some meconopsis flower each year but others are monocarpic – they flower and fruit just once, then die. For the first three to four years, the monocarpic species consist of a single, but very attractive and decorative rosette of leaves. Some of these rosettes are evergreen, turning russet, orange-brown or gold in autumn. Others are herbaceous and the foliage dies to a large, resting bud in winter. The seed capsules are oblong to oval and may be hairy, bristly or smooth.

RECOMMENDED SPECIES AND VARIETIES

M. betonicifolia♀ (syn. *M. baileyi*) (Himalayan blue poppy, blue poppy) Bright

sky-blue to lavender-pink flowers, up to 10 cm (4 in) across, are borne on stiff, bristly stalks from early to mid summer. The leaves, held in a whorl below the flowers, are oblong and hairy with a rather heart-shaped base. Bristly, elliptical seed capsules follow. In its preferred growing conditions, this plant usually flowers each year, especially in cooler, moister regions. Otherwise, it is monocarpic. It is usually easy to grow and often self-sows. HEIGHT & SPREAD 1.2 m×60 cm (4×2 ft).

White flowers distinguish var. *alba*.

M. cambrica (Welsh poppy) In bloom from spring to mid autumn, this yellow-flowered European species flourishes even in shaded, moist parts of the garden, and can become invasive. The flowers, about 6 cm (2½ in) across, are held almost upright on long stalks. The stems carry several dissected, pale green, almost hairless leaves. The seed-pods are smooth, narrow and pointed. HEIGHT & SPREAD 45×30 cm (1½×1 ft).

Orange flowers distinguish var. *aurantiaca*. 'Flore Pleno' can have double orange or yellow flowers, while 'Frances Perry' has scarlet flowers.

▼ *Meconopsis cambrica* var. *aurantiaca*

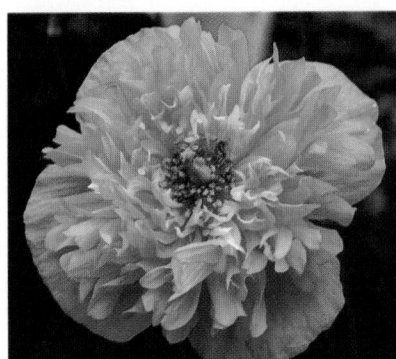
▼ *Meconopsis cambrica* 'Flore Pleno'

▼ *Meconopsis cambrica* 'Frances Perry'

m

M. grandis♀ Magnificent flowers ranging from rich blue to a wine-like reddish purple adorn this stout herbaceous perennial. The cup-shaped flowers, 7.5-12.5 cm (3-5 in) across, open in early and mid summer. The rough hairy leaves are lance-shaped to elliptical with a tapered base. The upper 3-5 leaves are held in a whorl beneath the flowers. The seed capsules are somewhat bristly. HEIGHT & SPREAD 1.2 m×80 cm (4 ft×32 in).

M. horridula With its blue, lilac, lavender, or occasionally reddish blue flowers, this plant is at home in a shady rock garden or peat bed. The flowers, up to 7.5 cm (3 in) across, are borne in a distinct spike in cultivation and appear from late spring to mid summer. This monocarpic plant has roughly elliptical, bristly leaves with dark purplish blotches. The plant sometimes self-sows. HEIGHT & SPREAD 80×30 cm (32×12 in).

M. integrifolia Bowl-shaped, upright, deep primrose yellow flowers, about 23 cm (9 in) across, appear from late spring to mid summer. Tinged russet or pink when young, the leaves are lance-shaped to elliptical, with 3 veins and stiff hairs. The upper 3-7 leaves are held in a whorl beneath the flowers. The bristly seed capsules are topped by a stigma shaped like a cartwheel. This is a herbaceous monocarpic species. HEIGHT & SPREAD 30-90×30 cm (1-3×1 ft).

M.. napaulensis Panicles of pink to red, occasionally purplish, flowers form loose spires on tall stout stems. The bowl-shaped flowers, up to 8 cm (3¼ in) across, appear from early to mid summer. This monocarpic species has magnificent rosettes of finely divided, hairy, evergreen leaves that are often russet in autumn, and bristly seed capsules. HEIGHT & SPREAD 2.5 m×60 cm (8×2 ft).

M. paniculata This is like a yellow-flowered *M. napaulensis*, also blooming from early to mid summer. The pale green hairy leaves are lobed and toothed and held in large handsome evergreen rosettes that turn

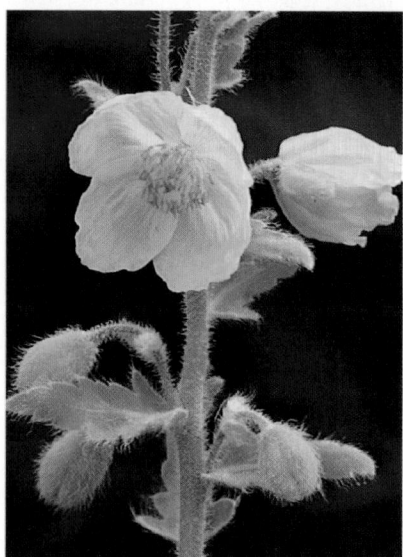
▲ *Meconopsis paniculata*

russet over winter. HEIGHT & SPREAD 2.5 m×60 cm (8×2 ft).

M. quintuplinervia♀ (harebell poppy) Solitary pale lavender flowers, about 3 cm (1¼ in) across, nod on slender stems throughout summer. Elliptical leaves covered with rust coloured hairs form a loose clump. This plant needs acid, humus-rich soil and does well in a rock garden. HEIGHT & SPREAD 45×45 cm (1½×1½ ft).

M. regia Large oblong panicles of deeply cupped, pale yellow flowers, up to 12.5 cm (5 in) across, appear in early to mid summer. A monocarpic species, its striking grey or silver leaf rosettes turn gold in autumn. The hairy leaves are lance-shaped to elliptical with fine edges; the seed capsules are bristly. HEIGHT & SPREAD 2 m×80 cm (6½ ft×32 in).

M. × sheldonii♀ The large, blue flowers of this magnificent hybrid are flushed with green, like shot silk. This long-lived, vigorous plant forms substantial clumps. HEIGHT & SPREAD 1.2 m×80 cm (4 ft×32 in).

Crewdson hybrids have mid blue, slightly transparent petals. **'Slieve Donard'**♀ has rich, deep blue flowers on plants about 75 cm (2½ ft) tall.

M. villosa see *Cathcartia villosa*

M. wallichii (syn. *M. napaulensis* 'Wallich's

▲ *Meconopsis wallichii*

form', *M. napaulensis* 'Blue form') Flowers of pale blue to purplish blue or lavender appear from mid summer to early autumn. The evergreen rosettes of bristly leaves are finely lobed and the seed capsules have spreading bristles. HEIGHT & SPREAD 2 m×80 cm (6½ ft×32 in).

CULTIVATION Plant in spring or summer in well-drained, moist, slightly acid to neutral, humus-rich soil. If planting in chalky soil, add plenty of humus. Choose a cool, sheltered site, preferably in the shade or partial shade. Mulch with well-rotted manure or compost, and dress with bone meal in spring and summer.

Protect plants with hairy winter green rosettes from excessive winter wet with a cloche or pane of glass.

PROPAGATION Sow seed as soon as it is ripe or in early spring. Prick out seedlings as soon as they are large enough to handle and plant them out by mid to late summer. Otherwise, leave them until the following

spring. Divide perennial species after flowering or in early spring.

PESTS AND DISEASES Slugs and snails may attack young shoots, and aphids may also infest young leaves and flower buds. Crown rot can kill plants in waterlogged soils and seedlings are prone to various fungal diseases.

Medlar see *Mespilus germanica*

Melaleuca
Myrtaceae

Suitable for a greenhouse or conservatory, these evergreen shrubs are grown for their bottlebrush flowerheads – the effect is produced by numerous, tiny, closely packed flowers made up of just a spray of stamens.

Native to Australasia, melaleucas are too tender to be grown outdoors in Britain, although most species can be brought out onto a patio for the summer – but keep them well-watered. They require a minimum temperature of 5°C (41°F).

RECOMMENDED SPECIES

M. gibbosa Purple flowerheads, in dense 3 cm (1¼ in) spikes, bloom from mid to late summer. The branches of this wiry shrub are crowded with light green, oval leaves about 5 mm (¼ in) long. HEIGHT & SPREAD 3×1.5 m (10×5 ft).

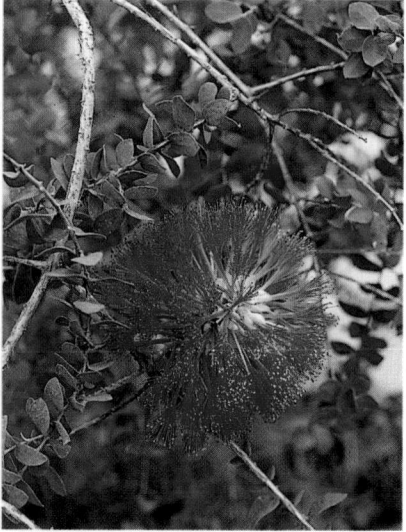
▲ *Melaleuca gibbosa*

M. hypericifolia Crimson flower spikes, up to 8 cm (3¼ in) long, appear from spring to late summer on this large graceful shrub. Mid green lance-shaped leaves, up to 4 cm (1½ in) long, cover the branches. HEIGHT & SPREAD 3×2 m (10×6½ ft).

M. squamea Purple, pink or mauve flowers, in spikes up to 2 cm (¾ in) long, are borne in early summer by this erect shrub. Narrow, mid green leaves, up to 1 cm (⅜ in) long, densely cover its branches. HEIGHT & SPREAD 1.5×1.2 m (5×4 ft).

▲ *Melaleuca squamea*

M. squarrosa Cream to yellow scented flowers, in spikes up to 5 cm (2 in) long, are borne from early to mid summer. This erect shrub has deep green oval leaves, up to 1.5 cm (½ in) long. HEIGHT & SPREAD 3 × 1.5 m (10 × 5 ft).

CULTIVATION Grow in neutral potting compost; keep moist during summer – less so in winter. Feed once a month in summer using a low-nitrogen fertiliser.

PROPAGATION Sow seed under glass in spring or take semi-ripe cuttings in summer.

PRUNING Cut back after flowering to keep within the bounds of the greenhouse.

PESTS AND DISEASES Red spider mite can be a nuisance.

Melandrium see *Silene*

Melianthus

Melianthaceae

Large, blue-green, serrated leaves give these tall plants their dramatic architectural grandeur. Curving down on slender grey and green stems, the deeply cut foliage is formed by up to 13 serrated leaflets. The leaves are about 50 cm (20 in) long. Native to southern Africa, melianthus can produce plumes of red flowers, but only during very hot British summers. Although a shrub, it is treated as a herbaceous perennial in Britain and the two recommended species are not reliably hardy. However, they will survive in a warm position in most parts of the country if protected in winter. Alternatively, melianthus can be grown in a conservatory.

RECOMMENDED SPECIES

M. major♀ (honey locust) About 11 oblong leaflets, each up to 13 cm (5¼ in) long, make this one of the most decorative foliage plants. It may bear brown-red flower plumes in late summer on 80 cm (32 in) stems. HEIGHT & SPREAD 2.4 × 2 m (8 × 6½ ft).

M. minor The leaves have up to 13 leaflets, each about 5 cm (2 in) long. Bright, brick-red flowers can appear on 40 cm (16 in) stems. HEIGHT & SPREAD 2 × 1 m (6½ × 3 ft).

CULTIVATION Plant in spring in fertile soil in a warm position. To encourage flowers, choose poor soil in full sun and do not feed. Plant at least 1 m (3 ft) apart to allow for

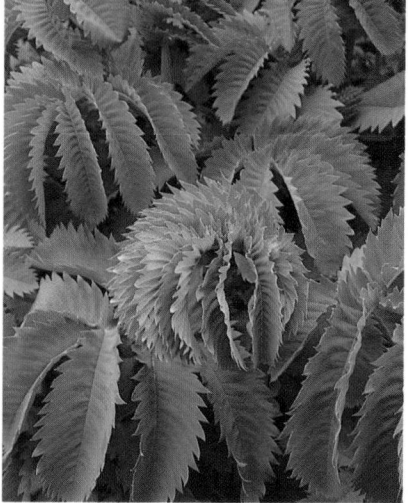

▲ *Melianthus major*

rapid root spread. Protect in winter with bracken, branches, coarse compost, or spun nylon netting. For conservatory plants, use a loam-based compost and 20 cm (8 in) pots.

PROPAGATION Remove and replant sections of rhizomatous root in spring or sow seed under glass in late winter.

PESTS AND DISEASES Usually trouble free, although red spider mite may attack conservatory plants.

Melissa

Bee balm, lemon balm
Labiatae

A delicious lemon scent is given off by the distinctive leaves of these hardy herbaceous perennials when they are crushed between the fingers. Although the white tubular flowers are insignificant, they crown the foliage with a light haze in summer and early autumn and are attractive to bees. The plant has a place in the garden both as a herb and as a decorative foliage plant, especially billowing out beside a path where the aroma of the leaves can be enjoyed.

Lemon balm does well in any type of soil and in any situation, including dry shade. An invasive habit in all but an acid soil in wet northern gardens makes it unsuitable for growing in small beds. The three species in the genus are natives of Europe. Only one is commonly grown.

RECOMMENDED SPECIES AND VARIETY

M. officinalis 'Aurea' Gold-splashed, strongly veined and tooth-edged, the hairy,

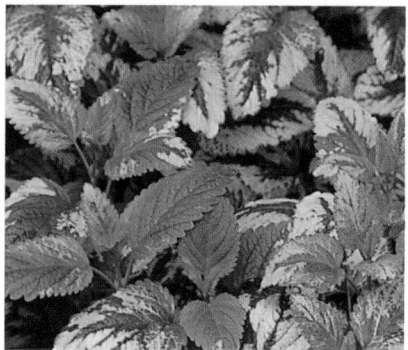

▲ *Melissa officinalis* 'Aurea'

aromatic leaves, up to 5 cm (2 in) long and broadly oval, are equally ornamental in a herbaceous border and in a herb garden. Numerous hairy upright and branched square stems are thrown up from slowly extending woody roots. As the flower stems develop, the variegation of the leaves starts to fade. The tiny white tubular flowers appear in whorls on spikes from mid summer to early autumn. HEIGHT & SPREAD 60-90 × 45 cm (2-3 × 1½ ft).

CULTIVATION Plant in spring or autumn in any ordinary garden soil in a dry sunny site or in partial shade. Plants flourish in limestone areas. Unless the flowers are wanted to attract bees to the garden, cut off flowering stems to about 15 cm (6 in) above ground level in mid summer to promote fresh growth, maintain variegation and prevent self-seeding.

PROPAGATION Divide the roots in spring or autumn. Take softwood cuttings and sow seeds in spring.

PESTS AND DISEASES Usually trouble free.

Melittis

Bastard balm
Labiatae

Tubular two-lipped flowers in shades of white, pink and purple, and often bicoloured, are borne by this herbaceous perennial. It is useful for the front of a border or a herb garden and effective in pockets on larger rock gardens. The sole species is native to W and central Europe and hardy to -25°C (-13°F).

M. melissophyllum Clusters of 2-6 flowers, each 3-4 cm (1¼-1½ in) long, appear at the upper leaf axils in late spring and early

▼ *Melittis melissophyllum*

summer. Bees are attracted to this aromatic plant which forms erect tufts of simple stems bearing pairs of oval, toothed, mid green and slightly shiny leaves. HEIGHT & SPREAD 30×20 cm (1 ft×8 in).

Selected forms include pink and white-flowered kinds.

CULTIVATION Plant in sun or part shade in well-drained soil that does not dry out rapidly.

PROPAGATION Sow seed in pots in a cold-frame during winter or early spring. Prick out seedlings once they are large enough to handle. Divide parent plants carefully in early spring or after flowering; they may take time to re-establish.

PESTS AND DISEASES Usually trouble free.

Mentha
Mint
Labiatae

A popular group of herbs grown for their decorative aromatic foliage. They can be invasive so plant them where their vigorous root systems do not swamp adjacent plants. (For culinary species, see HERBS p. 332.)

RECOMMENDED SPECIES AND VARIETIES
M. aquatica (water mint) An erect to spreading marginal aquatic plant. Oval or lance-shaped, aromatic mid or grey-green leaves are up to 6 cm (2½ in) long. Whorls of pinkish or lilac fluffy flowers are produced from late summer to autumn. HEIGHT & SPREAD 30×45 cm (1×1½ ft), or more.

M. × *gracilis* (syn. *M.* × *gentilis*) (ginger mint) Oval to lance-shaped aromatic leaves, up to 6 cm (2½ in) long are produced on erect reddish stems which during mid summer terminate in uninteresting tiny lilac flowers. HEIGHT & SPREAD 30×30 cm (1×1 ft) or more.

'**Variegata**' has leaves flecked with gold

▲ *Mentha* × *gracilis* 'Variegata'

and a scent that is reminiscent of ginger.
M. longifolia (horsemint) Strongly scented lance-shaped leaves are 8 cm (3¼ in) long. Terminal groups of insignificant white, lilac or mauve flowers are borne in summer. HEIGHT & SPREAD 60×30 cm (2×1 ft).

'**Variegata**' has hairy leaves splashed with yellow.

CULTIVATION Plant in a sunny, free-draining position. Lift and divide every third year to reduce the chances of mint rust.

PROPAGATION Divide roots in spring.

PESTS AND DISEASES Mint rust is the most likely problem.

Menyanthes
Bog bean
Menyanthaceae

A creeping, deciduous, aquatic marginal perennial is the only species in this genus. Hardiness and delightful flowers in spring recommend it for inclusion at the edge of a large pond – it is too vigorous for small ponds – where it tolerates up to 15 cm (6 in)

▲ *Menyanthes trifoliata*

of water and disguises the transition from the pond to the surrounding area throughout summer. At other times, creeping stems fulfil this role, but to a lesser extent. The plant is native to the Northern Hemisphere.
M. trifoliata (buck bean) Up to 20 fringed, star-like flowers form loose spikes, 7.5 cm (3 in) long, on the prominent stems of this aquatic marginal throughout spring. The petals are white with a pinkish flush in bud. Leaves divided into 3 separate bluish green, broadly lance-shaped leaflets, up to 8 cm (3¼ in) long and 4 cm (1½ in) wide, grow upright from fleshy scrambling stems. HEIGHT & SPREAD 25×60 cm (10 in×2 ft), or spreading much farther in rich mud.

CULTIVATION Plant at the pond margin in spring or early summer in a latticework container, filled with heavy loam soil or aquatic plant compost. Cover the soil surface with pea gravel to prevent fish disturbing the plants. Remove faded flowerheads.

PROPAGATION Divide overgrown clumps in spring. Take stem cuttings in late spring or summer and root them in a pot of mud.

PESTS AND DISEASES Usually trouble free.

Menziesia
Ericaceae

Nodding clusters of tubular, urn or bell-shaped flowers appear at the end of stems beneath deciduous leaves. The flowers are borne in late spring and early summer and are purple, pink to nearly white or sometimes bicolour. These compact, slow-growing small to medium-sized shrubs must have acid soil and are suited to a woodland garden. They are hardy, and native to N America and Japan.

RECOMMENDED SPECIES AND VARIETIES
M. ciliicalyx var. *purpurea* Flowers about 1.5 cm (½ in) long with a yellowish green base and purplish lobes are freely produced on this long-lived, rounded variety. It has a tidy habit and egg-shaped leaves, up to 5 cm (2 in) long, with fine hairs on the margins. HEIGHT & SPREAD 30×30 cm (1×1 ft) after 5 years, ultimately 60×60 cm (2×2 ft).

Var. *multiflora* has a slightly shorter flower which is often paler in colour.
M. taxifolia see *Phyllodoce caerulia*

▲ *Menziesia ciliicalyx* var. *multiflora*

CULTIVATION Plant in an open part of the garden in moist, well-drained acid soil that is rich in organic matter. Menziesia will remain compact in a sunny situation.

PROPAGATION This is an extremely difficult shrub to propagate. The most reliable method is division in early spring.

PRUNING Not necessary but cut back straggly shoots to improve habit.

PESTS AND DISEASES Usually trouble free.

Merrywort see *Ulvaria*

Mertensia
Boraginaceae

Clusters of pendent tubular or bell-like blue flowers, complemented by bluish green or grey foliage, crowd the stems of these hardy herbaceous and semi-evergreen perennials in spring and early summer. They embellish a shady part of a flower border or brighten dappled shade beneath deciduous trees, apart from *Mertensia maritima,* which needs an open sunny position. Grow the small species in a rock garden.

RECOMMENDED SPECIES

M. ciliata In early summer, pale pink buds, borne in lax clusters, open into pale blue flowers, up to 1 cm (⅜ in) long, on this herbaceous perennial. The bluish green leaves, up to 8 cm (3¼ in) long, are narrow, elliptical and tapering. Native to open woodlands in the Rocky Mountains, USA. HEIGHT & SPREAD 60×30 cm (2×1 ft).

M. maritima (oyster plant) Small clusters of bright blue flowers, about 1 cm (⅜ in) long, open from pink buds in late spring and early summer. This semi-evergreen has trailing stems and beautiful fleshy elliptical or oval grey-blue leaves, up to 8 cm (3¼ in) long. It does not mix well with other plants. Native to coastal habitats in E Asia, Europe and USA. HEIGHT & SPREAD 15×50 cm (6×20 in).

M. pulmonarioides♀, syn. *M. virginica* (Virginian cowslip) Deep blue flowers, about 2 cm (¾ in) long, appear in drooping

▲ *Mertensia maritima*

▲ *Mertensia pulmonarioides*

clusters from mid to late spring and contrast with narrow, tapering to oval, bluish green leaves, up to 7.5 cm (3 in) long. The stems of this herbaceous perennial die back in mid summer. Native to USA. HEIGHT & SPREAD 50×40 cm (20×16 in).

M. sibirica Clusters of 1 cm (⅜ in) long bluish purple flowers highlight the rounded or heart-shaped leaves, up to 8 cm (3¼ in) long. Native to Siberia. HEIGHT & SPREAD 45×30 cm (1½×1 ft).

CULTIVATION Plant all species in autumn or early spring in moist humus-rich soil in dappled shade, except *M. maritima*, which

thrives in poor, dry, gravelly soil in full sun.

PROPAGATION Sow seeds in pots as soon as they are ripe. Put in a coldframe and prick out the seedlings as soon as they are large enough to handle. Divide herbaceous plants in early spring or straight after flowering.

PESTS AND DISEASES Aphids may infest young shoots. *M. maritima* is easily damaged by slugs and snails.

Mesembryanthemum see *Dorotheanthus*

Mespilus
Medlar
Rosaceae

Mespilus germanica 'Nottingham'

Sweet fruit – which can be eaten raw when overripe or, more often, used to make jelly – is borne by this undemanding deciduous shrub, a single-species member of the rose family. It is fully hardy and makes a large, wide-spreading ornamental shrub that is good as a specimen plant, for example, on a lawn. Medlars are native to SE Europe and central Asia.

Mespilus germanica Solitary white flowers, up to 4 cm (1½ in) across, appear in late spring and early summer, often in small numbers. Oblong leaves, dull green above and hairy beneath, grow to 10 cm (4 in) long and can provide good autumn colour, depending on the individual. Stout spines arm the branches and the marble-shaped hard green fruits, which appear in autumn, grow to about 2.5 cm (1 in) across. They are best eaten at the end of the year when, after

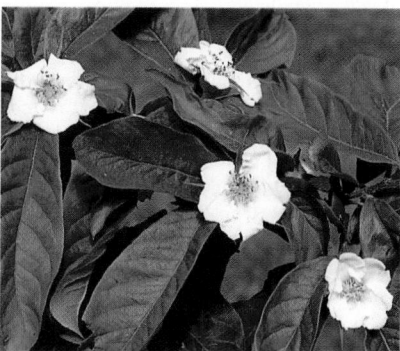
▲ *Mespilus germanica*

storing for about 3 weeks, they turn soft and brown and the overripe flesh very sweet. HEIGHT & SPREAD 2.4×1.8 m (8×6 ft) after 10 years, ultimately 5×3 m (16×10 ft).

'Nottingham' has bigger fruits, flowers

and leaves, and there are almost no spines.

CULTIVATION Grow anywhere, in any soil. Plant between late autumn and mid spring, avoiding frosty periods.

PROPAGATION Sow seed in early to mid spring. Cultivars must be grafted.

PRUNING None is required.

PESTS AND DISEASES Usually trouble free.

Metasequoia
Dawn redwood
Taxodiaceae

Metasequoia glyptostroboides

The sole, superb species of this genus grows into a majestic forest tree which, in a large garden, makes a striking, stand-alone specimen. The deciduous hardy conifer is well suited to acid soil in damp, dark corners, river banks or pond edges. It soon forms a neat, conical shape round a trunk that is buttressed at ground level. The cinnamon-brown bark flakes in long bootlace shreds.

Metasequoia glyptostroboides♀ The foliage resembles feathers, with pairs of opposite shoots close set with opposite rows of blunt-tipped needles some 2.5 cm (1 in) long and very soft to the touch. The leaves are bright light green when they open, then turn pink, gold and deep orange before dropping when there are hard winter frosts. Late spring frosts can damage the new leaves.

Yellow male flowers appear in large clusters with greener female flowers in small clusters close to them. The females develop into round, occasionally cylindrical, green cones up to 2 cm (¾ in) across; these hang on long stalks and ripen to dark brown. Native to China. HEIGHT & SPREAD 7×2 m (23×6½ ft) after 10 years, ultimately 40 m (130 ft) tall.

CULTIVATION Grow in fertile, moist, but not waterlogged soil. The tree grows much more slowly in alkaline soil than in its preferred acid conditions.

PROPAGATION Seed is the best method of propagation but is in short supply. Cuttings taken in mid to late autumn root easily with bottom heat.

PRUNING None is necessary, but the canopy can be raised by removing whole branches to clear the required length of trunk.

PESTS AND DISEASES Metasequoias are susceptible to root rot and butt rot if damaged round the base by mowing. Honey fungus can also strike.

m

Metrosideros
Myrtacae

These tender evergreen trees, shrubs and climbing plants are grown for their very showy flowers. The species listed below have flowers with only tiny, inconspicuous red petals, but their numerous crimson stamens give a fiery display in mid summer.

The branches and short leaf stalks on young plants grown from seed are glossy green and hairless. Older plants, together with younger plants grown from cuttings, have branches and leaf stalks covered with short white hairs. The oval leaves are thick and leathery, dark green above but densely felted and near white beneath.

The species in cultivation are best grown as shrubs. Native to Malaysia, Polynesia, Australia and New Zealand, they can only survive outside in Britain in frost-free gardens and are usually grown in pots and overwintered under glass.

RECOMMENDED SPECIES AND VARIETIES
M. excelsa (New Zealand Christmas tree) The flowers, with stamens as long as 4 cm (1½ in), are borne in broad, branched clusters up to 10 cm (4 in) across. The leaves are about 7 cm (2¾ in) long. HEIGHT & SPREAD 1×1 m (3×3 ft) after 5 years, ultimately 15 m (50 ft) tall.
M. kermadecensis Flowers in broad branched clusters up to 10 cm (4 in) wide display stamens about 1.5 cm (½ in) long. The leaves are as long as 5 cm (2 in). HEIGHT & SPREAD 1×1 m (3×3 ft) after 5 years, ultimately 15 m (50 ft) tall.

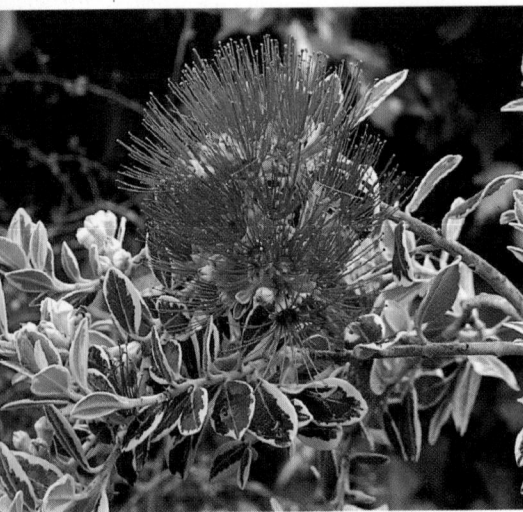

▲ *Metrosideros kermadecensis* 'Variegata'

'**Variegata**' is very showy, with dark green leaves broadly and irregularly edged with yellow. Flowers are often produced by young plants only 50 cm (20 in) tall. This cultivar grows to a height and spread of about 60 cm (2 ft) after 5 years.
CULTIVATION Grow in pots of a well-drained, general purpose compost and overwinter in a frost-free greenhouse. Move outside once the danger of frost has passed. Give an occasional extra feed with a good general fertiliser. Plant outside only in a very well-drained, frost-free site.
PROPAGATION Sow seed in spring under glass. Take semi-ripe cuttings in early autumn. They may take all winter to root.
PRUNING Cut back after flowering to maintain a compact shape.
PESTS AND DISEASES Usually trouble free.

Meum
Spignel
Umbelliferae

Feathery foliage and bold white flower-heads in summer secure a place in a wild garden for this hardy and aromatic herbaceous perennial. It is particularly successful when established with other wild-garden plants in well-drained soil and in an open, sunny position, such as in a grassy sward. There is only one species in the genus.

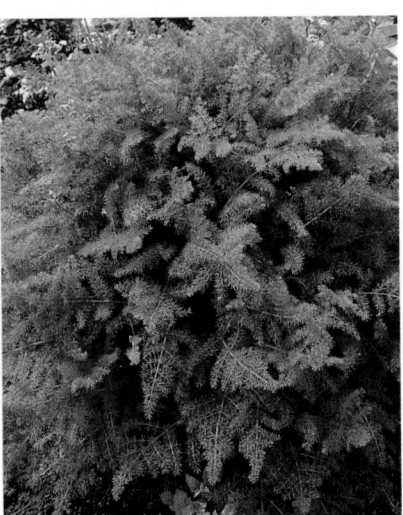

▲ *Meum athamanticum*

Meum athamanticum Prominent white flowerheads, 7.5 cm (3 in) across, consist of many tiny blossoms that are often tinged yellow and purple. They bloom from early to mid summer. The leaves are divided into 3 or 4 groups of thread-like bright green leaflets. Native to Europe. HEIGHT & SPREAD 60×30 cm (24×12 in).
CULTIVATION Plant in spring in well-drained soil. Grow in close association with other plants in a sunny spot in a wild garden. Remove the faded flowerheads, unless fresh seedlings are required for natural colonising.
PROPAGATION Sow seeds in open ground in permanent growing positions immediately they ripen or in early spring. Seedlings do not transplant well.
PESTS AND DISEASES Usually trouble free.

Mezereon see *Daphne mezereum*

Microbiota
Cupressaceae

microbiota decussata

This prostrate evergreen shrub provides excellent ground cover. The plant is native to SE Siberia and extremely hardy – it will thrive almost anywhere in the garden, including cold dark places where many other plants may not grow. The genus has only one species. It is closely related to juniperus, the main difference being that the berries are more woody than fleshy.

▲ *Microbiota decussata*

Microbiota decussata♀ Flattened sprays of trailing, dark green, scale-like foliage turn bronze in winter. The leaves sometimes go so brown in low temperatures that the plant could be mistaken as dead until the leaves recover their colour. Insignificant flowers in spring are followed by woody brown berries, 3 mm (⅛ in) across, in autumn. HEIGHT & SPREAD 10×30 cm (4×12 in) after 5 years, ultimately 30 cm×1.2 m (1×4 ft).
CULTIVATION Plant in spring in any well-drained soil in sun or shade.
PROPAGATION Ripewood cuttings taken in winter, early spring or early autumn will root easily. Use rooting hormone on autumn cuttings.
PRUNING None required.
PESTS AND DISEASES Usually trouble free. Avoid growing microbiota close to paths or other areas frequented by dogs and cats, because their urine can poison the plant.

Michaelmas daisy see *Aster*
Milium see GRASSES p. 301
Milkwort see *Polygala*
Miltoniopsis see ORCHIDS p. 466
Mimosa see *Acacia dealbata*

Mimosa

Leguminosae

Mimosa pudica

Fluffy heads of summer flowers are borne by plants belonging to this large genus of tropical, thorny, shrubby plants. The only species in general cultivation in Britain is a tender greenhouse pot plant usually raised as an annual. This plant is something of a curiosity, as its much divided foliage collapses temporarily if touched in daylight. Plants belonging to the genus *Mimosa* should not be confused with *Acacia dealbata*, which has the common name mimosa.

RECOMMENDED SPECIES

M. pudica (sensitive plant) Ball-like lilac-pink to mauve flowers up to 2 cm (¾ in) across appear throughout summer. The tiny, bright to greyish green, lance-shaped leaflets are borne in ranks of 25 or more, each arrangement making up divisions of a larger leaf up to 10 cm (4 in) long. This small shrub's prickly stems are generally erect, but can become loosely climbing unless pinched back from time to time, or supported. The plant is short-lived and is best replaced each spring. HEIGHT & SPREAD 60×60 cm (24×24 in).

▲ *Mimosa pudica*

CULTIVATION Grow in pots in a soil-based compost such as John Innes No. 2. Choose a warm humid place out of direct sunlight, with a temperature of at least 13°C (55°F). Keep plants moist at all times. Feed once a month in summer with a general liquid houseplant fertiliser. Provide support or pinch out wayward shoots to shape.

PROPAGATION Sow seed in a propagator in spring. Take semi-ripe cuttings in summer.

PESTS AND DISEASES Red spider mite can be a problem.

Mimulus

Monkey flower
Scrophulariaceae

Mimulus 'Whitecroft scarlet'

Dark patterns on the flowers of many of these plants give them a cheerful appearance that has been likened to the grinning face of a monkey. The flowers, borne from summer to early autumn, have two lips and a pouch and are particularly good at attracting bees and other insects to the garden. The pale green or grey-green leaves, 2-6 cm (¾-2½ in) long, held in pairs, may be oval, oblong or lance-shaped, with toothed edges.

Most species and varieties prefer moist, humus-rich, slightly acid soil, although alkaline soil will do. Bog gardens, the margins of ponds and streams, and damp, open woodland provide the best conditions. The larger varieties do well in informal borders, but can become invasive and smother less vigorous plants. Smaller varieties are ideal for moist, semi-shaded parts of a rock garden or for naturalising around ponds or streams. The more compact species – *Mimulus cardinalis* and *M. lewisii* – can grow in any moist garden soil, but really thrive in deep, fertile soil. *M cardinalis*, *M. cupreus* and *M. guttatus* also do well in containers provided they are well watered.

The genus includes annuals, herbaceous perennials and small shrubs. Native to N and S America, most plants are hardy in Britain. They mix especially well with water margin irises, hostas and rodgersias.

RECOMMENDED SPECIES AND VARIETIES

M. 'Andean Nymph'♀ Cream flowers, about 4 cm (1½ in) long, are flushed with rose-pink and spotted with a deeper pink on the throat and lower lip. They are produced throughout summer. This spreading perennial is not frost-hardy. HEIGHT & SPREAD 20×30 cm (8×12 in).

M. aurantiacus♀ (syn. *M. glutinosus*, *Diplacus aurantiacus*, *D. glutinosus*) (bush monkey flower) Orange or deep yellow, unmarked flowers, about 4 mm (⅛ in) long, with widely spread petal-lobes, are borne in pairs in late spring and summer. This shrub has a much-branched woody base and sticky stems and leaves. It is not frost-hardy. HEIGHT & SPREAD 1×1 m (3×3 ft).

Reddish purple flowers distinguish var. *puniceus* (syn. *M. atrosanguineus*).

M. cardinalis♀ (scarlet monkey flower) The flowers of this herbaceous perennial are brilliant scarlet with yellow in the throat and about 5 cm (2 in) long. They are borne

▲ *Mimulus aurantiacus* var. *puniceus*

in long spikes in summer on erect stems. HEIGHT & SPREAD 1 m×60 cm (3×2 ft).

M. cupreus Numerous small, golden yellow flowers with some patterning in the throat change to bright copper as they age. They are about 3 cm (1¼ in) long and are borne in short spikes. Impatiens make good planting companions for this hardy annual. HEIGHT & SPREAD 30×20 cm (12×8 in).

M. glutinosus see *M. aurantiacus*

M. guttatus (common monkey flower) Brilliant golden yellow flowers, about 4 cm (1½ in) long, with red to purple-brown blotches on the lower lip appear in profusion in late spring and summer. This clump-forming herbaceous perennial has bright green, obovate to rounded, toothed leaves and thick, erect to spreading stems. HEIGHT & SPREAD 60×60 cm (24×24 in).

M. lewisii♀ (great purple monkey flower) This handsome plant has magenta-purple or deep rose-pink flowers, up to 5 cm (2 in) long, carried in tall spikes. A downy, rather sticky-stemmed, clump-forming herbaceous perennial, it is not frost-hardy. HEIGHT & SPREAD 60×45 cm (24×18 in).

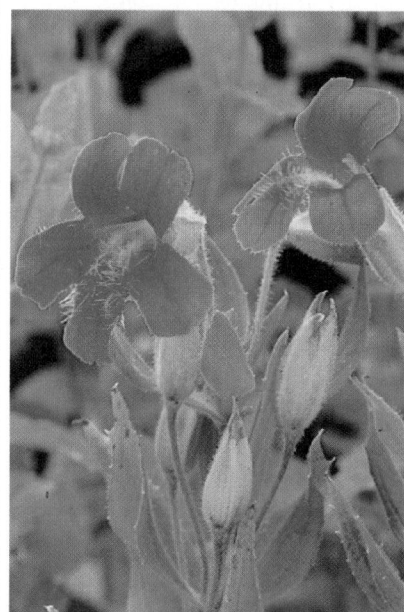

▲ *Mimulus lewisii*

M. longiflorus (salmon bush monkey flower) Salmon-flushed yellow or cream flowers give this sticky shrub its common name. Pairs of funnel-shaped flowers, about 6 cm (2½ in) long, appear in summer. This much branched, woody-stemmed plant is not frost-hardy. HEIGHT & SPREAD 70×70 cm (28×28 in).

M. luteus (monkey flower) Masses of small bright yellow flowers, about 4 cm (1½ in) long, appear throughout summer on this spreading herbaceous perennial, which is widely naturalised in Britain. HEIGHT & SPREAD 30×40 cm (12×16 in).

M. moschatus (musk or musk flower) Small, pale yellow, musk-scented flowers, about 2.5 cm (1 in) long, are produced by a spreading, mat-forming, herbaceous perennial all summer long. HEIGHT & SPREAD 20×30 cm (8×12 in).

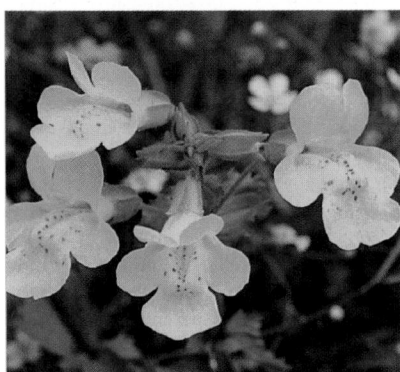
▲ *Mimulus primuloides*

M. primuloides This hairy, spreading, herbaceous perennial has most of its elliptical or oval leaves in basal rosettes. Small yellow flowers, up to 2 cm (¾ in) long, appear all through summer. HEIGHT & SPREAD 10×50 cm (4×20 in).

M. ringens (Allegheny monkey flower) Violet-blue flowers, about 3 cm (1¼ in) long, are borne in long erect clusters throughout summer. This is a herbaceous perennial with erect, leafy stems. HEIGHT & SPREAD 1 m×60 cm (3×2 ft).

M. tilingii (larger mountain monkey flower) Bright yellow flowers, about 3 cm (1¼ in) long, with brown patterns on the lower lip cover this dense, mat-forming, herbaceous perennial in summer. The spreading stems carry bright green, oval, toothed leaves, up to 3 cm (1¼ in) long. HEIGHT & SPREAD 20×40 cm (8×16 in).

More compact is var. *caespitosus*, which is no taller than 10 cm (4 in), and has smaller, elliptical leaves.

RECOMMENDED HYBRIDS

Some of the most showy and easy-to-grow monkey flowers are of hybrid origin. The following hybrids are perennials, although often short-lived, and hardy to -5°C (23°F). The flowers are usually 2-3 cm (¾-1¼ in) long. Plants grow to a height of about 30 cm (12 in) and spread to 40 cm (16 in).

▲ *Mimulus* 'Highland Orange'

'Bees' Scarlet' has bright scarlet flowers. 'Highland Orange' bears bright orange flowers. Those of 'Highland Pink' are rich pink. 'Highland Red'♀ has deep red blooms. 'Highland Yellow' produces flowers of bright yellow. The soft tan flowers of 'Hose in Hose' have a double corolla, one sitting inside the other. 'Inca Sunset' carries orange-red blossoms. The flowers of 'Inshriach Crimson' are deep crimson. Those of 'Whitecroft Scarlet'♀ are red to reddish orange. 'Wisley Red' produces velvety, blood-red flowers and grows to a height of not more than 15 cm (6 in).

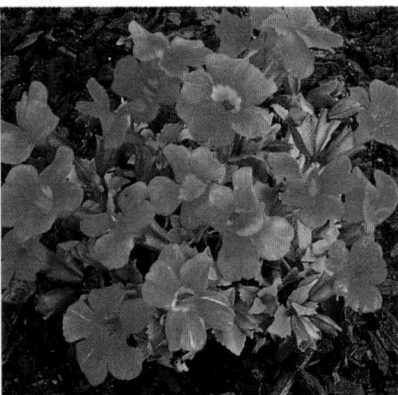
▲ *Mimulus* 'Whitecroft Scarlet'

CULTIVATION Plant in a moist, humus-rich soil, ideally slightly acid, that does not dry out. Plant hardy perennials in autumn or spring, and annuals in late spring or early summer. Thin larger varieties to prevent them becoming invasive.

PROPAGATION Sow seed in winter or early spring in pots under glass. Alternatively, sow annual varieties in their flowering position in early spring, or in a cool greenhouse in late summer or early winter for early spring displays of flowers.

Divide perennials in autumn or early spring. Take semi-ripe cuttings from shrubby species in late summer. Take softwood cuttings of the hybrid perennials in early summer.

PESTS AND DISEASES Usually trouble free. Some systemic sprays used against slugs, snails and aphids will turn leaves yellow.

Mint (culinary herb) see HERBS p. 332
Mint see *Mentha*
Mint bush see *Prostanthera rotundifolia*

Mirabilis
Nyctaginaceae

Clusters of narrow, trumpet-shaped flowers in a range of brilliant colours make this a decorative plant for a warm sunny position. Only one of the 45 species native to southeastern N America and to S America is commonly grown in British gardens. This is *Mirabilis jalapa*, a long-lived but tender herbaceous perennial. It can be grown as a half-hardy annual for summer bedding in a sunny border, or in a greenhouse or conservatory.

RECOMMENDED SPECIES

M. jalapa (marvel of Peru, four o'clock plant) Fragrant flowers appear from mid to late summer, opening from mid to late afternoon and fading the next morning. The blooms, up to 5 cm (2 in) long, can be purple, crimson, light orange, yellow, of mixed colours or striped. The ovate leaves are bright green and up to 10 cm (4 in) long. The small green fruits contain one large seed which is black when ripe. The plant has a bushy, erect habit and develops a large tuber, weighing up to 20 kg (44 lb). Native to Peru. HEIGHT & SPREAD 1×1 m (3×3 ft).

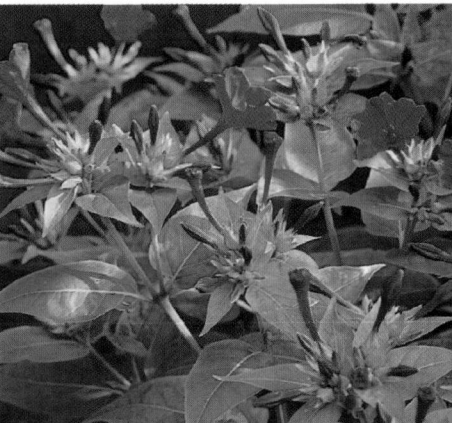
▲ *Mirabilis jalapa*

CULTIVATION Plant in any fertile, well-drained soil in a sheltered sunny position in the garden, after all danger of frost has passed. Lift the tubers in late autumn and store them in a frost-free place.

Alternatively, plant in containers filled with a soil-based potting compost and keep in a cool greenhouse or conservatory, placing the containers outside during summer if desired.

PROPAGATION Sow seeds every year in a warm greenhouse during early spring.

PESTS AND DISEASES Generally trouble free but the leaves may become infested by glasshouse whitefly.

Moltkia

Boraginaceae

Masses of pendent funnel-shaped blue or purple flowers cover these pretty evergreen shrubs or sub-shrubs in summer. They are particularly useful for a rock garden or for the top of a dry retaining wall. Although fully hardy, plants dislike prolonged cold winters and cold drying winds.

RECOMMENDED SPECIES AND VARIETIES
M. × *intermedia* The bright blue flowers, each about 1.5 cm (½ in) long, are borne in drooping clusters throughout summer. The numerous deep green narrow leaves, up to 10 cm (4 in) long, are covered underneath with whitish bristles. This is a shrub with an open dome-shaped habit of growth. HEIGHT & SPREAD 23×23 cm (9×9 in), ultimately 30 cm (1 ft) tall.
M. petraea Hanging clusters of violet or blue flowers, about 8 mm (⅜ in) long, appear in summer. The narrow deep green leaves, 1-5 cm (⅜-2 in) long, have undersides covered with whitish bristles. A semi-evergreen shrub native to the Balkans. HEIGHT & SPREAD 20×20 cm (8×8 in), ultimately 40 cm (16 in) tall.

▼ *Moltkia* × *intermedia*

▼ *Moltkia petraea*

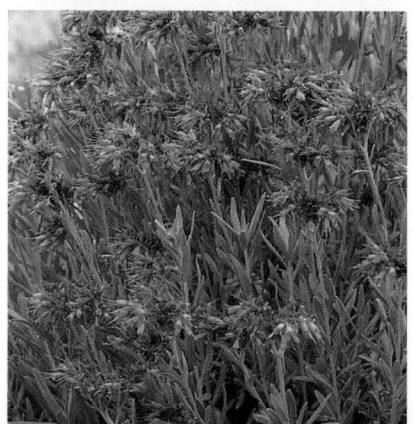

CULTIVATION Plant during spring in full sun in well-drained gritty soil, preferably neutral or alkaline. Choose a site sheltered from cold winds.
PROPAGATION Take semi-ripe cuttings or layer plants in late summer. Alternatively, sow seed in pots in a coldframe in winter or early spring.
PRUNING Not normally required. Remove straggly or dead branches in spring.
PESTS AND DISEASES Usually trouble free.

Molucella

Labiatae

Molucella laevis

Of the four species in this genus, the half-hardy annual *Molucella laevis* is by far the most widely grown. Its numerous tall stems bearing tall white flowers surrounded by prominent green calyxes (made up of sepals) add interest to a border and are a favourite among flower arrangers, both as cut flowers and dried for winter decoration.

RECOMMENDED SPECIES
M. laevis (bells of Ireland, shellflower) The common name is derived from the whorls of green bell-like calyxes which clothe the uppermost regions of the tall, upright stems. In late summer to early autumn each lime-green calyx forms an upturned collar, up to 5 cm (2 in) across, around a tiny white flower. The stems also carry rounded, lime-green leaves which are toothed and about 6 cm (2½ in) long. Native to W Asia. HEIGHT & SPREAD 60×30 cm (2×1 ft).
CULTIVATION Plant in a light, rich soil in an open, sunny situation after the spring frosts.
PROPAGATION Sow seed under glass in any seed compost in early spring at a temperature of 15°C (59°F). Harden off and plant out after the spring frosts. In mild areas you can scatter seed in the plant's flowering position in mid spring and thin out later.
PESTS AND DISEASES Usually trouble free.

▼ *Molucella laevis*

Monarda

Bergamot
Labiatae

Monarda didyma

These showy flowers, set against a backdrop of aromatic foliage, add colour and interest to a mixed herbaceous border. Monardas are also suitable for planting along the edge of water. Rounded whorls of narrow, tubular, two-lipped flowers appear in mid summer and attract bees and butterflies. The simple, opposite leaves can be dried and used in potpourri. Native to woodlands and watersides of N America.

RECOMMENDED SPECIES AND VARIETIES
M. citriodora (lemon mint) This annual bears white to pink or purple flowers, spotted darker purple, 2 cm (¾ in) long. Erect stems, often branched, carry serrated, lance-shaped, mid green leaves, to 6 cm (2½ in) long. HEIGHT & SPREAD 60×30 cm (2×1 ft).

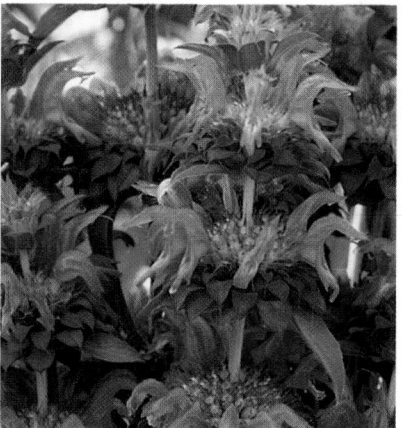

▲ *Monarda citriodora*

M. didyma (Oswego tea, sweet bergamot, bee balm) Red flowers with red or purple bracts are carried in dense heads 4 cm (1½ in) across. This herbaceous perennial carries pairs of mid green leaves, about 10 cm (4 in) long, on erect stems. HEIGHT & SPREAD up to 1.2 m×45 cm (4×1½ ft).
    '**Alba**' has white flowers.

▼ *Monarda didyma*

m

⚉ *Monarda fistulosa*

⚉ *Monstera deliciosa*

⚉ *Monarda 'Croftway Pink'*

M. fistulosa (wild bergamot, purple bee balm) The lavender, lilac or pink narrow-lipped and tubular flowers are carried in crowded heads, about 4 cm (1½ in) across, over a long season, lasting all summer. This is a herbaceous perennial, with triangular or lance-shaped mid green leaves, which are about 10 cm (4 in) long. HEIGHT & SPREAD 1 m × 40 cm (3 ft × 16 in).

M. menthifolia (mint-leaved bergamot) Pale pink flowers are borne in crowded heads 2.5 cm (1 in) across. The lance-shaped mid green leaves of this herbaceous perennial are 8 cm (3¼ in) long and often have serrated edges. HEIGHT & SPREAD up to 75 × 40 cm (30 × 16 in).

M. punctata (horsemint) The yellowish purple dotted flowers are carried in whorls up to 2.5 cm (1 in) across at the apex of the stem. Under each flower there are yellowish or purple bracts. This biennial or short-lived perennial has lance-shaped mid green leaves that are 1.5–10 cm (½–4 in) long. HEIGHT & SPREAD 1 m × 40 cm (3 ft × 16 in).

RECOMMENDED CULTIVARS

These cultivars usually bloom for a long period in summer. They grow to a height of 1–1.2 m (3–4 ft).

'Aquarius' has light mauve flowers with dark green foliage. **'Beauty of Cobham'**♀ bears pale pink flowers with a dark purplish calyx. **'Blaustrumpf'** ('Blue Stocking') with dark lilac flowers, is very vigorous. **'Cambridge Scarlet'**♀ has red flowers with a plum-red calyx. **'Capricorn'** has purple flowers. **'Croftway Pink'**♀ carries salmon-pink flowers. **'Fishes'** ('Pisces') has strong pink flowers with a green calyx. **'Kardinal'** has purple-tinted red flowers. **'Mahogany'** bears deep wine-red flowers. **'Prärienacht'** ('Prairie Night') carries dark lilac flowers. **'Schneewittchen'** ('Snow Maiden') is less robust, with small white flowers. **'Squaw'** is a vigorous grower with vermilion flowers.

CULTIVATION Plant in autumn or spring in sun or partial shade. Monardas prefer moist spots, but will grow in most soils if given adequate bulky organic manure or compost. The more vigorous cultivars can be invasive in wetter soils. Remove dead

flowerheads as the flowers fade. Mulch each year and replant every 3 years. Annual species should be sown directly into the flowering position in spring. Staking is not usually required.

PROPAGATION Divide species and cultivars in spring. Species can also be raised from seed sown under glass in spring and planted out later in the year.

PESTS AND DISEASES Usually trouble free.

Moneywort see *Lysimachia nummularia*
Monkey flower see *Mimulus*
Monkey puzzle see *Araucaria araucana*
Monkshood see *Aconitum*

Monstera
Araceae

The Swiss cheese plant is the only species of these evergreen scrambling plants to be widely grown in this country, as a house and greenhouse plant. *Monstera deliciosa* is grown for its very large, glossy leathery leaves, which have deeply cut margins and irregular holes. The arum-like flowers are rarely produced under domestic conditions, because plants do not achieve sufficient size and maturity. Plants need a warm environment out of direct sunlight with a minimum temperature of 15°C (59°F). Given the right conditions, Swiss cheese plants are easily cared for and can grow very rapidly.

RECOMMENDED SPECIES

M. deliciosa (Swiss cheese plant) A robust, woody-stemmed, scrambling plant with large rounded or heart-shaped leaves up to 30 cm (12 in) long and as much across carried on long stalks. The leaves have either regular or irregular perforations according to the maturity of a particular part of the plant. Older leaves have the most pronounced incisions and holes, while young leaves are heart-shaped and often unbroken. The leaves densely clothe the scrambling stem, which is generally grown attached to a moss-covered pole or framework. Apart from the usual compost roots the plant also

produces trailing aerial roots up to 60 cm (24 in) long. These should be left alone unless they become unsightly and must never be pushed into the compost. Native to tropical Central America. HEIGHT & SPREAD 3 m × 75 cm (10 × 2½ ft) under ordinary domestic conditions.

'Variegata' has leaves irregularly splashed with cream and yellow patches.

CULTIVATION Grow in a richly organic potting compost, such as John Innes No 3, plus as much as a third by volume of composted bark. Keep the soil moist but not waterlogged, and mist the foliage with clear water every day. If the plant is growing on a moss pole, ensure that the moss remains damp. Remove faded leaves and trim back wayward growths to maintain the desired shape.

PROPAGATION Take leaf-bud or stem-tip cuttings in summer. Air layering in summer is also successful.

PESTS AND DISEASES Scale insects and mealy bugs can be a nuisance.

Montbretia see *Crocosmia*

⚉ *Monstera deliciosa 'Variegata'*

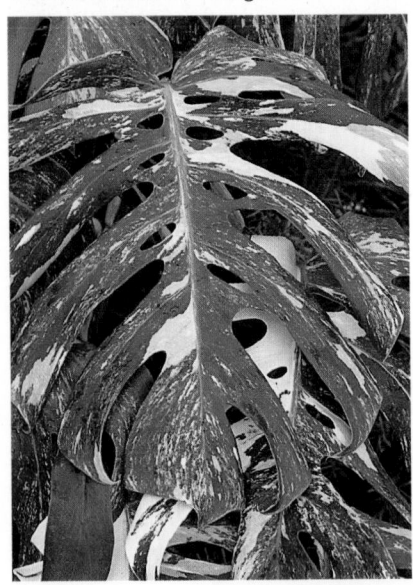

Morina
Whorlflower
Morinaceae

Prominent whorls of small tubular flowers spring from the axils of short, spiny bracts on this hardy perennial in summer. The elegantly arching, prickly, evergreen foliage forms a rosette at the base of the plant. Grow in a herbaceous border or as a single specimen in a bed of smaller plants. Plants are short-lived and require well-drained soil and protection from cold winds. Of the numerous European and central Asian species, only one species, native to the Himalayas, is commonly grown in British gardens.

RECOMMENDED SPECIES
M. longifolia Tubular flowers, up to 2.5 cm (1 in) long, each with 5 widely expanded petals, arch down from a circlet of 15-20 opening buds from early to mid summer. They are white on opening, then turn pink and deepen to crimson on fading. The dark green, narrowly oblong basal leaves, up to 30 cm (12 in) long, have wavy, spiny edges and a strong central vein. Shorter leaves are borne on the stems. HEIGHT & SPREAD 60-90 × 30-45 cm (24-36 × 12-18 in).

CULTIVATION Plant in spring in a sheltered sunny or partially shaded spot and in well-drained, moisture-retentive soil. In cold areas, protect plants in winter.

PROPAGATION Sow seeds as soon as they are ripe or in spring. Plants dislike disturbance, but young plants with multiple crowns may be carefully divided immediately after flowering. Or detach lateral growth with a narrow, pointed trowel or knife. Take root cuttings in spring.

PESTS AND DISEASES Poor drainage may cause plants to rot, otherwise trouble free.

❦ *Morina longifolia*

Morisia
Cruciferae

Bright and cheerful yellow flowers are clustered posy-like on this low-growing, hardy, evergreen perennial from the coastal sands of Corsica and Sardinia. It does well in a trough, a rock garden or in any sharply drained soil. It also makes an excellent pot specimen for an unheated, well-ventilated greenhouse. There is only one species.

Morisia monanthos (syn. *M. hypogaea*) Each plant bears many bright yellow, 4-petalled flowers, 1.5 cm (½ in) across, carried on short erect stalks in spring and early summer. Numerous radiating, deep green and shiny, pinnate leaves up to 8 cm (3¼ in) long form neat rosettes. HEIGHT & SPREAD 5 × 10 cm (2 × 4 in).

'Fred Hemingway' has flowers of a deeper yellow, that are also slightly larger.

❦ *Morisia monanthos* 'Fred Hemingway'

CULTIVATION Plant morisias in very well-drained, gritty soil or compost in full sunshine. Protect plants growing outdoors from excessive winter wet with a cloche or sheet of glass placed overhead.

PROPAGATION Sow seed in winter or early spring in a coldframe, or take root cuttings in early spring.

PESTS AND DISEASES Aphids may infest plants indoors. Red spider mite may be a problem when plants are grown under glass.

Morning glory see *Ipomoea purpurea*

Morus
Mulberry
Moraceae

There are few more permanent features in a garden than a mulberry tree, which may live for several hundred years. Hardy, deciduous and slow-growing, these trees form shapely, dense, spreading canopies of large, toothed leaves. They carry edible raspberry-like fruits in summer and autumn. After fast early growth, the bark becomes attractively knarled. Mulberries are self-fertile, with inconspicuous male and female flowers forming separate yellow-green catkins in spring. Both the white and black mulberry grow best in Britain in the south. In colder areas, plant mulberries against a south-facing wall. The black mulberry is the easier to grow and has sweeter fruit. If space is limited *Morus alba* 'Pendula' is best.

RECOMMENDED SPECIES AND VARIETIES
M. alba (white mulberry) The shiny, heart-shaped, light green leaves are about 12 cm (5 in) long and the fruits are white changing to light red. Native to China. HEIGHT & SPREAD 4 × 3 m (13 × 10 ft) in 20 years, ultimately 9 × 10 m (30 × 33 ft).

The weeping cultivar **'Pendula'**♀ is a smaller neater tree. The largest known specimen measures 4 × 4 m (13 × 13 ft).

❦ *Morus alba* 'Pendula'

M. nigra♀ (black mulberry) This picturesque, often leaning tree has coarse dark green leaves, heart-shaped, 15 cm (6 in) long, which turn golden yellow in autumn. The abundant red-black fruits, up to 2.5 cm (1 in) long, are delicious. Native to W Asia. HEIGHT & SPREAD 5 × 4 m (16 × 13 ft) after 20 years, ultimately 9 m (30 ft) tall.

CULTIVATION Cool well-drained soil and a sunny spot should produce robust mulberry

❦ *Morus nigra*

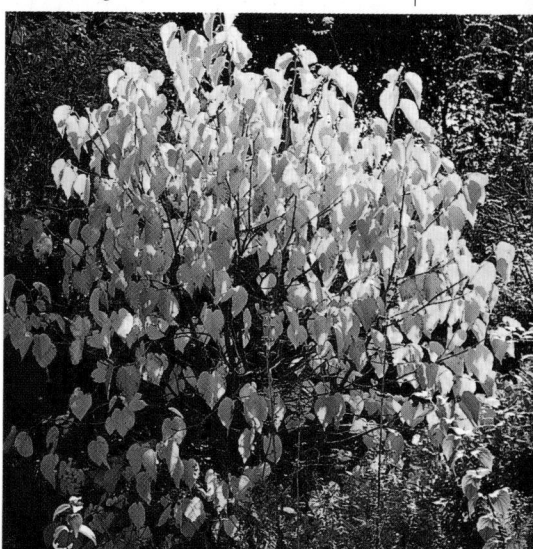

trees. They need protection from cold winds in exposed areas.

PROPAGATION Take care when planting not to damage or expose the fleshy roots. Hardwood cuttings taken in mid winter do well; use quite long shoots of the previous season's growth and dig them well in.

PRUNING Avoid pruning. If necessary for shaping or controlling size, prune between late autumn and late winter to prevent sap from bleeding.

PESTS AND DISEASES Die-back, often associated with nectria canker, can infect pruning wounds or storm-damaged branches.

Mother-in-law's tongue
see *Sansevieria trifasciata*
Mountain avens see *Dryas octapetala*
Mouse plant see *Arisarum proboscideum*

Muehlenbeckia

Polygonaceae

Clusters of tiny flowers are borne by these twiggy shrubs in summer. Both species included here are evergreen and hardy. *Muehlenbeckia axillaris* is a useful ground-cover plant and *M. complexa* forms a bushy shrub or twining climber. The flowers are followed by white, succulent fruits, which enclose small, three-sided, black nuts. Some plants bear flowers of only one sex, others of both. Native to New Zealand.

RECOMMENDED SPECIES

M. axillaris The slender wiry branches of this prostrate shrub are clothed with small, rounded leaves 5 mm (¼ in) across. In mid summer, racemes of yellowish to white flowers are borne on short stalks. HEIGHT & SPREAD 5 cm × 1 m (2 in × 3 ft) after 5 years, ultimately 30 cm (1 ft) tall.

M. complexa Greenish yellow flowers are carried on spikes up to 4 cm (1½ in) long in early and mid summer. Leaves are rounded and 1.5 cm (½ in) across. Plants vary: some are dense, tangled shrubs with stiff, wiry branches and leathery leaves, others have long, slender, trailing or twining branchlets and softer leaves. HEIGHT & SPREAD of the climber, 6 × 6 m (20 × 20 ft) after 5 years and ultimately; of the shrub, 1 × 1.5 m (3 × 5 ft) after 5 years, ultimately 1.8 m (6 ft) tall.

CULTIVATION Plant in well-drained soil in sun or partial shade. Provide support for the climbing form of *M. complexa*.

PROPAGATION Sow seed when ripe or in late winter. Layer or take semi-ripe cuttings in summer.

❧ *Muehlenbeckia axillaris*

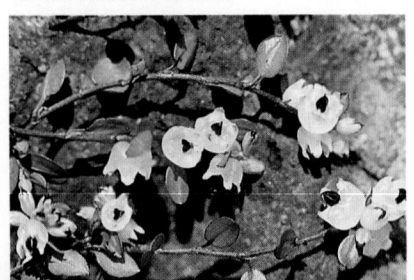

PRUNING Cut back in spring or summer if the plants become rampant.
PESTS AND DISEASES Usually trouble free.

Mugwort, white see *Artemisia lactiflora*
Mulberry see *Morus*
Mullein see *Verbascum*

Musa

Banana
Musaceae

Grown for the exotic appearance of their foliage, flowers and fruit, these tender ever-green perennials create a lush, tropical atmosphere in conservatories and large, brightly sunlit rooms. The fresh green leaves are up to 1.2 m (4 ft) long. Each oblong leaf has a stiff midrib with the rest of the leaf hanging slightly away from it as it arches out from the top of the 'trunk'.

RECOMMENDED SPECIES AND VARIETIES

M. acuminata 'Dwarf Cavendish'♀ (syn. *M. cavendishii*) Yellow flower spikes are borne in summer, with red or purple bracts on a drooping stem. Small yellow bananas follow, which may be eaten. HEIGHT & SPREAD 2.4 × 3 m (8 × 10 ft).

M. basjoo Flowerheads with brown bracts and yellow flowers appear in summer. As a conservatory plant, its eventual height may cause problems, so cut it back to encourage shooting from the base. HEIGHT & SPREAD 2.4 × 1.5 m (8 × 5 ft).

M. cavendishii see *M. acuminata* 'Dwarf Cavendish'

CULTIVATION Grow in a 60 cm (24 in) pot in full sunlight. Keep *M. acuminata* at a

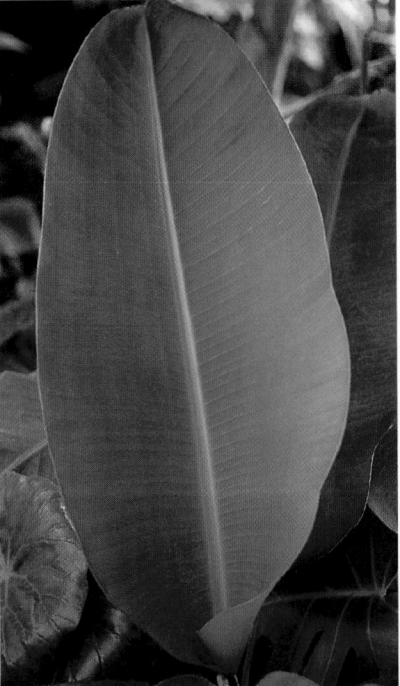

⚘ *Musa acuminata* 'Dwarf Cavendish'

temperature of around 21°C (70°F) during active growth and above 10°C (50°F) in winter. *M. basjoo* does best at slightly lower temperatures. Ensure good humidity and avoid draughts. Water generously in summer and sparingly in winter. Apply a high-potash feed weekly during the growing season. Repot young plants in spring, but fully grown plants just require regular feeding. Cut back to the base after flowering to stimulate new shoots.

PROPAGATION Divide plants with multiple crowns or sow seed (available from exotic-seed merchants) in spring. The seed is very hard and should be filed and soaked in warm water for 2 days before sowing.

PESTS AND DISEASES Red spider mite, the only serious pest, is aggravated by dry air.

Muscari

Grape hyacinth
Hyacinthaceae

Muscari armeniacum

These spring-flowering bulbs produce dense spikes of fragrant, globular, blue flowers. Most are very hardy and easy to grow. Grape hyacinths make ideal companion plants for all other bulbs that flower at the same time, particularly daffodils and tulips. The narrow, strap-shaped, mid green leaves are up to 30 cm (12 in) long.

Muscaris are best grown in a sunny well-drained position in a rockery or border; they tolerate light shade, but too shady a spot prevents flowering. Some multiply rapidly and some species, including *Muscari neglectum*, can be invasive. Native to the Mediterranean and SW Asia.

RECOMMENDED SPECIES AND VARIETIES

M. ambrosiacum see *M. muscarimi*

M. armeniacum♀ Densely packed, purple-blue flowers are borne in long unbranched clusters in mid spring among narrow semi-erect leaves. HEIGHT 15–20 cm (6–8 in).

'Blue Spike' is a double form with large heads of minute dark blue flowers tipped with greenish yellow. 'Cantab' has light blue flowers with a white rim and 'Saffier' has dark blue flowers with a white rim.

M. aucheri♀ (syn. *M. tubergenianum*) The bright blue, early spring flowers have white rimmed mouths and are almost spherical; they are paler at the top of the long, dense spikes. HEIGHT 20 cm (8 in).

M. azureum♀ Compact, bell-shaped flowers, pale to bright blue with a darker narrow

⚘ *Muscari azureum* 'Album'

stripe on the lobes, are carried on short dense spikes in early spring. The plant tolerates light shade and thrives in borders as well as rockeries. HEIGHT 10-15 cm (4-6 in).

'Album' has pure white flowers, which are sweetly scented.

M. botryoides Dense spikes of bright blue flowers with a white rim appear from early to mid spring; the leaves are narrow and erect. HEIGHT 20 cm (8 in).

'Album' has narrow clusters of pure white flowers.

M. comosum (tassel hyacinth) The lower flowers are brownish green and those at the top of the spike, on longer stalks, are bright violet to mauve. They are carried in loose clusters in late spring to early summer. HEIGHT 10-30 cm (4-12 in).

'Plumosum' bears a large open cluster of thread-like, mauve-blue, sterile florets.

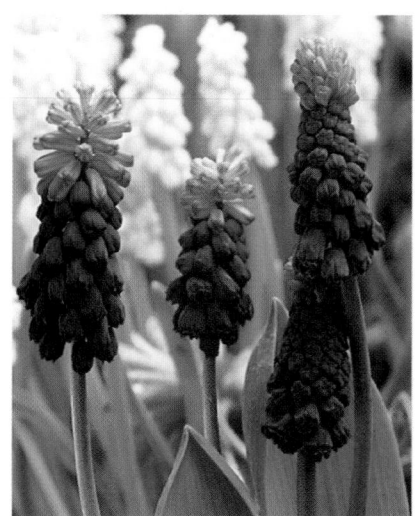

⚘ *Muscari latifolium*

M. latifolium The fragrant flowers are dark violet-blue at the bottom, paler at the top. They are carried in long clusters in mid to late spring. Each plant has one strap-shaped, grey-green leaf. HEIGHT 15-30 cm (6-12 in).

M. macrocarpum (syn. *M. muscarimi* var. *flavum*, *Muscarimia macrocarpum*) Clusters of sweetly scented bright yellow flowers appear in late spring among the broad

⚘ *Muscari muscarimi*

grey-green leaves. The plant requires a hot, sunny site. HEIGHT 15-20 cm (6-8 in).

M. muscarimi (syn. *M. ambrosiacum*, *M. moschatum*, *Muscarimia ambrosiacum*) The musky scented flowers, purplish at first, fading to yellowish green then ivory, are borne on lax racemes in late spring. Plant in a sunny position. The leaves, which emerge in autumn, are almost evergreen. HEIGHT 15 cm (6 in).

M. neglectum (syn. *M. racemosum*) This is the most common species. It grows freely and so is useful for naturalising in shrub borders. Fragrant flowers, in dense spikes in early and mid spring are dark blue with a white rim at the mouth; they are paler at the top of the spike. HEIGHT 30 cm (12 in).

M. tubergenianum see *M. aucheri*

CULTIVATION Grape hyacinths grow in almost any reasonably well-drained soil in sun or light shade. Plant the bulbs 5-8 cm (2-3¼ in) deep, between late summer and late autumn. Most species can be grown in pots, tubs or window boxes.

PROPAGATION Lift and divide the bulbs every 3-4 years during summer, when they are dormant. Sow from seed from mid summer onwards in a frame or outdoors. They should flower in 3-4 years.

PESTS AND DISEASES Usually trouble free.

Musk see *Mimulus moschatus*

Mutisia
Compositae

Showy daisy-like flowers are borne by these exuberant evergreen perennial climbers in summer and autumn. The plants cling and climb by means of tendrils. They are not fully hardy – grow them outdoors in a sheltered position, with their roots in well-drained soil in the shade and their heads in

the sun, or under the protection of a greenhouse or conservatory, where they will thrive more reliably. Native to S America.

RECOMMENDED SPECIES

M. decurrens Vivid orange flowers, up to 10 cm (4 in) across, bloom throughout summer. Lance-shaped mid green leaves, up to 12.5 cm (5 in) long, grow on untidy, multibranched stems. The plant is difficult to establish outdoors, where it needs the protection of a south or west-facing wall. HEIGHT & SPREAD 2×1 m (6½×3 ft).

M. ilicifolia Flowers up to 7.5 cm (3 in) across, with lilac pink petals raying from yellow discs, are produced throughout summer and into early autumn. Mid green oval leaves, up to 5 cm (2 in) long, cover vigorous scrambling stems. HEIGHT & SPREAD 3×1 m (10×3 ft).

CULTIVATION In spring plant in well-drained soil in a sheltered place outside or in a greenhouse border. If pot-grown, use a soil-based medium, such as John Innes No.3. In a conservatory provide shade; outdoors plant beneath an established shrub, which acts as a climbing frame. Trim back untidy growth in spring.

PROPAGATION Sow seeds under glass in spring or plant stem cuttings in summer. Layer semi-ripe stems in late summer or early autumn.

PESTS AND DISEASES Greenfly can often be a nuisance.

Myosotidium
Chatham Island forget-me-not
Boraginaceae

Myosotidium hortensia

Blue forget-me-not flowers and large, deep-veined shiny green leaves characterise this rare evergreen herbaceous perennial from Chatham Island, east of New Zealand. It is not reliably hardy, except in very sheltered gardens, but can be cultivated in a greenhouse or conservatory. There is only one species in the genus.

Myosotidium hortensia (syn. *M. nobile*) Dense heads of flowers up to 15 cm (6 in) across appear in early summer, carried high above the 30 cm (12 in) long oval to kidney-shaped leaves. This is not an easy plant to establish so, once growing, do not move. The plant needs protection from strong cold winds, which would damage the large leaves, and suits a cool, moist site, perhaps close to a water feature or under the light shade of trees or shrubs to offer protection from the midday sun. HEIGHT & SPREAD 45×60 cm (18×24 in).

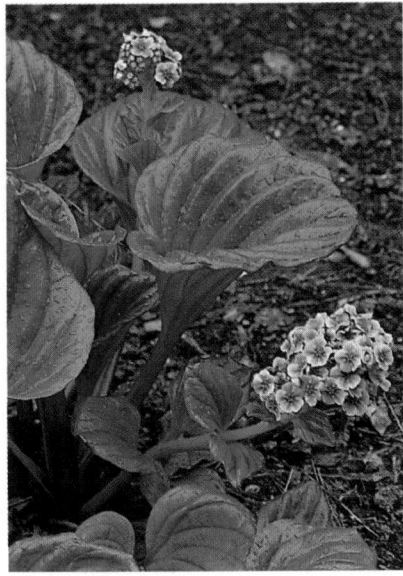

⚘ *Myosotidium hortensia*

CULTIVATION Plant in fertile moist soil in spring, in a sheltered site. Top-dress annually in spring with seaweed, if possible. During severe weather, protect with branches and coarse leaves and bracken.

In pots, plant in peat-based compost in spring as seedlings come into growth.

PROPAGATION Divide with care in spring. Sow seed under glass, as soon as it is ripe, or in autumn, and plant out the following spring, after the last frosts.

PESTS AND DISEASES Usually trouble free.

Myosotis
Forget-me-not
Boraginaceae

Carpets of these blue flowers are a favourite sight in late spring. The species described are short-lived perennials or biennials and make dwarf-tufted clumps or mats suitable for growing in beds or borders, in rock gardens or under glass. *Myosotis scorpioides* is a moisture-loving plant and thrives at the water's edge. The flowers, each about 1 cm (⅜ in) across, are carried in flat-topped clusters and the simple leaves are arranged alternately. The cultivars of *M. alpestris* and *M. sylvatica* are grown as biennials. Forget-me-nots thrive in any well-drained soil, in full sun or – preferably – in light shade.

RECOMMENDED SPECIES AND VARIETIES

M. alpestris (syn. *M. rupicola*) Azure-blue fragrant flowers with distinctive yellow eye are borne in dense sprays from mid to late spring. This tufted hardy perennial with oval to oblong leaves is suitable for a rock garden. Native to Europe. HEIGHT & SPREAD 10-20×20 cm (4-8×8 in).

'**Ruth Fischer**' has light blue flowers.

M. australis Small white or yellow flowers appear in early summer. The upright plant carries tufts of greenish brown hairy leaves.

This native of Australia and New Zealand is usually grown in a rock garden. HEIGHT & SPREAD 25×20 cm (10×8 in).

M. colensoi (syn. *M. decora*) White flowers are carried either singly or in clusters in early summer. This is a mat-forming perennial with narrowly oval to lance-shaped hairy leaves. It requires well-drained but not dry soil with adequate humus. Plant in a rock garden, a scree or an unheated well-ventilated greenhouse. Native to New Zealand. HEIGHT & SPREAD 5×20 cm (2×8 in).

M. decora see *M. colensoi*

M. palustris see *M. scorpioides*

M. rupicola see *M. alpestris*

M. scorpioides (syn. *M. palustris*) (water forget-me-not) Sky-blue flowers with yellow eyes are borne throughout summer. This perennial is for moist areas of the garden, especially pond margins. It is a loose-growing evergreen that spreads by rhizomes. The elongated spoon-shaped leaves are hairy. Native to Europe. HEIGHT & SPREAD 15-30×25 cm (6-12×10 in).

'**Mermaid**' produces small bright blue flowers on branching stems from tufts of shiny green leaves.

M. sylvatica Fragrant blue flowers are carried in open sprays from late spring to early summer. This tufted biennial has narrowly oblong to lance-shaped, mid green, hairy

⚘ *Myosotis scorpioides*

⚘ *Myosotis scorpioides* '**Mermaid**'

leaves. Native to Europe. HEIGHT & SPREAD 30×15 cm (12×6 in).

'**Blue Ball**'♀ is compact with blue flowers, growing to 15 cm (6 in) tall. '**Carmine King**', with carmine flowers, has an upright habit and grows to a height of 20 cm (8 in). '**Indigo**' and '**Royal Blue**' both have very deep blue flowers and are about 30 cm (12 in) tall. '**Spring Symphony Mixed**' is 20 cm (8 in) tall and '**Victoria Mixed**' reaches a height of 15 cm (6 in); blue, pink and white shades are available.

CULTIVATION Forget-me-nots are very hardy and will thrive in most situations, though they do best in light shade. Plant in early or mid autumn in any reasonable well-drained garden soil. Plant *M. scorpioides* in heavy fertile loam at water level or covered by up to 3 cm (1¼ in) of water. Position in sun or partial shade.

PROPAGATION Sow seed outdoors in early summer. Thin seedlings to 8 cm (3¼ in) apart once established. *M. scorpioides* can be divided in spring.

PESTS AND DISEASES Aphids may be troublesome. Powdery mildew can be very damaging in a dry spring.

Myrica
Myricaceae

myrica gale

The leaves of these plants release a delightful aroma when crushed. Male and female flowers, in the form of catkins, produced either on the same plant or on different plants, are borne in profusion in spring or summer. Most of the evergreen or deciduous plants in the genus are shrubs but some are small trees. They are very undemanding plants and will thrive under a wide range of conditions. The species described below tolerates extremely exposed sites and boggy conditions. Australia is the only place where the genus is not represented.

RECOMMENDED SPECIES

M. gale (sweet gale, bog myrtle) Sweetly fragrant, narrow, glossy, dark green leaves, up to 5 cm (2 in) long, are the chief feature of this hardy, deciduous, multistemmed, upright shrub. They are preceded by dense clusters of small golden brown catkins – up to 10 in a cluster – in late spring or early summer. Male and female catkins are most frequently on separate plants. Female catkins are the slightly fatter of the two. Native to Europe, N America and N Asia. HEIGHT & SPREAD 1 m×60 cm (3×2 ft) after 5 years, ultimately 1.5×2-3 m (5×6½-10 ft).

CULTIVATION Plant from late autumn to early spring in lime-free garden soil. Do not allow the plant to dry out immediately after planting. It thrives in very wet conditions and in full sun but will stand some shade.
PROPAGATION Sow seed in early to mid spring. Layer plants in autumn for planting the following autumn.
PESTS AND DISEASES Usually trouble free.

Myrrhis
Sweet cicely
Umbelliferae

Myrrhis odorata

Fern-like leaves surrounding umbrellas of white flowers are a pleasing spectacle near a pond or stream and in a wild garden. Prominent black seed heads, which provide a dramatic contrast to the pale green leaves, can be added to salads, when still green, and make excellent dried foliage once ripe. The leaves are also of culinary use. The scent of aniseed distinguishes this hardy perennial, which is native to the mountains of S Europe and prefers damp but not waterlogged conditions. There is only one species in the genus.
Myrrhis odorata A mass of tiny flowers with unequal petals open in tight clusters 5-7.5 cm (2-3 in) across from late spring to mid summer. They are supported on tall,

▼ *Myrrhis odorata*

hollow, branched stems with prominent basal sheaths. Long-stalked leaves up to 30 cm (12 in) high are produced in a clump at the base of the plant. Each has 2 or 3 soft green leaflets, usually blotched white at the bottom, with deeply cut lobes. HEIGHT & SPREAD 60-100×60-100 cm (2-3×2-3 ft).
CULTIVATION Plant between autumn and spring in moist but well-drained soil in sun or partial shade. Remove seeds to prevent self-seeding.
PROPAGATION Sow seed where required in spring, or when ripe. The main roots are difficult to divide so use any small plants that have self-sown.
PESTS AND DISEASES Watch for aphids, slugs and snails. Carrot flies are attracted by the aromatic foliage.

Myrtle see *Myrtus*
Myrtle, bog see *Myrica gale*

Myrtus
Myrtle
Myrtaceae

These evergreen shrubs are grown for their fragrant summer flowers and glossy foliage, which is aromatic when crushed. Each saucer-shaped, five-petalled flower has a prominent boss of slender stamens. Myrtus will not withstand prolonged periods of frost and flourishes in British gardens only in milder areas. It often does well in gardens close to the sea. In cooler regions, grow plants in pots in a frost-free greenhouse and take them outside for the summer.
RECOMMENDED SPECIES AND VARIETIES
M. apiculata see *Luma apiculata*

▼ *Myrtus communis*

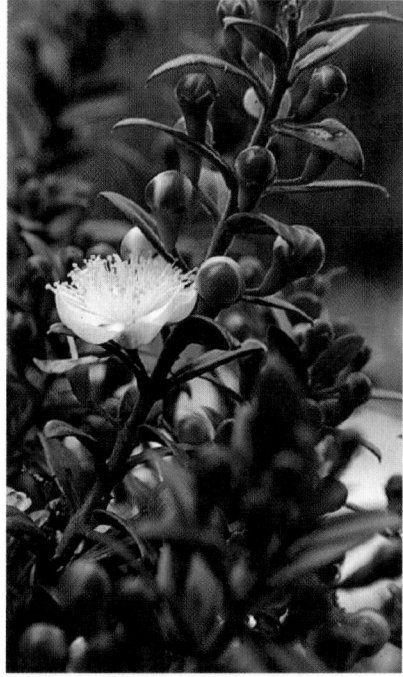

▲ *Myrtus communis* ssp. *tarentina*

M. communis♀ (common myrtle) This rounded many-stemmed shrub bears abundant white flowers in mid and late summer. The flowers measure up to 2 cm (¾ in) across. Small dark purple berries often follow in autumn. The deep green oval leaves grow to about 2.5 cm (1 in) long. Native to the Mediterranean and SE Europe. HEIGHT & SPREAD 1 m×60 cm (3×2 ft) after 5 years, ultimately 3 m (10 ft) tall.

A more compact plant, ssp. *tarentina*♀ (syn. 'Jenny Reitenbach', 'Microphylla', 'Nana') has smaller leaves, pink-tinged flowers and white berries. Its cultivar **'Microphylla Variegata'** has leaves that are variegated in colour.

'Variegata' is a cultivar of the species that has grey-green leaves edged with a narrow white band.
M. luma see *Luma apiculata*
CULTIVATION In milder regions, plant outdoors in late spring in any well-drained soil, choosing a sheltered position in full sun.

Alternatively, grow plants in pots of multipurpose compost in a cool greenhouse. Keep the compost just moist in winter, but in summer water more freely and provide plenty of ventilation. Plants grown in containers can be moved outside from late spring to early autumn, avoiding any periods of frost.
PRUNING Not normally required, but plants can be trimmed into shape in spring when frosts have passed.
PROPAGATION Sow seed under glass in early or mid spring or take semi-ripe cuttings in early or mid summer. Variegated varieties should be raised from cuttings if they are to come true to type.
PESTS AND DISEASES Usually trouble free.

Nandina
Sacred bamboo
Berberidaceae

Nandina domestica
'Firepower'

Grown chiefly for its beautiful and elegant foliage and autumn and winter colour, the one species in this genus also has attractive flowers and fruits. It is native to warm-temperate Asia.

Although the shrub is frost hardy, nandina needs a sheltered position in the garden. Somewhat similar to bamboo in appearance, nandina is actually closely related to berberis.

Nandina domestica♀ This evergreen or semi-evergreen shrub forms a clump of erect leafy stems. The leaves are divided into several narrow lance-shaped leaflets, up to 7 cm (2¾ in) long. They are green in summer, but reddish purple when young, turning a similar or brighter hue in the autumn and winter. In mid summer, large branched sprays of starry, creamy white flowers, each 1 cm (⅜ in) wide, appear at the tips of the stems. After a hot summer they are often followed by showy, spherical, bright red berries, 5 mm (¼ in) across. HEIGHT & SPREAD 1 m × 75 cm (3 × 2½ ft) after 5 years, ultimately 2 m (6½ ft).

'Firepower' is a smaller plant, growing to 1.2 m (4 ft) high and 60 cm (2 ft) wide. It has broader leaflets that colour more brightly in autumn.

'Richmond' is a large, vigorous, free-fruiting form with showy scarlet berries. It reaches a height of 2.4 m (8 ft) and spreads to 1.5 m (5 ft) wide.

CULTIVATION Plant in early spring, in fertile, well-drained, fairly moist soil in a sunny, sheltered position.

PROPAGATION Sow seed in early spring or take semi-ripe cuttings in summer.

PRUNING Cut out old and weak shoots to soil level in early spring.

PESTS AND DISEASES Nandina is usually trouble free.

Narcissus

Daffodil

Amaryllidaceae

———

These bold, cheerful harbingers of spring
dance in informal swathes in rough grass,
brighten banks and hedgerows, or stand
sentinel in formal borders

9 'Sabine Hay'
10 'Double Fashion'
11 'Tahiti'
12 'Sir Winston
Churchill'
13 'Acropolis'
14 'Unique'
15 'Ice Wings'
16 'Thalia'
17 'February Gold'
18 'Quail'
19 'Geranium'
20 'Soleil d'Or'
21 *N. pseudonarcissus*
ssp. *obvallaris*
22 'Mondragon'
23 'Cassata'
24 'Orangery'
25 'Tête-à-Tête'

1 'Dutch Master'
2 'Little Beauty'
3 'Bravoure'
4 'Salome'
5 'Rainbow'
6 'Carlton'
7 'Ipi Tombi'
8 'Saint Keverne'

Golden heads of daffodils among fresh green strap-like leaves are the epitome of spring. Although white daffodils are popularly referred to as narcissi, daffodil is the common name for all members of this genus. Almost all flower in late winter or early spring. Each bulb produces one or more flower stems, each with one or more blooms. Flowers range from 2.5-10 cm (1-4 in) across, with a central cup (corona) surrounded by six petals (perianth segments), which may be narrow and twisted or broad and flat. Colour varies from white to shades of yellow and orange-red or pink; daffodils are often bicoloured. In 'reversed bicolours', the cup is paler than the petals.

INDEX OF SPECIES & VARIETIES

———

In order to classify the many daffodil varieties they are grouped into 12 divisions.

(1) Trumpet daffodils
(2) Large-cupped daffodils
(3) Small-cupped daffodils
(4) Double daffodils
(5) Triandrus daffodils
(6) Cyclamineus daffodils
(7) Jonquilla daffodils
(8) Tazetta daffodils
(9) Poeticus daffodils
(10) Species and wild variants
(11) Split-corona daffodils
(12) Miscellaneous

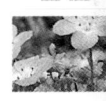

The following lists the daffodils covered in the book; the division appears in brackets.

'Acropolis' (4)
'Actaea' (9)
'Arctic Gold' (1)
'Arish Mell' (5)
'Bantam' (2)
'Bell Song' (7)
'Biscayne' (1)
'Bravoure' (1)
bulbocodium (10)
'Canaliculatus' (8)
'Cantabile' (9)
'Carlton' (2)
'Cassata' (11)
'Chanterelle' (11)
'Charity May' (6)
'Cheerfulness' (4)
cyclamineus (10)
'Daydream' (2)
'Dolly Mollinger' (11)
'Double Fashion' (4)
'Dove Wings' (6)
'Dutch Master' (1)
'Empress of Ireland' (1)

'February Gold' (6)
'February Silver' (6)
'Feeling Lucky' (2)
'Foundling' (6)
'Geranium' (8)
'Golden Aura' (2)
'Golden Rapture' (1)
'Hawera' (5)
'Ice Follies' (2)
'Ice Wings' (5)
'Ipi Tombi' (2)
'Irish Minstrel' (2)
'Jack Snipe' (6)
'Jenny' (6)
'Jetfire' (6)
jonquilla (10)
'Jumblie' (12)
'Kingscourt' (1)
'Liberty Bells' (5)
'Little Beauty' (1)
'Little Gem' (1)
'Little Witch' (6)
Loch Owskeich' (2)

'Merlin' (3)
'Minnow' (8)
'Mondragon' (11)
'Mount Hood' (1)
'Orangery' (11)
'Paper White' (8)
'Papillon Blanc' (11)
papyraceus (8)
'Passionale' (2)
'Peeping Tom' (6)
'Pencrebar' (4)
'Petrel' (5)
'Pinza' (2)
'Pipit' (7)
poeticus var. *recurvus* (10)
pseudonarcissus (10) ssp. *obvallaris* (10)
'Quail' (7)
'Rainbow' (2)
'Rijnveld's Early Sensation' (1)
'Rippling Waters' (5)
'Rip van Winkle' (4)
'Sabine Hay' (3)
'Saint Keverne' (2)
'Salome' (2)
'Segovia' (3)

'Sir Winston Churchill' (4)
'Soleil d'Or' (8)
'Spellbinder' (1)
'Sun Disc' (7)
'Sundial' (7)
'Suzy' (7)
'Sweetness' (7)
'Tahiti' (4)
'Telamonius Plenus' ('Van Sion') (4)
'Tête-à-Tête' (12)
'Thalia' (5)
'Trena' (6)
'Trevithian' (7)
triandrus (10)
'Tripartite' (11)
'Tuesday's Child' (5)
'Ulster Prince' (1)
'Unique' (4)
'Verona' (3)
'Vulcan' (2)
'W.P. Milner' (1)
'White Lion' (4)
'Xit' (3)
'Yellow Cheerfulness' (4)

▲ *Narcissus* 'White Lion'

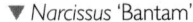

▲ *Narcissus* 'Arctic Gold'

Though mostly 40-60 cm (16-24 in) tall, there are shorter varieties and dwarf forms just 10-20 cm (4-8 in) high. The basal leaves appear at the same time as the flowers and are more or less strap-shaped. They elongate as the flowers fade and should not be removed until they begin to die back, to encourage the formation of a mature bulb for the following year. Most daffodils are suitable for massing under trees or shrubs; smaller varieties are ideal for the front of a border or a rock garden. The more vigorous varieties can be naturalised in grass.

With the exception of tazettas and some jonquils, most daffodils are hardy. Some, especially the smaller varieties, are suitable for containers. Do not, however, allow the pots to freeze right through.

(1) TRUMPET DAFFODILS
One flower is produced per stem with a trumpet that is as long or longer than the petals. HEIGHT 40-60 cm (16-24 in).

'Arctic Gold'♀ has well-shaped, clear yellow flowers with broad overlapping petals. 'Biscayne'♀ has yellow flowers. 'Bravoure'♀ is tall with white petals and a yellow trumpet. 'Dutch Master'♀ is a reliable golden hybrid with broad, smooth petals. 'Empress of Ireland'♀ has excep-

tionally large white flowers. 'Golden Rapture'♀ has large, well-shaped, golden-yellow flowers. 'Kingscourt'♀ is an excellent robust variety with rich golden yellow flowers. 'Little Beauty' is a perfect miniature, reaching just 15 cm (6 in) tall, with cream petals around a pale yellow trumpet. 'Little Gem'♀ is an early-flowering dwarf hybrid, reaching just 15 cm (6 in) tall with small yellow flowers. 'Mount Hood'♀ is vigorous with large, creamy white flowers.

'Rijnveld's Early Sensation'♀ is exceptionally early flowering (usually in mid or late winter). It has large yellow flowers on 30 cm (12 in) stems. 'Spellbinder'♀ bears flowers that open sulphur yellow, though the trumpet gradually fades to cream. 'Ulster Prince'♀ has golden yellow flowers. 'W.P. Milner' has very pale creamy yellow nodding flowers on 30 cm (12 in) stems and is excellent for naturalising.

(2) LARGE-CUPPED DAFFODILS
One flower is carried per stem with a cup that is more than one-third, but less than the whole length of the petals. HEIGHT is typically 40-60 cm (16-24 in).

'Bantam'♀, just 30 cm (12 in) tall, has well-rounded brilliant yellow flowers with an almost flat, bright red cup. 'Carlton'♀, vigorous and free flowering, has pale yellow flowers with a frilled cup. 'Daydream'♀ has white petals and a dark lemon yellow cup. 'Feeling Lucky'♀ is a striking hybrid with a bright red cup and yellow petals.

'Golden Aura'♀ bears well shaped golden flowers. The vigorous 'Ice Follies'♀ has creamy white petals around a widely flaring lemon yellow cup that gradually fades to cream. 'Ipi Tombi' is a large-flowered hybrid with yellow petals and a frilled orange cup. 'Irish Minstrel'♀ has white petals and a yellow cup.

'Loch Owskeich'♀ has large flowers with yellow petals and a clear orange cup.

'Passionale'♀ has broad, pointed white petals and a long, pale pink cup. 'Pinza'♀ has yellow petals and a deep orange-red cup. 'Rainbow'♀ has pure white petals and a pink-rimmed cup. 'Saint Keverne'♀ has golden yellow flowers and is resistant to basal rot. 'Salome'♀ has pure white petals and a pinkish orange cup. 'Vulcan'♀ has vivid yellow petals with an orange cup.

(3) SMALL-CUPPED DAFFODILS
One flower is carried per stem with a cup that is not more than one-third the length of the petals. HEIGHT 40-60 cm (16-24 in).

'Merlin'♀ has pure white petals and a red-rimmed yellow cup. 'Sabine Hay' has golden petals around a neat orange cup. 'Segovia' is a vigorous dwarf hybrid – just 20 cm (8 in) tall – with white petals and a lemon yellow cup. 'Verona'♀ has white flowers. 'Xit', a dwarf hybrid 18 cm (7 in) tall, has tiny 4 cm (1½ in) glistening white flowers. It is slightly tender.

(4) DOUBLE DAFFODILS
One or more flowers are carried on a stem. The petals, the cup or both may be double. HEIGHT 40-60 cm (16 in-2 ft).

'Acropolis' bears flowers whose broad outer petals are pure white while the inner petals are a mixture of white and orange-red. 'Cheerfulness'♀ bears 1-3 small, fully double, fragrant flowers of cream and pale yellow. 'Double Fashion' has large, well-shaped flowers with pale yellow outer petals and ruffled orange inner petals.

'Pencrebar' is a dwarf hybrid, reaching only 18 cm (7 in) tall, with 1-2 small double yellow flowers. 'Rip van Winkle' is an old cultivar valued for its ability to naturalise and its early flowering. It is 30 cm (12 in) tall and has rather uneven greenish yellow double flowers. 'Sir Winston Churchill'♀ bears multiple rounded blooms of white and pale yellow. 'Tahiti'♀ has strong stems of large, rounded, rich gold and orangey red blooms, good for cutting. 'Telamonius Plenus' ('Van Sion') is the common, early double yellow daffodil. Either the trumpet or the whole flower may be double.

'Unique'♀ has large rounded flowers with white outer petals and yellow inner ones. 'White Lion'♀ is a vigorous hybrid

▼ *Narcissus* 'Bantam'

Narcissus 'Ice Follies' ▼

Narcissus 'Cheerfulness' ▼

▼ *Narcissus* 'Pinza'

Narcissus 'Salome' ▼

Narcissus 'Vulcan' ▼

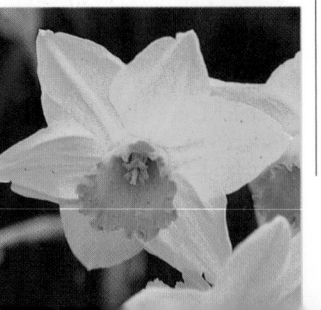

with pointed white petals interspersed with pale yellow ones. **'Yellow Cheerfulness'**♥ is a yellow version of 'Cheerfulness'.

(5) TRIANDRUS DAFFODILS
Resembling the parent species, *N. triandrus*, daffodils in this group usually have two or more pendent flowers, with reflexed petals, to a stem. HEIGHT 40-60 cm (16-24 in).

'Arish Mell' has up to 4 white flowers. **'Hawera'**♥ has 3-5 small, pale yellow nodding flowers. Each bulb produces a succession of 18 cm (7 in) stems. **'Ice Wings'**♥ bears 2-3 medium-sized white flowers with rather long trumpets. **'Liberty Bells'** has well-shaped lemon yellow flowers. **'Petrel'** has 3-7 small white nodding flowers on 30 cm (12 in) stems. **'Rippling Waters'**♥ has up to 3 white flowers and grey foliage. **'Thalia'** has rather star-like white flowers; it is good for naturalising. **'Tuesday's Child'**♥ has 1 or 2 well-shaped flowers with white petals around a yellow cup.

(6) CYCLAMINEUS DAFFODILS
The varieties in this group have the characteristics of *N. cyclamineus*, the parent species. There is usually one flower to a stem. The flower has a short pedicel (neck), is held at an acute angle to the stem, and its petals are strongly reflexed. Many of these hybrids are early flowering and are useful for growing under shrubs or for naturalising in grass. HEIGHT 30-60 cm (12-24 in).

'Charity May'♥ has early pale yellow flowers. **'Dove Wings'**♥ has white petals around a lemon yellow trumpet. **'February Gold'**♥ is early flowering with deep yellow flowers. **'February Silver'** has exceptionally long-lasting, large flowers with almost flat white petals around a yellow trumpet.

'Foundling'♥ has white petals and a salmon-pink cup. **'Jack Snipe'**♥ has white petals and short yellow cup. It is excellent

Narcissus 'Hawera'

▲ *Narcissus* 'Tuesday's Child'

for naturalising. **'Jenny'**♥ has pointed creamy white petals around a flared lemon trumpet that fades to cream. **'Jetfire'**♥ is a sturdy hybrid with yellow flowers. The trumpets gradually turn bright orange. **'Little Witch'** reaches 30 cm (12 in) tall at most, with small golden flowers. It is good in grass. Early-flowering **'Peeping Tom'**♥ has a long, golden yellow trumpet with a flared tip, surrounded by strongly reflexed petals. **'Trena'** has strongly reflexed white petals around a lemon yellow trumpet.

(7) JONQUILLA DAFFODILS
Resembling *N. jonquilla*, these daffodils carry 1-3, often fragrant, flowers per stem. The petals are spreading, but not reflexed. Daffodils within this group require full sun. HEIGHT 30-40 cm (12-16 in).

▲ *Narcissus* 'Pipit'

'Bell Song' bears up to 3 white flowers with small pink cups; **'Pipit'**♥, 1 or 2 reversed bicolour flowers in lemon yellow with paler cups; **'Quail'**♥, 2-3 scented yellow flowers, with rather long cups; **'Sun Disc'**♥, a tiny solitary yellow flower, which fades to cream, on a 20 cm (8 in) stem; **'Sundial'**♥, 1 or 2 small early yellow flowers on a 20 cm (8 in) stem; **'Suzy'**♥, 1-4 deep yellow flowers with orange cups; **'Sweetness'**♥, single, small, golden and very fragrant flowers; and **'Trevithian'**♥, which has pale lemon yellow flowers.

(8) TAZETTA DAFFODILS
Daffodils in this group resemble *N. tazetta*. There are 3-20 flowers to each stout stem, depending on the variety. The petals are spreading and the flowers are mostly fragrant. The leaves are broad. These daffodils are less hardy than most and are prone to frost damage. HEIGHT 40 cm (16 in).

'Canaliculatus' has grey leaves and up to 7 tiny pure-white flowers with yellow cups to each 25 cm (10 in) stem. **'Geranium'**♥ is a vigorous hybrid with 3-4 pure-white, broad flowers with orange cups. 'Minnow' has 2-4 tiny creamy yellow flowers on a 25 cm (10 in) stem. 'Paper White' (syn. *N. papyraceus*) is a well-known early tazetta, usually forced for early winter flowering. Each stem carries up to

▲ *Narcissus* 'Suzy'

Narcissus 'Sweetness' ▲

10 tiny, pure white, highly scented flowers. The fragrant but tender **'Soleil d'Or'** has many small, golden yellow flowers with orange cups.

(9) POETICUS DAFFODILS
These daffodils clearly show the characteristics of the *N. poeticus* group without admixture from any other. There is usually one fragrant flower to a stem with pure white petals and a flat, disc-shaped cup. This group is usually late flowering, and care must be taken to provide sufficient moisture. HEIGHT 30-40 cm (12-16 in).

'Actaea'♥ has an early large, round flower with white petals and small red-rimmed cup. **'Cantabile'**♥ has a small, perfectly round white flower with a red-rimmed cup and green eye.

(10) SPECIES AND WILD VARIANTS
This group covers all species and wild or reputedly wild variants and hybrids, including those with double flowers. All differ greatly in their cultural requirements, most being unsuitable for general garden use. They make excellent pot plants for an alpine house. Most are increased by seed.

N. bulbocodium♥ (hoop petticoat) The flowers of this variable species have round, expanded trumpets and tiny, narrow yellow petals. The leaves are grass like. The plant needs a moist acid soil that dries out in summer. HEIGHT 10-25 cm (4-10 in).

N. cyclamineus♥ has narrow, deep yellow trumpets and long, completely reflexed yellow petals. It self-seeds freely in a cool, acid soil. HEIGHT 25-30 cm (10-12 in).

N. jonquilla♥ Up to 4 tiny golden yellow flowers appear rather later than most in mid

▲ *Narcissus* 'Geranium'

▲ *Narcissus bulbocodium*

to late spring. This strongly fragrant species is easy to grow in well-drained, limy soils in full sun. HEIGHT 30-40 cm (12-16 in).

N. poeticus var. *recurvus*♀ (pheasant's eye narcissus) White, strongly scented flowers with slightly reflexed petals and tiny red-rimmed, green-eyed cups appear later than most in late spring. Bulbs may take a while to establish. Lack of moisture in late spring can cause blindness. HEIGHT 36 cm (14 in).

N. pseudonarcissus♀ (Lent lily) Narrow, twisted, sulphur-yellow petals almost clasp the creamy trumpets. It needs soil that is not too dry and can take years to become established. Once settled, it can self-sow to cover large areas. HEIGHT 25-36 cm (10-14 in).

The vigorous ssp. *obvallaris*♀ (Tenby daffodil) is early-flowering, up to 30 cm (12 in) tall, and ideal for naturalising in grass. The clone in cultivation is sterile.

N. triandrus♀ Up to 4 flowers are carried per stem, each with a rounded cup and fully reflexed petals. This species can be naturalised in dry, acid soils or grown in a pot in an alpine house. HEIGHT 10-20 cm (4-8 in).

(11) SPLIT-CORONA DAFFODILS
Sometimes referred to as collar, orchid or papillon daffodils, the cup is split, forming an inner coloured layer.

'Cassata' has flat flowers with yellow inner petals laid evenly over white outer ones. 'Chanterelle' has white flowers with yellow centres. 'Dolly Mollinger' has white petals and orange centres.

'Mondragon' has golden cups and pale yellow petals; 'Orangery', white petals and orange cups; 'Papillon Blanc', white flowers; and 'Tripartite', 2-3 yellow flowers.

(12) MISCELLANEOUS
Daffodils not falling into any other division are grouped here.

'Jumblie'♀ is a vigorous dwarf hybrid with up to 3 flowers per 18 cm (7 in) stem and many stems per bulb. A deep gold trumpet is surrounded by paler, narrow, fully reflexed petals. 'Tête-à-Tête'♀ is a dwarf hybrid with 1-3 small yellow flowers per 15 cm (6 in) stem.

CULTIVATION Plant bulbs in autumn. Most grow in any soil but will not tolerate waterlogged conditions. While in growth, they need sun for at least part of the day, and

late-flowering varieties should be watered in dry periods. Plant species narcissi, that naturally increase by self-seeding, singly, and hybrids in groups of one variety.

Deadhead hybrids as soon as the flowers fade, both for appearance and to encourage a larger bulb to form, but leave the seed heads of species to ripen.

PROPAGATION Remove offsets of hybrid daffodils in autumn or lift and divide the clumps as the leaves turn yellow after flowering. Increase species by sowing seed as soon as it is ripe in early summer. Seedlings can take up to 7 years to flower.

PESTS AND DISEASES Waterlogged soils can cause fungal attacks. Narcissus fly and stem and bulb eelworm can attack bulbs.

Nasturtium see *Tropaeolum*
Navelwort see *Umbilicus rupestris*
Nectarine see p.727

Nectaroscordum

Alliaceae

Bell-shaped flowers flushed flesh pink and dark red, with a greenish tinge towards the base, are borne in loose arrangements of up to 40 florets. These easily grown spring-flowering bulbs, hardy to -12°C (10°F), can become invasive. They have a pungent onion smell and the strap-shaped leaves give off a similar odour when crushed. After flowering, the stalks bend upwards to hold the off-white to brownish seedpods erect. Pods are 1 cm (⅜ in) long and diamond-shaped. The genus, formerly included in

▼ *Nectaroscordum siculum*

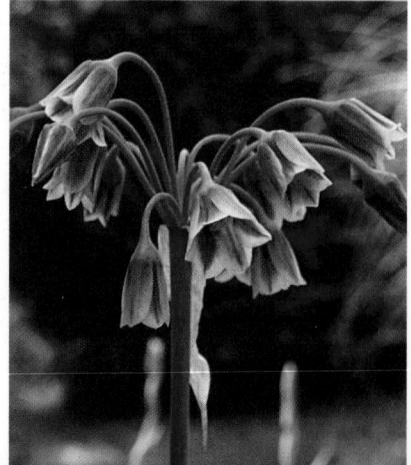

allium, is native to the E Mediterranean.
RECOMMENDED SPECIES AND VARIETIES
N. siculum (syn. *Allium siculum*) (Sicilian honey garlic) Pale greenish cream flowers, suffused with greenish red, appear from mid to late spring in rounded clusters 7.5 cm (3 in) across. HEIGHT 1 m (3 ft).
N. siculum bulgaricum Up to 30 flowers, larger and with less red than *N. siculum*, are carried in each cluster during late spring and early summer. HEIGHT 1 m (3 ft).
CULTIVATION Grow in any good garden soil in sun or partial shade. Plant between late summer and late autumn, 5 cm (2 in) deep and 25-40 cm (10-16 in) apart.
PROPAGATION Sow seed in sandy soil in late summer and plant out after two seasons.
PESTS AND DISEASES Can suffer from white onion rot.

Nemesia

Scrophulariaceae

Grown for their abundant, brightly coloured, trumpet-shaped flowers, this genus includes half-hardy annuals and herbaceous perennials. The annuals make good summer bedding plants; the perennial species can be grown in a cool greenhouse and moved outside in summer. Some will survive outdoors over winter in mild areas. All species have narrow, toothed, opposite leaves, that are usually pale green.
RECOMMENDED SPECIES AND VARIETIES
N. caerulea (syn. *N. foetens*, *N. fruticans* hort.) Yellow-centred lilac flowers, 1.5 cm (½ in) across, bloom from early summer to early autumn on this dwarf, half-hardy perennial. The leaves are up to 4 cm (1½ in) long. HEIGHT & SPREAD 30×75 cm (1×2½ ft).

'Joan Wilder' has deep lavender blue flowers; 'Innocence' has white flowers and 'Woodcote', purple flowers.
N. denticulata The scented, pinky-purple flowers of this perennial – which can survive winter outdoors – are about 1 cm (⅜ in) across; its leaves are up to 4 cm (1½ in) long. HEIGHT & SPREAD 25×30 cm (10×12 in).
N. foetens see *N. caerulea*
N. fruticans hort. see *N. caerulea*
N. strumosa Profuse yellow, white or

▼ *Nemesia caerulea* 'Joan Wilder'

purple flowers with yellow throats, about 2.5 cm (1 in) across, appear in summer. The leaves of this annual are up to 7.5 cm (3 in) long. HEIGHT & SPREAD 30×20 cm (12×8 in).

Varieties tend to be slightly smaller than the species: 'Blue Gem' has brilliant blue flowers with prominent white stamens; the mixed colours of **Carnival Series** include cream, orange, pink, purple and yellow; 'KLM' has blue and white flowers, and 'Mello Red & White' is also bicoloured.

CULTIVATION Plant in late spring or early summer, after the risk of frost, in moisture-retentive soil in a sunny, sheltered position. Water frequently in dry weather. Cut back hard after first flowering for repeat flowering. Lift perennials in early autumn and overwinter in pots in a cool greenhouse. If *N. denticulata* is left to winter outdoors, do not cut the old flowering stems until spring.
PROPAGATION Sow seeds under glass in early spring. Take softwood cuttings of perennials in early spring or semi-hardwood cuttings in late summer.
PESTS AND DISEASES Poor greenhouse hygiene may cause foot rot.

Nemophila
Hydrophyllaceae

Distinctively marked flowers characterise this Californian genus of hardy annuals. The two species described flower from summer into autumn – most profusely in cool wet weather. Their low-growing habit makes nemophilas suitable for the edges of borders, rock gardens and containers.

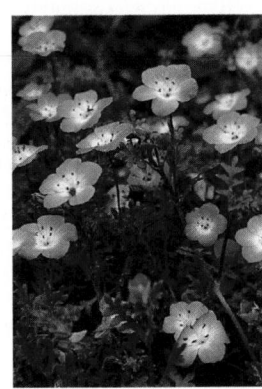

▲ *Nemophila maculata*
Nemophila menziesii ▲

RECOMMENDED SPECIES AND VARIETIES
N. insignis see *N. menziesii*
N. maculata (five spot) White flowers, up to 4 cm (1½ in) across, appear from early summer to mid autumn. Each of the 5 petals bears purple veins and a deep violet blotch at the tip. The spreading, semi-prostrate plant has pale green, deeply lobed leaves. HEIGHT & SPREAD 15×20 cm (6×8 in).
N. menziesii (syn. *N. insignis*) (baby blue eyes) Sky-blue, white-centred, 5-petalled flowers, up to 4 cm (1½ in) across, grow on

the long succulent stems of this spreading plant from early summer to mid autumn. The pale green, downy leaves are deeply lobed. HEIGHT & SPREAD 20×30 cm (8×12 in).

'Pennie Black' has deep purple-petalled flowers with white edges. 'Snowstorm' is finely spotted with black on the innermost two-thirds of each white petal.
CULTIVATION Nemophilas thrive in moisture-retentive soil, in sun or partial shade. Shelter the fragile, succulent stems from wind and support them with short twigs. Water generously in dry weather.
PROPAGATION Sow seed in mid spring where plants are to grow. Early autumn sowings – successful in all but the coldest areas of the country – result in larger plants which are early to flower.
PESTS AND DISEASES Attacked by aphids.

Neoregelia
Bromeliaceae

The shiny, strap-like foliage of these evergreen, rosette-forming, tropical plants changes colour when the flowers appear. The centre of the leaf rosette forms an urn-like hollow that holds water and from which the flowerheads emerge. These bromeliads can be grown as houseplants but are best cultivated in a heated greenhouse.
RECOMMENDED SPECIES AND VARIETIES
N. carolinae (blushing bromeliad) Arching, bright green, finely toothed leaves are about 45 cm (1½ ft) long. The centre of the rosette turns red in mid summer when the flowers are produced. These are purple-blue and tubular with 3 petals, up to 3 cm (1¼ in) long, and borne in a compact cluster among bright red bracts. HEIGHT & SPREAD 30×45 cm (1×1½ ft).

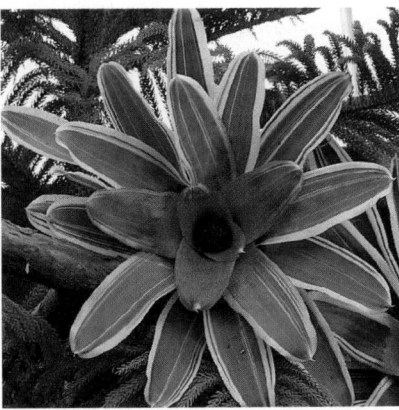

▲ *Neoregelia carolinae* Meyendorffii Group 'Flandria'

Meyendorffii Group 'Flandria' (syn. *Nidularium flandria*) has narrow leaves, up to 35 cm (14 in) long, radiating from the central urn. Each is striped green and cream ending with cream edges. The base of the leaf rosette turns crimson when the flowers appear. Bright blue-mauve flowers with red

bracts are 2.5 cm (1 in) long and only just emerge from the central urn. The most widely grown variety, f. *tricolor*♀, has yellow and green striped leaves.
CULTIVATION Plant in pots of equal parts loam-based compost and bark chips, or in soil-less compost. Place in a warm room or heated greenhouse with a minimum temperature of 10°C (50°F), high humidity, and plenty of light, but not full sun. Water by filling the central urn in the leaf rosette with soft water. Mist daily. Feed monthly from spring to late summer with a liquid houseplant feed. Remove faded flowers.
PROPAGATION Remove and replant offsets during spring and early summer.
PESTS AND DISEASES Usually trouble free.

Nepeta
Labiatae

Nepeta × faassenii 'Six Hills Giant'

Tiny flowers in shades of blue, purple, yellow and white are borne in summer in delicate, hazy spikes above often silvery foliage. These are formed of clusters of blooms along the upper part of the stems.

Individual flowers are tubular or funnel-shaped with two lips: the upper lip is upright, the lower lip more spreading, and both lips are prominently lobed. The leaves are often hairy with toothed edges and, in some species, are aromatic. Cats are particularly attracted to *Nepeta cataria*. The herbaceous perennials have a loose, spreading habit. Native to Europe, N Africa and Asia, most are hardy, but *N. nepetella* may need winter protection in colder districts.
RECOMMENDED SPECIES AND VARIETIES
N. 'Blue Beauty' see *N. sibirica* 'Souvenir d'Andre Chaudron'
N. cataria (catnip, catmint) White flowers are dotted with violet. Both the upright stems and aromatic foliage are hairy and greyish green with leaves up to 4 cm (1½ in) long. HEIGHT & SPREAD 1 m×60 cm (3×2 ft).
'Citriodora' has light blue flowers and is lemon-scented.
N. × faassenii This plant has pale lavender flowers and hairy, silver-grey, aromatic leaves about 3 cm (1¼ in) long. HEIGHT & SPREAD 60×60 cm (2×2 ft).
'Six Hills Giant' grows up to 1 m (3 ft) and has darker lavender flowers.
N. glechoma see *Glechoma hederacea*
N. govaniana Pale yellow flowers are borne in loose spikes. Pointed, mid green leaves are up to 10 cm (4 in) long. A more upright

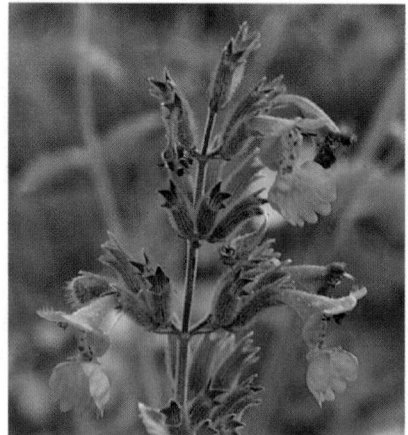

▲ *Nepeta × faassenii* 'Six Hills Giant'

plant, it prefers cool, moist conditions. HEIGHT & SPREAD 1m×60cm (3×2ft).

N. hederacea see *Glechoma hederacea*

N. lanceolata see *N. nepetella*

N. macrantha see *N. sibirica*

N. mussinii see *N. racemosa*

N. nepetella (syn. *N. lanceolata*) This compact plant has abundant pinkish white flowers and narrow grey-green leaves. HEIGHT & SPREAD 60×60cm (2×2ft).

N. nervosa This species has dense spikes of pale blue flowers and aromatic, narrow, mid green leaves up to 10cm (4in) long. HEIGHT & SPREAD 35×60cm (14in×2ft).

N. racemosa (syn. *N. mussinii*, *N. reichenbachiana*) A spreading plant with violet to lilac-blue flowers. The grey-green, aromatic leaves are about 3cm (1¼in) long. HEIGHT & SPREAD 30×60cm (1×2ft).

'Snowflake' has white flowers. 'Little Titch' is just 15cm (6in) tall.

N. sibirica (syn. *N. macrantha*) Large lavender blue flowers are borne in loose spikes on this upright plant. The aromatic, narrow, dark green leaves, are about 7cm (2¾in) long. HEIGHT & SPREAD 1m×60cm (3×2ft).

'Souvenir d'Andre Chaudron' (syn. *N.* 'Blue Beauty') reaches 50cm (20in) in height and spreads vigorously. It has grey-green leaves and soft blue flowers.

▲ *Nepeta nervosa*

Nepeta racemosa ▲

CULTIVATION Plant in early spring in any well-drained soil in full sun, although *N. govaniana* prefers moist soil and part shade. Deadhead to prolong flowering. Clip back plants used for edging after flowering.

PROPAGATION Divide in early spring or take softwood cuttings in late spring. Sow fresh seed in late summer or early autumn.

PESTS AND DISEASES Powdery mildew can be troublesome in hot, dry summers.

Nephrolepis see FERNS p.264

Nerine
Amaryllidaceae

Nerine bowdenii

Airy pink nerine trumpets adding a bright splash to a border in autumn are likely to be those of *Nerine bowdenii*. This is the hardiest species of this genus of autumn-flowering, bulbous perennials from southern Africa: most are frost tender and need greenhouse protection in Britain. The wavy petalled trumpets are carried in 7.5-13cm (3-5in) clusters on graceful stems. They are bright red, pink or white and bloom for several weeks. The strap-shaped, mid green leaves, 30-45cm (1-1½ft) long, usually appear after the flowers.

RECOMMENDED SPECIES AND VARIETIES

N. bowdenii♀ Stout stems bear umbels (umbrella-like clusters) of up to 8 pink to deep rose flowers. HEIGHT 45cm (1½ft).

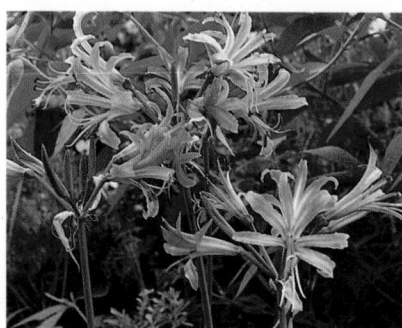

▲ *Nerine bowdenii*

'Mark Fenwick' is taller and more vigorous with soft pink flowers. 'Pink Triumph' has deep pink flowers.

CULTIVATION Grow most nerines in frost-free conditions in a cool greenhouse.

The hardier *N. bowdenii* can be planted outdoors in early to mid spring or late autumn in any free-draining garden soil, preferably near a warm wall. Plant bulbs

with their tips just below the soil surface; bury deeper in colder areas. Feed in early spring with a light dressing of fertiliser. Take bulbs grown in tubs indoors in winter.

PROPAGATION Nerines do best when left undisturbed, but if the bulbs become overcrowded, lift and divide in summer when the foliage dies down. Sow seeds in a sandy, well-drained soil. They will reach flowering size in 2-3 years depending on the species.

PESTS AND DISEASES Protect nerines from slugs and snails.

Nerium
Apocynaceae

Showy blossoms are produced throughout summer and into autumn on these tender evergreen shrubs. *Nerium oleander* is the only species in the genus, although there are many cultivated varieties. All parts of the plant are toxic; keep sap away from eyes.

▲ *Nerium oleander*

Nerium oleander (oleander) Papery pink or white flowers, up to 5cm (2in) across, and sometimes scented are usually borne in clusters on this upright shrub. The mid to deep green leaves are lance-shaped and up to 15cm (6in) long. HEIGHT & SPREAD 2×1m (6½×3ft) after 5 years, ultimately 6m (20ft).

'Géant des Batailles' has deep red double flowers; 'Luteum Plenum', large double yellow flowers; 'Peach Blossom', soft pink flowers; 'Professeur Granel'; semidouble orange-red flowers; 'Roseum Plenum', fully double rose-pink flowers; and 'Variegatum', cream-yellow and green variegated foliage with soft pink flowers.

CULTIVATION Grow in large pots of soil-based compost in a well-ventilated greenhouse and ensure a minimum temperature of 10°C (50°F). Move plants outside in summer and keep well watered. Feed with a liquid tomato feed from late spring until late summer. Remove any faded flowers.

PROPAGATION Take semi-ripe cuttings during summer.

PRUNING Trim out any unwanted shoots as they appear and cut back hard to the woody framework in spring so that the plant can be completely reclothed in fresh growth.

PESTS AND DISEASES Greenfly, mealy bugs and scale insects can cause problems.

Nertera
Bead plant
Rubiaceae

Freely produced, rounded or pear-shaped red or orange fruits can completely cover these creeping and readily rooting alpines or pot plants between late summer and mid autumn. Little yellow funnel-shaped flowers open in late spring but are stemless, and so small that they are hidden among the mats of tiny evergreen leaves. Not all the species are hardy and only three are commonly cultivated in Britain. These have an almost limitless spread once established but are not easy to grow: they are very shallow rooted and must be kept moist. The genus is native to Australia, New Zealand, Chile, the Pacific islands and central S America.

RECOMMENDED SPECIES AND VARIETIES
N. balfouriana Tiny bright green leaves form a compact mat. Pear-shaped orange berries are about 8 mm (⅜ in) long. Usually cultivated as an alpine house plant, it can be grown outdoors if kept constantly moist. HEIGHT & SPREAD 5 mm×25 cm (¼×10 in).
N. depressa Open mats of small spade-shaped shiny leaves have an offensive smell when crushed. This fast-growing species, which has rounded red berries about 4 mm (⅛ in) across, can be grown outside but is best moved to an alpine house in winter. HEIGHT & SPREAD 1×30 cm (⅜ in×1 ft).

▲ *Nertera granadensis*

N. granadensis Rounded, matt, light green leaves, and 8 mm (⅜ in) orange berries characterise this compact species which is often incorrectly sold as *N. depressa*. It is not fully hardy and is usually grown as a pot plant. HEIGHT & SPREAD 1×30 cm (⅜ in×1 ft).
CULTIVATION Plant in spring and summer in rich soil and keep moist to prevent the shallow roots from drying out. Move to a cool, well-ventilated greenhouse in winter.
PROPAGATION Divide in spring or sow ripe berries on the surface of the soil. Keep moist at all times.
PESTS AND DISEASES Slugs and snails may cause damage.

Nettle, flame see *Solenostemon*
Nettle, painted see *Solenostemon*
Nettle tree see *Celtis*
New Zealand bur see *Acaena*

Nicandra
Shoo fly plant
Solanaceae

Bell-shaped flowers open for a single day from summer to autumn on this showy hardy annual, followed by spherical green fruits, enclosed in a yellow winged calyx. The Peruvian genus consists of a single species, whose common name results from a reputation for repelling flies.

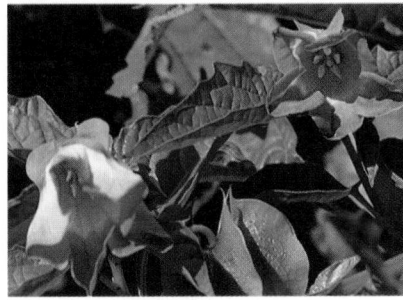

▲ *Nicandra physalodes*

N. physalodes Violet-blue, white-throated flowers, 4 cm (1½ ft) across, appear singly from mid summer to early autumn among mid green foliage. This fast-growing hardy annual has branching stems and elliptical or lance-shaped leaves up to 10 cm (4 in) long. Spherical green fruits, known as apples of Peru, up to 5 cm (2 in) across, follow the flowers. HEIGHT & SPREAD 90×30 cm (3×1 ft).
CULTIVATION Grow in a sunny spot in rich, well-drained soil where plants are to flower. Water freely in dry spells and feed occasionally with liquid tomato fertiliser.
PROPAGATION Sow seeds into open ground in spring. Thin crowded seedlings.
PESTS AND DISEASES Usually trouble free.

Nicotiana
Tobacco plant
Solanaceae

Profuse clusters of tubular, five-petalled flowers are borne for long periods during summer and autumn. The blooms of flowering tobacco, *Nicotiana alata*, only open in the evening to release their powerful scent. Modern hybrids have a less intense fragrance but their flowers open throughout the day. Most nicotianas have large, oval, mid green leaves. The plants recommended below are herbaceous perennials but are mostly grown as half-hardy annuals. All parts of these S American natives are toxic.

RECOMMENDED SPECIES AND VARIETIES
N. alata (syn. *N. affinis*) (flowering tobacco) White flowers, 10 cm (4 in) long, are borne on this sticky plant from mid summer to mid autumn. HEIGHT & SPREAD 1 m×40 cm (3 ft×16 in), or more.
'Lime green' has yellow-green flowers.
N. langsdorffii♀ Pale green, scentless flow-

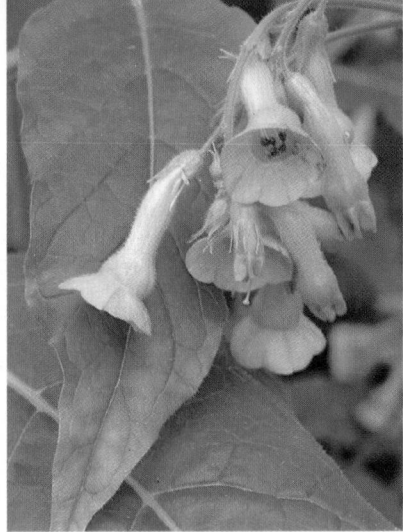

▲ *Nicotiana langsdorffii*

ers, 5 cm (1 in) long, are carried in drooping sprays from mid summer to mid autumn. HEIGHT & SPREAD 1.5 m×40 cm (5 ft×16 in).
N. x sanderae Slightly fragrant flowers, 7.5 cm (3 in) long, bloom in loose clusters from early summer until the first autumn frost. HEIGHT & SPREAD 60×30 cm (2×1 ft).
Domino Series comes in mixed colours or separately – in crimson, lime, salmon-pink and white. The flowers tilt upwards. Plants reach 30 cm (1 ft) tall. **'Havana Apple Blossom'**, 35 cm (14 in) tall, has flowers that are rose-pink outside and very pale pink inside. The flowers of **'Havana Lime Rose'**, 35 cm (14 in) tall, are yellow-green outside and rose-pink inside. **Merlin Series** seed is available in mixed colours only. Plants are 25 cm (10 in) high. **Nicki Series**, 40 cm (16 in) tall, is available as mixed colours or in pink. The **Sensation Series** is available in mixed colours only. The plants can reach 1 m (3 ft) in height.
N. sylvestris♀ Pendulous, slender, fragrant white flowers, 9 cm (3½ in) long, are borne in clusters in late summer. They close in full sun. The leaves are fiddle-shaped. HEIGHT & SPREAD 1.5 m×75 cm (5×2½ ft).
CULTIVATION Plant in spring, in moist, fertile soil, in a sheltered site in full sun or light shade, after the danger of frost has passed. Deadhead regularly. If treating plants as perennials, cut stems to just above ground level after the first hard autumn frosts and protect with a dry mulch.
PROPAGATION Sow seed in early spring in a heated greenhouse.
PESTS AND DISEASES Young plants are liable to attacks from aphids and slugs.

▲ *Nicotiana sylvestris*

Nidularium
Bromeliaceae

The foliage of these evergreen, rosette-forming, tropical bromeliads changes colour when plants are in flower. The leaves around the central urn-like hollow turn red. Within the hollow, small tubular flowers are borne from time to time, mostly in summer. Plants may be grown in the home, but the best results are obtained in humid conditions in a heated greenhouse or conservatory. Native to Brazil.

RECOMMENDED SPECIES AND VARIETIES

N. flandria see *Neoregelia carolinae* Meyendorffii Group 'Flandria'

N. innocentii (bird's nest bromeliad) The strap-shaped, finely toothed, mid green leaves, with purple or blood-red undersides, are up to 30 cm (1 ft) long. Papery red bracts encircle the white flowers. HEIGHT & SPREAD 30×45 cm (1×1½ ft).

'**Striatum**' has several narrow, yellow stripes down the length of each green leaf.

N. regelioides The mid green leaves are mottled with purple. Each leaf is strap-shaped, finely toothed and up to 35 cm (14 in) long. They surround a central rosette of shorter leaves that colour red when the plant bears its red flowers. HEIGHT & SPREAD 30×60 cm (1×2 ft).

▲ *Nidularium regelioides*

CULTIVATION Grow in pots of soil-less compost and feed twice during the growing season. Alternatively, grow in bark chips and feed monthly between late spring and late summer with a liquid houseplant feed. Keep in a heated greenhouse or conservatory or a warm room at a minimum temperature of 10°C (50°F). Nidulariums enjoy high humidity. Provide plenty of light but protect from exposure to full sun. Water freely into the centre of the rosettes, using soft water. Remove faded flowers.

PROPAGATION Remove and replant off-sets during spring and early summer.

PESTS AND DISEASES Usually trouble free.

Nierembergia
Cupflower
Solanaceae

Nierembergia repens

Cup-shaped blooms, in shades of blue, violet or white, bring charm to a sunny border for many weeks in summer. The herbaceous perennials described below will grow in any garden soil, generally preferring a moist but sunny situation. All can be grown in containers to make colourful edging to a patio or terrace. Two species – *Nierembergia caerulea* and *N. scoparia* – are tender and usually treated as annuals, grown each year from seed or from overwintered cuttings. Native to S America.

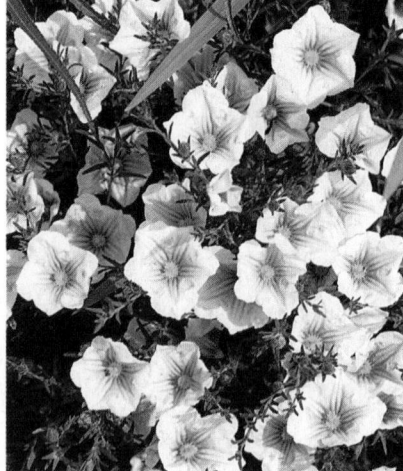

▲ *Nierembergia caerulea*

RECOMMENDED SPECIES AND VARIETIES

N. caerulea♀ (syn. *N. hippomanica*) This woody-based perennial bears a long succession of 2 cm (¾ in) wide, lilac-blue to pale violet flowers with a yellow throat from early summer to early autumn. Slender, branching stems also carry small, pointed, paddle-shaped, mid green leaves up to 8 cm (3¼ in) long. It is a very floriferous plant for a rock garden or border front. HEIGHT & SPREAD 30×20 cm (12×8 in).

N. frutescens see *N. scoparia*

N. hippomanica see *N. caerulea*

N. repens (syn. *N. rivularis*) This plant forms a low carpet of light green, spatular-shaped leaves up to 3 cm (1¼ in) long. From early to mid summer 3 cm (1¼ in) wide, white, cup-shaped flowers with yellow eyes are in bloom. The plant is hardy to -10°C (14°F). HEIGHT & SPREAD 5×60 cm (2×24 in).

'**Violet Queen**' has a similar habit, but the flowers are a deep violet.

N. rivularis see *N. repens*

N. scoparia (syn. *N. frutescens*) This bushy plant has a similar habit to *N. caerulea*, but is a little taller with narrower leaves and pale to deep violet flowers. HEIGHT & SPREAD 36×20 cm (14×8 in).

CULTIVATION Plant in spring in well-drained soil in a warm, sunny place. Propagate the tender species regularly or lift them for the winter. *N. repens* grows best in dry sandy soils and can spread excessively.

PROPAGATION The tender perennials are easily raised either from cuttings taken at any time during summer or from seed sown under glass in spring. Divide *N. repens* in spring.

PESTS AND DISEASES Aphids and whitefly cause problems under glass; slugs and snails damage plants out in the open.

Nigella
Ranunculaceae

Abundant, dainty, summer flowers are set against the feathery, deep green leaves of these hardy annuals. They also have inflated seed heads that are an attractive feature for some weeks after flowering has ended. Nigellas are easy to grow and self-seed readily. The flowers last well when cut and the seed heads can be used fresh or dried in floral arrangements. Each flower has a prominent cluster of stamens and styles at the centre. The leaves are finely divided.

RECOMMENDED SPECIES AND VARIETIES

N. damascena (love-in-a-mist) Blue, pink or white flowers, about 4 cm (1½ in) across, bloom on upright stems in early or mid summer. A ring of small, finely divided bracts extends, ruff-like, around the petals. HEIGHT & SPREAD 50×25 cm (20×10 in).

All the cultivars listed below have semi-double flowers. '**Dwarf Moody Blue**' has sky-blue flowers. It reaches a height of 20 cm (8 in) and a spread of 15 cm (6 in). '**Miss Jekyll**' has sky-blue flowers. '**Mulberry Rose**' has pale pink flowers, darkening as they age. '**Persian Jewels**' come in mixed colours. '**Shorty Blue**' has dark violet-blue flowers. It reaches 20 cm (8 in) in height and a spread of 15 cm (6 in).

▲ *Nigella damascena*

▲ *Nigella damascena* 'Persian Jewels'

N. hispanica (fennel flower) Blue, pink or white flowers, up to 6 cm (2½ in) across, appear on erect stems in early summer. HEIGHT & SPREAD 50×25 cm (20×10 in).

'Curiosity' has deep blue flowers with maroon stamens.

N. nigellastrum Star-shaped green-white flowers, tinged with red and about 1.5 cm (½ in) across, bloom in early summer. HEIGHT & SPREAD 40×20 cm (16×8 in).

'Summer Stars' has sky-blue flowers.

CULTIVATION Plant in spring in any garden soil in full sun. Deadhead to prolong the flower display.

PROPAGATION Sow seed where the plants are to grow in spring. In southern Britain and sheltered gardens elsewhere, sow seed in late summer where the plants are to grow. Thin the seedlings to 20 cm (8 in) apart. Move self-sown seedlings in spring. To grow *N. damascena* 'Dwarf Moody Blue' and *N. d.* 'Shorty Blue' as spring-flowering pot plants, sow seed in a cool greenhouse in early autumn.

PESTS AND DISEASES Usually trouble free.

Ninebark see *Physocarpus opulifolius*

Nomocharis
Liliaceae

Nomocharis aperta

Very showy lily-like flowers are borne by these hardy bulbous plants in mid summer. They can be a little tricky to grow, preferring partial shade and a rich organic soil which is damp but free draining. They grow best in areas of Britain where the climate is predominantly cool and moist.

Allow plants to become well established and avoid disturbing them. Plants in this genus are native to the Himalayas and W China.

RECOMMENDED SPECIES

N. aperta Pink flowers of a flattened star-shape, with red spotting on the petals and maroon blotches at the base, are up to 10 cm (4 in) across. There are as many as 6 on each stem, Lance-shaped leaves, up to 10 cm (4 in) long, clothe the elegant flower stems. HEIGHT & SPREAD 60×15 cm (24×6 in).

▲ *Nomocharis aperta*

N. farreri Soft pink saucer-shaped flowers with maroon spots and blotches towards the centre are up to 10 cm (4 in) across. The flowers are borne up to 10 each stem and start from a pendent position then turn upwards once fully open. The dark green lance-shaped leaves are 4 cm (1½ in) long and are produced in whorls up the flower stems. HEIGHT & SPREAD 90×15 cm (36×6 in).

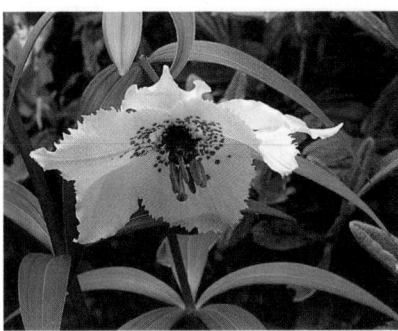

▲ *Nomocharis farreri*

N. pardanthina Nodding star-like flowers, up to 10 cm (4 in) across, have fringed petals which vary from white to pink and are blotched with maroon or dark purple at the base. There are up to 10 flowers on each stem. The dark green, lance-shaped leaves are up to 10 cm (4 in) long and are carried in whorls around the flower stems. HEIGHT & SPREAD 90×15 cm (36×6 in).

N. saluenensis This is the easiest species to grow. Up to 6 horizontal or star-like blooms are produced on each stem. The flowers are rose to pale rose-pink with dark central patches of maroon accompanied by small maroon spots. Dark green, lance-shaped leaves, up to 4 cm (1½ in) long, clothe the elegant flower stems. HEIGHT & SPREAD 75×15 cm (30×6 in).

CULTIVATION Plant bulbs 7.5–10 cm (3–4 in) deep in late autumn or spring in a richly organic moist soil with good drainage, in a semi-shaded area. Do not allow bulbs to dry out during the summer growing period. Apply a slow-release fertiliser in spring. Remove faded flowers.

PROPAGATION Sow seed in a coldframe in autumn and prick out into trays in late spring with the minimum of disturbance.

PESTS AND DISEASES Slugs and snails are the greatest problem, although greenfly can also be a nuisance. Lily beetle can be a problem in southern Britain.

Nothofagus
Southern beech
Fagaceae

Nothofagus obliqua

These deciduous or evergreen trees make fast-growing specimens suitable for a large lawn. The leaves are generally small. Insignificant flowers are produced in spring. The species listed here are from Argentina and Chile, except for *Nothofagus solandri*, from New Zealand. None of them are fully hardy in areas of prolonged or late frost.

RECOMMENDED SPECIES AND VARIETIES

N. alpina see *N. nervosa*

N. antarctica (Antarctic beech) The glossy green leaves of this upright, deciduous tree turn yellow in autumn. Just 2.5 cm (1 in) long, they are tightly clustered on the stems and have a very crinkled appearance. HEIGHT & SPREAD 5×2.4 m (16×8 ft) after 20 years, ultimately 15 m (50 ft) tall.

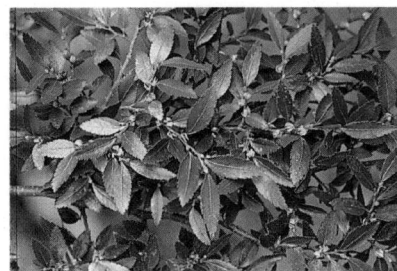

▲ *Nothofagus dombeyi*

N. dombeyi This upright, conical, semi-evergreen tree has small, dark green leaves, up to 2.5 cm (1 in) long. HEIGHT & SPREAD 10×4 m (33×13 ft) after 20 years, ultimately 20 m (66 ft) tall.

N. nervosa (syn. *N. procera*, *N. alpina*) (Rauli beech) This handsome, deciduous tree of upright habit has pale green leaves,

n

✦ *Nothofagus antarctica*

4-10 cm (1½-4 in) long, with prominent veins and a rather crinkled appearance. They turn pale gold and crimson in autumn. HEIGHT & SPREAD 8×3 m (26×10 ft) after 20 years, ultimately 20 m (66 ft) tall.

N. obliqua (Roble beech) The leaves of this upright, deciduous tree are pale green above, blue-green beneath, to 8 cm (3¼ in) long. HEIGHT & SPREAD 6×3 m (20×10 ft) after 20 years, ultimately 25 m (80 ft) tall.

N. procera see *N. nervosa*

N. pumilio This evergreen tree has a narrow, conical appearance with very open branches. The leaves, to 3 cm (1¼ in) long, are dark green, edged with small blunt teeth. HEIGHT & SPREAD 5.5×2.4 m (18×8 ft) in 20 years, ultimately 15 m (50 ft) tall.

N. solandri var. *cliffortioides* This evergreen tree bears small leaves, 1.5 cm (½ in) long, light green with a wavy edge. HEIGHT & SPREAD 4.5×2 m (15×6½ ft) after 20 years, ultimately 12 m (40 ft) tall.

CULTIVATION Plant in open ground from mid autumn to mid spring, avoiding frost or dry conditions. Do not plant in chalky soils.

PROPAGATION Sow seed in either early or mid spring.

PRUNING Not normally required.

PESTS AND DISEASES Usually trouble free.

Nuphar
Nymphaeaceae

Globular flowers, scattered over leathery floating foliage, highlight these hardy, deciduous deep-water aquatic perennials in summer. Versatility is a strong point – in addition to flourishing in full sun and still water, plants in this genus will also tolerate shade and moving water, unlike water lilies, their more showy relatives. A large wildlife pond is a suitable setting. The ideal water depth is 2 m (6½ ft) but plants can be grown in 1 m (3 ft) of water.

RECOMMENDED SPECIES

N. lutea (yellow water lily) Yellow waxy flowers, to 5 cm (2 in) across, with a strong alcoholic aroma bloom just above the water throughout summer. The leathery, mid green, floating leaves are oval to heart-shaped and up to 30 cm (12 in) long and 20 cm (8 in) wide. Translucent pale green leaves are produced under water in early

spring before the floating foliage appears. The rootstock is vigorous and invasive unless restricted by container cultivation. Native to Eurasia, N America, West Indies, N Africa. Plant in water 2 m (6½ ft) deep. SPREAD 2 m (6½ ft). If the plant is grown in shallower water the spread will be less.

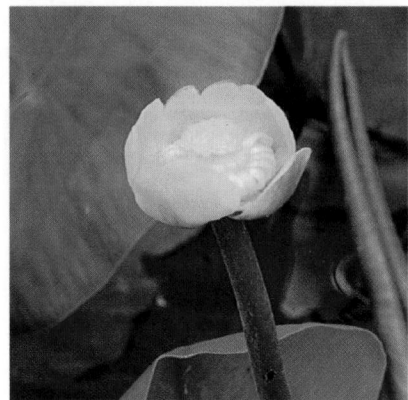

✦ *Nuphar lutea*

CULTIVATION Plant in an open-sided aquatic planting basket in either a heavy loam soil or an aquatic planting compost. Cover the surface with pea gravel to prevent fish disturbing the soil. Use an aquatic plant fertiliser in early spring. Divide the plants when they become crowded.

PROPAGATION Divide established crowns in spring and early summer.

PESTS AND DISEASES Water-lily aphids can be troublesome.

Nymphaea
Water lily
Nymphaeaceae

Nymphaea alba

Grown for their waxy, star or cup-shaped summer flowers and floating foliage, water lilies are deciduous, perennial aquatic plants. There are tender, night-blooming water lilies available but those recommended below are hardy and flower during the day.

The flowers are often pure white but they also range in colour from pastel pink to rich crimson or from pale yellow to deep orange. The flowers of some varieties, such as *Nymphaea* 'Aurora', change colour as they age; this particular variety turns from yellow to blood-red. Nearly all flowers have prominent yellow or orange stamens. The blooms float among oval, rounded or heart-shaped leaves that are green, purplish

green or green splashed with purple or maroon. If plants become crowded, the flowers rise above the leaves. The leaves shade the surface of the water and so help to reduce the amount of algae in a pond.

There are water lilies to suit every pond size. Those with a planting depth greater than 1.2 m (4 ft) are best for large ponds and those with a planting depth of less than 45 cm (1½ ft) are better in small pools or water tubs. The planting depths given below are the optimum for successful growth and the spreads given are what plants are likely to achieve if planted at the ideal depth.

RECOMMENDED SPECIES AND VARIETIES

N. alba (common white water lily) Snow-white, cup-shaped blossoms, up to 20 cm (8 in) across, float among circular mid green leaves, up to 30 cm (12 in) across. The ideal planting depth for this water lily is 3 m (10 ft). SPREAD 2 m (6½ ft).

N. 'Albatros' White, star-shaped flowers grow up to 20 cm (8 in) across and float among deep green, circular leaves, also 20 cm (8 in) across. Young leaves are a purplish colour when they first appear. Plant at a depth of 1 m (3 ft). SPREAD 1 m (3 ft).

N. 'Amabilis' Star-like, salmon-pink flowers, up to 25 cm (10 in) across, deepen to soft rose-pink with age. The yellow stamens become fiery orange. Deeply cleft, dark green, rounded leaves grow up to 25 cm (10 in) across. Plant this water lily at a depth of 1 m (3 ft). SPREAD 1 m (3 ft).

N. 'Andreana' Deep brick-red, cup-shaped blossoms, up to 20 cm (8 in) across, are streaked with cream and yellow. The glossy green leaves, up to 25 cm (10 in) across, are blotched with maroon. The ideal planting depth is 60 cm (2 ft). SPREAD 60 cm (2 ft).

N. 'Apple Blossom Pink' see
   N. 'Marliacea Carnea'

N. 'Atropurpurea' Deep crimson-purple blooms, with a satiny sheen, float amid dark green rounded leaves up to 25 cm (10 in) across. Each cup-shaped flower is up to 15 cm (6 in) across with distinctive incurving petals. Plant at a depth of 60 cm (2 ft). SPREAD 1 m (3 ft).

N. 'Attraction' Garnet-red flowers, flecked with white and up to 25 cm (10 in) across, have rich, mahogany-coloured stamens tipped with yellow and sepals that are off-white infused with rose-pink. They change from cup-shaped to star-shaped. The mid green oval leaves with overlapping lobes grow up to 30 cm (12 in) across. Plant at a depth of 1.2 m (4 ft). SPREAD 1.2 m (4 ft).

N. 'Aurora' Cup-shaped flowers, up to 7.5 cm (3 in) across, start cream in bud, opening to yellow, then deepen through orange to blood red. The rounded leaves, up to 10 cm (4 in) across, are dark green mottled purple. The planting depth for this variety is 45 cm (1½ ft). SPREAD 60 cm (2 ft).

N. 'Brakeleyi Rosea' Sweetly scented, star-shaped flowers, up to 15 cm (6 in) across, open rose-pink but age to flesh-pink or almost white. The deep green, rounded leaves are up to 25 cm (10 in) across. Plant at a depth of 75 cm (2½ ft). SPREAD 1 m (3 ft).

N. 'Caroliniana Nivea' The star-shaped, white, fragrant blossoms are up to 15 cm (6 in) across and the mid green rounded leaves are as wide as 20 cm (8 in). Plant at a depth of 75 cm (2½ ft). SPREAD 1 m (3 ft).

N. 'Charles de Meurville' Cup-shaped flowers, up to 25 cm (10 in) across, become star-shaped and the colour changes from plum, tipped and streaked with white, to deep wine red. The oval, olive-green leaves grow up to 30 cm (12 in) long. Plant at a depth of 1.2 m (4 ft). SPREAD 1.5 m (5 ft).

⚘ *Nymphaea* 'Colonel A.J. Welch'

N. 'Colonel A.J. Welch' The lemon yellow, star-shaped flowers, up to 15 cm (6 in) across, have a slight fragrance. The rounded, olive-green leaves grow up to 25 cm (10 in) across. The blossoms of this variety often transform into new plantlets. Plant this water lily at a depth of 75 cm (2½ ft). SPREAD 1 m (3 ft).

N. 'Colossea' Fragrant, cup-shaped, flesh-pink blossoms, up to 25 cm (10 in) across, sit among dull green, rounded leaves up to 30 cm (12 in). This is a vigorous, free-flowering variety and needs to be planted at a depth of 1.2 m (4 ft). SPREAD 1.2 m (4 ft).

N. 'Comanche' Cup-shaped, deep apricot to orange blossoms, up to 10 cm (4 in) across, fade to bronze with age. The rounded leaves, up to 15 cm (6 in) across, are purplish when young but change to

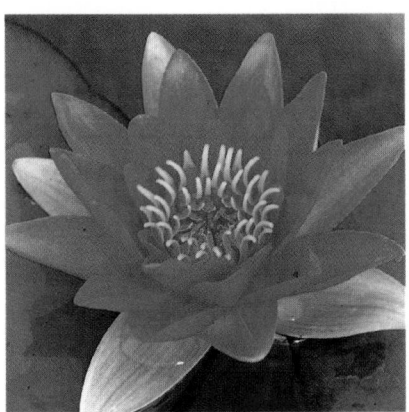

⚘ *Nymphaea* 'Escarboucle'

mid green as they unfurl, occasionally with purple spots. Plant this water lily at a depth of 60 cm (2 ft). SPREAD 1 m (3 ft).

N. 'Ellisiana' Small, wine-red, star-shaped flowers are up to 10 cm (4 in) across, with orange stamens. The oval, dark green leaves grow up to 15 cm (6 in) across. This free-flowering water lily needs to be planted at a depth of 45 cm (1½ ft). SPREAD 60 cm (2 ft).

N. 'Escarboucle' ♀ Scented, crimson, cup-shaped, becoming star-shaped, flowers grow up to 30 cm (12 in) across in a large open pond. The rounded mid green leaves, up to 30 cm (12 in) across, are often tinged with bronze or brown. Plant at a depth of 1.5 m (5 ft). SPREAD 1.5 m (5 ft).

N. 'Firecrest' Star-shaped, deep pink flowers, up to 10 cm (4 in) across, sport red-tipped stamens. The rounded leaves, up to 20 cm (8 in) across, are purplish when young, turning mid green with age. Plant at a depth of 60 cm (2 ft). SPREAD 1 m (3 ft).

⚘ *Nymphaea* 'Froebelii'

N. 'Froebelii' The deep blood-red, cup-like flowers, which become star-shaped, are up to 10 cm (4 in) across and are produced among dull, purplish green rounded leaves, up to 15 cm (6 in) across. Plant this water lily in 60 cm (2 ft) of water. SPREAD 1 m (3 ft).

N. 'Gloriosa' Star-shaped, fragrant, currant-red blooms, up to 15 cm (6 in) across, with bright orange stamens, float on the surface of the water. The dull bronze-green leaves are rounded and up to 15 cm (6 in) across. Plant at a depth of 60 cm (2 ft). SPREAD 1 m (3 ft).

N. 'Gonnère' ♀ The fully double, cup-shaped, white flowers, with conspicuous apple-green sepals, are up to 15 cm (6 in) across. Rounded bright green leaves grow up to 20 cm (8 in) across. The best planting depth is 60 cm (2 ft). SPREAD 1 m (3 ft).

N. 'Graziella' Orange-red, cup-shaped flowers, rarely more than 5 cm (2 in) across, are produced freely throughout summer. The olive-green rounded leaves, up to 10 cm (4 in) across, are heavily blotched with brown and purple. Plant at a depth of 30 cm (1 ft). SPREAD 45 cm (1½ ft).

N. x helvola ♀ (syn. *N. x pygmaea* 'Helvola') Star-like yellow flowers, up to 5 cm (2 in) across, are freely produced by this plant.

⚘ *Nymphaea* 'Gonnère'

The olive-green, oval to heart-shaped leaves, up to 6 cm (2½ in) long, are splashed with purple and brown. Plant at a depth of 20 cm (8 in). SPREAD 30 cm (12 in).

N. 'Indiana' Orange-red, cup-shaped flowers, up to 7.5 cm (3 in) across, age to deep red. The rounded leaves are dark green, up to 10 cm (4 in) across, and heavily blotched with purple. Plant at a depth of 60 cm (2 ft). SPREAD 75 cm (2½ ft).

N. 'James Brydon' ♀ The deep crimson, cup-shaped blossoms, up to 15 cm (6 in) across, smell of ripe apples. The dark purplish green, rounded leaves, up to 25 cm (10 in) across, are often flecked with maroon. This water lily should be planted at a depth of 1 m (3 ft). SPREAD 1 m (3 ft).

⚘ *Nymphaea* x *helvola*

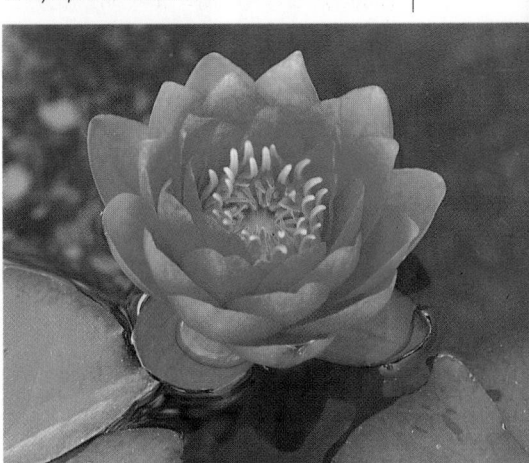

⚘ *Nymphaea* 'James Brydon'

N. **'Laydekeri Fulgens'** The bright crimson, scented, cup-shaped flowers, with reddish stamens, are up to 8 cm (3¼ in) across. Leaves are rounded, dark green with purple undersides, as wide as 15 cm (6 in). Plant at a depth of 45 cm (1½ ft). SPREAD 60 cm (2 ft).

N. **'Laydekeri Lilacea'** Soft pink flowers, up to 8 cm (3¼ in) across, age to deep rosy crimson. Glossy green leaves, up to 15 cm (6 in) across, are sparsely blotched with brown. Plant this water lily at a depth of 45 cm (1½ ft). SPREAD 60 cm (2 ft).

N. **'Laydekeri Purpurata'** Cup-shaped wine-red flowers, up to 8 cm (3 in) across, have bright orange stamens. The dark green leaves, up to 15 cm (6 in) across, are purple beneath and often marked on the upper surface with maroon or black splashes. Plant at a depth of 45 cm (1½ ft). SPREAD 60 cm (2 ft).

N. **'Madame Wilfon Gonnère'** The cup-shaped, almost double, white blossoms, up to 15 cm (6 in) across, are flushed and spotted with deep rose-pink and are soft pink at the centre. The rounded mid green leaves, up to 25 cm (10 in) across, have distinctive overlapping lobes. Plant at a depth of 75 cm (2½ ft). SPREAD 1 m (3 ft).

N. **'Marliacea Albida'** Scented, white flowers, up to 15 cm (6 in) across, are flushed with soft pink on the undersides of the petals. The rounded, deep green leaves, up to 20 cm (8 in) across have red or purplish undersides. Plant at a depth of 1 m (3 ft). SPREAD 1.2 m (4 ft).

N. **'Marliacea Carnea'** (syn. *N.* 'Apple Blossom Pink') Flesh-pink blossoms, up to 20 cm (8 in) across, become star-like when fully open. This variety has a vanilla fragrance. It is the best hardy water lily for cut flowers. The oval, deep green leaves, up to 20 cm (8 in) across, are purplish when young. Plant this water lily at a depth of 1 m (3 ft). SPREAD 1.2 m (4 ft).

Nymphaea
'Marliacea Carnea'

N. **'Marliacea Chromatella'** ♀ Rich canary-yellow flowers, up to 15 cm (6 in) across, float among olive green leaves, to 20 cm (8 in) across, splashed with maroon and bronze. Plant this variety at a depth of 1 m (3 ft). SPREAD 1.2 m (4 ft).

N. **'Masaniello'** Fragrant, rose-pink, cup-shaped flowers, up to 12.5 cm (5 in) across, are flecked with crimson and age to deep carmine. The leaves are mid green, rounded and to 20 cm (8 in) across. Plant at a depth of 75 cm (2½ ft). SPREAD 1 m (3 ft).

N. **'Moorei'** Soft yellow, star-like blossoms, up to 15 cm (6 in) across, are slightly scented. The pale green, rounded leaves, up to 25 cm (10 in) across, are sometimes splashed with purple spots. Plant at a depth of 45 cm (1½ ft). SPREAD 75 cm (2½ ft).

N. **'Mrs Richmond'** The cup-shaped, pale rose-pink flowers, up to 10 cm (4 in) across, are bright red at the base of the petals. The flowers age to crimson. Rounded, mid green leaves grow up to 15 cm (6 in) across. Plant at a depth of 75 cm (2½ ft). SPREAD 1 m (3 ft).

⚘ *Nymphaea* 'Mrs Richmond'

N. **odorata** (sweet-scented water lily) The fragrant, white flowers, up to 15 cm (6 in) across, are star-like. The bright green leaves are rounded and up to 25 cm (10 in) across. Plant 1 m (3 ft) deep. SPREAD 1.2 m (4 ft).

The white flowers of var. *minor* (millpond lily), up to 8 cm (3¼ in) across, float among soft green leaves as wide as 10 cm (4 in). Plant at a depth of 30 cm (12 in). This variety will spread to 45 cm (18 in). 'Sulphurea Grandiflora' has canary-yellow blooms, to 12.5 cm (5 in) across, held slightly above olive-green leaves, mottled with purple, up to 20 cm (8 in) across. Plant at a depth of 60 cm (2 ft). This plant spreads to 1 m (3 ft). 'Turicensis' has soft rose-pink flowers, up to 13 cm (5 in) across. The mid green leaves are up to 20 cm (8 in) across. Plant this water lily at a depth of 45 cm (18 in). It will spread to 60 cm (2 ft).

N. × *pygmaea* **'Alba'** see *N. tetragona*
N. × *pygmaea* **'Helvola'** see *N.* × *helvola*
N. × *pygmaea* **'Rubra'** The blood-red, star-like flowers, up to 2.5 cm (1 in) across, have orange stamens. Rounded to heart-shaped, purplish green leaves, with distinctive reddish undersides, are up to 8 cm (3¼ in) long. This variety needs planting at a depth of 20 cm (8 in). SPREAD 30 cm (12 in).

N. **'Rose Arey'** Star-like, rose-pink flowers, up to 20 cm (8 in) across, smell of aniseed. The rounded leaves, up to 25 cm (10 in) across, are red when young and age to mid green tinged with red. Plant at a depth of 60 cm (2 ft). SPREAD 1 m (3 ft).

N. **'Sioux'** Star-shaped flowers, up to 10 cm (4 in) across, start yellow, then turn orange, then crimson. The rounded leaves are 15 cm (6 in) across, dull green and mottled purple. Plant this variety at a depth of 60 cm (2 ft). SPREAD 1 m (3 ft).

N. **tetragona** (syn. *N.* × *pygmaea* 'Alba') White flowers no more than 5 cm (2 in) across float among oval or heart-shaped, dark green leaves, up to 8 cm (3¼ in) long. Plant this species in only 15 cm (6 in) of water. SPREAD 25 cm (10 in).

N. **tuberosa** (magnolia water lily) Cup-shaped, white flowers, 15–25 cm (6–10 in) across, rest among apple-green, rounded leaves, up to 40 cm (16 in) across. Plant at a depth of 1 m (3 ft). SPREAD 1.2 m (4 ft).

'Rosea' has pink flowers.

⚘ *Nymphaea* 'Marliacea Albida'
Nymphaea 'Madame Wilfon Gonnère' ⚘

⚘ *Nymphaea* 'Marliacea Chromatella'

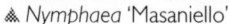

⚘ *Nymphaea* 'Masaniello'

⚘ *Nymphaea* 'Moorei'

⚠ *Nymphaea* 'Rose Arey'

⚠ *Nymphaea* 'Sioux'

⚠ *Nymphoides peltata*

N. 'William Falconer' Blood-red, cup-shaped flowers, to 10 cm (4 in) across, float among rounded leaves, to 15 cm (6 in) wide. The red-veined leaves start purplish green, then turn deep olive-green. Plant at a depth of 60 cm (2 ft). SPREAD 1 m (3 ft).

CULTIVATION Plant during spring and early summer, in aquatic planting compost or heavy loam soil in a plastic mesh basket. Cover the compost or soil with a layer of pea gravel to prevent fish from stirring it up. Apply slow-release aquatic fertiliser annually. To avoid congestion, divide water lilies every 3-5 years.

PROPAGATION Lift and divide the rootstock in spring every 3-5 years, apart from *N. tetragona*, which is propagated from ripe seed in summer. Alternatively, remove 'eyes', small growths on the creeping rootstock, during spring and early summer and grow on in small pots in a tank of water.

PESTS AND DISEASES Water lily aphids and, in southern Britain, water lily beetle can attack plants. Crown and root rot may cause stems and leaves to blacken and become slimy. Remove affected plants from the water at once and destroy.

Nymphoides
Menyanthaceae

Bright yellow, saucer-shaped blossoms with delicately fringed petals are produced all summer long on these deep-water aquatic plants. There are tender tropical species in this genus but it is the hardy deciduous perennials that are commonly grown in British garden ponds.

RECOMMENDED SPECIES AND VARIETIES
N. peltata (syn. *Villarsia nymphoides*) (water fringe) The flowers of this adaptable plant are up to 2.5 cm (1 in) across. Heart-shaped,

bright green leaves up to 10 cm (4 in) across are produced on numerous stringy stems, which grow up from the creeping, tangled rootstock. In ponds with a mud bottom, this plant can be very invasive. HEIGHT & SPREAD 5×60 cm (2×24 in).

'Bennettii' (syn. *Villarsia bennettii*) has leaves which are spotted with brown.

CULTIVATION Grow in an open sunny position in the deeper part of a pool, away from the planting shelf at the pond edge. Plant at a depth of 15-60 cm (6-24 in), in spring or early summer, in an open lattice-work container in heavy loam soil or an aquatic planting compost. Cover the surface of the container with pea gravel to prevent fish from disturbing the soil. Feed annually with a slow-release aquatic fertiliser. Divide plants to retain vigour, when the container becomes congested.

PROPAGATION Divide established plants during spring and early summer.

PESTS AND DISEASES Water lily aphids can be a problem.

Nyssa
Cornaceae

Nyssa sylvatica

These hardy deciduous trees are remarkable for the brilliant scarlet colour of their leaves in autumn. They look particularly effective planted in a group, beside water or against a background of evergreens. The lustrous, pointed, oval leaves, arranged alternately on the stem, are up to 15 cm (6 in) long. Small, insignificant flowers in spring and early summer are followed by fleshy blue-black berries in autumn.

RECOMMENDED SPECIES
N. sinensis♀ The leaves on this large shrub or small tree turn every shade of red in autumn. Green flowers appear in

⚠ *Nyssa sinensis*

rounded heads 1.5 cm (½ in) across. Plant in a sheltered position, as the species is only moderately frost-hardy. Native to central China. HEIGHT & SPREAD 2.4×1.2 m (8×4 ft) after 10 years, ultimately 9 m (30 ft) tall.

N. sylvatica♀ (tupelo) This tree has an upright, conical habit, which spreads with age. Leaves change to glorious shades of red, gold and yellow in mid or late autumn.

⚠ *Nyssa sylvatica*

The yellow-green flowers are borne in rounded clusters 1.5 cm (½ in) wide. Native to N and Central America. HEIGHT & SPREAD 4.5×2.4 m (15×8 ft) after 20 years, ultimately 15 m (50 ft) tall.

CULTIVATION Grow in a damp, lime-free soil, in sun or partial shade, but preferably sun. Plant specimens between late autumn and mid spring. Place them in their permanent positions while they are still small, because they may suffer if moved later on.

PROPAGATION Specimens are normally acquired as young plants, because they are not that easy to propagate. Sow seed in early or mid spring. Layer in autumn, and move rooted sections about 18 months later.

PRUNING No pruning required.

PESTS AND DISEASES Usually trouble free.

Oenanthe
Umbelliferae

This genus is characterised by fern-like foliage. It is seldom cultivated, apart from the colourful Japanese subspecies, *Oenanthe javanica* 'Flamingo'. A damp open setting, such as an informal bog garden, suits it best.

▲ *Oenanthe javanica* 'Flamingo'

RECOMMENDED SPECIES

O. javanica **'Flamingo'** (syn. *O. japonica*) Pink, cream and white splashes decorate the narrow oval toothed or lobed leaflets, many of which form compound leaves up to 15 cm (6 in) long. Dense heads of tiny white flowers appear throughout the summer. HEIGHT & SPREAD 30×25 cm (12×10 in).

CULTIVATION Plant in damp soil in spring. Remove flowerheads either as soon as they appear or immediately after flowering to retain the quality of the foliage.

PROPAGATION Divide carefully in spring.

PESTS AND DISEASES Slugs and snails may be troublesome.

Oenothera
Evening primrose
Onagraceae

Profuse, short-lived, showy flowers, often fragrant, distinguish this genus of annuals, biennials and perennials. Many bear flowers that open at twilight and fade by sunrise – to be replaced by new blooms the next evening; some have flowers that remain open all day. Evening primroses are not good as cut flowers, but they attract butterflies to the garden. Plant larger varieties in borders or a wild garden, and smaller ones in a rock garden. Most seed prolifically, and many self-sow. Native to the Americas.

Oenothera speciosa

RECOMMENDED SPECIES AND VARIETIES

O. acaulis (syn. *O. taraxacifolia*) White cup-shaped flowers that age to pink, up to 7.5 cm (3 in) wide, appear on this perennial throughout summer. The lance-shaped, 20 cm (8 in) long, grey-green leaves are lobed or deeply toothed. It is ideal in a rock garden. HEIGHT & SPREAD 15×20 cm (6×8 in).

'Aurea' has yellow flowers.

O. biennis (common evening primrose) A hardy biennial that self-sows easily and can become a nuisance, its seeds are the source of evening primrose oil. Fragrant yellow flowers, up to 7.5 cm (3 in) wide, appear from early summer to mid autumn. Rosettes of narrow oval to oblong leaves, up to 30 cm (1 ft) long, form at stem bases. Leaves farther up the stem are half as long. HEIGHT & SPREAD 1 m×40 cm (3 ft×16 in).

O. childsii see *O. speciosa*

O. fruticosa (syn. *O. linearis*) (sundrops) Fragrant yellow flowers, 5 cm (2 in) wide, borne on leafy spikes, open during the day from mid to late summer. This biennial or perennial has reddish upright stems and oval to lance-shaped green leaves, sometimes edged with red, up to 12.5 cm (5 in) long. HEIGHT & SPREAD 60×40 cm (2 ft×16 in).

'Fyrverkeri' ♀ ('Fireworks') has red buds on red stems that open to yellow flowers. This perennial grows to about 40 cm (16 in) tall.

The toothed leaves of ssp. **glauca** ♀ are broader and more or less grey-green.

O. linearis see *O. fruticosa*

O. macrocarpa ♀ (syn. *O. missouriensis*) (Ozark's sundrops) Yellow flowers, 10 cm (4 in) across, are borne close to the dark green foliage on this almost prostrate plant. The oval to lance-shaped leaves, 2.5-7.5 cm (1-3 in) long, have a silvery mid rib. HEIGHT & SPREAD 12.5×18 cm (5×7 in).

O. odorata see *O. stricta*

O. perennis (syn. *O. pumila*) (sundrops) Fragrant yellow blooms, about 1.5 cm (½ in) wide, flower in loose spikes during the day

▼ *Oenothera macrocarpa*

▲ *Oenothera perennis*

in summer and early autumn. A perennial, it has slender upright stems and narrow spoon-shaped leaves, about 4 cm (1½ in) long. HEIGHT & SPREAD 40×30 cm (16×12 in).

O. speciosa (syn. *O. childsii*, *O. speciosa* var. *childsii*) (white evening primrose) Fragrant summer flowers, 5 cm (2 in) wide, fade to delicate rose pink as they age. This perennial has creeping rhizomes and mid-green elliptical leaves, 5 cm (2 in) long. HEIGHT & SPREAD 30×45 cm (1×1½ ft).

'Pink Petticoats' has pale pink flowers, delicately veined and slightly frilled.

'Rosea' also has pale pink flowers and grows to no more than 30 cm (1 ft) tall.

O. stricta (syn. *O. odorata*) This sprawling plant has rich yellow tubular flowers, about 4 cm (1½ in) across, sparsely spread along the

▲ *Oenothera fruticosa* 'Fyrverkeri'
Oenothera speciosa 'Rosea' ▲

stems. The pale green leaves are lance shaped, up to 10 cm (4 in) long. HEIGHT & SPREAD 1 m×40 cm (3 ft×16 in).

'Sulphurea' has pastel yellow flowers that fade to peach.

O. taraxacifolia see *O. acaulis*

CULTIVATION Plant in autumn or spring in well-drained, sandy soil in a sunny position. Water generously during the growing season. Stake plants if required.

PROPAGATION Sow evening primrose seed in pots in a light sandy compost in early spring; or sow annuals and biennials in their growing position.

Divide perennials and replant in early spring, or take softwood cuttings in spring or early summer, grow under glass and plant out the following spring. Remove and replant rooted rhizomes of *O. speciosa* in late summer and keep in a cold frame over winter if necessary.

PESTS AND DISEASES Usually trouble free.

Old woman see *Artemisia stelleriana*

Olea
Olive
Oleaceae

Olea europaea

These half-hardy evergreen trees and shrubs have attractive silvery foliage. *Olea europaea* is hardy enough to survive outdoors in mild areas of Britain. Olives make excellent outdoor tub plants for the summer but rarely thrive unless grown under glass. In Britain, fruit is not borne on outdoor trees and is rarely edible on those grown under glass.

RECOMMENDED SPECIES AND VARIETIES
O. europaea♀ (wild olive) The grey-green, lance-shaped leaves, about 7cm (3¼in) long, have silvery undersides. Clusters of tiny white flowers appear in mid summer, followed by red or purple oval fruits up to 4cm (1½in) long. This Mediterranean tree has an upright freely-branching habit. HEIGHT & SPREAD 2×1m (6½×3ft) after 10 years, ultimately 5m (16ft) tall.

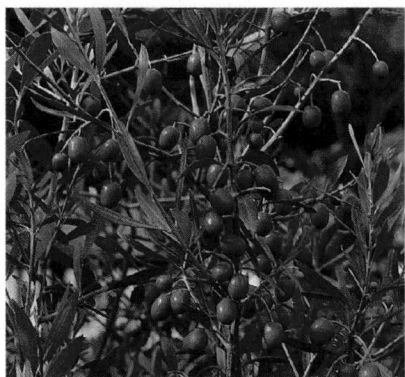

⚹ *Olea europaea*

The fruits of var. *europaea* 'El Greco' are larger with small stones.
CULTIVATION Grow in a greenhouse, a border or in a soil-based compost in large tubs; water regularly in summer and feed with a general-purpose liquid feed in early spring and again in mid summer.
PROPAGATION Take semi-ripe cuttings in summer.

PRUNING Cut out weak shoots and trim to shape in spring.
PESTS AND DISEASES Scale insects and mealy bugs may trouble plants under glass.

Oleander see *Nerium oleander*

Olearia
Daisy bush
Compositae

Olearia macrodonta

Cheerful, daisy flowers and evergreen leathery leaves give summer and winter value in this genus of fast-growing shrubs or small trees. The small flowers are usually white and may be solitary or borne in clusters up to 10cm (4in) across.

Mainly from Australia and New Zealand, olearias are sun-loving and many are resistant to strong winds and salt spray, making them ideal coastal hedging plants. Most of the plants listed are hardy in warmer areas, provided that they are planted in well-drained soil. *Olearia× haastii* tolerates pollution, making it useful for town hedging.
RECOMMENDED SPECIES AND VARIETIES
O. × haastii Numerous fragrant, daisy-like white flowers appear in mid to late summer on this dense, rounded bush. Alternate oval leaves grow to 2.5cm (1in) and open dark, shiny green above, ageing to a dull grey-green. HEIGHT & SPREAD 1×1m (3×3ft) after 5 years, ultimately 1.8m (6ft) tall.
O. 'Henry Travers'♀ (syn. *O. semidentata*) Only really suitable for gardens with little or no frost, the rounded bush bears large lilac flowers with a purple centre from early to mid summer. Slightly toothed lance-shaped dark green leaves grow to 6cm (2½in) long. HEIGHT & SPREAD 1.5×1m (5×3ft) after 5 years, ultimately 3m (10ft) tall.
O. macrodonta♀ A large, vigorous, upright shrub with peeling, papery bark, its numerous, tiny white flowers have a musky scent and appear in early summer in clusters up to 12cm (4¾in) across. The holly-like leaves are toothed and wavy and grow to 7.5cm (3in). Standing up well to salt winds it

⚹ *Olearia macrodonta*

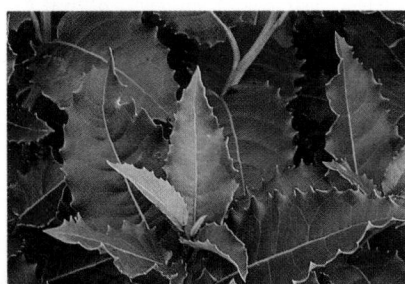

makes useful hedging in seaside gardens. HEIGHT & SPREAD 1×1m (3×3ft) after 5 years, ultimately up to 6m (20ft) tall.
O. × mollis This compact, rounded, hardy shrub has white-felted branchlets, clusters of small white flowers in spring and pale green oval alternate leaves, 12mm (½in) long. HEIGHT & SPREAD 30×30cm (1×1ft) after 5 years, ultimately 2m (6½ft) tall.
'Zennorensis'♀ has dark green, sharply toothed leaves up to 10cm (4in) long, and pale brown-felted branches. It is a fine plant for warm coastal areas.
O. nummularifolia Small, solitary fragrant white flowers appear in mid summer on this dense, rounded hardy shrub. Its alternate leathery leaves are 5mm (¼in) long. HEIGHT & SPREAD 1×1m (3×3ft) after 5 years, ultimately 3m (10ft) tall.
The dwarf variety *cymbifolia* has slightly longer grey-green leaves, erect branches and solitary white flowers.
O. oleifolia see *O.* 'Waikariensis'
O. semidentata see *O.* 'Henry Travers'
O. stellulata♀ Large clusters of white flowers appear in spring or early summer. The 8cm (3¼in) toothed leaves have sunken veins. HEIGHT & SPREAD 3×2m (10×6½ft) after 5 years, ultimately 5m (16ft) tall.
O. 'Waikariensis' (syn. *O. oleifolia*) White-felted angular branchlets carry grey-green alternate leaves, 5cm (2in) long. White flowers are borne in panicles on this freely flowering compact shrub in mid to late summer. HEIGHT & SPREAD 1×1m (3×3ft) after 5 years, ultimately 1.8m (6ft) tall.
CULTIVATION Grow in any well-drained soil. Most olearias thrive on chalk.
PROPAGATION Take semi-ripe cuttings

⚹ *Olearia* 'Waikariensis'
Olearia × mollis 'Zennorensis' ⚹

from late summer to late autumn.
PRUNING Prune after flowering, if necessary, to maintain a good shape.
PESTS AND DISEASES Usually trouble free.

Oleaster see *Eleagnus angustifolia*
Olive see *Olea*

Omphalodes
Navelwort
Boraginaceae

Omphalodes cappadocica

Sprays of blue or white flowers liven up the low clumps of foliage in spring or summer. Similar to forget-me-not blooms, each one opens to just 1 cm (⅜ in) across. *Omphalodes cappadocica* and *O. verna* are good spring-flowering plants for moist shady conditions. Their spreading habit makes them useful ground cover. Of some 25 species, only one annual and three herbaceous perennials and their varieties are widely grown.

RECOMMENDED SPECIES AND VARIETIES
O. cappadocica ♀ Branching sprays of bright blue flowers with whitish eyes are carried well above the leaves in spring. Glossy oval to heart-shaped leaves, up to 10 cm (4 in) long, rise in dense clumps from spreading rhizomes. Native to Asia Minor. HEIGHT & SPREAD 25×40 cm (10×16 in).

'Cherry Ingram' is more robust with larger deeper blue flowers. The blue petals of **'Starry Eyes'** have broad white margins.
O. linifolia ♀ White or very pale blue flowers are borne in erect branching sprays by this annual from early to mid summer. The grey-green lance-shaped leaves are up to 10 cm (4 in) long. The plant self-seeds freely in mild gardens. Native to SW Europe. HEIGHT & SPREAD 30 × 20 cm (12 × 8 in).

▲ *Omphalodes linifolia*

▲ *Omphalodes luciliae*

O. luciliae Loose sprays of powder blue flowers, often pink in bud, are carried in summer above pale grey-blue fleshy elliptic leaves up to 10 cm (4 in) long. Native to Turkish cliffs, it is difficult to establish except in scree, tufa, or in an alpine house. HEIGHT & SPREAD 10 × 15 cm (4×6 in).
O. verna (blue-eyed Mary) Lax clusters of pale blue flowers are produced in spring on stems up to 30 cm (12 in) tall. Dark green oval leaves are up to 15 cm (6 in) long. It spreads quickly by runners. Native to S European mountain woodland. HEIGHT & SPREAD 20×30 cm (8×12 in).

'Alba' has pure white flowers.
CULTIVATION Sow seed of *O. linifolia* thinly in its flowering position in spring. Plant *O. luciliae* in a very gritty alkaline compost or tufa under glass or in a trough. The other perennials thrive in moist humus-rich soils in full or partial shade.
PROPAGATION Sow seed of species in pots in autumn and keep in a cold frame. Divide named varieties of *O. cappadocica* in spring, or in late summer after flowering.
PESTS AND DISEASES Plants are particularly prone to slug and snail damage.

Oncidium see ORCHIDS p.467
Onion, edible see p.741
Onion, ornamental see *Allium*
Onoclea see FERNS p.264

Ononis
Rest harrow
Leguminosae

Showy heads of pink or white blooms are borne on these summer-flowering plants. The flowers have a characteristic pea shape, and the simple or trifolate leaves are abundant on tangled stems. The genus consists of annuals, herbaceous perennials and sub-shrubs. Those listed here are all sub-shrubs.
RECOMMENDED SPECIES
O. repens Rose-pink flowers, up to 1.5 cm (½ in) long, appear in small spikes in mid summer. The scrambling plant has tiny, mid green, oval, hairy leaflets on soft spiny stems. HEIGHT & SPREAD 30×60 cm (1×2 ft).
O. rotundifolia Pink or white flowers up to 1.5 cm (½ in) long are borne in loose spikes in summer. Erect stems are densely clothed with toothed, elliptical, mid green leaflets. HEIGHT & SPREAD 60×45 cm (2×1½ ft).

▲ *Ononis spinosa*

O. spinosa (spiny rest harrow) Reddish pink flowers up to 1.5 cm (½ in) long appear in small spikes at mid summer on this dwarf sub-shrub. The spiny stems are clothed with small, mid green leaflets of variable length. HEIGHT & SPREAD 45×60 cm (1½×2 ft).
CULTIVATION Plant in spring in a sunny, open situation in any free-draining soil.
PRUNING Trim untidy growth in spring.
PROPAGATION Sow seed directly in the open ground in spring, or sow under glass in late summer and plant out in spring.
PESTS AND DISEASES Usually trouble free.

Onopordum
Compositae

These tall, vigorous silver-leaved plants are grown for their dramatic appearance and look best near the back of wide borders when planted against a darker background of tall shrubs or a high hedge. They are also ideal for semi-wild areas of larger gardens. The two species commonly grown are biennials and, although they self-seed, the removal of young unwanted plants is easy as they are very conspicuous and any roots left behind in the soil die off once the foliage has been removed. *Onopordum acanthium* is native to Britain and is hardy, while *O. nervosum*, native to Spain and Portugal, is only reliably hardy in milder areas of Britain.

▲ *Onopordum acanthium*

RECOMMENDED SPECIES
O. acanthium (Scotch thistle, cotton thistle) Pinkish purple flowerheads, about 5 cm (2 in) across, often solitary but sometimes in small clusters, are borne in summer. Silvery grey hairy lobed leaves, up to 35 cm (14 in) long, first form a rosette at ground level

from which the upright branching stems develop. Both the leaves and the wings along the length of each stem are spiny. HEIGHT & SPREAD 2.5×1 m (8×3 ft).

O. *nervosum*♀ (syn. O. *arabicum*) Purple-red flowerheads, often solitary but sometimes in small clusters and up to 5 cm (2 in) across, are borne in summer. Silvery green leaves, up to 50 cm (20 in) long, are smooth above and patterned by a network of pale veins. The wings formed by the leaf bases and the under surfaces of the leaves are spiny. HEIGHT & SPREAD 2.5×1 m (8×3 ft).

⚘ *Onopordum nervosum*

CULTIVATION Plant in early autumn or very early spring in any good garden soil. O. *acanthium* thrives in sun or partial shade while O. *nervosum* prefers full sun. Deadhead to prevent self-seeding.

PROPAGATION Sow seed in small clusters where the plants are to grow and reduce the young plants to one at each position.

PESTS AND DISEASES Slugs and snails eat young plants, and aphids may be a problem.

Onosma
Boraginaceae

Dense nodding clusters of tubular flowers in yellow, white, pink or purple cover the small evergreen sub-shrubs in summer. They require a sunny, well-drained site and thrive on a hot bank or wall, where they can be planted on their sides so that their pendent flowers can be admired, while excessive moisture can quickly drain from their roots.

The narrow tubular flowers are 2 cm (¾ in) long, carried on woody, branching plants with numerous bristly leaves up to 10 cm (4 in) long. The species listed below are native to the Mediterranean and Asia Minor. They are hardy to -10°C (14°F) if protected from winter wet by planting them on their sides, or covering them with a cloche. In wetter regions, however, onosmas are better off in an alpine house.

RECOMMENDED SPECIES AND VARIETIES

O. *alborosea* Clusters of white, pink-tipped flowers appear amid a mound of branching hairy stems with lance-shaped to oblong

⚘ *Onosma alborosea*

leaves. The flowers age to pinkish purple. This is one of the hardiest of the genus. HEIGHT & SPREAD 25×40 cm (10×16 in).

O. *nana* This is a neat rock garden plant with clusters of pale yellow flowers and narrow lance-shaped leaves. It is often short-lived, but usually self-sows. HEIGHT & SPREAD 20×20 cm (8×8 in).

⚘ *Onosma taurica*

O. *taurica*♀ This vigorous species has bright yellow flowers up to 3 cm (1¼ in) long, which sometimes fade to white. HEIGHT & SPREAD 30×50 cm (12×20 in).

CULTIVATION Plant in very gritty well-drained compost in full sun. The plants also do well in a gritty compost in pots in an alpine house if watered sparingly in winter.

PROPAGATION Sow seed in pots in autumn, or take greenwood cuttings in summer.

PESTS AND DISEASES Usually trouble free in the garden, but in a greenhouse the plants may suffer infestations of aphids or whitefly.

Ophiopogon
Lily turf
Convallariaceae

Tiny white or purple bell-shaped flowers nestle among tufted clumps of handsome grass-like leaves in summer, later followed by blue, purple or black berries. These evergreen perennials make interesting ground cover plants for the front of a border, especially on dry soils. The flowers are often concealed by the foliage.

The species listed here are reasonably hardy, with the exception of *Ophiopogon jaburan* which is used for summer bedding or as a conservatory plant. Native to E Asia.

O. *jaburan* Dense spikes of white flowers, about 10 cm (4 in) long, appear in late summer; berries are violet-blue. The lustrous deep green leaves grow to 60 cm (2 ft) long. HEIGHT & SPREAD 60×30 cm (2×1 ft).

'Vittatus' has cream-striped leaves.

O. *japonicus* Loose 8 cm (3 in) spikes of white or pale purple flowers are followed by blue-black berries. The flowers are often hidden by the glossy dark green leaves that grow to about 30 cm (12 in) long. This species, suitable for moister sites, spreads by underground stolons and is good for carpeting. It may also be grown as an aquatic foliage plant, when it produces fewer flowers. HEIGHT & SPREAD 30×45 cm (1×1½ ft).

⚘ *Ophiopogon planiscapus*

O. *planiscapus* White flowers, sometimes tinted purple, appear crowded together on a more or less erect 8 cm (3 in) spike in late summer. The berries are blue-black and the deep green leaves grow to 30 cm (12 in) long. HEIGHT & SPREAD 25×30 cm (10×12 in).

⚘ *Ophiopogon planiscapus* 'Nigrescens'

'Nigrescens'♀ has distinctive purple-black leaves, darker flowers and black fruits.

CULTIVATION All plants thrive in well-drained soil in sun or partial shade, except for O. *japonicus* which requires more moisture. Top-dress with compost and in colder gardens protect with conifer branches or horticultural fleece in winter. Replant every 3 or 4 years.

PROPAGATION Divide in spring or early autumn; or sow seed under glass in autumn or spring.

PESTS AND DISEASES Usually trouble free.

O

463

ORCHIDS

THE EASIEST TYPES TO GROW

THESE ORNAMENTAL PLANTS PRODUCE SHOWY
OR DELICATE BLOOMS YEAR AFTER YEAR,
AS LONG AS THEIR BASIC NEEDS ARE MET

Intense colours, delicate markings and unusually shaped petals make orchids ideal display plants. There is a huge diversity of flowers, from the dainty white blooms of *Phalaenopsis amabilis* to the large waxy ones of *Stanhopea tigrina*. Typically, each orchid flower has three petal-like sepals and three petals. The third, usually the lower, petal is called the lip and is often differently shaped from the other petals. It is usually more flamboyant and more intensely marked. Some are inflated and form a pouch or slipper, as in *Cypripedium*.

The family Orchidaceae is one of the largest plant families and includes more than 20 000 different species. The plants are evergreen or herbaceous perennials and are native to every continent except Antarctica. Some readily interbreed and orchid growers frequently produce new hybrids.

Cultivated orchids do best in environments that imitate their native habitats. Hardy orchids such as *Bletilla*, *Dactylorhiza* and *Epipactis* (see separate genus entries) can be grown in the garden. But most orchids grown in Britain must be kept indoors. Some will thrive only if grown in a cool greenhouse, with a minimum temperature of 4°C (39°F); a warm greenhouse, heated to at least 10°C (50°F); or a hot greenhouse which has a minimum temperature of 15°C (59°F). Others can be kept in a conservatory or grown as houseplants. Many greenhouse orchids will not suffer if they are brought into the house for a few weeks while they are in flower.

RECOMMENDED PLANTS

Roughly a third of all orchid species are terrestrial, growing on the ground. The remainder are epiphytic and live on the branches of trees or on rocks. In the tropics, the majority of orchids are epiphytes, while in temperate regions almost all the orchids are terrestrial.

TERRESTRIAL ORCHIDS

Terrestrial orchids usually have either rhizomes or underground tubers. Herbaceous species have an annual dormant period, when they die down, enabling them to survive periods when the climate is inhospitable.

In general, herbaceous species with rhizomes

FASCINATING FLOWERS
Paphiopedilum, Oncidium *and* Vuylstekeara *show the variable but unmistakable blooms of exotic orchids.*

become dormant in winter and herbaceous species with tubers become dormant in summer. Evergreens may have a dormant period when growth slows down. This is often in winter, but may occur after flowering.

Cypripedium

The flamboyant blooms of these temperate slipper orchids have inflated lower petals.
C. formosanum (syn. *C. japonicum* var. *formosanum*) One or two pinkish white flowers, with red markings, are held on each stem. The lower, slipper-shaped petal is 7 cm (2¾ in) wide and spotted more densely than the other petals. The rhizomatous plant blooms in late spring. Its green, ribbed, fan-shaped

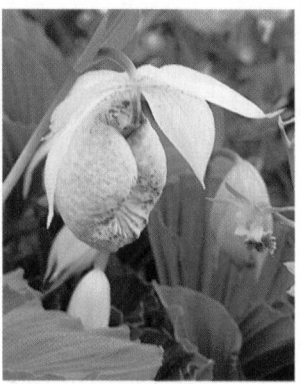

▲ *Cypripedium formosanum*

leaves are 15 cm (6 in) long. Grow the plant in a cold or cool, well-ventilated greenhouse. Pot in a shallow clay container at the end of winter, in compost made up of 2 parts grit, 1 part orchid bark, 1 part loam and 1 part leaf-mould. The growing bud of the rhizome should just protrude from the compost. Keep the compost moist, and each winter remove the top 3 cm (1¼ in) and replace with a mix of equal parts grit, bark and leaf-mould. Add bonemeal in early spring. Repot only if the plant outgrows its container. Native to Taiwan. HEIGHT & SPREAD 30×30 cm (12×12 in) after 5 years.
C. insigne see
Paphiopedilum insigne

Disa

Brightly coloured flowers are borne singly or in groups on these tuberous orchids.

▲ *Disa uniflora*

D. uniflora Spectacular scarlet (occasionally orange) flowers, 5 cm (2 in) across, appear in groups of up to 5 in summer. A veined upper petal, paler than the others, partially encloses a small inner petal, which is often splashed yellow and red. The plant has 10-20 cm (4-8 in) long, shiny, evergreen, lance-shaped leaves arranged in a basal rosette, or sheathing the 30-60 cm (12-24 in) stem.

Keep the plant in a plastic container, in a cool greenhouse. Choose a peat compost with added sphagnum moss. The compost must remain moist at all times. Use water that is not alkaline – rainwater if necessary. Native to South Africa. HEIGHT & SPREAD 45×40 cm (18×16 in) after 5 years.

Ophrys

Plants in this genus are collectively known as bee orchids because of the close resemblance of their flowers to bees, as well as other insects.

▼ *Ophrys tenthredinifera*

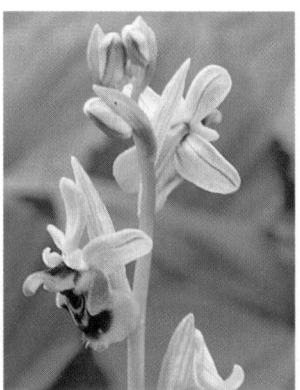

O. tenthredinifera (sawfly orchid) Six or more flowers, which are predominantly pink and 2 cm (¾ in) across, are produced in mid and late spring. They are carried on an erect central stem up to 30 cm (12 in) tall. The upper and side petals are spread open and flat. The fleshy lip is greenish yellow to pinkish brown, lobed and velvety, with a white-edged marking at the base. The pale green, lance-shaped leaves, which grow up to 8 cm (3¼ in) long, form a basal rosette round the 30 cm (12 in) tall central stem. The plant is tuberous.

Grow it in a shallow plastic pot in a cool greenhouse. Pot the tubers about 2.5 cm (1 in) deep in a compost made up of 3 parts grit, 2 parts loam, 1 part leaf-mould, and 1 part fine orchid bark. Repot the plant annually in late summer, when it is resting. Incorporate roughly a third of the old compost with the new compost.

Gradually increase watering as the plant grows in autumn and winter, keeping the compost moist but not wet – and allowing it to dry out to a depth of 2.5 cm (1 in) before each watering. Slowly reduce watering once flower buds have formed in spring. Water occasionally in summer. The plant does not need feeding. Native to Europe. HEIGHT & SPREAD 30×15 cm (12×6 in) after 3 years.

Orchis

Plants in this genus are tuberous and have single stems that bear many delicate flowers.
O. morio (green-winged orchid) Variably coloured flowers, in purple to white and

▼ *Orchis morio*

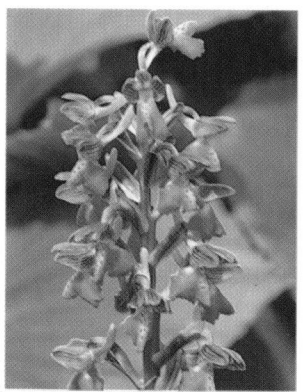

2.5 cm (1 in) wide, appear in mid and late spring. The pink to purple lip is broad, 3-lobed and white at the base. A central spike, which reaches 30 cm (12 in) tall, with up to 12 flowers, rises above a basal rosette of pale green, lance-shaped leaves, 8 cm (3¼ in) long.

Cultivate this species in the way described for *Ophrys tenthredinifera*. Native to Europe. HEIGHT & SPREAD 30×15 cm (12×6 in) after 3 years.

Paphiopedilum

These Asiatic slipper orchids are evergreen and have showy blooms that are long-lasting.
P. insigne♀ (syn. *Cypripedium insigne*) Each waxy flower has upper and lower petals that are spotted golden brown, oblong and pinched at the tip, and 2 narrow, golden brown side petals. The slipper-shaped lip is also golden brown, with a

▲ *Paphiopedilum insigne*

golden interior, speckled with brown. The flowers appear from autumn to spring. One or, occasionally, two blooms, 10 cm (4 in) long and 5 cm (2 in) wide, are carried on a 30 cm (12 in) tall stalk that rises from a clump of lax, dark green, strap-shaped leaves, which are up to 20-30 cm (8-12 in) long.

Grow in a warm greenhouse or conservatory, in a pot or plastic-coated hanging basket. Maintain high humidity and keep the compost moist. Plant in a compost made up of 2 parts coarse bark, 1 part fine bark and half a part finely chopped sphagnum moss. Repot annually to maintain the plant's health. Native to NE India and Nepal. HEIGHT & SPREAD 30×50 cm (12×20 in) after 3 years.

Phragmipedium

Originating from S America, these evergreen slipper orchids often bear several striking blooms on a stem.
P. besseae Vivid scarlet flowers have pouched lips with yellow markings. The blooms are softly hairy and 6 cm (2½ in) across.

▲ *Phragmipedium besseae*

They are held in groups of 1-4 on a 30 cm (12 in) tall spike between spring and autumn, and occasionally in winter. The 10-20 cm (4-8 in) long leaves are pale green and strap-shaped. The plant has a creeping rhizome from which it produces several leafy growths.

Keep the plant in a hot greenhouse, in the compost described for *Paphiopedilum insigne*. Pot in a shallow plastic pan to accommodate the rhizome. Native to Ecuador and Peru. HEIGHT & SPREAD 30×30 cm (12×12 in) after 3 years.

GROWING TERRESTRIAL ORCHIDS

CULTIVATION See the individual entries for each plant's cultivation requirements. In general, do not allow the potting compost to become waterlogged and water orchids less often when they are dormant.

PROPAGATION Divide established rhizomatous plants when they are dormant. Take care with cypripediums, which dislike being disturbed. Tuberous orchids may produce extra tubers which can be potted separately. Raising the plants from seed is not recommended.

PESTS AND DISEASES Aphids and whitefly can affect plants that are grown in a cool or warm greenhouse; red spider mite, scale insect and mealy bug can affect orchids grown in a hot greenhouse. Fungal diseases may result from overwatering or lack of air movement.

EPIPHYTIC ORCHIDS

These orchids use other plants, rocks and fallen trees for anchorage. They have specialised aerial roots that absorb moisture and nutrients from the air, rainwater and decayed plant matter.

Typically, an epiphytic orchid has a rhizome from which grow vertical swollen organs, called pseudobulbs. These are storage vessels for food and water. They are usually oval and are up to 10 cm (4 in) long. Some orchids, such as *Dendrobium chrysotoxum*, produce elongated cane-like pseudobulbs, which form the stems of the plant. New pseudobulbs are produced each year.

Vanda does not have a rhizome or pseudobulbs. Instead, it has an elongated, ever-lengthening stem. The leaves are fleshy to prevent water loss.

All the recommended epiphytic orchids described below are evergreens. Most epiphytic orchids have a dormant period when growth either slows down or stops altogether. This may occur in winter when there is not much daylight.

Cattleya

Spectacular, brightly coloured flowers are borne in groups on these tropical orchids.
C. bowringiana (syn. *C. skinneri* var. *bowringiana*) Lilac and purple flowers, 10 cm (4 in) across, are carried in groups of 10 or more in autumn on 20 cm (8 in) long spikes. Each 6 cm (2½ in) long, oblong pseudobulb is sheathed by a pair of stiff, oblong, pale green leaves, up to 20 cm (8 in) long. The plant forms a clump, which should be divided in winter or spring after 5 years. Grow it in a warm greenhouse in good light. Native to Central America. HEIGHT & SPREAD 40×40 cm (16×16 in) after 5 years.

▼ *Cattleya bowringiana*

Coelogyne

These orchids have glossy green leaves and their blooms are often highly scented.

C. cristata Showy white, fragrant flowers, boldly marked with yellow, are borne during winter and spring on arching, 20 cm (8 in) long stems. A stem

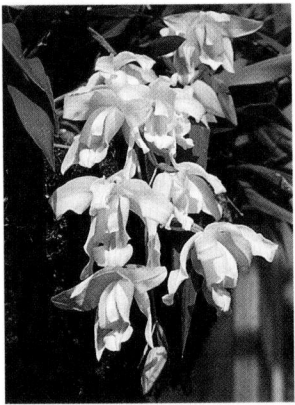

▲ *Coelogyne cristata*

bears 3-10 flowers, each of which is 8 cm (3¼ in) long by 5 cm (2 in) wide. The plant has green, rounded, wrinkled pseudobulbs, each with 2 dark green lance-shaped leaves, up to 30 cm (12 in) long. It is scrambling and can be grown in a pot or wooden-slatted basket.

Grow the plant in a warm greenhouse. It can also be kept indoors, on a windowsill, or in a conservatory, if humid enough. Native to the Himalayas. HEIGHT & SPREAD 10×30 cm (4×12 in) after 3 years.

Cymbidium

These orchids, which are popular houseplants, bear many flowers on their stems.

C. lowianum (syn. *C. giganteum* var. *lowianum*) Greenish sepals and petals surround a yellow flower centre and wide lip, which is splashed with red and white. The flowers are 8 cm

▼ *Cymbidium lowianum*

(3¼ in) long and wide, and appear in groups of up to 20 in late winter and throughout spring. They are carried on one or more arching spikes that can grow up to 1 m (3 ft) long. The plant forms large clumps and has clusters of green, strap-like leaves, up to 1 m (3 ft) long, arising from oval pseudobulbs.

Keep the plant in a warm greenhouse or conservatory in good indirect light. In summer, it can be moved into the garden and placed in dappled sunshine. Plant in a mixture of medium and fine bark. Divide in spring. This orchid is native to SW China, Burma and Thailand. HEIGHT & SPREAD 60×30 cm (24×12 in) after 3 years.

Dendrobium

Plants in this large genus vary greatly in appearance but they generally have showy and sometimes fragrant flowers.

D. chrysotoxum (syn. *D. suavissimum*) Yellow scented flowers, 5 cm (2 in) wide, have frilly lower petals partly coloured an

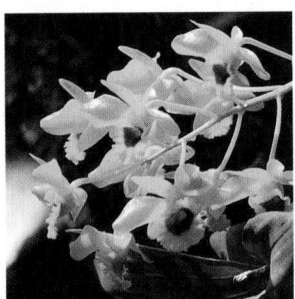

▲ *Dendrobium chrysotoxum*

intense orange-red. Flowers are borne in winter and spring on cane-like pseudobulbs. Bright green, leathery, oblong leaves are 10-15 cm (4-6 in) long. Grow the plant in a hot greenhouse. Native to Indochina. HEIGHT & SPREAD 20×20 cm (8×8 in) after 5 years.

Laelia

These plants have colourful and elegant blooms which are borne on one or more flower spikes.

L. anceps Lilac sepals and petals surround a tubular rose-pink lip with a yellow interior. Each arched flower spike, 75 cm (30 in) long, bears up to 6 flowers, 10 cm (4 in) across, in winter. The pseudobulbs, 7 cm

▲ *Laelia anceps*

(3 in) long, each produce one or two leathery green, oblong leaves, 20 cm (8 in) long. Grow in a hot or warm greenhouse in good light. Native to Mexico. HEIGHT & SPREAD 40×20 cm (16×8 in) after 3-4 years.

Masdevallia

Curiously shaped flowers are produced by these orchids which have no pseudobulbs.

M. coccinea (syn. *M. harryana, M. lindeni*) Brilliant white, yellow, orange, red or purple flowers are borne singly on one or more upright stalks in spring and early summer. Two or three flowers may be in bloom at a time. The flower is 2 cm

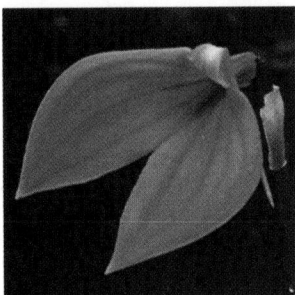

▲ *Masdevallia coccinea*

(¾ in) across and includes several partially fused, oval petals and a thread-like upper petal that arches behind the rest of the flower. The base of the flower is rolled into a tube which holds the tiny inner petals, including the lip. Glossy green, oblong leaves, 20 cm (8 in) long, grow from the top of the stems, which are 6 cm (2½ in) long. Grow the plant in a warm greenhouse. Native to Peru and Colombia. HEIGHT & SPREAD 18×15 cm (7×6 in) after 3 years.

Miltoniopsis

These orchids have pansy-like flowers and are native to South and Central America.

M. Anjou 'St Patrick' The fragrant flowers, 8 cm (3¼ in) wide, have deep red petals splashed with white, and orange and yellow centres. They are carried in clusters on spikes,

▲ *Miltoniopsis* Anjou 'St Patrick'

20 cm (8 in) long, in summer. Small pseudobulbs each bear 2 narrow, tapered pale green leaves, 40 cm (16 in) long. Grow in good indirect light in a warm greenhouse or as a houseplant. HEIGHT & SPREAD 30×20 cm (12×8 in) after 3 years.

Odontoglossum

The plants produce numerous star-shaped flowers on attractively arching stalks.

O. crispum Showy, white, blooms cluster on 50 cm (20 in) long stalks. Several spikes may be produced over autumn and winter. The flowers are 10 cm (4 in) long and 8 cm (3¼ in) wide. Narrow, green leaves are 40 cm (16 in) long, and egg-shaped pseudobulbs reach 10 cm (4 in). This is an easy orchid to grow in a warm greenhouse. Native to Colombia. HEIGHT & SPREAD 30×30 cm (12×12 in) after 3-4 years.

▼ *Odontoglossum crispum*

▲ *Oncidium sphacelatum*

Oncidium

Plants in this large genus usually produce sprays of small, sometimes fragrant blooms.

O. sphacelatum Each flower has petals that are yellow or reddish brown and yellow. The broad yellow lip has a red-brown, white and orange-red centre. Flowers measure 3 cm (1¼ in) across and are carried in branched clusters on arched stalks up to 1.5 m (5 ft) long, from winter until early summer. The plant has flattened pseudobulbs, and rigid linear leaves, 60 cm (2 ft) long. Grow in a hot greenhouse in good light. Native to Central America. HEIGHT & SPREAD 60×30 cm (2×1 ft) after 3-4 years.

Phalaenopsis

Striking moth-like flowers give the plants, which have no pseudobulbs, the common name of moth orchids.

P. amabilis♀ The white flowers, 8 cm (3¼ in) across, are held on a slender, arching spike up to 1m (3 ft) long. They are produced in winter. The plant has 3-5 leathery, oblong, mid green leaves, which are naturally drooping, and may be as long as

▲ *Phalaenopsis amabilis*

50 cm (20 in). Grow this plant in the shade, in a hot greenhouse, or on a draught-free windowsill in a house or conservatory, maintaining a high level of humidity. Native to Indonesia, New Guinea and NE Australia. HEIGHT & SPREAD 45×20 cm (18×8 in) after 4-5 years.

Stanhopea

The extraordinary blooms are waxy, heavily perfumed and hang below the plant.

S. tigrina♀ Up to 4 cream, red-splashed flowers, 12 cm (4¾ in) long, are held on each 5 cm (2 in) long stalk. They appear in summer and last only a few days. The plant has clusters of small, oval pseudobulbs and deep green lance-shaped leaves, 30 cm (12 in) long. Grow it in a shady part of a hot greenhouse, in a wooden-slatted or plastic-mesh hanging basket, lined with

▲ *Stanhopea tigrina*

moss. This allows the flower stalks to grow between the roots and hang down below the rest of the plant. Native to Mexico. HEIGHT & SPREAD 40×30 cm (16×12 in) after 3 years.

Vanda

These Asian climbing plants produce numerous spikes of flowers that are often fragrant.

V. Rothschildiana♀ This orchid flowers profusely, producing long spikes of spectacular purple and white marbled flowers in summer. Five large oval petals surround a small purple lip. Each 40 cm (16 in) long spike holds as many as 12 flowers, each measuring about 8 cm (3¼ in) across. The strap-shaped green leaves, which

grow up to 35 cm (14 in) long, are arranged alternately on a constantly elongating stem that grows upwards. The stem produces occasional side growths and both stem and shoots have whitish aerial roots that are tipped with green or purple when the orchid is in active growth.

Grow the plant in a wooden-slatted or plastic-mesh basket to enable the long aerial roots to grow through the container and hang below the plant. Support the main stem with a stake, and hang the container from wires attached to both container and stake. Keep it in a hot greenhouse, Mist the plant daily. HEIGHT & SPREAD 1 m×50 cm (36×20 in) after 3-4 years.

Vuylstekeara

These plants are hybrids. They produce spikes of showy, colourful flowers.

V. Cambria 'Plush' Pretty, star-shaped, crimson, white and yellow flowers, up to 8 cm (3¼ in) wide, last for 4 weeks or more. There are as many as 6 flowers on each 40 cm (16 in) long spike. The bi-lobed lip is wider than the other petals. The pseudobulbs are small and oval, and the leaves are dull green, oblong and up to 20-30 cm (8-12 in) long. The plant blooms after the current year's pseudobulb has finished growing, often in autumn. Keep the plant in a warm greenhouse, or grow it on a warm windowsill, where it will be slightly smaller. HEIGHT & SPREAD 40×30 cm (16×12 in) after 3 years.

▼ *Vuylstekeara* Cambria 'Plush'

▲ *Vanda*
Rothschildiana

GROWING EPIPHYTIC ORCHIDS

CULTIVATION Epiphytic orchids need a humid environment. Damp down the floors and benches or use a humidifier to maintain an air humidity of 90-95 per cent at night and 80-85 per cent during the day.

Maintain humidity for any orchids grown on windowsills in the house or in a conservatory by placing their containers on a tray of moist pebbles. Keep the plants out of direct sunlight and cold draughts.

Grow small, young plants in a compost made up of 5 parts fine grade orchid bark to 1 part perlite. For established plants, use a mixture of 5 parts medium grade orchid bark and 1 part perlag. Repot plants in late winter or early spring. Unless otherwise stated in the individual plant descriptions, water epiphytic orchids liberally when they are in active growth and apply a liquid fertiliser once a fortnight. Reduce waterings and do not feed during the plant's resting period.

PROPAGATION Divide well-established plants during their resting periods. For orchids that have an ever-increasing stem, such as *Vanda*, remove any new growths from the base when repotting, and pot them up separately. Remove offshoots from orchids that have cane-like stems, such as *Dendrobium*, and pot them up separately. Raising orchids from seed is not recommended.

PESTS AND DISEASES Thrips, mealy bugs, red spider mites, and scale insects may all affect epiphytic orchids.

467

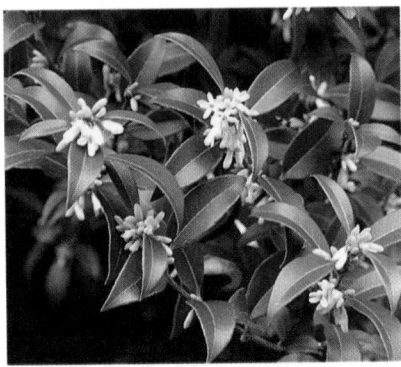

▲ *Osmanthus* × *burkwoodii*

O. × burkwoodii♀ (syn. × *Osmarea burk-woodii*) Small groups of short-tubed scented flowers, about 1 cm (⅜ in) across, appear in mid spring. This hybrid between *O. decorus* and *O. delavayi* grows slowly into a dense shrub with neat 2.5–5 cm (1–2 in) long ovate leaves that are finely toothed and dark glossy green. HEIGHT & SPREAD 1 m × 60 cm (3 × 2 ft) after 5 years, ultimately 3 × 3 m (10 × 10 ft).

O. decorus (syn. *Phillyrea decora*) Sweetly scented flowers are borne in mid spring by this rounded species of dense, upright habit. Its glossy, dark green, narrowly elliptic leaves are yellowish green beneath and 5–12 cm (2–4¾ in) long. The blackish purple oval fruits are 1.5 cm (½ in) long and appear in summer. HEIGHT & SPREAD 1 × 1 m (3 × 3 ft) after 5 years, ultimately 3 × 4 m (10 × 13 ft).

▲ *Osmanthus delavayi*

O. delavayi♀ Fragrant flowers 1.5 cm (½ in) long with reflexed lobes appear in mid and late spring. Broadly egg-shaped, 1 cm (⅜ in) long, blue-black fruits ripen in autumn on this usually compact, bushy species. It has neat, rounded or broadly ovate, dark green leaves that are stiff and glossy, up to 2.5 cm (1 in) long with a few small sharp teeth. HEIGHT & SPREAD 60 × 60 cm (2 × 2 ft) after 5 years, ultimately 1.8 × 2.4 m (6 × 8 ft).

O. forrestii see *O. yunnanensis*

O. heterophyllus (syn. *O. ilicifolius*) Fragrant flowers 6 mm (¼ in) wide with a short tube and recurved lobes are borne in early and mid autumn. They are followed

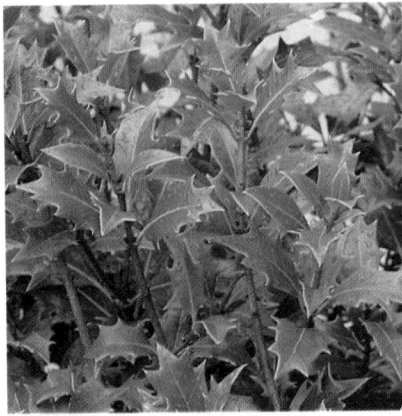

▲ *Osmanthus heterophyllus*

in early winter by oblong, 1.5 cm (½ in) long, purple-black fruits, which are seldom abundant. This holly-like species of compact, bushy habit has 4–6 cm (1½–2½ in) long, stiff, ovate leaves that are glossy dark green, paler beneath and usually with a few large, spine-tipped teeth. HEIGHT & SPREAD 1 × 1 m (3 × 3 ft) after 5 years, ultimately 3–6 × 3–6 m (10–20 × 10–20 ft).

'Argenteomarginatus' see 'Variegatus'; 'Aureomarginatus' ('Aureus') leaves with golden yellow margins; 'Aureus' see 'Aureomarginatus'; 'Goshiki' ('Tricolor') bronze young growth and strongly spined, heavily mottled leaves splashed with creamy yellow and green; 'Gulftide'♀ compact, to 2.4 m (8 ft) tall, with boldly spine-toothed, dark green leaves; 'Purpureus' glossy, deep blackish purple young leaves and shoots become green tinged with purple by summer; 'Tricolor' see 'Goshiki'; 'Variegatus'♀ ('Argenteomarginatus') popular compact variety grows to 3 m (10 ft) tall and 3 m (10 ft) wide, leaves broadly edged with creamy white.

O. ilicifolius see *O. heterophyllus*

O. yunnanensis (syn. *O. forrestii*) Creamy white flowers, 1 cm (⅜ in) across, with spreading lobes appear in mid and late spring. This large species has 8–15 cm (3¼–6 in) long dull, olive-green, narrowly oblong or lance-shaped leaves. Young growth is flushed with bronze and the margins smooth-edged or wavy with many spiny teeth. The 1.5 cm (½ in) long fruit is bloomy dark purple, borne in summer but not freely produced. HEIGHT & SPREAD 1.2 × 1 m (4 × 3 ft) after 5 years, ultimately 10 × 10 m (33 × 33 ft).

CULTIVATION Plant in autumn or winter in any fertile, well-drained soil in sun or shade. *O. yunnanensis* needs some shelter.

PROPAGATION Take semi-ripe cuttings in summer. Sow seeds of species in spring.

PRUNING Not normally needed but shorten excess growth in mid to late spring.

PESTS AND DISEASES Usually trouble free.

× Osmarea see *Osmanthus*
Osmunda see FERNS p. 264

Osteospermum
Compositae

Osteospermum 'Buttermilk'

The centres of these daisy-like flowers contrast strikingly with the colours of the petals. Each flowerhead, up to 5 cm (2 in) wide, has a centre, which is properly called a disc floret, surrounded by linear petals called ray florets. They make an eye-catching summer display in an open border, as ground cover, or in containers. The soft leaves mix well with plants with strong leaf outlines, such as phormium and yucca. Unless stated otherwise, the recommended plants have a spreading habit and linear to lance-shaped or reverse lance-shaped leaves, some with slightly serrated edges, about 8 cm (3¼ in) long. There are about 70 species of this semi-woody, evergreen from South Africa. They are not reliably frost hardy and survive best in free-draining soils in mild areas. Dry sunny conditions suit them best. The plants can tolerate dry conditions in shade but may flower sparsely as a result.

RECOMMENDED SPECIES AND VARIETIES

O. 'Blackthorn Seedling'♀ The dark brown centres of this plant contrast with the rose-magenta petals. HEIGHT & SPREAD 30 × 60 cm (12 × 24 in).

▲ *Osteospermum 'Buttermilk'*

O. 'Buttermilk'♀ Pale primrose and white petals with dark brown centres appear among the grey-green, egg-shaped leaves of this upright plant. HEIGHT & SPREAD 60 × 30 cm (2 × 1 ft).

O. 'Cannington John' Pink, spoon-shaped petals offset white centres in this prostrate plant. HEIGHT & SPREAD 30 × 60 cm (1 × 2 ft).

O. caulescens (syn. *O. ecklonis* var. *prostratum*)

O. ecklonis (syn. *Dimorphotheca ecklonis*) The petals are soft white above and striped, slate-blue underneath, while the centre is a

▲ *Osteospermum ecklonis var. prostratum*

dark, metallic blue. This plant is upright. HEIGHT & SPREAD 60×60 cm (2×2 ft).

The recumbent form, var. *prostratum*♀ (syn. *O. caulescens*), creeps along the ground to a height of 30 cm (12 in).

O. **'Gold Sparkler'** Gold-splashed, green leaves earn this upright plant its place in the garden. The flowers have pale pink petals and dark brown centres. HEIGHT & SPREAD 40×60 cm (16×24 in).

O. **'Hopleys'**♀ The yellow centres stand out against the mauvish pink petals with white bases and purple undersides. HEIGHT & SPREAD 30×60 cm (1×2 ft).

O. **'Jacarandum'**♀ The light purple petals have undersides streaked with yellow. HEIGHT & SPREAD 30×60 cm (1×2 ft).

O. jucundum♀ Black-purple centres are surrounded by petals that are mauve to rich purple above and dark purple underneath. The shiny, greyish green leaves are spoon-shaped. HEIGHT & SPREAD 20×60 cm (8×24 in).

O. **'Lady Leitrim'**♀ (syn. *O.* 'Pale Face') White petals shaded pink at the base and mauve underneath are set off by big, yellow centres. HEIGHT & SPREAD 30×60 cm (1×2 ft).

O. **'Langtrees'**♀ Yellow and blue centres contrast with pink petals that are bronze-coloured underneath. HEIGHT & SPREAD 30×60 cm (1×2 ft).

O. **'Merriments Joy'**♀ Yellowish green, lance to spoon-shaped leaves set off vivid reddish purple petals with pale, silvery purple undersides. HEIGHT & SPREAD 35×60 cm (14×24 in).

O. **'Pink Whirls'**♀ The spoon-shaped,

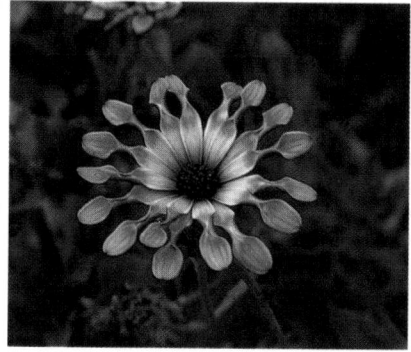

▲ *Osteospermum* 'Pink Whirls'

pink petals have mauve undersides, while the centres are also mauve. This plant is upright. HEIGHT & SPREAD 60×60 cm (2×2 ft).

O. **'Silver Sparkler'**♀ Variegated cream and green leaves are complemented by flowers with white petals and purple centres. This plant is upright. HEIGHT & SPREAD 60×60 cm (2×2 ft).

▲ *Osteospermum* 'Silver Sparkler'

O. **'Stardust'**♀ Dark purplish red petals with mauve undersides contrast with the yellow to green flower centres. The hairy leaves are olive-green. HEIGHT & SPREAD 45×60 cm (18×24 in).

O. **'Weetwood'**♀ The white flower petals are deep mauve underneath and have yellow-white centres. The leaves are soft green. This is one of the hardiest cultivars. HEIGHT & SPREAD 60×60 cm (2×2 ft).

▲ *Osteospermum* 'Weetwood'

O. **'Whirligig'**♀ Grey-green leaves complement white, rippled, paddle-shaped petals with mauve undersides. The centres of this upright plant are powder-blue. HEIGHT & SPREAD 60×60 cm (2×2 ft).

CULTIVATION Plant in well-drained soil and in a sunny position in late spring. Staking is not necessary.

PROPAGATION Take semi-ripe stem cuttings in late summer for rooting under glass. Grow on in pots and plant out in spring. Sow the seed of species in late winter for early summer flowering plants.

PESTS AND DISEASES Usually trouble free.

Ostrya
Hop hornbeam
Betulaceae

Ostrya carpinifolia

Ostryas are deciduous trees with good yellow foliage in autumn and moderately slow growth. They bear male and female flowers on the same plant, followed by curious hop-like fruits which are a large part of their appeal. Those listed below cast a pleasant amount of dappled shade which allows grass to grow underneath reasonably well.

▲ *Ostrya carpinifolia*

RECOMMENDED SPECIES AND VARIETIES

O. carpinifolia (hop hornbeam) This shapely broad-headed tree makes an ideal specimen for a large garden in sheltered parts of Britain. Male flowers are in 7.5 cm (3 in) long, hanging yellow catkins, usually in threes. Females are smaller at 5 cm (2 in) long and green and reddish at first. They develop into clusters of light brown nuts measuring 5 mm (¼ in), enclosed in a flat, papery husk. The alternate leaves, up to 8 cm (3¼ in) long, are broadly oval with a pointed tip, regularly toothed edges and distinct parallel veins. Native to lime-rich valleys and mountain slopes of W Asia and S Europe. HEIGHT & SPREAD 6×4 m (20×13 ft) after 20 years, ultimately 20 m (66 ft) tall.

O. virginiana (American hop hornbeam) This sun-loving woodland tree is remarkably tolerant of a range of soils and is also very hardy. It has brown scaly bark and

Oxydendrum
Sorrel tree, sourwood
Ericaceae

Oxydendrum arboreum

Vivid autumnal foliage in shades of red follows the slender, drooping flowerheads of this deciduous shrub or small tree. There is only one species in this genus. Although hardy, the plant needs summer heat to thrive and does best in warmer regions. It prefers an acid soil and produces the best leaf colour when planted in an open site.

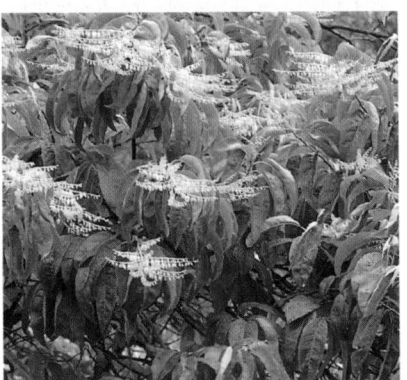

▲ *Oxydendrum arboreum*

Oxydendrum arboreum Drooping clusters of tubular white flowers appear in late summer. The plant is at its best in early autumn, when its leaves turn red. The lanceolate leaves have elongated tapering points and reach up to 20 cm (8 in) long. They sometimes have finely serrated edges. Clothed in deeply furrowed bark, this species usually forms a tree-like shrub, but occasionally develops into a tree 18 m (60 ft) tall. Native to eastern USA. HEIGHT & SPREAD 1.8×1.5 m (6×5 ft) after 10 years, ultimately 6 m (20 ft) tall.

CULTIVATION Plant in autumn or spring in loose, friable acid soil that is moist but well drained. Position in full sun or partial shade.

PROPAGATION Sow shop-bought seed in mid to late winter under glass in peat or sphagnum. Protect from strong sunlight and keep the growing medium moist. Plant out when 3 or 4 years old, keeping root disturbance to a minimum. Alternatively, take softwood cuttings in summer.

PRUNING Not usually necessary, but plants can be shaped or unwanted lower branches removed in winter or early spring.

PESTS AND DISEASES Usually trouble free.

Oxypetalum see *Tweedia*

Ozothamnus
Compositae

Ozothamnus ledifolius

The shrubs of this genus are valued for their dense, evergreen foliage. There are smaller species, which suit a rock garden, and larger species to grow in a sunny border. Natives of mountain and heathland in Australia and New Zealand, the plants vary somewhat in hardiness. The species listed below used to belong to *Helichrysum*.

RECOMMENDED SPECIES AND VARIETIES

O. coralloides♀ Erect, stout branchlets are covered with tiny, scale-like, shiny green leaves. The leaves' white, woolly undersurface shows at the margins and produces a coral-like effect. The flowers, infrequently produced in cultivation, are borne in 6 mm (¼ in) wide heads composed of tiny yellow florets. This compact shrub is hardy, but it requires perfect drainage. HEIGHT & SPREAD 30×40 cm (12×16 in) after 5 years, ultimately 40 cm (16 in) tall.

▲ *Ozothamnus ledifolius*

O. ledifolius♀ (kerosene bush) The flowers of this small, dense shrub are borne in clusters about 3 cm (1¼ in) across. In late spring the flower buds are brick-red, opening to white in early summer. The yellow branchlets have narrow, shiny, dark green, leathery leaves about 1 cm (⅜ in) long with the margins turned under. The uppermost leaves of the plant are erect, showing their yellow felted undersurface and giving the plant a golden effect. Hardy in the southern counties and often successful farther north. HEIGHT & SPREAD 50×40 cm (20×16 in) after 5 years, ultimately 80 cm (32 in) tall.

O. rosmarinifolius This is an erect shrub whose slender branchlets, white with woolly hairs, are densely clothed with

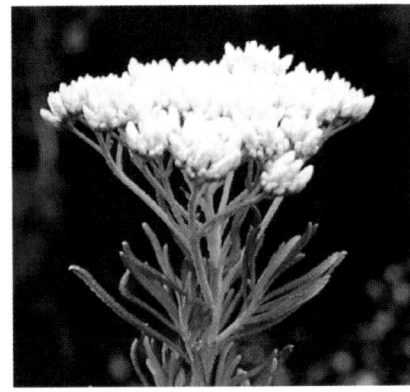

▲ *Ozothamnus rosmarinifolius*

needle-like leaves up to 3 cm (1¼ in) long. The leaves' rough or warty upper surface is bright green and hairless in some forms of the species; greyish and hairy in others. The leaf margins are rolled under and the underside is white. The numerous flower clusters, up to 5 cm (2 in) across, are purplish or pinkish in bud opening to white, and appear from early to mid summer. The plant is reasonably hardy in southern counties. HEIGHT & SPREAD 1.8×1.2 m (6×4 ft) after 5 years, ultimately 3 m (10 ft) tall.

▲ *Ozothamnus rosmarinifolius* 'Silver Jubilee'

'Silver Jubilee'♀ has white felted branchlets and 2.5 cm (1 in) long silvery leaves. The flowerheads are pinkish in bud opening to white.

O. selago This hardy rock-garden plant has erect branchlets clothed with small, scale-like, shiny green leaves, pressed flat against the twigs. The flowerheads, 6 mm (¼ in) across, are composed of numerous creamy white florets, and appear from late spring to early summer. HEIGHT & SPREAD 30×40 cm (12×16 in) after 5 years, ultimately 40 cm (16 in) tall.

CULTIVATION Plant in well-drained soil in an open, sunny situation.

PROPAGATION Take small cuttings of one-year-old wood, preferably with a heel, in early or mid spring.

PRUNING No pruning is necessary.

PESTS AND DISEASES Usually trouble free.

p-q

Pachyphragma
Cruciferae

The tiny white flowers begin to appear as winter yields to spring and continue until early summer. New leaves emerge almost as early from the mat formed by overwintering rosettes and the whole plant looks fresh and green by mid spring. This herbaceous perennial, with creeping rhizomes, provides excellent ground cover in shady parts of the garden. *Pachyphragma macrophyllum*, the only species in the genus, is hardy and will even tolerate heavy clay soils.

▲ *Pachyphragma macrophyllum*

Pachyphragma macrophyllum (syn. *Cardamine asarifolia*) Dense clusters of pure white, 4-petalled, 1.5 cm (½ in) wide flowers, are borne on erect stems. At close range the flowers emit a slightly unpleasant smell. The glossy, overlapping dark green leaves grow from the base. These are kidney-shaped with a scalloped edge and up to 10 cm (4 in) wide; 4 or 5 similar but smaller leaves grow from the flower stems. When ripe, the flattened pods, up to 12 cm (4¾ in) long, split open to release smooth brown seeds. HEIGHT & SPREAD 40×80 cm (16×32 in).

CULTIVATION Plant in autumn or spring in moist ground in partial to deep shade. Plants will thrive in clay or limy soils provided they are not allowed to dry out.

PROPAGATION Divide or take softwood cuttings in late spring. Sow seed in autumn.

PESTS AND DISEASES Usually trouble free.

Pachysandra
Buxaceae

A carpet of rich green or variegated leathery leaves, enlivened by small white flowers in late spring or early summer, provides excellent, weed-suppressing ground cover for shady places. These hardy, evergreen sub-shrubs are easily grown and particularly useful for the foot of shade-loving shrubs, such as rhododendrons and camellias. Native to E Asia and eastern USA.

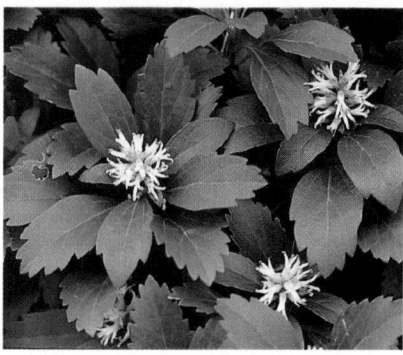

▲ *Pachysandra terminalis*

RECOMMENDED SPECIES AND VARIETIES

P. terminalis♀ Creeping, rooting stems produce short erect branches bearing clusters of deep green, coarsely toothed, oval or oblong leaves up to 10 cm (4 in) long. In early spring white flowers appear in 4 cm (1½ in) long spikes at the ends of the previous year's shoots. Each spike contains several male flowers with prominent stamens, 1 cm (⅜ in) long, and a few smaller female flowers at the base. These may be followed by fleshy, oval, white fruits, 1.5 cm (½ in) long. HEIGHT & SPREAD 20×40 cm (8×16 in).

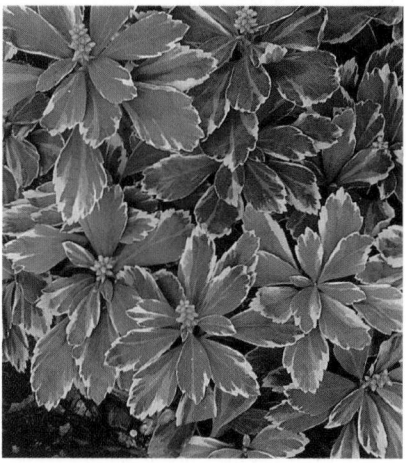

▲ *Pachysandra terminalis* 'Variegata'

'Green Carpet' is more compact, with smaller leaves and a height and spread of 10×20 cm (4×8 in). 'Variegata'♀ has green leaves edged in creamy white, with a height and spread of 15×40 cm (6×16 in).

CULTIVATION Plant in early autumn or spring in a fairly moist yet well-drained, leafy soil in partial or full shade. Do not plant on shallow, chalky soils.

PROPAGATION Divide established plants in early autumn or early spring.

PESTS AND DISEASES Usually trouble free.

Pachystachys
Acanthaceae

Pachystachys lutea

Tropical, evergreen shrubs from the Americas, these house or greenhouse plants are grown for their striking flowering spikes. They are usually raised from cuttings every year, although it is possible to grow one plant for several years.

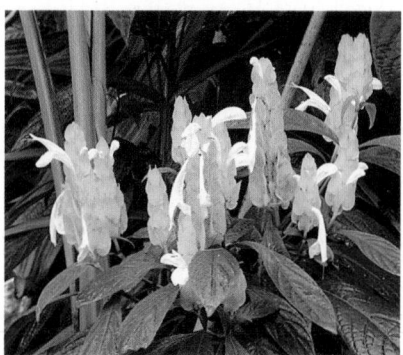

▲ *Pachystachys lutea*

RECOMMENDED SPECIES

P. lutea♀ (lollipop plant) Soft mid to deep green, lance-shaped leaves, up to 7.5 cm (3 in) long, are borne on upright stems. At the end of each stem is a 10 cm (4 in) spike of bright yellow bracts, from which emerge tubular, 2-lipped white flowers. HEIGHT & SPREAD 45×30 cm (18×12 in).

CULTIVATION Grow in the home or conservatory at a minimum temperature of 13°C (55°F) and in good but indirect sunlight. Use a soil-based compost, such as John Innes No. 2. Water freely in spring and summer, supplying a high potash liquid feed every 6 weeks. Water sparingly in winter.

PROPAGATION Take softwood cuttings in spring and early summer, then discard the old plant if you wish. Cuttings come into flower after about 3 months.

PRUNING In late winter or early spring cut back hard to encourage the development of vigorous young shoots suitable for cuttings.

PESTS AND DISEASES Red spider mite and whitefly may be troublesome.

Paeonia
Paeony, peony
Paeoniaceae

Paeonia delavayi var. lutea

The showy flowers of peonies are a striking sight in a mixed border and are often gloriously fragrant as well. The genus includes upright deciduous shrubs, also known as tree peonies, and herbaceous perennials which form compact clumps.

The blooms, which make excellent cut flowers, are borne in late spring and early summer. In the species they are single and globe-shaped, with up to ten petals and numerous stamens. The cultivars may be semidouble, with two or three rows of petals around a central boss of stamens; double, with a large number of petals, the inner ones usually smaller and obscuring the stamens; or anemone form, with one or two rows of outer petals and a centre of numerous densely arranged narrow petals derived from the stamens. Most of the cultivars are scented, and tend to flower more profusely than many of the species. The leaves are compound or lobed, some colouring to shades of yellow and red in the autumn, when the seedpods of a few species reveal brightly coloured seeds.

Peonies are tuberous-rooted plants and may take a year or two to become established. They should be allowed to remain where they are for many years as they resent disturbance. They do well in full sun on any fertile soil with plenty of organic material added at planting time. Although most peonies are hardy the shrubs can be caught by spring frost, and if they are planted in a location where early morning sun reaches them, the young growth may be damaged. Native to Europe, temperate Asia, China and NW America. The shrubs included below reach their full size in about five years.

RECOMMENDED SPECIES AND VARIETIES

P. arietina see *P. mascula* ssp. *arietina*

P. cambessedesii♀ (Majorcan peony) This herbaceous perennial has single deep rose-pink flowers, 10 cm (4 in) across, with red filaments and purple stigmas. The flowers appear in late spring. The glossy dark green leaves have purple-red veins, stalks and undersurfaces. Each leaf is 25 cm (10 in) across, made up of lance-shaped leaflets 10 cm (4 in) long. This species is not reliably hardy, so plant it in a warm part of the garden such as at the base of a south-facing wall. HEIGHT & SPREAD 45×45 cm (18×18 in).

▲ *Paeonia cambessedesii*

P. corallina see *P. mascula*

P. **'Defender'**♀ The single red blooms of this herbaceous perennial appear in late spring. The flowers are up to 15 cm (6 in) across with a central mass of yellow stamens. The glossy bright green leaves are 20 cm (8 in) wide, composed of elliptic to oblong leaflets up to 8 cm (3¼ in) long. HEIGHT & SPREAD 75×75 cm (2½×2½ ft).

▲ *Paeonia delavayi*

P. delavayi♀ This shrubby tree peony bears deep maroon-red single flowers, 8 cm (3¼ in) across, with yellow anthers in late spring. The stiff stems bear deeply cut shiny leaves, up to 30 cm (12 in) across, dark green above and blue-green beneath. Each leaflet is up to 10 cm (4 in) long. HEIGHT & SPREAD 1.8×1 m (6×3 ft).

The golden yellow flowers of var. *ludlowii*♀ (syn. *P. lutea* var. *ludlowii*) (Tibetan peony) are up to 12 cm (4¾ in) in diameter. They are unscented. The yellow flowers of var. *lutea* (syn. *P. lutea*) are unscented, up to 7.5 cm (3 in) across and carried in small clusters. The leaves are mid green.

P. emodi Fragrant, single white flowers, 12 cm (4¾ in) across with a central boss of golden yellow stamens, are borne in late spring. The glossy fresh green dissected foliage, up to 15 cm (6 in) wide, has 9 or more leaflets, each 17 cm (6¾ in) long. In cold gardens this herbaceous perennial needs winter protection. It tolerates light shade. HEIGHT & SPREAD 1×1 m (3×3 ft).

P. lactiflora This erect herbaceous perennial bears fragrant single white flowers, 6–10 cm (2½–4 in) across, in early summer. It has divided leaves up to 15 cm (6 in) wide with three stalks each carrying three leaflets up to 10 cm (4 in) long. HEIGHT & SPREAD 60×60 cm (2×2 ft).

'Adolphe Rousseau' has deep red double flowers, while those of 'Alexander Fleming' are bright rose-pink. 'Bowl of Beauty'♀ bears semidouble, soft pink flowers with conspicuous golden yellow stamens which look like narrow petals. 'Duchesse

▲ *Paeonia lactiflora* 'Bowl of Beauty'

de Nemours'♀ (syn. 'Mrs Gwyn Lewis') has strongly scented, double flowers with very large incurving outer petals, tinged with palest green and fading to white, and creamy yellow inner petals with irregular edges. The very fragrant double flowers of 'Félix Crousse'♀ (syn. 'Victor Hugo') are rich carmine with dark red centres, and ruffled, often white-tipped petals. 'Festiva Maxima'♀ produces scented, double flowers, composed of pure white outer petals, while the inner petals are white with a basal crimson blotch.

'Lady Alexandra Duff'♀ has scented, soft pink, double blooms. The flowers of 'Laura Dessert'♀ are scented and double, the outer petals a creamy blush white, the incurving inner petals a rich lemon-yellow, often with deeply cut edges. 'Monsieur Jules Elie'♀ has silvery rose, large and fully double blooms. 'Sarah Bernhardt'♀ has double, scented flowers with apple-blossom pink petals, ruffled at the edges. 'White

▲ *Paeonia lactiflora* 'Sarah Bernhardt'

▲ *Paeonia lactiflora* 'White Wings'

Wings' has single, scented, white blooms with prominent yellow stamens. The foliage of **'Whitleyi Major'**♥ (syn. 'The Bride') colours well in autumn. The single, ivory-white flowers have yellow anthers.
P. lutea see *P. delavayi* var. *lutea*.
P. lutea var. *ludlowii* see *P. delavayi* var. *ludlowii*

▲ *Paeonia mascula*

P. mascula (syn. *P. corallina*) Red, pink or occasionally white, single flowers are seen on this hardy herbaceous perennial from late spring to early summer. The flowers are 12 cm (4¾ in) across and have a central mass of yellow stamens. The glossy bright green leaves have 9-15 oval leaflets and are up to 25 cm (10 in) across. Position in full sun. HEIGHT & SPREAD 60 cm×1 m (2×3 ft).

▼ *Paeonia mascula* ssp. *arietina*

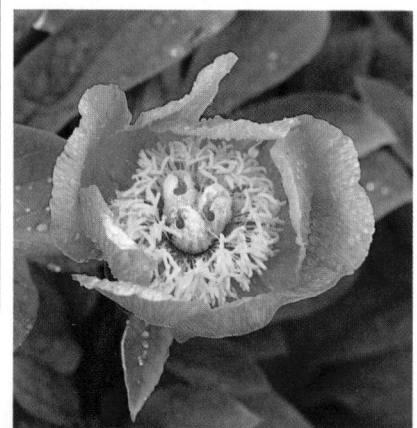

The leaves of ssp. *arietina* (syn. *P. arietina*) are glossy dark green with hairy undersides. The single pinky red flowers are borne in late spring. Its cultivar **'Northern Glory'** has grey-green leaves and deep magenta flowers.

▲ *Paeonia mascula* ssp. *arietina* 'Northern Glory'

P. mlokosewitschii♥ Soft bluish green foliage is topped by single lemon-yellow flowers, 12 cm (4¾ in) across, in mid to late spring. This herbaceous perennial is a dwarf plant suitable for the front of the border. The leaves, up to 12 cm (4¾ in) across, are composed of broadly oval leaflets 6 cm (2½ in) across, and often have good autumn tints. HEIGHT & SPREAD 75×75 cm (2½×2½ ft).
P. obovata♥ Rose-pink flowers, 7 cm (2¾ in) in diameter, are borne in late spring. The shiny dark green leaves, about 20 cm (8 in) across, are composed of leaflets 15 cm (6 in) long. This herbaceous perennial is better suited to semi-shade than full sun. HEIGHT & SPREAD 60×60 cm (2×2 ft).

The flowers of var. *alba*♥ have white petals with crimson bases and a central circle of golden stamens.
P. officinalis This herbaceous perennial is the parent of the traditional cottage-garden peonies. The fragrant single flowers are crimson, 15 cm (6 in) across, with yellow stamens. The glossy bright green leaves, 15 cm (6 in) across, are composed of elliptic to oblong leaflets up to 11 cm (4¼ in) long. HEIGHT & SPREAD 60×60 cm (2×2 ft).

Paeonia officinalis 'Rubra Plena'

'Anemoniflora Rosea'♥ has deep pink flowers with yellow stamens like small petals. **'Rosea Plena'**♥ has deep pink flowers. **'Rubra Plena'**♥ has crimson blooms.
P. peregrina **'Otto Froebel'**♥ In early summer, this herbaceous perennial has vermilion single flowers 12 cm (4¾ in) across.

▲ *Paeonia officinalis* 'Rosea Plena'

Its shiny green leaves, up to 12 cm (4¾ in) across, are composed of up to 17 segments, each 2 cm (¾ in) wide. This is generally a rather difficult plant to establish in gardens. It does best in a warm spot such as the base of a south-facing wall. HEIGHT & SPREAD 1 m×60 cm (3×2 ft).
P. suffruticosa (Moutan peony, tree peony) This species, the authentic tree peony, makes a stately plant for a shrub border. Bowl-shaped flowers, 15 cm (6 in) across, open in late spring. Colour varies but flowers are usually white with a magenta or pink blotch at the base of each petal; pink and red forms also occur. The deeply cut leaves, 30 cm (12 in) across, are glossy dark green above and blue-green beneath. Each of the lobed leaflets is up to 10 cm (4 in) long. HEIGHT & SPREAD 2×1.5 m (6½×5 ft).

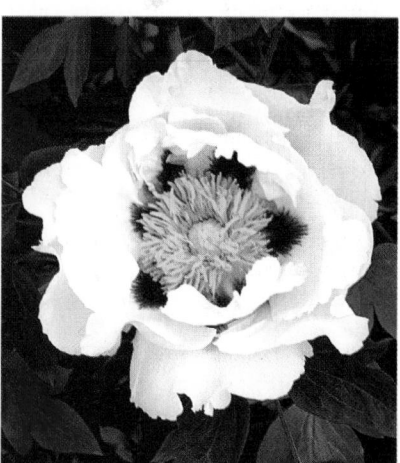

▲ *Paeonia suffruticosa*

'Rock's Variety' has large white flowers with a maroon blotch on the inner petals. There are also many double-flowered cultivars available in a range of colours.
P. veitchii A profusion of single crimson-purple flowers appear in late spring. Each flower is up to 10 cm (4 in) in diameter. With fresh green dissected leaves, about 12 cm (4¾ in) across, this herbaceous perennial makes a compact clump. Bluish seeds

▲ *Paeonia veitchii*

follow the flowers in autumn. HEIGHT & SPREAD 60×60 cm (2×2 ft).

The flowers of var. *woodwardii* are paler, in varying shades of pink.

CULTIVATION Plant herbaceous perennials from autumn to spring and shrubby peonies in autumn. All prefer a fertile, well-drained soil and a position in full sun.

Set the young plants of the herbaceous species so that the buds are about 2.5 cm (1 in) below the soil. Provide some support for the plants. Remove dead flowers as they fade. Cut down herbaceous perennials after the foliage has died in autumn.

PROPAGATION Sow ripe seed of species in pots of loam-based compost in a coldframe in autumn. Plant out in autumn if the seedlings are large enough, or grow on for another year.

Propagate cultivars of herbaceous perennials by careful division of existing clumps in autumn, cutting with a knife to ensure that the tuberous roots are not damaged too much in the process. Cultivars of shrubby species are propagated by grafting, usually carried out by specialists.

PRUNING Prune shrubby species after flowering occasionally to keep the shape and size required. Annual pruning is not necessary.

PESTS AND DISEASES Peonies can be attacked by chrysanthemum eelworms as well as swift moth caterpillars. The most widespread problem is peony wilt. Peony blotch produces grey-brown spots with reddish margins on the leaves and stems. Grey mould and viruses also afflict peonies.

Paeony see *Paeonia*
Pagoda tree see *Sophora japonica*
Painted lady see *Gladiolus carneus*
Painted tongue see *Salpiglossis sinuata*
Palm, Canary Island date
    see *Phoenix canariensis*
Palm, Chusan see *Trachycarpus fortunei*
Palm, date see *Phoenix*
Palm, kentia see *Howea fosteriana*
Palm, parlour see *Chamaedorea elegans*
Palm, sentry see *Howea*
Panicum see GRASSES p. 300
Pansy see *Viola*

Papaver
Poppy
Papaveraceae

Papaver alpinum

Bright-flowering favourites of cottage and rock gardens, poppies range from quick-growing annuals to robust herbaceous and evergreen perennials. They are mostly sun-loving, preferring a well-drained site, and are ideally suited to wildflower gardens or for filling gaps in herbaceous borders.

The flowers – usually with four petals but sometimes more – come in a large range of colours, including white, yellow, pink, purple, violet, orange, red and almost black. The pods, containing numerous seeds, vary in shape from globular to oval, with a distinctive ring of pores at the top. They are not particularly decorative except for those of *Papaver somniferum*, which can be dried and used in floral arrangements. When cut, most species exude an orange or yellowish latex which can irritate the skin.

RECOMMENDED SPECIES AND VARIETIES
P. alpinum hort. (alpine poppy) White, yellow, orange or occasionally salmon-pink flowers, up to 4 cm (1½ in) across, appear in late spring and until mid summer if dead-headed. These dainty little tufted evergreen perennials are short-lived and are often grown as annuals as they self-sow readily in the garden. They have grey or grey-green finely divided leaves. The pods are small, barrel-shaped and bristly. HEIGHT & SPREAD 20×20 cm (8×8 in).

'Alba' (syn. f. *album*) has white flowers with a boss of yellow stamens. 'Summer Breeze' provides a fine selection of F₁ hybrids with flowers in shades of red, orange, yellow and white above a mound of grey foliage.

P. atlanticum (Moroccan poppy) Dull orange, saucer-shaped flowers, about 6 cm (2½ in) across, are borne on wiry branched stems in late spring and throughout summer. An evergreen perennial, it has deeply divided, rough leaves mostly crowded into a basal rosette. The seedpod is club-shaped and smooth. The plant self-sows in the garden. HEIGHT & SPREAD 50×50 cm (20×20 in).

'Flore Pleno' has semidouble flowers. 'Double Orange' has semidouble and double, brick-red to tangerine blooms.

P. bracteatum see *P. orientale*
P. commutatum♀ In mid summer this annual species bears vivid scarlet flowers 6–9 cm (2½–3½ in) across with a large black

▲ *Papaver commutatum* 'Ladybird'

blotch in the centre of each petal. The fleshy, bristly leaves are deeply divided. The seed capsule is smooth and almost spherical. HEIGHT & SPREAD 45×45 cm (1½×1½ ft).

'Ladybird' is a particularly large-flowered form with a big black blotch in the middle of each petal.

P. heldreichii see *P. spicatum*
P. lateritium Small fiery orange flowers, up to 5 cm (2 in) across, appear in late spring and early summer. A rhizomatous patch-forming herbaceous perennial, this species has lance-shaped, coarsely toothed leaves. HEIGHT & SPREAD 50×50 cm (20×20 in).

The species is quite rare in gardens and is generally represented by the following cultivar. 'Fireball' (syn. 'Nanum', *P. orientale* 'Flore Pleno') is smaller, at only 30 cm (1 ft) tall, and has double orange flowers.

P. miyabeanum Pale yellow flowers up to 4 cm (1½ in) across are held on bristly stems in late spring and throughout summer. A delightful, little short-lived, evergreen perennial poppy, it has tufts of greyish, rough, deeply divided leaves and bristly round seedpods. It self-sows easily. HEIGHT & SPREAD 10×10 cm (4×4 in).

P. nudicaule (Iceland poppy) Bowl-shaped, bright yellow to orange or red flowers, 4–6 cm (1½–2½ in) across, appear in late spring and early summer if sown in autumn, or from mid to late summer if sown in spring. This annual or short-lived evergreen perennial forms basal tufts of yellowish or greyish green, deeply divided leaves. The seed capsule is club-shaped to oblong and covered with bristles. HEIGHT & SPREAD 45×45 cm (1½×1½ ft).

The cultivars mostly have large flowers, up to 12.5 cm (5 in) across. 'Aurora Borealis' has large flowers in a wide range of colours from white to yellow, orange, salmon and red. **Champagne Bubbles Group**, to 40 cm (16 in) tall, has large flowers in various shades from yellow to red. **Garden Gnome (Gartenwerg) Group**, a dwarf strain to 30 cm (12 in) only, has flowers in the full range of colours from white and yellow through salmon and orange to red. 'Kelmscott Giant' is about 80 cm (32 in) tall with flowers in pastel colours.

'Oregon Rainbows' has single or semi-double blooms, up to 18 cm (7 in) wide, in the full colour range from white and yellow through to red, including bicolors and picotees with a darker or paler rim. 'San Remo' produces single flowers which are mostly in yellows, oranges and reds. 'Unwins Giant Coonara' is up to 50 cm (20 in) tall, with flowers in yellow, orange and red. **Wonderland Hybrids** provide dwarf plants in the full colour range.

Papaver orientale

P. orientale (oriental poppy) The deep red flowers, 10–15 cm (4–6 in) across, usually have a violet-black blotch at the base of the 4–6 petals. They appear from early to mid summer. This robust, bristly, herbaceous perennial forms large clumps, generally spreading by underground runners and with bristly, deep green, oblong to lance-shaped, deeply divided leaves up to 30 cm (12 in) long. The seed pod is round and smooth. HEIGHT & SPREAD 90×70 cm (36×28 in).

The cultivars of *P. orientale* listed here are 60–75 cm (24–30 in) tall unless stated otherwise. 'Allegro' has bright scarlet petals with bold black blotches at their base. 'Beauty of Livermere'♀ is 1.2 m (4 ft) tall with scarlet flowers with a large black

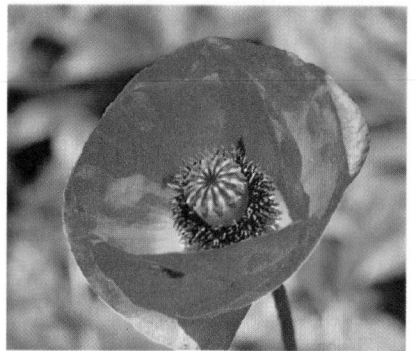

▲ *Papaver orientale*
Papaver orientale 'Allegro' ▼

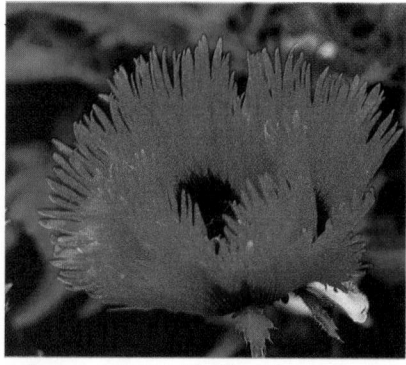

▲ *Papaver orientale* 'Curlilocks'

blotch at the base of each petal. 'Black and White'♀ has white petals with black blotches. 'Blue Moon' is 1 m (3 ft) tall with flowers up to 25 cm (10 in) across that are mauve-pink with black at the base of each petal and maroon veins on their reverse. 'Cedric's Pink' (syn. 'Cedric Morris') has soft pink petals with black blotches and is 1 m (3 ft) tall. 'Curlilocks' has orange-red petals with a black blotch at their base and distinctive lacerated edges. 'Doubloon' is 1 m (3 ft) tall with orange-red, unblotched double flowers. 'Indian Chief' has mahogany-red unblotched flowers. 'Ladybird' is 60 cm (2 ft) tall and its flowers are vermilion with a black blotch at the base of each petal. 'Marcus Perry' is a vigorous plant with orange-scarlet, unblotched blooms. 'Mrs Perry'♀ has rich salmon-pink flowers, each petal with a black blotch at the base. 'Perry's White', 1 m (3 ft) tall, has pure white flowers with a dark centre and a boss of violet-black stamens. 'Picotee' has frilled white petals with a distinctive orange edge.

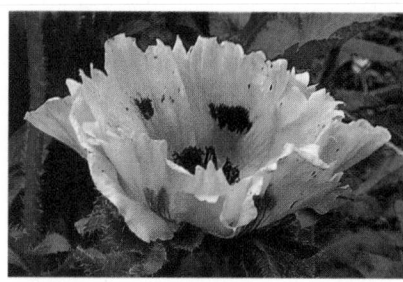

▲ *Papaver orientale* 'Mrs Perry'
Papaver orientale 'Perry's White' ▼

'Prinzessin Victoria Louise' has salmon-rose flowers, each petal with a black basal blotch. 'Salmon Glow' is 1 m (3 ft) tall, with double salmon-pink flowers; 'Scarlet King' has blood-red double flowers on stems 1 m (3 ft) high. 'Türkenlouis'♀ is 1 m (3 ft) tall. The petals are deep scarlet, with a black basal blotch and finely cut edges.

P. rhoeas (common poppy, corn poppy, Flander's poppy) The early to mid summer flowers of this annual species are rich scarlet, occasionally paler red, pink or white, up to 9 cm (3½ in) across, with broad, rounded, overlapping petals with or without a black basal blotch. The leaves are lobed, with narrow, toothed segments and the seed capsule is rounded and smooth. HEIGHT & SPREAD 60×30 cm (2×1 ft).

▲ *Papaver orientale* 'Picotee'
Papaver orientale 'Prinzessin Victoria Louise' ▲

'Mother of Pearl' has single flowers in pastel shades of pink, silvery white and white. **Shirley** poppies are single-flowered plants in shades of red, pink, mauve, lilac and white, including bicolors and picotees edged with a darker or lighter colour. **Double Shirley** poppies are also available.

P. rupifragum Brick-red flowers, up to 4.5 cm (1¾ in) across, appear on branched, leafy stems in late spring and summer. It is a herbaceous perennial with grey-green, more or less smooth, deeply divided leaves. HEIGHT & SPREAD 50×50 cm (20×20 in).

'Flore Pleno' has semidouble flowers.

P. somniferum♀ (opium poppy) This fleshy upright annual has cup-shaped flowers that are white to pink or purple, up to 12.5 cm (5 in) across, the base of each petal normally with a dark blotch. The flowers open in mid summer and are followed by large, smooth, rounded grey-green seedpods, widely used in dried flower arrangements. HEIGHT & SPREAD 1 m×30 cm (3×1 ft).

Many of the fully double forms are referred to as **Peony-Flowered Group**, named according to flower colour. Forms with double flowers and fringed petals are referred to as the **Carnation-Flowered Group**. Other cultivars include 'Hen and Chickens', with single pink flowers and large seedpods surrounded by numerous minor pods, 'Pink Chiffon', with pale pink flowers, and 'White Cloud', with large double white flowers with lacerated petals.

▲ *Papaver somniferum*

P. spicatum (syn. *P. heldreichii*) From early to mid summer spikes of flattish pale brick-red flowers are borne on stiff stems which rise out of a basal tuft of grey-green leaves. The flowers of this stout herbaceous perennial are up to 4.5 cm (1¾ in) across. HEIGHT & SPREAD 70×40 cm (28×16 in).

CULTIVATION Plant in a sunny well-drained site, though *P. atlanticum* and *P. rupifragum* will tolerate partial shade. Sow the annual species thinly where they are required to flower and provide some support when they come into bloom. With the exception of *P. nudicaule*, annuals dislike transplanting.

Plant the perennials in early spring. Dress the larger species with bone meal or mulch with well-rotted manure. Apart from *P. lateritium* and *P. orientale*, perennials resent disturbance once established.

PROPAGATION Sow seed in late autumn or early spring in pots in a coldframe. Divide *P. orientale* or take root cuttings after flowering in mid to late summer.

PESTS AND DISEASES Slugs and snails may attack seedlings. Aphids may attack plants in bud. *P. miyabeanum* and *P. spicatum* suffer from neck rot.

Paphiopedilum see ORCHIDS p. 465

p

q

Paradisea
Asphodelaceae

Fragrant white flowers adorn the slender stems of the two species in this genus in summer. Grey-green foliage offsets the almost translucent petals. These herbaceous perennials are suitable for growing in borders or at the edges of wooded areas and around shrubs.

RECOMMENDED SPECIES AND VARIETIES
P. liliastrum (paradise lily, St Bruno's lily) From 3–10 fragrant, funnel-shaped flowers, up to 5 cm (2 in) long and as wide at the mouth, bloom in loose, one-sided spikes from early to mid summer. Each of the 6 petal-like tepals (modified leaves fused with petals) has a green spot at the tip. The 4–7 linear leaves, up to 25 cm (10 in) long, arise from the base and tend to wither when flowering is over. Clusters of short, fleshy

▲ *Paradisea liliastrum*

rhizomes with fibrous roots form distinct clumps. The fruits have 3 compartments filled with plentiful, small, ridged seeds. Native to S Europe. HEIGHT & SPREAD 60×45 cm (2×1½ ft).

'**Major**'♀ is a strong-growing plant with slightly larger flowers than the species.
P. lusitanica Sweet-smelling, bell-shaped flowers, 4 cm (1½ in) across, are carried in 2 layers of loose clusters in early summer. Each stem bears 20–25 flowers. The leaves are up to 25 cm (10 in) long. This species can be grown in dappled shade as ground cover. Native to Portugal and Spain. HEIGHT & SPREAD 75 cm×1 m (2½×3 ft).

CULTIVATION Plant in early spring in well-drained, fertile soil that does not dry out and in a sunny or partially shaded spot.

PROPAGATION Divide in spring or after flowering. Sow seed when ripe or in spring.

PESTS AND DISEASES Slugs and snails may attack young plants.

Parahebe
Scrophulariaceae

Parahebe catarractae

Pretty white, pink or blue flowers bloom profusely all through summer and into autumn on these evergreen sub-shrubs. Plants are low-growing and bushy, with soft stems and woody bases. The hardy species are ideal for the rock garden and for edging borders and beds, and can also be grown in containers. The four-petalled flowers, up to

2 cm (¾ in) across, differ in shape from species to species, as do the leaves. All the species listed here are hardy. They all come from New Zealand, except *Parahebe perfoliata*, which is native to Australia.

RECOMMENDED SPECIES AND VARIETIES
P. × *bidwillii* '**Kea**' White flowers with purple-red veining are borne in racemes up to 25 cm (10 in) long. The green leaves, about 6 mm (¼ in) long, are oval, with incised edges. The prostrate branches with upturned ends often root at the nodes. HEIGHT & SPREAD 15×15 cm (6×6 in).
P. catarractae♀ White, pink or blue flowers are borne among leaves that are green or bronze, oval to lance-shaped, toothed and up to 7 cm (2¾ in) long. This is a variable species, ranging from prostrate to bushy and erect in growing habit. HEIGHT & SPREAD 6–50×50 cm (2½–20×20 in).

'**Delight**'♀ carries 20 cm (8 in) long clusters of violet-blue flowers with reddish purple centres and veining. The leaves are slightly bronzed and about 2.5 cm (1 in) long. This cultivar grows up to 25 cm (10 in) tall. The flowers of ssp. *diffusa* are white, pink or blue, and the plant has a prostrate habit. The white form of *P. catarractae* is similar to 'Delight', its white flowers with reddish purple centres and veins.

▲ *Parahebe catarractae* 'Delight'

P. decora Widely spaced white flowers, decorated with pink veins, grow in stiffly erect racemes up to 15 cm (6 in) tall. The leaves of this tiny, creeping, rooting species are green to purplish and only 3 mm (⅛ in) long. HEIGHT & SPREAD 15×30 cm (6×12 in).
P. lyallii The most common form has cup-shaped, white flowers with red centres and veins. Racemes up to 7 cm (2¾ in) long carry as many as 20 flowers. The leaves are broad, toothed and up to 1.5 cm (½ in) long. HEIGHT & SPREAD 15×60 cm (6×24 in).

'**Clarence**' bears lilac flowers.
P. '**Mervyn**' Violet-blue flowers grow in racemes up to 10 cm (4 in) long, among green to purplish, rounded, toothed leaves. HEIGHT & SPREAD 10×25 cm (4×10 in).

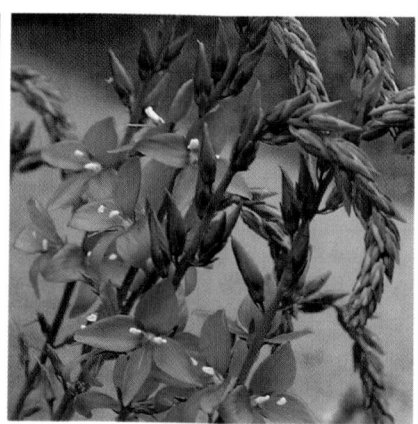

▲ *Parahebe perfoliata*

P. perfoliata♀ (digger's speedwell) The violet-blue flowers are widely spaced on the 10 cm (4 in) long racemes. Sprawling, wiry branches, 1 m (3 ft) or more in length, bear rounded, glaucous, blue-green leaves, sometimes toothed, up to 3 cm (1¼ in) wide. HEIGHT & SPREAD 1×1.5 m (3×5 ft).
CULTIVATION Plant in any soil that is well drained but not too dry at any time of year. Choose an open situation, in the sun or half shade. Cut back straggling growth after flowering and shear off old seed capsules.
PROPAGATION Small softwood cuttings taken at any time will root easily.
PESTS AND DISEASES Aphids may occasionally attack. Downy mildew can be troublesome in early autumn or spring.

Paris
Herb Paris
Trilliaceae

These shade-loving, hardy, herbaceous, woodland perennials are grown for their unusual flowers and prominent seed capsules. A single flower is borne at the top of each upright, unbranched stem which arises from the underground rhizomes. The flowers have green, leaf-like sepals, narrow petals and long stamens, and bloom in early summer. Immediately below each flower is a symmetrical whorl of leaves. A rounded, green or purple seed capsule, 2 cm (¾ in) wide, develops at the centre of each flower. The capsule turns brown and splits in late summer, revealing fleshy, black or red (poisonous) seeds. Plants suit a mixed or shrub border, perhaps within a woodland edge.
RECOMMENDED SPECIES AND VARIETIES
P. polyphylla (syn. *Daiswa polyphylla*) Green flowers, 15 cm (6 in) wide, are composed of 4–6 green sepals, equally long yellow petals and about 20 shorter greenish stamens. At the base of each flower is a whorl of deep green lance-shaped to oval leaves up to 15 cm (6 in) long. The seeds are bright red. Native to China and the Himalayas. HEIGHT & SPREAD 30–90×30 cm (12–36×12 in).

P. thibetica (syn. *Daiswa thibetica*) This plant has flowers slightly smaller than those of *P. polyphylla*, with yellowish green sepals, 5 linear petals and about 10 conspicuous creamy yellow stamens elongated into threads. The leaves are ovate, mid green and about 5 cm (2 in) long. The seeds are red. Native to the Himalayas. HEIGHT & SPREAD 20×15 cm (8×6 in).

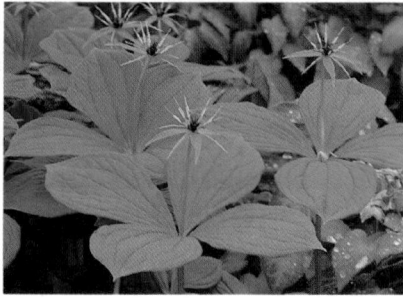

▲ *Paris quadrifolia*

P. quadrifolia Each flower, about 6 cm (2½ in) wide, has 4 lance-shaped green sepals, up to 3 cm (1¼ in) long, and 4 petals. The mid green ovate leaves are up to 8 cm (3¼ in) long. The seed capsule is also green and the seeds are black. Native to Europe. HEIGHT & SPREAD 30×15 cm (12×6 in).
CULTIVATION Plant in partial shade in humus-rich soil, keeping plants moist at all times. Mark their position well, as they only come into growth in late spring.
PROPAGATION Divide clumps in spring. Sow seed in autumn and keep cool. If grown from seed, top growth may not appear until the second spring after sowing and flowering takes 5 years or more.
PESTS AND DISEASES Slugs and snails may attack young growth.

Parodia see CACTI p.106

Parrotia
Persian ironwood
Hamamelidaceae

Parrotia persica

There is just one species in this genus, a hardy deciduous tree, which brings spectacular autumn colour to the garden with its amber, crimson and gold foliage. Then, in mid winter, the bare, spreading branches become studded with tiny red flowers. An additional bonus is the attractive flaking bark seen on older trees.

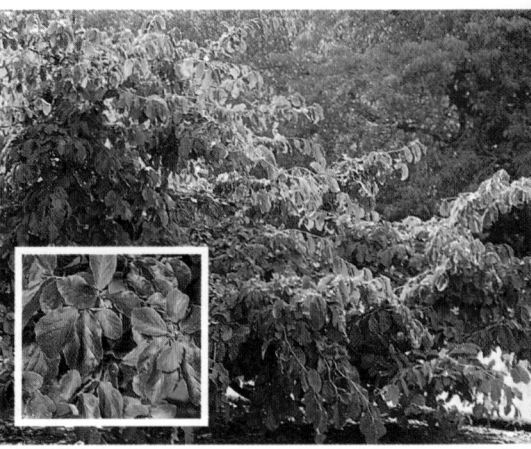

▲ *Parrotia persica*

Parrotia persica♀ The tree has a rounded habit, being almost as broad as it is tall. The flowers, consisting of red stamens only, emerge in dense clusters 1.5 cm (½ in) across, one cluster from each chocolate-brown bud case, in mid to late winter. The leaves are ovate with wavy edges and up to 12.5 cm (5 in) long. As the smooth, grey bark flakes away, an attractive pink and creamy yellow pattern develops on the trunk, shown to best advantage if the lower branches are removed. Native to N Iran and the Caucasus. HEIGHT & SPREAD 4×3 m (13×10 ft) after 20 years, ultimately 12 m (40 ft) tall.

▲ *Parrotia persica* 'Pendula'

'Pendula', with a domed habit and pendulous branches, is a smaller tree.
CULTIVATION Plant in well-drained, loamy soil between late autumn and mid spring. Site in sun, preferably, or light shade.
PROPAGATION Layer in autumn, digging up and transplanting rooted sections to new sites about 18 months later. Alternatively, sow seed in mid or late spring.
PRUNING No pruning is required, except to control the shape or size of the tree, best done between late autumn and early spring.
PESTS AND DISEASES Usually trouble free.

Parrot's bill see *Clianthus puniceus*
Parsley (culinary herb)
see HERBS p.332
Parsnip see p.742
Pasqueflower see *Pulsatilla*
Passionflower see *Passiflora*

p
q

481

Pericallis
Compositae

Daisy-like flowers typify these herbaceous perennials and shrubs, which are mostly native to the Canary Islands. They are not hardy in Britain.

The pericallis recommended here has plenty of impact and brings a summery splash to late winter and early spring. It is short-lived and suitable only as a temporary conservatory plant or houseplant, but if kept cool and moist the flowering season can extend to several weeks.

▲ *Pericallis × hybrida*

RECOMMENDED SPECIES AND VARIETIES
P. × hybrida (syn. *Senecio hybridus, S. cruentus*) (cineraria) A mass of showy flowers each 2.5–5 cm (1–2 in) across are grouped into a tight, flattish or slightly domed head that almost hides the foliage. Blue, maroon, pink, purple, red or white petals contrast with the darker flower centres, which can be any of these colours. The triangular to heart-shaped fresh green leaves are up to 15 cm (6 in) long. This rough-textured foliage is shallowly lobed and toothed, with downy undersides. Although this is herbaceous it is grown as an annual. HEIGHT & SPREAD 25×10 cm (10×4 in).

Seed is available only in mixed colours. Established strains of compact growth habit include **Amigo Hybrids** (very dwarf), **Cindy Mixture, Mini-Starlet Mixture** and **'Spring Glory'** (syn. 'Dwarf British Beauty'). **Moll Hybrids** have flowers 4 cm (1½ in) wide and are taller and very spreading, reaching 40–45 cm (16–18 in) high and 50 cm (20 in) wide.
CULTIVATION Grow in pots of John Innes No. 2 at a temperature of 7–15°C (45–59°F). Shade plants in spring and summer but provide full light in autumn and winter. Water regularly. Liquid feed once the final pot is filled with roots, but stop when the plant is in bud.

PROPAGATION Sow seed in spring for autumn flowering, and in mid to late summer for flowering in late winter and early spring. Ensure a temperature of around 15–20°C (59–68°F) for germination. Prick out seedlings 7 cm (2¾ in) apart. When they begin to crowd one another, move them to final pots in a cool, well-ventilated greenhouse, conservatory or light windowsill. Keep cool in winter and bring indoors when the flowers open if desired.
PESTS AND DISEASES Aphids can cause great damage, especially to young growth. Chrysanthemum leaf miners also attack.

Perilla
Labiatae

The striking, dark red-purple foliage of perillas provides a dramatic contrast to the floral display of many other summer bedding plants. These fast-growing, half-hardy annuals of branching, bushy habit look good as part of mixed plantings in large containers, as well as in beds and borders. The leaf colour complements pale pink flowers especially well.
RECOMMENDED SPECIES
P. frutescens var. *crispa*♀ (syn. var. *nankinensis*) (beefsteak plant) The slightly curved leaves, reddish purple with a bronze sheen, are broadly oval and up to 12 cm (4¾ in) long. The margins of the leaves are very deeply cut. Short spikes of small, white or pale violet flowers appear in late summer and early autumn. HEIGHT & SPREAD 50×25 cm (20×10 in).
CULTIVATION Plant in late spring in fertile, moist soil in full sun with some shelter from wind. Pinch out the growing points of the

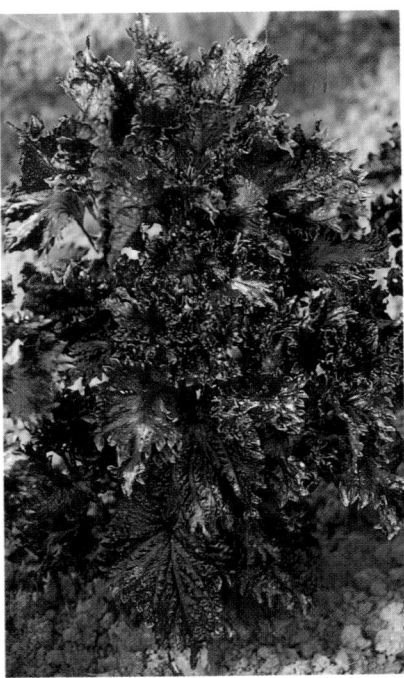

▲ *Perilla frutescens* var. *crispa*

strongest shoots during the first month after planting to encourage good plant shape.
PROPAGATION Sow seed in late winter under glass.
PESTS AND DISEASES Perillas attract aphids.

Periwinkle see *Vinca*
Pernettya see *Gaultheria*

Perovskia
Russian sage
Labiatae

Prominent, grey stems in winter, aromatic leaves in spring and flowers that last from mid summer until autumn make Russian sage a plant for all seasons. Deeply cut, grey, narrowly oval leaves, up to 6 cm (2½ in) long, are covered in white hairs. Their aroma is similar to culinary sage. The stiff, upright stems give a strong, vertical shape. Widely grown in herbaceous and mixed borders, this hardy sub-shrub or herbaceous perennial needs full sun. The recommended plants have pale violet-blue, tubular, lipped flowers, each about 3 mm (⅛ in) wide.
RECOMMENDED SPECIES AND VARIETIES
P. atriplicifolia♀ The flowers are held in spires. HEIGHT & SPREAD 1.2×1 m (4×3 ft).
P. 'Blue Spire'♀ Robust spikes of flowers appear on this plant. HEIGHT & SPREAD 1.2×1 m (4×3 ft).
CULTIVATION Plant in spring on well-drained soil in full sun.
PROPAGATION Divide and replant or take basal cuttings in spring.
PRUNING Cut back the previous year's stems to the ground in spring.
PESTS AND DISEASES Usually trouble free.

▲ *Perovskia* 'Blue Spire'

p
q

Persicaria
Knotweed
Polygonaceae

Persicaria bistorta 'superba'

Flowers in shades of pink or white appear mostly late in the season on these hardy, herbaceous perennials. Excellent for the border or as ground cover, persicarias are easy to grow, although the taller species prefer slightly moist conditions. The low-growing plants will tolerate dry situations. They grow in full sun or partial shade but the best flower and leaf colour is obtained in a sunny position.

RECOMMENDED SPECIES AND VARIETIES

P. affinis (syn. *Polygonum affine*) Small pink or red flowers carried in dense, upright spikes about 8 cm (3¼ in) long appear in late summer. They often persist through autumn into winter, gradually fading in colour. The dark green, elliptic leaves, about 10 cm (4 in) long, turn to shades of red and bronze in autumn. A compact, low-growing plant, it can be grown in a rock garden or as edging to a path. It is native to the Himalayas. HEIGHT & SPREAD 60×60 cm (2×2 ft).

'Darjeeling Red'♀ has long-lasting pinky red flowers. Its lanceolate leaves turn russet brown as winter approaches. 'Donald Lowndes'♀ is more compact and has salmon pink flowers which darken as the plant ages. 'Superba'♀ (syn. 'Dimity') has pale pink flowers which turn crimson and striking rich brown leaves in autumn.

▲ *Persicaria affinis* 'Donald Lowndes'

P. amplexicaulis (syn. *Polygonum amplexicaule*) Small, pale pink or purple flowers in loose, tapering spikes up to 8 cm (3¼ in) long, appear in late summer to early autumn. Its dense habit and tall flowering stems make this a good plant for the herbaceous border. Native to the Himalayas. HEIGHT & SPREAD 1.2×1.2 m (4×4 ft).

'Firetail'♀ has bright crimson flowers.

P. bistorta (syn. *Polygonum bistorta*) (bistort, snakeweed, Easter ledges) Dense, cylindrical spikes, up to 9 cm (3½ in) long, consisting of a mass of small pale pink or white flowers appear in early summer and last for a long time. The ovate to oblong light green leaves, up to 20 cm (8 in) long, form thick, fast-growing ground cover. This plant does well in a mixed border or at the damp edges of a pond, although it can become invasive there. Native to Europe and W Asia. HEIGHT & SPREAD 75×60 cm (2½×2 ft).

▲ *Persicaria bistorta* 'Superba'

'Superba'♀ has clear pink flowers.

P. campanulata (lesser knotweed) A compact, mat-forming plant grown as much for its foliage as its tiny, bell-shaped, fragrant pale pink flowers. It has lance-shaped, ribbed, mid green leaves, 20 cm (8 in) long, with rounded ends and buff-coloured backs. The flowers are carried in branching clusters up to 8 cm (3¼ in) across which appear in late summer to early autumn. Native to the Himalayas. HEIGHT & SPREAD 1×1 m (3×3 ft).

There are 2 white-flowered selections, **Alba Group** and **'Southcombe White'**, which can be more invasive.

P. filiformis see *P. virginiana*

P. milletii Crimson flowers carried in dense round or cylindrical heads, 4 cm (1½ in) long, appear in mid to late summer. The slender, oblong, basal leaves are up to 30 cm (1 ft) long. A clump-forming species, it can be planted in a border or large rock garden and grows best in a rich, moist soil. Native to Nepal and China. HEIGHT & SPREAD 60×60 cm (2×2 ft).

P. mollis (syn. *Polygonum molle*) Very small, creamy white flowers are carried in dense

clusters, up to 30 cm (1 ft) long, on branching stems in late summer. It is a tall-growing, bushy plant with dark green, wavy leaves up to 20 cm (8 in) long. It grows best in moist areas. Native to the Himalayas. HEIGHT & SPREAD 2.4 m×75 cm (8×2½ ft).

P. tenuicaulis Tiny white flowers are produced in loose spikes up to 10 cm (4 in) long in early spring. A low-growing plant used for ground cover or in a rock garden, it has ovate, mid green leaves up to 8 cm (3¼ in) long that are flushed with red underneath. This species is native to Japan. HEIGHT & SPREAD 15×20 cm (6×8 in).

P. vacciniifolia♀ Heather-pink flowers in spikes, 5 cm (2 in) long, appear from late summer to early autumn. The pointed, leathery leaves up to 2.5 cm (1 in) long change colour in autumn. The attractive trailing mats of foliage make this species good for ground cover, especially over

▲ *Persicaria milletii*

▲ *Persicaria virginiana* 'Painter's Palette'

rocks, walls or paved areas. This plant is native to the Himalayas. HEIGHT & SPREAD 20×60 cm (8 in×2 ft).

P. virginiana (syn. *P. filiformis*) Creamy white and sometimes pink-tinged flowers, carried in spikes, 40 cm (16 in) long, appear in summer. The bright green, ovate leaves are 15 cm (6 in) long. This species is native to Japan and the Himalayas. HEIGHT & SPREAD 1.2 m×60 cm (4×2 ft).

'Painter's Palette' has variegated leaves with gold and pinky brown blotches.

'Lloyd's Variety' has densely hairy, grey, oval leaves, up to 12.5 cm (5 in) long. It does not flower, and spreads up to 75 cm (2½ ft).

P. bovei ssp. *maroccana* The flowers are purple-pink and up to 4 cm (1½ in) long. They are borne in whorls in loose spikes. The leaves are mid green, lance to heart-shaped and up to 7.5 cm (3 in) long. HEIGHT & SPREAD 1.5×1.5 m (5×5 ft).

▲ *Phlomis bovei* ssp. *maroccana*

P. cashmeriana The pale lilac flowers, up to 2.5 cm (1 in) long, are held in whorls. The narrow, oval, mid green leaves are up to 20 cm (8 in) in length. HEIGHT & SPREAD 60×45 cm (2×1½ ft).

P. chrysophylla ♀ Golden yellow flowers, up to 5 cm (2 in) long, are borne in spikes or scattered in pairs along the stems. The oval leaves, up to 7.5 cm (3 in) long, are grey-green when young and take on a golden flush with age. HEIGHT & SPREAD 1×1 m (3×3 ft).

P. **'Edward Bowles'** Soft golden yellow flowers, up to 4 cm (1½ in) long, are produced in whorls. The coarse, lance-shaped, silvery green leaves are up to 15 cm (6 in) long. HEIGHT & SPREAD 1.2×1.2 m (4×4 ft).

P. fruticosa ♀ (Jerusalem sage) Bright yellow flowers up to 4 cm (½ in) long, are borne in clusters. This is a sturdy low-growing shrub with dull green, oval or lance-shaped leaves, up to 10 cm (4 in) long. HEIGHT & SPREAD 1×1 m (3×3 ft).

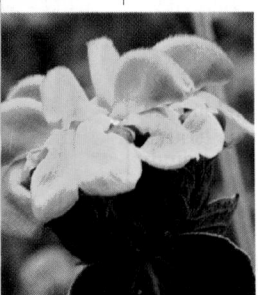

▲ *Phlomis fruticosa*   *Phlomis italica* ▲

P. italica Dull purple or pink flowers, up to 2.5 cm (1 in) long, are produced in small whorls at the ends of the branches. The rough, dull green, lance-shaped leaves are up to 10 cm (4 in) long. This is a stiff, upright, rather untidy-looking plant. HEIGHT & SPREAD 1 m×60 cm (3×2 ft).

▲ *Phlomis longifolia*

P. lanata The orange-yellow flowers, up to 2.5 cm (1 in) long, appear in whorls on this dwarf shrub. The rounded, woolly, golden-green leaves, 2.5 cm (1 in) long, clothe stems that are conspicuously golden when young. HEIGHT & SPREAD 45×45 cm (1½×1½ ft).

P. longifolia Yellow flowers, up to 4 cm (1½ in) long, appear in clusters on this low-growing shrub. The lance-shaped, heart-shaped or oval leaves are up to 7.5 cm (3 in) long. Dull green above, the leaves are grey or yellowish beneath. HEIGHT & SPREAD 1.2×1.2 m (4×4 ft).

The basal leaves of var. *bailanica* are oval.

P. purpurea Flowers in shades of pink to purple or white, up to 2.5 cm (1 in) long, appear in whorls against the lance-shaped, mid green leaves, up to 10 cm (4 in) long. HEIGHT & SPREAD 60×60 cm (2×2 ft).

The flowers of var. *alba* are white.

P. russeliana ♀ (syn. *P. samia*, *P. viscosa* hort.) Numerous stout upright stems bear clusters of golden yellow flowers, up to 4 cm (1½ in) long. The rough, heart-shaped greyish green leaves are up to 20 cm (8 in) long. HEIGHT & SPREAD 1 m×60 cm (3×2 ft).

P. samia see *P. russeliana*

P. viscosa hort. see *P. russeliana*

CULTIVATION Plant in spring in well-drained soil in full sun.

PROPAGATION Take softwood cuttings in summer or semi-ripe cuttings in autumn.

PRUNING None is normally required.

PESTS AND DISEASES Usually trouble free.

Phlox
Polemoniaceae

Phlox douglasii

Varying in size and habit, these annuals and hardy perennials from N America all have abundant and colourful flowers. Each flower has a narrow tube opening into five widely spreading petals, usually notched at their tips. There is often a contrasting colour in the throat. The recommended plants are divided into four groups: low-growing perennials, woodland perennials, border perennials and annuals.

RECOMMENDED SPECIES AND VARIETIES
LOW-GROWING PERENNIALS
A profusion of stemless or short-stemmed flowers, up to 2.5 cm (1 in) across, appears from early spring to early summer above evergreen, needle-like leaves, up to 2 cm (¾ in) long. These cushion-forming or low, mat-forming plants make a colourful carpet at the edge of a well-drained border or in a rock garden.

P. amoena hort. see *P.* × *procumbens*

P. bifida (sand phlox) Loose cushions of foliage bear clusters of flowers from white to deep lilac. There is also a blue-flowered form. This plant needs sharp drainage, and is best in a rock garden. HEIGHT & SPREAD 8×30 cm (3¼×12 in).

'Colvin's White' is a vigorous plant with pure white flowers, while 'Starbrite' is compact with pale blue flowers.

P. caespitosa (cushion phlox) A tight cushion of foliage bears white or pale blue flowers, usually solitary but occasionally in small clusters. This plant needs to be grown in a greenhouse or on scree. HEIGHT & SPREAD 5×20 cm (2×8 in).

P. douglasii Flowers in white, lavender or pink appear singly, in pairs or in threes. HEIGHT & SPREAD 8×30 cm (3¼×12 in).

'Apollo' has good-sized violet-pink flowers, while 'Boothman's Variety' ♀ has lavender flowers with a deep blue centre. 'Crackerjack' ♀ is a compact plant bearing

▼ *Phlox douglasii* 'Crackerjack'

▲ *Phlox douglasii* 'Eva'
   Phlox douglasii 'Iceberg' ▲

brilliant magenta blooms in great abundance. 'Eva' is a compact plant with pinkish lavender flowers. 'Galaxy' is also compact with darker violet flowers, while 'Iceberg' ♀ has white blooms flushed with the palest violet. 'Kelly's Eye' ♀ bears

▲ *Phlox douglasii* 'Red Admiral'

▲ *Phlox subulata* 'McDaniel's Cushion'

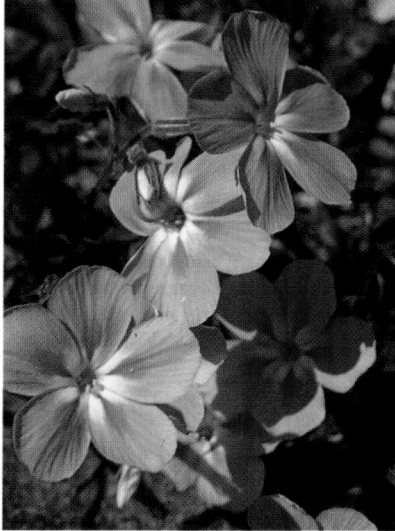

▲ *Phlox adsurgens* 'Red Buttes'

masses of pale pink flowers with deeper coloured eyes, and **'Red Admiral'**♈ has flowers of deep crimson. **'Rose Cushion'** makes a very compact plant with rose-pink flowers, while **'Rosea'** has deep rose flowers. **'Violet Queen'** forms a very compact plant with flowers of darkest violet, and **'Waterloo'** bears purplish pink flowers.

P. kelseyi **'Rosette'** Abundant clusters of rounded deep pink flowers are borne by this plant, which forms a low shrubby mound. HEIGHT & SPREAD 5×20 cm (2×8 in).

P. nivalis (trailing phlox) Forming a small dense mat, this phlox has small clusters of purple to pink or white flowers. HEIGHT & SPREAD 5×20 cm (2×8 in).

'Camla' has pale pink flowers.

P. subulata (moss phlox) Clusters of red, purple, violet, lilac, pink or white flowers appear in late spring and early summer. HEIGHT & SPREAD 8×30 cm (3¼ in×1 ft).

'Alexander's Surprise' has large pinkish white flowers, while **'Amazing Grace'** has

▲ *Phlox subulata* 'Alexander's Surprise'

▲ *Phlox subulata* 'Amazing Grace'

pink flowers with a purple eye. **'Betty'** has large, deep pink flowers, and **'Bonita'** is a vigorous plant with large, purplish lilac flowers. **'Brightness'** has deep pink flowers with a crimson eye. **'Emerald Cushion Blue'** is a compact grower with lavender-

blue flowers, while the large flowers of **'G. F. Wilson'** are pale lavender. The flowers of **'Maischnee'** ('May Snow', 'Snow Queen') are pure white, while those of **'Marjorie'** are rose-pink. **'McDaniel's Cushion'**♈ is a vigorous plant with bright pink flowers. **'Oakington Blue Eyes'** bears lavender flowers, and **'Red Wings'**♈

▲ *Phlox subulata* 'Oakington Blue Eyes'

makes a vigorous plant bearing rose-red blooms with a darker eye. **'Samson'** has large, salmon-pink flowers with a red eye. **'Scarlet Flame'** has large, carmine blooms. **'Tamaongalei'** bears white blooms, streaked with reddish pink. **'Temiskaming'** is a very reliable plant with vivid deep magenta flowers. **'White Delight'** has pure white flowers.

WOODLAND PERENNIALS

These colourful, low carpeting or clump-forming, evergreen plants need a moist humus-rich soil in part shade, and are ideal between shrubs or taller plants, such as lilies, meconopsis, polygonatums and disporums. They have semi-prostrate stems, which root at the nodes, and oval or lance-shaped leaves, up to 3 cm (1¼ in) long. Loose flowerheads, each up to 2.5 cm (1 in) across, appear on upright stems in late spring and early summer. Height and spread measurements vary widely.

P. adsurgens♈ Soft pink flowers have a pale eye and a dark central streak on each petal. The leaves are ovate. This temperamental plant requires perfect conditions to thrive. HEIGHT & SPREAD 25×60 cm (10 in×2 ft).

'Red Buttes' has pink and white flowers with deeper pink markings. Its overlapping petals give a rounded appearance. The narrow petalled flowers of **'Wagon Wheel'** are dark pink streaked with pale pink.

P. amoena hort. see *P.* × *procumbens*

P. **'Chattahoochee'** see *P. divaricata* ssp. *laphamii* 'Chattahoochee'

▲ *Phlox adsurgens* 'Wagon Wheel'

P. divaricata♈ (blue phlox) This vigorous and spreading phlox bears clusters of flowers with notched petals, usually violet-blue with a darker eye. HEIGHT & SPREAD 20 cm×1 m (8 in×3 ft).

'Blue Dreams' has scented, lavender-blue flowers, and **'Charles Ricardo'** has fragrant, pale lavender flowers. **'Dirigo Ice'** bears large, very pale blue flowers. The flowers of ssp. *laphamii* are lilac with longer tubes and more rounded petals. Its cultivar, **'Chattahoochee'**♈, the most popular phlox, is very compact, bearing deep lilac flowers with a contrasting reddish purple eye. **'May Breeze'** is a vigorous plant with pale ice-blue flowers.

P. × *procumbens* (syn. *P. amoena* hort.) This plant, which forms a loose carpet, has purple flowers. HEIGHT & SPREAD 12×60 cm (4¾ in×2 ft).

'Millstream'♈ makes a dense mat bearing deep pink flowers with white centres

p

q

long. Plants in the **Purpureum Group**♀ have leaves in various shades of purple. **'Variegatum'**♀ has mid green leaves with creamy yellow stripes of varying widths on the edges, and plum-red flowering spikes.

GARDEN HYBRIDS

These plants have been selected for leaf colour as the flowers are not generally regarded as a feature. They reach a height of up to 3 m (10 ft) and spread to 1 m (3 ft).

The outer red-bronze leaves of **'Bronze Baby'** are arching. **'Duet'**♀ is a dwarf plant with bright green leaves with a creamy white stripe, up to 30 cm (12 in) long. **'Sundowner'**♀ has erect bronze leaves tipped purple and pink. **'Yellow Wave'**♀ has bright yellow-and-green leaves.

CULTIVATION Plant in any soil provided that it can be kept fairly moist throughout summer. Do not feed the plants as this encourages soft growth which may kill the plant in winter. If attempting to grow plants outdoors, protect them in winter with bracken, old branches of conifers or horticultural fleece. Deadhead in autumn to prevent winter rocking which can damage or even kill the plant. For container plants placed outside in spring and summer in a windy position or by the sea, consider trimming the leaves to a third of their length to diminish wind resistance.

PROPAGATION Divide in spring, making sure that each piece of root has 4–5 strong leaves. Alternatively, sow seed in spring under glass and grow on in individual pots under cover. Plant out, if appropriate, the following spring.

PESTS AND DISEASES Usually trouble free.

Photinia
Rosaceae

Photinia x fraseri 'Robusta'

Brilliant year-round leaf colour on the evergreens, and spectacular autumn fruit and foliage on the deciduous plants distinguish these hardy Asian shrubs. Clusters of white flowers in spring are followed by berries, 5–10 mm (¼–⅜ in) wide, in summer. The young evergreen leaves are red.

RECOMMENDED SPECIES AND VARIETIES

P. beauverdiana♀ Glorious bronze-red autumn leaves grace this deciduous shrub. The narrow oval leaves, up to 12.5 cm (5 in) long, have prominent veins underneath. Flower clusters, 5 cm (2 in) across, appear in late spring followed by dark red fruit. HEIGHT & SPREAD 1.5×2 m (5×6½ ft) after 5 years, ultimately 8 m (26 ft) tall.

▲ *Photinia beauverdiana*

P. davidiana (syn. *Stransvaesia davidiana*) This sprawling, semi-evergreen shrub has leathery, egg-shaped to pointed dark green leaves, up to 11 cm (4¼ in) long. They turn orange and red, and fall in early winter. The flower clusters, up to 10 cm (4 in) across, give way to red berries. HEIGHT & SPREAD 2.4×2.4 m (8×8 ft) after 5 years, ultimately 4 m (13 ft) tall.

P. × fraseri The bronze to red young leaves of this evergreen hybrid turn glossy green later. They are toothed, egg-shaped and up to 9 cm (3½ in) long. The flowers appear in clusters up to 12 cm (4¾ in) wide. HEIGHT & SPREAD 1.5×2 m (5×6½ ft) after 5 years, ultimately 4 m (13 ft) tall.

'Birmingham' has deep coppery red young leaves. **'Red Robin'**♀ has glossy, sharply toothed, bright red foliage at first.

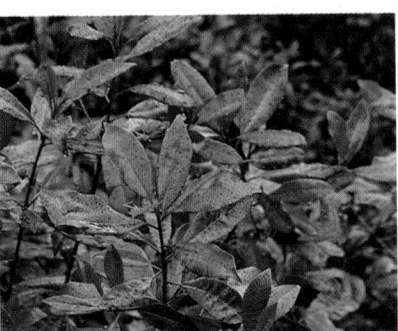

▲ *Photinia × fraseri* 'Red Robin'

'Robusta'♀ displays thick, leathery, oblong leaves that are bright coppery red at first. It is one of the hardiest cultivars. **'Rubens'** (syn. *P. glabra* 'Rubens') has glossy bright red young foliage.

P. glabra **'Parfait'** (syn. *P.* 'Pink Lady', *P.* 'Variegata') This evergreen has smooth, bronze-red young leaves, up to 8 cm (3 in) long, initially edged in pink. The margins turn cream as the leaf becomes green flecked with grey-green. In a mild spring flower clusters, up to 10 cm (4 in) across, may appear, followed by red to black berries. HEIGHT & SPREAD 1.5×2 m (5×6½ ft) after 5 years, ultimately 3 m (10 ft) tall.

P. glabra **'Rubens'** (syn. *P. × fraseri* 'Rubens')

P. **'Pink Lady'** see *P. glabra* 'Parfait'

P. **'Redstart'**♀ Red young leaves turn

▲ *Photinia serratifolia*

glossy green later on this vigorous evergreen. Clusters of white flowers on purplish red stalks in early summer are then followed by orangey red berries. HEIGHT & SPREAD 1.5×2 m (5×6½ ft) after 5 years, ultimately 5 m (16 ft) tall.

P. serratifolia Leathery, toothed, mature leaves, up to 18 cm (7 in) long, are dark green above and yellowish below. The young growth is red tinted. Flower clusters are up to 18 cm (7 in) wide. HEIGHT & SPREAD 1.5×2 m (5×6½ ft) after 5 years, ultimately 5 m (16 ft) tall.

P. **'Variegata'** see *P. glabra* 'Parfait'

P. villosa♀ The leaves of this deciduous shrub turn orange and red in autumn. They are pointed, ovate to oblong and up to 3 cm (1¼ in) long. Flower clusters, 5 cm (2 in) across, are followed by egg-shaped fruits. HEIGHT & SPREAD 1.5×2 m (5×6½ ft) after 5 years, ultimately 5 m (16 ft) tall.

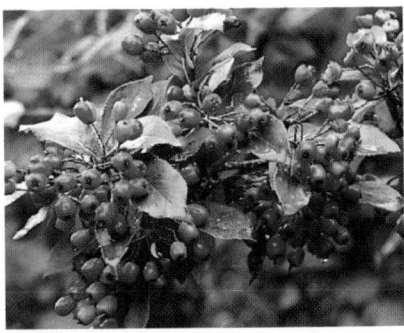

▲ *Photinia villosa*

CULTIVATION Plant on a sheltered site in well-drained fertile soil, except *P. davidiana* and *P. × fraseri* which prefer moist soil. Evergreens are lime tolerant, while deciduous plants prefer acid to neutral soil, although *P. beauverdiana* will withstand some lime.

PROPAGATION Sow ripe seed in autumn in a coldframe or take ripewood cuttings in mid to late autumn.

PRUNING None is necessary for deciduous plants. Cut back evergreens each year to encourage the growth of young red leaves.

PESTS AND DISEASES Fire blight may be a problem, especially in *P. davidiana*. Honey fungus may be troublesome and powdery mildew may appear on leaves in summer.

Phuopsis
Rubiaceae

A pink carpet of summer flowers attracts butterflies to this low-growing hardy perennial from the Caucasus Mountains. It is ideal for the front of a border, or beneath a wall or on a bank. The genus has only one species which usually dies back in winter, but might retain its leaves in a mild weather.
Phuopsis stylosa (syn. *Crucianella stylosa*) Pink, five-lobed, tubular flowers, about 2 cm (¾ in) across, form dense round heads. Pungent smelling, pale green leaves, up to 5 mm (¼ in) long, appear in whorls. HEIGHT & SPREAD 15×50 cm (6×20 in).
'Purpurea' has deeper purplish pink flowers.

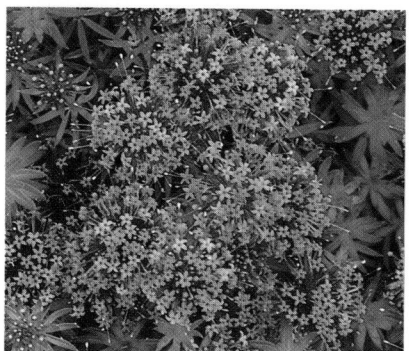

▲ *Phuopsis stylosa 'Purpurea'*

CULTIVATION Plant plants in spring in any well-drained soil in full sun or light shade. Cut back after flowering to prevent the plant becoming too straggly.
PROPAGATION Divide plants in spring or take semi-ripe cuttings in early summer. Alternatively, sow the seed of the species in a coldframe in autumn.
PESTS AND DISEASES Usually trouble free.

Phygelius
Scrophulariaceae

Phygelius aequalis 'Yellow Trumpet'

Spikes of pendulous tubular flowers, up to 4 cm (1½ in) long, in yellow, orange, pink, red and scarlet adorn these short-lived shrubs for most of summer and early autumn. The plants can tolerate temperatures as low as -10°C (14°F), and in mild winters they are evergreen. However, in long periods of frost they lose their leaves and die back to the ground, although new growth usually emerges in spring. The toothed oval to pointed leaves, up to 10 cm (4 in) long, are deep to pale green. Native to South Africa, they are drought-tolerant but prefer free-draining soil and a sunny site. The recommended plants reach their ultimate size within the first year.
RECOMMENDED SPECIES AND VARIETIES
P. aequalis Dusky red-pink flowers form dense spikes on this compact bushy shrub. Each flower is flared at the mouth with an attractive yellow throat. HEIGHT & SPREAD 1 m×60 cm (3×2 ft).
'Yellow Trumpet' has yellow flowers.
P. capensis (Cape fuchsia, Cape figwort) Orange to deep-red flowers are carried in loose spikes on this sparsely branched shrub. HEIGHT & SPREAD 1 m×60 cm (3×2 ft).
P. × rectus Flowers of varying colours are arranged in loose spikes on this spreading, sparsely branched shrub. HEIGHT & SPREAD 1.5 m×75 cm (5×2½ ft).
'African Queen' has red flowers with orange and red lips, while the deep reddish pink flowers of 'Devil's Tears' have yellow throats. 'Moonraker' has pale yellow flowers, while those of 'Salmon Leap' are orange. The dusky red-pink flowers of 'Winchester Fanfare' have a scarlet tip.
CULTIVATION Plant in free-draining soil in a sunny but sheltered situation protected by a south or west-facing wall. Mulch the plants well. Remove early spikes after flowering to promote the growth of sideshoots.
PROPAGATION Take greenwood cuttings in mid to late summer or sow seed in spring.
PRUNING Cut dead stems to ground level in spring.
PESTS AND DISEASES Usually trouble free.

▲ *Phygelius × rectus 'African Queen'*

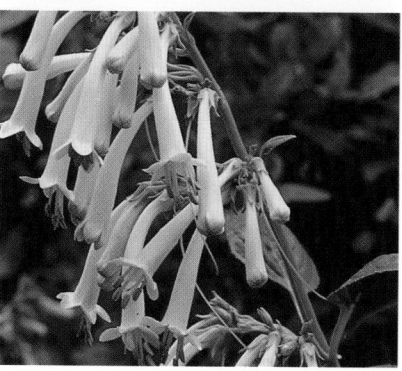

▲ *Phygelius aequalis 'Yellow Trumpet'*

X Phylliopsis
Ericaceae

x Phylliopsis hillieri 'Pinocchio'

Loose spikes of many bell-shaped flowers appear above the foliage of this dwarf evergreen shrub. The leaves, up to 2 cm (¾ in) long, are a lustrous dark green. The plants do well in a peat bed or rock garden.
RECOMMENDED SPECIES AND VARIETIES
X *P.* 'Askival' Showy pink flowers appear in mid to late spring. HEIGHT & SPREAD 20×40 cm (8×16 in) after 5 years, ultimately 60 cm (2 ft) tall.
X *P.* 'Coppelia' Pink flowers appear in mid to late spring on this vigorous and easy to grow plant. HEIGHT & SPREAD 20×40 cm (8×16 in) after 5 years, ultimately 60 cm (2 ft) tall.
X *P. hillieri* 'Pinocchio' Elongated, upright spikes of rich pink flowers are open for a long period in mid to late spring. HEIGHT & SPREAD 20×40 cm (8×16 in) after 5 years, ultimately 60 cm (2 ft) tall.
CULTIVATION Grow in well-drained, acid, humus-rich soil in a sunny position.
PROPAGATION Take semi-ripe cuttings in late summer or early autumn.
PRUNING Remove any long shoots after flowering.
PESTS AND DISEASES Usually trouble free.

▲ *x Phylliopsis 'Coppelia'*

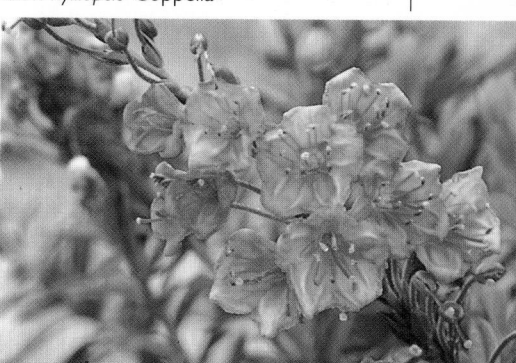

▲ *x Phylliopsis hillieri 'Pinocchio'*

Phyllodoce
Mountain heath, blue heather
Ericaceae

Phyllodoce caerulea

In mid spring and early summer, the pink, purple, red or white flowers of these hardy dwarf evergreen shrubs bring splashes of colour to the garden. The shrubs are particularly suitable for rockeries in areas with a high rainfall and they prefer acid soil. Although hardy, they need protection against frost when there is no snow cover, and against drying winds and strong sunlight, especially when covered in frost.

RECOMMENDED SPECIES

P. aleutica Nodding heads, up to 5 cm (2 in) wide, of rounded, yellowish white flowers appear in mid and late spring. The narrow, bright green leaves are up to 1 cm (⅜ in) long. A mat-forming species native to NE Asia and W Alaska. HEIGHT & SPREAD 20×30 cm (8×12 in) after 5 years, ultimately 25 cm (10 in) tall.

▲ *Phyllodoce aleutica*

P. breweri The purplish pink flowers of this prostrate shrub are dish-shaped and deeply split with conspicuous pink stamens. They form heads up to 7.5 cm (3 in) across that appear in late spring and early summer, and again, sometimes in autumn. Glossy dark green leaves, 1 cm (⅜ in) long, are narrow and densely arranged on the stem. Native to the Rocky Mountains of N America. HEIGHT & SPREAD 23×30 cm (9×12 in) after 5 years, ultimately 30 cm (12 in) tall.

P. caerulea♀ (syn. *Menziesia taxifolia*) Purplish pink, urn-shaped blooms which turn blue with age, appear from mid spring to early summer. They are held in flowerheads up to 5 cm (2 in) across. This bushy shrub has dense, glossy dark green foliage with narrow leaves up to 1 cm (⅜ in) long. Native to arctic and alpine Europe. HEIGHT & SPREAD 15×15 cm (6×6 in) after 5 years, ultimately 30 cm (12 in) tall.

▲ *Phyllodoce empetriformis*

P. empetriformis Bell-shaped, 5-lobed, rose-red flowers in heads up to 5 cm (2 in) wide, are borne on thin, nodding stalks between mid spring and mid summer. The narrow, bright green leaves of this small, spreading shrub are up to 1.5 cm (½ in) long. It is more tolerant of dry conditions than other species. Native to the Rocky Mountains of N America. HEIGHT & SPREAD 15×20 cm (6×8 in) after 5 years, ultimately 25 cm (10 in) tall.

P. nipponica♀ (syn. *P. caerulea* ssp. *japonica*) White, often pink-tinged flowers appear from mid spring to early summer, borne in spikes up to 5 cm (2 in) long. The narrow, dark green leaves, up to 1 cm (⅜ in) long, are grey beneath. A compact shrub native to Japan. HEIGHT & SPREAD 10×10 cm (4×4 in) after 5 years, ultimately 20 cm (8 in) tall.

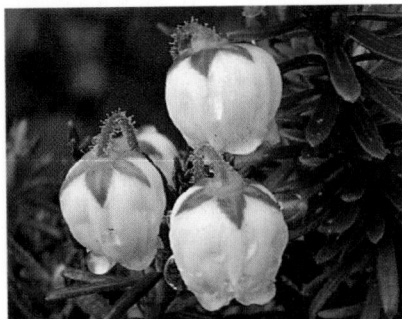

▲ *Phyllodoce nipponica*

CULTIVATION Plant in spring or autumn in moist but well-drained, lime-free, humus-rich soil, choosing a spot in partial shade. Protect plants by covering with conifer twigs or sacking in winter.
PRUNING Not usually necessary but plants can be cut into shape after flowering.
PROPAGATION Take semi-ripe heeled cuttings in mid summer.
PESTS AND DISEASES Usually trouble free.

Phyllostachys see BAMBOOS p. 77

✕ Phyllothamnus
Ericaceae

This hardy evergreen shrub with clusters of spring flowers is the sole species in this hybrid genus. It is a cross between *Phyllodoce* and *Rhodothamnus*, and is suitable for semi-shaded sites on acid soil.

✕ *Phyllothamnus erectus* Bell-shaped, rosy purple flowers, up to 1.5 cm (½ in) long and wide, are borne in clusters of 8 or more at the ends of stems. The short, dark green, needle-like leaves are crowded together on tough, wiry stems to form a plant with a compact habit. HEIGHT & SPREAD 25×25 cm (10×10 in) ultimately after 5 years.

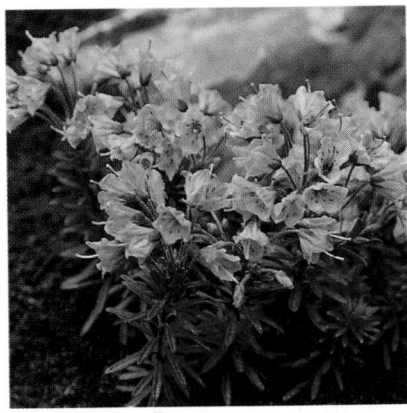

▲ ✕ *Phyllothamnus erectus*

CULTIVATION Plant in spring in moisture-retentive, lime-free soil that is enriched with liberal quantities of organic matter. Feed established plants annually in spring with a slow-release fertiliser. Water regularly in dry weather and, once flowering is over, clip off the spent flowers.
PROPAGATION Take semi-ripe cuttings during late summer.
PESTS AND DISEASES Usually trouble free.

Physalis
Chinese lantern
Solanaceae

Physalis alkekengi

Bright orange, papery lanterns in late summer and early autumn are the main attraction of these plants. The genus contains hardy and tender annuals and herbaceous perennials but as the plants tend to be invasive only the two hardy perennials described are commonly cultivated. As well as adding colour to an informal border in autumn, the fruits retain their colour when dried for use in winter floral arrangements. The genus is widely distributed around the world, particularly in the Americas.

RECOMMENDED SPECIES AND VARIETIES
P. alkekengi♀ (bladder cherry, winter cherry) A hardy plant with insignificant creamy white flowers which appear on rather floppy, unbranched stems in summer. They are carried in the upper leaf axils among pointed, lance-shaped, mid green leaves up to 12 cm (4¾ in) long. Bright red papery calyxes develop after the flowers, each one puffing out around an edible orange-red berry. Each lantern may be up to 5 cm (2 in) in diameter. For dried flower arrangements cut the stems as the calyxes begin to colour, and hang upside-down in an airy shed or attic to dry. HEIGHT & SPREAD 60×60 cm (24×24 in).

More pointed lanterns are seen on var. *franchetii*. The plant is larger than the parent species with mid green leaves and an intense orange-red calyx.

CULTIVATION Plant in any soil from autumn to spring, choosing a sunny site. To control the spreading roots, plant in a large pot and bury it in the ground. Alternatively, cut round the roots of the plant each autumn with a sharp spade to remove surplus material which can be used to increase the plant elsewhere in the garden.

PROPAGATION Divide in the dormant season, which is winter or early spring. Alternatively sow seed in a coldframe in early spring and plant out in early summer when the plants are large enough for the conditions in the particular garden.

PESTS AND DISEASES Usually trouble free.

▲ *Physalis alkekengi* var. *franchetii*

Physocarpus
Rosaceae

Physocarpus opulifolius 'Dart's Gold'

Abundant clusters of small white flowers appear in early summer on these hardy deciduous shrubs. Rounded and many-stemmed in habit, they are good plants for the back of the border. They do best in full sun and moist acid soil.

RECOMMENDED SPECIES AND VARIETIES
P. opulifolius (ninebark) Tiny white flowers, which may be tinged with pink, have 5 petals and numerous stamen. The flowers form clusters up to 5 cm (2 in) across. Small red berries follow in autumn. Mid green, ovate leaves have 3 lobes and are up to 6 cm (2½ in) long and wide with very serrated edges. The pale brown bark of the medium-sized deciduous shrub peels attractively after 5-10 years to reveal lighter shades of wood beneath. Native to N America. HEIGHT & SPREAD 1×1 m (3×3 ft) after 5 years, ultimately 3 m (10 ft) tall.

The leaves of **'Dart's Gold'** are bright yellow in mid spring, fading to dull green in the following 6-8 weeks. It is slightly smaller and denser than the species. **'Luteus'** does not keep its young yellow leaf colour for such a long time and leaves become olive green or tinged with bronze.

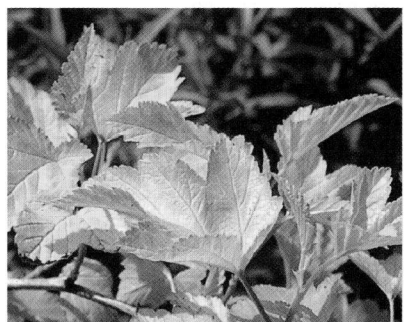

▲ *Physocarpus opulifolius* 'Luteus'
▼ *Physocarpus opulifolius* 'Dart's Gold'

CULTIVATION Plant between late autumn and mid spring in moist soil and a sunny position avoiding chalky ground.

PRUNING Little pruning is required, but plants can be trimmed between late autumn and early spring to keep them in shape and prevent straggling.

PROPAGATION Sow seed in late autumn or early spring in a coldframe. Position the coldframe in full sun and use a moist, fertile, acid soil. Alternatively, take semi-ripe cuttings in early or mid summer and plant them in a coldframe, or plant hardwood cuttings outdoors in late autumn.

PESTS AND DISEASES Usually trouble free.

Physoplexis
Campanulaceae

Unusual flask-shaped flowers in dense clusters are borne by this hardy tufted perennial from the SE Alps. A long stigma projects from the spiky top of the flower, where the petals are joined together at the tip. In the wild, the plant grows in rock crevices; in cultivation it can be grown outside in scree or tufa, a porous rock suited to lime-loving crevice plants. There is one species.

P. comosa♀ (syn. *Phyteuma comosum*) Pale violet flowers with deep violet tips, 2 cm (¾ in) long, are borne in round, stemless clusters in early to mid summer. The dark green oval leaves are deeply toothed. HEIGHT & SPREAD 8×10 cm (3¼×4 in).

CULTIVATION Plant in very well-drained compost, preferably alkaline, in a pot in an alpine house, or outside in a trough, scree, or a hole in tufa.

PROPAGATION Sow seed in autumn or winter in a coldframe and keep cool through winter.

PESTS AND DISEASES Slugs, snails and aphids may prove troublesome.

p
q

Physostegia
Labiatae

Physostegia virginiana

Flower spikes crowded with dainty tubular flowers characterise these hardy herbaceous perennials. The species cultivated in British gardens makes a delightful show in the middle of a border in summer and autumn. Moist, rich soil and a position in sun or light shade suit the plant best and it may become

Picea glauca var. albertiana 'Conica'

very hardy but slow-growing tree is perfectly conical, densely clothed with dusky green needles 1 cm (⅜ in) long. The new growth each spring is a bright, light green. HEIGHT & SPREAD 1.5×1.5 m (5×5 ft) after 20 years, ultimately 4×2 m (13×6½ ft).

P. mariana 'Nana'♀ This cultivar forms a fine rounded, flattened, cushion. It has blunt, blue-green needles, 1.5 cm (½ in) long, on yellow-brown shoots. HEIGHT & SPREAD 60×40 cm (24×16 in) after 20 years, ultimately 75 cm×3 m (2½×10 ft).

P. omorika♀ (Serbian spruce) An almost columnar tree which grows to a tapering point, with pendulous branches turning up at the tips. Needles are glossy dark green above and blue-white beneath, 2 cm (¾ in) long. Red flowers produce narrow cones, 6 cm (2½ in) long, ultimately brown. This spruce is very hardy, tolerant of atmospheric pollution and one of the few that grow well in chalky soils. HEIGHT & SPREAD 7×2.4 m (23×8 ft), ultimately 30 m (100 ft) tall.

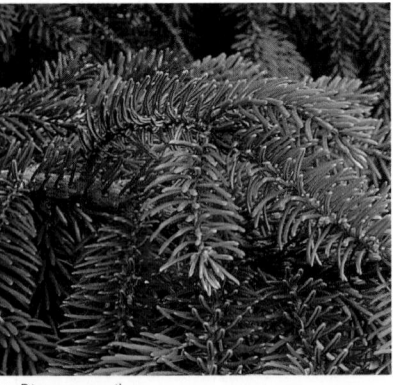

▲ *Picea omorika*

'Pendula'♀ has branches that hang nearly straight down from the trunk, their tips twisting upwards to reveal the silvery underside of the needles.

P. orientalis♀ (Oriental spruce) The tree has glossy, deep green, blunt needles lying tightly pressed along the shoots, only 8 mm (⅜ in) long. Many crimson flowers bloom in spring. The cylindrical cones which are purple ripening to rich brown, 10 cm (4 in) long, appear in autumn. HEIGHT & SPREAD 6×3 m (20×10 ft) after 20 years, ultimately 50 m (165 ft) tall.

The annual spring growth of **'Aurea'**♀ is bright yellow, ripening to pale green.

P. pungens (Colorado spruce) This very hardy tree with narrowly conical habit has sharp, stiff, grey-green needles, 3 cm (1¼ in) long. Flowers are red and green. The egg-shaped, pale brown cones are 10 cm (4 in) long. The aromatic and long-lasting foliage is good for decorations and flower arrangements. HEIGHT & SPREAD 3×1.5 m (10×5 ft) after 20 years, ultimately 35 m (115 ft) tall.

'Erich Frahm', with blue foliage, forms a regular cone, 6 m (20 ft) tall, spreading to 2 m (6½ ft), at 20 years old, ultimately reaching a height of 15 m (50 ft).

The following cultivars, with blue needles, all fall within the var. *glauca* group. All measurements are for plants after 20 years. The very hardy **'Glauca Prostrata'** has ground-creeping branches spreading to 1.5 m (5 ft), but is only 25 cm (10 in) high. **'Globosa'**♀ forms a vivid blue, flattened dome, 80 cm (32 in) high and wide.

▲ *Picea pugens 'Globosa'*

'Hoopsii'♀, bluish white, with dense branches forming a narrowly conical shape, is 5 m (16 ft) tall, spreading to 1.5 m (5 ft). **'Hoto'** has grey-blue needles and a regular, narrow, conical shape with dense branches and foliage. It is the same size as the species. **'Koster'**♀ is a slow-growing, narrowly conical tree with curving, silver-blue needles, 3 m (10 ft) tall and 1 m (3 ft) wide. **'Procumbens'**♀ is silver-grey and spreads irregularly, some branches drooping while others ascend. If ascending branches are removed, as is recommended, it reaches 1.5 m (5 ft) high and spreads to 3 m (10 ft).

P. smithiana♀ (West Himalayan spruce) This large tree has noticeably pendulous side branches, with dark green needles, 4 cm (1½ in) long. Flowers are green. Cigar-shaped cones, 20 cm (8 in) long, eventually glossy brown, appear in late autumn. This tree does not stand cold winds well, the needles soon becoming a sickly yellow brown. HEIGHT & SPREAD 3×2 m (10×6½ ft) after 20 years, ultimately 40 m (130 ft) tall.

CULTIVATION Plant in late spring in fertile, deep, neutral or acid soil that remains moist but is well drained. Choose a sunny site, sheltered from cold winds. Trees in general do not like shallow, chalky or dry soils. *P. abies* tolerates slightly more waterlogged soils. Late spring frosts can damage young trees and new growth.

PROPAGATION Sow seed of any species under glass in late winter, in pots or deep

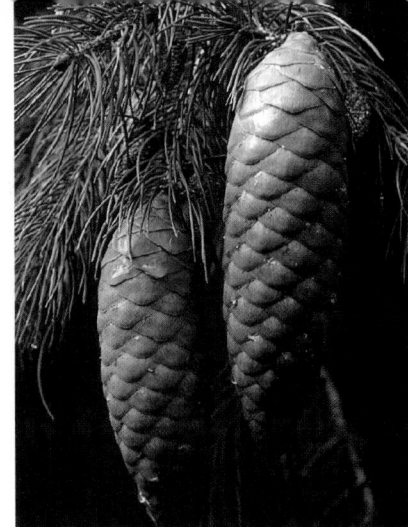

▲ *Picea smithiana*

boxes of seed compost. Line out the seedlings in rows the following spring, and grow on for 2 or 3 years before planting out in their final positions.

Of the listed species, *P. abies, P. glauca, P. orientalis* and *P. pungens* can also be propagated by taking hardwood cuttings in early or mid autumn, and *P. breweriana, P. omorika* and *P. smithiana* can be propagated by grafting. For cultivars, the blue forms of *P. pungens* in particular, grafting is the only recommended method.

PRUNING Cutting back trees will disfigure rather than control the growth of most spruces. Confine pruning to removing dead twigs, branches that have reverted to green on coloured varieties and unwanted branches. Prune in winter as resin bleeding can occur attracting disease. Cut out branches growing the wrong way on prostrate varieties, or peg them out in the required direction.

PESTS AND DISEASES Red spider mite attacks most dwarf *P. abies* and *P. glauca* var. *albertiana* cultivars. Honey fungus and various root and butt rots also attack spruces, most commonly conifer root rot (*Phaeolus schwinitzii*) and conifer heart rot (*Fomes annosus*, syn. *Heterobasidion annosum*).

Pieris
Ericaceae

Pieris 'Forest Flame'

On acid soil pieris are among the most widely grown of evergreen shrubs, justly popular for their abundant flowers, the colourful new growth and the often attractive flower buds that form in autumn. The white to red flowers are pitcher-shaped and sometimes scented. Shrubs are generally

p
q

long-lived and may be compact, upright or spreading in habit. Most are hardy but *P. formosa* and its varieties may be severely cut back or killed in the worst winters in cold areas and the young growth may be damaged by late frosts. They enjoy acid soil conditions similar to those required by rhododendrons, but are more tolerant of drought, dense shade and the presence of tree roots in the soil.

RECOMMENDED SPECIES AND VARIETIES

P. floribunda In early and mid spring, pure white flowers are produced in upright sprays up to 12.5 cm (5 in) long. The dull green leaves are oval with a pointed tip and about 7.5 cm (3 in) long. This is the hardiest species. It is compact in habit. Native to SE United States. HEIGHT & SPREAD 30×30 cm (1×1 ft) after 5 years, ultimately 1.5 m (5 ft) tall.

P. **'Forest Flame'** The showy, red young growth on this compact, bushy plant fades to pink, cream or yellowish white, before gradually turning green. The rarely produced flowers are white, borne in large, spreading sprays, 15 cm (6 in) long, in mid to late spring. The lance-shaped leaves are about 12 cm (4¾ in) long. The first flush of new growth invariably gets frosted but this is a reliably hardy plant. HEIGHT & SPREAD 45×45 cm (1½×1½ ft) after 5 years, ultimately 2.1 m (7 ft) tall.

P. formosa The showy young growth is red at first before turning bronze and then deep green. The pointed, oval or spoon-shaped leaves are up to 18 cm (7 in) long. In late spring, pure white flowers are borne in upright or drooping sprays up to 15 cm (6 in) long. This is the least hardy of recommended species but if cut back by a harsh winter, it will usually regenerate. A dense shrub or small tree, native to W China and Burma. HEIGHT & SPREAD 60×60 cm (2×2 ft) after 5 years, ultimately 5 m (16 ft) tall.

The flowers of var. *forrestii* are lightly fragrant and the red young growth is particularly fine. Among the cultivars of this variety are **'Jermyns'**♥, with red winter buds that open white, and **'Wakehurst'**♥, which has bright red young growth, fading to pink and then to green. It tends to be early into growth and is therefore liable to have its new growth frosted.

▲ *Pieris japonica*

P. japonica (lily of the valley bush) White or occasionally pink or nearly red flowers are borne in upright or slightly drooping sprays, 15 cm (6 in) long, in early to mid spring. The glossy, mid green, oval to lance-shaped leaves are up to 6 cm (2½ in) long. A shrub of bushy habit, clothed to the ground with branches. Hardiness is variable. Native to Japan, E China, Taiwan. HEIGHT & SPREAD 60×60 cm (2×2 ft) after 5 years, ultimately 3 m (10 ft) tall.

Most cultivars come into growth late in the year and so are good for cold gardens. **'Blush'**♥ is of rather open habit, with pink flowers. **'Christmas Cheer'** (syn. 'Wada's Pink') has pink to white flowers, some of

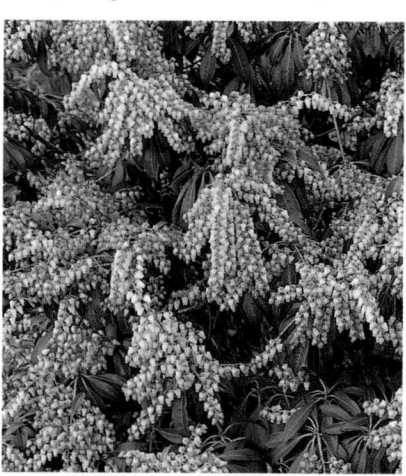
▲ *Pieris japonica* 'Pink Delight'

which open in winter. **'Debutante'**♥ has white flowers and is compact with bronzy new growth. The upright **'Dorothy Wyckoff'** has white flowers. **'Flamingo'** is tall and upright in habit, with deep pink flowers. The showy red young growth of **'Firecrest'**♥ fades to pink, cream or yellowish white, then gradually turns green. **'Grayswood'**♥ is dome-shaped, with long drooping sprays of white flowers. The non-flowering **'Little Heath'**♥ has yellowish green variegated leaves. **'Little Heath Green'**♥ is a dwarf spreading plant with bronzy red new growth. It rarely flowers. **'Mountain Fire'**♥ is one of the best cultivars for deep red new growth. The flowers are white. **'Pink Delight'**♥ has pink flowers fading to blush. **'Purity'**♥ is dense and compact, with bronzy new growth and abundant white flowers. **'Pygmaea'** (syn. 'Don') is slow-growing, with very narrow leaves that are bronzy when new. The white flowers are rarely produced. **'Red Mill'** is a hardy, tall-growing plant with dark red new growth. **'Sarabande'** is compact, with bronzy new growth and white flowers. **Taiwanensis Group** have upright or drooping white flowerheads. **'Tilford'** has white flowers. **'Valley Rose'** is tall and open-growing, with pink flowers fading to off-white. **'Valley Valentine'**♥ has deep rose to red flowers. **'Variegata'** is slow-growing and less vigorous with white variegated leaves. The flowers are white. **'White Pearl'** bears upright white flowerheads. **'White Rim'**♥ has showy creamy white variegation and white flowers.

CULTIVATION Plant in autumn or spring in a lime-free soil rich in organic matter. Plant those grown for their young foliage in partial shade. *P. japonica* needs a sunny site. Deadhead to encourage new flower buds.

PROPAGATION Take semi-ripe cuttings in late summer or layer low branches in early to late autumn. Alternatively, sow the seed of species under glass in spring or autumn.

PRUNING Cut back old straggly specimens in late winter. In late summer or autumn, cut off the dead wood on plants that have been frosted.

PESTS AND DISEASES Leaf spot may occur in wet seasons.

p
q

▲ *Pieris formosa* var. *forrestii* 'Wakehurst'

▲ *Pieris japonica* 'Valley Rose'

▲ *Pieris japonica* 'Valley Valentine'

Pilea
Urticaceae

The patterned foliage of these tropical ever-green perennials is their chief attraction. The species described here are popular as houseplants and for growing in a warm greenhouse or conservatory. The best-looking foliage is produced on young plants, which are easily raised from cuttings.

RECOMMENDED SPECIES AND VARIETIES
P. cadierei ♀ (aluminium plant) The oval, glossy, dark green leaves, up to 4 cm (1½ in) long, are marked with many silver patches between the veins. Forms a bushy plant. HEIGHT & SPREAD 30×30 cm (1×1 ft).

'**Minima**' has pink stems and olive-green foliage with silvery markings. The leaves are small and scalloped. It reaches a height of 15 cm (6 in) and a spread of 20 cm (8 in).
P. involucrata (friendship plant) Oval, downy dark green leaves up to 6 cm (2½ in) long are marked bronze, silver or red around the veins. A loosely branching plant. HEIGHT & SPREAD 25×25 cm (10×10 in).

'**Bronze**' has strong-growing bronze-copper foliage. '**Moon Valley**' has leaves up to 10 cm (4 in) long tinged with bronze, dark bronze veins and scalloped edges.

▲ *Pilea involucrata* 'Moon Valley'

'**Norfolk**' is a smaller plant with a height of 20 cm (8 cm) and a spread of 15 cm (6 in). The oval leaves are bronze to black-green marked with prominent, raised silver bands.
P. microphylla (syn. *P. muscosa*) (artillery plant) Tiny, oval, mid green leaflets form compound, mossy-looking leaves. Myriad tiny flowers are heavily laden with pollen and if the plant is shaken or water droplets fall on it, clouds of pollen erupt like tiny explosions, hence the common name. This fleshy stemmed, densely branched species is treated as an annual and raised from cuttings. HEIGHT & SPREAD 25×25 cm (10×10 in).
P. peperomioides The fleshy, rounded mid green leaves, up to 10 cm (4 in) long, have prominent darker green veins. The leaf stalks are 10–15 cm (4–6 in) long. HEIGHT & SPREAD 30×30 cm (1×1 ft).
CULTIVATION Grow under glass or indoors at a minimum temperature of 10°C (50°F). Plant in well-drained, soil-based compost. Protect from direct sunlight and draughts.

Water regularly in summer and feed with a liquid houseplant feed every 4-6 weeks. Water sparingly during winter. Pinch back plants as they develop in spring.
PROPAGATION Take softwood cuttings during spring and summer.
PESTS AND DISEASES Red spider mite can be troublesome.

Pimelea
Rice flower
Thymelaeaceae

Pimelea prostrata

Small, white or pink tubular flowers with four spreading petals are produced, usually in clusters, on these small evergreen shrubs. They are followed by white, pink, red or black berries, which are sometimes hard and nut-like. Male forms do not produce fruit. These plants can be bushy, erect or prostrate. All are native to Australia and New Zealand. The listed species is the only one widely available in Britain.
RECOMMENDED SPECIES
P. prostrata (syn. *P. coarctata*) White flowers with orange anthers are produced from mid spring to early summer in groups of about 10, forming a head 1 cm (⅜ in) across. This hardy alpine is very free flowering and prostrate, ideal for trailing over stones and walls in a rock garden. It has tiny grey-green leaves and forms patches. Conspicuous berry-like, fleshy white fruit appear in mid to late summer. Each bears one seed. HEIGHT & SPREAD 4×60 cm (1½×24 in).

▲ *Pimelea prostrata*

CULTIVATION Plant anytime from spring to autumn in well-drained gravelly, preferably lime-free soil in full sun.
PROPAGATION Sow seed in pots in autumn and leave outside to germinate in spring. Take semi-ripe cuttings in late summer.
PESTS AND DISEASES Usually trouble free.

Pimpernel see *Anagallis*

Pimpinella
Umbelliferae

Flat spreading heads of tiny creamy, white or pink summer flowers and delicate filigree foliage contribute an airy quality to any planting scheme that includes the hardy annuals and herbaceous perennials of this genus. The plants require an open, sunny position in a border or wild-flower garden and a free-draining soil. They are native to Eurasia and N Africa.
RECOMMENDED SPECIES AND VARIETIES
P. anisum (aniseed, anise) Myriad tiny creamy flowers on spreading heads, up to 10 cm (4 in) across, are produced from early to mid summer by this aromatic annual plant which is grown as a herb. Its delicate leaves are used as a culinary herb. Tiny, oval, greenish, aromatic fruits appear in late summer after the flowers have faded. The seeds are ripe and ready for culinary use when the tips of the fruits turn from green to grey. HEIGHT & SPREAD 45×25 cm (18×10 in).
P. major '**Rosea**' Spreading heads of minute pink flowers, up to 10 cm (4 in) across, crown the tall stems of this strong-growing perennial plant in early to mid summer. The divided fern-like leaves are mid green. HEIGHT & SPREAD 75–90×45 cm (2½–3×1½ ft).

▲ *Pimpinella major* 'Rosea'

CULTIVATION Grow in any well-drained soil and in an open, sunny situation. Remove faded flowerheads from perennial plants to prevent seeding.
PROPAGATION Sow seed directly into the open ground in spring where the plants are to grow. Thin the seedlings as soon as they are large enough to handle. The thinnings do not transplant successfully. Alternatively, sow seeds in pots in early spring and plant out seedlings in late spring. Divide *P. major* 'Rosea' in early spring.
PESTS AND DISEASES Usually trouble free.

Pincushion flower see *Scabiosa*
Pine see *Pinus*
Pineapple see *Ananas comosus*
Pineapple flower see *Eucomis*

Pinellia
Araceae

Hooded spathes, leaf-like open-sided tubes, wrap around upright pencil-like flower spikes, or spadices, to create an unusual effect in summer. These hardy, herbaceous, tuberous perennials thrive at the front of a partially shaded border.

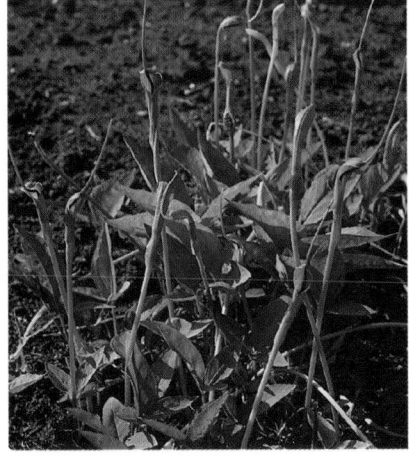

▲ *Pinellia ternata*

RECOMMENDED SPECIES
P. ternata A leafless stem produces a small, hooded, tubular, green spathe, 5 cm (2 in) long, surrounding the spadix which is greenish with a purple base. The flat, oval, dull green leaflets up to 12.5 cm (5 in) long are borne in groups of 3 on erect stems. HEIGHT & SPREAD 20×15 cm (8×6 in).
CULTIVATION Plant tubers in spring 10 cm (4 in) deep in a rich organic soil in partial shade. Apply a slow-release fertiliser once yearly in spring when growth commences.
PROPAGATION Divide young tubers in the spring or collect bulbils from the leaf axils in late summer.
PESTS AND DISEASES Greenfly are sometimes troublesome.

Pinguicula
Butterwort
Lentiburiaceae

Pinguicula grandiflora

The broad, pale green, sticky leaves of these insectivorous plants trap small insects that alight on them. Handsome violet-like flowers appear in late spring and summer. Pinguiculas are small herbaceous evergreen perennials widespread in boggy areas of the Northern Hemisphere. The only species that is readily available is hardy and can be grown either outside in sunny, boggy conditions or in a cool greenhouse. Under glass, pinguiculas can be helpful in catching whitefly and aphids on their sticky leaves.

RECOMMENDED SPECIES
P. grandiflora The solitary funnel-shaped dark blue flowers, up to 4 cm (1½ in) across, have long slender spurs, white throats and spreading lobes. The pale green leaves, up to 4 cm (1½ in) long, form flattish rosettes. HEIGHT & SPREAD 15×10 cm (6×4 in).
CULTIVATION Plant outdoors in humus-rich, boggy soil and in sun or partial shade. Alternatively, grow under glass in pots of peat-based compost. Keep plants very wet in summer, but relatively drier in winter.
PROPAGATION Divide plants in late winter or sow ripe seed on sphagnum moss.

▲ *Pinguicula grandiflora*

PESTS AND DISEASES Liable to attack by slugs and snails. Birds may remove over-wintering buds outdoors.

Pink see *Dianthus*

Pinus
Pine
Pinaceae

Pinus parviflora

These evergreen conifers range from semi-prostrate shrubs to tall forest trees 75 m (245 ft) high, but most are 15-50 m (50-165 ft) tall with stems up to 2 m (6½ ft) thick. These sizes are reached in 70-100 years, depending on the species and conditions. Young trees are conical, maturing to flat-topped specimens which can still be quite bushy. There are also many dwarf or slow-growing forms which are good for a rock garden or large landscaped area.

Some of these versatile trees are chosen for decorative purposes while others, particularly *Pinus sylvestris*, provide wind shelter. All have long, needle-like leaves in groups of two, three or five held on to the twigs by a sheath. The bark is an attractive feature on many, as are cones and flowers.

Male and female flowers appear in separate clusters on new shoots, usually in spring but in summer on *P. montezumae*, producing cones that ripen two years after setting. The male flowers, at the base of the new shoots, are generally catkin-like and 1.5-5 cm (½-2 in) long. The female flowers, on the growth tips, are immature cones, usually pea-sized.

The cones can be round, conical or even banana-like. They may crack open in strong sunshine, releasing winged seeds for wind dispersal, but some open only when forced to by the extreme heat of a forest fire.

Most pines prefer acid soils in a dry site; some tolerate poor, infertile soil and water-logged conditions. They are native to temperate zones of the Northern Hemisphere, as far south as Central America and Indonesia. All those listed thrive in Britain but some are too tall to be suitable for anything but an extremely large garden.

Pinus bungeana

RECOMMENDED SPECIES AND VARIETIES
P. bungeana (lace bark pine, chequer bark pine) This large, slow-growing species has beautiful flaking bark, blotched with grey-green and creamy white when stems are 10 cm (4 in) thick. Mature trees have multiple stems, creating a broadly conical bush, devoid of branches to a height of 2 m (6½ ft). Rigid, sharply pointed, dark green needles are 7.5 cm (3 in) long in sparse groups of 3 and smell of turpentine when crushed. Male flowers are yellow and female flowers are green. The latter mature into yellow-brown, egg-shaped, stalkless cones 7 cm (2¾ in) long with a spine on each scale. They become foxy brown with age. This tree suits dry, stony soil. HEIGHT & SPREAD 2×1 m (6½×3 ft) after 10 years, ultimately 20×4 m (66×13 ft).
P. cembra ♀ (arolla pine) Very dark foliage adorns this tidy but austere, narrowly conical, sometimes columnar tree. This is a very hardy pine. Needles 5-9 cm (2-3½ in) long, in groups of 5, are dark glossy green on the

outside, blue-grey on the inside. The male flowers are purple. The red female flowers ripen into 7.5 cm (3 in) long blue-purple to red-brown banana-shaped cones. They never fully open. This species is too large for many gardens. HEIGHT & SPREAD 1.5×1 m (5×3 ft) after 10 years, ultimately 20×2.4 m (66×8 ft).

P. coulteri♀ (big cone pine) Everything about this tree is large, but it is slow-growing in Britain and difficult to establish and propagate. Most trees are bushy although some are tall and slender with long, branchless stems. The cones, 30 cm (12 in) long and 20 cm (8 in) thick, weighing up to 3 kg (6 lb 8 oz), are the largest borne by any pine, but only about 10 are produced by a tree in a lifetime. They are egg-shaped, more pointed at one end, with a slight curve in the longer axis. Each scale has a viciously pointed barb. The cones remain on the tree for many years, and stay closed. The seeds are up to 1.5 cm (½ in) across. Thumb-size purple male flowers and red female flowers the size of walnuts appear high up in the crown. The grey-green 30 cm (12 in) long needles are held in groups of 3. Young shoots, up to 2 cm (¾ in) thick, have an attractive dusting of grey. HEIGHT & SPREAD 2 m×50 cm (6½ ft×20 in) after 10 years, ultimately 25×12 m (80×40 ft).

P. densiflora 'Umbraculifera' This is a very slow-growing, multistemmed form, with a dense head of branches resembling an umbrella. It is good for a rock garden but needs room with age. Salmon-pink young bark matures into fissured grey-red plates. Slender bright green needles up to 5 cm (2 in) long grow in pairs and point forwards. Male flowers are yellow-brown and female flowers are red. The ripe cones, often in bunches of 3 or more, are about 4 cm (1½ in) long, pale brown, stalkless and conical. They open in their second summer to release the winged seed. HEIGHT & SPREAD 2×1 m (6½×3 ft) after 10 years, ultimately 4×6 m (13×20 ft).

P. heldreichii var. *leucodermis*♀ A slow-growing two-needle pine, of narrow, conical habit, with closely clustered, prickly 8 cm (3¼ in) long stiff dark green needles. A shoot covered with needles resembles a series of bottle brushes. Female flowers are purple-red and the male flowers open yellow. Deep blue cones are pointed, egg-shaped, 10 cm (4 in) long, and produced in pairs. They turn yellow-brown, then pale brown with age. This variety is best on gravelly dry soils and will even grow on chalk. HEIGHT & SPREAD 2.4×2 m (8×6½ ft) after 10 years, ultimately 25×8 m (80×26 ft).

'Compact Gem' is a very slow-growing, dense, compact bush with a rounded habit that reaches its full size of 1 m (3 ft) tall, with a spread of 50 cm (20 in), in 40 years. It is suited to a rock garden. 'Satellit' has steeply ascending branches, making a good narrow, columnar form that takes 50 years to reach

▲ *Pinus heldreichii* var. *leucodermis*

its full size of 15 m (50 ft) tall with a spread of 3 m (10 ft). Densely packed needles lie against the shoots when young, later spreading and becoming brush like. 'Schmidtii'♀ is a very slow-growing dwarf form, taking 100 years to reach 3 m (10 ft) high and wide. This compact, very dense, mound-shaped bush is an excellent choice for a garden with dry or chalk-based soil.

P. montezumae Dramatic foliage distinguishes this tender species which has a broadly spreading crown over a 2 m (6½ ft) tall main stem. It needs a sheltered site to thrive and reach full size. Each branch is laden with numerous groups of 5 grey-green needles at least 30 cm (12 in) long and spread in flue-brush fashion on thick, smooth red-brown shoots. Serrated edges make the needles rough and sharp to the touch. Male flowers are purple and female flowers are red. The latter grow into 15 cm (6 in) long, prickly, blue-purple cones, ripening red to yellow-brown. Young trees have single cones; older trees bear clusters. HEIGHT & SPREAD 3×1.5 m (10×5 ft) after 10 years, ultimately 20×20 m (66×66 ft).

P. mugo (mountain pine) Plentiful red female flowers, in groups of 2 or 3, are the best feature of this very hardy, slow-growing, 2-needle species which can be a large shrubby bush or, more rarely, a small upright tree. Its many stems hug the ground then turn upwards from obvious knees. The green male flowers are often hidden by the pairs of densely packed 3-4 cm (1¼-1½ in) long dark green needles, which are curved and rigid, sometimes twisted. Blackish brown young cones ripen to yellow-brown. They are egg-shaped but very pointed, 6 cm (2½ in) long, stalkless and usually erect. They sometimes hang in groups of 3 or 4, but young trees always have single cones.

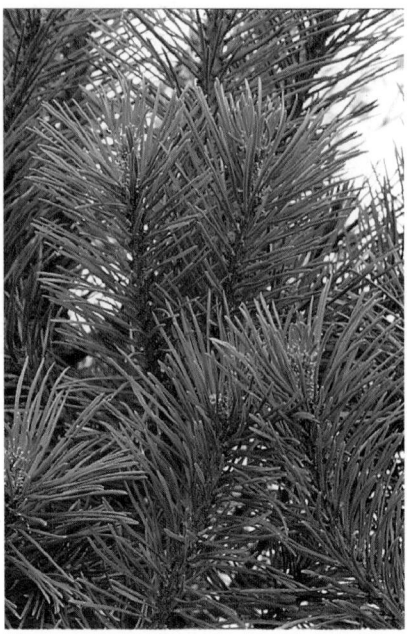

▲ *Pinus mugo*

This is a good maintenance-free plant for awkward places but will look untidy until very old. In tree form it reaches no more than 9 m (30 ft) with a bushy spread of 2-3 m (6½-10 ft). HEIGHT & SPREAD 1×1 m (3×3 ft) after 10 years, ultimately 3×9 m (10×30 ft).

'Gnom' is a compact, densely branched plant with tightly packed pairs of radially arranged 4.5 cm (1¾ in) long deep green needles. In 70 years it forms a dense rounded mound 2 m (6½ ft) high and wide. Older plants may be more conical. 'Humpy' is a compact form suited to containers. It reaches 1 m (3 ft) in height and width in 40 years and is conical with 1.5 cm (½ in) long needles and noticeable red-brown winter buds. 'Mops'♀ is a densely branched, dwarf, rounded bush similar to a mop head. It reaches 1 m (3 ft) in height and spread in 30 years and is suited to any situation. In winter it displays attractive resinous brown buds. 'Ophir' is a flattened bun-

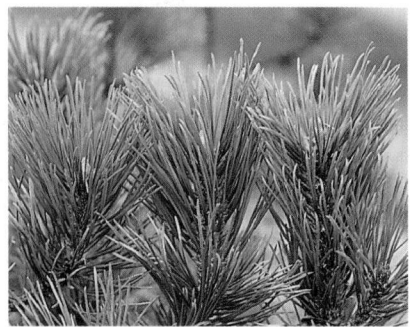

▲ *Pinus mugo* 'Mops'

shaped shrubby dwarf with pleasing golden yellow winter foliage, which reaches 60 cm (2 ft) high and 30 cm (1 ft) wide in 10 years. The slightly twisted 4-7 cm (1½-2¾ in) long needles are light green in summer. The

▲ *Pinus mugo* var. *pumilio*

shrubby, usually creeping, var. *pumilio*♀ reaches perhaps 2m (6½ft) in height and 3m (10ft) in width in 100 years. Striking purple cones, which ripen dark brown, are more rounded than those of the species and only about 2.5cm (1in) long. Almost pure white winter buds coated with resin are conspicuous against very dark foliage. **'Winter Gold'** has 7cm (2¾in) long widely spread, twisted needles, with golden tips in winter. It is an open spreading dwarf bush, seldom exceeding 1m (3ft) in height and 2m (6½ft) in spread in over 50 years. Showy 1cm (⅜in) long, 4mm (⅛in) wide, resinous buds appear in winter.

▲ *Pinus mugo* 'Winter Gold'

P. parviflora♀ (Japanese white pine) Abundant soft green-blue foliage makes this tree an ideal centrepiece for a large lawn. The 6cm (2½in) needles, held in groups of 5, all have a vivid blue-white stripe on the inside. These groups stay closed for years, opening only when 4 or 5 years old. Male flowers are purple-red and female flowers start bright red. In early summer an 18cm (7in) long pale green, slightly upturned spiky candle of new growth protrudes from the pale yellow-brown spent male flowers, and the female blooms, purple by now, grace the tip of the 'candles'. The latter mature into blue-green, egg-shaped cones 3-4cm (1¼-1½in) long. The spreading branches are fairly horizontal, with short

branchlets. The bark is smoother than that of other species. HEIGHT & SPREAD 3×2m (10×6½ft) after 10 years, ultimately 15×10m (50×33ft).

'Adcock's Dwarf'♀ is more of a compact bush than a conical tree, and slow-growing, reaching 2.4m (8ft) high and 1.2m (4ft) across in 30 years. Tightly packed bunches of greyish green needles up to 2.5cm (1in) long appear at the tips of young shoots. Smaller than the species, but similar in other ways, f. *glauca* reaches 12m

▲ *Pinus parviflora* 'Adcock's Dwarf'

(40ft) in 50 years. The foliage, blue-green rather than green-blue, is densely packed at the growth tips. Young trees have no branches but those on older trees can spread 3m (10ft) or more in all directions.

P. patula♀ (Jelecote pine) Only the south-west of Britain or very sheltered conditions suit this tender species, which has drooping needles, often in threes, sometimes fours or fives, that can be 30cm (12in) long on slightly grey shoots. This weeping shiny blue-green foliage, long, spreading branches and, frequently, multiple stems give the tree a graceful habit. It seldom flowers in Britain but when it does, clusters of 5 banana-shaped cones, each up to 9cm (3½in) long, are evenly spaced around the twigs. Tiny thorns can be seen on the larger cone scales. HEIGHT & SPREAD 2m×50cm (6½ft×20in) after 10 years, ultimately 20×9m (66×30ft).

P. pinea♀ (stone pine, umbrella pine) Gnarled and twisted heavy branches radiating from a 6m (20ft) clear main stem culminate in a dense umbrella-shaped canopy of needles on thin shoots and branches. The branches have orange-brown bark, while the main stem, which usually leans, shows regular ring bulges on deeply fissured dark grey to black bark. Stiff, 12cm (4¾in) long grey-green needles are smooth and in pairs. Male flowers are yellow and female flowers are green. The roundish 12cm (4¾in) long cones resemble a handful of green-brown pebbles glued together. Seeds, too, look and feel like small rounded stones. HEIGHT & SPREAD 2×2m (6½×6½ft) after 10 years, ultimately 10-15×10m (33-50×33ft).

P. pumila 'Glauca'♀ This pine often lacks a main stem. All the branches are densely covered with grey-blue foliage and sweep upwards, unlike the species, which has lower branches that sometimes sprout roots where they touch the ground, causing the tree to spread widely. This very slow-growing pine has dark green 10cm (4in) long needles held in fives, sometimes more, each with a rich blue-green stripe on the inside. Only the red male flowers are visible. Rounded 3.5cm (1⅜in) cones ripen from purple-violet to dull brown and are held in delicate bunches that are easily shed. HEIGHT & SPREAD 1×1m (3×3ft) after 10 years, ultimately 2×6m (6½×20ft).

P. strobus 'Radiata'♀ A compact, dwarf form that eventually makes a rounded, almost spherical, plant. It has the smooth and silver-grey bark of the species, which becomes fissured only when old. Crowded slender twigs are covered with 9cm (3½in) long blue needles pointing upwards at the branch tips. They are borne in fives and have a grey-white inner surface. Male flowers are yellow. The pink female flowers grow into green banana-shaped hanging cones 15cm (6in) long and 5cm (2in) thick, which ripen to brown. HEIGHT & SPREAD 30×30cm (1×1ft) after 10 years, ultimately 1.5×1.5m (5×5ft).

P. sylvestris♀ (Scots pine) This species, the only true British native pine, is very fast-growing when young but slows down with age, when it develops a rounded, flattened crown above a tall clean main stem which can be over 20m (66ft) tall before branching begins. With a mature trunk over 2m (6½ft) thick, this tall forest tree is not suited to an average garden. Needles in radially arranged pairs are stiff, somewhat twisted, 7cm (2¾in) long and blue-grey or blue-green. Beautiful salmon-pink papery bark peels from the upper stem of older trees, while much thicker bark at the stem base is fissured into regular plates that flake off, leaving deep pink or russet-red, scars. Male flowers are yellow and female flowers are red. Egg-shaped cones 7.5cm (3in) long ripen from green to brown. They crack open in late summer to release their seed.

p
q

▲ *Pinus sylvestris*

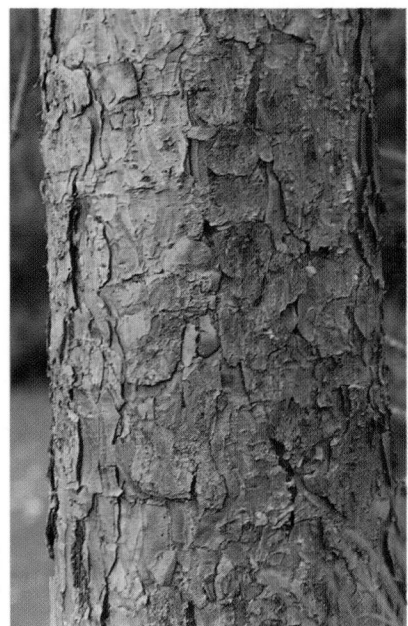

▲ *Pinus sylvestris* bark

HEIGHT & SPREAD 3×2m (10×6½ft) after 10 years, ultimately 35×4m (115×13ft).

'**Aurea**'♀ turns a rich golden yellow after the first hard frost. '**Beuvronensis**'♀ is covered with 1.5cm (½in) long bright blue-green needles. It makes a superb rockgarden plant, growing into a small, tidy dome seldom taller or wider than 1m (3ft) after 60 years. '**Chantry Blue**' is a slow-growing tree with blue needles. It is very conical in shape. In 30 years it reaches 4m (13ft) in height and is half as wide at ground level. Majestic '**Fastigiata**' resembles a tall, straight feather in silhouette. A medium to large garden is a suitable setting for this tree, which reaches 15m (50ft) in over 70 years but is never wider than 2m (6½ft). '**Gold Coin**' has striking bright yellow foliage. It is slow-growing, eventually reaching 2m

▼ *Pinus sylvestris* 'Beuvronensis'

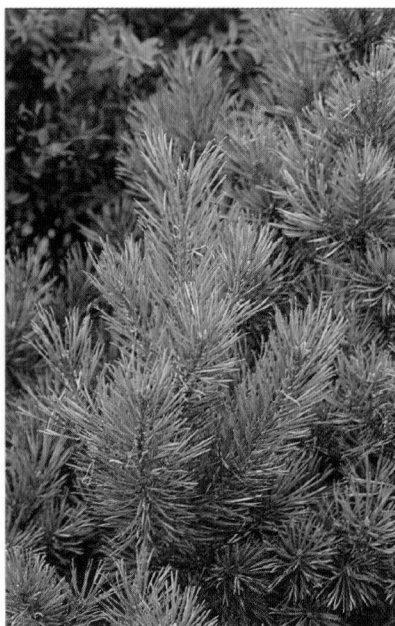

▲ *Pinus sylvestris* 'Watereri'

(6½ft) in height and spread. '**Inverleith**' is identical to the large-growing species, apart from the distinction of creamy white variegations in the needles, and is suitable only for exceptionally large gardens. '**Lodge Hill**' is a compact dwarf plant with dense blue-grey foliage. Each branch ends with very dark terminal buds in winter. In 40 years it reaches 80cm (32in) in height with a spread of 60cm (2ft). '**Watereri**' is a dwarf form. An upright, conical tree when young, it becomes rounded with age, reaching 4m (13ft) high and almost as wide in over 100 years. The blue-grey needles are 3cm (1¼in) long, very stiff, somewhat twisted and borne in pairs. This pine is suited to a heather garden but will eventually outgrow the position.

CULTIVATION Plant in the tree's final position, in good light, during mid to late autumn. Grow in well-drained acid soil, unless otherwise stated. Do not use strimmers or mowers near the tree base, as they can damage roots just under the surface.

PROPAGATION Sow seed in late winter under glass, or in late spring in the open. Plant out when 2 years old, or more. Graft cultivars in autumn with grafting scions about half the thickness of a pencil. Side grafting onto pencil-thick rootstocks is best.

PRUNING Seldom necessary. Remove any spindly lower branches. Pruning disfigures the conical shape of most pines.

PESTS AND DISEASES Plants are prone to infection by honey fungus, phytophthora and rusts. Adelgids, sawflies and pine shoot moth caterpillars can also cause damage. The caterpillars of the pine shoot moth, brown and about 2cm (¾in) long, can seriously damage young trees by boring into and killing shoots. Treat the problem with a contact insecticide.

Piptanthus
Leguminosae

Piptanthus nepalensis

Clusters of showy, bright yellow flowers above semi-evergreen foliage distinguish these slightly tender shrubs from the Himalayas and China. Only one of the two species is usually grown in Britain, and the plants benefit from the protection of a sunny wall in cold areas. In a hard winter, the erect stems may be killed, but established shrubs will usually make strong new growth from the base.

RECOMMENDED SPECIES
P. nepalensis (*P. forrestii*, *P. laburnifolius*) The flowers, like sweet peas, and about 3cm (1¼in) long, appear in spring at the tips of erect, dark green stems. The glossy dark green leaves have 3 elliptical leaflets, up to 10cm (4in) long, which usually last well into winter. Many conspicuous, flat, green or blackish seedpods appear in late summer. HEIGHT & SPREAD 1.2×1m (4×3ft) after 5 years, ultimately 2.4m (8ft) tall.

CULTIVATION Plant in early spring in a sheltered, sunny position in any well-drained, fairly fertile soil. Provide the protection of a south or west-facing wall in cold areas.

PROPAGATION Sow seeds under glass or in a coldframe in autumn or early spring.

PRUNING Cut out the oldest stems every 2 to 3 years and remove any frost-damaged stems in spring.

PESTS AND DISEASES Usually trouble free.

▲ *Piptanthus nepalensis*

p
q

Pittosporum
Pittosporaceae

*Pittosporum tenuifolium
'Tom Thumb'*

Often used as the backbone of borders or for hedging, these small trees and shrubs are admired for their evergreen foliage. Some are showy in flower. The tubular or bell-shaped blooms are up to 2 cm (¾ in) across, often with reflexed petals. They may be white, yellow or red, carried in clusters or singly and usually carry a pleasant honey fragrance. Many species carry male and female flowers on separate plants. If fertilised, the female plants go on to display globular or oval seed capsules which may be green, grey, yellow or red. The leaves are very variable in shape, ranging from linear to obovate. The foliage of *Pittosporum tenuifolium* is good for cutting.

Most of the species described below are reasonably hardy across Britain, but grow best in mild, southern areas. In more northerly regions improved vigour can be attained by providing a windbreak in the form of a hedge or wall. *P. anomalum, P. dallii* and *P. tenuifolium* are the hardiest species. *P. crassifolium* is particularly suited to mild, coastal areas since it is resistant to salt-laden winds. Native to Australasia.

RECOMMENDED SPECIES AND VARIETIES
P. anomalum Rigid, interlacing, near-black branches, sparsely clothed with tiny dark green toothed leaves, make the whole bush appear black. This shrub bears tiny solitary white or pale yellow flowers in spring. HEIGHT & SPREAD 60×60 cm (2×2 ft) after 5 years, ultimately 1 m (3 ft) tall.

P. crassifolium Leathery obovate leaves, 7.5 cm (3 in) long, are borne by this erect shrub or small tree. The leaves are grey-green above and densely white or brownish beneath. Clusters of red flowers appear in spring. Female and hermaphrodite plants go on to produce pale green seed capsules. HEIGHT & SPREAD 3×2 m (10×6½ ft) after 5 years, ultimately 10 m (33 ft) tall.

'Variegatum' has pale green leaves edged with creamy white. It bears female flowers and is slower growing than the species.

P. dallii This large shrub or small tree has dark green leathery leaves about 10 cm (4 in) long, distinctly toothed in the upper half. Clusters of white flowers in summer are only seen on mature plants. HEIGHT & SPREAD 1×1 m (3×3 ft) after 5 years, ultimately 3 m (10 ft) tall.

P. eugenioides (lemonwood) A near white trunk and branches clothed with glossy green, wavy-edged leaves, 12.5 cm (5 in)

▲ *Pittosporum eugenioides* 'Variegatum'

long, distinguish this tree. Mature plants produce numerous clusters of small yellow flowers in spring. When grown in a container it will reach up to 3 m (10 ft) tall, and makes a fine conservatory plant. HEIGHT & SPREAD 3×1 m (10×3 ft) after 5 years, ultimately 10 m (33 ft) tall.

'Variegatum'♀ bears male flowers and has broad cream edges to its leaves.

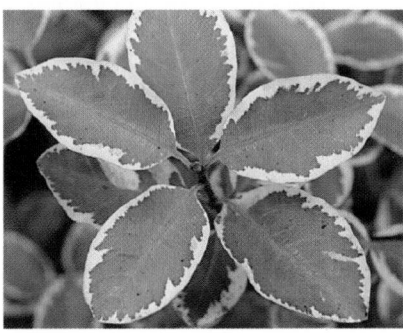

▲ *Pittosporum* 'Garnettii'

P. 'Garnettii'♀ This large shrub or small tree with a conical habit has greyish green leaves about 6 cm (2½ in) long. The leaves have an irregular cream border and are tinted and spotted purplish pink in winter. Solitary dark red flowers are produced in spring. It is a hermaphrodite plant. HEIGHT & SPREAD 2×1 m (6½×3 ft) after 5 years, ultimately 4 m (13 ft) tall.

P. 'Margaret Turnbull' Yellowish, slightly wavy leaves, about 4 cm (1½ in) long, have dark green margins while young, and

▼ *Pittosporum tenuifolium*

become totally dark green with age. This female shrub produces dark red flowers from mid to late spring. HEIGHT & SPREAD 1.8×1 m (6×3 ft) after 5 years, ultimately 3 m (10 ft) tall.

P. tenuifolium♀ Dark young branches are clothed with thin wavy-edged leaves of various colours and sizes up to 7.5 cm (3 in) long, depending on the variety. The flowers are dark red, usually highly fragrant and borne singly in late spring. *P. tenuifolium*

▲ *Pittosporum tenuifolium* 'Abbotsbury Gold'

can be grown as a hedge or as a small tree and some of the colourful leaf forms make admirable tub plants for the patio. HEIGHT & SPREAD 5×1 m (16×3 ft) after 5 years, ultimately 10 m (33 ft) tall.

'Abbotsbury Gold' is a reasonably hardy variety. Its leaves, about 4 cm (1½ in) long, are yellowish green with paler midribs and an irregular broad margin of darker green. Its female flowers are dark red and fragrant. 'Golden King' see 'Warnham Gold'.

'Irene Paterson'♀ is a popular variety with very pale green leaves usually heavily blotched and spotted white – as the leaves age they become greener. The dark red flowers are male. Although it is pleasing to the eye, it is slower growing than most

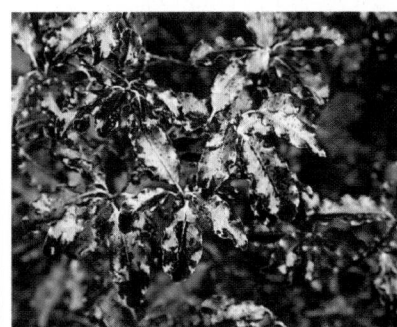

▲ *Pittosporum tenuifolium* 'Purpureum'

other varieties and less hardy. 'Purpureum' has pale green young leaves which become dark purple. The dark red flowers are male with yellow anthers. It is a less hardy cultivar than the others.

'Silver Queen'♀ is deservedly the most popular cultivar. A pyramidal tree with 3 cm (1¼ in) long, pale silvery green leaves with white wavy edges. Dark red flowers (mainly female) are produced in mid and

p
q

▲ *Pittosporum tenuifolium* 'Silver Queen'

Pittosporum tenuifolium 'Silver Queen'

late spring. This variety is hardy near London and worth trying farther north. **'Tom Thumb'**♀ is a dwarf, rounded shrub only reaching about 1m (3ft) tall. The young leaves are pale green becoming dark purple through winter. The dark red flowers have conspicuous yellow anthers.

'Warnham Gold' has a rather open habit. The leaves are about 4cm (1½in) long. They are pale green while young becoming bright yellow in autumn and winter. This beautiful large shrub is at its best in semi-shade – it can be scorched by the sun. The same or a very similar plant is sold under the name 'Golden King'. **'Wendle Channon'** is a bushy male variety with shiny green leaves, broadly and irregularly edged in yellow while young, the edges becoming creamy white later.

P. tobira♀ The 9cm (3½in) long, leathery mid green leaves of this bushy shrub are obovate with the base narrowed to a stout petiole. Clusters of creamy white, highly fragrant flowers in summer are followed by yellow seed capsules. Suitable for warmer gardens. HEIGHT & SPREAD 3×1m (10×3ft) after 5 years, ultimately 6m (20ft) tall.

▼ *Pittosporum tenuifolium* 'Wendle Channon'

▲ *Pittosporum tobira* 'Variegatum'

'Nanum' is a compact dwarf form, reaching a height of only 3m (10ft). **'Variegatum'**♀ has grey-green leaves with conspicuous creamy white edges.

CULTIVATION Plant in well-drained soils in spring or summer. Pittosporums do not object to lime. All benefit from a deep dry mulch applied around the base in winter to provide some protection. *P. crassifolium* makes an excellent windbreak in warm, coastal gardens. *P. tenuifolium* prefers semi-shade but usually does well in the open. Good ventilation is important for plants grown under glass.

PROPAGATION Sow seed in autumn or spring under glass. Grow on in pots in a coldframe for 2 years before planting out in late spring. The cultivars are best grown from semi-ripe cuttings taken in mid summer, overwintered in pots under glass and planted out the following spring.

PRUNING Prune as required to keep a good shape. Cut back *P. tenuifolium* in summer to keep it compact or to form a hedge.

PESTS AND DISEASES Scale insects and aphids are occasionally troublesome.

Plane see *Platanus*

Plantago
Plantain
Plantaginaceae

Plantago major 'Rubrifolia'

The neat rosettes of leaves, often covered in a silvery down, make useful additions to a rock garden or crevice. These hardy annual, biennial or perennial plants – some of which are persistent weeds – tolerate most soils and situations except dense shade. Spikes of tiny flowers appear in summer.

▲ *Plantago major* 'Rosularis'

▲ *Plantago major* 'Rubrifolia'

RECOMMENDED SPECIES AND VARIETIES
P. asiatica **'Variegata'** The lance-shaped, variegated leaves grow up to 10cm (4in) long. The insignificant flowers are borne on stout stems and are usually removed when they appear. This reliably perennial plant is suitable for planting in a damp, but free-draining sunny spot. HEIGHT & SPREAD 15×20cm (6×8in).

P. major Rosettes of oval or roughly heart-shaped leathery green leaves, up to 20cm (8in) long, appear on this hardy perennial. This plant is represented in the garden by the following cultivars. HEIGHT & SPREAD 25×25cm (10×10in).

'Atropurpurea' see 'Rubrifolia'
'Rosularis' (syn. *P. rosea*) (rose plantain) has tufts of green leaves growing up to 7.5cm (3in) across. The cultivar **'Rubrifolia'** (syn. 'Atropurpurea') bears maroon leaves. The short spikes of greenish purple flowers are up to 25cm (10in) tall and have an architectural quality. **'Variegata'** produces green and cream variegated leaves.

P. nivalis The neat rosettes of lance-shaped leaves, up to 7cm (2¾in) long, are covered in silver hairs. The short spikes of insignificant grey summer flowers are best removed as they detract from the architectural quality of the leaves. This small perennial, suitable for a rock garden, requires a free-draining soil. HEIGHT & SPREAD 5×10cm (2×4in).

P. rosea see *P. major* 'Rosularis'

p
q

CULTIVATION Plant in spring in an open, sunny position. *P. nivalis* requires a top dressing of coarse grit in order to protect the hairy leaves from the soil. In very wet winters protect with a small square of glass resting on 2 bricks or 4 small stakes just above the foliage. Remove flower spikes of all varieties before seed sets.
PROPAGATION Sow seed or divide in spring.
PESTS AND DISEASES Usually trouble free.

Plantain SEE *Plantago*

Platanus
Plane tree
Platanaceae

Platanus orientalis

With their distinctively mottled bark and deciduous lobed leaves, planes are handsome trees, although few ordinary gardens are large enough to accommodate their monumental size. They are a familiar feature in parks and in streets and are tolerant of atmospheric pollution. However, little will grow under their spreading branches and their durable leaves can be a nuisance in autumn. The dappling on the trunks and branches occurs when irregular-sized plates of olive-green to light grey-brown bark are shed each spring to reveal pale gold inner layers. Insignificant spring flowers develop into conspicuous bristly globe-like clusters of nutlets, up to 6cm (2½in) across, borne on pendulous stalks that persist among bare branches all through winter. The species in cultivation are hardy in lowland Britain.

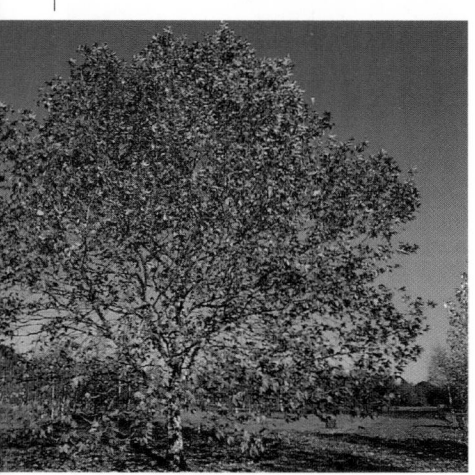

▲ *Platanus × hispanica*

RECOMMENDED SPECIES AND VARIETIES
P. × hispanica♀ (syn. *P. × acerifolia*) (London plane) The bright green, shallowly lobed leaves, with 3 or 7 segments, are about 20cm (8in) broad and long. This tree has a straight trunk and forms a rounded head. HEIGHT & SPREAD 10×6m (33×20ft) after 20 years, ultimately 45m (150ft) tall.
P. orientalis♀ (oriental plane) The deeply lobed, glossy dark green leaves are up to 20cm (8in) broad and long. This tree has a wide-spreading head of sinuous branches. HEIGHT & SPREAD 8×6m (26×20ft) after 20 years, ultimately 30m (100ft) tall.

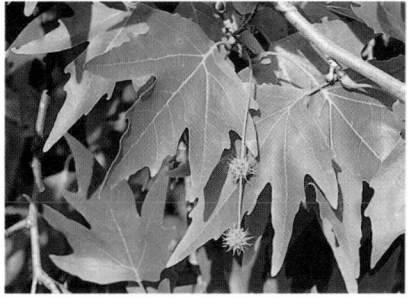

▲ *Platanus orientalis*

The leaves of f. *digitata* (syn. 'Laciniata') have 3 or 5 exaggerated lobes.
CULTIVATION Plant from late autumn to early spring in sun or shade in any garden soil. Plane trees will even grow in poor soils or soils with restricted drainage.
PROPAGATION Take hardwood cuttings in early winter. After one year cut back the young plants to a strong bud and grow on for another 3-4 years before planting out.
PRUNING Plane trees can be pollarded in spring, by a professional tree surgeon.
PESTS AND DISEASES *P. × hispanica* can suffer from anthracnose die-back.

Platycerium SEE FERNS p.264
Platycladus SEE *Thuja*

Platycodon
Balloon flower
Campanulacea

Platycodon grandiflorus

Flower buds like small balloons develop into bells, making this tuberous rooted herbaceous perennial a fascinating plant for a large rock garden or a border. There is only one species in the genus, but the varieties and cultivars recommended increase the choice of flower colours.

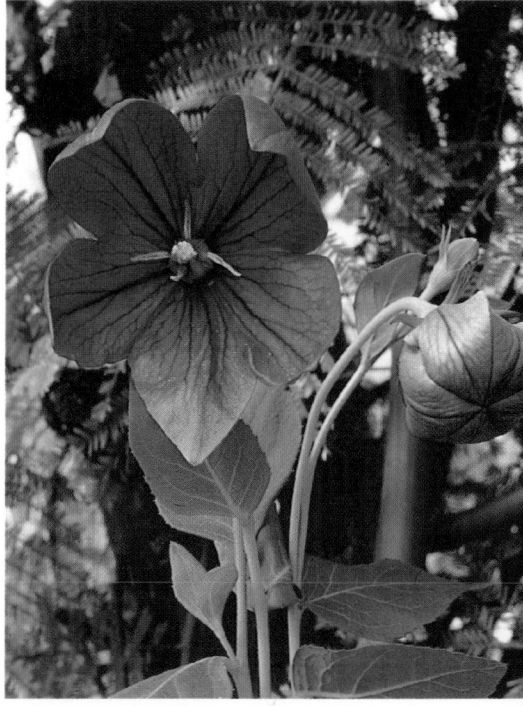

▲ *Platycodon grandiflorus*

Platycodon grandiflorus The stiff, upright stems are flushed purple as they emerge in spring. From mid summer to autumn, they bear one or more blue flowers, up to 6cm (2½in) wide, with flared lobes. The bluish green, ovate to lance-shaped leaves, up to 10cm (4in) long, are held in whorls. HEIGHT & SPREAD 60×25cm (24×10in)

White flowers, sometimes faintly flushed with blue, appear on var. *albus,* while var. *apoyama*♀ has large, blue flowers on a dwarf plant. The compact plant var. *apoyama albus*, which is about 25cm (10in) high, has white flowers.

'Florist Rose' has rose-pink blooms, and 'Florist Snow' has white flowers. The flowers of 'Fuji Pink' are pale pink, while 'Fuji White' has white blooms. 'Hakone' has double, very deep blue flowers. The earlier flowering var. *mariesii*♀, which is usually less than 40cm (16in) tall, has particularly dark blue flowers, while var.

▼ *Platycodon grandiflorus* 'Fuji Pink'

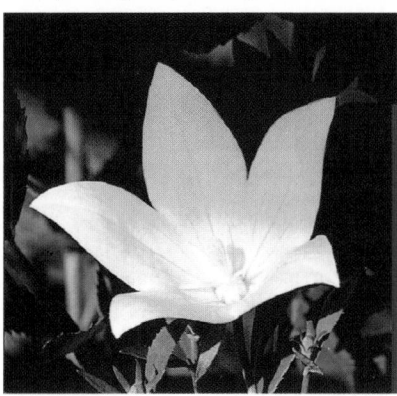

p
q

517

mariesii albus has pure white flowers. **'Parks Double Blue'** has double blue flowers. **'Perlemutterschale'** ('Mother of Pearl') is a vigorous plant with large, silvery pink flowers. The dwarf var. *pumilus* has blue flowers while var. *roseus* is pink flowered.

CULTIVATION Plant, ideally in spring, in any reasonably well-drained soil in a sunny or very lightly shaded position.

PROPAGATION Sow the seed of species in pots outside in autumn. Divide varieties and cultivars in spring or take softwood or semi-ripe cuttings in early summer.

PESTS AND DISEASES Usually trouble free, but may be attacked by slugs and snails.

Plectranthus
Swedish ivy
Labiatae

Trailing stems bearing soft evergreen foliage make these tender perennials a popular choice for growing in containers in warm conditions, where they tolerate dry air conditions successfully. *Plectranthus forsteri* is also frequently used in outdoor displays in summer as a ground-cover plant.

RECOMMENDED SPECIES AND VARIETIES
P. forsteri (syn. *P. coleoides* hort.) The oval, scallop-edged, dark green leaves are up to 5 cm (2 in) long and aromatic when rubbed. Tubular flowers, 3 cm (1¼ in) long, are white or light purple. The stems are prostrate and trailing. HEIGHT & SPREAD 20×60 cm (8×24 in).

'Marginatus' has dark green leaves with a white, cream or golden edge. The small tubular flowers are white, and are borne in upright sprays.

▲ *Plectranthus forsteri* 'Marginatus'

P. oertendahlii♀ The leaves are rounded, attractively patterned by conspicuous white veins, dark green above and reddish below. The tiny flowers, white or pale mauve, are borne on erect spikes. The stems of this species have a trailing habit, although the tips curve upwards. HEIGHT & SPREAD 20×60 cm (8×24 in).

CULTIVATION Grow in hanging baskets or pots of potting compost and keep in a greenhouse, conservatory or on a warm windowsill. Maintain a minimum winter temperature of 10°C (50°F) and protect

from exposure to direct sunlight. Plectranthus will tolerate dry air conditions. Alternatively, plant *P. forsteri* outdoors, once the danger of frost has passed, in any fertile, well-drained soil in a semi-shaded situation. Overwinter the plants under glass. Pinch out shoot tips if a bushy growth habit is required.

PROPAGATION Take stem cuttings in spring and summer; these will root very easily.

PESTS AND DISEASES Usually trouble free.

Pleioblastus see BAMBOOS p.78

Pleione
Orchidaceae

Pleione formosana

These Asian orchids with their big, showy flowers are easily grown in a frost-free greenhouse or on a cool, shaded windowsill. In warm parts of the country, some species will grow outdoors if they are given adequate winter protection.

These members of the orchid family have pseudobulbs – swollen basal stems which act as the plants' storage organs. Each year, a new stem emerges from the base of the previous season's pseudobulb. Both flowers and leaves are borne on this stem which then swells to become a new pseudobulb. Usually pear-shaped and purplish or green, the pseudobulbs are about 2.5 cm (1 in) long. The flowers, borne singly or in pairs, are made up of a central tube with a large lower lip, usually ridged and fringed and marked with coloured blotches, which is surrounded by five spreading tepals. Those plants described here flower in spring. Pleiones usually bear just one mid green, oval, pleated leaf, 7.5-15 cm (3-6 in) long, that emerges with or just after the flowers and continues to grow once the blooms have faded.

RECOMMENDED SPECIES AND VARIETIES
P. bulbocodioides This species has pale to deep rose flowers, 5-7 cm (2-2¾ in) across, with dark reddish purple spots and several ridges on the flower lip. *P. bulbocodioides* can be grown outdoors if protected. HEIGHT & SPREAD 10×10 cm (4×4 in).

Limprichtii Group♀ has slightly smaller, generally deep pink to magenta flowers with 4 white ridges and deep red blotches on the lips. **Pricei Group** (see *P. formosana* Pricei Group).

P. × confusa Clear yellow flowers, 6-9 cm (2½-3½ in) across, have purple-blotched

lips. HEIGHT & SPREAD 10×10 cm (4×4 in).
P. formosana The rose-pink or white flowers are 5-7 cm (2-2¾ in) across. On the lip there are abundant red or yellow markings and 2-5 ridges. The easiest species to grow, *P. formosana* can be grown outdoors in milder regions given adequate protection. HEIGHT & SPREAD 10×10 cm (4×4 in).

▲ *Pleione formosana* 'Alba'

'Alba' has white flowers with yellow lip markings. **'Avalanche'** has pure white flowers. **'Lilac Beauty'**, which flowers early in the season, has lilac-pink flowers with a paler lip, spotted with dark red. **'Oriental Grace'** has pinky violet flowers with a pale rose lip, spotted brown and yellow. The purplish pink flowers of **'Oriental Jewel'** have a very pale lip marked in yellowish brown. **'Oriental Splendour'** often bears 2 deep purplish rose flowers with a paler lip, marked with brown and yellow. The flowers of **Pricei Group** (syn. *P. bulbocodioides* Pricei Group) are similar to 'Oriental Splendour' but appear slightly earlier. **'Snow White'** bears white flowers with lemon-yellow markings on the lip that also appear early in the season.

▲ *Pleione formosana* 'Snow White'

P. forrestii This species carries large flowers 6-9 cm (2½-3½ in) across, varying in colour from pale to deep orange-yellow. The lip has deep red or brown blotches and several ridges. HEIGHT & SPREAD 10×10 cm (4×4 in).
P. speciosa (syn. *P. pogonioides* hort.) The rose-purple flowers, 5-7 cm (2-2¾ in) across, have lips with many reddish brown spots and 2-4 white or yellow ridges. HEIGHT & SPREAD 10×10 cm (4×4 in).

p
q

▲ *Pleione forrestii*

P. yunnanensis The rose-pink flowers, 5-7 cm (2-2¾ in) across, have lips with 5 ridges that are heavily blotched with purple. HEIGHT & SPREAD 10×10 cm (4×4 in).

OTHER HYBRIDS
There are many hybrids and hybrid groups available. The name grex is applied to a group of plants that may be difficult to separate individually. In most cases the flowers are 6-9 cm (2½-3½ in) across.
Alishan has pink flowers with white-tipped tepals and a white lip heavily spotted with reddish purple. **Eiger** has 2 white flowers to a stem and its tepals are very faintly flushed with pink. In **Hekla** the deep pinkish purple flowers have red markings on the lip.

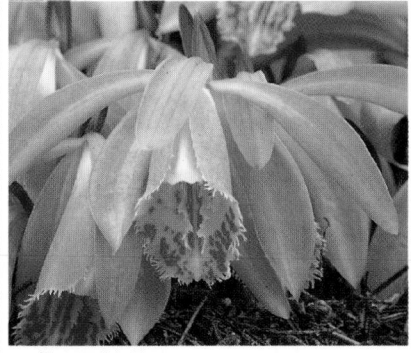

▲ *Pleione* Hekla

Shantung has flowers in a range of colours from yellow to peach with lips usually fringed and spotted red. **'Muriel Harberd'**♀ is a cultivar of Shantung that has large peach-coloured flowers, up to 10 cm (4 in) across. Their lip is deep orange-red with conspicuous ridges. Another cultivar of Shantung is **'Ridgeway'**, a vigorous variety with pale apricot flowers whose deep yellow lip is heavily spotted orange-red.
Stromboli has deep reddish purple flowers. **Tolima** has deep rose-purple flowers with lips heavily spotted darker red and ridged in yellow or white. It often bears 2 flowers to a stem.
The vigorous **Versailles** is variable, but generally has very large rose-pink flowers up to 10 cm (4 in) across with a paler lip. Among the finest and most readily available cultivars of Versailles is **'Bucklebury'**♀. Its flowers are purple with a lip blotched brownish red.

▲ *Pleione* Shantung 'Ridgeway'

CULTIVATION Grow pleiones under glass or indoors in shallow containers of well-drained open compost, made up of chopped sphagnum moss, fine bark chips, a little loam and charcoal pieces, for example. Plant the pseudobulbs so that their bases are just covered by the compost. Keep in a cool greenhouse or alpine house. Pleiones can be

▲ *Pleione* Versailles 'Bucklebury'

grown indoors on a shady windowsill where summer temperatures do not exceed 25°C (77°F) but they need to be kept cool during their dormant period and are best overwintered in a cool greenhouse or alpine house. Do not water plants during their dormancy. Only begin watering when new growth appears, and then increase the amounts of water used gradually. During summer mist overhead daily and give a mild liquid feed weekly. Keep well-watered until leaf-fall when the dormant period begins.
Alternatively, in milder regions plant *P. bulbocodioides* and *P. formosana* outdoors in mid to late spring, choosing a shady spot in free-draining soil to which leaf-mould and fine bark chips have been added. Ensure that the base of the pseudobulbs are just covered by the soil. Cover them with a cloche or pane of glass in winter to protect them from excessive winter wet.
PROPAGATION Divide plants in early spring before the new growth begins.
PESTS AND DISEASES Red spider mite, voles, slugs and aphids may be troublesome.

Plum see p. 728
Plum, ornamental see *Prunus*

Plumbago
Leadwort
Plumbaginaceae

Abundant sprays of pale, sky-blue flowers and a long flowering period earn *Plumbago auriculata* its place in conservatories, greenhouses and summer beds. This fast-growing, decorative shrub from South Africa is the only species commonly grown in Britain, although other species, with different coloured flowers, can sometimes be seen in warm greenhouses at botanical gardens. In the wild, plumbago plants support themselves by growing their whip-like shoots over and through other shrubs. In cultivation, they need support.

RECOMMENDED SPECIES AND VARIETIES
P. auriculata♀ (syn. *P. capensis*) Terminal clusters of slender-tubed sky-blue flowers, measuring 1.5 cm (½ in) across, appear from summer to early winter. The blooms have 5 spreading, rounded, lobes and are carried on slender, arching, creamy brown stems. The narrow, oblanceolate, thin-textured leaves are up to 8 cm (3¼ in) long. HEIGHT & SPREAD 1.5×1.5 m (5×5 ft) after 5 years, ultimately 3-4 m (10-13 ft) tall.

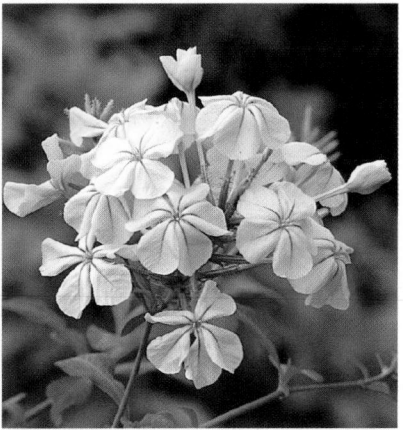

▲ *Plumbago auriculata*

Pure white flowers distinguish var. *alba*.
P. larpentae see *Ceratostigma plumbaginoides*
CULTIVATION Plant in pots or in a greenhouse border in well-drained, fertile compost in sun or dappled shade. Tie selected main shoots to supports. If desired, move conservatory plants onto a patio in summer and return them in autumn. For summer bedding, move the plants outside after all danger of frost has passed. Reduce watering when the plants are not in active growth.
PROPAGATION Take semi-ripe cuttings in summer.
PRUNING Cut back shoots that flowered the previous year by two-thirds in early spring.
PESTS AND DISEASES Glasshouse whitefly may infest the foliage of plants under glass.

Plumbago, Chinese
see *Ceratostigma willmottianum*

p
q

Podocarpus
Podocarpaceae

Podocarpus salignus

This genus of evergreens includes shrubs suitable for a rock garden or for using as ground cover, as well as medium to large trees for larger gardens in warmer, southerly regions of Britain. These slow-growing plants are clothed with stiff, leathery, yew-like leaves, usually arranged spirally.

Where several plants are grown together – as ground cover, for example – fruits are produced if mainly female plants are used with an occasional male for pollination. Male and female plants can only be identified when in flower or fruit. From late spring to early summer, male plants bear erect catkin-like flowers and female plants have discreet cones. The cones, if pollinated, are followed by fleshy, red berries.

RECOMMENDED SPECIES AND VARIETIES
P. macrophyllus (Japanese yew, Buddhist pine) Commonly grown as a houseplant,

▼ *Podocarpus nivalis*

this species grows up to 8 m (26 ft) tall in the wild, but makes a small, compactly conical shrub when grown in a container. The flat leaves, up to 10 cm (4 in) long, are bright green and bluish beneath. Their shape is needle-like, although broader and softer in appearance than pine needles. Native to Japan. HEIGHT & SPREAD 1.8×1 m (6×3 ft).

P. nivalis Foliage colour varies greatly between specimens of this generally low-growing, spreading shrub which is suitable for ground cover. The leathery leaves may be green, yellow, bluish or purple to bronze. It is hardy and variable in size. Native to New Zealand. HEIGHT & SPREAD 60×80 cm (24×32 in) after 5 years, ultimately 1-2 m (3-6½ ft) tall.

▲ *Podocarpus salignus*

P. salignus♀ Glossy, dark green, willow-like leaves are carried on the drooping branches of this slow-growing tree. The plant does best in sheltered situations in warmer regions of Britain. Native to Chile. HEIGHT & SPREAD 5.5×3 m (18×10 ft) after 25 years, ultimately 12 m (40 ft) tall.

CULTIVATION Plant *P. nivalis* in well-drained soil and an open situation in spring. *P. salignus* is not fussy about soil and grows in sun or shade. Both tolerate alkaline soils. Keep *P. macrophyllus* in good indirect sunlight at a temperature above 4°C (39°F). Repot in spring only when the plant has completely filled its pot with roots.

PROPAGATION Take semi-ripe cuttings in early autumn, root during winter, preferably under glass with bottom heat.

PRUNING Shear plants into shape between mid summer and autumn if necessary.

PESTS AND DISEASES Usually trouble free, but scale insects can sometimes infest plants.

Podophyllum
May apple
Berberidaceae

Used medicinally for centuries, this small genus is now of interest for the treatment of certain types of cancer. There are just five species in the genus, all rhizomatous perennials. With handsome leaves, simple flowers

▲ *Podophyllum hexandrum*

and colourful fruits, they give garden value for several months. The plants have a characteristic habit with erect stems bearing one or a few leaves at the top plus a single white or pink bowl-shaped flower in spring. Late summer brings forth a plum-like, fleshy but inedible fruit.

Woodland plants in nature, the May apples do best in a moist, somewhat shaded position in the garden. Native to eastern N America and NE Asia.

RECOMMENDED SPECIES AND VARIETIES
P. emodi see *P. hexandrum*
P. hexandrum (syn. *P. emodi*) A solitary white flower, up to 6 cm (2½ in) wide, appears to sit on the unfolding leaves in mid spring, developing into a 4 cm (1½ in) long red fruit by late summer. The deeply lobed leaves, up to 25 cm (10 in) wide, are often mottled with purplish brown. HEIGHT & SPREAD 45×30 cm (1½×1 ft).

Light pink flowers are produced by var. *chinense*.

P. peltatum (May apple, wild mandrake) A single, nodding white flower, up to 5 cm (2 in) across, is borne with the partly folded young leaves in mid spring. The shiny dark green leaves, up to 30 cm (1 ft) wide, are divided into several deep lobes which are often forked at the tips. An egg-shaped pale yellow fruit, 4 cm (1½ in) long, ripens in late summer or early autumn. HEIGHT & SPREAD 45×30 cm (1½×1 ft).

CULTIVATION Plant in a moist, leafy soil in autumn in a partially shaded spot. Strong sun or dry conditions may scorch the leaves.

PROPAGATION Sow seed in autumn and raise in a nursery bed, planting out in the spring of the second year, or carefully divide well-established clumps in late winter.

PESTS AND DISEASES Usually trouble free.

Poinsettia see *Euphorbia pulchemima*
Pokeweed see *Phytolacca americana*

Polemonium
Jacob's ladder
Polemoniaceae

Polemonium caeruleum

Clusters of cup-shaped summer flowers appear above distinctive basal rosettes that are composed of pairs of leaflets resembling the rungs of a ladder. Suitable for borders, rock gardens or the alpine house, these hardy perennials may be short-lived, but they self-seed readily. Native to Europe, Asia, Central and S America.

RECOMMENDED SPECIES AND VARIETIES

P. boreale The blue, purple or white flowers are about 1 cm (⅜ in) across. The plant is useful for a rock garden where it appreciates sandy or gravelly soil. HEIGHT & SPREAD 25×20 cm (10×8 in).

P. brandegeei Straw-yellow flowers, 2.5 cm (1 in) across, appear in terminal clusters of up to 12 in summer or early autumn. The leaves are sticky and have an unpleasant smell. The plant is best grown under glass but even there it is short-lived. HEIGHT & SPREAD 20×15 cm (8×6 in).

Sweetly scented white or yellow flowers are seen on ssp. *mellitum*.

P. caeruleum Lavender-blue flowers, borne in early summer, have deep yellow stamens and are 2.5 cm (1 in) across. HEIGHT & SPREAD 60×60 cm (2×2 ft).

'Album' bears white flowers and 'Brise d'Anjou' has clumps of yellow-edged, finely divided leaves and violet-blue flowers throughout summer.

P. carneum Clusters of salmon-pink, cup-shaped flowers, 2.5 cm (1 in) across, appear on this clump-former throughout summer. HEIGHT & SPREAD 45×45 cm (1½×1½ ft).

'Apricot Delight' has pinky apricot-coloured flowers.

▼ *Polemonium carneum 'Apricot Delight'*

▲ *Polemonium foliosissimum*

P. foliosissimum The lavender-blue or white flowers of this upright plant grow up to 2 cm (¾ in) wide and are enhanced by bright orange stamens. HEIGHT & SPREAD 75×60 cm (2½×2 ft).

P. 'Lambrook Mauve' ♀ This spreading plant bears pale mauve flowers that are about 2 cm (¾ in) across. HEIGHT & SPREAD 45×45 cm (1½×1½ ft).

P. pauciflorum Soft yellow tubular flowers, about 3 cm (1¼ in) long, are borne in loose clusters; some with a reddish tinge. This short-lived perennial is suitable for a rock garden and can also be used in the front of a herbaceous border in well-drained soil. HEIGHT & SPREAD 30×15 cm (12×6 in).

P. pulcherrimum Blue flowers, 1.5 cm (½ in) long, are borne in loose clusters and have a yellow or white eye. This plant is suitable for growing in a rock garden. HEIGHT & SPREAD 50×30 cm (20×12 in).

P. reptans This slightly woody-based plant carries pale blue pendulous tubular flowers about 1.5 cm (½ in) long. It does best in a shady, moist spot at the edge of woodland. HEIGHT & SPREAD 45×45 cm (1½×1½ ft).

CULTIVATION Plant from autumn to spring in sun or partial shade in any soil, but preferably moist. Deadhead to prevent too many seedlings arising and to encourage a possible second crop of flowers. Stake taller

▼ *Polemonium reptans*

plants if necessary. Grow *P. brandegeei* in pots in a coldframe or in an alpine house in a gritty mixture with leaf-mould, and provide shade from summer sun.

PROPAGATION Divide plants in spring. Division every 2 or 3 years ensures vigorous growth. Sow seed in autumn and plant out the seedlings in spring.

PESTS AND DISEASES Usually trouble free.

Polyanthus
see *Primula* Polyanthus Group

Polygala
Milkwort
Polygalaceae

Polygala calcarea

Unusual flowers, with two wing-like sepals and a lip, adorn the milkworts in late spring and summer. The genus contains annuals, perennials and shrubs but it is mainly the small low-growing shrubs that are cultivated. *Polygala calcarea* is good for rock gardens and *P. chamaebuxus* is suitable for growing in partial shade among woodland bulbs or small ericaceous shrubs.

Polygala myrtifolia and *P.* × *dalmaisiana* are too tender for any but the mildest of British gardens, and are generally grown in containers in a cool greenhouse or conservatory and brought outside in summer. Native to Europe and South Africa.

RECOMMENDED SPECIES AND VARIETIES

P. calcarea Upright spikes of brilliant deep blue flowers with a white fringe on the lip pierce the low mat of deep green spatulate

▼ *Polygala calcarea*

▲ *Polygala calcarea* 'Lillet'

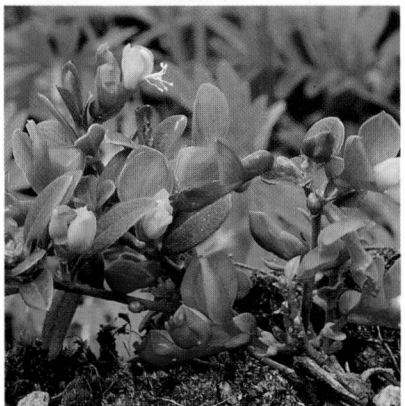

▲ *Polygala chamaebuxus* var. *grandiflora*

leaves in early summer. HEIGHT & SPREAD 5×20cm (2×8in) after 5 years, ultimately spreading to 60cm (2ft).

Bulley's form has larger flowers in a deeper shade of blue. **'Lillet'**♀ is more compact with flowers in a brighter blue.

P. chamaebuxus♀ Clusters of flowers with yellow or white lips and bright yellow wings appear in late spring or early summer. The wings darken to brown with age. This hardy, suckering plant has glossy, dark green, oval leaves. HEIGHT & SPREAD 15×30cm (6×12in) after 5 years, ultimately spreading to 1m (3ft).

More colourful is var. *grandiflora*♀ (syn. 'Purpurea', 'Rhodoptera'), bearing larger flowers with bright yellow lips and deep rosy purple wings. **'Loibl'** is a low-growing mat-former, reaching just 10cm (4in) high, and ultimately spreading to 60cm (2ft), with darker leaves than the species and deep purple-and-yellow flowers.

P. × dalmaisiana Similar in habit to *P. myrtifolia*, this tender shrub has lanceolate to ovate blue-green leaves and purplish red flowers. The flowers are borne from late spring to late summer. HEIGHT & SPREAD 1×1m (3×3ft) after 5 years, ultimately spreading to 2m (6½ft).

P. myrtifolia Greenish white flowers veined with purple, appear in clusters from late spring to late summer. This tender, branching shrub has blue-green, ovate leaves.

HEIGHT & SPREAD Up to 1×1m (3×3ft) after 5 years, ultimately spreading to 2m (6½ft).

'Grandiflora' has larger deep violet-purple flowers with a white-crested lip. It flowers throughout the summer months.

CULTIVATION Plant in autumn or early spring. *P. calcarea* does best in gritty, limy soil with plenty of humus and in full sun. *P. chamaebuxus* does better in acid woodland soil, in partial shade.

Grow the tender species in ordinary well-drained compost in large containers in a cool greenhouse or conservatory.

PROPAGATION Take softwood heel cuttings of outdoor plants in early summer or sow seed of the species in autumn and keep cool through winter. Take cuttings from greenhouse species in mid spring.

PESTS AND DISEASES Aphid and whitefly are problems under glass.

Polygonatum
Solomon's seal
Liliaceae

Pendent, bell-like, and sometimes fragrant flowers appear in spring and early summer. These and glossy, architectural foliage characterise the herbaceous perennials in this genus. The plants described below are all hardy and rhizomatous. They look highly ornamental when planted among shrubs in a mixed border. Exceptionally among the recommended species, *Polygonatum hookeri* is suitable for growing in a rock garden and bears solitary, erect flowers. Plants generally grow best in partial shade and enjoy a moist, well-drained soil, rich in organic matter. Native to northern USA, Europe and Asia.

RECOMMENDED SPECIES AND VARIETIES

P. biflorum (syn. *P. canaliculatum*, *P. commutatum*) (great Solomon's seal) Greenish white drooping flowers, up to 1.5cm (½ in) long, are borne beneath bold, arching stems in pairs, and occasionally alone or in groups of 3 or 4, on this strong-growing plant in late spring. The stems are further clothed in bright, glossy, mid green, oval to elliptical leaves, up to 20cm (8in) long, with distinctive bluish undersides. HEIGHT & SPREAD 2m×60cm (6½×2ft).

P. canaliculatum see *P. biflorum*

P. commutatum see *P. biflorum*

P. falcatum Small white drooping blossoms, up to 1.5cm (½in) long, are liberally produced in early summer beneath upright stems, which arch at the ends. The stems bear narrow, lance or sickle-shaped mid green leaves, up to 23cm (9in) long. HEIGHT & SPREAD 1m×45cm (3×1½ft).

'Variegatum' has foliage variegated with creamy yellow at the margins.

P. hookeri Solitary pinkish or white flowers, up to 2cm (¾in) long, peep from crowded groups of lance-shaped, mid green leaves, up to 1.5cm (½in) long, during late spring to early summer. This small plant is suitable

▲ *Polygonatum hookeri*

for a damp, shady spot in a rock garden. HEIGHT & SPREAD 7.5×30cm (3×12in).

P. humile Solitary or paired, green-tipped, white, pendent flowers, up to 2cm (¾in) long, bloom in late spring. Lance-shaped or oval, mid green, downy leaves, up to 15cm (6in) long and 2.5cm (1in) wide, are arranged alternately on erect stems. HEIGHT & SPREAD 1m×60cm (3×2ft).

P. × hybridum♀ (syn. *P. multiflorum*) In late spring clusters of tubular to bell-shaped white flowers with a greenish flush and up to 2cm (¾in) long, are produced from the leaf axils beneath this leafy plant's gently arching stems. The mid green, roughly oval and occasionally undulating leaves are up to 7.5cm (3in) long and 4cm (1½in) wide. HEIGHT & SPREAD 1.2×1m (4×3ft).

▲ *Polygonatum × hybridum*

'Striatum' (syn. 'Variegatum') has undulating leaves striped with cream. It reaches 60×30cm (2×1ft) in height and spread.

P. multiflorum see *P. × hybridum*

P. odoratum (angled Solomon's seal) Pendent, fragrant white flowers with greenish tips, up to 2cm (¾in) long, bloom in groups of 2 or 3 in the leaf axils in spring.

p
q

▲ *Polygonatum × hybridum* 'Striatum'

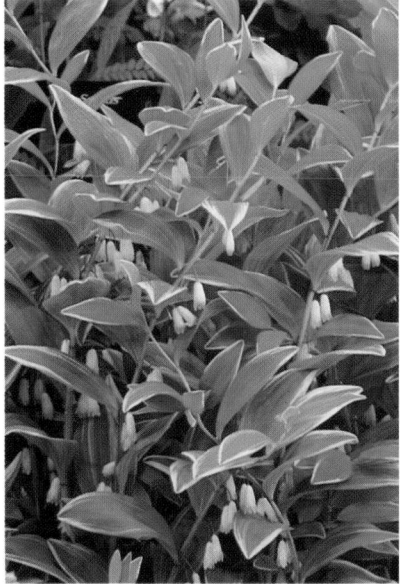

▲ *Polygonatum odoratum* 'Variegatum'

The mid green, lance-shaped or oval leaves, up to 12.5 cm (5 in) long, are borne on angular, arching stems. HEIGHT & SPREAD 60×30 cm (2×1 ft).

'Flore Pleno'♀ carries double flowers; 'Variegatum' has leaves edged with cream and stems slightly flushed with red.

P. verticillatum (whorled Solomon's seal) Drooping, narrowly bell-shaped, greenish white flowers, about 1.5 cm (½ in) long, are produced in the upper leaf axils of this upright plant in early summer. The narrow leaves are mid green and up to 15 cm (6 in) long. HEIGHT & SPREAD 1 m×45 cm (3×1½ ft).

'Rubrum' has pink-tinged shoots and dusky pink bell-shaped flowers.

CULTIVATION Plant from late autumn to early spring in a partially shaded position and in a well-drained soil that is rich in organic matter. Lift and divide in early spring every few years to maintain vigour.

PROPAGATION Divide during early spring.

PESTS AND DISEASES Solomon's seal sawfly can strip plants bare.

Polygonum see *Fallopia, Persicaria*
Polypodium see FERNS p. 265
Polystichum see FERNS p. 265

Poncirus
Japanese bitter orange
Rutaceae

Poncirus trifoliata

This slow-growing spiny shrub or very small tree, is the nearest thing to an orange tree that can be grown outdoors in Britain, if only in sheltered lowland areas. It bears edible, but sour, fruit and has been crossed with *Citrus* to produce a type of orange called citrange, and with *Fortunella* to create the kumquat.

The only species in its genus, this tough deciduous shrub is native to N China and Korea and hardy to -10°C (14°F). It forms a sturdy thorn hedge and lives to a good age, as records of an 80-year-old specimen will testify.

Poncirus trifoliata White scented flowers, about 5 cm (2 in) across with 5 longish, often twisted petals, appear in early spring amid a tangle of thorns and smooth, vivid green, compressed branches. Each leaf consists of 3 leaflets: the terminal leaflet is obovate and up to 6 cm (2½ in) long, while the side pair are smaller and elliptic-ovate in shape. Small fruit up to 5 cm (2 in) across are produced in autumn and last throughout winter. HEIGHT & SPREAD 50×50 cm (20×20 in) after 5 years, ultimately 4 m (13 ft) tall.

CULTIVATION Plant during late spring in any well-drained soil, preferably in full sun.

PROPAGATION Cuttings are difficult and seed is unpredictable. It is best to buy the readily available plants.

PRUNING Seldom required and hazardous because of the spines.

PESTS AND DISEASES Usually trouble free.

Pondweed see *Potamogeton*
Pondweed, Cape
   see *Aponogeton distachyos*
Poplar see *Populus*

▼ *Poncirus trifoliata*

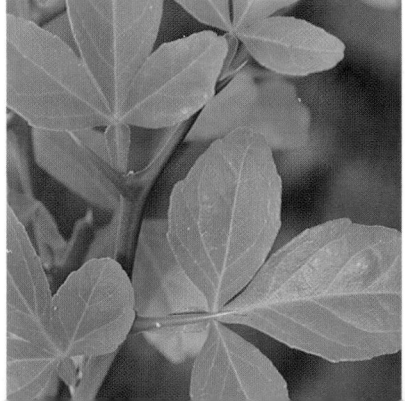

Poppy see *Papaver*
Poppy, blue see *Meconopsis betonicifolia*
Poppy, California see *Eschscholzia*
Poppy, Himalayan
   see *Meconopsis betonicifolia*
Poppy, horned see *Glaucium*
Poppy, Mexican
   see *Argemone mexicana*
Poppy, plume see *Macleaya*
Poppy, tree see *Romneya*
Poppy, Welsh see *Meconopsis cambrica*

Populus
Poplar
Salicaceae

Populus alba 'Raket'

These hardy, fast-growing, generally slender trees are grown for their deciduous foliage and pleasing habit. They are suitable only for larger gardens where they make effective windbreaks. They are tolerant of pollution and have the open head and pliable branches that withstand coastal winds. Be careful when choosing a tree, as many species grow very tall at an alarming rate and may become expensive to remove. For example, the Lombardy poplar, *Populus nigra* 'Italica', can grow to 35 m (115 ft) and the aspen, *P. tremula*, reaches 24 m (79 ft). The massive dimensions of these two trees have precluded them from this book.

All poplars have spreading roots that pull enormous amounts of water from the soil. They should never be planted near buildings, particularly those built on clay soil which shrinks as it dries, as they are likely to cause subsidence. Some species produce suckers when cut back or even cut down, which continue the demand for water.

Reddish male catkins appear on the bare shoots in early spring and grow to about 5 cm (2 in) long. The slender, greenish, female catkins are borne on separate trees;

▼ *Populus alba* 'Richardii'

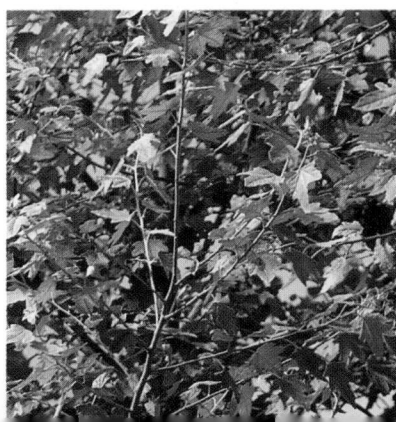

p
q

523

they are up to 10 cm (4 in) long and develop into strings of green capsules from which the tiny seeds disperse on cotton-like filaments, sometimes leading to unwelcome seedlings on neighbouring land.

RECOMMENDED SPECIES AND VARIETIES
P. alba 'Raket' (syn. 'Rocket') Upright grey branches form a narrow, columnar tree. Glossy green leaves, 7 cm (2¾ in) long, are usually 5-lobed and have silvery white undersides that give a shimmering effect when they stir in summer breezes. Suckering can become a problem and on a windy site young trees need staking if they are to grow upright. HEIGHT & SPREAD 15×5 m (50×16 ft) after 20 years, ultimately 20 m (66 ft) tall.

P. alba 'Richardii' The golden yellow leaves of this less vigorous poplar are 6-12 cm (2½-4¾ in) long and have silvery felted undersides. HEIGHT & SPREAD 10×6 m (33×20 ft) after 20 years, ultimately 15 m (50 ft) tall.

P. × canadensis 'Aurea'♀ Clear yellow leaves turn golden in autumn. They are 8 cm (3¼ in) long and almost triangular. The tree is extremely vigorous. HEIGHT & SPREAD 16×12 m (52×40 ft) in 20 years, ultimately 20 m (66 ft) tall.

P. × candicans 'Aurora' Cream, pink and green mingle on the variegated, broadly ovate leaves which can grow to 12 cm (4¾ in) long and are pine-scented. Canker usually causes die-back in middle age. HEIGHT & SPREAD 16×8 m (52×26 ft) in 20 years, ultimately 18 m (60 ft) tall.

▼ *Populus × canadensis* 'Aurea'

▼ *Populus tremula* 'Pendula'

P. nigra 'Lombardy Gold' Triangular yellow leaves are up to 8 cm (3¼ in) long on this narrow, slow-growing tree. HEIGHT & SPREAD 5×1.5 m (16×5 ft) after 20 years, ultimately 8 m (26 ft) tall.

P. tremula 'Pendula' This is one of the best and most robust weeping trees available in Britain, and more suitable for the average garden than its massive parent species. It tolerates a vast range of soil types and grows well in towns, though it does best on a moist, fertile site. Greyish purple catkins are borne in early spring before the balloon-shaped leaves. Suckers might appear so the planting position must be carefully chosen. HEIGHT & SPREAD 8×7 m (26×23 ft) after 20 years, ultimately 10 m (33 ft) tall.

CULTIVATION Poplars are easy to grow, but require ample space and moisture. Plant well away from buildings – twice as far away as the tree's ultimate height.

PROPAGATION Most poplars strike easily from mid winter hardwood cuttings planted outdoors or late summer semi-ripe cuttings reared under glass.

PRUNING Pruning is usually needed only if a tree becomes top heavy and unsafe. Many poplars react to pruning by suckering.

PESTS AND DISEASES Usually trouble free, except for *P. × candicans* 'Aurora' which is susceptible to canker.

Portulaca
Portulacaceae

Of the 40 species in this genus of mostly succulent annual plants, *Portulaca grandiflora* is by far the most popular. This brilliantly coloured and showy half-hardy annual adds a flourish to summer bedding schemes. It will thrive on a dry bank or as a filler in sunny spots in a rock garden. The flowers tend to close in shade or dull weather.

The other species described below, *P. oleracea*, is not showy but has edible leaves. Native to sub-tropical and tropical regions of the world.

RECOMMENDED SPECIES AND VARIETIES
P. grandiflora (rose moss, sun plant) A succession of saucer-shaped flowers, in shades of orange, pink, red, yellow or white, appear from mid summer to early autumn. The flowers have a silky sheen and are up to 5 cm (2 in) across. Reddish stems carry

▼ *Portulaca grandiflora*

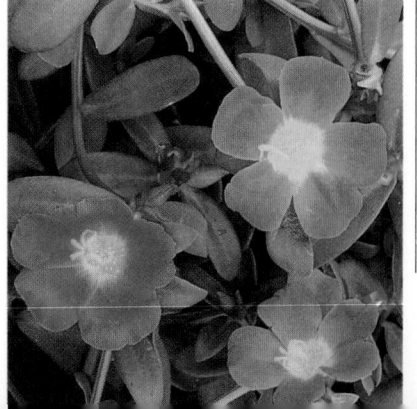

cylindrical leaves, up to 2.5 cm (1 in) long. HEIGHT & SPREAD 10-20×20 cm (4-8×8 in).

The following varieties, all with double blooms, have been bred so that their flowers close less readily in dull weather. 'Cloudbeater' and 'Sundance' have flowers in the same colour range as the species. 'Peppermint' bears white flowers with pink stripes. 'Swan Lake' bears white flowers.

P. oleracea (purslane) Small yellow flowers are produced on thick erect stems from mid summer to early autumn. The flat, spatula-shaped leaves are fleshy and up to 2.5 cm (1 in) across. They can be used in salads and soups. HEIGHT & SPREAD 30×20 cm (12×8 in).

CULTIVATION Plant in a sunny spot in well-drained, low-nutrient soil when all risk of frost has passed.

PROPAGATION Sow seed in a heated greenhouse in early spring. Prick out the seedlings into small pots or cellular trays. Alternatively, sow seed in mid to late spring in the flowering site.

PESTS AND DISEASES Aphids may be troublesome. Seedlings and young plants are susceptible to damping off.

Potamogeton
Pondweed
Potamogetonaceae

Potamogeton crispus

These hardy aquatic plants with submerged and floating leaves are often considered to be weedy and invasive, but at least one species (described below) is more restrained and has come to be highly regarded by pond-keepers. Though the flower spikes are decidedly unspectacular, the decorative foliage enhances any water garden and the plant will help to oxygenate the water.

RECOMMENDED SPECIES
P. crispus (curled pondweed) Brittle, branching stems are densely clothed with narrow, lance-shaped leaves up to 5 cm (2 in) long with crinkly edges. The dark green seaweed-like leaves are attractively flushed with copper. Tiny spikes of flowers appear above the surface of the water in summer but they have no decorative merit. The plant will grow in 60-100 cm (2-3 ft) of water. SPREAD 60 cm (2 ft).

CULTIVATION Plant in spring as bunches of cuttings fastened together at the base with narrow strips of lead. Push into a container of clean heavy garden soil or aquatic planting compost, being sure to bury the lead

p
q

strips. Top dress the container with pea gravel and place in water at least 60 cm (2 ft) deep. Remove decaying foliage in autumn and repot if necessary the following spring.
PROPAGATION Take softwood cuttings in summer and grow in a tray of mud placed in an unheated aquarium.
PESTS AND DISEASES Usually trouble free.

Potato see p.744
Potato, duck see *Sagittaria latifolia*
Potato vine see *Solanum jasminoides*

Potentilla
Cinquefoil
Rosaceae

Potentilla
'Gibson's scarlet'

Flowers resembling small wild roses, in yellow, orange, red, pink or white, bring an abundance of colour to the garden from late spring through summer and into autumn. The five-petalled flowers are usually about 2.5 cm (1 in) across and carried in loose clusters. There are species for the rock garden, shrubbery or border, all bearing vibrant blooms that contrast attractively with their green, greyish or silvery, divided leaves.

This widely distributed genus contains 500 species, including annuals, perennials and shrubs. The annuals are of little garden value, but several herbaceous to semi-evergreen perennials and one shrub (*P. fruticosa*) and its many varieties are popular additions to British gardens; these are described below. All are hardy and easy to grow if given a sunny spot.

RECOMMENDED SPECIES AND VARIETIES
P. alba White, yellow-eyed flowers appear in mid summer. The flowers are borne on 10 cm (4 in) stems above a mat of palmate leaves. The leaves are silver-grey beneath and dark green above. This low-growing perennial is a good ground-cover plant. HEIGHT & SPREAD 10×15 cm (4×6 in).
P. ambigua see *P. cuneata*
P. arbuscula see *P. fruticosa* 'Elizabeth'
P. atrosanguinea Loose clusters of flowers, each bloom up to 4 cm (1½ in) across, are produced throughout the summer by this upright perennial. The blooms vary in colour from yellow to orange and dark red. The dark green ternate leaves are silvery haired and toothed. HEIGHT & SPREAD 45×60 cm (1½×2 ft).
Yellow-orange flowers are borne by var. *argyrophylla*.

P. aurea Bright yellow flowers, often with a darker centre, are carried in summer and early autumn above a compact mat of mid green, silky-edged leaves made up of 5 radiating leaflets. This low-growing plant is suited to a rock garden. HEIGHT & SPREAD 20×30 cm (8×12 in).
'Plena' has deep yellow, semidouble flowers.
P. cinerea (syn. *P. tommasiniana*) Light yellow flowers appear in late spring and early summer just above the palmate, greygreen leaves, which are composed of 3 or 5 narrow, toothed leaflets. The rooting stems of this perennial spread into a compact mat and it is well suited to a sunny rock garden. HEIGHT & SPREAD 10×40 cm (4×16 in).
P. crantzii (syn. *P. villosa*) Bright yellow, orange-eyed flowers appear in summer above the 3-5 fingered, dark green leaves. This plant forms a low mound with arching or prostrate stems coming up from a woody base and is suitable for a rock garden. It is more compact and free-flowering in poor soils, but may become lush and leafy in rich conditions, with few flowers. HEIGHT & SPREAD 20×40 cm (8×16 in).
P. cuneata♀ (syn. *P. ambigua*) Solitary bright yellow flowers are borne just above the low mat of foliage. Prostrate stems come up from a woody base clothed in small, mid green leaves, composed of 3 oval or wedgeshaped leaflets, coarsely toothed at the tip. This plant suits a rock garden. HEIGHT & SPREAD 10×20 cm (4×8 in).
P. eriocarpa Bright yellow, mostly solitary flowers in late summer are followed by attractive silky seed heads. The small, bluegreen leaves are composed of 3 wedgeshaped leaflets and have reddish stalks. The plant forms a low mat and is suitable for a rock garden. HEIGHT & SPREAD 10×40 cm (4×16 in).

▼ *Potentilla atrosanguinea*

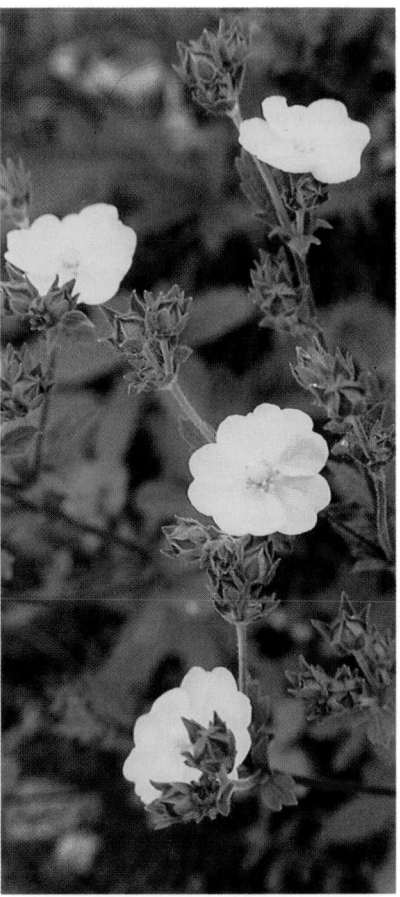

▲ *Potentilla atrosanguinea* var. *argyrophylla*

P. fragiformis see *P. megalantha*
P. fruticosa (shrubby cinquefoil) Yellow or white flowers, 2-5 cm (¾-2 in) wide, are borne freely in summer and often well into autumn, among small, pinnate, mid green, grey-green or sometimes silvery leaves. These compact, twiggy deciduous shrubs are useful in a sunny border. There are many varieties to choose from. HEIGHT & SPREAD 30-50×45 cm (12-20×18 in) after 5 years, but the ultimate size varies. Dwarf and spreading varieties reach up to 75 cm×1 m (2½×3 ft); the taller ones may grow to 1.8×1.5 m (6×5 ft).
'Abbotswood'♀ is low and spreading with dark foliage and white flowers appearing over a long period. 'Abbotswood Silver' is similar, with white-edged leaves, but tends to revert to all-green foliage. 'Beesii'♀ (syn. 'Argentea Nana') is dwarf with silvery leaves and large, bright yellow flowers. 'Daydawn'♀ is a low-grower with small leaves and creamy peach-pink flowers. 'Elizabeth'♀ (syn. *P. arbuscula*) makes a rounded bush ultimately 1×1.2 m (3×4 ft), with large, rich canary-yellow flowers.
'Goldfinger'♀ is dwarf with blue-green leaves and large, rich yellow flowers. 'Goldstar' makes a dwarf, upright bush with large deep yellow flowers. 'Hopley's Orange' is compact, with small leaves and dark-centred, orange flowers. 'Jackman's

p
q

Variety' is vigorous and upright in growth, with large, light yellow flowers. **'Katherine Dykes'**♀ is similar in size and habit to 'Jackman's Variety', but has small primrose-yellow flowers. **'Klondike'**♀ is a compact, dwarf variety with golden yellow flowers.

'Longacre Variety'♀ forms a low mat with small leaves and vivid, light yellow flowers. **'Maanelys'**♀ (also sold as **'Moonlight'**) has light yellow flowers that are paler beneath. **'Manchu'** (syn. *P.* 'Mandshurica') is low and spreading with grey-green leaves and white flowers. The flowers are borne rather sparsely but over a long period. **'Mount Everest'** has narrow, yellowish green leaves and white flowers. It is an upright plant, up to 1 m (3 ft) tall.

'Pretty Polly' is low-growing, with pale pink flowers. **'Primrose Beauty'**♀ has grey-green leaves and pale primrose-yellow flowers on low, arching branches. **'Princess'** (also sold as **'Blink'** or **'Pink Panther'**) is low and spreading, with

▲ *Potentilla fruticosa* 'Princess'

▲ *Potentilla fruticosa* 'Red Ace'

yellow-centred, pale pink flowers. **'Red Ace'** is a low spreading bush with bright vermilion flowers that are pale creamy yellow on the back. The flowers fade in hot, dry weather. **'Royal Flush'** is almost prostrate, with rose-pink flowers, some with a few extra petals.

'Sunset' is low-growing with light to deep orange flowers. **'Tangerine'**♀ is low-growing, with large, light coppery yellow flowers. **'Tilford Cream'**♀ is a small, spreading shrub with large creamy white flowers. White flowers are seen on var. *veitchii*, carried on arching branches. The plant ultimately grows up to 1 m (3 ft) tall.

Potentilla 'Vilmoriniana'

'Vilmoriniana' is tall and upright with silvery leaves and cream blooms.

P. megalantha♀ (syn. *P. fragiformis*) Rich yellow flowers, up to 4 cm (1½ in) wide, appear in summer on stems up to 30 cm (12 in) long, above glossy mid green leaves composed of 3 broad, strongly toothed and heavily veined leaflets. This perennial is suitable for a rock garden. HEIGHT & SPREAD 30×60 cm (1×2 ft).

P. nepalensis Glowing red or orange flowers appear in early summer. The leaves are made up of 5 radiating, boldly toothed leaflets. This plant is good for borders. HEIGHT & SPREAD 45×60 cm (1½×2 ft).

'Miss Willmott'♀ bears rose-pink flowers with a darker centre and reaches just 35 cm (14 in) in height. **'Roxana'** has orange-scarlet blooms.

P. neumanniana **'Nana'** (syn. *P. verna* 'Pygmaea') Small, deep yellow flowers are borne from late spring to early summer. The bright green palmate leaves are composed of 5 or 7 sharply toothed leaflets. Spreading, woody-based stems form low mats well suited to a rock garden or dry wall. HEIGHT & SPREAD 10×30 cm (4×12 in).

P. nitida Almost stemless flowers in an unusual light rosy pink with a darker centre appear in mid to late summer. They contrast beautifully with the small, silvery leaves, which are made up of 3 wedge-shaped leaflets, toothed at the tips. This low mat-forming plant is suitable for a rock garden, alpine house, or unheated greenhouse. It flowers most freely in poor, gritty soil. HEIGHT & SPREAD 10×20 cm (4×8 in).

'Rubra' displays its deep rose-pink blooms more freely than the species.

P. recta Yellow flowers appear in mid summer. The plant makes a loose clump in borders with wiry stems that usually need staking. The shiny green palmate leaves are

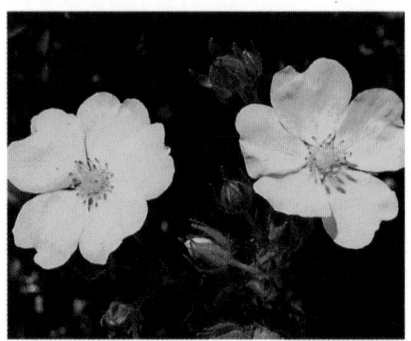

▼ *Potentilla recta* 'Warrenii'

composed of 5 or 7 leaflets. HEIGHT & SPREAD 60×30 cm (2×1 ft).

Pale yellow flowers are borne by var. *pallida*♀ (syn. var. *sulphurea*). **'Warrenii'** (syn. 'Macrantha') has rich yellow blooms. Both plants flower throughout the summer as long as it is not too hot and dry.

P. rupestris White flowers are borne on erect or sprawling, sparsely leafy stems, above a rosette of pinnate leaves with 5 or 7 coarsely toothed, oval or rounded leaflets. Plant at the front of a perennial border. HEIGHT & SPREAD 45×30 cm (1½×1 ft).

P. tommasiniana see *P. cinerea*

P. × *tonguei*♀ Soft apricot-yellow flowers with a crimson centre are borne on spreading stems from mid to late summer. Dark green leaves composed of 3 or 5 oblong, toothed leaflets contrast well with the flowers. This plant suits a rock garden. HEIGHT & SPREAD 15×40 cm (6×16 in).

P. verna **'Pygmaea'** see *P. neumanniana* 'Nana'

P. villosa see *P. crantzii*

GARDEN VARIETIES
There are several plants for which the parentage cannot be exactly determined. These perennials flower throughout the summer, adding colour to a border, but they can also be grown in large blocks as ground-cover plants. Each flower is up to 4 cm (1½ in) across and held in a loose cluster. All have soft green leaves. HEIGHT & SPREAD 45×60 cm (1½×2 ft).

'Flamenco' bears scarlet flowers with frilled edges. **'Gibson's Scarlet'**♀ has bright scarlet flowers. **'Gloire de Nancy'** has orange-brown flowers flushed with deep coral-red. **'Helen Jane'** carries mid pink flowers. **'Melton'** has pinky red flowers. **'Monsieur Rouillard'** bears mahogany-red,

▼ *Potentilla* 'Flamenco'

▲ *Potentilla* 'Gibson's Scarlet'

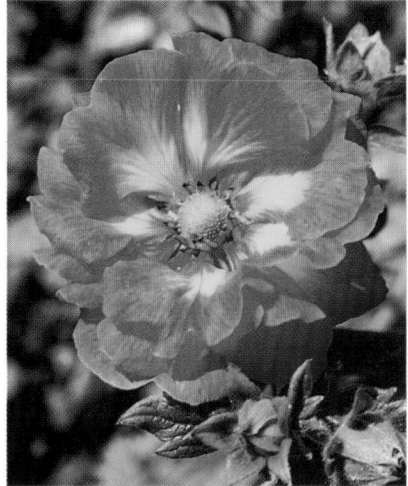

▲ *Potentilla* 'William Rollison'

semidouble flowers. It is one of the darkest varieties and looks best in light shade. **'William Rollison'**♥ bears orange-red, semidouble flowers with yellow reverse.

CULTIVATION Plant from autumn to spring in any moderately fertile and well-drained soil, except *P. crantzii*, *P. cuneata* and *P. nitida*, which need a gritty, poor soil if they are to produce a good display of flowers. All potentillas prefer a sunny situation. All, except the 3 species already mentioned, benefit from a spring mulch of organic material or compost.

Cut back flower stems (except those of *P. fruticosa*) as flowers fade.

PROPAGATION Sow seed of the species in a coldframe in spring and plant out seedlings in autumn. Divide and replant herbaceous perennials in early spring every 3-4 years, but this period can be extended if plants are given a good mulch each year. The woody-based perennials are increased by division or by cuttings taken in late spring or summer. Take cuttings of *P. fruticosa* and its varieties in late summer.

PRUNING The shrub *P. fruticosa* seldom requires pruning.

PESTS AND DISEASES Usually trouble free.

Pratia
Campanulaceae

Pratia pedunculata

Long-lasting carpets of small flowers cover the small leaves of these creeping evergreen perennials in summer. The flowers, up to 1.5 cm (½ in) across, are followed by fleshy berries. The plants are useful as rock plants, for ground cover, or even to make a lush, unusual lawn. Indeed, given favourable conditions of moist soil and shade, *Pratia angulata* and *P. pedunculata* can become invasive and so need a carefully chosen site.

RECOMMENDED SPECIES AND VARIETIES

P. angulata White flowers are produced over a long period in summer and followed by purplish red fleshy berries. Creeping branches carry rather fleshy leaves. Native to New Zealand. HEIGHT & SPREAD 5 cm (2 in) high with an indefinite spread.

'Treadwellii' is extremely vigorous, with

▼ *Pratia angulata*

▼ *Pratia angulata* 'Treadwellii'

long, trailing branches and larger leaves and larger white flowers than the species.

P. pedunculata Mats of creeping, small-leaved branches carry blue flowers on erect 3 cm (1¼ in) long stalks. Flowers appear throughout the summer. The species bears small green berries but these are not produced by most cultivated forms. Native to Australia. HEIGHT & SPREAD 10 cm (4 in) high with an indefinite spread.

'County Park' has violet-blue, fragrant flowers about 1.5 cm (½ in) across.

P. perpusilla This compact plant has small leaves and fragrant almost stemless white flowers followed by inconspicuous green berries. HEIGHT & SPREAD 1.5 cm (½ in) high with an indefinite spread.

CULTIVATION The plants grow best in a moist soil. Some forms can be invasive.

PROPAGATION Lift and divide during spring or summer.

PESTS AND DISEASES Slugs and snails may devour small plants in spring and autumn.

Prayer plant see *Maranta leuconeura*
Pride of India
see *Koelreuteria paniculata*
Primrose see *Primula*
Primrose, Cape see *Streptocarpus*
Primrose, evening see *Oenothera*

▼ *Pratia pedunculata*

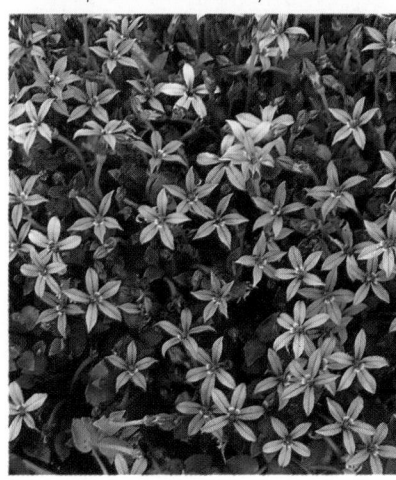

▼ *Pratia pedunculata* 'County Park'

p
q

Primula

Primulaceae

The wild species of primula provide some of the loveliest plants for an informal garden. Selective breeding has discovered bedding plants of sparkling colour and specimens of gem-like perfection for growing under glass

A huge genus of perennial plants, primulas are widely distributed throughout the temperate regions of the Northern Hemisphere, in mountain and lowland, woodland and meadow. They vary in habit, from tiny cushions and low-growing mats to vigorous clump-forming plants up to 80 cm (32 in) high.

They all form rosettes of leaves at ground level and grow flowering stems (scapes) bearing one to many five-petalled flowers, often with a white or yellow eye. In some species the stem is so reduced that the flowers are borne above the foliage only by their individual stalks (pedicels). In other species, the 'candelabra' types, flowers are borne in several whorls up a strong stem.

One feature of the genus is the appearance of 'farina', a silvery, powdery wax, secreted by glands on the leaves, stems and even flowers of some species. It is also called paste or meal. Some people are allergic to it.

RECOMMENDED SPECIES AND VARIETIES

The plants are divided into five groups:
(1) Indoor species
(2) Alpine species
(3) Species for border and bog
(4) Primrose and polyanthus cultivars
(5) Auricula cultivars
All are hardy except the first group.

INDOOR SPECIES

These tender primulas are grown as annuals in pots for indoor decoration – to flower in a greenhouse or conservatory or in the house in winter and spring.

P. kewensis ♀ Fragrant, soft yellow, salver-shaped flowers, 2 cm (¾ in) wide, are closely borne on the stem in several whorls. The oval or spoon-shaped evergreen leaves have a light dusting of white farina. HEIGHT & SPREAD 30×25 cm (12×10 in).

P. malacoides (fairy primrose) Whorls of 4-6 small, single, or occasionally double, flowers are borne in shades of red, pink, purple or white with a small yellow eye. An easily grown species, generally grown as an annual, with oval, hairy, evergreen leaves, contact with which can cause an allergic skin reaction in some people. HEIGHT & SPREAD 30×20 cm (12×8 in).

'Bright Eyes' is a mixed selection covering the full range of colours. Each flower has a large, contrasting, dark eye, and sometimes a yellow throat. 'Carmine Pearl' is a dwarf strain, 15-20 cm (6-8 in) tall, with carmine flowers. 'Fire Chief' has brick-red flowers. 'Jubilee' has cherry-red flowers. 'Lilac Queen' has double flowers of soft lilac. 'Mars' is a plant to 12 cm (4¾ in) high with deep lavender flowers. 'Ninette' has deep crimson flowers. 'Rose Bouquet' bears deep carmine blooms.

P. obconica Large clusters of 2.5 cm (1 in) wide flowers are borne in a range of colours, white, pink, red, pale lavender to deep purple, all with a greenish eye. Contact with the hairy, rounded, evergreen leaves can cause a severe skin allergy. HEIGHT & SPREAD 30×20 cm (12×8 in).

Giant-Flowered and **Juno** are mixed selections, but several excellent individual coloured varieties are available. 'Caerulea' has purplish blue flowers. 'Giant White' has large, pure white flowers. 'Salmon King' bears reddish salmon-pink flowers. 'Snowstorm' has pure white flowers.

ALPINE SPECIES

Suitable for growing in rock gardens or in an alpine house, these small clump-forming species grow to 15 cm (6 in) high. They have open-faced, salver-shaped, primrose-type, or occasionally more bell-shaped flowers, to 2 cm (¾ in) across, carried either singly, in trusses or in spikes in spring and early summer. European and Asiatic species have different cultural requirements.

P. allionii A dense cushion of evergreen foliage is smothered in early and mid spring with pink to reddish purple or white flowers with white eyes, 1.5 to 3 cm (½-1¼ in) wide. The sticky, fleshy, spoon-shaped to rounded leaves grow to 4 cm (1½ in) long.

▲ *Primula kewensis*

1 *Primula vialii*
2 *Primula denticulata* var. *alba*
3 *Primula denticulata*
4 *Primula auricula*
5 *Primula capitata*
6 *Primula auricula* 'Andrea Julie'
7 *Primula vulgaris* 'Lilacina Plena'
8 *Primula auricula* 'Lovebird'
9 *Primula auricula* 'Rolts'
10 *Primula marginata* 'Prichard's Variety'
11 *Primula × pubescens* 'Cream Viscosa'
12 *Primula × pubescens* 'Faldonside'
13 *Primula × pubescens* 'Boothman's Variety'
14 *Primula vulgaris*

This is one of the most popular alpine house plants, growing wild on shady cliffs in the Maritime Alps, with many varieties and hybrids. All need special care in cultivation, as they resent overhead water especially in winter, and are subject to botrytis unless dead leaves are removed meticulously. HEIGHT & SPREAD 5×20 cm (2×8 in) or more in many cultivars.

'Anna Griffith' is flat-growing and slow, and has pale lavender-pink petals with a fringed margin. 'Austen' is purplish pink and slow-growing. 'Avalanche' has large, creamy white flowers. 'Crowsley Variety' has small leaves and very dark purplish red flowers with a white eye. 'Ken's Seedling' (syn. 'KRW') is vigorous, bearing large, violet-purple flowers with notched petals. 'Marion' has large, pale pink flowers with a large white eye. 'Martin' has pink to reddish purple or white flowers with white eyes. 'Mrs Dyas' has small violet-pink flowers. 'Pennine Pink' has purplish pink flowers. Easy to grow. 'Praecox' is very early flowering, often in late autumn, with lilac-pink flowers. 'Snowflake' is a superb alpine primula with large, pure white flowers. 'William Earle' is vigorous, has dark purplish pink flowers with a white eye and very broad, wavy-edged petals.

P. auricula ♀ (bear's ear) Clusters of bright yellow, trumpet-shaped flowers with a white farinose eye appear from mid spring to early summer. The leathery, evergreen, pointed leaves grow to 12 cm (4¾ in) and may be with or without farina, toothed or untoothed. Growing in the wild from the French Alps to the Tatras, this is a good garden primula and the mother plant from which the auricula cultivars derive. HEIGHT & SPREAD 15×15 cm (6×6 in).

P. 'Beatrice Wooster' This European hybrid has large clusters of deep rose-pink flowers with white eyes in mid spring and fleshy evergreen leaves to 15 cm (6 in) long. Fairly easy to grow and good in troughs. HEIGHT & SPREAD 10×20 cm (4×8 in).

P. capitata Dense, flat or conical heads of small, deep purplish blue flowers appear in mid and late summer. A native of the

p
q

Himalayas, with rosettes of mealy, toothed, semi-evergreen leaves up to 15 cm (6 in) long, it is one of the more easily grown of the Asiatic species and self-seeds readily. HEIGHT & SPREAD 25×15 cm (10×6 in).

P. chionantha♀ Fragrant, creamy white, yellow-eyed flowers are borne in whorls up the stem in early summer. With long, farinose deciduous leaves, this Chinese species is one of the easiest of the Asiatics to grow. HEIGHT & SPREAD 40×20 cm (16×8 in).

P. clarkei Clear rose-pink flowers, to 2 cm (¾ in) across, are borne in mid spring by this fine, very dwarf primula from Kashmir. With short, rounded, toothed, deciduous leaves, it is usually short-lived unless divided and replanted frequently. HEIGHT & SPREAD 5×10 cm (2×4 in).

P. concholoba Dense clusters of violet flowers, with exceptionally long tubes and farinose backs to the petals, appear in mid to late spring. This uncommon Himalayan species has toothed, lance-shaped, deciduous leaves up to 8 cm (3 in) long. HEIGHT & SPREAD 15×10 cm (6×4 in).

P. 'Ethel Barker' Small, purplish pink flowers are borne in mid spring by this cushion-forming, evergreen European hybrid. HEIGHT & SPREAD 10×20 cm (4×8 in).

P. farinosa (bird's-eye primrose) Clusters of small lavender-pink, or occasionally white, flowers with a yellow eye appear in early spring. It has farinose rosettes of 2–10 cm (¾–4 in) long deciduous leaves with rolled edges. A British native, it needs the same treatment as the Asiatic species. It tends to be short-lived but is easily raised from seed. HEIGHT & SPREAD 10×8 cm (4×3¼ in).

P. flaccida♀ (syn. *P. nutans*) Dense clusters of nodding, funnel-shaped, deep lilac-purple flowers are borne by this beautiful Chinese species in early summer. Its hairy deciduous leaves have waved margins and grow to 15 cm (6 in) long. It is usually short-lived but well worth maintaining from seed. HEIGHT & SPREAD 30×10 cm (12×4 in).

P. × *forsteri* (syn. *P. minima* × *hirsuta*) This variable hybrid of two European species forms cushions of rounded, glossy, evergreen leaves with toothed margins, and bears short-stalked deep pink flowers with a pale eye in mid and late spring. HEIGHT & SPREAD 10×20 cm (4×8 in).

'Bileckii' has deep rose flowers with a white eye and small rosettes of glossy triangular leaves with an irregular tip. 'Dianne' has deep crimson flowers and larger rosettes of glossy leaves, toothed at the tip.

P. frondosa♀ Large clusters of small, lilac-pink to red-purple flowers are borne in early spring by this Bulgarian species. The dark green, oval to spoon-shaped, toothed deciduous leaves are white and farinose on the underside and grow to 9 cm (3½ in) long. HEIGHT & SPREAD 12×10 cm (4¾×4 in).

P. glaucescens Small clusters of reddish purple flowers appear in late spring. This shy-flowering Italian evergreen alpine has

short, glossy and leathery, finely-toothed leaves. HEIGHT & SPREAD 10×15 cm (4×6 in).

P. halleri Trusses of up to 19 small, lilac, yellow-eyed flowers appear in mid and late spring. The deciduous leaves have a dense covering of farina on the underside. Although native to SE Europe, it has the same cultural requirements as the Asiatic species. HEIGHT & SPREAD 15×20 cm (6×8 in).

P. juliae This parent of many of the modern primrose cultivars bears small, very short-stemmed trusses of deep magenta flowers with a yellow eye in mid and late spring. It is a creeping, stoloniferous plant, very easy to divide, with rounded and toothed semi-evergreen leaves. Native to the Caucasus. HEIGHT & SPREAD 15×20 cm (6×8 in).

P. marginata♀ Flowerheads with as many as 20 shallow trumpet-shaped flowers, up to 2.5 cm (1 in) across, with a mealy white eye and varying in colour from pale to deep lilac, sometimes pinkish, are borne from early to late spring. A fine species from the Maritime Alps, it forms clusters of rosettes from gradually lengthening woody stems. The attractive evergreen leaves are covered with white farina and have jagged margins. HEIGHT & SPREAD 15×30 cm (6×12 in).

The flowers of var. *alba* are rather small and white or off-white. 'Beatrice Lascaris' is a compact plant having clear blue flowers

▲ *Primula marginata* 'Beatrice Lascaris'

with a white eye and yellow-farinose, regularly toothed leaves. 'Caerulea' has clear blue flowers and leaves covered with white farina. 'Clear's Variety' has deeply toothed, yellow-farinose leaves, and small lilac flowers. 'Drake's Form' is a strong-growing plant, with large, pale lilac flowers and handsome, white-farinose leaves. 'Holden Variety' is very compact, with narrow, white-farinose leaves and small lilac-blue flowers. 'Hyacinthia' is an easily grown, robust hybrid with toothed green leaves, only slightly farinose at their margins, and large, rounded, deep lilac flowers. 'Kesselring's Variety' carries large clusters

p
q

of deep lavender flowers and has leaves and stems covered with farina. **'Linda Pope'**♀ is the finest of all, with large, white-powdered, toothed leaves and exceptionally large, well-rounded, soft lilac-blue flowers with a white eye. **'Prichard's Variety'** has broad leaves edged with white farina, and large trusses of lilac-purple flowers.

P. minima Pink, occasionally white, flowers with a white eye and deeply notched, narrow petals appear singly or in pairs in late spring and early summer. The small, shiny, dark evergreen leaves are deeply toothed. Widely distributed from the E Alps to the Tatras, but not free-flowering. HEIGHT & SPREAD 5×15cm (2×6in).

P. minima × hirsuta see *P. × forsteri*

P. **'Peter Klein'** Trusses of white-eyed pink flowers are borne in mid spring. A hybrid of two Asiatic primulas, it has finely toothed, narrow, semi-evergreen leaves. HEIGHT & SPREAD 15×15cm (6×6in).

P. petiolaris Dense trusses of pink flowers, with a yellow eye surrounded by a white ring, appear in early and mid spring. The spoon-shaped evergreen leaves of this Himalayan primula grow to 15cm (6in) long. Requires acid to neutral, humus-rich soil. HEIGHT & SPREAD 10×20cm (4×8in).

P. × pubescens♀ Large flattish heads of up to 15 flowers, possibly 2.5cm (1in) across, in various colours are borne from mid spring to early summer. This very variable European hybrid typically makes compact clumps of evergreen rosettes of thick, hairy, toothed, oval to lance-shaped leaves. An excellent free-flowering plant for the rock garden. HEIGHT & SPREAD 10×15cm (4×6in).

'Bewerley White' is a vigorous plant, with heads of creamy white flowers. **'Boothman's Variety'** (syn. **'Carmen'**) is a compact plant and easy to grow, with deep crimson, white-eyed flowers. **'Christine'** is a compact plant with yellowish green leaves and deep rose flowers with a white eye. **'Cream Viscosa'** is easy to grow, with loose clusters of slightly funnel-shaped cream flowers. **'Faldonside'** is a compact variety with white-eyed, pinkish red flowers. **'Freedom'** is very vigorous and tall, with large leaves and heads of deep purplish lilac flowers. **'Harlow Carr'** is vigorous with large creamy white flowers. **'Mrs J.H. Wilson'** is compact but vigorous with deep violet-purple flowers with white eyes. **'Rufus'** has very large, brick-red flowers with a yellow eye. **'The General'** is vigorous, with sparse trusses of yellow-eyed, velvety red flowers.

P. reidii Fragrant, creamy white flowers, nodding and broadly bell-shaped, are borne in clusters of up to 10 in late spring. An exquisite Himalayan species with hairy, oblong to lance-shaped, deciduous leaves up to 15cm (6in) long. HEIGHT & SPREAD 15×10cm (6×4in).

More robust than the species, var. *williamsii* has pale blue to white flowers.

P. scotica Clusters of up to 6 small dark purple flowers with white eyes are borne from late spring to early summer. This diminutive Scottish species has small, spoon-shaped deciduous leaves, thickly covered with farina on the underside. It needs rich but well-drained soil, like the Asiatic species, and is short-lived, but easy to propagate from seed. HEIGHT & SPREAD 8×5cm (3¼×2in).

P. vulgaris (primrose) The other parent of the modern primrose cultivars is our native primrose, widely distributed throughout Europe. From early to late spring it bears fragrant, pale yellow flowers with orange markings at the base of the petals, occasionally these may be white or pink. The semi-evergreen leaves are deeply veined. HEIGHT & SPREAD 12.5×25cm (5×10in).

The flowers of var. *alba* are pure white. **'Alba Plena'** is vigorous with double white flowers. **'Lilacina Plena'** (quaker's bonnet) is fairly vigorous with double lilac blue flowers. The flowers of ssp. *sibthorpii*♀, a native of the E Balkans, are usually pink or purple, occasionally white, and the leaves are wedge shaped.

P. warshenewskiana Small bright pink flowers, with a yellow eye surrounded by a zone of white, are borne in trusses in late spring. A rhizomatous, creeping plant from central Asia and Afghanistan with short, toothed, deciduous leaves. HEIGHT & SPREAD 5×18cm (2×7in).

SPECIES FOR BORDER AND BOG
Most of these larger primulas are native to the Himalayas and E Asia, and grow into clumps 20cm (8in) or more wide. The leaves are 10-20cm (4-8in) long, and the flowers are borne in spikes or clusters or, in the candelabra species, in whorls up the stem. Some demand boggy conditions. The others thrive in humus-rich, moisture-

retentive soil. They flower from late spring to mid summer, unless stated otherwise.

P. alpicola Fragrant, nodding, funnel-shaped flowers are borne in trusses. They are farinose and may be white, cream, yellow, or purple. The deciduous leaves are narrow oval. HEIGHT & SPREAD 15-40×20cm (6-16×8in).

In var. *alba* the flowers are white, in var. *violacea* pink to purple.

P. aurantiaca Deep brownish orange flowers are carried in whorls on dark purple stems. The oval, slightly farinose, dark green, deciduous leaves of this candelabra species often have a purple midrib. HEIGHT & SPREAD 30×20cm (12×8in).

P. beesiana Deep rose flowers with a yellow eye are borne in candelabra-type clusters covered with farina. The large semi-evergreen leaves are finely toothed. HEIGHT & SPREAD 30×20cm (12×8in).

P. bulleyana♀ In this candelabra species golden yellow flowers emerge from red buds. The semi-evergreen leaves have a purple midrib and the stems are coated with white farina. HEIGHT & SPREAD 50×20cm (20×8in).

P. burmanica The flowers of this deciduous candelabra type are purple with an orange eye. HEIGHT & SPREAD 30×20cm (12×8in).

P. chungensis This vigorous candelabra type has coarsely toothed deciduous leaves and produces small, fragrant, pale orange flowers from red buds. HEIGHT & SPREAD 60×20cm (24×8in).

P. cockburniana Bright orange-red flowers are carried in small whorls on white-farinose stems. A beautiful but very short-lived deciduous plant, easily kept going from seed. HEIGHT & SPREAD 25×15cm (10×8in).

P. denticulata♀ (drumstick primrose) The flowers are carried in dense, round clusters from early spring to early summer. They

▲ *Primula beesiana*

▲ *Primula bulleyana*

▲ *Primula denticulata*

come in shades of pink to purple, lavender and red, all with a yellow eye. The plant has finely toothed, slightly hairy deciduous leaves. Easily grown, it makes a colourful edging to a border or among shrubs. HEIGHT & SPREAD 40×20 cm (16×8 in).

The flowers of var. *alba* are pure white. **Ruby** has deep purplish red flowers.

P. elatior♀ (oxlip) One-sided clusters of up to 10 funnel-shaped, primrose-yellow flowers appear in mid and late spring. This British native has conspicuously veined, hairy, semi-evergreen leaves with toothed margins, and is a plant that establishes well in grass. HEIGHT & SPREAD 15×20 cm (6×8 in).

P. florindae♀ (giant cowslip) Large trusses of nodding, bell-shaped, fragrant, yellow flowers are borne in summer on stout stems. It is a magnificent plant needing very wet conditions. Deciduous. HEIGHT & SPREAD 80×30 cm (32×12 in).

P. helodoxa see *P. prolifera*

P. Inshriach Hybrids Whorls of very bright flowers in shades of yellow, orange, pink and red are borne on plants of robust candelabra type. Deciduous. HEIGHT & SPREAD 50×20 cm (20×8 in).

P. 'Inverewe' ♀ Bright orange-red flowers are borne by this strong-growing, semi-evergreen candelabra hybrid. HEIGHT & SPREAD 75×60 cm (2½×2 ft)

P. ioessa Nodding trusses of fragrant, large, cream or lilac, funnel-shaped flowers appear in early summer. Deciduous. HEIGHT & SPREAD 25×15 cm (10×6 in).

P. japonica♀ Reddish purple, sometimes white or pink, flowers with a dark eye are carried in whorls on green or reddish stems. A candelabra type with pale green, coarsely toothed deciduous leaves, it is easily grown and does not need very damp conditions. HEIGHT & SPREAD 40×20 cm (16×8 in).

'Fuji' has white flowers. 'Miller's Crimson' is vigorous with dark red flowers. 'Postford White' has large white flowers with a yellow eye. An easily grown plant that comes true from seed.

P. littoniana see *P. vialii*

P. poissonii Deep purplish pink flowers with a yellow or white eye are carried in 2–6 whorls up the stem. An evergreen candelabra type primula with bluish green

leaves. HEIGHT & SPREAD 40×20 cm (16×8 in).

P. polyneura Trusses of pale pink to crimson flowers, with a greenish yellow eye and notched petals, are borne in early summer. This deciduous primula has dark green, hairy lobed leaves and hairy stems, and grows well in woodland conditions. HEIGHT & SPREAD 40×20 cm (16×8 in).

P. prolifera♀ (syn. *P. helodoxa*) Slightly pendent, short-stalked, bright yellow fragrant flowers are carried in whorls. A candelabra type with dark evergreen leaves. HEIGHT & SPREAD 60×20 cm (24×8 in).

P. pulverulenta♀ Deep reddish purple flowers with a darker eye are carried in large whorls. The irregularly toothed deciduous leaves have a pale midrib. It is the most vigorous and long-lasting of the candelabras and is striking with its very white-farinose stems. HEIGHT & SPREAD 80×20 cm (32×8 in).

▲ *Primula pulverulenta*

Bartley Hybrids♀ come in shades from pink to purple, with pale or dark eyes.

P. rosea♀ The large flowers are vivid rose with a yellow eye, and borne in trusses in late spring. A bog-loving species, with glossy, oval, deciduous leaves, it is very good for pond margins, combining well with calthas, lysichitons and other bog plants. HEIGHT & SPREAD 15×20 cm (6×8 in).

'Grandiflora' is a large-flowered variety.

P. secundiflora Deep purple, funnel-shaped, pendent flowers are carried in a one-sided cluster, occasionally in 2–3 whorls. It is an easy species to grow, tolerating drier conditions than others in this group, and has smooth, narrow, evergreen or semi-evergreen leaves on white-farinose stalks. HEIGHT & SPREAD 40×20 cm (16×8 in).

P. sieboldii♀ Large flowers in shades of pink

and purple with a white eye, the petals usually notched or frilled, are carried in trusses. This spreading rhizomatous primula has pale green, hairy, oval deciduous leaves with wavy, blunt-toothed margins. The species and cultivars are excellent easily grown plants for moist borders, in the shade of rhododendrons and other woodland shrubs. HEIGHT & SPREAD 20×20 cm (8×8 in).

The flowers of var. *alba* are white. 'Dancing Ladies' has pale pink or white flowers with a pink, occasionally blue, reverse. 'Manankoora' has blue and white flowers. 'Mikado' has lilac-blue flowers with a white eye. 'Pago-Pago' has flowers in shades of red and pink. 'Snowflake' has white flowers with unnotched petals.

P. sikkimensis (Himalayan cowslip) Narrow-tubular, cream or yellow flowers appear in large pendent clusters. A deciduous species that needs very damp ground. HEIGHT & SPREAD 40×20 cm (16×8 in).

P. veris♀ (cowslip) Fragrant, deep yellow flowers, with an orange spot at the base of each petal, appear in one-sided trusses in late spring and early summer. A British semi-evergreen native, it is easily grown and can be established in grass. HEIGHT & SPREAD 25×20 cm (10×8 in).

P. vialii♀ (syn. *P. littoniana*) Small, deep lavender flowers, opening from scarlet buds, form a dense cylindrical spike, vivid red above and blue below. An easily grown but short-lived plant, it is worth growing from seed as a biennial to replace any losses. Deciduous. HEIGHT & SPREAD 40×15 cm (16×6 in).

P. waltonii Deep purple, funnel-shaped flowers hang down in trusses. Deciduous. HEIGHT & SPREAD 50×20 cm (20×8 in).

P. wilsonii Purplish red flowers are carried in whorls by this evergreen, candelabra type. HEIGHT & SPREAD 60×20 cm (24×8 in).

PRIMROSE AND POLYANTHUS CULTIVARS
A large number of primrose cultivars has been developed as a result of selection and of crossing the European primrose, *P. vulgaris*, with the Caucasian primrose, *P. juliae*. Crossing *P. vulgaris* and the cowslip, *P. veris*, has produced the polyanthus cultivars. The primrose cultivars bear their flowers singly on elongated stalks. Many double-flowered varieties have been bred. The polyanthus cultivars carry their flowers in a cluster on stout upright stems.

Primrose and polyanthus cultivars are widely sold as mixed seed selections, including some for greenhouse use or for bedding that are more tender than those raised for garden use. There is a large range of vegetatively propagated cultivars, of which some of the best are described below.

Primrose
Flowering from early to mid spring. Semi-evergreen, ranging in height from 10–15 cm (4–6 in) and spreading about 25 cm (10 in).
'Alan Robb' has double pale apricot flowers. 'April Rose' has double deep pink

p
q

flowers. **'Captain Blood'** has double blood-red flowers. **'Chocolate Soldier'** has double flowers; the gold-edged petals are chocolate-brown becoming purple. **'Corporal Baxter'** has velvety crimson double flowers. **'Dawn Ansell'** is a 'jack-in-the-green' type: its double white flowers are surrounded by a ruff of large leaflets. **'Eugénie'** has double dark blue flowers, reddish purple towards the base of the petals. **'Freckles'** has double dark red flowers dotted with white. **'Groeneken's Glory'** has bright bluish pink flowers with a green eye. **'Ken Dearman'** has double flowers, yellow at the base, shading to reddish orange towards the petal tips. **'Lilian Harvey'** has double purplish pink flowers. **'Marianne Davey'** has double pale yellow and cream flowers. **'Marie Crousse'** has violet double flowers, edged with white. **'Miss Indigo'** has double deep violet-blue flowers edged with white. **'Olive Wyatt'** has deep reddish pink double flowers. **'Rose O'Day'** has light rose-red double flowers. **'Roy Cope'** has red, scented, double flowers. **'Schneekissen'** (syn. 'Snow Cushion') has small, pure white flowers. **'Sue Jervis'** has double, soft salmon-pink flowers. **'Sunshine Susie'** has double, bright yellow flowers, partly flushed with pink. **'Val Horncastle'** has double, yellow and cream flowers. **'Wanda'**♀ has dark leaves and very deep reddish purple flowers; easy to grow. **'White Wanda'** has dark leaves and white flowers; easy to grow.

Polyanthus

Flowering from early to late spring. Semi-evergreen, ranging in height from 15–20 cm (6–8 in) and spreading about 25 cm (10 in).
Cowichan is a range of very dark reds, purples, and blues, with no central eye. The leaves are very dark green, tinged with purple. **Gold-laced Group** has very dark brownish purple flowers with a deep golden eye and each petal margined with gold. **'Guinevere'**♀ carries large heads of pink flowers on reddish stems. The leaves are bronze-tinged. **Hose-in-Hose** Two rows of petals give the appearance of one flower inside another. Plants may be of polyanthus or primrose habit, with flowers in shades of yellow, pink or red. **Jack-in-the-Green Group** Flowers in shades of yellow are each encircled by a ruff of small green leaves. Plants may be of primrose or polyanthus type. **'Kinlough Beauty'** has flowers of salmon-pink with a cream stripe down each petal. **'Lady Greer'**♀ has small, pale yellow flowers. **'McWatt's Claret'** has small, deep brownish red flowers. **'McWatt's Cream'** has small, pale cream flowers. **Silver-laced Group** has dark brownish purple flowers with a golden eye; the petals have a narrow white margin. **'Tawny Port'** is a compact plant with red-tinged foliage, bearing deep purplish red flowers.

AURICULA CULTIVARS

These highly bred, evergreen hardy plants are mostly grown under glass to protect the foliage and flowers from damage by rain. The rosettes of broad, fleshy, usually farinose, pointed leaves eventually form a dense clump if not divided. Growing to 15 cm (6 in) high, the flowers appear in mid spring in trusses of 2 to 20 on stout stems. They are mainly flat-faced or very slightly trumpet-shaped, with several concentric circles of colour. The colouring and amount of farina vary in the four different groups into which auriculas are divided: alpine, border, double and show.

Alpine auriculas

These have no farina on the leaves or flowers. Around the eye of the flower is a light-coloured (white or cream) or gold-coloured ring, surrounded by a deep colour which often turns paler towards the edge.

▲ *Primula* 'Lady Greer'

▲ *Primula auricula* 'Argus'

'Andrea Julie' gold-centred, light red; easy to grow. **'Applecross'** gold-centred, rich crimson. **'Argus'** light-centred, deep plum shading to purplish red. **'Beatrice'** light-centred, blue. **'Blossom'** gold-centred, red. **'Bookham Firefly'** gold-centred, red. **'C.W. Needham'** light-centred, dark purple; with attractive toothed leaves. **'Elsie May'** light-centred, deep velvety plum. **'Jenny'** gold-centred, dull red. **'Joy'** light-centred, deep velvety crimson. **'Lisa'** light-centred, deep purple shading to lilac; a vigorous alpine auricula. **'Mark'** light-centred, bright pink; a vigorous plant. **'Prince John'** gold-centred, red. **'Rowena'** light-centred, purple shading to pale lilac. **'Sandra'** mauve with a small light centre. **'Sandwood Bay'** gold-centred, bright crimson. **'Sirius'** gold-centred, deep maroon shading to pale primrose. **'Valerie'** light-centred, dark mauve shading to light mauve. **'Winnifrid'** gold-centred, crimson shading to bright scarlet.

Border auriculas

These may have green leaves with little or no farina or they may be markedly farinose. The flowers also vary greatly, some with a farinose centre and some without, the latter usually also having leaves with no farina and flowers that are paler towards the edge. They make good border plants in rich but well-drained soil in partial shade.
'Blairside Yellow' is compact-growing with small, clear yellow flowers. **'Blue Velvet'** has purplish blue flowers with a cream centre fading to white. **'Broadwell Gold'** has farinose leaves and large, golden yellow flowers; a good increaser. **'Old Red Dusty Miller'** has farinose leaves and deep red flowers. **'Old Yellow Dusty Miller'** has very farinose leaves and bright yellow

▲ *Primula* 'Dawn Ansell'

▲ *Primula* 'Groeneken's Glory'

▲ *Primula* 'Kinlough Beauty'

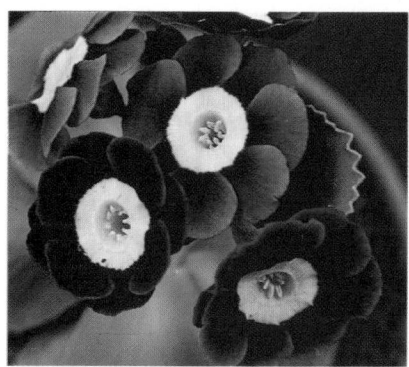

▲ *Primula auricula* 'C.W. Needham'

▲ *Primula auricula* 'Prince John'

flowers; a vigorous border auricula. **'Paradise Yellow'** has large trusses of yellow flowers; a vigorous plant.

Double auriculas

These have 8 or more petals in a variety of colours – usually cream or yellow but also brown, crimson, lavender, pink or purple. The foliage is usually farinose.
'Camelot' has dark red flowers and is a vigorous and freely increasing plant. **'Catherine'** has lemon-yellow flowers and long, narrow leaves. **'Devon Cream'** has cream flowers with a deep yellow centre. **'Doublet'** is dark red and vigorous. **'Trouble'** includes mixed shades of yellow, pink, and green.

Show auriculas

The flowers have a ring of 'paste' (farina) round the central eye. The show auriculas are divided into three types. 'Selfs', where the petals are of only one colour, red, yellow or blue, apart from the paste. 'Edged' and 'fancy' show auriculas exhibit a mutation, where the outer edge of petal tissue is replaced with leaf tissue. Where there is no farina on the edge it is green. With a light covering of farina it is grey. With a heavy covering it is white. In the edged types, the petal colour (body colour) between the ring of paste and the outer edge of the petal is black. In the fancy types, it is a colour other than black.
'Alice Haysom' is a deep red self. **'Blue Nile'** is a good blue self. **'Brazil'** is a yellow self and increases well. **'C.G. Haysom'** is grey-edged. **'Chorister'** is a yellow self,

fast-growing and prolific. **'Fanny Meerbeck'** is a red self. **Gildersome Green'** is green-edged. **'Gizabroon'** is a dark brownish red self. **'Gleam'** is a yellow self. **'Guinea'** is a bright yellow self and a vigorous plant. **'Lechistan'** is a strong-growing red self. **'Lovebird'** is grey-edged. **'Mojave'** is a red self. **'Moonglow'** is a creamy green self. **'Neat and Tidy'** is a dark red self. **'Nocturne'** is a dark red self. **'Orb'** is green-edged, an unusual shade of olive-green. **'Pot o' Gold'** is a yellow self with yellowish paste; freely increasing. **'Prague'** bears large trusses of green-edged flowers. **'Rajah'** is a green-edged fancy with bright scarlet body colour. **'Red Gauntlet'** is a scarlet self; freely increasing. **'Remus'** a dark blue self; freely increasing. **'Rolts'** is a green-edged fancy with red body colour. **'Stant's Blue'** is a bluish mauve self. **'Sweet Pastures'** is a green-edged fancy with yellow body colour.

CULTIVATION

INDOOR SPECIES Grow in peat-based or loam-based compost in 13 cm (5 in) pots. Feed regularly and shade from hot sun.
ALPINE SPECIES Plant the European alpines in a very well-drained bed with plenty of humus, or in a similar compost in pots, in a sunny position. Most of the Asiatic species need a richer and moister but still well-drained soil, with plenty of leaf mould or other humus, in partial shade. In pots, the Asiatic species do best in a peat-based or humus-rich compost, the European species in loam-based compost, both with good drainage. Apply liquid feed monthly in the growing season.

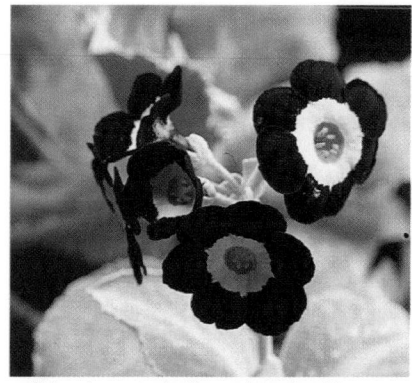

▲ *Primula auricula* 'Fanny Meerbeck'

SPECIES FOR BORDER AND BOG Plant in any moisture-retentive soil enriched with plenty of humus, leaf mould, compost or well-rotted manure. In dry areas grow in partial shade, but grow in full sun in damper ground. The candelabra species generally need more moisture than the others and should be watered in dry weather. Grow *P. florindae*, *P. rosea* and *P. sikkimensis* in very wet, even boggy, ground.
PRIMROSE AND POLYANTHUS CULTIVARS Plant in early spring in humus-rich soil, preferably with abundant, well-rotted

▲ *Primula auricula* 'Lovebird'

manure, compost or leaf mould. In the south plants benefit from partial shade. Divide frequently, at least every two years, and replant in freshly treated soil. A rich, peat-based compost is ideal for plants grown indoors. A light, cool, airy windowsill suits them, and plenty of moisture.
AURICULA CULTIVARS Grow alpine, double and show auriculas in pots of soil-based compost with grit added to improve drainage. Water freely during the growing periods of autumn and spring and feed monthly, keeping water off the foliage and flowers. Repot in early summer. Keep partially shaded in hot weather. Grow border auriculas and the more robust alpine auriculas, such as 'Argus', 'Lisa' and 'Mark', in humus-rich, well-drained soil in full sun, partial sun in the south.

PROPAGATION

INDOOR SPECIES Sow seed in a peat-based compost, from early summer to autumn to give a succession of flowers. Transplant seedlings into separate small pots when 2 true leaves have appeared. Repot when full of roots into final 13 cm (5 in) pots and grow on in a cool, shaded frame. Bring into a cool greenhouse, minimum temperature 5-7°C (41-45°F), before the onset of frosts.
ALPINE SPECIES Sow species in autumn and keep cold through the winter. Remove offsets in spring and root them as cuttings.
SPECIES FOR BORDER AND BOG Sow seed in peat-based compost in autumn in a cold greenhouse or in heat in early spring. Divide strong plants in early spring.
PRIMROSE AND POLYANTHUS CULTIVARS Sow seed in peat-based compost in early spring at 15-18°C (59-64°F). Divide plants in early spring.
AURICULA CULTIVARS Remove offsets in early summer. Those with roots can go straight into individual 5 cm (2 in) pots. Treat those without roots as cuttings.
PESTS AND DISEASES Viruses and vine weevils are the main enemies of primulas. Grey mould, brown core, leaf spot, aphids (including root aphids), whitefly and red spider mite (especially under glass) and slugs and snails are problems too.

p
q

Prostanthera
Labiatae

Prostanthera cuneata

Peppermint-scented leaves and abundant flowers earn these evergreen shrubs their place in a garden. The short, tubular flowers have two lips. The upper lip is usually upright and may be lobed, while the lower lip is spreading and often divided into several lobes. Of the recommended plants, *Prostanthera cuneata* is hardy, except in the coldest gardens, whereas *P. rotundifolia* can be grown only in a frost-free garden or in pots that are overwintered under glass.

RECOMMENDED SPECIES AND VARIETIES
P. cuneata♀ (alpine mint bush) White or pale violet flowers, about 2 cm (¾ in) across, with their throats heavily dotted in purple and orange-yellow, appear in summer. The short upper lip is slightly split and the lower lip is divided into 4 lobes. Highly aromatic, almost stalkless, dark green, rounded leaves, about 6 mm (¼ in) across, crowd the stems of these dense bushes, which may grow wider than they are high. HEIGHT & SPREAD 45×45 cm (1½×1½ ft) after 5 years, ultimately 60 cm (2 ft) tall.

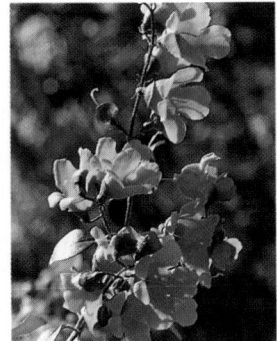

▲ *Prostanthera cuneata*
Prostanthera rotundifolia ▲

'**Alpine Gold**' has yellowish leaves while '**Fastigiata**' has a more upright habit than other types of prostanthera.
P. rotundifolia (mint bush) Bell-shaped purple flowers, about 1.5 cm (½ in) wide, cover this upright shrub in early spring. Each flower has an upper lip with 2 lobes and a hairy lower lip with 3 lobes. The shiny, mid green, almost rounded, aromatic leaves, about 1 cm (⅜ in) across, usually have notched edges. This is a very showy plant for a frost-free garden or for a greenhouse or conservatory. HEIGHT & SPREAD 2×1 m (6½×3 ft) after 5 years, ultimately 2 m (6½ ft) tall.

CULTIVATION Plant *P. cuneata* in spring in well-drained, acid or neutral, humus-rich soil. Choose a site in full sun. Grow *P. rotundifolia* in pots of peaty compost and place in partial shade. During periods of frost keep the pots in a cool greenhouse or conservatory in a partly shaded position.
PROPAGATION Sow seed under glass in early spring. Alternatively, take semi-ripe cuttings in autumn.
PRUNING No pruning is normally required, but *P. rotundifolia* can be cut back hard immediately after flowering to encourage bushy growth.
PESTS AND DISEASES Usually trouble free.

Protea
Proteaceae

Striking bracted flowerheads, that are often brightly coloured, appear on these half-hardy evergreen trees and shrubs in spring and summer. Native to Africa, these are among the trickiest plants to grow in Britain. Proteas can be tried outside in a sheltered spot in the West Country, the Channel Islands and south-west Scotland, but they are generally more successful in a greenhouse or conservatory. Standard potting composts are rarely successful as proteas demand neutral to acid soil with low phosphate and nitrogen levels.

RECOMMENDED SPECIES AND VARIETIES
P. compacta The roughly egg-shaped flowerheads, up to 10 cm (4 in) across, have

▲ *Protea compacta*

bright pink and white ribbon-like bracts in spring and early summer. This erect shrub has hard, somewhat leathery, elliptical leaves up to 12.5 cm (5 in) long. HEIGHT & SPREAD 3×2 m (10×6½ ft).
P. cynaroides (king protea) Goblet-like flowerheads roughly resembling a globe artichoke grow up to 20 cm (8 in) across in spring and early summer. They have many silky-haired, petal-like, pink to red bracts. The dark green oval leaves of this bushy,

▲ *Protea cynaroides*

rounded shrub are up to 15 cm (6 in). HEIGHT & SPREAD 1.5×1.5 m (5×5 ft).
P. eximia The rounded, oblong flowerheads, up to 15 cm (6 in) long, have numerous pink bracts which are often flushed with red. This erect shrub or, rarely, small tree is clothed with oval or elongated, heart-shaped, bluish green leaves, up to 10 cm (4 in) long, that are tinged purple. HEIGHT & SPREAD 3×2 m (10×6½ ft).

CULTIVATION Plant in large pots in a mixture of equal parts of peat and acid, or neutral, loam. Place under glass at a minimum temperature of 5°C (41°F) in the coolest and brightest position possible. In summer stand the pots outside. During the active growing season water regularly and feed with a liquid tomato feed diluted to half strength.
PROPAGATION Sow seed under glass in spring or take semi-ripe cuttings in summer.
PRUNING No regular pruning is necessary, but remove any weak or unwanted shoots.
PESTS AND DISEASES Usually trouble free.

Prunella
Self heal
Labiatae

Prunella grandiflora
'*Pink Loveliness*'

The pink to purple or white flowers of these creeping herbaceous perennials provide a colourful and long-lasting display in summer. Prunellas are excellent for ground cover at the front of a border, or for splashes of colour among shrubs or under trees. The flowers, which are tubular with an upright upper lip and a spreading lower lip, are

▲ *Prunella grandiflora*

▲ *Prunella grandiflora* 'White Loveliness'

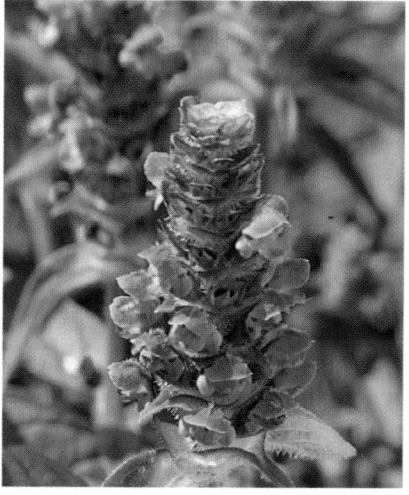

▲ *Prunella vulgaris*

long, form a spreading carpet. HEIGHT & SPREAD 30 cm × 1 m (1 × 3 ft).

P. × webbiana see *P. grandiflora*

CULTIVATION Plant in early spring in any garden soil in sun or partial shade. Avoid rich soils which may encourage leafiness.

PROPAGATION Divide plants in autumn or during spring.

PESTS AND DISEASES Usually trouble free.

Prunus
Rosaceae

Prunus avium 'Plena'

Dazzling displays of blossom enliven these well-loved trees in spring or summer. There are also species and varieties with good autumn leaf colour or attractive bark. Others are grown specifically for fruit, including almonds, apricots, plums, peaches and edible cherries. (See FRUIT p. 720.)

Ranging from pure white through pink to deep red, the profuse, five-petalled, cup-shaped flowers look particularly attractive in spring on bare branches. Some varieties bear semidouble or double flowers. Few are particularly fragrant. Unless stated otherwise, the leaves, 5–15 cm (2–6 in) long, are oval. Most have slightly serrated edges. This large genus is native mostly to temperate regions. All the recommended plants are frost-hardy, although their tolerance varies.

RECOMMENDED SPECIES AND VARIETIES

All the ornamental trees listed here are deciduous, except the cherry laurels, which are evergreen.

ORNAMENTAL ALMONDS

P. dulcis (common almond) Although it will produce almonds in Britain, this tree is grown mainly for its pink blossom in early to mid spring. The flowers, up to 5 cm (2 in) across, usually appear singly or in pairs. The fine-toothed leaves are lance-shaped. This tree is only moderately frost-hardy. HEIGHT & SPREAD 2.4 × 1.2 m (8 × 4 ft) after 10 years, ultimately 6 m (20 ft) tall.

'Roseoplena' has double pink flowers.

P. glandulosa (Chinese bush cherry) Abundant white or pink flowers, about 1.5 cm (½ in) across, appear singly or in pairs in mid spring. The pale green ovate leaves are about 6 cm (2½ in) long. This small rounded shrub prefers a sunny position. HEIGHT & SPREAD 1.5 × 1 m (5 × 3 ft) after 10 years and ultimately.

The cultivars produce an even better show of flowers than the species. 'Alba Plena'♀ has double white flowers in late spring, while 'Sinensis'♀ (syn. *P.* 'Rosea Plena') produces double pink flowers.

▲ *Prunus glandulosa* 'Alba Plena'

▲ *Prunus glandulosa* 'Sinensis'

P. tenella (dwarf Russian almond) Bright pink flowers, 2 cm (¾ in) across, wreath the branches in mid spring. The leaves are up to 9 cm (3½ in) long. This is the smallest prunus. It suckers freely and produces a good number of stems. HEIGHT & SPREAD 1 × 1 m (3 × 3 ft) after 10 years and ultimately.

'Fire Hill'♀ has pinkish red flowers.

P. triloba Pinkish white flowers, 2.5 cm (1 in) across, appear in profusion in early and mid spring on this small tree or large

grouped in whorls amid conspicuous bracts. The plants are hardy and easy to grow in any soil, including poor types.

RECOMMENDED SPECIES AND VARIETIES

P. grandiflora (syn. *P. × webbiana*) Deep violet flowers, about 2.5 cm (1 in) long, are borne in dense spikes up to 4 cm (1½ in) long. The oval leaves, up to 10 cm (4 in) long, may be shallowly toothed. HEIGHT & SPREAD 30 cm × 1 m (1 × 3 ft).

Several named varieties have flower spikes up to 6 cm (2½ in) long. 'Alba' has pure white flowers. 'Blue Loveliness' has deep lilac-blue flowers while 'Loveliness'♀ has pale violet-blue flowers. 'Pink Loveliness' has soft pink flowers while those of 'Rotkäppchen' (syn. *P.* 'Little Red Riding Hood') are deep carmine. The flowers of 'White Loveliness' are white.

P. incisa see *P. vulgaris*

P. laciniata The cream flowers, sometimes flushed pink, are about 2.5 cm (1 in) long. The deeply cut leaves are about 5 cm (2 in) long. HEIGHT & SPREAD 30 cm × 1 m (1 × 3 ft).

P. vulgaris (syn. *P. incisa*) This plant has deep purple flowers about 2.5 cm (1 in) long. Deeply cut leaves, up to 5 cm (2 in)

p
q

▲ *Prunus tenella*

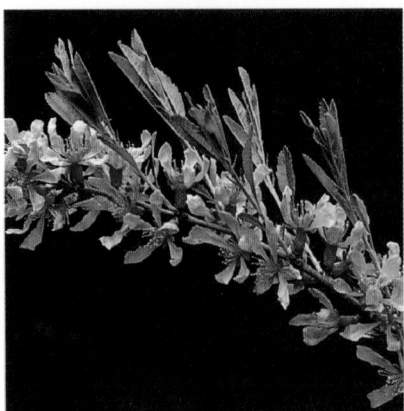

▲ *Prunus tenella* 'Fire Hill'

▲ *Prunus* 'Accolade'

shrub of spreading habit. HEIGHT & SPREAD 2.4×1.2m (8×4ft) after 10 years, ultimately 4m (13ft) tall.

'Multiplex'♀ has large double flowers in peachy pink.

ORNAMENTAL PEACHES

P. persica (peach) Pale rose-pink flowers, about 4cm (1½in) wide, appear in mid spring. The rather pointed leaves of this small tree or large multistemmed shrub are up to 15cm (6in) long. HEIGHT & SPREAD 2.4×1.2m (8×4ft) after 10 years, ultimately 3m (10ft) tall.

This species needs the protection of a wall or unheated greenhouse if grown for its fruit (see PEACHES AND NECTARINES p.727). However, several cultivars have been developed for their flowers. 'Iceberg' has pure white semidouble flowers and 'Klara Mayer' has deep pink semidouble flowers. Both grow to medium-sized shrubs, with flowers up to 4cm (1½in) across.

ORNAMENTAL PLUMS

P. × blireana♀ Double pink, slightly fragrant flowers, about 2.5cm (1in) across, appear in mid spring on this large shrub or small, spreading tree. The ovate leaves, 7.5cm (3in) long, emerge a rich coppery purple and take on a more greeny tinge later. HEIGHT & SPREAD 2.4×1.2m (8×4ft) after 10 years, ultimately 4m (13ft) tall.

P. cerasifera A profusion of small white flowers appear in early spring followed, when pollination is good, by yellow or red fruits, up to 3cm (1¼in) long. The ovate leaves are up to 6cm (2½in) long. This large shrub or small tree has a spreading habit. HEIGHT & SPREAD 3×2m (10×6½ft) after 10 years, ultimately 6m (20ft) tall.

Plants in the **Myrobalan Group** have dark bronze, red or purple leaves. 'Nigra'♀ has blackish purple leaves preceded by small pink flowers. The new leaves and stems of 'Pissardii' are flushed dark red at first and deepen to dark purple later. The flowers are whitish. Both cultivars make good hedging.

P. × cistena♀ White flowers, 4cm (1½in) across, appear in late spring. Glossy leaves, 6cm (2½in) long, emerge red and deepen to reddish brown. HEIGHT & SPREAD 2×1.5m

(6½×5ft) after 10 years and ultimately.

P. mume (Japanese apricot) Fragrant pink or white flowers, about 3cm (1¼in) wide, appear in late winter on this small upright tree. The broadly ovate leaves are 10cm (4in) long and tapering. HEIGHT & SPREAD 3×1.5m (10×5ft) after 10 years, ultimately 6m (20ft) tall.

'Beni-chidori' (syn. *P.* 'Beni-shidori') has deep pink, strongly scented, cup-shaped double flowers. The double white blooms of 'Omoi-no-mama' are also very fragrant. *P. spinosa* (blackthorn, sloe) Small, white, short-lived flowers appear in early spring followed in autumn by small blue-black fruits that can be used to make sloe gin. The leaves are up to 5cm (2in) long. This very hardy native shrub is armed with stout thorns. HEIGHT & SPREAD 3×2m (10×6½ft) after 10 years, ultimately 6m (20ft) tall.

'Plena' is double-flowered. 'Purpurea' has purple leaves which fade to pale green.

ORNAMENTAL CHERRIES

P. 'Accolade'♀ Semidouble rich pink flowers, up to 4cm (1½in) across, appear in clusters or singly in early spring. The dark green leaves, up to 10cm (4in) long, are deeply serrated. HEIGHT & SPREAD 2.4×1.2m (8×4ft) after 10 years, ultimately 6m (20ft) tall.

P. 'Amanogawa'♀ The late-spring flowers are semidouble, pale pink and slightly fragrant, borne on upright branches. The toothed leaves, 10cm (4in) long, tapered at the tips, are flushed greenish bronze at first.

▲ *Prunus cerasifera* 'Nigra'

They turn mid green later, then colour well in autumn. HEIGHT & SPREAD 2.4×1m (8×3ft) after 10 years, ultimately 4.5m (15ft) tall.

P. avium♀ (wild cherry) This vigorous upright tree bears profuse clusters of pendulous white flowers, about 2.5cm (1in) across, in mid spring. Small blackish red cherries sometimes appear in autumn. The leaves, 12.5cm (5in) long, are rather tapered at the tips and coarsely and irregularly toothed. They turn red and yellow in autumn. The bark is at first smooth but becomes fissured with age. HEIGHT & SPREAD 4×1.8m (13×6ft) after 10 years, ultimately 15m (50ft) tall.

'Plena'♀ blossoms even more freely in late spring.

P. cerasus (sour cherry) Dense clusters of white flowers, 2.5cm (1in) wide, in mid spring are often followed by black or red fruits in autumn. This plant makes a small bushy tree. HEIGHT & SPREAD 2.7×1.5m (9×5ft) after 10 years, ultimately 6m (20ft) tall.

The cultivars tend to produce bigger, more abundant flowers than the species. 'Rhexii' has profuse double white flowers up to 4cm (1½in) across.

P. 'Cheal's Weeping'
see *P.* 'Kiku-shidare-zakura'

P. 'Choshu-hizakura'♀ Deep pink flowers are produced in profusion, one to a stem, in mid spring. The young leaves emerge coppery red and take on a green tinge later. HEIGHT & SPREAD 2.4×1.2m (8×4ft) after 10 years, ultimately 6m (20ft) tall.

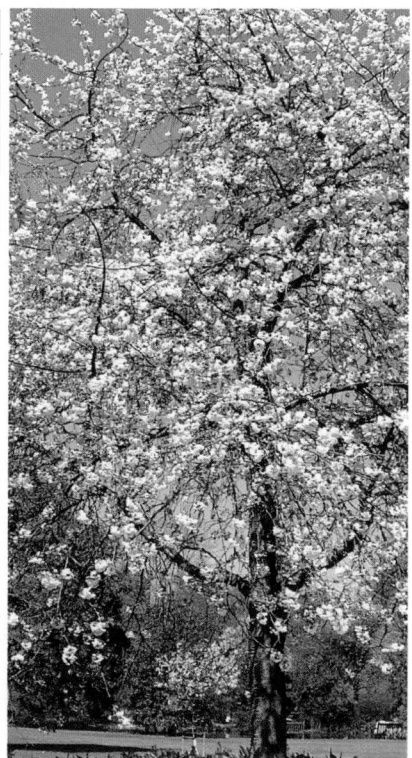
▲ *Prunus avium* 'Plena'

P. **'Hillieri Spire'** see *P.* 'Spire'

P. *incisa* (Fuji cherry) This cherry tree flowers profusely in early spring before the leaves appear. The flowers, 2 cm (¾ in) wide, are white, flushed with pink. The leaves, up to 6 cm (2½ in) long, are double-toothed. Reddish at first, the leaves become green later in the season and turn shades of red and orange in autumn. This large shrub or small tree has an upright habit at first but becomes rounded with age. HEIGHT & SPREAD 3×1.8 m (10×6 ft) after 10 years, ultimately 6 m (20 ft) tall.

The flowers of **'Praecox'**♀ are more pink and open as early as mid winter if the weather is mild.

P. **'Kanzan'**♀ Masses of large, double, deep pink flowers, 5 cm (2½ in) across, appear in late spring. The leaves are up to 12.5 cm (5 in) long with tapering tips. When young,

▲ *Prunus* 'Kanzan'

the leaves are flushed a coppery colour, but this is lost as the season progresses. In autumn they turn orange and yellow. The branches have an ascending habit, giving the tree a somewhat top-heavy appearance. HEIGHT & SPREAD 3×2 m (10×6½ ft) after 10 years, ultimately at least 6 m (20 ft) tall.

P. **'Kiku-shidare-zakura'**♀ (syn. *P.* 'Cheal's Weeping') The arching branches of this weeping tree are covered in deep pink, double flowers, 3 cm (1¼ in) across, in early spring. The leaves, about 7.5 cm (3 in) long, are flushed bronzy green at first and turn glossy green later. HEIGHT & SPREAD 2×1 m (6½×3 ft) after 10 years, ultimately 4 m (13 ft) tall.

P. **'Kursar'**♀ Clusters of 4 cm (1½ in) wide deep pink flowers appear in great profusion in mid to late spring. The leaves are up to 10 cm (4 in) long with pointed tips. When young they are bronzy in colour, turning green later in the summer. HEIGHT & SPREAD 2.4×1.2 m (8×4 ft) after 10 years, ultimately 5 m (16 ft) tall.

P. *maackii* (Manchurian cherry) Shiny bronzy gold bark is the outstanding feature of this hardy tree that becomes rounded with age. White flowers, 1.5 cm (½ in) wide, appear in spikes in mid spring. The ovate leaves are up to 10 cm (4 in) long. HEIGHT & SPREAD 3×1.5 m (10×5 ft) after 10 years, ultimately 9 m (30 ft) tall.

P. **'Okame'**♀ This decorative tree has abundant carmine coloured flowers, 2.5 cm (1 in) wide, in early spring. The leaves, 7.5 cm (3 in) long, turn red and orange in autumn. HEIGHT & SPREAD 2.4×1.2 m (8×4 ft) after 10 years, ultimately 5 m (16 ft) tall.

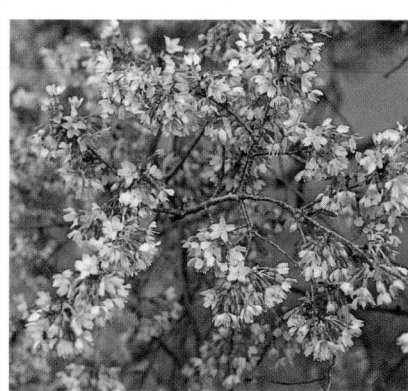
▲ *Prunus* 'Okame'

P. *padus* (bird cherry) Small, white, slightly almond-scented flowers appear on 15 cm (6 in) long spikes in late spring after the foliage has emerged. The leaves, which are up to 12.5 cm (5 in) long, are dark green above and bluish green beneath. HEIGHT & SPREAD 3×1.5 m (10×5 ft) after 10 years, ultimately 9 m (30 ft) tall.

The shoots of **'Colorata'**♀ are purple-brown and the leaves are at first coppery purple, fading to a dull green with purple veins. The flowers are pale pink. **'Watereri'**♀ has the same colour flowers as

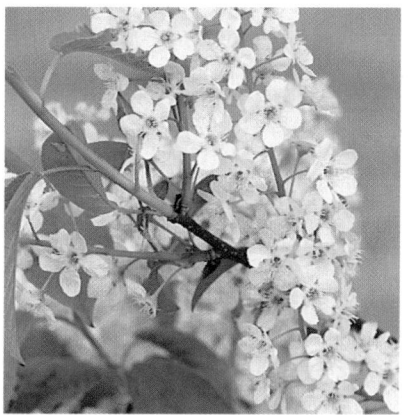
▲ *Prunus padus*

the species on spikes up to 20 cm (8 in) long.

P. **'Pandora'**♀ Ascending branches are covered in pale pink flowers, up to 2.5 cm (1 in) across, in early to mid spring. The leaves are up to 7.5 cm (3 in) long with tapering tips. Bronzy green as they emerge, they turn shades of red and yellow in autumn. HEIGHT & SPREAD 2.4×1.2 m (8×4 ft) after 10 years, ultimately 6 m (20 ft) tall.

P. *pendula* The weeping habit of this tree makes it look like the shape of an umbrella. Pale pink flowers, up to 1.5 cm (½ in) wide, appear in profusion in late spring. The leaves are up to 7.5 cm (3 in) wide. If a grafted plant, it will not grow much taller than the trunk. HEIGHT & SPREAD 2.4×1.8 m (8×6 ft) after 10 years, ultimately 4 m (13 ft).

P. **'Pink Perfection'**♀ Abundant double flowers, 4 cm (1½ in) wide, open deep pink but fade to white with age. The leaves, 10 cm (4 in) long and rather pointed, emerge pale bronze and gradually become green. The ascending branches give this tree a vase-shaped appearance. HEIGHT & SPREAD 2.7×1.8 m (9×6 ft) after 10 years, ultimately 6 m (20 ft) tall.

P. **'Pink Shell'**♀ The slender branches give this tree a delicate, slightly pendulous appearance, especially when it is in flower. The pale pink flowers, 2.5 cm (1 in) across, complement the pale green of the new foliage. The leaves, up to 11 cm (4¼ in) long, become darker green later. HEIGHT & SPREAD 2.4×1.5 m (8×5 ft) after 10 years, ultimately 5 m (16 ft) tall.

P. *pumila* ssp. *depressa* Small white flowers appear in abundance before the leaves emerge. Greyish green above and bluish white beneath, the leaves turn various shades of red in autumn. This small shrub makes good ground cover. HEIGHT & SPREAD 15 cm×1 m (6×36 in) after 10 years, and ultimately.

P. *sargentii*♀ (Sargent's cherry) Pink flowers, 4 cm (1½ in) across, are freely borne in mid spring. The pointed leaves, about 10 cm (4 in) long, emerge bronzy green before turning plain green. In autumn, the leaves give a magnificent display of crimson and orange. The bark of this spreading tree

p
q

▲ *Prunus 'Pink Shell'*

p
q

is chestnut-brown. HEIGHT & SPREAD 3×1.8m (10×6ft) after 10 years, ultimately 15m (50ft) tall.

P. serrula♀ This tree's outstanding feature is its shiny red-brown bark which peels off in strips that appear golden when they catch the light. The small white flowers are insignificant. The dull green leaves are narrowly lance-shaped and up to 10cm (4in) long. HEIGHT & SPREAD 2.4×1.2m (8×4ft) after 10 years, ultimately 5m (16ft) tall.

P. 'Shirofugen'♀ The abundant double flowers, 4cm (1½in) across, emerge white but turn purplish pink with age. This is one of the latest cherries to blossom and the flowers may not appear until early summer. The leaves are up to 9cm (3½in) long with pointed tips. Emerging an attractive bronze

▲ *Prunus serrula*

which persists into summer, the leaves turn mid green in late summer. HEIGHT & SPREAD 2.7×2m (9×6½ft) after 10 years, ultimately 10m (33ft) tall.

P. 'Shirotae'♀ Semidouble pure white flowers, up to 5cm (2in) across, appear in abundance in mid spring. The large pale green leaves have long thread-like ends to their teeth, giving them a very feathery appearance. This small tree has a spreading, pendulous habit, and is often broader than it is tall. HEIGHT & SPREAD 1.8×1.8m (6×6ft) after 10 years, ultimately 4m (13ft) tall.

P. 'Shogetsu'♀ An abundance of white semidouble flowers, 5cm (2in) across, with frilled edges are borne during late spring. The leaves, which have attractive thread-like points to their teeth, emerge brown-green and turn pale green as they age. This small tree with spreading branches is often broader than it is tall. HEIGHT & SPREAD 2.4×1.8m (8×6ft) after 10 years, ultimately 6m (20ft) tall.

P. 'Spire'♀ (syn. *P.* 'Hillieri Spire') Pale pink flowers, 2.5cm (1in) across, are freely borne in mid spring. These are followed by a wonderful display of autumn tints as the pointed leaves, 9cm (3½in) long, turn orange and red. The tree's upright habit gives it a vase-like appearance. HEIGHT & SPREAD 2.7×1m (9×3ft) after 10 years, ultimately 10m (33ft) tall.

P. x subhirtella Pale pink flowers, about 2cm (¾in) across, appear before the pale green leaves in early or mid spring. The double-toothed leaves are 7.5cm (3in) long and taper to a point. This small upright tree and its cultivars provide a good display of autumn colour. HEIGHT & SPREAD 2.7×1.8m (9×6ft) after 10 years, ultimately 9m (30ft) tall.

'Autumnalis Rosea'♀ has plentiful, small, pale pink flowers in late winter. The small white flowers of **'Autumnalis'**♀ appear in early winter. **'Fukubana'**♀ has abundant deep pink flowers in mid spring.

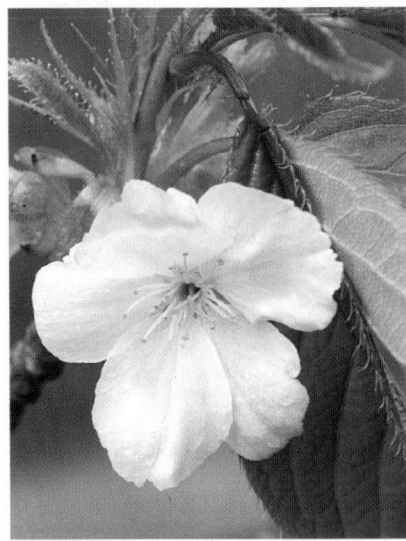

▲ *Prunus 'Taihaku'*

P. 'Taihaku'♀ (great white cherry) The large white flowers, 6cm (2½in) across, are produced in great clusters during mid spring. They provide an attractive contrast to the new foliage which emerges coppery green. The leaves, which gradually become plain mid green, are 15cm (6in) long and taper with thread-like ends to the serrated edges. This small tree has a spreading habit and is often as broad as it is tall. HEIGHT & SPREAD 2.7×1.5m (9×5ft) after 10 years, ultimately 10m (33ft) tall.

P. 'Ukon'♀ The abundant, semidouble, white flowers, 4cm (1½in) across, open with a green tinge that is lost as the season progresses. The leaves, 10cm (4in) long, are bronzy green when they emerge but mature to dark green. In autumn the leaves give an attractive display of reds and purples. HEIGHT & SPREAD 2.4×1.2m (8×4ft) after 10 years, ultimately 7m (23ft) tall.

▲ *Prunus 'Ukon' in autumn*

P. x verecunda (Korean hill cherry) White or pink flowers, 2.5cm (1in) across, appear in mid or late spring. The leaves emerge green-bronze, turn mid green later in the season and finally become red in autumn. HEIGHT & SPREAD 2.4×1.2m (8×4ft) after 10 years, ultimately 5m (16ft) tall.

P. virginiana 'Shubert' Pendulous spikes of white flowers, 1cm (⅜in) across, are produced in mid spring. The broad leaves, 10cm (4in) long, are glossy green at first but quickly change to deep purple-red. This large shrub or small tree has a conical habit. HEIGHT & SPREAD 2.4×1.2m (8×4ft) after 10 years, ultimately 4m (13ft) tall.

P. x yedoensis♀ A profusion of slightly almond-scented flowers, 2cm (¾in) across, is carried on arching branches in early spring. At first the flowers are flushed with pink but they turn pure white soon after opening. The double-toothed leaves, 11cm (4¼in) long, give a good display of autumn colour. HEIGHT & SPREAD 3×2.4m (10×8ft) after 10 years, ultimately 12m (40ft) tall.

The weeping branches of 'Shidare-Yoshino', covered in pink blossom in early spring, often brush the ground.

ORNAMENTAL CHERRY LAURELS

P. laurocerasus (common or cherry laurel) The glossy mid green leaves of this vigorous large shrub or multistemmed small tree are up to 20 cm (8 in) long. White flowers, 1 cm (⅜ in) across, appear on upright spikes in mid spring followed by black fruits in early autumn. The berries, up 2 cm (¾ in) long, are often produced in great profusion. This species makes an excellent screen or windbreak. HEIGHT & SPREAD 3×2 m (10×6½ft) after 10 years, ultimately 6 m (20 ft) tall.

'Camelliifolia', which reaches only 4 m (13 ft) tall, has leaves with a curled appearance. 'Castlewellan' (syn. *P.* 'Marbled White') bears mid green leaves with grey-green patches and white marbling. It is a slow-growing plant which makes a dense shrub of rounded habit. The leaves of 'Otto Luyken' are deep glossy green and up to 10 cm (4 in) long. This dense shrub is about

▲ *Prunus laurocerasus* 'Otto Luyken'

1 m (3 ft) tall and broad. It is a good plant for a border of small shrubs or for hedging. The erect stems are covered in spikes of small white flowers in mid spring. 'Zabeliana' makes good ground cover. It often spreads to 3 m (10 ft) but may grow only 1 m (3 ft) tall. It flowers freely in late spring. The shiny narrow leaves are 11 cm (4¼ in) long. *P. lusitanica* (Portugal laurel) Glossy green ovate to elliptic leaves, about 12 cm (4¾ in) long, appear on attractive red stalks. Cup-shaped, fragrant white flowers, 1.5 cm (½ in) wide, are borne in long, ascending spikes in early to mid summer. Small red fruits, ripening to black, may follow. A small, multistemmed tree of rounded habit, this is good for windbreaks and hedging. It grows better on shallow chalk soils than does *P. laurocerasus*. HEIGHT & SPREAD 2.7×2 m (9×6½ft) after 10 years, ultimately 6 m (20 ft) tall.

The leaves of ssp. *azorica* are slightly larger than those of the species. They have a reddish tinge when young but turn dark green with age. It makes a tree about 4 m (13 ft) tall.

'Variegata' has white margins to its leaves. This plant is really a large shrub rather than a tree.

CULTIVATION Plant in moisture-retentive but well-drained fertile soil between late autumn and mid spring, avoiding frosty periods. Most prunus do best in a reasonably sunny position, but *P. laurocerasus*, which will not thrive on chalky soils, will be fine in shade.

PROPAGATION Sow the seed of species in a gritty compost in a coldframe in early spring. Alternatively, take greenwood cuttings of deciduous species in early summer and semi-ripe cuttings of evergreens in mid summer. Buy grafted cultivars.

PRUNING The deciduous trees rarely need pruning. However, they may be trimmed in mid summer to maintain their shape and size. When used as hedging, *P. lusitanica* and *P. laurocerasus* and their cultivars may be pruned to shape at any time, although late spring or early summer is best.

PESTS AND DISEASES Usually pest free, but susceptible to bacterial canker, silver leaf, wither tip and spur blight.

Pseudofumaria see *Corydalis*

Pseudolarix
Chinese golden larch
Pinaceae

Pseudolarix amabilis

These slow-growing but breathtakingly colourful trees from China come into their own in autumn, when the foliage steadily turns orange. Pseudolarix are hardy deciduous larches with beautiful cones that are pale green when they first appear and turn a

▼ *Pseudolarix amabilis*

yellowy orange later. Chinese golden larches make superb trees for any garden with acid soil. There is just one species in this genus.

Pseudolarix amabilis This conical tree has downward curving needles, 6 cm (2½ in) long, fanning out from a central bud. Male and female flowers appear together on the same tree in spring, long before the needles appear. The green female flowers look like tiny broccoli spears, while the male flowers are small and yellow about the size of a pea. Upright, stalkless cones, up to 3 cm (1¼ in) long, with fleshy scales appear in late autumn. The flowers and cones, however, are not produced until the tree is at least 40 years old. HEIGHT & SPREAD 2×1.5 m (6½×5ft) after 20 years, ultimately 12 m (40 ft) tall.

CULTIVATION Plant in full sun or partial shade between mid autumn and early spring in moist but well-drained acid soil.

PROPAGATION Raising pseudolarix is difficult, and it is best to buy a young plant from a specialist nursery.

PRUNING Remove badly shaped branches in winter.

PESTS AND DISEASES Usually trouble free.

Pseudopanax
Araliaceae

The foliage of these hardy or half-hardy evergreen shrubs and trees is striking for its shapes and colours. The summer flowers are small, greenish and of no decorative merit. Male and female flowers are usually borne on separate plants and both need to be grown if the small rounded fruit are to appear. Native to Chile, New Zealand and Tasmania, some plants in the genus are used as conservatory plants. However, most will grow outdoors at the base of a wall with a south or west-facing aspect, provided they have a sunny position and free-draining soil.

RECOMMENDED SPECIES AND VARIETIES

P. Adiantifolius Group 'Cyril Watson' Tough, leathery, 3-lobed, spreading leaves,

▼ *Pseudopanax* Adiantifolius Group 'Cyril Watson'

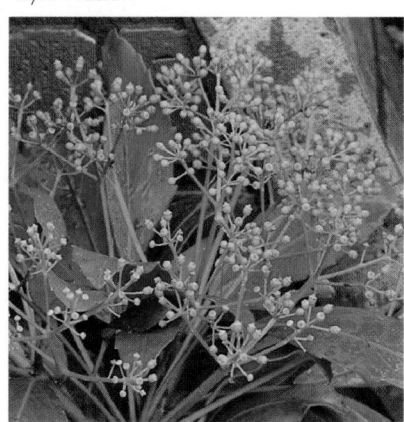

p
q

up to 25 cm (10 in) long, are produced on this compact multistemmed shrub. They are mid green with pale conspicuous veins. This plant is usually grown in a pot or border in a greenhouse or conservatory and can only be grown outdoors in mild areas of Britain. HEIGHT & SPREAD 1.5×1 m (5×3 ft) after 5 years, also the ultimate size.

P. lessonii (houpara) The bright green leaves are divided into 3-5, coarsely toothed, lance-shaped leaflets, up to 10 cm (4 in) long. This plant can be grown both as a conservatory plant and in a sheltered spot outdoors. A small tree or large shrub, it will reach only about half its size if confined to a pot. HEIGHT & SPREAD 5×3 m (16×10 ft) after 5 years, also the ultimate size.

Leaves variegated with gold distinguish **'Gold Splash'**♀, while **'Purpureus'** has glossy bronze-green foliage in summer, turning purplish bronze in winter.

▲ *Pseudopanax lessonii* 'Gold Splash'

CULTIVATION Plant outdoors in a sheltered spot, preferably in full sun, in well-drained soil. Alternatively, grow in pots of free-draining potting compost, such as John Innes No.3, in a cool greenhouse or conservatory. Water freely during summer and sparingly in winter. Apply a slow-release fertiliser in spring.
PROPAGATION Take semi-ripe cuttings in summer.
PRUNING Remove any wayward shoots as they appear.
PESTS AND DISEASES Usually trouble free.

Pseudosasa see BAMBOOS p.78

Pseudotsuga
Pinaceae

Pseudotsuga menziesii

Given the right spot, these stately evergreen conifers with a broadly conical habit make handsome specimen trees. Only one of the four species is grown in Britain. *Pseudotsuga menziesii*, native to western N America, is a tall forest tree which grows quickly, so is suitable only for the largest gardens. However, the cultivars are smaller. The trees have a noticeable aroma of caramel in strong afternoon sunshine.

RECOMMENDED SPECIES AND VARIETIES
P. menziesii♀ (Douglas fir) The soft, dense, fragrant foliage is made up of needles, 2.5 cm (1 in) long, that are green above with 2 white bands underneath. Abundant cones, up to 10 cm (4 in) long, with protruding seed bracts, appear after about 10 years. HEIGHT & SPREAD 7×1.5 m (23×5 ft) after 20 years, ultimately 60 m (200 ft) tall.

'Fletcheri' will suit any garden with moist acid soil. As it grows only 2 m (6½ ft) tall, it is also suitable for small gardens. This is a flat-topped, rounded, bushy shrub with sweet-smelling, blue-green leaves.

The most hardy tree is var. *glauca* (blue Douglas fir), a narrow, conical variety with striking blue foliage. The needles grow to 5 cm (2 in) and the cones are up to 7 cm (2¾ in) long. This tree, which grows up to 40 m (130 ft) tall, does not tolerate lime.

'Glauca Pendula'♀ is a small, weeping tree with elegant silver-blue foliage that looks superb in winter and ultimately grows 10 m (33 ft) tall.
CULTIVATION Grow in moist but well-drained soil on a site in morning shade and afternoon sun to prevent frost damage to early new growth.
PROPAGATION Sow the seed of species in spring outdoors. Cultivars, which are nor-

▲ *Pseudotsuga menziesii* 'Glauca Pendula'

mally grafted in late winter, are best bought ready grafted from a reputable nursery.
PRUNING Remove any broken branches right back to the main stem. If young plants have 2 leading shoots, remove one at the base. The remaining shoot will then straighten up quickly, even if it was quite crooked at first.
PESTS AND DISEASES Usually trouble free.

Psylliostachys
Plumbaginaceae

Dainty summer flowers dot the slender spikes of these annuals. The plants are suitable for drying as everlasting flowers. Well-drained soil and a position in a sunny border meet their growing requirements. They are particularly suitable for growing in the salt-laden air of coastal areas.

RECOMMENDED SPECIES AND VARIETIES
P. suworowii (syn. *Limonium suworowii*, *Statice suworowii*) (pink poker, rat's tail statice) Tiny, tubular, pink to purple flowers appear from mid to late summer on erect spikes, up to 30 cm (12 in) long, that often curl at the top. The dull green lance-shaped leaves are up to 15 cm (6 in) long. This upright plant, native to W and central Asia, is half-hardy. HEIGHT & SPREAD 45×30 cm (18×12 in).
CULTIVATION Plant in well-drained soil once the risk of frost has passed. Choose a position in full sun. Weed and water regularly. Flower spikes intended for drying are best harvested when the tiny blossoms first open.
PROPAGATION Sow seeds in early spring in a propagator at 21°C (70°F) and plant outside in late spring to early summer.
PESTS AND DISEASES Aphids are often troublesome on young plants. Botrytis and powdery mildew sometimes affect plants establishing themselves outdoors.

▲ *Psylliostachys suworowii*

Ptelea
Rutaceae

Ptelea trifoliata

Just one species of this N American genus of deciduous shrubs or small trees is grown in British gardens. *Ptelea trifoliata* is a spreading shrub with aromatic leaves and winged fruit. Although hardy, it needs a sheltered position to thrive.

RECOMMENDED SPECIES AND VARIETIES
P. trifoliata♀ (hop tree) The yellowish green leaves are made up of 3-5, pointed oval leaflets, 10 cm (4 in) long. They are clammy to the touch because of the secretions from their glands. Rounded clusters of fragrant, greenish white, star-shaped flowers, each 1 cm (⅜ in) long, bloom in early summer and are followed by pale, lime-green fruits in late summer. Each fruit, about 2.5 cm (1 in) across, has 2 flattened seeds surrounded by an almost circular wing. The seeds are fertile in mid summer after warm summers. This large wide-spreading shrub has smooth red-brown stems. HEIGHT & SPREAD 1.5 × 1.5 m (5 × 5 ft) after 5 years, ultimately 4 m (13 ft) tall.

▲ *Ptelea trifoliata*

▲ *Ptelea trifoliata* 'Aurea'

'Aurea'♀ has soft yellow foliage that contrasts with the lime-green fruits.
CULTIVATION Plant in autumn or spring in any moist fertile soil, choosing a sheltered site in semi-shade.
PROPAGATION Sow the seed of species under glass as soon as it is ripe in mid to late autumn. Alternatively, take softwood cuttings from species and cultivars.
PRUNING Cut back lightly in early to mid spring to control unruly specimens.
PESTS AND DISEASES Usually trouble free.

Pterocarya
Wing-nut tree
Juglandaceae

Where there is light and space enough in the garden, these big, fast-growing deciduous trees offer a show of attractive feathery foliage. They develop a short thick trunk and a mass of heavy, spreading branches. Insignificant, greenish yellow, male and female flowers appear in drooping catkins in early summer on the previous year's growth. The pale green winged fruits follow in early autumn. The trees are hardy, but need a sheltered sunny site to thrive.

RECOMMENDED SPECIES AND VARIETIES
P. fraxinifolia♀ (Caucasian wing-nut) The glossy, bright green, pinnate leaves, 30-60 cm (1-2 ft) long, turn yellow in autumn. Each has 7-27, pointed, oblong leaflets up to 12 cm (4¾ in) long. The winged nuts dangle in distinctive pendulous strings up to 40 cm (16 in) long. Native to Iran and the Caucasus. HEIGHT & SPREAD 12 × 8 m (40 × 26 ft) after 20 years, ultimately 30 m (100 ft) tall.

▲ *Pterocarya fraxinifolia*

P. stenoptera (Chinese wing-nut) The pinnate leaves are 20-40 cm (8-16 in) long with 11-23 rounded oblong leaflets, each up to 10 cm (4 in) long. A glossy bright green in summer, the leaflets turn yellow in autumn. The winged nuts are borne in strings

▲ *Pterocarya stenoptera*

20-30 cm (8-12 in) long. Native to China. HEIGHT & SPREAD 12 × 8 m (40 × 26 ft) after 20 years, ultimately 30 m (100 ft) tall.
CULTIVATION Plant in spring in any moist but well-drained rich soil. Choose a site in full sun with shelter from the wind. Remove suckers as soon as they appear.
PROPAGATION Sow seed under glass in spring. Alternatively, either layer plants or take semi-ripe cuttings in late summer.
PESTS AND DISEASES Usually trouble free.

Pterocephalus
Dipsacaceae

In summer the pinkish purple flowers of these mat-forming plants bring colour to a rock garden. In its native Mediterranean and Asia, this genus includes annuals and perennials, but just one species of semi-evergreen plants is usually grown in British gardens.

RECOMMENDED SPECIES AND VARIETIES
P. perennis Pale pinkish purple flowers are held in rounded clusters, up to 4 cm (1½ in) across. The oval leaves are 4 cm (1½ in) long and covered with white downy hairs. HEIGHT & SPREAD 12 × 25 cm (4¾ × 10 in).
The leaves of ssp. *belldifolius* are green.
CULTIVATION Plant in spring in well-drained soil in a rock garden or sunny bed.
PROPAGATION Sow ripe seed in a cold-frame. Alternatively take softwood cuttings in early summer.
PESTS AND DISEASES Usually trouble free.

p
q

Pterostyrax
Styracaceae

Pterostyrax hispida

Between late spring and mid summer, fragrant five-lobed white flowers droop in abundant clusters from the gracefully spreading branches of these deciduous trees from E Asia. They have handsome, mid green, oval leaves that are edged with fine bristly teeth. Pterostyrax are quite hardy, and will grow anywhere except in shallow, chalky soils.

RECOMMENDED SPECIES

P. corymbosa♀ In late spring and early summer, small flowers in pendulous branched clusters, 8–15 cm (3¼–6 in) long, open beneath the branches. These are followed in late summer by downy, spindle-shaped fruits with 5 longitudinal ribs. The leaves are 7.5–18 cm (3–7 in) long. HEIGHT & SPREAD 3×3 m (10×10 ft) after 10 years, ultimately 8.5 m (28 ft).

⚠ *Pterostyrax hispida*

P. hispida♀ (epaulette tree) Drooping flower clusters, up to 23 cm (9 in) long, hang beneath the branches in early and mid summer. The spindle-shaped fruits are densely covered in stiff pale brown hairs. The leaves are 7.5–20 cm (3–8 in) long. HEIGHT & SPREAD 3×3 m (10×10 ft) after 10 years, ultimately 12 m (40 ft) tall.

CULTIVATION Plant in autumn or early spring in deep, fertile loamy soil choosing a position in full sun or part shade.

PROPAGATION Sow seed under glass in early spring or take softwood or semi-ripe cuttings in summer.

PRUNING Not usually required.

PESTS AND DISEASES Usually trouble free.

Pulmonaria
Lungwort
Boraginaceae

Pulmonaria officinalis

Distinctive foliage and long-lasting spring flowers make these low-growing, hardy herbaceous perennials ideal as ground cover. They are particularly useful in shady garden areas. The leaves, 15–30 cm (6–12 in) long, are deep green or spotted or marbled with silvery white and are covered in fine bristles. The funnel-shaped flowers, to 2 cm (¾ in) long with spreading lobes, appear from early to late spring. Colours range through shades of blue, pink to purple, and white. The plants grow best in humus-rich moist soil, in partial or full shade. Native to Europe and Asia.

RECOMMENDED SPECIES AND VARIETIES

P. angustifolia♀ Very deep blue flowers are borne in dense heads among long, narrow, unspotted dark green leaves. HEIGHT & SPREAD 30×45 cm (1×1½ ft).

The flowers of ssp. *azurea* are deeper blue and the plant is a little taller. 'Munstead Blue' has reddish violet flowers turning to rich blue. 'Rubra' see *P. rubra*

P. 'Beth's Blue' Loose heads of deep blue flowers open from red buds. The leaves are mid green with white streaks and blotches. HEIGHT & SPREAD 30×45 cm (1×1½ ft).

P. 'Blue Ensign' Dark violet-blue flowers in compact heads are carried among narrow, unmarked, dark green leaves. HEIGHT & SPREAD 30×45 cm (1×1½ ft).

P. 'Glacier' Pale pink flowers eventually turn to white on this well-spreading plant. Long leaves are sparsely spotted with paler green. HEIGHT & SPREAD 30×45 cm (1×1½ ft).

P. 'Lewis Palmer'♀ (syn. *P.* 'Highdown') Dark blue flowers are held in large dense heads. The long, narrow, dark green leaves are heavily blotched with greenish white. HEIGHT & SPREAD 30×45 cm (1×1½ ft).

P. longifolia A densely clump-forming plant with long narrow leaves that are dark green and vividly spotted with white. The bright blue flowers open from dark buds. HEIGHT & SPREAD 30×45 cm (1×1½ ft).

'Bertram Anderson' has especially well-marked leaves and brightly coloured flowers. It is more compact.

P. 'Mawson's Blue' Deep blue flowers are borne among narrow dark green leaves. A low-growing plant, it spreads slowly. HEIGHT & SPREAD 30×45 cm (1×1½ ft).

P. mollis Large violet-blue flowers are carried in dense heads. The large, downy,

unspotted leaves are deep green. HEIGHT & SPREAD 45×60 cm (1½×2 ft).

P. 'Mournful Purple' Rich purple flowers are borne in drooping clusters. The dark green leaves are blotched with pale green. HEIGHT & SPREAD 30×45 cm (1×1½ ft).

P. officinalis The flowers, borne in compact clusters, are deep pink in bud, then pink and finally violet-blue when mature. Heart-shaped leaves are spotted pale green or white. HEIGHT & SPREAD 30×45 cm (1×1½ ft).

'Bowles' Blue' has pale blue flowers early in the season and leaves that are moderately marked with white and pale green. The flowers of **Cambridge Blue Group** are light blue and the leaves are variably spotted with silver. 'Sissinghurst White'♀ is a very vigorous plant with flowers that open white from pale pink buds. The leaves are spotted with silver. For ssp. *rubra* see *P. rubra*. 'White Wings' has white flowers with pink eyes. It is a more compact plant with sparsely pale-spotted leaves.

P. 'Roy Davidson' The long, narrow leaves of this compact plant are heavily spotted with white. Pale blue to violet flowers are borne in dense heads. HEIGHT & SPREAD 30×45 cm (1×1½ ft).

P. rubra♀ (syn. *P. angustifolia* 'Rubra', *P. officinalis* ssp. *rubra*) The pinkish red flowers of this vigorous, ground-covering plant are carried in large open heads that bloom very early and keep their colour unchanged. The large, pale green leaves are unspotted and very hairy. HEIGHT & SPREAD 45 cm×1 m (1½×3 ft).

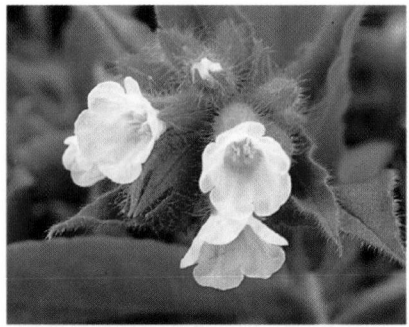

⚠ *Pulmonaria rubra* var. *albocorollata*

The leaves of the less vigorous var. *albocorollata* (syn. var. *alba*) are paler and the small white flowers are carried on shorter stems. 'Barfield Pink' has white and pink-striped flowers and is less vigorous and floriferous. 'Bowles' Red' has faintly spotted leaves and the flowers are orangey. The grey-green leaves of 'David Ward' have cream edges and the flowers are pale coral. The large red flowers of the vigorous 'Redstart' are carried on upright stems among soft green leaves.

P. saccharata (syn. 'Picta') The leaves of this strong-growing clump-former have variable white spots and blotches, sometimes almost completely covering the whole leaf. The flowers are pink in bud, changing to a

⚘ *Pulmonaria saccharata* Argentea Group

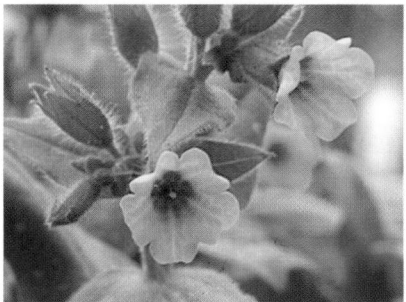

⚘ *Pulmonaria saccharata* 'Dora Bielefeld'

⚘ *Pulmonaria saccharata* 'Mrs Moon'

pale reddish violet. HEIGHT & SPREAD 30×60 cm (1×2 ft).

'Alba' has paler leaf spots, and white flowers from pink buds. The leaves of Argentea Group♀ are silvery white and narrow with mottled green edges. The strong-growing 'Dora Bielefeld' is one of the best varieties for flower colour. Its blooms open clear pink and darken to violet among pale, sparsely spotted leaves. 'Frühlingshimmel' has brightly spotted leaves and pale blue flowers with a darker eye. The leaves of 'Leopard' are dark green, spotted and blotched with white. The reddish pink flowers are borne on upright stems. 'Mrs Moon' has leaves spotted pale green, and pink to violet flowers. 'Pink Dawn' is a compact plant with wavy-edged leaves blotched with pale whitish green. The large flowers are deep pink becoming violet.

P. vallarsae Violet flowers are borne amid wavy-edged, blotched, downy leaves. HEIGHT & SPREAD 25×60 cm (10×24 in).

'Margery Fish'♀ has whitish grey leaves with green spotted margins. The reddish pink flowers mature to violet.

CULTIVATION Plant from autumn to spring in any reasonably moist, humus-rich soil in partial or even full shade.

PROPAGATION Divide in late autumn.

PESTS AND DISEASES Liable to attack by slugs and snails, and some varieties may develop powdery mildew during summer.

Pulsatilla
Pasqueflower
Ranunculaceae

Pasqueflowers are some of the loveliest of all alpine plants. Their foliage is feathery and the large flowers are covered with soft down on the outside. The flowers are followed by long-lasting, decorative, silky seedheads. These clump-forming, hardy evergreen or herbaceous perennials grow best in the well-drained situation of a rock garden or raised bed, in full sun and well away from more vigorous and invasive rock plants. They can also be grown in pots in an unheated greenhouse or alpine house.

The solitary bell or goblet-shaped flowers vary from nodding to erect. Colours may be white or shades of yellow, pink, lavender, purple or red. There are usually six petal-like sepals which surround a boss of conspicuous golden stamens. The plants recommended below are herbaceous tuft-forming perennials except for the evergreen *Pulsatilla vernalis*. Height is given for plants in flower; most increase in height slightly when in fruit.

RECOMMENDED SPECIES AND VARIETIES

P. alpina (alpine pasqueflower) Erect bowl to saucer-shaped flowers, up to 6 cm (2½ in) across, are white with a bluish or lilac flush on the outside. They are borne from late spring to early summer among mid green, ferny leaves covered with silky hairs. The plant is slow to flower from seed, taking 8 or more years to build up to a good flowering clump. Native to central and S Europe. HEIGHT & SPREAD 45×45 cm (18×18 in).

The bell-shaped flowers of ssp. *apiifolia*♀ (syn. ssp. *sulphurea*, syn. *Anemone sulphurea*) are primrose yellow.

⚘ *Pulsatilla alpina* ssp. *apiifolia*

P. halleri♀ Bell-shaped flowers, up to 9 cm (3½ in) across, are lavender to violet-purple and appear in spring before the leaves unfurl. The ferny leaves are densely silky. Native to central and E Europe. HEIGHT & SPREAD 20×20 cm (8×8 in).

The flowers of ssp. *slavica*♀ are violet and the leaves are less finely divided.

P. pratensis Nodding bell-shaped flowers, 3–4 cm (1¼–1½ in) long, are dark purple to reddish purple and occasionally greenish yellow. They are borne in late spring and

⚘ *Pulsatilla halleri* ssp. *slavica*

early summer above finely divided silky leaves. HEIGHT & SPREAD 15×15 cm (6×6 in).

P. vernalis♀ (syn. *Anemone vernalis*) (spring pasqueflower) Bell-shaped flowers up to 6 cm (2½ in) across, are white flushed with blue or lilac outside. The erect to semi-erect flowers appear in early to mid spring above leathery, deep green, divided leaves. An evergreen, it is excellent for an alpine house or unheated greenhouse. Outdoors, it needs protection from winter wet. Native to Europe and Siberia. HEIGHT & SPREAD 10×20 cm (4×8 in).

P. vulgaris♀ (syn. *Anemone pulsatilla*) (common pasqueflower) Slightly nodding, bell-shaped flowers borne in spring are up to 9 cm (3½ in) across and are pale to dark purple, red or white. The pale green leaves are very finely cut. Native to England, France and central Europe. HEIGHT & SPREAD 20×20 cm (8×8 in).

The flowers of ssp. *alba*♀ are white. 'Barton's Pink' has flowers of delicate rose. 'Eva Constance' has deep reddish black flowers. 'Papageno' has semidouble, cut-petal flowers ranging from white to pink, lavender and red shades. 'Rode Klokke' ('Rote Glocke') has deep red flowers. The flowers of var. *rubra* are in shades of red.

CULTIVATION Plant in spring or autumn in gritty well-drained neutral to chalky soil in

⚘ *Pulsatilla vulgaris*

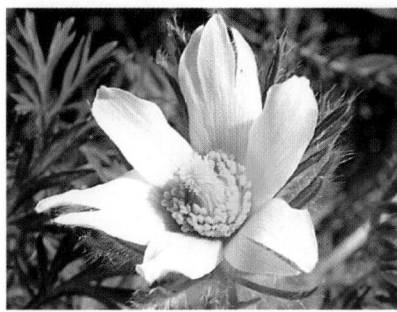

⚘ *Pulsatilla vulgaris* ssp. *alba*

p
q

full sun, although *P. alpina* ssp. *apiifolia* prefers acid soil. Remove dead leaves on herbaceous species in autumn. Avoid disturbance once plants are established.

PROPAGATION Sow seed when ripe or in autumn. Take root cuttings in winter or early spring.

PESTS AND DISEASES Usually trouble free.

Pumpkin see p.741

Punica
Pomegranate
Lythraceae

Only one variety of this genus is commonly grown in Britain, *Punica granatum* var. *nana*, a summer-flowering, tender, semi-evergreen shrub. Native to western Asia, it can be grown in a greenhouse, conservatory or very sunny, warm room, where it makes a good specimen plant. Its fruits rarely ripen. Pot-grown plants can be moved outside once the danger of frost has passed.

RECOMMENDED VARIETY

P. granatum var. *nana* (dwarf pomegranate) Bright orangey scarlet flowers, up to 4 cm (1½ in) across, are produced throughout the summer by this bushy shrub. Round, pale orange fruits, about 3 cm (1¼ in) across, follow the flowers in early autumn. The fresh green, broadly lance-shaped leaves are 2–4 cm (¾–1½ in) long. HEIGHT & SPREAD 1×1 m (3×3 ft).

▲ *Punica granatum* var. *nana*

CULTIVATION Grow in pots of potting compost and place in direct sunlight in a warm greenhouse or conservatory or well-lit room. Provide a minimum winter temperature of 7°C (45°F). If wished, move plants outside in summer. Water regularly in summer, but only occasionally in winter. Feed fortnightly during the growing season. Pot on annually in spring until the plant reaches the desired size.

PROPAGATION Take semi-ripe cuttings during summer.

PRUNING Cut back in spring to reduce the size of the plant, if required.

PESTS AND DISEASES Usually trouble free.

Purslane see *Portulaca oleracea*

Puschkinia
Liliaceae

Dense spikes of flowers appear in spring on this hardy bulbous perennial. It is ideal for the rock garden, where it will spread freely, and is a good choice for naturalising in short grass. It can also be used in dry soil conditions around shrubs, although it does need full sun. There is only one species.

Puschkinia scilloides (striped squill) Star-shaped pale blue flowers with a darker blue stripe running down the centre of each

▲ *Puschkinia scilloides*

petal are borne in spikes about 10 cm (4 in) long. The dark green strap-like leaves are up to 15 cm (6 in) long. HEIGHT 15 cm (6 in).

CULTIVATION Plant in autumn in an open position in any soil, provided it is not waterlogged. Apply a slow-release general fertiliser as the leaves start to emerge in spring. Remove faded foliage when it has died back completely.

PROPAGATION Divide and replant mature clumps in autumn or sow seed in late summer in a coldframe.

PESTS AND DISEASES Usually trouble free.

Pussy toes see *Antennaria*
Pygmaea see *Chionohebe*

Pyracantha
Firethorn
Rosaceae

Pyracantha rogersiana

Long-lasting berries in brilliant shades of red, orange, or yellow adorn these hardy evergreen shrubs. Generally lasting from late summer to autumn, they are up to 1 cm (⅜ in) in diameter and grow in dense clusters. Frothy clusters of tiny, white, five-petalled flowers appear in early summer. The oval leaves, up to 7.5 cm (3 in) long,

have toothed edges. Generally mid to dark green, some varieties have variegated leaves. Pyracanthas are armed with sharp thorns and should be handled with care. They will grow in almost any well-drained fertile soil, although in chalky conditions the foliage may yellow. They may sometimes be defoliated in a severe winter, but usually recover quickly. Fire blight and pyracantha scab can be problems, but new disease-resistant strains are now available. Pyracanthas are effective when grown as freestanding specimen shrubs and also make excellent hedges. They are, however, mainly grown as wall shrubs and are invaluable for brightening up a shady site. With the exception of *P.* Alexander Pendula, heights and spreads given below refer to wall-grown plants. Freestanding shrubs are usually 10 to 15 per cent smaller. Native to E Europe and Asia.

RECOMMENDED SPECIES AND VARIETIES

P. Alexander Pendula Sparse yellow berries turn red later on. If grown as a free-standing specimen, this shrub forms a dense hummock with weeping branches. Trained against a wall it forms a graceful cloak. HEIGHT & SPREAD 50 cm×1.5 m (20 in×5 ft) after 5 years, ultimately 60 cm (2 ft) tall.

P. atalantioides (syn. *P. gibbsii*) Crimson berries appear from summer until the following spring. Upright at first, the almost thornless stems arch over later on. It is very hardy but particularly susceptible to fire blight. HEIGHT & SPREAD 1.8×1.5 m (6×5 ft) after 5 years, ultimately 4.5 m (15 ft) tall.

'Aurea' (syn. *P. gibbsii* 'Flava') has large clusters of rich yellow berries.

P. coccinea This species bears bright red berries. The plant forms a dense shrub. HEIGHT & SPREAD 1.5×1.5 m (5×5 ft), ultimately 3.5 m (12 ft) tall.

'Red Column' has reddish shoots and masses of berries which ripen early. It is upright in habit. 'Red Cushion' has vivid red berries. This densely leafy variety reaches a spread of 1.8 m (6 ft).

P. gibbsii see *P. atalantioides*

P. gibbsii 'Flava' see *P. atalantioides* 'Aurea'

P. 'Golden Charmer' Large clusters of yellowish orange berries ripen early. Upright at first, the branches arch over as the plant ages. HEIGHT & SPREAD 1.5×1.2 m (5×4 ft) after 5 years, ultimately 3 m (10 ft) tall.

P. 'Golden Sun' see *P.* 'Soleil d'Or'

P. 'Harlequin' The decorative foliage is variegated with cream and pink. It has small red berries. HEIGHT & SPREAD 1×1 m (3×3 ft) after 5 years, ultimately 1.8 m (6 ft) tall.

▼ *Pyracantha coccinea* 'Red Column'

⚘ *Pyracantha* 'Golden Charmer'

P. **'Mohave'** The berries are reddish orange. This dense shrub is resistant to disease, and birds avoid the berries. HEIGHT & SPREAD 1.8×1.5m (6×5ft) after 5 years, ultimately 4.5m (15ft) tall.

 'Mohave Silver' is a less vigorous sport of 'Mohave' with silver-edged leaves

P. **'Navaho'** Small reddish orange berries ripen slowly. The plant has a dense, spreading habit. It is particularly resistant to fire blight. HEIGHT & SPREAD 1×1.2m (3×4ft) after 5 years, ultimately 3.5m (12ft) tall.

P. **'Orange Glow'**♀ Red-orange berries ripen in early autumn and last into winter. A dense, upright shrub, resistant to scab disease. HEIGHT & SPREAD 1.8×1.8m (6×6ft) after 5 years, ultimately 4.5m (15ft) tall.

P. **rogersiana**♀ Masses of reddish orange berries appear in mid summer. Upright at first, the stems eventually arch over. HEIGHT & SPREAD 1.8×1.2m (6×4ft) after 5 years, ultimately 3m (10ft) tall.

 'Flava'♀ has bright yellow berries.

P. **'Shawnee'** Yellow to light orange berries

⚘ *Pyracantha* 'Navaho'

ripen in mid summer. This plant is densely branching, spreading at the base. It is fairly resistant to fire blight and scab. HEIGHT & SPREAD 1.8×1.2m (6×4ft) after 5 years, ultimately 3m (10ft) tall.

P. **'Soleil d'Or'** (syn. P. 'Golden Sun', P. 'Yellow Sun') This plant carries large clusters of deep golden yellow berries. The plant has reddish stems and a semi-spreading habit. HEIGHT & SPREAD 1.5×1.5m (5×5ft) after 5 years, ultimately 3m (10ft) tall.

P. **'Sparkler'** The white-mottled leaves become pink-tinged in autumn and winter. Not reliably hardy, this is best grown against a sheltered wall or in a cold green-

❦ *Pyracantha* 'Shawnee'

house. HEIGHT & SPREAD 1.2×1.2m (4×4ft) after 5 years, ultimately 2.4m (8ft) tall.

P. **'Teton'** Yellowish orange berries are borne in profusion. A vigorous upright shrub with reddish shoots, resistant to fire blight. HEIGHT & SPREAD 1.8×1.2m (6×4ft) after 5 years, ultimately 3m (10ft) tall.

P. **'Yellow Sun'** see P. 'Soleil d'Or'

⚘ *Pyracantha* 'Soleil d'Or'

CULTIVATION Plant in any fertile, well-drained soil that is not too chalky in sun or shade. If using as hedging, set young plants 50cm (20in) apart. Water all plants until established. Feed occasionally. Support wall-grown plants with trellis or wires and tie in vigorous shoots each year from early summer to autumn.

PROPAGATION Take semi-ripe cuttings in mid to late summer.

PRUNING Trim established plants to shape from early spring to mid summer. Prune before flowering for maximum berry production. For hedging plants, lightly trim sideshoots at time of planting, leaving leading shoots untouched. Cut back sideshoots of established plants from early spring to late summer. Only shorten leaders if few sideshoots are produced.

PESTS AND DISEASES Aphids may infest stems and leaves. Woolly aphids may be troublesome. Fire blight and pyracantha scab can be problems. Birds may eat the berries.

Pyrethrum see *Tanacetum coccineum*

Pyrus
Ornamental pear
Rosaceae

Pyrus salicifolia 'Pendula'

Ornamental pears are hardy deciduous trees valued for their habit, white blossom and decorative foliage. Individual flowers are 2–4cm (¾–1½in) across and are borne in clusters. The fruits have no ornamental

value and most are not suitable for eating. (For fruiting pear trees, see p.728.)

RECOMMENDED SPECIES AND VARIETIES

P. **callyerana 'Chanticleer'**♀ Clusters of flowers appear from early to mid spring and again, occasionally, in summer. The leathery, glossy green leaves, up to 10cm (4in) long, are roughly oval, with pointed tips. In autumn, they turn to shades of red and sometimes persist through winter. This tree is narrowly pyramidal. HEIGHT & SPREAD 5×2.4m (16×8ft) after 10 years, ultimately 15m (50ft) tall.

P. **communis 'Beech Hill'** Bunches of flowers are carried from early to mid spring. The mid green leaves, about 10cm (4in) long, are oval with somewhat pointed tips and usually curled. The foliage sometimes takes on attractive autumn colouring. This tree forms a lofty spire that casts little shade. HEIGHT & SPREAD 4×2.4m (13×8ft) after 10 years, ultimately 10m (30ft) tall.

P. **nivalis** (snow pear) Clusters of white flowers appear in late spring. The roughly oval leaves, 7.5cm (3in) long, are white, with a felted texture when young. Older leaves are green above, remaining white and felted beneath. This forms a small tree with upright branches that become more spreading. HEIGHT & SPREAD 5×3m (16×10ft) after 10 years, ultimately 10m (30ft) tall.

⚘ *Pyrus nivalis*

P. **salicifolia 'Pendula'**♀ Dense clusters of creamy blossom appear in mid spring. The narrow leaves, up to 9cm (3½in) long, are white and felted until early summer, turning greyish green later. This tree forms a dense mound of weeping branches. HEIGHT & SPREAD 5×2.7m (16×9ft) after 10 years, ultimately 8m (26ft) tall.

CULTIVATION Plant from mid autumn to early spring in full sun or partial shade, preferably in heavy, but well-drained and well-cultivated soil.

PROPAGATION It is advisable to buy a healthy specimen from a reputable supplier.

PRUNING Not normally necessary, but trim trees lightly into shape in summer if desired.

PESTS AND DISEASES Usually trouble free.

Quamash see *Camassia*
Queen of the prairie
 see *Filipendula rubra*
Queen's tears see *Billbergia nutans*

p
q

Reseda
Mignonette
Resedaceae

The flowers of reseda plants are often sweetly fragrant and are most attractive to bees. The genus comprises hardy and half-hardy annuals, biennials and herbaceous perennials, native to the Mediterranean, E Africa and SW Asia. They are popular bedding and wild-garden plants and some make interesting cut flowers. All enjoy an open, sunny position in a free-draining soil.

RECOMMENDED SPECIES AND VARIETIES
R. lutea (wild mignonette) Short, slender spikes of tiny 6-petalled, almost scentless, yellowish green blossoms, each no more than 6mm (¼in) across, appear in mid to late summer. It is a sparingly branched plant with mid-green leaves, up to 15cm (6in) long, that are roughly lance-shaped and deeply divided. This is a short-lived perennial which often behaves as a biennial. HEIGHT & SPREAD 30×15cm (12×6in).
R. luteola (dyer's weld) The slender, upright, flower spikes of this species are up to 60cm (2ft) long, mostly unbranched, but occasionally producing sub-spikes. The flowers are tiny, only 5mm (¼in) in diameter, and are greenish yellow on white. They are produced from mid to late summer. This strong-growing biennial has lance-shaped, wavy-edged, mid-green leaves up to 10cm (4in) long. HEIGHT & SPREAD 1m×45cm (3×1½ft).
R. odorata (sweet mignonette) Conical heads of tiny buff or whitish green flowers, each with petals no more than 5mm (¼in) long surrounding conspicuous orange-brown stamens, are borne from midsummer to autumn. They are intensely fragrant. The oval mid green leaves grow up to 10cm (4in) long. It is a fast-growing, erect-branching annual. HEIGHT & SPREAD 45×30cm (1½×1ft).

'Machet' is a traditional garden variety with large, dense whitish green flower spikes tinged with red.
CULTIVATION Plant in spring in an open sunny position in free-draining soil. Remove faded flowerheads. Dig up annual

▼ *Reseda lutea*

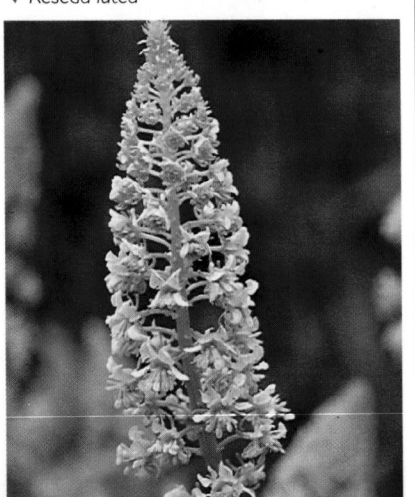

and biennial plants when the foliage starts to turn brown at the end of the summer. Retain true perennials, cutting back their foliage in autumn. *R. odorata* is also sometimes grown in a pot as a houseplant.
PROPAGATION Sow seed during the spring where the plants are to flower, except for *R. odorata* which is best started off in pots in a coldframe.
PESTS AND DISEASES Greenfly can be a problem.

Rhamnus
Buckthorn
Rhamnaceae

Rhamnus alaternus
'Argenteovariegata'

Handsome foliage and abundant black berries in autumn provide the main features of these deciduous, sometimes evergreen, trees and shrubs. Small greenish white flowers are carried in clusters in summer. The berries are poisonous.
RECOMMENDED SPECIES AND VARIETIES
R. alaternus 'Argenteovariegata'♀ The leaves, up to 5cm (2in) long, are variegated green and grey and have creamy margins. They are elliptic to ovate, finely toothed and have 3-5 pairs of veins. The black berries are 6mm (¼in) across. This evergreen shrub is one of the finest variegated plants for the medium to large-sized garden. Native to the Mediterranean. HEIGHT & SPREAD 1×1m (3×3ft) after 5 years, ultimately 4m (13ft) tall.
R. catharticus A deciduous spiny tree with ovate toothed leaves up to 8cm (3¼in) long. These have 3-5 pairs of veins and are bright green above, paler beneath. The numerous black berries are 6mm (¼in)

▼ *Rhamnus frangula*

across. The bark on the shoots has a pungent smell if scraped. This British native species is important to wildlife. HEIGHT & SPREAD 4×3m (13×10ft) after 20 years, ultimately 6m (20ft) tall.
R. frangula (syn. *Frangula alnus*) The alternate, lustrous deep green, untoothed leaves, no more than 6cm (2½in) long, are ovate and pointed and have 8-9 pairs of veins. The berries, about 6mm (¼in) across, are orange-red at first and then turn purple-black. This deciduous shrub is a British native. HEIGHT & SPREAD 2×1.5m (6½×5ft) after 5 years, ultimately 6m (20ft).
CULTIVATION Plant in spring or autumn in any soil in sun or partial shade. *R. catharticus* tolerates lime.
PROPAGATION Sow seed in spring.
PRUNING None required.
PESTS AND DISEASES Usually trouble free.

Rheum
Ornamental rhubarb
Polygonaceae

Rheum palmatum 'Atrosanguineum'

Though they are best known for their large and handsome foliage, these hardy clump-forming herbaceous perennials are also sometimes grown for their unusual flower spikes. Particularly useful for waterside or bog garden plantings, ornamental rheums must have a damp, organic-rich soil, but will otherwise prosper in most situations except heavy shade. The genus also includes the culinary rhubarb, *R.* × *hybridum* and its cultivars, which are grown for their colourful, edible stems (see p. 730).
RECOMMENDED SPECIES AND VARIETIES
R. 'Ace of Hearts' (syn. 'Ace of Spades') The roughly heart-shaped leaves are mid-green with a strong crimson flush and conspicuous crimson veins beneath. They reach up to 45cm (18in) long and 30cm (12in) across. Tall, slender sprays of tiny pink flowers appear in early to mid summer. HEIGHT & SPREAD 1.2×1.2m (4×4ft).
R. 'Ace of Spades' see *R.* 'Ace of Hearts'.
R. alexandrae Slender flower stalks bearing sparse creamy yellow flowers and pendent, broadly lance-shaped, yellowish green bracts up to 10cm (4in) long appear in early and mid summer. The glossy, dark green, roughly heart-shaped leaves, up to 25cm (10in) long and 15cm (6in) wide, are neatly arranged in a rosette at the base. HEIGHT & SPREAD 1.5×1m (5×3ft).
R. australe (Himalayan rhubarb) The

r

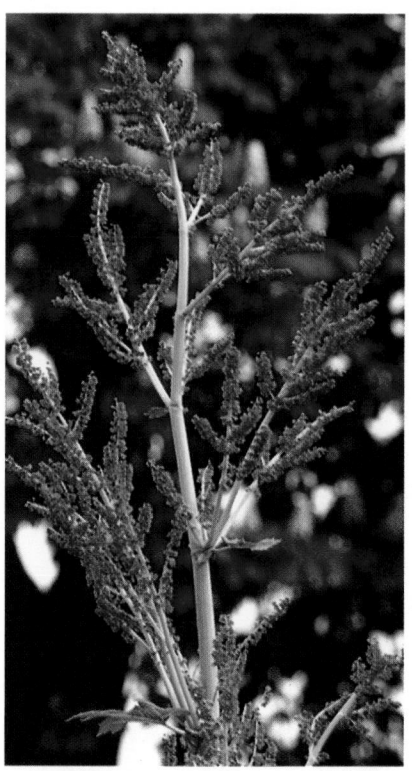

▲ *Rheum palmatum* 'Atrosanguineum'

broadly heart-shaped, strongly veined leaves grow to 75 cm (30 in) long and 60 cm (24 in) across, mostly with wavy edges and distinct hairiness beneath. The red-tinged leaf stalks are up to 1 m (3 ft) long. The tiny flowers vary in colour from plant to plant and can be white or shades of pink through to burgundy. They are borne in dense, narrow spikes. HEIGHT & SPREAD 2×2 m (6½×6½ ft).

R. palmatum♀ The hairy or downy mid-green to bluish-green leaves are up to 60 cm (24 in) long and wide, deeply lobed and with coarsely toothed edges. They have strong green or reddish purple stems. Tall sprays of tiny flowers appear in early and mid summer. Most gardeners retain the flowers, although removing them results in larger leaves. HEIGHT & SPREAD 2.5×1.8 m (8×6 ft).

'Atrosanguineum' (syn. 'Atropurpureum') has leaves suffused with red, while **'Bowles' Crimson'** produces foliage with crimson undersides. The leaves of var. *rubrum* are strongly flushed with deep maroon-red, while var. *tanguticum* has leaves which are much more deeply incised and lobed.

CULTIVATION Plant from autumn to spring in a moist, humus-rich soil in full sun or partial shade. Water regularly in dry seasons. Remove faded flower spikes and any yellowing leaves immediately.

PROPAGATION Divide plants in autumn. Alternatively, sow the seed of species and natural varieties under glass in spring.

PESTS AND DISEASES Usually trouble free.

Rhipsalis see CACTI p. 109

Rhodiola
Crassulaceae

Fleshy, succulent leaves and flat, clustered flower heads characterise these low, clump-forming herbaceous perennials which flower in early summer. Grow rhodiolas in rock gardens, raised beds or containers. They mingle well with small sedums.

The flowers are star-shaped, with five petals, and have especially prominent stamens that are often twice as long as the petals. In the past, rhodiolas were included in the genus *sedum*.

RECOMMENDED SPECIES AND VARIETIES
R. heterodonta This hardy plant produces an open tuft of slightly arching stems, sparingly clad in ovate, toothed leaves that are 1.5 cm (½ in) long and grey-green, with a bluish bloom. Yellow flowers in shallow rounded heads, 3 cm (1¼ in) across, are generously displayed at the shoot tips from late spring to early summer. Native to the Himalayas. HEIGHT & SPREAD 30×20 cm (12×8 in).

▲ *Rhodiola rosea*

R. rosea (rose root) This robust, erect, clump-forming species carries 2.5 cm (1 in) long, oblong leaves of glaucous green held alternately on sturdy stems. Terminal heads, 7 cm (2¾ in) across, of pale yellow flowers bloom in early and mid summer. The hardy plant is attractive to butterflies and bees. Native to Britain and Arctic regions. HEIGHT & SPREAD 30×30 cm (12×12 in).

CULTIVATION Grow in most medium-to-light soils, but add plenty of grit to heavy ground. Over-moist and heavy soils can cause the rootstock to rot. Sunny positions promote good leaf colour and bloom, whereas shade can result in lax growth and poor flowering. The best time to plant out is mid spring. Lengthy periods of drought will stress the foliage, turning it yellow or red, but full recovery usually follows a generous watering.

PROPAGATION Sow fresh seed in mid autumn in pots in a cold frame. Established plants can be divided. Alternatively, cuttings from non-flowering shoots can be taken in late spring. However, the root growth achieved may be insufficient for winter dormancy.

PESTS AND DISEASES Aphids can attack the plants.

Rhodochiton
Scrophulariaceae

These elegant climbers will cling with twining leaf-stalks to any suitable support. They produce striking tubular flowers surrounded by umbrella-like calyxes over a long period in summer and autumn. Although the plants are in fact rather tender perennials, they are usually grown as half-hardy annuals. The leaves are deciduous when the plant is in the garden, deciduous or semi-evergreen when the plant is grown indoors. The species described here makes a useful climber for a cool greenhouse or conservatory as well as for summer bedding. Native to Mexico.

RECOMMENDED SPECIES AND VARIETIES
R. atrosanguineus♀ (syn. *R. volubilis*) The maroon to purple tubular flowers are flared abruptly at the mouth and hang down from slender stems. Each flower, up to 6 cm (2½ in) long, hangs within a bowl-shaped, red-purple calyx. The dark green leaves grow to 7.5 cm (3 in) long and are ovate, sometimes slightly lobed. HEIGHT & SPREAD 3 m×50 cm (10 ft×20 in).

▲ *Rhodochiton atrosanguineus*

r

CULTIVATION Plant in well-drained soil in full sun in early summer. Support plants with wires against a wall or in a greenhouse, with a narrow pyramid of canes or with trimmed conifer thinnings. Alternatively, grow the plant through a shrub.

PROPAGATION Sow seed in early spring in a cool greenhouse and plant out in early summer, when the danger of frost is past.

PESTS AND DISEASES Usually trouble free.

Rhododendron

Rhododendron and Azalea
Ericaceae

———

For those who garden on acid soil, rhododendrons are among the most prized ornamental shrubs. Trusses of translucent flowers are borne in profusion in a vast range of delicate and striking colours, while the mostly evergreen foliage gives year-round form and texture to the garden. Plants can be grown en masse, as single specimens or in containers

———

INDEX OF SPECIES AND VARIETIES

———

Forest giants 30 m (100 ft) tall, with leaves longer than a man's arm, are at one extreme of the diverse and outstandingly ornamental rhododendron genus. At the other extreme are alpine creepers only 5 cm (2 in) tall, with leaves smaller than a fingernail. There are hundreds of species and hybrids in between, including dramatic specimen plants, border shrubs, rock garden miniatures and houseplants, most needing acid, moist soil with an open structure. Where the soil is alkaline, containers or a raised bed of acid soil allow gardeners to grow rhododendrons.

Most rhododendrons are evergreen, but a few are semi or fully deciduous. Rhododendrons grow wild in much of the Northern Hemisphere, including the moister parts of arctic and temperate N America, the arctic and mountainous regions of Europe, Papua New Guinea and much of SE Asia. If eaten in large quantities, the leaves and flowers are poisonous.

Breeders have now produced virtually

◄ *Rhododendron* 'Percy Wiseman'

---

edgeworthii (RSM)
'Egret' (RHD)
'Electra' (RSL)
'Elisabeth Hobbie' (RHM)
'Elizabeth' (RHM)
'Exquisitum' (AHO)
'Fabia' (RHM)
falconeri (RSL)
fastigiatum (RSD)
'Fastuosum Flore Pleno' (RHL)
'Favorite' (AHJ)
'Fireball' (AHK/E)
flavum (AS)
'Florida' (AHJ)
formosum (RSM)
fortunei (RSL)
  ssp. *discolor* (RSL)
'Fragrantissimum' (RHM)
'Fred Peste' (RHM)
fulvum (RSL)
'Furnivall's Daughter' (RHM)
'Geisha Orange' (AHJ)
'Gibraltar' (AHK/E)
'Gigha' (RSD)
'Ginny Gee' (RHD)
'Glowing Embers' (AHK/E)
'Golden Torch' (RHM)
'Goldsworth Orange' (RHM)
'Gomer Waterer' (RHM)
'Grace Seabrook' (RHL)

'Grumpy' (RHD)
'Haida Gold' (RHM)
'Halfdan Lem' (RHM)
'Harvest Moon' (RHM)
'Hatsugiri' (AHJ)
'Hino-crimson' (AHJ)
'Hinode-giri' (AHJ)
'Hino-mayo' (AHJ)
'Homebush' (AHG/R)
'Hoppy' (RHM)
'Hotei' (RHM)
'Hydon Dawn' (RHM)
'Idealist' (RHL)
'Irene Koster' (AHO)
'Irohayama' (AHJ)
'Jean Marie de Montague' (RHM)
'Johanna' (AHJ)
'John Cairns' (AHJ)
johnstoneanum (RSM)
keiskei (RSD)
'Kermesina' (AHJ)
'Kilimanjaro' (RHL)
'Kirin' (AHJ)
'Klondyke' (AHK/E)
'Kluis Sensation' (RHM)
'Kuri-no-Yuki' (AHJ)
'Lady Alice Fitzwilliam' (RHM)

r

every flower colour except a true blue. Two or more colours blend in the flowers of newer varieties, while spots and blotches of another colour, or flares of a deeper colour on the centre of the upper lobe widen the choice. Many white and pale pink flowers are scented. Flower shape varies from a narrow tube to almost flat; some are lobed, frilled or scalloped at the rim. The largest are trumpets 12.5 cm (5 in) long. Flowers are generally borne in clusters, some with up to 50 in a truss.

The usual flowering time in Britain is mid spring to early summer but the flowers of *R. moupinense* are borne in mid winter, 'Christmas Cheer' flowers in late winter to early spring, and 'Polar Bear' flowers at the end of summer. The foliage adds form and texture. Leaf shape is almost round to long and narrow, and young growth may be red, purple or grey as well as shades of green; red bud scales often give extra colour. Leaf surfaces may be shiny or may have hairs that form either a thick felt or a smooth, shiny mat, both known as indumentum. Several species have aromatic foliage.

RHODODENDRON SPECIES, LARGE

The largest-growing rhododendron species are most often seen in botanic gardens, and in large woodland gardens which have the soil and shelter plants need. Yet a smaller garden can use just one to spectacular effect as a specimen plant that is of interest all year.

The typical large species reaches 3 m (10 ft) or more in both height and spread in 15 years. Many are valued for their handsome foliage as well as for their flowers, with leaves that are on average 12.5×5 cm (5×2 in). In the plants listed, the flower size is given only when it is outside what is usual for this group; flowers described as small are

Rhododendron arboreum

5 cm (2 in) long and all others are an average of 7.5 cm (3 in) long.

R. arboreum Only milder areas or sheltered sites are suitable for this plant, whose flowers are crimson-scarlet to pink and white, usually spotted, and borne in early to late spring. Scarlet-flowered plants tend to be the most tender. If growth is cut back by frost, it is often renewed from the trunk. The upright, narrow plant is 5 m (16 ft) or more tall with stiff leaves.

The clone **'Tony Schilling'**♀ has deep pink flowers.

▲ *Rhododendron* 'Tony Schilling'

r

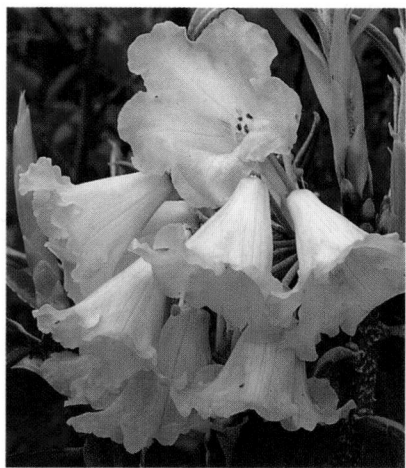

▲ Rhododendron argyrophyllum
'Chinese Silver'

R. argyrophyllum ssp. **nankingense** The small, pink flowers are borne in late spring on a plant hardy enough for sheltered gardens. The dark green leaves are shiny on top with white indumentum beneath.

R. a. 'Chinese Silver' ♀ is a selection with rich, clear pink flowers.

Rhododendron augustinii

R. augustinii The bluest flowers of any rhododendron, varying from light to dark lavender-blue, are only 4 cm (1½ in) long and carried in plentiful trusses in late spring. The narrow, upright plant has pointed leaves, about 7.5×2.5 cm (3×1 in). It thrives in moderate climates but young growth can be damaged by late frosts.

'Electra' ♀ has dark blooms.

R. calophytum ♀ The large white to pink flowers, blotched with maroon, open in late winter to mid spring. The plant makes a rounded shape, often wider than it is high. One of the hardiest of the large species, it needs shelter for its early flowers and for the large leaves which are long and narrow, up to 30×8 cm (12×3¼ in).

R. davidsonianum ♀ Pink flowers, 3 cm (1¼ in) long, with or without a deep pink blotch, are very freely produced from a young age in late spring. The plant is variable in flower colour and hardiness. It is

▼ Rhododendron augustinii

fairly upright with long arching shoots and scaly leaves about 7.5×2.5 cm (3×1 in). It needs plenty of light to avoid becoming straggly, but responds well to pruning.

R. decorum Wide open, white to pale pink, fragrant flowers are borne in late spring to early summer. The easily grown, upright plant with a rough bark is one of the few species that has scented flowers and is hardy enough for most gardens.

▲ Rhododendron decorum

R. falconeri ♀ Creamy white, long-lasting flowers are borne in large compact trusses in mid to late spring. Matt, veined leaves, up to 35×17 cm (14×6¾ in), have rust coloured indumentum on the lower surface. The plant forms a tree and does best in mild, well-sheltered gardens in the south and west; it takes 10–20 years to flower.

R. fortunei Scented white to pink flowers are borne in late spring to early summer amid leaves with purplish stalks. This is the hardiest of the scented species.

In ssp. **discolor** ♀ the flowers are later.

R. fulvum ♀ Pink to white flowers, blotched or spotted with deep maroon, about 4 cm (1½ in) long, appear in mid to late spring. The rounded shrub or small tree has upright shoots bearing dark green leaves with cinnamon-coloured indumentum on the underside. It is hardy in all but the coldest gardens if sheltered from wind.

▲ Rhododendron macabeanum

R. macabeanum ♀ Yellow flowers, usually with a reddish blotch, appear in early or late spring. The vigorous, upright plant has leaves that measure 38×20 cm (15×8 in) and have whitish woolly indumentum beneath. It does best in milder or sheltered gardens.

R. morii ♀ The small, white (occasionally pink) flowers are blotched and spotted red or purple. They are borne from early to late spring. This is a free-flowering and easily grown species with narrow leaves. Grow in a sheltered position as new growth may be harmed by spring frosts.

R. oreodoxa Freely produced, frost-hardy flowers, usually pale pink, are 4 cm (1½ in) long and borne in early to mid spring. The upright but well-branched plant has leaves up to 9×4 cm (3½×1½ in).

The commoner var. **fargesii** ♀ is easily grown.

R. ponticum This is the very vigorous, common purple rhododendron, naturalised in numerous parts of Britain and invasive in many western areas. The flowers are pale to deep pinkish purple and spotted or blotched with a deeper shade and appear in late spring to mid summer. The leaves are up to 20×7.5 cm (8×3 in) on a plant that is compact in the open but straggly in shade. The plant tolerates severe winds but is not fully hardy in the coldest inland areas. It clips into a sturdy hedge.

'Variegatum' has white leaf markings.

R. rex White to pink flowers with a crimson blotch and spots are borne in early to late spring. The broad, large bush, hardy enough for any sheltered garden, has leaves measuring up to 38×14 cm (15×5½ in) that are dark green above with thick, woolly, fawn indumentum below.

▲ Rhododendron rubiginosum

R. rubiginosum Profuse pink to mauve-pink flowers up to 4 cm (1½ in) long are borne in early to mid spring. The leaves, measuring up to 11×5 cm (4¼×2 in), are dark green on top, brown and scaly beneath. The fast-growing, erect species is hardy in most areas and is suitable for growing as an informal hedge.

R. sinogrande ♀ This has the largest leaves of any rhododendron species at 70×30 cm (28×12 in) or more; they are dark green and shiny on top with a thin fawn indumentum beneath. Large trusses of creamy white flowers with a crimson blotch are borne in mid to late spring. The plant is not reliably hardy away from the west or south coasts and needs a sheltered woodland site.

r

▲ *Rhododendron thomsonii*

R. thomsonii The fleshy, blood-red flowers open in loose trusses in early to late spring. An upright-growing plant, it has smooth or peeling reddish brown bark and rounded leaves that are often bluish grey when young. It is suitable for all but the coldest areas but is susceptible to mildew.

R. yunnanense The pink to white, late spring flowers, are variously blotched with deep pink, red, yellow or green. Flowers are only 3 cm (1¼ in) long but the trusses are very numerous and often open from multiple buds enhancing the display. Scaly leaves, up to 10×2.5 cm (4×1 in), may be semi-deciduous, especially after a hard winter. The plant does best in a fairly open site but is prone to bark split in the coldest areas.

'Openwood'♀ is a clone with mauve-lavender flowers speckled with red.

RHODODENDRON SPECIES, MEDIUM
These plants reach 1-2.4 m (3-8 ft) in both height and spread in 15 years. Many eventually grow much larger but, because they are fairly slow-growing, they are suitable for smaller gardens, where they make fine specimen plants. Most need a position sheltered from the wind and not in a frost pocket.

In the plants listed leaves are, on average, 7.5×4 cm (3×1½ in). Flowers average 4 cm (1½ in) long; those described as large are 5 cm (2 in) and any other sizes are given.

R. anwheiense♀ (syn. *R. maculiferum* ssp. *anwheiense*) Pink flowers in late spring are fairly frost-resistant on a very hardy, compact bush with mid green leaves.

R. bureaui♀ White to rose flowers are borne in late spring. The hardy plant is rounded and compact in an open site, more straggly in shade. It is renowned for its foliage: the leaves are a shiny dark green when mature with thick, rust-red, woolly indumentum underneath and on the stems.

The closely related *R. bureavioides* has shorter leaf stalks and larger flowers.

R. cinnabarinum This variable species has waxy, semi-pendent, tubular flowers that range from yellow through orange and pink to red and purple. They are borne in mid spring to mid summer. The plant varies from erect and sparse to dense and compact.

Its scaly, usually evergreen leaves (often greyish-blue when young) are up to 11.5×5.5 cm (4½×2¼ in). Many of the plants are susceptible to mildew.

The most commonly grown are **Blandfordiiflorum Group** with bicoloured yellow and red flowers, **Concatenans Group** and 'Conroy'♀, both with orange flowers, **Purpurellum Group** with purple flowers, **Roylei Group** with red flowers, and ssp. *xanthocodon*♀ with yellow flowers.
R. concinnum The deep red, purplish red or pink flowers, only 2.5 cm (1 in) long, are borne in mid to late spring. The plant, with leaves that are dark green above and very scaly below, is hardy in a sheltered garden.

Pseudoyanthinum Group♀ has the richest flower colour.
R. dauricum The small, rosy purple or white flowers, in early winter to mid spring, often come from multiple buds. The plant is usually erect and rather narrow, but may be dwarf. It is hardy (although late frosts may damage young growth) and semi-evergreen with leaves 3×1.5 cm (1¼×½ in).

▲ *Rhododendron dauricum*

The tall 'Midwinter'♀ is one of the earliest species to flower and the blooms are moderately frost-resistant.
R. degronianum see *R. yakushimanum*
R. edgeworthii♀ The sweetly scented white flowers, often flushed rose, are up to 7.5 cm (3 in) long and are borne in late spring. The plant has a spreading to upright habit and is one of the few with both scales and fawn brown indumentum on its leaves which measure about 3×1.5 cm (1¼×½ in). The plant needs well-drained soil and a mild climate. Alternatively, it can be grown in a greenhouse or conservatory.
R. formosum♀ White flowers, up to 7.5 cm (3 in) long, are often flushed pink and may be scented. They open in late spring to early summer. The plant varies from fairly compact to more open, and has scaly leaves up to 12.5×5 cm (5×2 in). It does best in milder areas but may survive for years on a sheltered wall in moderately cold gardens.
R. johnstoneanum♀ The sometimes fragrant flowers are white to greenish yellow and are freely borne in mid to late spring. The fairly vigorous plant is rather an untidy grower, especially when young. It is an easy species for milder gardens.

R. maddenii♀ Fragrant flowers in white, often flushed pink or purple, and sometimes greenish yellow at the base appear in late spring to mid summer. Scaly, dark green leaves reach 20×7.5 cm (8×3 in) on a variable plant which may be compact, upright or sprawling; it needs a mild climate.

More tolerant of a harsher climate if grown in a sheltered spot is ssp. *crassum*♀.
R. makinoi♀ Rose-pink flowers open in early summer on a compact plant. The dark green, narrow leaves, 18×2.5 cm (7×1 in), curve back at the edges. They often have whitish indumentum above, and thick, tawny indumentum below. The plant grows best in a neutral, near-alkaline soil.
R. moupinense♀ The white to pink flowers are among the earliest to open, in mild spells from mid winter to mid spring, and they are fairly frost hardy. The plant is upright or spreading with a cinnamon-brown, peeling bark and stiff, scaly leaves up to 5×2.5 cm (2×1 in). It needs good drainage and resists drought well.
R. mucronulatum Deep rosy purple to pink or occasionally white flowers are carried singly, but often from clustered buds. They open from mid winter to mid spring and are quite frost-resistant. The deciduous plant is upright with an open habit and has leaves up to 7.5×3 cm (3×1¼ in).

'Cornell Pink' has bright pink flowers. 'Winter Brightness'♀ has purplish rose flowers. The lower growing var. *chejuense* has purple to pink flowers.
R. niveum♀ The tight trusses of large, smoky lilac to deep mauve flowers are borne in early to mid spring. The compact, rounded bush has leaves that are dark above with white to fawn wool known as indumentum on the under surface. It is hardy enough for most sheltered gardens.
R. orbiculare Large, rose-coloured bell-shaped flowers open in mid to late spring on a bush that is broad and domed, but can become straggly in a shady spot. The plant, which is hardy in most areas, has almost round, bright green leaves that measure up to 12.5×7.5 cm (5×3 in).
R. oreotrephes The variable flowers in shades of pale pink to rose-purple are borne in mid to late spring. The plant is rounded to upright with scaly leaves that are glaucous green when young and sometimes semi-deciduous. It is hardy in most areas.

▼ *Rhododendron orbiculare*

R. *pachysanthum*♀ Bell-shaped, white to pale rose-pink flowers are freely produced on mature plants in early to mid spring. Given some shelter, the dense, rounded shrub with upright growth is hardy enough for all parts of Britain. The leaves are just over 10×5 cm (4×2 in) with silvery to brown indumentum above and thick indumentum on the under surface that turns from white to brown.

R. *pseudochrysanthum*♀ White to pale pink flowers spotted with red are freely borne in early to late spring. The plant is usually wider than high. It enjoys partial shade and is intolerant of fertiliser.

▲ *Rhododendron racemosum*

R. *racemosum* Flowers in shades of pink and white, just under 2.5 cm (1 in) long, are freely borne in early to late spring. The small, scaly leaves are up to 5×3 cm (2×1¼ in) and dark green above, milky-grey below. The plant varies from compact to upright and is often leggy. Variable in hardiness, it does best in a fairly open position.

'Rock Rose'♀ is a tall plant with clear pink flowers.

R. *veitchianum*♀ This greenhouse species has large white flowers, often blotched yellow, that open in late winter to mid summer. They are scented and often frilly. The plant varies from compact to somewhat straggly and may be taller than wide.

Cubittii Group♀ has similar flowers but with a pink flush in mid to late spring. The plant is hardy enough to grow outside in the mildest western gardens.

R. *wardii* Saucer-shaped yellow flowers are borne in late spring to early summer. The leaves are up to 12.5×6 cm (5×2½ in) and often milky-green when young. This variable species makes a compact or open plant and often becomes leggy in shade. It is hardy enough for most sheltered gardens.

R. *yakushimanum* (syn. R. *degronianum* ssp. *yakushimanum*) Flowers that usually open pink and fade to white are borne in late spring. Recurved leaves have semi-persistent indumentum above lasting into their second year, and thick, tawny woolly indumentum below. The plant usually forms a very compact, broad dome. This very hardy species grows well in sun or shade. (See also Rhododendron hybrids, Medium.)

Rhododendron yakushimanum

RHODODENDRON SPECIES, DWARF

These plants typically reach up to 1 m (3 ft) in 15 years but spread wider, forming a low mass of growth. Most are alpine plants and do best in an open position in northern areas of Britain, and with only light shade in the south. The leaf size averages 2.5×1.5 cm (1×½ in) and the typical flower size is 2.5 cm (1 in) long; in the plants listed, flower size is given only when it differs from this.

R. *calostrotum* This variable species has an erect to creeping habit. In ssp. *calostrotum*, which is usually mound-shaped with grey-green scaly leaves, the saucer-shaped flowers, about 4 cm (1½ in) across, are held up singly or in pairs. They are sometimes purple but in 'Gigha'♀ the flowers are rich rose-crimson and smother the plant in late spring. In ssp. *keleticum*♀, which forms a lower mound with narrower, dark green leaves, the flowers are purplish crimson and bloom in late spring to early summer. Radicans Group is near-prostrate in habit with very small leaves.

R. *campylogynum* The bell-shaped, long-stalked flowers, 1-2.5 cm (⅜-1 in) long, appear in late spring and early summer. The scaly leaves are dark to medium green, and greyish white below (except in the Cremastum Group). Most of the variable but usually compact plants are hardy, but if they are to grow well they need a soil that does not dry out and coolish summers. Charopoeum Group is compact in habit with the largest rose-coloured flowers; 'Claret' has dark shiny leaves and claret-coloured flowers; Cremastum Group 'Bodnant Red' is an upright grower with red flowers; Leucanthum Group has white flowers; Myrtilloides Group has the smallest leaves and purple flowers; in 'Patricia' the flowers are plum red.

R. *ciliatum*♀ White to pale pink, bell-shaped flowers, up to 5 cm (2 in) long, are borne in early to late spring. The hairy, scaly leaves are up to 9×3 cm (3½×1¼ in). The compact plant can sometimes become leggy when grown in a shady position; it is easy to grow but is slightly too tender for the coldest gardens.

R. *fastigiatum* Abundant purple to blue-purple flowers, up to 2 cm (¾ in) long, are borne in mid to late spring. Blue-grey, scaly leaves up to 15×6 mm (½×¼ in) clothe the compact, low, easily grown plant.

R. *keiskei* Pale yellow flowers are borne in early to late spring. The scaly leaves are about 5×2 cm (2×1 in) on a plant that varies from straggly to very low and compact. Cordifolia Group, usually sold under the

▲ *Rhododendron fastigiatum*

▲ *Rhododendron keiskei*

name 'Yaku Fairy'♀, is the most dwarf form and is exceptionally free-flowering.

R. *lepidostylum*♀ Yellow flowers, borne in early summer, tend to be lost amid the new growth. The scaly, bristly leaves are 4×2 cm (1½×¾ in) and are glaucous. The compact, broad plant prefers light sandy soil.

R. *leucaspis* Freely produced, flat-faced white flowers, 5 cm (2 in) across, are borne singly or in pairs in early to mid spring. Hairy, scaly, roundish leaves up to 6×3 cm (2½×1¼ in) clothe the compact plant, which is suited only to mild areas.

R. *pemakoense* Pinkish purple flowers, up to 4 cm (1½ in) long, are borne singly or in pairs with great abundance in early to late spring. The very compact plant is easily grown in most areas, but the swelling flower buds are often damaged by frost.

R. *polycladum* Scintillans Group♀ Dark purple-blue flowers, perhaps the nearest to true blue in dwarf species, appear in mid to

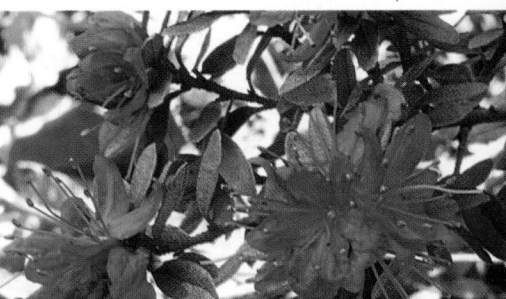

▲ *Rhododendron polycladum* 'Scintillans Group'

late spring in the most usual form of this plant. Flowers are 1.5 cm (½ in) long. Scaly, dark leaves up to 20×6 mm (¾×¼ in) clothe the very hardy but rather straggly plant, which is susceptible to mildew.

R. russatum ♀ Flowers, to 2 cm (¾ in) long, in shades of reddish purple, deep indigo-blue or almost black-purple open in mid to late spring. The scaly leaves, up to 4×1.5 cm (1½×½ in), are dark green. The hardy, easily grown plant can vary from compact and spreading to upright and straggly.

R. saluenense Large, usually reddish purple flowers, about 4 cm (1½ in) across, are borne in mid spring to early summer. The dark, shiny leaves are up to 4×1.5 cm (1½×½ in) on a plant varying from compact and spreading to straggly.

The leaves of ssp. *chameunum* ♀ are coppery purple in winter and the hardy plant is more compact.

R. trichostomum ♀ White to rose flowers, 1.5 cm (½ in) long, open in profuse trusses in late spring to early summer. The aromatic, narrow leaves, 3×1 cm (1¼×⅜ in), are dark green and scaly. The plant is erect but compact in the open, straggly in shade, and usually hardy enough for most areas.

▲ *Rhododendron williamsianum*

R. williamsianum ♀ Rose to almost white, bell-shaped flowers, up to 4 cm (1½ in) long, are borne in mid to late spring. The almost round leaves are bronze-coloured when young and the new growth is susceptible to frost damage, although the plant is hardy. It forms a dense, spreading shrub, becoming dome-shaped with age.

RHODODENDRON HYBRIDS, LARGE

These plants reach 2.4–3 m (8–10 ft) high or more in 15 years. They vary in habit from upright with a bare trunk to domed and clothed to the ground with foliage. The leaf size averages 15×5 cm (6×2 in) and the flower size averages 6 cm (2½ in) long. Flowers are borne on plants five or more years old. Although plants are large for small gardens, a single one makes a specimen that gives interest all year round. The hardy plants are suitable for an open position in all but the severest climates. The woodland plants need shelter from wind and cold.

'Albert Schweitzer' Hardy. Flowers of rose-pink with a dark red blotch are borne

in large, rounded trusses in late spring to early summer on a vigorous, upright plant.

'Alice' ♀ Hardy. Large, deep pink flowers, lighter at the centre, fade to off-white in sun. They are borne in full, upright trusses in late spring on a tidy, upright plant.

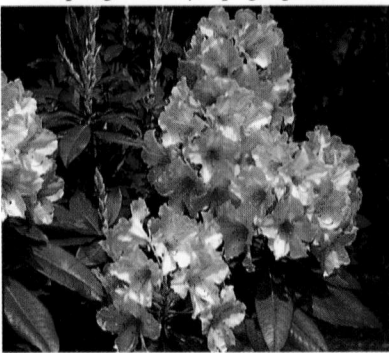

▲ *Rhododendron 'Alice'*

'Anna Rose Whitney' Hardy. Bright, deep rose-pink flowers in large, open-topped trusses appear in late spring. The upright shrub is vigorous and often untidy, needing pruning to control and shape it. It is susceptible to powdery mildew.

'Beauty of Littleworth' ♀ Hardy. The huge, upright trusses of white flowers, speckled crimson, weigh down the branches of the upright, leggy, vigorous shrub in late spring.

'Betty Wormald' Hardy. Rose-pink flowers with a paler centre are borne in conical trusses in late spring to early summer. The upright shrub is fairly tidy.

'Crest' ♀ Woodland. Orange buds open to large trusses of long-lasting primrose flowers in late spring. The upright but fairly open shrub is rather slow to start flowering.

'Cynthia' ♀ Hardy. Large, pyramidal trusses of deep rose-pink flowers spotted with crimson open in late spring to early summer. A leggy plant when young, the plant is fairly tidy when mature if grown in plenty of light. It is susceptible to mildew.

'David' ♀ Woodland. Rounded trusses of frilly, blood-red flowers with deeper spots bloom in late spring. The very upright plant flowers when quite young – after 4–5 years.

'Fastuosum Flore Pleno' ♀ Hardy. Light bluish mauve, semidouble flowers are borne in early to mid summer and are long-lasting. The plant is upright but compact.

'Grace Seabrook' Hardy. The blood-red flowers are in large full trusses in mid to late spring and can be damaged by late frosts. The broad shrub has upright growth bearing handsome, pointed, dark green leaves. It takes 4–5 years before it flowers.

'Idealist' ♀ Woodland. Pink buds open into pale yellow, pink-tinged flowers with a small red blotch. Trusses appear in mid to late spring. The upright, vigorous bush with glossy leaves is easy to grow.

'Kilimanjaro' ♀ Woodland. Large, compact trusses with luminous red flowers with

crimson spotting are borne in late spring to early summer. They are beautiful but the upright plant has a straggly, sparse habit.

'Lady Clementine Mitford' ♀ Hardy. Pinkish white flowers edged in peach-pink are borne in late spring to early summer. The vigorous, spreading but dense plant is easily grown. It is broader than tall with dark leaves that are silvery when young.

'Lady Eleanor Cathcart' ♀ Hardy. Clear pink flowers with a maroon flare are borne in late spring to early summer. The vigorous and upright plant forms a domed bush with long, greyish green leaves. The plant resists cold and is heat resistant but does not flower freely when young.

'Lem's Monarch' ♀ Woodland. Huge trusses of pale pink flowers ringed with deeper pink open in late spring to early summer. The strong-growing plant is often wider than it is high with large, thick leaves. It is hardy in most of Britain if given shelter.

'Loderi King George' ♀ Woodland. The huge, scented, blush-pink flowers, fading to pure white, are in loose, tall trusses in late spring to early summer. This plant, which needs plenty of room in a sheltered spot, has a vigorous, open growth habit with large leaves that are sometimes prone to yellow veining. **'Loderi Venus'** ♀ is similar but with slightly later, light pink flowers.

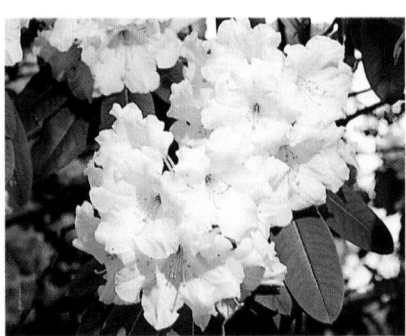

▲ *Rhododendron 'Loderi King George'*

'Loder's White' ♀ Woodland or hardy. Mauve-pink buds open to white flowers in late spring. The well-branched and fairly compact plant, which grows as wide as it is high, can be damaged in very hard winters, but is capable of making a good recovery.

'Lord Roberts' Hardy. The dark red flowers with a small dark flare appear in early to mid summer on a dense upright plant.

'Markeeta's Prize' ♀ Woodland or hardy. Large, bright scarlet flowers open in late spring. The stiff, upright shrub has thick, dark leaves and is hardy in most areas.

'Mrs A.T. de la Mare' ♀ Hardy. The flowers open from pale pink buds to pure white with a green throat in late spring and early summer. The compact, upright plant has glossy leaves. It is hardy enough for cold areas, but the flowers are thin in texture so are prone to weather damage.

'Mrs Charles E. Pearson' ♀ Hardy. Mauve-pink buds open to pale pinkish

▲ *Rhododendron* 'Bruce Brechtbill'

▲ *Rhododendron* 'Mrs A.T. de la Mare'

mauve flowers with brown spots and are carried in tall trusses in late spring. The plant is strong and upright-growing but reasonably compact, and it is easy to grow.

'Mrs G.W. Leak' Hardy. Showy flowers, freely produced after a few years, are pink with a large brown and crimson flare in late spring. The upright, compact plant has dull green leaves that are prone to leaf spot.

'Pink Pearl' Hardy. Large pink flowers with brown speckling are borne in tall trusses in late spring and early summer. The vigorous shrub can become leggy and sparse, and tends to be straggly in shade.

'Polar Bear'♀ Woodland. Strongly scented, large white flowers are borne in loose trusses in mid to late summer. The plant is strong-growing and eventually very big, with large leaves that are often a rather pale green. It needs shelter to protect the flowers and the late growth.

'Taurus'♀ Hardy. The flowers are rich blood-red and appear in mid to late spring. The plant forms an upright, fairly rigid shrub with showy red buds that contrast with the deep green, pointed leaves. It is very hardy but needs shelter from late frosts.

'Virginia Richards' Hardy. Trusses of flowers open rosy pink and fade to soft apricot-cream with a darker centre. The rounded bush has glossy, dark green foliage but is susceptible to mildew.

RHODODENDRON HYBRIDS, MEDIUM
These plants reach a height of 1-2.4 m (3-8 ft) in 15 years and are often about as wide as they are high. On average the leaves measure 10×4 cm (4×1½ in) and the flowers are 4 cm (1½ in) long. Many of the plants are crosses of *R. yakushimanum* and are familiarly called 'yak' hybrids. These are compact, low-growing, free-flowering shrubs and are suitable for small gardens. The flower colour tends to fade a few days after opening in most varieties.

In the plants listed, those described as hardy or as 'yak' hybrids are hardy enough for most gardens; those described as woodland need shelter from wind and frosts; those described as small-leaved hybrids have scaly leaves and masses of small flowers. Tender hybrids are suitable only for growing in a greenhouse or the mildest gardens.

The plants in the category *forrestii* hybrids are hardy and have smallish leaves and red flowers on a fairly compact bush to 1-1.2×1 m (3-4×3 ft). Plants in *williamsianum* hybrid category are all hardy and form plants of a rounded shape with roundish leaves and abundant loose trusses of pink or cream flowers.

'Alison Johnstone' Woodland. The bell-shaped flowers are golden amber, flushed pink, and are borne in late spring. The plant makes a compact and rounded shrub in an open situation. The grey-green leaves may develop a yellow edge, especially in sun. It is easily grown but is susceptible to mildew.

▲ *Rhododendron* 'Alison Johnstone'

▲ *Rhododendron* 'Blue Diamond'

'Blue Diamond' Small-leaved hybrid. Fine violet-blue flowers bloom in large clusters of 4-5 in mid to late spring. The fairly compact plant is hardy in most of Britain but has leaves susceptible to chlorosis and leaf spot.

'Blue Peter'♀ Hardy. Pale lavender-blue flowers with a large purple flare are borne in late spring. The shrub is spreading, even sprawling, and grows wider than high.

'Bo-peep'♀ Small-leaved hybrid. Dainty, pale yellow flowers open in twos and threes, often from multiple buds, during early spring. The upright shrub makes a very pretty plant for milder gardens.

'Bow Bells'♀ *williamsianum* hybrid. Deep pink buds open to light pink flowers borne in lax trusses during late spring. The shrub is upright and compact when grown in the open, but may become leggy in shade. Its young foliage is reddish bronze.

'Brocade'♀ *williamsianum* hybrid. Frilly, peach-pink, bell-shaped flowers are borne in loose trusses in late spring. It forms a large

plant but takes a few years to flower freely.

'Bruce Brechtbill' Hardy. Compact trusses of pink flowers have yellow tinges. The very compact rounded plant, about as wide as high, has shiny, tough foliage.

'Buttermint' Hardy. Pink and yellow shades blend to give the flowers a good orange effect, which is rare in rhododendrons. The compact shrub, hardy in most of Britain, is wider than high, even when grown in shade. Young leaves are tinged bronze, but may scorch in strong sunlight. The growth may become rather congested.

'Caroline Allbrook'♀ 'yak' hybrid. Frilly, lavender-rose flowers are borne in late spring to early summer. The broad, compact shrub starts flowering at a young age.

'Cheer' Hardy. The shell-pink flowers have a prominent red blotch and are borne in abundant trusses in mid to late spring. The dense shrub is very hardy, and so is a useful rhododendron for cold gardens.

'Christmas Cheer' Hardy. The flowers, in small, conical trusses, open blush-pink and fade to near white. This rugged, free-flowering plant has frost-resistant buds that open during mild winter spells with a final flush in mid to late spring. The compact shrub, about as wide as high, has medium-green leaves with a thin brown indumentum below on the underside.

▲ *Rhododendron* 'Cheer'
Rhododendron 'Christmas Cheer' ▼

r

▲ *Rhododendron* 'Countess of Haddington'

'Countess of Haddington'♀ Tender. White flowers, flushed rose, are slightly scented and open in mid spring. The compact plant, often wider than high, has hairy leaves. It is suitable only for mild gardens or indoors as its buds cannot withstand more than a few degrees of frost.

'Cowslip' *williamsianum* hybrid. Bell-shaped, hanging flowers, pale primrose-yellow to cream, are marked with pink or red. Flowers are borne in mid to late spring. The fairly compact plant with rounded leaves is hardy enough for most of Britain if given some protection.

'Creamy Chiffon' Hardy. Double, creamy yellow flowers are borne in long-lasting, compact trusses in late spring. The upright plant, usually taller than wide, is fairly hardy but tends to die off after a few years.

'Cunningham's White'♀ Hardy. Pink buds open to white flowers with yellow to green or brown markings in late spring to early summer. Different clones of this hybrid exist, usually compact with dark foliage, but some forms are untidy. It is easy to grow and hardy enough for exposed sites; it makes an informal flowering hedge.

'Doncaster' Hardy. Flowers that are dark red, with a slight blue cast as they fade, have black spots and are borne in late spring to early summer. The compact and spreading shrub is usually wider than high.

'Dopey'♀ 'yak' hybrid. Deep red flowers which may bleach a little on the lobes but do not fade, are long-lasting and open in late spring to early summer. The compact plant, as wide as it is high, is quite hardy and easy to grow.

▲ *Rhododendron* 'Dopey'

▲ *Rhododendron* 'Dusty Miller'

'Dusty Miller' 'yak' hybrid. The flowers open pale pink flushed red but soon fade out to cream. The compact, quite hardy plant has a silvery indumentum on both surfaces of the leaf.

'Elisabeth Hobbie'♀ *forrestii* hybrid. Scarlet-red flowers open in mid to late spring. The rounded, tight bush which is best in full exposure is tough, reliable and suitable for severe climates.

'Elizabeth' *forrestii* hybrid. Large, bright red flowers are freely produced in mid spring, and sometimes in autumn. The dome-shaped plant, wider than high, has mid green leaves that are extremely susceptible to mildew, and the plant is not quite hardy in the coldest gardens.

'Fabia'♀ Woodland. Freely produced, variable flowers are in various shades of pink through orange to red, usually giving an overall effect of orange. They are borne in late spring and early summer on a plant that is often wider than high, sometimes fairly compact in the open but invariably loose and floppy in shade. The leaves have a thin light fawn indumentum beneath. The plant is not hardy enough for colder gardens.

'Fragrantissimum'♀ Tender. The large flowers are white tinged with pink and are strongly scented. They open in mid to late

▲ *Rhododendron* 'Elizabeth'

Rhododendron 'Fabia' ▼

spring on a very straggly bush with small, hairy leaves. The plant is hardy enough only for mild coastal areas but can be grown in a container, pruned frequently to make a better shape, and moved under cover for the winter.

'Fred Peste' 'yak' hybrid. Strong red flowers, which do not fade much, are borne in a fairly lax truss in late spring to early summer. The compact plant, wider than tall, has dark foliage with brownish indumentum on the leaf's underside.

'Furnivall's Daughter'♀ Hardy. Showy, bright pink flowers with a large strawberry-red flare are borne in late spring to early summer. The rounded plant is often wider than high, with rather rough leaves.

'Golden Torch'♀ 'yak' hybrid. Pink buds open to very pale yellow flowers which fade to off-white. They are borne in compact trusses in early summer on a low and compact shrub, wider than high, which starts flowering when about 3 years old.

'Goldsworth Orange' Hardy. Salmon-pink flowers with orange shading and brown spots are borne in early summer. The upright shrub is compact in sun but can become open with age in the shade. It is a little slow to start flowering, at about 6 years old, but is hardy and easy to grow.

'Gomer Waterer'♀ Hardy. Rosy lilac buds open to white flowers flushed with mauve-pink in early summer. The vigorous but dense and compact shrub has dark, leathery leaves. It is very free-flowering and hardy.

'Haida Gold' Woodland. Greenish yellow flowers open in late spring. This fairly compact, upright plant with bluish green foliage starts to flower quite young at 4–7 years old, but new growth comes early so is easily damaged by late frosts.

'Halfdan Lem' Hardy. Rich red flowers that tend to fade are borne in late spring in big trusses. Large, thick, deep green leaves and red buds enhance the vigorous plant, which is often wider than high and apt to sprawl with age. It needs a lot of room, but is hardy in most of Britain.

'Harvest Moon' Hardy. Full trusses of cream-coloured flowers with a small reddish brown flare open in late spring on a fairly compact plant with heavily veined leaves. It is hardy in most of Britain.

▲ *Rhododendron* 'Golden Torch'

'Hoppy' 'yak' hybrid. Plentiful, frilly flowers are pale lilac-pink fading to near white. They are borne in late spring to early summer on quite a tall plant with long, dark leaves. It starts flowering at 3 years old.

'Hotei' ♀ Woodland. Heavy-textured flowers are deep yellow, each one encircled with a large yellow calyx. They are borne in mid to late spring on a well-branched plant which flowers when about 6 years old and requires some shade and good drainage. It is hardy enough for most of Britain.

▲ *Rhododendron* 'Hydon Dawn'

'Hydon Dawn' ♀ 'yak' hybrid. Freely borne, frilled flowers of pale pink, deeper at the centre and fading to near white, open in late spring to early summer on a very compact bush. It is hardy and easy to grow.

'Jean Marie de Montague' (syn. 'The Hon. Jean Marie de Montague') Hardy. Bright red flowers open in late spring on an upright plant. It is hardy enough for all but the most severe conditions.

'Kluis Sensation' ♀ Hardy. Dark red flowers spotted with crimson open in tight trusses in early summer. The slow-growing, fairly compact plant, as wide as it is high, is quite hardy but its dark crinkled foliage tends to turn yellowish.

'Lady Alice Fitzwilliam' ♀ Tender. Scented flowers are pink in bud and open to white with some yellow in the throat. They are borne in mid to late spring on a fairly compact plant, about as wide as it is high. It is hardy enough for milder gardens and may do well on a sheltered wall in colder places.

'Lavender Girl' ♀ Hardy. Lightly scented, lavender-pink flowers, paler in the centre, are borne in late spring. The vigorous, easily grown plant, as wide as it is high, is hardy throughout Britain.

'Linda' ♀ *williamsianum* hybrid. Frilled, rose-pink flowers open in late spring. Pale green leaves do not appear early so are not vulnerable to frost damage. The very hardy plant is compact and as wide as it is high.

'Madame Masson' Hardy. Star-shaped, white flowers with a bold yellow flare are borne in tight, rounded trusses in early summer. The dense, spreading plant, which is easy to grow, has shiny leaves.

'May Day' ♀ Woodland. Red to orange-red flowers are borne in mid to late spring.

▲ *Rhododendron* 'May Day'

The compact, rounded or flat-topped shrub is not suitable for the coldest gardens because it is vulnerable to bark-split.

'Mrs Furnival' ♀ Hardy. Light rose-pink flowers with a bold, deeper flare open in late spring on a compact, rounded shrub.

'Mrs T.H. Lowinsky' Hardy. White flowers with a large orange-brown flare open from mauve pink buds in dense trusses in early summer. The compact, rounded plant is very hardy and easy to grow.

'Nancy Evans' ♀ Woodland. Orange-red buds open to profuse, rounded trusses of deep yellow flowers in late spring. The neat, rounded plant with bronzy new growth needs good drainage and is then hardy in most gardens with a little shelter.

'Nobleanum' Hardy. This is usually the first rhododendron to open its flowers, at the end of autumn in mild areas, and in mid to late winter in cold areas. Several clones are available: 'Nobleanum' and 'Nobleanum Coccineum' have scarlet-rose flowers; 'Nobleanum Album' has white flowers and 'Nobleanum Venustum' produces white to pink flowers. The plant is hardy enough for most of Britain.

'Odee Wright' Woodland. Yellow flowers with pink tinges and light red spotting are borne in late spring. The slow-growing, neat plant with shiny, dark leaves is suitable for all but the coldest British gardens.

'Penheale Blue' ♀ Small-leaved hybrid. Profuse, bright violet-blue flowers open in mid spring on a neat, rounded plant. The leaves seldom suffer from the leaf spot that afflicts many 'blue' hybrids. The plant is hardy but the flowers are borne early in the season and may be caught by frost.

▲ *Rhododendron* 'Nancy Evans'

▲ *Rhododendron* 'Penheale Blue'

'Percy Wiseman' 'yak' hybrid. The flowers, freely produced in late spring, are peach-pink and cream, fading to cream. The compact plant has pale green, rounded leaves. It is hardy anywhere in Britain.

'Pink Cherub' ♀ 'yak' hybrid. Pale pink flowers that fade to near white open in late spring. The compact, rounded plant is free-flowering, hardy and easy to grow.

'Pink Pebble' ♀ *williamsianum* hybrid. Bell-shaped, pink flowers open in mid to late spring on a plant with rounded leaves. It needs full light and is not hardy enough for the coldest gardens.

'Praecox' ♀ Small-leaved hybrid. Rosy purple flowers are borne in clusters from multiple buds in early spring, but they are not frost resistant. The upright plant itself is hardy enough for any British garden.

'President Roosevelt' Hardy. Bright red flowers paling to near white in the centre are borne in rounded trusses in late spring. The leaves of this sprawling plant are variegated with yellow; leaves and branches that revert to green must be removed.

'Princess Alice' ♀ Tender. Lightly lemon-scented, white flowers with a yellow flare open in mid spring. The plant is hardy enough to grow outside in mild areas and then keeps a neat shape, but if grown indoors it becomes straggly.

'St Breward'/'St Tudy' ♀ Small-leaved hybrid. The two virtually indistinguishable sister seedlings bear masses of showy, violet-

▲ *Rhododendron* 'Pink Pebble'

▲ *Rhododendron* 'Scintillation'

▲ *Rhododendron* 'Surrey Heath'

▲ *Rhododendron* Temple Belle'

▲ *Rhododendron* 'Susan'

blue flowers in mid to late spring. The leaves, reddish when young, tend to suffer from leaf spot. These upright plants are hardy in all but the coldest British gardens.

'Scintillation'♀ Hardy. Pastel pink flowers with brown spotting are borne in early summer. The broad plant has glossy leaves and is hardy enough for any British garden.

'Sleepy' 'yak' hybrid. The pale purple flowers fading to off-white open in late spring. The plant tends to be untidy.

'Sneezy'♀ 'yak' hybrid. Pink flowers spotted with red and fading to pale pink open in late spring. This fairly neat, compact shrub is as wide as it is high.

'Snow Lady'♀ Small-leaved hybrid. Pure white flowers with black anthers open in clusters in early spring. The small, rounded plant is not hardy enough for the coldest gardens and is susceptible to mildew.

'Surrey Heath'♀ 'yak' hybrid. The pink flowers have paler centres that give a two-toned effect. They open in late spring on a compact, dense plant.

'Susan'♀ Hardy. Bluish mauve flowers, fading to pale lavender, open in late spring. Dark green leaves, with a thin layer of light fawn indumentum below, clothe a plant that is susceptible to mildew.

'Temple Belle'♀ *williamsianum* hybrid. Pendulous pink flowers are borne in mid to late spring. The neat, dense bush with rounded leaves is generally hardy, but its early growth may be caught by late frosts.

'The Hon Jean Marie de Montague' see 'Jean Marie de Montague'.

'Titian Beauty' 'yak' hybrid. Bright red flowers are freely produced in loose trusses in early summer and, unlike many other red 'yak' hybrids, these flowers do not fade out. The upright but neat and compact shrub is hardy in all but the coldest gardens.

'Tortoiseshell Orange'♀ has orange-red flowers and 'Tortoiseshell Wonder'♀ has pale salmon-pink flowers. Woodland hybrids. A group of moderately hardy hybrids with a rather open habit and pastel-shaded flowers. These shrubs are not suitable for cold gardens.

'Unique'♀ Hardy hybrid. Pale ochre-yellow flowers, blushed pink fading to ivory

white are borne in mid to late spring. It is a very tidy shrub with a dense habit and hardy enough for any British garden.

'Vanessa Pastel'♀ Woodland hybrid. The creamy pink and red flowers open in late spring to early summer. Suitable for moderately cold areas or a sheltered site, the beautiful hybrid has a fairly low habit and grows wider than its height. Its sister 'Vanessa' has pinker flowers and a more sparse, upright habit. Not suitable for cold gardens.

'Venetian Chimes' 'yak' hybrid. Red flowers, borne in fairly compact trusses in late spring to early summer, fade to deep pink. The poor, rather thin foliage is easily damaged by sun and cold and the plant itself is not for very cold gardens.

'Vintage Rose'♀ 'yak' hybrid. Pale pink flowers in late spring to early summer are easily weather damaged. This compact plant with fine foliage grows wider than high. Not suitable for the coldest gardens.

'Vulcan'♀ Hardy hybrid. A vigorous plant bearing bright red flowers in domed trusses in early summer with narrow leaves. Hardy enough for any British garden, but its late growth can suffer frost damage in autumn.

'Wilgen's Ruby'♀ Hardy hybrid. Bright red flowers appear in late spring on this low, almost spreading bush. The red shade is not one of the best, however.

'Winsome'♀ Woodland hybrid. Bright pink flowers open in late spring. The com-

▲ *Rhododendron* 'Vanessa'

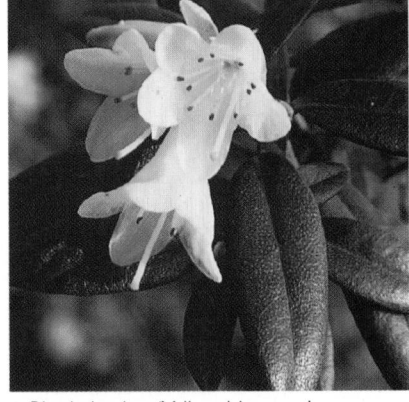

▲ *Rhododendron* 'Yellow Hammer'

pact plant has bronzy new growth and dark leaves. Not suitable for very cold gardens.

'Yellow Hammer'♀ Small-leaved hybrid. Masses of tiny yellow flowers, some of which often open in autumn as well as in mid spring, combine with an abundance of tiny leaves. The straggly, upright hybrid benefits from pruning either when in flower or a few weeks later.

RHODODENDRON HYBRIDS, DWARF

This group of hybrids, reaching a height of up to 1m (3ft) in 10-15 years, includes the alpine types, generally with small leaves and a spreading habit. The flowers are about 2cm (¾in) long and the leaves grow up to 2.5cm (1in) long. Dwarf hybrids are at their best when planted in clumps.

'Anna Baldsiefen'♀ Small-leaved hybrid. Bright pink flowers open in early to mid spring on this neat, erect, columnar plant. Hardy, but rather early flowering for frost hollows and also subject to rust fungus.

'Bengal' *forrestii* hybrid. Bright red flowers open in mid to late spring. The low, dense, mounding hybrid, with smooth leaves, is very hardy and easy to please.

'Carmen'♀ *forrestii* hybrid. The deep red flowers are borne in mid to late spring. This popular and widely grown plant bears small, deep green leaves and has a tidy, compact habit. Not suitable for very cold gardens.

'Chikor' Small leaved hybrid. Masses of relatively large yellow flowers are borne in

▲ *Rhododendron* 'Bengal'

▲ *Rhododendron* 'Cilpinense'

▲ *Rhododendron* 'Moerheim'

▲ *Rhododendron* 'Princess Anne'

▲ *Rhododendron* 'Ramapo'

late spring on this upright, but low-growing, twiggy plant with small leaves. It dislikes hot summers and resents fertiliser.

'**Cilpinense**'♀ Small leaved hybrid. Blush pink flowers cover the bush in early spring. The vigorous but fairly tidy grower has hairy leaves. Opening buds and flowers are very frost sensitive, so the plant is best suited to milder western areas.

'**Curlew**'♀ Small-leaved hybrid. Clear yellow flowers with red spotting are borne in mid to late spring on this dwarf hybrid. Not for the coldest gardens or frost pockets.

'**Dora Amateis**'♀ Small-leaved hybrid. Pure white flowers are borne in abundance in mid to late spring. The foliage of this semi-dwarf American hybrid can get rather yellowish, but the plant is very hardy and suitable for any British garden.

'**Egret**'♀ Small-leaved hybrid. Tiny, bell-shaped white flowers open in profusion in late spring amid small deep green leaves. The plant is hardy and easy to grow.

'**Ginny Gee**'♀ Small-leaved hybrid. Masses of pink and white flowers obscure the small leaves in mid to late spring. This very dense shrub, wider than it is tall, is hardy and easy to grow.

'**Grumpy**' 'yak' hybrid. Cream-coloured flowers, tinged pink at first, open in late spring to early summer and contrast well with the handsome dark leaves. This is one of the lowest-growing 'yak' hybrids and is wider than it is high. The late second growth sometimes gets frosted.

'**Merganser**'♀ Small-leaved hybrid. Primrose-yellow, bell-shaped flowers are freely produced in late spring. The compact plant, wider than it is high, bears dark green, narrow leaves that are glaucous white below. Hardy and easy to grow in most of Britain.

'**Moerheim**'♀ Small-leaved hybrid. A low and compact shrub, wider than it is high, with small leaves and plentiful pale violet flowers in mid spring. The plant is a hardy and easy-to-grow hybrid.

'**Patty Bee**'♀ Small-leaved hybrid. The pale yellow flowers of this mound-forming plant are freely produced in mid to late spring. This shrub is one of the best hardy yellow-flowered dwarfs.

'**Pink Drift**' Small-leaved hybrid. A very dense-growing dwarf, usually wider than high, that bears an abundance of pinkish mauve flowers in late spring. The leaves are tiny. Hardy and easy to grow. The plant is susceptible to mildew.

'**Princess Anne**'♀ Small-leaved hybrid. Masses of pale yellow flowers appear in late spring. The hardy plant forms a compact spreading mound and the light green leaves are bronze when young.

'**Ptarmigan**'♀ Small-leaved hybrid. Plentiful pure white flowers, resembling a mantle of snow, are borne in early to mid spring. A little straggly when young, the plant soon forms a tight mound with tiny dark leaves. Although hardy, a favourable site is required to enjoy the early flowers.

'**Ramapo**'♀ Small-leaved hybrid. The pale violet flowers appear in mid to late spring. Fine grey-blue leaves cover this compact, vigorous plant that is wider than it is high. Exceptionally hardy.

'**Razorbill**'♀ Small-leaved hybrid. The long-lasting, bright pink tubular flowers open from multiple buds and are carried in upright clusters in mid to late spring. The attractive crinkled leaves cover a fairly vigorous, mound-forming plant. The shrub is sufficiently hardy for most of Britain.

'**St Merryn**'♀ Small-leaved hybrid. The plentiful rich violet-blue flowers open in mid to late spring. Growing wider than high, this is one of the smallest 'blue' hybrids and has dark foliage.

'**Sapphire**'♀ Small-leaved hybrid. A spreading, open shrub that produces light purple-blue flowers in mid spring and small leaves. Reasonably hardy.

'**Sarled**'♀ Small-leaved hybrid. Long-lasting tubular flowers open pale pink and fade to creamy white in late spring. This upright, neat, compact plant has tiny, narrow leaves. It is easy to grow and quite hardy.

'**Scarlet Wonder**'♀ *forrestii* hybrid. An abundance of bright red flowers are borne in late spring. This fairly compact and spreading shrub grows wider than high. One of the most popular dwarf red-flowered shrubs, it is very hardy.

'**Snipe**'♀ Small-leaved hybrid. Masses of lavender-pink flowers, fading to pale pink, open in early to mid spring and completely hide the foliage. The compact rounded plant grows as wide as it is high. The flowers are vulnerable to frost and the plant is

r

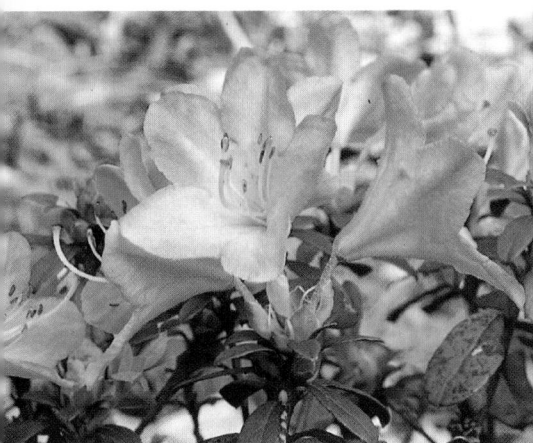

▲ Rhododendron 'Snipe'

rather susceptible to powdery mildew.

'Teal' Small-leaved hybrid. Relatively large yellow flowers appear in late spring on this upright but tidy shrub. The plant is not suitable for very cold gardens.

'Wee Bee' Small-leaved hybrid. Two-toned dark and light pink flowers are borne in abundance in mid to late spring. This very compact and low-growing plant is hardy, but the flowers may be frost-damaged in colder areas.

'Wren' Small-leaved hybrid. The yellow flowers, spotted red, are freely produced in late spring on this slow-growing, spreading, very dwarf hybrid. It is hardy enough for all but the coldest gardens, but needs good soil conditions with organic matter and must not be allowed to dry out.

Azaleas

AZALEA SPECIES

The deciduous azaleas are mostly very hardy, tolerate full sun or light shade and will stand cutting back hard after flowering (except in the rare cases when they are grafted). Their flowering season begins from late spring to mid summer, often with scented flowers. The plants reach a height and spread of 1–2.5×1–2.5 m (3–8×3–8 ft) in 10–15 years and have light green leaves which develop fine autumn colour in some species. Azalea mildew affects the leaves of some species and their hybrids.

R. albrechtii♀ Flat-faced flowers in bright rose-purple to deep rose are 4 cm (1½ in) across and are borne in mid to late spring. The upright, tidy, twiggy shrub has leaves 11 cm (4¼ in) long. Although very hardy, its flowers and growth are early so it does best sheltered by light woodland.

R. dilatatum see R. reticulatum

R. luteum♀ (syn. A. ponticum, R. flavum) (common yellow azalea, Pontic azalea). The bright yellow flowers, 5 cm (2 in) across, are strongly fragrant, and are borne in late spring to early summer. The upright, spreading, sometimes suckering plant is

very hardy and has leaves 12.5 cm (5 in) long that colour brilliantly in autumn.

R. occidentale♀ Fragrant white flowers, 10 cm (4 in) across, are sometimes flushed pink and have a yellow blotch. The flowers are borne in mid to late summer on a tall plant which is hardy in most areas. The shiny leaves, 10 cm (4 in) long, need watching for mildew. (See also Azalea hybrids, Occidentale.)

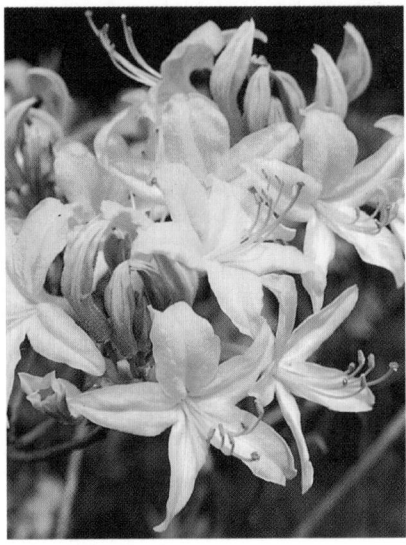

▲ Rhododendron luteum

R. reticulatum♀ (syn. R. dilatatum, R. wadanum) Flowers, 5 cm (2 in) across, are borne singly or in pairs, in shades of purple or white in mid spring to early summer on a broad plant that has tiered branches. The leaves are 6 cm (2½ in) long, usually in groups of 3 and often turn purple in autumn. The plant is very hardy in areas with hot summers where wood is well-ripened, but it is less successful in the north.

R. schlippenbachii♀ (royal azalea) The almost flat flowers, 8 cm (3¼ in) across, vary from rose-pink to white and are borne in late spring. The symmetrical bush has leaves 12 cm (4¾ in) long. Although hardy, it needs shelter to protect its early growth.

R. vaseyi♀ (pink shell azalea) Flowers in shades of pink or white, 5 cm (2 in) across,

▲ Rhododendron reticulatum

appear in mid to late spring. The narrow, willow-like leaves, 12.5 cm (5 in) long, of this hardy broad plant turn red in autumn.

R. viscosum♀ (swamp azalea) The flowers are usually white and sticky with a spicy fragrance. They are up to 4 cm (1½ in) across with a narrow tube and are borne in early to late summer. The leaves are 7.5 cm (3 in) long on a hardy, upright, suckering plant. It needs moist soil.

R. wadanum see R. reticulatum

Rhododendron schlippenbachii

AZALEA HYBRIDS, GHENT/RUSTICA

The flowers on these very hardy plants are 6 cm (2½ in) across with long tubes, and are carried in trusses in late spring to early summer. Most have no scent. The shrubs reach a height and spread of 2.4 m (8 ft).

'Coccineum Speciosum'♀ bears brilliant orange-red flowers. **'Daviesii'♀** has white flowers with a yellow blotch. Two plants are sold by this name, one of them scented. In **'Homebush'♀** the double, deep carmine flowers are in rounded trusses. **'Narcissiflorum'** has double flowers of pale yellow.

AZALEA HYBRIDS, KNAPHILL/EXBURY

The largest and brightest azalea flowers are found in this group of plants, and some are scented. They come into flower between late spring and early summer. Some have red or bronze-tinted foliage, some have fine autumn colour, and some have both. Seedlings are often sold unnamed, simply by colour. The plants listed are very hardy and in a favourable site reach a height and spread of 2.4 m (8 ft) in 15 years.

'Berryrose'♀ has deep pink flowers with a yellow blotch and coppery young leaves. **'Cecile'♀** bears salmon-pink flowers with a deep blotch; it is not a strong grower. **'Fireball'** has deep orange-red flowers and bronzy foliage. **'Gibraltar'♀** bears vivid

▲ Rhododendron 'Narcissiflorum'

▲ *Rhododendron* 'Gibraltar'

▲ *Rhododendron* 'Satan'

orange flowers. **'Glowing Embers'** has reddish orange flowers with an orange blotch. The flowers of **'Klondyke'**♀ are scented, large and golden yellow, and the young foliage is coppery red. **'Persil'**♀ has a yellow flare on the white flowers. In **'Satan'**♀ the flowers are scarlet and there is good autumn colour. **'Silver Slipper'**♀ has white flowers that are flushed pink and have a yellow blotch. **'Strawberry Ice'**♀ bears pale pink flowers shaded with yellow. In **'Sun Chariot'**♀ the buttercup-yellow flowers have a deep orange eye. **'Surprise'** has large, frilled flowers of orange-yellow.

AZALEA HYBRIDS, MOLLIS

These azaleas are selections or seedlings of the Japanese species *R. molle* ssp. *japonicum*. The unscented flowers in late spring are usually available in red, orange, salmon or yellow. Flowers are funnel-shaped, about 6cm (2½in) long and held in trusses. The plants are very hardy with an upright, bushy habit, and grow to about 1.4m (4½ft).

AZALEA HYBRIDS, OCCIDENTALE

All these plants, derived from the species *R. occidentale* (see Azalea species), are sweetly scented and flower very freely in late spring to early summer, bearing blooms up to 7.5cm (3in) across in trusses. They are

▲ *Rhododendron* 'Strawberry Ice'

hardy, reach a height of 2.1-2.4m (7-8ft), and usually spread wider than high. They need watching for mildew.

'Delicatissimum'♀ has cream flowers tinged pink and with a yellow flare. **'Exquisitum'** is cream flushed pink and with an orange flare. **'Irene Koster'** is pale pink inside, fading to white, with a deeper pink outside.

AZALEA HYBRIDS, JAPANESE (EVERGREEN)

The name used to refer to these plants is not strictly accurate since they are not all from Japan and not all completely evergreen. These azaleas can generally stand hotter and drier sites than dwarf rhododendrons. They should be planted in full sun in the north and light shade in the south. There are numerous tender varieties grown as houseplants and frequently brought into flower for Christmas – *R. simsii* for example; they are seldom sold as named cultivars. Although evergreen azaleas are easy to grow, they need watching for the unsightly

▲ *Rhododendron* 'Exquisitum'

swellings caused by galls, which form on leaves and young shoots (also occasionally on flowers) soon after new growth unfurls.

The average size of the plants listed is 60cm-1m (2-3ft) tall and the same in spread; those described as low or creeping seldom exceed 30cm (1ft). The plants have small, dark, glossy leaves and bear masses of wide funnel flowers, about 4cm (1½in) across, in shades of red, purplish pink, salmon and white, and held in trusses. Some have 'hose-in-hose' flowers with one flower inside another. Varieties described as 'early' flower in late spring, 'mid season' flower in late spring to early summer, and 'late' flower in early to mid summer.

'Addy Wery'♀ is upright with vermilion flowers borne early. **'Alexander'** is creeping and bears its reddish orange blooms very late. **'Amoenum'** makes a low plant with rosy purple, hose-in-hose blooms in mid season. **'Beethoven'**♀ is of medium height with large lilac-mauve flowers in mid season. **'Blaauw's Pink'**♀ has salmon-pink hose-in-hose flowers early on a medium plant. **'Blue Danube'** has large bluish lilac flowers in early to mid season on a low plant. **'Buccaneer'** is an upright plant whose warm orange flowers are early. **'Chippewa'** has bright pink flowers late and is good in the north. **'Diamant'**, a range of very low, dense plants that do well in the north, has early blooms in white, pink, rosy red or lilac-purple. **'Favorite'** has deep rosy pink, early flowers on a medium shrub. **'Florida'**♀ has deep red, hose-in-hose blooms in mid season on a medium plant. **'Geisha Orange'** is low with reddish orange early blooms and is good in the north. The low, spreading **'Hatsugiri'**♀ has early, magenta flowers. **'Hino-crimson'**, a low to medium grower, bears strong red blooms in early to mid season. **'Hinode-giri'** carries bright crimson, early flowers on a low to medium plant. **'Hino-mayo'**♀ is low and nearly deciduous, with bright pink, early to mid season flowers. **'Irohayama'**♀ has mauve-pink, white-centred blooms in

▲ *Rhododendron* 'Hino-crimson'

▲ *Rhododendron* 'Hinode-giri'

▲ *Rhododendron* 'John Cairns'

mid season on a medium bush. **'Johanna'**, also medium, has carmine-red flowers in mid season and handsome foliage. The medium to tall **'John Cairns'**♀ has large scarlet flowers in mid season. **'Kermesina'** makes low, compact growth, thrives in the north and has mid season, deep pink blooms. **'Kirin'**♀ has hose-in-hose, mid season flowers in two shades of pink on a medium plant that is not very hardy. **Kure-no-Yuki'**♀ is low, with white flowers in mid season. **'Lemur'** does well in the north, with pink flowers in mid season. **'Leo'**♀ has orange-pink, mid season blooms on a low, spreading shrub. **'Mother's Day'**♀, also low and spreading, carries its large crimson flowers in early to mid season. *R. naka-*

▲ *Rhododendron* 'Kirin'

▲ *Rhododendron* 'Leo'

harae is a creeping plant that does well in the north and flowers late; the form sold as **'Mariko'** has scarlet flowers. **'Orange Beauty'**♀ flowers are early and salmon-orange on a medium shrub that is good in the north. **'Palestrina'**♀ has white, early to mid season flowers on an erect, medium plant. **'Panda'** does well in the north, with pure white blooms borne in mid season on a low plant. **'Pink Pancake'** is low, spreading and late to bear its blooms of strong pink. **'Purple Triumph'** has purple flowers in early to mid season on a low shrub. **'Rosebud'**♀ has double pink blooms in mid season on a medium shrub. **'Squirrel'** is low to medium and does well in the north, bearing its bright red blooms late. **'Stewartstonian'**♀ has large red flowers in early to mid season on a medium plant.

'Vida Brown', a low grower, has crimson, hose-in-hose blooms in mid to late season. **'Vuyk's Rosy Red'**♀ bears large reddish pink flowers in mid season on a low to medium shrub. **'Vuyk's Scarlet'**♀, of similar size, has early crimson flowers and does well in the north. **'Wombat'**, also good in the north, is low and spreading with pink flowers in mid season.

CULTIVATION Rhododendrons thrive only in an acid soil that is moist but well drained. Their fibrous root system appreciates a relatively loose, friable soil that the roots can easily penetrate. Open up clay soil by working in plenty of gritty sand and also organic matter such as oak or beech leaf-mould; or instead use conifer needles or a compost of bracken, bark, straw or garden and household waste. Alternatively, make a raised bed to lift the roots partly above the normal surface. Mix the original soil with lighter soil from elsewhere, or use new soil entirely.

If the soil is alkaline, build an isolated raised bed lined with permeable woven plastic and fill it with suitable soil or ericaceous (lime-free) compost. In very wet areas plant on a mound and in a dry area plant in a slight hollow.

Rhododendrons must be planted at the correct depth. The rootball needs covering with no more than 2-3 cm (about 1 in) of soil. Planting too deeply can stunt or kill the plant. Plants from open ground establish better and faster in a garden than those grown in containers. The usual age on sale is a 2 to 5-year-old plant. Plants 6-10 years old or more are sold but are much more expensive. Rhododendron planting can be

▲ *Rhododendron* 'Rosebud'

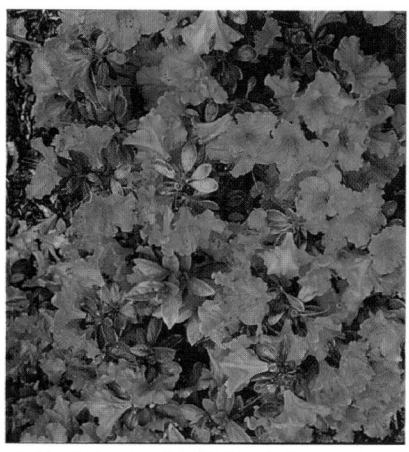

▲ *Rhododendron 'Vuyk's Scarlet'*

done at any time, particularly from containers, but autumn planting is best. It gives the plant time to form new roots before growth starts in spring. Spring planting entails much more aftercare with watering, and even more care is needed by plants put in during the growing season.

If it is necessary to transplant a rhododendron, do it in autumn or early spring. The shallow root ball is easy to lift intact. Put the plant on a sheet of thick polythene and pull it to the new position.

Generally the larger the leaf of a plant, the more shade and shelter from wind the rhododendron needs. Shade from early morning sun helps to reduce frost damage to early flowering varieties. Young plants are especially vulnerable to frost and cold. To protect them, cover them overnight at risky periods with cloches, or with garden fleece or light sacking supported on canes to keep it clear of the plants. Remove covers in the morning once the frost has gone.

It is also worth giving longer protection to young plants in mid winter, especially over their first season. Make a wigwam from evergreen conifer branches pushed in the ground and tied at the top; or with a circle of wire netting, kept in place with canes and covered with branches, or filled with loose bracken fronds or conifer shoots.

Protection from wind and sun can be provided by widely spaced trees that have open crowns, and these do not take too much of the ground's moisture. A building gives shade but can produce harmful air turbulence. The best wind shelter is a permeable windbreak that filters wind and reduces its strength. Woven plastic netting makes a temporary windbreak but the best long-term solution is a hedge or a belt of trees.

Water rhododendrons in dry weather, especially in the first season after planting and when they are making new growth. Soak the soil well occasionally rather than watering little and often. Fine mist, small drops or water from a seep hose is best.

Keep the ground under and close to rhododendrons free of plants that compete for moisture and nutrients. Plants that like the same conditions as rhododendrons but will not compete include primulas, lilies, meconopsis, gentians, trilliums and erythroniums put in groups between the rhododendrons. Shrubs and smaller-leaved trees that are suitable include camellias, cornus, some maples, viburnums and cotoneasters.

Mulching helps to conserve moisture, reduce weed growth, moderate soil temperature and eventually add humus to the soil. Mulching with leaf-mould, garden compost or rotted bracken is best as they help provide nutrients that plants require and do not use up the soil's nitrogen, which other mulches such as pulverised bark and wood chips, often do as they break down. Many dwarf plants are intolerant of fertilisers and are easily scorched.

Apply 2.5 cm (1 in) of a fine mulch every year, or apply up to 7.5 cm (3 in) of a coarse mulch of bark or wood chips every 2-3 years. Do not build up a mulch too deep and bury the rhododendron roots. Do not use fresh grass mowings. They keep out water and a thick layer generates enough heat to kill rhododendron roots.

Deadheading faded flower trusses brings on better new growth and more flower buds for the next season. Young plants and those that have flowered very freely should have preference if time is limited. Take care not to break off or damage the buds or young shoots just below the flowers.

Growing in containers 'Yak' hybrids are perhaps the best choice for containers; they are hardy, free-flowering, leafy and fairly slow-growing. Evergreen azaleas are suitable for smaller pots if space is limited.

Use an acid, free-draining compost such as peat mixed with composted bark, good garden soil, leaf-mould or grit. Add slow-release fertiliser. Wrap the pot to protect the roots in cold weather, and shade it in hot weather.

Tender rhododendrons and azaleas can also be grown in containers to bring into the house when in flower and put outside in the shade for the summer. They need careful watering. When the pots are outside, plunge them into cool, moist soil if possible. Indoors, they cannot tolerate hot, dry air for long so keep them in a cool porch or unheated room as much as possible.

The plants can stay in containers for years. Repot smaller ones into a slightly larger pot every second year and give liquid or slow-release food in the growing season. Remove part of the roots of large plants every 2 to 3 years and put them back in the same pot with fresh compost added.

PROPAGATION For species, reliable seed collected in the wild or from hand-pollinated plants is available from rhododendron societies, but vegetative reproduction is easier. Always propagate hybrids vegetatively; seedlings from them vary greatly from the parent and are usually inferior.

If seed is used, sow it in spring or, if heat and artificial light are available, sow as soon as it is ripe when the capsules turn brown and start to split open. Sow in peat or sifted fresh sphagnum moss. Water from beneath to avoid botrytis. When large enough to handle, prick seedlings out into a tray of pure peat or an acidic humus-rich compost leaf-mould mixture. Keep seedlings in the protection of a greenhouse or frame for their first winter.

Rhododendrons vary in their readiness to root from cuttings. The easiest are cuttings of evergreen azaleas and dwarf rhododendrons, which root more quickly with bottom heat. If using bottom heat, keep the temperature at 21°C (70°F) or lower, as too high a temperature encourages rotting. Remove well-rooted cuttings from bottom heat. Take cuttings from mid summer onwards as shoots become springy when bent instead of breaking. Wound thicker cuttings on one or both sides to encourage rooting. Grafting is needed to raise those plants that are almost impossible to root, but this is better left to professionals.

Layering is an easy way to propagate a plant in the garden. Help layers of larger varieties to root by wounding the bark underneath. Keep the layer moist throughout the growing season. It takes a few years for an adequate root system to develop.

PRUNING Most rhododendrons need no pruning, but old or straggly specimens benefit from being cut back. The best times to prune are late winter, especially for late-flowering plants, or just after flowering.

As a rule, smooth-barked rhododendrons — mostly species — do not respond well to being cut back but the commoner hybrids do. Carry out severe pruning in two or three stages, leaving some foliage each time. Remove the thick branches first and, if these put out new growth, cut back or remove altogether the thinner branches.

Most small-leaved species and hybrids can be trimmed after flowering to maintain a compact shape, without loss of flowering. Most deciduous azaleas can be invigorated or reduced in size by pruning.

PESTS AND DISEASES Vine weevil larvae eat plants at and below soil level and are especially injurious to young plants in containers. Adult vine weevils, greenfly (aphids), caterpillars and slugs eat new leaves. Rabbits and deer feed on azaleas and dwarf rhododendrons.

Grey mould (botrytis) afflicts seedlings in autumn and winter. Powdery mildew may be troublesome on established plants. Honey fungus is the worst killer of rhododendrons. Phytophthora, root rot, mostly affects plants that have been kept too wet and too warm; plants grown in containers are especially at risk. Rust fungus attacks plants but is rarely fatal. Unsightly galls may occur on evergreen azaleas and some rhododendron hybrids.

r

Rhodohypoxis
Hypoxidaceae

Rhodohypoxis baurii 'Fred Broome'

These dwarf bulbs produce a continuous display of flowers from spring to the end of summer. The six-petalled flowers offer a range of pastel colours from warm white to dusky ruby, and each flower lasts for several weeks. The velvety petals are arranged in two sets of three, one set above the other. Although not fully hardy, they may be grown in warm spots where little frost occurs, or in a container that can be moved to a frost-free place. All put up tufts of grassy, linear to lance-shaped foliage, and have corm-like rootstocks. Plants are usually grouped together. Native to SE Africa.

RECOMMENDED SPECIES AND VARIETIES
R. baurii♀ Flowers varying from white to red, 1.5-2 cm (½-¾ in) wide, rise singly on hairy stems, amid prominently hairy, dull green leaves that are about 5 cm (2 in) long. HEIGHT & SPREAD 10×5 cm (4×2 in).

'Alba' has white flowers. 'Albrighton' bears flowers of a deep pink. Red or deep pink flowers are borne by var. *baurii*. 'Dawn' produces large, pale pink flowers that fade to white. 'Douglas' has flowers of a rich, deep red. 'Eva-Kate' is a large form with deep pink flowers. 'Fred Broome' produces rich, shell-pink flowers with firm,

▲ *Rhodohypoxis baurii* 'Fred Broome'

▲ *Rhodohypoxis baurii* 'Picta'

broad petals. 'Harlequin' is a pink and white bi-coloured form. 'Margaret Rose' has well-shaped, large pink flowers. 'Perle' has clear white flowers. 'Picta' bears large white flowers tipped with pink. 'Ruth' is a large, white-flowered form. 'Stella' has deep pink flowers. 'Susan Garnett-Botfield' is very free-flowering, with pink blooms. 'Tetra Red' has red flowers.

R. milloides Red to magenta, occasionally white or pink, flowers up to 4 cm (1½ in) across are borne singly on hairy stems. This is a taller, erect species with almost hairless bright green leaves up to 15 cm (6 in) across, spreading readily by stolons. HEIGHT & SPREAD 18×15 cm (7×6 in).

CULTIVATION Plant in a light, sandy, neutral to acid soil with added humus in early autumn. The soil must retain moisture without becoming clammy in summer. Grow in full sun in northern Britain, but in southern Britain plants benefit from light shade. Provide a warm, sheltered position with winter protection from excessive wetness, and guard against spring frosts. Water in warm, dry weather. Divide plants every 3-4 years, in late spring, to keep them healthy and flowering freely.

PROPAGATION Sow seed in early spring. Alternatively, divide clustered corms in late spring, during their growing season.

PESTS AND DISEASES Mice unearth and eat corms. Wireworms can also cause damage.

Rhoeo see *Tradescantia*

Rhoicissus
Vitaceae

Rhoicissus capensis

These tender, evergreen, climbing shrubs produce lustrous large-leaved foliage, held on twining stems. They climb by means of tendrils. *R. capensis* is ideal for the house, conservatory or greenhouse. It is easily grown, not harmed by gas or oil fumes and may be set in a fairly shaded, but not dark, position. Grow in a pot, supported by canes or a moss stick, or in a border, allowing the plant to climb a trellis or screen. Native to tropical and southern Africa.

RECOMMENDED SPECIES AND VARIETIES
R. capensis♀ This ornamental plant has shiny, dark green, tooth-edged leaves that grow to 20 cm (8 in) long and consist of 3-5 diamond-shaped leaflets. Pale reddish brown hairs cover the leaves and stems when young. HEIGHT & SPREAD 1 m×50 cm

(3 ft×20 in) after 5 years, ultimately 2 m×50 cm (6½ ft×20 in) in a pot; ultimately 6×1 m (20×3 ft) in a greenhouse border.

CULTIVATION Grow plants in John Innes No. 2 potting compost, or in a greenhouse border in a similar compost. Rhoicissus species require a minimum temperature of 7-10°C (45-50°F). Give plants plenty of light in winter, but move them to a lightly shaded spot in summer. Water carefully in summer and apply liquid feed every 2 weeks. Water sparingly in winter, never allowing a plant to become waterlogged. Mist plants occasionally in summer. Repot annually in mid spring.

PROPAGATION Take 10 cm (4 in) cuttings in mid or late spring.

PRUNING Pinch back growths 2 or 3 times in the first spring or summer to encourage bushy growth. If plants become too large, cut them back by up to two-thirds.

PESTS AND DISEASES Usually trouble free.

Rhubarb, edible see p. 730
Rhubarb ornamental see *Rheum*

Rhus
Sumac
Anacardiaceae

Rhus typhina

Brilliant shades of red, orange and yellow colour these hardy deciduous shrubs or small trees in autumn. Grown for their large pinnate leaves, some sumacs produce unusual fruit in autumn. Insignificant green flowers appear in spring. The sap of some species can be an irritant. Sumacs will grow in any soil but may be invasive.

RECOMMENDED SPECIES AND VARIETIES
R. glabra 'Laciniata' hort. see *R. × pulvinata* Autumn Lace Group
R. hirta see *R. typhina*
R. × pulvinata Autumn Lace Group (syn. *R. glabra* 'Laciniata' hort.) The leaves, 45 cm (1½ ft) long, have 11-31, deeply cut, mid green leaflets that turn to orange or yellow in autumn. The plant has a suckering habit. HEIGHT & SPREAD 3×3 m (10×10 ft) after 10 years, ultimately 4 m (13 ft) tall.

'Red Autumn Lace' has dissected leaflets that turn a fiery red in autumn.
R. typhina♀ (syn. *R. hirta*) (stags-horn sumac) The leaves, up to 45 cm (1½ ft) long, have 11-13, mid-green leaflets with toothed edges. These change to shades of yellow, orange, red and purple in autumn. Upright,

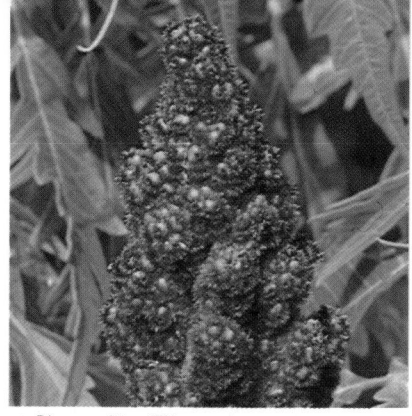
▲ Rhus typhina 'Dissecta'

furry crimson fruit, up to 20 cm (8 in) long, appear in autumn. It has a suckering habit and can spread widely. HEIGHT & SPREAD 3.5×5 m (12×16 ft) after 10 years, ultimately 8 m (26 ft) tall.

In autumn, the deeply cut leaves of 'Dissecta'♥ (syn. 'Laciniata') turn to shades of yellow and red.

CULTIVATION Plant in spring in any well-drained garden soil, preferably in full sun.

PROPAGATION Dig up and transplant suckers in autumn or spring. Alternatively, take root cuttings in early winter.

PRUNING Cut plants back hard in winter, although this will have the disadvantage of stimulating those with a suckering habit.

PESTS AND DISEASES Verticillium wilt may be a problem.

Ribes
Ornamental currant
Grossulariaceae

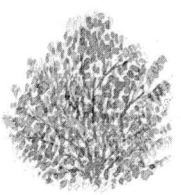

Ribes sanguineum 'Brocklebankii'

Clusters of spring flowers shaped like fuchsias, and lobed, green or gold leaves that may colour vividly in autumn give a long period of interest to the ornamental currant. The alternate leaves have three to five lobes and grow to 7.5 cm (3 in) long. The small, five-petalled flowers grow in racemes up to 10 cm (4 in) long and are very showy on some species. The plants sometimes bear small round black or red fruits in summer. Some are evergreens, all are hardy.

RECOMMENDED SPECIES AND VARIETIES

R. alpinum (mountain currant) The leaves of this tall shrub turn bright yellow in autumn. The small greenish yellow flowers appear in mid spring. Native to N Europe. HEIGHT & SPREAD 1×1 m (3×3 ft) after 5 years, ultimately 2 m (6½ ft) tall.

'Aureum' has golden leaves that blaze in full sun. It is smaller than the species, often broader than it is tall.

R. americanum Red, orange and yellow tints light up the autumn foliage. The leaves have a number of coarse teeth on their outer edge and emit a strong odour when crushed. The spring flowers are yellow. Native to eastern N America. HEIGHT & SPREAD 1×1 m (3×3 ft) after 5 years, ultimately 1.5 m (5 ft) tall.

'Variegatum' has cream and pale green streaks on the leaves. The autumn colour is not as bright as the species.

R. × *gordonianum* Long, drooping clusters of small red flowers with a yellow centre are carried on the rounded shrub in mid spring. HEIGHT & SPREAD 1×1 m (3×3 ft) after 5 years, ultimately 2 m (6½ ft) tall.

R. laurifolium This small evergreen shrub has greenish yellow flowers in late winter. The dark green leaves, lighter underneath, have small teeth rather than lobes and are up to 12.5 cm (5 in) long. Native to China. HEIGHT & SPREAD 50×50 cm (20×20 in) after 5 years, ultimately 1 m (3 ft) tall.

▲ Ribes laurifolium

R. odoratum (buffalo currant) Bright yellow, clove-scented flower clusters bloom in mid to late spring on the small, spreading shrub. Pale green leaves, usually deeply toothed, turn red and purple in autumn. Native to central USA. HEIGHT & SPREAD 1×1 m (3×3 ft) after 5 years, ultimately 2 m (6½ ft) tall.

▲ Ribes odoratum

R. sanguineum (flowering currant) Small rosy-red flowers appear in mid spring. They have a rather pungent smell. The shrub has a rounded, spreading habit and is the most commonly grown ornamental currant. Native to western N America. HEIGHT &

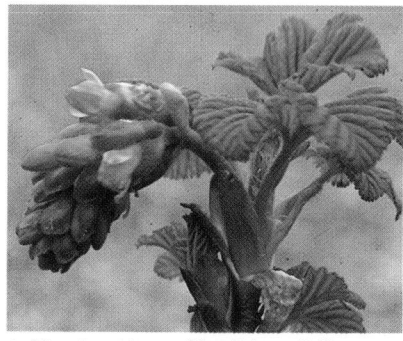
▲ Ribes sanguineum 'King Edward VII'

SPREAD 1.2×1.2 m (4×4 ft) after 5 years, ultimately 2 m (6½ ft) tall.

'Brocklebankii'♥ has pale yellow leaves and pale pink flowers in mid spring. It does not grow as big as the species. 'King Edward VII' has deep red flowers which appear in drooping bunches in early spring. It has a lower, more spreading habit than

▲ Ribes sanguineum 'Brocklebankii'

the species and is slower growing. 'Pulborough Scarlet'♥ has a profusion of deep red flowers on drooping racemes in mid spring. It is the best of the red-flowered varieties. 'Tydeman's White'♥ is the best white-flowering variety, producing clusters of white flowers in mid spring.

R. speciosum♥ Profuse pendulous clusters of deep red flowers bloom in mid to late spring on the rounded shrub. The glossy green leaves are semi-evergreen. This Californian plant is only moderately frost hardy and usually needs the protection of a wall. HEIGHT & SPREAD 1×1 m (3×3 ft) after 5 years, ultimately 3 m (10 ft) tall.

CULTIVATION Ribes tolerate a wide range of soil types and growing conditions.

PROPAGATION Raise deciduous species from hardwood cuttings taken in autumn. Raise evergreen species from semi-ripe cuttings taken in autumn.

PRUNING Flowers are carried on the previous season's growth, so trim the plant immediately after flowering to maintain good shape. At the same time, cut back some of the older stems to ground level. This encourages new growth and better flowering, but any berries are lost.

PESTS AND DISEASES Usually trouble free.

Ricinus
Castor-oil plant
Euphorbiaceae

Ricinus communis

This fast-growing tropical shrub from Africa is grown as a half-hardy annual or as a conservatory plant for its striking foliage. Most varieties usually reach a height of 1.2-1.8m (4-6ft). The seed coats are extremely poisonous and are best removed as they ripen. *Ricimus communis* is the only species in the genus.

Ricinus communis This branching shrub carries long-stalked leaves that are 25cm (10in) or more across. The leaves are deeply lobed in 5-11 segments which are toothed, glossy and deep bronze when young. Insignificant green and red flowers are borne in clusters. Female plants bear clusters of spiny fruits which burst open to reveal hard black seeds. HEIGHT & SPREAD 1m×60cm (3×2ft) as an annual outdoors, 1.8×1.5m (6×5ft) in containers.

Heights given for cultivars are for plants in their first season's growth. **'Carmencita'** has shiny dark brown leaves and bright red flower buds and seed pods. It reaches 1.8m (6ft) tall. **'Gibsonii'** has dark purple-red foliage with a metallic sheen and grows to 1.5m (5ft) tall. The lower leaves of **'Impala'** are bronze-green and the upper

▼ *Ricinus communis 'Carmencita'*

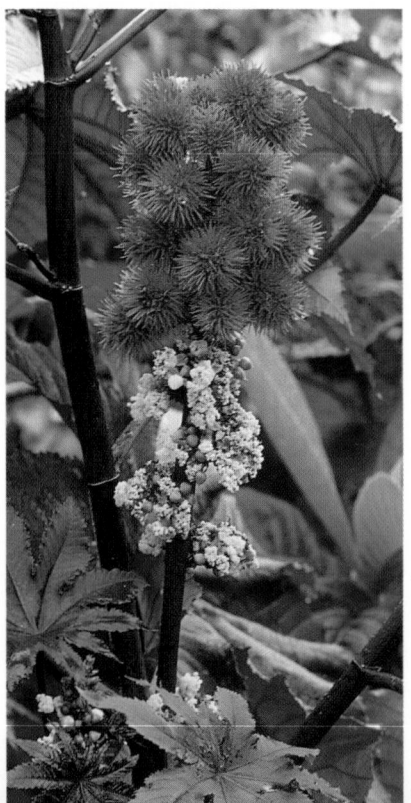

leaves are bronze-carmine. Creamy yellow flowers are followed by maroon seed pods. It grows to 1.2m (4ft) tall. **'Zanzibarensis'** has large white-veined green to reddish purple leaves. It grows to 2.4m (8ft) tall.

CULTIVATION Plant in moist fertile soil in sun when all risk of frost has passed. Water and feed in dry weather. For conservatories plant in pots 20cm (8in) across, or in beds.

PROPAGATION Sow seeds individually in 10cm (4in) pots in early spring. Soak the seeds for 24 hours before sowing. Germinate in warm conditions and grow on in a heated greenhouse or conservatory.

PESTS AND DISEASES Young plants are susceptible to damping off and stem rot.

Robinia
Leguminosae

Robinia pseudoacacia 'Frisia'

Hanging clusters of white or pink, often scented, sweetpea-like flowers add to the decorative value of the light and airy foliage of these small to medium deciduous trees and shrubs. The delicate leaves, made up of numerous small leaflets, are borne alternately on slender branches that tend to be of angular appearance and are often thorny; they can be quite brittle and are prone to break in heavy winds. A native of N America and Mexico.

RECOMMENDED SPECIES AND VARIETIES

R. hispida♀ (rose acacia) Small pink flowers appear in early to mid summer on pendulous racemes up to 7.5cm (3in) long. The dark green, pinnate leaves grow to 25cm (10in). The rounded shrub is moderately frost hardy, but needs protection from winds. HEIGHT & SPREAD 1×1m (3×3ft) after

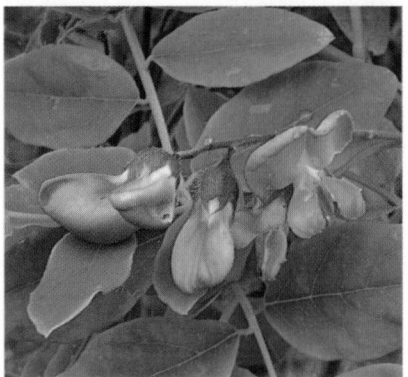

▲ *Robinia hispida*

5 years, ultimately about 2.4m (8ft) tall.

R. × margaretta Pale pink flowers are produced on 15cm (6in) racemes in early summer on this frost-hardy large shrub or small tree. The pale green leaves grow to 25cm (10in) long and have rounded leaflets. HEIGHT & SPREAD 2×2m (6½×6½ft) after 5 years, ultimately about 4m (13ft) tall.

The cultivar **'Pink Cascade'** has larger flowers that are deeper in colour. It grows slightly larger than the species.

R. pseudoacacia♀ (false acacia) The elegant, upright tree has an open habit and 30cm (12in) long delicate leaves that are light green above and pale blue-green beneath. The shoots are well armed with thorns. The small white flowers in 20cm (8in) long racemes appear in early summer and are slightly scented. The plant is extremely hardy. HEIGHT & SPREAD 1.5×1m (5×3ft) after 5 years, ultimately 20m (66ft) tall.

▲ *Robinia pseudoacacia*
Robinia pseudoacacia 'Bessoniana' ▼

'Bessoniana' is smaller than the species and has a narrower crown. It is almost thornless, but does not flower as well as the species. **'Frisia'** is an elegant small tree reaching an ultimate height of only 9m (30ft). In spring the leaves emerge a bright yellow-gold. It retains its leaf colour better if planted in full sun.

R. × slavinii Pale pink flowers are borne in racemes 10cm (4in) long in early summer on this elegant small tree. It is a good choice for a small garden. HEIGHT & SPREAD 120×60cm (4×2ft) after 5 years, ultimately 6m (20ft) tall.

'Hillieri'♀ has small, slightly scented lilac-pink flowers.

CULTIVATION Robinias thrive under a wide range of conditions.
PROPAGATION Seed of the species can be sown in spring, but the cultivars need to be grafted. *R. pseudoacacia* suckers freely, and the suckers can be transplanted.
PRUNING Not generally necessary.
PESTS AND DISEASES Usually trouble free.

Rockcress see *Arabis*
Rock jasmine see *Androsace*

Rodgersia
Saxifragaceae

Large, divided leaves, held well above ground level on long stalks, give these hardy perennials architectural value in the garden, particularly beside ponds and in boggy ground. The foliage can be subtly coloured with bronze tints. Plumes of tiny star-like flowers appear in mid summer carried well above the foliage, though they are not always reliably produced. The plants are native to China, Japan and Korea.

RECOMMENDED SPECIES AND VARIETIES
R. aesculifolia♀ Green and bronze-tinged crinkled leaves, 5 cm (10 in) across, resemble large horse-chestnut leaves with coarsely toothed, deep lobes. Plumes of very small, fragrant flowers are white with a pink tinge. HEIGHT & SPREAD 1.2 m×90 cm (4×3 ft).
R. pinnata Deep green leaves are arranged in pairs of leaflets with each leaflet 20 cm

▼ *Rodgersia pinnata*

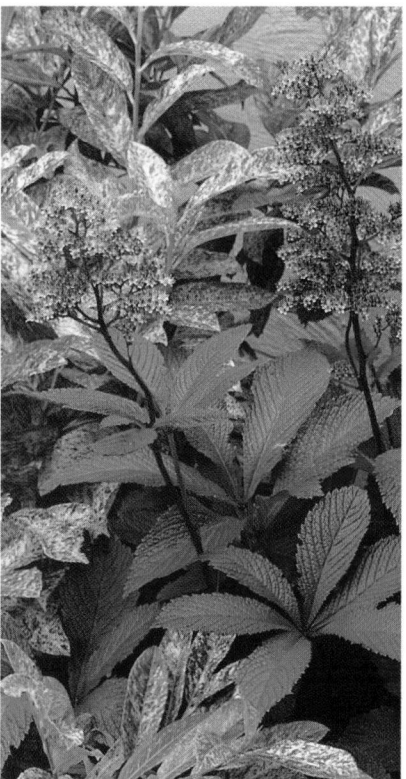

▲ *Rodgersia pinnata* 'Superba'

(8 in) long. Tall plumes carry a mass of flowers in shades of white, yellow or pink.
   'Elegans' has cream flowers with a pink tinge. The green leaves of **'Superba'**♀ are tinted bronze and the branched sprays of rose-pink flowers are over 50 cm (20 in) long. HEIGHT & SPREAD 1×1 m (3×3 ft).
R. podophylla♀ Deeply veined leaves are bronze when young, becoming green and fading to copper tints in autumn. They are palmate in shape with 5 large triangular leaflets divided and toothed at the ends. Plumes of small, creamy white flowers are 30 cm (1 ft) long and are carried well above the leaves. HEIGHT & SPREAD 1×1.2 m (3×4 ft).
R. sambucifolia The emerald-green, bronze-tinged pinnate leaves have distinct veining and are each up to 60 cm (2 ft) long. Creamy white flowers are borne in sprays with arching tips above the foliage in mid summer. HEIGHT & SPREAD 1×1 m (3×3 ft).
R. tabularis see *Astilboides tabularis*
CULTIVATION Rodgersias grow best in humus-rich, moist soil. In other soils add a generous mulch in spring and water freely in dry spells. They prefer a shaded site, protected from strong winds which can damage the leaves. Plant from autumn to spring in soil with added well-rotted compost or manure. Mulch in subsequent seasons.
PROPAGATION Divide rhizomes in spring or autumn. Sow seed of species in autumn and plant out seedlings the following year. The flower and leaf colour of resulting plants may be variable.
PESTS AND DISEASES Usually trouble free.

Romneya
Californian tree poppy
Papaveraceae

Huge white poppy heads with papery petals around central golden stamens, and backed by jagged grey leaves, make exotic additions to the garden from mid summer to early autumn. Despite their Californian origin, Romneyas are hardy in well-drained sunny borders or in a sheltered spot against a sunny wall in cold areas. They are perennial sub-shrubs which dislike disturbance or competition from nearby plants, but once established their roots can be invasive.

RECOMMENDED SPECIES AND VARIETIES
R. coulteri♀ The 6 almost round petals form 2 overlapping layers around golden stamens. Petals unfold crinkled and filmy from the smooth buds in mid summer to early autumn to become silken and almost translucent as the flowers open out to a width of 10-15 cm (4-6 in). The solitary flowers are slightly fragrant. Bristly ovoid pods, up to 3 cm (1¼ in) long and packed with brown seeds, form after flowering.

▲ *Romneya coulteri*

The large grey leaves have 5-9 lobes and are roughly hand-shaped. Native to California and Mexico. HEIGHT & SPREAD 2.5×2 m (8×6½ ft).
   Growing to a height of 1.5 m (5 ft) var. *trichocalyx* has more finely divided leaves and somewhat thinner stems. **'White Cloud'** has bold flowers, very grey foliage and spreads vigorously.
CULTIVATION Plant in spring in a sunny well-drained site, with minimal root disturbance until established. Provide frost protection for young plants in cold areas. Flowering occurs on the current season's stems, so prune in spring, or in winter to prevent rocking.
PROPAGATION Take 7.5-10 cm (3-4 in) long root cuttings in early spring. Cover with soil to a depth of about 1.5 cm (½ in) and keep in a cold frame until growth begins. Alternatively, sow seeds when fresh or in spring at a temperature of 15°C (59°F), or take basal cuttings in early spring.
PESTS AND DISEASES Usually trouble free.

r

ROCK PLANTS
Gems of form and colour

DELICATELY FORMED ALPINE PLANTS BRING THE FASCINATION OF THE MINIATURE TO GARDENS OF ALL SIZES

Small and usually slow-growing, rock plants offer a vast array of shape, colour and texture. Their carpets, rosettes or domes of foliage, and abundant and often brightly coloured flowers can transform a garden. Most produce their best displays in spring or summer but a careful choice of plants ensures a colourful show throughout the year.

Many rock plants are true alpines and originate from rocky slopes and mountain meadows above the tree line. Most thrive in full sun and require a free-draining and gritty soil. The term alpines is also often used for other plants that grow well in similar conditions, including many dwarf conifers, shrubs and bulbs. Some small woodland dwellers, such as *Erythronium, Hepatica* and *Trillium*, are also used as rock plants. However, these plants need a humus-rich soil and a shady site.

Given the right planting conditions, alpines are easy to grow and need minimal attention. Rock features require no hoeing or digging and little general maintenance other than regular weeding.

▼ CREATIVE CASCADE *Brightly coloured* Aurinia *and* Aubrieta *tumble down the rocks in spring.*

ROCK FEATURES

The small size of rock plants means that they are best appreciated when grown in a self-contained site. The traditional rock garden, a sloping feature with outcrops of rocks, provides excellent conditions. Plants grow in pockets of soil between rocks, or in ledges and crevices. A peat bed or water feature can be incorporated to further extend the range of plants grown.

Alpines also grow well in a scree bed, an area with very gritty soil. It is constructed on a slope or as a slightly raised area, and may form part of a rock garden. A self-contained scree bed takes up less space than a traditional rock garden so can be a good choice for a smaller garden.

Raised beds too have naturally good drainage and display rock plants well. They are particularly useful in those gardens with poor drainage, or can be filled with ericaceous compost and used to grow lime-haters in gardens with limy soil.

Rock plants look equally attractive displayed in less formal settings. Gaps in paving or the top of a retaining wall are useful places. Containers, including old kitchen sinks and troughs, make excellent planting sites which suit the miniature scale of the plants and look highly attractive, particularly in a small garden or patio area.

Alpines also grow well in an unheated greenhouse or an alpine house, which provides cool, airy conditions.

THE RIGHT PLACE

Vigorous carpeting plants, such as *Acaena* (New Zealand bur) and some *Campanula* and *Thymus* (thyme) species, are best grown in a rock garden or scree bed, where they have plenty of space to spread. They also look good when planted on top of a wall and allowed to cascade over the bricks or stones, or grown in gaps left between slabs of paving.

Small alpines that form cushions, such as some *Saxifraga,* are

▶ GROWING ON GRIT
Many alpines thrive in the free-draining conditions of a scree bed.

▲ MIX AND MATCH *Contrast shapes, textures and colours for interest throughout the year.*

better off in containers or raised beds, isolated from any strong-growing competitors. Larger cushion-forming plants grow well in scree beds or in vertical rock crevices, where water cannot collect in leaf rosettes and cause rotting.

Some alpines may rot and develop fungal diseases if they are exposed to prolonged rain. They include *Asperula* (woodruff), *Draba* (whitlow grass) and some species of *Primula*.

If possible, keep these plants under glass, where they produce their best displays. When grown outdoors, protect each plant from winter wet by placing a brick on either side of it and laying a sheet of glass on top to keep off rain.

YEAR-ROUND COLOUR

There are a host of alpines that provide colour in spring, making a rock feature a bright focal point in the garden. *Aurinia* (yellow alyssum), *Aubrieta, Daphne, Gentiana* (gentian), *Pulsatilla* (pasque flower) and *Primula* species are good choices and associate well with small spring-flowering bulbs, such as *Crocus* and *Narcissus*.

Follow on with the pinks of *Dianthus*, blues of *Campanula* and snowy white plumes of the silver saxifrages. *Armeria* (thrift), *Chiastophyllum* (lamb's tail), *Geranium* (cranesbill), *Helianthemum* (rock rose) and *Sedum* (stonecrop) all add to a blaze of summer colour.

Grow late-flowering *Carlina* (carline thistle) and *Gentiana* with autumn-flowering *Crocus, Cyclamen, Colchicum* (autumn crocus) and *Origanum* for elegant autumn displays. Include plants with interesting leaves that last through winter. Some sedums, silver saxifrages and *Sempervivum* (houseleek) provide valuable colour. Choose cushion saxifrages, which have pink, yellow or white blooms, and dwarf cyclamen, such as *Cyclamen coum*, for floral colour in late winter.

Intersperse different types of plants to provide longer seasons of interest in each area of the rock garden. For example, grow dwarf bulbs through carpeting plants that flower in summer, and place autumn

▼ IN PROPORTION *An old sink is just the right size to show off a few favoured alpines.*

▲ LATERAL PLANTING *Low-growing New Zealand bur and thyme spill across stone steps.*

crocuses and colchicums to distract the eye from faded summer leaves. Use plants with vivid winter foliage to hide any empty spaces left by the herbaceous species.

Conifers make excellent contrasts to low-growing plants and provide interest throughout the year. Some conifers do not stay dwarf when planted out so choose reliable miniature varieties. *Chamaecyparis pisifera* 'Nana Aureovariegata', *Juniperus communis* 'Compressa', *Picea abies* 'Little Gem' and *Pinus mugo* 'Gnom' are good choices for a rock feature.

THE RIGHT SOIL

Rock plants thrive in a well-draining and gritty soil, set on a drainage layer of rubble. Top dress plants with a layer of gravel, grit or stone chippings.

In a rock garden, use equal parts of soil and small stone chippings or gravel, and add an equal part of organic matter if the soil is sandy. Use three parts chippings or gravel and two parts soil for rock plants that prefer a stony ground, and three parts chippings or gravel with one part soil for a scree bed.

Use equal parts of good quality soil or John Innes No. 2 compost and chippings or gravel in a raised bed. In a container, use the same mixture on a layer of broken crocks. Raise the pot on bricks to improve drainage.

Use a fibrous, humus-rich soil for a peat bed. Leafmould or equal parts of composted bark, coir and garden compost, with a little sand, are suitable alternatives to peat. Top dress with bark chips or coco shell.

ROCK PLANTS FOR EVERY SEASON

SPRING

- *Aurinia saxatilis* Dense clusters of golden yellow flowers and silvery grey, oval leaves.
- *Draba aizoides* Lemon yellow flower clusters above dense tufts of deep green, bristly leaves.
- *Gentiana acaulis* Blue trumpet-shaped flowers and mats of dark green, oval, evergreen leaves.
- *Primula marginata* Lilac trumpet-shaped blooms and rosettes of grey-green scalloped leaves.
- *Pulsatilla vulgaris* Purple, pink or white, bell-shaped flowers and light green, feathery foliage.

SUMMER

- *Armeria juniperifolia* Dense heads of purple or pink blooms and mounds of deep green foliage.
- *Chiastophyllum oppositifolium* Bell-shaped, yellow flowers and bright green succulent leaves.
- *Dianthus alpinus* Rose to crimson single flowers and lance-shaped green leaves.
- *Helianthemum* hybrids Clusters of flowers in a wide range of colours and oval to lance-shaped green leaves.

AUTUMN

- *Carlina acaulis* Round, off-white or pale brown flowerheads and rosettes of spiny grey-green leaves.
- *Gentiana septemfida* Deep blue or purplish trumpet-shaped flowers and tufts of mid green pointed leaves.
- *Origanum rotundifolium* Large apple green bracts and low mounds of bright green leaves.

WINTER

- *Cyclamen coum* Pink flowers with reflexed petals, and kidney-shaped, green or silvery, patterned leaves.
- *Saxifraga* 'Cranbourne' Shallow, cup-shaped, rose-purple flowers and cushions of dark green leaves.
- *Sempervivum tectorum* Rosettes of fleshy evergreen leaves tipped with rich red-brown.

Rosa

Rose

Rosaceae

———

Most beautiful and romantic of flowers, inspiring not only gardeners but also lovers and poets, roses have been cultivated for more than 4000 years – and remain the world's most popular garden shrubs

Whether they are massed in traditional formal beds, trained on a fence, trellis or tree, or combined with other plants in a mixed bed, there are roses for almost any garden. They can stand alone as billowing or weeping specimens in a lawn, or serve as an informal flowering hedge. Some roses make neat rock-garden plants, some spread low and wide for ground cover, while smaller types do well in containers.

Some 150 species of rose have been found in the wild – all in the Northern Hemisphere. There are some distinctions between the species native to Europe and the Middle East, to the Far East, and to North America. These distinctions, and the additional ones shown by hybrids that occurred naturally between species, have given plant breeders numerous features to blend and develop over the last 100 years or more. The result is several thousands of rose varieties for gardeners to choose from, with new ones being added every year.

• THE MAIN GROUPS •

Traditionally, roses were grouped according to the parent species or place of origin but as new varieties have been developed

1 *R.* 'Arthur Bell'
2 *R.* Anna Livia
3 *R.* 'Fountain'
4 *R.* Iceberg
5 *R.* Red Ace
6 *R.* 'Fountain'
7 *R.* Painted
   Moon
8 *R.* Polar Star
9 *R.* Bonica
10 *R.* Alberic Barbier
11 *R.* 'Southampton'

the grouping has become complex. All roses recommended here are listed alphabetically in the index overleaf and the group that each belongs to is indicated in brackets after its name. Each one of these groups is then treated separately, with descriptions given for the roses belonging to them. The groups are:

> Species Roses and their hybrids
> Old Garden Roses (including Gallica, Damask, Alba, Centifolia, Moss, Bourbon, Portland, Hybrid Perpetual, and China Roses)
> Large-flowered Bush Roses (or Hybrid Tea Roses)
> Polyantha Roses
> Cluster-flowered Bush Roses (or Floribunda Roses)
> Modern Shrub Roses
> Rugosa Roses
> Patio Roses (or Dwarf Cluster-flowered Bush Roses)
> Miniature Roses (including Miniature Climbing Roses)
> Ground-cover Roses
> Climbing Roses
> Rambler Roses

The care of roses is treated on pp. 599–601. Nearly all roses are hardy everywhere in Britain. They grow on almost any soil provided that it is not waterlogged and not virtually pure sand, chalk or blue clay. A few species and some old hybrids and sports developed from them do well on fairly poor soil, but most roses thrive on a rich soil containing plenty of organic matter. All flower better and are more vigorous with regular pruning, but the method, severity and timing vary according to type.

Roses holding the Award of Garden Merit of the Royal Horticultural Society and the Royal National Rose Society are indicated by the symbol ♀. Roses awarded the RNRS Gold Medal are indicated by +. This award is based on three-year trials at the RNRS trial grounds, during which the roses are assessed by a panel of experts every week throughout the summer and autumn.

SPECIES ROSES AND THEIR HYBRIDS

All roses are descended from the wild or species roses. These have long, arching shoots that bear along their entire length single, five-petalled flowers, often sweetly scented. Most species roses flower only in early summer, some in late spring, but several have decorative hips in autumn. In the plant descriptions here, the hips are mentioned only if they are particularly showy.

Species roses are vigorous deciduous shrubs whose pinnate leaves vary in the number of leaflets and range from light to mid green, sometimes with a purple tinge. The plants are hardy, often resistant to pests and diseases and not as demanding in their soil requirements as modern roses. They make superb specimen or border plants.

Original species are the only roses to come true from seed. Natural or cultivated hybrids, or selected named forms of wild roses retain most of the characteristics of a species but seedlings from them do not reproduce reliably the parents' features.

R. californica 'Plena' see *R. nutkana* 'Plena'

R. 'Canary Bird' see *R. xanthina* 'Canary Bird'

▲ *Rosa* 'Dupontii'

R. 'Dupontii' The scented, white, single blooms, faintly flushed pink and with pale yellow stamens, are up to 10 cm (4 in) across. They are set off by grey-green leaves. HEIGHT & SPREAD 2.1×2.1 m (7×7 ft).

R. ecae Golden yellow, single flowers, about 3 cm (1¼ in) across, show well against the ferny foliage. This rose suits smaller gardens. HEIGHT & SPREAD 1.5×1.2 m (5×4 ft).

'Helen Knight' see *R.* 'Helen Knight'

R. fedtschenkoana Spasmodic blooms over the summer follow the first flush of single white flowers that are 5 cm (2 in) across. A sprawling, suckering plant with grey-green leaves. HEIGHT & SPREAD 2.1×2.1 m (7×7 ft).

R. foetida 'Bicolor' Orange-red, single blooms with bright yellow on the back of the petals are 7.5 cm (3 in) across and have a musty smell. The leaves are glossy. This open-growing shrub is susceptible to black spot. HEIGHT & SPREAD 1.5×1.5 m (5×5 ft).

R. 'Geranium' ♀ (syn. *R. moyesii* 'Geranium') Bright crimson, single flowers 5 cm (2 in) across are followed by long-lasting, flagon-shaped scarlet hips on tall, arching growth. The dainty leaves are rounded. HEIGHT & SPREAD 2.4×2.1 m (8×7 ft).

R. glauca ♀ (syn. *R. rubrifolia*) The clusters of single, pink flowers 2 cm (¾ in) across are very fleeting but are followed by red hips that last up to 4 months. Long, arching, plum-red shoots, almost thornless when young, bear leaves with a purplish bloom. HEIGHT & SPREAD 2.1×1.8 m (7×6 ft).

R. × harisonii 'Harison's Yellow' ♀ (syn. *R. pimpinellifolia* 'Harisonii') Bright yellow, semidouble blooms, up to 7.5 cm (3 in) across, appear in mid to late spring on a plant of upright, rather uneven growth. HEIGHT & SPREAD 1.8×1.2 m (6×4 ft).

R. 'Helen Knight' ♀ (syn. *R. ecae* 'Helen

r

Knight') The flowers are bright yellow. This hybrid is not completely hardy, but with the protection of a wall it thrives and climbs well. HEIGHT & SPREAD 2.4×2.4 m (8×8 ft).

R. 'Highdownensis' (syn. *R. moyesii* 'Highdownensis') Reddish pink, single flowers 5 cm (2 in) across bloom on this strong-growing, arching plant. In autumn it carries flagon-shaped, orange-red hips. HEIGHT & SPREAD 2.7×1.8 m (9×6 ft).

R. hugonis see *R. xanthina* f. *hugonis*

R. macrophylla 'Master Hugh' Cerise single flowers, 7.5 cm (3 in) across, and purplish green leaves distinguish this rose. Most striking are the very large, orange-red hips that last for several months. HEIGHT & SPREAD 4.5×2.4 m (15×8 ft).

R. moyesii 'Geranium' see *R.* 'Geranium'

R. moyesii 'Highdownensis' see
  R. 'Highdownensis'

R. moyesii 'Sealing Wax' see
  R. 'Sealing Wax'

R. multibracteata Bright pink, single flowers, 4 cm (1½ in) across, bloom against small, grey-green leaves on a shrub that makes a mound of twiggy growth. HEIGHT & SPREAD 2.1×2.1 m (7×7 ft).

R. nitida Bristly reddish stems carry vivid lilac-pink flowers, 5 cm (2 in) across, followed by hips. A low, compact shrub that suckers freely, spreading virtually as far as it is allowed. HEIGHT & SPREAD 1×1 m (3×3 ft).

R. nutkana 'Plena' (syn. *R. californica* 'Plena') Abundant, bright pink, semi-double flowers 4 cm (1½ in) across spangle the large mound of tangled growth in late spring. HEIGHT & SPREAD 1.8×1.8 m (6×6 ft).

R. omeinensis f. *pteracantha* see *R. sericea* ssp. *omeinensis* f. *pteracantha*

R. 'Paulii' (syn. *R.* 'Paulii Alba') White, single flowers, 7.5 cm (3 in) across, and veined grey-green leaves are carried on strong, arching shoots. A wide-spreading bush. HEIGHT & SPREAD 1.2×1.5 m (4×5 ft).

R. pimpinellifolia (syn. *R. spinosissima*) White, single flowers 5 cm (2 in) across are borne on a low, twiggy, dense plant that spreads by suckers and is very prickly. HEIGHT & SPREAD 60 cm×1.2 m (2×4 ft).

'Harisonii' see *R.* × *harisonii* 'Harison's Yellow'

R. primula (incense rose) Pale primrose-yellow, single flowers 4 cm (1½ in) across bloom in small clusters on reddish stems. The small, glossy leaves have a sweet aroma, especially after rain. An arching, open plant. HEIGHT & SPREAD 1.8×1.8 m (6×6 ft).

R. roxburghii (burr rose, chestnut rose) Lilac-pink, single or double flowers, 5 cm (2 in) across, are borne on angular growth with grey, flaking bark. The flowers are followed by distinctive, prickly green hips that resemble chestnuts. HEIGHT & SPREAD 1.8×1.8 m (6×6 ft).

R. rubrifolia see *R. glauca*

R. 'Sealing Wax' (syn. *R. moyesii* 'Sealing Wax') Single, bright pink flowers, 5 cm (2 in) across, are followed by long-lasting, flagon-shaped scarlet hips. Dainty, rather rounded leaves are borne on tall arching growth. HEIGHT & SPREAD 2.4×2.1 m (8×7 ft).

R. sericea ssp. *omeinensis* f. *pteracantha* (syn. *R. omeinensis* f. *pteracantha*) White 4-petalled blooms, borne in late spring, are

▲ *Rosa primula*

4 cm (1½ in) across. Large, flattened, translucent thorns are borne on reddish shoots. HEIGHT & SPREAD 2.4×2.4 m (8×8 ft).

R. spinosissima see *R. pimpinellifolia*

R. 'Stanwell Perpetual' Blush-pink, double blooms, 7.5 cm (3 in) across, open out flat and are repeat-flowering on a thorny shrub with grey-green leaves that spreads widely by suckers. HEIGHT & SPREAD 1×1.2 m (3×4 ft).

R. virginiana Single, bright pink flowers, 6 cm (2½ in) across, are followed by red hips. The shiny green leaves develop striking autumn colour. A bushy, rounded shrub that suckers freely. HEIGHT & SPREAD 1.2×1.5 m (4×5 ft).

R. xanthina 'Canary Bird' (syn. *R.* 'Canary Bird') Vivid yellow, single flowers,

---

INDEX OF PLANTS

The letters in brackets after each plant name indicate the section where the plant is described. (Cl)=Climbing Roses; (Flor)=Cluster-flowered Bush Roses; (GrC)=Ground Cover Roses; (HT)=Large-flowered Bush Roses (Hybrid Teas); (Min)=Miniature Roses; (MC)=Miniature Climber; (MS)=Modern Shrub Roses; (OGG)=Old Garden Roses – Gallicas; (OGD)=Old Garden Roses – Damasks; (OGA)=Old Garden Roses – Albas; (OGCe)=Old Garden Roses – Centifolias; (OGM)=Old Garden Roses – Moss; (OGB)=Old Garden Roses – Bourbons; (OGP)=Old Garden Roses – Portland; (OGHP)=Old Garden Roses – Hybrid Perpetuals; (OGCh)=Old Garden Roses – China; (Pat)=Patio Roses (Dwarf Cluster-flowered Bush Roses); (Poly)=Polyantha Roses; (Ra)=Rambler Roses; (Rug)=Rugosa Roses; (Sp)=Species Roses and their Hybrids.

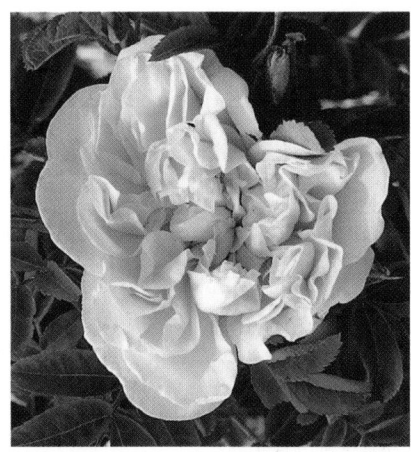

▲ *Rosa* 'Stanwell Perpetual'

about 4 cm (1½ in) across, appear in late spring on arching shoots. This shrub is less rampant when grown as a weeping standard. HEIGHT & SPREAD 2.4×2.4 m (8×8 ft).

The pale yellow blooms of f. **hugonis**♀ (syn. *R. hugonis*) (golden rose of China) are 5 cm (2 in) across and appear in late spring on a dense bush with dainty, ferny foliage. This rose spreads to 1.8 m (6 ft).

OLD GARDEN ROSES

Some very ancient Gallica, Damask and Alba roses are included in this group, but most are hybrids raised from the ancient roses in the 19th century. They vary widely in habit, some making arching shrubs up to 2.1 m (7 ft) tall, others twiggy, upright and no more than 1.2 m (4 ft), and a few growing into airy bushes less than 1 m (3 ft) tall.

Although both single and semidouble flowers are found among Old Garden Roses, double flowers are far more typical – indeed the blooms are packed with petals and often quartered, that is arranged in 4 whorls. Most are sweetly fragrant. Of the nine families, Gallicas, Damasks, Albas, Centifolias and Moss roses flower, almost without exception, only at mid summer. The China Roses, Bourbons, Portlands and Hybrid Perpetuals are generally repeat-flowering, though some varieties are a great deal more so than others.

The leaves of most Old Garden Roses are matt or semi-glossy, looking rather rough in comparison with the glossy foliage of modern varieties. The foliage of China Roses is rather different, always smooth and much more pointed. Whether smooth or rough, Old Garden Rose foliage is reasonably healthy and if affected by disease, most plants are vigorous enough to shrug it off.

Gallica Roses

All the listed Gallica Roses bear flowers 7.5-10 cm (3-4 in) across, unless stated otherwise. They bloom in mid summer only, have a sweet scent and are borne in small clusters, or occasionally singly, on bushes with few thorns and plenty of leaves.
R. 'Belle de Crécy'♀ The double, quartered blooms that open flat are deep cerise-pink, fading to soft purple. The leaves are grey-green on a bushy plant. HEIGHT & SPREAD 1.2×1 m (4×3 ft).
R. 'Camaïeux' A striking combination of crimson-purple and lilac-pink streaks the petals of the rather loosely formed, semi-

double blooms. This rose bears grey-green leaves on its arching stems HEIGHT & SPREAD 1×1 m (3×3 ft).
R. 'Cardinal de Richelieu'♀ The rich, warm purple, double blooms have petals that curve back rather loosely with age. The flowers are well set off by dark green leaves on a bushy, rather arching plant. HEIGHT & SPREAD 1×1.1 m (3×3½ ft).

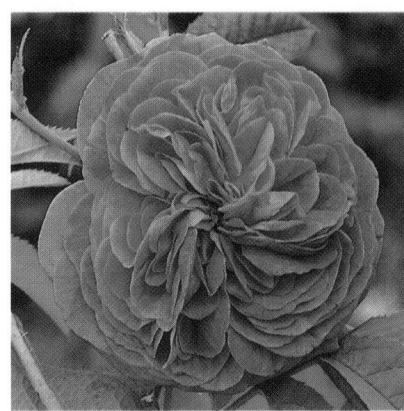

▲ *Rosa* 'Charles de Mills'

R. 'Charles de Mills'♀ Very full, double, quartered flowers, up to 11 cm (4¼ in) across, are a light beetroot-purple and bloom with great freedom. The twiggy bush sometimes gets top-heavy and needs support. HEIGHT & SPREAD 1.2×1 m (4×3 ft).
R. 'Complicata'♀ (syn. *R. gallica* 'Complicata') The spectacular single, bright pink, white-eyed blooms with a boss of golden stamens open flat all along the arch-

Darling Flame (Min)
'Dawn Chorus' (HT)
'De Meaux' (OGCe)
'De Rescht' (OGP)
'Dicbar' (Flor)
Dortmund (Cl)
Doctor McAlpine (HT)
Dream Girl (Cl)
'Dreaming Spires' (Cl)
Drummer Boy (Flor)
'Du Maître d'Ecole' (OGG)
Dublin Bay (Cl)
'Duc de Guiche' (OGG)
'Duchesse de Montebello' (OGG)
'Duchess of Portland' (OGP)
'Dupontii' (Sp)
Dutch Gold (HT)
'Easter Morning' (Min)
R. ecae (Sp)
R. ecae 'Helen Knight' (Sp)
'E.H. Morse' (HT)
Edith Holden (Flor)
Elina (HT)
Elizabeth of Glamis (Flor)
'Emily Gray' (Ra)
'Empress Josephine' (OGG)

'Ena Harkness, Climbing' (Cl)
English Garden (MS)
'English Miss' (Flor)
'Ernest H. Morse' (HT)
Escapade (Flor)
Essex (GrC)
'Etoile de Hollande, Climbing' (Cl)
Evelyn (MS)
Eye Paint (Flor)
'F.E. Lester' (Ra)
'F.J. Grootendorst' (Rug)
R. fedtschenkoana (Sp)
Felicia (MS)
'Félicité Parmentier' (OGA)
'Félicité Perpétue' (Ra)
Fellowship (Flor)
Festival (Pat)
'Fimbriata' (Rug)
Flower Carpet (GrC)
R. foetida 'Bicolor' (Sp)
'Fountain' (MS)
Fragrant Cloud (HT)
Fragrant Delight (Flor)
Fragrant Dream (HT)
'Francesca' (MS)
'Francis E. Lester' (Ra)

R. × francofurtana (Sp)
'François Juranville' (Ra)
'Frau Karl Druschki' (OGHP)
'Fred Loads' (MS)
Freedom (HT)
'Fru Dagmar Hastrup' (Rug)
Frühlingsgold (MS)
'Frühlingsmorgen' (MS)
R. gallica var. *officinalis* (OGG)
R. gallica var. *officinalis* 'Complicata' (OGG)
R. gallica var. *officinalis* 'Versicolor' (OGG)
Galway Bay (Cl)
'Gaujard' (HT)
Gentle Touch (Pat)
'Geranium' (Sp)
Gertrude Jekyll (MS)
Gingernut (Pat)
'Gipsy Boy' (MS)
R. glauca (Sp)
'Glenfiddich' (Flor)
'Gloire de Dijon' (Cl)
'Gloire des Mousseuses' (OGM)
Golden Celebration (MS)

Golden Jubilee (HT)
Golden Showers (Cl)
Golden Wedding (Flor)
'Golden Wings' (MS)
Golden Years (Flor)
'Goldfinch' (Ra)
Graham Thomas (MS)
'Grandpa Dickson' (HT)
'Great Maiden's Blush' (OGA)
Greenall's Glory (Flor)
'Gruss an Aachen' (Flor)
'Guinée' (Cl)
Gwent (GrC)
'Gypsy Boy' (MS)
Hampshire (GrC)
Handel (Cl)
Hannah Gordon (Flor)
R. × harisonii 'Harison's Yellow' (Sp)
Harry Wheatcroft (HT)
Harvest Fayre (Flor)
'Helen Knight' (Sp)
'Henri Martin' (OGM)
Heritage (MS)
Hertfordshire (GrC)
'Highdownensis' (Sp)
Highfield (Cl)
High Hopes (Cl)

'Honey Bunch' (Pat)
Honeymoon (Flor)
'Honorine de Brabant' (OGB)
R. hugonis (Sp)
Iceberg (Flor)
'Iceberg, Climbing' (Cl)
Ice Cream (HT)
'Iced Ginger' (Flor)
Ingrid Bergman (HT)
Invincible (Flor)
'Irène Watts' (OGCh)
'Ispahan' (OGD)
Jacqueline du Pré (MS)
Jane Asher (Pat)
Jardins de Bagatelle (HT)
'Jenny Duval' (OGG)
'Judy Fischer' (Min)
Julia's Rose (HT)
Just Joey (HT)
Keepsake (HT)
Kent (GrC)
King's Ransom (HT)
'Königin von Dänemark' (OGA)
'Korresia' (Flor)
L.D. Braithwaite (MS)
'Lady Hillingdon, Climbing' (Cl)

ing shoots. Unlike other Gallicas, this large bush is thorny and has grey-green leaves. HEIGHT & SPREAD 2.1×2.4m (7×8ft).

R. 'Comtesse de Lacépède' see
R. 'Du Maître d'Ecole'

R. 'Crimson Damask' see R. gallica var. officinalis

R. 'Duc de Guiche'♥ Crimson-purple, globular double blooms are slightly quartered, showing a green eye. The leaves are dark green. A shrubby, spreading plant. HEIGHT & SPREAD 1.2×1.2m (4×4ft).

R. 'Duchesse de Montebello'♥ Large, blush-pink, very double blooms flower early in summer. The leaves are grey-green. HEIGHT & SPREAD 1.5×1.2m (5×4ft).

R. 'Du Maître d'Ecole'♥ (syn. R. 'Comtesse de Lacépède', R. 'Rose du Maître d'Ecole') Quartered double flowers in a mixture of rose-pink and purple, fading to lilac, are 11cm (4¼in) across and show a green eye when they open flat. The leaves are greyish green on lax shoots that droop under the weight of bloom. HEIGHT & SPREAD 1×1.2m (3×4ft).

R. × francofurtana (syn. R. 'Empress Josephine') Deep pink petals with darker veining and wavy edges make up the semi-double cupped flowers, which are striking but loosely formed. The spreading bush has dark leaves and narrow autumn hips. HEIGHT & SPREAD 1.2×1.2m (4×4ft).

R. gallica var. officinalis♥ (syn. R. 'Crimson Damask', R. officinalis) (apothecary's rose, red rose of Lancaster) Deep pink, large, semidouble flowers cover this neat, upright plant with dark green leaves.

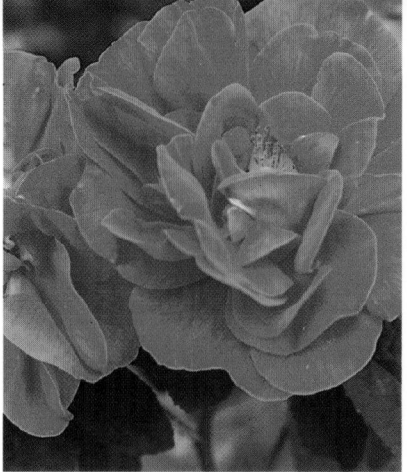
▲ Rosa gallica var. officinalis

HEIGHT & SPREAD 1×1m (3×3ft).

'Complicata' see R. 'Complicata'. **'Versicolor'**♥ (syn. R. mundi, R. m. ssp. versicolor, R. versicolor) has pale blush-pink, semidouble flowers, striped and splashed with reddish pink and up to 11cm (4¼in) across. They are borne on a twiggy plant.

R. 'Jenny Duval' see R. 'Président de Sèze'

R. officinalis see R. gallica var. officinalis

R. mundi see R. gallica 'Versicolor'

R. mundi ssp. versicolor see R. gallica 'Versicolor'

R. 'Président de Sèze'♥ (syn. R. 'Jenny Duval') The double, quartered blooms in deep magenta-pink edged with lilac-pink make a vivid show. The bushy growth bears rich green leaves. HEIGHT & SPREAD 1.2×1m (4×3ft).

R. 'Rose du Maître d'Ecole' see R. 'Du Maître d'Ecole'

R. 'Scharlachglut'♥ (syn. R. 'Scarlet Fire',

R. 'Scarlet Glow') Bright cherry-red, single blooms with golden stamens are large and borne abundantly in clusters or singly, but they have no scent. Large, pear-shaped orange hips hang on into winter on the sprawling growth, which makes a semi-climber. HEIGHT & SPREAD 3×1.8m (10×6ft).

▲ Rosa 'Tuscany Superb'

R. 'Tuscany Superb'♥ Velvety, maroon, double flowers, up to 8cm (3in) across, are often quartered and are lightly scented. Dark green leaves clothe the upright, bushy plant. HEIGHT & SPREAD 1×1m (3×3ft).

R. versicolor see R. gallica 'Versicolor'

Damask Roses
The plants listed have richly fragrant flowers, most about 7.5cm (3in) across, borne in loose clusters in mid summer only. The bushes are open-growing with small, rather rounded leaves on bristly stems. Some have hips but they are small and not showy.

R. 'Celsiana' (syn. R. 'Amélia') The pale pink, semidouble blooms with crinkled petals open wide to show golden stamens.

The grey-green leaves are aromatic. HEIGHT & SPREAD 1.5×1.2m (5×4ft).

R. 'Ispahan' ♀ Large, blush-pink, double blooms are freely borne over a long period, giving good value from the single flowering. The tall, generally upright plant has comparatively large leaves with a blue tinge. HEIGHT & SPREAD 1.8×1.4m (6×4½ft).

R. 'La Ville de Bruxelles' ♀ The wealth of petals gives a domed centre to the beautiful clear pink, double flowers. The upright but bushy plant carries luxuriant, fresh green leaves. HEIGHT & SPREAD 1.5×1m (5×3ft).

R. 'Madame Hardy' ♀ Pure white, double blooms open flat from the palest pink buds, showing petals exquisitely arranged round a green eye. The well-branched, erect plant has plentiful mid green foliage. HEIGHT & SPREAD 1.5×1.5m (5×5ft).

R. 'Marie Louise' The mauve-pink, double flowers are 10cm (4in) across and so full-petalled that they weigh down the dark-leaved, rather lax shoots. The outer petals curve back as the flower opens out flat. HEIGHT & SPREAD 1.2×1m (4×3ft).

Alba Roses

All the plants listed have fragrant flowers, borne in clusters only in mid summer. They vary in size, from 5–11cm (2–4¼in) across. The vigorous, upright plants, with few thorns and plenty of grey-tinged leaves, do well in poor soil and partial shade.

R. × alba 'Alba Maxima' ♀ (syn. R. 'Maxima') Profuse double flowers are creamy white with a hint of buff in the bud. HEIGHT & SPREAD 2.1×1.5m (7×5ft).

'Alba Semiplena' ♀ (syn. R. 'Semiplena') has semidouble flowers.

R. 'Cuisse de Nymphe' see R. 'Great Maiden's Blush'

R. 'Félicité Parmentier' ♀ Rounded, pale yellow buds open into small, light pink flowers that are double and sometimes quartered. The plant puts out suckers if it is grown on its own roots instead of grafted. HEIGHT & SPREAD 1.2×1m (4×3ft).

R. 'Great Maiden's Blush' (syn. R. 'Cuisse de Nymphe', R. 'Maiden's Blush, Great') The double flowers are open cups, blush-pink at the centre and creamy pink at the edge. They are rather loosely formed and are freely borne. HEIGHT & SPREAD 2.1×1.5m (7×5ft).

R. 'Königin von Dänemark' ♀ (syn. R. 'Queen of Denmark') The soft pink of the double blooms deepens towards the centre. The flowers open flat and are quartered. The plant is less upright than other Albas. HEIGHT & SPREAD 1.5×1.2m (5×4ft).

R. 'Madame Legras de Saint Germain' The large, white, double blooms look like powder-puffs on this large, arching shrub. HEIGHT & SPREAD 1.8×1.8m (6×6ft).

R. 'Maiden's Blush' Open cup-shaped double flowers are pink at the centre, fading to creamy pink at the edge. HEIGHT & SPREAD 1.2×1m (4×3ft).

R. 'Maiden's Blush, Great' see R. 'Great Maiden's Blush'

R. 'Maxima' see R. × alba 'Alba Maxima'

R. 'Queen of Denmark' see R. 'Königin von Dänemark'

R. 'Semiplena' see R. × alba 'Alba Semiplena'

Centifolia Roses

The crowded petals of these double, globular blooms, which are often called cabbage roses, make the clusters so heavy that they tend to droop and the arching, thorny stems need some support. The plants listed bloom once only, are richly scented and do not produce hips.

R. × centifolia (Provence rose, cabbage rose) The numerous, rich pink, mid summer blooms are 10cm (4in) across on this lax shrub with drooping, grey-green leaves. HEIGHT & SPREAD 1.5×1.2m (5×4ft).

'Cristata' ♀ (syn. R. Chapeau de Napoléon, R. 'Cristata') has buds enclosed by an enlarged, bristly, crested green calyx. The rich pink mid summer blooms are 10cm (4in) across.

R. 'De Meaux' (syn. R. 'Rose de Meaux') The rich pink blooms, paler round the edge, are little pompoms only about 4cm (1½in) across but abundant on the arching stems. They open in early summer. HEIGHT & SPREAD 1×1m (3×3ft).

Moss Roses

The buds and stems of these roses have a soft bristly green covering with a spicy aroma, known as moss. Full-petalled double flowers, usually fragrant and 7.5–10cm (3–4in) across, bloom in clusters in mid summer only, on arching plants with mid green leaves. There are no hips.

R. 'Capitaine John Ingram' ♀ The dark crimson blooms are lighter on the back of the petals and fade to purple. The bristly moss is tinged red. HEIGHT & SPREAD 1.2×1.2m (4×4ft).

'Poulmuti' (GrC)
'Precious Platinum' (HT)
'Président de Sèze' (OGG)
Pretty Polly (Pat)
R. primula (Sp)
Princess Royal (HT)
Pristine (HT)
Purple Tiger (Flor)
Queen Elizabeth (Flor)
Queen Mother (Pat)
'Queen of Denmark' (OGA)
'Rambling Rector' (Ra)
Ray of Sunshine (Pat)
Red Ace (Min)
Redgold (Flor)
'Red Grootendorst' (Rug)
Red Rascal (Pat)
Red Sunblaze (Min)
'Reine des Violettes' (OGHP)
Remember Me (HT)
Remembrance (Flor)
Renaissance (HT)
Robin Redbreast (Pat)
Rob Roy (Flor)
'Rose de Meaux' (OGCe)
'Rose de Rescht' (OGP)

'Rose du Maître d'Ecole' (OGG)
Rose Gaujard (HT)
Rosemary Harkness (HT)
'Roseraie de l'Haÿ' (Rug)
'Rosy Cheeks' (HT)
'Rosy Mantle' (Cl)
R. roxburghii (Sp)
'Royal Gold' (Cl)
Royal William (HT)
R. rubrifolia (Sp)
'Ruby Wedding' (HT)
R. rugosa 'Alba' (Rug)
R. rugosa var. *rubra* (Rug)
R. rugosa 'Scabrosa' (Rug)
Saint Cecilia (MS)
Sally Holmes (MS)
'Sanders' White Rambler' (Ra)
Sarah (HT)
Savoy Hotel (HT)
'Scarlet Fire' (OGG)
'Scarlet Glow' (OGG)
Scarlet Queen Elizabeth (Flor)
'Scharlachglut' (OGG)

Schneewittchen (Flor)
'Schoolgirl' (Cl)
'Seagull' (Ra)
'Sealing Wax' (Sp)
'Semiplena' (OGA)
R. sericea ssp. *omeinensis* f. *pteracantha* (Sp)
Sexy Rexy (Flor)
'Shailer's White Moss' (OGM)
Sheila's Perfume (Flor)
Shine On (Pat)
Shocking Blue (Flor)
'Shot Silk, Climbing' (Cl)
Silver Jubilee (HT)
'Silver Lining' (HT)
'Silver Wedding' (HT)
Snow Carpet (GrC)
'Snow Queen' (OGHP)
Solitaire (HT)
'Southampton' (Flor)
'Souvenir de Claudius Denoyel' (Cl)
'Souvenir de la Malmaison' (OGB)
'Souvenir de Saint Anne's' (OGB)
'Souvenir du Docteur Jamain' (Cl)

'Spanish Beauty' (Cl)
Sparkling Scarlet (Cl)
R. spinosissima (Sp)
'Stacey Sue' (Min)
'Stanwell Perpetual' (Sp)
Starina (Min)
Strawberry Fayre (Pat)
Suffolk (GrC)
Suma (GrC)
Summer Wine (Cl)
Sunblest (HT)
Super Star (HT)
Surrey (GrC)
Sussex (GrC)
'Swan Lake' (Cl)
Swany (GrC)
Sweet Dream (Pat)
Sweet Juliet (MS)
Sweet Magic (Pat)
Sympathie (Cl)
Tall Story (Flor)
Tango (Flor)
Tear Drop (Pat)
Tequila Sunrise (HT)
The Countryman (MS)
'The Fairy' (Poly)
The McCartney Rose (HT)
'The New Dawn' (Cl)

The Pilgrim (MS)
The Prince (MS)
The Times Rose (Flor)
Topsi (Flor)
Troika (HT)
Trumpeter (Flor)
'Tuscany Superb' (OGG)
Uncle Walter (HT)
'Veilchenblau' (Ra)
Velvet Fragrance (HT)
Vidal Sassoon (HT)
R. virginiana (Sp)
'Viridiflora' (OGCh)
Warm Welcome (MC)
Warm Wishes (HT)
'Wee Jock' (Pat)
'Wendy Cussons' (HT)
'Whisky Mac' (HT)
'White Bath' (OGM)
'White Cockade' (Cl)
'White Pet' (Poly)
Wiltshire (GrC)
Wishing (Flor)
R. xanthina 'Canary Bird'
'Yellow Doll' (Min)
'Yesterday' (Poly)
'Yvonne Rabier' (Poly)
'Zéphirine Drouhin' (Cl)
'Zigeunerknabe' (MS)

r

R. × *centifolia* '**Muscosa**'♀ (common moss rose) Clear pink blooms open from buds covered with a reddish moss. HEIGHT & SPREAD 1.5×1.2m (5×4ft).

R. '**Gloire des Mousseuses**' The lilac-pink blooms, fading to pale pink, are mossy in bud. The leaves are bright green. The flowers have good scent. HEIGHT & SPREAD 1.2×1m (4×3ft).

R. '**Henri Martin**'♀ Profuse crimson blooms open flat on a branching shrub with vivid green moss. This plant needs support. HEIGHT & SPREAD 1.5×1.2m (5×4ft).

▲ *Rosa* 'Nuits de Young'

R. '**Nuits de Young**' Velvety, deep maroon-purple blooms that are globular at first, open into loose cups showing golden stamens. This wiry plant has sparse, dark leaves. HEIGHT & SPREAD 1.2×1m (4×3ft).

R. '**Shailer's White Moss**'♀ (syn. *R.* 'White Bath') The white, urn-shaped blooms have plenty of moss. The drooping leaves are dark green. HEIGHT & SPREAD 1.2×1m (4×3ft).

R. '**White Bath**' see *R.* 'Shailer's White Moss'

Bourbon Roses

The plants listed, mainly repeat-flowering, have well-scented, double, cupped blooms with incurved petals opening to 7.5–10cm (3–4in) across. The vigorous open growth bears dark green leaves. There are no hips.

R. '**Blairii Number Two**'♀ Pale pink flowers, even paler at the petal edges, are borne only in mid summer. A vigorous plant that can be grown as a climber. HEIGHT & SPREAD 3.5×2.4m (12×8ft).

R. '**Boule de Neige**' Small white flowers with just a touch of pink open from pink buds. The petal edges curve back, giving the blooms a globular shape. HEIGHT & SPREAD 1.5×1.2m (5×4ft).

R. '**Honorine de Brabant**' Pale pink, quartered blooms are striped with deeper pink and mauve. They last from mid summer until the autumn frosts. There are large, leathery leaves and few thorns. HEIGHT & SPREAD 1.8×1.8m (6×6ft).

R. '**Madame Isaac Pereire**'♀ Fragrant,

▲ *Rosa* 'Madame Isaac Pereire'

deep pink blooms tinged with purple are 12.5cm (5in) across. They are rather loosely formed with some quartering. The autumn display is magnificent, but if the weather is cold at the first flush some flowers are malformed. HEIGHT & SPREAD 2.1×1.5m (7×5ft).

R. '**Madame Pierre Oger**' The tightly cupped, rosy crimson blooms have thin, papery petals with a pearly sheen. There is a good repeat-flowering. A loose plant which needs some support. HEIGHT & SPREAD 1.8×1.1m (6×3½ft).

R. '**Souvenir de la Malmaison**' Shell-pink flowers deepen to blush-pink at the raised, quartered centre. They reach 12.5cm (5in) across and weigh down the dark-leaved shrub in fine weather, but may fail to open properly during wet spells. HEIGHT & SPREAD 1.2×1.2m (4×4ft).

R. '**Souvenir de Saint Anne's**'♀ Fragrant, semidouble, creamy white flowers, up to 10cm (4in) across, bloom with great freedom and good continuity on this sturdy plant. HEIGHT & SPREAD 1.2×1.2m (4×4ft).

Portland Roses

The compact, upright bushes with light green leaves have their main flowering in

▼ *Rosa* 'Souvenir de Saint Anne's'

mid summer, with some repeat flowering until the autumn frosts. The blooms are in clusters and generally have good fragrance.

R. '**Comte de Chambord**' see *R.* 'Madame Knorr'

R. '**De Rescht**'♀ (syn. *R.* 'Rose de Rescht') Deep fuchsia-pink, pompom-shaped flowers, 6cm (2½in) across and packed with petals, are carried in numerous clusters on this short, upright-growing plant. HEIGHT & SPREAD 1m×60cm (3×2ft).

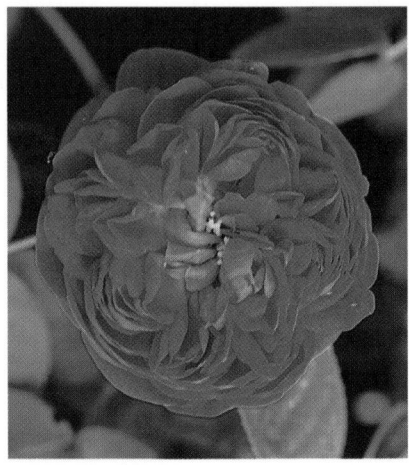

▲ *Rosa* 'De Rescht'

R. '**Duchess of Portland**' see *R.* 'Portlandica'

R. '**Madame Knorr**'♀ (syn. *R.* 'Comte de Chambord') Quartered, rich pink blooms, double and 10cm (4in) across, develop a hint of lilac as they fade. There is an abundant second flowering. The light green leaves are tinged with grey. HEIGHT & SPREAD 1.2×1m (4×3ft).

R. '**Portlandica**' (syn. *R.* 'Duchess of Portland') The single to semidouble blooms are a deep pinky scarlet. They are up to 10cm (4in) across and make a good repeat display on this bushy, upright plant. HEIGHT & SPREAD 1.5×1m (5×3ft).

R. '**Rose de Rescht**' see *R.* 'De Rescht'

Hybrid Perpetual Roses

These vigorous, upright, rather leggy plants with dark green leaves bear globular, shapely blooms about 9cm (3½in) across, which are the forerunners of the Large-flowered Bush Roses (Hybrid Teas). The flowers, borne singly or in small clusters from mid summer to autumn, include some with strong colours, except yellow, and these fade less if grown in some shade.

R. '**Baron Girod de l'Ain**' The cupped, double blooms have bright crimson, waved petals edged with white. They are strongly fragrant and borne both in clusters and singly. A bushy plant. HEIGHT & SPREAD 1.2×1m (4×3ft).

R. '**Baronne Prévost**'♀ Bright pink, quartered double blooms with a moderate scent open wide and flat on this freely branching plant with plentiful foliage. HEIGHT & SPREAD 1.2×1m (4×3ft).

R. 'Frau Karl Druschki' (syn. *R.* 'Snow Queen') Dazzling white, double flowers open from pink-tinged buds on the arching stems. The blooms are not affected by rain. They have little scent. This leggy plant bears plentiful leathery foliage. HEIGHT & SPREAD 1.5×1 m (5×3 ft).

R. 'Mrs John Laing' Beautifully formed, double, rosy lilac flowers with a rich scent are freely borne, singly and in clusters, on stout stems. An upright plant. HEIGHT & SPREAD 1.2×1 m (4×3 ft).

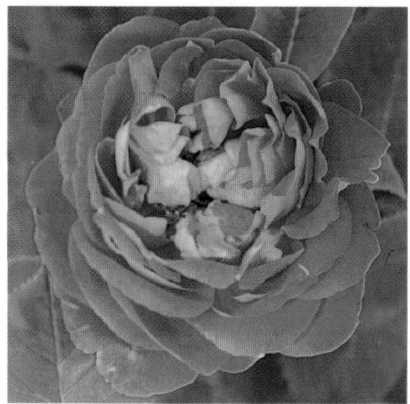
▲ *Rosa* 'Paul Neyron'

R. 'Paul Neyron' Globular, 12.5 cm (5 in) wide flowers, mostly carried singly, are a deep raspberry-pink. They have only a slight scent. The leaves are dark green and leathery on a vigorous, upright plant. HEIGHT & SPREAD 1.5×1 m (5×3 ft).

R. 'Reine des Violettes' The velvety, rosy violet flowers fade to lilac and are double, with quartering at the centre, and held in clusters. The plant has arching shoots and grey-green leaves. HEIGHT & SPREAD 1.5×1 m (5×3 ft).

R. 'Snow Queen' see *R.* 'Frau Karl Druschki'

China Roses

The dainty flowers are varied in form and appear from early summer to autumn, but they have very little scent. They are carried in clusters of 3-4, with each flower opening to about 7.5 cm (3 in) across. These open-growing, airy shrubs have small dark leaves, almost always shiny.

R. x *chinensis* 'Mutabilis' see *R.* x *odorata* 'Mutabilis'

R. 'Irène Watts'♀ Abundant ivory-white, double flowers, 8 cm (3¼ in) across, are shaded with pale orange-pink. There is a generous repeat on a plant that is small and bushy with matt leaves. HEIGHT & SPREAD 45×45 cm (1½×1½ ft).

R. x *odorata* 'Mutabilis' (syn. *R.* x *chinensis* 'Mutabilis', *R.* 'Mutabilis') Numerous, single blooms, 6 cm (2½ in) across, open from coppery buds to ochre-yellow flowers that turn pink, crimson and finally slate-purple as they age. All these colours can be seen at the same time. The plum-red stems and dark green leaves have a coppery

tinge when new. The plant needs a warm spot to thrive. HEIGHT & SPREAD 1.2×1.2 m (4×4 ft).

'Viridiflora' (syn. *R.* 'Viridiflora') has unusual, green double flowers, 5 cm (2 in) across, sometimes with brownish tints. (The petals are actually modified leaves.) They turn purple as they age and become rather untidy. This rose reaches a height of 1 m (3 ft) and a spread of 75 cm (2½ ft).

R. 'Viridiflora' see *R.* x *odorata* 'Viridiflora'

LARGE-FLOWERED BUSH ROSES (HYBRID TEA ROSES)

The flowers of the hundreds of Hybrid Teas available include all shades, except blue. Most hold their flower colour well, apart from a few that fade or discolour in hot sun or rain. Almost all varieties are double but some have fewer or thicker petals. These are less weighed down and damaged by rain, but they do tend to open fast and be over quickly.

The classic Hybrid Tea flower shape has a high, conical centre amid outer petals that reflex as they open. A fully opened flower is generally about 10 cm (4 in) across. Some varieties open to a more cupped shape. The first flowers appear in early summer and flowering continues well into autumn, with two main flushes and scattered blooms between. Most varieties have some scent and a number are richly fragrant. The blooms are on long, strong stems either singly or in small clusters. These plants need well-cultivated, moist soil and pruning, deadheading, and a careful watch for black spot, powdery mildew, rust and aphids.

Hybrid Teas are hardy and deciduous, generally with mid green leaves that have 5 ovate leaflets. They make upright growth and each variety's reliably uniform height makes them ideal for massing in formal beds. However, it is now common to mix varieties of different colours and heights, or to plant a group of Hybrid Teas in a mixed border that includes winter foliage to compensate for the bare rose bushes. Tall narrow varieties can make informal hedges.

R. Abbeyfield Rose♀ Freely borne deep rosy pink flowers with high centres are loosely formed and lightly scented. The foliage is dark and glossy on this low, bushy plant. HEIGHT & SPREAD 60×60 cm (2×2 ft).

R. Alexander♀+ The deep vermilion, lightly scented blooms are well shaped, and often have scalloped petals. A rose of upright growth with healthy, glossy foliage. HEIGHT & SPREAD 1.5 m×60 cm (5×2 ft).

R. Alpine Sunset Soft yellow with a peachy flush, the blooms are full-petalled and sweetly scented. Plentiful light green, glossy leaves are borne on strong, upright stems. HEIGHT & SPREAD 60×60 cm (2×2 ft).

R. Barkarole Heavily perfumed and full-petalled, the deep red, large blooms are set off by dark, glossy foliage on a spreading bush. HEIGHT & SPREAD 1 m×60 cm (3×2 ft).

R. Big Purple The flowers are a rich purple, full-petalled and sweetly scented. They are set off by dark, semi-glossy leaves. HEIGHT & SPREAD 1 m×60 cm (3×2 ft).

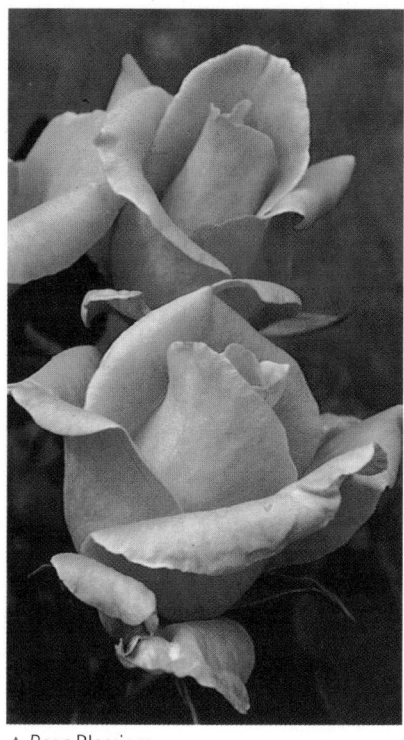
▲ *Rosa* Blessings

R. Blessings♀ A long display of rosy, salmon-pink blooms are produced. The large, loosely formed flowers appear, often in clusters, on a sturdy, bushy plant. HEIGHT & SPREAD 1 m×60 cm (3×2 ft).

R. Blue Moon The abundant lilac-mauve, fragrant flowers are elegantly formed. This rather narrow plant is short of leaves and often uneven in growth. HEIGHT & SPREAD 1 m×60 cm (3×2 ft).

R. Cherry Brandy Scented blooms in blends of orange and salmon-pink make a fine display against glossy leaves on plants of an uneven growth. HEIGHT & SPREAD 75×60 cm (2½×2 ft).

▲ *Rosa* 'Cheshire Life'

R. 'Cheshire Life' The profuse vermilion flowers are loosely formed. The growth is strong and well branched. HEIGHT & SPREAD 75×60 cm (2½×2 ft).

▲ *Rosa* Congratulations

▲ *Rosa* 'Dawn Chorus'

▲ *Rosa* Fragrant Cloud

▲ *Rosa* Julia's Rose

R. Chicago Peace Full yellow blooms, flushed orange and pink, are freely borne. The dark, glossy leaves are normally very healthy and the growth strong and bushy. HEIGHT & SPREAD 1.2m×60cm (4×2ft).

R. Congratulations Light pink, beautifully shaped blooms are carried profusely on long stems. The bush is rather lanky and has healthy, dark leaves. HEIGHT & SPREAD 1.5m×60cm (5×2ft).

R. 'Dawn Chorus' Deep orange blooms are set off particularly well by red-tinged leaves. The flowers offer only moderate scent and size but the plant is vigorously bushy. HEIGHT & SPREAD 75×60cm (2½×2ft).

R. Doctor McAlpine Deep pink, well-scented blooms are borne singly and in clusters on a healthy plant that is spreading and bushy. HEIGHT & SPREAD 45×60cm (1½×2ft).

R. Dutch Gold Deep yellow blooms keep their colour well and show to advantage against handsome dark leaves. The scent is moderate, the plant bushy and the growth strong. HEIGHT & SPREAD 1m×60cm (3×2ft).

R. Elina♀ (syn. *R.* Peaudouce) Abundant shapely, creamy white blooms are borne one to a stem. They have a light scent, long stems and petals that withstand rain. A strong grower with dark leaves that may be affected by mildew in late summer. HEIGHT & SPREAD 1.2m×60cm (4×2ft).

R. 'Ernest H. Morse'+ (syn. *R.* 'E.H.Morse') Sweetly scented, rich crimson flowers, bloom with great freedom and a good repeat. Open-centred, they fade with age. This healthy, bushy plant has hand-some, glossy leaves. HEIGHT & SPREAD 1m×60cm (3×2ft).

R. Fragrant Cloud+ Well-scented, dusky scarlet flowers are densely petalled but neatly formed, and carried in numerous trusses. The colour dulls a little in the sun. The dark leaves need watching for black spot. HEIGHT & SPREAD 75×60cm (2½×2ft).

R. Fragrant Dream The blend of apricot shades in the profuse, fragrant, full-petalled blooms is enhanced by abundant, healthy leaves. The plant is an upright grower. HEIGHT & SPREAD 75×60cm (2½×2ft).

R. Freedom♀+ Shapely, deep butter-yellow flowers that keep their colour are freely borne but have only a slight scent. A bushy uniform plant with plenty of glossy leaves. HEIGHT & SPREAD 75×60cm (2½×2ft).

R. 'Gaujard' see *R.* Rose Gaujard

R. Golden Jubilee Well-formed, lightly scented yellow blooms are flushed pink at the petal edges. The growth is bushy and the leaves large and glossy. HEIGHT & SPREAD 75×60cm (2½×2ft).

R. 'Grandpa Dickson'+ The well-formed, full-petalled, light yellow blooms pale and the rolled-back petal edges turn pink. An upright, very thorny plant. HEIGHT & SPREAD 75×60cm (2½×2ft).

R. Harry Wheatcroft Golden yellow in bud, these well-formed blooms have petals striped scarlet and yellow on their upper sides; the scent is light. The leaves on the bushy growth are dark and glossy. HEIGHT & SPREAD 75×60cm (2½×2ft).

R. Ice Cream Ivory-white blooms show well against dark, bronze-tinted foliage on a bushy plant. The full flowers are fragrant. HEIGHT & SPREAD 75×60cm (2½×2ft).

R. Ingrid Bergman♀ The abundant velvety blooms of dusky red have little scent. This sturdy plant has dark, leathery foliage and fairly even growth. HEIGHT & SPREAD 1m×60cm (3×2ft).

R. Jardins de Bagatelle see *R.* Sarah

R. Julia's Rose The loosely formed flowers are an unusual, light pinkish brown. They have little scent. This well-branched plant has rich green foliage but is not a robust grower. HEIGHT & SPREAD 60×60cm (2×2ft).

R. Just Joey♀ Copper-pink blooms that fade to creamy orange have wavy-edged petals. The flowers are pleasantly scented but the foliage tends to be sparse. HEIGHT & SPREAD 75×60cm (2½×2ft).

R. Keepsake The immaculately formed, globular, cerise-pink flowers have a lighter shading at the base of the petals. This vigorous plant has healthy, dark foliage. HEIGHT & SPREAD 1m×60cm (3×2ft).

R. King's Ransom Plentiful, rich yellow, well-shaped blooms are held upright over glossy dark foliage on this vigorous, branching, healthy plant. The scent is light. HEIGHT & SPREAD 75×60cm (2½×2ft).

▲ *Rosa* 'La France'

R. 'La France' Pleasantly scented, semi-double, silvery pink blooms appear profusely in clusters. This plant is vigorous. HEIGHT & SPREAD 75×60cm (2½×2ft).

R. L'Oréal Trophy The lightly scented, orange-salmon flowers hold their colour well. HEIGHT & SPREAD 1.2m×60cm (4×2ft).

R. Lovely Lady♀ The abundant well-formed blooms of pure, clear pink are moderate in fragrance. There is plenty of

r

▲ *Rosa* 'Lovers' Meeting'

▲ *Rosa* Polar Star

R. Pascali Shapely white flowers with a hint of buff at the centre and little scent are borne profusely, rarely in clusters. The leaves are dark on a very narrow, upright plant. HEIGHT & SPREAD 1m×60cm (3×2ft).

R. Paul McCartney see *R.* The McCartney Rose

R. Paul Shirville♀ Beautifully formed, soft pink blooms, tinged amber at the heart, are sweetly scented and carried with great freedom, sometimes in extra-large clusters. This well-branched bush has abundant dark leaves, though black spot may afflict them. HEIGHT & SPREAD 75×60cm (2½×2ft).

R. Peace♀+ The superb, full blooms of pale yellow have waved petals, often tinged pink at the edge. The lightly scented flowers, usually borne one to a stem, are profuse in mid summer and in autumn. Glossy foliage clothes this vigorous, branching plant. HEIGHT & SPREAD 1.2m×60cm (4×2ft).

R. Peaudouce see *R.* Elina

R. Peer Gynt Bright yellow blooms with a reddish flush, deeper on the outer petals, are full, globular, and mostly in large clusters. The scent is light. A bushy plant. HEIGHT & SPREAD 75×60cm (2½×2ft).

R. Piccadilly Scarlet petals with yellow on the outer side merge to orange as the profuse, shapely blooms open. They withstand rain well, but fade in the sun. There is little scent. The bushy plant has handsome, dark foliage, sometimes affected by black spot. HEIGHT & SPREAD 75×60cm (2½×2ft).

R. 'Pink Favourite' Bright pink, full-petalled high-centred blooms are profusely

borne with a good repeat. The colour fades slightly and the scent is light. Strong and branching growth bears plentiful glossy leaves. HEIGHT & SPREAD 1m×60cm (3×2ft).

R. 'Pink Peace' The deep pink, sweetly scented blooms are rather loosely formed. This plant flowers freely and is vigorous, with plenty of dark, leathery foliage. HEIGHT & SPREAD 1.1m×60cm (3½×2ft).

R. Polar Star Beautifully formed, fragrant blooms are borne on strong, upright stems. The flowers are not easily spoiled by rain and the large dark leaves are usually healthy. HEIGHT & SPREAD 75×60cm (2½×2ft).

R. Pot o' Gold The golden yellow, well-scented, full blooms have slightly scalloped petals. The abundant flowers appear singly and in sprays on a bushy plant with glossy leaves. HEIGHT & SPREAD 75×60cm (2½×2ft).

R. 'Precious Platinum' The vibrant blood-red flowers are large, well-shaped, lightly scented and freely produced. The leaves are dark and glossy on a bushy. healthy plant. HEIGHT & SPREAD 75×60cm (2½×2ft).

healthy, dark foliage on this bushy plant. HEIGHT & SPREAD 1m×60cm (3×2ft).

R. 'Lovers' Meeting' The shapely, warm orange blooms are lightly scented and appear in clusters. The bronze-tinted leaves are held on red shoots. This spreading plant is healthy but likely to suffer die-back from frost. HEIGHT & SPREAD 75×60cm (2½×2ft).

R. Loving Memory The plentiful, vivid crimson-red blooms hold their colour well and are shapely with a light fragrance. The plant is vigorous, tall and upright. HEIGHT & SPREAD 1.1m×60cm (3½×2ft).

R. 'Madame Butterfly' The very fragrant, pale pink flowers are soft yellow at the heart and fade to cream. They are dainty but full-petalled and numerous on a firm-stemmed, upright plant with small leaves. HEIGHT & SPREAD 60×60cm (2×2ft).

R. 'National Trust' The bright red well-shaped blooms have little scent. There is plentiful, dark foliage. HEIGHT & SPREAD 60×60cm (2×2ft).

R. 'Ophelia' Light pink flowers are especially profuse later in the season. The foliage is not too plentiful. HEIGHT & SPREAD 60×60cm (2×2ft).

R. Painted Moon Flowers in blends of light yellow, crimson and pink, are carried in large clusters, but have little scent. The bushy plant has plentiful glossy foliage. HEIGHT & SPREAD 75×60cm (2½×2ft).

▼ *Rosa* Painted Moon

▲ *Rosa* 'National Trust'

r

583

▲ *Rosa* Rosemary Harkness

R. Princess Royal Large, shapely blooms in deep golden yellow suffused with apricot are very profuse. The scent is slight. Healthy leaves clothe this strong, bushy plant. HEIGHT & SPREAD 75×60 cm (2½×2 ft).

▲ *Rosa* Pristine

R. Pristine Strongly fragrant, large-petalled blooms in ivory-white shade to blush pink at the edges. Dark leaves are carried on the strong stems of this robust plant. HEIGHT & SPREAD 1.1 m×60 cm (3½×2 ft).

R. Remember Me Coppery orange flowers with some vivid red tints bloom singly and in clusters on the dense, upright growth that carries ample healthy, dark foliage. HEIGHT & SPREAD 75×60 cm (2½×2 ft).

R. Renaissance The shapely, delicate, blush-pink blooms are very fragrant. They are carried with freedom and continuity. The bush is upright with plenty of foliage. HEIGHT & SPREAD 75×60 cm (2½×2 ft).

R. Rose Gaujard+ (syn. *R.* 'Gaujard') The numerous, bright cerise blooms with silvery-backed petals are full and, though shapely in bud, usually have a split, muddled centre as they open. They are borne singly among plentiful glossy dark leaves on a branching, vigorous, healthy plant. HEIGHT & SPREAD 1 m×60 cm (3×2 ft).

R. Rosemary Harkness Orange, salmon and yellow blend in well-formed, large, fragrant blooms, that pale as they age. This freely branching plant has glossy dark leaves. HEIGHT & SPREAD 75×60 cm (2½×2 ft).

R. 'Rosy Cheeks' The large, well-scented, carmine-pink flowers are yellow on the petals' underside. This plant is bushy with bright, glossy leaves. HEIGHT & SPREAD 60×60 cm (2×2 ft).

R. Royal William♀ Blood-red, fully fragrant, gracefully formed blooms are carried in great profusion on strong shoots. The leaves are dark on this healthy, vigorous plant. HEIGHT & SPREAD 1 m×60 cm (3×2 ft).

R. 'Ruby Wedding' The warm crimson, lightly scented blooms are full-petalled, shapely and held on strong stems. This well-branched plant has dainty foliage. HEIGHT & SPREAD 75×60 cm (2½×2 ft).

R. Sarah (syn. *R.* Jardins de Bagatelle) Richly perfumed, cream blooms with blush-pink round the petal edges are borne on strong upright stems. The foliage is plentiful on a well-branched plant of even growth. HEIGHT & SPREAD 60×60 cm (2×2 ft).

R. Savoy Hotel♀ Large, full-petalled blooms are light pink with deeper shading at the centre. They are lightly scented. The leaves are dark on the spreading plant. HEIGHT & SPREAD 60×60 cm (2×2 ft).

R. Silver Jubilee♀+ Continuous and abundant large, shapely blooms have a pale pink centre tinged salmon at the base and set among deeper pink petals. The colour lasts well but there is little scent. The normally healthy plant is sturdy with a wealth of glossy dark leaves. HEIGHT & SPREAD 75×60 cm (2½×2 ft).

R. 'Silver Lining'+ Pale pink, strongly fragrant blooms are silvery white on the back of the very dense petals, which develop a deeper pink rim as they age. The plant is an upright grower with glossy leaves. HEIGHT & SPREAD 75×60 cm (2½×2 ft).

R. 'Silver Wedding' Ivory blooms with a light scent are cream at the centre, neatly formed and borne in clusters. The dark-leaved plant is not a strong grower. HEIGHT & SPREAD 60×60 cm (2×2 ft).

R. Solitaire+ The clear yellow, pink-edged fragrant blooms are set off by dark bronze-tinted, glossy foliage. The plant is healthy and very vigorous but uneven in growth. HEIGHT & SPREAD 1.2 m×60 cm (4×2 ft).

R. Sunblest Golden yellow, moderately full blooms hold their colour in sun and rain. The bushy, healthy plant is an even grower with small, shiny, light green leaves. HEIGHT & SPREAD 75×60 cm (2½×2 ft).

R. Super Star+ The vivid vermilion blooms are well formed, full and borne abundantly in clusters. There is a light scent. The blooms withstand rain and do not fade. The upright plant grows robustly but its dark foliage is susceptible to mildew. HEIGHT & SPREAD 1 m×60 cm (3×2 ft).

R. Tequila Sunrise♀ Brilliant yellow petals edged with scarlet form full, well-shaped blooms. They are plentiful, lightly scented and retain their colour to make a striking

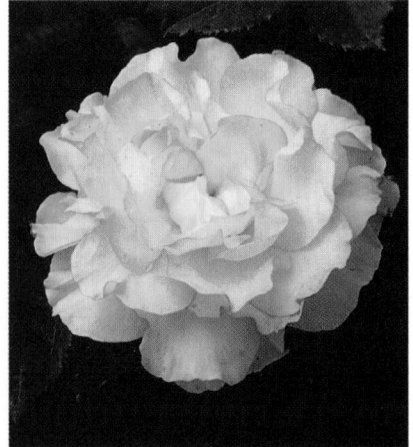

▲ *Rosa* Solitare

Rosa Tequila Sunrise ▼

▲ *Rosa* 'Wendy Cussons'

▲ *Rosa* 'Whisky Mac'

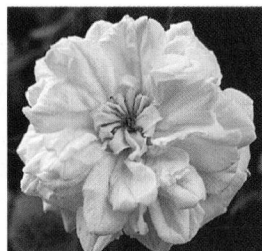

▲ *Rosa* 'Cécile Brunner'

show against dark, glossy leaves on a sturdy plant. HEIGHT & SPREAD 75×60cm (2½×2ft).

R. The McCartney Rose (syn. *R.* Paul McCartney) Deep candy-pink, elegant flowers are richly perfumed and carried on a robust upright plant with gleaming, dark foliage. HEIGHT & SPREAD 1m×60cm (3×2ft).

R. Troika ♀ Scarlet buds open to shapely coppery orange flowers with golden centres; they age to creamy pink. They are almost rainproof but only lightly scented. This vigorous, normally healthy bush has plenty of glossy leaves. HEIGHT & SPREAD 1.1m×60cm (3½×2ft).

R. Uncle Walter Bright scarlet flowers with the classic, high-centred shape, but little scent, are borne profusely in clusters. This plant is spindly and it needs support. It does well on a pillar. HEIGHT & SPREAD 1.5m×60cm (5×2ft).

R. Velvet Fragrance The heavily scented, deep crimson-pink blooms are beautifully formed and set off by glossy, dark leaves. This plant is vigorous with upright growth. HEIGHT & SPREAD 1.1m×60cm (3½×2ft).

R. Vidal Sassoon The large flowers are lavender-pink with brown overtones, and have a rich, slightly lemony scent. The leaves are glossy on a strong-stemmed plant. HEIGHT & SPREAD 75×60cm (2½×2ft)

R. Warm Wishes Shapely, well-scented blooms of a pale orange-pink are borne over a long period on a well-branched bush with glossy leaves. HEIGHT & SPREAD 75×60cm (2½×2ft).

R. 'Wendy Cussons'+ Very fragrant, elegantly formed, deep pink flowers are freely borne and withstand rain well. Leathery leaves are dark and glossy on this well-branched and wide-spreading plant. HEIGHT & SPREAD 1m×60cm (3×2ft).

R. 'Whisky Mac' Profuse, richly scented, yellow blooms with an orange flush are full-petalled and finely formed. They show well against abundant dark leaves, bronze-tinged when young, on an upright-growing plant. This rose is marred by die-back from frost, and by susceptibility to rust and mildew. HEIGHT & SPREAD 75×60cm (2½×2ft).

POLYANTHA ROSES
One parent of Polyantha Roses was *R. multiflora*, a vigorous, cluster-flowered wild rose. The short, generally upright, early Polyanthas carried numerous flower clusters but tended to produce different-coloured sports and their health was suspect. Only a

few of these early Polyantha plants are still available.

Most of the roses sold as Polyanthas now are the result of crossing true Polyanthas with Teas and other roses from China. They retain the bushy growth of the originals and make successful, free-flowering shrubs with two main flushes of clustered bloom, usually faintly scented. They are suitable for foreground planting and small gardens or patios.

R. 'Ballerina' ♀ Pale pink, single flowers, 2.5cm (1in) across, shading to a white centre, are borne in big, mop-head clusters on this spreading shrub. The generous repeat flowering is followed by an autumn crop of small hips. The mid green leaves are plentiful, small, narrow and shiny. HEIGHT & SPREAD 1×1m (3×3ft).

R. 'Cécile Brunner' ♀ (syn. *R.* 'Maltese Rose') Lightly scented, flesh-pink, double flowers, deepening in colour at the heart, are high-centred at first, then open loosely to 4cm (1½in) across. This airy plant has dark green, pointed healthy leaves. HEIGHT & SPREAD 1.1m×60cm (3½×2ft).

R. 'Little White Pet' see *R.* 'White Pet'
R. 'Maltese Rose' see *R.* 'Cécile Brunner'
R. 'Mevrouw Nathalie Nypels' ♀ (syn. *R.* 'Nathalie Nypels') Clear pink, semidouble, lightly scented blooms, 6cm (2½in) across, are borne in abundant clusters. The small, light green leaves are plentiful. HEIGHT & SPREAD 75×75cm (2½×2½ft).

R. 'The Fairy' ♀ Pale pink, double, rosette-shaped blooms, 5cm (2in) across, are in profuse clusters; they come into flower late but then make a continuous show on stiff but spreading shoots. The glossy leaves need watching for black spot. HEIGHT & SPREAD 76cm×1m (2½×3ft).

R. 'White Pet' ♀ (syn. *R.* 'Little White Pet') Clusters of creamy white, double pompom blooms, 5cm (2in) across, appear all summer. The dark leaves stay on the plant late. HEIGHT & SPREAD 45×45cm (1½×1½ft).

R. 'Yesterday' ♀ Deep rosy lilac flowers, white at the centre, bloom all summer in small trusses. They are scented, semidouble and 2.5cm (1in) across on an airy bush with small, shiny, mid-green leaves. HEIGHT & SPREAD 1.1×1.1m (3½×3½ft).

R. 'Yvonne Rabier' ♀ Sweetly scented, white, double, rosette-shaped, 5cm (2in) wide blooms, tinged yellow at the heart,

flower all summer in small clusters. The deep green leaves stay on into winter. HEIGHT & SPREAD 45×45cm (1½×1½ft).

CLUSTER-FLOWERED BUSH ROSES
(FLORIBUNDA ROSES)
Crosses between cluster-flowered Polyantha Roses and Hybrid Teas produced the Floribundas, which became popular during the 1930s – and the number of varieties still increases yearly. Because their parents had little scent, most Floribundas also lacked scent until recently, when more care has been taken to breed new varieties from the more fragrant strains.

In their size, habit of growth and uses in the garden the Floribundas do not differ from Hybrid Teas. The main difference between these two groups lies in the flowers and the way in which they are carried on the plant. The individual flowers of Floribundas are smaller and they are borne in large clusters or trusses, some having 20 or more blooms. Because the flowers in each truss do not all open at once, the flowering period is lengthened considerably – and as the old clusters fade, new ones are forming to continue the display. There is not the gap of a few weeks that occurs between the flushes of bloom in the case of many Hybrid Teas.

▼ *Rosa* 'Ballerina'

Since most Floribundas have fewer, and more substantial, petals than Hybrid Teas, water drains more easily from the flowers and they withstand wet weather better.

In the plants listed below, flower size is given only if it is very different from the average 6 cm (2½ in). The flowers are double, semidouble or single according to variety, and have a light scent unless stated otherwise. The spread is generally a little less than the height, and is given only when it differs markedly.

Rosa Allgold

R. Allgold+ Shapely, bright yellow, double blooms hold their colour in sun and rain, making a vivid show all summer. The small, healthy leaves are bright green on this bushy plant. HEIGHT 60 cm (2 ft).
R. Amber Queen♀ Amber-yellow, fragrant double blooms, suffused with soft orange, are carried in large clusters with good continuity of flowering. This spreading, healthy plant has dark foliage, red-tinted when young. HEIGHT 60 cm (2 ft).
R. Anna Livia♀ Soft salmon-pink, double blooms in big clusters are rainproof and carried above bushy growth whose leathery, glossy foliage is among the healthiest of all roses. HEIGHT 75 cm (2½ ft).
R. Anne Harkness The huge heads of light apricot, rosette-shaped flowers appear later than other roses and continue well into autumn. A tall plant with dark, semi-glossy, healthy leaves. HEIGHT 1.2 m (4 ft).
R. 'Arthur Bell'♀ Golden yellow, shapely double blooms that are larger than most floribundas and fade to cream. They are strongly scented. This plant is upright with healthy, shiny leaves. HEIGHT 1 m (3 ft).
R. Bright Smile Sparkling clear yellow, semidouble flowers in small clusters come into bloom early on a bushy, spreading plant whose glossy leaves are usually healthy. HEIGHT 60 cm (2 ft).
R. Bucks Fizz Light, warm orange, well-formed, double blooms on an upright plant are set off by healthy foliage that is red-

▲ *Rosa* Anna Livia

▼ *Rosa* Bright Smile

▲ *Rosa* Anne Harkness

▲ *Rosa* Champagne Cocktail

tinged when young, then a glossy, dark green. HEIGHT 1 m (3 ft).
R. By Appointment The double flowers have creamy petals round the close-furled, deep apricot centre. They come in large, well-spaced trusses and are enhanced by the dark, shiny leaves. HEIGHT 75 cm (2½ ft).
R. Champagne Cocktail Large, fragrant, semidouble flowers of pale yellow are flecked with rich pink and are deeper pink on the back of the petals. They are abundant on this erect plant with dark, glossy, healthy leaves. HEIGHT 1 m (3 ft).
R. 'Chanelle' Shapely and fragrant double blooms in creamy pink and apricot are freely borne and unspoiled by rain. The leaves are normally very healthy. HEIGHT 75 cm (2½ ft).
R. Chinatown♀+ The very large, sweetly scented, bright yellow, double flowers in medium-sized clusters are sometimes edged with pink. This tall plant has bright green, glossy leaves. HEIGHT 1.2 m (4 ft).
R. City of London♀ Blush-pink, fragrant, double blooms are borne in graceful sprays against bright green, glossy leaves. HEIGHT 1.1 m (3½ ft).
R. Dame Wendy The abundant, full, bright peach-pink, double flowers hold their colour well. A spreading plant with purplish young foliage that matures to dark

▲ *Rosa* Elizabeth of Glamis

grey-green. HEIGHT 75 cm (2½ft).

R. **'Dicbar'** see *R.* Memento

R. **Drummer Boy** This short, spreading plant bears clusters of bright blood-red, semidouble blooms, displayed against abundant foliage. HEIGHT 45 cm (1½ft).

R. **Edith Holden** Warm brownish gold, semidouble flowers open wide, showing a bright yellow eye. The blooms are numerous on a strong, bushy plant with dark green leaves. HEIGHT 75 cm (2½ft).

R. **Elizabeth of Glamis+** Large, shapely, double blooms in salmon-pink with an orange tint are carried in well-spaced clusters and are strongly fragrant. The colour withstands rain but the plant does not thrive in heavy, cold soils. HEIGHT 75 cm (2½ft).

R. **'English Miss'** The delicate, blush-pink, strongly scented blooms, shading to white, are cupped and full-petalled. The leaves are dark, purplish and semi-glossy. HEIGHT 75 cm (2½ft).

R. **Escapade**♀ The fragrant, pale rosy violet, semidouble blooms, which open wide to show the white centre, hold their colour well and make a long, generous display. The vigorous plant has shiny, light green, very healthy leaves. HEIGHT 1 m (3ft).

R. **Eye Paint** The showy, wide-open, single flowers are small and scarlet with a

▼ *Rosa* 'English Miss'

▼ *Rosa* Escapade

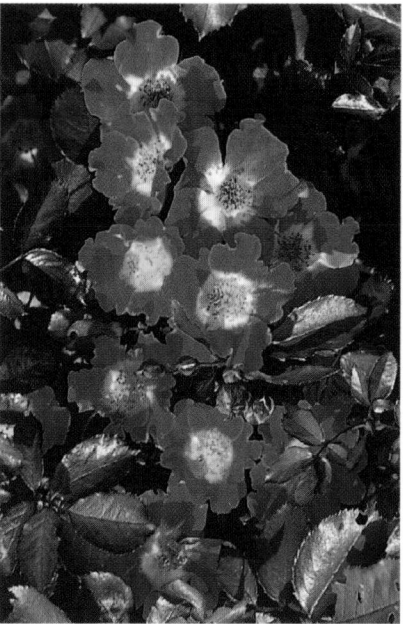

▲ *Rosa* Eye Paint

white eye, golden stamens and white backs to the petals. They are carried in huge clusters against dark, glossy leaves. The flowers have little scent. HEIGHT 1.4 m (4ft).

R. **Fellowship+** Scented, cupped, deep orange, double blooms are carried singly and in clusters with great freedom on an upright, well-branched plant with glossy, dark green leaves. HEIGHT 75 cm (2½ft).

R. **Fragrant Delight**♀ The glowing, orange-tinted, salmon-pink, double flowers fade to a pale pink. They have a rich scent and are numerous, shapely and semi-double. The large open sprays show well against red stems and dark green, bronze-tinted leaves. HEIGHT 1 m (3ft).

R. **'Glenfiddich'** The rich amber-yellow, double flowers are shapely and bloom with good continuity on this upright plant with dark, glossy leaves. HEIGHT 75 cm (2½ft).

R. **Golden Wedding** Bright yellow, high-centred, full-petalled and shapely flowers bloom in small clusters on a vigorous, healthy plant with glossy, dark foliage. HEIGHT 75 cm (2½ft).

R. **Golden Years** Golden yellow flowers open to wide, full-petalled cups and are carried in profusion on an upright plant with dark, glossy leaves. HEIGHT 75 cm (2½ft).

R. **Greenall's Glory** The semidouble blooms are blush-pink at the centre and silvery white towards the edge. This low, spreading plant has bronze-tinged, glossy leaves. HEIGHT 45 cm (1½ft).

R. **'Gruss an Aachen'** The very large, full-petalled blooms are creamy white to blush-pink. The sprays are shown off well by the dark, leathery foliage. HEIGHT 45 cm (1½ft).

R. **Hannah Gordon** Freely borne, semi-double, shapely white blooms have their petals edged with cherry-pink. This tall, open-growing bush has healthy, glossy,

dark leaves. HEIGHT 1 m (3ft).

R. **Harvest Fayre** Large clusters of light golden orange, well-formed, double flowers glow against the light green leaves densely clothing the bushy, strong plant. HEIGHT 75 cm (2½ft).

R. **Honeymoon** Full-petalled, canary-yellow, rosette-shaped blooms show beautifully against the semi-glossy leaves of this very vigorous plant. HEIGHT 1 m (3ft).

▲ *Rosa* Iceberg

R. **Iceberg**♀+ (syn. *R.* 'Schneewittchen') The double white blooms, which are sometimes stained pink by rain, are carried in large clusters on slender shoots. The pointed leaves are light green. Flowering often continues until Christmas on this vigorous, gracefully spreading, almost thornless plant. HEIGHT 1 m (3ft).

R. **'Iced Ginger'** The flowers are ivory-buff at the centre and coppery pink towards the edge. They are double, profuse and stiff-stemmed on a strong-growing bush. HEIGHT 1 m (3ft).

R. **Invincible** The nonstop, bright scarlet-crimson, double blooms, which hold their colour well in sun and rain, are shapely on a robust, upright plant with dark green, semi-glossy leaves. HEIGHT 75 cm (2½ft).

R. **'Korresia'** The sparkling bright yellow, double flowers with wavy-edged petals hold their colour and are sweetly perfumed. They are ideal for bedding and bloom continuously in well-spaced trusses enhanced by bright green, shiny leaves on a tidy plant. HEIGHT 75 cm (2½ft).

R. **Lilli Marlene** Deep scarlet, double blooms, opening wide and rather loose, hold their colour and are profusely borne in

r

▲ Rosa 'Korresia'

▲ Rosa Many Happy Returns

▲ Rosa Margaret Merril

large, stiff-stemmed trusses. They have very little scent. This dense, branching plant is well covered with glossy, mid green leaves. HEIGHT 75 cm (2½ ft).

R. 'Macrexy' see *R. Sexy Rexy*

R. Many Happy Returns♀ Abundant clusters of finely formed, blush-pink, large double blooms cover a dense, spreading plant, which has large, glossy, pointed leaves. HEIGHT 1 m (3 ft).

R. Margaret Merril♀ Richly fragrant, pearly white, double blooms, with a faint blush at the centre and pinkish gold stamens, are exquisitely formed. They are abundantly borne in clusters. The dark leaves are glossy. HEIGHT 75 cm (2½ ft).

R. 'Masquerade'+ Small, semidouble blooms that change from yellow to flame to pink and then red as they age are borne in huge trusses that show all the colours at the

same time and repeat well if assiduously deadheaded. This tall, freely branching bush has dark, glossy leaves. HEIGHT 1.1 m (3½ ft).

R. Matangi+ The orange-red, double blooms have a white eye and are silvery white on the back of the petals They are carried on a bushy plant with dark, glossy leaves. HEIGHT 1.1 m (3½ ft).

R. Melody Maker Light vermilion, full-petalled blooms with a silvery sheen in the centre are held in large trusses on a bushy, dark-leaved plant. HEIGHT 75 cm (2½ ft).

R. Memento (syn. *R.* 'Dicbar') Seldom out of flower, this rose bears its orange-red, double blooms in clusters. The flowers hold their colour well and open out wide against this bushy plant's plentiful dark leaves. HEIGHT 75 cm (2½ ft).

R. Mountbatten♀ Sunny soft yellow, full-petalled flowers bloom in large clusters and singly on a tall plant with dark glossy leaves. HEIGHT 1.2 m (4 ft).

R. 'Oranges and Lemons' Orange-yellow petals striped with scarlet make eye-catching large, double blooms that are well displayed in open clusters on this upright plant. New leaves have a coppery tinge. HEIGHT 1 m (3 ft).

R. Peppermint Ice Pale green shades in the ivory-white petals make the full-petalled, shapely blooms unusual. They are profuse, and set off by the glossy leaves on this well-branched plant. HEIGHT 75 cm (2½ ft).

R. Perestroika As the shapely, golden

▼ Rosa Matangi

▼ Rosa Memento

▲ Rosa 'Oranges and Lemons'

yellow, double flowers open, the petals roll back at the edges. The blooms shine out from this low, rounded plant clothed with dark, glossy, usually healthy foliage. The flowers are virtually unscented. HEIGHT 45 cm (1½ ft).

R. 'Pink Parfait'+ The satin-pink, double blooms, rich cream at the petal base, are very shapely as they open and are held in profuse clusters. The open, rather slender growth has dark green foliage. HEIGHT 75 cm (2½ ft).

R. Purple Tiger Very striking mauve blooms with variable purple striping and touches of ivory are full-petalled and open out wide. This plant has few thorns and is well filled out with dark leaves. HEIGHT 75 cm (2½ ft).

R. Queen Elizabeth♀+ Clear pink, cupped blooms that are well formed and double are held singly and in small clusters at the top of the bush on strong stems with few thorns. This tall, upright plant is rather narrow with an ample covering of very large, healthy leaves. HEIGHT 1.8 m (6 ft).

R. Redgold Double blooms with a variable red edging merging with the bright gold centre are held in large sprays. They age to a pinky orange. The tall, strong shoots have rather sparse leaves. HEIGHT 1 m (3 ft).

R. Remembrance Deep scarlet, double flowers are carried with abundance in large trusses and over a long season. This compact and bushy plant has glossy, dark leaves. HEIGHT 60 cm (2 ft).

R. Rob Roy The rich crimson-scarlet, well-formed, double blooms are large and

▼ Rosa Purple Tiger

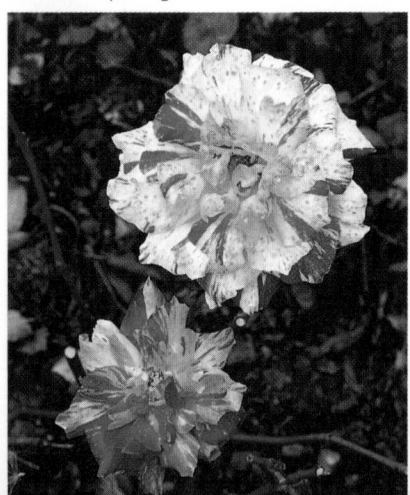

borne both singly and in small clusters. The growth is upright, with sparse, semi-glossy, dark green foliage. HEIGHT 1 m (3 ft).

R. Scarlet Queen Elizabeth Large, globular, deep scarlet blooms appear in great profusion on a stiff, upright plant with plenty of dark foliage. HEIGHT 1.2 m (4 ft).

R. Schneewittchen see *R.* Iceberg

▲ *Rosa* Sexy Rexy   *Rosa* Trumpeter ▲

R. Sexy Rexy♀ (syn. *R.* 'Macrexy') Palest coral-pink, small but full-petalled blooms with slightly frilled petals are borne in large clusters over a long period. They are shown off by plentiful dark, glossy leaves. HEIGHT 75 cm (2½ft).

R. Sheila's Perfume Well-formed, golden yellow, double blooms, their large petals edged with pinky red, are richly fragrant. The foliage is glossy, dark green and healthy on a strong-stemmed, well-branched plant. HEIGHT 75 cm (2½ft).

R. Shocking Blue The numerous and unusually coloured, vivid magenta-mauve, double blooms are carried in medium clusters. They are well formed and rich in fragrance. The leaves are a good dark green but the plant is not a strong grower. HEIGHT 75 cm (2½ft).

R. 'Southampton'♀ Apricot, large, double blooms are fragrant and borne in big clusters on an upright bush with shiny, very healthy leaves. HEIGHT 1 m (3 ft).

R. Tall Story Soft yellow, semidouble flowers are carried among light green, semiglossy leaves along arching branches, which make the plant so wide-spreading that it can

▼ *Rosa* Sheila's Perfume

▲ *Rosa* 'Southampton'

▲ *Rosa* Tango

be used for ground cover. The flowers give a good repeat display. HEIGHT & SPREAD 75 cm×1.5 m (2½×5 ft).

R. Tango♀ In these unique orange-scarlet blooms, each petal has a fine white rim, a yellow base and a yellow back. The flowers are profuse and full-petalled, opening wide on an upright plant with glossy, dark leaves. HEIGHT 75 cm (2½ft).

R. The Times Rose♀+ The continuous display has trusses of dark crimson-red, very full blooms that open to flat rosettes showing golden stamens. This sturdy, spreading plant is well clothed with healthy, coppery tinged, shiny leaves that turn dark green as they age. HEIGHT 75 cm (2½ft).

R. Topsi+ Orange-scarlet, semidouble blooms that keep their colour flower with great profusion. Both flowers and leaves are large on the short but sturdy bush. It may be subject to die-back. HEIGHT 45 cm (1½ft).

R. Trumpeter♀ Heavy trusses of orange-scarlet double blooms may make this plant rather sprawling. The flowers, which have little scent, are well shown off by plenty of glossy healthy leaves. HEIGHT 75 cm (2½ft).

R. Wishing Peach and salmon shades blend in the shapely double blooms, which are borne in well-spaced clusters. They stand out against the gleaming leaves that fill out this bushy plant. HEIGHT 60 cm (2 ft).

▲ *Rosa* Wishing

MODERN SHRUB ROSES

Some of the most free-flowering of all roses are among the Modern Shrubs, whose branching stems bear generous clusters of blooms in a full palette of colours. The diversity of the plants reflects the variety of parents used to produce roses with the vigour and free growth of the old and the long flowering period and bright tints of the new. The flowers can be single, semidouble or double, and are mostly carried in clusters. There are sprawling growers that make mounds more than 3 m (10 ft) tall, upright shrubs resembling Floribunda bush roses, and spreading, freely branching ones like the sweetly scented Hybrid Musks. The English Roses combine the flower form and scent of old roses with a modern range of colour. Rugosa Roses belong here but are treated separately below.

The bigger Modern Shrubs make beautiful specimen plants, and most of the others are successful as hedging. These plants' informal habit of growth suits mixed borders better than carefully pruned bush roses. With few exceptions Modern Shrub Roses are repeat flowering, a later blooming being encouraged by diligent deadheading.

R. Abraham Darby Apricot-pink double blooms that are fragrant, cup-shaped and

▼ *Rosa* Abraham Darby

589

▲ *Rosa* 'Buff Beauty'

10cm (4in) across, are borne on this English Rose, which makes spreading growth. HEIGHT & SPREAD 1.5×1.5m (5×5ft).

R. 'Buff Beauty'♀ Large clusters of buff to apricot, lightly scented, double flowers that fade to pale cream are 7.5cm (3in) across and extremely profuse. Dark, glossy foliage clothes this spreading Hybrid Musk shrub. HEIGHT & SPREAD 1.2×1.2m (4×4ft).

R. Constance Spry♀ The outstanding, clear pink blooms are 10cm (4in) across, double, urn-shaped and richly perfumed. Although not repeat flowering, they are carried very freely over a long period in mid summer. The long, arched shoots need support and look well on a dome-shaped frame. HEIGHT & SPREAD 1.8×1.5m (6×5ft).

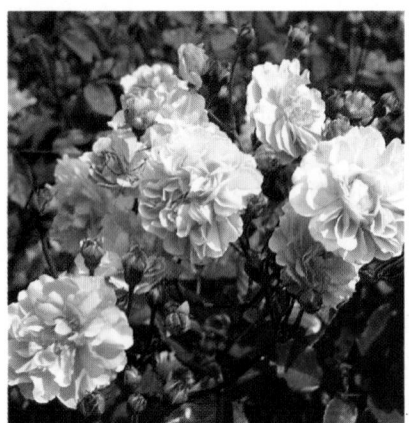

▲ *Rosa* 'Cornelia'

R. 'Cornelia'♀ The apricot-pink, scented, double blooms are only 5cm (2in) across and are borne in large trusses. They are set off by the dark green leaves. This robust, arching Hybrid Musk has a generous repeat flowering in autumn. HEIGHT & SPREAD 1.5×1.5m (5×5ft).

R. English Garden The ivory-white, quartered, double blooms, shading to yellow in the centre, are fragrant and open to 10cm (4in) across. A short, upright English Rose. HEIGHT & SPREAD 1m×60cm (3×2ft).

▲ *Rosa* English Garden

R. Evelyn Light apricot-pink, double blooms with a full fragrance are 9cm (3½in) across. This English Rose is fairly small but bushy. HEIGHT & SPREAD 1.1×1m (3½×3ft).

R. Felicia♀ Many sprays of double, light pink flowers that open flat to 7.5cm (3in) across have the sweet Hybrid Musk scent. They show well against dark, shiny leaves on this spreading plant. HEIGHT & SPREAD 1.5×2.1m (5×7ft).

R. 'Fountain' Small clusters of crimson double flowers are abundantly borne throughout the season on this upright shrub with dark green foliage. HEIGHT & SPREAD 1.5×1.5m (5×5ft).

R. 'Francesca' Apricot-yellow, semi-double flowers with a light scent are 7.5cm (3in) across. There is plentiful dark, glossy foliage on the spreading Hybrid Musk bush. HEIGHT & SPREAD 1.2×1.2m (4×4ft).

R. 'Fred Loads'♀+ Large trusses of bright orange-vermilion blooms 10cm (4in) across are borne on light green stems above bright green, glossy leaves. The flowers are semidouble and lightly scented, and the plant is a strong, upright grower. HEIGHT & SPREAD 1.8×1.1m (6×3½ft).

R. 'Frühlingsgold'♀ Very large and fragrant semidouble blooms of primrose-yellow cover the long, arching shoots – but in early summer only. The flowers open to 10cm (4in). The leaves are markedly small. HEIGHT & SPREAD 2.4×2.1m (8×7ft).

R. 'Frühlingsmorgen' The glowing single blooms are pink with a primrose centre and amber stamens. They open to 10cm (4in) across, making a magnificent display in spring but without much of a repeat flowering. The arching shoots carry small, matt grey-green leaves. HEIGHT & SPREAD 1.8×1.8m (6×6ft).

▲ *Rosa* Felicia

R. Gertrude Jekyll♀ Full-scented, rich pink blooms that are very double in form and up to 12.5cm (5in) across make a generous display on this rather open-growing English Rose shrub. HEIGHT & SPREAD 1.5×1.1m (5×3½ft).

R. 'Gipsy Boy'♀ see *R.* 'Zigeunerknabe'

R. Golden Celebration Huge, golden yellow, double flowers form cups some 12.5cm (5in) across and have a rich fragrance. There are dark, glossy leaves on this nicely rounded bush. HEIGHT & SPREAD 1.2×1.2m (4×4ft).

R. 'Golden Wings'♀ Great quantities of single, pale yellow blooms with amber stamens are produced by this rose throughout the summer. The flowers are 10cm (4in)

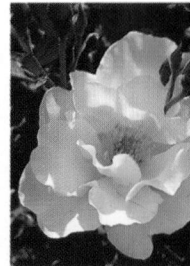

▲ *Rosa* Gertrude Jekyll

Rosa 'Golden Wings' ▲

across and lightly scented. This spreading plant branches freely. HEIGHT & SPREAD 1.5×1.5 m (5×5 ft).

R. Graham Thomas♥ The fragrant, golden yellow, cupped flowers are 10 cm (4 in) across, very double and borne abundantly. Shown off against glossy, healthy leaves, they make an outstanding English Rose with tall, upright growth. HEIGHT & SPREAD 1.5×1.2 m (5×4 ft).

R. 'Gypsy Boy'♥ see R. 'Zigeunerknabe'

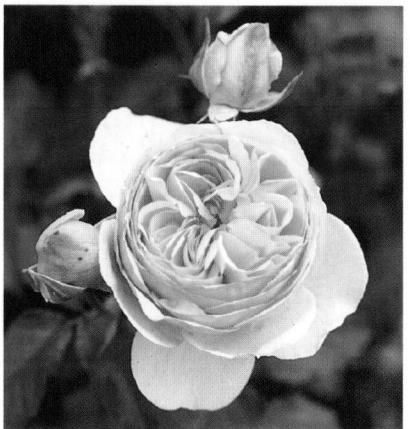

▲ *Rosa* Heritage

R. Heritage The clusters of very large, fragrant, light pink blooms are 12.5 cm (5 in) across and full-petalled, with petals curving in to form a globular flower. This fairly upright English Rose has dark green leaves. HEIGHT & SPREAD 1.2×1.2 m (4×4 ft).

R. Jacqueline du Pré♥ Blush-pink, semidouble flowers with scalloped petals show well against the dark, shiny leaves. The fragrant flowers, 10 cm (4 in) across, give an excellent repeat blooming. Branching growth fills out the vigorous shrub. HEIGHT & SPREAD 1.5×1.5 m (5×5 ft).

R. L.D. Braithwaite Cupped, full-petalled, crimson flowers bloom in profusion among greyish green leaves. They are fragrant, double and 10 cm (4 in) across. This quite short English Rose is upright but filled out with bushy growth. HEIGHT & SPREAD 1×1.1 m (3×3½ ft).

R. 'Lavender Lassie'♥ Enormous heads of double, bright pink flowers weigh the strong shoots down to the ground unless this plant is staked. These plentiful, well-scented, rosette-shaped blooms are 9 cm (3½ in) across and show well against the healthy, shiny leaves. HEIGHT & SPREAD 1.5×1.2 m (5×4 ft).

R. 'Marguerite Hilling'♥ The outstandingly profuse early summer show of semidouble, mid pink flowers is followed by a lesser display later in the season. The scented flowers, 7.5 cm (3 in) across, are borne on the arching shoots of a dense, spreading shrub with matt leaves. HEIGHT & SPREAD 2.1×2.1 m (7×7 ft).

R. Mary Rose Pink double flowers with a hint of lilac in them and a light scent are

▲ *Rosa* Mary Rose

carried on this short, shrubby English Rose. The flowers are 10 cm (4 in) across. HEIGHT & SPREAD 1.1×1.1 m (3½×3½ ft).

R. 'Nevada'♥ The huge and profuse creamy white flowers with golden stamens open to 12.5 cm (5 in) across. They are semidouble, lightly scented and smother the arching stems of this large, spreading shrub. HEIGHT & SPREAD 2.1×2.1 m (7×7 ft).

Rosa 'Nevada'

R. 'Penelope'♥+ Clusters of abundant, light peach-pink, semidouble flowers 7.5 cm (3 in) across fade to cream. This sweet-scented Hybrid Musk has broad, glossy, dark green leaves on a well-branched, bushy plant. HEIGHT & SPREAD 1.2×1.2 m (4×4 ft).

R. Saint Cecilia Double, full-scented blooms in blends of pink and orange eventually open out flat, reaching 10 cm (4 in) across. This English Rose makes a bushy plant. HEIGHT & SPREAD 1.1×1.1 m (3½×3½ ft).

R. Sally Holmes♥ Dense clusters of large, single, ivory-white flowers are almost too crowded to display themselves fully but make a spectacular display against the dark, glossy leaves. The scented blooms are 12.5 cm (5 in) across and borne on a strong-growing upright plant. HEIGHT & SPREAD 2×1 m (6½×3 ft).

R. Sweet Juliet Apricot blooms that are double and quartered with a rich fragrance open to 10 cm (4 in) across and are carried on arching stems on this English Rose. HEIGHT & SPREAD 1.2 m×75 cm (4×2½ ft).

R. The Countryman Rich pink flowers with a full fragrance are carried on a spreading shrub. The double blooms are 7.5 cm (3 in) across and as well as an early summer show, make a generous second display in autumn. HEIGHT & SPREAD 1×1 m (3×3 ft).

R. The Pilgrim Double yellow blooms, the colour darkening in the centre, open to

7.5 cm (3 in) across and have a full scent. The plant is upright and bushy. HEIGHT & SPREAD 1×1 m (3×3 ft).

R. The Prince The crimson flowers open cupped and the outer petals reflex until they form a rosette. The colour darkens to purple as the blooms age. The fragrance is strong and the growth low and bushy with dark green leaves. HEIGHT & SPREAD 60×60 cm (2×2 ft).

R. 'Zigeunerknabe' (syn. R. 'Gipsy Boy', R. 'Gypsy Boy') The large clusters of double crimson blooms open to show golden stamens and are 9 cm (3½ in) across. They cover the very vigorous, tangled shrub at mid summer but there is no repeat flowering and the blooms have little scent. The leaves are rather coarse. HEIGHT & SPREAD 1.8×1.8 m (6×6 ft).

RUGOSA ROSES

The robust descendants of R. rugosa now grown in gardens were raised about 1900 – which classifies them as Modern Shrub Roses. They are, however, distinctive enough to justify a section on their own.

These roses do well in most soils, even poor ones. They are shrubby, upright, very spiny and generally well clothed to the ground with bright green, glossy, deeply veined and notably healthy foliage. As well as being vigorous, colourful border plants, they make excellent hedges.

Rugosa flowers, borne in early summer and then more or less continuously until early autumn, are usually about 8 cm (3½ in) across and purplish pink or white. They are mostly in clusters and are single, semidouble or double. Single and semidouble flowers are usually followed by round orange-red hips that can be very striking.

R. 'Agnes' The scented, pale amber blooms, paler at the edge, are double and have crinkled petals. The autumn flowering is only half-hearted. The foliage is rather dark. HEIGHT & SPREAD 1.8×1.5 m (6×5 ft).

▲ *Rosa* The Countryman

▲ Rosa 'Agnes'

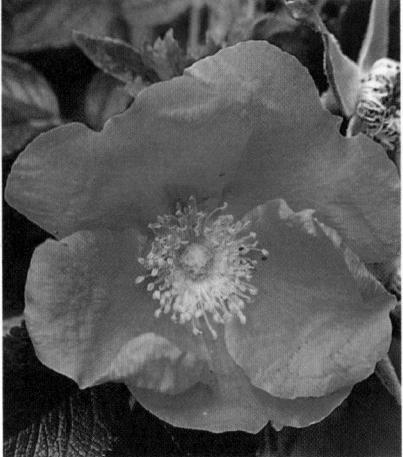

▲ Rosa rugosa var. rubra

▲ Rosa Boys' Brigade

▲ Rosa 'Blanche Double de Coubert'

R. 'Blanche Double de Coubert'♀ Pure white, very fragrant, semidouble blooms are 10 cm (4 in) across on an open plant and have papery petals that do not withstand rain. They do not produce hips. HEIGHT & SPREAD 1.5×1.2 m (5×4 ft).

R. 'F.J. Grootendorst' (syn. *R.* 'Red Grootendorst') Fringed petals distinguish the bright crimson-red, double blooms, only 4 cm (1½ in) across. They are carried in large clusters but have no scent. HEIGHT & SPREAD 1.5×1.2 m (5×4 ft).

R. 'Fimbriata' The pale blush-pink, semidouble blooms have prettily fringed petals and a moderate scent. HEIGHT & SPREAD 1.2×1 m (4×3 ft).

R. 'Fru Dagmar Hastrup'♀ Fragrant, light pink single blooms with creamy yellow stamens are freely borne with good continuity. Large hips appear while the flowers are still on this spreading shrub. HEIGHT & SPREAD 1.2×1.2 m (4×4 ft).

R. 'Pink Grootendorst'♀ The scentless double blooms are bright pink and held in clusters. HEIGHT & SPREAD 1.5×1.2 m (5×4 ft).

R. 'Red Grootendorst' see
   R. 'F.J. Grootendorst'

R. 'Roseraie de l'Haÿ'♀ Velvety, light purple-red blooms, 10 cm (4 in) across, are borne freely. They are fragrant and double,

and open flat and rather loose on a plant well covered with healthy foliage that turns golden in autumn. There are no hips. HEIGHT & SPREAD 1.8×1.8 m (6×6 ft).

R. rugosa 'Alba'♀ White, scented, silky single flowers are followed by orange-red hips, borne alongside late flowers. The bright green leaves turn gold in autumn. HEIGHT & SPREAD 1.8×1.8 m (6×6 ft).

The flowers of var. *rubra*♀ are purple-red. **'Scabrosa'**♀ has single blooms, 14 cm (5½ in) across, with velvety, purplish pink petals and yellow stamens. There is a fine crop of hips. It reaches a height of 1.5 m (5 ft) and a spread of 1.2 m (4 ft).

PATIO ROSES (DWARF CLUSTER-FLOWERED BUSH ROSES)
Breeders have crossed Floribundas with Miniatures to create a group of roses halfway between the two – too big in flower and leaf to be Miniatures and too short for Floribundas. Patio roses have the upright bushy growth and clustered blooms of the Floribundas, a resemblance reflected in their alternative name, given in brackets above.

Patio roses tend to be more widespreading than the Floribundas, forming cushions of floral colour over a long season as the blooms in the early clusters open in succession and fresh flower clusters follow on. Their short stature suits cultivation in planters, tubs and other containers, but if pot-grown, these roses need extra feeding to keep up such enthusiastic flowering.

Unless stated otherwise, the patio roses included here have mid green leaves and clusters of double, slightly scented blooms, generally about 3 cm (1¼ in) across when fully open but with some larger ones opening to 5 cm (2 in).

R. Angela Rippon The full-petalled, large, rosy salmon blooms are immaculately formed and set off by plenty of matt leaves HEIGHT & SPREAD 45×45 cm (1½×1½ ft).

R. Anna Ford♀+ Deep orange-red blooms that fade to orange open wide and flat. They are semidouble, freely and continuously produced and set off by very shiny,

bright green leaves. HEIGHT & SPREAD 45×45 cm (1½×1½ ft).

R. Boys' Brigade Large clusters of small, crimson-red, white-eyed flowers with little scent are in bloom over a long period. The leaves are plentiful and glossy. HEIGHT & SPREAD 45×45 cm (1½×1½ ft).

R. Buttons Clusters of well-spaced, salmon-red flowers make a bright display against the abundant, glossy foliage. HEIGHT & SPREAD 45×45 cm (1½×1½ ft).

R. Cider Cup♀ The high-centred, beautifully formed, deep apricot-pink blooms are enhanced by glossy foliage. HEIGHT & SPREAD 45×45 cm (1½×1½ ft).

R. Festival Large, shapely, bright crimson-scarlet flowers are made striking by silvery white on the back of the petals. They are semidouble and bloom with good continuity, against dark green, glossy foliage. HEIGHT & SPREAD 45×45 cm (1½×1½ ft).

▲ Rosa Gentle Touch

R. Gentle Touch♀ Neatly furled buds, open flat into small, pale pink flowers, tinged acid-yellow in the middle. This plant has healthy dark green, semi-glossy leaves. HEIGHT & SPREAD 45×45 cm (1½×1½ ft).

R. Gingernut Flowers in bronze-orange with a reddish back to the petals are well spaced in trusses that cover the plant evenly. There is plenty of glossy foliage. HEIGHT & SPREAD 45×45 cm (1½×1½ ft).

R. 'Honey Bunch' The small but full-petalled and shapely flowers are a muted soft yellow suffused with salmon-pink. They are sweet-scented, freely borne and held against healthy bright green, glossy leaves. HEIGHT & SPREAD 45×45 cm (1½×1½ ft).

R. Jane Asher Small, bright scarlet blooms are freely produced over a long season on a small but very tough plant with glossy leaves. HEIGHT & SPREAD 40×45 cm (16×18 in).

R. Little Bo-Peep♀+ Small, full-petalled, blush-pink buds, delicately formed and very numerous, open out flat to show the yellow stamens in the pale pink blooms. The spreading plant has tiny glossy leaves. HEIGHT & SPREAD 30×50 cm (12×20 in).

R. Minilights Continuously flowering clusters of pale yellow, single blooms blend with the abundant light green leaves on this spreading plant. HEIGHT & SPREAD 25×50 cm (10×20 in).

R. Peek A Boo Masses of apricot-pink blooms are borne in graceful sprays over a long period, making a cushion of bloom on a background of small, dark leaves. HEIGHT & SPREAD 45×45 cm (1½×1½ ft).

R. Pretty Polly+ The small, soft pink blooms are well formed, long-lasting and very freely borne. They show a deeper pink centre as they open. There is a dense covering of glossy foliage. HEIGHT & SPREAD 40×45 cm (16×18 in).

R. Queen Mother♀ The numerous, light pink, semidouble flowers, which open flat, give a continuous display, enhanced by healthy dark, glossy leaves on a rather spreading plant. HEIGHT & SPREAD 45×45 cm (1½×1½ ft).

R. Ray of Sunshine Golden yellow, semidouble flowers that hold their colour well are neatly furled at first, then open out flat. The leaves are small and glossy. HEIGHT & SPREAD 40×45 cm (16×18 in).

▼ *Rosa* Queen Mother

R. Red Rascal Bright crimson-scarlet flowers that are full-petalled, shapely and unfading bloom abundantly, set off by dark, glossy foliage. HEIGHT & SPREAD 40×45 cm (16×18 in).

R. Robin Redbreast Single blooms the colour of redcurrants and with a whitish eye are carried in large trusses on a dense plant with dark, glossy leaves. HEIGHT & SPREAD 45×45 cm (1½×1½ ft).

R. Shine On Shapely full-petalled flowers in warm pinky orange shades bloom profusely and with good continuity on this neat plant with small, glossy leaves. HEIGHT & SPREAD 45×45 cm (1½×1½ ft).

R. Strawberry Fayre The flowers are blood-red at the petal edges, striped and mingled red and white within. They are set off by dark green, glossy leaves. HEIGHT & SPREAD 45×45 cm (1½×1½ ft).

R. Sweet Dream♀ The peachy pink blooms, tightly cupped and crammed with petals, appear in many clusters on a plant well covered with healthy glossy foliage. HEIGHT & SPREAD 45×45 cm (1½×1½ ft).

R. Sweet Magic♀ Well-formed, orange flowers with gold highlights open out flat and flush pink as they age. They bloom profusely all season against glossy leaves. HEIGHT & SPREAD 45×45 cm (1½×1½ ft).

R. Tear Drop Clusters of semidouble, blush-white blooms with yellow stamens give a continuous display. They are unmarked by rain and complemented by the tiny, glossy leaves. HEIGHT & SPREAD 30×45 cm (1×1½ ft).

R. 'Wee Jock' Bright crimson-scarlet, neatly formed blooms are freely borne on a dense plant with glossy foliage. HEIGHT & SPREAD 45×45 cm (1½×1½ ft).

MINIATURE ROSES

Thin, twiggy shoots and tiny leaves and flowers distinguish true Miniature Roses from Patio Roses. Miniatures are about 38 cm (15 in) tall at most, some much smaller, and little more than half as wide. They are probably descended from *R. chinensis* 'Minima', a dwarf Chinese cultivated rose, introduced to the West in the 19th century. Most early Miniatures had flowers in shades of red and pink, or white but breeders have now raised hundreds of varieties and greatly extended the colour range.

Miniatures are often thought of as houseplants because they are so often sold in pots, but they are quite hardy outdoor plants that cannot survive long in a dry, indoor atmosphere. They need watching carefully for mildew and black spot, to which some are very susceptible. In a border they make the best effect in a group or as an edging. Their size suits pots, planters and window boxes but in such confinement, they must be fed and watered.

The flowers are borne in clusters with the blooms opening to about 2.5 cm (1 in) across, and rather less on the tiniest plants. Unless stated otherwise, the Miniatures

▲ *Rosa* Baby Masquerade

▲ *Rosa* Shine On

Rosa 'Cinderella' ▲

listed below have mid green leaves, and double or semidouble flowers that are slightly scented and repeat flowering. Conscientious deadheading will encourage continuity of flowering.

R. Apricot Sunblaze Cupped blooms of light orange-red appear over a long flowering period among glossy, dark leaves. HEIGHT 38 cm (15 in).

R. Baby Masquerade The profuse flowers change from yellow to orange to pink to red as they age, with all colours on show together. The bush is dense with shiny, dark green leaves. HEIGHT 38 cm (15 in).

R. Benson and Hedges Special Golden yellow blooms are borne prolifically and combine well with the light green, glossy leaves on a plant that bushes out more than most miniatures. HEIGHT 38 cm (15 in).

R. Bush Baby Full and neatly formed, light salmon-pink blooms show amber at the heart as they open wide. The leaves are glossy. HEIGHT 25 cm (10 in).

R. 'Cinderella' Exquisite, full-petalled, white blooms tinged with pink grace the tiny, thornless bush which has very healthy leaves. HEIGHT 23 cm (9 in).

R. Darling Flame Vivid vermilion flowers with yellow shading and golden anthers are carried in numerous clusters on a plant with dark, glossy leaves. HEIGHT 38 cm (15 in).

r

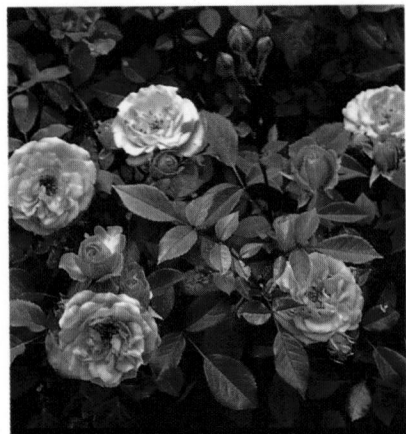

▲ *Rosa* 'Judy Fischer'

R. 'Easter Morning' Ivory-white blooms, up to 4 cm (1½ in) across, are unspoiled by rain. They are luminous against the dark, glossy foliage. HEIGHT 38 cm (15 in).

R. 'Judy Fischer' Rich ruby-red blooms are well matched by the fine dark leaves. HEIGHT 38 cm (15 in).

▲ *Rosa* 'Little Buckaroo'

R. 'Little Buckaroo' Blooms are scarlet with white centres and gold stamens. The leaves are dark green. HEIGHT 38 cm (15 in).

R. Magic Carrousel Rosette-shaped, creamy white blooms are edged with warm pink and make a fine show against the glossy leaves. HEIGHT 38 cm (15 in).

R. 'Mr Bluebird' Lavender-purple flowers are held against dark green leaves. HEIGHT 30 cm (12 in).

R. 'New Penny' The abundant, coppery orange flowers open flat and become pinker as they age. The leaves are dark and glossy. HEIGHT 25 cm (10 in).

R. Peace Sunblaze Tiny pink-and-white blooms are carried in numerous compact clusters. A leafy bush. HEIGHT 38 cm (15 in).

R. Peach Sunblaze Peachy apricot, cupped blooms with abundant repeat flowering are enhanced by plenty of leaves on this bushy plant. HEIGHT 25 cm (10 in).

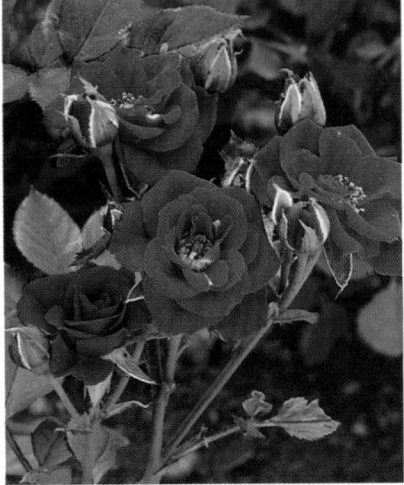

▲ *Rosa* Red Ace

R. Red Ace The dark crimson-scarlet blooms are velvety and shapely. An upright plant. HEIGHT 30 cm (12 in).

R. Red Sunblaze Bright blood-red flowers open wide but full and are quick to repeat. The matt leaves are a fresh green. HEIGHT 30 cm (12 in).

R. 'Stacey Sue' This free-flowering plant bears prettily shaped, light pink, full-petalled blooms above glossy foliage. HEIGHT 25 cm (10 in).

R. Starina Scarlet and gold blooms that are shapely and lasting make a fine show, set off to perfection by glossy, light green leaves. HEIGHT 38 cm (15 in).

R. 'Yellow Doll' Tiny, light yellow blooms with narrow petals are freely borne on a bushy plant with glossy leaves. HEIGHT 30 cm (12 in).

MINIATURE CLIMBING ROSES
Some of these varieties are climbing sports of the Miniature bush roses. Others, which grow rather larger, have been specially developed as small climbers for confined spaces such as patios. They need a position in full sun and all do well in containers if well fed and watered.

R. Laura Ford♀ Strong yellow flowers, even deeper in the late-summer blooms, take on a pink flush in hot sun. This vigorous plant has plenty of dark, shiny leaves. HEIGHT 2.1 m (7 ft).

R. Nice Day Soft salmon-pink, full-petalled flowers with a sweet scent open wide to form loose rosettes, profusely borne. A freely branching plant with plenty of dark, glossy foliage. HEIGHT 2.1 m (7 ft).

R. Orange Sunblaze, Climbing Bright vermilion blooms appear with good continuity on a short plant with glossy foliage. HEIGHT 1.5 m (5 ft).

R. Warm Welcome♀+ Bold orange-vermilion blooms with yellow at the heart are fragrant and borne with great freedom, starting early and continuing until the frosts. The glossy leaves have a coppery tone when young. HEIGHT 2.1 m (7 ft).

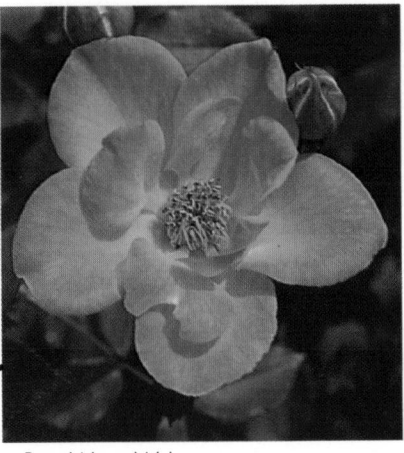

▲ *Rosa* Warm Welcome

GROUND-COVER ROSES
Low-growing but spreading shrubs, each covering a lot of ground, make up the group known as Ground-cover Roses. However, despite the name, permanent, weed-smothering cover for the soil is not possible with roses. They give no leaf cover in winter so weeds can grow in the bare ground and, since roses are thorny, removing weeds from beneath them is not easy.

Ground-cover Roses vary in height and spread. Most branch much more freely than Hybrid Teas or Floribundas, and they are well clothed to the base with leafy shoots. They carry their flowers in clusters. A sunny position at the front of a border or lining a path or drive suits these plants, but their spreading habit lends itself to tumbling over a wall, drooping gracefully over the side of a tub, or sprawling down a sloping bank.

Unless stated otherwise, the plants listed are repeat-flowering with blooms that have little scent, and the leaves are mid green.

R. Avon (syn. *R.* 'Poulmuti') Numerous pale pink buds open to pearly white, semi-double flowers, 2.5 cm (1 in) across, and show prominent golden stamens. The bushy growth bears glossy leaves. HEIGHT & SPREAD 30 cm × 1 m (1 × 3 ft).

R. Bonica♀ Sprays of pink, cup-shaped, semidouble flowers are borne throughout summer on this bushy, hardy plant. The leaves are dark leathery green. HEIGHT & SPREAD 1 × 1.5 m (3 × 5 ft).

R. Essex Single, rich pink blooms, 2.5 cm (1 in) across, with a white eye flower continuously in large clusters. The dense growth of trailing shoots bears glossy leaves. HEIGHT & SPREAD 60 cm × 1.2 m (2 × 4 ft).

R. Flower Carpet♀ Glowing bright pink, double blooms, 4 cm (1½ in) across, appear in heavy trusses all summer. This plant is healthy with glossy leaves that stay on late. HEIGHT & SPREAD 1 × 1.2 m (3 × 4 ft).

R. Gwent Bright lemon-yellow, cupped, semidouble blooms, 5 cm (2 in) across, are profusely borne over a long season. The leaves are dark and glossy. HEIGHT & SPREAD 45 cm × 1 m (1½ × 3 ft).

r

▲ *Rosa* Flower Carpet

▲ *Rosa* Hampshire

R. Hampshire The deep scarlet, yellow-eyed, single blooms, up to 2.5 cm (1 in) across, are extremely showy. This plant produces small, glossy, bright green leaves that are usually healthy. HEIGHT & SPREAD 30×75 cm (1×2½ ft).

R. Hertfordshire The carmine-pink, single blooms, 2.5 cm (1 in) across and borne in large clusters, open wide showing vivid yellow stamens. There is an ample coverage of healthy bright green leaves. HEIGHT & SPREAD 45 cm×1 m (1½×3 ft).

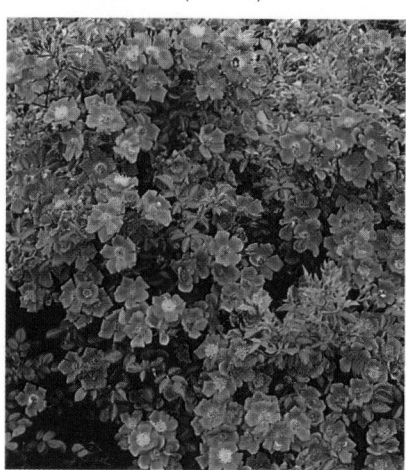
▲ *Rosa* Hertfordshire

R. Kent+ White semidouble flowers, 4 cm (1½ in) across, are borne in great profusion. They are not spoiled by rain and give a generous repeat flowering. The neat shrub has shiny leaves. HEIGHT & SPREAD 45×75 cm (1½×2½ ft).

R. Laura Ashley Light magenta-pink, single flowers, 4 cm (1½ in) across, with pale yellow centres are lightly scented. They are freely borne against small, glossy leaves. HEIGHT & SPREAD 60 cm×1.2 m (2×4 ft).

R. Northamptonshire Pearly pink, semidouble flowers, 6 cm (2½ in) across, are held in large clusters. The dense leaves are shiny. HEIGHT & SPREAD 45 cm×1.1 m (1½×3½ ft).

R. 'Nozomi'♀ Dainty, single, pearly pink flowers, 2 cm (¾ in) across and fading to white, are borne in huge clusters along the dense shoots. The leaves are small, shiny and dark. HEIGHT & SPREAD 1×1.8 m (3×6 ft).

R. Pearl Drift Elegant pink buds open to white, semidouble blooms with a pearly blush and golden stamens. They are 10 cm (4 in) across, freely and continuously borne, and shown off by the dark, glossy leaves. HEIGHT & SPREAD 1×1.2 m (3×4 ft).

R. Pheasant Full-petalled, deep pink, double flowers, 2.5 cm (1 in) across, hold their colour well and have a sweet scent. They are held in large trusses along the trailing shoots, but in early summer only. The leaves are small and glossy. HEIGHT & SPREAD 30 cm×3 m (1×10 ft).

R. 'Poulmuti' see *R*. Avon

R. Snow Carpet♀ Dainty but very double, white pompom blooms, 2.5 cm (1 in) across, flower with good continuity over a very long season. The ground-hugging shoots bear little, dark green leaves. HEIGHT & SPREAD 15×45 cm (6×18 in).

R. Suffolk Bright scarlet, single flowers, 4 cm (1½ in) across, bloom profusely all summer. They open wide to show prominent golden stamens and are followed by orange-red hips in autumn. There are plenty of light green leaves. HEIGHT & SPREAD 45 cm×1 m (1½×3 ft).

R. Suma♀ Massed ruby-red, very double blooms, 2.5 cm (1 in) across, open all along the spreading shoots. The small dark leaves turn red in autumn. HEIGHT & SPREAD 1×1.8 m (3×6 ft).

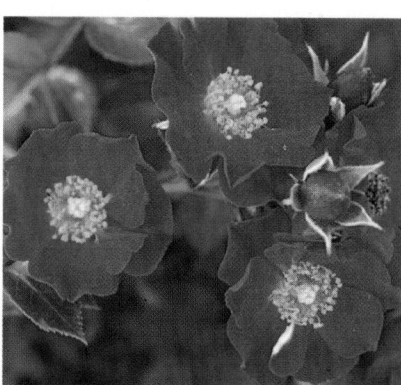
▲ *Rosa* Suffolk

R. Surrey♀+ The frilly-edged, double blooms, 6 cm (2½ in) across, are deep pink at the centre, paler at the edge and moderately fragrant. They are borne in large trusses throughout the summer. This plant is generously clothed with glossy leaves. HEIGHT & SPREAD 1×1.2 m (3×4 ft).

R. Sussex The lightly scented, buff-apricot blooms, gradually fading, are 5 cm (2 in) across and flower all season. The dark bronzy green leaves are glossy. HEIGHT & SPREAD 60 cm×1.2 m (2×4 ft).

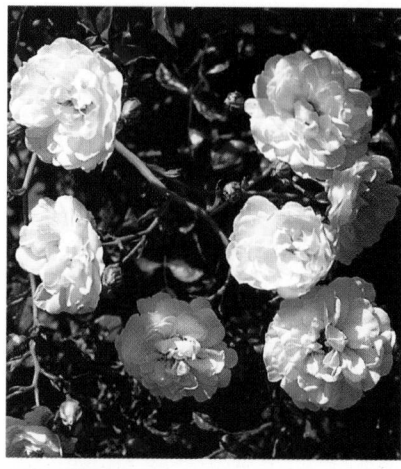
▲ *Rosa* Swany

R. Swany♀ White, very full-petalled double blooms, 4 cm (1½ in) across, are held with great freedom on the sprawling flexible shoots. The leaves are dark, glossy and healthy. HEIGHT & SPREAD 1×1.2 m (3×4 ft).

R. Wiltshire Profuse, deep pink, double blooms, 6 cm (2½ in) across, flower early and go on well into autumn. This wide-spreading bush has tiny, dark, glossy leaves. HEIGHT & SPREAD 60 cm×1.2 m (2×4 ft).

CLIMBING ROSES
The typical Climbing Rose sends out long shoots which either scramble up through shrubs or trees by hooking their thorns over twigs and branches, or have to be tied to a frame or to fixed wires. Climbing Roses generally have small clusters of quite large blooms, are repeat-flowering, and form a permanent framework of strong, fairly stiff shoots. But a few do not conform. There are some that flower only once a season and some that have flexible shoots bearing huge heads of small blooms – all typical features of Ramblers, for there is some confusion and overlap between the two.

Climbers grown on walls or fences need to have their shoots trained and tied in to grow as near to horizontal as possible. This encourages the production of flowering sideshoots. On pillars and obelisks, shoots can be spiralled round and tied to the support to achieve the same effect. Vigorous climbers grown through trees need training only in their early stages.

Deadheading helps Climbers to produce a better second flowering, although the task may be difficult to carry out on the stronger growers. Lack of deadheading does not mean that there is no second blooming at all, but it will usually be less profuse.

In the varieties listed, those with the word 'Climbing' at the end of the name are climbing sports that first occurred spontaneously from bush varieties and have been reproduced by breeders. The flowers look like those on the bush versions, but the continuity of flowering is often not as good.

The blooms of Climbing Roses can be double, semidouble or single. Sometimes, especially in climbing sports, they are very large and shapely, reaching 10 cm (4 in) across. Those which are not sports of bush roses are generally 7.5–10 cm (3–4 in) across. The blooms of *R. banksiae* 'Lutea' and some of the other tree-climbers, however, are no more than 2.5 cm (1 in) across but make up for it by massing together, 100 or more to a single truss. Unless stated otherwise the flowers are lightly scented and the leaves, usually with 5 leaflets, are mid green.

R. **Agatha Christie** Clear pink, double blooms show well against the dark, glossy leaves. The bushy grower is a convenient size for a pillar or obelisk. HEIGHT 3 m (10 ft).

▲ *Rosa* 'Alchymist'

R. **'Alchymist'** The well-scented, very full-petalled blooms are a light buff-yellow with orange shading; there is no second flowering. The growth is upright and the leaves are bronze-green when young. HEIGHT 2.4 m (8 ft).

R. **'Allgold, Climbing'** Unfading, bright yellow, double flowers appear in clusters. The stiff growth is covered with healthy, bright green leaves. HEIGHT 4.2 m (14 ft).

R. **'Aloha'** Very large, bright pink, double blooms have an orange flush at the heart and a sweet fragrance. The dark, bronzy foliage has been troubled by rust in some areas. The upright habit is suitable for growing up a pillar. HEIGHT 2.4 m (8 ft).

R. **Altissimo** ♀ Deep scarlet, single blooms with large petals open wide to reveal orange

stamens. The dark, glossy leaves are held on stiff, upright growth. HEIGHT 3 m (10 ft).

R. banksiae **'Lutea'** ♀ This plant does best in a site protected from frost and cold spring winds, such as a warm wall, which must be extensive to accommodate it. Even then it may be slow to become established. It bears sweetly scented, rounded, double blooms, 2.5 cm (1 in) across, that are light yellow and carried in large clusters, in early summer only. HEIGHT 6 m (20 ft).

R. **Bantry Bay** Bright pink, semidouble blooms are generously borne over a long season and with a good repeat. The plant is freely branching with dark, glossy leaves. HEIGHT 3.5 m (12 ft).

R. **'Bobbie James'** ♀ Huge, fragrant sprays of small, creamy white, semidouble blooms are borne in early summer only. The rampant grower has shiny, dark green leaves with copper tinges. HEIGHT 9 m (30 ft).

R. **'Céline Forestier'** ♀ Fragrant, buff-yellow, double blooms with pink undertones that open out flat are carried in small clusters. The plant is moderately vigorous but not completely hardy and needs a sheltered position. HEIGHT 2.4 m (8 ft).

R. **'Compassion'** ♀ Fragrant, pink, shapely

▲ *Rosa* 'Compassion'

flowers with apricot shading bloom with great continuity. Dark, shiny leaves are held on stiff, branching shoots. HEIGHT 3 m (10 ft).

R. **'Crimson Glory, Climbing'** Strongly perfumed, dark crimson blooms that are large and double make a sumptuous display on this extensive plant, but the foliage is rather sparse and may be attacked by mildew. HEIGHT 4.5 m (15 ft).

R. **Dortmund** Showy clusters of single, bright red blooms with a white eye are carried on an upright grower with healthy, dark green, glossy leaves. HEIGHT 3 m (10 ft).

R. **Dream Girl** ♀ The double, warm pink flowers have a fine scent and are abundant but appear only at mid summer with no repeat. They are well set off by glossy leaves. HEIGHT 2.7 m (9 ft).

R. **'Dreaming Spires'** Large, double, richly scented blooms are in a clear yellow which shows up well against the dark green, glossy foliage that covers the stiff, branching growth. HEIGHT 3 m (10 ft).

R. **Dublin Bay** ♀ Showy clusters of blood-red, double blooms are enhanced by the handsome, dark green, glossy leaves. The flowers are virtually scentless. This climber has bushy growth that makes it very like a shrub. HEIGHT 2.1 m (7 ft).

R. **'Ena Harkness, Climbing'** The bright crimson, double blooms are inclined to droop – an advantage since this large climber is seen mostly from below. The flowers are large, shapely and double, with a good repeat. The stiff, branching plant has glossy, healthy foliage. HEIGHT 4.5 m (15 ft).

R. **'Etoile de Hollande, Climbing'** ♀ Large, dark crimson blooms with a rich, sweet scent are carried on the vigorous, well-branched grower whose foliage is dark green. HEIGHT 5 m (16 ft).

R. **Galway Bay** Beautifully formed double blooms, with mid pink petals that are darker

▲ *Rosa* Dortmund

▲ *Rosa* Galway Bay

▲ *Rosa* Bantry Bay

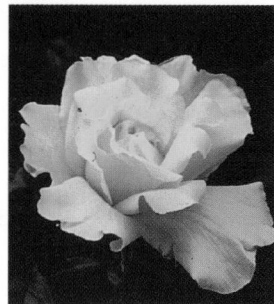

Rosa Golden Showers ▲

on the back, are borne abundantly in medium-sized clusters. The growth is stiff and branching. HEIGHT 3 m (10 ft).

R. **'Gloire de Dijon'** ♀ The buff-yellow, very double blooms are sometimes quartered and give a continuous display, but they are only lightly scented. The plant is well branched with dark green leaves. HEIGHT 4.5 m (15 ft).

R. **Golden Showers** ♀ Shapely yellow buds open to rather loosely formed, scented double flowers with large petals, the yellow coloration fading quite quickly to cream. Upright growth and moderate size makes this a successful plant for a pillar. HEIGHT 2.4 m (8 ft).

R. **'Guinée'** The darkest of dusky red blooms and a delicious perfume distinguish this rose. The flowers are well formed, large and double. They make a profuse first flowering but give only a slight repeat. The leaves, too, are dark on a well-branched plant, but they are susceptible to mildew. HEIGHT 4.5 m (15 ft).

R. **Handel** ♀ Cupped, double blooms of creamy white edged with cerise are carried in large clusters and have a good repeat. There is dark, shiny foliage on the vigorous, freely branching plant, which will spread well on a wall. HEIGHT 3 m (10 ft).

▼ *Rosa* Handel

R. **High Hopes** Light pink, shapely, double blooms combine elegantly with the dark green, glossy foliage. The flowers have little scent. HEIGHT 3 m (10 ft).

R. **Highfield** Light yellow, double blooms with a sweet fragrance are freely borne on this stiff, well-branched plant with big, glossy, dark green leaves. HEIGHT 3 m (10 ft).

R. **'Iceberg, Climbing'** ♀ Profuse clusters of double white flowers with a reliably abundant repeat. Mildew sometimes affects the glossy leaves. HEIGHT 3 m (10 ft).

R. **'Lady Hillingdon, Climbing'** ♀ The richly tea-scented, apricot-orange double blooms are beautifully shaped and carried on a well-branched plant. This rose performs at its best with some protection from a south or west-facing wall or fence. HEIGHT 4.5 m (15 ft).

R. **'Lady Sylvia, Climbing'** Light pink, large double blooms are carried singly and in small clusters on stiff growth. This climber rarely produces flowers after the first flush. HEIGHT 3.5 m (12 ft).

R. **Lavinia** ♀ Large and fragrant, mid pink, double blooms are enhanced by the background of fine dark leaves on a freely branching plant. HEIGHT 3.5 m (12 ft).

R. **Leaping Salmon** Full-scented, salmon-pink blooms that are large and double stand out well against handsome, glossy leaves on a branching plant. HEIGHT 3 m (10 ft).

R. **'Leverkusen'** Pale yellow, long-stemmed, semidouble blooms, deepening in colour at the centre, are held in small clusters and give a good repeat. The dark, glossy leaves may develop mildew. HEIGHT 3 m (10 ft).

R. **'Madame Alfred Carrière'** ♀ The clusters of white, blush-tinted, double blooms are very freely produced and have a good repeat. This is a rose of great vigour which easily covers the wall of a large house, and tolerates a shady wall. The pale green leaves may develop mildew. HEIGHT 5.5 m (18 ft).

R. **'Madame Grégoire Staechelin'** ♀ (syn. *R.* 'Spanish Beauty') The first flowering, in late spring, is very early and spectacular with large, carmine-pink, semidouble blooms carried extraordinarily freely. The display extends over several weeks but there is no repeat flowering. HEIGHT 6 m (20 ft).

R. **'Maigold'** ♀ Orange-yellow, fragrant, semidouble blooms are profuse and first appear in late spring, but there is only spasmodic blooming after that. The stiff, very thorny shoots are well covered with shiny, bronze-green leaves. HEIGHT 2.4 m (8 ft).

R. **'Masquerade, Climbing'** Showy, double flowers change from yellow to pink to a strong red, just as in the Floribunda bush version, and give a good display after the first flush. HEIGHT 3 m (10 ft).

R. **'Meg'** The clusters of very large, apricot-pink flowers have orange stamens and a strong fragrance. The blooms are semi-double and 10 cm (4 in) across but appear only spasmodically after the first flush in

▲ *Rosa* 'Leverkusen'

early summer. This sturdy grower forms hips in autumn, but they remain green. HEIGHT 3.5 m (12 ft).

R. **'Mermaid'** ♀ + Large, luminous light yellow blooms with amber stamens are borne in clusters on a branching, very thorny plant which, though vigorous, is a slow grower when first planted. It is not completely hardy, needing a sheltered situation, and the shiny leaves are not entirely resistant to mildew. HEIGHT 6 m (20 ft).

R. **Morning Jewel** ♀ Sparkling, bold pink, semidouble flowers cover the plant with early and late displays, making a bright contrast with the shiny, dark green leaves on the branching plant. HEIGHT 3.5 m (12 ft).

R. **'Mrs Sam McGredy, Climbing'** ♀ The large, double blooms in a coppery red with a hint of salmon are unlike those of any other rose. There is rather sparse, dark green foliage but vigorous growth. HEIGHT 3.5 m (12 ft).

Rosa
'New Dawn'

R. 'New Dawn' ♀ (syn. *R.* 'The New Dawn') Thriving anywhere, even on a north wall, this vigorous plant has its slender shoots laden with a tremendous profusion of strongly scented, light satin-pink, double blooms which are very shapely and borne in small sprays. The leaves are healthy and glossy. HEIGHT 3m (10ft).

R. Night Light Red-gold buds open to large, golden yellow, double flowers with little scent. The plant is stiff and branching with dark, glossy leaves. HEIGHT 3m (10ft).

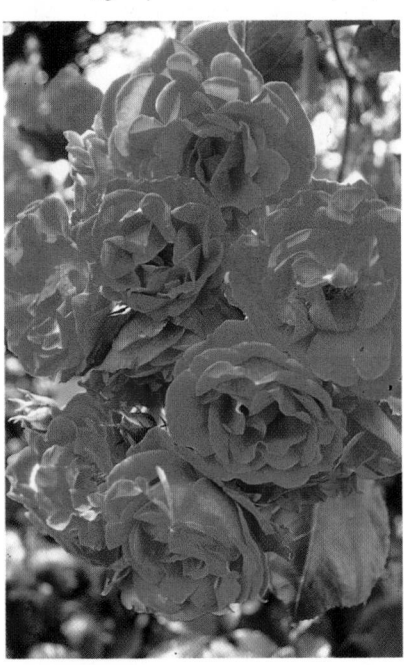

▲ *Rosa* 'Parade'

R. 'Parade' ♀ There is a continuous show of heavy flower clusters, whose carmine-pink, double blooms tend to droop. A reddish tinge warms the dark, glossy leaves. HEIGHT 3m (10ft).

R. Parkdirektor Riggers Bright red, semi-double, well-formed blooms with a touch of white at the heart are carried in numerous clusters and give a good repeat. The flowers show to advantage against the dark green, glossy leaves. HEIGHT 3.5m (12ft).

R. 'Paul's Scarlet Climber' + Fairly small, bright red, double flowers give a reliably generous display, though at mid summer only. The well-branched plant has abundant foliage. HEIGHT 3m (10ft).

R. 'Phyllis Bide' ♀+ A combination of fawn, pink and yellow distinguishes the

▲ *Rosa* 'Pink Perpétué'

small, double blooms, which are borne in clusters with great freedom. The growth is slender and branching with glossy leaves. HEIGHT 2.4m (8ft).

R. 'Pink Perpétué' Pink blooms with a deeper pink reverse are carried in large clusters and with great freedom. Deadheading is necessary to get a good second show. The plant has an abundance of glossy leaves. HEIGHT 2.7m (9ft).

R. 'Rosy Mantle' Rather loosely formed, double blooms in bright rose-pink with lighter shading are sweetly scented and freely borne over a long season. The open growth is clothed with glossy, dark foliage. HEIGHT 3m (10ft).

R. 'Royal Gold' Shapely, large, double blooms of deep golden yellow are borne singly or in small clusters and with a good repeat. The plant easily becomes gaunt and leggy and could do with its glossy leaves being more numerous. It is best grown as a pillar rose. HEIGHT 2.4m (8ft).

R. 'Schoolgirl' The light orange to apricot blooms are very large, double and beautifully formed. The plant is open-growing and leggy, and the glossy leaves, though large, are sparse. HEIGHT 3m (10ft).

R. 'Shot Silk, Climbing' ♀ An abundant first flush produces strongly fragrant, large, double blooms of salmon-pink blended with yellow. They are rather loose when opened and the repeat flowering is unreliable. There are handsome, glossy leaves. HEIGHT 3m (10ft).

R. 'Souvenir de Claudius Denoyel' ♀ Cupped, loosely formed, double flowers with a full fragrance make a great splash of bright crimson in early summer, and a more subdued show later. The plant is a vigorous grower. HEIGHT 5.5m (18ft).

R. 'Souvenir du Docteur Jamain' Velvety dark red, perfumed, double flowers bloom in profusion and make a continuous display set off by dark leaves. HEIGHT 3m (10ft).

R. 'Spanish Beauty' see *R.* 'Madame Grégoire Staechelin'

R. Sparkling Scarlet Small, semidouble scarlet flowers are carried in large trusses on a plant with stiff, well-branched growth. HEIGHT 3m (10ft).

R. Summer Wine ♀ Single coral-pink flowers with orange stamens are borne in small clusters. This stiff, branching plant has large, glossy leaves. HEIGHT 3m (10ft).

▲ *Rosa* 'Swan Lake'

R. 'Swan Lake' The shapely, high-centred white blooms tinged with pink are double. This plant is well branched with shiny, dark green leaves that need watching for black spot. HEIGHT 3m (10ft).

R. Sympathie Clusters of blood-red, double blooms are carried on stiff, branching growth, well furnished with glossy leaves. This rose will easily cover a wall. HEIGHT 4.5m (15ft).

R. 'The New Dawn' see *R.* 'New Dawn'

▲ *Rosa* 'White Cockade'

R. 'White Cockade' ♀ Sprays of white, double flowers are shown off against very dark green, glossy leaves. This short plant is useful for a patio, pillar or obelisk. HEIGHT 2.1m (7ft).

R. 'Zéphirine Drouhin' ♀ Profuse clusters of well-scented, deep pink, double blooms are borne over a long period and with a good repeat. This almost thornless plant has

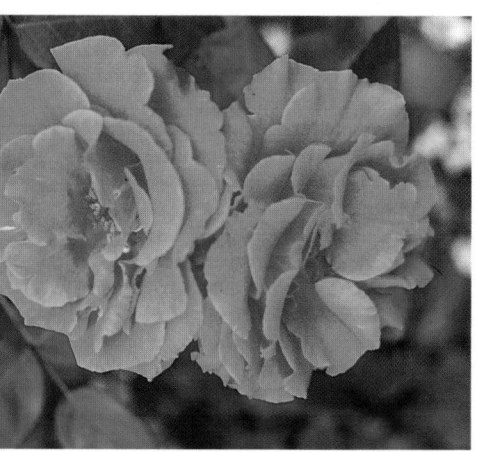

▲ *Rosa* 'Zéphirine Drouhin'

open growth but its leaves are susceptible to mildew. HEIGHT 2.4m (8 ft).

RAMBLER ROSES

Ramblers bear large clusters of small blooms and come into flower only once a year, in early to mid summer. They have flexible shoots, and send up fresh ones from ground level each year; a number of the old shoots can be pruned away to maintain the plant's vigour. Like Climbing Roses, Ramblers have to be trained on supports but they are less suitable for growing against walls, where the air is frequently still and mildew is more likely to develop on the dense growth. Their very pliable shoots, however, are ideal for training round pillars, over arches and wherever curving shapes are needed. Ramblers' flexibility is also an advantage in weeping standards because the shoots hang down or 'weep' naturally.

The flowers can be double or semidouble and are carried in clusters that often contain as many as 20. The blooms are generally about 5cm (2in) across; in the plants listed, flower size is given only if it differs from this. Unless stated otherwise, the flowers are lightly scented and the leaves, with 5 or 7 leaflets, are mid green.

R. 'Adélaïde d'Orléans' ♀ Delicate blushpink, semidouble blooms are set off by plenty of leaves and these stay on the bushy plant well into winter. HEIGHT 4.5m (15ft).

R. 'Albéric Barbier' ♀ The flowering

▲ *Rosa* 'Albertine'

comes in early summer and is exquisite, with small clusters of light orange buds opening to creamy white, double blooms. The plant is almost evergreen, with fine, glossy leaves and rampant growth. HEIGHT 4.5m (15ft).

R. 'Albertine' ♀ Very fragrant, double flowers that are large for a Rambler, at 9cm (3½in) across, are a warm pink and shapely at first but they become loose as they open. The young shoots are plum-red, and the leaves dark green and prone to develop mildew. HEIGHT 4.5m (15ft).

R. 'Alexandre Girault' Scarlet, double flowers with 'quilled' petals, each reflexed to form a point, have a white eye round a boss of yellow stamens. The scarlet deepens as the flower ages. There are few thorns on the long, whippy shoots which carry dark, glossy leaves. HEIGHT 6m (20ft).

R. 'Crimson Shower' ♀ The large flower clusters come after mid summer and, although not repeating, make a display over a long period. The flowers are crimson, small and double, and are borne on lax shoots with an abundance of little, shiny leaves. HEIGHT 2.4m (8ft).

R. 'Emily Gray' + The buttery yellow blooms have a pleasing scent, are semidouble and open to 9cm (3½in) across, becoming loose as they do so. The bright green, shiny leaves stay on the plant for a long time. HEIGHT 4.5m (15ft).

R. 'Félicité Perpétue' ♀ (syn. *R.* 'Little White Pet, Climbing') Enormous heads of creamy white, very double pompom flowers sometimes have their petals tipped with red. Small, dark leaves cover stems that are plum-red when young. The vigorous plant sends up new shoots freely from the base. HEIGHT 4.5m (15ft).

R. 'Francis E. Lester' ♀ (syn. *R.* 'F.E. Lester') This free-flowering rose has no repeat but displays its large trusses of small, blush-pink, single blooms over a long period. The flowers have a rich fragrance. HEIGHT 4.5m (15ft).

R. 'François Juranville' ♀ Fragrant, warm salmon-pink, double blooms are numerous, well formed and full-petalled. They are large, opening up to 9cm (3½in) across and making a glowing display against the dark leaves. HEIGHT 5m (16ft).

R. 'Goldfinch' Each creamy yellow, semidouble bloom has a cushion of bright orange-yellow stamens in the centre – the reason for the plant's nickname 'poached egg rose'. The dense, vigorous growth bears leaves that are a conspicuously bright, glossy green. HEIGHT 2.7m (9ft).

R. 'Little White Pet, Climbing' see *R.* 'Félcité Perpétue'

R. 'Paul's Himalayan Musk' ♀ Lilac-pink, double blooms are carried in large sprays on long, enormously vigorous shoots that can swarm up a tree. The shoots bear large, greyish olive leaves that are rather drooping. HEIGHT 9m (30ft).

▲ *Rosa* 'Félicité Perpétue'

R. 'Paul Transon' ♀ Unusually among the Ramblers, the numerous blooms are mixed shades of coppery orange and salmon-pink. In a warm season the plant gives a limited second flowering. HEIGHT 3m (10ft).

R. 'Rambling Rector' ♀ This vigorous grower, suitable for training up a small tree, has very large trusses of creamy white, semidouble blooms. HEIGHT 6m (20ft)

R. 'Sanders' White Rambler' ♀ Sweetly scented, white, double blooms of rosette shape are carried in plentiful clusters. The glossy, bright green, outstandingly healthy foliage makes a superb, dense background for them. HEIGHT 3.5m (12ft).

R. 'Seagull' ♀ White, single and semi-

▲ *Rosa* 'Seagull'

double flowers are held in huge clusters. The very strong shoots are stiffer than in most Ramblers and carry leaves of a greyish green. HEIGHT 6m (20ft).

R. 'Veilchenblau' ♀ Semidouble flowers of an unusual violet-blue are white at the centre. The clusters are carried on shoots that have few thorns and are well covered with bright green, shiny leaves. HEIGHT 4.5m (15ft).

CULTIVATION

Site and soil Roses need a position where they have plenty of sun – preferably for at least three-quarters of the day. They never do as well in a shady site; a position under a tree is worst of all, not only because of the shade, but because the tree's roots compete for nutrients. The only roses that put on any show without direct sunlight are climbers recommended for north walls, but even

▲ *Rosa 'Veilchenblau'*

these always do better on a south or west wall. An exposed, windy position is another to avoid. Wind rocks the plants and makes the roots loose in the soil so they cannot take up nutrients. Wind also makes the shoots whip about and damage the blooms.

Slightly acid soil, with a pH of 6.5, is best for roses. A medium loam retains the water they need but does not become water-logged. The claim that roses prefer clay is not true where the clay does not let water drain away reasonably well. Roses do not like their roots to stand in water because this deprives them of the air they need to thrive. They do not like growing in chalk either; the only exceptions are some of the Old Garden Roses, for instance the Hybrid Perpetuals, which do tolerate chalk. There are also some roses, the Rugosas for example, that cope well with light, sandy soils. But light soils, whether chalky or sandy, are always made better for roses by adding as much humus-forming matter as possible.

Since roses like a moist soil, apply a mulch round them regularly. It reduces evaporation, suppresses weeds and can improve the soil and provide some nutrients if it is made up of well-rotted stable manure, garden compost, chipped bark, or some other organic matter. Put it on in late spring when the soil has begun to warm up, applying a layer about 7.5 cm (3 in) thick.

Unless roses are grown for exhibition, they require an application of a powdered or granular rose fertiliser only twice a year. Scatter a small handful round each plant in spring, immediately after pruning, and again soon after mid summer, when the first flush of bloom is over. Work it gently into the top 2.5 cm (1 in) of soil, taking care not to damage the roots. Do not make a later application; this would encourage the growth of late shoots that have no time to ripen before the first frost and would be destroyed. A fertiliser rich in potash used for the second application helps shoots to ripen.

Planting Before planting, cut out any damaged or diseased shoots from the top growth and trim back tough, not fibrous, roots by about a third. Make the planting hole wide enough for the roots to be spread out and deep enough for the budding union (the swelling at the base of the main stem) to be 2.5 cm (1 in) below the soil surface. Work a small handful of rose fertiliser into the soil at the bottom of the hole, then set the plant in the hole. Place a cane across the hole to check that the depth is right. Container-grown roses often have the budding union well above the soil because the pots are too small for them. Make sure that this is rectified in the actual planting. Work in soil round the roots so that there are no air pockets round them, then fill in the hole and tread the soil down firmly.

When planting roses in spring, cut the shoots hard back to about 3 or 4 buds immediately after firming the soil – except with climbing roses, whose shoots should be left just as they came from the nursery.

Plant Climbing Roses at least 45 cm (1½ ft) away from a wall or fence (and even farther from a tree), with the roots fanned outwards away from the support. Soil near a wall, fence or tree is liable to be very dry.

Training climbing roses Some of the more lax-growing shrub roses may be better displayed if trained on a frame, but for most gardeners the only roses that need training are Climbers and Ramblers. These are not true climbing plants because they do not have tendrils, suction pads, or other means of attaching themselves to supports – in nature they scramble up surrounding trees or shrubs by hooking their thorns over branches and twigs. On an artificial support such as a wall, arch, pillar, fence or pergola, there is little for the thorns to gain purchase on and the shoots always have to be tied to the support.

When growing a rose on a wall, tie the shoots to wires threaded through vine eyes driven into the brickwork and stretched horizontally about 45 cm (1½ ft) apart up the wall. Tie the shoots into positions as horizontal as possible; this encourages flower-bearing sideshoots to break into life along their entire length. If it is not done, the blooms come mainly at the top. Garden twine is satisfactory for tying-in, but plastic ties are stronger and last much longer.

When training a Climber or Rambler up a pillar, spiral it round the support rather than letting it go straight up. The comparatively stiff shoots of a Climber are more difficult to train than the flexible shoots of Ramblers.

For training into trees, one of the loveliest ways of growing climbing roses, choose the Ramblers *R.* 'Paul's Himalayan Musk' or *R.* 'Rambling Rector', for example, or a vigorous Climber such as *R.* Sympathie or *R.* 'Souvenir de Claudius Denoyel'. Bear in mind, however, that the weight of such a rose when fully grown, to say nothing of the extra wind resistance of its leaves, means that only a large, strong tree in prime condition can support it. Do not be tempted to use an old and half decayed apple tree, which a gale may bring down. For growing up a full-grown, healthy apple tree, or something of similar size, choose a more modest size of rose, such as *R.* 'New Dawn'.

Plant the Climber or Rambler far enough out from the tree trunk to avoid the major tree roots, both for convenience in digging the hole and to reduce competition for water and nutrients. Set away from the tree trunk, the rose will not be completely deprived of rain by the tree's leaves.

Train the rose towards the tree along a stout cane or rope tied at an angle between the tree trunk and a long peg driven into the ground beside the rose. Tie the rose shoots to the support for a year or two until they make their way up through the lower branches, and then leave them to find their own way upwards. It is best to plant on the windward side of the tree so that the rose shoots tend to be blown into it rather than out. Pruning is not possible, but the roses used for this kind of planting get along very well without it, as they would in the wild; the old shoots are replaced by new, but much more slowly than they would be if the old were pruned out each year.

Rose hedges Many shrub roses make excellent hedges, but some take up a lot of space. Hybrid Musks such as *R.* 'Felicia' and *R.* 'Penelope' send out long flowering shoots at awkward angles, which is a nuisance if the hedge runs alongside a path. The answer is to train such spreading shrub roses either along horizontal wires strung between posts or on a chain-link fence. The Rugosas and upright-growing shrub roses such as *R.* 'Fred Loads', or Floribundas such as *R.* Chinatown and *R.* Queen Elizabeth, rarely need such training when used for hedges.

Deadheading The natural yearly cycle of a rose is to produce flowers in early summer which, once they have been pollinated, form hips containing the seeds from which new plants could grow. If hips are allowed to develop, much of a plant's energy goes into forming them and the seeds they contain, instead of into producing new flowers. Deadheading – the removal of spent blooms before hips start to form – induces a repeat-flowering rose to try again to produce hips and seeds, starting the cycle off by producing more flowers. Do not deadhead species roses or any other roses you are growing for their decorative hips. Old Garden Roses need no deadheading unless blooms become waterlogged by rain and form soggy, unsightly balls that will not open but turn brown. Ramblers need deadheading only to clear the plant of spent blooms.

All other roses are generally repeat-flowering and deadheading stimulates the production of later blooms. It needs doing at least twice a season, that is after each main flush. In practice, however, it is best done whenever a faded flower is seen, simply by snipping off the spent flower. With Hybrid Teas and Floribundas it is best not just to snap off the flower but to cut back to 2 or 3 leaves below the old flowerhead. This can produce stronger new shoots with bigger flowers, though it may take longer for them to appear.

If individual blooms in a Floribunda truss shed their petals neatly as they are spent, wait for the whole cluster to be over before deadheading. If blooms become unsightly with withered petals, snip off the individual spent flowers and when the whole cluster is over, cut back the shoot.

Suckers Almost all the roses on sale are budded or grafted onto wild rose roots known as understocks or rootstocks. These give the cultivated variety extra vigour and, according to the type of stock, other desirable qualities such as a longer life, or greater ability to cope with heavy clay soils or light, sandy ones. Any shoot coming from below the budding union – the point where the cultivated rose was budded onto the stock – is a sucker that is coming from the stock itself and will have the features of the wild rose, not of the cultivated variety. If it is allowed to develop, other dormant buds at the base of the sucker are stimulated into growth, and gradually the stronger-growing stock will take over from the cultivated rose. A sucker must not simply be cut back; this would be the equivalent of pruning and make it grow more vigorously. Pull it away whole from the rootstock, clearing back the soil if necessary to see its point of origin; this removes its dormant buds as well.

A sucker is generally a lighter green than the other shoots with thorns of a different shape, and the leaves may have 7 leaflets rather than the 5 of most cultivated roses. But as some cultivated roses have 7 leaflets, the number of leaflets is not a reliable guide. To be certain that a suspect shoot is a sucker, scrape back a little soil at the base of the rose to find the spot from which the sucker originates; if it comes from below the budding union, remove it.

The stem of a standard rose is part of the rootstock; any shoots coming from below the head are suckers and must be pulled off.

PROPAGATION Seed is produced in the hips of species roses but it is not bound to come true because the flowers may have been cross-pollinated with other roses by visiting insects. Protecting and hand-pollinating plants may guarantee true seed but cuttings taken in autumn are an easier method of propagation. They take 3 or 4 years to make full-sized plants sturdy enough to be allowed to flower. In the first year, flower buds should be nipped out, energy being diverted to root growth. Budding or grafting onto rootstocks establishes plants more quickly but is best left to professionals.

The less highly bred a rose is, the more easily does it root, but actual species tend to make a great deal of leafy growth instead of flowering. Hybrid Teas do not always make such vigorous plants on their own roots as they do on selected rootstocks, but Floribundas are generally the most easily rooted. Miniatures, Ramblers and Modern Shrub Roses are generally the most successful. Shrubs are especially worth raising for an inexpensive flowering hedge as many may be needed.

PRUNING Rose shoots have a much more limited life span than those of many shrubs. They need renewing if worthwhile flowers are to be produced each year, especially on the more highly bred modern kinds such as Hybrid Teas and Floribundas. The pruning of roses is primarily to encourage new shoots to grow, but also to remove dead and diseased wood, to shape a nicely balanced bush and to open up its centre so as to improve air circulation, which helps the plant to remain healthy.

Pruning is not the exacting task it was once made to seem. Even a quick cut with a hedge trimmer promotes the production of essential new shoots, but diseased growth still has to be removed. Even using secateurs, roses should generally be pruned much less severely than traditional methods recommended.

Species Roses These need no pruning except for the removal of any dead wood as soon as it is noticed.

Old Garden Roses Most of these bloom only once each season and any pruning should be done in summer after the flowering to give time for plenty of new wood to develop and ripen before the frosts start. Ripe shoots are needed to carry the next year's blooms. Cut out any unhealthy growth, then cut back main shoots by about one-third and sideshoots by two-thirds. Some growers recommend only every other year or so, and others advocate no pruning at all. But regular attention to the bushes does maintain long-term vigour.

Large-flowered and Cluster-flowered Bush Roses (Hybrid Teas and Floribundas) Prune in spring. Cut out any unhealthy wood, then shorten the main shoots of Hybrid Teas to about 20 cm (8 in) and those of Floribundas to 25-38 cm

(10-15 in). Treat Polyanthas in the same way as Floribundas.

Modern Shrub Roses and Rugosas Prune in spring, first removing any dead or diseased wood, then cutting back main shoots by about one-third and sideshoots by two-thirds. Shrubs with very upright growth, reflecting the habit of their Floribunda parentage, need the main shoots cutting back by about half to prevent them from becoming leggy.

Climbers Do not prune them during their first year. After that, prune in mid autumn when the blooming of the repeat-flowering types is over. Prune the sideshoots only, cutting each back by about two-thirds. Leave the main stems alone, but if one is exceeding its allotted space cut it back to size. The only other reason to cut main shoots is if the rose becomes very bare at the base. In that case, cut 1 or 2 main shoots hard back to about 1m (3ft) and new growth should come from low down.

Ramblers Do not prune in the first year. After that, remove 2 or 3 entire main stems each year after flowering. It is usually easier to remove them in sections. Cut back each remaining main stem by about one-quarter, and sideshoots by two-thirds.

Miniature and Patio Roses There are two methods. The first is to give the bushes a light trim to keep them shapely and balanced. The second is to treat them in the same way as Hybrid Teas and Floribundas, removing any unhealthy wood, then cutting back main shoots by a third on smaller plants and a half on larger ones.

Ground-cover Roses These need a minimum of pruning. Trim lightly to keep them tidy and cut back more strongly any vigorous shoots that may unbalance the shape of the bush.

PESTS AND DISEASES Good cultivation of roses is the best defence. Strong plants in the right situation, well tended and pruned to ensure a flow of air through them are better able to resist or recover from pests and diseases. An increasing number of roses are bred with healthy growth as one of their characteristics. Rugosas and many of the Species have always been healthy, and the Old Garden Roses manage to cope with disease better than many modern roses.

The main diseases that afflict roses, all of them passed from rose to rose by airborne spores, are black spot, powdery mildew and rose rust.

The most troublesome pests are greenfly (aphids), caterpillars including those of tortrix moths and lackey moths, and leaf-rolling sawflies. A number of other insects can damage roses, though fortunately they never seem to attack all at the same time, and they may not appear at all in some years. They include froghoppers, chafers and other beetles, leaf miners, rose slug-worms, red spider mites, leafhoppers, thrips and capsid bugs.

601

Roscoea
Zingiberaceae

Roscoea cautleyoides

These handsome, hardy, herbaceous perennials are suitable for a rock garden or the front of a border. Most species bloom all summer, die down in autumn, then rest for an unusually long period, emerging only in late spring. The roots are tuberous. Native to China and the Himalayas.

RECOMMENDED SPECIES AND VARIETIES

R. alpina A single, somewhat floppy stem bears a succession of flowers, one at a time, from mid summer through to autumn. The flowers are deep rose to purple and up to 2.5 cm (1 in) long. Two to four unstalked, oval leaves, up to 10 cm (4 in) long, are arranged in a single tuft around the stem base. HEIGHT & SPREAD 15×15 cm (6×6 in).

R. auriculata A succession of purple flowers, 5 cm (2 in) long, appear on 6-10 erect stems. Each stem bears one flower at a time. Linear to lance-shaped leaves, about 25 cm (10 in) long, grow in sparse tufts. HEIGHT & SPREAD 40×30 cm (16×12 in).

'Beesiana' has flowers entirely yellow or yellow stained with purple.

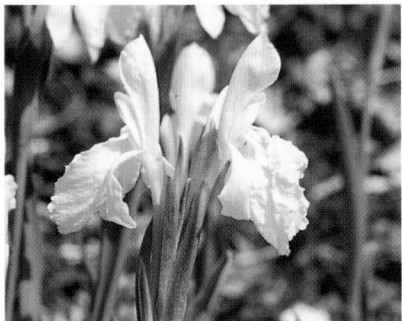

▲ *Roscoea cautleyoides*

R. cautleyoides♀ Daffodil-yellow flowers 4 cm (1½ in) long grow in spikes on top of upright stems from mid to late summer. The plant has 2-3 stems. Four or so flowers are in bloom at any one time. The lance-shaped leaves are as long as 35 cm (14 in). HEIGHT & SPREAD 30×20 cm (12×8 in).

R. humeana♀ Two to five, or more, purple or lilac-pink flowers, about 5 cm (2 in) long, open simultaneously in late spring or early summer. The plant has a single, stout stem, which bears 5-7 ovate leaves 20 cm (8 in) long that often emerge after the flowers have begun to bloom. HEIGHT & SPREAD 30×20 cm (12×8 in).

▲ *Roscoea humeana*

R. purpurea Purple, purple-and-white or all white flowers are 6 cm (2½ in) long. They open one at a time on a strong stem, which bears 20 cm (8 in) long lance-shaped leaves. HEIGHT & SPREAD 30×20 cm (12×8 in).

▲ *Roscoea purpurea*

R. scillifolia A cluster of 2-5 lilac-pink or purple flowers grows at the top of a single, slender, erect stem. Each flower is about 2.5 cm (1 in) long. On the lower half of the stem are set the 12 cm (4¾ in) long rectangular leaves. HEIGHT & SPREAD 40×30 cm (16×12 in).

CULTIVATION Plant tubers in autumn or early spring, no less than 15 cm (6 in) deep, in a humus-rich, well-drained soil, preferably neutral or slightly acid. Choose a position in good light. Remove faded flowers.

PROPAGATION Species will self-seed in favourable conditions, such as after a good summer. Sow seed any time in spring, or divide and replant the tubers as soon as the foliage has died down.

PESTS AND DISEASES Soil pests, including wireworms and vine weevil larvae, may cause root damage. Slugs eat young foliage. Wet, clammy soils encourage fungal diseases in the rootstock.

Rose, Christmas see *Helleborus niger*
Rose, guelder see *Viburnum opulus*
Rose, Lenten see *Helleborus orientalis*
Rose, rock see *Helianthemum*
Rose, sun see *Cistus*
Rosemary (culinary herb)
  see HERBS p. 332
Rosemary see *Rosmarinus*
Rosemary, bog see *Andromeda*
Rose of Sharon
  see *Hypericum calycinum*

Rosmarinus
Rosemary
Labiatae

Rosmarinus officinalis

Grown for its dense, strongly aromatic, evergreen foliage, this native of dry coastal areas around the Mediterranean thrives in full sun and well-drained soil. Small clusters of flowers, in shades of mauve and blue, pink and white, appear on shoots of the previous year. Valued as a culinary herb, rosemaries range in height from a medium-sized shrub to a low-growing, trailing plant. They also make a fine, informal hedge. Some varieties are half-hardy and should be grown in containers that can be moved to a sheltered spot or under glass in winter. The rest are hardy to -5°C (23°F) or just below.

RECOMMENDED SPECIES AND VARIETIES

R. officinalis The blunt-ended, needle-like leaves are 2-5 cm (¾-2 in) long, dark green and rather glossy above, white felted below. Mauve and dark blue, tubular, 2-lipped flowers, up to 2 cm (¾ in) long, are borne from mid spring to early summer and spasmodically until early autumn. HEIGHT & SPREAD 75×75 cm (2½×2½ ft) after 5 years, ultimately 1.5 m (5 ft) tall.

▲ *Rosmarinus officinalis*

White-flowered var. *albiflorus* is sought after as a herb and for flower arranging. The half-hardy and fairly prostrate var. *angustissimus* **'Corsican Blue'** has blue flowers. **'Aureus'** (syn. 'Aureovariegatus', 'Gilded', 'Variegatus') has leaves with irregular yellow variegation. **'Benenden Blue'** (syn. 'Collingwood Ingram') is a smaller variety of dense, semi-erect then cascading habit, with gentian-blue flowers. It reaches a final height of 1 m (3 ft). **'Fota Blue'** is a half-hardy, free-flowering variety with very dark blue flowers. Semi-prostrate in habit, it has a mature height of 60 cm (2 ft).

'Jackman's Prostrate' has pale blue flowers from early spring onwards and reaches a final height of only 30 cm (1 ft).

'Lady in White' has white flowers. 'Majorca Pink' is of columnar habit and has short, relatively broad, dull green leaves and lilac-pink flowers which open from early spring onwards. It is moderately hardy and reaches a final height of 1.2m (4ft). 'McConnell's Blue' is a spreading and prostrate plant with broad leaves and blue flowers. Half-hardy, it has an ultimate height of 40cm (16in). 'Miss Jessopp's

▲ *Rosmarinus officinalis* 'McConnell's Blue'

Upright'♀ (syn. 'Fastigiatus', f. *pyramidalis*) is a vigorous, erect variety with narrowly oblong leaves and light mauve-blue flowers. Good for hedging, it may grow to a height of 1m (3ft) after 5 years, ultimately reaching a height of 1.8m (6ft).

'Primley Blue' (syn. 'Frimley Blue') is an upright, tidy variety with clear blue flowers. Mature height 1m (3ft). **Prostratus Group**♀ (syn. *R. corsicus* 'Prostratus', *R.* × *lavandulaceus* hort., *R. officinalis* var. *lavandulaceus*, *R. o.* var. *repens*, *R. repens*) forms large, dense, trailing mats, up to 60cm (2ft) high, of fresh green leaves, studded with light blue flowers. Plants are half-hardy.

'Roseus' has lilac-pink flowers. 'Severn Sea'♀, a plant of spreading, arching habit, with violet-blue flowers, grows to 1m (3ft) tall. 'Sissinghurst Blue'♀ is of upright habit, very free-flowering with rich blue blossom, and reaches a height of 1.2m (4ft). 'Sudbury Blue' is of upright habit, with dense, blue-green foliage and mid blue flowers. 'Tuscan Blue' is a fast-growing, upright plant with reddish brown stems. The light green, rather broad leaves smell of nutmeg. The large blue flowers often appear in winter.

CULTIVATION Plant in mid spring, or late spring for the less hardy forms, in a sunny position in any ordinary, well-drained soil. For hedging, use 'Miss Jessopp's Upright', spacing the plants 60cm (2ft) apart.

PROPAGATION Take semi-ripe cuttings in mid to late summer and insert in a cold-frame. Pot up the rooted cuttings and over-winter in a frost-free frame or greenhouse.

PRUNING Cut out dead wood and shorten straggly shoots in early spring. Overgrown bushes may be cut by half in mid spring.

PESTS AND DISEASES Usually trouble free.

Rowan see *Sorbus aucuparia*
Rubber plant see *Ficus elastica*

Rubus
Rosaceae

Rubus arcticus

As well as producing raspberries, blackberries, loganberries and tayberries, this genus also includes plants grown for their ornamental value. These include hardy, erect or scrambling, evergreen and deciduous shrubs and climbers. Although some of them bear edible fruit, they are valued more for their flowers, foliage and attractive stems. (For fruiting species, see p.723.) In spring or summer, five-petalled flowers are borne either singly or in clusters.

RECOMMENDED SPECIES AND VARIETIES
The species here are divided into two groups – evergreen and deciduous. Unless otherwise stated, all the plants bear prickles.

EVERGREEN SPECIES AND VARIETIES
R. arcticus (crimson bramble) A semi-evergreen alpine creeper, useful for a rock garden or as ground cover. Pink or red flowers, up to 2.5cm (1in) wide, are borne singly on short thornless stems, from time to time through summer. Each mid green leaf has 3–5 serrated leaflets. Plant in lime-free soil. HEIGHT & SPREAD 2×25cm (¾×10in).

R. calycinoides see *R. pentalobus*

R. henryi var. *bambusarum* Grown for its foliage, this elegant climber has leaves, as long as 12.5cm (5in), with 3 distinct lance-shaped leaflets. Sprays of pink flowers, up to 7.5cm (3in) long, appear in early summer. Edible black fruit, about 1.5cm (½in) across, carried in clusters, are sometimes produced in autumn. HEIGHT & SPREAD 3.5×1.8m (12×6ft) after 5 years, ultimately 6m (20ft).

R. pentalobus (syn. *R. calycinoides*) Oval, 3–5 lobed leaves, to 4cm (1½in) long, form a mat of foliage over the stems of a spreading, prostrate shrub. Wrinkled leaves covered with grey down partially conceal white flowers, up to 2cm (¾in) wide, in early summer. Red berries may follow. The plant self-roots from branches along the ground. HEIGHT & SPREAD 5×20cm (2×8in) after 5 years, ultimately 60cm (2ft) or more across.

'Betty Ashburner' is a popular form.
R. tricolor This scrambling carpeter, with long trailing stems that self-root readily, will spread indefinitely unless curbed. The heart-shaped leaves, up to 10cm (4in) long, are dark green above and whitish beneath. White flowers, up to 2.5cm (1in) wide, carried in mid summer, are sometimes followed by red, raspberry-like, edible fruits. The stems are covered in red bristles. HEIGHT & SPREAD 60cm×3m (2×10ft) after 5 years.

DECIDUOUS SPECIES AND VARIETIES
R. 'Benenden'♀ (syn. *R. Tridel* 'Benenden') In late spring and early summer, this shrub carries saucer-shaped,

▲ *Rubus* 'Benenden'

pure white flowers, up to 6cm (2½in) across, with a tuft of golden stamens. The broadly oval, mid green, 3–5 lobed leaves are up to 8cm (3¼in) long. The upright thornless stems with peeling bark arch with age. HEIGHT & SPREAD 2×2m (6½×6½ft) after 5 years, ultimately 3m (10ft) tall.

R. cockburnianus♀ Purple shoots overlaid with a white bloom make this arching shrub a spectacular feature in winter. Dark green leaves, up to 20cm (8in) long, have 5–9 oval leaflets and are white beneath. Sprays of purple flowers, up to 12cm (4¾in) long, are produced in early summer. Inedible black fruits follow the flowers. HEIGHT & SPREAD 1.8×1.2m (6×4ft) after 5 years, ultimately 2.4m (8ft).

The glowing yellow, fern-like foliage of 'Golden Vale' mellows to lime-green as the season progresses. This plant reaches a maximum height of about 1.8m (6ft).

▼ *Rubus cockburnianus* 'Golden Vale'

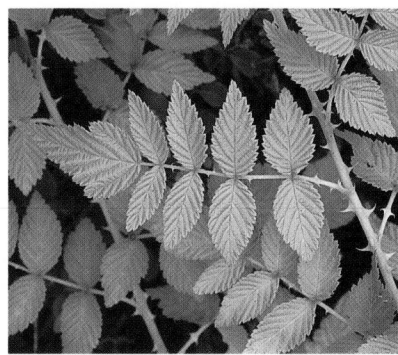

R. phoenicolasius (Japanese wineberry) Spreading, biennial stems are densely covered with reddish bristles and a few prickles. Each mid green leaf, to 18cm (7in) long, is whitish beneath and has 3–5 toothed oval leaflets. Pale pink flowers appear in spikes up to 20cm (8in) long in mid summer. Edible, conical, red berries, to 2cm (¾in) long, follow in late summer; they will ripen better if the plant is grown against a wall. HEIGHT & SPREAD 1.5×1.5m (5×5ft) after 5 years, ultimately 3m (10ft) tall, if supported.

R. thibetanus♀ This erect shrub has purple biennial stems which are white-bloomed in winter. Dark green pinnate leaves, up to 23cm (9in) long, with many leaflets, are covered with silky hairs and are white beneath. Purple flowers, up to 1.2cm (½in) wide, are followed by edible, round black fruits. HEIGHT & SPREAD 1.8×1m (6×3ft) after 5 years, ultimately 2.4m (8ft) tall.

r

R. **Tridel 'Benenden'** see *R.* 'Benenden'
CULTIVATION Plant in spring in any well-drained soil in sun or shade. Grow *R. phoenicolasius* against a sunny wall.
PROPAGATION Take semi-ripe cuttings of evergreens and semi-evergreens in mid to late summer. Take softwood cuttings of deciduous species in spring or hardwood cuttings in late autumn. Layer *R.* 'Benenden' in spring.
PRUNING Cut back the previous season's growth of *R. cockburnianus* and *R. thibetanus* to ground level in spring, as soon as new shoots appear. Alternatively, remove a proportion of the flowered shoots at ground level after flowering. Thin out the other species and varieties annually, as necessary.
PESTS AND DISEASES Usually trouble free.

Rudbeckia
Coneflower
Compositae

Rudbeckia
'Goldquelle'

These hardy herbaceous perennials and annuals are grown for their brightly coloured daisy-like flowers, which brighten the garden from late summer to early autumn. The blooms are in shades of yellow and orange and all have prominent cone-shaped centres in contrasting colours, surrounded by gracefully drooping petals. The erect stems of rudbeckias form sturdy clumps. Native to N America.
RECOMMENDED SPECIES AND VARIETIES
R. **echinacea** var. *purpurea* see *Echinacea purpurea*
R. **fulgida** This herbaceous perennial bears flowers up to 7 cm (2¾ in) across with yellow to orange petals and purplish brown centres. The mid green lance-shaped leaves reach a length of 12 cm (4¾ in). The original species is not usually grown in gardens, where selected varieties are preferred. HEIGHT & SPREAD 60×45 cm (24×18 in).

The narrow, deep yellow petals of var. *deamii*♀ surround a black centre. The petals of var. *sullivantii* 'Goldsturm'♀ are golden, also around a black centre.
R. **gloriosa** see *R. hirta*
R. **'Goldquelle'**♀ Double flowers, up to 10 cm (4 in) across, have deep yellow petals surrounding green centres. The mid green leaves are divided, hairy beneath and up to 10 cm (4 in) long. The plant is a herbaceous perennial. HEIGHT & SPREAD 75×50 cm (30×20 in).

▲ *Rudbeckia fulgida* var. *deamii*

R. **'Herbstsonne'** ('Autumn Sun') Discs, up to 10 cm (4 in) across, of floppy golden yellow petals surround green centres. The oval, mid green leaves of this herbaceous perennial grow to 15 cm (6 in) long. Both flowers and leaves are borne on wavy stems. HEIGHT & SPREAD 2 m×60 cm (6½×2 ft).

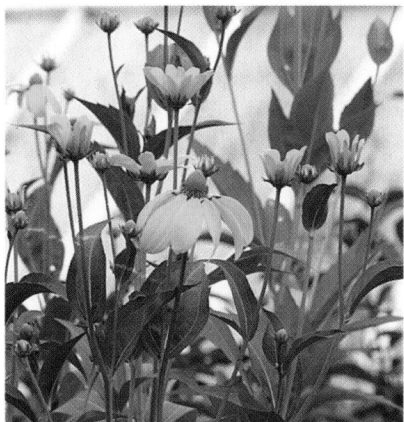

▲ *Rudbeckia* 'Herbstsonne'

R. **hirta** (syn. *R. gloriosa*) (black-eyed Susan) Pale yellow petals surround dark red centres. The blooms are up to 7.5 cm (3 in) across. The narrow, pointed, deep green, bristly leaves are ribbed and grow to 10 cm (4 in) in length. This short-lived herbaceous perennial is usually grown as an annual. The flowers last well in water when cut. HEIGHT & SPREAD 30-100×50 cm (1-3 ft×20 in).

The double or semidouble flowers of the cultivar **'Goldilocks'** have deep golden petals and black centres. The petals of **'Marmalade'** are a rich gold and the small centres are jet-black.
R. **laciniata** The blooms, up to 10 cm (4 in) across, have bright yellow petals and yellowish green centres. The mid green pinnate leaves grow to 10 cm (4 in) long, with as many as 10 leaflets. This tall herbaceous perennial is ideal for the back of the border. HEIGHT & SPREAD 1.8 m×60 cm (6×2 ft).

'Hortensia' (syn. 'Golden Glow') has bright golden yellow, double flowers on branching stems.
R. **maxima** The golden flowers, up to 5 cm (2 in) across, have black conical centres. The

greyish green, oval to oblong leaves grow to 12 cm (4¾ in) in length. This herbaceous perennial enjoys slightly damper situations than most rudbeckias. HEIGHT & SPREAD 1.5 m×60 cm (5×2 ft).
R. **purpurea** see *Echinacea purpurea*
R. **subtomentosa** Golden flowers, up to 10 cm (4 in) across, are produced by this herbaceous perennial. The flattish centres are purplish black. The soft oval leaves grow to 12.5 cm (5 in) long and have toothed edges and a covering of grey hairs. This species likes rather moister conditions than most other rudbeckias. HEIGHT & SPREAD 75×50 cm (30×20 in).
CULTIVATION Plant from autumn to mid spring in any reasonably fertile, moisture-retentive soil, choosing an open sunny situation. In drier conditions apply a moisture-retaining mulch in spring, to prevent the plants from wilting in hot sun when in flower. Deadhead faded flowers and stake taller plants.
PROPAGATION Divide established plants in spring or autumn. Alternatively, sow the seed of herbaceous perennials on open ground in spring. Sow the seed of *R. hirta* where they are to flower in early spring.
PESTS AND DISEASES Usually trouble free.

Rue see *Ruta graveolens*
Rue, meadow see *Thalictrum flavum*
Rue anemone
  see *Anemonella thalictroides*

Ruscus
Butcher's broom
Ruscaceae

Ruscus aculeatus

Attractive foliage and showy red berries earn these tough evergreen perennials a place under a tree or in any dry shady area. The foliage is distinctive in that the true leaves are reduced to minute scales and the shoots are flattened into the shape of leaves, known as cladodes. Tiny greenish flowers are borne on the cladodes in spring or autumn, with male and female flowers usually on separate plants. When fertilised, the female flowers develop into bright red berries which last well into winter.

The listed species are all hardy and can be used to provide ground cover in dry, shady places. The cut foliage lasts well in water and is used by flower arrangers. Native to Europe, W Asia and the Azores.

r

▲ *Ruscus aculeatus*

RECOMMENDED SPECIES AND VARIETIES

R. aculeatus Wiry green stems bear stiff, spine-tipped, ovate or lance-shaped cladodes up to 2.5 cm (1 in) long. Starry pale green flowers are borne on the upper surface of the cladodes. Brilliant scarlet berries, 1 cm (⅜ in) across, may be abundant on female plants where both sexes are grown in proximity. The plant has a variable habit, but is often rather erect. HEIGHT & SPREAD 1×1 m (3×3 ft).

The compact, self-fertile clone 'Sparkler' is free-fruiting.

R. hypoglossum Arching stems bear soft, ovate cladodes up to 10 cm (4 in) long. Starry light green flowers sit in the axil of a green bract on the upper surface of each cladode. Bright red globular berries, 1.5 cm (½ in) across, follow the flowers. HEIGHT & SPREAD 60 cm×1 m (2×3 ft).

R. racemosus see *Danae racemosa*

▲ *Ruscus hypoglossum*

CULTIVATION Plant in autumn in any well-drained soil, in shade or sun. Butcher's brooms are very tolerant of dry, shady conditions. To encourage fruiting, plant a mixture of male and female plants, or a hermaphrodite variety if available.
PROPAGATION Divide in spring.
PESTS AND DISEASES Usually trouble free.

Rush, flowering
see *Butomus umbellatus*

Russelia
Scrophulariaceae

Clusters of brightly coloured blossoms embellish these tender evergreen shrubs and sub-shrubs in summer and autumn. They perform best when growing unrestricted in a conservatory or a greenhouse border, but display their lax habit well in hanging baskets. Plants need a minimum temperature of 10°C (50°F). The genus is native to Central and S America.
RECOMMENDED SPECIES
R. equisetiformis♀ (coral plant) Narrow, tubular red flowers, up to 2.5 cm (1 in) long, bloom in cascading clusters, from mid summer to early autumn on this branching evergreen shrub. It has strange, slender rush-like stems and tiny mid green scale-like leaves. HEIGHT & SPREAD 1×1 m (3×3 ft).

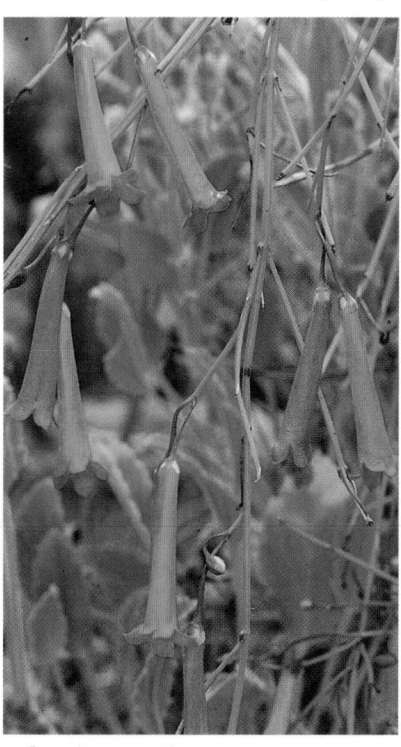

▲ *Russelia equisetiformis*

CULTIVATION Plant in spring in well-drained soil that has been enriched with organic matter. The plants require great cultural care if grown in the confined conditions of hanging baskets. Stake plants growing in a conservatory or greenhouse border. Cut out any untidy shoots as they appear. Deadhead the flowers when practicable. Water well in summer and keep much drier during autumn and winter. Apply a slow-release fertiliser in spring.
PROPAGATION Take stem cuttings during spring and summer.
PESTS AND DISEASES Mealy bugs can be a nuisance.

Russian vine see *Fallopia baldschuanica*

Ruta
Rue
Rutaceae

These hardy evergreen sub-shrubs are mainly grown for their aromatic leaves which are sometimes used as medicinal or culinary herbs. The S European species described below will grow happily in poor chalky soils in a sunny position.
RECOMMENDED SPECIES AND VARIETIES
R. graveolens (common rue) Deeply divided, blue-green leaves, about 4 cm (1½ in) long, clothe this compact, rounded bush. Terminal clusters of small, starry yellow flowers appear in mid summer. HEIGHT & SPREAD 45×30 cm (1½×1 ft).

▲ *Ruta graveolens*

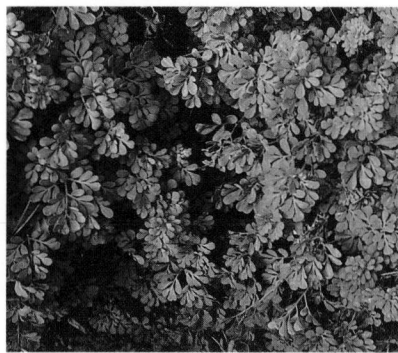

▲ *Ruta* 'Jackman's Blue'

'Jackman's Blue'♀, more compact, bears distinctly glaucous leaves, but is rather more reluctant to flower.
CULTIVATION Plant in spring in an open, sunny site in free-draining soil. Trim back in spring to the old wood to maintain the shape of the plants. Some people are allergic to the foliage so wear gloves when pruning. Do not apply fertiliser as soft growth will be induced, leading to winter damage.
PROPAGATION Sow seed of species, including *R. graveolens*, in trays under glass as soon as it is available in late summer. Pot on seedlings and plant out in early summer of the following year. For cultivars, such as 'Jackman's Blue', take semi-ripe cuttings in summer and root in coarse, gritty compost in a coldframe. Pot on and keep in a coldframe over winter.
PESTS AND DISEASES Usually trouble free.

605

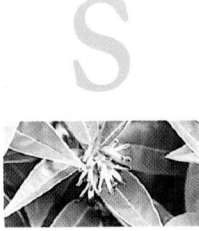

Sagina
Pearlwort
Caryophyllaceae

The low mound of *Sagina subulata* 'Aurea' and the glossy cushion of *S. boydii*, both evergreens, provide year-round interest. These decorative and slow-growing hardy perennials are worthy of a place in a trough or raised bed. 'Aurea' does well in the cracks in paving in the company of small thymes and other sun-loving crevice plants.

RECOMMENDED SPECIES AND VARIETIES
S. boydii The deep green, highly glossed foliage is made up of tight rosettes of narrow, pointed leaves, up to 1.5 cm (½ in) long, which form a dense hump. The white flowers in summer are tiny and sparse. HEIGHT & SPREAD 5×10 cm (2×4 in).

▲ *Sagina subulata* 'Aurea'

S. subulata 'Aurea' Golden, linear leaves up to 2 cm (¾ in) long are carried in loose clusters and form soft mounds. A profusion of tiny, star-like, white flowers appears in early summer. It is hardy, but not usually long-lived in cultivation. HEIGHT & SPREAD 10 × 30 cm (4 × 12 in).

CULTIVATION Plant in well-drained gritty soil. *S. boydii* benefits from winter protection or from growing in an alpine house.

PROPAGATION Increase by cuttings or by careful division in spring. Use coarse sand to promote root growth with both cuttings and – in the initial stage – divisions.

PESTS AND DISEASES Moulds may attack pearlworts during winter. *S. boydii* is frequently infested with aphids.

Sagittaria
Arrowhead
Alismataceae

Elegant, arrow-shaped leaves and loose clusters of decorative flowers grace these submerged and emergent aquatic plants. Widely grown in ponds and aquaria, sagittarias require a well-lit position, preferably in still water. The species described are hardy marginals, and require a water depth of up to 15 cm (6 in), but will tolerate a little more. Both spread by underground runners and quickly form dense colonies. In winter they produce dormant buds, or turions, resembling small tubers, that detach themselves from the parent plant. Sagittarias are native to the USA.

RECOMMENDED SPECIES AND VARIETIES
S. japonica see *S. sagittifolia*
S. latifolia (duck potato) White 3-petalled flowers, up to 2.5 cm (1 in) across and with a conspicuous yellow centre, are borne in mid to late summer. The soft green leaves grow up to 60 cm (24 in) long. HEIGHT & SPREAD 1.2 m×60 cm (4×2 ft).

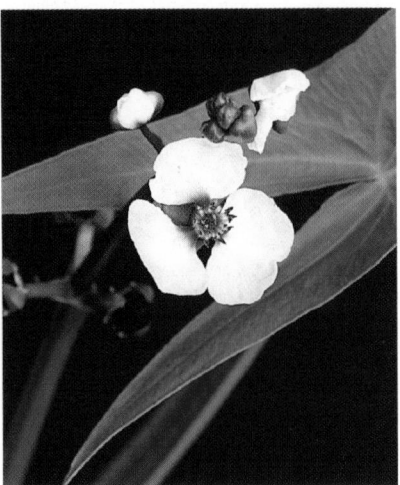

▲ *Sagittaria sagittifolia*

S. sagittifolia (syn. *S. japonica*) (arrowhead, water archer) Loose spikes of white 3-petalled flowers, each up to 2.5 cm (1 in) across and with a purplish brown centre, are borne in mid to late summer. Upright mid green leaves grow to 45 cm (18 in) in length. HEIGHT & SPREAD 45×30 cm (18×12 in).
'Flore Pleno' is a fine double variety.

CULTIVATION Plant from late spring to mid summer in clean, heavy garden soil or a proprietary aquatic planting compost either in an aquatic planting basket or on the marginal shelf of a pool. Cover the soil with a layer of pea gravel to prevent fish from disturbing it. And if ducks are likely to be a nuisance, cover with fine wire-netting. Remove faded foliage in autumn.

PROPAGATION Divide in spring.

PESTS AND DISEASES Water-lily aphids are often troublesome.

Saintpaulia
African violet
Gesneriaceae

saintpaulia ionantha

Brightly coloured, star-shaped flowers are produced almost all year round by these tender perennials, native to E Africa. They have soft, velvety, rounded leaves – those of the plants recommended here are up to 5 cm (2 in) across. They make ideal house-plants and greenhouse specimens for warm humid conditions out of direct sunlight.

RECOMMENDED SPECIES AND VARIETIES
S. 'Bright Eyes'♀ A profusion of single deep violet flowers, up to 1.5 cm (½ in) across and with conspicuous yellow centres, are produced on short stalks. The leaves are dark green and form a compact rosette. HEIGHT & SPREAD 10×25 cm (4×10 in).
S. 'Colorado'♀ The single magenta flowers are up to 2 cm (¾ in) across with neatly frilled edges and bright yellow centres. The plant forms a neat rosette of dark green leaves. HEIGHT & SPREAD 10×25 cm (4×10 in).
S. 'Garden News'♀ Beautiful fully double white flowers up to 2 cm (¾ in) across are produced above rosettes of bright green leaves. HEIGHT & SPREAD 10×25 cm (4×10 in).
S. ionantha The main parent of the modern African violet cultivars bears single flowers, violet-blue or white with a violet throat. Up to 2.5 cm (1 in) across, they are produced just above the leaves in loose clusters of 2-8. The rather fleshy leaves are rounded or scalloped, usually hairy and dull green, often with reddish undersides. HEIGHT & SPREAD 10×25 cm (4×10 in).
S. 'Rococo Pink'♀ Fully double iridescent

▼ *Saintpaulia* 'Bright Eyes'
Saintpaulia 'Garden News' ▼

▲ *Saintpaulia* 'Rococo Pink'

pink blooms, up to 2.5 cm (1 in) across, are produced on this tidy rosette-forming plant. The leaves are mid green. HEIGHT & SPREAD 10×25 cm (4×10 in).

S. 'Starry Trail'♀ This trailing variety has blue flowers up to 2.5 cm (1 in) across with a distinctive white edge to the petals. Mid green leaves are borne on drooping stems. HEIGHT & SPREAD 10×30 cm (4×12 in).

S. 'Wonderland'♀ This plant has semi-double, light blue, ruffled flowers up to 2 cm (¾ in) across, and mid-green leaves. HEIGHT & SPREAD 10×25 cm (4×10 in).

CULTIVATION Grow in pots of rich free-draining compost, preferably soil-less. Maintain a minimum temperature of 15°C (59°F). Place in a well-lit position protected from full sun. Allow the plants to become slightly pot-bound. Water sparingly and liquid feed in spring and summer, preferably from beneath; water occasionally in winter. Remove faded leaves and flowers.

PROPAGATION Leaf cuttings in summer.

PESTS AND DISEASES Whitefly and mealy bug can cause trouble.

Salal see *Gaultheria shallon*

Salix
Willow
Salicaceae

salix alba var. sericea

Fluffy catkins, slender shoots and coloured bark are among the many attractive features of these trees and shrubs. Willows are predominantly deciduous and totally hardy. Most are undemanding about site and soil and tolerate the British climate perfectly well, but excessive heat in southern gardens harms a few sub-alpines. In most species there are separate male and female trees, with showier catkins on the males.

The larger willows have wide-spread-

ing, moisture-seeking roots, which can damage nearby buildings, walls or drains. For these, 40 m (130 ft) is the minimum recommended planting distance from a house.

The smallest willows are creeping shrubs no more than 2.5 cm (1 in) in height, while the largest trees reach 30 m (100 ft). The larger trees and coppice shoots may grow as much as 2.5 cm (1 in) a day in early summer.

RECOMMENDED SPECIES AND VARIETIES In the garden, willows have five distinct uses, and they are grouped here as follows:
(1) Landscape, feature and shelter plants
(2) Willows grown for buds and catkins
(3) Willows grown for winter twig colour
(4) Summer-foliage feature plants
(5) Alpine and shrubby willows

LANDSCAPE, FEATURE AND SHELTER
Large willows create a leafy summer backdrop to other plants or to water. The flexible branches and twigs rapidly form a good windbreak.

S. alba (white willow) Slender branches droop slightly on this large spreading tree. The narrow, pointed, matt green leaves have blue-grey undersides covered with fine hairs, giving the tree a silvery appearance. Native to Britain. HEIGHT & SPREAD 6×3 m (20×10 ft) after 20 years, ultimately 20 m (66 ft) or more tall.

The smaller var. *sericea*♀ has a brilliant silver crown and is slower growing. Final height is 10 m (33 ft), reached after 15 years.

S. caprea (goat willow) Although not suitable for a small garden, this woodland willow makes a good windbreak. It has broadly oval, fresh green leaves, finely toothed with a short point. Silvery green female catkins or bright yellow male catkins appear before the leaves. Native to Britain. HEIGHT & SPREAD 15×10 m (50×33 ft) – final size, reached in less than 20 years.

salix caprea 'Kilmarnock'

More suitable for small gardens are the small weeping cultivars. The male form is often sold as 'Kilmarnock'♀ and the female form as 'Weeping Sally'. They are elegant trees with a narrow head of weeping shoots, often no taller than 1.5 m (5 ft), and some 2 m (6½ ft) across, after 10-15 years. They require some pruning to keep their shape.

S. × pendulina 'Elegantissima' Cascades of weeping shoots form a spectacular large specimen tree, especially beside a pond that catches its reflection. The narrow pendulous leaves are fresh green. Disease resistant. HEIGHT & SPREAD 8×6 m (26×20 ft) after 10-15 years, ultimately 25×25 m (80×80 ft).

WILLOWS FOR BUDS AND CATKINS
Pussy willow buds, held upright against the rather erect stems, last for several weeks in late winter and early spring. Then they open fully into powder-puff male catkins, 1-2 cm (⅜-¾ in) long and usually yellow, or female catkins, which are less fluffy and a silvery green. Some plants have coloured or textured stems.

S. aegyptiaca (musk willow) Long, yellow male catkins make this large rounded shrub or small tree a haze of colour in late winter before the broad, deep green leaves appear. Native to Turkey, Armenia and Iran. HEIGHT & SPREAD 6×4 m (20×13 ft) after 10-15 years, ultimately 12 m (40 ft) tall.

S. daphnoides 'Aglaia'♀ Long, pearly grey pussy willow buds are borne on the plum-purple shoots of this male tree early in the year. The species, native to central Europe, is often short lived. HEIGHT & SPREAD 5×4 m (16×13 ft) after 10-15 years, ultimately 10 m (33 ft) tall.

S. gracilistyla♀ This ornamental spreading shrub has furry stems and silky pink catkins. Native to Japan, China and Korea. HEIGHT & SPREAD 80×80 cm (32×32 in) after 5 years, ultimately 2 m (6½ ft) tall.

'Melanostachys'♀, a male clone, has unusual black catkins in early spring, which turn brick-red and then gold. The stems are a rich plum-purple colour.

S. udensis 'Sekka' (syn. *S. sachalinensis* 'Sekka') Numerous pearly buds develop into large, silky, pink male catkins in early spring on this sprawling shrub. The shoots are often flattened. Native to Japan and E Russia. HEIGHT & SPREAD 3×8 m (10×26 ft) after 10-15 years, ultimately 5 m (16 ft) tall.

WILLOWS FOR WINTER TWIG COLOUR
Brilliantly coloured young stems are obtained by regularly cutting back these willows to near ground level. If this is done at the end of winter in alternate years, good colour is combined with catkins on the yearling stems. Older shoots are not brightly coloured. Leaves are narrow and 5-15 cm (2-6 in) long. The plants listed grow to 1 m (3 ft) in one year and to 1.5-2 m (5-6½ ft) after two years. After 10-15 years a plant has a spread of about 3 m (10 ft) with some 50 stems. The roots spread widely even on plants that are cut back.

S. acutifolia 'Blue Streak'♀ Shiny, deep purplish violet shoots are dusted with a silver-grey bloom. The young silvery buds make a striking contrast though the catkins are dull yellow.

S. alba var. *vitellina*♀ (golden willow) The young shoots are a striking orange-yellow.

'Britzensis'♀ has orange-red stems.

S. × rubens 'Basfordiana'♀ The yellow stems of this male plant bear slender yellow catkins with glossy leaves in spring. 'Sanguinea' is a red-stemmed female variety.

ALPINE AND SHRUBBY WILLOWS
Several of these plants are suitable for beds or permanent containers. Some are spread-

S

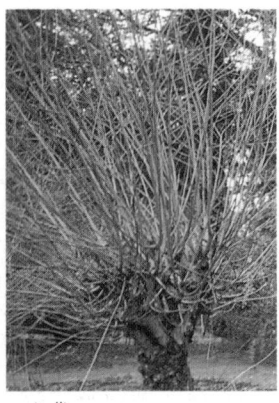

▲ *Salix alba* var. *vitellina*
Salix alba var. *vitellina* 'Britzensis' ▲

ing but their roots are not invasive. The true alpines do not thrive in hot conditions nor in competition with other plants.

S. alpina (syn. *S.* 'Jacquinii') This is a low spreading shrub with glossy round leaves. Male plants have purplish catkins, which turn golden yellow, females have greenish catkins. Native to the Alps and Carpathians. HEIGHT & SPREAD 25×20 cm (10×8 in).

▲ *Salix exigua*

S. exigua (coyote willow) Very narrow, long, silvery, pale green leaves distinguish this open-growing shrub with its graceful, slender branches. Yellow male catkins appear in spring at the same time as the leaves; the green female catkins, on separate plants, are hidden by the leaves. Native to western N America and N Mexico. HEIGHT & SPREAD 4 m (13 ft) tall, spreading 30 cm (1 ft) a year by suckers.

S. hastata 'Wehrhahnii' ♀ White woolly catkins maturing to a brilliant yellow are borne on stout, dark reddish purple stems by this small multistemmed shrub. The rounded leaves are dark green. Native to Japan, China and Korea. HEIGHT & SPREAD 80×80 cm (32×32 in) after 5 years, ultimately 2 m (6½ ft) tall.

S. lindleyana A mat of tiny, glossy, pale green leaves trails over rocks and scree. Male catkins are browny green, female catkins reddish brown. Native to the Himalayas. HEIGHT & SPREAD 10×30 cm

(4×12 in) after 5 years.

S. repens var. *argentea* ♀ Silver leaves are borne on an ornamental, low and sprawling bush. Roundish silver catkins are small but often numerous. Native to Britain. HEIGHT & SPREAD up to 70×120 cm (28×48 in).

'Voorthuizen' is a completely prostrate cultivar of *S. repens*, with trailing stems and tiny silvery leaves.

S. reticulata ♀ The summer catkins on this minute prostrate plant may be as tall as the whole plant at 4 cm (1½ in). They vary in colour from brown to purple and yellow. The stalked, round, deciduous leaves are leathery and heavily veined. Native to N Asia, N America and Europe. HEIGHT & SPREAD 4×20 cm (1½×8 in) after 15 years.

WILLOWS FOR SUMMER FOLIAGE

Curious or brightly coloured foliage is a feature of several medium-size willows that enliven a garden bed. Larger curiosities serve as dramatic specimen plants.

S. babylonica 'Crispa' (syn. *S. babylonica* 'Annularis') Spiralling narrow leaves on this erect shrub often form complete rings. Shoots tend to die back. HEIGHT & SPREAD 1.5×1 m (5×3 ft) after 10–15 years.

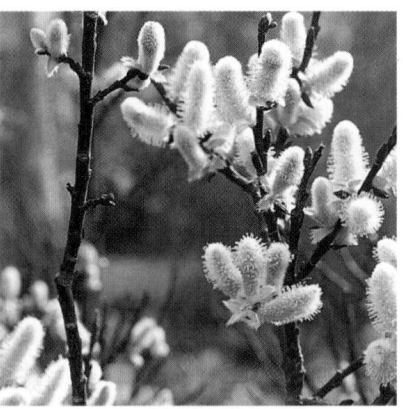

▲ *Salix hastata* 'Wehrhahnii'

S. babylonica var. *pekinensis* 'Tortuosa' ♀ (syn. *S. matsudana* 'Tortuosa') This curiously twisted, fast-growing tree has contorted greenish twigs and leaves. Even large branches and trunks are bent and often they split because of it. Female catkins appear before the leaves. HEIGHT & SPREAD 10×7 m (33×23 ft) when mature at about 15 years.

S. elaeagnos ♀ (hoary willow) Slender purple-brown shoots, bearing yellow catkins in spring, form a dense shrub. The very narrow, long, graceful leaves are grey-green above, silvery below. Native to S Europe and Turkey. HEIGHT & SPREAD 2×2 m (6½×6½ ft) after 6 years and ultimately.

S. fargesii Large glossy leaves and long erect catkins succeed the brilliant red winter buds. Glossy green new shoots mature to a polished red-brown in the second year. In cold areas the spectacular foliage sometimes suffers damage. Native to SE Asia. HEIGHT & SPREAD 1.5×1.5 m (5×5 ft) after 5 years, ultimately 5 m (16 ft) tall.

▲ *Salix integra* 'Hakuro-Nishiki'

S. helvetica ♀ (Swiss willow) Glaucous, thickly woolly leaves make this small rounded bush into a bright blue-green ball of colour. In early spring the catkins are silvery green, the male flowers turning golden yellow with pollen. Native to the Alps, it relishes an exposed position. HEIGHT & SPREAD 1×1 m (3×3 ft) in 6 years.

S. integra 'Hakuro-Nishiki' (syn. 'Albomaculata') Slender catkins are followed by the pink and white, variegated leaves of this graceful branched shrub. Prune in early spring to encourage new growth. A willow bred from a Japanese species, it is often grown as a 1 m (3 ft) high standard. HEIGHT & SPREAD 1.5×1.5 m (5×5 ft) as a shrub.

salix lanata

S. lanata ♀ (woolly willow) Grey-green, downy, rounded leaves form a low spreading bush suitable for a rock garden. The erect catkins become fluffy and turn yellow in summer. Native to Scotland. HEIGHT & SPREAD 30×30 cm (1×1 ft) after 5 years, ultimately 90 cm×2 m (3×6½ ft).

CULTIVATION Though tolerant of a wide range of soils, willows generally prefer damp heavy soil and thrive least on shallow chalk. They do best in full light. Alpine types grow best in dry air, low temperatures and moist rocky ground.

PROPAGATION Semi-ripe or hardwood cuttings root readily. Grafting is needed to reproduce exactly the named varieties.

PRUNING Only plants grown for twig colour need hard pruning. Cut them down to the ground at the end of winter, cutting half the shoots in alternate years. Trim other willows sparingly, otherwise excessive growth is stimulated.

PESTS AND DISEASES Aphids, moths, beetles and weevils occasionally cause damage. Midges and mites cause galls but these are usually best left alone. *S. alba* sometimes suffers from watermark disease caused by the bacterium *Erwinia salicis*.

Salpiglossis
Solanaceae

Funnel-shaped, strikingly marked flowers are freely produced on these upright branching plants. Only one species, a half-hardy annual, is normally cultivated in Britain, and this has given rise to numerous hybrids. The plants thrive in a sunny sheltered position in mild dry areas. A bed or large container on a patio with a southerly aspect suits them well and they flower from mid summer to early autumn. In cooler regions, they can be grown as pot plants in a greenhouse or conservatory, flowering in spring and early summer. The flowers are ideal for cutting and last well in water.

RECOMMENDED SPECIES AND VARIETIES
S. sinuata (painted tongue) This Chilean species is rarely grown, but seed of dwarf hybrids in mixed colours is widely available. The flowers, up to 7 cm (2¾ in) long, range in colour from yellow to orange, red, rose, purple and blue. The petals are often overlaid by another colour, usually gold, though darker veins are also a feature. The slender stems are covered in sticky hairs. The narrow, lance-shaped, pale green leaves have wavy, toothed edges and grow to 10 cm (4 in) long.

Bolero grows to 60 cm (2 ft) tall. **Carnival** reaches a height of 45 cm (1½ ft). **Casino**♀, **Festival** and **Flamenco** reach a height of 35 cm (14 in).

CULTIVATION Plant after all risk of frost has passed in moist but well-drained soil, choosing a sheltered spot in full sun. Alternatively, grow in pots of general purpose or potting compost and keep in a greenhouse or conservatory; plants can be moved outside in summer. In winter, maintain a temperature of 10°C (50°F).

Provide support for taller varieties, and removed faded flowers on all varieties to prolong flowering.

PROPAGATION For plants grown outside, sow seed in late winter or early spring in a heated greenhouse. For pot plants, sow seed in a heated greenhouse in late summer for

▲ *Salpiglossis* Casino

spring flowering, and in late winter for late spring and early summer flowering.

PESTS AND DISEASES Soil-borne fungal attack may cause wilt and die-back.

Salvia
Sage
Labiatae

salvia argentea

The upright flower spikes of this large genus of annuals, perennials and shrubs provide some of the brightest colours for summer borders or for winter displays in a greenhouse or conservatory. Many salvias have soft hairy leaves and some species, including the herb sage (*Salvia officinalis*), are grown for their decorative and aromatic foliage. The individual flowers are tubular with two lips, the upper lip often elongated and pulled forward to form a hood. The flower spikes are formed by whorls of flowers along the stems. Most salvias prefer drier conditions in well-drained soil in full sun.

RECOMMENDED SPECIES AND VARIETIES
Salvias vary in hardiness and can be divided into 3 groups accordingly; there are hardy, half-hardy and tender species and varieties.

HARDY SPECIES AND VARIETIES
These can be grown outdoors all year round in Britain.
S. argentea♀ A mass of woolly, silver, oval to oblong leaves, up to 20 cm (8 in) long, form a basal rosette. White flowers, 1.5 cm (½ in) long, appear in branching spikes on strong upright stems in early summer. This herbaceous perennial or biennial often dies after the plant has flowered. It is mainly

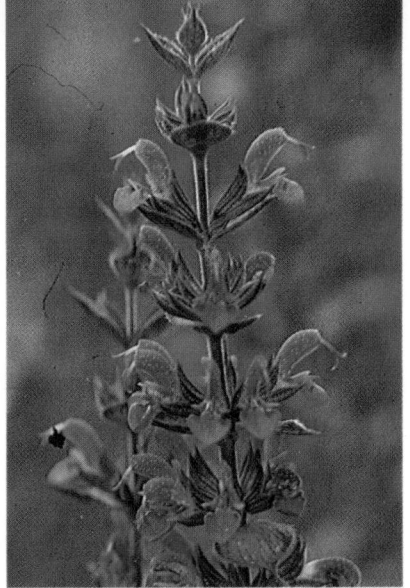
▲ *Salvia nemorosa* 'Ostfriesland'

grown for its decorative leaf rosettes. Native to the Mediterranean. HEIGHT & SPREAD 60–90×45 cm (2–3×1½ ft).
S. haematodes
see *S. pratensis* Haematodes Group
S. horminum see *S. viridis*
S. nemorosa 'Ostfriesland'♀ ('East Friesland') Dense upright spikes of purple flowers, each about 6 mm (¼ in) long, cover these bushy herbaceous perennials in mid summer. The rough, narrow oval leaves, 10 cm (4 in) long, are mid green. HEIGHT & SPREAD 45×45 cm (1½×1½ ft).
S. officinalis (common sage) This aromatic evergreen sub-shrub is widely cultivated for its ornamental foliage as well as for use as a culinary herb. The rough, grey-green, pointed oval to oblong leaves are up to 7.5 cm (3 in) long. Flowers in shades of blue and purple, 2 cm (¾ in) long, appear in short spikes intermittently throughout the summer. Native to the Mediterranean. HEIGHT & SPREAD 60 cm×1 m (2×3 ft).

The leaves of 'Icterina'♀ are marbled with primrose yellow and gold. 'Kew Gold'♀ has bright golden yellow leaves but flowers sparsely. **Purpurascens Group**♀ has soft purple leaves that gradually darken through the summer. 'Tricolor'♀ has white, deep pink and purple leaves which

Salvia officinalis Purpurascens Group ▼
▼ *Salvia officinalis* 'Icterina'

▲ *Salpiglossis sinuata*

▲ *Salvia przewalskii*

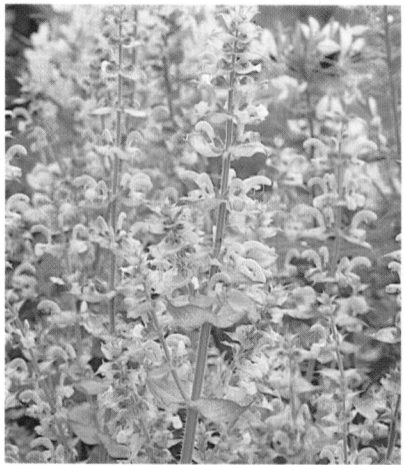

▲ *Salvia sclarea var turkestanica*

darken as summer progresses.

S. pratensis **Haematodes Group**♀ (syn *S. haematodes*) Light lavender-blue flowers, 3 cm (1¼ in) long, are borne in loose panicles in early summer. The dark green, rough leaves, 15 cm (6 in) long, have wavy, toothed edges and form a basal rosette. *S. pratensis* (meadow clary) is a short-lived herbaceous perennial, native to Europe, including Britain. HEIGHT & SPREAD 1 m×38 cm (3 ft×15 in).

S. przewalskii Violet to purple or blue flowers, 2 cm (¾ in) long, appear on branching stems in late summer. The heart-shaped leaves, up to 10 cm (4 in) long, are mid-green above, beige beneath. They form a clump at the base of the plant. A herbaceous perennial, native to China, with tuberous roots. HEIGHT & SPREAD 1.2×1 m (4×3 ft).

S. sclarea var. *turkestanica* (clary sage) White and purple flowers, 3 cm (1¼ in) long, appear in mid summer on branching spikes. Prominent purple bracts persist after the flowers fade. The dark green, hairy, aromatic leaves are up to 23 cm (9 in) long and, if touched, their unpleasant smell can cling to clothing. A short-lived evergreen perennial or biennial that seeds itself freely.

Native to central Asia. HEIGHT & SPREAD 1 m×30 cm (3×1 ft).

S. × *superba*♀ Masses of violet-blue flowers, 1.5 cm (½ in) long, are borne on numerous branching spikes in mid summer. Crimson-purple bracts persist after the flowers have faded. The rough, narrow pointed leaves of this herbaceous perennial are mid-green and grow to 10 cm (4 in) long. HEIGHT & SPREAD 60-90×45 cm (2-3×1½ ft).

salvia × superba

'**Rubin**' has pink flowers and claret-striped bracts. '**Superba**' has purple flowers.

S. × *sylvestris* '**Rose Queen**' Pale pink flowers, about 1.5 cm (½ in) long, with red bracts appear on branching spikes in early summer. The narrow pointed, dark green, veined leaves of this herbaceous perennial are up to 7 cm (2¾ in) long. HEIGHT & SPREAD 1.2 m×60 cm (4×2 ft).

S. verticillata In late summer, long arching spikes carry tiny, vivid violet flowers with crimson-tinted bracts that persist after the flowers fade. The oval to oblong, mid-green leaves, 10 cm (4 in) long, form a large clump. A herbaceous perennial, native to Europe and W Asia. HEIGHT & SPREAD 75 cm×45 cm (2½×1½ ft) or more.

The flowers of '**Alba**' are white.

S. viridis (syn. *H. horminum*) White or lilac flowers, 1.5 cm (½ in) long, appear in spikes in early summer and their colourful bracts last throughout summer. These can be blue, pink, purple or white, with darker veins. The flowerheads can be dried. The mid-green oval leaves are up to 5 cm (2 in) long. An annual, native to the Mediterranean, of very upright habit. HEIGHT & SPREAD 45×20 cm (1½ ft×8 in).

The cultivar of *S. viridis*, '**Claryssa**', has larger bracts of more intense colour, and grows to 40 cm (16 in).

HALF-HARDY SPECIES AND VARIETIES
These are half-hardy herbaceous perennials and sub-shrubs which can be grown outdoors in summer and overwintered under glass. These can also be treated as annuals by raising new plants from cuttings or seed each year. There are also half-hardy annuals available.

S. cacaliifolia♀ Bright blue flowers, 2 cm (¾ in) long, appear on loose spikes in late summer. The shiny mid green leaves grow to 10 cm (4 in) long. A herbaceous perennial of loose habit, native to Central America. HEIGHT & SPREAD 1 m×45 cm (3×1½ ft).

S. candelabrum♀ Violet-blue flowers, 4 cm

(1½ in) across and flecked with white, appear in mid summer on branching spikes. The dark grey-green, aromatic leaves grow to 9 cm (3½ in) long. This herbaceous perennial or sub-shrub, native to Spain, may survive outside in more protected gardens. HEIGHT & SPREAD 90×60 cm (3×2 ft).

S. cardinalis see *S. fulgens*

S. coccinea Long spikes of red flowers, each about 2 cm (¾ in) long, appear from early to mid summer. Dark green, downy, heart-shaped leaves, about 6 cm (2½ in) long, are also borne by this annual of graceful habit, native to tropical S America. HEIGHT & SPREAD 60-90×30 cm (2-3×1 ft).

'**Coral Nymph**' has pink and white flowers, '**Lady in Red**'♀ has scarlet.

S. confertiflora Deep red flowers, 12 mm (½ in) long, appear in spikes in late summer or autumn. The yellowy green, ovate leaves, 20 cm (8 in) long, are rough and densely woolly. They give off a foetid smell when crushed. A herbaceous perennial, native to Brazil. HEIGHT & SPREAD 1.2 m×60 cm (4×2 ft).

S. discolor♀ Deep purple, almost black flowers, 3 cm (1¼ in) long and with hooded white calyxes, appear in late summer. The pointed, oval, grey to whitish green leaves are 10 cm (4 in) long. All parts of the plants are covered with white hairs. A herbaceous perennial, native to Peru. HEIGHT & SPREAD 45×30 cm (1½×1 ft).

S. farinacea (mealy sage) Tiny blue, lavender or purple flowers appear in slender spikes throughout summer. The narrow, mid or dark green leaves are up to 8 cm (3 in) long. The densely branched stems of this herbaceous perennial are covered with a white dust. A plant of upright habit usually raised from seed. Native to Texas and N Mexico. HEIGHT & SPREAD 50×25 cm (20×10 in).

'**Strata**' has clear blue flowers with contrasting silver calyxes, which are prominent when the flowers are in bud. It reaches 40 cm (16 in) in height. '**Victoria**'♀ has

▼ *Salvia farinacea*

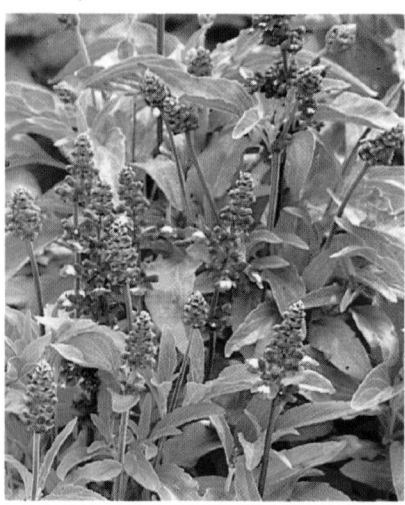

deep purple-blue flowers and grows 50 cm (20 in) tall. **'White Victory'**♀ has silvery white blooms and reaches 35 cm (14 in) tall.

S. fulgens♀ (syn. *S. cardinalis*) Scarlet flowers, up to 3 cm (1¼ in) long, appear in branching spikes towards the end of summer. The pointed oval leaves, 12 cm (4¾ in) long, are bright green above and white-hairy underneath. A herbaceous perennial, native to Mexico, with upright stems which are woody at the base. HEIGHT & SPREAD 1.2 m×75 cm (4×2½ ft).

S. grahamii hort.
  see *S. microphylla* var. *neurepia*

S. greggii (autumn sage) Flowers 1.5 cm (½ in) across, ranging in colour from red to purple, appear in clusters on thin wiry stems in late summer. The narrow oblong leaves, matt and deep green, grow to 3 cm (1¼ in) in length. An upright evergreen sub-shrub from Texas and Mexico. HEIGHT & SPREAD 1×1 m (3×3 ft).

The hybrid × *lycioides* (syn. *S. lycioides*) has deep purple flowers. **'Peach'** see *S. × jamensis* 'Pat Vlasto'.

S. guaranitica♀ Dark gentian-blue flowers, 5 cm (2 in) long, appear in terminal spikes in late summer. The dark green, ovate leaves are 12.5 cm (5 in) long. This evergreen perennial, also grown as an annual, can survive outside in warmer gardens if protected with horticultural fleece or a dry mulch. Native to S America. HEIGHT & SPREAD 1.2 m×45 cm (4×1½ ft).

S. involucrata♀ In late summer, pinky crimson flowers, 3-5 cm (1¼-2 in) long, are carried in compact spikes. The oval mid green leaves are 25 cm (10 in) long. A herbaceous perennial with woody-based stems, native to Mexico. HEIGHT & SPREAD 1.5 m×60 cm (5×2 ft).

'Bethellii' has larger, dark cerise blooms.

S. × jamensis **'Pat Vlasto'** (syn *S. greggii* 'Peach' hort.) Deep pink, tubular flowers, 2.5 cm (1 in) long, appear in spikes from mid summer onwards. The ovate leaves, 3 cm (1¼ in) long, are mid green. An evergreen sub-shrub. HEIGHT & SPREAD 75×45 cm (2½×1½ ft).

S. lycioides see. *S. greggii × lycioides*

S. microphylla var. *neurepia*♀ (syn *S. grahamii* hort., *S.* 'Kew Red') Vibrant scarlet flowers, 2.5 cm (1 in) long, are carried in spikes and last from early summer to the first frosts. The pale green, ovate leaves are up to 4 cm (1½ in) long. An upright-growing, evergreen sub-shrub of rounded habit, native to Mexico. HEIGHT & SPREAD 1.2 m×75 cm (4×2½ ft).

The flowers of **'Newby Hall'**♀ are brighter scarlet.

S. patens♀ (gentian sage) Pale or deep blue flowers, 2.5 cm (1 in) across, are borne on long slender spikes in late summer and autumn. The oval leaves, 10-20 cm (4-8 in) long, are pale green. An upright, branching herbaceous perennial which has tuberous roots that can be lifted and stored over the

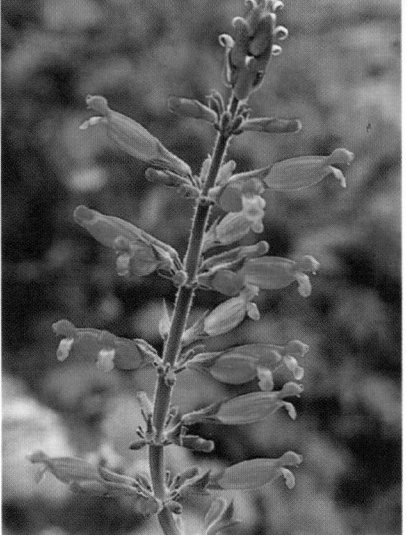
▲ *Salvia involucrata*

winter. In warm sheltered gardens with well-drained soil, the tubers will usually survive the winter outdoors if left undisturbed. Often raised from seed. Native to Mexico. HEIGHT & SPREAD 60-75×30 cm (2-2½×1 ft).

'Cambridge Blue'♀ has pale blue flowers and is available as seed strain. **'Chilcombe'** has mauve-blue flowers.

S. splendens (scarlet sage) Scarlet flowers, each up to 5 cm (2 in) long, appear from early to mid summer on dense flower spikes. Conspicuous red bracts persist after the flowers fade. The pointed oval, mid to dark green leaves, up to 7 cm (2¾ in) long, have toothed edges. This is the bushy annual, native to Brazil, that is widely grown as a bedding plant. HEIGHT & SPREAD 30×25 cm (12×10 in).

'Blaze of Fire' has red flowers. **'Laser Purple'** and **'Phoenix Purple'** both produce purple blooms. **Sizzler Series** has flowers in shades of pink, red and purple as well as white. **'Vanguard'**♀ has red flowers.

S. uliginosa♀ Azure flowers, 1½ cm (½ in) across, open from purple buds in late summer and continue well into autumn. The shiny, narrow, mid green leaves are 9 cm (3½ in) long. This herbaceous perennial prefers moister conditions and may survive the winter outside in mild areas. It often breaks into growth late in spring, so it should not be presumed dead till then. Native to S America. HEIGHT & SPREAD 1.5-2.5 m×60 cm (5-8×2 ft).

TENDER SPECIES AND VARIETIES

These plants are best grown in a greenhouse or conservatory with a minimum temperature of 7°C (45°F). They flower so late in the year that, grown outside even in mild areas, they risk being killed by the first frosts before flowering has finished.

S. buchananii♀ (syn. *S. bacheriana*) Spikes of purple flowers, up to 5 cm (2 in) long, appear from mid summer to mid autumn. The dark green lanceolate leaves, up to 6 cm (2½ in) long, have a leathery shiny surface. A herbaceous perennial with woody-based stems, native to Mexico. HEIGHT & SPREAD 60×30 cm (2×1 ft).

S. leucantha♀ (Mexican sage bush) White

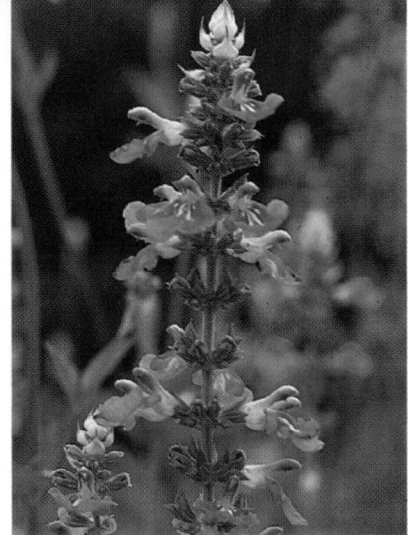
▲ *Salvia uliginosa*

flowers, 2 cm (¾ in) long with purple calyxes, appear from mid summer to mid autumn on spikes up to 50 cm (20 in) long. The mid green lanceolate leaves grow to 10 cm (4 in) long. Leaves, stems and flowers of this herbaceous perennial are covered in dense white wool. HEIGHT & SPREAD 1-1.5 m×45 cm (3-5×1½ ft).

S. oppositiflora♀ Spikes of brilliant red flowers, tinged with orange and up to 4 cm (1½ in) long, appear in mid summer. The heart-shaped hairy leaves, about 5 cm (2 in) long, are pale green above with dense white wool beneath. A herbaceous perennial, native to Peru. HEIGHT & SPREAD 60×45 cm (2×1½ ft).

CULTIVATION Plant hardy salvias from autumn to spring in any free-draining soil in full sun. Some staking will be needed for taller plants. Cut back the flowering stems of hardy herbaceous perennials after the first flowers fade to encourage a second crop of blooms later in the season.

Plant half-hardy salvias in late spring after danger of frosts has passed, choosing a warm, protected spot. Lift plants in autumn before the first hard frosts and overwinter in a cool greenhouse or conservatory. Alternatively, grow in containers of compost and move outside during the summer.

Grow tender salvias in pots of compost in a greenhouse or conservatory. Maintain a minimum winter temperature of 7°C (45°F). Water freely during the growing season and feed every 3 weeks.

PROPAGATION Divide hardy plants in autumn or spring, or sow the seed of species in open ground in spring.

Take softwood or tip cuttings of half-hardy and tender perennials in summer and grow on under glass through the winter. Alternatively, sow seed in early spring in a heated greenhouse – salvias for bedding out are always propagated in this way.

PRUNING If necessary, control the size of *S. officinalis* by cutting back in spring. Other shrubby salvias do not need pruning.

PESTS AND DISEASES Red spider mites and leafhoppers can be a problem under glass. Capsid bugs and powdery mildew may attack the leaves of plants grown outside.

S

Sambucus
Elder
Caprifoliaceae

sambucus racemosa

Familiar residents of English hedgerows, elders have long been cultivated for their colourful foliage and scented flowers. Although they are not particularly showy, the flat creamy white clusters of starry flowers possess a delicate charm. The flowers are borne in early summer and can be used to make wine as can the small black berries which ripen in early autumn.

All elders bear pinnate leaves with 5-7 toothed, ovate leaflets, each up to 12.5 cm (5 in) long. When allowed to grow freely the plants develop an untidy habit. However, they can be cut back almost to ground level every 2 or 3 years, to which they respond by producing brightly coloured regrowth. There are 20 hardy species of elder but generally the cultivars of only two species – *Sambucus nigra* and *S. racemosa* – are grown in Britain. They make a colourful summer feature in a large, informal garden. Native to Europe.

RECOMMENDED SPECIES AND VARIETIES
S. nigra (European elder) This rampant, invasive species with mid green leaves has little appeal to most gardeners, but there are several cultivars that make attractive garden subjects. HEIGHT & SPREAD 6×4 m (20×13 ft) after 10 years, ultimately 8 m (26 ft) tall.

'**Aurea**'♀ (golden elder) is a very hardy variety. It needs full sun for its leaves to develop the best golden colour, which deepens as summer ends. It can be coppiced

▼ *Sambucus nigra* 'Marginata'
Sambucus nigra 'Pulverulenta' ▼

to good effect every 1-3 years. '**Aureomarginata**' has bright yellow-edged foliage and should be treated in the same way as 'Aurea'. '**Guincho Purple**'♀ bears green foliage to begin with, which develops into purple-black growth in summer, finally turning red in autumn. The flowers are pinkish in bud on purple stalks. If it is shaded or coppiced, it tends to stay quite green all year. Finely divided green leaflets distinguish f. *laciniata*♀ (fern-leaved elder). It can be coppiced to resemble a clump of ferns, or allowed to grow into a small tree of 4×3 m (13×10 ft) in 20 years. '**Linearis**' has variably shaped leaflets often cut to the midrib. The plant seldom exceeds a height and spread of 2×2 m (6½×6½ ft). '**Marginata**' is a silver to white variegated variety. It is vigorous and produces coppice regrowth of around 1.5 m (5 ft) in the first year. The green leaves have creamy edges. Full sun is needed to produce good colour. '**Pulverulenta**' is a small slow-growing plant with white-mottled leaves.

▲ *Sambucus nigra* 'Aurea'

S. racemosa (European red elder) Roughly conical heads of yellowish white flowers are borne by this spreading shrubby tree. The berries are bright, glossy scarlet. HEIGHT & SPREAD 3×3 m (10×10 ft) after 10 years, ultimately 4 m (13 ft) tall.

'**Sutherland Gold**'♀ is a deeply cut, golden variety with yellowish flowers. It needs full light to develop good foliage colour but often suffers from heat in southern Britain. '**Tenuifolia**'♀ is a slow-growing, cut-leaved variety that grows well on lime-rich soils. It seldom exceeds a height and spread of 1.5×1.5 m (5×5 ft).

CULTIVATION Plant in any well-drained soil, ensuring that the golden and variegated forms have plenty of sunlight.

PROPAGATION Plant hardwood cuttings outdoors in winter, or semi-ripe heel cuttings in late summer under glass.

PRUNING Left unpruned, elders tend to become untidy and unstable. They may be pruned to the ground in winter, losing flowers and fruit, or old wood may be cut out and young shoots reduced by a half.

PESTS AND DISEASES Aphids and mosaic virus may occasionally strike.

Sanguinaria
Bloodroot
Papaveraceae

There is just one species in this genus, a hardy herbaceous perennial bearing short-lived anemone-like flowers in spring. After the flowers have faded, the grey-green leaves open to their full extent forming a dense canopy. Bloodroot with its rhizomatous roots is a useful plant for naturalising in leafy woodland. It is also good for a shady spot in a rock garden or a peat border. The name of this woodland plant from N America refers to the crimson sap that oozes from its rhizomes when they are cut.
Sanguinaria canadensis Solitary white, 8-petalled flowers, 5 cm (2 in) across, are held at the top of stout upright stems, 10 cm (4 in) tall, in spring. The rounded, lobed and scalloped leaves, carried on stiff stalks, grow to 10 cm (4 in) across. HEIGHT & SPREAD 30×45 cm (1×1½ ft) after 3 or 4 years.

▲ *Sanguinaria canadensis* 'Plena'

'**Plena**'♀, the most widely grown cultivar, and the best for gardens, has double flowers. '**Rosea**' (also sold as '**Pink**') has blooms flushed with rose pink.

CULTIVATION Plant in cool, humus-rich soil in light shade in spring or autumn.

PROPAGATION Lift and divide plants every few years in autumn.

PESTS AND DISEASES Usually trouble free, though wireworm or cutworm may damage the rhizomes.

Sanguisorba
Burnet
Rosaceae

Striking flowers and attractive foliage enhance the perennial border throughout the summer. The tiny flowers with protruding stamens are packed into spherical or oblong heads held at the top of slender stems, producing a bottlebrush effect. These hardy rhizomatous perennials have pinnate leaves, divided into several rounded or oblong, serrated leaflets. The genus is naturally distributed in Europe, Asia and N America.

RECOMMENDED SPECIES AND VARIETIES

S. albiflora (syn. *S. magnifica alba*) Nodding white flower heads, up to 6 cm (2½ in) long, are borne from mid summer to early autumn. The grey-green leaves are composed of 11-15 rounded, 5 cm (2 in) long, clearly stalked leaflets. HEIGHT & SPREAD 75×40 cm (30×16 in).

S. canadensis Creamy white flowers, carried in erect, narrowly cylindrical heads up to 20 cm (8 in) long, appear from mid summer to mid autumn. The pale green leaves have up to 8 pairs of narrow, 10 cm (4 in) long leaflets. HEIGHT & SPREAD 1.8 m×60 cm (6×2 ft).

S. magnifica alba see *S. albiflora*

S. minor (salad burnet) Spherical green flowerheads, 1.5 cm (½ in) across, are borne in early summer and early autumn. The flowerheads are often tinged with purple and become reddish in fruit. The pinnate leaves have 9-25 rounded leaflets, about 2 cm (¾ in) long. HEIGHT & SPREAD 1 m×45 cm (3 ft×18 in).

S. obtusa Nodding, rich rose-pink flowerheads, up to 7.5 cm (3 in) long, appear from mid summer to early autumn. The grey-green leaves are composed of 13-17 thick-textured, 5 cm (2 in) long, rounded leaflets. HEIGHT & SPREAD 60×40 cm (24×16 in).

S. officinalis (great burnet) Oblong or globular, dull crimson flowerheads, up to 2 cm (¾ in) across, appear in early summer to early autumn on branched leafy stems. This erect plant bears leaves with up to 7 pairs of 5 cm (2 in) long, ovate leaflets. HEIGHT & SPREAD 1 m×60 cm (3×2 ft).

CULTIVATION Plant in any moderately moist soil, in full sun or light shade, in autumn. Taller plants may need support from twigs pushed in around the clump.

PROPAGATION Lift and divide in early spring. Alternatively, sow seed in autumn or early spring.

PESTS AND DISEASES Usually trouble free.

▼ *Sanguisorba officinalis*

Sansevieria
Dracaenaceae

sansevieria trifasciata 'Laurentii'

Erect, sword-like leaves, often patterned and variegated, make this tropical evergreen perennial one of the most popular house plants. Mature plants produce rather insignificant fragrant, lily-like flowers. These are creamy, white or greenish and may be removed when they first appear, though they are quite pleasing and may be followed by red berries. Sansevierias are extremely easy to grow, but avoid overwatering, especially in winter, and maintain a minimum temperature of 10°C (50°F).

RECOMMENDED SPECIES AND VARIETIES

S. trifasciata (mother-in-law's tongue) The stiff, upright, dull green leaves grow up to 75 cm (30 in) long. They are beautifully patterned and splashed with dark green and resemble a snakeskin. Native to W Africa. HEIGHT & SPREAD 25×15 cm (10×6 in).

'Gigantea' grows to a height of 75 cm (2½ ft) and has green-patterned leaves with yellow margins. 'Golden Hahnii'♀ has rosettes of pale green foliage, marked and marbled with darker green and with bold yellow, informally banded edges. 'Hahnii' is a dwarf plant that forms rosettes of broadly lance-shaped, leathery leaves, up to 15 cm (6 in) long. 'Laurentii'♀ has erect, fleshy, sword-like, dark green leaves with gold edges and cross bands of dark green.

▼ *Sansevieria trifasciata 'Golden Hahnii'*

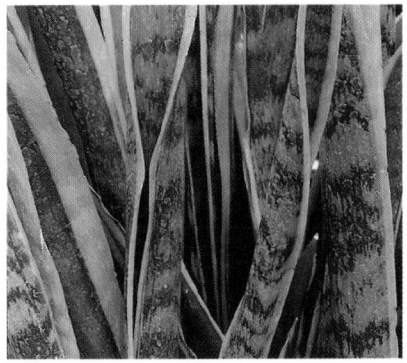

▲ *Sansevieria trifasciata 'Laurentii'*

CULTIVATION Grow sansevierias in free-draining gritty compost, preferably in a sunny position, though some shade is tolerated. Never overwater. Feed occasionally with a liquid house-plant fertiliser in summer. Keep the foliage free from dust, especially where light levels are low and in winter. Sansevierias are slow-growing, making only a few fresh leaves each year. They tolerate neglect but grow faster and better if their compost is replaced regularly.

PROPAGATION Take leaf cuttings in spring and summer. Divide variegated plants in spring and summer.

PESTS AND DISEASES Usually trouble free.

Santolina
Compositae

santolina chamaecyparissus

These summer-flowering, dwarf evergreen shrubs are grown for their mounds of aromatic, finely divided foliage and pale button-like flowers. They are suitable for growing in large rock gardens, at the front of shrub borders or as low hedging. The species below bear 2 cm (¾ in) wide flowerheads, held singly on long stems. The plants are frost hardy but relatively short-lived and need replacing every 5-10 years. The measurements given below are for full-grown 5-year-old plants.

RECOMMENDED SPECIES AND VARIETIES

S. chamaecyparissus♀ (syn. *S. incana*) (cotton lavender) Silvery, finely dissected, woolly leaves, up to 4 cm (1½ in) long, form a dense leafy mass. Bright lemon-yellow flowers appear in mid summer. HEIGHT & SPREAD 60×60 cm (2×2 ft) or more.

The following cultivars are slightly smaller than the species. 'Lambrook Silver' has silver, thread-like foliage and deep

S

▲ *Santolina chamaecyparissus* 'Lemon Queen'

yellow flowers. Its neat tight habit makes it good for hedging. **'Lemon Queen'** has grey-green foliage and, despite the name, cream flowers. With a height and spread of just 20×20 cm (8×8 in), var. *nana*♥ is a good rock garden plant. **'Pretty Carol'** has greyish leaves.

S. pinnata The smooth, divided, mid green leaves grow up to 4 cm (1½ in) long. White flowers appear in mid to late summer. HEIGHT & SPREAD 60 cm×1 m (2×3 ft).

The widely grown ssp. *neapolitana*♥ has longer and more feathery leaves than the species and lemon-yellow flowers. Its cultivar **'Edward Bowles'** has greenish-grey leaves and pale primrose-yellow flowers. It reaches a height and spread of about 45×50 cm (18×20 in).

S. rosmarinifolia (syn. *S. virens*, *S. viridis*) Bright green, thread-like leaves grow up to 5 cm (2 in) long. Lemon-yellow flowers are borne in mid to late summer. HEIGHT & SPREAD 60 cm×1 m (2×3 ft).

'Primrose Gem'♥ has feathery mid green foliage and pale primrose-yellow flowers.

CULTIVATION Plant in spring or early autumn in full sun in any well-drained soil. For hedges, plant about 30 cm (1 ft) apart.

PROPAGATION Take semi-ripe cuttings from mid to late summer. Pot on in spring and move outdoors. Plant out in early autumn or the following spring.

PRUNING Cut back by at least half every spring to maintain a bushy neat habit. Trim lightly after flowering. For hedges, shear to shape after flowering once a year.

PESTS AND DISEASES Usually trouble free.

Sanvitalia
Compositae

Sanvitalia procumbens

The bold flowers of *Sanvitalia procumbens* spread a bright cover over the ground from summer to autumn. The plant is a hardy annual, flourishing in well-drained soil in a sunny spot edging a bed or border or hugging a path, though its exuberant trailing habit is best displayed in a container, such as a hanging basket or a window box.

RECOMMENDED SPECIES AND VARIETIES
S. procumbens (creeping zinnia) The flowers, appearing from mid summer to early autumn, are 2.5 cm (1 in) across and made up of bright yellow ray florets (petals) and dark purple centres of flattened cone shape. The mid green leaves, up to 6 cm (2½ in) long, are borne in pairs. Native to Mexico. HEIGHT & SPREAD 15×40 cm (6×16 in).

'Mandarin Orange' has golden orange ray florets. **'Irish Eyes'** has ray florets of the same colour, but the centres are greenish.

CULTIVATION Grow in a sunny situation in well-drained, preferably light, soil.

PROPAGATION Sow seeds in mid spring where the plants are to grow, thinning the seedlings to 25-30 cm (10-12 in) apart. On light soils, early autumn sowing is also successful but defer the final thinning until mid spring to allow for winter losses. For container culture or for earlier flowering, sow seeds in early spring in a heated greenhouse. Prick out the seedlings into cell trays, to minimise root disturbance at planting.

PESTS AND DISEASES Usually trouble free.

Saponaria
Soapwort
Caryophyllaceae

This genus of hardy summer-flowering plants includes popular rock-garden species and plants for borders. The recommended species are low-growing evergreen perennials, except *Saponaria officinalis*, a herbaceous perennial, and the border annual, *S. vaccaria*. Soapwort's five-petalled flowers are pink, unless stated otherwise. The leaves are roughly lance-shaped. The plants thrive in dry, sunny, sheltered locations.

RECOMMENDED SPECIES AND VARIETIES
S. **'Bressingham'**♥ Almost stemless flowers smother the low, dense, foliage mounds of this dwarf plant. The flowers, about 1 cm (⅜ in) across, appear in early summer. Deep green, bunched leaves grow to 2 cm (¾ in) long. HEIGHT & SPREAD 5×15 cm (2×6 in).

S. caespitosa Pink to purple flowers, about 1.5 cm (½ in) across, bloom on slender, upright stems in early summer. The leaves are rather fleshy and about 2.5 cm (1 in) long. The plant may not be hardy in colder districts and benefits from winter protection. HEIGHT & SPREAD 12.5×15 cm (5×6 in).

▼ *Saponaria ocymoides*

▲ *Saponaria officinalis*

S. ocymoides♥ (tumbling Ted) Abundant loose clusters of pink flowers, about 1 cm (⅜ in) wide, smother the foliage mat in early summer. This robust, fairly vigorous, but short-lived plant has hairy leaves about 2 cm (¾ in) long and self-seeds readily. HEIGHT & SPREAD 10×45 cm (4×18 in).

'Rubra Compacta'♥ is a tight, slower-growing plant with profuse, rich carmine blooms. The white-flowered **'Alba'** is neither as robust nor as abundant in flower.

S. officinalis (bouncing Bet) Flowers about 2.5 cm (1 in) across are borne in small clusters from late summer to mid autumn. With leaves up to 8 cm (3 in) long, it is a robust hairless plant with erect stems. It self-seeds freely (not the double-flowered varieties, though) and spreads invasively by thick underground stolons. Native to Britain. HEIGHT & SPREAD 80×50 cm (32×20 in).

'Alba Plena', **'Rosea Plena'** and **'Rubra Plena'** are double-flowered forms, white, pink and red. **'Dazzler'** has leaves variegated gold to cream and pink flowers.

S. × *olivana*♥ A profusion of 2.5 cm (1 in) wide flowers are borne above tufts of leaves, about 2 cm (¾ in) long in early summer. HEIGHT & SPREAD 5×15 cm (2×6 in).

S. pumilio (syn. *S. pulvinaris*) Pale pink to carmine flowers, about 2.5 cm (1 in) across, appear in mid summer over a dense pad of foliage. The leaves are about about 2 cm (¾ in) long. Often a short-lived plant. HEIGHT & SPREAD 7.5×20 cm (3×8 in).

S. vaccaria (syn. *Vaccaria hispanica*) This hardy annual has graceful sprays of flowers, 1 cm (⅜ in) across, which appear from late spring to mid summer. HEIGHT & SPREAD 80×25 cm (32×10 in).

CULTIVATION Plant the low-growing alpine species in early spring in gritty, well-drained, lime-free soil or scree in a sheltered, sunny position. *S. ocymoides* is an easily grown plant for sunny walls and path edges. Plant *S. vaccaria* in a sunny position in a mixed border in spring or early autumn. Grow *S. officinalis* in full sun or partial shade in any well-drained soil.

PROPAGATION Take semi-ripe cuttings of the alpines. *S. ocymoides* may also be raised from seed, sown outdoors in early summer. Sow seed of *S. vaccaria* in early spring or early autumn where it is to flower. Divide *S. officinalis* in spring or sow seed in situ in early spring or early autumn.

PESTS AND DISEASES Slugs and aphids can be troublesome, so too can leaf spot.

Sarcococca

Christmas box, sweet box
Buxaceae

sarcococca hookeriana
var. digyna

Providing abundant fragrant flowers in winter and glossy evergreen foliage, these hardy, many stemmed, small shrubs are good for the front of the border. Most species spread by suckers and, although invasive, they make good edging plants. The cut stems are useful for winter flower arrangements, though the sweet heady scent can be overpowering when blooms are brought indoors. The tiny, cream or white flowers are petal-less but with prominent anthers and are gathered in tassel-like clusters, 1-2 cm (⅜-¾ in) long, where the leaves join the branches. All species bear attractive berries about 6 mm (¼ in) wide. These and all other parts of the plant are harmful if eaten. Sarcococcas are native to W China.

RECOMMENDED SPECIES AND VARIETIES

S. confusa♀ Clusters of cream flowers are borne on the new season's growth in mid winter, the same time that the berries of the previous year turn black and become noticeable. The pointed elliptic leaves, 3-5 cm (1¼-2 in) long, are mid-green above and lighter beneath. A non-suckering species, and therefore less invasive. HEIGHT & SPREAD 1×1 m (3×3 ft) after 5 years, ultimately 1.5 m (5 ft) tall.

S. hookeriana var. *digyna*♀ White flowers with pink sepals are borne in clusters in mid to late winter. The black fruits appear in summer. Bright green and narrowly elliptic, the leaves are 6 cm (2½ in) long. HEIGHT & SPREAD 75×75 cm (2½×2½ ft) after 5 years, ultimately 1.2 m (4 ft) tall.

'Purple Stem' has reddish purple flower buds and young shoots.

S. hookeriana var. *humilis* Similar to *S. h.* var. *digyna*, this lower-growing variety makes an excellent ground-cover plant. HEIGHT & SPREAD 60×60 cm (2×2 ft) after 5

▼ *Sarcococca hookeriana* var. *humilis*

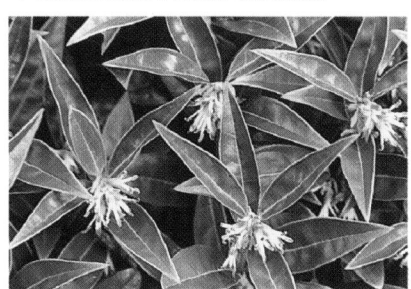

years, when it will have reached full size.

S. ruscifolia Clusters of ivory-white flowers appear in late winter and early spring, the blood-red berries in summer. The pointed ovate leaves, 2.5-6 cm (1-2½ in) long, are dark green above, paler beneath. HEIGHT & SPREAD 75×75 cm (2½×2½ ft) after 5 years, ultimately 1.2 m (4 ft) tall.

CULTIVATION Plant in early spring in moist but well-drained, loamy soil in partial shade. If plants become invasive, dig up suckers using a sharp spade.

PROPAGATION Transplant rooted suckers or take hardwood cuttings in autumn.

PRUNING Not necessary except to shape or restrict the spread of a plant.

PESTS AND DISEASES Usually trouble free.

Sasa see BAMBOOS p.76
Sasaella see BAMBOOS p.76

Sassafras

Lauraceae

sassafras albidum

These handsome deciduous trees have aromatic distinctively shaped leaves and give fine autumn colour. Not completely hardy, they prefer a sheltered position and require lime-free soil.

RECOMMENDED SPECIES

S. albidum The aromatic, dark green leaves have paler undersides and turn brilliant shades of red and gold in autumn. The leaves are alternate and ovate and grow to 15 cm (6 in) long. Some are entire, some 2-lobed, some 3-lobed. Tiny yellow flowers are borne in 3-5 cm (1¼-2 in) long racemes in late spring, and in autumn blue-black, ovoid berries, 1 cm (⅜ in) long, are carried on bright red, fleshy stalks. The bark is deeply fissured and the twigs and branches zigzag. In Britain it often grows as a multi-

▼ *Sassafras albidum*

stemmed shrub, but is still ornamental. Native to the USA. HEIGHT & SPREAD 2×1 m (6½×3 ft) after 5 years, ultimately up to 17 m (56 ft) tall.

CULTIVATION Grow in well-drained, lime-free soil in a position sheltered from late spring frosts, which can kill young growth.

PROPAGATION Sow fresh seed in autumn, take root cuttings in winter or transplant the suckers that are freely produced by sassafras.

PESTS AND DISEASES Usually trouble-free.

Satsuma see *Citrus reticulata*

Saururus

Lizard's tail
Saururaceae

saururus cernuus

Remarkable tail-like spikes of flowers emerge in summer from the decorative foliage of the two species in this genus. These hardy herbaceous perennials require an open sunny position in a bog garden or at the edge of a pond, where they disguise the transition to the surrounding ground. The recommended species quickly colonises bare ground round taller and more vigorous, upright-growing marginal and bog-garden plants.

RECOMMENDED SPECIES

S. cernuus (swamp lily, water dragon) Tiny, fragrant, cream-coloured flowers appear from mid to late summer, massed on arching spikes, which look rather like white pipe cleaners. The mid green, heart-shaped leaves, up to 7.5 cm (3 in) long, turn copper or red in autumn if frost has not damaged them. A clump-forming species, native to eastern N America. HEIGHT & SPREAD 23×30 cm (9×12 in).

CULTIVATION Plant in spring or early summer directly into a bog garden or shelf at the margin of a pond. Preferably (because swamp lilies are so invasive) plant in heavy loam or aquatic planting compost in an aquatic planting basket and stand the basket on a marginal shelf. Do not submerge plants by more than 2.5 cm (1 in) of water. If planting at the margin of a pond, cover the soil with a layer of pea gravel to prevent fish stirring up the mud.

PROPAGATION Divide plants in spring.

PESTS AND DISEASES Water-lily aphids can be a nuisance.

Savory see HERBS p.332

S

Saxifraga
Saxifrage
Saxifragaceae

saxifraga cebennensis

Complex cushions or mats of leaf rosettes are smothered in colour when saxifrages burst into flower. This large genus is the mainstay of a rock garden, offering a plant for almost every position and the choice of a succession of flowers from late winter to autumn. Many plants can also be grown in pots in an unheated, well-ventilated greenhouse or frame and the genus includes the trailing houseplant *Saxifraga stolonifera*.

Saxifrages usually have low-growing rosettes of leaves that may be stiff, fleshy or feathery. The shallow, cup or saucer-shaped flowers have five petals and come in all colours except blue. Native to mountainous and arctic areas of Europe, Asia and N and S America, saxifrages grow in a variety of soils.

The recommended plants are divided into four groups: silver saxifrages, cushion saxifrages, mossy saxifrages, and a group of miscellaneous plants. All are hardy evergreen perennials, except for *S. fortunei* 'Wada', which is semi-evergreen, and *S. granulata*, which dies back in winter.

RECOMMENDED SPECIES AND VARIETIES
SILVER SAXIFRAGES

Beads of lime decorate the silver-grey or green foliage of these plants. Most silver saxifrages prefer limy soil which increases this beading. The encrusted leaves, formed into flattish rosettes, are fleshy or leathery and usually narrow and roughly linear. Plumes of countless flowers – white unless stated otherwise – arch over mounds of leaf rosettes in late spring and early summer. The individual flowers are 1-1.5 cm (⅜-½ in) wide. Most can tolerate shade and dry conditions. Long-lived and vigorous, they make good companions for ramondas and haberleas but are unsuitable for planting with slower-growing saxifrages.

▼ *Saxifraga* × *burnatii*

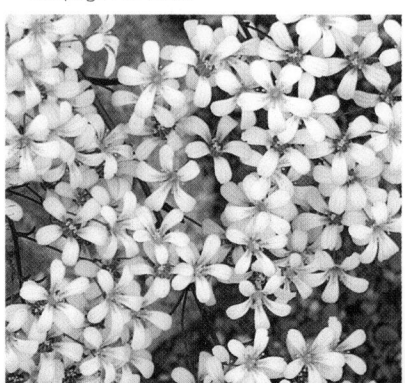

S. aizoon see *S. paniculata*

S. × *burnatii* Upright flower clusters appear on reddish stems over neat rosettes. Each silver-green rosette is about 4 cm (1½ in) across. HEIGHT & SPREAD 20×15 cm (8×6 in).

S. callosa♀ (syn. *S. lingulata*) Irregular grey-green rosettes, each up to 7.5 cm (3 in) across, give a tousled appearance to this plant. Flower clusters, 30-40 cm (12-16 in) long, appear on each arched stem. HEIGHT & SPREAD 30×40 cm (12×16 in).

S. cochlearis Silvery rosettes, each about 2.5 cm (1 in) wide, of outward-curving, spoon-shaped leaves form cushions. Open, arching spikes of flowers appear on pale brown or mahogany-red stems. HEIGHT & SPREAD 25×15 cm (10×6 in).

'Major'♀ is a larger-leaved version of *S. cochlearis,* while 'Minor'♀ is a compact, dwarf version.

S. cotyledon A central rosette, to 12 cm (4¾ in) wide, of fleshy, toothed, dark green leaves is surrounded by smaller rosettes. The flowers, sometimes spotted pink or red, are carried in conical clusters. HEIGHT & SPREAD 30-60×20 cm (12-24×8 in).

S. 'Doctor Ramsay' Rosettes, each about 5 cm (2 in) across, of spoon-shaped leaves distinguish this plant. HEIGHT & SPREAD 20×15 cm (8×6 in).

S. 'Esther' Sprays of pale yellow flowers, which later fade to almost white, arch over leaf rosettes. The leaves, predominantly dark green, are about 2.5 cm (1 in) across. This plant is slow-growing. HEIGHT & SPREAD 30×20 cm (12×8 in).

S. 'Kathleen Pinsent' Wands of pink flowers appear above silvery rosettes of spoon-shaped leaves. This is a short-lived plant. HEIGHT & SPREAD 40×10 cm (16×4 in).

▼ *Saxifraga* 'Esther'

▼ *Saxifraga paniculata*

⬥ *Saxifraga* 'Southside Seedling'

S. paniculata (syn. *S. aizoon*) (lifelong saxifrage) This easy-to-grow plant has silver-green rosettes, each up to 2.5 cm (1 in) wide, with inward-curving leaves. The flowers appear in loose, upright sprays. HEIGHT & SPREAD 5-30×20 cm (2-12×8 in).

There are two dwarf varieties – var. *baldensis* and 'Munitifolia'. The flowers of 'Lutea'♀ are pale yellow, while those borne by 'Rosea' are shell-pink.

S. 'Southside Seedling'♀ Clusters of white flowers heavily spotted with crimson appear above bright green rosettes, each up to 10 cm (4 in) wide. HEIGHT & SPREAD 30×15 cm (12×6 in).

S. 'Tumbling Waters'♀ Arching spires of flowers appear above silvery green leaf rosettes, each up to 10 cm (4 in) across, on an easy-to-grow, hummock-forming plant. HEIGHT & SPREAD 75×30 cm (30×12 in).

S. 'Whitehill' Violet tinted leaf rosettes, each about 3 cm (1¼ in) wide, have heavy beads of lime encrustation. The abundant flowers are creamy white. HEIGHT & SPREAD 30×40 cm (12×16 in).

CUSHION SAXIFRAGES

Flowering from late winter to mid spring, these slow-growing, dwarf plants form dense, rounded mounds of leaf rosettes. The foliage includes neat rosettes of densely packed, needle-like leaves, as well as more open rosettes with broader, blunter leaves, and uneven humps of fleshy leaves. The flowers, 5-25 mm (¼-1 in) wide, have rich yellow or orange centres and can sit almost stemless on the cushion or be raised on stalks up to 15 cm (6 in) high.

Cushion saxifrages are often grown in a greenhouse or frame, where they are easy to see, but will thrive in a scree garden, raised bed or trough as well as in a rock garden, provided they have good light and protection from hot sun.

S. × *apiculata* see *S.* 'Gregor Mendel'

S

S. **'Aretiastrum'** (syn. *S.* 'Valerie Finnis') Elegant, pale yellow flowers appear over grey-green rosettes. HEIGHT & SPREAD 10×7.5 cm (4×3 in).

S. **'Boston Spa'** Masses of yellow flowers appear above a bright green cushion. HEIGHT & SPREAD 4×20 cm (1½×8 in).

S. **'Bridget'** This plant forms a loose hump of spiny, silvered rosettes. Pink-tinted stems bear pale mauve flowers. HEIGHT & SPREAD 10×7.5 cm (4×3 in).

S. **'Buttercup'** Glossy rosettes and bright yellow flowers distinguish this slow-growing plant. HEIGHT & SPREAD 6×6 cm (2×2 in).

S. **'Carmen'** (syn. *S.* × *elisabethae*) Abundant clusters of yellow flowers are carried over a low, dull green cushion on this vigorous plant. HEIGHT & SPREAD 5×15 cm (2×6 in).

S. **'Cranbourne'**♀ (syn. *S.* 'Valborg', *S.* 'Valentine') Abundant, deep rose-pink flowers fade to a paler hue with age on this plant with a dome of dark green rosettes. HEIGHT & SPREAD 4×10 cm (1½×4 in).

S. **'Crenata'** Scallop-edged, saucer-shaped, white flowers distinguish this plant. HEIGHT & SPREAD 10×7.5 cm (4×3 in).

S. × *elisabethae* see *S.* 'Carmen'

❦ *Saxifraga* 'Cranbourne'

❦ *Saxifraga federici-augusti*

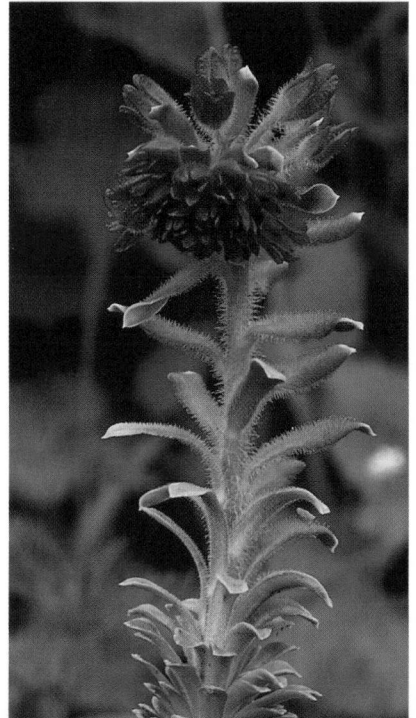

S. **'Faldonside'**♀ Rich yellow flowers appear in profusion over a hard, grey-green cushion. This plant is vulnerable to various moulds. HEIGHT & SPREAD 7.5×7.5 cm (3×3 in).

S. **federici-augusti**♀ (syn. *S.* *frederici-augusti*) This plant has striking claret coloured hairs on the stems, and bears purple-red flowers. Spoon-shaped, silver-grey leaves form a tight cluster of rosettes. HEIGHT & SPREAD 20×10 cm (8×4 in).

S. **ferdinandi-coburgi**♀ This tough, easy-to-grow plant has grey-green leaf rosettes with clusters of golden yellow flowers. HEIGHT & SPREAD 7.5×10 cm (3×4 in).

S. **'Gloria'**♀ Many saucer-shaped, white flowers appear above a spiky-leafed cushion. HEIGHT & SPREAD 7.5×7.5 cm (3×3 in).

S. **'Gold Dust'** Profuse clusters of golden flowers appear on this vigorous plant. HEIGHT & SPREAD 9×15 cm (3½×6 in).

S. **'Grace Farwell'** Burgundy flowers appear over a dull green cushion. HEIGHT & SPREAD 6×10 cm (2½×4 in).

S. **'Gregor Mendel'**♀ (syn. *S.* × *apiculata*) Abundant clusters of primrose-yellow flowers are borne over a bright green cushion. This is a vigorous, easy-to-grow plant. HEIGHT & SPREAD 15×30 cm (6×12 in).

❦ *Saxifraga ferdinandi-coburgi*

❦ *Saxifraga* 'Grace Farwell'

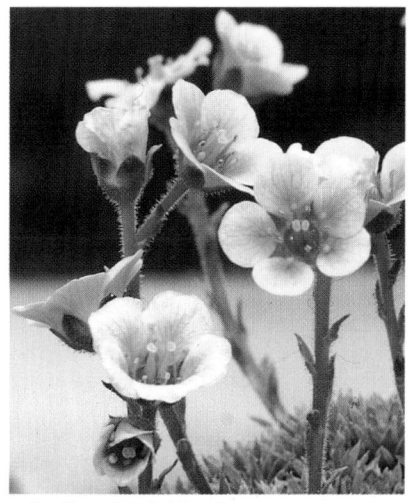

⚑ *Saxifraga* 'Iris Prichard'

S. **'Haagii'** Dark green rosettes set off the golden flowers on this tough hybrid. HEIGHT & SPREAD 10×15 cm (4×6 in).

S. **'Hindhead Seedling'** From its grey-green cushion, this plant sends up yellow flowers early in the year. HEIGHT & SPREAD 5×7.5 cm (2×3 in).

S. **'Iris Prichard'** Apricot coloured flowers rise above a hard cushion of silvery, spiny leaves. HEIGHT & SPREAD 10×10 cm (4×4 in).

S. × *irvingii* see *S.* 'Walter Irving'

S. **'Jenkinsiae'**♀ Abundant lilac-pink flowers appear just above a hard, dark green cushion. HEIGHT & SPREAD 5×7 cm (2×2¾ in).

S. **'Johann Kellerer'** (syn. *S.* × *kellereri*) One of the earliest to flower, in mid winter, the plant has lilac-pink flowers above a compact, grey-green cushion. HEIGHT & SPREAD 10×15 cm (4×6 in).

S. **'Joy'** see *S.* 'Kaspar Maria Sternberg'

S. **juniperifolia** A very prickly, bright green cushion carries sparse, spindly stems of up to 10 yellow flowers. HEIGHT & SPREAD 7.5×10 cm (3×4 in).

S. × *kellereri* see *S.* 'Johann Kellerer'

S. **'Kaspar Maria Sternberg'** (syn. *S.* 'Joy') Pure white flowers appear over a solid grey-green cushion. HEIGHT & SPREAD 7.5×6 cm (3×2½ in).

S. **'Maria Luisa'** Dense clusters of white flowers appear early in the year above a grey-green cushion. HEIGHT & SPREAD 7.5×7.5 cm (3×3 in).

S. × *megasaeflora* see *S.* 'Robin Hood'

S. **'Moonlight'** see *S.* 'Sulphurea'

S. **'Myra'** Carmine flowers emerge above a dark green cushion of squat rosettes. HEIGHT & SPREAD 2×7.5 cm (¾×3 in).

S. **'Penelope'** Amber blooms are accentuated by the green cushion. HEIGHT & SPREAD 5×7.5 cm (2×3 in).

S. **poluniniana** Almost stemless flowers, which open white and then age to pink, smother a strong-growing dark green cushion. HEIGHT & SPREAD 5×10 cm (2×4 in).

S. **'Primrose Dame'** A hard, prickly cushion and clusters of lemon-yellow flowers

S

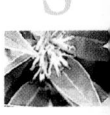

617

distinguish this plant. HEIGHT & SPREAD 10×10 cm (4×4 in).

S. **'Riverslea'**♀ Grey-green foliage complements rich claret flowers. HEIGHT & SPREAD 5×7.5 cm (2×3 in).

S. **'Robin Hood'** (syn. *S.* × *megasaeflora)* Unusual flowers with widely separated pink petals distinguish a plant of tousled appearance. HEIGHT & SPREAD 7×7.5 cm (2¾×3 in).

S. **'Salomonii'** Clusters of white flowers appear above a grey-green cushion. HEIGHT & SPREAD 5×7.5 cm (2×3 in).

S. ***sancta*** Clusters of yellow flowers sit on the light green cushion of this easy-to-grow plant. HEIGHT & SPREAD 10×15 cm (4×6 in).

S. ***sempervivum*** Stems bearing rosy purple hairs and rosy purple flowers rise above an uneven mound of silver-grey rosettes. HEIGHT & SPREAD 12×10 cm (4¾×4 in).

▼ *Saxifraga sempervivum*

▼ *Saxifraga cebennensis*

S. **'Sulphurea'** (syn. *S.* 'Moonlight') Sulphur-yellow flowers nod over a firm mound of grey-green rosettes. HEIGHT & SPREAD 15×15 cm (6×6 in).

S. **'Valborg'** see *S.* 'Cranbourne'

S. **'Valentine'** see *S.* 'Cranbourne'

S. **'Valerie Finnis'** see *S.* 'Aretiastrum'

S. **'Vesna'** Dense, rounded cushions of dark green rosettes are topped by abundant clusters of pale yellow flowers. HEIGHT & SPREAD 5×6 cm (2×2½ in).

S. **'Walter Irving'** (syn. *S.* × *irvingii*) Dark-eyed, pale lilac flowers rise above a tight, grey-green cushion. HEIGHT & SPREAD 3×6 cm (1¼×2½ in).

MOSSY SAXIFRAGES

Most of these plants form spongy hummocks of soft, feathery foliage and have a mass of slender-stalked flowers in late spring and early summer.

S. ***cebennensis*** ♀ Open, sticky, mid to dark green rosettes, about 2 cm (¾ in) wide, form tight domes. White flowers, about 1 cm (⅜ in) wide appear in abundance. This plant is best kept in a greenhouse. HEIGHT & SPREAD 10×15 cm (4×6 in).

S. ***exarata*** White, cream, yellow or occasionally red flowers appear above a compact cushion of dark green rosettes on this dwarf plant which survives best in a greenhouse. HEIGHT & SPREAD 15×15 cm (6×6 in).

The recommended hybrids are easy-to-grow plants with flowers 1.2-2.5 cm (½-1 in) wide, carried in small groups on upright stems, 3-15 cm (1¼-6 in) tall. Dwarf hybrids form a mound about 15 cm (6 in) wide. More vigorous plants reach about 30 cm (12 in) wide.

S. **'Bob Hawkins'** has variegated leaves in green, cream and pink with white flowers. *S.* **'Cloth of Gold'**, a slow-growing plant vulnerable to dry spells and hot sun, has mainly yellow foliage, arranged in rosettes, and white flowers. *S.* **'Dartington Double'** has double white flowers. *S.* **'Findling'** (syn. *S.* 'The Foundling') also has white flowers. The vigorous *S.* **'Four Winds'** has rich crimson flowers. *S.* **'Gaiety'** bears deep pink flowers. *S.* **'Hi-Ace'** is a slow-growing dwarf plant with rose-pink blooms over green and white variegated foliage. *S.* **'Pixie'** has cream and pink flowers. The vigorous, compact *S.* **'Silver Cushion'** bears variegated leaves in silver-grey and green that complement shell-pink flowers. Crimson blooms appear on *S.* **'Triumph'**. Pure white flowers give *S.* **'White Pixie'** its name.

OTHER SAXIFRAGES

The plants in this diverse group each have different growing requirements, which are given after the individual plant descriptions. *S.* ***cuneifolia*** (spoon-leafed saxifrage) Open clusters of about 12 star-shaped, white flowers, with yellow and sometimes red spots, appear from late spring to mid

▼ *Saxifraga* 'Cloth of Gold'

▼ *Saxifraga* 'Pixie'

▼ *Saxifraga* 'White Pixie'

summer. The long-stalked leaves, mid green, roughly wedge-shaped, with blunt teeth, form mats of flat rosettes, about 7 cm (2¾ in) wide. This plant requires fairly moist, neutral to acid, humus-rich soil and dappled shade. HEIGHT & SPREAD 10-25×30 cm (4-10×12 in).

'Variegata' has yellow and green foliage.
S. fortunei 'Wada' Bright green, glossy leaves mature to bronze-red on a semi-evergreen plant that thrives in sheltered woodland conditions. The rounded, lobed leaves, to 8 cm (3¼ in) wide, form clumps. White flowers, about 2 cm (¾ in) across, appear in autumn. This plant needs lime-free soil and shade. It is not hardy in severe winters. HEIGHT & SPREAD 30×30 cm (1×1 ft).
S. granulata (meadow saxifrage) Long-stalked, grey-green kidney-shaped leaves, to 5 cm (2 in) wide, form a tuft. Branched stems carry a loose cluster of white flowers, each about 3 cm (1¼ in) wide, from mid spring to early summer. This easy-to-grow, herbaceous plant dislikes dry soil. It looks good naturalised in grass. HEIGHT & SPREAD 30×20 cm (12×8 in).

saxifraga granulata

'Plena' is a double-flowered plant.
S. oppositifolia (purple saxifrage) Rosy-purple flowers, to 2.5 cm (1 in) wide, borne singly, cover this exceptionally hardy plant in spring. A dense mat of creeping shoots is clad in tiny, congested, deep green leaves. Favouring a limy soil, this plant is ideal for a rich scree bed, a raised bed or a trough. HEIGHT & SPREAD 5 cm×20 cm (2×8 in).

'Alba' has pure white flowers. 'Latina' has rose-pink flowers and slightly encrusted foliage. **'Ruth Draper'** produces large blooms of rich crimson. The vigorous **'Splendens'**♀ bears deep pink flowers.

▼ *Saxifraga* 'Ruth Draper'

S. × primulaize Pale carmine flowers appear in late spring over mid green, fleshy, roughly oblong, lobed leaves. This plant prefers moist soil in partial shade. HEIGHT & SPREAD 20×20 cm (8×8 in).
S. stolonifera (syn. *S. sarmentosa*) (mother of thousands, strawberry geranium) The thin, reddish runners of this houseplant carry plantlets that root on contact with moist soil. The hairy leaves, to 10 cm (4 in) wide, are rounded and toothed. They are dark green with silver markings on the leaf surface and reddish beneath. White flowers appear in summer. The plant needs a temperature of at least 5°C (41°F). It spreads as wide as the pot. LENGTH 1 m (3 ft).
S. umbrosa Upright, branched stems carry clusters of tiny, white, star-shaped flowers with pink centres in early summer. This plant, which does best in moist soil in partial shade, forms a close mat of flat, leathery rosettes of bluntly elliptic, scalloped-edged, mid to dark green leaves, up to 3 cm (1¼ in) long. HEIGHT & SPREAD 25×30 cm (10×12 in).

The compact **'Clarence Elliott'**♀ has rose-pink flowers.

saxifraga umbrosa

S. × urbium♀ (London pride) From its long-lived mat of rather fleshy rosettes, each about 7.5 cm (3 in) across, the plant raises delicate, airy clusters of star-like, pinkish, white flowers in early summer. It is easy to grow in a damp soil, with some shade. This

▼ *Saxifraga umbrosa*

plant is good for edging paths. HEIGHT & SPREAD 25×60 cm (10×24 in).

Rich, yellow blotches decorate the fleshy-leaved rosettes of S. × **'Variegata'**.
S. 'Winifred Bevington' Slender sprays of rose-centred, white flowers, each about 8 mm (⅜ in) wide, appear in early summer above a tight hump of leaf rosettes, each about 2.5 cm (1 in) wide. This plant thrives in light soil in partly shaded positions. HEIGHT & SPREAD 10×20 cm (4×8 in).

▲ *Saxifraga × urbium*

S

CULTIVATION For silver saxifrages, with the exception of *S. cotyledon,* which needs lime-free soil, plant in well-drained, gritty, limy soil, ideally with partial shade in the middle of the day. For cushion saxifrages, plant in gritty, limy soil in good light but with protection from hot sun. For pot-grown plants, use a mixture of John Innes No. 2 compost and about one-third sharp sand or stone chippings. For mossy saxifrages, plant in well-drained soil, ideally neutral to slightly acid, and protect from hot sun. Cover *S. cebennensis* and *S. exarata* with glass from autumn to early spring to protect them from winter wet.

PROPAGATION Separate young rosettes and root them as individual cuttings in sharp sand. The best times for this are from mid to late summer for silver saxifrages, throughout summer for cushion saxifrages, and from early to mid summer for mossy saxifrages. Sow the ripe seed of species under glass and plant out when the seedlings are large enough to handle.

PESTS AND DISEASES Vine weevil can damage silver saxifrages, especially pot-grown plants. Stem eelworm sometimes damages cushion saxifrages, while the roots of plants grown in wet conditions may rot. Aphids, red spider mite and botrytis can affect mossy saxifrages.

Saxifrage see *Saxifraga*

Scabiosa
Scabious, pincushion flower
Dipsacaceae

Showy flowerheads with centres resembling pincushions make these hardy annuals and perennials attractive components of summer beds and borders. *Scabiosa columbaria, S. graminifolia* and *S. lucida* are sufficiently dwarf for a rock garden. The plants attract bees and butterflies. They are native to Europe, Asia and Africa.

RECOMMENDED SPECIES AND VARIETIES
S. atropurpurea (sweet scabious) Dark crimson flowerheads 5 cm (2 in) across are held on slender stems from mid summer to early autumn. The mid green leaves of this erect annual are narrow, deeply lobed and held in a compact rosette. HEIGHT & SPREAD 1 m×23 cm (3 ft×9 in).
S. banatica see *S. columbaria*
S. caucasica Pale blue blooms, 7.5 cm (3 in) across, appear for a long period over the summer. They are good for cutting. The grey-green leaves of this herbaceous perennial form a tight cluster at the base of the plant. Each leaf is lance-shaped with tips cut into narrow segments. HEIGHT & SPREAD 60×60 cm (2×2 ft).
'Clive Greaves'♥ bears an abundance of lavender-blue flowerheads. '**Miss Willmott**'♥ has off-white flowerheads.

▲ *Scabiosa graminifolia*

S. columbaria (syn. *S. banatica*) Lilac-blue flowerheads, 4 cm (1½ in) across, are carried on tall, wiry, branched stems in summer. This evergreen perennial forms a mat of grey-green leaves beneath the flowerheads. HEIGHT & SPREAD 30×30 cm (1×1 ft).
'Nana' reaches just 15 cm (6 in) high.
S. graminifolia Lilac to pink flowerheads, 4 cm (1½ in) across, rise on 25 cm (10 in), branched stems, from late spring to early summer. This evergreen perennial has grassy silvery grey leaves. It is best grown in a rock garden or the front of a border. HEIGHT & SPREAD 25×30 cm (10 in×1 ft).
'Rosea' has rich pink flowerheads.
S. lucida The unbranched flower stems and flower colour of pale carmine to purple are the only differences between this species and *S. columbaria*. HEIGHT & SPREAD 30×30 cm (1×1 ft).

CULTIVATION Plant in spring in a light, well-drained soil in a sunny situation.

PROPAGATION Sow seed of the annuals in the flowering site in early autumn or late spring. Autumn-sown annuals need the protection of a cloche through winter. Lift and divide perennial species in early spring.

PESTS AND DISEASES Slugs damage young foliage. Powdery mildew can be a problem.

Scabious see *Scabiosa*
Scarborough lily see *Cyrtanthus*
Scarlet pimpernel see *Anagallis arvensis*

Scaevola
Fan flower
Goodeniaceae

Large numbers of flowers are borne throughout summer on these tender evergreen perennials. *Scaevola aemula* is the only species commonly grown in Britain. It can only be grown outdoors all year round in the warmest districts. Elsewhere, it is best overwintered in a frost-free greenhouse or

▲ *Scaevola aemula* 'Blue Fan'

conservatory. Its naturally sprawling habit makes it particularly useful for containers, especially hanging baskets and window boxes. Native to Australia.

RECOMMENDED SPECIES AND VARIETIES
S. aemula Blue, purple-blue, lilac or white flowers, about 3 cm (1¼ in) across, each have 5 lobes, that radiate outwards on one side to form a fan shape. Sharply toothed, oblong, dark green leaves, up to 5 cm (2 in) long, are borne on thick, short-jointed stems. HEIGHT & SPREAD 30×60 cm (1×2 ft).
'**Blue Fan**' has purple-blue flowers with a white eye. '**Petite**' has smaller leaves and flowers than the species. '**Alba**' has white flowers and more slender stems.

CULTIVATION Plant out after the risk of frost has passed in any well-drained soil in full sun or light shade. Lift plants before first frosts and overwinter in a frost-free greenhouse or conservatory. Alternatively, grow in pots of general purpose or potting compost in a cool greenhouse or conservatory. Move outside in late spring and summer.

PROPAGATION Take softwood cuttings in late summer.

PESTS AND DISEASES Usually trouble free.

Schefflera
Umbrella tree
Araliaceae

These evergreen trees and shrubs are popular foliage plants in homes, conservatories and offices. Native mainly to tropical Australasia, scheffleras are fairly adaptable but rarely flower in cultivation. The dimensions are for a plant in a 20 cm (8 in) pot.

RECOMMENDED SPECIES AND VARIETIES
S. actinophylla♀ (syn. *Brassaia actinophylla*) (umbrella tree) Five to seven leaflets fan out from each long stalk. The leathery textured mid green leaflets, up to 30 cm (12 in) long, are oval with pointed tips. HEIGHT & SPREAD 1.5-2×1 m (5-6½×3 ft) after 5 years, ultimately 2 m (6½ ft) tall.

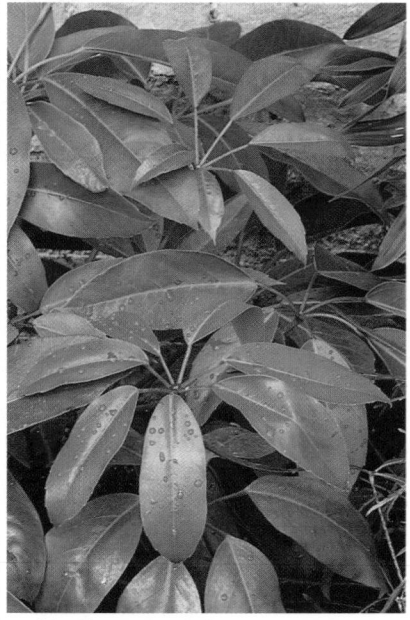

⚘ *Schefflera actinophylla*

S. arboricola♀ (syn. *Heptapleurum arboricola*) (parasol plant) Dark green glossy leaflets, 7-15 to a stalk, are held on a plant with largely upright habit. Young foliage is often slightly bronze. The elongated oval leaflets, to 15 cm (6 in) long, have pointed tips. HEIGHT & SPREAD 3×1.5 m (10×5 ft) after 10 years, ultimately 3 m (10 ft) tall.

The deep green leaves of '**Trinetta**' are splashed bright yellow.
S. elegantissima♀ (syn. *Aralia elegantissima, Dizygotheca elegantissima*) (false aralia) Narrow, bronze, toothed leaflets distinguish this graceful plant. With age, the leaflets, to 18 cm (7 in) long, become wider with fewer teeth. The plant needs constant conditions. Overwatering, dryness, sudden changes in temperature or dry air can prompt leaf loss. HEIGHT & SPREAD 3 m×70 cm (10 ft×28 in) after 5 years, ultimately 3 m (10 ft) tall.

CULTIVATION Place *S. actinophylla* and *S. arboricola* in full sun or bright, indirect light. Position *S. elegantissima* in good indirect light or direct sun for half the day. Keep a plant at a minimum temperature of 10°C (50°F) if possible, although they will tolerate cooler temperatures for short periods. Water whenever the soil begins to dry out, decreasing watering in winter. Repot every year until the plant reaches the desired size. From then on, give an annual top dressing.

PROPAGATION Scheffleras are not easy to propagate at home. Try taking softwood cuttings in early summer and use rooting powder and bottom heat.

PRUNING Pinch out the tips or cut the top part of the main stem down to the lowest leaves to encourage branching.

PESTS AND DISEASES Scale insects can damage all plants, while red spider mites can affect *S. elegantissima*.

Schisandra
Schisandraceae

schisandra rubriflora

These woody climbing plants are grown for their flowers and sometimes showy fruit. They climb by means of twining stems to a height of 4 m (13 ft) or more. Native to India and Burma, they are best grown on a south or west wall. In milder areas they can be trained on free-standing structures such as arches or pergolas.

RECOMMENDED SPECIES
S. rubriflora (syn. *S. grandiflora* var. *rubriflora*) Clusters of bright or dark red, bowl-shaped flowers are carried along the stems of this deciduous climber in early summer. The 2.5 cm (1 in) wide male and female flowers are carried on separate plants. Grow male and female plants together for a display of bright red berries in autumn. The pendulous clusters of berries are up to 12 cm (4¾ in) long. The narrowly oval leaves are mid green, up to 15 cm (6 in) long and 7 cm (2¾ in) wide. This species does well outside in a sheltered spot. HEIGHT 5-8 m (16-26 ft).

CULTIVATION Plant out in spring in any well-drained, moisture-retaining soil, out of direct sunlight. Avoid lime-rich soil. Mulch annually in spring. Water well in dry periods, especially wall-trained plants. Give plants a framework to climb over. They may need tying in until established. Prune only to retain desired shape, in late winter.

PROPAGATION Sow seed when ripe or propagate by layering. Semi-ripe cuttings taken in mid summer are less successful.

PESTS AND DISEASES Aphids can be a problem on leaves and young shoots.

Schizanthus
Poor man's orchid, butterfly flower
Solanaceae

Exotic flowers and handsome, bright green foliage make these tender annuals popular as pot plants. They can be grown outdoors as summer bedding in a warm sheltered spot or in a greenhouse or conservatory. The orchid-like flowers come in a mixture of rich colours often with contrasting markings inside. The leaves are deeply dissected and often feathery. Native to Chile.

RECOMMENDED SPECIES AND VARIETIES
S. pinnatus Pink flowers, up to 4 cm (1½ in) across, with a yellow throat and violet markings are produced in dense clusters from late summer to winter. The bright green leaves are up to 13 cm (5 in) long. HEIGHT & SPREAD 60×30 cm (2×1 ft).

The following varieties have a spread of 20-30 cm (8-12 in) and, unless otherwise stated, reach a height of 30-45 cm (12-18 in). '**Butterfly Mixture**' has a wide range of colours from deep red and purple with yellow or white throats marked with violet to orange and buff. It can reach a height of 60 cm (2 ft). '**Dwarf Bouquet**' has flowers in shades of pink, purple and yellow. It reaches a height of 30 cm (12 in) and a spread of 15 cm (6 in). Variously coloured, '**Giant Hybrids**' reach a height of 1.2 m (4 ft). '**Hit Parade**' has large, well-marked flowers in red, pink, lilac, violet, purple and white. '**Star Parade**' is a compact plant with large flowers in almost any combination of colours.
S. × *wisetonensis* The flowers vary in colour from lavender and white to pink and brown and are often flushed with yellow. They are up to 2.5 cm (1 in) across and are

❦ *Schizanthus* 'Hit Parade'

❦ *Schizanthus* 'Star Parade'

S

621

carried in bold clusters in late summer and autumn. The bright green leaves are as long as 15cm (6in). HEIGHT & SPREAD 45×30cm (18×12in).

CULTIVATION Grow in pots of John Innes No. 2 and keep in a greenhouse or conservatory with a minimum temperature of 5°C (41°F). Plants can be moved outside when the danger of frost has passed and planted in any moisture-retentive, well-drained soil in full sun. When the taller varieties reach a height of 15cm (6in) pinch out the growing points to encourage bushy growth. They may need support.

PROPAGATION Sow seed under glass in late spring for late summer and autumn flowering. Sow during late summer for winter and early spring flowering.

PESTS AND DISEASES Greenfly can be troublesome.

Schizophragma
Hydrangeaceae

Few climbers can match the elegant, creamy white flowerheads of these vigorous, deciduous plants. Large, flattened flower sprays like old-fashioned lace caps are formed from an outer ring of sterile flowers – each with an enlarged, petal-like sepal – and an inner circle of small, densely packed, fertile flowers. The plants are in bloom in mid summer. Clinging by their aerial roots, they can clamber high into a tree or up a tall wall, although they grow slowly at first. They are shade-tolerant and like a cool root run, but flower more freely in full sun. There are four species, all native to Asia, where they climb into deciduous trees and sometimes grow up cliffs. Two species, both hardy, are grown in Britain.

RECOMMENDED SPECIES

S. hydrangeoides Flowerheads about 25cm (10in) wide have sterile flowers with sepals about 3cm (1¼in) long. The coarsely toothed leaves, which turn yellow in autumn, are broadly oval or rounded and up to 12cm (4¾in) long. Native to Japan. HEIGHT & SPREAD 2×1m (6½×3ft) after 5 years, ultimately 10m (33ft) tall.

S. integrifolium♀ The flowerheads of this plant are about 30cm (1ft) wide, while the sepals of the sterile flowers are about 8cm (3¼in) long. The dark green, ovate leaves, 10–18cm (4–7in) long, have a rounded base and pointed apex. The leaf edges may have a few small teeth. This plant is native to central and W China. HEIGHT & SPREAD 2×1m (6½×3ft) after 5 years, ultimately 12m (40ft) tall.

CULTIVATION Plant in fertile, well-drained soil at the foot of a tall wall or large tree, preferably where the plants can have their heads in the sun. As they are slow starters, tie young plants to wires, canes or some other support until the aerial roots take hold of the tree or wall.

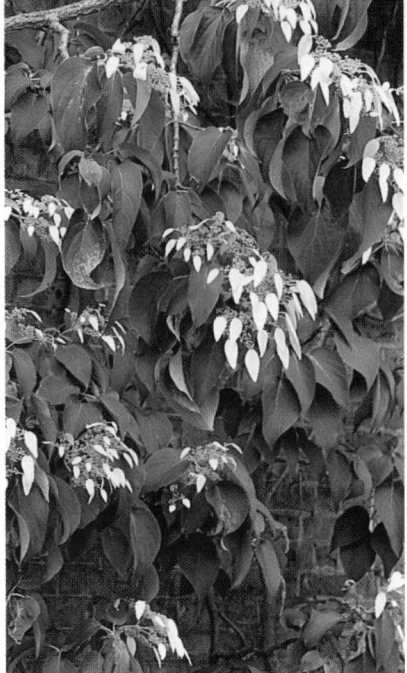

▲ *Schizophragma integrifolium*

PROPAGATION Take softwood or semi-ripe cuttings in summer.

PRUNING None usually necessary. Cut back some of the long shoots to a lateral shoot in winter to limit growth.

PESTS AND DISEASES Usually trouble free.

Schizostylis
Kaffir lily
Iridaceae

schizostylis coccinea

Star-shaped, red, pink or white flowers appear above narrow, sword-shaped leaves from late summer to early autumn. This genus of hardy perennials likes an open, sunny position and moist soil. In cold districts plants may be short-lived, so protect their crowns in winter once flowering has finished. The flowers are good for cutting.

RECOMMENDED SPECIES AND VARIETIES

S. coccinea Between 4 and 10 bright red blossoms, about 2.5cm (1in) across, are carried on each slender stem. The leaves are light green, prominently ribbed and up to 40cm (16in) long. The plant has a fleshy root, which is vulnerable to drying out. Native to southern Africa. HEIGHT & SPREAD 60×25cm (24×10in).

'Alba' produces pretty white flowers, but tends to be short-lived and less hardy. 'Jennifer'♀ has large pink flowers. 'Major'♀ (syn. 'Gigantea', 'Grandiflora') is a very free-flowering, robust plant with

▲ *Schizostylis coccinea*

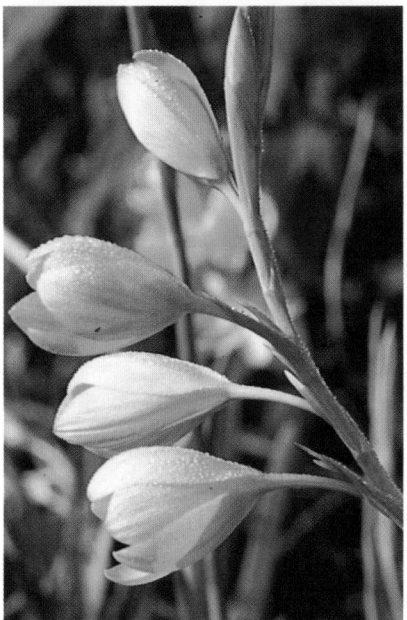

▲ *Schizostylis coccinea* 'Sunrise'

bright red flowers. '**Mrs Hegarty**', with pink blooms, is late flowering. '**Sunrise**'♀ bears large soft pink blossoms. '**Viscountess Byng**' has bright red flowers, which bloom later than other schizostylis, in mid autumn.

CULTIVATION Plant in spring or autumn in an open, sunny position in moist soil beside a pool or stream would be fine, provided that the soil does not become waterlogged for more than a month or two of the year. Remove flowers as they fade and rake off dead foliage in late autumn, after plants have died back. Lift and divide crowded clumps in spring every 3–4 years.

PROPAGATION Divide and replant established clumps in spring.

PESTS AND DISEASES Usually trouble free, but slugs and snails may damage shoots.

Schlumbergera see CACTI p. 109

S

Scilla
Hyacinthaceae

Small starry or bell-shaped flowers, usually in shades of blue or purple, decorate rock gardens or containers mainly in spring. The flowers are held on leafless stems among glossy mid green, strap-shaped leaves, 10-20 cm (4-8 in) long. This genus of dwarf bulbous perennials is distributed worldwide. All listed plants are hardy in Britain, except *Scilla peruviana* which only tolerates temperatures as low as -5°C (23°F).

RECOMMENDED SPECIES AND VARIETIES
S. amethystina see *S. litardierei*
S. autumnalis (autumn squill) Loose racemes of starry pale pinkish lilac flowers appear in late summer or early autumn. HEIGHT 25 cm (10 in).
S. bifolia♀ Fragrant bluish violet, starry flowers are borne in late winter and early spring. This species will grow in semi-shade. HEIGHT 15 cm (6 in).
   'Rosea' has pink flowers.
S. campanulata see *Hyacinthoides hispanica*
S. litardierei (syn. *S. amethystina, S. pratensis*) Some 15 to 30 pale-lilac to lavender-blue, starry flowers appear in mid to late spring. HEIGHT 25 cm (10 in).
S. mischtschenkoana (syn. *S. tubergeniana*) Open bell-shaped flowers, 2 cm (¾ in) across, very pale blue with a darker blue stripe, appear in late winter. Each stem

▼ *Scilla peruviana*

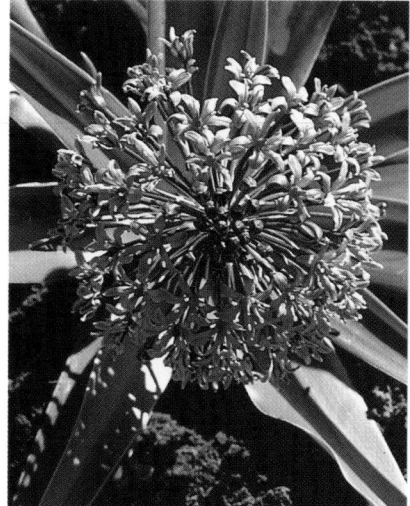

▼ *Scilla siberica* 'Spring Beauty'

bears up to 6 flowers. Plant among other early-flowering bulbs, such as snowdrops. HEIGHT 10 cm (4 in).
S. non-scripta see *Hyacinthoides non-scripta*
S. nutans see *Hyacinthoides non-scripta*
S. pratensis see *S. litardierei*
S. peruviana Dense flowerheads of starry, violet-blue flowers appear in late spring and early summer. The broad deep green leaves are almost evergreen. HEIGHT 25 cm (10 in).
   'Alba' has pure white flowers, blue-violet anthers and a blue ovary.
S. siberica♀ (siberian squill) Stems bearing bright azure-blue, bell-shaped flowers appear in early spring. HEIGHT 20 cm (8 in).
   'Alba' has pure-white flowers. 'Spring Beauty' is a deeper blue and very vigorous.
S. tubergeniana see *S. mischtschenkoana*
CULTIVATION Plant bulbs in late summer, in humus-rich, fast-draining soil, 5-7.5 cm (2-3 in) deep and 5-7.5 cm (2-3 in) apart for larger bulbs. Position in dappled shade. *S. peruviana* needs a dry sunny situation to flower and should be protected with a dry mulch in winter.
PROPAGATION Lift and divide every 4-5 years in late summer. Alternatively, sow seed in early summer in trays in a greenhouse. Plant out at the end of the second year and they should flower 2-3 years later.
PESTS AND DISEASES Stored bulbs can suffer from various moulds if not kept dry.

Scindapsus see *Epipremnum*
Scottish maple see *Acer pseudoplatanus*

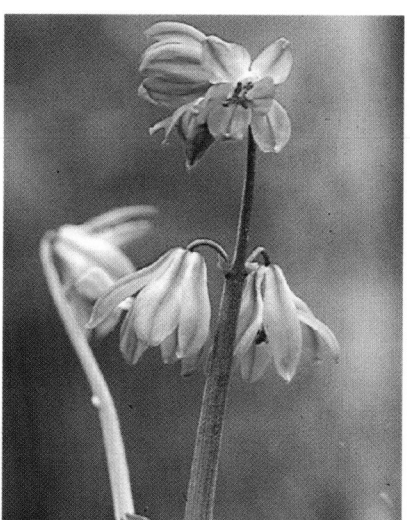

▲ *Scilla siberica*

Scrophularia
Scrophulariaceae

Striking foliage or unusual flowers in summer earn some of the hardy herbaceous or semi-evergreen plants in this genus a place in the garden. Most have strong-smelling leaves. The recommended species is best confined to a wild garden. Give the variety 'Variegata' a prominent position, allowing it to show off its remarkable leaves, in a bed or border, beside a pond or in a bog garden. Both plants flourish in damp, partially shaded places.

RECOMMENDED SPECIES AND VARIETIES
S. auriculata (syn. *S. aquatica*) (water fig-wort) Strong, vigorously growing, winged stems are clothed with coarse, dark green, lance-shaped leaves up to 25 cm (10 in) long. The leafy flowering stems die back in autumn and new leaf tufts develop, which overwinter. Strange pouch-like maroon flowers, up to 1 cm (⅜ in) long, are borne sparingly on branching flower spikes throughout summer. Native to W Europe. HEIGHT & SPREAD 90×60 cm (36×24 in).

▲ *Scrophularia auriculata* 'Variegata'

'Variegata' has decorative green and cream leaves that are at their best in spring and early summer. Remove the flower spikes as soon as they emerge to retain the quality of the foliage as long as possible.
CULTIVATION Plant at any time between autumn and early spring in moist soil and preferably in a little shade. Remove the flowering spikes either immediately they appear or as the blossoms fade – if they are retained, they will seed freely.
PROPAGATION Divide and replant at any time between autumn and spring.
PESTS AND DISEASES Usually trouble free.

623

Scutellaria
Skullcap
Labiatae

scutellaria alpina

Colourful snapdragon-like flowers grace these shrubby plants in summer and autumn. They may be annuals, perennials or sub-shrubs, evergreen or deciduous and vary from hardy to tender. It is mainly species from mountain habitats that are of interest, since they are suitable for rock gardens. The listed plants are all hardy perennials and all, except *S. altissima*, *S. hastifolia* and *S. incana*, are evergreen. *S. hastifolia* and *S. scordiifolia*, too vigorous for association with slower-growing rock plants, are best placed on the fringes of the rockwork. The genus is distributed worldwide.

RECOMMENDED SPECIES AND VARIETIES
S. alpina Clusters of pale-lipped, purple flowers, 2.5 cm (1 in) long, are held on erect stems, 20 cm (8 in) tall, from early to late summer. The plant bears mid green oval, bluntly toothed, 2 cm (¾ in) long leaves. HEIGHT & SPREAD 20×30 cm (8×12 in).

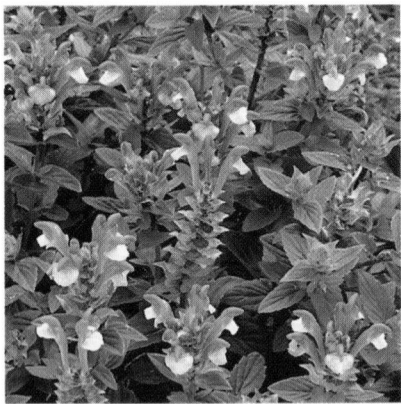

▲ *Scutellaria alpina*

'Alba' has white flowers.
S. altissima Loose spikes of cream or pale lilac, 2 cm (¾ in) long flowers appear in mid summer. The erect plant has simple or branched stems bearing 15 cm (6 in) long, broadly spear-shaped, mid green leaves. HEIGHT & SPREAD 75×30 cm (2½×1 ft).
S. hastifolia (syn *S. hastata*) Violet flowers, sometimes pink, 2 cm (¾ in) long, decorate the 45 cm (18 in) tall stems in summer. The leaves are lance-shaped, moderately toothed and up to 5 cm (2 in) long. HEIGHT & SPREAD 45×45 cm (18×18 in).
S. incana Loose, flat-topped clusters of violet flowers tinged with blue appear in mid summer. The flowers are up to 2.5 cm (1 in) long. The upright, hairy stems also bear heart-shaped, dull green leaves, as long

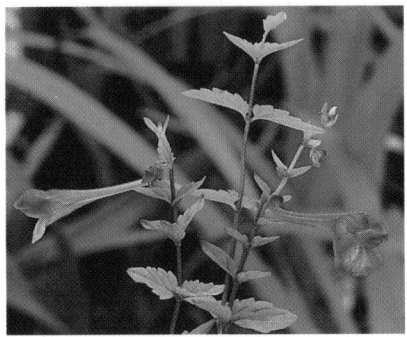

▲ *Scutellaria indica* var. *parvifolia*

as 10 cm (4 in) with serrated edges. This plant is too big for a rock garden. HEIGHT & SPREAD 1 m×60 cm (3×2 ft).
S. indica var. *parvifolia* (syn. *S. i.* var. *japonica*) Pale purple flowers, about 2 cm (¾ in) long, are held in sprays during early summer. The plant has a spreading habit with its stems forming a low mound of shoots clad in 1 cm (⅜ in) wide, rounded, hairy leaves with bluntly toothed edges. HEIGHT & SPREAD 5×25 cm (2×10 in).
'Alba' has pure white flowers.
S. nana var. *sapphirina* Short, loose heads of 2 cm (¾ in) long, clear blue 'snapdragon' flowers are produced through the summer. The ascending stems bear ovate, toothed leaves, up to 3 cm (1¼ in) long. HEIGHT & SPREAD 10×20 cm (4×8 in).
S. orientalis Yellow flowers, occasionally spotted or stained red, to 3 cm (1¼ in) long, appear in summer. They can also be pure purple, pink or red. This variable plant makes a shrub-like clump of woody stems bearing rounded, 1.5 cm (½ in) broad leaves with deep narrow lobes. HEIGHT & SPREAD 30×30 cm (12×12 in).
The leaves of ssp. *pinnatifida* are even more deeply lobed than the species.
S. prostrata In late summer 1.5 cm (½ in) long flowers, yellow flushed with violet, decorate a mat of foliage. Tiny rounded leaves cover the creeping shoots. HEIGHT & SPREAD 7.5×30 cm (3×12 in).
S. scordiifolia Leafy spikes, up to 30 cm (12 in) tall, rise from tufts of 3 cm (1¼ in) long elliptical leaves to bear 2 cm (¾ in) long flowers in a range of blues, through summer. This robust plant is inclined to be invasive on good soils. HEIGHT & SPREAD 30×60 cm (12×24 in).

CULTIVATION Plant in a sunny but not too dry situation in early spring. A rich soil can produce rank, invasive growth in those species noted for vigour. To curb this spread and improve flowering, trim the stems back to about 10 cm (4 in) in late winter or after flowering.
PROPAGATION Divide clumps in early spring or sow seed in pots in a coldframe at a similar time, and plant out the following spring. Cuttings of lateral shoots, taken in late spring, root readily.
PESTS AND DISEASES Usually trouble free.

Sedum
Stonecrop
Crassulaceae

sedum acre

These succulent plants bring pleasant variations of form and colour to less hospitable parts of the garden, where there is little shade and the soil is poor and tends to parch. They are for the most part very easy to grow. Sedums range from tiny mats or mounds to plants as tall as 1 m (3 ft). Grow smaller sedums in rock gardens, troughs and raised beds, tucked into the cracks between paving stones, or in containers. Larger sedums are often found in mixed borders.

Foliage varies from grey-green to deep purple. The star-like flowers, nearly always with five petals, are generally yellow, pink, purple or white. Some species bloom well into autumn. A few sedums are notorious for spreading excessively, but the majority need little curbing.

All the plants listed here are hardy perennials, except the half-hardy *Sedum sieboldii*.
RECOMMENDED SPECIES AND VARIETIES
S. acre (biting stonecrop) A creeping, pale green mat of crowded shoots distinguished by scaly, overlapping, triangular leaves, 4 mm (⅛ in) long, is covered with 1.5 cm (½ in) wide yellow flowers in early summer. The flowers are arranged in loose, flat clusters, each containing 3-5 blooms. The plant is an evergreen. It originates from the Balkans and is now naturalised in parts of Britain. HEIGHT & SPREAD 5×15 cm (2×6 in).
'Aureum' has a neater habit and a golden tint to its leaf tips in spring.
S. aizoon Several upright stems bear alternate, oblong to lance-shaped, toothed leaves, 5 cm (2 in) long, which are mid green and velvety. Pale yellow flowers, 1.5 cm (½ in) wide, appear in dense, terminal clusters in mid summer. This robust, herbaceous perennial is native to Siberia, China and Japan. HEIGHT & SPREAD 30×25 cm (12×10 in).
'Euphorbioides' has rich yellow flowers, borne in somewhat larger clusters.
S. alboroseum 'Mediovariegatum' The pale green leaves have yellow centres on this striking herbaceous perennial. A strong, clumped growth of upright stems carries paired, oval leaves, 5 cm (2 in) long, smooth and velvety to the touch, and 3 cm (1¼ in) wide terminal clusters of white flowers in early autumn. Native to China and Japan. HEIGHT & SPREAD 30×12 cm (12×4¾ in).
S. album This vigorous and somewhat untidy plant has a sprawling tangle of shoots that easily spreads to 30 cm (12 in) in a single season, and will continue to spread year

S

after year. The leaves are typically cigar-shaped, up to 1.5 cm (½ in) long, smooth and shiny, and arrayed 'bottle brush' fashion on 8 cm (3¼ in) long shoots. The white flowers, 1 cm (⅜ in) across, are carried in flattish heads on stems up to 15 cm (6 in) tall in mid summer. The plant is evergreen, but must be cut back hard every autumn. Found in Europe, Scandinavia and W Asia, *S. album* is firmly naturalised in Britain. HEIGHT & SPREAD 15×30 cm (6×12 in).

'**Chloroticum**' has very clear green foliage. '**Coral Carpet**' has leaves that turn red in hot, dry conditions. The leaves of ssp. *teretifolium* '**Murale**' take on a purple hue.

S. anacampseros Lax stems sprouting from creeping tubers form a vigorous mat. There is no real limit to its spread. Alternate leaves, 2 cm (¾ in) long, fleshy, broadly spatulate and blue-green, clothe the upper half of the stems. They are semi-deciduous. Purple flowers arranged in globular heads 4 cm (1½ in) wide top the stems from mid to late summer. Native to S Europe. HEIGHT & SPREAD 10×100 cm (4×40 in).

S. cauticolum♀ A herbaceous perennial of somewhat straggling habit, with creeping stems terminating in 2.5 cm (1 in) wide heads of purple flowers in early and mid autumn. The slightly toothed, fleshy leaves are rounded, 2.5 cm (1 in) long, bluish green rimmed purple-red. Native to Japan, HEIGHT & SPREAD 10×30 cm (4×12 in).

'**Bertram Anderson**' is more upright and branching, with purple-blue leaves and red flowers. '**Lidakense**' has a smaller, neater habit of growth.

S. dasyphyllum A dwarf evergreen perennial, whose foliage has year-round beauty. Little egg-shaped, polished leaves, 3 mm (⅛ in) long, clasp 4 cm (1½ in) long crowded shoots, producing a pale grey mound suffused with pink. The 6 mm (¼ in) wide flowers, white ridged with pink, spangle the

▼ *Sedum* 'Bertram Anderson'

plant in early and mid summer. Native to the Mediterranean. HEIGHT & SPREAD 7×15 cm (2¾×6 in).

S. ewersii The rounded leaves of this prostrate, herbaceous perennial are sparsely toothed, fleshy, 2 cm (¾ in) long, blue-green and in opposed pairs, on floppy stems that root down from their nodes. Branching heads, 4 cm (1½ in) wide, of rose-pink flowers bloom in late summer and early autumn. Widely distributed through the Himalayas, Mongolia and China. HEIGHT & SPREAD 10×30 cm (4×12 in).

S. forsterianum see *S. rupestre*

S. '**Herbstfreude**'♀ ('Autumn Joy') Stout, upright stems carry pale green, fleshy, oval, toothed leaves, about 5 cm (2 in) long, and terminal heads, up to 8 cm (3¼ in) across, of pink flowers that deepen to bronze-red. The flowers bloom in early and mid autumn. This herbaceous perennial is usually grown in flowerbeds, being too large for most rock gardens. HEIGHT & SPREAD 45×45 cm (18×18 in).

S. hispanicum var. *minus* This evergreen mat-forming plant has bunched, linear leaves, 6 mm (¼ in) long, at the tops of almost bare, 5 cm (2 in) stems, which crowd together to form a dense, spreading mat. Purplish pink flowers, 1 cm (⅜ in) across, are borne in loose heads in early and mid summer. The plant grows in the wild in S Europe and as far east as Iran, but not in Spain, despite its name. HEIGHT & SPREAD 5×30 cm (2×12 in).

'**Aureum**' is slow-growing, compact and has a yellow tinge to its foliage.

S. kamtschaticum♀ Lax, fleshy stems radiate from stumps of previous growth, bearing mid green, toothed, elliptic, widely spaced leaves, up to 6 cm (2½ in) long, and flattish, terminal clusters of deep yellow flowers, from early summer to early autumn. Each flower is about 1.5 cm (½ in)

▼ *Sedum* 'Herbstfreude'

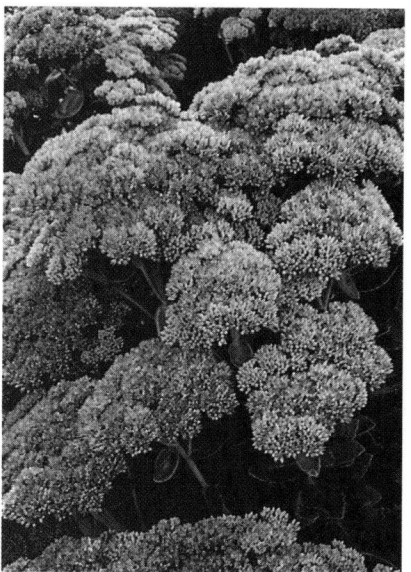

▼ *Sedum kamtschaticum*

Sedum kamtschaticum 'Variegatum' ▼

▲ *Sedum middendorffianum*

wide. This tough, vigorous, semi-evergreen perennial is usually planted in a border. Native to NE Siberia, China and Japan. HEIGHT & SPREAD 10×60 cm (4×24 in).

var. *ellacombeanum*♀ has pale yellow flowers and neater, more compact growth. var. *floriferum* '**Weihenstephaner Gold**'♀ has extra flowering shoots, giving an extended display, until mid autumn. '**Variegatum**'♀ is eye-catching, with pale orange flowers and gold-rimmed leaves.

S. lydium Densely tufted, 5 mm (¼ in) long, linear leaves, bright green tinged with red and fleshy, borne at the tips of creeping stems, form an evergreen mat. Sparse, rounded, 2 cm (¾ in) wide clusters of white flowers appear on erect 2.5 cm (1 in) stalks from early to mid summer. This sedum prefers partial shade and moister, cooler conditions than most other species. It is native to Asia Minor. HEIGHT & SPREAD 2.5×15 cm (1×6 in).

S. middendorffianum A neat herbaceous perennial, forming a crowded clump of 15 cm (6 in) long stems carrying narrowly oblong, 2 cm (¾ in) long, sparsely toothed leaves that are a fresh green and fleshy. Bright yellow flowers bloom in 2 cm (¾ in) wide terminal clusters between mid and late summer. This vigorous plant is native to N Asia. HEIGHT & SPREAD 15×45 cm (6×18 in).

S. oppositifolium see *S. spurium* var. *album*

S. oreganum An evergreen with richly coloured, glossy foliage, the plant makes a moderately vigorous creeping hummock.

S

Blunt, wedge-shaped leaves, 2cm (¾in) long, bright green suffused with deep red, clad creeping stems, with terminal heads, 2.5cm (1in) across, of rich yellow flowers, in mid summer. Native to NW America. HEIGHT & SPREAD 8×30cm (3¼×12in).

S. pachyclados (syn. *Rhodiola pachyclados*) The plant consists of packed rosettes of fresh green, rounded, fleshy 1cm (⅜in) long leaves. Creamy white flowers, 1cm (⅜in) across, sit almost stemless on the mat in mid and late summer. This plant dies back to resting buds in winter, when it can be damaged by excessive wet. Native to Afghanistan. HEIGHT & SPREAD 5×15cm (2×6in).

S. pilosum Spear-shaped, fleshy, 1cm (⅜in) long leaves form a single, squat, barrel-shaped rosette of grey-green, downy, overlapping leaves. From this, in late spring and early summer of the second year, rise pink flowers in dense heads up to 5cm (2in) across, on upright leafy stems some 10cm (4in) long. Although biennial, the plant is persistent due to self-sown seedlings. Several plants tend to grow together. Native to Asia Minor, the Caucasus and Iran. HEIGHT & SPREAD 10×4cm (4×1½in).

S. pluricaule Grey-green, oval leaves, 1cm (⅜in) long, clad the upper third of stems that creep then rise to hold domed clusters, 5cm (2in) wide, of crowded purple flowers in mid and late summer. This is a bushy semi-deciduous plant. Native to Siberia. HEIGHT & SPREAD 8×20cm (3¼×8in).

S. populifolium This open, bushy herbaceous perennial has stalked, pale green, heart-shaped leaves, unevenly edged in deep, blunt toothing and about 2.5cm (1in) long. Pink-tipped, white flowers, 1.5cm (½in) long, held in branched terminal clusters, appear all through summer. Native to Siberia. HEIGHT & SPREAD 20×30cm (8×12in).

S. reflexum see *S. rupestre*

S. 'Ruby Glow'♀ Deep green leaves and ruby-red flowers suffused with purple appear on this upright plant. The fleshy, oval leaves, 5cm (2in) long, grow in pairs along the stems. The flowers 1.5cm (½in) across, are borne in globular heads about 7.5cm (3in) wide. The plant, a herbaceous perennial, blooms in early and mid autumn. HEIGHT & SPREAD 20×25cm (8×10in).

S. rupestre (syn. *S. forsterianum, S. reflexum*) A robust, evergreen mat-former of rather untidy habit, this plant is too invasive for most rock gardens. Wandering shoots carry massed, 1.5cm (½in) long, awl-shaped, fleshy, blue-grey leaves. Flower stems rise to 20cm (8in), with dense heads, 2.5cm (1in) across, of yellow blooms in mid summer. Native to W Europe. HEIGHT & SPREAD 20×60cm (8×24in).

S. sediforme This strong-growing evergreen makes an upright, 15cm (6in) tall clump of branching stems, with terminal spikes of 1.5cm (½in) long, oval, pale blue-green, fleshy leaves. In mid and late summer, blooming stems rise to 30cm

(12in) or more, carrying white flowers, 1.5cm (½in) wide, in branching clusters. Native to S Mediterranean and N Africa. HEIGHT & SPREAD 30×30cm (12×12in).

S. sexangulare A vigorous, soft mat of slender, creeping stems is densely clad in fresh green, cylindrical, 4mm (⅛in) long leaves that are evergreen. Tall stems bear branched clusters, 3cm (1¼in) wide, of yellow flowers through summer. Native to E Europe. HEIGHT & SPREAD 7×60cm (2¾×24in).

S. sieboldii This straggling herbaceous perennial, almost prostrate has fresh green leaves rimmed with red. They are rounded, smooth, fleshy and 1.5cm (½in) long. Pale pink flowers appear in autumn, 4-6 together in loose, broadly conical clusters, about 3cm (1¼in) across. The plant is hardy only in mild areas. From Japan. HEIGHT & SPREAD 10×60cm (4×24in).

Sedum sieboldii 'Mediovarigatum'

'Med1ovarigatum'♀ has grey-green leaves with creamy centres; give the plant some protection in winter.

S. spathulifolium This evergreen perennial typically forms a spreading mound, 5cm (2in) tall, of crowded leaf rosettes 2cm (¾in) wide, on brittle stems, with leaves fleshy, grey-green, spoon-shaped and 1cm (⅜in) wide. Alternatively, foliage may be silvery, pale grey or purple dusted with grey. Bright yellow flowers, 1.5cm (½in) wide, are borne in branched heads on 10cm (4in) stems in early summer. Native to parts of western N America. HEIGHT & SPREAD 10×20cm (4×8in).

The foliage of **'Aureum'** turns yellow in summer. **'Cape Blanco'**♀ is more compact, with leaves powdered silver-grey. **'Purpureum'**♀ is a strong spreading plant, with leaves flushed plum-red in summer.

S. spectabile♀ (ice plant) A profusion of pink flowers with purple centres, carried in dense, domed clusters 10cm (4in) across,

Sedum spectabile

top the stems of this robust, upright, clump-forming plant in early autumn. The oval, shallow-toothed leaves, 5cm (2in) long, pale blue-green, smooth and fleshy, grow in pairs. The plant is often found in a border. It dies down to resting buds over winter. Native to China. HEIGHT & SPREAD 40×40cm (16×16in).

▲ *Sedum spectabile* 'Brilliant'

▲ *Sedum spectabile* 'Iceberg'

'Brilliant'♀ has flowers coloured deep rose; **'Carmen'** has carmine flowers; those of **'Iceberg'** are white; **'Meteor'** has flowers of deep carmine.

S. spurium A mass of partly naked, creeping stems hold tufts of dark green, broadly spatulate, toothed, smooth and fleshy leaves, 2.5cm (1in) long, which form a mat about 5cm (2in) high. Deep mauve flowers are borne in loose heads 6cm (2½in) across on 10cm (4in) tall flower stems in mid and late summer. Use this semi-deciduous plant as ground cover, because of its invasive spreading habit. Native to the Caucasus. HEIGHT & SPREAD 10×90cm (4×36in).

The flowers of var. **album** (syn. *S. oppositifolium*) are white; **'Atropurpureum'** has dark red leaves and red flowers; **'Coccineum'** has bright red flowers; **'Erdblut'** has green leaves edged with crimson and crimson flowers; **'Fuldaglut'** has dark red leaves and flowers; **'Purpurteppich'** ('Purple Carpet') has purple leaves and flowers; **'Schorbuser Blut'**♀ ('Dragon's Blood') has older leaves tinged bronze and deep red flowers; **'Variegatum'** has leaves edged with pink and cream.

S. telephium A herbaceous perennial which is similar in many respects to *S. spectabile*.

▼ *Sedum spurium*

S

⚘ *Sedum spurium* 'Fuldaglut'
Sedum spurium 'Purpurteppich' ⚘

⚘ *Sedum telephium*

Diamond-shaped leaves with blunt-toothed edges, bright green, waxy and 4 cm (1½ in) long, grow alternately up the stems. Red-purple or whitish flower heads, 7.5 cm (3 in) across, bloom in late summer and early autumn. Native to Europe. HEIGHT & SPREAD 20×30 cm (8×12 in).

'Atropurpureum'♀ has all growth suffused with purple. 'Munstead Dark Red' has dark red flowers. 'Variegatum' has leaves coloured green, cream and pink.
S. 'Vera Jameson'♀ This sprawling clump has rounded leaves, slightly toothed, fleshy, smooth, purple-hued, 3 cm (1¼ in) long. Pale, dusky pink flowers carried in 5 cm (2 in) wide panicles are borne in autumn, before the plant dies down for winter. HEIGHT & SPREAD 20×30 cm (8×12 in).
CULTIVATION Sedums accept a wide range of soil types, but not cold, heavy, wet soils. S. lydium and the telephium types require some moisture-retentive material at their roots; for other species quite dry soils are satisfactory. Most sedums require a sunny location. Some will thrive in sun or partial shade, including S. alboroseum 'Mediovariegatum', S. cauticolum and S. 'Herbstfreude'. S. lydium prefers partial shade. Leave dead growth of herbaceous species in place over winter, to be cleared away in early spring.
PROPAGATION Increase perennial species by division in late autumn, or by taking cuttings of non-flowering shoots in spring. Sow seed in early spring, grow on in pots and plant out in mid spring of the following year.
PESTS AND DISEASES Aphids and mealy bugs are the major pests. Over-wet soils promote rotting of the rootstock.

Sea buckthorn
see *Hippophaë rhamnoides*
Sea kale see *Crambe maritima*
Sea lavender see *Limonium*
Sea pink see *Armeria*

Selaginella
Selaginellaceae

Though many look rather like mosses, selaginellas are related to ferns, and are flowerless. They are tender plants which thrive in shady, damp situations and make ideal plants for a bottle garden, terrarium or humid conservatory.
RECOMMENDED SPECIES AND VARIETIES
S. kraussiana♀ This ground-hugging perennial forms a moss-like mat up to 60 cm (24 in) across. The stems, which root as they spread, are covered with tiny bright green overlapping oval leaves. HEIGHT & SPREAD 5×60 cm (2×24 in).
'Aurea' has leaves that are golden green. 'Variegata' has leaves splashed with cream.
S. martensii This species, less moss-like, has stems as long as 30 cm (12 in) long bearing bright green oval leaves up to 1 cm (⅜ in) long. The stems start off growing upright, and then arch over. Stiff roots grow vertically downwards into the compost. HEIGHT & SPREAD 30×80 cm (12×32 in).
CULTIVATION Site in shade or soft, indirect light in a humid atmosphere and at a minimum winter temperature of 7°C (45°F). Water to keep plants damp but not wet, using soft water if possible. Repot when plants reach the edge of the container.
PROPAGATION Take a cutting of a section of stem that has started to produce roots and pot on. Larger plants can also be carefully divided in spring.
PESTS AND DISEASES Usually trouble free.

Self-heal see *Prunella*

Selinum
Umbelliferae

Bold, spreading heads of tiny white or, occasionally, purplish flowers emerge from the decorative foliage of these strong-growing hardy perennials in summer. The plant described here brings height to a border and distinction to a wild-flower garden.
RECOMMENDED SPECIES
S. wallichianum (syn. S. tenuifolium) The finely divided, lacy green leaves of this vigorous hardy perennial are about 25 cm

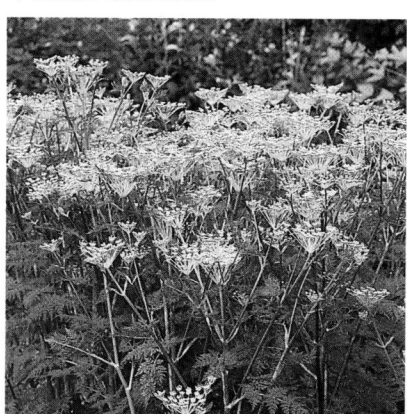

❧ *Selinum wallichianum*

(10 in) long. Tiny white blossoms massed in flat, spreading heads, up to 20 cm (8 in) across, are carried on tall, greenish bronze stems in mid summer. HEIGHT & SPREAD 1.5×1 m (5×3 ft). Native to central Asia.
CULTIVATION Plant in early summer in free-draining soil and in a sunny or partially shaded position. Remove faded flower-heads and cut back dying foliage in autumn.
PROPAGATION Sow seeds in mid spring in the open ground where they are to grow or in small pots in early spring for careful transplanting in early summer. Plants do not transplant well unless they have a rootball.
PESTS AND DISEASES Usually trouble free.

Semiaquilegia
Ranunculaceae

These elegant upright, hardy, herbaceous perennials mix well with alpine meadow plants. They are closely related to the genus aquilegia, but the nodding, bell-shaped flowers do not have the characteristic spurs of that genus. They can be short-lived, particularly when summers bring long periods of hot dry weather. Native to E Asia.
RECOMMENDED SPECIES AND VARIETIES
S. adoxoides Pink to purple flowers, up to 2.5 cm (1 in) wide, appear on widely branching stems in late spring to early summer. The narrow, mid green, lobed leaves are 3 cm (1¼ in) long. HEIGHT & SPREAD 20×15 cm (8×6 in).
S. ecalcarata Loose, pendulous clusters of chocolate-brown to purple-brown flowers, each about 2.5 cm (1 in) wide, appear in spring and early summer. This vigorous plant has grey-green leaves, made up of 3 leaflets, each 2.5 cm (1 in) long. HEIGHT & SPREAD 30×30 cm (1×1 ft).
'Flore Pleno' has double flowers.
CULTIVATION Plant in early spring or mid autumn in a light, well-drained soil in an open situation shaded from midday sun.
PROPAGATION Sow ripe seed in pots under glass in late summer and plant out the following autumn. Plants will self-sow freely in the garden and will hybridise readily with species of aquilegia.
PESTS AND DISEASES Usually trouble free, although aphids may be a problem.

Semiarundinaria see BAMBOOS p.79

S

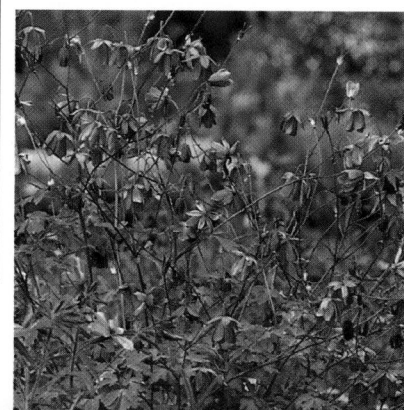

❧ *Semiaquilegia ecalcarata*

627

Sempervivum
Houseleek
Crassulaceae

sempervivum tectorum

These evergreen succulents are grown for their dense mats of fleshy foliage since most produce only a smattering of flowers in summer. The starry flowers, about 2.5 cm (1 in) across, are held in clusters well above the leaf rosettes at the top of fat, leafy stems. After flowering, the leaf rosettes at the base of the stems die, but the plant lives on, aided by offsets on rooting stolons. Native to Europe and N Africa, most are hardy in Britain, doing well in a rock garden, though a few need protection from winter wetness.

RECOMMENDED SPECIES AND VARIETIES

S. andreanum Rich green rosettes of brown-tipped leaves form a spreading mat. Each rosette is up to 4 cm (1½ in) across. The pink flowers are held on 15 cm (6 in) stems. HEIGHT & SPREAD 2.5×20 cm (1×8 in).

S. arachnoideum♀ (Cobweb houseleek) Light green, globular rosettes, up to 2 cm (¾ in) across, with their leaf tips criss-crossed by cobweb-like hairs, form a tight, shallow mound. The rose-red flowers are held on 12.5 cm (5 in) stems. Protect in winter. HEIGHT & SPREAD 2.5×20 cm (1×8 in).

'Stansfieldii' has a crimson flush to its leaves, while slightly larger rosettes are formed by ssp. *tomentosum*♀ with the leaves more heavily covered in 'cobwebs'.

⚘ *Sempervivum arachnoideum* ssp. *tomentosum*

S. calcareum This variable species typically forms a flat clump of 7.5 cm (3 in) wide rosettes. The tips of the blue-green leaves have purple-brown blotches. Pale pink flowers grace stems up to 25 cm (10 in) tall. HEIGHT & SPREAD 5×30 cm (2×12 in).

'Greenii' forms rosettes no more than 4 cm (1½ in) wide.

S. ciliosum Prized for the symmetry of its globular rosettes, each up to 5 cm (2 in) across, this species forms a grey-green mound. The lemon-yellow flowers are carried on stems up to 10 cm (4 in) tall. HEIGHT & SPREAD 5×25 cm (2×10 in).

The leaves of var. *borisii* develop attractive red tints in full sun.

S. grandiflorum Fleshy, sticky, open rosettes, 2.5 cm (1 in) wide, form loose mats with offsets on long stolons. The large yellow flowers are held on 20 cm (8 in) stems. The plant does best in acid soils. HEIGHT & SPREAD 5×30 cm (2×12 in).

S. marmoreum This variable species forms mats of spiky-tipped, dark green rosettes, up to 6 cm (2½ in) across. The red flowers are carried on 20 cm (8 in) stems. HEIGHT & SPREAD 5×30 cm (2×12 in).

⚘ *Sempervivum marmoreum*

'Brunneifolium' has a denser habit, with brownish leaves that turn red in winter.

S. montanum Fleshy, semi-open, fresh green rosettes, up to 7.5 cm (3 in) wide, with long-stoloned offsets, make a broad mat. The large 'starfish' flowers are a deep claret held on 10 cm (4 in) stems. HEIGHT & SPREAD 6×36 cm (2½×14 in).

Smaller rosettes, up to 5 cm (2 in) across, tipped with reddish brown are formed by ssp. *stiriacum*.

S. pittonii Grey-green, downy rosettes, up to 5 cm (2 in) across, form a spreading clump. The flowers are pale yellow and held on 12.5 cm (5 in) stems. This species benefits from winter cover. HEIGHT & SPREAD 5×15 cm (2×6 in).

S. tectorum♀ The rosettes of this variable species can be up to 18 cm (7 in) across, forming into large clumps. The flowers are among the most attractive of the genus with heads of up to 100 dusky pink blooms on stems as much as 50 cm (20 in) tall. HEIGHT & SPREAD 7.5×30 cm (3×12 in).

The densely packed ssp. *alpinum* has small rosettes. 'Atropurpureum' has rich red-purple foliage. 'Atroviolaceum' has purple-violet leaves. 'Nigrum' has bright green foliage tipped with purple. The leaves of 'Sunset' have orange-red tips in autumn.

S. thompsonianum Small, 2 cm (¾ in), globular rosettes, which turn reddish in full sun, make a dense mat. On rare occasions pink-and-yellow flowers are seen on 7.5 cm (3 in) stems. This species requires winter protection. HEIGHT & SPREAD 2.5×15 cm (1×6 in).

GARDEN HYBRIDS

These are grown for their rosette colouring: 'Alpha', green and crimson with hairy tips; 'Blood Tip', green and crimson; 'Commander Hay'♀, green flushed with red; 'Director Jacobs', deep red with silvery hairs; 'Jubilee', hairy, light green flushed with maroon in summer; 'King George', like 'Jubilee' but with persistent colour; 'Mahogany', rich reddish brown; 'Rosie', flushed pink; 'Royal Ruby', deep red; 'Rubin', bronze-red.

⚘ *Sempervivum* 'Rosie'

⚘ *Sempervivum* 'Rubin'

CULTIVATION Plant in spring or early summer in a well-drained, light soil and sunny situation (they tolerate periods of drought). Some prefer acid soils and in wet regions the cobwebbed types need to be covered with a pane of glass or brought into an alpine house for the winter.

PROPAGATION Plant the ready-rooted off-shoots in spring or summer or sow seed in trays in a coldframe in early spring and plant out the following year.

PESTS AND DISEASES Rust can be a problem. Plants may rot in cool, wet soils.

Senecio
Compositae

Senecio cineraria 'White Diamond'

The yellow-flowered weeds of this genus are well known, but it also contains excellent annuals, perennials, pot plants, sub-shrubs and climbers, that are suitable for a garden or conservatory. They range from the tender to the very hardy. Most have daisy flowers, usually bright yellow but sometimes purple or white. The genus is widely distributed, with species found in all continents except Antarctica.

RECOMMENDED SPECIES AND VARIETIES
S. cineraria (syn. *Cineraria maritima*) Egg-shaped, often deeply lobed, grey leaves are up to 15 cm (6 in) long and covered in grey-ish woolly hairs, as are the stems. This ever-green sub-shrub, which forms a mound of foliage, is best treated as a half-hardy annual but may survive winters in milder areas. It can be raised annually from seed. Yellow daisies to 2.5 cm (1 in) across appear in clusters in mid summer, but are best removed. HEIGHT & SPREAD 50×50 cm (20×20 in).

'White Diamond'♀ looks much whiter than the species.
S. compactus see *Brachyglottis compacta*
S. cruentus see *Pericallis × hybrida*
S. greyii hort. see *Brachyglottis* 'Sunshine'
S. × hybridus see *Pericallis × hybrida*
S. leucostachys see *S. viravira*
S. macroglossus 'Variegatus'♀ (Cape ivy, waxvine) Triangular, slightly succulent leaves up to 7.5 cm (3 in) across are ivy-like with 3–5 lobes. Leaves are bright, deep green and glossy with an irregular creamy white margin; others are entirely cream. This tender evergreen climber is suited to a house or conservatory. Solitary pale creamy yellow daisies, 6 cm (2½ in) across with darker yellow centres, appear rarely, usually in winter. The purple-toned twining stems grow rapidly and need the support of wires or canes. They become woody with age. HEIGHT & SPREAD 1.8 m×50 cm (6 ft×20 in).
S. monroi see *Brachyglottis monroi*

S. pulcher Loose sprays of rich reddish purple daisies, up to 7.5 cm (3 in) across with a yellow centre, are produced in autumn. They are carried on erect stems above rosettes of elliptic, slightly toothed, dark green leaves, which taper to a narrow base. Grow this herbaceous perennial in a sheltered site outdoors, or in a conservatory. HEIGHT & SPREAD 60×45 cm (2×1½ ft).
S. rowleyanus (string of beads) Prostrate strings of tiny, succulent, spherical pale green leaves, each about 8 mm (⅜ in) across, are produced by this tender perennial. It grows best in a conservatory but may be situated in a well-lit window, cascading from a jardinière or hanging basket. Small, daisy-like white flowers up to 1.5 cm (½ in) across are produced intermittently throughout summer and into autumn. HEIGHT & SPREAD 5×30 cm (2×12 in).
S. scandens Large branched clusters of yellow daisies, each 1.5 cm (½ in) wide, open in winter. This robust, woody-based evergreen perennial produces long arching or trailing stems, clothed in thin-textured narrowly triangular, mid to bright green leaves, up to 10 cm (4 in) long. It needs to be grown in a conservatory and is best treated as a climber, given support on trellis or wires. HEIGHT & SPREAD 5×2 m (16×6½ ft).
S. smithii Large, rounded clusters of yellow-centred white daisies, up to 5 cm (2 in) wide, appear in summer at the end of erect, leafy stems. The long-stalked, oblong or oval basal leaves are dark greyish green and up to 25 cm (10 in) long. This hardy herbaceous perennial grows best in a moist situation. HEIGHT & SPREAD 1.2×1 m (4×3 ft).
S. 'Sunshine' see *Brachyglottis* 'Sunshine'
S. viravira♀ (syn. *S. leucostachys*) Deeply divided greyish leaves, densely covered in white hairs, are the main feature of this semi-evergreen perennial. They are up to 7.5 cm (3 in) long, with several pairs of narrow segments. The plant is shrubby and often grown as a half-hardy annual for bedding but in sheltered gardens it survives most winters. It usually produces clusters of small, button-like, pale yellow flowers of little ornamental value. These appear from mid to late summer. HEIGHT & SPREAD 75×75 cm (2½×2½ ft).

CULTIVATION Treat *S. cineraria* and *S. viravira* as half-hardy annuals and plant out on well-drained soil in full sun after the spring frosts. *S. macroglossus* 'Variegatus', *S. rowleyanus* and *S. scandens* need to be

grown in a greenhouse or conservatory and kept at a minimum temperature of 7°C (45°F). In cold areas grow *S. pulcher* under glass, too. *S. smithii* prefers moist peaty soil in a cool situation. Trim perennials each spring to maintain their shape.
PROPAGATION Sow seed in late winter or early spring. Tender species need to be raised in a greenhouse; *S. smithii* in a cold-frame. Alternatively, take semi-ripe cuttings in late summer, root under a coldframe and grow on, under protection, for planting out the following spring. Divide herbaceous perennials in early spring.
PESTS AND DISEASES Slugs and snails.

Senna
Leguminosae

Senna corymbosa

These tropical and sub-tropical trees, shrubs and sub-shrubs are grown for their pleasing, much divided foliage, clusters of brightly coloured sweet-pea flowers and curious pod-like fruits. They are usually kept in a conservatory or greenhouse, in pots or tubs. They grow very quickly, so it is a good idea to propagate them regularly to ensure compact, well-formed plants. The listed plants are fully grown within five years.

RECOMMENDED SPECIES AND VARIETIES
S. artemisioides♀ (syn. *Cassia artemisioides*) (wormwood senna, feathery cassia) Grey-green, downy, narrowly linear leaflets arranged in pairs, make up the leaves, which are up to 6 cm (2½ in) long. Small, fragrant, rich yellow flowers, carried in unbranched clusters up to 7.5 cm (3 in) long, bloom from mid winter until early summer. The fruits are oblong, flattened pods, up to 10 cm (4 in) long, mid green but often burnished brown. Keep this erect to spreading evergreen shrub in a minimum temperature of 13°C (55°F). Native to Australia. HEIGHT & SPREAD 3×2 m (10×6½ ft).
S. corymbosa (syn. *Cassia corymbosa*) The leaves, up to 60 cm (2 ft) long, consist of many small, pointed, broadly lance-shaped,

❦ *Senecio macroglossus* 'Variegatus'

❦ *Senecio viravira*

❦ *Senna corymbosa*

629

dull yellow-green leaflets. Golden yellow flowers are held in clusters up to 15 cm (6 in) long from mid summer to early autumn. The green, bean-like pods are straight or curved and up to 12.5 cm (5 in) long. This evergreen may grow into a small tree in the wild, but remains shrubby in a pot. Grow at a temperature of at least 10°C (50°F). Native to N and S America. HEIGHT & SPREAD 3×2 m (10×6½ ft).

S. marilandica (syn. *Cassia marilandica*) (wild senna) This is a shrubby and somewhat unruly plant with several stems that start erect, then tumble over. The stems are clothed with dull greenish yellow leaves up to 25 cm (10 in) long, made up of a number of pairs of small oval leaflets. Flowers are brown and yellow, in clusters as long as 7.5 cm (3 in), appearing between mid summer and mid autumn. The stiff, downy, green fruits are up to 10 cm (4 in) long. This deciduous plant requires a minimum temperature of 1°C (34°F). Native to N America. HEIGHT & SPREAD 1×1 m (3×3 ft).

CULTIVATION Grow in a well-ventilated greenhouse or conservatory, where plants will get plenty of sun, in pots of a soil-based compost such as John Innes No. 3. Water freely throughout summer and apply a liquid houseplant feed regularly. Water sparingly in winter. Repot as necessary.

PROPAGATION Sow seed in spring or take semi-ripe heel cuttings during summer.

PRUNING Trim back regularly during the growing season to maintain an attractive shape. If a plant is allowed to become overgrown, its regrowth will not be satisfactory.

PESTS AND DISEASES Red spider mite is a nuisance and can cause rapid defoliation.

Sensitive plant see *Mimosa pudica*
Serviceberry see *Amelanchier*
Shallon see *Gaultheria shallon*
Shallot see p. 741
Shamrock see *Trifolium*
Sheep's bit see *Jasione*
Shibataea see BAMBOOS p. 79
Shoo fly see *Nicandra physalodes*
Shooting star see *Dodecatheon*

Shortia
Diapensiaceae

shortia soldanelloides

Pink or white flowers appear in spring above glossy, bronze-tinted foliage. Spreading slowly, these deciduous, evergreen or semi-evergreen sub-shrubs form mats of long-stemmed, rounded leaves. Native to N America and E Asia, shortias grow best in

the shade, thriving in cool, moist areas of NW England, Scotland and Ireland. The recommended plants are hardy provided they have humus-rich, acid soil and dappled shade – a position near trees is ideal. Dwarf rhododendrons and cassiopes make good planting companions. Shortias resent disturbance once established.

RECOMMENDED SPECIES AND VARIETIES
S. galacifolia Pure white or faintly pink-tinged flowers with delicately scalloped petals complement finely scalloped leaves, about 5 cm (2 in) wide. The flowers, 2 cm (¾ in) long, are almost bell-shaped. The plant dies down to resting buds in winter. HEIGHT & SPREAD 10×30 cm (4×12 in).

S. soldanelloides (fringebell) Deeply frilled, trumpet-shaped flowers stand above a low clump of bright green, broadly toothed leaves that are often stained mahogany red. Ranging from rich to pale pink and occasionally white, the flowers are about 2 cm (¾ in) long. The attractive evergreen leaves are about 3 cm (1¼ in) across. HEIGHT & SPREAD 5×20 cm (2×8 in).

With fewer teeth on its leaves, var. *ilicifolia* is available in named forms including 'Askival Sunrise' with pink flowers and 'Askival Iceberg' with pure white flowers.
S. uniflora Pale pink, flared, bell-shaped flowers, about 3 cm (1¼ in) wide, are borne

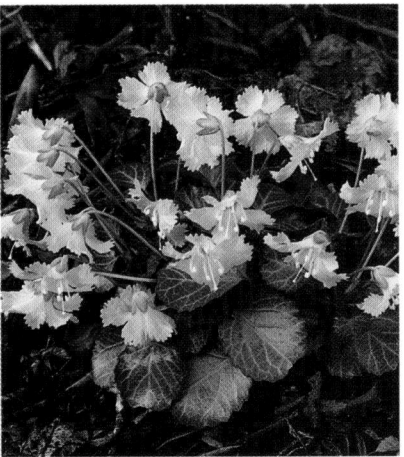

▲ *Shortia uniflora*

on this semi-evergreen plant. It has heavily veined leaves, about 2.5 cm (1 in) wide. HEIGHT & SPREAD 15×30 cm (6×12 in).

The flowers of 'Grandiflora' are about 4 cm (1½ in) wide.

CULTIVATION Plant in late spring in moist but well-drained, peaty, acid soil in partial shade. In warm, dry regions ensure that the plants do not dry out.

PROPAGATION Sow seed in a coldframe or greenhouse in early spring and protect from frost. Plant out in the second spring after germination. Alternatively, take basal cuttings in early summer.

PESTS AND DISEASES Usually trouble free.

Shrimp plant see *Justicia brandeegeana*

Sidalcea
Prairie mallow, checker mallow
Malvaceae

sidalcea 'Elsie Heugh'

Tall spires of long-lived silky flowers are borne by these hardy herbaceous perennials in mid summer. The open, funnel-shaped blooms are found in white and shades of pink, held on stems which rise above the rosettes of rounded, mid green leaves. The leaf rosettes are produced early in the season and are an effective weed suppressor.

These elegant plants often extend their garden value by producing a second flush of blooms in autumn. Sidalceas prefer fairly cool, moist conditions but may not survive very hard winters. Both the species listed below are native to N America.

RECOMMENDED SPECIES AND VARIETIES
S. candida The pure white flowers of this species are up to 2.5 cm (1 in) across. The leaves may reach 20 cm (8 in) across. HEIGHT & SPREAD 75×50 cm (30×20 in).

S. malviflora The pink blossoms are up to 5 cm (2 in) in diameter. The leaves grow to 6 cm (2½ in) across. HEIGHT & SPREAD 1 m×50 cm (36×20 in).

GARDEN VARIETIES
The more commonly grown garden varieties have flowers up to 5 cm (2 in) across and leaves about 6 cm (2½ in) wide. Unless otherwise stated, they reach a height of 1 m (3 ft) and a spread of 50 cm (20 in).

The flowers of 'Croftway Red' appear in early summer. 'Elsie Heugh' has fringed,

▼ *Sidalcea 'Elsie Heugh'*

△ *Sidalcea* 'Rose Queen'

pale pink blossoms. It may reach a height of 60 cm (2 ft). **'Loveliness'** has pale pink petals and the plant has a compact habit. The blossoms of **'Party Girl'** are a delicate rose-pink. **'Puck'** has deep pink flowers and it grows to 60 cm (2 ft) high. The flowers of **'Rose Queen'** are deep rose-pink. It has a rather bushy appearance. **'Sussex Beauty'** has clear pale pink blooms. The petals of **'William Smith'**♀ are bright rose-pink, flushed with salmon.

CULTIVATION Plant from autumn to spring in any reasonably fertile soil. Choose a sunny spot, but in hot, dry gardens plant in light shade and apply a mulch of well-rotted compost to help to keep the roots cool and moist. Cut off faded flowering stems to encourage a second flush of blooms. Do not allow plants to set seed as this weakens them. Stake in windy, exposed spots.

PROPAGATION Divide named cultivars in spring or autumn. Sow seed of species in a coldframe in late winter or early spring. Plant out in early summer in their permanent positions.

PESTS AND DISEASES Usually trouble free.

Silene
Campion, catchfly
Caryophyllaceae

silene acaulis

Salver-shaped flowers with a swollen calyx, which in some species is very pronounced, make an attractive addition to a rock garden, although *Silene dioica* and *S. fimbriata* are better suited to a woodland environment. The genus is native to much of the Northern Hemisphere and includes annuals, biennials and perennials. Those listed below are hardy perennials.

RECOMMENDED SPECIES AND VARIETIES
S. acaulis A mass of pale pink to deep rose flowers, up to 1.5 cm (½ in) across, appear on very short stems over a dense cushion of foliage in late spring. This species can, however, be reluctant to flower well. The evergreen rosetted leaves are linear, up to 1 cm

(⅜ in) long, and bright green. HEIGHT & SPREAD 5×15 cm (2×6 in).

The flower stems of ssp. *acaulis* are up to 5 cm (2 in) tall. **'Alba'** has white flowers. **'Frances'** has yellow leaves. **'Mount Snowdon'** is very compact.

S. alpestris White flowers, up to 2 cm (¾ in) across, appear from early to mid summer with petals bearing several prominent blunt teeth. Sparse light green leaves are narrowly tapering and up to 5 cm (2 in) long. This herbaceous species makes an upright, airy clump of slender, branched stems. HEIGHT & SPREAD 30×20 cm (12×8 in).

'Flore Pleno'♀ is multipetalled.
S. dioica **'Flore Pleno'** Red double flowers, 2 cm (¾ in) across, open in early summer, held in lax, branched clusters. Long-stalked, egg-shaped leaves are bright green and up to 5 cm (2 in) long. HEIGHT & SPREAD 60×30 cm (24×12 in).

S. elisabethae In mid to late summer a single stem, normally holding a solitary flower, rises from a ruff of mid green leaves. The deep rose to pink bloom is 3 cm (1¼ in) wide. The plant is semi-evergreen. HEIGHT & SPREAD 15×20 cm (6×8 in).

S. fimbriata Clusters of white flowers, up to 4 cm (1½ in) across with heavily fringed petals, appear on the arched branches of this herbaceous plant in early summer. The attractive inflated calyx is exposed after the flower has perished. Hairy, dark green leaves are egg-shaped and up to 10 cm (4 in) long. Cut back after flowering to encourage a second crop of flowers later in the year. HEIGHT & SPREAD 60×60 cm (2×2 ft).

S. keiskei Pink flowers, 1.5 cm (½ in) wide, appear from mid summer to early autumn on the wiry, branched stems of this herbaceous species. Elliptic 2 cm (¾ in) long, mid green leaves make a delicate, rather tangled clump. HEIGHT & SPREAD 15×20 cm (6×8 in).

Smaller than the species, var. *minor* is just 5 cm (2 in) tall.
S. maritima see *S. uniflora*
S. schafta♀ Light pink flowers, 2 cm (¾ in) across, appear in a succession of open sprays from mid summer to mid autumn. This

▽ *Silene schafta* 'Shell Pink'

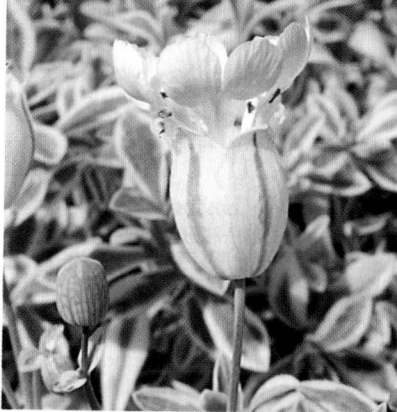

△ *Silene uniflora* 'Druett's Variegated'

△ *Silene uniflora* 'Robin Whitebreast'

easy-to-please semi-evergreen produces a tuft of slender shoots bearing 2 cm (¾ in) long, narrowly oval, pale green leaves. HEIGHT & SPREAD 15×30 cm (6×12 in).

'Abbotswood' (see *Lychnis* × *walkeri* 'Abbotswood Rose'); **'Shell Pink'** is as its name suggests.

S. uniflora (syn. *S. maritima*) (sea campion) White flowers, 2 cm (¾ in) wide with deeply notched petals, appear on this herbaceous species in late spring. They are held in a few clusters crowning a straggly mat of grey-green foliage. The sparse, oval leaves are up to 4 cm (1½ in) long. HEIGHT & SPREAD 10×15 cm (4×6 in).

'Druett's Variegated' has creamy leaf margins. **'Robin Whitebreast'** (syn. 'Flore Pleno') bears double flowers.

CULTIVATION Plant between autumn and spring in well-drained fertile soil. Most enjoy a sunny site, while *S. dioica* and *S. fimbriata* thrive in partial shade. *S. keiskei* needs a cool, moist site and acid soil. *S. uniflora* suits a seaside garden.

PROPAGATION Sow seed in early spring, and put out young plants in autumn. Take cuttings of single rosettes of *S. acaulis* in early to mid summer. Take basal cuttings of *S. dioica* 'Flore Pleno' and *S. fimbriata* in early summer, or divide in autumn.

PESTS AND DISEASES Usually trouble free.

Silk tassel bush see *Garrya elliptica*
Silver berry see *Elaeagnus angustifolia*
Silver bush see *Convolvulus cneorum*
Silver inch plant
  see *Tradescantia zebrina*

S

Skimmia

Rutaceae

skimmia japonica 'Rubella'

Star-like, white or yellow flowers, sometimes tinged pink, appear in dense, oval sprays at the end of stems in spring. The small blooms have four or five petals. Aromatic leaves are closely set and semi-glossy. There are male and female forms of these mound-forming evergreen shrubs, with a male pollinating up to five females. The female forms bear berries, which often persist through winter.

Skimmias, which are native to the Himalayas and E Asia, prosper in seaside gardens and tolerate atmospheric pollution. All require moist soil and most need shade or semi-shade from trees as protection from sun and frost.

RECOMMENDED SPECIES AND VARIETIES

S. × confusa 'Kew Green'♀ Sweet-scented off-white or cream flowers are borne in trusses up to 10 cm (4 in) long. Narrowly oblong to egg-shaped rich green leaves are 6–10 cm (2½–4 in) long and aromatic when crushed. This male plant tolerates full sun. HEIGHT & SPREAD 45×60 cm (18×24 in) after 5 years, ultimately 1 m (3 ft) tall.

▲ *Skimmia × confusa 'Kew Green'*

S. japonica. Sprays up to 7.5 cm (3 in) long of small white flowers appear into late spring. On female plants, these are followed by 8 mm (⅜ in) wide, bright red berries, if plants of both sex are planted close together. Dense foliage is pale to mid green or yellowish. Narrowly egg-shaped or oval leathery leaves are up to 10 cm (4 in) long. HEIGHT & SPREAD 50×50 cm (20×20 in) after 5 years, ultimately 1.2 m (4 ft) tall.

'Bowles Dwarf' has dark green, slender leaves, up to 4 cm (1½ in) long. There are male plants, that reach a height and spread of

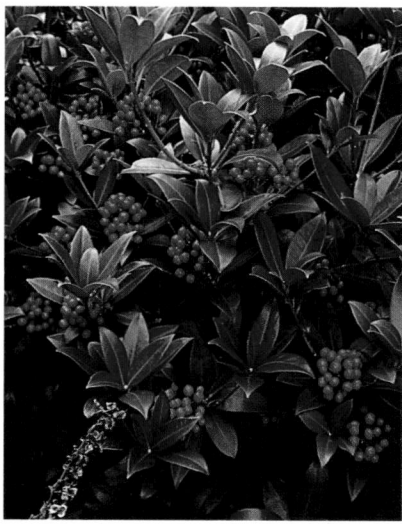

▲ *Skimmia japonica*

30 cm (1 ft), and female plants, that reach 23 cm (9 in) tall and wide. The berries are up to 1.5 cm (½ in) across. **'Fragrans'**♀ is a dome-shaped male plant that grows to 1 m (3 ft) tall and wide. Its flowers are scented like lily-of-the-valley and borne in sprays up to 10 cm (4 in) long. **'Kew White'** is an open-growing female plant with a good show of white berries. It reaches a height and spread of 1 m (3 ft) tall and wide and does best in shade. **'Nymans'**♀ has off-white flowers and red-tinged stalks with bluntly pointed leaves up to 6 cm (2½ in) long. It is female and extremely free fruiting, with 1 cm (⅜ in) wide berries, and is of slender,

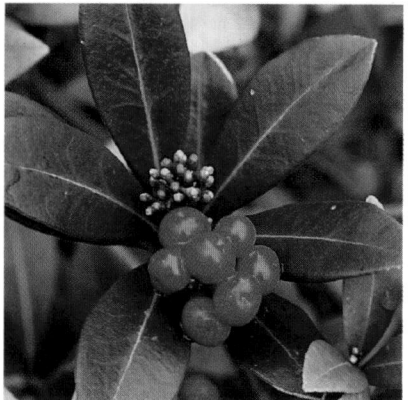

▲ *Skimmia japonica 'Nymans'*

open growth. **'Redruth'** is an hermaphrodite but is best pollinated by 'Fragrans' to give open sprays of berries. It reaches a height of 1 m (3 ft) and a spread of 75 cm (2½ ft), with upright shoots carrying broad, bright green leaves.

Clusters of creamy white flowers appear in sprays up to 7.5 cm (3 in) long on the hermaphrodite ssp. *reevesiana* in late spring. Dark green leaves, 7.5 cm (3 in) long and narrowly lance-shaped, often have a pale edge. Matt, deep red berries, which ripen in late summer, are oval or pear-shaped. This

low, compact plant grows 75 cm (2½ ft) tall and wide. It dislikes chalky soils. Its cultivar **'Robert Fortune'**♀ is more widely grown.

'Rubella'♀ has coppery stalks bearing 7.5 cm (3 in) long open sprays of pink buds all winter. These open in early spring into richly scented male flowers with yellow anthers. Red-rimmed, bright green leaves are 10 cm (4 in) or more long. This dense, upright plant grows 1.5 m (5 ft) tall and wide.

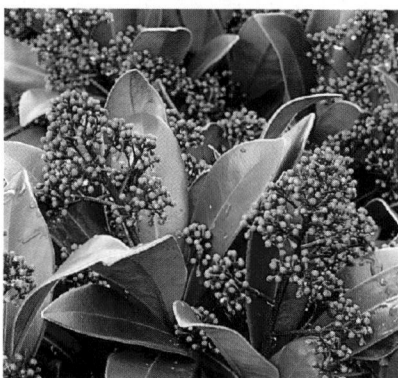

▲ *Skimmia japonica 'Rubella'*

'Ruby King' is a male plant with large conical sprays of reddish flowers opening from deep red buds. Narrow taper-pointed leaves are dark green. **'Veitchii'** (syn. 'Foremanii') has fragrant, creamy white flowers in 5 cm (2 in) sprays into late spring. Large bunches of spherical fruits persist throughout winter. Rich green leaves are distinctly broad, oval to egg-shaped. This vigorous, upright plant of dense habit reaches 1.5 m (5 ft) tall and

▲ *Skimmia 'Veitchii'*

wide. **'Wakehurst White'** (syn. 'Fructu Albo') has pleasantly fragrant, pale creamy white flowers in clusters up to 3 cm (1¼ in) across. Up to 25 ivory white berries, each 6 mm (¼ in) long and 3 mm (⅛ in) wide, are held in groups. Leathery egg-shaped to elliptic leaves are 8 cm (3¼ in) long and dark yellow-green above, paler beneath. This low, spreading evergreen reaches 50 cm (20 in) tall and 1 m (3 ft) wide. **'Wisley Female'** has whitish flowers. Narrow, pointed berries show well below slender dull green leaves, which are 7.5 cm (3 in)

long and also pointed and narrow. It has a spread of 1 m (3 ft).

S. laureola Fragrant, hermaphrodite or unisexual greenish ochre flowers appear in 5–7.5 cm (2–3 in) sprays into late spring. The purplish black fruits are rarely seen in cultivation. This low compact species has very dark green leaves of variable shape up to

▲ *Skimmia laureola*

10 cm (4 in) long. HEIGHT & SPREAD 40×45 cm (16×18 in) after 5 years, ultimately 1×1 m (3×3 ft).

CULTIVATION Plant container-grown specimens any time, ideally in early autumn or spring. Choose well-drained soil in partial shade. *S. japonica* ssp. *reevesiana* prefers lime-free soil.

PROPAGATION Take semi-ripe or ripewood cuttings in late summer or early autumn.

PRUNING None required.

PESTS AND DISEASES Usually trouble free. Yellow leaves and shoot die-back are caused by heavy, poorly drained, cold soil or very limy soil. Whitened foliage is a sign of frost damage.

Skullcap see *Scutellaria*
Slipper flower, slipperwort
  see *Calceolaria*

Smilacina
False Solomon's seal
Convallariaceae

Sprays or clusters of small, star-shaped flowers are carried at the ends of the shoots of these elegant, herbaceous perennials, whose foliage resembles Solomon's seal. *Smilacina racemosa* is the only one of the 25 species native to the Himalayas, E Asia and N America recommended for British gardens. It is quite hardy and easily cultivated in any lime-free, fairly moist soil in light shade. The smaller *Smilacina stellata* may be invasive, particularly on light soils.

RECOMMENDED SPECIES
S. racemosa♀ Fluffy-looking, creamy white flowers in a densely packed cluster, up to

▲ *Smilacina racemosa*

15 cm (6 in) long, appear from mid spring to mid summer, often becoming slightly pink as they age. Arching stems bear almost stalkless, elliptic, light green leaves, about 15 cm (6 in) long. The leaves, which turn yellow in autumn, are alternate with prominent parallel veins. The small berries are red or greenish red and finely speckled with dark red or purple. This rhizomatous plant forms clumps. HEIGHT & SPREAD 75×75 cm (2½×2½ ft).

CULTIVATION Plant in autumn or spring in fairly moist, humus-rich, acid or neutral soil in partial shade.

PROPAGATION Divide in spring.

PESTS AND DISEASES Usually trouble free.

Smilax
Smilacaceae

Grown for their foliage and fruit, these evergreen or deciduous climbing perennials are useful for covering the walls of a greenhouse or conservatory. Those species most commonly grown are tender, requiring a minimum temperature of 3°C (37°F). Their tough, prickly stems, clothed in shiny, leathery green leaves, scramble up supports or wires. The pale yellowish green flowers are insignificant but are sweetly scented. Male and female flowers are borne

▲ *Smilax aspera*

on separate plants and both types need to be grown if the brightly coloured berries are to be seen at all, which is why the fruit is rare in Britain.

RECOMMENDED SPECIES AND VARIETIES
S. aspera Spiny stems, growing in a zigzag pattern, are liberally clothed with lance or narrowly heart-shaped dark green leaves, up to 10 cm (4 in) long, with prickly edges and main veins. Fragrant flowers appear in late summer, followed by black or red berries. A vigorous, handsome evergreen climber. HEIGHT & SPREAD 3×1 m (10×3 ft).
S. china Rounded or oval, mid green leaves, up to 10 cm (4 in) long, often turn red in autumn. Flowers appear in late spring usually followed by bright red berries in autumn. A deciduous scrambling climber. HEIGHT & SPREAD 5×2 m (16×6½ ft).

CULTIVATION Plant in pots of a soil-based compost such as John Innes No. 2. Water freely throughout summer, but sparingly in winter. Feed with a liquid houseplant fertiliser during summer. Repot every 18 months. Plants can be grown outdoors in frost-free areas in well-drained soil against a warm wall.

PROPAGATION Sow seed in spring under glass or divide well-established plants in spring when repotting.

PRUNING Cut back excessive growth regularly throughout the growing season.

PESTS AND DISEASES Red spider mite and mealy bugs can cause problems.

Smoke tree, smoke bush see *Cotinus*
Snakeroot, black
  see *Cimicifuga racemosa*
Snakeroot, button see *Liatris spicata*
Snapdragon see *Antirrhinum*
Sneezeweed see *Helenium autumnale*
Snowbell see *Soldanella, Styrax*
Snowberry see *Symphoricarpus*
Snowdrop see *Galanthus*
Snowdrop tree see *Halesia*
Snowflake see *Leucojum*
Snow-in-summer
  see *Cerastium tomentosum*
Snowy mespilus see *Amelanchier*
Soapwort see *Saponaria*

S

Solandra
Chalice vine
Solanaceae

solandra maxima

Richly fragrant at night, large flowers bloom freely among the handsome shiny foliage of these tender evergreen, woody-stemmed climbers. Grown as specimen plants in the conservatory or greenhouse they like a light position but need shading from intense sunlight.

RECOMMENDED SPECIES AND VARIETIES
S. hartwegii see *S. maxima*
S. maxima (syn. *S. hartwegii*) The large, tubular to funnel-shaped flowers are golden with purple veins, up to 20 cm (8 in) long, and with undulating petals. They bloom from late spring to mid summer. The mid green leaves, produced during winter and early spring, are shiny but downy beneath, elliptical and up to 10 cm (4 in) long. It requires a minimum temperature of 7°C (45°F). HEIGHT & SPREAD 12×5 m (40×16 ft).

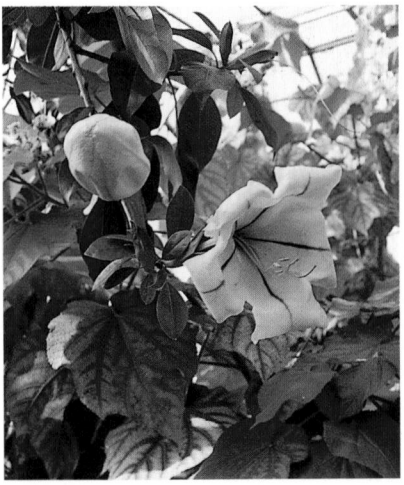

▲ *Solandra maxima*

CULTIVATION Plant in spring in pots of soil-based compost such as John Innes No. 2. Water freely during summer and sparingly in winter. Feed monthly with a high-potash liquid feed during the growing season. Tie in stems to supports. Regularly remove fading foliage and dead flowerheads.
PROPAGATION Take semi-ripe cuttings during summer.
PRUNING Cut out any wayward shoots as they appear and thin out crowded growth after flowering.
PESTS AND DISEASES Red spider mite and mealy bug can be troublesome.

Solanum
Solanaceae

solanum jasminoides 'Album'

This wide-ranging genus includes annuals, perennials, trees, sub-shrubs and shrubs both hardy and tender, deciduous and evergreen. It contains plants that are poisonous, such as bittersweet (*Solanum dulcamara*), but also useful plants such as the aubergine (*S. melongena*, see p.733) and the potato (*S. tuberosum*, see p.744). The flowers have a prominent yellow centre and the leaves are lance or oval-shaped and sometimes downy.

RECOMMENDED SPECIES AND VARIETIES
S. crispum (Chilean potato tree) Fragrant lilac to violet flower clusters, 10 cm (4 in) across, appear from mid summer to early autumn. The dark green leaves, up to 15 cm (6 in) long, can be slightly downy. Round white fruits are flushed yellow. A semi-evergreen vine hardy in mild areas, it prefers shelter. HEIGHT & SPREAD 4×1 m (13×3 ft).
'Glasnevin'♀ has deep blue flowers.
S. jasminoides (potato vine) Star-like white and lilac-tinged blooms in clusters up to 10 cm (4 in) across, cover this half-hardy evergreen or semi-evergreen vine in summer. The deep green, 3-5 lobed leaves

▼ *Solanum crispum*

▼ *Solanum crispum* 'Glasnevin'

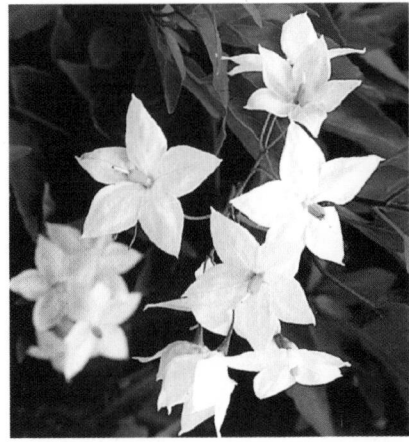

▲ *Solanum jasminoides* 'Album'

are up to 5 cm (2 in) long. It requires a minimum of 3°C (37°F) but may stand some frost. HEIGHT & SPREAD 3 m×60 cm (10×2 ft).
'Album'♀ has white long-lasting flowers and darker leaves tinged with purple.
S. pseudocapsicum (Jerusalem cherry, winter cherry) Bright orange-red, round fruits, up to 2 cm (¾ in) across, appear in autumn and winter on this tender, shrubby pot plant. White star-like flowers, up to 1.5 cm (½ in) across, bloom in summer. The dark to mid green leaves, up to 8 cm (3¼ in) long, can have undulating edges. This plant needs a minimum of 5°C (41°F). HEIGHT & SPREAD 45×45 cm (1½×1½ ft).
S. sisymbriifolium (viscid nightshade) Round orange berries, up to 2 cm (¾ in) wide, are enclosed in a papery covering. Stout, yellow spiny stems have divided leaves, up to 8 cm (3¼ in) long. The spiny, violet-blue or white, star-like, summer flowers are about 3 cm (1¼ in) across. A half-hardy annual. HEIGHT & SPREAD 1 m×60 cm (3×2 ft).
S. wendlandii (giant potato creeper) Lilac-blue flowers in drooping clusters up to 15 cm (6 in) across, appear in summer on this tender, semi-evergreen vine. The stout woody stems have short hook-like spines and bright green leaves up to 25 cm (10 in) long. HEIGHT & SPREAD 5×1 m (16×3 ft).
CULTIVATION Plant hardy species and varieties in spring in an open sunny position in a free-draining soil. Plant tender solanums in pots of John Innes No.3, and keep in a greenhouse or conservatory with plenty of light but shaded from intense sunshine. Water freely in spring and summer, sparingly in winter. Feed monthly in summer with a liquid houseplant feed. Mist above the open flowers of species grown for their decorative fruits with water to aid setting.
PROPAGATION Sow seed in spring under glass or take semi-ripe cuttings in summer.
PRUNING Cut back wayward growths in summer. Prune climbing shrubs hard during spring if they become untidy.
PESTS AND DISEASES Indoor plants can suffer from red spider mite.

S

Soldanella

Snowbell
Primulaceae

soldanella alpina

Delicate, fringed bell-shaped flowers about 1.5 cm (½ in) long, emerge in spring on upright, springy stems. The leaves of this hardy, evergreen perennial are generally 1-4 cm (⅜-1½ in) wide. Native to mountains of S Europe and the Balkans, snowbells spread by runners. They may be difficult to grow in warmer, drier regions of Britain, but do well in Northern Ireland and W Scotland where they need winter cover.

RECOMMENDED SPECIES AND VARIETIES
S. alpina Lilac to purple-blue flowers, are carried in clusters of 2-4 on abundant, upright stems. The leaves are dark green. HEIGHT & SPREAD 15×15 cm (6×6 in).
S. carpatica♀ The leaves of this plant have violet undersides. The flowers, carried up to 5 to a stem, are lilac to purple-blue. HEIGHT & SPREAD 15×20 cm (6×8 in).
S. cyanaster The pure blue, widely flared flowers have exceptionally deep fringing. Up to 4 flowers are carried on each stem. HEIGHT & SPREAD 15×20 cm (6×8 in).
S. hungarica Violet-blue flowers are carried 2-8 to a stem. The leaves can be smooth or crinkled and may be violet underneath. HEIGHT & SPREAD 15×30 cm (6×12 in).

▲ *Soldanella carpatica*

▲ *Soldanella hungarica*

S. minima Dainty, white flowers with violet markings in the throat appear over a carpet of dull green leaves. HEIGHT & SPREAD 8×20 cm (3¼×8 in).
'Alba' is white without throat colour.
S. montana Slightly flared, purple-blue flowers are held 3-4 to a stem. This vigorous plant develops a mat of distinctly veined, light green leaves, up to 6 cm (2½ in) wide, with a prominent notch at the tip. HEIGHT & SPREAD 20×30 cm (8×12 in).
S. pindicola The blue-grey underside of the leaves help to distinguish this plant, which has lilac to purple-blue flowers. HEIGHT & SPREAD 15×15 cm (6×6 in).
S. villosa Purple-blue flowers in clusters of 3-4 appear over prominently veined leaves, to 7 cm (2¾ in) wide. The leaves and flower stalks are very hairy. HEIGHT & SPREAD 25×45 cm (10×18 in).
CULTIVATION Plant in fairly rich, peaty, well-drained soil in spring in a position with some summer shade. *S. montana*, *S. pusilla* and *S. villosa* need neutral to acid soil. Water regularly to prevent the roots from drying out. In wet areas, cover resting plants with a cloche in winter to protect them from rotting.
PROPAGATION Divide or remove rooted runners after flowering and grow them on in pots. Plant out the following spring. Alternatively, sow seed in pots in spring.
PESTS AND DISEASES Slugs and aphids attack this plant. It is also vulnerable to rot.

Solenopsis see Laurentia

Solenostemon

Coleus, painted nettle
Labiatae

Grown for their brightly coloured, nettle-like foliage, the garden varieties of solenostemons are cultivars or hybrids of the tropical, evergreen perennial, *Solenostemon scutellarioides*. Their leaves are broadly lance-shaped, up to 10 cm (4 in) long, and variously crinkled and scalloped. The short spikes of insignificant, blue flowers are usually removed. For best results replace plants annually, except those grown as standards.

RECOMMENDED VARIETIES
The species is seldom grown and cultivated varieties are more readily available. Unless stated otherwise, plants reach a height of 60 cm (2 ft). They require a minimum temperature of 10°C (50°F).
'Autumn' has maroon and green leaves with scalloped edges. 'Beauty' has crimped leaves, pinkish purple darkening towards the centre and with yellow edges. 'Black Prince' has almost black leaves and is good for growing as a standard. 'Buttermilk'♀, with a neat upright habit, has bright green leaves mottled and spotted with cream. 'Carnival' has green and red leaves with brown marks. 'Crimson Ruffles'♀ has rich beetroot-red leaves with purple veins and a faint green edge. 'Freckles' has leaves of red and green in irregular patterns. 'Funfair' has large, irregular-edged leaves of yellow dappled with pink and white. 'Kentish Fire' bears small leaves, salmon-pink with a brown halo and green scalloped edges. It reaches a height of 45 cm (1½ ft). 'Kiwi Fern' has finely cut leaves of dark maroon with a green and ivory edge. 'Picturatus'♀ has crimson-red and brown leaves with a green margin. 'Pineapple Beauty'♀ bears large leaves of lime-green to gold with a dark maroon centre. The leaves of 'Pineapplette'♀ have a frilled edge and are yellow with red speckles.

▲ *Solenostemon* 'Pineapplette'

Rainbow Mixed is a seed-raised selection, producing a wide range of leaf shapes and colours. 'Royal Scot'♀ has small, pointed leaves, orange-red with a bright golden edge. **Wizard Mixed** is a seed-raised selection, up to 25 cm (10 in) tall, branching freely from the base and with leaves combining pink, red, black and white.
CULTIVATION Grow in John Innes No.3. Remove faded foliage regularly and pinch out the growing points of leggy plants to encourage bushy development. Remove flowers as they appear.
PROPAGATION Sow seed of the mixed selections under glass in spring and summer. Take softwood cuttings of these and of the named varieties in spring and summer.
PRUNING To grow as a standard, choose a thick-stemmed plant and remove the side-

S

shoots. When the stem is 1 m (3 ft) high, pinch out the top to develop a bushy crown. Later, remove leaves on the stem.
PESTS AND DISEASES Red spider mite and mealy bugs can be troublesome.

Solidago
Golden rod
Compositae

solidago 'Goldenmosa'

The bright yellow flowers of golden rod enliven a border from summer into autumn; the smaller members of the genus are ideal for a rock garden. Tiny, daisy-like flowers form frothy flowerheads on upright stems. The leaves are generally lance-shaped, mid green and 8-12.5 cm (3¼-5 in) long. The plants recommended here are hardy herbaceous perennials. Native to the Americas and Eurasia.
RECOMMENDED SPECIES AND VARIETIES
S. brachystachys see *S. cutleri*
S. caesia Clusters of small bright yellow flowers are borne from late summer to mid autumn. The flower stems are wiry. HEIGHT & SPREAD 1 m×60 cm (3×2 ft).

▲ *Solidago caesia*

S. canadensis Tiny, bright yellow flowers are produced in massed clusters on strong stems in late summer and early autumn. HEIGHT & SPREAD 1.5×1 m (5×3 ft).
S. 'Cloth of Gold' Bright yellow flowers are borne in profusion in late summer on this dwarf plant with strong upright stems. HEIGHT & SPREAD 45×25 cm (18×10 in).
S. cutleri (syn. *S. brachystachys*) Bright yellow flower clusters appear from late summer to autumn. The elliptical leaves, up to 15 cm (6 in) long, are sometimes toothed. HEIGHT & SPREAD 45×30 cm (1½×1 ft).
S. flexicaulis Short yellow flower clusters

appear from late summer into early autumn. Strong, erect stems carry oval or elliptical, 15 cm (6 in) long leaves with toothed edges. HEIGHT & SPREAD 1.2 m×60 cm (4×2 ft).
    'Variegata' (syn. *S. latifolia*) has brown and gold stippled leaves and reaches a height of 60 cm (2 ft) and a spread of 30 cm (1 ft).
S. 'Golden Baby' ('Gold Kind') Clusters of soft yellow flowers appear from late summer into autumn. HEIGHT & SPREAD 45×45 cm (1½×1½ ft).
S. 'Golden Dwarf' ('Goldzwerg') Bright yellow flowerheads appear during late summer on strong stems. HEIGHT & SPREAD 30×30 cm (1×1 ft).
S. 'Golden Thumb' see *S. 'Queenie'*
S. 'Goldenmosa'♀ Deep golden-yellow flowerheads appear from late summer to autumn. The leaves are yellowish green. HEIGHT & SPREAD 75×45 cm (2½×1½ ft).
S. hybrida see × *Solidaster luteus*
S. latifolia see *S. flexicaulis* 'Variegata'
S. 'Lemore' see × *Solidaster luteus* 'Lemore'
S. 'Queenie' (syn. *S. 'Golden Thumb'*) Dense, bright yellow flowerheads appear in late summer. The leaves are pale green and gold. HEIGHT & SPREAD 30×30 cm (1×1 ft).
S. virgaurea Loose heads of bright yellow flowers appear throughout late summer and into autumn on strong, erect stems. HEIGHT & SPREAD 1 m×60 cm (3×2 ft).
    A dwarf form, ssp. *alpestris* var. *minutissima* reaches 10 cm (4 in) in height and spread and has small leaves.
CULTIVATION Plant from autumn to spring in any moist but well-drained soil in sun or partial shade. Deadhead and cut back dying foliage in autumn. Lift and divide every 3 years, replanting the outside shoots.
PROPAGATION Divide in autumn or spring.
PESTS AND DISEASES Usually trouble free.

× Solidaster
Compositae

A profusion of small, yellow daisy-like flowers are borne in clusters on tall stems by this hardy herbaceous perennial in late summer. It thrives in well-drained soil, in an open sunny situation. There is only one species in this hybrid genus between aster and solidago.

▼ × *Solidaster luteus*

× *Solidaster luteus* (syn. × *S. hybridus*, *Solidago hybrida*) Canary-yellow flowers, are held in rounded, branching clusters. The upright stems bear narrow mid green leaves, up to 15 cm (6 in) long. HEIGHT & SPREAD 1 m×45 cm (3×1½ ft).
    'Lemore'♀ (syn. *Solidago* 'Lemore') is shorter and has lemon-yellow blooms.

▲ × *Solidaster luteus* 'Lemore'

CULTIVATION Plant between autumn and spring in full sun in any well-drained soil. Remove faded flowerheads and cut back old foliage in autumn. Divide every 3 years.
PROPAGATION Divide and replant in autumn or spring.
PESTS AND DISEASES Usually trouble free.

Sollya
Pittosporaceae

Clusters of bell-shaped flowers nod on this frost-tender evergreen climber. Native to Australia, it is suitable for conservatories and sheltered positions in warm gardens.
RECOMMENDED SPECIES
S. heterophylla♀ (syn. *S. fusiformis*) (blue-bell creeper, Australian bluebell) Sky-blue

▼ *Sollya heterophylla*

occasionally white or mauve flowers, about 1.5 cm (½ in) wide, are held in drooping clusters from mid summer to early autumn. The small cylindrical fruits have many seeds. The linear leaves are up to 7 cm (2¾ in) long. HEIGHT & SPREAD 1.8×1.8 m (6×6 ft) after 5 years, also the ultimate size.

CULTIVATION Plant in full sun in gritty soil in a conservatory, greenhouse or warm garden where there is little or no frost. Water generously in summer. Grow garden specimens on trellis or among shrubs.

PROPAGATION Take greenwood cuttings in summer or autumn.

PRUNING Cut out any dead wood in winter or early spring and prune to restrict growth.

PESTS AND DISEASES Usually trouble free.

Solomon's seal see *Polygonatum*

Sophora
Leguminosae

sophora japonica

These hardy deciduous and evergreen trees and shrubs, with their handsome pinnate leaves, give an airy grace to the garden. After several years, they bear hanging clusters of unusual tubular yellow or white flowers. These are followed by long seedpods that resemble a string of beads. The leaves are composed of pairs of oval leaflets. All parts of the plants are poisonous.

RECOMMENDED SPECIES AND VARIETIES
S. japonica♀ (pagoda tree) Rich green leaves clothe this deciduous, round-headed

▼ *Sophora japonica*

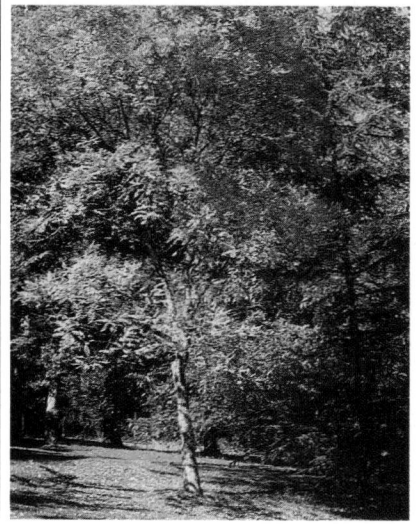

tree. Creamy white flowers are borne during late summer and autumn on mature trees, 30 or more years old. Native to China. HEIGHT & SPREAD 4×3 m (13×10 ft) after 20 years, ultimately 15 m (50 ft) tall.

S. microphylla Striking yellow flowers borne in dangling clusters, appear on mature trees in late spring. The narrow evergreen leaves, up to 15 cm (6 in) long, are dark green. This shrub or small tree is native to New Zealand. HEIGHT & SPREAD 2.4×2.4 m (8×8 ft) after 10 years, ultimately 6 m (20 ft) tall.

S. tetraptera♀ Large bright yellow flowers appear before the new leaves in late spring. This deciduous shrub or small tree does best planted against a sunny sheltered wall. Native to New Zealand. HEIGHT & SPREAD 3×3 m (10×10 ft) after 10 years, ultimately 6 m (20 ft) tall.

▼ *Sophora tetraptera*

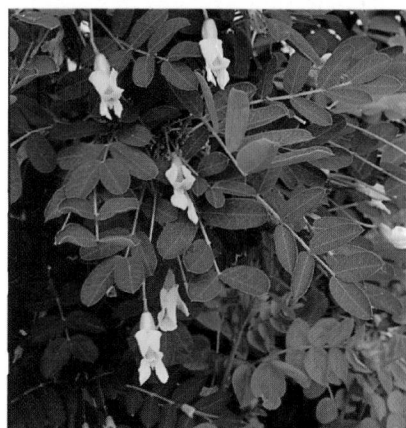

CULTIVATION Plant in early or mid spring in any fertile, well-drained soil. Choose a site in full sun, sheltered from north and east winds. If training plants against a wall, tie in shoots to supports.

PROPAGATION Sow seed under glass in early or mid spring, or take semi-ripe cuttings in early autumn.

PRUNING None is required.

PESTS AND DISEASES Red spider mite may be a problem, especially on wall-trained plants. Scale insects attack occasionally.

Sorbaria
False spirea
Rosaceae

*sorbaria tomentosa
var. angustifolia*

Sorbarias are grown for their long, decorative clusters of tiny white flowers with prominent stamens, which appear during the summer. These deciduous, frost-hardy shrubs have a rounded, multistemmed habit. The handsome leaves are long, pinnate and alternate. They are native to E Asia and the Himalayas.

RECOMMENDED SPECIES AND VARIETIES
S. aitchisonii see *S. tomentosa* var. *angustifolia*

S. arborea see *S. kirilowii*

S. kirilowii (syn. *S. arborea*, *Spiraea arborea*) Flower clusters, up to 30 cm (1 ft) long, are produced in mid summer. Leaves consisting of 13–17 toothed leaflets grow up to 30 cm (1 ft) long. Native to central and W China. HEIGHT & SPREAD 1.5×1 m (5×3 ft) after 5 years, ultimately 4.5 m (15 ft) tall.

S. lindleyana see *S. tomentosa*

S. sorbifolia Tiny white flowers appear in clusters up to 25 cm (10 in) long in mid and late summer. The doubly serrated leaves with 13–25 leaflets grow up to 30 cm (1 ft) long. HEIGHT & SPREAD 1 m×60 cm (3×2 ft) after 5 years, ultimately 1.8 m (6 ft) tall.

▼ *Sorbaria sorbifolia*

S. tomentosa♀ (syn. *S. lindleyana*) Clusters of flowers produced in mid and late summer reach up to 45 cm (1½ ft) in length. Heavily toothed leaves, comprising 11–23 leaflets, grow up to 45 cm (1½ ft) long. HEIGHT & SPREAD 1.5×1 m (5×3 ft) after 5 years, ultimately 4.5 m (15 ft) tall.

There are more flowers produced by var. *angustifolia*♀ (syn. *S. aitchisonii*).

▼ *Sorbaria tomentosa* var. *angustifolia*

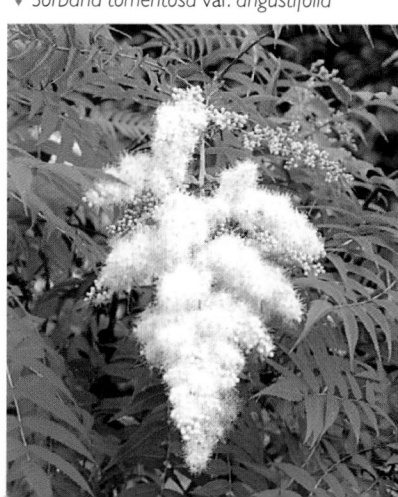

S

CULTIVATION Plant from mid autumn to mid spring, avoiding dry or frosty periods, in any good, fairly moist soil. They flower best in a sunny position.

PROPAGATION Divide plants, dig up suckers or take root cuttings in late autumn to early spring, avoiding frosty periods. Sow seed in early to mid spring.

PRUNING Remove dead wood in late winter or early spring or cut back plants at the same time to promote strong shoots and better flowering.

PESTS AND DISEASES Usually trouble free.

Sorbus
Rosaceae

sorbus aria 'Majestica'

Autumn berries and graceful foliage earn a place for these easily grown, hardy deciduous shrubs or trees in many gardens. They range in size from *Sorbus reducta* at 60cm (2ft) tall to *S. thibetica* 'John Mitchell' at 20m (66ft). Many of the small trees have open foliage which casts little shade, making them well suited to small gardens. The foliage often displays outstanding autumn colour, and clusters of red, orange, yellow, pink or white berries, about 1cm (⅜in) across, add to the decorative effect. The berries do attract birds, although white and yellow berries are reputedly eaten less and so remain on the trees longer. The leaves are either pinnate (divided into many leaflets) or simple (undivided) in shape. The pinnate leaves are between 10-30cm (4-12in) long, while most simple leaves are 5-15cm (2-6in) long with a serrated edge. The flat-topped clusters of small flowers, between 5-20cm (2-8in) across, are usually white or cream, occasionally flushed with pink. They are borne in late spring or early summer and tend to be short-lived. The bark is usually smooth and grey, becoming rougher with age.

RECOMMENDED SPECIES AND VARIETIES

S. aria (whitebeam) Silver-white when young, the leaves become a glossy green above but remain silvery white beneath. The ovate, toothed, simple leaves turn brown and gold in autumn. The berries are deep crimson. A multistemmed, rounded tree. Native to Europe. HEIGHT & SPREAD 6×4m (20×13ft) after 20 years, ultimately 15m (50ft).

'Lutescens'♀ has a more conical habit than the species. The young leaves are covered with creamy white hairs. 'Majestica'♀ (syn. 'Decaisneana') has larger leaves and fruits than the species. It is a vigorous grower particularly when young.

S. aucuparia (mountain ash, rowan) Large clusters of brilliant red berries are always plentiful. The pinnate leaves give rich coppery autumn tones. Clusters of creamy white flowers in late spring have a pervasive fragrance. This neat tree, often multistemmed, is open and graceful with an upright habit. Native to Europe. HEIGHT & SPREAD 5×2m (16×6½ft) in 20 years, ultimately 12m (40ft).

'Aspleniifolia' has more deeply cut and toothed leaflets. The ascending branches of 'Sheerwater Seedling'♀ give this tree a narrow crown and make it a good choice where space is limited. The large clusters of fruits colour orange-red during autumn.

▲ *Sorbus aucuparia* 'Sheerwater Seedling'

▲ *Sorbus cashmiriana*

S. cashmiriana♀ (Kashmir rowan) The flowers of this small tree are flushed pale pink. The delicate, finely toothed pinnate leaves are rich green above, grey-green beneath. Drooping clusters of large white fruit stay on the tree after leaf-fall. A spreading tree of rounded habit, native to W Himalayas. HEIGHT&SPREAD 4×3m (13×10ft) in 20 years, ultimately 7m (23ft) tall.

S. intermedia (Swedish whitebeam) The large berries are shiny red and the white spring flowers have pale pink stamens.

▲ *Sorbus intermedia*

Simple, slightly lobed leaves are glossy dark green above and grey-green beneath. The stems are grey and scaly and the bark flakes on older trees. A small rounded tree of spreading habit. Native of NW Europe. HEIGHT & SPREAD 7×5m (23×16ft) after 20 years, ultimately 12m (40ft) tall.

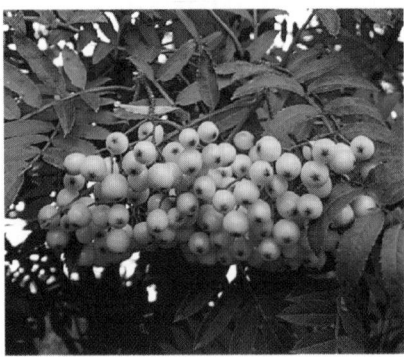

▲ *Sorbus* 'Joseph Rock'

'Brouwers'♀ is more upright in habit. *S.* 'Joseph Rock'♀ The red, purple and orange autumn colour is outstanding on this small upright tree. The large clusters of berries are a creamy yellow ripening to pale orange-yellow. The pinnate leaves have sharply toothed, narrow leaflets, bright green above, dull green beneath. Native to China. HEIGHT & SPREAD 6×3m (20×10ft) after 20 years, ultimately 9m (30ft) tall.

S. × kewensis♀ Abundant brilliant red fruit hang in dense bunches. The pinnate leaves also give good autumn colour. This tree has an upright habit. HEIGHT & SPREAD 4×2m (13×6½ft) after 20 years, ultimately 6m (20ft) tall.

S. koehneana♀ Drooping clusters of berries

▼ *Sorbus × kewensis*

ripen to brilliant white on reddish stalks. The small pinnate leaves on this upright shrub are bright green. Native to W China. HEIGHT & SPREAD 1m×80cm (36×32in) after 5 years, ultimately 3m (10ft) tall.

S. reducta♀ Clusters of small flowers in spring give way to rose-pink berries. The small pinnate leaves give strong red-bronze colouring in autumn. This dwarf multi-stemmed shrub makes a good rockery plant. Native of W China. HEIGHT & SPREAD 60×60cm (2×2ft) after 5 years, ultimately 60cm×1m (2×3ft).

S. sargentiana (Sargent's rowan)♀ White spring flowers in wide clusters mature to abundant large bunches of small orange-scarlet fruits. This large tree of rounded habit has distinctive big sticky leaf buds in winter. Matt green, pinnate leaves, up to 30cm (1ft) long, turn a brilliant orange-red in autumn. Native to SW China. HEIGHT & SPREAD 5×4m (16×13ft) in 20 years, ultimately 10m (33ft) tall.

Sorbus sargentiana

S. thibetica 'John Mitchell'♀ (syn. S. aria 'Mitchellii') Green berries ripen to orange or yellow in late summer. The simple leaves, up to 20cm (8in) long, can be nearly circular. Lustrous dark green above with bright silver hairs beneath, the leaves turn yellow in autumn. This large tree has a rounded crown. Native to SW China. HEIGHT & SPREAD 6×3m (20×10ft) after 20 years, ultimately 20m (66ft) tall.

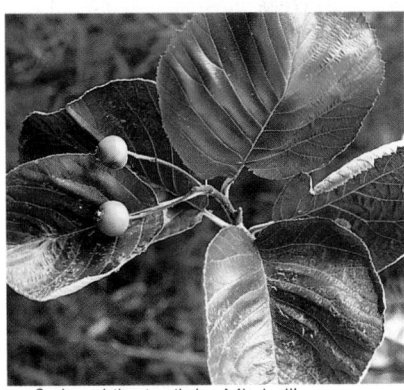

▲ *Sorbus thibetica 'John Mitchell'*

S. vilmorinii (Vilmorin's rowan) The delicate pinnate leaves have a fern-like appearance. They are rich red and purple in autumn. Fruits ripen through shades of carmine and pink to white flushed with pink. This large shrub or small tree is rounded and spreading with slender, arch-ing branches and often grows as broad as it is tall. Native to W China. HEIGHT & SPREAD 3.5×2.4m (12×8ft) after 20 years, ultimately 4.5m (15ft) tall.

CULTIVATION Plant in any well-drained soil from autumn to spring in sun or part shade.

PROPAGATION Growing from seed can have varying results – buy a grafted plant if particular qualities are desired.

PRUNING None required.

PESTS AND DISEASES Usually trouble free, but fire blight can be a problem.

Sorrel (culinary herb)
 see HERBS p.333
Sorrel, wood see *Oxalis acetosella*
Southernwood
 see *Artemesia abrotanum*
Spanish dagger see *Yucca gloriosa*

Sparaxis
Iridaceae

sparaxis tricolor

Brilliantly coloured, six-petalled flowers appear in early and mid summer. These tender, bulbous perennials need full sun and a well-drained soil. They can also be grown in pots and kept under glass or moved outdoors into a sunny spot in summer.

RECOMMENDED SPECIES AND VARIETIES

S. tricolor (harlequin flower) Wiry stems carry loose heads of star-like, multi-coloured flowers, up to 5cm (2in) wide, ranging from red, orange and yellow to white. Some have striking gold and red or black throats. The plants have narrow, strap-like leaves up to 25cm (10in) long. HEIGHT & SPREAD 30cm (1ft).

CULTIVATION Plant corms in spring in well-drained soil, covered to their own depth. A south-facing pocket on a rock garden is ideal. Lift after the first frost has blackened the leaves and store in a cool, frost-free place. In mild districts, it may be safe to plant in autumn and leave corms in the ground over winter if protected by straw. Alternatively, plant in pots of gritty, soil-based compost in late autumn or early spring. Keep under glass in a cool but frost-free position in plenty of light.

PROPAGATION Sow seed in spring for flowers appearing from mid summer, or sow in late autumn for flowers appearing from early to mid summer. Alternatively, separate and replant the corms in spring or autumn.

PESTS AND DISEASES Usually trouble free, although autumn-planted specimens are vulnerable to frost damage and soft rot.

Sparrmannia
Tiliaceae

Sculptural, pale green leaves earn *Sparrmannia africana* its place in cool conservatories and greenhouses. This vigorous South African tender evergreen shrub has white summer flowers with prominent red and yellow stamens. *S. africana* prefers cool conditions in winter, but freezing temperatures damage leaves and may kill the plant.

RECOMMENDED SPECIES

S. africana♀ (African hemp) The distinctly veined leaves, about 15cm (6in) long, are roughly triangular with shallow lobes. They are hairy and almost coarse to the touch. HEIGHT & SPREAD 1.5×1.8m (5×6ft) after 5 years, ultimately 6m (20ft) tall.

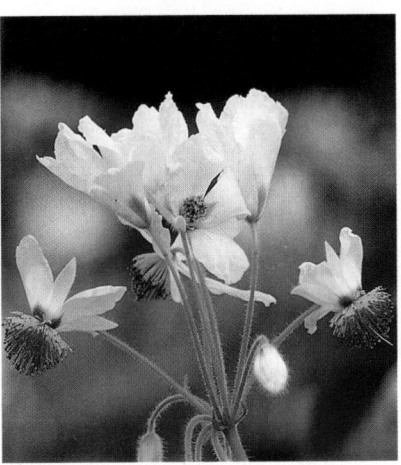

▲ *Sparrmannia africana*

CULTIVATION Grow in soil-based compost in good light in a cool greenhouse or conservatory. Water regularly when in growth and feed every 2 weeks. Repot each year until the desired size is reached – use a 30cm (12in) pot to keep the plant about 1.5m (5ft) tall. Train on a trellis if desired.

PRUNING Cut back if necessary to maintain the desired size, but avoid summer pruning which may limit flowering. Pinch out the tips to encourage bushiness.

PROPAGATION Take semi-ripe cuttings in early summer.

PESTS AND DISEASES Prone to whitefly and red spider mite.

Spartium
Leguminosae

spartium junceum

There is only one species in this genus, a hardy deciduous shrub with rush-like green stems. It grows best in sandy or alkaline soil, and is an especially good plant for coastal gardens. Its tall slender stems make it excellent for the back of a border.

Spartium junceum♀ (Spanish broom) A profusion of fragrant, yellow, hooded flowers cover this shrub from early summer through to early autumn. The flowers appear in loose sprays, up to 45 cm (1½ ft) long, on the current season's dark green shoots. The inconspicuous, mid green, linear leaves are up to 2 cm (¾ in) long. HEIGHT & SPREAD 1.5×1.5 m (5×5 ft) after 5 years, ultimately 3 m (10 ft) tall.

▲ *Spartium junceum*

CULTIVATION Plant in spring or early autumn, in an open sunny position in sandy soil. Deadhead to prevent self-seeding.

PROPAGATION Sow seed in early spring in sandy compost. Prick out singly into 10 cm (4 in) pots for the first growing season, then pot into 13 cm (5 in) pots. Transfer plants to their permanent sites after the second growing season.

PRUNING Cut out any weak growths and snip off the tips of the main shoots during the first season. In early spring of the second season, cut back last summer's shoots by a half. In subsequent seasons cut back all new shoots to about 2 buds annually. Trim shrubs lightly in autumn to encourage early flowering and trim in spring to encourage a compact habit.

PESTS AND DISEASES Usually trouble free.

Spathiphyllum
Peace lily
Araceae

White or greenish arum-like flowers and handsome leaves characterise these tropical, evergreen perennials, grown indoors or in a conservatory or greenhouse. Each sail-like spathe partially surrounds a spike made up of tiny flowers. Plants flower at intervals throughout the year. They do well in warm, humid conditions out of direct sunlight, and so make excellent houseplants for

▲ *Spathiphyllum* 'Mauna Loa'

shady corners where many other plants will not thrive. Keep in a temperature of 15°C (59°F) or more.

RECOMMENDED SPECIES AND VARIETIES
S. **'Mauna Loa'** This robust, beautiful plant has leaves up to 30 cm (12 in) long. White, oval spathes, 8 cm (3¼ in) long, surround fragrant white flower spikes. HEIGHT & SPREAD 1 m×60 cm (3×2 ft).
S. wallisii A compact plant with wavy-edged, bright green leaves up to 30 cm (12 in) long, and white spathes and fragrant flowers. The spathes are up to 8 cm (3¼ in) tall. Native to Central America. HEIGHT & SPREAD 60×45 cm (2×1½ ft).

CULTIVATION Grow in a warm, humid atmosphere in a moist, soil-less potting compost. Repot about once a year. Water freely in summer and regularly apply a liquid houseplant feed. Water only sparingly in winter to keep compost moist. Regularly clean the leaves with a little warm milk applied with cotton wool and mist frequently with clear water, especially during summer.

PROPAGATION Divide plants in spring.

PESTS AND DISEASES Mealy bugs can be troublesome, and sometimes scale insects.

Speedwell see *Veronica*

Sphaeralcea
Malvaceae

These hardy and half-hardy perennials and sub-shrubs with an unruly habit bear profuse, colourful cup-shaped flowers. Well-drained, rich soil and an open, sunny site are necessities. Native to N and S America.

RECOMMENDED SPECIES AND VARIETIES
S. fendleri Pale red-orange flowers, up to 2.5 cm (1 in) across, bloom in clusters in late summer and early autumn. This half-hardy sub-shrub has roughly oval, deeply 3-lobed grey-green leaves up to 4 cm (1½ in) long. HEIGHT & SPREAD 1.2 m×50 cm (4 ft×20 in).
S. munroana Apricot-pink to pale red or orange flowers, up to 2.5 cm (1 in) across,

▲ *Sphaeralcea munroana*

are produced in summer. The heart-shaped grey-green leaves are up to 5 cm (2 in) long. Hardy in milder areas. HEIGHT & SPREAD 1 m×50 cm (3 ft×20 in).
'Pale Pink' has pale pink flowers.

CULTIVATION Plant in spring in fertile, well-drained soil and in a warm, sunny spot. Remove growth with faded blooms. Cut back dead growth on *S. fendleri* in spring.

PROPAGATION Divide plants or sow the seed of species in spring.

PESTS AND DISEASES Usually trouble free.

Spider flower see *Cleome*
Spider plant
 see *Chlorophytum comosum*
Spike heath
 see *Bruckenthalia spiculifolia*
Spinach see p.745
Spindle tree see *Euonymus*

Spiraea
Rosaceae

Spiraea 'Arguta'

These hardy deciduous shrubs are invaluable for their abundant heads of tiny, starry flowers. Spiraeas may be grown as specimen shrubs and because of their dense growth most also make attractive hedging plants. All are native to the Northern Hemisphere.

Spiraeas fall into two categories: early flowering varieties that flower in spring or early summer on the previous year's growth and late flowering varieties that flower from mid summer or later, on the current season's growth.

RECOMMENDED SPECIES AND VARIETIES
S. aborea see *Sorbaria kirilowii*
S. palmata ssp. *elegans* see *Filipendula palmata* 'Elegantissima'
S. ulmaria see *Filipendula ulmaria*
S. venusta **'Magnifica'** see *Filipendula rubra* 'Venusta'

EARLY-FLOWERING VARIETIES
S. **'Arguta'** (syn. *S.* × *arguta* 'Bridal Wreath') Tight clusters, up to 5 cm (2 in)

S

across, of dainty white-petalled flowers appear from mid to late spring. The tapering, pointed leaves, up to 4cm (1½in) long, are a bright, fresh green. A dense, rounded shrub with arching stems. It can produce suckers. HEIGHT & SPREAD 1.2×1m (4×3ft) after 5 years, ultimately 1.8m (6ft) tall.

S. × *arguta* 'Bridal Wreath' see *S.* 'Arguta'
S. × *arguta* 'Compacta' see *S.* × *cinerea*
S. × *arguta* 'Nana' see *S.* × *cinerea*
S. betulifolia Dense white flowerheads, up to 7.5cm (3in) across, appear in mid summer. The grey-green leaves are broadly oval and grow to 4cm (1½in) in length. This shrub forms mounds of reddish brown stems. HEIGHT & SPREAD 50×50cm (20×20in) after 5 years, ultimately 85cm (34in) tall.

The leaves of var. *aemiliana* have rounded toothed edges and it reaches a height and spread of about 30cm (1ft).
S. × *cinerea* (syn. *S.* × *arguta* 'Compacta', *S.* × *arguta* 'Nana') Dense white flower clusters, up to 2.5cm (1in) across, appear in late spring. The narrow pale green leaves, up to 3cm (1¼in) long, have grey-green, downy upper surfaces when young. Downy, arching stems form a densely branched shrub. HEIGHT & SPREAD 1.2×1m (4×3ft) after 5 years, ultimately 1.5m (5ft) tall.

'Grefsheim'♥ blooms in mid spring. The leaves are about 4cm (1½in) long.
S. nipponica Clusters, up to 4cm (1½in) across, of white flowers with green centres appear in early summer. Grey-green leaves, up to 3cm (1¼in) in length, clothe long, arching stems. The plant forms a dense, bushy shrub. HEIGHT & SPREAD 1×1m (3×3ft) after 5 years, ultimately 1.8m (6ft) tall.

'Snowmound'♥ (syn. var. *tosaensis* hort.) has abundant, dense clusters of flowers. The leaves are dark green.
S. prunifolia Dense clusters, up to 6cm (2½in) across, of small double white flowers appear from mid to late spring. The 5cm (2in) long, mid green leaves, turn yellow in autumn. Arching stems form a graceful shrub. HEIGHT & SPREAD 1.2×1m (4×3ft) after 5 years, ultimately 1.8m (6ft) tall.
S. thunbergii♥ White flowerheads, up to 2.5cm (1in) across, are borne in early spring before the foliage. The narrow pale green leaves, up to 4cm (1½in) long, may persist until late autumn or even winter. A shrub with a twiggy habit and slender, arching branches. HEIGHT & SPREAD 1×1m (3×3ft) after 5 years, ultimately 1.5m (5ft) tall.
S. × *vanhouttei*♥ Flattish white flower clusters, up to 5cm (2in) across, appear in early summer. The coarsely toothed, diamond-shaped leaves, dark green above and greenish blue beneath, are up to 4cm (1½in) long. This shrub forms thickets of gracefully arching branches. HEIGHT & SPREAD 1.2×1.2m (4×4ft) after 5 years, ultimately 1.8m (6ft) tall.

Pink Ice has shrimp-pink new growths and flower buds in spring. The pale green leaves have cream variegation.

▲ *Spiraea* × *vanhouttei*

LATE-FLOWERING VARIETIES
S. albiflora see *S. japonica* var. *albiflora*
S. × *billiardii* 'Triumphans' Crowded plumes, up to 20cm (8in) long, of purplish pink flowers are carried from mid to late summer. The oval mid green leaves are up to 5cm (2in) long, with finely toothed edges. HEIGHT & SPREAD 1.5×1m (5×3ft) after 5 years, ultimately 1.8m (6ft) tall.
S. callosa 'Alba' see *S. japonica* var. *albiflora*
S. crispifolia see *S. japonica* 'Bullata'
S. japonica Flattish rosy pink flowerheads, up to 30cm (1ft) across, appear from mid to late summer. The coarsely toothed mid green leaves are up to 8cm (3¼in) long. HEIGHT & SPREAD 1.2×1m (4×3ft) after 5 years, ultimately 1.5m (5ft) tall.

The flowerheads of var. *albiflora* (syn. *S. albiflora*, *S. callosa* 'Alba', *S. japonica* 'Alba') are white. Slender, light green leaves grow to 4cm (1½in) long. This compact shrub reaches a height and spread of 80cm (32in). The dusky purple buds of 'Anthony Waterer'♥ open to crimson flowers, produced until autumn. Some shoots and leaves are variegated pink and cream. It forms a low twiggy shrub spreading to 1.2m (4ft). 'Bullata' (syn. *S. crispifolia*) has pinkish scarlet flowerheads up to 7.5cm (3in) across, which appear in mid summer. The oval, dark green leaves reach a length of 2.5cm (1in). This variety forms a compact shrub, with a height and spread of 45cm (1½ft). 'Crispa' bears deep pink flowerheads in mid summer. The strongly toothed and twisted leaves, up to 10cm (4in) long, are reddish when young, turning to dark glossy green. This shrub has a height of 1.5m (5ft) and spread of 1.2m (4ft). 'Goldflame'♥ bears reddish orange young foliage, turning yellow as it matures. Some of the leaves become variegated, others turn pale yellowish green. Slightly arching stems form a bushy shrub, reaching a height and spread of up to 1m (3ft). 'Gold Mound'♥ has bright gold foliage and forms a compact shrub with a height and spread of 25cm (10in). 'Little Princess' bears pinkish crim-

▲ *Spiraea japonica* 'Nana'

son flowerheads, up to 4cm (1½in) across, from mid summer to early autumn. The leaves, 3cm (1¼in) long, are bronze when young, turn mid green as they mature, and take on red tints in autumn. This variety forms a low compact mound, reaching a height of 60cm (2ft) and spread of 1m (3ft). 'Nana'♥ (syn. 'Alpina', 'Nyewoods') produces masses of flowerheads, up to 4cm (1½in) across, from late spring to late summer. The oval leaves, 3cm (1¼in) long, are pale green, turning coppery red in autumn. The shrub forms a dense, compact mound, reaching a height of 45cm (1½ft) and spread of 1.2m (4ft). 'Shirobana'♥ has flowerheads up to 5cm (2in) across, from mid to late summer. Most blooms are white, with some pink ones mixed in, sometimes on the same head. The leaves are pale green. This bushy shrub attains a height and spread of 1.2m (4ft).

CULTIVATION Plant from autumn to spring in any reasonably fertile soil with the exception of *S.* × *billiardii* 'Triumphans' which dislikes shallow, chalky soils. All spiraeas thrive in full sun but can tolerate light shade. For hedging, set plants at intervals a third of their ultimate height.

PROPAGATION Take semi-ripe cuttings in late summer. Plants with a suckering habit can be divided during the dormant season.

PRUNING Prune early-flowering spiraeas after flowering by cutting out any weak or old wood. Cut back all growth of late-flowering spiraeas hard in early spring. For hedging plants, cut back previous year's growth to 15cm (6in) above ground in the second season. Remove tips of all subsequent shoots when they are 7.5-10cm (3-4in) long. Thereafter, shear to shape annually, after flowering is over.

PESTS AND DISEASES Usually trouble free.

Spiraea, false see *Sorbaria*
Spring snowflake see *Leucojum vernum*
Spruce see *Picea*
Spurge see *Euphorbia*
Squash see p.741
Squill, autumn see *Scilla autumnalis*

S

Stachys
Labiatae

stachys byzantina

These clump or mat-forming perennials are valuable for their carpets of foliage and their spikes of flowers in summer. Plant them as ground cover, as edging, or in borders and rock gardens. Most species are best in well-drained soil in full sun. *Stachys coccinea* may not be fully hardy in cold exposed gardens. Native to temperate regions of the world.

RECOMMENDED SPECIES AND VARIETIES
S. byzantina (syn. *S. lanata*) (lamb's ears, lamb's tongue) Thick, woolly, grey leaves, up to 10 cm (4 in) long, form dense mats. Whorls of tiny mauve-pink flowers are carried in leafy spikes during summer. HEIGHT & SPREAD 40×50 cm (16×20 in).

'Cotton Ball' is a good carpeting foliage plant that produces spikes of round, silver-white bobbles. 'Silver Carpet' has distinctive velvety silver leaves with no flowers.

S. coccinea Two lipped, scarlet flowers are borne in the leaf axils in slender spikes

▼ *Stachys byzantina*

▼ *Stachys coccinea*

▲ *Stachys corsica*

during summer. The heavily veined, oval, mid green leaves are up to 5 cm (2 in) long. HEIGHT & SPREAD 60×45 cm (24×18 in).

S. corsica A hardy prostrate, creeping ever-green plant, suitable for the rock garden, with pale green, rounded leaves up to 1 cm (⅜ in) long. Pale purple to creamy white, almost stemless flowers, 1.5 cm (½ in) long, are borne in mid summer. HEIGHT & SPREAD 2.5×30 cm (1×12 in).

S. grandiflora see *S. macrantha*
S. lanata see *S. byzantina*
S. macrantha (syn. *S. grandiflora*) Mauve-pink, 2-lipped flowers, 3 cm (1¼ in) long, are carried in whorls in erect stems on this clump-forming plant in mid summer. It needs moisture-retentive soil to produce the green, scalloped-edged, crinkled, oval leaves, up to 5 cm (2 in) across. HEIGHT & SPREAD 60×25 cm (24×10 in).

'Robusta'♀ has deep mauve flowers on a compact spike.

S. officinalis (wood betony) Two-lipped, reddish purple, pink or white flowers, 2 cm (¾ in) long, are borne in mid summer. The plant forms a mat of foliage from which emerge erect flower spikes. The oval or oblong leaves with rounded teeth are up to 15 cm (6 in) long. HEIGHT & SPREAD 60×30 cm (24×12 in).

'Rosea Superba' has rose-pink flowers and corrugated leaves.

CULTIVATION Plant in autumn or early spring in any ordinary, well-drained garden soil and in a sunny spot, except for *S. corsica* which prefers moist soil and a lightly shaded position.

PROPAGATION Sow seed in early spring to produce plants to set out later in the year. Divide mature plants in autumn or spring. Take cuttings of non-flowering shoots of *S. corsica* in late summer and pot up the rooted cuttings to grow on for planting out the following spring. Provide protection from winter frosts. Remove rooted stems from *S. corsica* in mid spring and grow them on for autumn planting.

PESTS AND DISEASES Usually trouble free.

Stachyurus
Stachyuraceae

stachyurus praecox

A graceful, arching habit and catkin-like drooping clusters of pale yellow flowers give these hardy shrubs or small trees, which can be trained as wall shrubs, their garden value. Yellow buds first appear in mid autumn and persist until opening in late winter or early spring. Native to E Asia.

RECOMMENDED SPECIES
S. praecox♀ Pendulous clusters, up to 10 cm (4 in) long, of pale yellow, urn-shaped flowers hang from shiny red-brown stems. Clusters of yellow globular berries follow. The glossy leaves are narrowly ovate and pointed, up to 14 cm (5½ in) long. HEIGHT & SPREAD 1.5×1.8 m (5×6 ft) after 5 years, ultimately 2.4 m (8 ft) tall.

CULTIVATION Plant in autumn in any well-drained, fertile soil in sun or partial shade. Plants do best in humus-rich acid soil, though some lime is tolerated. Provide shelter from cold winter winds.

PROPAGATION Take semi-ripe cuttings in mid summer with gentle bottom heat in a greenhouse. Layering is also successful.

PRUNING Cut weak shoots back to the ground after flowering.

PESTS AND DISEASES Usually trouble free.

Stanhopea see ORCHIDS p. 467

Stapelia
Carrion flower
Asclepiadaceae

Large, malodorous flowers at the base of fleshy stems distinguish these greenhouse perennials. Native to the hot, arid climate of east, central and southern Africa, they must be grown in a warm greenhouse. The striking five-petalled flowers, in late summer and early autumn, look attractive but are pungent. The succulent, angled stems branch from the base to form a clump.

RECOMMENDED SPECIES AND VARIETIES
S. gettleffii Yellow flowers, up to 15 cm (6 in) across, have purple blotches in the centre and purple staining inside the spreading petals. Greyish green stems are toothed. HEIGHT & SPREAD 20×30 cm (8×12 in).

S. variegata (syn. *Orbea variegata*) Pale yellow flowers with brown blotches and bands inside, and maroon spotting on the

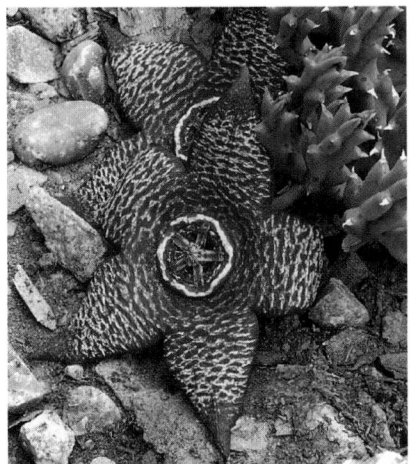

▲ *Stapelia variegata*

petals appear freely on this clump-forming plant. The particularly pungent flowers are 10 cm (4 in) across. The erect, grey-green toothed stems are sometimes tinged with purple. HEIGHT & SPREAD 10×20 cm (4×8 in).
CULTIVATION Plant in a free-draining compost in a greenhouse with a minimum winter temperature of 10°C (50°F). Feed fortnightly in spring and summer. Water sparingly in winter. Repot in mid spring.
PROPAGATION Sow seed shallowly in early to mid spring at 18-21°C (64-70°F). Take stem cuttings in summer, brush the cut surface with flowers of sulphur and leave to dry for a few days before potting. Divide established plants in spring.
PESTS AND DISEASES Mealy bugs and root mealy bugs may be troublesome.

Staphylea
Bladder nut
Staphyleaceae

staphylea colchica

Loose clusters, up to 12.5 cm (5 in) long, of small white or pink flowers are borne on these deciduous shrubs or small trees from mid to late spring. In autumn the plant produces curious and decorative seedpods that when ripe look like an inflated bladder. These frost-hardy plants are native to temperate parts of the Northern Hemisphere.
RECOMMENDED SPECIES AND VARIETIES
S. colchica ♀ Erect sprays, up to 12.5 cm (5 in) long, of small, fragrant, yellowish white tubular flowers are borne during mid to late spring. Flowers are followed by seedpods. The bright green leaves have 3 or 5 leaflets with shiny undersides and are up to

▲ *Staphylea colchica*

15 cm (6 in) long. The multistemmed shrub has a rounded, spreading habit. HEIGHT & SPREAD 1×1 m (3×3 ft) after 5 years, ultimately 3 m (10 ft) tall.
S. holocarpa Hanging clusters, up to 10 cm (4 in) long, of white flowers appear in profusion on this large shrub or small tree. Flowers sometimes take on a pinkish tinge. Blue-green leaves, up to 20 cm (8 in) long, have 3 leaflets. Seedpods are often not very numerous. HEIGHT & SPREAD 1.5×1 m (5×3 ft) after 5 years, ultimately 6 m (20 ft) tall.
'Rosea' ♀ is very decorative with slightly larger pale pink flowers.
CULTIVATION Plant during mild damp spells from mid autumn to mid spring in moist, fertile soil, on a sunny site.
PROPAGATION Sow seed in compost from early to mid spring. Propagation from seed and cuttings is relatively easy but plants will be variable and if a particular feature is required take semi-ripe cuttings from early to mid summer.
PRUNING None usually required except to shape and remove any dead wood.
PESTS AND DISEASES Usually trouble free.

Star of Bethlehem see *Ornithogalum*
Statice see *Limonium sinuatum*

Stephanandra
Rosaceae

stephanandra incisa

Admired for their elegant foliage and graceful spreading habit, these hardy deciduous shrubs have alternate toothed or lobed leaves that often give a colourful display in autumn. In early to mid summer, the plants bear tiny creamy or greenish white flowers in branched clusters which are followed by small seed capsules. Their beauty lies more in their foliage and general habit than in the flowers. Native to NE Asia.
RECOMMENDED SPECIES AND VARIETIES
S. incisa (syn. *S. flexuosa*) A graceful deciduous shrub forming a low, rounded bushy plant with a mass of thin zigzag branches whose reddish brown colour is conspicuous in winter. The leaves are up to 7.5 cm (3 in) long and turn orange-brown in autumn. HEIGHT & SPREAD 1×2 m (3×6½ ft) after 5 years, ultimately 1.5 m (5 ft) tall.
'Crispa' (syn. *S.* 'Prostrata') is low-growing, forming a wide mat of interlaced shoots. The leaves are smaller and more deeply cut. It reaches 60 cm (2 ft) high with an ultimate spread of about 3 m (10 ft).
S. tanakae A broad deciduous shrub with arching orange-brown branches. Leaves, up to 12.5 cm (5 in) long, have 3 pointed lobes and are deeply incised and turn orange in autumn. HEIGHT & SPREAD 1.5×2 m (5×6½ ft) after 5 years, ultimately 2.4 m (8ft) tall.

▲ *Stephanandra tanakae*

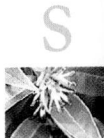

CULTIVATION Plant in fairly moist, fertile, acid or neutral soil in sun or partial shade in autumn or early spring.
PROPAGATION Take softwood cuttings in summer, alternatively divide established plants in autumn.
PESTS AND DISEASES Usually trouble free.

Stephanotis
Asclepiadaceae

stephanotis floribunda

Sweetly scented flowers and attractive glossy foliage make this climbing plant ideal for a warm conservatory. It flowers freely if its needs, regarding temperature, humidity and soil moisture, are met.

RECOMMENDED SPECIES

Stephanotis floribunda♀ (Madagascar jasmine, wax flower) White waxy flowers, 4 cm (1½ in) long, have 5 petals flaring from a tubular base in summer. Dark green, glossy, evergreen leaves clothe the twining stems. HEIGHT & SPREAD 1–2 m×50 cm (3–6½ ft×20 in) in a 20 cm (8 in) pot.

CULTIVATION Place in good, indirect light, with a minimum growing temperature of 17°C (63°F) and 13°C (55°F) in winter. Keep the compost and air moist but reduce watering in winter. Regular feeding is important for bud formation. A potash-rich feed will stimulate flowers.

PROPAGATION Take softwood cuttings from non-flowering shoots in early summer. Bottom heat, humidity and rooting powder help rooting which may take months.

PRUNING Trim after flowering if needed.

PESTS AND DISEASES Scale insects, red spider mites and mealy bugs can cause problems.

Sternbergia
Amaryllidaceae

sternbergia lutea

Crocus-like flowers characterise these bulbous perennials from the dry mountains of the eastern Mediterranean. In most cases the long, basal, strap-shaped leaves are produced at the same time as the flowers. Most species open their generally deep yellow flowers in mid to late autumn and although they are reasonably hardy in Britain, all need a warm summer dormancy to flower. Only *Sternbergia lutea* is reliable as a garden plant, doing best in a well-drained limy soil against a sunny wall. Others are best grown in an alpine house or unheated greenhouse.

▲ *Sternbergia candida*

RECOMMENDED SPECIES AND VARIETIES

S. candida Solitary white funnel-shaped flowers, up to 5 cm (2 in) long, stand on 20 cm (8 in) stems in late winter to early spring at the same time as the grey-green leaves appear. HEIGHT 10–20 cm (4–8 in).

S. clusiana (syn. *S. macrantha*) The 7 cm (2¾ in) long, rather pointed yellow flowers are almost stemless and appear before the leaves. HEIGHT 7.5 cm (3 in).

S. fischeriana Narrow, 4 cm (1½ in) long, funnel-shaped yellow flowers appear in early spring. The basal leaves are grey-green. HEIGHT 10 cm (4 in).

S. lutea The most easily grown plant with yellow funnel-shaped flowers, 5 cm (2 in) long, in early autumn among bright green leaves. HEIGHT 15 cm (6 in).

Angustifolia Group plants are similar to the species, but with narrower leaves.

S. macrantha see *S. clusiana*

S. sicula Star or funnel-shaped yellow flowers, up to 4 cm (1½ in) long, appear in autumn, with or just before the narrow leaves on this variable plant. HEIGHT up to 7.5 cm (3 in).

CULTIVATION Plant the bulbs in late summer. Plant *S. lutea* 10 cm (4 in) deep and 7.5 cm (3 in) apart in a free-draining soil in full sun – the sunny base of a wall is an ideal spot. *S. sicula* can also be grown outdoors in similar conditions.

Pot bulbs intended for an alpine house or unheated greenhouse in a gritty, loam-based compost. Water sparingly when in growth, taking care to avoid overwatering which can cause the bulbs to rot. Dry off completely when dormant.

PROPAGATION As leaves die back in spring, lift and divide overcrowded clumps. Do not disturb established plants unnecessarily.

PESTS AND DISEASES Usually trouble free but may suffer basal rot or narcissus fly.

Stewartia
Theaceae

stewartia pseudocamellia

Long-lasting displays of white summer flowers and brightly coloured, smooth, flaking bark give these evergreen and deciduous trees interest for many months of the year. The foliage of deciduous species produce brilliant autumn colour. Native to SE Asia and SE United States.

RECOMMENDED SPECIES AND VARIETIES

S. pseudocamellia♀ (Japanese stewartia) The bright green, finely toothed, elliptic leaves, up to 8 cm (3¼ in) long, turn yellow, red and purple in autumn. Solitary, 5-petalled white flowers, about 6 cm (2½ in) across, are cup-shaped and have orange-yellow anthers. As the bark matures it becomes dark red and brown and flakes off in irregular patches. This deciduous shrub

▲ *Stewartia pseudocamellia*

or small tree is fairly hardy. HEIGHT & SPREAD 4.5×3 m (15×10 ft) after 20 years, ultimately 20 m (66 ft) tall.

Koreana Group♀ has the best claret-red autumn colour.

S. sinensis♀ (Chinese stewartia) A large shrub or small tree with bright green oval leaves, up to 10 cm (4 in) long, that turn red in autumn. The red-brown bark flakes to light grey or pale greenish cream. The fragrant white flowers are 5 cm (2 in) across, and have yellow anthers. HEIGHT & SPREAD 6×5 m (20×16 ft) after 20 years, ultimately 9 m (30 ft) tall.

CULTIVATION Grow in a neutral to acid, well-drained soil in semi-shade. Protect roots from the sun. Shelter from cold winds and frost. Avoid disturbance once planted.

PROPAGATION Sow seed in autumn or early spring or take semi-ripe cuttings of sideshoots, using bottom heat for both.
PRUNING None necessary.
PESTS AND DISEASES Usually trouble free.

Stipa see GRASSES p.302
Stock see *Matthiola*
Stock, Virginian see *Malcomia maritima*

Stokesia
Stokes' aster
Compositae

Fringed lavender, blue or white petals radiate from the disc florets of this hardy perennial, which is the only species in the genus. The flowers make a summer show in a sunny border and the narrow evergreen leaves form an overwintering rosette. A well-drained soil is necessary for the plant to flourish. Native to SE United States.
Stokesia laevis Blue, many-petalled flowers with white centres, 6-10cm (2½-4in) across, are borne from mid to late summer. Strong branching stems are clothed with narrow, lance-shaped mid green leaves, up to 20cm (8in) long. HEIGHT & SPREAD 90×60cm (36×24in).
  'Alba' has white flowers. 'Blue Star' has deep blue flowers and reaches only 45×45cm (18×18in) in height and spread.

▲ *Stokesia laevis* 'Alba'

'Wyoming' has cornflower-blue flowers. It grows to just 35×35cm (14×14in). Varieties of *S. laevis* have whitish centres.
CULTIVATION Plant in autumn or spring in well-drained soil and in a sunny spot. Apply a slow-release fertiliser each spring.
PROPAGATION Divide plants in spring, alternatively raise from seed sown during late summer or early spring.
PESTS AND DISEASES Slugs and snails may damage the overwintering rosettes of leaves. Otherwise usually trouble free.

Stone cress see *Aethionema*
Stonecrop see *Sedum*
Storax see *Styrax*
Stork's bill see *Erodium*
Stransvaesia see *Photina*

Stratiotes
Water soldier
Hydrocharitaceae

---

stratiotes aloides

This hardy, evergreen perennial is a free-floating aquatic plant with decorative spiky leaves. Large colonies of plants are produced on creeping runners. There is only one species in this genus. Native to Europe.
Stratiotes aloides The rosettes of distinctive spiky leaves are rather like those of a pineapple. They are narrow and lance-shaped and up to 45cm (18in) long with sharply toothed or spined edges. Small, white, 3-petalled flowers, up to 3cm (1¼in) long, appear in mid to late summer.
CULTIVATION Place in a pond in spring or summer, allowing plants to float freely, in water to a depth of 30cm (12in) or more. Thin overcrowded colonies. Older plants do not overwinter as well as young ones. In spring when plants reappear from their winter dormancy on the floor of the pond, discard those that are least attractive.
PROPAGATION Divide plantlets in summer.
PESTS AND DISEASES Usually trouble free.

Strawberry see p.730
Strawberry, Indian see *Duchesnea indica*
Strawberry tree see *Arbutus*

Strelitzia
Strelitziaceae

Grown for their brightly coloured, beak-like flowers, held within boat-shaped bracts, these tender evergreen perennials should be kept in a conservatory or greenhouse.
RECOMMENDED SPECIES
S. reginae♀ (bird of paradise) Each orange and blue flower emerges from a 12.5cm (5in) long, green, orange-bordered bract, which produces several flowers in succession, as spring progresses. The bracts are carried at the top of tall, erect stems. Leaves are somewhat bluish green and up to 75cm (2½ft) long. Native to South Africa. HEIGHT & SPREAD 1-1.8×1m (3-6×3ft).
CULTIVATION Grow plants in pots of John Innes No.3 compost, or in a greenhouse border with fertile soil. Ensure plenty of light, but give shade from full, direct summer sun. Keep plants in a temperature of at least 10°C (50°F). Water freely in spring and summer and feed regularly with a general liquid fertiliser. In winter, keep

▲ *Strelitzia reginae*

compost barely damp, especially if only the minimum temperature can be maintained. Remove faded flowers and dead leaves.
PROPAGATION Divide plants in spring. Sow seed in seed compost in early or mid spring at a temperature of 18-21°C (64-70°F).
PESTS AND DISEASES Mealy bugs and scale insects can be troublesome.

Streptocarpus
Cape primrose
Gesneriaceae

---

streptocarpus 'Constant Nymph'

Clusters of elegant flowers in a wide range of colours are borne on these tender perennials. The funnel-shaped flowers on delicate stems have five flared lobes. Some have dark veins radiating outwards while others have contrasting white or yellow throats. In Britain, Cape primroses need to be grown in pots indoors or in a cool greenhouse or conservatory. Native to Africa.
RECOMMENDED SPECIES AND VARIETIES
The recommended plants are divided into 2 groups: rosette-forming and stemmed.
ROSETTE-FORMING PLANTS
Rosette-forming plants have basal rosettes of strap-shaped, wrinkled leaves. The flowers are held well above the foliage in clusters at the ends of bare stems. Unless otherwise stated, leaves are about 30cm (1ft) long.
S. candidus Fragrant white flowers, up to 4cm (1½in) across, are freely produced in summer. The leaves grow to 60cm (2ft) long. HEIGHT & SPREAD 25×50cm (10×20in).

S

S. cyaneus The pink flowers, borne in spring and summer, are 6 cm (2½ in) across. HEIGHT & SPREAD 25×50 cm (10×20 in).

S. primuliformis ssp. *formosus* Pale mauve flowers with a yellow throat grow to about 6 cm (2½ in) across in summer. HEIGHT & SPREAD 25×50 cm (10×20 in).

S. rexii This compact species produces pale violet or white flowers, about 7.5 cm (3 in) across, in summer. Each bloom has 7 distinct stripes in a deep shade of violet. HEIGHT & SPREAD 25×50 cm (10×20 in).

Hybrids

Many excellent hybrids are available with abundant blooms and a flowering season which may last from mid spring to early autumn. The following varieties have flowers up to 6 cm (2½ in) across.

'Albatross'♥ has white flowers, with a yellow throat. The blooms of 'Catrin' are deep pink, with a white throat. The flowers of 'Constant Nymph' are violet-blue, with darker veins and a creamy yellow throat. 'Cynthia'♥ is a free-flowering variety with magenta flowers. 'Heidi'♥ is a compact plant. Its blue flowers have deep purple

▲ *Streptocarpus* 'Falling Stars'

markings on the lower lobes. 'Helen'♥ has pale blue flowers. The shell-pink flowers of 'Lisa'♥ have a white throat and are produced in abundance. The blooms of 'Paula'♥ have reddish purple petals and a yellow throat. The flowers of 'Ruby'♥ are a rich red. 'Sarah'♥ has dark purple flowers. The petals of 'Stella'♥ are pink, with red veining. 'Susan'♥ has magenta flowers with golden yellow centres. 'Tina'♥ is a vigorous, compact-growing variety. The pink blooms have darker lower petals.

▼ *Streptocarpus* 'Gloria'

▲ *Streptocarpus* 'Kim'

The following varieties have small flowers, up to 3 cm (1¼ in) across. The abundant sky-blue blooms of 'Falling Stars'♥ have white throats and dark veining. This plant looks particularly delicate. 'Gloria'♥ has masses of pale pink flowers, with slightly darker veining and a white throat. The blooms of 'Happy Snappy' are deep magenta. 'Kim'♥ has velvety, deep inky blue flowers with a white throat, and a compact habit. 'Laura' is an extremely free-flowering variety with pale pink flowers with deep pink veining on the lower petals. The profuse, upturned blooms of 'Snow White'♥ have yellow throats.

STEMMED PLANTS

These plants produce mostly round or oval leaves, which are attached to the long, slender, main stems in pairs. Unless otherwise stated, the blooms are borne in spring and summer. The sprawling habit of some stemmed species makes them ideal for hanging baskets or in pots on shelves.

S. caulescens Deep purple flowers, up to 2 cm (¾ in) across, are borne in profusion. The dark green, softly hairy leaves grow to 6 cm (2½ in) in length. This shrubby plant is upright in habit. HEIGHT & SPREAD 40×30 cm (16×12 in).

S. 'Concord Blue'♥ Numerous blue flowers, about 3 cm (1¼ in) across, are produced. The leaves are small and round. This plant has a bushy habit. HEIGHT & SPREAD 30×30 cm (1×1 ft).

S. glandulosissimus This species bears violet-blue flowers, up to 3 cm (1¼ in) across. The oval leaves reach a length of 12.5 cm (5 in). This is a good plant for a hanging basket. HEIGHT & SPREAD 20×75 cm (8×30 in).

▲ *Streptocarpus saxorum*

S. saxorum♥ (false African violet) Mauve flowers, up to 4 cm (1½ in) across, with a white throat, appear from early spring to autumn. The round leaves, up to 3 cm (1¼ in) across, are blue-green, hairy and succulent. This almost prostrate plant is ideal for hanging baskets. HEIGHT & SPREAD 30×60 cm (1×2 ft).

CULTIVATION Grow in pots of houseplant or potting compost in a greenhouse or conservatory. Situate in good light but protect against strong, direct sunlight during spring and summer. Indoor plants do well in an east or west-facing window. Ventilate well on warm days to prevent temperatures rising above 21°C (70°F). Maintain a minimum winter temperature of at least 4°C (39°F) for rosette-forming types and 10°C (50°F) for stemmed kinds. Plants flower best if root-bound, so repot only when pots are full of roots. Water generously from spring to autumn, sparingly in winter. Avoid splashing leaves with water to avoid marking. Cut stems when flowering is finished. Snap off yellow leaf tips in autumn.

PROPAGATION Take leaf cuttings from established rosette-forming plants in spring or early summer. Take stem cuttings of stemmed plants, ideally in late spring. Sow seed under glass in early spring.

PESTS AND DISEASES Aphids, mealy bugs and vine weevil grubs may prove troublesome. Grey mould can affect plants in autumn and winter. Powdery mildew may be a problem.

Strobilanthes
Acanthaceae

A large group of hardy and tender perennials and sub-shrubs, a few of which are grown for their striking tubular flowers borne in summer above coarse, often hairy or downy leaves. The plants do best in a rich, well-drained soil and in an open or partially shaded situation. Plant in a mixed border, shrubbery or alongside a pond or stream. The genus is native to Asia.

RECOMMENDED SPECIES

S. atropurpureus The tubular flowers are indigo to deep purple and are up to 4 cm

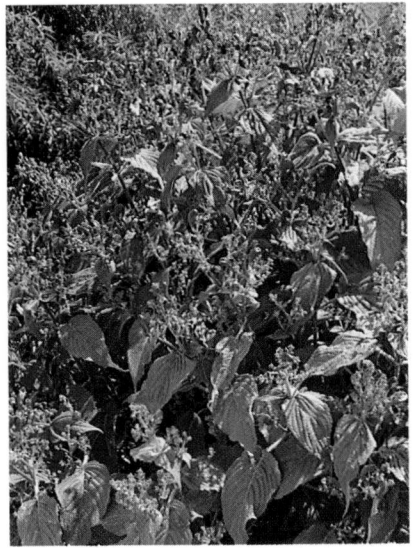

▲ *Strobilanthes atropurpureus*

(1½ in) long. Flowers are borne in dense, branching clusters on this hardy perennial plant from mid to late summer. The erect, branching stems are clothed with oval to heart-shaped, coarse, mid green leaves with serrated edges. The leaves are up to 10 cm (4 in) long and 8 cm (3¼ in) across. HEIGHT & SPREAD 1.2 m×60 cm (4×2 ft).

CULTIVATION Plant in spring in moisture-retentive, rich but free-draining soil and in an open or partially shaded position. Cut off faded blossoms. Apply a slow-release fertiliser in spring.

PROPAGATION Divide and replant in early spring. Alternatively take basal stem cuttings in late spring.

PESTS AND DISEASES Usually trouble free.

Stylophorum
Papaveraeae

Papery yellow petals unfold into saucer or cup-shaped flowers from spring to summer, showing the prominent styles from which this genus is named. These hardy perennial poppies need moist, well-drained, leafy soil and a shady site. The rosettes of lobed leaves may be scorched in sunny sites. *Stylophorum lasiocarpum* needs shelter from wind.

▼ *Stylophorum diphyllum*

RECOMMENDED SPECIES

S. diphyllum (celandine poppy) Four-petalled yellow flowers, up to 5 cm (2 in) across, open from late spring to early summer. Flowers may be solitary on the top of branched, erect stems or in small loose bunches, with leafy bracts below. The basal leaves are bluish green and grow on stalks up to 50 cm (20 in) long and form a loose rosette. They are up to 15 cm (6 in) across and cut into 5-7 deep, oblong lobes, irregularly scalloped round the edges. Hairy, seed cases, 2.5 cm (1 in) long, droop when ripe. Native to eastern N America. HEIGHT & SPREAD 30-45×45 cm (12-18×18 in).

S. lasiocarpum Clusters of pale yellow, cup-shaped flowers, up to 4 cm (1½ in) across, bloom on branched stems from late spring to early summer. The sharply lobed and toothed basal leaves are paired and are mid green and whitish on the undersides. The plant lives for only 2-4 years, often behaving as a biennial. Native to central and E China. HEIGHT & SPREAD 45×30 cm (18×12 in).

CULTIVATION Plant from spring to autumn in moist, well-drained, leafy soil and in a shady site.

PROPAGATION Sow seeds when ripe or in spring. Seeds may be sown where plants are to flower or seedlings can be transplanted. Divide *S. diphyllum* in spring.

PESTS AND DISEASES Usually trouble free.

Styrax
Snowbell
Styracaceae

styrax obassia

Profuse clusters of dangling, white, bell-shaped flowers appear in early summer among fine glossy foliage on these graceful deciduous small trees or shrubs. Fairly slow-growing, they produce flowers after about 10-15 years. Rounded, pale green fruits often hang from the branches well into winter. The plants dislike lime and thrive on acid soil. They need a sheltered position.

RECOMMENDED SPECIES

S. hemsleyana♀ Long bunches of flowers, up to 15 cm (6 in), appear in early summer. The small flowers have conspicuous yellow anthers. The pale green leaves, about 15 cm (6 in) long, have fine serrated edges. The species is fairly tender, especially when young, and in colder areas needs a sheltered position such as a south or west-facing wall protected by other shrubs. HEIGHT & SPREAD

2.4×1.8 m (8×6 ft) after 10–15 years, ultimately 6 m (20 ft) tall.

S. japonica♀ The most reliable of the snowbells has wide-spreading, slightly drooping branches below which numerous clusters of flowers hang in early summer. White flowers have prominent yellow stamens and are seen to best advantage from below. The leaves are oval and glossy. HEIGHT & SPREAD 2.4×1.2 m (8×4 ft) after 10 years, ultimately 9 m (30 ft).

S. obassia♀ Large rounded leaves, up to 15 cm (6 in) long, are softly felted below. The lax clusters, up to 20 cm (8 in) long, of fragrant flowers appear in early summer. Though fairly hardy the plant needs shelter and should be protected from early morning sun. HEIGHT & SPREAD 4×2 m (13×6½ ft) after 10-15 years, ultimately 9 m (30 ft) tall.

▲ *Styrax obassia*

CULTIVATION Plant in lime free, moist but well-drained soil in a sheltered position.

PROPAGATION Sow seed or take semi-ripe cuttings in mid summer.

PESTS AND DISEASES Usually trouble free.

S

Symphoricarpos
Snowberry
Caprifoliaceae

Symphoricarpos x chenaultii 'Hancock'

These hardy deciduous shrubs are grown chiefly for their graceful habit and long-lasting, ornamental berries. The inedible fruits are produced in white or in shades of pink or red. Appearing in mid autumn, the berries may last into winter. The insignificant summer flowers are rich in nectar and popular with bees. The oval leaves are up to 3 cm (1¼ in) long. Snowberries are easy to grow and thrive in sun or shade. They may be grown as specimen shrubs or used as hedging. The majority sucker freely. Most are native to N America.

RECOMMENDED SPECIES AND VARIETIES
S. × chenaultii 'Hancock' The tiny, spherical berries are a deep lilac-pink. The young bronze leaves turn bright green as they age. This dense, sprawling shrub is suckering and useful as ground cover under trees. HEIGHT & SPREAD 60 cm × 1.5 m (2×5 ft) after 5 years, ultimately 1 m (3 ft) tall.
S. orbiculatus (coralberry, Indian currant) Hanging clusters of white or pink flowers are followed by bunches of tiny, deep purplish red berries. After hot summers these may persist into late winter. This species forms a densely bushy shrub. HEIGHT & SPREAD 1.2×1.2 m (4×4 ft) after 5 years, ultimately up to 1.8 m (6 ft) high.
   The leaves of **'Foliis Variegatis'** (syn. 'Variegatus') are bright green, edged with yellow. It spreads to 1.5 m (5 ft). **'Taff's Silver Edge'** (syn. 'Albovariegatus', 'Argenteovariegatus') has leaves with silvery white margins. It reaches a height and spread of 1.2 m (4 ft).

CULTIVATION Plant bare-rooted specimens between late autumn and early spring and container-grown specimens at any time. Plant in any ordinary, well-drained soil, choosing a sunny or shady situation.
PROPAGATION Detach large, rooted suckers between late autumn and early spring and replant in new situations. Take hardwood cuttings in late autumn.
PRUNING In late autumn and early spring, thin out overgrown specimens and occasionally remove unwanted suckers. Cut hedging plants back to 30 cm (12 in) above ground level after planting. When subse-

▲ *Symphoricarpos orbiculatus* 'Variegatus'

quent shoots reach a length of 15 cm (6 in), shear back to encourage bushiness. Trim established hedges 2 or 3 times during summer, to maintain a good shape. After about 4 years, cut a few older shoots down to the ground in late winter.
PESTS AND DISEASES Usually trouble free.

Symphyandra
Campanulaceae

Symphyandra wanneri

These sun-loving, hardy herbaceous perennials are native to E Europe. Nodding bell-shaped flowers, produced in late summer, are borne above loosely clumped or rosetted foliage. The plants are often short-lived in cultivation and several species behave as biennials, dying after their summer flowering, but they set plenty of viable seed, which germinates readily. Symphyandra need to be grown in very well-drained soil and are ideal for a sunny crevice in a rock garden or scree bed.

RECOMMENDED SPECIES
S. armena A succession of nodding, white flowers, 2 cm (¾ in) long and with blunt lobes, are held on leafy and rather floppy flowering stems. The 4 cm (1½ in) long

▲ *Symphyandra hofmannii*

leaves are heart-shaped, coarsely toothed and form a clump at the base of the plant. HEIGHT & SPREAD 30×30 cm (1×1 ft).
S. hofmannii A strong-growing species that develops a large rosette of sharp-tipped, oval leaves, that are up to 15 cm (6 in) long and coarsely toothed. From the rosette of leaves rises usually one leafy, branching stem that bears pendent, creamy white flowers 3 cm (1¼ in) long. HEIGHT & SPREAD 60×30 cm (2×1 ft).
S. ossetica The pale blue flowers are up to 5 cm (2 in) long and hang from upright, leafy, branching stems. The rounded leaves are up to 6 cm (2½ in) long and have coarsely toothed edges. The leaves form lax rosettes at the base of the plant. It is reliably perennial in mild areas. HEIGHT & SPREAD 40×30 cm (16×12 in).
S. pendula Trusses of pendent, creamy white flowers, up to 5 cm (2 in) long, are held on branched, leafy stems. They have deep, pointed lobes at the mouth. The coarsely toothed, crinkled, narrowly heart-shaped leaves, up to 15 cm (6 in) long, form a basal clump. HEIGHT & SPREAD 45×30 cm (18×12 in).
S. wanneri The pendent, mid blue flowers, 2 cm (¾ in) long, are held in lax clusters on branching stems. The pointed, oval, toothed leaves, up to 10 cm (4 in) long, form a basal rosette. HEIGHT & SPREAD 30×20 cm (12×8 in).
S. zanzegura The nodding or pendent, violet flowers, up to 5 cm (2 in) long, are deeply lobed. They hang from slender, arching leafy stems. The rounded, deeply lobed leaves, about 6 cm (2½ in) long, form a basal clump. This plant is reliably perennial in milder districts. HEIGHT & SPREAD 15×30 cm (6×12 in).
CULTIVATION Plant in mid spring in a sunny site in a light, very well-drained soil.
PROPAGATION Sow seed in seed compost in winter or early spring. Alternatively, take cuttings of non-flowering shoots in late summer and place in sharp sand. Pot seedlings on in a potting compost mixed with an equal amount of grit.
PESTS AND DISEASES Slugs and aphids may be a problem.

S

Symphytum
Comfrey
Boraginaceae

Symphytum x uplandicum 'Variegatum'

These vigorous, coarse-leaved, hardy herbaceous perennials are grown for both their flowers and foliage. The individual blooms are tubular or bell-shaped. Comfrey is mostly cultivated in the wilder parts of the garden, although the variegated foliage varieties are excellent for general border decoration. They are tolerant of most soil conditions and situations.

RECOMMENDED SPECIES AND VARIETIES

S. asperum (prickly comfrey) Showy flowers, up to 1 cm (⅜ in) long, appear in early and mid summer, opening pink and then turning blue or lavender. This is an untidy branched plant with bristly stems clothed in coarse, mid green, oval or lance-shaped leaves up to 25 cm (10 in) long. HEIGHT & SPREAD 1-1.5×1 m (3-5×3 ft).

S. caucasicum A soft, hairy plant with oval or lance-shaped mid green leaves up to 20 cm (8 in) long. The arching spikes of reddish purple then blue flowers, up to 8 cm (3¼ in) long, appear in early summer. HEIGHT & SPREAD 60×60 cm (2×2 ft).

'Eminence' has velvety leaves which are mid green, tinted with grey and short branched spikes of rich blue flowers. It reaches 45 cm (1½ ft) in height and spread.

S. 'Goldsmith' This hybrid is grown for its broadly lance-shaped leaves, up to 15-25 cm (6-10 in) long, which are dark green, edged and splashed with gold and cream. In early spring, pink and white or blue flowers, 1 cm (⅜ in) long, appear. HEIGHT & SPREAD 30×45 cm (1×1½ ft).

▼ *Symphytum* 'Goldsmith'

S. 'Hidcote Blue' The soft blue flowers start red in bud and eventually turn white. They are produced in profusion during late spring and early summer. This vigorous plant has rough oval or lance-shaped leaves up to 20 cm (8 in) long. HEIGHT & SPREAD 45×45 cm (1½×1½ ft).

S. 'Langthorn's Pink' Bright pink flowers, 1 cm (⅜ in) long, are produced in clusters all summer long on this tall plant. The coarse elliptical or lance-shaped mid green leaves are up to 20 cm (8 in) long. HEIGHT & SPREAD 1.2×1 m (4×3 ft).

S. officinale (common comfrey) The leaves of this plant can be added in layers to the compost heap rather like a compost activator. They are oval to broadly lance-shaped, coarse, mid green and up to 25 cm (10 in) long. The small, late spring and summer flowers are yellowish cream, pink or purple. HEIGHT & SPREAD 1.2×1 m (4×3 ft).

The flowers of var. *ochroleucum* are pale yellow.

S. orientale A profusion of white flowers, up to 2 cm (¾ in) long, are borne in forked clusters in late spring and summer. The oval or heart-shaped, dull green leaves are hairy and up to 15 cm (6 in) long. A resilient plant for difficult soil conditions. HEIGHT & SPREAD 60×60 cm (2×2 ft).

S. peregrinum see *S.* × *uplandicum*

S. 'Rubrum' Small red flowers are produced freely throughout summer. The mid green leaves are broadly lance-shaped to oval and up to 20 cm (8 in) long. This coarse plant makes good ground cover. HEIGHT & SPREAD 60×45 cm (2×1½ ft).

S. × *uplandicum* (syn. *S. peregrinum*) Hairy, lance-shaped or oval, coarse mid green leaves, up to 30 cm (12 in) long, are carried on stout bristly stems. Flowers, 1 cm (⅜ in) long, are rose in bud and turn blue-purple. They appear in late spring and early

▲ *Symphytum* × *uplandicum*

summer. A tall, branching plant. HEIGHT & SPREAD 90-120×60 cm (3-4×2 ft).

'Variegatum' has leaves boldly edged with cream-white. It reaches a height of 1 m (3 ft) and spread of 45 cm (1½ ft) or more.

CULTIVATION Plants are easily grown in any soil that retains moisture during summer. Plant at any time from autumn to spring in sun or partial shade. Remove faded flowers and foliage. Feed sparingly with a slow-release fertiliser each spring.

PROPAGATION Divide established plants in spring. Sow seed of the species in a cold-frame during late summer or spring.

PESTS AND DISEASES Usually trouble free.

Symplocos
Symplocaceae

Symplocos paniculata

This large, sub-tropical genus has only one reliably hardy species, *Symplocos paniculata*. A deciduous shrub or small tree, it is grown for its fragrant flowers and decorative fruits. Native to E Asia from the Himalayas to China and Japan.

RECOMMENDED SPECIES

S. paniculata Small, scented, 5-petalled, white flowers are borne in rounded clusters, 2.5-5 cm (1-2 in) wide, in late spring and

▲ *Symplocos paniculata*

early summer. The oval, bright blue or black berries, 6 mm (¼ in) long, ripen in autumn, but only occur where 2 or more bushes are planted together. Oval, slightly hairy, light yellowish green leaves, up to 9 cm (3½ in) long, have deeply marked veins and finely toothed margins. HEIGHT & SPREAD 1 m×60 cm (3×2 ft) after 5 years, ultimately 3 m (10 ft) tall.

CULTIVATION Plant in a warm, sheltered position in full sun in any fertile, deep soil.

PROPAGATION Sow seed in autumn; germination may be slow.

PRUNING None usually required.

PESTS AND DISEASES Usually trouble free.

Syngonium
Goosefoot plant
Araceae

These tropical, evergreen, scrambling and climbing plants are grown for their decorative foliage, as pot plants in a house, conservatory or greenhouse. They enjoy a position out of direct sunlight. A high level of humidity is desirable along with a minimum temperature of 15°C (59°F). Native to Central and S America.

RECOMMENDED SPECIES AND VARIETIES

S. podophyllum (syn. *Nephythytis triphylla*) A scrambling, woody stemmed climbing plant popularly grown as a houseplant on a mossed pole or trellis. The leaves are bright green with prominent pale green veins. They are arrow-shaped when young, becoming lobed as they mature, and can grow very large – as much as 30 cm (12 in) long and 20 cm (8 in) across or more. Plants occasionally produce greenish white to cream or rarely yellow arum-like flowers up to 11 cm (4¼ in) long, at which time the rest of the plant sometimes develops a reddish tinge. HEIGHT & SPREAD 2 m × 60 cm (6½ × 2 ft).

▲ *Syngonium podophyllum*

S

'Emerald Gem' has dark green, fleshy, shiny leaves that are strikingly arrow-shaped when young. **'Silver Knight'** has silvery green leaves. **'Variegatum'** has bright green leaves splashed with pale green.

CULTIVATION Grow in pots out of direct sunlight in a richly organic, soil-less compost. Repot in fresh compost at least every other year. Provide a support for the climbing stems. Mist plants regularly with clear water, especially in spring and summer. Clean the leaves regularly with a little warm milk and water applied with cotton wool. Water moderately in spring and summer, sparingly in autumn and winter. Feed during summer with a liquid houseplant fertiliser. Remove faded leaves.

PROPAGATION Take leaf-bud or stem-tip cuttings during summer.

PESTS AND DISEASES Mealy bugs and scale insects can be a nuisance, along with red spider mites, especially when growing conditions are too dry.

Synthyris
Kittentails
Scrophulariaceae

Synthyris stellata

Small bluish purple flowers crowded on the narrow spikes of these plants make a decorative impact in the spring garden. The genus is composed of alpines and woodland evergreen perennials and many are fairly easy to grow. The plants retain appealing basal rosettes of toothed and rounded leaves throughout the winter. The recommended species is a woodland plant that flourishes in well-drained, moist soil in partial shade at the edge of a shrub border, in a peat garden or in an open wooded area. The genus is native to western N America.

RECOMMENDED SPECIES

S. stellata Dense, narrow flower spikes, up to 15 cm (6 in) long, are carried on erect stems in mid spring. The small, bluish purple flowers form shallow bells on short tubes and the 4 deep lobes are irregularly and finely toothed round the edges, almost as if they had been gnawed by a tiny rodent. Two prominent stamens protrude beyond the tubular mouths of the flowers and stand out noticeably as they are whitish against the blue petals. The stems of the clump-forming plant are almost leafless, the few leaves that do grow are almost stalkless. Basal rosettes of heart or kidney-shaped, thick mid green leaves, up to 5 cm (2 in) across, are deeply and doubly toothed or shallowly divided and taper gradually towards the tip. The seed capsule, up to 8 mm (⅜ in) across, is almost round. In its native habitat it grows on stream banks and at the edges of woodland. HEIGHT & SPREAD 15–30 × 30 cm (6–12 × 12 in).

CULTIVATION Plant in spring in leafy soil that is moist and well drained. The addition of grit to the soil is beneficial. Woodland plants grow best in a partially shaded position, alpine plants do best in a rock garden in sun. Plants will grow in dry, poorish soil but are less robust and make less of a show.

PROPAGATION Divide the fibrous roots after flowering. Alternatively, sow seeds in spring or when ripe.

PESTS AND DISEASES Usually trouble free.

Syringa
Lilac
Oleaceae

Syringa microphylla 'Superba'

A glorious display of late-spring flowers is provided by these hardy deciduous shrubs and small trees. The small tubular flowers, borne in clusters, are available in a wide palette of colours and many are sweetly scented. All the species listed have mid to dark green leaves. Easy to grow in a sunny position and thriving in town gardens, lilacs make good specimen or border shrubs. Bushier species and varieties can also be grown as informal hedges and screens. Native to E Asia and SE Europe.

RECOMMENDED SPECIES AND VARIETIES

S. meyeri **'Palibin'**♀ The lavender-pink flowers of this rounded, compact shrub are borne in numerous small clusters, about 5 cm (2 in) across, in late spring to early summer. The elliptic leaves grow to 3 cm (1¼ in) long. This dense shrub is slow-growing and is suitable for any garden. HEIGHT & SPREAD 30 × 20 cm (12 × 8 in) after 5 years, ultimately 1.2 m (4 ft) tall.

S. microphylla **'Superba'**♀ A slender-branched bush that bears small, erect heads of deliciously fragrant, rosy pink flowers that are deeper in bud; these appear in late to early spring, then often again in early autumn. The mid green leaves, up to 5 cm (2 in) long, are oval and pointed. HEIGHT & SPREAD 1 × 1 m (3 × 3 ft) after 5 years, ultimately 1.8 m (6 ft) tall.

S. × *persica*♀ (Persian lilac) The fragrant, soft-lilac flowers are carried in small, erect

▼ *Syringa microphylla 'Superba'*

▲ *Syringa reflexa*

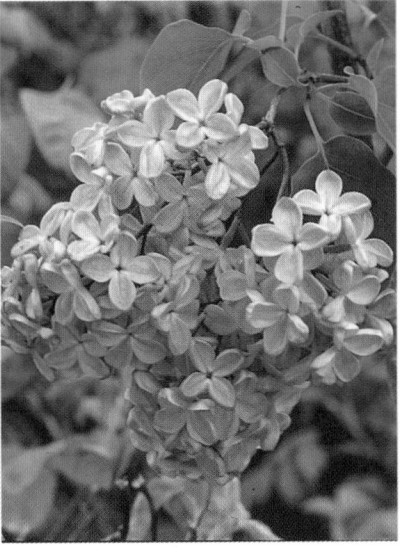

▲ *Syringa × hyacinthiflora* 'Esther Staley'

heads up to 7.5 cm (3 in) across in late spring and early summer. Tightly packed, narrow leaves, up to 5 cm (2 in) long, are often lobed. This rounded, slender-branched shrub is free-flowering and has a semi-arching habit. HEIGHT & SPREAD 1.2×1 m (4×3 ft) after 5 years, ultimately 1.8 m (6 ft) tall.

'**Alba**' has white flowers and the branches are more slender.

S. reflexa♀ The flowers are rich purplish pink outside, whitish within. These are borne in abundance in late spring to early summer in densely packed, drooping, cylindrical plumes up to 20 cm (8 in) long. This very free-flowering, upright shrub has oval to lance-shaped, dark green leaves, up to 20 cm (8 in) long, that have a rough texture. HEIGHT & SPREAD 1.5×1.2 m (5×4 ft) after 5 years, ultimately 3.5 m (12 ft) tall.

Syringa vulgaris

S. vulgaris (common lilac) Richly scented, lilac-coloured flowers are borne erect in dense, pyramidal panicles, between 15–25 cm (6–10 in) long, in late spring to early summer. The ovate to heart-shaped leaves grow to 12 cm (4¾ in) long. A large, upright shrub or small tree. This species and its cultivars are the most commonly grown members of the genus. HEIGHT & SPREAD 1.5×1.2 m (5×4 ft) after 5 years, ultimately 3.5 m (12 ft) tall.

'**Andenken an Ludwig Späth**'♀ (syn. 'Souvenir de Louis Spaeth') Deep wine-red, scented, single flowers are carried in large heads in mid to late spring. This shrub has a strong, spreading habit.

'**Charles Joly**'♀ Dark purplish red, double, scented flowers in mid to late spring. Dark green leaves and an erect habit.

'**Congo**' Dark lilac-red in bud opening to rich pink, single flowers that are strongly scented. The small, graceful heads are very freely produced. Mid to late spring. A rounded bush reaching an ultimate height of 1.8 m (6 ft).

'**Esther Staley**'♀ (× *hyacinthiflora*) Carmine-red buds open to single, fragrant, bright pink flowers in late spring. This

▼ *Syringa vulgaris*

large, free-flowering shrub has numerous slender, erect stems.

'**Firmament**'♀ Pinkish mauve in bud opening to beautiful, fragrant lilac-blue single flowers. Mid spring. Compact habit.

'**Katherine Havemeyer**'♀ Highly fragrant, deep purple-lavender flowers fading to pale lilac-pink are borne in dense pyramidal heads. Late spring. Fairly open habit.

'**Madame Lemoine**'♀ Compact heads of creamy white buds opening to pure white, scented double flowers are carried in compact heads. Mid spring. A broad bush.

'**Michel Buchner**' Large heads of clear lilac, sweetly scented, double flowers. Late spring. Broad, open habit.

'**Mrs Edward Harding**'♀ Semidouble, lilac-red scented flowers. Mid to late spring. Very free-flowering and the best red in this group. Tall and rather loose habit.

'**Primrose**' Graceful, slightly scented heads of small, single, primrose-coloured flowers. Mid spring. Very free-flowering with a compact habit.

'**Sensation**' Narrow heads of purple-red, single flowers that are edged with white are

▼ *Syringa vulgaris* 'Madame Lemoine'

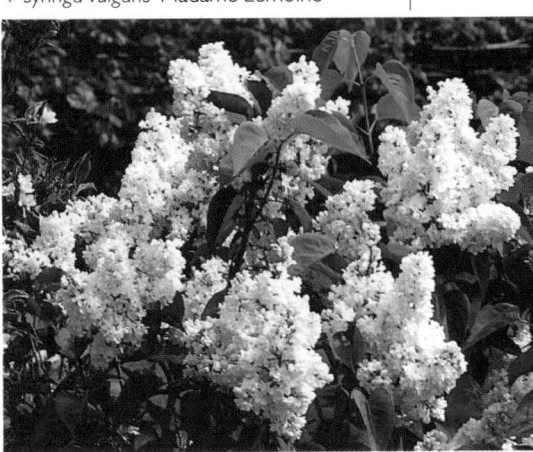

PESTS AND DISEASES Tagetes are susceptible to slug and snail attack, especially during the period immediately after planting if the weather is wet. Aphids may infest the plants. In hot summers, red spider mite may become troublesome.

Grey mould may infect the centres of the flowers of African marigolds in prolonged wet weather, causing the flowerheads to decay and turn brown.

Taiwania
Taxodiaceae

Taiwania cryptomerioides

These conical to columnar, slow-growing evergreen conifers make ideal specimen trees. Their upward-curving branches bear drooping branchlets, covered in needles. Not fully hardy, taiwanias need a warm, humid sheltered site, such as at the foot of a slope or in a moist valley. There is only one species, native to Taiwan, in this genus.

T. cryptomerioides This very beautiful tree grows into a column of silver-grey foliage. The drooping whip-like branchlets are covered with sharp, pointed needles that curve forwards towards the branch tip. Male and female flowers are borne together on the same tree in spring. The male flowers are tiny, tight green clusters, often bunched together, while the female flowers are tiny single green clusters. The round cones rarely appear in Britain but if seen, they are 1.5 cm (½ in) across, green at first, ripening to brown in the autumn. The reddish brown bark peels off the trunk in loose strips. Long cold spells can kill the foliage but the tree will recover given time. HEIGHT & SPREAD 2.7×1.2 m (9×4 ft) after 20 years, ultimately 12 m (40 ft).

CULTIVATION Plant specimens that are at least 30 cm (1 ft) tall in late spring. The trees prefer soil that is acid and moist but well drained, although they will grow on the heaviest of clay soils.

Choose a site sheltered from the morning sun in winter but which is particularly warm and humid in summer. A position sheltered from cold winds is also necessary.

PROPAGATION Sow seed in a coldframe in spring. Alternatively take hardwood cuttings in autumn.

PRUNING None usually required except the removal of dead or frost-damaged wood.

PESTS AND DISEASES Usually trouble free.

▲ *Taiwania cryptomerioides*

Tamarix
Tamarisk
Tamaricaceae

Tamarix tetrandra

Tiny pink flowers in slender plume-like sprays cover these hardy, deciduous small trees and shrubs. Small, scale-like leaves are carried on fine, slender branches that bend easily in the wind. These plants are ideal for seaside locations as they tolerate salt and strong winds and can act as effective windbreaks. They are unsuitable for heavy soil but are tolerant of drought.

RECOMMENDED SPECIES AND VARIETIES

T. ramosissima (syn. *T. pentandra*) Feathery pink flowers in tresses 7.5 cm (3 in) long are borne on the current season's shoots in late summer. The tiny leaves are pale grey-green. Young branches are green but soon age to red-brown. Plants grow rapidly to their maximum height then spread sideways by arching outwards. They have a suckering habit. HEIGHT & SPREAD 5×6 m (16×20 ft) after 10 years, also the ultimate size.

'**Pink Cascade**' produces a spectacular display of pink flowers which can obscure all the mid green foliage in late summer.

'**Rubra**'♀ (syn. 'Summer Glow') produces a mass of deep pink flowers.

T. tetrandra♀ Numerous feathery sprays, 5 cm (2 in) long, of light pink flowers are borne on the previous season's wood during

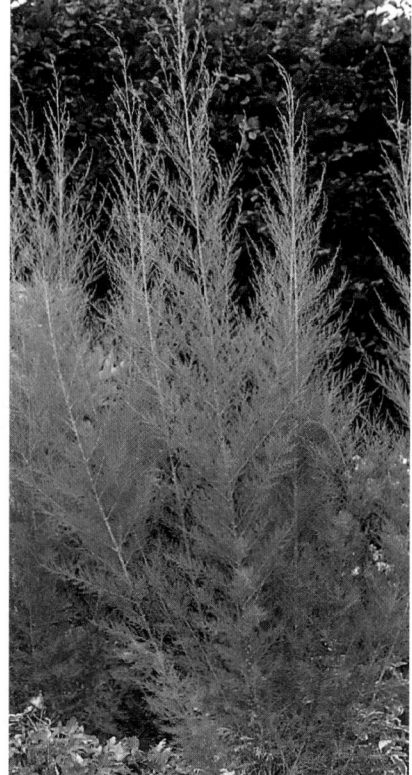

▲ *Tamarix ramosissima*

spring and early summer. The shrub forms a loose, open bush with arching branches, covered in tiny, pale green leaves. HEIGHT & SPREAD 4×4 m (13×13 ft) after 10 years, also the ultimate size.

CULTIVATION Plant between late autumn and early spring. The plants grow best in full sun in any well-drained soil.

PROPAGATION Take hardwood cuttings in autumn, preferably using a sandy rooting medium. Plant out the following spring.

PRUNING For use as a windbreak, cut back *T. ramosissima* hard in spring once new growth commences and cut back *T. tetrandra* after flowering. This will also encourage strong flowering shoots.

PESTS AND DISEASES Usually trouble free.

▲ *Tamarix tetrandra*

Tanacetum
Compositae

Tanacetum coccineum 'Brenda'

Yellow disc florets and white, pink, purple or red ray florets (petals) or button-like yellow flowers highlight the hardy annual and perennial plants in summer. Many have decorative and scented leaves. All the plants require well-drained soil and an open sunny position. Some, including invasive tansy, contribute character to a wild garden or herb garden, while the neat habit of others fits them for a place in a rock garden. The majority embellish a mixed border.

RECOMMENDED SPECIES AND VARIETIES

T. argenteum A mass of small, white, daisy-like flowers with yellow centres is produced from mid to late summer. This low-growing, mat-forming perennial has finely cut and crimped silvery grey leaves, up to 7.5 cm (3 in) long. HEIGHT & SPREAD 20×30 cm (8×12 in).

The finely cut, silvery foliage of ssp. *canum* forms tight, low mounds. The plant, ideal for a rock garden, grows to 15 cm (6 in) tall. Remove the flowers to retain the quality of the foliage.

T. balsamita (alecost, costmary) Tiny yellow disc flowers, surrounded by white ray florets, bloom in profusion in late summer on this aromatic herbaceous perennial, which is suitable for a herb garden. The elliptical mid green leaves, up to 25 cm (10 in) long, have rounded toothed edges. HEIGHT & SPREAD 75×45 cm (30×18 in).

The flowers of ssp. *balsamita* (syn. var. *tanacetoides*) look like tiny yellow buttons because there are no white ray florets round the yellow centres. The leaves and stems of ssp. *balsamitoides* (syn. *tomentosum*) are hairy. It has yellow, button-like flowers.

T. cinerariifolium (Dalmatian pyrethrum) White ray florets fan out from yellow centres on flowers, up to 2.5-4 cm (1-1½ in) across, that bloom from mid to late summer. This slender-stemmed herbaceous perennial has deeply cut, lance-shaped, pungent, grey-green leaves, up to 20 cm (8 in) long, with white downy undersides. HEIGHT & SPREAD 45×30 cm (18×12 in).

T. coccineum (syn. *Pyrethrum roseum*) (pyrethrum) Bold yellow centres contrast with white, pink, purple and red ray florets on single flowers, up to 7.5 cm (3 in) across, produced in late spring and early summer. Robust, erect stems carry finely divided,

▲ *Tanacetum coccineum 'James Kelway'*

bright green, aromatic leaves, up to 10 cm (4 in) long, on this hardy herbaceous perennial. HEIGHT & SPREAD 75×60 cm (30×24 in).

'Brenda'♀ carries magenta-pink flowers; 'Bressingham Red' has bright red flowers; 'Eileen May Robinson'♀ produces pink flowers; 'James Kelway'♀ displays deep scarlet flowers; 'Robinson's Pink' has pink flowers; 'Robinson's Red' has red flowers; 'Snow Cloud' has white flowers. Apart from 'Eileen May Robinson', which grows to 75 cm (30 in) tall, all these varieties reach a height of 60 cm (24 in) tall.

T. corymbosum Groups of 3-15 yellow-centred white flowers, up to 1 cm (⅜ in) across, appear in mid summer on this herbaceous perennial. Much divided and sharply toothed, mid green leaves, up to 5 cm (2 in) long, are borne on erect branching stems. HEIGHT & SPREAD 60×45 cm (24×18 in).

▲ *Tanacetum densum*

T. densum Tiny, yellow, daisy-like flowers, bloom on heads, 7.5 cm (3 in) across, from mid to late summer. This shrubby, clump-forming perennial is evergreen in sheltered areas. The oval silvery grey-green leaves, up to 5 cm (2 in) long, are deeply cut. HEIGHT & SPREAD 30×30 cm (18×18 in).

The leaves of ssp. *amani* are grey and hairy. Remove the yellow flowers to retain the quality of the foliage. The plant reaches a height of 20 cm (8 in).

T. haradjanii Terminal clusters of small, bright yellow, button-like late-summer flowers are supported by broadly lance-shaped and much divided silvery grey

leaves, up to 5 cm (2 in) long. A rock garden is a suitable place to grow this hardy, shrubby, mat-forming evergreen perennial. HEIGHT & SPREAD 30×30 cm (12×12 in).

T. macrophyllum Small white blossoms with a yellowish tinge appear in dense clusters in mid summer. This hardy herbaceous perennial, suitable for a wild garden, has coarsely toothed lance-shaped leaves, up to 20 cm (8 in) long, HEIGHT & SPREAD 90×60 cm (36×24 in).

T. parthenium 'Aureum' (syn. *Chrysanthemum parthenium*) (golden feverfew) The profuse single, daisy-like white blossoms, up to 1 cm (⅜ in) across, are tinged with gold and appear throughout summer. Remove them to retain the quality of the bright golden, deeply cut, oval leaves, up to 7.5 cm (3 in) long. This shrubby perennial is short-lived. HEIGHT & SPREAD 45×30 cm (18×12 in).

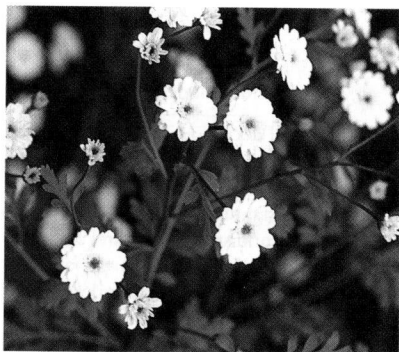

▲ *Tanacetum parthenium 'Plenum'*

'Plenum' has white double flowers. 'White Bonnet' has ivory white double flowers and grows to 30 cm (12 in) tall.

T. vulgare (tansy) Clusters of tiny button-like mustard-yellow flowers appear from late summer to autumn. This strongly aromatic hardy herbaceous perennial has much divided and deeply toothed, bright green, lance-shaped leaves, up to 15 cm (6 in) long. It spreads prettily in a wild garden, but needs careful placing in a herb garden. HEIGHT & SPREAD 1.2 m×60 cm (4×2 ft).

Up to 60 cm (24 in) tall, var. *crispum* (crisp-leafed tansy) has crisp, fern-like leaves. 'Silver Lace' has silvery variegated foliage that fades as summer progresses.

▲ *Tanacetum vulgare*

Tellima
Fringe cup
Saxifragaceae

A hardy, herbaceous perennial, flowering in late spring and early summer, tellima is a woodland native of western N America, as far north as Alaska. Suited to cool, shady conditions, it associates well with hardy ferns. Easily grown and forming compact clumps, tellima plants can be massed to create good ground cover. The genus has only one species.

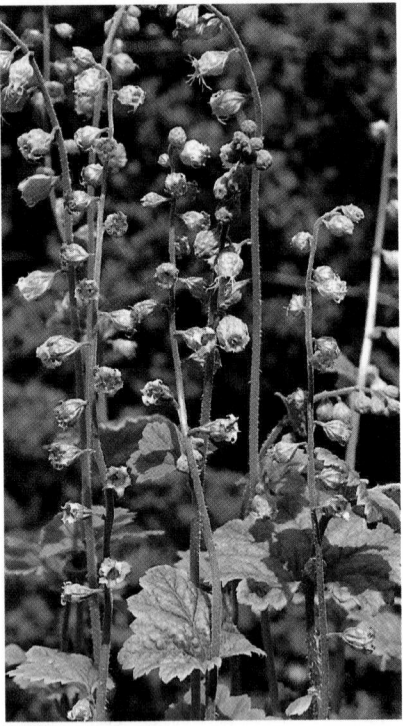

▲ *Tellima grandiflora*

Tellima grandiflora Upright stems are dotted with small, bell-shaped flowers, about 6 mm (¼ in) across, with fringed, yellow-green petals, which turn deep pink with age. The fruit is a small green capsule. The light green, hairy leaves at the base of the stems are rounded with several triangular lobes and grow to 10 cm (4 in) wide. Tellima is frost-hardy but may be damaged in cold northern gardens. HEIGHT & SPREAD 75×30 cm (2½×1 ft).

Odorata Group has flowers with a slight but distinct sweet scent. **Rubra Group** (syn. 'Purpurea') contains forms in which the foliage is tinged with purplish red especially in winter.

CULTIVATION Plant in any well-drained soil in a cool, partially shaded position. Tellimas are fairly tolerant of dry soil but do better in slightly moist conditions. They tolerate fairly deep shade but produce fewer flowers.
PROPAGATION Divide plants in early autumn or spring.
PESTS AND DISEASES Usually trouble free.

Teucrium
Germander
Labiatae

Teucrium polium

Noted for their aromatic foliage, these summer-flowering, evergreen shrubs or sub-shrubs have a neat habit. The flowers have a prominent five-lobed lower lip, but lack an upper lip. Small species make excellent rock-garden plants while taller plants make good hedging or specimen plants in a warm border. Not all species are reliably hardy and they thrive in the warmer parts of Britain. Most are native to the Mediterranean region.

RECOMMENDED SPECIES AND VARIETIES

T. aroanium The silver-grey leaves of this sub-shrub are up to 2.5 cm (1 in) long. Dull purple-blue flowers, up to 2 cm (¾ in) long, are borne in plentiful clusters at the leaf nodes. Frost hardy. HEIGHT & SPREAD 10×30 cm (4×12 in).

T. chamaedrys The lustrous green, holly-like leaves, 2 cm (¾ in) long, are grey-felted beneath. The rosy-purple flowers, up to 1.5 cm (½ in) long, are held in loose spikes. It is a hardy sub-shrub, with an upright habit. HEIGHT & SPREAD 30×30 cm (1×1 ft).

'Nanum' is a compact, dwarf plant. 'Rose Carpet' has rich bluish rose flowers. 'Variegatum' has yellow-blotched leaves.

T. fruticans Loose spikes of pale blue flowers, 2.5 cm (1 in) long, appear in summer. The aromatic grey-green leaves are up to 2.5 cm (1 in) long. Both the leaves and arching stems are covered in silver-grey down. This bushy shrub is not reliably hardy. HEIGHT & SPREAD 1.2×4 m (4×13 ft).

'Azureum'♀ has rich purple flowers.

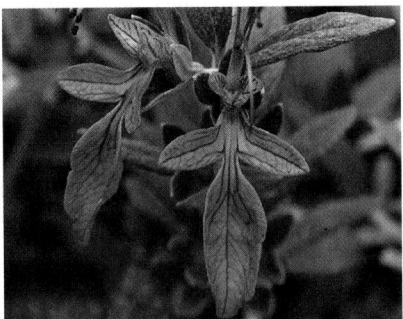

▲ *Teucrium fruticans*
▼ *Teucrium fruticans* 'Compactum'

'Compactum' reaches a height of 45 cm (1½ ft) and a spread of 30 cm (1 ft).

T. hircanicum The stems of this hardy sub-shrub are clad in shaggy hairs, and hold greyish, broadly lanceolate leaves 2.5 cm (1 in) long. The reddish purple flowers, 2 cm (¾ in) long, in short dense spikes appear in late summer to early autumn. HEIGHT & SPREAD 60 cm×1 m (2×3 ft).

▲ *Teucrium polium*

T. polium The deep green oak-like leaves of this low hummock-forming sub-shrub are about 2 cm (¾ in) long. The flowers are red-purple, yellow or white. They are about 6 mm (¼ in) long and borne in dense heads at the tips of the shoots. Not reliably hardy. HEIGHT & SPREAD 20×30 cm (8×12 in).

'Album' has white flowers.

T. pyrenaicum The almost circular, bristly and bluntly toothed dull green leaves of this semi-evergreen sub-shrub grow to 3 cm (1¼ in) across. Bicoloured purple and cream flowers 2 cm (¾ in) long are held in profuse dense terminal heads. This hardy plant has a creeping habit. HEIGHT & SPREAD 10×30 cm (4×12 in).

T. scorodonia The crinkled, triangular grey-green leaves are up to 7 cm (2¾ in) long. Greenish yellow, occasionally pure white flowers, up to 2 cm (¾ in) long, are held in one-sided spikes. This is one of the few species to favour acid soils and cool places, and spreads on woody rhizomes. It is only reliably hardy in mild areas. HEIGHT & SPREAD 30×45 cm (1×1½ ft).

'Crispum' has puckered leaf edges. In 'Crispum Marginatum' these are coloured white to pink.

T. subspinosum Dark green leaves, 5 mm (¼ in) long, grow on spiny silver-grey branches. The clear pink flowers are 3 mm (⅛ in) long and are borne in pairs at the shoot tips. This congested, rounded bush is fully hardy, but shoot tips may die back in winter. HEIGHT & SPREAD 15×20 cm (6×8 in).

CULTIVATION Plant in autumn or spring in

▼ *Teucrium scorodonia* 'Crispum'

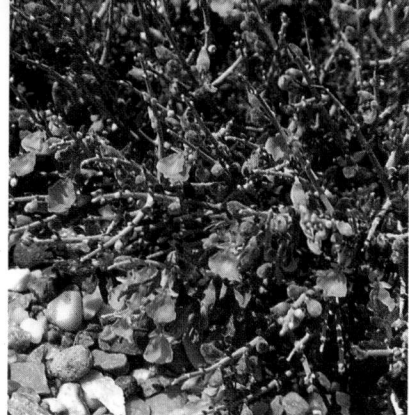

▲ *Teucrium subspinosum*

almost any reasonably light soil in a sunny position. Grow the smaller, less hardy species in pots of John Innes No.2 in a cool greenhouse or alpine house.

PROPAGATION Take semi-ripe cuttings in mid to late summer. Alternatively, divide *T. scorodonia* in early spring or sow seed in late winter or early spring.

PRUNING Trim *T. fruticans* to shape in spring. Otherwise none is required.

PESTS AND DISEASES Usually trouble free.

Thalictrum
Ranunculaceae

Lacy grey-green summer foliage highlights these hardy herbaceous perennials. Airy clusters of flowers appear from early to mid summer. The stamens often form prominent tassels, which impart a charming fluffy aspect. Among the recommended species are tall plants for a mixed border or woodland edge, and small plants for a rock garden or trough.

The plants are slender and generally upright, with leaves made up of many small, lobed leaflets. Most do best in a well-drained soil and a sunny or lightly shaded site. *Thalictrum kiusianum* requires an acid soil and a cool spot. *T. minus* may become invasive in a rich, very fertile soil.

RECOMMENDED SPECIES AND VARIETIES

T. aquilegiifolium A mass of fluffy lilac-purple flowers, 20-30cm (8-12in) across, appear on stiff, erect stems. The coarsely divided grey-green leaves grow up to 30cm (12in) long. HEIGHT & SPREAD 1m×30cm (3×1ft).

The flowers of var. *album* are creamy white. 'Thundercloud' ('Purple Cloud')♀ has violet-purple flowers.

T. chelidonii **dwarf form** The rose-lilac flowers, 2cm (¾in) across, are borne in branched clusters up to 5cm (2in) across. Mid green leaves, up to 45cm (18in) long, are composed of multitoothed leaflets. HEIGHT & SPREAD 30×20cm (12×8in).

T. delavayi♀ (syn. *T. dipterocarpum*) Small, semi-pendulous purple flowers with protruding yellow stamens are borne in loose branched clusters. The thin stems of this plant are often grown over shrubs rather than supported by stakes. The grey-green leaves, up to 36cm (14in) long, consist of

many 3-lobed leaflets. HEIGHT & SPREAD 1.5m×60cm (5×2ft).

'Hewitt's Double'♀ has masses of deep purple double flowers.

T. dipterocarpum see *T. delavayi*

T. diffusiflorum Large semi-pendent lilac flowers, 2cm (¾in) across, are borne on branched stems. This short-lived species does best in cool, moist northerly gardens. The grey leaves are deeply divided and up to 20cm (8in) long. HEIGHT & SPREAD 1m×30cm (3×1ft).

T. flavum (meadow rue) Tiny pale yellow flowers are held in fluffy clusters up to 5cm (2in) across. The glaucous blue-green leaves, up to 40cm (16in) long, are composed of lobed leaflets. HEIGHT & SPREAD 1.5m×60cm (5×2ft).

The leaves of ssp. *glaucum*♀ (syn. *T. speciosissimum*) are more glaucous.

T. isopyroides Tiny brown and yellow flowers are held in loose spikes, about 7.5cm (3in) long, on this clump-forming species. The finely divided blue-green leaves grow up to 10cm (4in) long. HEIGHT & SPREAD 20×20cm (8×8in).

T. kiusianum Tiny fluffy pink-mauve flowers are borne in open clusters, up to 5cm (2in) across, on this dainty, low-growing plant. The mid green, 3-lobed leaflets form leaves up to 12.5cm (5in) long. The plant spreads slowly by stolons. HEIGHT & SPREAD 7×20cm (2¾×8in).

T. minus Small, nodding, creamy yellow, occasionally pale purple, flowers are carried in fluffy clusters, about 7.5cm (3in) across, on tall stems. The pale green leaves, up to 25cm (10in) long, are made up of many deeply lobed leaflets. HEIGHT & SPREAD 30×20cm (12×8in).

The var. *adiantifolium* has insignificant purple-green flowers on stems up to 1m (3ft) high and grey-green foliage.

T. speciosissimum
see *T. flavum* ssp. *glaucum*

▼ *Thalictrum minus* var. *adiantifolium*

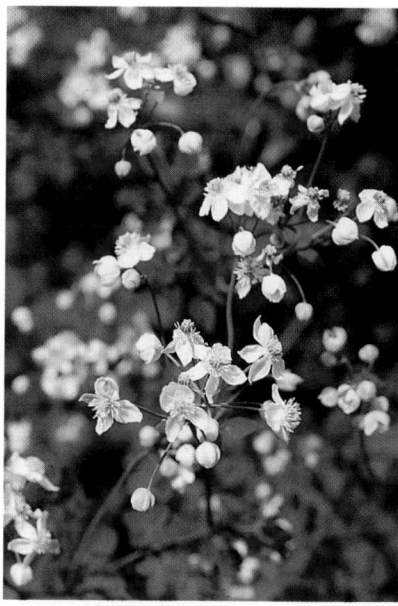

▲ *Thalictrum tuberosum*

T. tuberosum Distinctive creamy white flowers, 3cm (1¼in) across, form open clusters, up to 15cm (6in) long, on tall stems. Mid green, 3-lobed leaflets make up the 12.5cm (5in) long leaves. HEIGHT & SPREAD 30×20cm (12×8in).

CULTIVATION Plant from autumn to spring in reasonably fertile, well-drained soil, in a sunny or lightly shaded spot. *T. kiusianum* needs to be planted in fibrous, acid soil and in a cool, moist spot. Stake tall species.

PROPAGATION Divide clumps and replant in early spring; young plants may take 2 years to become established. Sow fresh seed in autumn in pots. Keep in a coldframe over winter and plant out in spring. Alternatively, sow seed in early spring and grow on the young plants in pots for the first year.

PESTS AND DISEASES Usually trouble free.

Thamnocalamus see BAMBOOS p.79

Thermopsis
Leguminosae

The curious name comes from *thermos*, a Greek word meaning 'hot' which was also an ancient name for the lupin, to which thermopsis flowers bear some resemblance. All are tough and vigorous rhizomatous perennials with erect stems bearing mid green leaves about 6cm (2½in) long, divided into three leaflets, and yellow or purple, pea-type flowers. The species listed below produce 10-20cm (4-8in) spikes of 2.5cm (1in) long bright yellow flowers in summer. They are reliably hardy and easy to grow in a sunny herbaceous border. Native to temperate parts of N America and E Asia.

RECOMMENDED SPECIES AND VARIETIES

T. caroliniana see *T. villosa*

t

T. fabacea see *T. lupinoides*

T. lanceolata Dense spikes of flowers are carried at the top of erect, hairy stems from late spring to early summer. The flowers are followed by curved woolly pods. The leaves are almost stalkless and woolly beneath. HEIGHT & SPREAD 75×60 cm (2½×2 ft).

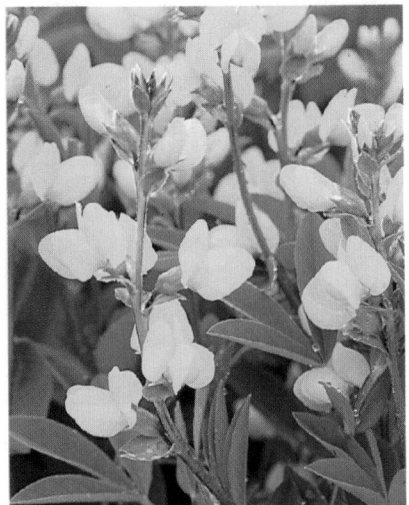

▲ *Thermopsis lupinoides*

T. lupinoides (syn. *T. fabacea*) Spikes of flowers are produced from early to mid summer, followed by straight pods. This plant spreads vigorously, producing stems that are hairy at first, later becoming smooth. The leaves are slightly hairy. HEIGHT & SPREAD 75 cm×1.5 m (2½×5 ft).

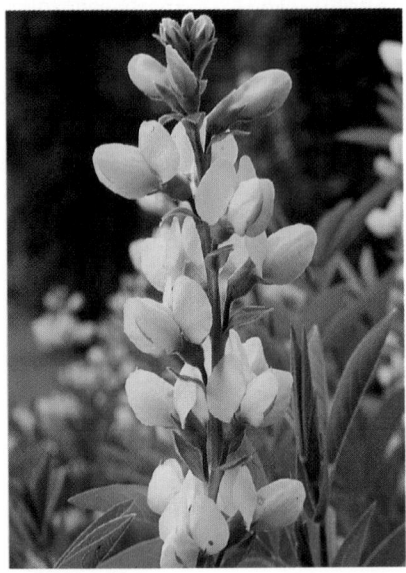

▲ *Thermopsis montana*

T. montana Open flower spikes appear in mid summer. The flowers are followed by straight, hairy pods. The clumps of erect, hairless stems also bear leaves made up of ovate leaflets. HEIGHT & SPREAD 60×60 cm (2×2 ft).

T. villosa (syn. *T. caroliniana*) Dense spikes of flowers appear in early or mid summer,

followed by hairy pods. The robust, erect stems also bear leaves with grey-green undersides. HEIGHT & SPREAD 1.5×1 m (5×3 ft).

CULTIVATION Plant in autumn in any fertile, well-drained soil in a sunny position.

PROPAGATION Divide in spring or sow seed in pots under a coldframe in spring and plant out when large enough to handle.

PESTS AND DISEASES Usually trouble free.

Thistle, carline see *Carlina acanthifolia*
Thistle, Scotch see *Onopordum acanthium*

Thlaspi
Pennycress
Cruciferae

Thlaspi cepaeifolium ssp. rotundifolium

Some of the scree-dwelling alpine species of this genus carry blooms which rival daphnes in the sweetness of their perfume. The four-petalled flowers appear from mid to late spring. In their natural habitat the plants are hardy, evergreen perennials, but they can be difficult to cultivate.

RECOMMENDED SPECIES AND VARIETIES

T. alpinum White flowers, 6 mm (¼ in) across, open successively in loose spikes. The stalked oval leaves, about 1.5 cm (½ in) long, are borne in basal rosettes. This tufted, mat-forming plant dislikes limy soils. Native to the central Alps. HEIGHT & SPREAD 10-15×20 cm (4-6 in×8 in).

The ssp. *brevicaule* is more compact.

T. cepaeifolium ssp. *rotundifolium* Sweetly fragrant, rosy lilac flowers, 1 cm (⅜ in) across, are borne in flattened heads just above the foliage. This is a variable species, but it typically produces tufted rosettes of grey-green, paddle-shaped and fleshy leaves that are 2 cm (¾ in) long. The plant spreads by creeping shoots. Native to an area from the Alps to the Balkans. HEIGHT & SPREAD 5×15 cm (2×6 in).

CULTIVATION Plant in early spring in a raised bed in well-drained soil containing a mixture of two parts fine gravel to one part fibrous soil. Position in a sunny spot. *T. alpinum* does not perform well in limy soil.

PROPAGATION Sow seed in winter and grow the young plants on in pots for the first year.

PESTS AND DISEASES Aphids may attack.

Thorn apple see *Datura*
Thrift see *Armeria*

Thuja
Arbor vitae
Cupressaceae

Thuja occidentalis 'Rheingold'

Trees belonging to this small genus of evergreen conifers are clothed to the ground with densely covered slender branches. Juvenile foliage has a soft, feathery appearance, maturing into flattened sprays of scale-like leaves. The foliage is aromatic when crushed. The larger conical thujas are suitable only for a spacious garden or for hedging, while the dwarf, rounded varieties suit smaller gardens, rockeries or containers.

Native to temperate regions of the Northern Hemisphere, thujas prefer a sunny position in a moist, acid, well-drained soil. Although most withstand shade, particularly *Thuja plicata* and its varieties, the foliage tends to be less vibrant and will not be variegated. Prolonged drought can kill these trees, especially specimens 50-70 years old. All recommended plants are hardy, although *T. orientalis* and its cultivars do best in a sheltered position.

RECOMMENDED SPECIES AND VARIETIES

T. occidentalis (American arbor vitae, white cedar) Slender branches are covered with flattened sprays of small scale-like foliage, glossy yellowish green above and matt green below. Oblong, upright cones consist of 8-10 overlapping scales joined at the base and measuring 1 cm (⅜ in) long. Yellow-green at first, the cones turn brown in autumn. This is a tidy tree when young, taking on a more open, conical shape within 5 years. HEIGHT & SPREAD 2×1 m (6½×3 ft) after 20 years, ultimately 20 m (66 ft) tall.

'Danica'♀ quickly becomes an almost round, dwarf bush. After 20 years it is just 50 cm (20 in) high and wide. The branches are all vertically arranged, bearing erect sprays of bright green foliage. It is useful for rock gardens and containers. 'Ericoides' has soft juvenile foliage which is a dull grey-green in summer and turns brown, sometimes purple, in winter. This is a good plant for adding subtle colour and texture variation to a rock garden, and it is very effective with heathers. It grows into a willowy rounded or conical bush, reaching a height of 1 m (3 ft) and spread of 50 cm (20 in) in 20 years. It is easily damaged by snow. 'Golden Globe' forms a rounded dwarf bush bearing golden yellow foliage throughout the year. In 20 years it reaches a diameter of 50 cm (20 in). Probably the

▲ *Thuja occidentalis* 'Golden Globe'

smallest dwarf and rounded thuja of all is **'Hetz Midget'**, which reaches a height and spread of just 25 cm (10 in) in 20 years. Its bright green foliage is carried on stout shoots. **'Holmstrup'**♀ forms a pointed spire of rich green foliage, remaining glossy throughout the year. It is best grown in pots for at least 5 years to establish its shape before planting in its final position. In 20 years it reaches 2.4 m (8 ft) high and 50 cm (20 in) wide. **'Lutea Nana'**♀ produces

▲ *Thuja occidentalis* 'Holmstrup'

dense yellow foliage that bronzes in winter. It will reach 1 m (3 ft) high and 50 cm (20 in) wide in 20 years.

'Rheingold'♀ is a slow-growing bush that varies from egg-shaped to conical. In 20 years it attains a height and spread of 2×1.5 m (6½×5 ft). The colour is a deep gold with amber tints, giving good value in winter. **'Smaragd'** is very similar in size,

▼ *Thuja occidentalis* 'Smaragd'

shape and growth to 'Holmstrup' except that it has bright almost emerald-green foliage. **'Spiralis'** grows into a brilliant blue-green column with spirally arranged branches covered with twisted sprays of foliage. It reaches a height and spread of 3×1.5 m (10×5 ft) after 20 years. The dense foliage of **'Sunkist'** is golden yellow. In summer it has glowing yellow tips. After 20 years it achieves a height and spread of 2×1.5 m (6½×5 ft), eventually growing into a narrowly conical tree, 20 m (66 ft) high and 4 m (13 ft) across at ground level.

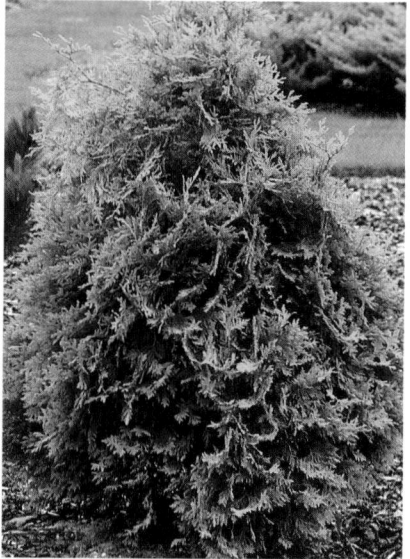

▲ *Thuja occidentalis* 'Sunkist'

T. orientalis (syn. *Platycladus orientalis*) (Chinese arbor vitae) This species grows into a large shrub or small tree with dense erect sprays of pale greeny yellow foliage on almost vertical branches. In mid autumn the plant bears the largest cones in the genus, measuring 2 cm (¾ in) long. They are generally egg-shaped and always upright, with a ring of hooked barbs pointing back around the top. The colour is silvery green ripening to brown. This species is the slowest grow-

▲ *Thuja orientalis* 'Aurea Nana'

ing of all the thujas. HEIGHT & SPREAD 1 m×75 cm (3×2½ ft) after 20 years, ultimately 3 m (10 ft) tall.

'Aurea Nana'♀ forms a bright yellow-green, densely packed globe, reaching 30 cm (12 in) all round after 20 years. The foliage of **'Elegantissima'**♀ is golden yellow at first, then tinged with bronze and eventually greenish yellow in winter. It has a conical shape and reaches 75 cm (2½ ft) high and 50 cm (20 in) wide in 20 years. **'Meldensis'** is egg-shaped and densely clothed with sea-green foliage that turns a deep purple in winter. In 20 years it reaches only 30 cm (12 in) high and 20 cm (8 in) wide, making it suitable for containers. The foliage of **'Rosedalis'** is initially bright yellow, turning sea-green in mid summer and almost plum-purple in winter. It is a dense, slow-growing plant with soft juvenile foliage. In 20 years this egg-shaped bush will be 80 cm (32 in) high with a spread that is about half its height.

▲ *Thuja orientalis* 'Rosedalis'

T. plicata (western red cedar) If left unpruned this species rapidly grows into a large tree, but with regular trimming it makes an excellent, easily controlled, dense hedge. The bright green leaves are marked with a white cross beneath. The upright, egg-shaped cones are about 1.5 cm (½ in) long. HEIGHT & SPREAD 10×2 m (33×6½ ft) after 20 years, ultimately 30 m (100 ft) tall.

The foliage of **'Atrovirens'**♀ is the darkest and shiniest green of all *T. plicata* cultivars. This strictly conical tree is slightly slower growing than the species, but it can still reach a large size, attaining a height and spread of 8×2 m (26×6½ ft) after 20 years. It is very hardy and makes an excellent hedge. **'Aurea'**♀ has yellow-green foliage with an attractive scattering of pure yellow splashes. In 20 years it reaches 10 m (33 ft) high and 2 m (6½ ft) wide. **'Copper Kettle'** is similar to *T. orientalis* 'Aurea Nana' but slightly smaller and the tips of the branches turn

t

coppery in winter. **'Fastigiata'** is the best cultivar for hedging because of its tidy habit. In 20 years a height of 8 m (26 ft) can be attained with a spread of 2 m (6½ ft). However, if left unpruned the tree will eventually be 30 m (100 ft) high and 5 m (16 ft) wide at ground level, ably forming the centrepiece to a large lawn or lining a formal avenue. **'Rogersii'** has dense gold and bronze foliage, becoming more bronzed in winter. It grows into a low, compact and conical bush. In 20 years it will be 1 m (3 ft) high and 1 m (3 ft) wide. The straggly branched young **'Stoneham Gold'**♀ develops into a narrowly conical

Thuja plicata 'Stoneham Gold'

tree after 40 years. Broad sprays of foliage look heavier and coarser than those of the species. The tree is green with coppery gold young shoots. In 20 years it will be 3 m (10 ft) high and 1 m (3 ft) across. A good plant for rock gardens and containers.

The colour of **'Zebrina'** depends on the amount of sunlight it receives, but is typically an alternating pattern of green and golden stripes. The stripes are not as pronounced in the shade.

CULTIVATION Plant young trees between late autumn and early spring in a moist, well-drained acid soil in a sheltered position. For hedges, space the trees 60 cm (2 ft) apart and pinch out growing tips when the required height is reached.

PROPAGATION Take semi-ripe cuttings at any time from autumn to early summer. Insert them in a mixture of equal parts peat and sharp sand and keep them well watered.

PRUNING Older trees can spread by layering as the weight of the foliage causes the lower branches to bow down. If necessary, prune the lower branches right back to the main stem in early spring or mid autumn. Raise the crown by continuing this process to the desired height. If the tree gets too large it can be topped, with professional assistance, but it will continue to grow with an even heavier crown. *T. plicata* and its cultivars used as hedging need to be clipped once a year in early spring.

PESTS AND DISEASES Rabbits eat thujas, and dogs' urine turns the foliage rusty brown. Honey fungus and a newly recognised disease known as canker rot also damage thujas. Canker rot usually infects trees via wounds made by storm damage or pruning: the branches turn yellow and then brown. Remove and burn affected branches as they occur and sterilise all pruning tools.

Thujopsis
Cupressaceae

Thujopsis dolabrata

The branching foliage of this tidy-looking, hardy coniferous tree is highly distinctive, and so dense that the main stem cannot be seen, even in young plants. The tree is conical and is most suitable for large gardens as it will overwhelm anything near it. It can be trained to form a dense hedge. There is only one species in the genus. Native to Japan.

Thujopsis dolabrata♀ (hiba, false arbor vitae) The foliage is made up of tightly packed overlapping scales about 4 mm (⅛ in) across, forming flattened sprays. The upper surface is dark green to yellow, quite polished and waxy looking. Underneath each leaf scale is a pure white, comma-shaped mark. Cones are produced in autumn. HEIGHT & SPREAD 2×1 m (6½×3 ft) after 10 years, ultimately 15 m (50 ft) tall.

▲ *Thujopsis dolabrata*

'Aurea' usually has golden yellow variegated foliage, although some specimens have only slight variegation that can revert to green. **'Nana'** has smaller, more tightly packed leaf scales than the species. It reaches a height of 45 cm (1½ ft) and a spread of 2 m (6½ ft), and forms a flat-topped, ground-hugging dwarf plant. The foliage sprays spread outwards from the centre then curve sharply upwards towards the tips. It is a good plant for rock gardens or as ground cover. **'Variegata'** has creamy white variegation, but it often reverts to pure green.

CULTIVATION Plant in spring or autumn on any moist but well-drained soil. Site variegated plants in full sun, although the green varieties are shade tolerant.

PROPAGATION Take semi-ripe cuttings in late summer and early autumn.

PRUNING Little pruning is required. Topping should be avoided.

PESTS AND DISEASES Usually trouble free.

Thunbergia
Clock vine
Acanthaceae

These strongly growing annual and perennial climbers bear abundant, brightly coloured tubular flowers from spring to autumn. All are tender in Britain and, with the exception of *Thunbergia alata*, need to be grown in a greenhouse or conservatory all year round. Native to Africa and Asia.

RECOMMENDED SPECIES AND VARIETIES

T. alata (black-eyed Susan) Cream to orange flowers, up to 4 cm (1½ in) across and often with a dark purple-brown throat, appear from early summer to mid autumn. The dark green leaves grow up to 7.5 cm (3 in) long. Although perennial, the plant is usually treated as an annual. HEIGHT & SPREAD 2 m×25 cm (6½ ft×10 in).

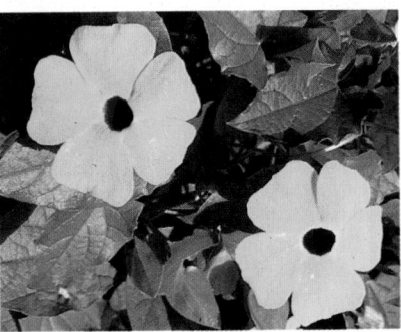

▲ *Thunbergia alata*

T. fragrans **'Angel Wings'** Fragrant white flowers, up to 5 cm (2 in) across, are borne in succession throughout summer. The dark green leaves are triangular, sometimes toothed and up to 7.5 cm (3 in) long. HEIGHT & SPREAD 1.5 m×25 cm (5 ft×10 in).

T. grandiflorum♀ (blue trumpet vine, Bengal clock vine) This vigorous species has sprays of sky-blue, yellow-throated flowers, up to 7.5 cm (3 in) across, from summer to early autumn. The oval mid green leaves, up to 20 cm (8 in) long, have pointed tips. HEIGHT & SPREAD 6×4.5 m (20×15 ft).

'Alba' has white flowers.

T. mysorensis♀ Flowers in hanging sprays, up to 40 cm (16 in) long, appear from spring to autumn. The blooms of this very vigorous species are yellow, with reddish purple, backward-curving lobes. The deep green narrow leaves grow to 15 cm (6 in) long. HEIGHT & SPREAD 6×4.5 m (20×15 ft).

CULTIVATION Grow in pots of loam-based potting compost in a greenhouse or conservatory and provide a minimum winter temperature of 10°C (50°F). Place in full light. Water frequently in spring and summer. Feed weekly with a general-purpose liquid fertiliser. Keep plants dry in winter. Give them wires or canes to climb up. *T. alata* can be grown as a houseplant on a sunny windowsill. It can be moved outdoors in summer to a sunny, sheltered position.

PROPAGATION Sow seed of *T. alata* and *T. fragrans* under glass in early spring. Take softwood cuttings of other species and varieties in spring or early summer. Alternatively, layer them in mid summer.

PRUNING Prune lightly in late winter to early spring, before growth resumes.

PESTS AND DISEASES Aphids and red spider mite may attack plants.

Thyme (culinary herb) see HERBS
    p.333
Thyme see *Thymus*

Thymus
Thyme
Labiatae

Thymes are sun-loving evergreen perennials, grown for their aromatic and often colourful foliage and tiny blooms. All species have two-lipped, tubular flowers, flared at the mouth, and most bloom in mid summer. Thymes are widely used in pavement plantings, rock gardens and at the front of borders; they can also be grown in containers. The prostrate species look good planted where their creeping stems can drape over the edge of a trough or raised bed. *Thymus vulgaris*, *T. × citriodorus*, *T. herba-barona* and *T. pulegioides* are also grown as culinary herbs (see Herbs, p.333). Most thymes are hardy, but replacement is often necessary after three to four years when growth becomes excessive or straggly. They grow throughout the Northern Hemisphere, especially in hot, dry areas.

RECOMMENDED SPECIES AND VARIETIES

T. caespititius This spreading, prostrate plant is grown for its purple to pale pink flowers, borne in loose spikes, 2 cm (¾ in) tall. It has bright green, narrowly spoon-shaped leaves, up to 1 cm (⅜ in) long. HEIGHT & SPREAD 5×36 cm (2×14 in).

'Aureus' has yellow-variegated foliage.

T. cilicicus Profuse lilac-pink to purple flowers are borne in rounded heads, 2 cm (¾ in) across. The narrow, mid green leaves are 6 mm (¼ in) long. This low, shrubby plant is only fully hardy in sheltered gardens. HEIGHT & SPREAD 10×30 cm (4×12 in).

T. × citriodorus (lemon thyme) This upright shrubby hybrid bears lance-shaped, mid green, lemon-scented leaves, 1 cm (⅜ in) long. Lilac flowers are borne in 2.5 cm (1 in) spikes. HEIGHT & SPREAD 15×15 cm (6×6 in).

▼ *Thymus cilicicus*

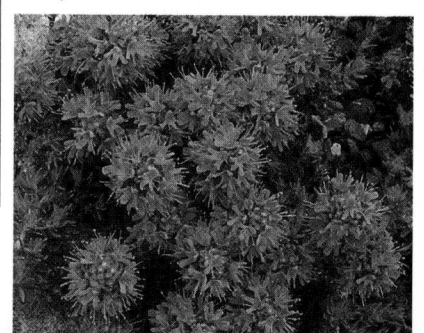

'Archer's Gold', 'Aureus'♀, 'Bertram Anderson'♀, 'Golden King', 'Golden Lemon' and 'Golden Queen' all have leaves suffused with yellow of differing shades. They may suffer from harsh frosts and cold winds. 'Fragrantissimus' has lemon-scented leaves. 'Silver Queen'♀ is variegated with grey and creamy white. 'Variegatus' has green and cream foliage.

T. 'Doone Valley' Dark green leaves, 3 mm (⅛ in) long and blotched with yellow, cover this shrubby plant. The flowers are purple-pink and borne in dense heads. HEIGHT & SPREAD 10×20 cm (4×8 in).

T. 'Hartington Silver' The dark green leaves are 3 mm (⅛ in) long and blotched with cream. Purple-pink flowers are borne in dense heads. The plant has a bushy habit. HEIGHT & SPREAD 10×20 cm (4×8 in).

▲ *Thymus* 'Hartington Silver'

T. herba-barona (caraway thyme) Dark green leaves, up to 6 mm (¼ in) long and scented of caraway, cover this mat-forming plant. The flowers are lilac-pink, in clusters 2 cm (⅛ in) across, on upright stems. HEIGHT & SPREAD 5×45 cm (2×18 in).

T. 'Porlock' The dark, glossy leaves of this mat-forming, prostrate plant are narrowly lance-shaped, and about 1 cm (⅜ in) long. They are densely borne and very fragrant. Abundant mauve, purple or occasionally white flowers are borne in 1.5 cm (½ in) spikes. HEIGHT & SPREAD 5×30 cm (2×12 in).

T. pulegioides (broad-leaf thyme) This shrubby plant forms a low tussock covered with dark green oblong leaves about 1.5 cm (½ in) long. The flowers are purple to pink, in blunt spikes 5-25 cm (2-10 in) long. HEIGHT & SPREAD 7.5×20 cm (3×8 in).

T. serpyllum (creeping thyme, wild thyme) Dense, dark, narrowly lance-shaped leaves clothe this mat-forming species. Squat spikes of purple, mauve or, rarely, white

▼ *Thymus pulegioides*

▲ *Thymus serpyllum* var. *albus*

flowers are profusely borne. HEIGHT & SPREAD 5×30 cm (2×12 in).

The flowers of var. *albus* are white. 'Annie Hall' has shell-pink blooms. Bright crimson flowers appear on var. *coccineus*♀, of which there is a vigorous form, 'Major'. The small and dense 'Elfin' has emerald-green foliage, bearing only a few purple flowers. 'Goldstream' has yellow-variegated foliage. 'Minimus' and 'Minor' (syn. 'Minus') are dwarf forms. 'Pink Chintz'♀ has profuse pink flowers. 'Rainbow Falls' and 'Russetings' have bronzed foliage.

T. vulgaris (common thyme) This wiry-stemmed shrubby plant has very dark green leaves about 1.5 cm (½ in) long. Pink or white flowers are borne in oblong clusters. This species can be quite variable in size. HEIGHT & SPREAD 25×30 cm (10×12 in).

The flowers of var. *albus* are white. 'Erectus' is an upright form. 'Silver Posy' has pale grey foliage.

CULTIVATION Plant in spring or early summer in well-drained, light or gritty soil in a sunny, sheltered spot. Clip back the shrubby types lightly after flowering.

PROPAGATION Divide low-growing species in early spring. Take semi-ripe heeled cuttings from shrubby species in early summer and place in sharp sand. Seed can be sown in pots in autumn or early spring, in a coldframe.

PESTS AND DISEASES Usually trouble free.

Tiarella
Foam flower
Saxifragaceae

Tiarella cordifolia

These hardy evergreen perennials produce small, white or pink flowers in elegant, frothy spires. The foliage is useful as ground cover at the edge of a shady rock garden, shrub bed or rocky bank. The creeping tiarellas, such as *Tiarella cordifolia*, can be too vigorous for all but the largest of rock gardens. The species included here flower from late spring to early summer. Cultivars are valued mainly for variation of foliage.

t

RECOMMENDED SPECIES AND VARIETIES

T. collina see *T. wherryi*

T. cordifolia♀ Spires of white blooms, 23 cm (9 in) tall, rise from the distinctive foliage. The leaves of this mat-forming plant are shallowly lobed, about 7.5 cm (3 in) wide and pale green. They develop a bronze tint with the onset of winter. HEIGHT & SPREAD 23 cm×1 m (9×36 in).

T. polyphylla Nodding spikes of creamy white flowers, 20 cm (8 in) tall, are held above the leaves. Each 3-lobed, mid green leaf is about 5 cm (2 in) wide with toothed edges. The plant spreads on rhizomatous roots to form a clump. HEIGHT & SPREAD 20×30 cm (8×12 in).

'Pink' has pale pink flowers.

T. trifoliata Spires of white blooms, 25 cm (10 in) tall, rise above a strong tuft of leaves. The clump-forming, mid green leaves are 3-lobed and about 4 cm (1½ in) long. HEIGHT & SPREAD 45×30 cm (18×12 in).

▲ *Tiarella wherryi*

T. wherryi♀ (syn. *T. collina*) Pink or white flowers are held in spires, 23 cm (9 in) tall, above the leaves. The clump-forming, palmate leaves are about 7.5 cm (3 in) long, and frequently bear handsome deep claret mottling. HEIGHT & SPREAD 15×30 cm (6×12 in).

'Bronze Beauty' has coppery foliage.
'Pink Foam' has clear pink flowers.

CULTIVATION Plant during autumn or spring in any moisture-retentive, humus-rich garden soil. Tiarellas do best in a cool, shady situation.

PROPAGATION Divide plants in mid autumn or early spring. Alternatively, sow seed in a coldframe in early spring.

PESTS AND DISEASES Usually trouble free.

Tibouchina
Melastomataceae

Brightly coloured flowers highlight this shrub which needs to be grown in a conservatory or greenhouse. Well-drained soil-based compost, indirect sunlight and a minimum of 7°C (45°F) are all essential.

RECOMMENDED SPECIES

T. urvilleana (syn. *T. semidecandra*) (glory bush) Satiny, blue-purple, saucer-shaped flowers, up to 7.5 cm (3 in) across, are produced in clusters from mid summer to early winter. The slender-branched, evergreen

▲ *Tibouchina urvilleana*

shrub has oval, mid to deep green leaves, up to 10 cm (4 in) long. They are soft and velvety and have prominent veins. Native to Brazil. HEIGHT & SPREAD 5×2 m (16×6½ ft) after 5 years. Prune regularly, to restrict size to 2×1 m (6½×3 ft).

CULTIVATION Plant tibouchinas at any time of the year except winter in a pot of John Innes No. 3 compost, or directly into a conservatory or greenhouse border. Water freely in summer but sparingly in winter. Feed with a general liquid fertiliser during spring and summer. Remove faded flowers and foliage.

PROPAGATION Take softwood cuttings in spring or semi-ripe cuttings in summer.

PRUNING Cut back stems which have flowered to within 2 buds of the main branch each spring and remove any unwanted wood. Pinch out the tips of young growths in early summer to encourage branching.

PESTS AND DISEASES Mealy bugs and glasshouse red spider mites are troublesome.

Tickseed see *Bidens frutilolia, Coreopsis*
Tiger flower see *Tigridia pavonia*

Tigridia
Tiger flower
Iridaceae

These frost-tender bulbs produce a succession of short-lived but vividly coloured flowers in summer. Upright or slightly pendulous, the flowers have three large outer tepals that form a bowl, with three much smaller petals inside. Each plant has three to five, flattened, sword-shaped leaves. Native to Guatemala and Mexico.

RECOMMENDED SPECIES

T. pavonia Brightly coloured flowers, 10 cm (4 in) across, are produced in shades of yellow, orange, red, pink and white, with purplish spots and blotches on the bowl, from mid summer to early autumn. HEIGHT 50 cm (20 in).

▲ *Tigrida pavonia*

CULTIVATION Plant bulbs about 10 cm (4 in) deep and 15 cm (6 in) apart in any well-drained soil in a sunny spot when the danger of frost has passed. Dig well-rotted manure into the soil before planting, and keep moist during the growing season. Lift bulbs in autumn after the leaves have died down, and store them in dry sand in a well-ventilated place, with a minimum temperature of 10°C (50°F). Alternatively, plant in containers of well-drained compost. Keep well watered and in a very sunny position. Overwinter the pots in a frost-free place.

PROPAGATION Separate offsets from the bulbs when they are lifted in autumn. Offsets should flower in 2-3 years.

PESTS AND DISEASES Usually trouble free.

Tilia
Lime, linden
Tiliaceae

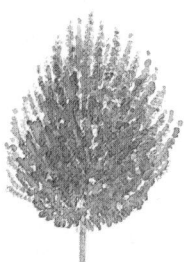

Tilia cordata

Limes are large, stately deciduous trees that are native throughout the temperate regions of the Northern Hemisphere. They are best suited to large gardens. The bright green leaves are generally heart-shaped with a serrated edge and turn pale yellow in autumn. The new shoots often grow in a characteristic zigzag pattern. Numerous small, fragrant pale yellow flowers hang in clusters in summer. Only a few seeds develop fully into hard-shelled grey-green round fruits about 8 mm (⅜ in) across.

RECOMMENDED SPECIES AND VARIETIES

T. cordata♀ (small-leaved lime) This upright tree develops a rounded crown after many years. The heart-shaped leaves grow up to 7.5 cm (3 in) long, and are glossy dark green above, lighter beneath. HEIGHT & SPREAD 7×3 m (23×10 ft) after 20 years, ultimately 20 m (66 ft) tall.

'Greenspire'♀ is a vigorous tree with a narrowly conical habit.

T. × euchlora♀ (Crimean lime) This is a semi-pendent tree with arching branches. The rounded leaves, 10 cm (4 in) long, are dark green above and paler blue-green beneath. They have toothed edges. HEIGHT & SPREAD 7.5×3 m (25×10 ft) after 20 years, ultimately 20 m (66 ft) tall.

T. × europaea (common lime) Much favoured in parks and avenues, this tree can be grown only in the largest gardens. The heart-shaped leaves grow up to 7.5 cm (3 in) long. HEIGHT & SPREAD 7.5×3 m (25×10 ft) after 20 years, ultimately 40 m (130 ft) tall.

'Wratislaviensis'♀ is smaller, with pale yellow young leaves.

T. mongolica♀ (Mongolian lime) This compact, graceful tree of upright habit develops a rounded crown in old age. New leaves open coppery bronze before turning glossy green, then bright yellow in autumn. They are rounded, 7 cm (2¾ in) long and so coarsely toothed that when young they appear to be lobed. It requires a sheltered garden. HEIGHT & SPREAD 5×3 m (16×10 ft) after 20 years, ultimately 10 m (33 ft) tall.

T. 'Petiolaris'♀ (weeping silver lime) This large stately tree with a graceful weeping habit has long arching branches. The leaves, 6–12 cm (2½–4¾ in) long, are rounded, toothed and sometimes almost lobed. They are silvery underneath and are at their most attractive when ruffled by the wind. HEIGHT & SPREAD 14×8 m (46×26 ft) after 20 years, ultimately 32 m (105 ft) tall.

T. platyphyllos (large-leaved lime) This species grows into a monumental tree of rounded habit. The rounded leaves, up to

▼ *Tilia platyphyllos*

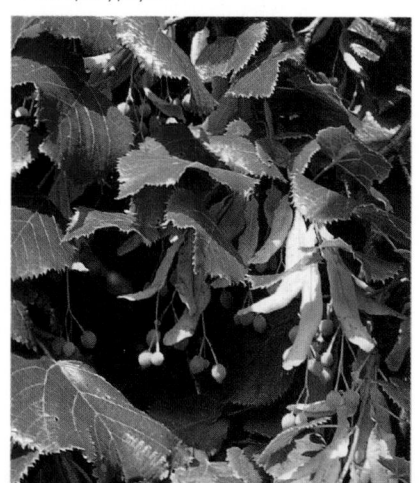

12 cm (4¾ in) long, are dark green above and slightly silvery beneath, with sharply toothed margins. They have soft bristly hairs above and below. HEIGHT & SPREAD 7.5×3 m (25×10 ft) after 20 years, ultimately 35 m (115 ft) tall.

'Fastigiata' has a very upright, rather conical habit and is smaller, reaching an ultimate height of about 13 m (43 ft). 'Rubra'♀ (red-twigged lime) bears bright red-brown new shoots that are very decorative in winter. The effect can be enhanced by frequent pollarding or annual clipping.

T. tomentosa (silver lime) This tree is upright at first and then develops a slightly weeping habit with a rounded crown in old age. The rounded, sharply toothed leaves, up to 10 cm (4 in) long, are dark green above and silvery felted beneath. HEIGHT & SPREAD 7.5×3 m (25×10 ft) after 20 years, ultimately 35 m (115 ft).

'Brabant'♀ has a more upright habit and a dense conical head.

CULTIVATION Plant in late spring – or in autumn in mild gardens – in moist, fertile soil. Lime trees tolerate partial shade, but develop best in full sun.

PROPAGATION Take semi-ripe cuttings in summer or layer in winter.

PRUNING Not generally required, but hard pruning is tolerated in winter. Remove basal shoots from *T. × europaea*.

PESTS AND DISEASES Aphids are attracted to *T. × europaea* and *T. platyphyllos*. Caterpillars eat lime leaves and gall mites attack in late summer. Fungi and canker can cause die-back in older trees, and honey fungus can also occur. Leaf spot may cause trees to defoliate in warm, wet weather.

Tillandsia
Air plant
Bromeliaceae

These tropical evergreen perennials bear exotic flowers at intervals throughout summer. The plants listed are all epiphytes. With the exception of *Tillandsia usneoides*, they have long, narrow leaves that form single rosettes and bear tubular flowers with prominent bracts. Native to tropical and sub-tropical regions of N, Central and S America. Grow in a warm conservatory or greenhouse.

RECOMMENDED SPECIES AND VARIETIES

T. argentea The leaves, covered with white scales and up to 10 cm (4 in) long, form an almost spherical rosette, with a fleshy base. The bright red flowers, up to 2.5 cm (1 in) long, are enclosed by greenish red bracts. HEIGHT & SPREAD up to 25×20 cm (10×8 in).

T. balbisiana The plant forms a dense, bulbous rosette. The tough, whip-like leaves, up to 45 cm (18 in) long, are mid green and edged with purple. Bright red bracts surround violet flowers up to 4 cm (1½ in) long. HEIGHT & SPREAD 45×30 cm (18×12 in).

▲ *Tillandsia balbisiana*

▲ *Tillandsia bulbosa*

T. bulbosa This is a rosette-forming plant with a swollen base and coarse, thread-like leaves, green flushed with dark red and up to 30 cm (12 in) long. Violet-blue flowers, about 4 cm (1½ in) long, partially enclosed by red bracts, are carried in an erect spike. HEIGHT & SPREAD 20×45 cm (8×18 in).

T. caput-medusae Twisted, rolled leaves arise from a hollow, bulb-like base on this bizarre, contorted, rosette-forming plant. The leaves, up to 15 cm (6 in) long, are dark green and covered in grey scales. The plant freely produces long spikes of violet-blue flowers, surrounded by papery red, pink or green bracts, each flower up to 4 cm (1½ in) long. HEIGHT & SPREAD 20×20 cm (8×8 in).

T. lindenii The pointed, arching leaves are mid green lined with reddish brown, grooved, have scaly undersides and are up to 40 cm (16 in) long. The flat, paddle-shaped flower spike, up to 30 cm (12 in) tall, largely consists of compressed, pinkish green leafy bracts from which emerge, 1 or 2 at a time, deep blue pansy-like flowers with white throats. HEIGHT & SPREAD 45×50 cm (18×20 in).

T. usneoides (Spanish moss) This pendulous plant has dense festoons of long, wiry, multibranched stems and linear leaves, about 3 cm (1¼ in) long. Both stems and leaves are covered with silvery white, moisture-retaining scales. The fragrant, greenish yellow or pale blue flowers, 1 cm (⅜ in) long, are borne singly in the leaf bracts. HEIGHT & SPREAD 1 m×15 cm (36×6 in).

CULTIVATION Attach plants to a pad of moss wired to a piece of wood and hang them from the wall or roof of a warm greenhouse or conservatory. Alternatively, grow plants in pots filled with bark chippings. Suspend *T. usneoides* from a wire, without moss or wood. Plants require indirect sunlight, high humidity and a mini-

mum temperature of 10°C (50°F). Water throughout the year and mist regularly.
PROPAGATION Detach offsets in spring.
PESTS AND DISEASES Mealy bugs are sometimes troublesome.

Tithonia
Mexican sunflower
Compositae

Vivid flowers from summer to autumn and striking height are the main characteristics of the Mexican sunflower. This half-hardy annual makes most impact at the back or centre of a wide bed.

RECOMMENDED SPECIES AND VARIETIES
T. rotundifolia (syn. *T. speciosa*) Slightly scented orange flowers, up to 8 cm (3¼ in) across, appear from mid summer to mid autumn. The plant is strong-growing and erect with dark green hairy stems and mid green simple or 3-lobed leaves, up to 30 cm (12 in) long. Seeds of the species are not readily available and cultivars represent it in gardens. HEIGHT & SPREAD 3×1 m (10×3 ft).

'Goldfinger' has rich orange ray florets (petals) round a golden yellow centre. It

▲ *Tithonia rotundifolia*

reaches a height and spread of 75×50 cm (30×20 in). 'Torch' has flame-red ray florets round a golden yellow centre. It reaches 120×50 cm (48×20 in) in height and spread.

T. speciosa see *T. rotundifolia*
CULTIVATION Plant 50 cm (20 in) apart in well-drained soil in a sheltered site in full sun when all risk of frost has passed. Incorporate organic matter, such as garden compost, into very poor soil. In exposed situations, some support should be given to the plants, especially the taller variety 'Torch'. Deadhead regularly.
PROPAGATION Sow seed in early spring. Prick out the strong-growing seedlings individually into 8 cm (3 in) pots. Plant out in the garden when frosts are over.
PESTS AND DISEASES Slugs and aphids may be troublesome.

Ti tree see *Leptospermum scoparium*
Toadflax see *Linaria*
Toadflax, ivy-leaved
  see *Cymbalaria muralis*
Tobacco plant see *Nicotiana*

Tolmiea
Pickaback plant
Saxifragaceae

The single species of this genus is an easy-to-grow evergreen perennial for a shady corner of the garden. Useful for ground cover, it can also be grown indoors on a north-facing windowsill. Native of the cool coniferous forests of western N America.

▲ *Tolmiea menziesii*

Tolmiea menziesii Nodding, dull greenish brown, tubular flowers, about 1.5 cm (½ in) long, are borne in narrow racemes on erect stems from late spring to early summer. The mid green leaves, up to 10 cm (4 in) wide, often produce a small plantlet at the junction of the leafstalk and blade. HEIGHT & SPREAD 60×30 cm (2×1 ft).

'Taff's Gold' ♀ (also sold as 'Variegata') bears leaves that are variably mottled and splashed with yellow and cream.
CULTIVATION Plant in a leafy, moist, acid or neutral soil in full or partial shade in autumn or early spring. Repot houseplants every 1–2 years in early spring. Water freely when actively growing, and feed monthly in spring and summer.
PROPAGATION Divide in spring or detach well-developed plantlets in summer.
PESTS AND DISEASES Usually trouble free.

Tomato see p. 747

Trachelium
Campanulaceae

Tiny tubular flowers mass into showy blossoms on these hardy and half-hardy perennials, enlivening a border or rock garden in spring and summer. *Trachelium caeruleum* is most successful when grown as an annual. Native of the Mediterranean area.
RECOMMENDED SPECIES AND VARIETIES
T. caeruleum ♀ The pale blue or mauve flowers are produced in clusters as wide as 15 cm (6 in) from mid to late summer. The oval to broadly lance-shaped mid green leaves grow to 10 cm (4 in) long. It is good for an annual or mixed border. HEIGHT & SPREAD 90×30 cm (36×12 in).

▲ *Trachelium caeruleum*

T. jacquinii Dense, rounded heads of small, bluish lilac flowers, 10 cm (4 in) across, appear from mid to late summer. The mid green leaves of this woody based perennial grow up to 7.5 cm (3 in) long. This species is best for a crevice in a rock garden. HEIGHT & SPREAD 15×20 cm (6×8 in).
CULTIVATION Plant in late spring in well-drained soil and in a sunny, sheltered position. Remove faded flowers.
PROPAGATION Sow seed in early spring or take basal cuttings in late spring .
PESTS AND DISEASES Usually trouble free.

Trachelospermum
Apocynaceae

Trachelospermum asiaticum

Sprays of small, sweetly scented flowers make these vigorous, twining evergreen climbers a delight in summer. Although frost-hardy, they benefit from a warm, sheltered position against a south or west-facing wall if grown outdoors. In the coldest areas they can be grown in a cool greenhouse or conservatory, but they need space to spread.
RECOMMENDED SPECIES AND VARIETIES
T. asiaticum ♀ The creamy white flowers have an orange throat and age to buff yellow. Each flower is 2 cm (¾ in) across with 5 spreading lobes. They are sometimes followed by pairs of slender pods up to 23 cm (9 in) long, containing silky plumed seeds. Some of the 2–5 cm (¾–2 in) long lance-shaped leaves turn red in winter. Native to Japan and Korea. HEIGHT & SPREAD 1.8×1.5 m (6×5 ft) after 5 years, ultimately 6 m (20 ft) tall.
T. jasminoides ♀ (syn. *T. majus*) White, fragrant flowers 2.5 cm (1 in) wide open in mid to late summer and age to cream. Pods are produced occasionally. The lance-shaped leaves are up to 7.5 cm (3 in) long. Less hardy than *T. asiaticum*, it is best grown under glass in colder regions. Native to S China and Taiwan. HEIGHT & SPREAD 2×1.8 m (6½×6 ft) after 5 years, ultimately 8 m (26 ft) tall.

'Variegatum' ♀ has leaves which are boldly splashed and edged with creamy white, often tinged with coppery red in winter. The leaves of 'Wilsonii' vary from lance-shaped to oval and are strongly tinged with deep coppery red in winter.

CULTIVATION Plant in early spring in well-drained soil against a sheltered, sunny south or west-facing wall. Tie in to horizontal wires. Alternatively, grow in pots of fertile, well-drained compost in a cool greenhouse or conservatory, positioned in partial shade and supported by wires or a trellis.

PROPAGATION Take semi-ripe cuttings in late summer.

PRUNING During winter tie in or prune out any long shoots that are growing away from the wall to keep the shrub tidy.

PESTS AND DISEASES Usually trouble free.

Trachycarpus
Chusan fan, windmill palm
Palmae

These slow-growing specimen evergreens have a distinctive habit. Large, fan-shaped leaves top a tall, single trunk that is covered in fibre. Large, downward-curving sprays of numerous small yellow flowers with many bracts at the base are borne among the foliage near the top of the stem. Although frost-hardy, these trees need full sun and a sheltered position. They are not suitable for gardens in the north-east of Britain.

RECOMMENDED SPECIES

T. fortunei♀ (syn. *Chamaerops excelsa* hort.) Dense sprays, up to 60 cm (2 ft) long, of small yellow flowers appear in early summer. Mid green, pleated leaves, up to 1.2 m (4 ft) wide, are carried on sharply toothed stalks, up to 1 m (3 ft) long. The leaves last for many years. Trees bear either male or female flowers and so it is necessary to grow plants of either sex for the small, spherical, blue-black fruits to be produced. HEIGHT & SPREAD 1×1 m (3×3 ft) after 5 years,

▼ *Trachycarpus fortunei*

ultimately to 4 m (13 ft) tall or more.

CULTIVATION Plant in mid to late spring in well-drained soil in a position sheltered from north and east winds. During the first 3 years, protect with a screen of matting or hessian and a deep mulch of bracken or straw in severe weather.

PROPAGATION Remove basal suckers with 2 or 3 leaves in mid to late spring and pot into 15 cm (6 in) pots of multipurpose potting compost. Place in a coldframe or greenhouse with a minimum temperature of 10°C (50°F). Grow on under glass for a year before hardening off and planting out.

PRUNING None required.

PESTS AND DISEASES Usually trouble free.

Tradescantia
Spider lily, spiderwort
Commelinaceae

Tradescantia x andersoniana
'J.C. Weguelin'

With their leafy, wandering stems, tradescantias make good houseplants. Vigorous and easy to grow, they cascade out of pots and hanging baskets. There are also hardy, clump-forming plants for the mixed or herbaceous border. All have three-petalled triangular flowers, about 2.5 cm (1 in) across, which are usually short-lived.

RECOMMENDED SPECIES AND VARIETIES

OUTDOOR PLANTS

These hardy perennials suit the front of a border. *T. brevicaulis* is also useful for a rock garden. The linear-lanceolate, mid green leaves are up to 35 cm (14 in) long. The solitary flowers are short-lived, but new blooms appear as the old ones fade.

T. × andersoniana Clusters of blue, purple or white flowers, each up to 4 cm (1½ in) across, appear from early summer to early autumn. The lance-shaped leaves grow to 40 cm (16 in) long. HEIGHT & SPREAD 60×45 cm (24×18 in).

'Isis'♀ carries deep blue blooms. 'J.C. Weguelin'♀ has lavender-blue flowers. 'Osprey'♀ bears white flowers with purple-blue stamens.

T. brevicaulis Narrow, fleshy leaves cover the branched flower stems which carry rose-red flowers in early summer. HEIGHT & SPREAD 24×15 cm (9½×6 in).

T. virginiana From a compact clump of fleshy, grass-like foliage this species produces flowers throughout the summer. HEIGHT & SPREAD 60×45 cm (24×18 in).

'Caerulea Plena' produces double royal blue flowers.

▲ *Tradescantia x andersoniana* 'Osprey'

INDOOR PLANTS

There are several tradescantias, commonly known as wandering Jews, which thrive in average room temperatures and though they require good light, they do not need high humidity. The stems trail to about 60 cm (24 in) or more.

T. fluminensis 'Quicksilver'♀ (inch plant) The pointed oval leaves, up to 7 cm (2¾ in) long, are evenly striped green and white. Pure white flowers are carried in clusters at the ends of the stems in mid summer.

T. pallida 'Purpurea'♀ (purple heart) A robust plant with red-purple broadly lance-shaped leaves. The flowers in mid summer are bright magenta pink.

T. zebrina♀ (syn. *T. pendula*, *Zebrina pendula*) (silvery inch plant) A vigorous plant for hanging baskets or as ground cover for a conservatory border. The stems carry closely packed leaves on either side. The 5 cm (2 in) long leaves have a green central stripe with a glistening silvery band on either side. The undersides are purple. The mauve-pink flowers appear in mid summer.

'Purpusii'♀ (bronze inch plant) has olive-green leaves to 7 cm (2¾ in) long with a rich bronze-purple flush if grown in good light. The flowers are mauve-pink. 'Quadricolor'♀ bears leaves with irregular longitudinal bands in pink, olive green, cream and silver. It is prone to leaf drop.

CULTIVATION Plant out garden species from autumn to spring in any fertile soil in full sun. Houseplants require full sunlight, especially the variegated types. Keep them above 17°C (63°F), although they will survive down to a few degrees above freezing in winter. Water generously in summer but more sparingly in winter. Repot small plants annually in spring, but large plants can be fed once a week instead. Pinch out regularly to promote bushy growth. Houseplants are best replaced after 2 or 3 years.

PROPAGATION Divide garden plants between autumn and spring. Take tip cuttings of houseplants at any time of the year.

PESTS AND DISEASES Slugs attack the young leaves of garden plants.

Treasure flower see *Gazania rigens*

t

TOPIARY

The art of garden sculpture

CREATE EYE-CATCHING FEATURES BY CLIPPING AND TRAINING PLANTS INTO FORMAL OR FANCIFUL SHAPES

Topiaries lend elegance, humour or rustic charm to gardens, patios, balconies and entrances. Ranging in shape from cubes and spirals to abstract designs and animals, these living sculptures can be created in lawns, containers and borders or from hedges.

A tree or shrub with dense, small-leaved foliage and pliable, thin stems is ideal for topiary. The evergreen *Buxus sempervirens* (box), *Taxus baccata* (yew) and *Ligustrum ovalifolium* (oval-leaved privet) are particularly suitable; the hollies *Ilex × altaclerensis* and *I. aquifolium* also

BIRD LIFE *A whimsical topiary shape can add humour to a garden.*

make long-lived topiaries. Site them in a sheltered area in fertile and free-draining soil, to promote vigorous and even growth. In an exposed site or a heavy soil, use tough plants such as *Carpinus betulus* (hornbeam) or *Crataegus monogyna* (hawthorn). Like all deciduous plants, they are best used to fashion simple shapes.

The topiarist's tool kit includes sharp hand shears and secateurs. For large areas that lack detail, a powered hedge-trimmer saves time and heavy-duty loppers or a pruning saw are useful for renovating old topiaries. Most topiaries

take five to ten years to form their shapes, but *Hedera helix* (ivy) can be trained over a framework to create a feature in two to four years. Green varieties are most effective; topiaries made from variegated ivies often lack definition because of the breaks in colour.

CREATING TOPIARY

Simple shapes may be cut free-hand, provided that you have a good eye. Clip a little at a time and stand back to view your work regularly. A framework is useful if accuracy is vital or the shapes are complicated. For example, pairs of cones are more likely to match and animals will look more convincing if they are cut to outlines.

Frames for simple shapes can be made with canes and galvanised wire. Otherwise, they can be bought from garden centres or made up by a blacksmith. Place the frame over the shrub. As the plant develops, prune any leaves and branches that grow outside the framework. This can be left in place or cut out once the shape has formed.

SIMPLE STYLES

Cubes, cones and other geometric shapes introduce a formal note to their setting. They are especially effective in pairs, framing a view or gateway, or multiples of pairs, set along a pathway.

Spheres are simple to execute, either by eye or using a framework. Box is particularly suitable because its new shoots

◄ WELCOMING ARCH *Two box trees create an abstract frame for a cottage doorway.*

▲ SHAPELY BOUNDARY *Regular columns enliven a hedge of* Chamaecyparis lawsoniana.

develop from the plant's centre, and yew and *Lonicera nitida* (box-leaved honeysuckle) also form dense rounded mounds. To create a standard – a sphere on a clear stem – train a single leader up a cane then pinch out the top growth regularly until it forms a rounded bush.

Trees that grow naturally in a conical pattern, such as yew and the cypress *Cupressus macrocarpa* 'Goldcrest', can be shaped easily into geometric cones. Make a template out of a wigwam of canes and place it over the plant to form an outline against which to cut.

A spiral can be created from an established cone (see facing page). Alternatively, train the leader shoot of a young plant round a cane, winding like a corkscrew as it develops.

To make a cube, place four young plants in a square; they will knit together to form a base. Mark the precise shape

▼ SIMPLE SPHERES *A line of symmetrical box topiaries makes an unusual surround for a border.*

with canes and string for accurate clipping. If possible, use four cuttings from the same plant to ensure even growth.

To create a pyramid or obelisk from the square base, clip the sides at oblique angles, allowing the inner shoots to form a central point.

HUMOROUS SHAPES

An animal, train or freeform design adds a whimsical air to the garden. Use a framework to create the shape from a young plant, or exploit the natural form of a growing plant. For example, after two or three years' growth, a bushy yew will have several branches that can be coaxed into a new shape by trimming, bending or tying. To create a topiary pheasant or a squirrel, use upright branches to form a body and head, and peg a long, wispy branch to the ground to make a tail. A plant that is naturally conical, such as holly, often has evenly arranged branches which can be adapted into a tiered 'cakestand'.

HEDGE-TOP TOPIARY

Many topiary effects can be created on the top of a hedge. For a quick result, clip the top of a mature deciduous or evergreen hedge into a simple scalloped or castellated design. Use string to measure and mark out the pattern before you cut.

Columns, pilasters or buttresses fashioned on a long run of hedging create a pleasing architectural effect. Allow the sides of the hedge to grow out at regular intervals and trim to shape over three to five years, again using string to measure and mark out the pattern.

Windows can be cut into hedges to give peephole views into the landscape beyond. While the hedge is growing, train pliable young branches round an iron frame firmly staked into the ground.

Evergreen hedges are best for creating elaborate shapes, such as small animals. Allow some leader shoots to grow out of the hedge top, then shape them either freehand or to the outline of a framework.

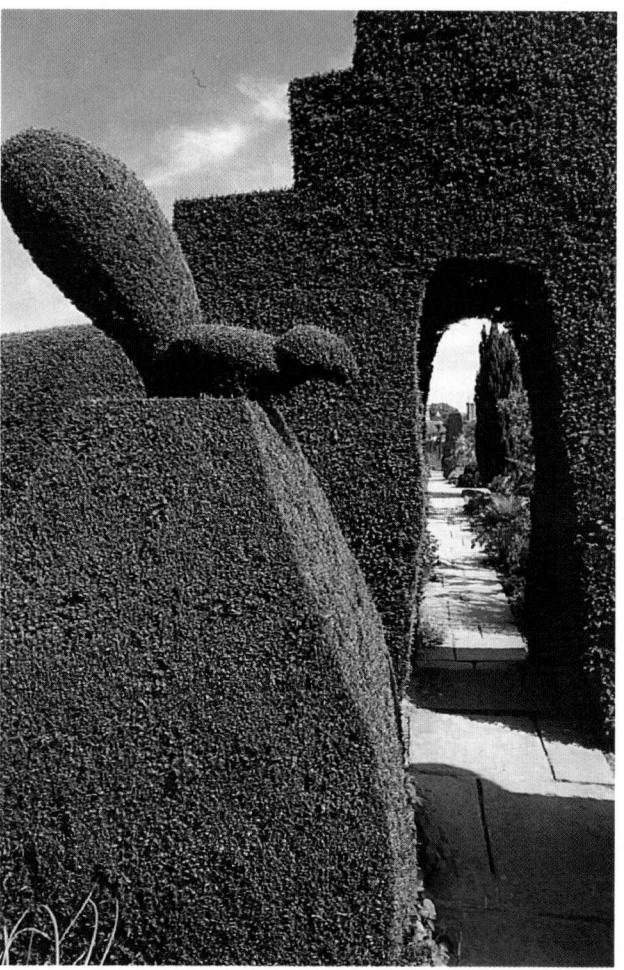

CARING FOR TOPIARIES

Feed topiaries with a slow-release fertiliser in spring, and water during dry spells until the plants are two or three years old. Topiaries in containers need watering all year round because the dense foliage prevents rainwater reaching the soil.

Clip once a year, in late summer or more often if the shrub is fast-growing. Privet and hawthorn shapes, for example, may need three trims in the growing season.

At the onset of winter, insulate the roots of pot-grown topiaries from frost by wrapping hessian sacking or bubble-wrap polythene round the container. The trunks of standards are vulnerable and also need to be insulated. Brush any heavy snow off topiary shapes.

Old, neglected topiaries can sometimes be renovated, particularly those created from yew which stands hard pruning. Clip in stages over three years, cutting one side of the plant at a time.

• CREATING A SPIRAL •

A cone-shaped topiary can be quickly adapted into an elegant, slender spiral by the following method. The best results are obtained from plants that are at least 1m (3 ft) in height, and the spiral looks most effective when the central trunk is revealed as the pattern winds up to the top.

1 Tie a length of string to the apex of the plant and wind it in a loose spiral round the foliage. Secure the end of the string to the stem or a branch at the bottom of the shrub.

2 Carefully following the spiral marked by the string, cut away the outer branches of the plant with a pair of secateurs. Aim to keep the tiers even all the way round.

Tricyrtis
Toad lily
Liliaceae

Tricyrtis formosana

Spectacular flowers are produced by the hardy herbaceous perennials in this genus during summer and autumn. The flowers stand out well against light green foliage plants in a mixed border.

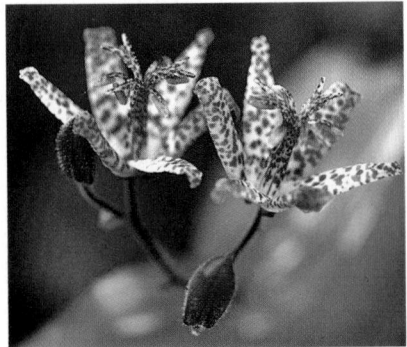

▲ *Tricyrtis formosana*

RECOMMENDED SPECIES AND VARIETIES

T. *formosana* ♀ (syn. *T. stolonifera*) Heavily spotted, purplish pink, spurred flowers with yellow-tinged throats appear in early autumn. They are up to 7.5 cm (3 in) across. The dark green, lance-shaped leaves, 10 cm (4 in) long, are sparingly produced. HEIGHT & SPREAD 60×45 cm (24×18 in).

▲ *Tricyrtis hirta*

T. *hirta* (Japanese toad lily) Bell-shaped flowers, up to 2.5 cm (1 in) across, bloom in clusters in late summer or early autumn. They are white, spotted with purple. Dark green, narrow leaves, up to 15 cm (6 in) long, are carried on strong stems densely clothed with white down. HEIGHT & SPREAD 90×45 cm (36×18 in).

'**Alba**' has white flowers flushed green.
T. *latifolia* Yellow or yellowish green, purple-spotted flowers, up to 5 cm (2 in) across, are produced sparingly in mid summer. The leaves are up to 15 cm (6 in) long and borne on an erect, hairy stem. HEIGHT & SPREAD 90×45 cm (36×18 in).

T. *macrantha* ssp. *macranthopsis* Bell-shaped, chocolate-spotted yellow flowers, up to 7.5 cm (3 in) across, are borne at the tips of arching stems in late summer or autumn. The dark green, oval leaves are up to 10 cm (4 in) long and 5 cm (2 in) wide. HEIGHT & SPREAD 90×45 cm (36×18 in).

T. *macropoda* Beautiful cup-shaped whitish purple flowers, up to 5 cm (2 in) across, are sprinkled with small purple spots. They appear in late summer, offset by dark green leaves, up to 12.5 cm (5 in) long. HEIGHT & SPREAD 75×45 cm (30×18 in).

T. *ohsumiensis* Faintly spotted, cup-shaped primrose-yellow flowers, up to 5 cm (2 in) across, are borne in late summer. The dark green leaves are up to 15 cm (6 in) long. HEIGHT & SPREAD 45×30 cm (18×12 in).

T. *stolonifera* see *T. formosana*

CULTIVATION Plant in spring in soil enriched with organic matter and in a sheltered place. Remove faded flowerheads.

PROPAGATION Sow seed in autumn or spring or divide plants in spring.

PESTS AND DISEASES Slugs and snails can be troublesome, especially in early spring. Powdery mildew may affect foliage.

Trifolium
Clover
Leguminosae

Rounded heads of tiny flowers in summer and leaves with three leaflets are the familiar features of these pretty plants. Occasionally a leaf may be composed of four or even up to seven leaflets. The genus includes hardy annuals, biennials and perennials, a few of which are evergreen. Clover makes good ground cover, but some species can become invasive. Native to all temperate and subtropical regions outside Australasia.

RECOMMENDED SPECIES AND VARIETIES

T. *incarnatum* (crimson clover) Tiny bright red flowers borne in heads up to 7.5 cm (3 in) long appear over mid summer. Slender erect stems carry dark green leaves, up to 4 cm (1½ in) across, with rounded leaflets. This annual is often grown for its value as a green manure. HEIGHT & SPREAD 30×30 cm (12×12 in).

T. *ochroleucum* (sulphur clover) Sulphur yellow, oval flowerheads, up to 3 cm (1¼ in) wide, bloom in early and mid summer. The brightly coloured flowers are complemented by mid green, oval to lance-shaped leaflets. These semi-evergreen leaves are up to 3 cm (1¼ in) long, on stalks up to 15 cm

▲ *Trifolium ochroleucum*

(6 in) long. As a short-lived perennial, the plant will last 3-4 years. HEIGHT & SPREAD 30×30 cm (12×12 in).

T. *pratense* (purple clover) This is a bushy, short-lived, semi-evergreen perennial bearing reddish purple to pink, occasionally cream, flowerheads, up to 2.5 cm (1 in) across, in mid summer. The dark green, oval leaflets are up to 2.5 cm (1 in) long. The plant is commonly grown as a forage crop or for green manure. HEIGHT & SPREAD 30×60 cm (12×24 in).

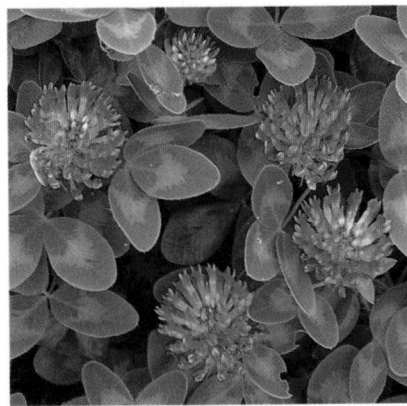

▲ *Trifolium pratense*

'**Green Ice**' has cream flowers and two-toned green leaves. '**Susan Smith**' has dark pink flowers and leaflets with golden veins.

T. *repens* (white clover, shamrock) Tiny white blossoms, in fragrant heads up to 2.5 cm (1 in) across, are produced from late spring until early autumn. The plant, a semi-evergreen perennial, has dark green leaves on creeping stems, each rounded leaflet up to 2 cm (¾ in) long. HEIGHT & SPREAD 15×60 cm (6×24 in).

'**Purpurascens**' is a robust plant with reddish brown leaflets edged with green. '**Purpurascens Quadrifolium**' is similar but many leaves have 4 or more leaflets.

CULTIVATION Grow in an open, sunny position in a free-draining soil, although plants will tolerate most other conditions found in the garden, with the exception of

▲ *Trifolium repens* 'Purpurascens'

dense shade. Deadhead as required. To use clover as green manure, dig the plant into the soil in late summer or early autumn.
PROPAGATION Sow seed or divide plants in spring. Clover self-seeds freely.
PESTS AND DISEASES Usually trouble free.

Trillium
Wood lily
Trilliaceae

Trillium chloropetalum

Each stem of these herbaceous perennials is topped by a cluster of three leaves and a single three-petalled flower. Most trilliums are hardy but a few can be damaged by late frosts. Plants are sometimes slow to become established and once settled resent disturbance at the roots. As woodland dwellers in their native N America, trilliums are ideal for moist, shady sites.

RECOMMENDED SPECIES AND VARIETIES
T. catesbyi (syn. *T. stylosum*) (bashful wake-robin) Nodding flowers, up to 5 cm (2 in) across, appear from late spring to early summer. The pink petals are flushed with red and curl elegantly upwards. The leaves are up to 10 cm (4 in) long and have wavy edges. HEIGHT & SPREAD 20×10 cm (8×4 in).
T. cernuum (nodding trillium) Pendent white or pinkish flowers, 4 cm (1½ in) across, appear in mid spring. The petals curl up at the tips and the prominent anthers are

▲ *Trillium chloropetalum*

purple. The leaves are up to 10 cm (4 in) long. HEIGHT & SPREAD 60×30 cm (24×12 in).
T. chloropetalum♀ The upright flowers, which appear from mid to late spring, can be white, white with a pink flush, greenish orange, brown or maroon. Narrow petals, 9 cm (3½ in) long, are set off by a ruff of bright green leaves, up to 20 cm (8 in) long. HEIGHT & SPREAD 45×45 cm (18×18 in).
T. cuneatum (toad trillium) Purple or brownish purple upright flowers are borne above round leaves from mid to late spring. The leaves are blotched with bronze and up to 10 cm (4 in) across. HEIGHT & SPREAD 40×30 cm (16×12 in).
T. erectum♀ (birthroot, lamb's quarters, wet-dog trillium) Slightly nodding, deep claret flowers, 5 cm (2 in) across, appear in

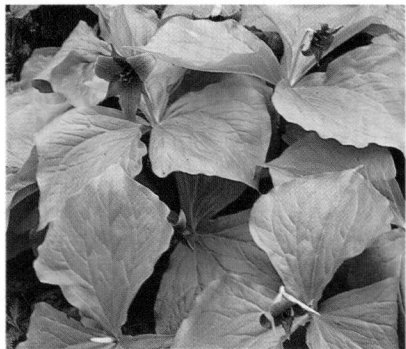

▲ *Trillium erectum*

mid spring. The pointed oval, pale green leaves are up to 15 cm (6 in) long. HEIGHT & SPREAD 40×30 cm (16×12 in).
The flowers of f. *albiflorum* are white, tinged with green. The petals of f. *luteum* are a rich yellow, veined with deep red.
T. grandiflorum♀ (wake-robin) Showy, pure white, outward-facing flowers appear in late spring. The petals have wavy edges.

▲ *Trillium grandiflorum*

and are up to 7.5 cm (3 in) long. The flowers sometimes open pink. The leaves are 10 cm (4 in) long, with pointed tips. HEIGHT & SPREAD 45×45 cm (18×18 in).
Double flowers are seen on f. *flore-pleno*.
T. luteum♀ (syn. *T. sessile* var. *luteum*) Greenish yellow upward-facing flowers, 5 cm (2 in) across, appear on upright stems

in mid spring. The almost circular leaves are up to 12 cm (4¾ in) across. They are mid green, blotched with dark bronze-green. HEIGHT & SPREAD 40×30 cm (16×12 in).
T. ovatum var. *hibbersonii* Pinkish upward-facing flowers, about 5 cm (2 in) across, that turn white with age, are produced in spring. They are flanked by diamond-shaped mid green leaves, 7.5 cm (3 in) long. HEIGHT & SPREAD 20×45 cm (8×18 in).
T. recurvatum Reddish brown to purple-green, upright flowers, up to 6 cm (2½ in) across, appear in spring. The leaves are mottled in bronze and up to 12 cm (4¾ in) long. HEIGHT & SPREAD 40×30 cm (16×12 in).
T. rivale♀ Nodding white or pink flowers, spotted with purple and about 3 cm (1¼ in) across, appear from early to mid spring. The dark green leaves with carmine spots are 4 cm (1½ in) long. This species can be damaged by late frost and is best grown in pots so that it can be overwintered under glass. HEIGHT & SPREAD 15×10 cm (6×4 in).
T. sessile Upright, scented flowers appear in early spring. The dark reddish brown petals are about 5 cm (2 in) long. The leaves are marbled with grey and are 12 cm (4¾ in) long. HEIGHT & SPREAD 20×30 cm (8×12 in).
T. sessile var. *luteum* see *T. luteum*
T. stylosum see *T. catesbyi*
CULTIVATION Plant in autumn in moist, but well-drained, fibrous soil that is acid or neutral. Position in moderate shade.
PROPAGATION Sow seed in autumn in a coldframe or take root cuttings in autumn.
PESTS AND DISEASES Slugs and snails may be troublesome.

Triteleia
Alliaceae

A cluster of funnel-shaped flowers is held by a single stem in early summer. Long, narrow leaves grow from the base of the plant. Triteleias are useful for rock gardens or borders and can be grown in containers. The flowers are good for cutting. Native to western parts of the USA.

RECOMMENDED SPECIES AND VARIETIES
T. laxa 'Queen Fabiola' ('Koningin Fabiola') As many as 20 violet-blue flowers,

▲ *Triteleia laxa* 'Queen Fabiola'

up to 5 cm (2 in) long, are carried in a loose umbel on a stout, upright flower spike that may attain a height of 50 cm (20 in). The plant produces only 1 or 2 narrow leaves, up to 30 cm (12 in) long. HEIGHT & SPREAD 50×15 cm (20×6 in).

CULTIVATION Plant the corms in early autumn, 7.5 cm (3 in) deep and 10 cm (4 in) apart, in a free-draining position in an open, sunny spot. In very cold weather cover with straw or a mulch. Supply a high potash liquid feed in early summer. Remove faded blossoms and allow foliage to die back.

For indoor pot plants, bury corms in four parts John Innes No.2 compost to one part sharp grit. Leave pots in sand inside a coldframe, cool but frost-free and with plenty of light, until shoots begin to appear, then bring them indoors.

PROPAGATION Remove offsets in autumn. It will be 2 or 3 years before they flower.

PESTS AND DISEASES Usually trouble free.

Tritonia

Iridaceae

These half-hardy, bulbous perennials are grown for their summer spikes of brightly coloured, funnel-shaped flowers. They can also be grown as pot plants. Native to tropical and southern Africa.

RECOMMENDED SPECIES AND VARIETIES

T. disticha ssp. *rubrolucens* (syn. *T. rosea*, *Crocosmia rosea*) Funnel-shaped, deep pink flowers, up to 4 cm (1½ in) long, appear in late summer or early autumn. The mid-green, grassy leaves grow to 30 cm (1 ft) long. HEIGHT 45 cm (1½ ft).

T. rosea see *T. disticha* ssp. *rubrolucens*

CULTIVATION Plant corms 5 cm (2 in) deep and 15 cm (6 in) apart during spring in free-draining soil in a warm, sunny position. In winter, cover with a mulch of bark chips, removing it when the danger of severe frost has passed. Remove faded flowerheads and old foliage in autumn.

Grow pot plants in four parts John Innes No.2 compost to one part sharp grit. Overwinter pots in a frost-free greenhouse or conservatory and keep the compost dry.

PROPAGATION Divide in autumn or spring.

PESTS AND DISEASES Usually trouble free.

Trochodendron

Trochodendraceae

The solitary species of this genus is an evergreen shrub or small tree grown for its striking, spirally arranged foliage and unusual green flowers. Native to E Asia.

T. aralioides The vivid green flowers, 2 cm (¾ in) across, are made up of numerous stamens radiating from green discs, giving a wheel-like appearance. Clusters of flowers are borne in late spring and early summer. The lustrous leaves, up to 12.5 cm (5 in)

Trochodendron aralioides

▲ *Trochodendron aralioides*

long, grow on long stalks. They are apple-green or yellowish green with scalloped margins. HEIGHT & SPREAD 1.2×1 m (4×3 ft) after 5 years, ultimately 8 m (26 ft) tall.

CULTIVATION Plant out container-grown stock in spring in moist, well-drained soil, choosing a sunny place sheltered from cold winds. Do not plant in dry or chalky soil.

PROPAGATION Take semi-ripe cuttings in late summer or sow seed in autumn.

PRUNING None required.

PESTS AND DISEASES Usually trouble free.

Trollius

Globeflower
Ranunculaceae

Trollius europaeus

The common name aptly describes the large rounded blooms of the majority of the species in this genus, although the flowers of *T. acaulis* and *T. pumilus* are flatter and more buttercup-like. The flower colours range from pale cream to orange, with varieties flowering from late spring to early summer. The flowers are generally about 5 cm (2 in) across. Deeply divided leaves provide lush ground cover.

Globeflowers are hardy clump-forming perennials. They are easy to grow, as long as the soil does not dry out during summer. They thrive around pond edges or along the banks of a stream and can also be grown

successfully in a herbaceous border, given liberal watering and a mulch to prevent the soil drying out in hot weather. Small species, such as *T. acaulis* and *T. pumilus* suit rock gardens, troughs and peat beds. Native to Europe, Asia and N America.

RECOMMENDED SPECIES AND VARIETIES

T. acaulis Small and neat, this species has bright yellow flowers in early summer and 5 cm (2 in) wide leaves which grow on short stalks from the crown. HEIGHT & SPREAD 25×25 cm (10×10 in).

T. chinensis (syn. *T. ledebourii*) In early and mid summer showy, orange-yellow flowers bloom on tall stems. The leaves are up to 12 cm (4¾ in) long. HEIGHT & SPREAD 75×45 cm (30×18 in).

▲ *Trollius chinensis* 'Golden Queen'

'Golden Queen'♀ and 'Imperial Orange' both have orange flowers.

T. × cultorum see Garden Varieties

T. europaeus (common globeflower) Pale yellow flowers, 4 cm (1½ in) across, show up well against bright green, deeply divided leaves, up to 12 cm (4¾ in) across. HEIGHT & SPREAD 75×45 cm (30×18 in).

▲ *Trollius europaeus*

'Superbus'♀ is more free-flowering with deeper yellow flowers.

T. ledebourii see *T. chinensis*

T. pumilus Yellow flowers, 4 cm (1½ in) across, appear from late spring to early summer on this neat, slow-growing small plant. HEIGHT & SPREAD 23×23 cm (9×9 in).

T. yunnanensis The neat clump of leaves is brightened by yellow flowers, 4 cm (1½ in) across, from early to mid summer. HEIGHT & SPREAD 75×45 cm (30×18 in).

t

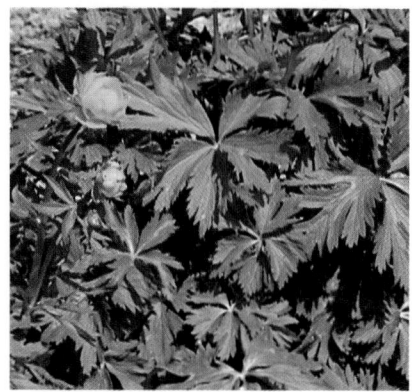

▲ Trollius 'Orange Princess'

GARDEN VARIETIES

These plants are often listed under *T. × cultorum*. All flower from late spring to early summer. The figure given is the height, the spread is usually slightly less.

'Alabaster', pale creamy yellow, 60 cm (2 ft); 'Canary Bird', lemon yellow, 75 cm (2½ ft); 'Earliest of All', yellow, 75 cm (2½ ft); 'Etna', deep orange, 60 cm (2 ft); 'Golden Cup', golden yellow, 75 cm (2½ ft); 'Goldquelle'♀, bright yellow, 60 cm (2 ft); 'Helios', pale yellow, 60 cm (2 ft); 'Lemon Queen', lemon yellow, 60 cm (2 ft); 'Orange Princess'♀, orange yellow, vigorous in growth, 1 m (3 ft).

CULTIVATION Plant from autumn to early spring, but not in frosty weather. Best grown in rich, moist soil, trollius will thrive in sun or partial shade. Cut off old flowering stems to encourage a second flush.

PROPAGATION Lift and divide clumps in autumn if they have outgrown their space or are not flowering well.

PESTS AND DISEASES Usually trouble free, although mice and voles sometimes eat the leaves and buds in early summer.

Tropaeolum

Tropaeolaceae

Tropaeolum speciosum

These hardy and half-hardy herbaceous perennials or tender annuals are grown for their brightly coloured, trumpet-shaped flowers. They include climbers and scramblers that are ideal for training on walls or trelliswork or for growing through shrubs. Native to Central and S America.

RECOMMENDED SPECIES AND VARIETIES

T. canariense see *T. peregrinum*

T. majus (common nasturtium) These tender annuals are used in borders, for climbing up trelliswork and also in pots and hanging baskets. The yellow, orange or red flowers, up to 5 cm (2 in) across and with a distinctive long spur, appear in summer. The leaves, up to 7.5 cm (3 in) across, are circular, with wavy edges. HEIGHT & SPREAD 2×2.3 m (6½×7½ ft).

'Alaska' has cream and green variegated foliage and orange or red flowers. It reaches a height and spread of 25 cm (10 in). 'Empress of India' has dark bluish green foliage and crimson-scarlet blossoms. It reaches 25 cm (10 in) in height and spread. Gleam Series have semi-double flowers in yellow, red and orange. They reach a height and spread of 35 cm (14 in). 'Hermine Grashoff'♀ has double orange-scarlet blooms. It reaches a height and spread of 20 cm (8 in). 'Jewel Mixed' is early flowering with semi-double blooms from yellow through orange to crimson. It reaches 30 cm (1 ft) in height and spread. 'Tom Thumb' is compact with yellow, orange or red flowers. It reaches a height and spread of 25 cm (10 in). 'Whirlybird' has yellow to red, single flowers without spurs. It reaches 25 cm (10 in) in height and spread.

T. peregrinum (syn. *T. canariense*) (canary creeper) Bright yellow, spurred flowers, up to 2.5 cm (1 in) across, appear in summer and autumn. The blue-green, lobed leaves are up to 7.5 cm (3 in) across. A fast-growing, tender annual climber. HEIGHT & SPREAD 4×1 m (13×3 ft).

T. polyphyllum (wreath nasturtium) This hardy, scrambling, herbaceous perennial produces yellow, spurred flowers, up to 2.5 cm (1 in) long, during early to mid summer. Grey-green leaves, up to 5 cm (2 in) long, are borne on fleshy stems. This species particularly dislikes winter wet. HEIGHT & SPREAD 10×60 cm (4×24 in).

T. speciosum♀ (Scottish flame flower, flame creeper) Bright red flowers, up to 2.5 cm (1 in) across, are produced from mid to late summer. Bright blue berries surrounded by purplish red, papery scales often appear in autumn. The plant's vibrant green leaves, up to 5 cm (2 in) long, have 5-7 lobes. A hardy, herbaceous perennial climber. HEIGHT & SPREAD 3 m×60 cm (10×2 ft).

T. tuberosum Bright orange-scarlet flowers, up to 4 cm (1½ in) long and with a prominent spur, are borne from mid summer into autumn. Greyish green leaves, up to 4 cm (1½ in) long, are held on strong purplish stems. This half-hardy herbaceous perennial climber grows from a potato-like tuber. HEIGHT & SPREAD 3 m×60 cm (10×2 ft).

The distinctive flowers of var. *lineamaculatum* 'Ken Aslet'♀ are red and orange.

CULTIVATION Plant in spring in a moisture-retentive but well-drained soil in full sun. *T. majus* and its cultivars prefer poor soil. Keep well watered in summer. Lift the tubers of *T. tuberosum* in winter and store them in peat in a cool, dry, frost-free place.

▲ *Tropaeolum speciosum*

▲ *Tropaeolum tuberosum*

PROPAGATION Sow seed under glass in autumn or spring or divide roots in early spring before any growth appears. Separate the tubers of *T. tuberosum* in autumn.

PESTS AND DISEASES Aphids may attack.

Trout lily see *Erythronium americanum*
Trumpet creeper see *Campsis*

t

TREES

A living framework for the garden

TAKE THE LONG VIEW AND GROW TREES
TO BRING STRUCTURE AND A SENSE OF
PERMANENCE TO A PLANTING SCHEME

Even when young, trees give a garden a feeling of maturity. Planted singly or in groups, they provide scale and structure, act as focal points and frame views. Their silhouettes, leaves, fruits, flowers and barks enrich all planting schemes. These tall, woody plants are often the most prominent and long-lived species in the garden. They are usually single-stemmed, though a few are multistemmed.

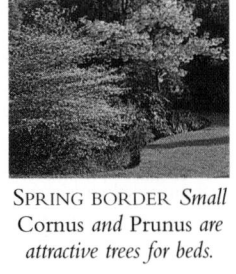

SPRING BORDER *Small Cornus and Prunus are attractive trees for beds.*

Apart from their aesthetic value, trees are of great practical benefit, providing shelter from cold winds and sun glare, giving privacy and hiding unsightly areas from view. Many trees, particularly *Quercus robur* (English oak) and other native species, benefit wildlife (see WILDLIFE GARDENS p.710).

Choose a tree that suits the particular conditions and requirements of your garden and site it where it has enough room to spread. Once a tree starts to outgrow its setting, it needs to be pruned regularly, which can destroy its natural form and grace.

Plant and stake a tree with care (see p.810). For the first three years after planting, water during dry spells, mulch and carry out any formative pruning and training. Keep a 1m (3ft) wide area round the tree free from weeds or other plants in these early years. Once the tree has established a good root system, it will usually require very little attention.

SIZE AND SHAPE

The immense range of tree sizes means that there is a tree for most gardens. The genus *Acer* (maple), for example, includes *A. pseudoplatanus* (sycamore), which can reach 30m (100ft) in height, and *A. palmatum* (Japanese maple), which grows to only 4m (13ft) after 20 years.

There is a wide range of species under 15m (50ft) tall, which are suitable for many gardens. They include the colourful *Robinia pseudoacacia* 'Frisia' and *Cercis siliquastrum* (Judas tree). Crab apples, such as *Malus × zumi* 'Golden Hornet', or ornamental plums, such as *Prunus × blireana*, grow to a maximum height of 4m (13ft), which makes them ideal for small gardens.

When choosing a tree, consider the spread of its branches

◀ FOLIAGE AND FLOWERS *Cherry blossom, maple leaves and rhododendron flowers mingle.*

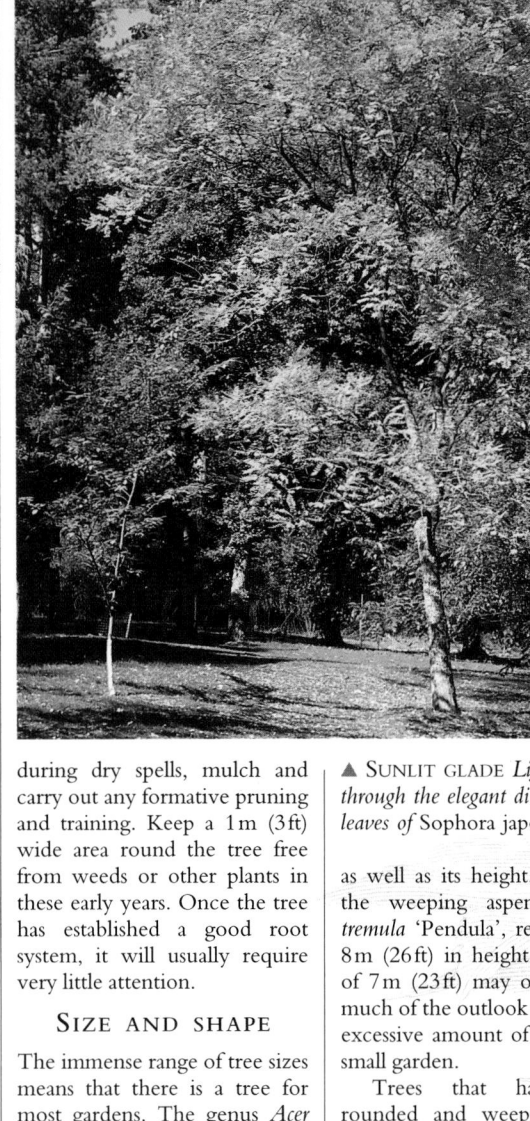

▲ SUNLIT GLADE *Light filters through the elegant divided leaves of* Sophora japonica.

as well as its height. Although the weeping aspen, *Populus tremula* 'Pendula', reaches only 8m (26ft) in height, its spread of 7m (23ft) may obscure too much of the outlook and cast an excessive amount of shade in a small garden.

Trees that have oval, rounded and weeping shapes generally take up more space than those that are columnar, conical or pyramidal. The weeping katsura, *Cercidiphyllum japonicum* f. *pendulum*, for example, is three times the width of the narrow Lawson cypress *Chamaecyparis lawsoniana* 'Grayswood Pillar'.

DECORATIVE FOLIAGE

After size and shape, the foliage is often the most significant feature to consider when choosing a tree. Evergreens, which include the majority of conifers, give colour throughout the year. Deciduous trees, which include most broad-leaved trees and a few conifers, such as *Larix* (larch) and *Metasequoia* (dawn redwood), burst into exhilarating life in spring and are often brightly tinted in autumn.

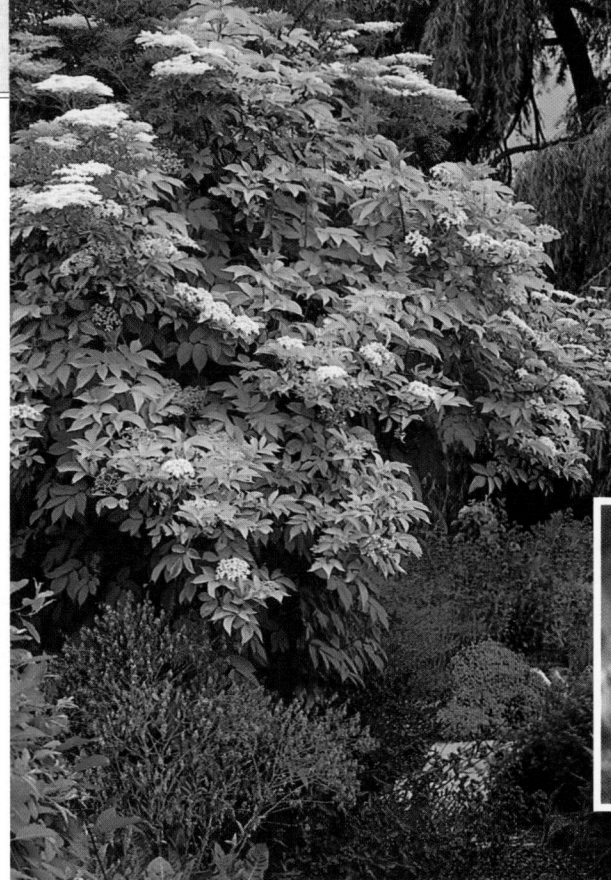

► GOLDEN ELDER *The bright leaves of* Sambucus nigra *'Aurea' lighten a dark corner.*

Trees with green leaves bring a restful air to the garden and provide foils to vividly coloured flowers. Green-leaved species growing at the end of a garden magnify its size, while species with coloured leaves tend to bring the background nearer. If planted in the foreground, these trees make strong features. Variegated foliage, such as that of the holly *Ilex × altaclerensis* 'Golden King', brightens up shady corners.

Many deciduous trees have foliage that offers a variety of beautiful colours. For example, the rowan *Sorbus thibetica* 'John Mitchell' emerges silvery white and then turns from green to yellow in autumn; and the bronze leaves of *Cercidiphyllum japonicum* turn blue-green and then pink, yellow and purple.

Autumn colour can be a major feature of trees, providing a bright display in the garden when many plants have finished flowering. *Nyssa sylvatica*, with its gold, scarlet and russet tones, and *Amelanchier lamarckii*, a snowy mespilus with brilliant yellow and red foliage, are good choices.

The shape of leaves also adds to the interest of some trees. The almost square leaves of *Liriodendron tulipifera* (tulip tree) are fine examples, as are the fan-shaped leaves of *Ginkgo biloba* (maidenhair tree). The frond-like foliage of *Gleditsia triacanthos* (honey locust) has a delicate appeal.

FLOWERS AND FRUITS

The flowering season of trees is often short-lived but the blooms can be outstandingly beautiful. Large pale *Magnolia* flowers are a magnificent sight after winter, and clouds of blossom make the ornamental fruit trees, *Malus* and *Pyrus*, real attractions in spring. *Cercis* is covered in clusters of pink flowers in late spring. The pendulous catkins of *Betula* (birch) and papery bracts of *Cornus* (dogwood) have their own distinctive charm.

Many trees produce fruits that are highly ornamental. Edible varieties, such as apples and pears, add their highlights to the garden in autumn. Striking fruits are also produced by *Sorbus* 'Joseph Rock', with its orange-yellow berries, and *S. vilmorinii*, which has pink-flushed white berries.

The fruits of some trees are poisonous, including those of laburnum and *Taxus baccata* (yew). These trees should not be planted in gardens where young children play.

▲ BURNISHED COPPER *The polished bark of* Prunus serrula *gives colour all year round.*

CHOOSING THE BEST-SHAPED TREE FOR YOUR GARDEN

The outline and branch structure of a tree adds form to a garden throughout the year and can affect the way it is used. Examples of the main shapes are given below.

COLUMNAR
Columnar trees provide distinct vertical emphasis and smooth outlines. Plant them as focal points, to frame views or in groups or avenues.

Acer rubrum Scanlon
Chamaecyparis lawsoniana
  'Grayswood Pillar'
Cupressus sempervirens
Prunus 'Amanogawa'
Sorbus aucuparia
  'Sheerwater Seedling'
Taxus baccata 'Fastigiata'

CONICAL
The ascending branches of conical trees form upswept outlines. They blend well in mixed designs, as well as making good screens or focal points.

Carpinus betulus 'Fastigiata'
Cupressus arizonica
  'Pyramidalis'
Fagus sylvatica 'Dawyck'
Magnolia × kewensis
  'Wada's Memory'
Prunus 'Spire'
Tilia cordata 'Greenspire'

OVAL
Taller than they are broad, these trees make attractive specimen plants, look good in mixed plantings and provide protection from wind and sun.

Fraxinus ornus
Ilex × altaclerensis
Laurus nobilis
Liriodendron tulipifera
Magnolia grandiflora
Quercus coccinea
Sorbus 'Joseph Rock'
Tilia cordata

PYRAMIDAL
The horizontal branches of these trees form pyramid shapes at maturity. Use them as single specimens, in mixed plantings or as screens.

Abies koreana
Alnus glutinosa 'Laciniata'
Chamaecyparis pisifera
  'Boulevard'
Corylus colurna
Juniperus scopulorum
  'Blue Heaven'
Ilex aquifolium 'Pyramidalis'

ROUNDED
Often spreading as broad as they are high, rounded trees make good specimens, focal points and screens, and provide shelter from wind and sun.

Amelanchier lamarckii
Arbutus × andrachnoides
Catalpa bignonioides
Eucryphia × intermedia
Malus × zumi 'Golden Hornet'
Paulownia tomentosa
Sorbus aria
Styrax japonica

WEEPING
Weeping trees have pendent main branches and side stems. Use them as specimens, particularly by water, or in mixed plantings.

Betula pendula 'Youngii'
Fagus sylvatica 'Pendula'
Morus alba 'Pendula'
Sophora japonica 'Pendula'
Picea breweriana
Pyrus salicifolia 'Pendula'
Salix caprea 'Kilmarnock'
Tsuga canadensis 'Pendula'

BARKS AND OUTLINES

The bark of some trees cracks, flakes or peels as their trunks and branches grow, forming patterns, textures and colours which provide interest in winter after the leaves have fallen. *Prunus serrula* has a peeling, polished trunk. The trunk of *Acer rufinerve* (snake-bark maple) has distinctive lengthwise stripes and the new bark of *A. griseum* (paper-bark maple) is a rich cinnamon colour.

In winter, the skeletons of most deciduous trees make gauntly attractive features. The airy crown of a birch is particularly elegant, *Nyssa sylvatica* has a handsome conical shape and the contorted branches of *Salix babylonica* var. *pekinensis* 'Tortuosa' are best appreciated after the leaves fall.

SMALL GARDENS

In a small garden, choose a tree that has two or more seasons of interest. Look for a species or cultivar which is naturally small or takes a long time to reach a substantial height. Consider also the size of its leaves, flowers and fruits; if these are large the tree may look out of scale.

The slow-growing *Acer griseum*, *A. davidii* 'George Forrest', the hawthorn *Crataegus persimilis* 'Prunifolia' and *Betula utilis* var. *jacquemontii* are all good trees for confined areas. Many ornamental fruit trees also make excellent choices.

Provided there is enough light, a tree can thrive in even a tiny garden or on a patio or balcony. Grow it in a large tub and water and feed regularly. A small apple tree grafted onto dwarfing rootstock is ideal for growing in a container, and the narrowly columnar holly *Ilex aquifolium* 'Green Pillar' or cultivars of *Cupressus sempervirens* (Italian cypress), such as the golden-leaved 'Swane's Gold', will also do well.

FOCAL POINTS

A tree makes a handsome specimen, particularly in the centre or at the edge of a lawn, where it provides a tall contrast to the even surface of the turf. Species that have spreading branches, including the round-headed *Morus nigra* (mulberry), or a weeping habit, such as *Fraxinus excelsior* 'Pendula' (weeping ash) or *Pyrus salicifolia* 'Pendula' (weeping pear), are particularly effective; their forms are often displayed to best advantage in open sites.

Specimen trees also look attractive planted beside a water garden. Weeping species are excellent because their pendent branches have a flowing appearance; the willow *Salix* × *pendulina* 'Elegantissima' and the beech *Fagus sylvatica* 'Pendula' make eye-catching features but need plenty of room.

Trees can make commanding features in borders, giving distinct vertical accents. A strong, narrow silhouette, such as that of *Acer rubrum* Scanlon, looks especially good here.

A pair of columnar or conical trees placed one either side of a gateway provides a natural framework for a view, and a tree can make an excellent focal point at the end of a hedge or a pathway.

GROUPING TREES

Where there is space, plant several trees in a group to create a strong feature or provide a backdrop of form, colour and texture. Plant an odd number of trees to create a natural-looking grouping and use both evergreen and deciduous trees. The evergreens provide a permanent show, while the deciduous trees offer a changing display.

◀ PLANTING EFFECT *Shapely trees create a strong, contrasting backdrop to flowering plants.*

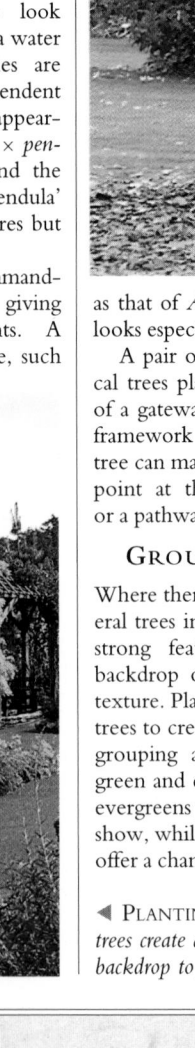

▲ YEAR'S TURNING Nyssa sylvatica *glowing with autumn colour is a spectacular centrepiece.*

Use a combination of contrasting leaf shapes or foliage colours to add interest. A creamy variegated tree adds lightness to a group of dark-foliaged trees; for example, the silver-leaved weeping pear and the purple-foliaged *Acer palmatum* 'Bloodgood' make a striking combination. However, avoid using too many trees with differently coloured leaves as they may compete with each other for attention.

Groups of trees are central to the design of a woodland garden. The upright, round-headed *Prunus* × *subhirtella* 'Autumnalis' or the open *Cercidiphyllum japonicum* are well suited to informal schemes. Tall trees, such as ashes or oaks, add height to a group of smaller ones, including dogwoods, birches and hollies.

In a small garden use silver birches, snake-bark maples and *Arbutus × andrachnoides* (strawberry tree), underplanted with several shrubs, to create an attractive grouping.

In a large and formal setting a double line of neatly clipped columnar trees, such as *Taxus baccata* 'Fastigiata', makes an impressive avenue.

WINDBREAKS AND SCREENS

Trees are useful as windbreaks and screens and many species make excellent hedging when they are densely planted (see p. 318). A line of beech or yew, for example, can provide a substantial boundary.

Use trees to create a screen which offers privacy, filters noise or hides ugly sights. Round-headed or pyramidal species, including the hazel *Corylus colurna* and *Catalpa bignonioides* (Indian bean tree), are particularly suitable because of their widths.

A row of trees can be used to create a shelterbelt, but in a small garden a single tree can be sufficient to break the force of the wind. Conifers with foliage that is not too dense, such as *Pinus sylvestris* (Scots pine), the false cypress *Chamaecyparis obtusa* and *Thuja plicata* 'Zebrina', are excellent choices for windbreaks. The deciduous *Crataegus monogyna*, *Laburnum* and *Sorbus thibetica* 'John Mitchell', will also provide shelter from harsh winds.

▼ FLORAL FOCUS *This well-placed* Pyrus salicifolia *'Pendula' makes a delicate centrepiece.*

HOW FAR FROM THE HOUSE?

Before planting a tree, consider its impact on neighbouring plants, houses and walls. Make sure the mature branches will not shade windows, and do not plant the tree close to a building or underground pipes or cables.

Trees may damage the foundations of a nearby building by direct pressure or by absorbing water from soils that shrink as they dry out. Root damage by direct pressure is most likely to be caused by trees with very vigorous root systems, such as ash, willow, poplar and large species of oak. These trees may cause particular problems on a shrinkable clay or peat soil.

It is worth seeking professional advice before planting a tree. As a general guide, leave a distance between a tree and building of a third to a half of the tree's ultimate height. Where the spread will be greater than the height, leave a distance equal to the radius of the spread. If planting on shrinkable peat or clay, place the tree farther away, at least as far as its ultimate height.

If your soil is shrinkable and you have a thirsty tree growing in your garden, take specialist advice before attempting any work on it. Severe pruning may reduce the tree's uptake of water and cause the surrounding soil to swell which may affect nearby buildings.

TREES FOR ALL SEASONS IN SMALL AND LARGE GARDENS

SMALL GARDENS

- *Abies koreana* Wide-spreading pyramidal evergreen with glossy, dark green needles, silver-white underneath, and purple to blue cones in autumn.
- *Acer davidii* 'George Forrest' Rounded and deciduous with spreading branches and a purplish red, white-striped trunk. Red-gold foliage and winged seeds in autumn.
- *Amelanchier lamarckii* Rounded, deciduous and multistemmed with clusters of white flowers in spring and leaves that emerge copper-bronze and turn yellow and red in autumn.
- *Crataegus persimilis* 'Prunifolia' Rounded, spreading and deciduous with clusters of white flowers in early summer. Orange and scarlet-tinted foliage in autumn and dark red berries.
- *Cryptomeria japonica* 'Elegans Aurea' Columnar evergreen with yellow-green foliage, turning bronze in winter, and brownish red peeling bark.
- *Malus coronaria* var. *dasycalyx* 'Charlottae' Oval, upright and deciduous with pink, semidouble, scented flowers in late spring. Bright red leaves and yellow-green fruit in autumn.
- *Picea pungens* 'Koster' Narrowly conical evergreen with scaly grey bark and silver-blue needles.
- *Pyrus salicifolia* 'Pendula' Rounded and deciduous with grey-silver leaves on weeping branches, clusters of white flowers in spring and green to brown fruits in autumn.
- *Salix daphnoides* 'Aglaia' Oval and deciduous with purple shoots and long, grey, pussy-willow buds in winter and early spring, and dark green foliage.
- *Sorbus vilmorinii* Rounded and deciduous with small white flowers in spring, ferny foliage turning rich red and purple, and small pink fruit in autumn.

LARGE GARDENS

- *Aesculus indica* 'Sydney Pearce' Rounded and deciduous with bronze-tinged leaves turning yellow to orange in autumn. White or pink flower candles in summer and conkers in autumn.
- *Betula albosinensis* var. *septentrionalis* Oval and deciduous with peeling, pink, brown and copper bark. Catkins in early spring and yellow leaves in autumn.
- *Betula pendula* 'Laciniata' Narrowly conical and deciduous with silver-white bark and deeply cut foliage turning yellow in autumn.
- *Carpinus betulus* 'Fastigiata' Conical and deciduous with a grey trunk, and yellow-green catkins in spring. Dark green leaves turning gold and winged seeds in autumn.
- *Ilex × altaclerensis* 'Camelliifolia' Dense pyramidal evergreen with glossy dark green leaves and plentiful red berries.
- *Picea breweriana* Pyramidal evergreen with weeping branches, blue-green needles and green cones ripening to purple in autumn.
- *Sophora japonica* Rounded and deciduous with cream tubular flowers on mature trees in late summer and autumn, and divided leaves turning yellow in autumn.
- *Sorbus aria* 'Lutescens' Oval and deciduous with silver-white foliage in spring turning mid green then bright yellow in autumn. Small white flowers in late spring and red to brown fruits in autumn.
- *Stewartia pseudocamellia* Oval and deciduous with brown flaking bark. Large white flowers in summer and green leaves turning orange, red and purple in autumn.
- *Tilia cordata* 'Greenspire' Conical and deciduous with clusters of cream flowers in mid summer and shiny green heart-shaped leaves turning gold in autumn.

Tsuga
Hemlock
Pinaceae

The graceful, sweeping branches of these broadly conical evergreen conifers are densely clothed in drooping or arched branchlets. Needle-like leaves, arranged in ranks on the shoots, are short, blunt and flat, and often have pure white undersides which contrast well with the dark green, sometimes blue-green, upper surface. Small, pendulous cones ripen the same year in which they form and remain on the tree for two or three years. Male and female flowers appear in separate clusters on the same tree in spring. The trees listed here are hardy and make fine specimen trees or hedges. Native to the forests of N and E Asia and N America.

RECOMMENDED SPECIES AND VARIETIES
T. canadensis (eastern hemlock) The dark green leaves have white undersides. The egg-shaped cones are 2 cm (¾ in) long and hang gracefully from the tips of the shoots. This multi-stemmed, broad-crowned tree is rather too large for most gardens, but there are a number of smaller cultivars. HEIGHT & SPREAD 6×2 m (20×6½ ft) after 20 years, ultimately 15 m (50 ft).

'Cole's Prostrate' forms a dense blue-green carpet and is suitable for a rock garden. This spreading plant reaches a height of only 30 cm (12 in). 'Fantana' is a small, slow-growing bushy plant with foliage and branches that radiate out like a fan. The plant, growing up to 2 m (6½ ft) tall, makes a good rock-garden plant and is also useful for containers. 'Jeddeloh'♀ does well in any garden situation and grows into a dense complete umbrella, up to 1 m (3 ft) tall, with fresh light green foliage. 'Minuta' is an extremely slow-growing, bun-forming dwarf conifer that seldom exceeds a height of 50 cm (20 in). It is suitable for the smallest of gardens, including window boxes. Best planted when it is at least 10 years old.

Tsuga canadensis 'Pendula'

'Pendula'♀, up to 2 m (6½ ft) tall, displays a low, wide-spreading canopy of overlapping branches and leaves, and makes a superb centrepiece for a lawn or large rock garden. Plant when it is at least 20 years old.
T. heterophylla♀ (western hemlock) A broadly conical tree that bears dense, dark green foliage hanging from slightly ascending branches. Some needles twist upwards to display silvery white undersides. Flowers are bright red; the pendulous green cones are tinged purple. This makes a majestic specimen tree, but is too large for most gardens. HEIGHT & SPREAD 18×7 m (60×23 ft) after 20 years, ultimately 40 m (130 ft) tall.
T. mertensiana (mountain hemlock) A tight, densely branched conical tree with beautiful blue-grey foliage and large pendulous cigar-shaped cones up to 7 cm (2¾ in)

Tsuga mertensiana

long. The needles are radially arranged, rather than ranked. This superb garden tree can be clipped and pruned regularly if required. HEIGHT & SPREAD 6×1.5 m (20×5 ft) after 20 years, ultimately 15 m (50 ft).
CULTIVATION Plant from mid autumn to mid spring in a moist, loamy soil. Shade and cold positions are tolerated and *T. canadensis* and its cultivars will also do well over chalk. *T. heterophylla* tolerates some waterlogging.
PROPAGATION Sow seed of the species in spring or take ripewood cuttings in autumn.
PRUNING Very little required, although specimens, especially *T. heterophylla,* can be clipped into handsome hedges. Remove branches back to the main stem if wide-spreading canopies need to be controlled.
PESTS AND DISEASES Prone to honey fungus and sensitive to sulphur dioxide.

Tulbaghia
Society garlic
Alliaceae

These hardy and half-hardy semi-evergreen perennials and bulbs are grown for their star-like summer flowers. They demand an open, sunny position in a free-draining soil and a mulch in winter in cold areas.

RECOMMENDED SPECIES AND VARIETIES
T. violacea This bulb produces lilac-pink to purplish pink, 6-petalled flowers, up to 2.5 cm (1 in) across, during late summer and early autumn. The strong flower spikes will remain upright even in adverse weather. This is a vigorous, clump-forming plant with long, narrow, mid green to bluish green leaves which often remain for much of the winter. HEIGHT 60 cm (2 ft).

▲ *Tulbaghia violacea*

'Silver Lace' has variegated foliage and larger flowers. It is not fully hardy.
CULTIVATION Plant in spring in full sun and in any well-drained soil that does not dry out totally. Remove faded flowerheads. Apply a slow-release fertiliser in spring.
PROPAGATION Divide plants in spring.
PESTS AND DISEASES Usually trouble free.

Tulip tree see *Liriodendron tulipifera*

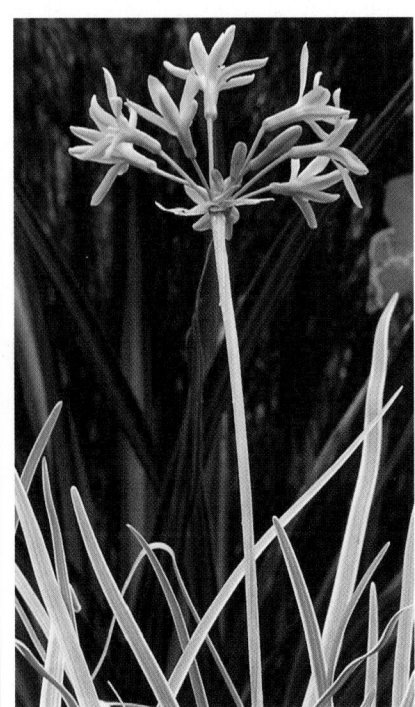

▲ *Tulbaghia violacea 'Silver Lace'*

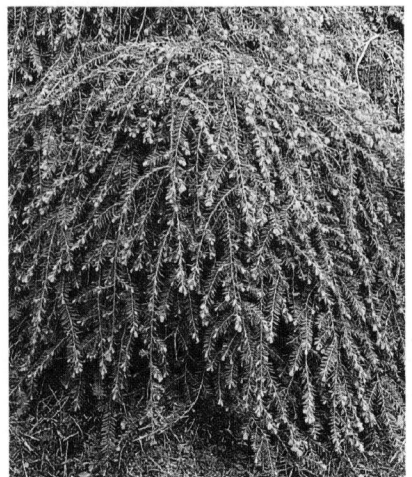

▲ *Tsuga canadensis 'Cole's Prostrate'*

Tulipa

Tulip

Liliaceae

———

Jewel-coloured flowers burst into life in spring. Whether forming stately processions across a border or ornamenting a bed in vivid patches, the presence of tulips in the garden lifts the spirits

Since their introduction from Turkey 400 years ago, tulips have been one of the most popular and rewarding bulbs for late spring displays. They are grown for their elegant flowers which are available in nearly every conceivable colour except true blue.

The six-petalled flowers are generally cup or goblet-shaped – although some may be rather starry – and mature blooms tend to open so wide in the sun that they are almost flat. Each erect stem normally carries a single flower but some varieties bear two or three flowers per stem. There are usually two or more lance-shaped basal leaves and smaller stem leaves which are often greyish green. The bulbs, which vary greatly in size, have a pointed tip and a brownish skin.

The genus as a whole is very varied, from the tiny mountain species suitable for the rock garden or greenhouse, through to the gaudy modern hybrids that are planted in huge beds in public parks and gardens. Around 100 species of tulip are known, mostly from W and central Asia, and there are thousands of garden hybrids that have been developed over the years.

The small species tulips are best planted in clumps towards the front of a border and they make colourful rock garden residents.

1 'Don Quichotte'
2 'Yokohama'
3 'Casablanca'
4 'Arabian Mystery'
5 'Rococo'
6 'Golden Apeldoorn'
7 'Kees Nelis'
8 'Attila'
9 'Prinses Irene'

INDEX OF SPECIES AND VARIETIES

Tulips are grouped into 15 divisions, with the last division covering the species tulips:

A list of tulips covered in this book follows in alphabetical order with the relevant division in brackets.

The larger-flowered hybrids can be used for general garden display either in formal beds – planted with forget-me-nots (*Myosotis*) or wallflowers (*Erysimum*) – or in clumps planted among herbaceous plants. Tulips can also be grown in containers for display on a patio or terrace.

All require a heavy loam soil that is nevertheless free-draining and a warm, dry summer dormant period to ripen the bulb. It is normal practice to lift the bulbs of the modern hybrids as the leaves fade and store them until replanting in autumn. Species tulips can be left in the ground where they may spread to form large patches, particularly *T. saxatalis*, *T. sprengeri* and *T. sylvestris*. If the bulbs dwindle, new bulbs can be added annually to boost the display.

RECOMMENDED SPECIES AND VARIETIES
Holland is traditionally associated with the tulip – the country's national flower – and hundreds of varieties, old and new, have been developed there. As early as 1600, faced with an ever-increasing choice of tulip hybrids, the Dutch introduced a system of classification according to flower-

▲ *Tulipa* 'Apricot Beauty'

▲ *Tulipa* 'Bellona'

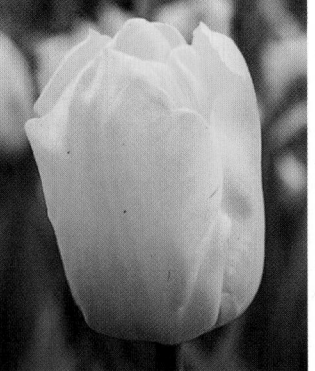

Tulipa 'Prinses Irene' ▲

ing time. This is still in use today and has been expanded to include new groups containing hybrids with similar characteristics. The garden hybrids are currently grouped into 14 recognised divisions. The 15th division in this book covers the species tulips.

(1) SINGLE EARLY TULIPS
Tulips within this division are the earliest to flower and can therefore be lifted earlier than most other tulips, making room for early summer bedding schemes. They are in bloom from early spring and are viewed to full advantage among forget-me-nots (*Myosotis*) and early bulbs, such as scillas and puschkinnias. They will flower in late winter under glass and many are excellent for forcing. HEIGHT 20-35 cm (8-14in).

'Apricot Beauty', salmon-rose with a

t

reddish flush. 'Bellona', scented with pure golden yellow flowers. 'Brilliant Star', scarlet. 'Christmas Marvel', cherry pink. 'Couleur Cardinal', plum with a scarlet interior. 'Diana', pure white. 'Flair', feathers of orange on a buttercup-yellow background. 'Generaal de Wet', bright orange. 'Grand Duc' see 'Keizerskroon'. 'Keizerskroon'♀, a red blaze on a yellow background. 'Prinses Irene'♀, orange with purple feathering.

(2) DOUBLE EARLY TULIPS

These tulips generally flower just a little later than those in the single early division. The blooms are large, often up to 10 cm (4 in) across, and fully double. They are suitable for large bedding schemes where bold, vivid swathes of colour are required, such as those seen in public parks. The shorter Murillo types (marked M) can also be planted in pots, tubs and window boxes. HEIGHT 25-40 cm (10-16 in).

'Carlton', deep red. 'Electra' (M), deep cherry red. 'Monte Carlo'♀, sulphur yellow. 'Orange Princess', soft orange flamed with purple and green. 'Oranje Nassau' (M), blood red flushed with fiery red. 'Peach Blossom' (M), deep rose pink.

▲ *Tulipa* 'Peach Blossom'

'Schoonoord' (M), pure white. 'Stockholm'♀, scarlet with a yellow base. 'Willemsoord' (M), carmine and white.

(3) TRIUMPH TULIPS

This group usually flowers from mid to late spring. Many of the Mendel tulips, which had their own division before the reclassification by the Tulip Committee in 1981, are now included here. The division contains many cultivars that are excellent for forcing. Available in a wonderful selection of colours, the triumph tulips are most effective when interplanted with winter pansies (*Viola*) and polyanthus. HEIGHT 40-50 cm (16-20 in).

'Abu Hassan', glowing cardinal red with crimson stripes on buttercup yellow edges. 'African Queen', deep ruby red with feathery white edges. 'Arabian Mystery', deep bluish purple edged in white. 'Athleet', pure white. 'Attila', light purple-violet. 'Cassini', deep red; excellent for forcing. 'Don Quichotte', deep rose pink. 'Douglas Bader', deep rose pink on

the outside; paler inside. 'Garden Party', glowing carmine edged in white; feathers of carmine against a white background inside. 'Golden Melody', buttercup yellow. 'Kees Nelis', blood red edged in orange-yellow. 'Merry Widow' (syn. 'Lustige Witwe'), deep glowing red edged in pure white; excellent for forcing. 'Negrita', doge purple with beetroot-purple veining and a bluish grey base. 'New Design', pale yellow fading to pinkish white with red edges. The leaves have pinkish white edges. 'Yokohama' bears strong yellow, rather pointed flowers.

(4) DARWIN HYBRID TULIPS

This is a comparatively new division, the first cultivar being introduced in 1936. The tulips have large flowers at the top of tall, sturdy stems. They make excellent cut flowers. In the garden they flower from mid to late spring. They are stunning when planted in large drifts and equally effective planted among wallflowers (*Erysimum*). HEIGHT 50-60 cm (20-24 in).

'Apeldoorn', cherry red edged with scarlet. 'Apeldoorn's Elite'♀, cherry red edged with buttercup yellow. 'Beauty of Apeldoorn', an exterior flushed with magenta and edged in golden yellow; golden yellow inside with a black base. 'Big Chief'♀, a rose-pink exterior with an orange-red edge; the inner petals flamed cream. 'Elizabeth Arden', dark salmon pink flushed with violet and a yellow and white base. 'Golden Apeldoorn', golden yellow with black anthers. 'Gordon Cooper', deep reddish pink, edged with scarlet and a blue and yellow base. 'Gudoshnik', deep yellow spotted and flushed with shades of orange-red; the base and anthers are black. 'Holland's Glorie'♀, deep carmine, edged in poppy-red with a yellow base; orange-red inside and a greenish black base. 'Jewel of Spring'♀, sulphur yellow with a reddish edge. 'Oranjezon' ('Orange Sun'), bright pure orange. 'Oxford'♀, scarlet flushed with blood red; capsicum red inside. 'Parade'♀, scarlet edged in yellow; black base and anthers. 'President Kennedy'♀, buttercup yellow spotted red and a deep bronzy-green base.

(5) SINGLE LATE TULIPS

These tulips flower from mid to late spring. They are tall – up to 70 cm (28 in) – with classically shaped flowers in a wide range of colours, making them excellent for large spring bedding schemes and they are often used in parks. HEIGHT 50-70 cm (20-28 in).

'Aristocrat'♀, soft purplish violet edged with white. 'Bleu Aimable', bluish lilac. 'Clara Butt', salmon pink. 'Georgette', a multiflowered variety in red with yellow edges and just 45 cm (18 in) tall. 'Greuze', violet purple. 'Halcro'♀, carmine-red with a yellow base and green edging. 'Landseadel's Supreme'♀, glowing cherry red with a creamy yellow base.

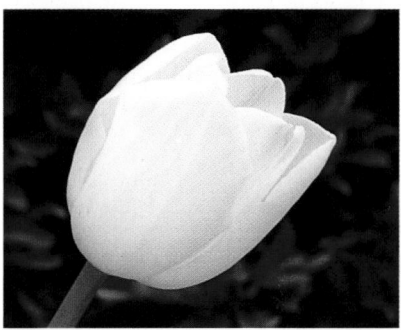
▲ *Tulipa* 'Maureen'

'Maureen'♀, marble white. 'Mrs John T. Scheepers'♀, yellow. 'Orange Bouquet'♀ is a multiflowered variety bearing deep orange flowers with a pale yellow base and greenish yellow anthers. Just 40 cm (16 in) tall. 'Queen of Bartigons', salmon pink with a whitish base. 'Queen of Night', deep velvety maroon. 'Red Georgette'♀ is a multiflowered variety in glowing scarlet and just 40 cm (16 in) tall. 'Shirley', ivory white with a fine purple edge, a white base spotted with pale purple and brownish violet anthers. 'Sorbet'♀, rosy white flamed with carmine-red and a creamy white base. Up to 70 cm (28 in) tall. 'Sweet Harmony'♀, lemon yellow edged in ivory white and yellow anthers. 'Temple of Beauty'♀, lily-shaped salmon-rose flowers. The leaves are slightly mottled. 'Union Jack', raspberry red on an ivory white

▲ *Tulipa* 'Apeldoorn's Elite'

▲ *Tulipa* 'Big Chief'

Tulipa 'Oxford' ▲

background. The base is white edged in blue.

(6) LILY-FLOWERING TULIPS

The tall, stately flowers of this group have pointed and reflexed petals. Opening in late spring, they are excellent for bedding schemes or interplanting in herbaceous borders. HEIGHT 50–60 cm (20–24 in).

'Aladdin', scarlet edged in yellow. 'Ballade'♀, reddish magenta edged in white and a yellow base. 'Ballerina', marigold-orange, slightly scented. 'China

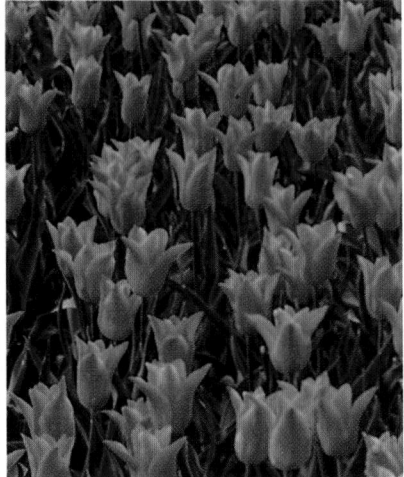

▲ *Tulipa* 'China Pink'

Pink', pink with a white base. 'Mariette', deep satin rose with a white base. 'Marilyn', white with fuchsia-purple feathering; ivory white flamed with red inside. 'Maytime', reddish violet with narrow white edges and a yellow base. 'Queen of Sheba', bright red with a fine yellow edge. 'Red Shine', deep ruby red. 'West Point', primrose yellow. 'White Triumphator', pure white.

(7) FRINGED TULIPS

The petals of this charming group of tulips have fringed edges, often in a contrasting colour. The showy flowers, which appear in late spring, are excellent for cutting. Like the single early and Darwin tulips, they look good among wallflowers (*Erysimum*) and forget-me-nots (*Myosotis*). HEIGHT 45–60 cm (18–24 in).

'Blue Heron', violet purple with a purplish fringe. 'Burgundy Lace', fringed wine red flowers. 'Fancy Frills', ivory-white flame on a rich, deep pink with a whitish to rose-pink fringe. 'Fringed Beauty', vermilion with golden yellow fringed edges and just 25 cm (10 in) tall. 'Hamilton', rich buttercup yellow. 'Redwing', glowing cardinal red with a lighter red fringe.

(8) VIRIDIFLORA TULIPS

An interesting group of tulips, with slender, urn-shaped flowers striped or flamed with green. They were put in their own division in 1981. The subtle colour combinations are much sought after by flower arrangers.

▲ *Tulipa* 'Hamilton'

Blooming in late spring, they make an effective display when planted in clumps at the front of a herbaceous border. HEIGHT 35–45 cm (14–18 in).

'Artist', purplish and salmon rose; salmon rose and green inside. 'Esperanto', mid pink flamed with green, fading to reddish brown with a greenish-yellow base. Variegated leaves. 'Golden Artist', golden orange with broad green stripes through the petals. 'Groenland' (syn. 'Greenland'), green edged with rose. 'Hollywood', red tinged with green. 'Humming Bird', mimosa yellow feathered green on the outside; mimosa yellow and green inside. 'Pimpernel', purple-red and green. 'Spring Green'♀, ivory white feathered green with light green anthers.

▲ *Tulipa* 'Spring Green'

(9) REMBRANDT TULIPS

Greatly prized by the tulip fanciers of old, these tulips are often depicted in paintings by the Dutch old masters. They display the characteristic mottled and flecked flowers in late spring. The distortion of the colours is caused by a virus which can be transmitted to other varieties by aphids. As a result, very few varieties are now cultivated and they are sold in mixtures only. The old Bizarre and Bijbloemen tulips belong to this group.

(10) PARROT TULIPS

Fringed and twisted petals in bright primary colours means that this division contains some of the showiest tulip blooms of all. The mid to late spring flowers are long lasting and can be up to 20 cm (8 in) across. HEIGHT 50–60 cm (20–24 in).

'Apricot Parrot'♀, pale apricot yellow tinged with creamy white and deep rose; purple anthers. 'Black Parrot', as its name suggests, a deep purple exterior and blackish purple interior. 'Blue Parrot', bright violet-blue tinged with bronze; purple inside. 'Estella Rijnveld' (syn. 'Gay Presto'), red flamed with white. 'Fantasy'♀, salmon pink feathered and striped green. 'Flaming Parrot', deep,

▲ *Tulipa* 'Fantasy'

strong yellow, lightening to the edges, flamed with bright crimson; primrose yellow flamed with blood red inside. 'Orange Favourite', orange with green blotches and a yellow base. 'Rococo', red with a crinkled yellow-green edge. 'Texas Gold', deep yellow with a red feathering at the edges. 'White Parrot', pure white.

(11) DOUBLE LATE TULIPS

Tulips in this division flower in late spring or a little earlier in warmer districts. They have large, peony-like flowers, often up to 10 cm (4 in) across. Although they are prone to damage from heavy rain, they make up for it with a long flowering period. HEIGHT 40–45 cm (16–18 in).

'Allegretto', red edged in yellow.

▼ *Tulipa* 'White Parrot'

'Angélique', pale pink, lighter at the edges. 'Carnaval de Nice', white flamed and feathered deep red. The leaves have a fine white edge. 'Casablanca', ivory white with a dark yellow mark on outer petals. 'Maywonder', deep rose pink. 'Mount Tacoma', pure white. 'Uncle Tom', deep maroon red.

(12) KAUFMANNIANA TULIPS

These small tulips, often with bicoloured flowers, are ideal for early spring bedding displays. They are also useful for planting in rockeries, tubs, pots and window boxes. Some have attractively mottled foliage. HEIGHT 15-20 cm (6-8 in).

'Alfred Cortot'♀, carmine red; deep scarlet inside with a black base. Mottled foliage. 'Ancilla'♀, soft pink flushed with red; a central red ring inside. 'Early Harvest'♀, deep red with yellow edges and a yellow base. Mottled leaves. 'Giuseppe Verdi', carmine edged in yellow; golden yellow blotched red inside. 'Heart's Delight', carmine red edged in pale rose and a golden yellow base with red blotches. Mottled leaves. 'Jeantine'♀, carmine edged in apricot with a golden yellow base. 'Johann Strauss', dark red edged in sulphur yellow; white inside with a golden yellow base. Mottled leaves. 'Love Song', orange-red flushed with carmine and a deep buttercup-yellow base with bronze green blotches. Mottled leaves. 'Showwinner'♀, scarlet with a buttercup-yellow base. Mottled leaves. 'Shakespeare', carmine red edged in yellow; salmon flushed with scarlet inside and a golden-yellow base. Just 15 cm (6 in) tall. 'Stresa'♀, currant red edged in yellow. Mottled leaves.

(13) FOSTERIANA TULIPS

Ideal for bedding schemes, the fosteriana tulips are generally taller and have much larger flowers than those in the kaufmanniana or greigii divisions. They flower in mid spring. HEIGHT 20-40 cm (8-16 in).

'Candela', pure yellow with black anthers. 'Cantata', vermilion red with a yellow-rimmed black basal blotch. 'Madame Lefeber' (syn. 'Red Emperor'), very large fiery red flowers. 'Orange Emperor', carrot orange with a pale buttercup-yellow base. 'Princeps', red with a greenish bronze base. Only 20 cm (8 in) tall. 'Purissima' (syn. 'White Emperor'), large creamy white flowers.

(14) GREIGII TULIPS

Perhaps these tulips offer the best value as their foliage is also a feature. The leaves are beautifully marked with maroon mottling. If the flowers are deadheaded as soon as they are finished they can be left in the ground until it is time to plant the summer bedding. The shorter varieties are ideal for pots and window boxes as well as borders, beds and rockeries, flowering from mid to late spring. HEIGHT 25 cm (10 in).

'Cape Cod', apricot edged in yellow with a black and red base. Only 20 cm (8 in)

▲ *Tulipa* 'Angélique'

▲ *Tulipa* 'Princeps'

▲ *Tulipa* 'Purissima'

tall. 'China Lady', carmine rose edged in white; ivory white inside and a greenish-bronze base with red blotches. 'Corsage'♀, pale rose-pink edged in yellow; inside deep pink with yellow feathering, bronze base and 35 cm (14 in) tall. 'Donna Bella'♀, carmine edged in cream; creamy yellow inside and a black base with scarlet blotches. 'Oratorio', rose-pink; apricot pink inside with a black base. 'Oriental Splendour'♀, carmine red edged in lemon yellow and a green-ringed red base. It is 35 cm (14 in) tall. 'Pandour', pale yellow flamed with carmine red. 'Plaisir'♀, carmine red; vermilion red inside edged in pale sulphur yellow and a black and yellow base. Just 15 cm (6 in) tall. 'Red Riding Hood'♀, carmine red with a black base. Just 20 cm (8 in) tall. 'Toronto'♀, rose red tinged with vermilion, 2-3 blooms to a stem. 'United States', fiery red feathered to the edges on a buttercup-yellow background. 'Zampa'♀, primrose yellow, flushed red, bronze-and-green base and just 15 cm (6 in) tall.

▲ *Tulipa* 'Zampa'

(15) SPECIES TULIPS

T. acuminata Spindly, twisted flowers in red or yellow, with red markings appear in mid spring. The leaves are grey-green. This species tends to be short lived. HEIGHT 30-40 cm (12-16 in).

T. aucheriana♀ A solitary, 5 cm (2 in) pink flower with a yellow centre arises from a

▲ *Tulipa aucheriana*

basal rosette of leaves in mid spring. This species is easily grown on a well-drained, sunny rock garden. HEIGHT 7.5 cm (3 in).

T. biflora (syn. *T. polychroma*) This easy-to-grow bulb flowers in early spring, bearing 1-3 tiny, star-like flowers of white with a yellow eye, which are suffused with green on the outside. The narrow, upright leaves are grey-green. HEIGHT 8-10 cm (3-4 in).

T. clusiana var. *chrysantha*♀ Slender, 7.5 cm (3 in) yellow flowers with red marks on the outside, are carried on thin stems with narrow, grey-green leaves in mid spring. HEIGHT 20-30 cm (8-12 in).

T. c. 'Cynthia' has paler, creamy yellow flowers.

T. eichleri see *T. undulatifolia*

T. humilis Violacea Group Tulips within this very variable group are easy to grow, producing one, rarely 2 or 3, large, rounded flowers of rich violet pink with a black or yellow centre in late winter or early spring. The narrow, grey-green leaves form a rosette. HEIGHT 15 cm (6 in).

T. kolpakowskiana♀ Pointed yellow flowers, suffused with red, orange or green on the outside, are borne in mid spring. This slender tulip has narrow, grey-green leaves. HEIGHT 10-20 cm (4-8 in).

T. linifolia♀ Brilliant red open flowers, 7.5 cm (3 in) across, appear in late spring. The grey-green leaves are narrow. This species is easily grown in a sunny, well-drained soil. HEIGHT 12.5 cm (5 in).

Batalinii Group 'Bright Gem' is a vigorous and long-lived hybrid. The rounded, sulphur-yellow flowers have pointed tips. This tulip increases freely in a well-drained

▲ *Umbilicus rupestris*

RECOMMENDED SPECIES

U. rupestris (navelwort, pennywort) Up to 50 small drooping flowers, in the shape of tubular bells and up to 1 cm (⅜ in) long, bloom from early to late summer on a tapered spire, 20-40 cm (8-16 in) tall. They have a toothed edge and are greenish white, sometimes flushed with pink. The circular, round-toothed, dark green fleshy leaves, up to 5 cm (2 in) across, are dimpled in the centres, accounting for one of the plant's common names. They form a basal rosette on pink-tinged, succulent stalks, from 2-10 cm (¾-4 in) long. The few smaller leaves along the flowering stem are more kidney-shaped than round. Narrow tubular seed capsules, enclosed within the flower bell, produce tiny brown seeds. Plants grow in the wild over rocks and banks. HEIGHT & SPREAD 30×15 cm (12×6 in).

CULTIVATION Plant in spring or autumn in moist, gritty, well-drained soil, in sun or partial shade. Limy soil is unsuitable.

PROPAGATION Sow seed as soon as it is ripe or in spring, preferably where you wish the plants to flower.

PESTS AND DISEASES Usually trouble free.

Umbrella plant see *Darmera peltata*
Umbrella tree see *Schefflera actinophylla*
Urn plant see *Aechmea fasciata*

Ursinia
Jewel of the Veldt
Compositae

Eye-catching daisy flowers bring sunshine colours to sunny beds and borders. Foiled by attractive lacy foliage, the vivid orange or yellow blooms can be seen through most of the summer, although they tend to close up during dull weather. The species of this South African genus grown in Britain are treated as half-hardy annuals. Those described below have a bushy habit, producing flowers up to 5 cm (2 in) across on wiry stems from mid to late summer.

RECOMMENDED SPECIES AND VARIETIES

U. anthemoides Orange 'petals' (ray florets) have a purple-brown base making a dark ring round the centre of the daisy. Pale green leaves are finely divided and scented. HEIGHT & SPREAD 30×20 cm (12×8 in).

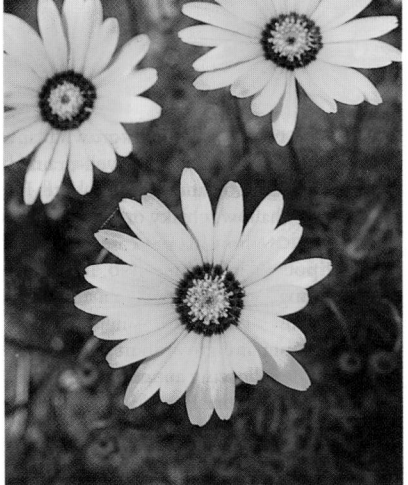

▲ *Ursinia anthemoides*

'Solar Fire' has orange flowers without the dark ring.

U. calenduliflora This species differs from *U. anthemoides* in having yellow flowers and less finely divided foliage. HEIGHT & SPREAD 30×20 cm (12×8 in).

U. speciosa This species produces yellow or orange-yellow, purple-centred daisy flowers. HEIGHT & SPREAD 30×20 cm (12×8 in).

CULTIVATION Plant out in spring, once the risk of hard night frosts has passed, choosing a sunny, sheltered situation. Ursinias flower best in poor, dry soil – a dry, sunny bank is an ideal setting. Deadhead to prolong the flowering period.

Ursinia also makes an attractive summer-flowering pot plant for a cool greenhouse or a sunny position in a conservatory. Put 3 plants in a 15 cm (6 in) pot.

PROPAGATION Sow seed in early spring in trays in the greenhouse. Sowing directly into the flowering positions in mid spring is also successful, though plants will commence flowering later.

PESTS AND DISEASES Usually trouble free.

Uvularia
Bellwort
Convallariaceae

Uvularia grandiflora

The fresh green foliage and nodding yellow flowers of these herbaceous perennials bring colour and grace to a cool shady site in spring and early summer. The flowers are narrowly bell-shaped, with six, usually twisted, petals. The leaves are borne on erect or arching stems.

These rhizomatous plants are native to deciduous woodland in N America and are best planted in a woodland edge or beside a pond. They also suit a shady situation in a large rock garden.

RECOMMENDED SPECIES AND VARIETIES

U. grandiflora ♀ Nodding, bright yellow flowers adorn this species in late spring and early summer. Each flower is up to 5 cm (2 in) long, with narrow, twisted petals. The flowers hang down on slender stalks that emerge from the point where the upper leaves join the stems. The bright green leaves are ovate, 7.5-13 cm (3-5¼ in) long, and hairy beneath. They are fused together in pairs around the stem. The plant has a clump-forming habit. HEIGHT & SPREAD 75×45 cm (2½×1½ ft).

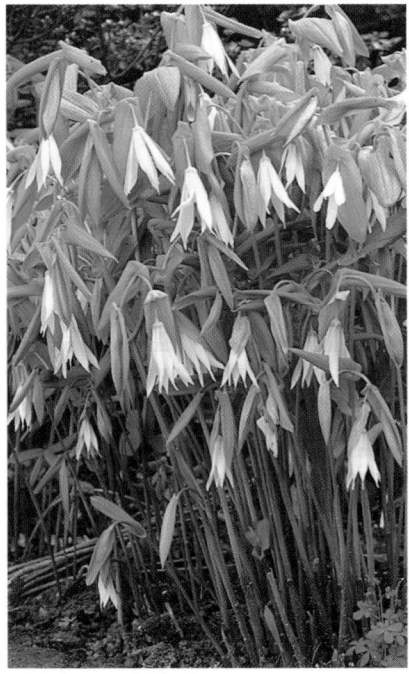

▲ *Uvularia grandiflora*

The flowers produced by var. **pallida** are pale yellow.

U. perfoliata Pale yellow, nodding flowers up to 3 cm (1¼ in) long, with twisted petals, appear in late spring and early summer. The thin flower stalks emerge where the upper leaves join the stems. The light greyish green elliptic to oval leaves are about 7.5 cm (3 in) long. The plant has a clump-forming habit. HEIGHT & SPREAD 60×30 cm (2×1 ft).

U. sessilifolia Nodding, creamy yellow flowers, about 2.5 cm (1 in) long, appear in late spring and early summer. They hang from the leaf axils near the arching tips of the upright leafy stems. The fresh green leaves are narrowly oblong and about 7.5 cm (3 in) in length. This species has a creeping habit. HEIGHT & SPREAD 40×40 cm (16×16 in).

CULTIVATION Plant in early autumn or early spring in a partially shaded situation in well-drained, fairly moist, humus-rich soil.

PROPAGATION Divide in autumn or early spring. Sow seed in pots in a coldframe as soon as it is ripe.

PESTS AND DISEASES Slugs and snails may attack young growth.

u
v

Vaccinium

Ericaceae

Vaccinium corymbosum

The decorative shrubs in this large genus are valuable in areas with acid soils. Most will grow in moist soil and can tolerate exceptionally acid, peaty or sandy soil. The genus includes deciduous plants, whose leaves turn colour before falling, and evergreens. The alternate leaves have smooth or serrated edges. Widespread throughout the Northern Hemisphere, the plants generally produce pretty but small urn-like, bell-shaped or tubular flowers. The many-seeded berries include blueberry and cranberry, but some of the other berries are insipid or sour. The recommended plants are fairly hardy, but *Vaccinium delavayi, V. floribundum, V. glaucoalbum* and *V. nummularia* are unsuitable for cold areas.

RECOMMENDED SPECIES AND VARIETIES

V. corymbosum♀ (blueberry) Deciduous ovate to lance-shaped leaves, up to 8 cm (3¼ in) long, turn orange to scarlet in autumn. The rounded, blue-black berries ripen in late summer and early autumn, attracting birds unless the shrub is protected by netting. This plant will grow in wet ground. HEIGHT & SPREAD 1 m×60 cm (3×2 ft) after 5 years, ultimately 1.5 m (5 ft) tall.

V. delavayi Shiny, dark green, obovate leaves, about 1.5 cm (½ in) long, grow on this dwarf evergreen with a compact habit. HEIGHT & SPREAD 20×20 cm (8×8 in) after 5 years, ultimately up to 1 m (3 ft) tall.

V. floribundum (syn. *V. mortinia*) Red-tinted young growth helps to earn this low, spreading evergreen its place in the garden. The leaves, to 1.5 cm (½ in), partly hide the red berries. HEIGHT & SPREAD 50 cm×1.2 m (20 in×4 ft) after 5 years, ultimately up to 1.2 m (4 ft) tall.

V. glaucoalbum♀ Stiff, oval leaves, up to 8 cm (3¼ in) long, have attractive waxy white undersides. A profusion of black

▼ *Vaccinium glaucoalbum*

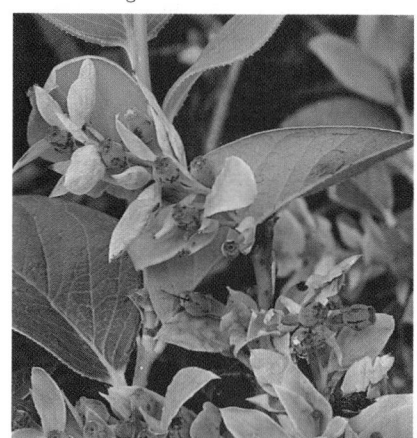

berries with a bluish white bloom appear in autumn on this compact, evergreen shrub. HEIGHT & SPREAD 1×1 m (3×3 ft) after 5 years, ultimately 1.2 m (4 ft) tall.

V. mortinia see *V. floribundum*

V. nummularia This dwarf evergreen is grown for its thick, shiny, oval leaves, up to 2.5 cm (1 in) long, that are bronzy when young. The shoots are hairy and the pinkish flowers appear in late spring and early summer. The berries are black. HEIGHT & SPREAD 20×20 cm (8×8 in) after 5 years, ultimately 40 cm (16 in) tall.

▲ *Vaccinium nummularia*

V. ovatum The leathery, evergreen foliage of this bushy, erect shrub is a glossy, pinkish brown when young. The oval to oblong leaves are up to 3 cm (1¼ in) long. This plant thrives in woodland conditions and tolerates shade. Its size is rather variable. HEIGHT & SPREAD 60×45 cm (2×1½ ft) after 5 years, ultimately up to 4 m (13 ft) tall.

V. vitis-idaea (cowberry, mountain cranberry) Lustrous green, egg-shaped leaves, up to 2.5 cm (1 in) long, give excellent ground cover and make this dwarf, creeping evergreen the best choice for a small garden. Bright red, sharp-tasting berries follow the summer flowers. HEIGHT & SPREAD 15×20 cm (6×8 in) after 5 years, ultimately 30 cm (12 in) tall.

Plants in the vigorous 'Koralle Group'♀ may be invasive, while ssp. *minus* is less so.

CULTIVATION Plant in autumn or spring in acid soil that does not dry out in summer. Provide shelter for *V. nummularia* and *V. glaucoalbum* in cold gardens.

▼ *Vaccinium vitis-idaea*

PROPAGATION Take softwood cuttings, including a heel of the old wood, in late summer and grow in a peat-sand mixture with bottom heat. Sow seed of species in moist peat in a coldframe in autumn. If using a propagator, sow seed in winter. Layer ground-hugging plants.

PRUNING Cut back the tips of vigorous shoots once a year in spring if necessary to keep the plant tidy.

PESTS AND DISEASES Usually trouble free, but rabbits and deer will eat unprotected plants and birds will eat unprotected berries of *V. corymbosum*.

Valerian, common see *Valeriana officinalis*
Valerian, red see *Centranthus ruber*

Valeriana

Valerian
Valerianaceae

Rounded clusters of tiny pink or white, tubular to flat flowers are borne above the foliage from spring to mid summer. The genus includes hardy herbaceous perennials, shrubs and sub-shrubs. Common valerian, *Valeriana officinalis*, has been cultivated for centuries for its medicinal properties. It is now more often grown as an ornamental. All the valerians described below are native to the Northern Hemisphere.

RECOMMENDED SPECIES AND VARIETIES

V. 'Alba' see *Centranthus ruber albus*

V. alliariifolia Tiny pink flowers, in clusters about 4 cm (1½ in) across, appear from early to mid summer. The bright green, heart-shaped leaves grow to 20 cm (8 in) across. Fluffy ornamental seed heads follow the flowers in autumn. This species is ideal for woodland gardens or other moist, shady areas. HEIGHT & SPREAD 1×1 m (3×3 ft).

V. 'Coccinea' see *Centranthus ruber*

V. officinalis (common valerian, garden heliotrope) Flower clusters, up to 4 cm (1½ in) across, are borne in mid summer. They may be white or shades of pink. The blooms rise above a mass of mid green, much divided foliage. The leaves may be up to 5 cm (2 in) long. The plant forms a clump. HEIGHT & SPREAD 1.2×1 m (4×3 ft).

▼ *Valeriana officinalis*

u
v

Veronica
Speedwell
Scrophulariaceae

Veronica prostrata

Tiny, mostly blue flowers, carried in slender spikes or held singly, make these hardy perennials valuable for summer colour. A number of species make fine border plants while other species are suitable for the rock garden. There are ground-hugging plants and shrubby clump-formers, most growing best in sunny, well-drained soils, though *Veronica beccabunga* requires a moist soil. The four-petalled, saucer-shaped flowers are 6–20 mm (¼–¾ in) across. Pink and white flowered varieties are also available. The leaves are narrowly to broadly oval.

RECOMMENDED SPECIES AND VARIETIES

V. austriaca Loose spikes of clear blue flowers are borne from early to mid summer. This evergreen plant has a semi-upright, but rather floppy habit, vigorously forming a clump with downy, 2.5–5 cm (1–2 in) long, oval leaves. It can be grown in a rock garden but needs winter cover in cold wet areas. Native to E Europe. HEIGHT & SPREAD 20×60 cm (8×24 in).

Corfu Form and **'Ionian Skies'** have particularly bright blue flowers.

Loose spikes of clear blue flowers are borne by ssp. *teucrium* (syn. *V. teucrium*) in early to mid summer among rounded leaves that are up to 3 cm (1¼ in) long. **'Crater Lake Blue'**♀ has vivid sky-blue flowers,

▼ *Veronica austriaca* ssp. *teucrium*

both **'Kapitän'** and **'Royal Blue'**♀ have deep blue flowers.

V. beccabunga (brooklime) Starry, blue flowers veined with violet are carried in slender spires in late spring and mid summer by this hardy perennial. Dark green oval leaves are up to 4 cm (1½ in) long. The plant is found in the wild, growing in or near water, but will grow on moist soils in the garden where its rather floppy habit can mask any unsightly low features round a pool. HEIGHT & SPREAD 60×60 cm (2×2 ft).

V. bombycina China-blue flowers are borne in short spikes during late spring above a loose mound of oval, almost white leaves with a dense, downy covering. This evergreen can be damaged by winter wet and cold and is best grown in an alpine house. Native to S Turkey and the Lebanon. HEIGHT & SPREAD 5×20 cm (2×8 in).

V. chamaedrys (germander speedwell) Narrow spikes of white-eyed, bright blue flowers sprout from upper leaf joints over a long period from early spring to mid summer. This rather untidy, sprawling plant is suitable for a rock garden. The oval to tri-angular evergreen leaves are unevenly toothed, 1–2.5 cm (⅜–1 in) long and dull green. Native to Britain. HEIGHT & SPREAD 15×30 cm (6×12 in).

V. cinerea♀ Unusual, ash-grey, broadly strap-shaped evergreen leaves, up to 2 cm (¾ in) long, set off the clusters of purplish blue or pink flowers in early summer on this tough and rather invasive carpeting plant. Flowering shoots rise over a broad mat of woody stems. It is hardy and suitable only for a large rock garden. Native to Turkey. HEIGHT & SPREAD 10×30 cm (4×12 in).

V. exaltata Spikes of tiny clear blue flowers are carried in mid summer. This hardy perennial will stand upright without the need for staking. The dark green, lance-shaped leaves, up to 10 cm (4 in) long, have jagged edges. Native to Europe. HEIGHT & SPREAD 1.2 m×30 cm (4×1 ft).

▼ *Veronica chamaedrys*

V. fruticans (rock speedwell) Deep blue flowers are enhanced by a reddish eye, and rise in short, loose spikes during mid summer to early autumn. The hardy rock plant is of bushy growth with fine, partly woody stems and evergreen, 1 cm (⅜ in) long, oval leaves. Native to Europe. HEIGHT & SPREAD 15×30 cm (6×12 in).

V. gentianoides♀ A stately hardy perennial, suitable for a rock garden, this species has spires of flowers resembling small holly-hocks and is undemanding and generous with bloom. The 20 cm (8 in) spikes of

Veronica gentianoides

powder-blue flowers are borne in early summer. The dark green, glossy, evergreen leaves, 2.5 cm (1 in) long, form a clump. Native to SE Europe. HEIGHT & SPREAD 30×40 cm (12×16 in).

'Nana' is more compact with pale blue flowers. **'Variegata'** is slightly less vigorous than the species with pale blue flowers and leaves marked with broad cream stripes.

V. incana see *V. spicata* ssp. *incana*

V. longifolia Bright blue, saucer-shaped flowers are carried in dense, slender spikes 25 cm (10 in) long. A hardy perennial, this rather floppy plant has stems with whorls of mid green leaves up to 8 cm (3¼ in) long. Native to Europe and Russia. HEIGHT & SPREAD 1 m×30 cm (3×1 ft).

'Schneeriesin' bears deep blue flowers on longer spikes.

▼ *Veronica longifolia*

V. nummularia (Pyrenean speedwell) Dense clusters of blue or pink flowers are held at the tips of shoots which rise from bare stems along the ground. The shoots of this mat-forming hardy rock plant are packed with 1 cm (⅜ in) long, rounded, fleshy evergreen leaves. Native to the Pyrenees. HEIGHT & SPREAD 5×30 cm (2×12 in).

V. pectinata Profuse clusters of pale blue flowers cover a mass of velvety shoots and deeply toothed, small, rounded evergreen leaves during late spring to early summer. This hardy rock plant forms a mat of creeping stems. Native to Iran and Turkey. HEIGHT & SPREAD 10×30 cm (4×12 in).

'Rosea' has rose-lilac blooms.

V. peduncularis Small spikes of bright blue flowers with white eyes are borne in early spring and summer on this hardy perennial. It is a plant suitable for rock gardens and paving because of its mat-forming habit, its prostrate stems clothed with small, glossy evergreen leaves up to 2.5 cm (1 in) long. Native to Turkey and the Caucasus. HEIGHT & SPREAD 10×40 cm (4×16 in).

'Georgia Blue' is more spreading.

V. prostrata♀ Small dense spikes of bright blue flowers are borne in late spring to early summer on this mat-forming, hardy rock plant with small, dark green, evergreen leaves. Native to S Europe. HEIGHT & SPREAD 10×45 cm (4×18 in).

'Blue Sheen' has bright blue flowers. 'Lodden Blue' has dusky blue flowers. 'Mrs Holt' has deep pink flowers. 'Rosea' has pink-lilac flowers. 'Spode Blue' has china-blue flowers. 'Trehane' has violet-blue flowers. The dwarf form 'Nana' has deep blue flowers.

V. 'Shirley Blue'♀ This is a reliable dwarf plant for growing at the front of a border. The bright blue flowers are carried on stiff stems among deep green leaves. HEIGHT & SPREAD 25×25 cm (10×10 in).

▼ *Veronica prostrata* 'Rosea'

V. spicata Profuse dense spikes of blue flowers are seen in mid to late summer on this hardy compact perennial. It is a good plant for the front of a mixed border with tussocks of mid green lance-shaped leaves up to 8 cm (3¼ in) long. Native to Europe, Turkey and central and E Asia. HEIGHT & SPREAD 45×45 cm (18×18 in).

'Erika' has pink flowers and grows to just 30 cm (12 in) tall.

V. spicata ssp. *incana*♀ (syn. *V. incana*) Dense spikes of mid blue flowers are borne in mid to late summer among the bright, silver-grey leaves of this hardy perennial. HEIGHT & SPREAD 45×45 cm (18×18 in).

'Nana' has starry, violet-blue flowers in mid summer that are crowded in narrow spires on upright shoots. A dwarf plant, the stems creep along the ground and bear greyish, oval leaves, 2 cm (¾ in) long, and bluntly toothed. Native to the Caucasus. HEIGHT & SPREAD 7.5×20 cm (3×8 in).

'Wendy'♀ has a looser habit with bright blue flowers and grey leaves. 'Romiley Purple' has a bushy habit and dark blue flowers and 'Rotfuchs' ('Red Fox') has deep pink flowers.

V. stelleri see *V. wormskjoldii*
V. teucrium see *V. austriaca* ssp. *teucrium*
V. wormskjoldii (syn. *V. stelleri*) Short spikes of violet-blue, cup-shaped flowers are borne in late summer on this easily grown, hardy perennial. A clump-forming plant for the rock garden or path edge, the semi-erect stems are clothed with oval, evergreen leaves up to 3 cm (1¼ in) long. Native to N America and Greenland. HEIGHT & SPREAD 20×40 cm (8×16 in).

CULTIVATION Plant from autumn to spring. Any reasonably light soil with some humus content will suffice. Choose locations for planting where there is plentiful sun but shelter from cold, harsh winds. Remove spent flowers to encourage compact habit and good flowering in the following year. Plants soon become weak because of the

growth of too many stems, so split them up every 2 or 3 years. Many of the taller types will need staking. Feeding is not required.

PROPAGATION Divide clump or mat-forming species from autumn to early spring, replanting the offsets in the required places. Some species, for example *V. bombycina* and *V. chamaedrys*, are too slender and loose in habit for division. For these species take semi-ripe cuttings of non-flowering shoots in mid to late summer. Grow on in pots in the shelter of a coldframe, and plant them out in late spring.

Species can be raised from seed sown in early spring to produce plants for setting out later in the year.

PESTS AND DISEASES Powdery mildew may attack the foliage in summer.

Veronica, shrubby see *Hebe*
Vervain see *Verbena*
Vetch see *Vicia*
Vetch, kidney see *Anthyllis vulneraria*
Vetch, spring see *Lathyrus vernus*

Viburnum
Caprifoliaceae

Viburnum plicatum 'Mariesii'

These hardy evergreen and deciduous shrubs offer a tremendous diversity of foliage, flowers and fruit, providing year-round colour and interest. Seldom exceeding a height of 4.5 m (15 ft), viburnums are easy to grow and make handsome features in a mixed border or can be grown as individual specimens in a lawn. They are also useful hedging and ground-cover plants.

The flowers are mainly white or cream, but can be entirely pink or flushed pink. They are borne in dense round clusters or flat wide heads and are often deliciously scented. The leaves vary considerably from species to species, but all are opposite and toothed and between 5-18 cm (2-7 in) in length. Some species produce brilliantly coloured autumn foliage. Fleshy fruits, often seen in great profusion from late summer and lasting into late winter or early spring, are about 8 mm (⅜ in) across and can be red, orange, yellow, blue or black.

RECOMMENDED SPECIES AND VARIETIES
V. x *bodnantense* The clusters of sweetly scented pink to white flowers open continuously from early winter to early spring. This erect, twiggy deciduous shrub has dull green ovate leaves – the young foliage is

695

tinged with bronze. HEIGHT & SPREAD 1.8×1.5 m (6×5 ft) after 5 years, ultimately 3 m (10 ft) tall.

'Charles Lamont'♀ carries flowers that are bright pink in bud, opening to a silvery pink. 'Dawn' has rose-red flowers in bud, opening flushed pink. This is the most commonly seen variety. 'Deben' has apple blossom pink buds that open to white.

V. × *burkwoodii* Sweetly scented pink buds open to white in mid to late spring. The leaves are a rich lustrous green above and covered with a pale brown down on the underside. This evergreen develops into a dense, twiggy, round-headed shrub. HEIGHT & SPREAD 1×1.2 m (3×4 ft) after 5 years, ultimately 2.4 m (8 ft) tall.

'Anne Russell'♀ is a more compact shrub with slightly larger clusters of fragrant flowers that are pink in bud, opening to pure white. 'Fulbrook' flowers later and has larger, conical clusters of flowers that are pink in bud, opening to pure white. 'Park Farm Hybrid'♀ has a more spreading habit and larger, pinker flower clusters.

V. × *carlcephalum*♀ Large, dense clusters of intensely fragrant white flowers (that are pink in bud) appear in late spring on this fast-growing, upright deciduous shrub with a rather stiff appearance. The light green, broadly ovate leaves often have red tints in autumn. HEIGHT & SPREAD 1.5×1.2 m (5×4 ft) after 5 years, ultimately 3 m (10 ft) tall.

V. carlesii Rounded clusters of very fragrant, waxy white flowers, pink in bud, open in mid to late spring. This is a dense, round-headed deciduous shrub with mid green leaves that offer red tints in autumn. HEIGHT & SPREAD 1×1 m (3×3 ft) after 5 years, ultimately 2 m (6½ ft) tall.

'Aurora'♀ has intense red buds opening to pale pink. The leaves are bright green with a hint of copper on opening. 'Charis' is a vigorous variety with red buds that open to pale pink and then white. 'Diana' is purplish red in bud, opening to pink and fading to almost white.

V. cinnamomifolium♀ This round-headed evergreen shrub is grown for its elegant oval

▼ *Viburnum cinnamomifolium*

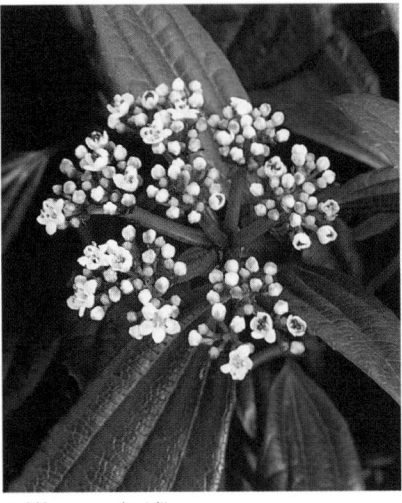

▲ *Viburnum davidii*

leaves that are dark green and leathery. Small dull white flowers appear in mid summer and are followed by blue fruits. Plant in a sheltered position. HEIGHT & SPREAD 1×1 m (3×3 ft) after 5 years, ultimately 4.5 m (15 ft) tall.

V. davidii♀ A low-growing, densely branched evergreen shrub grown primarily for its leathery, dark green leaves with 3 conspicuous veins. Small white flowers, borne in flat heads in early summer, are followed by iridescent blue fruits that last throughout winter. HEIGHT & SPREAD 30×40 cm (12×16 in) after 5 years, ultimately 1.5 m (5 ft) tall.

V. farreri♀ This densely branched, upright deciduous shrub bears drooping clusters of pale pinkish white scented flowers from late autumn to early spring. The bright green leaves are bronze when young. HEIGHT & SPREAD 1 m×75 cm (3×2½ ft) after 5 years, ultimately 2.4 m (8 ft) tall.

'Candidissimum' (syn. 'Album') is less densely branched with pure white fragrant flowers and lighter green leaves. 'Nanum', a compact, densely twiggy shrub, reaches an ultimate height of 1 m (3 ft). The pale pink scented flowers are less abundant.

▼ *Viburnum farreri* 'Candidissimum'

▲ *Viburnum opulus*

V. henryi Dull white, slightly fragrant flowers in early to mid summer are followed by rich red, oval fruits that turn black in winter. This stiffly branched evergreen shrub has dark green shiny leaves with paler undersides. HEIGHT & SPREAD 1×1 m (3×3 ft) after 5 years, ultimately 2.4 m (8 ft) tall.

V. × *juddii*♀ Clusters of scented flowers in spring are pink and open to white. This bushy deciduous shrub has dark green oval leaves. HEIGHT & SPREAD 1×1 m (3×3 ft) after 5 years, ultimately 1.8 m (6 ft) tall.

V. opulus (guelder rose) A dense, multistemmed deciduous shrub grown primarily for its display of bright red oval fruits in early to mid autumn. Flattened clusters of small creamy white flowers are produced in early summer. The dark green maple-like leaves sometimes produce brilliant orange and red autumn colour, but this is quite variable. HEIGHT & SPREAD 1.5×1.5 m (5×5 ft) after 5 years, ultimately 4.5 m (15 ft) tall.

'Aureum' has bright yellow leaves that turn pale green. This plant requires a sheltered situation preferably in shade for part of the day otherwise leaf scorch occurs. 'Compactum'♀ is a dense, twiggy shrub, growing to 1.5 m (5 ft) tall, that produces a

▼ *Viburnum opulus* 'Compactum'

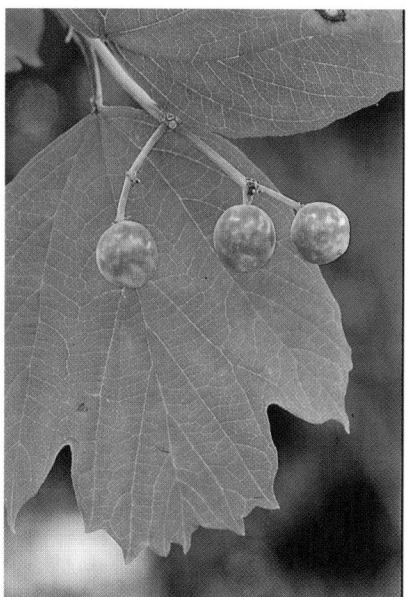

▲ *Viburnum opulus* 'Notcutt's Variety'

▲ *Viburnum opulus* 'Roseum'

▲ *Viburnum opulus* 'Xanthocarpum'

▲ *Viburnum plicatum* 'Lanarth'

good display of flowers, bright red fruits and occasionally autumn colour. **'Notcutt's Variety'** is vigorous with large flowers and fruit and attractive red autumn colour. **'Roseum'** (snowball tree) has pure white globular flowerheads that are apple green on opening and often fade to a dull pink. **'Xanthocarpum'** produces a conspicuous display of translucent yellow fruits.

V. plicatum Grown for their spectacular flowers, these deciduous shrubs can be compact and upright in habit, or can have horizontal branches that create an elegant tiered effect. The flowerheads, borne in late spring and early summer, are made up of masses of creamy white flowers surrounded by white ray florets. Autumn colour is not predictable, but can be rich reddish purple. HEIGHT & SPREAD 1×1.2m (3×4ft) after 5 years, ultimately 3m (10ft) tall.

Large, globular flowerheads of white sterile flowers are seen on **'Grandiflorum'**, fading to pink as they age. Branches are horizontally arranged. **'Lanarth'** is a vigorous variety with large white flowerheads and both ascending and horizontal branches. **'Mariesii'** attractively combines tiers of horizontal branches and abundant white flowers. **'Nanum Semperflorens'** is a compact, slow-growing shrub with ascending branches. It reaches a height of only 1.5m (5ft). Small white flowers are borne over a long period of time from early to late summer. **'Pink Beauty'** is compact with ascending and horizontal branches. The white flowers turn pink with age. **'Shasta'** is a broad-spreading plant with horizontal branches that are covered in a profusion of large pure white flowers.

V. **'Pragense'** This large, round-headed evergreen shrub is grown for its shiny dark green leaves that are felted beneath. Clusters of creamy white flowers are borne in late spring. HEIGHT & SPREAD 1×1m (3×3ft) after 5 years, ultimately 2.4m (8ft) tall.

V. rhytidophyllum A densely branched, round-headed evergreen shrub with shiny, dark green, wrinkled leaves that are felted beneath. Clusters of yellowish white flowers appear in late spring and early summer. The bright red fruits turn black in autumn and winter. HEIGHT & SPREAD 1×1m (3×3ft) after 5 years, ultimately 4.5m (15ft) tall.

V. sargentii This upright, multistemmed deciduous species has maple-like leaves that are bronze when young, turning rich yellow-green. Clusters of creamy white flowers in spring are followed by bright red translucent fruits that last from early autumn through to early winter. HEIGHT & SPREAD 1.2×1m (4×3ft) after 5 years, ultimately 4.5m (15ft) tall.

'Onondaga' bears pink fertile flowers surrounded by white sterile flowers in late spring and early summer. The flowers contrast well with the dark purple-maroon young foliage. The plant is more upright in habit than the species.

V. tinus (laurustinus) This evergreen shrub has a dense, bushy, rounded habit and shiny dark green leaves. The flowers, carried in large flat heads, are pink to pure white, ageing to whitish pink or white fading to pink. Buds appear from mid autumn onwards and open progressively from mid winter. The fruits are deep blue turning black. HEIGHT & SPREAD 1.2×1.2m (4×4ft) after 5 years, ultimately 3.5m (12ft) tall.

Viburnum tinus

'Eve Price' is a compact shrub with flowers that are pink in bud, opening to pale pink. The intensity of flower colour varies from year to year. **'French White'** is vigorous with large pure white flowers. **'Gwenllian'** has masses of pink flowers, deep pink in bud. **'Variegatum'** is a creamy yellow variegated form with small pink flower buds opening white.

CULTIVATION Viburnums do well in sun or light, dappled shade in most soils including those that are thin and chalky. The evergreen species tend to be more shade tolerant. *V. rhytidophyllum* and other large-leaved evergreens do not tolerate wind exposure, and deciduous winter flowerers require some frost protection. Viburnums flower well from an early age, generally between 1–3 years. Species grown for their decorative berries usually do best when planted in groups of 2 or 3.

U
V

PROPAGATION Raise evergreen species from semi-ripe cuttings in early to mid autumn. For deciduous species take soft-wood cuttings in early to mid summer. Berries can be sown in a coldframe in autumn or spring after a cold period in the fridge. Seedling variation will occur.

PRUNING Cut out old central branches of specimen plants to ground level in early spring to allow regeneration to take place from the centre of the plant.

PESTS AND DISEASES Aphids attack the deciduous species with *V. carlesii*, *V. opulus* and *V. sargentii* particularly susceptible. *V. tinus* is affected by sooty mould after an attack of either aphids or whiteflies. Honey fungus may occur in older species.

Vicia
Vetch
Leguminosae

These hardy herbaceous perennials have small, brightly coloured, two-lipped flowers and fern-like foliage. They are best suited to informal or wild areas in a garden as their creeping, clambering habit can make them invasive. Native to the woods and hedge-rows of the British countryside.

▼ *Vicia cracca*

RECOMMENDED SPECIES

V. cracca (tufted vetch) Small violet-blue flowers are carried in one-sided, 5-10 cm (2-4 in) long spikes throughout summer. The tendril-tipped shoots bear paired rows of narrowly oval, dark green leaflets 2 cm (¾ in) long. The shoots scramble across the ground and through other plants. HEIGHT & SPREAD 30 cm×1 m (1×3 ft).

V. sepium (bush vetch) Purple, or occasionally yellow, flowers are borne in short spikes, 1.5 cm (½ in) long, in mid summer. The 1 cm (⅜ in) long, oval leaves are dark green. HEIGHT & SPREAD 45×60 cm (1½×2 ft).

V. sylvatica Loose spikes, 1.5 cm (½ in) long, of pale lilac flowers are borne by this vigorous species in mid summer. Leaves with 6-12 pairs of mid green, oblong leaflets are carried along the shoots. HEIGHT & SPREAD 1×2 m (3×6½ ft).

CULTIVATION Plant in autumn or early spring in any soil as long as it contains little clay. Choose a site in full sun or partial shade. Provide twiggy supports for the plants to scramble over.

PROPAGATION Sow seed in the garden where the plants are to grow from late autumn to early spring.

PESTS AND DISEASES Powdery mildew may affect the foliage during dry spells.

Vinca
Periwinkle
Apocynaceae

Vinca major

These vigorous trailing plants form extensive carpets of foliage and produce five-petalled, propeller-shaped flowers mainly in spring and early summer and intermittently throughout the growing season. The hardy sub-shrubs or perennials listed here make good ground-cover plants in shrubberies and mixed beds or in wild gardens. Periwinkles grow well in shade provided it is not too dry and are useful for growing under deciduous trees and shrubs. However, flower production is more profuse in full sun. The plants are poisonous. Native to N Africa, central Asia and Europe.

RECOMMENDED SPECIES AND VARIETIES

V. difformis The glossy dark green leaves are narrowly lance-shaped and grow up to 7 cm (2¾ in) long. The violet-blue or white saucer-shaped flowers are 2.5 cm (1 in) across. This sub-shrub requires a moister, more protected site than the other species, but given the right conditions it will grow well and flower throughout the later part of the year. The plant may be evergreen in more protected gardens. HEIGHT & SPREAD 30×60 cm (1×2 ft).

V. herbacea A herbaceous perennial that bears trailing shoots with mid green leaves up to 5 cm (2 in) long. The pale blue or white flowers, 3 cm (1¼ in) across, are well spaced along the stems. HEIGHT & SPREAD 30×60 cm (1×2 ft).

V. major An evergreen sub-shrub with long prostrate shoots covered with ovate to lance-shaped leaves that grow up to 9 cm (3½ in) long. The bright blue flowers are 3 cm (1¼ in) across. HEIGHT & SPREAD 36×36 cm (14×14 in).

'Aureomaculata' see 'Maculata'. Pure

▼ *Vinca minor* f. *alba*

u v
u v

▲ *Vinca major* var. *oxyloba*

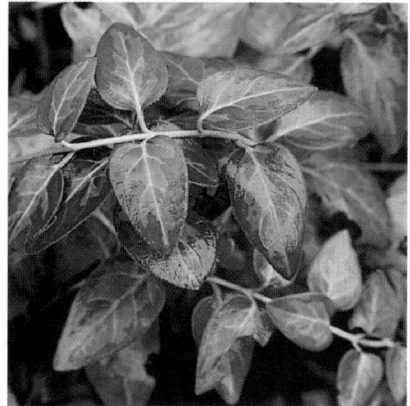

▲ *Vinca major* 'Maculata'

white flowers are seen on var. **alba**, while ssp. *hirsuta* has hairy leaf stalks and violet-blue flowers with hairy sepals.

'**Maculata**' (syn. 'Aureomaculata') has pale blue flowers. The leaves are dark yellowish green in the centre and have light yellowish green margins. Dark green leaves and narrow, pointed dark violet flowers with narrow lobes distinguish var. *oxyloba*.

▼ *Vinca minor* 'Alba Variegata'

▲ *Vinca minor* 'Burgundy'

'**Variegata**'♡ carries light green leaves with pale yellow margins and is decorated with rich lavender-blue flowers in early summer. *V. minor* This is an evergreen sub-shrub with long trailing shoots and blue-pink or purplish flowers. The glossy dark green leaves, up to 5cm (2in) long, are lance-shaped or elliptic. The flowers are 3cm (1¼in) across. This plant is usually found in gardens as one of the following selections. HEIGHT & SPREAD 20×80cm (8×32in).

White flowers are seen on f. *alba*. '**Alba Variegata**' has yellow variegation on its leaves and white flowers. '**Argenteo-variegata**'♡ produces violet-blue flowers and dull green leaves which have pale yellow-striped margins and midribs. '**Atro-purpurea**'♡ carries dark green leaves and purple flowers. '**Aureovariegata**' has blue flowers and leaves that are striped and edged with yellow. '**Azurea Flore Pleno**'♡ bears dark green leaves and carries dark blue double flowers.

'**Burgundy**' has dark green leaves and reddish purple flowers. '**Gertrude Jekyll**'♡ produces medium green leaves and narrow

▼ *Vinca minor* 'Argenteovariegata'

▲ *Vinca minor* 'Multiplex'

creamy white flowers carried well above the foliage. '**La Grave**'♡ is a compact plant with dark green leaves and lavender-violet flowers. '**Multiplex**' has double purple flowers. '**Silver Service**' carries grey-green leaves with silver variegation and double mid blue flowers.

CULTIVATION Plant from autumn to spring in any well-drained garden soil in a partially shaded or sunny spot. On dry soils mulch in spring to conserve moisture. Cut back in spring to control the size of the plants.

PROPAGATION Divide or remove trailing stems which have rooted into the ground from autumn to spring. Take softwood cuttings in summer and plant out at any time after they have rooted.

PESTS AND DISEASES Usually trouble free, but sometimes rust can appear on the leaves and reduce the plant's vigour.

▼ *Vinca major* 'Variegata'

U
V

Viola

Violaceae

Steeped in mythology and folklore, violas have an enduring place in British gardens for the cheerful splashes of colour they can bring throughout the year. Some have a sweet fragrance or can be used for culinary flavouring

Violas include the well-loved cottage-garden plants pansies and violets, as well as a wide range of cultivated varieties. They are all good at the front of borders and in rock gardens, often flowering throughout summer. *Viola* × *wittrockiana* and its varieties, known as the 'winter-flowering' pansies, are excellent in containers and can remain in flower during mild spells in winter and spring. Most violas are native to northern temperate areas. They are generally hardy evergreen perennials which are often treated as annuals or biennials. Most thrive in any soil and many do equally well in sun or partial shade. Only a few need special protection.

All have flat, roundish, five-petalled flowers, but these exhibit a diverse range of size, colour and patterning. Some have a tube or spur projecting from the back of the flower. Most violas have mid green, oval to heart-shaped leaves, 2-4cm (¾-1½in) long, sometimes with toothed edges.

RECOMMENDED SPECIES AND VARIETIES

V. alba (syn. *V. obliqua* ssp. *alba*) White flowers, 2cm (¾in) across, with violet veins appear in late spring and early summer. This plant will grow in shade. HEIGHT & SPREAD 10×30cm (4×12in).

V. bertolonii Patterned with violet and yellow, the spurred flowers, 2.5cm (1in) wide, appear from mid to late summer. HEIGHT & SPREAD 10×30cm (4×12in).

V. biflora (yellow wood violet) Bright yellow flowers, 2cm (¾in) across, are produced from mid to late spring. This plant tolerates some shade. HEIGHT & SPREAD 5×30cm (2×12in).

V. cornuta♀ (horned pansy) Fragrant white or lilac flowers, 2.5cm (1in) across, with pointed spurs appear from early to mid summer on this clump-forming plant. HEIGHT & SPREAD 15×30cm (6×12in).

Plants in the **Alba Group**♀ produce white flowers, as does the dwarf plant **'Alba Minor'**, while **'Belmont Blue'** has pale sky-blue flowers and those of the **Lilacina Group** are shades of lilac. **'Minor'**♀ is a compact lavender-blue variety. **'Rosea'** has pinkish violet flowers and **'Victoria Cawthorne'** has purplish pink flowers.

V. elatior Pale blue flowers, up to 3cm (1¼in) across, are borne from late spring to early summer. The leaves are lance-shaped. HEIGHT & SPREAD 30×30cm (12×12in).

V. gracilis Deep purple flowers, 2.5cm (1in) across, appear from mid to late spring above a low mound of tangled stems. HEIGHT & SPREAD 10×30cm (4×12in).

'Lutea' has yellow flowers.

V. hederacea (syn. *V. reniforme*) Twisted violet-blue flowers, 2cm (¾in) across, with white-tipped petals appear from summer to early autumn against kidney-shaped leaves. This plant is best grown under glass in equal quantities of compost and grit. HEIGHT & SPREAD 5×30cm (2×12in).

V. hirta (hairy violet) White or violet flowers, 1.5cm (½in) across, appear from spring to early summer. Loose bunches of leaves are held on hairy stems. HEIGHT & SPREAD 7×10cm (2¾×4in).

V. jooi Reddish purple flowers, 2cm (¾in)

u
v

1 Universal yellow
2 Universal hybrid
3 Universal violet blotch
4 Universal red blotch
5 Universal rose
6 Viola 'Sorbet Plum Velvet'
7 Universal apricot
8 Universal white blotch
9 Universal true blue
10 Universal yellow blotch

across, appear from mid to late spring. HEIGHT & SPREAD 5×15 cm (2×6 in).

V. labradorica hort. see *V. riviniana* Purpurea Group

V. obliqua ssp. *alba* see *V. alba*

V. odorata (sweet violet) Violet flowers, 1.5 cm (½ in) across, appear from early to late spring and again from late summer to early autumn. HEIGHT & SPREAD 7.5×15 cm (3×6 in).

V. pedata Flowers, 2.5 cm (1 in) across, appear from late spring to early autumn. The upper petals are purple, the lower ones pale lilac. The leaves are deeply divided. HEIGHT & SPREAD 15×15 cm (6×6 in).

V. pedatifida (prairie violet) Reddish violet flowers, 2 cm (¾ in) across, with dark veins appear in spring and summer. The leaves are deeply cut. HEIGHT & SPREAD 10×15 cm (4×6 in).

V. reniforme see *V. hederacea*

V. riviniana (dog violet) Spurred blue-violet flowers, 2 cm (¾ in) across, are borne from early spring to early autumn. This European native can be rather invasive. HEIGHT & SPREAD 10×30 cm (4×12 in).

The **Purpurea Group** (syn. *V. labradorica* hort.) have flowers of purple and violet. The leaves are often tinged purple.

V. septentrionalis (northern violet) Pale to deep violet flowers, up to 3 cm (1¼ in) across, appear from spring to early summer. HEIGHT & SPREAD 20×25 cm (8×10 in).

The flowers of f. *alba* are white.

V. tricolor (heartsease, wild pansy) Flowers, 1.5 cm (½ in) across, appear from spring to summer on this annual or biennial. Some flowers are yellow with white markings, while others are purple, marked with white. Colour combinations also occur. HEIGHT & SPREAD 10×30 cm (4×12 in).

V. × wittrockiana (pansy) Flowers, up to 10 cm (4 in) across, in a range of colours and often with a central blotch, appear from early summer to early autumn. These hybrids are grown as annuals or biennials. HEIGHT & SPREAD 15×20 cm (6×8 in).

The following plants produce flowers in spring and summer. A range of bright colours without a central blotch distinguish the flowers of **Clear Crystal Series**. The flowers of '**Joker Light Blue**' are pale blue with a white central blotch, while the **Joker Series**♀ has bicoloured flowers in a mixture

▲ *Viola cornuta*

of colours, all with central markings. '**Jolly Joker**' has rich purple flowers with vivid orange centres, while '**Padparadja**' has deep orange flowers without markings. **Super Chalon Giants** has ruffled flowers in deep red, yellow and purple with darker central blotches. **Swiss Giant Series** produces a range of brightly coloured flowers, all with purple-black central blotches.

The 'winter-flowering' pansies include the **Delta Series** with flowers in a range of colours, with or without central blotches. **Ultima Mixed**♀ has brightly coloured flowers that may be marked with contrasting colours, while those of the **Universal Series**♀ are available in single colours – red, orange, yellow, blue, purple and white – or in mixed colours, often with a central blotch.

OTHER HYBRIDS

VIOLAS

These plants have rounded flowers, 3-5 cm (1¼-2 in) across, with a central blotch. They are usually scented. The plants grow to 15 cm (6 in) tall and 33 cm (13 in) wide.

'**Ardross Gem**' has pale pink to dark

▼ *Viola* 'Maggie Mott'

mauve flowers with a golden central blotch. '**Huntercombe Purple**'♀ has spurred purple flowers. '**Irish Molly**' has yellowy bronze flowers. '**Jackanapes**'♀ has spurred flowers with brown upper petals and yellow lower petals, streaked brown. '**Julian**' has scented, pale lilac-blue flowers with yellow centres, while '**Maggie Mott**'♀ has silvery mauve blooms with cream centres. '**Martin**'♀ has rich, velvety purple flowers with a golden eye. '**Moonlight**'♀ has creamy yellow scented flowers, and '**Nellie Britton**'♀ has spurred mauve-pink flowers.

VIOLETS

Nodding, spurred flowers, up to 2.5 cm (1 in) across, with narrowly oval petals distinguish these plants. This group includes the sweetly scented Parma violets that are not very hardy and need protection in winter. Violets have a height and spread of 30 cm (12 in).

'**Coeur d'Alsace**' has scented salmon-pink flowers. '**Comte de Brazza**' is a Parma violet with white double flowers, shaded with pale blue. '**Duchesse de Parme**' has double, mauve, scented flowers. '**Marie Louise**' is a Parma violet with double mauve flowers, while the flowers of '**Sulphurea**' are apricot-yellow with a cream centre.

VIOLETTAS

These plants have sweetly fragrant, oval flowers, up to 2 cm (¾ in) across, each with a central yellow blotch. They grow to 10 cm (4 in) tall and spread to 25 cm (10 in).

'**Buttercup**' has heavily scented, pale yellow flowers, while '**Dawn**' has primrose-yellow flowers. The scented flowers of '**Little David**'♀ are cream with frilled petals, and '**Rebecca**' has heavily scented white flowers with purple streaked edges.

▼ *Viola gracilis* 'Lutea'

Viola 'Huntercombe Purple' ▼

▼ *Viola* 'Jackanapes'

Viola 'Little David' ▼

CULTIVATION Plant in spring in any reasonably fertile well-drained soil, ideally on a sunny site. Deadhead regularly.

PROPAGATION Take basal cuttings in mid summer. Alternatively, sow seed in spring.

PESTS AND DISEASES Mosaic virus, pansy sickness and rust can cause problems.

Violet see *Viola*
Violet, African see *Saintpaulia*
Violet, dog's tooth
  see *Erythronium dens-canis*
Violet, water see *Hottonia palustris*
Viper's bugloss see *Echium vulgare*
Virginia creeper
  see *Parthenocissus quinquefolia*
Virgin's bower see *Clematis*

Viscum
Viscaceae

This evergreen shrub that is mentioned in folklore is parasitic, growing on the branches of host trees such as *Malus*, *Populus* and *Tilia*. It is easy to grow the native species, *Viscum album*, although it takes seven years to fruit.

RECOMMENDED SPECIES

V. album (mistletoe) Branching yellowy green stems form a globular hanging bush. The stems carry pairs of pale green oblong-shaped leaves, up to 10 cm (4 in) long. Male and female flowers are borne on separate plants, and both are needed to produce the pearly berries from autumn to mid winter.

PROPAGATION In late winter or early spring remove mature berries and rub the seed into bark crevices or under a sliced flap of bark. Choose a healthy, mature host and a branch of at least 10 cm (4 in) diameter, and at least 1.5 m (5 ft) off the ground. The tree should ideally be the same species as the host of the parent plant.

PRUNING None is required.

PESTS AND DISEASES Usually trouble free.

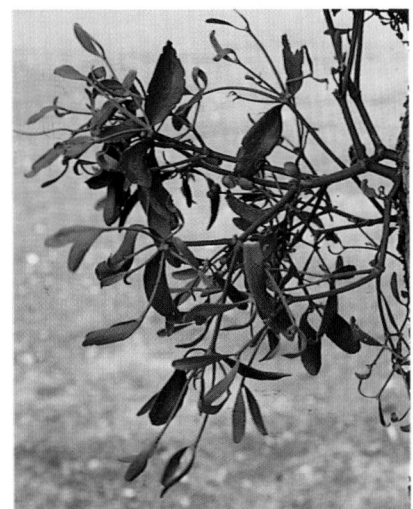
▲ *Viscum album*

Vitaliana
Primulaceae

In spring primrose-like flowers stud the dense cushions or mats of this native of the Alps, Apennines and mountains of Spain. It is excellent in a rock garden, scree bed or trough. Although frost-hardy, this plant needs some protection from winter wet. The genus contains only one species.

V. primuliflora (syn. *Androsoce vitalliana*, *Douglasia vitaliana*) Bright lemon-yellow, stemless flowers, up to 2 cm (¾ in) across, appear above greyish green needle-like leaves, up to 1 cm (⅜ in) long, which often form rosettes. HEIGHT & SPREAD 5 × 25 cm (2 × 10 in).

The oblong leaves of ssp. *praetutiana* are white underneath.

▲ *Vitaliana primuliflora* ssp. *praetutiana*

CULTIVATION Plant in early spring in well-drained neutral or acid soil, ideally in full sun. Improve heavy soil with coarse grit or stone chippings, but avoid limestone. Protect from winter wet with a cloche, or sheet of glass or transparent plastic. Alternatively, grow in pots of gritty compost in an unheated greenhouse.

PROPAGATION Detach rooted shoots from the parent plant in summer and grow in 7.5 cm (3 in) pots in an unshaded coldframe. Water well during warm dry spells.

PESTS AND DISEASES Aphids sometimes infest young leaves.

Vitex
Verbenaceae

Grown for its scented blossoms and handsome foliage, this genus includes evergreen and deciduous shrubs and trees.

RECOMMENDED SPECIES

V. agnus-castus (chaste tree) Clusters of fragrant, tubular, violet or lilac-coloured flowers, up to 15 cm (6 in) long, cover this spreading shrub in autumn. The dark green

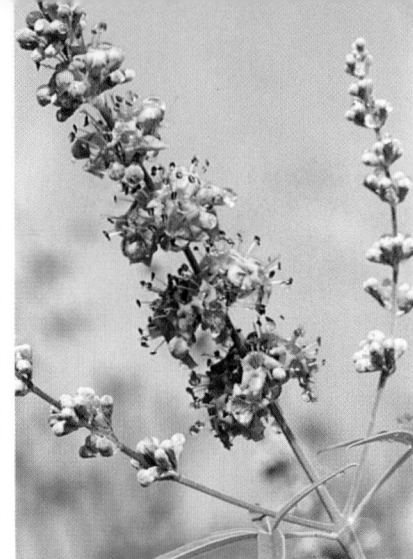
▲ *Vitex agnus-castus*

leaves, borne on grey downy shoots, are divided into oval or lance-shaped leaflets, about 12.5 cm (5 in) long. HEIGHT & SPREAD 2.4 × 2.4 m (8 × 8 ft) after 5 years, also the ultimate size.

CULTIVATION Plant in spring in free-draining soil in a warm, sheltered spot, preferably against a wall. Water well in summer and apply a slow-release fertiliser in spring.

PROPAGATION Take semi-ripe cuttings in summer or sow seed under glass in spring.

PRUNING If necessary, trim back the previous year's growth in spring. Remove any weak, crossing or damaged shoots.

PESTS AND DISEASES Usually trouble free.

Vitis
Grapevine
Vitaceae

Vitis coignetiae

Covering pergolas and trellises with colourful leaves and fruit, ornamental grapevines are at their best in autumn. The leaves are rounded, often with pointed lobes, and turn brilliant shades of orange, red and yellow in autumn. Inconspicuous greenish flowers appear in early or mid summer followed, after a good summer, by bunches of small grapes. (For plants grown for their fruit, see p. 726.)

The plants are native to the Northern Hemisphere. Most are hardy and deciduous, climbing by means of twining tendrils. The vines grow straight up before branching, but will spread nearer to the ground if cut back at planting time.

Only heights are given for the recommended plants as spread depends on the way the plant is trained.

u
v

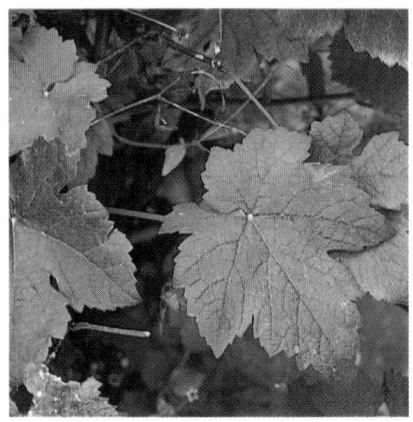

▲ *Vitis vinifera* 'Purpurea'

RECOMMENDED SPECIES AND VARIETIES

V. amurensis (Amur grape) Red, downy, young growth in spring gives way to dark green leaves, up to 30 cm (12 in) long with 5-7 lobes, that turn purple and red in autumn. Small black grapes appear in early or mid autumn. HEIGHT 3 m (10 ft) after 5 years, ultimately 6 m (20 ft) tall.

V. 'Brant'♀ has palmate, deeply lobed, mid green leaves, turning deep bronze-red, pink and orange in autumn, although the veins remain green. Purple-black fruits are borne in cylindrical bunches in mid or late autumn. HEIGHT 3 m (10 ft) after 5 years, ultimately 9 m (30 ft) tall.

V. coignetiae♀ (crimson glory vine) Smooth, rounded, dark green leaves, up to 30 cm (12 in) long, with rust-red hairs underneath thickly cover the stems of this vigorous species. Heart-shaped at the base, the leaves have 3 or 5 short, pointed, coarsely toothed lobes. In autumn they turn spectacular shades of yellow, orange-red and purple-crimson, especially when grown on poor soil. The inedible, 1.5 cm (½ in) wide black grapes have a purple bloom. Perhaps the finest of the ornamental vines, this species is best grown over trees or old buildings. HEIGHT 3.5-4.5 m (12-15 ft) after 5 years, ultimately 25 m (80 ft) tall.

V. vinifera (grape vine, wine grape) The 3 or 5-lobed leaves are up to 15 cm (6 in) long and wide with woolly undersides. Panicles of small flowers appear in late spring, followed by edible fruit. HEIGHT 3 m (10 ft) after 5 years, ultimately 9 m (30 ft) tall.

Ornamental varieties include the following plants. 'Incana' (dusty miller grape) bears 3-lobed or unlobed pale green leaves covered in pale down, especially when young. Black fruits appear in mid or late autumn. 'Purpurea'♀ (Teinturier grape) has ovate to round leaves with 3 or 5 coarsely serrated lobes. Young leaves are pale and downy, turning claret-red and eventually rich purple in autumn. Purple-black fruits with a blue bloom are borne in early or mid autumn.

CULTIVATION Plant in mild weather from late autumn to early spring. For autumn colour, choose a poor soil (which will also restrict growth) and a site facing south or west. Trim plants to within 25 cm (10 in) of the ground, and tie in the young growths.

PROPAGATION Sow seed in late autumn in trays of seed compost kept in a coldframe or greenhouse. Except for *V. coignetiae*, take cuttings of single buds of the previous summer's shoots in late winter and grow under glass. Alternatively, take 30 cm (12 in) hardwood cuttings in late autumn and plant out when rooted. Layer one-year-old growths of *V. coignetiae* in mid autumn.

PRUNING Thin out old growth and shorten young growth in late summer.

PESTS AND DISEASES Scale insects, especially brown scale, may infest stems and foliage, and weevils and caterpillars may eat the leaves.

Vriesea
Bromeliaceae

With eye-catching flowerheads and attractive leaf rosettes, these tropical perennials make bold, colourful houseplants and conservatory specimens. Vibrant spikes of flowers rise above funnel-shaped rosettes formed by plain or patterned, sword-shaped evergreen leaves. Native to S America, these epiphytic plants need high humidity, warmth and shade from direct sunlight.

RECOMMENDED SPECIES AND VARIETIES

V. carinata (lobster claws) In summer or autumn, yellow tubular flowers, up to 5 cm (2 in) long, enclosed by shorter red bracts, are held in short spikes above pale green leaves, up to 20 cm (8 in) long. HEIGHT & SPREAD 30×45 cm (12×18 in).

▲ *Vriesea fosteriana*

V. fosteriana Mid green leaves, up to 45 cm (18 in) long, have maroon bands on the undersides. A bold spike of flowers, up to 1 m (3 ft) tall, is produced in late summer or autumn. The flower spike has yellow leathery bracts, about 4 cm (1½ in) long, embracing yellow petals tipped with reddish brown. HEIGHT & SPREAD 1 m×60 cm (3×2 ft).

V. hieroglyphica (king of the bromeliads) Broad strap-shaped leaves, up to 80 cm (32 in) long, are yellowish green, cross-banded and chequered with dark brownish green. Summer spikes of tubular yellow flowers, each up to 4 cm (1½ in) long, are enclosed by yellow-green papery bracts. HEIGHT & SPREAD 60×75 cm (24×30 in).

V. saundersii♀ Ash-grey, scaly, strap-like leaves blotched with maroon, up to 30 cm (1 ft) long, form neat rosettes. Sword-shaped flower spikes appear from late summer to autumn carrying 5-7 sulphur-yellow flowers, up to 5 cm (2 in) long, enclosed by pale green or yellow-green bracts. HEIGHT & SPREAD 70×45 cm (28×18 in).

V. splendens♀ (flaming sword) Arching, strap-shaped leaves, up to 60 cm (2 ft) long, are olive-green with purple-brown cross-bands. A bold orange-red, sword-like flower spike appears from late summer to late autumn. It has flattened red bracts, up to 7.5 cm (3 in) long, embracing smaller yellow tubular flowers. HEIGHT & SPREAD 90×45 cm (36×18 in).

▲ *Vriesea splendens*

CULTIVATION Grow indoors or under glass in semi-shade at 15-18°C (59-64°F) during active growth, and at a minimum winter temperature of 15°C (59°F). Plant in 10 cm (4 in) pots in John Innes No.2 compost mixed in equal parts with bark chips or perlite. Pour water, ideally soft water, into the centre of the rosette. Water freely in spring and summer but sparingly in winter. Feed monthly from spring to autumn with a general liquid fertiliser. Repot as necessary in spring.

PROPAGATION Separate suckering rosettes in spring and leave to dry off for 2 days before potting on.

PESTS AND DISEASES Mealy bug and scale insects can be troublesome.

Vuylstekeara see ORCHIDS p.467

Wahlenbergia
Campanulaceae

Wahlenbergia saxicola

Single, upturned bell-shaped flowers on slender stalks appear in summer on these annuals or perennials. The plants listed here can be grown in a cold greenhouse or, given the right conditions, in a rock garden.

RECOMMENDED SPECIES AND VARIETIES
W. albomarginata White or pale blue flowers, 2 cm (¾ in) across, rise above a creeping mat of rosetted, spoon-shaped leaves up to 4 cm (1½ in) long. Although hardy, this evergreen perennial benefits from winter cover. Native to New Zealand. HEIGHT & SPREAD 5×15 cm (2×6 in).

▲ *Wahlenbergia albomarginata*

'Blue Mist' has pale blue flowers with deeper blue veining.
W. congesta Pale blue, delicate cupped flowers, 1.5 cm (½ in) across, are held on frail stalks in summer. This little rambling perennial evergreen sends up from creeping stems densely tufted rosettes of 2.5 cm (1 in) long, rounded leaves. Native to Australasia. HEIGHT & SPREAD 2.5×20 cm (1×8 in).
W. gloriosa Purple bell-shaped flowers, 4 cm (1½ in) across, are held on wiry upright stems from mid summer to early autumn. This evergreen perennial forms a low clump with crowded tufts of 3 cm (1¼ in) long strap-shaped leaves. Native to Australia. HEIGHT & SPREAD 15×20 cm (6×8 in).

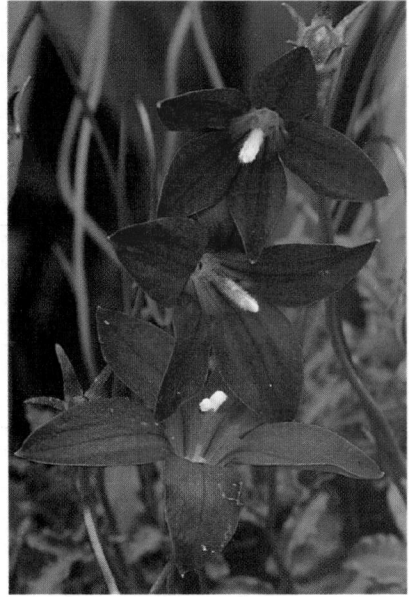

▲ *Wahlenbergia gloriosa*

W. pumilio see *Edrianthus pumilo*
W. saxicola Pale blue flowers, about 2 cm (¾ in) wide, appear on erect stalks in early summer. Spoon-shaped leaves, up to 2.5 cm (1 in) long, are borne in loose, flat mat-forming clusters. This evergreen perennial is easy to grow and hardy in all but the coldest of gardens. Native to Tasmania. HEIGHT & SPREAD 10×25 cm (4×10 in).
W. serpyllifolia see *Edrianthus serpyllifolius*
CULTIVATION Plant in a sheltered sunny position in a light, humus-rich, non-limy well-drained soil. Add plenty of coarse grit if the soil is inclined to heaviness.
PROPAGATION Sow seed or take softwood cuttings in late spring. Alternatively, take rooted tufts from the main growth after flowering and grow in a cold frame.
PESTS AND DISEASES Slugs can cause serious damage to young leaves.

Wake robin see *Trillium*

Waldsteinia
Rosaceae

Waldsteinia ternata

The creeping habit of this evergreen perennial makes it useful as ground cover planted with shrubs, or underplanted with bulbs. Wide-open, broad-petalled, potentilla-like flowers have a mass of golden stamens.
RECOMMENDED SPECIES
W. ternata Lax clusters of 2-4 upward-facing yellow flowers, 2 cm (¾ in) across, appear in early summer. A hardy, evergreen perennial, it spreads by rooted runners. The tufted, 3-lobed leaves, up to 7.5 cm (3 in) wide, have jagged, toothed edges and form dense cover. Found wild from S Alps to Japan. HEIGHT & SPREAD 15×45 cm (6×18 in).
CULTIVATION Plant in spring or autumn in fertile, well-drained soil. Position in partial shade in hotter, drier parts of the country.
PROPAGATION Snip off rooted shoots in late summer for growing on in pots.
PESTS AND DISEASES Usually trouble free.

Wallflower see *Erysimum cheiri*
Walnut see *Juglans*
Wandering Jew
 see *Tradescantia fluminensis*
Wand flower see *Dierama*
Wandflower see *Galax urceolata*
Water arum see *Calla palustris*
Water hawthorn
 see *Aponogeton distachyos*
Water lily see *Nymphaea*
Water soldier see *Stratiotes aloides*

Watsonia
Iridaceae

The elegant, upright spikes of flowers produced by these half-hardy perennials in mid to late summer make them good border plants. They look very effective when associated with grey-leafed plants. Each stem carries a branching spike of tubular flowers that have six lobes spreading out into a star shape. The leaves along the stems and at the base of the plant are narrow, upright and sword-like. Native to southern Africa, they like a sunny position in free-draining soil.
RECOMMENDED SPECIES
W. beatricis see *W. pillansii*
W. borbonica (syn. *W. pyramidata*) Rich pink flowers grow up to 4 cm (1½ in) long. The mid green leaves grow up to 60 cm (2 ft) long. HEIGHT 1 m (3 ft).
 The flowers of ssp. *ardernei* are normally white but may, rarely, be pink.
W. meriana Flowers may be orange, pinky-red, purple and, rarely, yellow, depending on the variety. The blooms, each up to 5 cm (2 in) long, branch irregularly from strong

▼ *Watsonia meriana*

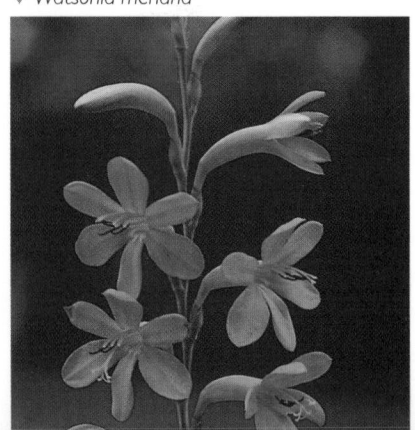

spikes. The mid green leaves are about 45 cm (18 in) long. HEIGHT 1 m (3 ft).

W. pillansii (syn. *W. beatricis*) Orange or orange-red flowers grow up to 5 cm (2 in) long. The mid green leaves grow up to 60 cm (2 ft) long. HEIGHT 1 m (3 ft).

W. pyramidata see *W. borbonica*

CULTIVATION Plant corms 10 cm (4 in) deep and 20 cm (8 in) apart in well-drained soil in a sunny position. In cold areas, plant in spring and after flowering gently lift and store for the winter. In mild areas, plant in autumn or spring and overwinter in the ground, under a generous layer of bark-chip mulch. Remove the mulch in early spring before the shoots appear.

Apply a slow-release fertiliser in spring. Remove faded flowerheads and rake off dead foliage at the end of the season.

PROPAGATION Sow seed in spring under glass. Although the corms do not like to be disturbed, they can occasionally be divided.

PESTS AND DISEASES Apart from occasional damage from earwigs and thrips, they are usually trouble free.

Wattle see *Acacia*
Waxberry see *Gaultheria hispida*
Wax flower see *Stephanotis floribunda*

Weigela
Caprifoliaceae

Weigela florida

Clusters of funnel-shaped flowers – mostly in shades of red, pink or white – are borne in late spring and early summer by these long-lived, deciduous plants. Among the easiest and most popular of all summer-flowering shrubs, weigelas are stalwarts of the shrubbery and are also suitable for a mixed border. The foxglove-like flowers are borne on the previous season's wood, so for the best display weigelas should be pruned straight after flowering. They are mostly native to E Asia, and are hardy in all parts of Britain, thriving in any fertile soil.

RECOMMENDED SPECIES AND VARIETIES

W. florida Rose-pink flowers, paler inside and 2.5 cm (1 in) long, are borne in clusters along arching branches. The light green, ovate leaves are up to 10 cm (4 in) long. They are wrinkled and prominently veined. HEIGHT & SPREAD 1 × 1 m (3 × 3 ft) after 5 years, ultimately 2.1 m (7 ft) tall.

'Aureovariegata' has cream-edged leaves and rose-pink flowers. 'Bristol Snowflake' has white flowers. 'Foliis

'Purpureis'♀ (also sold as 'Purpurea') is a slow-growing, compact variety with purplish leaves and dark pink flowers.

W. japonica Dense down covers the undersides of the mid green oval, tapering leaves, that are up to 10 cm (4 in) long. It is mainly grown in the guise of the cultivar 'Dart's Colourdream'♀, which bears both pink and cream blooms. HEIGHT & SPREAD 1 × 1 m (3 × 3 ft) after 5 years, ultimately growing to 2.4 m (8 ft) tall.

W. maximowiczii Pale yellow or greenish yellow flowers, up to 4 cm (1½ in) long, appear in small clusters in mid spring. The narrow mid green leaves are up to 10 cm (4 in) long. HEIGHT & SPREAD 1 × 1 m (3 × 3 ft) after 5 years, ultimately 1.5 m (5 ft) tall.

W. middendorffiana Pale yellow bell-shaped flowers with orange blotches in the centre appear in mid to late spring. The blooms are up to 4 cm (1½ in) long, held in small clusters at the end of the branches. The bright green, ovate leaves are wrinkled and rather narrow. This species is hardy but starts into growth early and may be frost-damaged unless given a sheltered position. HEIGHT & SPREAD 1 × 1 m (3 × 3 ft) after 5 years, ultimately 1.5 m (5 ft) tall.

▲ *Weigela middendorffiana*

GARDEN HYBRIDS
The garden hybrids are mostly derived from and have superseded *W. florida*, and are sometimes listed with it. They are generally showy and free flowering. Most have mid green ovate leaves with a slender tip and prominent veins. The clusters of 2.5 cm (1 in) long flowers cover the branches. HEIGHT & SPREAD 1 × 1 m (3 × 3 ft) after 5 years, ultimately 1.8 m (6 ft) tall.

'Abel Carriere'♀ has large rose-carmine flowers, fading later, with a gold flare. 'Briant Rubidor' (also sold as 'Olympiade' or 'Rubidor') has soft yellow leaves and red flowers. 'Bristol Ruby' has an upright habit and crimson flowers. 'Candida' is a compact variety with white flowers.

'Eva Rathke' is slow-growing with crimson flowers. 'Evita' is dense and broad, bearing red flowers. 'Fiesta' is vigorous with an open habit and red flowers. 'Looymansii Aurea' has yellow-green young leaves and does best in light shade. It bears pink flowers.

'Minuet' has small, rounded leaves. It

bears fragrant pink flowers and is compact and very hardy. 'Mont Blanc'♀ bears large white fragrant flowers which age to pink. 'Nana Variegata' is a dwarf, rounded shrub with cream-edged leaves and pale pink flowers. 'Newport Red' has dark red flow-

▲ *Weigela* 'Newport Red'
Weigela 'Praecox Variegata' ▼

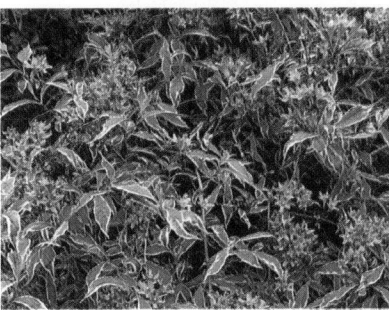

ers. 'Praecox Variegata'♀ has smooth, yellow-variegated leaves that turn white in summer. Its crimson buds open into pink flowers. 'Snowflake' is compact with white flowers often tinged with pink. 'Victoria' has purple-flushed leaves and red flowers.

CULTIVATION Plant from mid autumn to early spring in any well-drained fertile soil that does not dry out. Choose a sunny or partially shaded site. Mulch generously and feed in spring.

PROPAGATION Take softwood cuttings in early summer, or semi-ripe cuttings in mid summer and root in a coldframe. Alternatively, grow from hardwood cuttings taken after late autumn.

PRUNING Trim back just after flowering to maintain vigour. Thin out a few old shoots to the ground and shorten the strongest new shoots to a few buds above old wood.

PESTS AND DISEASES Usually trouble free.

Whitebeam see *Sorbus*
Whitlow grass see *Draba*
Wild angelica see *Angelica sylvestris*
Wild ginger see *Asarum*
Willow see *Salix*
Willow bell see *Campanula persicifolia*
Willowherb see *Epilobium*
Windflower see *Anemone*
Winged spindle see *Euonymus alatus*
Wintergreen see *Gaultheria procumbens*
Winter's bark see *Drimys winteri*
Wintersweet see *Chimonanthus praecox*
Wire netting bush
see *Corokia cotoneaster*

W

Water Plants
for ponds & bog gardens

WATER GARDENS PROVIDE CONDITIONS
THAT SUIT A WEALTH OF BEAUTIFUL PLANTS,
AND MAKE ARRESTING FOCAL POINTS

A water feature introduces a unique play of movement and light into the garden and enables the gardener to grow a wide range of plants which thrive in water or in the moist soil at the water's edge.

The smallest space can accommodate a trough filled with miniature plants, such as *Acorus gramineus* 'Variegatus' and the water lily *Nymphaea × pygmaea* 'Rubra'. In a larger garden, a pond provides a unique focus, and can set the garden's style. It may incorporate a moving-water feature, such as a fountain or waterfall, for added interest.

FLOATING GRACE
Exquisite water lilies suit every pond.

Site a pond in a flat sunny area of the garden, away from overhanging trees. For a formal pond, choose a design with a geometric shape, defined edges and a neat surround of stone or brickwork. Select plants with simple architectural outlines, such as the stiffly upright *Typha minima*, and be restrained in your planting.

A pond with an irregular, curving shape looks good in an informal garden, and also provides a valuable habitat for wildlife. See WILDLIFE GARDENS (p. 710). Soften its edges with turf or stones and incorporate a bog garden to provide a visual link

▶ EYE-CATCHING *Upright* Iris ensata *makes a bold display of purple beside a tranquil pool.*

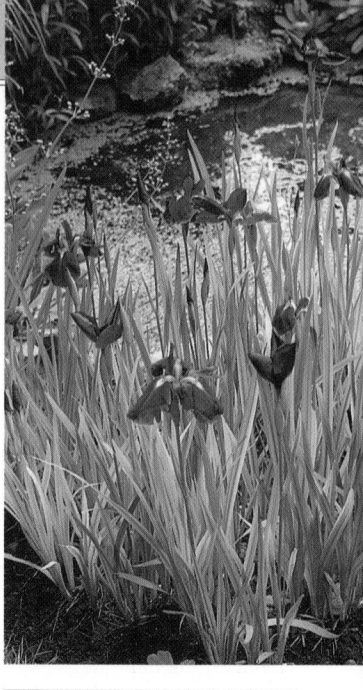

between the pond and the rest of the garden. Water plants with relatively loose habits, such as *Mimulus* (monkey flower), *Caltha* (marsh marigold) and *Myosotis scorpioides* (water forget-me-not) are particularly well suited to an informal pond. Allow their foliage to entwine for a natural effect.

NATURAL BALANCE

For a balanced and healthy ecology in a pond, include plants that grow at different levels. Submerged plants, such as *Potamogeton crispus* (curled pondweed) and *Hottonia palustris* (water violet) are essential because they produce oxygen and absorb nutrients that encourage algae.

Plants whose foliage floats on the water surface are also necessary because they reduce the amount of light reaching lower levels and so discourage algae. They include plants which are entirely floating, such as *Eichhornia crassipes* (water hyacinth), and deep-water aquatics, including water lilies, which have floating leaves and flowers but whose roots are below the surface of the water. Use these plants to cover between a third and a half of the pond and leave the rest clear.

Marginal plants, which grow in shallow water at the pond's edges, do not greatly affect the clarity and balance of the water. However, along with bog plants, they provide shelter for wildlife and help to create a lush effect.

COLOURFUL SCHEMES

The waxy star-like flowers and softly rounded or heart-shaped leaves of water lilies make these plants central to any water planting scheme.

Plain green-leaved varieties with single-colour flowers, such as the pure white *Nymphaea* 'Albatros' and the bright red *N.* 'Froebelii', are good choices and there are many attractive varieties which have

◀ HARMONIOUS GROUPING
A lavish mix of water plants results in a soothing scene.

PLANTING UP A
WATER GARDEN

PLANTING UP A WATER GARDEN

Plant up a water garden in late spring or early summer. Slide floating plants carefully onto the water surface and dig bog-garden plants directly into the soil. Use fine-mesh aquatic baskets for any other water plants, to contain growth.

Fill the basket with clean, heavy garden soil, free from weeds, sticks and stones, or use an aquatic-planting compost. Insert the plant then soak the soil to expel any air. Top up the basket and cover the surface with pea gravel.

Lower the basket carefully into place. Plant marginals so that the roots are covered by 2.5-15 cm (1-6 in) of water, and deep-water aquatics in a depth of 25-90 cm (10-36 in), depending on the plant. Place young deep-water aquatics in a depth of 25-30 cm (10-12 in) at first and move to the correct planting depth once they are established. Submerged plants grow in any depth of water. Keep deep-water and floating plants away from moving water.

Water gardens need little maintenance. During the growing season, thin out vigorous plants and divide rhizomes when necessary. Use a hooked stick to pull out blanket weed. Remove dead foliage in autumn.

▶ SHADES OF GREEN *Arching foliage of ferns and grasses leads the eye to the water in a stream.*

blotched or marked foliage, including *N.* 'Indiana'. The forked flowers of *Aponogeton distachyos* (water hawthorn), the fringed blooms of *Nymphoides peltata* and the upright flower spikes of *Orontium aquaticum* also make striking and colourful displays in deep water.

Round the margins, include flowering species and plants with architectural foliage or outlines. The flowering rush *Butomus umbellatus*, for example, has unusual twisted narrow leaves, and also produces pink blooms from mid summer to autumn. The sword-like cream and green *Acorus calamus* 'Variegatus' is an excellent choice and combines well with the blue-flowered *Myosotis scorpioides*; the upright *Iris laevigata* (water iris) makes a fine match with the creeping, green-leaved *Lysimachia nummularia*.

Integrate the pond margins with a bog garden by growing plants that thrive in both sites; the yellow-flowered *Mimulus guttatus* and *Lythrum salicaria* (purple loosestrife), with its slender purple spires, make an impressive display. Alternatively, adopt a single-colour scheme using, for example, a mass planting of white *Iris*

▼ PAIRED UP Lysichiton *(bog arum) and marsh marigolds combine well in a bog garden.*

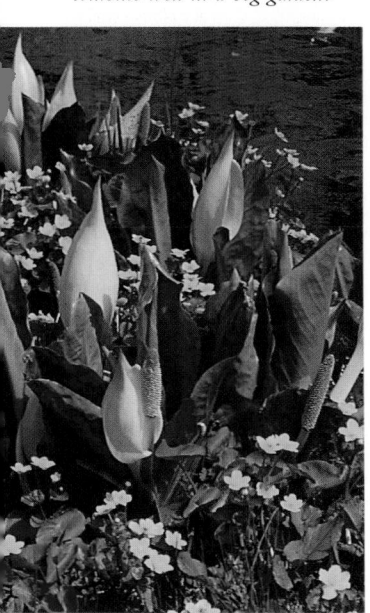

laevigata 'Alba' to complement a show of *Zantedeschia aethiopica* (arum lily).

LONGER SEASON

Create strong drifts of colour in a bog garden by grouping together several plants of the same species. Include *Caltha palustris* (kingcup) and *Primula denticulata* for spring colour, followed by the waterside irises *Iris ensata* and *I. pseudacorus*, and candelabra primulas, such as *Primula bulleyana*.

Many flowering water plants produce their best displays in summer, so include

foliage plants that have extended seasons of interest. The umbrella plant *Darmera peltata*, whose main feature is large, dark green leaves that turn a soft pinky bronze in autumn, is a good choice. The ornamental rhubarb *Rheum palmatum* 'Bowles' Crimson', with its colourful leaves, and the feathery *Athyrium felix-femina* (lady fern) are also useful, making fine backdrops and providing textured interest.

▼ STATELY FOCUS *Creamy white arum lilies stand out among other bog-loving plants.*

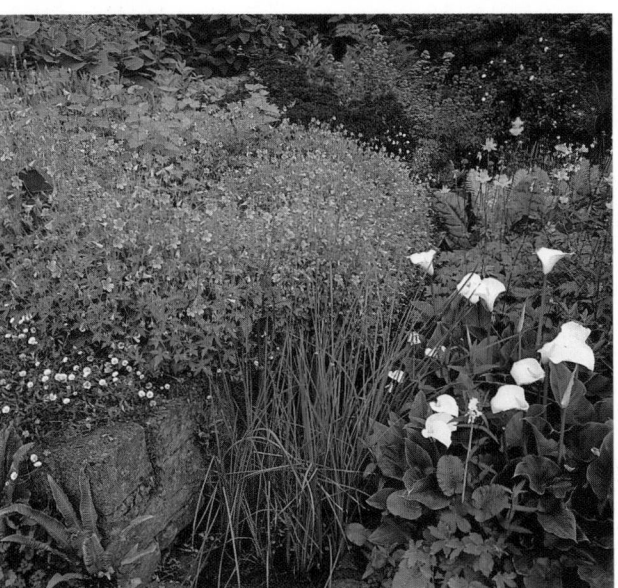

PLANTS IN AND AROUND THE POND

DEEP-WATER AQUATICS
• *Aponogeton distachyos* Spikes of white forked flowers from late spring to autumn and dark green, strap-like leaves.
• *Nymphaea* 'Froebelii' Deep red, starry flowers in summer and purple-green rounded leaves.
• *Nymphaea* 'Marliacea Chromatella' Yellow flowers in summer and olive-green, streaked, rounded leaves.
• *Nymphoides peltata* 'Bennettii' Fringed yellow flowers in summer and spotted heart-shaped leaves.

FLOATERS
• *Eichhornia crassipes* Spikes of lavender-blue flowers in summer and dark green, rounded leaves.
• *Stratiotes aloides* Spiky rosettes of dark green leaves.

MARGINALS
• *Butomus umbellatus* Clusters of pale pink flowers in mid summer and early autumn, and twisted bronze to mid green leaves.
• *Iris laevigata* Mid blue flowers in early summer and green sword-like leaves.
• *Lythrum salicaria* Spires of purple flowers from mid to late summer and mid green, lance-shaped foliage.
• *Mimulus guttatus* Hooded yellow blooms, dotted red, all summer and bright green, toothed, oval leaves.
• *Myosotis scorpioides* Sky-blue clusters in summer and spoon-shaped green leaves.

BOG-GARDEN PLANTS
• *Caltha palustris* Deep yellow, cup-shaped flowers in spring and dark green, rounded foliage.
• *Darmera peltata* White or pink clusters in spring and parasol-like, dark green leaves which turn bronze.
• *Primula japonica* 'Postford White' White flowers in early summer and pale green, toothed leaves.
• *Rheum palmatum* 'Bowles' Crimson' Tall red spikes in summer and green leaves with red undersides.

Wisteria
Leguminosae

Wisteria sinensis

Though their flowering season is of short duration, wisterias are among the most beautiful of all climbers for walls, fences, pergolas, arches and old trees. Their violet-blue, purple, pink or white flowers – all in the typical pea-family shape, and often beautifully scented – hang in long, elegant trails in late spring and early summer before the attractive feathery foliage is fully expanded. The bean-like seedpods that follow the flowers are distinctive. The pinnate leaves are divided into seven to nineteen narrow leaflets. All wisteria species are twining, woody, deciduous climbers. Given

▼ *Wisteria floribunda* 'Rosea'

something for the stems to twine around – those of some species twine clockwise, others anticlockwise – wisterias climb vigorously to a considerable height and need plenty of room to look at their best. They can live to be 100 years old and a mature plant will be very heavy so careful thought is required when positioning a young plant.

Wisterias can be trained as self-supporting, tree-like standards when they are supported during training (perhaps for 20 years) after which the supports are taken away to leave a free-standing specimen. They can be grown in large containers and can also be forced into early flower under glass.

Most wisterias are hardy throughout the British Isles, but will flourish best in a sunny, sheltered spot facing south or west. Buy a grafted or layered plant, or one grown from a cutting; a seed-raised plant may take 15 to 20 years to flower.

For a good flowering display, careful pruning and training is essential.

RECOMMENDED SPECIES AND VARIETIES

W. floribunda (Japanese wisteria) Fragrant violet-blue flowers appear with the early leaves in hanging trails 25–30 cm (10–12 in) or more long. Flowers open in sequence from the base of the cluster to the tip. Each leaf has 11–19 light to mid green leaflets. Native to Japan. HEIGHT up to 9 m (30 ft).

'Alba'♀ (syn. *W. multijuga* 'Alba') has white flowers tinged with lilac. 'Burford'

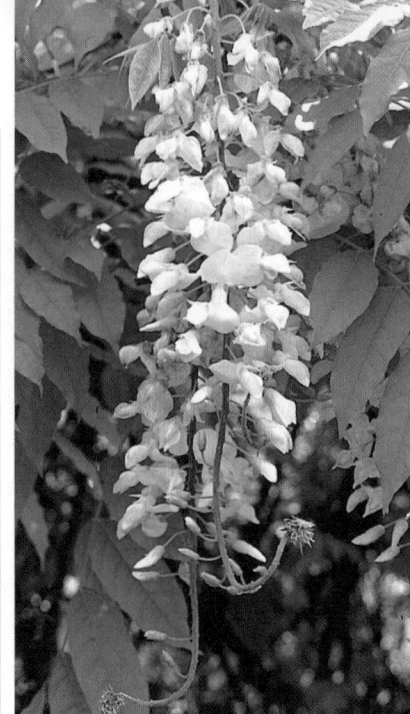

▲ *Wisteria floribunda* 'Alba'

has strongly scented lilac-blue flowers in pendent clusters that reach 60 cm (2 ft) or more long. The flowers of 'Kuchi-beni' ('Peaches and Cream') are pink and white. 'Multijuga'♀ (syn. 'Macrobotrys') has long flower trails, 60 cm (2 ft) or more, of purple and violet flowers. The flowers of 'Purple Patches' are violet-purple. 'Rosea'♀ has

▲ *Wisteria floribunda* 'Multijuga'

pale pink flowers with a rose pink throat. The flowers of 'Snow Showers' are pure white. 'Violacea Plena' has violet-blue, double flowers.

W. x formosa The strongly fragrant pale violet flowers hang in 25–30 cm (10–12 in) trails and nearly the whole length of cluster opens at one time as the leaves are emerging. Each leaf usually has 13 leaflets. HEIGHT up to 9 m (30 ft).

W

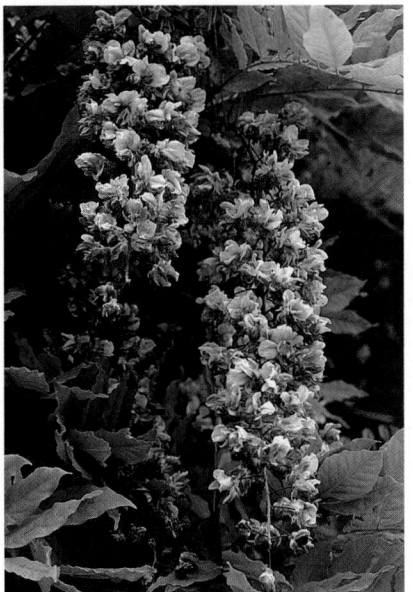

▲ *Wisteria × formosa* 'Kokkuryu'

▲ *Wisteria sinensis* 'Alba'

▲ *Wisteria venusta*

▲ *Wisteria sinensis*

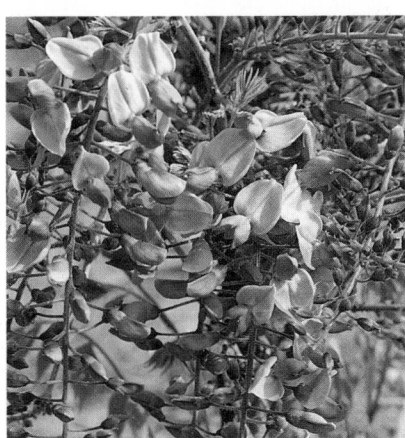

▲ *Wisteria sinensis* 'Caroline'

More commonly grown than the hybrid are the varieties **'Issai'**, which flowers as a young plant, producing lilac-blue flowers, and **'Kokkuryu'** ('Black Dragon'), which has double purple flowers.

W. sinensis♀ (Chinese wisteria) This fast-growing and vigorous climber bears dense trails, 15–30 cm (6–12 in) long, of slightly fragrant blue-violet flowers, all of which open together, before the leaves unfurl. Each leaf has 7–13 dark to mid green leaflets. Native to China. HEIGHT 10–15 m (33–50 ft) or more.

'Alba'♀ ('Shiro-capital) has white flowers. **'Caroline'** is a free-flowering climber with strongly scented, deep blue-purple flowers. **'Prolific'** is very free-flowering with blue-lilac flowers.

W. venusta (silky wisteria) Fragrant white flowers in hanging clusters, 10–15 cm (4–6 in) long, have a yellow blotch at the base of the upright petals. The flowers open all at once as the leaves unfurl. The silky-haired leaves are divided into 9–13 leaflets. Native to Japan. HEIGHT up to 9 m (30 ft).

The wild form, f. *violacea,* has violet-purple flowers.

CULTIVATION Most soils are suitable, but planting in a rich, moist loam will give the best results. Position the plant out of cold winds and early morning sun to avoid frost and wind damage to flower buds. Mature plants can become heavy so it is essential to provide strong trellis or wires for support. Thread new shoots behind the wires and do not try to twine them as the shoots snap easily. Do not tie them tightly. Feed plants with high potash fertiliser and mulch them in spring if the soil is not very fertile. Foliage will be produced at the expense of flowers if wisterias are overfed.

To force a tub-grown plant into early flower, move it under glass in mid to late winter at a minimum temperature of 10°C (50°F). Spray the plant twice daily with water, and keep it indoors until all danger of frost has passed.

PROPAGATION Wisteria is a very difficult plant to propagate, though it can be attempted in the following ways. To raise one or two new plants, layer low-growing lateral shoots between mid autumn and late spring. Alternatively, take 7.5–10 cm (3–4 in) semi-ripe heel or nodal cuttings in late summer and root in a propagating frame, preferably with bottom heat.

PRUNING For the first few years, train new growth to form a main stem and several horizontal side branches. After that cut back most of the long shoots not needed as new main branches to about 5 or 6 buds in mid summer. Prune all sideshoots back to 2 or 3 buds from the previous year's growth in late winter to form flowering spurs.

PESTS AND DISEASES Birds may attack the buds and flowers. Aphids may infest young growths and also spread a virus disease that causes leaf mottling. Thrips may damage the foliage. In warm conditions, red spider mites may attack the leaves, causing fine mottling. Drought or low night temperatures may cause bud-drop, and very alkaline soil can cause chlorosis. Fungal infections can cause brown or black leaf spots – rarely serious – but honey fungus can kill wisterias, particularly old plants.

Witch hazel see *Hamamelis*
Woad see *Isatis*
Wood anemone see *Anemone nemorosa*
Woodbine see *Lonicera*
Woodruff see *Asperula*
Woodwardia see FERNS p. 265
Wormwood see *Artemisia*

W

WILDLIFE GARDEN
PROVIDING MATERIAL HABITATS

ENTICE A HOST OF BIRDS, BUTTERFLIES AND OTHER CREATURES INTO THE GARDEN BY OFFERING THE FOOD AND SHELTER THEY NEED

C reating a welcoming area for wildlife is possible in any garden, no matter where it is sited or what its size. Given appropriate conditions, a wide range of creatures will soon appear, providing an endless source of fascination and entertainment for the gardener. In addition, a wildlife garden can play a valuable role in conservation, supporting native plants and creatures that may no longer easily survive in the countryside.

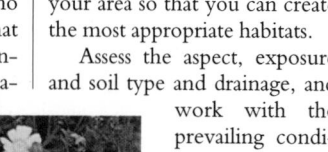

SUMMER SCARLET
Corn poppies complement a meadow or flowerbed.

Ideally a wildlife garden should contain a woodland area, wild-flower meadow and a pond – features which can be adapted to suit a small garden. Find out about the wildlife in your area so that you can create the most appropriate habitats.

Assess the aspect, exposure and soil type and drainage, and work with the prevailing conditions in your garden. A poor soil, for example, is an advantage in sustaining a wildflower meadow. A damp, shady spot suits many woodland plants, including *Euphorbia amygdaloides* (wood spurge), *Oxalis acetosella* (wood sorrel) and *Sorbus aucuparia* (rowan tree).

Brightly coloured, scented single flowers that produce plenty of pollen and nectar attract a wide range of insects, which encourages insect-eating birds, such as wrens, to visit the garden. Night-flowering nectar plants, including *Nicotiana alata* (flowering tobacco) and *Matthiola longipetala* (night-scented stock), are a valuable source of food for night-flying insects, which may in turn attract bats.

Whirligig beetles and pond skaters quickly turn up in a new pond, followed by dragonflies, diving beetles and frogs and toads. Hedges and nesting boxes will encourage wrens, finches, blackbirds, dunnocks, song thrushes and the tit family to make their homes in your garden. A woodland area may attract hedgehogs, bats and a range of other creatures.

Do not use chemical sprays as they disrupt the natural food chain and create an imbalance. A garden that is wildlife friendly will encourage natural predators and help to keep down pests and diseases. See ALLIES IN THE GARDENER'S WORLD (p. 32).

NATIVE PLANTS

Growing native plants helps to conserve species that are now rarely found in the wild. Many native plants look attractive combined with cultivated flowers in beds and borders. For example, red-flowered *Papaver rhoeas* (corn poppy) and the deep pink *Agrostemma githago* (corn cockle) make pretty additions to an annual flowerbed.

Although native plants such as *Digitalis purpurea* (foxglove), *Viola tricolor* (heartsease) and some *Geranium* (cranesbill) species may earn a place in the garden by appearance alone, many are also rich sources of seeds, nectar and pollen, and support a range of creatures.

Bees, butterflies and hoverflies, for example, depend on nectar-rich flowers, such as those of the attractive herb *Origanum vulgare* (marjoram). Pollen-rich plants, including *Achillea millefolium* (yarrow) and *Taraxacum officinale* (dandelion), are also much appreciated by insects. Once the creamy

◀ SECLUDED SPOT *A thicket of plants including (from front) cowslips, heartsease and foxgloves creates an informal attraction in the garden and provides a sheltered retreat for wildlife.*

▲ BIRD SANCTUARY *Roses and honeysuckle surround a nesting box on a wooden fence.*

white flowers of *Filipendula ulmaria* (meadowsweet) set their seed, they attract many birds, including siskins, as will *Rumex* (dock) and *Cirsium* (plume thistle). Goldfinches find *Dipsacus fullonum* (teasel) irresistible and yellowhammers eat the seeds of most large grasses.

Native plants can be bought from a mail-order supplier, garden centre or nursery.

WILD-FLOWER MEADOWS

A grassy meadow that is studded with a variety of native flowering plants not only looks beautiful, but also provides a haven for insects, and thus their predators. In addition, many grasses provide food for butterflies, caterpillars and bees.

Choose either a spring-flowering meadow or a late summer-flowering meadow as they are mowed at different times of the year.

A spring-flowering meadow may include plants such as *Cardamine pratensis* (cuckoo flower) and *Primula veris* (cowslip) as well as bulbs, including *Narcissus pseudonarcissus* (Lent lily) and *Leucojum aestivum* (summer snowflake).

For a summer-flowering meadow, select plants such as *Centaurea scabiosa* (greater knapweed), *Knautia arvensis* (field scabious) and *Rumex acetosa* (sorrel), which provide a bright show and combine well with *Colchicum autumnale* (meadow saffron) which provides some later colour.

To achieve a successful meadow, you first need to reduce the fertility of the soil. This ensures that grasses grow at a slower rate, which allows flowering plants to thrive.

If you are starting with bare soil, remove the richer topsoil and sow onto the less fertile subsoil, preferably in autumn. Use a mixture of fine grasses and native plants. Make up your own mixture, or buy one ready-made from a garden centre, nursery or a specialist supplier. These mixtures usually consist of 80 per cent grasses with 20 per cent flowering plants and are available to suit different soils and situations. Check to make sure that the seed is of native origin and the grasses are non-invasive and low-growing.

To convert a lawn into a meadow, strip off the turf then remove the topsoil and sow. Alternatively, mow the grass very closely and at frequent intervals for at least two seasons, removing all the grass clippings, which would otherwise add nutrients to the soil. Then introduce the flowering plants, either raised from seed or bought as plants from a garden centre or nursery.

The simplest way to create a meadow, however, is to leave a

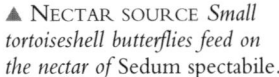

▲ NECTAR SOURCE *Small tortoiseshell butterflies feed on the nectar of* Sedum spectabile.

section of the lawn unmowed. A whole range of lawn weeds, including yarrow, *Bellis perennis* (daisy) and *Ranunculus* (buttercup), look attractive when they are left to flower. However, you may need to introduce more flowering plants to achieve a good balance between flowers and grasses.

Delay cutting a spring-flowering meadow until mid summer. This gives the flowers time to set seed. Mow a summer-flowering meadow in late spring, then leave it uncut until mid autumn. Always remove the mowings.

Each year, leave a different section of a summer-flowering meadow uncut in autumn. This

will provide valuable shelter for insects and small mammals throughout the winter.

BUTTERFLY BORDERS

As butterflies like to bask in sunny sheltered spots, make sure there are clumps of nectar-rich plants in sunny parts of the garden that are protected from winds. Have a succession of plants in flower to provide food for butterflies from the spring through to the autumn. Late summer is a very active time for butterflies so include plenty of plants that bloom then.

In a perennial border, grow *Aubrieta* to attract the painted lady, red admiral, brimstone and small tortoiseshell. The same butterflies use *Lavandula* (lavender) as a nectar source, as do the small copper, common blue, meadow brown and small skipper. *Aster* (Michaelmas daisy), *Centranthus* (valerian), *Phlox*, and *Sedum* also attract a wide range of butterflies.

Shrubs, such as *Cornus alba* (red-barked dogwood) and *Escallonia*, are useful additions to a mixed border, while *Buddleja davidii* (butterfly bush) is a favourite in summer.

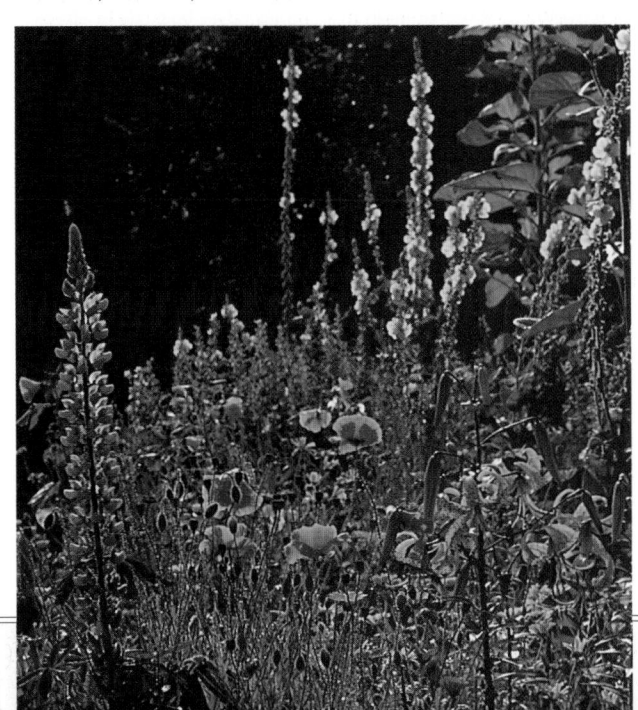

◄ WILD CORNER Calendula *and* Verbascum *combine with lilies and lupins in a natural area.*

Annuals that provide nectar include *Centaurea cyanus* (cornflower), *Helichrysum bracteatum* (strawflower), *Iberis umbellata* (candytuft), *Lobularia maritima* (sweet alyssum) and *Reseda odorata* (sweet mignonette).

Food plants for the next generation must also be provided as butterflies lay their eggs on plants that the emerging caterpillars will eat. Establish a patch of nettles in an out-of-the-way spot to provide food for the caterpillars of many butterflies, including the small tortoiseshell, red admiral, peacock, comma and painted lady. Cut some of the nettles down to the ground at different times of the year so that there are young leaves available.

Other useful food plants include cuckoo flowers, which support the caterpillars of the orange tip butterfly, and the common holly, *Ilex aquifolium*.

WOODLAND EDGE

A woodland edge provides a rich natural habitat for wildlife. Re-creating this environment, even on a small scale, will bring rewards in the diversity of creatures that it attracts.

The woodland area consists of various layers of vegetation – tall trees, smaller trees, a lower canopy of shrubs, and ground-cover plants and early bulbs. If there is insufficient room to grow tall trees, such as *Salix caprea* (goat willow) and

Quercus robur (English oak), choose a mixture of smaller trees and large shrubs to create the top layer. *Corylus avellana* (hazel), *Crataegus monogyna* (hawthorn), *Prunus padus* (bird cherry) and *Viburnum opulus* (guelder rose) are all of value in supporting wildlife.

In a smaller garden, use a mixed hedge as the top layer, or substitute climbing plants, including *Lonicera periclymenum* (woodbine) and *Hedera helix* (ivy), grown up a trellis. Do not trim hedges during the nesting season.

For the next layer down, select several small shrubs, especially those that produce berries. These include *Berberis* (barberry), *Cotoneaster*, *Pyracantha* (firethorn), *Euonymus* (spindle tree) and *Ligustrum vulgare* (privet).

Excellent ground cover for the woodland edge is provided by the shade-tolerant *Vinca* (periwinkle), *Ajuga* (bugle) and *Galium odoratum* (sweet woodruff). Some spring-flowering bulbs, such as *Galanthus* (snowdrop) and *Hyacinthoides nonscripta* (bluebell), also grow well here. Other useful plants include *Angelica sylvestris* (wild angelica), *Arum maculatum* (lords-and-ladies), *Ranunculus ficaria* (lesser celandine) and wood spurge.

A thick mulch of shreddings, bark, wood chippings or leaf-mould will complete the woodland habitat. Do not be too tidy in this area – leave dead stems and flowerheads to create a litter layer similar to that in a natural wood. This layer provides food and shelter for hundreds of tiny creatures, which all play a part in creating a balanced food chain. However, remove any diseased matter.

SUPPLEMENTING HABITATS

A woodland edge, or a quiet and secluded area of the garden, is the ideal place to encourage hedgehogs to take up residence and reduce the slug population.

A pile of logs covered with long grass and dead twigs or leaves makes a good place for them to hibernate and attracts many insects too. Alternatively, buy or make a wooden box to house hedgehogs. Provide a tunnel, 10 cm (4 in) high and 30 cm (12 in) long, as the

▼ TOWN GARDEN *Pink* Lavatera *and purple* Buddleja *frame an overgrown path.*

▶ WETLAND *An informal pond surrounded by plants provides water and shelter for wildlife.*

entrance to prevent foxes from gaining access. Cover the box with a layer of polythene to keep it dry and use a heap of dry leaves and sticks to provide some camouflage.

Encourage birds to nest in your garden by providing artificial nesting boxes. These are best put up in autumn or mid winter so that the birds can explore them thoroughly before the nest-building season begins.

The larger the entrance hole, the wider the range of birds that can make use of the nesting box, but you will probably find that the largest species become the most successful occupants. A diameter of 3 cm (1¼ in) allows smaller birds like tits, nuthatches and tree sparrows to use it. The entrance hole should be near the top to prevent cats or squirrels from reaching in. An open-fronted box or a simple platform, such as half a coconut shell, provides a nesting site for other birds, such as spotted flycatchers.

Position a nesting box in a place where it has shelter from wind, rain and strong sunlight, and away from bird tables. If fixing the box to a house, choose a wall facing north, north-east, east or south-east. Keep the box well away from branches to prevent predators from gaining easy access.

A bird table will attract many birds but food must be put out regularly. Seeds will bring finches, nuts attract tits and siskins, and fruit will be eaten by thrushes, fieldfares and blackbirds. You can also put out fat for tits and nuthatches.

Bats will take up residence in a nesting box. As these creatures are particularly susceptible to pesticides, boxes should be made from untreated wood and left unpainted and unvarnished. Rough-sawn timber is best because it allows the bats to get a good grip when they land. A bat box is similar in shape to a bird box, but smaller and with an entrance slit in the base. Make sure that there are no branches or other obstructions within 1 m (3 ft) of the box.

A WILDLIFE POND

A pond is one of the most important features that you can provide for wildlife. Many water-living species make their homes there, small mammals, bees, butterflies and other insects come to drink and birds use the shallow water for drinking and bathing.

Site a pond in an open, sunny position away from trees. Use a flexible sheet liner to make it as the sides of pre-formed plastic ponds are too steep and slippery for many creatures. The pond should include some sloping sides and areas of shallow water round the edges so that wildlife has easy access. Make sure that one area is at least 60 cm (2 ft) deep to prevent the water from freezing solid in winter.

Create a border of plants round part of the pond edge. A marsh or bog garden, which provides ideal conditions for a range of moisture-loving plants, is easily formed by extending the pond liner at one end.

Many bog-garden plants are attractive to bees and butterflies. For example, the red-barked dogwood, *Primula* and *Lobelia* produce nectar and will also provide shelter for amphibians and other creatures.

Pond-side features, such as rocks, a grassed area and a gentle slope covered with sand or gravel, are useful to a variety of different creatures – and a paved area is helpful for access and maintenance.

To colonise the new habitat, obtain a few buckets of water and pond sludge from an existing pond to introduce hundreds of creatures. You can also buy water snails and water fleas from garden centres to help to keep the water clear of algae.

Many other creatures will turn up of their own accord. Expect to see damselflies, pond-skaters, water boatmen and diving beetles. Frogs, toads and newts may also appear. If you want amphibians to use the pond, it is inadvisable to stock fish – especially goldfish.

Plants grow at different levels within a pond and together create a balanced ecology. Submerged aquatic plants, such as *Potamogeton crispus* (curled pondweed) and *Hottonia palustris* (water violet), are oxygenators. Floating plants or plants with floating leaves, such as the native *Nymphaea alba* (white water lily), help to shade the lower levels from light and thus discourage algae. Marginal plants, which include *Iris pseudacorus* (yellow water flag) and *Carex* (sedge), provide useful hiding places for wildlife. See also WATER PLANTS (p.706).

In a small garden where there is no space for a pond, substitute a birdbath. A stone one is best – plastic birdbaths are too slippery, although adding a layer of stones or wood provides a foothold. Break any ice that forms daily.

WALLS, ROCKS AND PAVING

Bare walls, fences and paved surfaces can be adapted to benefit wildlife. Fix a trellis 8-10 cm (3¼-4 in) in front of a wall or fence. Build ledges behind the trellis to create nesting sites for robins, wrens and other birds.

Grow climbers or wall shrubs over the trellis. Common ivy is particularly useful. It is often used for cover and nest sites by birds, and camouflage by moths and butterflies, which may also hibernate there. In addition, its flowers provide late pollen and nectar and its fruit is a source of food for birds in late winter and spring. *Cotoneaster franchetii* is another good choice because it produces orange-red berries in autumn, which attract birds.

Use the tops or cracks and crevices in walls as sites for plants like the stonecrop *Sedum acre*, or *Aubrieta* and *Aurinia*. On a patio or in a small town garden, plant up containers and hanging baskets with plants that are rich in nectar and pollen or produce seeds and berries, and include some evergreens, such as ivy, to provide winter shelter.

When laying paving slabs, leave large gaps between them and sow wild-flower seed there. Omit some slabs altogether, to create sites for plants that thrive in hot, dry conditions. These include *Thymus serpyllum* (wild thyme), *Linum perenne* (perennial flax) and *Dianthus deltoides* (maiden pink).

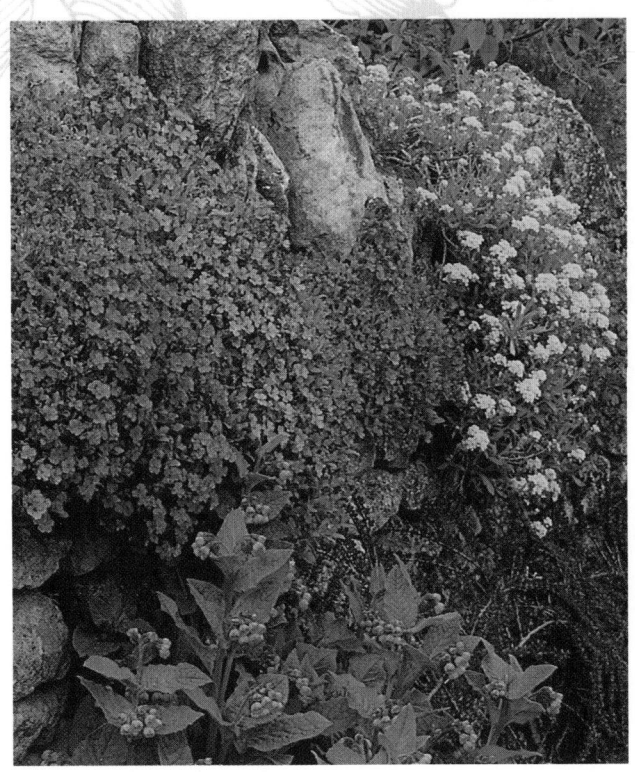

◀ WALL PLANTS Aubrieta *and* Aurinia *tumble down a wall above* Symphytum *(comfrey).*

X-Z

Xanthoceras

Sapindaceae

Xanthoceras sorbifolium

There is only one species in this genus, a large deciduous shrub or small tree grown for its upright spikes of fragrant flowers. Moderately frost hardy, it grows best in southern Britain, where warmer weather will ripen the wood and encourage abundant flowering. This is an excellent plant for chalky soils.

Xanthoceras sorbifolium♀ White flowers with a carmine centre, up to 3 cm (1¼ in) across, are produced in mid spring. The flower spikes at the ends of branches can be up to 20 cm (8 in) long, while the rest are about half that length. The compound leaves have 9-17 leaflets and grow to around 20 cm (8 in) long. They are pale green at first but darken with age. The plant has a rather upright habit of growth and can make a small tree in milder parts of Britain. Native to N China. HEIGHT & SPREAD 1.8×1 m (6×3 ft) in 10 years, ultimately 5 m (16 ft) tall.

CULTIVATION Plant from mid autumn to mid spring, avoiding dry or frosty periods, in any fertile soil, preferably chalky. Choose a sheltered position in full sun.

PROPAGATION Sow seed in pots in early to mid spring.

PRUNING Remove any dead wood in early spring before leaves emerge.

PESTS AND DISEASES Usually trouble free, but coral spot fungus can be a problem.

Xanthorhiza

Ranunculaceae

Xanthorhiza simplicissima

This deciduous frost-hardy shrub is grown for its impressive autumn colour. It is also a good ground cover plant. There is only one species in the genus.

Xanthorhiza simplicissima (yellow root) Bright green leaves, up to 30 cm (12 in) long, with 3-5 deeply cut leaflets, turn to shades of purple, red and yellow during autumn. Tiny, deep purple, five-part flowers appear in early to mid spring. These are produced in abundance on drooping plumes up to 20 cm (8 in) long. This multistemmed shrub produces many suckers from underground roots. When cut, the stems and roots are a brilliant yellow, which gives the plant its common name. A suckering habit makes propagation easy. Native to E United States. HEIGHT & SPREAD 1 m×60 cm (3×2 ft) after 5 years and ultimately.

CULTIVATION Plant from early autumn to late spring in any good, relatively moist soil, avoiding thin soils over chalk. Choose a shady position.

PROPAGATION Divide the plants in early spring.

PESTS AND DISEASES Usually trouble free.

Yarrow see *Achillea*
Yesterday-today-and-tomorrow see *Brunfelsia pauciflora*
Yew see *Taxus*
Yew, plum see *Cephalotaxus*
Youth and old age see *Zinnia*

Yucca

Agavaceae

Yucca gloriosa

These striking evergreen shrubs are grown for the architectural value of their long, sword-like, often rigid leaves. The leaves are held in clumps or rosettes from which tall, exotic-looking flower stems rise in mid to late summer, bearing numerous 10 cm (4 in) wide, bell-shaped flowers.

Native to S United States and Central America, most species are hardy enough for hot sunny sites in British gardens. *Yucca aloifolia* and *Y. elephantipes* are too tender to be grown outside, but make excellent container plants for a conservatory or house.

RECOMMENDED SPECIES AND VARIETIES
Y. aloifolia (Spanish bayonet) A strong erect stem bears a crown of rigid, 45 cm (1½ ft) long leaves. The leaves have finely toothed edges and end in a sharp point. The flowers are white, sometimes flushed with purple and held in 60 cm (2 ft) high panicles, but are rarely seen on containerised plants. HEIGHT & SPREAD 75×75 cm (2½×2½ ft) after 5 years, ultimately 3 m (10 ft) tall or more.

'Variegata' has yellow-edged leaves.
Y. elephantipes♀ Strong stems bear bright green spineless leaves up to 1.2 m (4 ft) long. White, pendent, cup-shaped flowers are carried in erect, branched clusters in mid and late summer. Flowers are rarely seen, however, on plants grown indoors. This

▲ Xanthoceras sorbifolium

▲ Xanthorhiza simplicissima

▲ Yucca filamentosa

▲ Yucca flaccida 'Golden Sword'

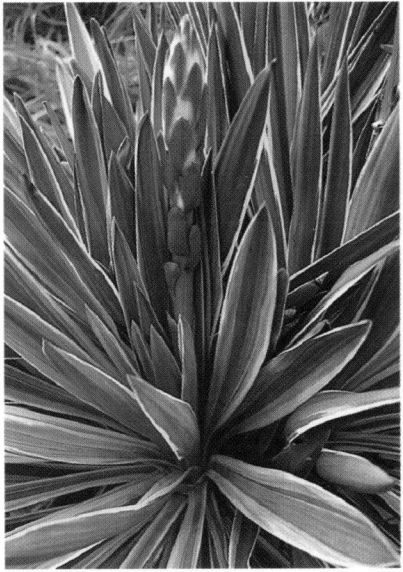

▲ Yucca gloriosa 'Variegata'

species makes a small tree in its native Mexico, but is much smaller when grown in a container as a houseplant, as it is in Britain. HEIGHT & SPREAD 100×30 cm (3×1 ft) after 5 years, ultimately 1.8 m (6 ft) tall.

'Variegata' has bright green leaves with creamy white edges.

Y. filamentosa♀ (Adam's needle) Narrow mid green leaves form rosettes. The stiffly erect leaves, up to 75 cm (2½ ft) long, are adorned with numerous wavy white threads. Creamy white, tulip-shaped flowers are carried in plumes up to 1.8 m (6 ft) high that stand above the foliage. HEIGHT & SPREAD 60×75 cm (2×2½ ft) after 5 years, ultimately 1 m (3 ft) tall.

'Bright Edge'♀ has leaves that are emerald green with wide yellow edges. 'Garland's Gold' has broad leaves with edges striped creamy yellow. The smaller 'Variegata'♀ has cream streaks and pink-tinged edges to its glaucous green leaves.

Y. flaccida Mid green or glaucous leaves, curving downwards at the tips, form low clumps. The leaves are up to 60 cm (2 ft) long with many short white threads along the edges. Creamy white flowers are carried in erect panicles up to 1.5 m (5 ft) tall. This species spreads by short basal side growths. HEIGHT & SPREAD 60×75 cm (2×2½ ft) after 5 years, ultimately 75 cm (2½ ft) tall.

'Golden Sword'♀ has leaves banded with creamy yellow. 'Ivory'♀ is a free-flowering variety bearing creamy white, green-stained flowers.

Y. glauca This low-growing, short-stemmed evergreen species forms rounded heads of spiky greyish leaves, up to 60 cm (2 ft) long, with white edges and some hanging threads. Well-established plants bear nodding greenish white flowers in erect panicles up to 1.5 m (5 ft) tall. HEIGHT & SPREAD 60×75 (2×2½ ft) after 5 years, ultimately 1 m (3 ft) tall.

Y. gloriosa♀ (Adam's needle, Spanish dagger) Stout semi-woody stems are topped by a cluster of straight, fiercely spiny, glaucous green leaves, up to 60 cm (2 ft) long. Creamy white flowers sometimes tinged with red are carried in panicles up to 2.1 m (7 ft) tall. The species may not flower for 5 or more years. HEIGHT & SPREAD 60×60 cm (2×2 ft) or more after 5 years, ultimately 1.5 m (5 ft) or more tall.

'Variegata'♀ has leaves edged and striped with creamy yellow.

▲ Yucca gloriosa

Y. recurvifolia♀ Spiky leaves, up to 75 cm (2½ ft) long, rise from a short stem that eventually branches. All but the upper central leaves are recurved. Creamy flowers are borne in dense, erect panicles up to 2.1 m (7 ft) high. HEIGHT & SPREAD 1×1 m (3×3 ft) after 5 years, ultimately 2.4 m (8 ft) tall.

'Marginata' has leaves edged with pale yellow. 'Variegata' bears leaves with a yellowish green band down the centre.

Y. whipplei Long, narrow, rigid, spine-tipped leaves form a dense, almost globular cluster. The leaves are grey-green, glaucous and finely toothed. Tall plumes of large milky green, purple-edged, scented bells are held in densely packed panicles on long stout stems. Plant this slightly tender garden plant in a sunny, well-drained site, where temperatures remain above -5°C (23°F). HEIGHT & SPREAD 40×40 cm (16×16 in) after 5 years, ultimately 1 m (3 ft) tall.

CULTIVATION Plant hardy species in spring in any well-drained garden soil in full sun. Plant the tender Y. aloifolia and Y. elephantipes in a 25 cm (10 in) pot of John Innes compost No. 2 or 3 in spring and maintain a minimum night-time temperature of 7°C (45°F). Place in a sunny position. Repot as necessary in spring.

PROPAGATION Remove well-rooted suckers in early or mid spring and replant in permanent positions. Alternatively, lift the plants in late spring and remove small buds from the base of the stem. Dip in dry wood ashes to stop excessive bleeding. Line out in sandy soil, 1.5 cm (½ in) below the surface, in a coldframe; the buds slowly grow into young plants.

PRUNING None required.

PESTS AND DISEASES Leaf spot can damage the foliage.

Yulan see *Magnolia denudata*
Yushania see BAMBOOS p. 79

X
y
z

Zantedeschia
Arum lily, calla lily
Araceae

Zantedeschia aethiopica
'Crowborough'

A petal-like, modified leaf called a spathe enfolds a fleshy spike of tiny flowers (called a spadix) at the top of a long stem on these stately plants. Blooming in late spring and early summer these lilies are much prized as cut flowers. Plants have arrow-shaped leaves and large rhizomes. Native to South Africa, the genus zantedeschia includes both hardy and tender plants. All species and varieties prefer damp or wet soil and so may be grown at the side of a pond. Some plants can be grown in water.

RECOMMENDED SPECIES AND VARIETIES

Z. aethiopica♀ A creamy white spathe, up to 25 cm (10 in) long, surrounds a yellow spadix. This plant is the hardiest zantedeschia, being able to withstand several degrees of frost. It can be grown in water as

▼ *Zantedeschia aethiopica*

▲ *Zantedeschia aethiopica* 'Crowborough'

▲ *Zantedeschia aethiopica* 'Green Goddess'

an aquatic plant, provided that the water does not freeze solid. HEIGHT & SPREAD 1 m×50 cm (3 ft×20 in).

'Crowborough' is even hardier than the species. 'Green Goddess'♀ has a white spathe heavily marked with green.

Z. elliottiana♀ The broad leaves, up to 28 cm (11 in) long, of this tender plant have translucent white spots. The spathe and spadix are yellow. The plant should be brought indoors for winter. There are many named, coloured forms available. HEIGHT & SPREAD 75×30 cm (2½×1 ft).

Z. rehmannii♀ Pink to maroon spathes with whitish flowers distinguish this plant which should be brought indoors for winter. The leaves are up to 20 cm (8 in) long. HEIGHT & SPREAD 80×30 cm (32×12 in).

CULTIVATION Plant the rhizomes of *Z. aethiopica* and its cultivars 10 cm (4 in) deep and about 40 cm (16 in) apart in moist or wet, fertile soil. If treating as an aquatic plant, place in a planting basket at a depth of 15-30 cm (6-12 in).

Plant *Z. elliottiana* and *Z. rehmannii* in 20-25 cm (8-10 in) pots, in John Innes No. 2 or No. 3 or in a moist, peat-based compost. Keep in a greenhouse over winter, then in late spring or early summer plant outside or place the pots outside. Feed regularly and reduce watering in late summer before bringing the plants inside once more.

PROPAGATION Best done by dividing the rhizomes in late summer.

PESTS AND DISEASES Leaf spot can mark and damage the leaves.

Zauschneria
Onagraceae

The abundance of flowers produced by these evergreen perennials will brighten the front of a border in late summer and early autumn. The funnel-shaped flowers grow in clusters on the ends of slender stems. The lance-shaped, rich green or grey-green leaves are mostly downy. Zauschnerias need a sunny position in order to thrive and are hardy when grown on a free-draining soil; the greatest threat to their survival is winter wet. Native to California and Mexico.

RECOMMENDED SPECIES AND VARIETIES

Z. californica (syn. *Epilobium californicum* hort.) (Californian fuchsia, humming-bird flower) The rich scarlet flowers are about 3 cm (1¼ in) long. The lance-shaped, greyish green leaves, up to 4 cm (1½ in) long, have a downy texture. HEIGHT & SPREAD 45×45 cm (1½×1½ ft) or more.

The flowers of ssp. *cana* (syn. *Epilobium canum, E. microphyllum*) are vermilion to scarlet. Its cultivars 'Albiflora' and 'Dublin'♀ (syn. 'Glasnevin') have white flowers and slightly longer, bright orange-red flowers respectively. 'Dublin' rarely exceeds 30 cm (1 ft) in height or spread.

The flowers of ssp. *latifolia* have more prominent stamens than the species and the leaves are smaller.

The flowers of ssp. *mexicana* (syn. *Epilobium villosum, Z. cana* ssp. *villosa*) are red. Its cultivar 'Solidarity Pink' has pale pink flowers.

Z. cana ssp. *villosa* see *Z. californica* ssp. *mexicana*

CULTIVATION Plant in late spring in an open sunny position in very well-drained soil. In cold areas a site at the foot of a south or west-facing wall is best. When

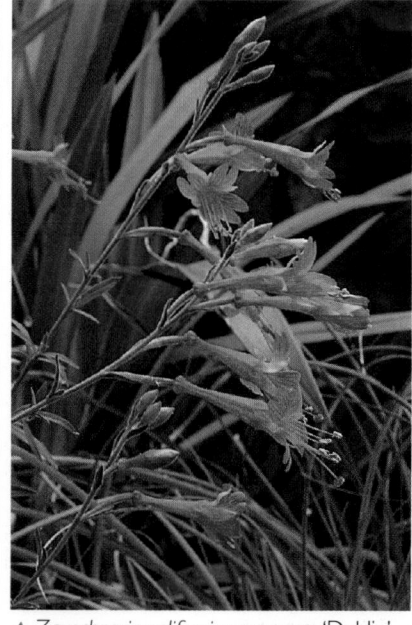

▲ *Zauschneria californica* ssp. *cana* 'Dublin'

established, apply a slow-release fertiliser during early spring. To protect plants from winter weather, do not cut back the foliage until late spring.

PROPAGATION Take softwood cuttings in summer, sow seed under glass in early spring, or divide in late spring.

PESTS AND DISEASES Usually trouble free.

Zea see GRASSES p.302
Zebra plant see *Aphelandra squarrosa*
Zebra plant see *Calathea zebrina*
Zebrina see *Tradescantia*

Zelkova
Ulmaceae

Zelkova serrata

These stately trees with upswept branches make an impressive focal point in a large garden. They are particularly valued for their distinctive goblet-like outline and splendid autumn colour. Fairly hardy and shade tolerant, they will grow in any soil and can live for over 100 years. The recommended trees have insignificant flowers.

RECOMMENDED SPECIES

Z. carpinifolia (Caucasian elm) A dense aerial forest of upright branches develops above a short, thick trunk, which is as much as 1 m (3 ft) across and often reinforced by

▲ *Zelkova carpinifolia*

buttress-like thickened sections at the base. The bark is pale grey. The pointed, elliptic-oblong leaves, 4-7.5 cm (1½-3 in) long, have rough, toothed edges. They turn yellow and then warm orange-brown in autumn. The species is native to mountainous forests of the Caucasus and N Iran. HEIGHT & SPREAD 6×4 m (20×13 ft) after 20 years, ultimately 30 m (100 ft) tall.

Z. serrata♀ (Japanese zelkova, saw leaf zelkova) Toothed, ovate-oblong leaves, about 5 cm (2 in) long, turn yellow, orange and red in autumn. The smooth, flaky, brownish grey bark sometimes reveals small patches of pale orange. This tree is often pruned as a bonsai. Native to SE Asia. HEIGHT & SPREAD 6×4 m (20×13 ft) after 20 years, ultimately 30 m (100 ft) tall.

▲ *Zelkova serrata*

CULTIVATION Plant in spring in any soil, ideally fertile, in partial shade. If you wish to restrict the growth rate, plant in poor soil and do not feed.

PROPAGATION Store seed in a paper bag in a refrigerator in winter and sow under glass in spring. Harden the seedlings outside in summer.

PESTS AND DISEASES Dutch elm disease is sometimes a problem. Otherwise, these trees are usually trouble free.

Zenobia
Ericaceae

Aniseed-scented, bell-like flowers hang from the long stalks of this bushy deciduous or semi-evergreen shrub for acid soils. There is one species in the genus.

Zenobia pulverulenta White flowers, up to 1 cm (⅜ in) long, arranged in unbranched clusters, open from early to mid summer. The alternate, ovate-oblong to broadly elliptic leaves, 2-7 cm (¾-2¾ in) long, have a blue-white bloom when young. The plant spreads by suckers. It is hardy, but young growth is occasionally damaged by frost. Native to eastern N America. HEIGHT & SPREAD 1.2 m×60 cm (4×2 ft) after 5 years, ultimately 1.8 m (6 ft) tall.

CULTIVATION Plant out in autumn or spring, if possible, in a moist, acid soil in sun

▲ *Zenobia pulverulenta*

or partial shade. Remove the developing seed heads if desired.

PROPAGATION Take semi-ripe cuttings in summer. Alternatively, sow the seed under glass in late winter.

PRUNING Cut back after flowering to near ground level about every 5 years, or more frequently if the plant becomes straggly.

PESTS AND DISEASES Usually trouble free.

Zephyranthes
Amaryllidaceae

Beautiful erect, cup-shaped blossoms crown the stems of the hardy to half-hardy bulbs in this genus in spring or autumn. It is essential to grow these clump-forming plants in a well-drained soil and in an open sunny position, such as the edge of a border or at the base of a south or west-facing wall. Cloche protection from the worst of the winter rain is necessary for most species and beneficial for the recommended plant. The bulbs are also easily grown in pots in an unheated greenhouse or conservatory. Native to N and S America.

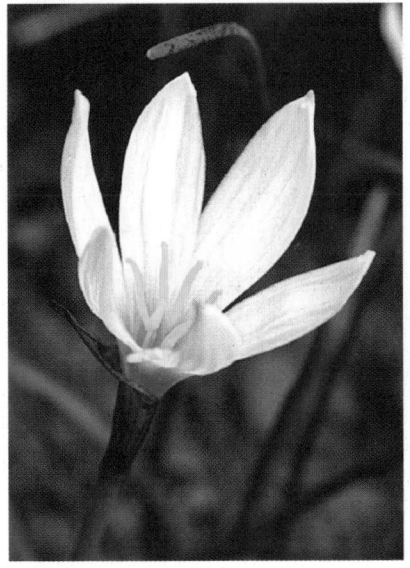

▲ *Zephyranthes candida*

x
y
z

717

RECOMMENDED SPECIES

Z. candida (zephyr flower) Pure white or, occasionally, rose-tinged petals open into starry flowers, up to 5cm (2in) across, in late summer and autumn. They are carried on individual leafless stems up to 15cm (6in) long. The dark green leaves, virtually evergreen, are narrow and rush-like and up to 25cm (10in) long. HEIGHT & SPREAD 25×10cm (10×4in).

CULTIVATION Plant *Z. candida* in spring in very well-drained soil and in a sunny spot, or pot in John Innes No.3 compost with up to 25 per cent of sharp grit added. Plunge the pot in sand in a coldframe. Dry off pot-grown plants in late spring and repot or top-dress them with fresh compost. Water well in late summer.

PROPAGATION Divide bulbs of *Z. candida* in late spring. Alternatively, sow seed in early spring in a coldframe.

PESTS AND DISEASES Usually trouble free.

Zephyr flower see *Zephyranthes candida*

Zigadenus
Melanthiaceae

Small, star-like blossoms highlight the hardy bulbs and rhizomes in this genus in summer. They require well-drained, rich soil and an open position, but one that is not baked by the sun. A place in a mixed border or a shrub border is suitable. The plants, which are poisonous, are native to N America and N Asia.

RECOMMENDED SPECIES

Z. elegans (white camass) Spikes of greenish white star-like, 6-petalled blossoms, up to 2cm (¾in) across, each with a distinctive yellowish green basal nectary, are produced

▲ *Zigadenus elegans*

throughout summer. The grey-green, semi-erect leaves of this clump-forming plant are narrow and strap-like and grow up to 30cm (12in) long. HEIGHT & SPREAD 45×15cm (18×6in).

CULTIVATION Plant in spring in cool, moist, well-drained soil that has been enriched with organic matter and in an open position. Water freely throughout spring and summer. Apply a slow-release fertiliser in early spring.

PROPAGATION Divide in early spring or sow seeds in a coldframe in autumn.

PESTS AND DISEASES Usually trouble free.

Zinnia
Youth and old age
Compositae

Zinnia elegans

Showy dahlia-like flowers, available in a wide range of brilliant colours, appear from mid summer until the first frosts. The longer-stemmed plants make very good cut flowers, while the smaller varieties are suitable for planting at bed and border edges and in containers. Zinnias perform best in hot, dry summers and tend to be disappointing when grown in cool, wet climates.

The plants described below are half-hardy annuals of erect habit. They have more or less stalkless leaves, undivided and smooth-edged, arranged in pairs along the stems. Native to S United States and Mexico, the plants are not frost hardy.

RECOMMENDED SPECIES AND VARIETIES

Z. angustifolia This short, small-flowered species makes an excellent summer ground-cover plant and is also useful as a filler for a sunny position in a rock garden. The single, star-shaped flowers are about 4cm (1in) across and in favourable conditions are borne in great abundance. HEIGHT & SPREAD 25-35×30cm (10-14×12in).

'**Starbright Mixed**' has gold, orange and white flowers. '**Tropical Snow**' carries white flowers.

Z. elegans Purple flowers, about 6cm (2½in) across, appear on coarse, upright stems in summer. The ovate or lance-shaped leaves, about 8cm (3¼in) long, are light to mid green. HEIGHT & SPREAD 100×30cm (40×12in).

Z. haageana (syn. *Z. mexicana*) Upright stems bear light green lance-shaped leaves, about 4cm (1½in) long, that are lightly covered in hairs. The single flowers grow to 4cm (1½in) across and are bright orange. HEIGHT & SPREAD 60×30cm (24×12in).

▲ *Zinnia haageana*

OTHER VARIETIES

Z. elegans and *Z. haageana* are the parent species of almost all the most commonly grown varieties. The flower colour range, unless otherwise stated, includes orange, pink, purple, red, white and yellow.

'**Chippendale**' has single deep red flowers with golden tips on the ray florets and grows as tall as 60cm (2ft). **Dahlia-Flowered Mixed** and **Giant Double Mixed** both have semidouble flowers up to 12cm (4¾in) across and grow to a height of about 60cm (2ft). '**Envy**' produces lime-green flowers, grows to 60cm (2ft) tall and will tolerate some shade.

'**Persian Carpet**' has semidouble flowers, about 5cm (2in) across, which are bicoloured in chocolate, cream, gold, maroon, purple and yellow, and grows to a height of about 40cm (16in). This variety performs better than the larger-flowered ones in cooler, wetter summers. **Sun Bow Mixed** has fully double, almost spherical flowers about 3cm (1¼in) across, which resemble pompon dahlias. The plant grows up to 50cm (20in) tall.

'**Thumbelina**' is a very compact dwarf plant growing to 10-15cm (4-6in) tall with double and semidouble flowers about 4cm (1½in) across. Of all zinnias, this performs best in wet summers. '**Whirligig Mixed**', about 50cm (20in) tall, has large single flowers about 8cm (3in) across with the ray florets tipped with a contrasting colour.

CULTIVATION Plant in full sun in a fertile, well-drained soil after all risk of frost has passed. Water in after planting, but avoid any further watering. Deadhead throughout the flowering period.

PROPAGATION Zinnias resent root disturbance, and if treated as half-hardy annuals they should be raised in pots. Sow seed in a greenhouse in mid spring about six weeks before planting out. Alternatively, sow in late spring in the final planting position and thin out the seedlings to the required spacing as soon as they are well established.

PESTS AND DISEASES Aphids, capsid bugs, chrysanthemum eelworms and earwigs may attack the plants. Seedlings are susceptible to damping off, and in wet conditions fungal foot and root rots may cause subsequent losses. Grey mould may infect the flowers in wet seasons.

Zinnia, creeping
see *Sanvitalia procumbens*

Food
from the
garden

Even in a small garden, fruit will grow against a sunny wall and vegetables can be sown among flowering plants. With a larger space, a kitchen garden can make a real contribution to both your eating enjoyment and the household budget

The Fruit Garden

Fruit trees and bushes can be as rewarding as any ornamental plant. Trees trace decorative shapes against a sunny wall – as well as giving fruit. And strawberries, raspberries and currants provide delicious summer tastes

Tree fruit and soft fruit

The fruits that grow in British gardens are divided into 'tree fruit' and 'soft fruit', which mostly grow on bushes. Soft fruit can be more rewarding as they produce their fruit more quickly after planting and also need no cross-pollination, which can result in more reliable cropping. Most varieties of tree fruit must be pollinated by another variety growing in your own or a neighbour's garden. Trees can be grown in a variety of shapes, including bush trees, pyramids, cordons, espaliers and fans. The choice depends on whether the tree will be grown against a wall or fence (a restricted form) or if it will be free-standing (unrestricted). The charts of varieties on the following pages will help you to choose the varieties of fruit that are most suitable to your garden – and to your palate.

PLANTING A YOUNG FRUIT TREE

The best time to plant a fruit tree is on a fine day in autumn, when the soil is not wet and sticky. Free-standing trees need to be staked for four years. Free-standing trees on dwarfing rootstocks, which have a small root system, need a permanent stake. First, drive the stake into position and then dig the hole next to it. For the full method of planting a tree, see page 808.

Restricted trees require a supporting framework – either horizontal wires or trellis – which may be fixed to a wall or fence or may stand alone. Wires are spaced 15 cm (6 in) apart for fan trees, with the lowest wire 38 cm (15 in) above the soil. Espaliers need stronger wire spaced 38-45 cm (15-18 in) apart and coinciding with the 'arms' of the tree, with the lowest wire 45 cm (18 in) above

the soil. The wires for cordons are spaced 60 cm (24 in) apart, with the bottom wire 60 cm (24 in) above the soil. Plant fruit trees no more than 15 cm (6 in) from a wall or fence so that they benefit from the extra warmth.

HOW TO TRAIN AND PRUNE A NEW TREE

Fruit trees are pruned for two reasons – in the early years to form the desired shape, in later years to allow maximum light to get in and to maintain the balance between growth of new wood and fruit production.

Winter pruning directs energy to the growth buds at the expense of flower buds, and should be kept to the minimum in the early years so as not to delay cropping. Early fruiting of unrestricted forms can be encouraged by bending new shoots outwards and tying them down, as horizontal shoots will

produce more flower buds.

Summer pruning is less stimulating to growth and also removes unwanted shoots. Stone fruits, such as plums and peaches, are usually pruned in summer because silver leaf disease may occur at other times.

Starting with a feathered maiden – a one-year-old tree with laterals (or feathers) – it is possible to train any shape. But two-year-old trees can be bought partly trained.

Unrestricted trees can be trained as 'bush' trees, which have an open centre, or as 'spindlebush' or 'pyramid' trees which have a central trunk and tiers of horizontal branches. Restricted trees can be trained

as cordons, espaliers, step-overs or fans. The eventual size of each shape depends on the type of rootstock it is grown on (see the chart of varieties for each type of fruit).

Spur-forming and tip-bearing varieties

Most varieties of fruit trees develop fruiting spurs which carry the flower buds each year. However, some types develop a flower bud at the end of each year's new growth, and are called 'tip bearers'. The different types are identified in the charts.

Always ensure that sufficient flower buds are left after pruning.

• TRAINING A BUSH TREE •

A 'bush' has a stem 75 cm (30 in) high. A higher stem gives a 'standard' which is too large for small gardens. A bush is easy to grow but can have poor light penetration.

Good hygiene with fruit pruning

After pruning a fruit tree – especially if diseased wood has been removed – clean the tools with a sterilant by spraying them with a small hand sprayer or by dipping them into a bucket of sterilant solution.

There is no need to paint cuts unless there is a high incidence of canker and silver leaf diseases in the neighbourhood, in which case paint the wounds with pruning paint within 30 minutes of making the cut.

When cutting wood out of a

REMOVING A BRANCH

tree, unless cutting to a bud or shoot, always leave the basal 5 mm (^{1}/$_4$in) intact. This will ensure that the tree's natural protection mechanism is able to shut out diseases.

1 FIRST WINTER After planting a feathered maiden (a one-year-old tree with laterals), cut back the main stem to 75 cm (30 in) above soil level to leave four laterals.

These laterals provide the basic framework of the adult tree. Shorten them by two-thirds of their length, each to a bud pointing away from the centre of the tree.

Remove any laterals on the main stem lower than the selected laterals. During spring and summer, the four laterals will grow longer and sub-laterals will sprout from them.

2 FIRST SUMMER In August on apples and pears remove all upright sub-lateral shoots longer than 23 cm (9 in).

Similar shoots on plum and cherry trees are shortened to 10 cm (4 in) by breaking them off between your finger and thumb (see left). Leave all the other sub-lateral shoots intact.

3 SECOND WINTER Shorten the leading laterals by half of their new growth to an outward facing vegetative bud (one that is flat and pointed and will produce a new shoot).

• TRAINING A SPINDLEBUSH TREE •

A spindlebush has one central stem with side branches growing from it, so that the tree looks like a capital 'A'. It takes up less space and is more light-efficient than a bush.

1 FIRST WINTER After planting a feathered maiden (a one-year-old tree with laterals), cut the main stem back to a bud 25 cm (10 in) above the top lateral. Then remove the top lateral so that it does not compete with the main stem for leadership. Remove all laterals on the main stem lower than 45 cm (18 in) above soil level. In spring the main stem will extend and more laterals will grow below the cut.

2 FIRST SUMMER In August on apples and pears remove all upright sub-lateral shoots longer than 23 cm (9 in). Similar shoots on plums and cherries are shortened to 10 cm (4 in) by breaking them off between finger and thumb.

Tie or weigh down to the horizontal all laterals that are growing upwards (see right). Laterals at the top of the tree are likely to be too vigorous and should be weighed down below the horizontal. The overall tree shape now resembles a capital 'A' and is very efficient at intercepting sunlight.

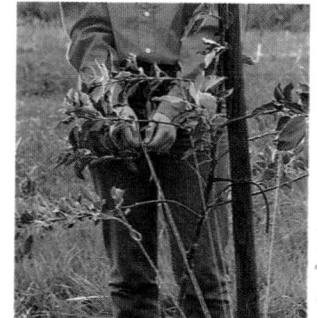

▶ Tie down upright laterals so that the tree looks like a capital 'A'.

3 SECOND WINTER Prune the tree in the same way as in the first winter.

• TRAINING A PYRAMID •

Like a spindlebush, a pyramid tree has a central stem. But the laterals of a pyramid are tied down less severely – to about 30 degrees above the horizontal.

1 FIRST WINTER After planting a feathered maiden (a one-year-old tree with laterals), prune as for a spindlebush but also shorten all the laterals by half. For stone fruits, wait until April before pruning.

2 FIRST SUMMER In August, cut back the current season's extension growth on laterals to 20 cm (8 in) and sublaterals to 15 cm (6 in). Tie or weigh down laterals to 30 degrees above the horizontal. Remove the ties in the autumn.

3 SECOND WINTER Cut back the extension growth on the main stem by two-thirds. For stone fruits (plums and cherries), wait until April before pruning.

• CORDON •

A single stem bears fruit all along it on short spurs. Double or triple-stemmed cordons can also be grown. Cordons take the least space.

1 FIRST WINTER After planting a feathered maiden (a one-year-old tree with laterals), cut back the main stem between the topmost lateral and its tip by half.

Tie the main stem to a cane along its entire length and then tie the cane to the support wires at an angle of 45 degrees (see right). Shorten all laterals to a length of 7.5-10 cm (3-4 in).

If you wish to cover an archway, train the stem vertically instead of at 45 degrees in order to release its full vigour.

2 FIRST SUMMER In August, shorten all new laterals longer than 23 cm (9 in) to 5 cm (2 in). Then shorten to 2.5 cm (1 in) all the sub-laterals that have grown from the laterals that were pruned in the first winter (see right).

3 SECOND WINTER Cut the leader as in the first winter.

4 SECOND SUMMER Prune the tree in the same way as in the first summer. Once the required height has been reached, cut the top of the stem back to a lateral in June.

• TRAINING AN ESPALIER •

The vertical stem has three or more horizontal tiers of branches growing from it at right angles. Ideally, the pairs of branches should be opposite each other. This is a decorative shape for a wall.

1 FIRST WINTER After planting a feathered maiden (a one-year-old tree with laterals), select two of the laterals that are growing at the height of the bottom support wire – 45 cm (18 in) above soil level. They will form the first tier of branches.

Shorten these laterals by half their length, each to an upward facing bud (see left).

Tie the laterals to bamboo canes and then tie the canes to the horizontal support wires.

CHOOSING THE RIGHT ROOTSTOCK

When buying a new tree choose one with the most suitable rootstock. It will decide the even- tual size of the tree, when and how heavily it will crop, and the shape into which it can be trained.

ROOTSTOCK	1ST FRUIT YEAR	FULL-CROP YEAR	SIZE OF CROP	AFTER 10 YEARS HEIGHT	SPREAD	POSSIBLE SHAPE OF TREE
MM 106	3-5	7-8	41-50kg (90-110lb)	4-5.5m (13-18ft)	5m (16ft)	Cordon, fan, spindlebush, espalier, bush, pyramid.
M 26	3-4	5-6	30-34kg (65-75lb)	3-3.5m (10-12ft)	3.5m (12ft)	Cordon, fan, spindlebush, espalier, bush, pyramid.
M 9	3-4	5-6	16-20kg (35-45lb)	2.4-3m (8-10ft)	3m (10ft)	Step-over, cordon, fan, spindlebush, bush, pyramid.
M 27	2-3	4-5	7-11kg (15-25lb)	1.5-1.8m (5-6ft)	1.8m (6ft)	Spindlebush, bush, cordon, step-over, tub, limited area.

HARVESTING AND STORAGE

Allow the apples to ripen on the tree and pick them when they detach easily. Don't allow them to over-ripen; it will affect the number of flowers next year.

On a free-standing tree, ripening starts on the south side which receives the most sun.

Fruit for storing needs to be slightly under-ripe. You can judge the correct degree of ripeness by painting iodine on a cut cross-section of one of the apples. If 50-60 per cent of the surface turns blue-black, the fruit should store safely until Christmas at least. If the fruit is not ripe enough, the stain will cover a greater area; if it is over-ripe the stain will be smaller.

For storage, put unblemished fruit in clear polythene bags – a maximum of 2kg (4½lb) per bag for easy handling. Tie the bags at the top and use a knitting needle to puncture each bag – two holes for every kilogram of fruit (one hole per pound). This will allow the fruit to breathe and ripen without rotting.

Place the bags in a dark, cool but frost-free place such as a cellar or garage. The bags will ensure that the apples do not shrivel through loss of water. Inspect the fruit occasionally and remove any rotting ones.

PESTS AND DISEASES

The main pests of apple trees are apple sawfly and codling moth (see Pests, p.824). Nest boxes put out close to fruit trees will encourage birds which will eat the caterpillars. Pheromone traps placed in the tree in early May kill some of the male codling moths, reducing the next generation. The increase in trapped moths also indicates the best time to spray.

You can provide a hibernation site for overwintering caterpillars by wrapping sacking or corrugated cardboard around the tree trunk in July. After the fruit has been picked, caterpillars in these traps can be destroyed by boiling the sacking or burning the cardboard.

The main diseases of apple trees are canker, brown rot, powdery mildew and apple scab (see Diseases and Disorders, p.838). To avoid them, clear up dead leaves and other plant material in autumn, remove any mummified fruit during winter pruning and water regularly during dry spells.

Blackberries see *Raspberries and Blackberries* p.729

Cherries
Prunus avium (Sweet cherry)
Prunus cerasus (Acid cherry)
Rosaceae

Cherry growing has entered a new phase with the introduction of dwarfing rootstocks which allow free-standing (unrestricted) trees to be netted against birds when the fruit is ripening. Previously, cherry trees were too large. They can also now be grown as restricted forms such as espaliers and fans.

CULTIVATION

Cherries will grow in most soils that have good drainage. In cool areas they are best trained as fans on a south-to-west-facing wall or fence for extra warmth. The acid variety 'Morello' is more hardy than sweet cherries and is often grown on a north-facing wall.

Buds may need to be netted against finches in winter.

Feed sweet cherries in February, using a compound fertiliser at the rate recommended on the label (the same as for apples). Acid cherries may need higher rates because of the amount of pruning.

Ripening fruit should be sheltered from the rain to prevent splitting. Apply netting against birds as the fruit starts to colour.

Water cherry trees in the same way as apples.

PROTECTION AGAINST WIND AND FROST

Cherries flower in April, so the blossom needs to be protected from cold winds and frost. Grow hedging to keep out cold winds, or put up open-mesh fencing. Avoid frost pockets,

RECOMMENDED VARIETIES OF CHERRY TREES

Old varieties need pollination from a variety in a different incompatibility group, but the same flowering group. Universal donors (UD) can pollinate any other variety, provided it is in the same flowering group. Self-fertile varieties will grow alone.

VARIETY	SEASON OF USE (PICK AND USE)	INCOMPATIBILITY GROUP	FLOWERING GROUP
Sweet Cherry			
Early Rivers	Mid to late June	1	1
Merchant	Early July	UD	3
Vega	Mid July	UD	3
Stella	Late July	UD. Self-fertile	4
Sunburst	Late July	UD. Self-fertile	4
Noir de Guben	Late July	UD	1
Van	Late July	2	3
Lapins	Early August	UD. Self-fertile	4
Acid cherry			
Morello	August	Self-fertile	5

CHERRY ROOTSTOCKS

The vigour of the rootstock will decide the size of the tree and the shapes in which it can be trained. Both Colt and Inmil rootstocks can be used for bush, espalier, pyramid, spindlebush and fan trees.

ROOTSTOCK	1ST FRUIT YEAR	FULL CROP YEAR	AFTER 10 YEARS YIELD	HEIGHT	SPREAD
Colt	3	7	9-16kg (20-35lb)	5m (16ft)	5m (16ft)
Inmil	3	6	5-11kg (11-25lb)	3.5m (12ft)	3.5m (12ft)

which are areas of low-lying ground or places where cool air flowing downhill becomes trapped by a solid fence. Draping the tree with hessian, supported off the flowers, will give protection against frost, but allow access for insects to pollinate the flowers during the day.

HARVESTING AND STORAGE

Pick cherries when they are ripe, with the stalk attached. Eat them as soon as possible, although they can be frozen.

If they are picked slightly under-ripe, cherries can be stored in a refrigerator for up to two weeks, but they must be picked with the stalk attached. Tie them up in a polythene bag and puncture the bag with a knitting needle – two holes per kilogram of fruit (one hole per pound).

PESTS AND DISEASES

Slugworms graze away the leaf surface to leave a skeleton. The damage is seen in May-June and July-August. Spray with derris, fenitrothion, permethrin or malathion. Cherry blackflies can attack young leaves (see Pests, p. 824).

Cherry trees can also suffer from bacterial canker and silver leaf (see Diseases and Disorders, p. 838).

Currants and Gooseberries

Ribes nigrum (Blackcurrant)
Ribes sativum
(Redcurrant/white currant)
Ribes grossularia
(Gooseberry)

Blackcurrants, redcurrants, white currants and gooseberries are cultivated in a similar way. Blackcurrant bushes have the stems growing from soil level; the other currants and gooseberries have a clean stem, called a 'leg', below the branches. Red and white currants and gooseberries are usually grown as bushes, but can also be cordons or fans. Currants are eaten fresh; gooseberries include both dessert and culinary varieties.

CULTIVATION

Currants and gooseberries will grow on most soils, provided a pH level of 6.5 is maintained. All of them, particularly gooseberries, need good drainage.

RECOMMENDED VARIETIES OF CURRANTS AND GOOSEBERRIES

Most of the new varieties have considerable resistance to frost, either through later flowering or resistance bred into the plants. The season for currants and gooseberries is from late June to August.

SEASON OF USE	VARIETY	CHARACTERISTICS
Blackcurrants Pick/use mid-late July	Ben Sarek	Small, compact bush. Heavy crops of large berries. Resistant to mildew. Tolerant of frost at flowering time.
	Ben Lomond	Good crops of large berries. Flavour good but acidic. Some frost and mildew resistance.
	Wellington	Heavy crops of sweet, medium-sized berries. Vigorous but spreading bush.
	Ben Nevis	Thick-skinned, medium-sized berries. Heavy cropping. Flavour fair. Some mildew resistance.
	Ben More	Heavy cropping. Large fruit with sharp flavour. Some mildew resistance.
Pick/use early August	Baldwin (Hilltop strain)	Medium-sized berries which hang well without splitting. Acid flavour. Good cropper and fairly compact bush.
Redcurrants Pick early July	Jonkheer van Tets	Heavy cropper. Long to very long bunches of good-flavoured fruit. Vigorous, upright growth; often damaged by wind.
Pick/use mid July	Laxton's No. 1	Good-quality, bright-red fruit of good flavour and small seeds.
Pick late July	Red Lake	Heavy crops of very large, bright-red fruit. Good flavour.
	Stanza	Heavy crops of firm, dark-red fruit borne on a short bunch. Good flavour. Vigorous growth.
Pick/use August	Redstart	High-yielding, reliable cropper. Rather acid flavour. Ripe fruit will hang on the bush for some time.
White currants Pick mid July	White Grape	Excellent sweet flavour. Medium yield and fruit size.
	White Versailles	Large, sweet fruit. Heavy cropper.
Gooseberries Pick/use late June	Early Sulphur	Good flavour. Heavy cropper. Makes excellent jam.
Pick mid July	Careless	Moderately vigorous and spreading bush. Green berries with fair flavour. Culinary.
	Jubilee	Heavier cropping selection of 'Careless'. Dual-purpose fruit.
	Greenfinch	Vigorous, upright bush. Resistant to mildew and leaf spot. Fair flavour. Only suitable for cooking.
Pick late July	Invicta	Well-flavoured pale-green berries. Vigorous, spreading and thorny. Resistant to mildew. Train as a fan-shape because of weak joints between branches and stem. Dual-purpose.
	Whitesmith	Very heavy crops of large, very well-flavoured white berries. Vigorous upright bush but spreading with age. Dual-purpose.
	Leveller	Very large, yellow-green berries. Good flavour. Weak on poor soils and needs good drainage. Dessert.
	Whinham's Industry	Heavy crops of red berries. Excellent flavour. Very vigorous; tolerates poor soils but susceptible to mildew. Dual-purpose.

Protect the buds of gooseberries and red and white currants from finches in winter, using nets. Blackcurrants are not usually attacked.

Blackcurrants need more fertiliser and water than other bush fruits. Feed them in February with a compound fertiliser at the rate recommended on the label.

Between May and August blackcurrants need up to 50 litres per m² (9 gal per sq yd) of water possibly every five to seven days. The other bush fruits need only 25 litres per m² (4½ gal per sq yd). Apply fertilisers and water within a circle 45 cm (18 in) around each plant.

Protect flower buds from frost (see Cherries).

• Blackcurrants

Plant in October or November while the soil is still warm and gaining moisture. Two-year-old bushes can be bought from garden centres, and hardwood cuttings root easily (see p.819), particularly if pushed through a black plastic sheet anchored to the soil.

Plant bushes with the base of the stems buried to encourage new shoots to emerge from below soil level. On normal soil, cut off the stems to leave stubs 2.5 cm (1 in) long. On good soil which will give quick growth, half of the stems can be left intact.

Each year, in November/December, cut back some of the stems to a stub 2.5 cm (1 in) long to encourage new growth. Count the stems and divide by four, then cut out that number. Remove diseased, old and low-lying stems first.

• Red and white currants and gooseberries

The plants are usually grown on a clean stem 20 cm (8 in) long.

After planting, cut off half of the one-year-old wood on the leading laterals to encourage new extension growth and sideshoots.

In later years, prune out whole branches to let in light that will ripen the remaining wood and deter disease.

In July cut back all sideshoots to 5 cm (2 in) to form fruiting spurs and avoid overcrowding. Gooseberries can be cut back immediately before picking to allow easier access past the spines to reach the fruit.

In later years when the crop decreases, cut out whole spurs to make way for new shoots.

Red and white currants and gooseberries can also be grown as single-stem or multi-stem cordons and fans on wires.

HARVESTING AND STORAGE

As currants ripen, they change colour from green to black, red or white. Pick entire stalks when fully ripe.

Culinary gooseberries will lighten in colour and dessert varieties will turn yellow-gold or red when ready to pick.

All fruits can be kept in the salad tray of a refrigerator for up to two weeks.

PESTS AND DISEASES

Gooseberry sawfly caterpillars may attack in April (see Pests, p. 824). Gall mites can cause blackcurrant buds to swell in spring and lead to a disease called reversion. Other possible diseases include botrytis, leaf spot, gooseberry mildew and coral spot (see Diseases and Disorders, p. 838).

Gooseberries see *Currants and Gooseberries*

Grapes
Vitis vinifera
Vitaceae

With the increased popularity of conservatories, grapevines can now be grown for dessert fruit throughout Britain. Grapes grown outdoors north of the Midlands are only suitable for wine-making, and then only if grown on a south or west-facing wall. In the Midlands and the South, grapes can be grown outdoors for both eating and wine-making.

CULTIVATION

In November/December plant the vine in the greenhouse soil. Alternatively, plant it outside so that the roots can grow unhindered, and train the stem through the wall.

For outdoor growing, plant vines against a south or west-facing wall. Good soil drainage is needed, so clay soils will need the addition of sand and organic material. Chalk soil usually drains well, but the pH may be too high, so add organic mater-

ial to the planting hole. Avoid making the soil too rich – the plant will produce too much growth at the expense of flowers. Plant 15 cm (6 in) away from the wall and mulch indoor vines to conserve moisture.

Each March apply a compound fertiliser according to the instructions on the label. A high-potash liquid feed should be applied every two weeks from when the flower buds start to open until the fruit is picked.

Vines can be grown in pots, which will restrict the roots and produce smaller plants. Indoor and potted vines need up to 50 litres of water per m² (9 gal per sq yd) weekly. After the first year, vines growing in a garden can find enough water as long as the roots are not restricted.

Indoors, flower pollination can be encouraged by gently shaking the stem at midday. Alternatively, if you have the time, hand pollinate by using a ball of cotton wool or a soft-bristled brush daily.

Shade the glass of a green-

▲ A greenhouse can be insulated with bubble plastic until late spring.

house from June to late August. When dessert grapes reach pea-size, they should be thinned if the bunches are tightly packed with little room to grow. Use long-bladed scissors in one hand and a small forked stick in the other. Never touch the fruit with your fingers.

On several occasions over about ten days, remove some of the fruit from within the bunch, plus any small fruits, leaving a 1.5 cm (½ in) gap between

RECOMMENDED VARIETIES OF GRAPES		
SEASON OF USE	VARIETY	CHARACTERISTICS
Greenhouse (unheated) Pick in July/ August	Black Hamburgh	Large dark red/purple fruit. Good flavour. Ripens freely without heat.
Greenhouse (heated) Pick in July	Muscat Hamburgh	Large dark red/purple fruit. Excellent flavour. Needs heat, and another variety that flowers at the same time to cross-pollinate.
	Muscat of Alexandria	Requires heat to crop well. Superb quality amber-coloured fruit.
Outdoor types Pick in September	Siegerrebe	Excellent muscat flavour. Highly recommended for dessert and wine. Protect from wasps. White.
	Mueller-Thurgau	Grow against south-facing wall for best performance. White.
	Madeleine Sylvaner	Consistent cropper. Reasonably hardy. Only fair flavour. White.
Pick in October	Madeleine Angevine	Heavy-cropping wine grape. Vigorous. Only fair quality. White.
	Seyval Blanc	Vigorous and resistant to mildew. Heavy cropper. Some frost resistance. White.
Pick in late October	Brandt	Masses of small red grapes for eating and wine. Resistant to mildew.

▲ Using long-bladed scissors and a forked stick, thin out grape clusters.

fruits. Remove diseased fruits as the bunches ripen.

Ripening fruit outdoors will need to be netted against birds.

PRUNING VINES

Grapevines grown indoors or outdoors on a wall are trained by the cordon system, which consists of a main stem (the rod) with fruiting laterals (spurs) 30 cm (12 in) apart along it.

After planting, shorten the stem by two-thirds, to a bud.

First spring and summer On indoor vines, select a strong shoot to become the rod and tie it to the underside of horizontal wires fixed 38 cm (15 in) from the glass and 30 cm (12 in) apart.

Outdoors, select two shoots and tie them to wires or trellis to create a double cordon.

Pinch back any laterals as they grow to five leaves, and sub-laterals to one leaf. Remove flowers and tendrils.

Second winter By the end of January, cut back last season's stem growth by two-thirds, and all laterals to one bud.

Second summer Indoors, train rods as in the first summer and select only one lateral every 30 cm (12 in) on last season's wood. Rub off unwanted laterals. Pinch back laterals as before.

Outdoors, train rods horizontally left and right. Select one lateral every 30 cm (12 in) on last season's wood. Rub off unwanted laterals. Pinch back laterals as before.

Both indoors and outdoors, allow three or four laterals to produce a bunch of flowers each and pinch them back to two leaves beyond the flowers.

Later seasons Prune last season's stem growth by two-thirds until long enough, and then back to one bud of last season's growth each winter. Treat laterals and sub-laterals as before. Increase fruiting laterals by four to six each year.

To stimulate laterals to grow along the full length of the rod as it grows longer, detach the rod from the wires in late January and lay it on the floor. When growth has started again, reattach it.

If the vine is creating a lot of work by growing too vigorously, select a lateral low down and train it as an extra rod.

Warning Vines become heavy, so monitor the greenhouse or conservatory roof for possible collapse.

HARVESTING AND STORAGE

Taste rather than colour is the only reliable way to decide when to pick grapes, both dessert and wine-making types. Dessert grapes are cut from the vine with a 'handle' of 5 cm (2 in) of stem both sides of the bunch. Treat bunches gently.

PESTS AND DISEASES

Birds will eat outdoor grapes before they are ripe. Netting is the only protection. Wasps are attracted to early outdoor fruit when it becomes ripe and sweet. Pick the fruit as it ripens.

Vines can be attacked by grey mould and powdery mildew (see Diseases and Disorders, p. 838). Powdery mildew is a particular problem of cold greenhouses. Outdoor vines are only affected in a dry place. Use resistant varieties and prune the canopy to aid ventilation.

Peaches and Nectarines

Prunus persica
Rosaceae

Peaches and nectarines will fruit successfully in Britain outdoors but only in a warm, sheltered position. Leaves must be kept clean from peach leaf curl to ensure survival of the tree. The late-ripening varieties must be grown in a greenhouse.

CULTIVATION

Peaches and nectarines will grow in most soils. They flower early so need protection from cold winds and frosts (see Cherries). Nectarines are less hardy than peaches and should only be grown on a south-to-west-facing wall or fence.

Hand pollination is necessary both outdoors and in a greenhouse. Dab the flowers

RECOMMENDED VARIETIES OF PEACHES AND NECTARINES

SEASON OF USE	VARIETY	CHARACTERISTICS
Peaches Pick/use mid July	Duke of York	Large fruit size. Juicy and refreshing flavour. Heavy cropper.
Pick/use mid July	Garden Lady	Compact habit. Ideal for growing in pots on a patio.
Pick/use mid to late July	Hale's Early	Heavy cropper but usually needs thinning. Average flavour but melting flesh.
Pick/use early August	Peregrine	Large fruit size. Juicy with excellent flavour. Reliable and high yielding.
Pick/use mid August	Rochester	Flowers late, misses early frosts. Reliable cropper outdoors. Juicy and good flavour.
Pick/use early to mid September	Bellegarde	Large to very large fruit size. Extremely good flavour. Must be grown in greenhouse.
Nectarines Pick/use late July	Early Rivers	Large fruit size. Juicy and good flavour.
Pick/use mid August	Lord Napier	Large fruit size. Regular and heavy cropper for outdoor growing. White aromatic flesh.
Pick/use mid August	Garden Delight	Compact habit. Ideal for growing in pots on a patio.
Pick/use early September	Pine Apple	Medium to large fruit. Grow in greenhouse. Outstandingly rich flavour and melting flesh.

ROOTSTOCKS FOR PEACHES AND NECTARINES

The rootstock of a tree decides the size of the tree and the shapes in which it can be trained. Both St Julien A and Pixy rootstocks can be used to train bush and fan-shape trees.

ROOT-STOCK	1ST FRUIT YEAR	FULL CROP YEAR	AFTER 10 YEARS YIELD	HEIGHT	SPREAD
St Julien A	4	7	22 kg (40 lb) Fan: 11 kg (25 lb)	5 m (16 ft)	5 m (16 ft)
Pixy	2	4	11 kg (25 lb) Fan: 5 kg (11 lb)	2.4 m (8 ft)	2.4 m (8 ft)

with a ball of cotton wool or a soft brush every two days from flower-opening to petal-fall.

Fertiliser rates are higher than most other tree fruit as a lot of wood is cut out each year. Use a compound fertiliser in February at the rate recommended on the label. Water as for apples if grown outdoors. In

a greenhouse, give 25–50 litres of water per m² (4½–9 gal per sq yd) during the growing season, depending on the heat of the sun and whether the roots are inside or outside.

A fan-trained tree is easier to maintain than a free-standing tree. Whether growing a tree from a one-year-old or from a

▲ A fan-trained peach tree grown against a wall or fence.

ready-trained fan, remove all blossoms in the first year.

The fruit is borne on wood of the previous year's growth, so wood that has borne fruit should be cut off after fruiting and new growths tied in. Select the strongest new growths as they grow, and pinch out all other unwanted shoots.

Within four weeks of petal-fall, thin the fruit to leave one per 15-20 cm (6-8 in). In a dry summer, more thinning may be needed as the fruit ripens.

HARVESTING AND STORAGE

The flesh around the stalk softens as it ripens and the skin takes on a reddish flush. Lift the fruit in your palm and twist it gently; ripe fruit will detach easily. Store in a cool place for up to a week, but fruit fresh from the tree tastes best.

PESTS AND DISEASES

Brown scale are sap-sucking insects protected by dark brown shells up to 6 mm (¼ in) long. In large numbers they will affect the vigour of the tree, and are most serious on greenhouse trees. Spray with tar oil in December, or use malathion or pirimiphos-methyl in early July.

The main diseases of peach trees are bacterial canker, peach leaf curl and silver leaf (see Diseases and Disorders, p.838).

A physiological disorder called split stone rots the kernel. Acid soil and drought cause a deep crack to show at the stalk end of the fruit. Correct the pH and mulch over moist soil – but not before April or May.

Pears

Pyrus communis
Rosaceae

Pears require more sun and warmth than apples but will grow well in various conditions. In colder areas, grow cor-

---

RECOMMENDED PEAR VARIETIES

Most varieties are dessert fruit for eating raw. Choose varieties from the same pollination group. Quality is out of a maximum of 5.

PICKING TIME	EATING TIME	VARIETY	POLLINATION GROUP	FRUIT QUALITY
Dessert pears				
Pick late August	Sept	Beth	4	4
	Sept	Williams' Bon Chretien	3	5
Pick mid-late September	Oct	Beurre Hardy	3	4
	Sept	Onward	4	5
	Oct	Conference	3	4
Pick October	Oct	Concorde	4	4
	Dec	Josephine de Malines	3 Tip bearer (see p. 720)	4
	Oct	Doyenne du Comice	4	5
Culinary pears				
Pick late October	Feb- Apr	Catillac	4	Hard flesh

ROOTSTOCKS FOR DIFFERENT PURPOSES

Rootstocks control the size of the tree and the shapes in which it can be trained. Both Quince A and C rootstocks can be used to train bush, pyramid, spindlebush, espalier, fan and cordon trees.

ROOT-STOCK	1ST FRUIT YEAR	FULL CROP YEAR	AFTER 10 YEARS YIELD	HEIGHT	SPREAD
Quince A	4	7	16-40 kg (35-88 lb)	3.5 m (12 ft)	3.5 m (12 ft)
Quince C	3	5	11-35 kg (24-77 lb)	3 m (10 ft)	3 m (10 ft)

dons, espaliers or fans against a south or west-facing wall or fence. Young leaves are easily damaged by wind, so trees need to be in a sheltered position.

Pear trees must be cross-pollinated so there has to be a nearby variety which flowers at the same time.

CULTIVATION

Pears will grow in most soils, but need protection from frosts and wind in April and May (see Cherries). The protection will increase temperatures and encourage pollinating insects.

Feed and water as for apples. During a drought pears can develop drooping yellow leaves, early leaf-drop and poor growth, so watering is critical.

Thin out the fruitlets to one per cluster as they swell and turn downwards.

On all forms of tree, lateral branches should not descend lower than the horizontal to ensure a balance between growth and fruiting.

In winter, remove very thin new shoots. Thicker shoots will produce flower buds in their second year on spur-bearing varieties and can be pruned back to these flower buds in winter. Prune restricted forms in summer (see pp. 721-2).

Old wood can be a site for pear scab to overwinter, so wood should be removed every five to six years and replaced with new shoots.

HARVESTING AND STORAGE

Early varieties, except Concorde which is yellow when unripe, are picked when the background colour changes from green to almost yellow, and its stalk comes away from the tree. Varieties harvested from September onwards are picked under-ripe and stored in a cool dark place in polythene bags (see Apples). They should not ripen on the tree as this will reduce next year's blossom.

PESTS AND DISEASES

Pear leaf blister mite, codling moth and pear midge are all major pests of pears (see Pests, p.824). Slugworms graze away the leaf surface in May-June and July-August. Spray with derris, fenitrothion, permethrin or malathion.

Canker, fireblight, pear scab, brown rot and honey fungus can all attack pear trees (see Diseases and Disorders, p.838).

Plums

Prunus domestica
Rosaceae

Plums include gages, damsons and bullaces. Dried plums are known as prunes. In small gardens plum trees can be grown as espaliers, cordons or fans on dwarfing rootstocks that keep the tree to a small size.

CULTIVATION

Plums will grow in most soil, provided it has good drainage. The flowers must be protected from cold winds and frosts in April (see Cherries). In colder areas, grow the trees as cordons, espaliers or fans on a south-to-west-facing wall. Feed and water as for apples.

Plum trees often produce root suckers which should be cut off or burnt off in summer with glyphosate weedkiller when 20 cm (8 in) high.

Like apples and pears, plums need to be thinned to improve the fruit and to encourage flower buds next year. Before late June, thin out the fruitlets to leave one every 5 cm (2 in).

Do not allow the soil to dry out as the stone may split inside the fruit. Water in dry spells and mulch when the weather warms up in late spring.

Summer prune (see pp. 721-2) in July, earlier than apples, by

RECOMMENDED PLUM VARIETIES

Some varieties are self-fertile – another variety is not needed for pollination. In practice, another variety flowering at the same time will ensure a crop in difficult seasons. Two varieties can be relied on to flower regularly and act as pollen donors – 'Denniston's Superb' for early flowerers and 'Oullins Gage' for late flowerers.

SEASON OF USE	VARIETY	POLLINATION GROUP
Dessert plums Late July	Opal	3 Self-fertile
Early to mid August	Blue Tit	5 Self-fertile
	Oullins Gage	4 Self-fertile
Late August	Denniston's Superb	2 Self-fertile
	Victoria	3 Self-fertile
Early September	Reeves Seedling	3
	Jefferson	1 Denniston's Superb will donate pollen
Culinary plums Early August	Czar	3 Self-fertile
Mid August	Pershore	3 Self-fertile
Late September	Marjorie's Seedling	5 Self-fertile
	Shropshire Prune (A damson that can be eaten fresh)	5

ROOTSTOCKS FOR DIFFERENT PURPOSES

Rootstocks control the size of the tree and the shapes in which the tree can be trained. St Julien A and Pixy rootstocks can be used to train bush, cordon, espalier, fan, spindlebush and pyramid trees.

ROOT-STOCK	1ST CROP YEAR	FULL CROP YEAR	AFTER 10 YEARS YIELD	HEIGHT	SPREAD
St Julien A	4	7	11–25 kg (24–55 lb)	5 m (16 ft)	5 m (16 ft)
Pixy	2	4	7–11 kg (15–24 lb)	2.4 m (8 ft)	2.4 m (8 ft)

snapping the unwanted shoots between finger and thumb to avoid disease infection. Spurs will then develop.

HARVESTING AND STORAGE
When the plums part easily from the tree they are ripe. Pick over the tree three to five times to collect the fruit as it ripens.

If plums are picked slightly under-ripe, with the stalk on the fruit, they will keep for up to four weeks in a refrigerator. Put them in a polythene bag tied at the neck and punctured with a knitting needle – two holes for every kilogram of fruit (one hole per pound). Take

them out of the refrigerator and allow them to develop colour for 24 hours before eating.

PESTS AND DISEASES
Caterpillars of plum fruit moth tunnel into fruit, often causing premature ripening. Pheromone traps reduce the caterpillars and also act as a guide to the best spraying time. Spray in late June with fenitrothion, pirimiphos-methyl or permethrin. A second spray two or three weeks later kills late hatchings.

The main diseases of plum trees are bacterial canker, brown rot and silver leaf (see Diseases and Disorders, p. 838).

Raspberries and Blackberries
Rubus idaeas (Raspberry), *Rubus fruticosus* (Blackberry) *Rosaceae*

Raspberries are the most widely grown cane fruit, but blackberries and the hybrids – such as tayberries and loganberries – are planted for their flowers, leaves and autumn colours as well as for fruit. They make an attractive display on an archway.

Canes are cut out each year after fruiting, and the new canes grow on to fruit next year. The new canes should be limited to 10 per metre of raspberries and 6–8 per plant of blackberries and hybrid berries.

However, the new canes can provide a home for diseases that overwinter in them. Two-yearly cropping will avoid the disease problem and eliminates the need to spray. Cutting off all canes after fruiting also makes pruning and training easier. Tie in new canes as they grow.

Cane fruit can be grown in a greenhouse or conservatory to extend fruiting at the start and the end of the season, but as raspberries are woodland plants their roots should be kept cool by growing them in white pots and watering regularly.

CULTIVATION
Cane fruits will grow on most soil. However, growth is hampered by poorly drained clay soil (especially raspberries) and by sandy soil where watering in the growing season is essential.

Each March apply a compound fertiliser according to the instructions on the label.

Water the canes throughout summer, especially as the berries start to colour, and again after picking. Always water at soil level rather than overhead to lessen the risk of infection.

The usual method of training is between pairs of wires 30 cm (12 in) apart, starting 90 cm (36 in) above the soil and spaced to a height of 1.8 m (6 ft).

• **Raspberries**
Most raspberries fruit in July and August, and their production of cane and fruit follows a two-year cycle. Each autumn

after the fruit has been picked, the cane that has borne the fruit is cut off at soil level. The new cane is then tied to the wires to fruit next year. Tops of canes can be bent over and tied to the top wire. If you cut them off you will lose fruiting spurs.

Autumn-fruiting varieties grow and fruit in the same season. All canes are cut off at soil level each February, and a greater number of new canes are allowed to grow than for summer raspberries. The row is usually 45 cm (18 in) wide.

Raspberries will not tolerate even temporary waterlogging. In wet places they can be planted on a ridge of soil.

▲ The tops of raspberry canes can be wound around the top wire.

• **Blackberries and hybrid berries**
Growth and fruiting follows a two-year cycle, so canes that have finished fruiting are cut out at soil level.

The canes need to be tied to the wire supports either in the shape of a fan or woven between the top wire and the bottom wire. Alternatively, tie the cane vertically and then horizontally along each wire to the left and right of the plant.

HARVESTING AND STORAGE
Raspberries and blackberries are usually picked without stalks, but most of the hybrid berries are picked with the stalk intact.

The fruit can be frozen, but warm fruit fresh from the plant has the best flavour.

PESTS AND DISEASES
The main pests of cane fruit are raspberry beetles, raspberry cane midges and aphids (see Pests, p. 824). Nets or a fruit cage will deter birds.

Possible diseases include cane blight, cane spot and spur blight (see Diseases and Disorders, p. 838). They can be avoided by cropping all cane fruit only once every two years, and cutting out all the canes after fruiting.

VARIETIES OF RASPBERRIES AND OTHER CANE FRUIT

SEASON OF USE	VARIETY	CHARACTERISTICS
Raspberries		
SUMMER-FRUITING		
Pick early to mid July	Glen Moy	Spine-free canes. Some resistance to aphids. Avoid planting with 'Malling Promise' or 'Malling Jewel' to reduce virus infection.
	Glen Clova	Heavy cropper. Vigorous cane growth. Avoid planting with 'Malling Promise' or 'Malling Jewel'.
	Malling Delight	Large orange-red fruits. Some aphid resistance. Heavy cropper.
Pick mid July to mid August	Malling Admiral	Good cropper. Vigorous canes. Some resistance to spur blight, mildew, cane botrytis.
	Malling Jewel	Good cropper. Sparse cane production. Tolerant of virus.
	Glen Prosen	Spine-free canes. Susceptible to spur blight and cane botrytis. Good crops.
Pick late July to late August	Leo	Large bright orange-red fruit. Very vigorous. Good resistance to spur blight, cane botrytis and aphids. Susceptible to cane spot. Some frost resistance.
AUTUMN-FRUITING		
Pick mid August to October	Autumn Bliss	Very good crops. Prolific canes requiring minimal support. Good resistance to aphids.
Blackberries		
Pick/use late July	Bedford Giant	Large, sweet fruit. Thorny. Plant 4.5 m (15 ft) apart.
Pick/use mid August	Ashton Cross	Good crops. Excellent flavour. Moderate vigour. Very spiny. Plant 3 m (10 ft) apart.
Pick late August to September	Loch Ness	Thornless. Well-flavoured. Plant 2.4 m (8 ft) apart. Fairly hardy.
	Fantasia	Vigorous canes; strong thorns. Heavy crops; good flavour.
	Oregon Thornless	Thornless. Mild flavour. Ornamental parsley-leaved blackberry. Fairly disease-free.
Hybrid berries		
Pick mid July to August	Tayberry	Heavy crops of long conical fruit. Excellent for jam.
	Loganberry LY59	Good crops of long berries. Plant 2.7 m (9 ft) apart.
	Loganberry LY654	Thornless. Otherwise as LY59.

Rhubarb
Rheum x hybridum
Polygonaceae

The stems of rhubarb are long, succulent and red with an acid taste, and must be cooked. Established plants can be forced into early growth to give sweeter stems for harvesting from early March. A range of varieties will produce suitable stems until September.

CULTIVATION
Rhubarb will grow in most soil, but not poorly drained clay. It prefers full sun but will tolerate shade for 25 per cent of the day. Each March, apply a compound fertiliser following the instructions on the label. First-year plants need watering in early summer, but rainfall normally gives enough water for established plants.

Rhubarb is grown from 'setts' which should be the size of a person's fist and have at least one prominent bud. Plant setts from late autumn to late March with the crown slightly above soil level. Space them 90 cm (3 ft) apart each way.

Rhubarb responds well to annual dressings of rotted compost applied in May.

Do not harvest any stems in the first year, and keep the soil weed-free to allow plants to become established. In the second year, harvest only two or three stems from each plant. In subsequent years stems can be removed when they are big enough. Any flower stems should be cut out.

To maintain vigour, lift plants every three years and divide them into 'setts' before replanting. Healthy established plants can be cut up with a spade or knife.

Rhubarb plants die down in winter. Established plants can be 'forced' into early growth the following spring. Cover selected plants in December or January with either wooden boxes or plastic bins. Specially made terracotta forcers which have lids to give access to the stems can also be used. Start harvesting stems in early March.

After being forced, plants need to be grown in the normal way for a year before being forced again.

Plants will crop well for six or seven years.

HARVESTING AND STORAGE
Pull the stems from the plant by holding them towards the base and twisting outwards and upwards. Ideally the stems should be cooked immediately, but they can be stored in a refrigerator for up to three days wrapped in a plastic bag to avoid loss of moisture.

PESTS AND DISEASES
Rhubarb is not usually attacked by pests. The crown of the plant may rot because of cold wet weather, poor drainage or being planted too deep.

Strawberries
Fragaria x ananassa
Rosaceae

Strawberries are the quickest fruit to produce a harvest after planting. They can be grown in a small garden and will do well in a patio container, growing bag or even a hanging basket. Their season of fruiting can be extended from March through to November by using different varieties, together with protection from rain and cold weather in the spring and autumn.

To ensure good crops, buy plants from a reputable source, and where possible plants that have been 'certified' by the Ministry of Agriculture, Fisheries and Food (MAFF).

RECOMMENDED VARIETIES OF RHUBARB

SEASON OF USE	VARIETY
April/May (suitable for forcing)	Early Victoria Timperly Early
May/June (main crop)	Cawood Delight
July/Sept	The Sutton Strawberry rhubarb

WHERE AND HOW TO PLANT

Strawberries will grow on most soil, but sandy soil needs watering in summer and clay needs good drainage – perhaps by building a raised bed or a ridge of soil. Chalky soil can cause deficiency of iron and manganese which can be rectified by using a chelated-iron compound. Strawberry plants need full sun, except for alpines which tolerate some shade.

Before planting, ensure a pH level of 6.5 (see p.803). Apply 35g of sulphate of potash per m² (1 oz per sq yd) and 17g of superphosphate per m² (½ oz per sq yd). Alternatively, use well-rotted farmyard manure at one barrowload to 5 m² (6 sq yd). Every February apply 17g of sulphate of potash per m² (½ oz per sq yd).

Bare-root and container-grown plants are both available. Bare-root plants need a period of establishment after planting before they are able to carry a crop successfully. If you plant them between July and September, a full crop can be picked the following year; but if they are planted at any other time the first flush of flowers has to be removed. Early planting with cold-stored runners in May gives the earliest crop. Plants sold in containers can be planted all year round, even when carrying flowers and fruit. Replace plants after four years, or sooner if growing poorly.

Roots of bare-root plants should be soaked in water before planting. The roots must point downwards in the hole and the 'crown' buried to half its depth. If planted too deep it will rot and if too shallow new roots will not grow.

Rows should be 30–36 in (75–90 cm) apart. Depending on the vigour of the variety, place

▲ Planting a bare-root strawberry plant, roots downwards.

the plants 15–24 in (38–60 cm) apart in each row.

Planting through a polythene sheet reduces weeds and keeps the fruit clean. And if you build up a ridge or wide bed of soil beneath the polythene, it will improve soil drainage, improve root growth and cause water to run off the sheet, reducing rotting of the fruit.

CULTIVATION

After planting, water through the holes in the polythene. As the flowers open, more water is needed but avoid wetting the flowers – it will encourage grey mould. In order for the water to get to the soil, spike some holes in the polythene. Low-pressure trickle irrigation is particularly useful beneath polythene.

On frosty nights in spring, protect the flowers with straw or sheets of perforated polythene, hessian or fleece.

As the fruits grow, protect them from soil splash by tucking straw or strawberry mats under them. To maintain fruit size remove runners (side-shoots) as they appear.

After picking, cut back the foliage to 10 cm (4 in) from the crown. Remove it, together with straw and debris, and burn it to kill pests and diseases. Add a general fertiliser to the soil and fork it in. Liquid feed plants growing through polythene. Water the plants if the soil is dry to encourage new leaves.

To maintain good fruit size, reduce the number of 'crowns' in each plant (where the leaves and flowers grow) to two or three. Pull the excess away from the edge of the plant.

HARVESTING

Pick the fruit only when dry by pinching the stalk between thumb and fingernails. Handle the fruit by the stalk to avoid bruising. Fruit for jam can be picked without a stalk.

Strawberries can be stored cool for up to two days, but warm strawberries fresh from the plant have the most flavour.

PROPAGATING STRAWBERRIES

The easiest method of producing new plants is to encourage the runners to root into pots of compost sunk into the soil around the parent plant.

A quicker method is to cut off the tips of the runners, complete with a 2.5 cm (1 in) piece of stem, when roots start to show. Insert them into small pots of compost and keep them under a polythene tent or in a propagator until fully rooted in about six weeks.

PESTS AND DISEASES

The main pests of strawberries are aphids, slugs, glasshouse red spider mite and strawberry beetles (see Pests, p.824). The most common diseases are grey mould and powdery mildew (see Diseases and Disorders, p.834).

RECOMMENDED VARIETIES OF STRAWBERRIES

Summer-fruiting varieties are most popular because they used to be the only varieties available to amateur growers. Perpetual (or remontant) varieties fruit later and extend the season into autumn. The table shows flavour, cropping and fruit size of each variety with scores out of 5.

SEASON OF USE	VARIETY	FLAVOUR	CROPPING	FRUIT SIZE	COMMENTS
Summer fruiting Pick early June	Honeoye	5	4	3	Some resistance to botrytis.
	Tamella	3	5	5	Very heavy cropper. Big fruit size. Moderate flavour.
	Elvira	4	5	4	Susceptible to mildew.
	Cambridge Vigour	4	4	3	Cropping and size better in first year.
	Royal Sovereign	5	3	4	Susceptible to diseases.
Pick mid June	Redgauntlet	1	5	5	Possible second crop in autumn. Disease resistant.
	Cambridge Favourite	3	4	3	Disease resistant but buy plants free of June Yellows disease.
	Elsanta	5	4	5	Vigorous. Poor disease resistance except mildew.
	Hapil	4	4	5	Vigorous. Crops well on all soils and dry conditions.
Pick mid July	Bogota	3	4	4	Fruit freezes well. Moderate disease resistance.
Perpetuals (Remontants) Pick late July	Rapella	4	5	4	Freeze well. Prone to mildew.
Alpines Pick mid summer to autumn	Baron Solemacher	–	–	–	Small fruit but excellent flavour.

The Vegetable Garden

In a large garden, enough vegetables can be grown to support a household through the year. Even a small patch can provide special treats

Artichoke, Globe
Cynara cardunculus Scolymus Group
Compositae

Globe artichokes are large perennial plants growing to 1.2-1.5 m (4-5 ft) tall and highly suitable for the back of a herbaceous border where the striking thistle-like green leaves make a good backdrop for contrasting flowers. The base of the scales around the flower and the base of the flower itself (called the fond) are the edible parts of the plant.

TYPES AND VARIETIES

Globe artichokes are usually grown from offsets (rooted suckers). They may also be raised from seeds, but the results are more variable and less predictable.

GRAND CAMUS DE BRETAGNE Large heads of good flavour; southern counties only.

GREEN GLOBE IMPROVED Reduced spines and consistent quality. Widely available.

PURPLE GLOBE Hardier with purple flowerheads. Offsets obtained from a garden centre may give better results than seeds.

VERT DE LAON The best for flavour, but suitable for southern counties only.

CULTIVATION AND HARVESTING

Globe artichokes need a sunny and sheltered position in fertile, well-drained soil.

In April, plant offsets 1m (3ft) apart and about 5cm (2in) deep. Protect them from full sun in the early stages. Keep them watered and mulch well with manure or compost once established. In the first year, remove flowerheads or harvest them small to encourage growth.

In the second and third years, allow 4-6 stems to develop and harvest the king head (on the leading stem) first when it is still green and tightly folded; harvest the lateral heads in June and July.

▲ Harvest the king head when it is still green.

Plants will need protection over winter. Cut down the stems and cover the rootstock with straw to protect from frost. Remove the straw in spring.

Plants should be renewed every three years by taking root offsets. In November

or April, select a strong shoot and cut down into the rootstock with a spade or knife. If growing from seed, sow the seeds indoors in February or outdoors in March, thin to 23×30 cm (9×12 in), and plant out in May. Transplant the following year and use the best plants for division for later crops.

PESTS AND DISEASES

Aphids and slugs may cause trouble.

Asparagus
Asparagus officinalis
Asparagaceae

Asparagus is a hardy perennial plant with tall, wispy, fern-like shoots and leaves. During spring tender spears emerge from beneath the soil and it is these that are eaten. Once established, asparagus is simple to grow, requiring very little attention except for feeding and weeding. However, an asparagus bed takes up a lot of room for only six weeks of harvesting each year.

TYPES AND VARIETIES

Asparagus may be grown from seed or from one-year-old crowns. Newer varieties are 'all male'; they give higher yields since their energy is not spent in producing seed.

CONNOVER'S COLOSSAL A traditional variety which has thick stalks and crops early.

FRANKLIM F_1 All male, heavy crops of thick spears.

LUCULLUS F_1 All male with long slim spears.

CULTIVATION

Take care over preparing an asparagus bed, as it may be productive for up to 20 years. Sandy soils are most suitable but heavier soils can be used if the drainage can be improved by, say, creating a raised bed. The bed should be dug and well manured. Remove all perennial weeds. The site should preferably be open and sheltered from strong winds.

Seed may be sown under glass in February-March, hardened off and transplanted into the prepared bed in June. Alternatively, sow in the open in April for transplanting the following year. Crowns (preferably one-year-old roots) must be kept moist and handled carefully.

Asparagus may be grown in a trench and earthed up, or on the flat. Earthing up produces a longer blanched stem; on the flat – which is easier – the stems are shorter.

Why rotate crops of vegetables?

If the same vegetables are grown in the same place year after year, the soil will become exhausted of its fertility and pests and diseases will increase. If space is available, divide the garden into three plots, growing different crops on each plot in consecutive years. For a three-year rotation, the crops could be grown as follows – although the order is not essential.

	FIRST PLOT	SECOND PLOT	THIRD PLOT
First year	Brassicas	Potatoes	Peas, beans, salad crops
Second year	Potatoes	Peas, beans, salad crops	Brassicas
Third year	Peas, beans, salad crops	Brassicas	Potatoes

Some plants provide benefits for those that follow them. Leguminous vegetables (peas, beans) enrich the soil with nitrogen, leaving it ideal for nitrogen-dependent brassicas the following year. Similarly, the earthing up of potatoes and their dense foliage, which help to keep weeds down, can benefit onions and carrots that struggle to survive in weedy ground. At the very least, try to avoid planting the same crop in the same place for at least two years.

▲ When planting asparagus, spread out the roots.

Plant them out in April – 10 cm (4 in) deep at 38 cm (15 in) intervals, spreading the roots out from the crown.

The spears may be harvested from the second year after planting. In late April cut with a knife below the soil surface when the spears are about 15 cm (6 in) above ground.

The traditional date for the end of the season is June 21. After that, fern must be allowed to grow to develop the crown for the next year.

A mulch of chopped straw put on in early spring will help to suppress weeds and conserve moisture. Apply a top dressing of fertiliser in summer and add compost or manure in autumn to maintain fertility. Keep asparagus weed-free, taking care to avoid damaging the shallow roots.

PESTS AND DISEASES
Asparagus beetle and slugs may be a problem; violet root rot and rust are the only likely diseases.

Aubergines
Solanum melongena
Solanaceae

Aubergines are shrubby sub-tropical plants related to tomatoes and potatoes and more distantly to sweet peppers. They became known as eggplants in Britain because the first types grown here had oval white fruits. Modern varieties generally have large, dark and shiny purple fruits, which may be 15-20 cm (6-8 in) long and around 450 g (1 lb) in weight, depending on variety. These follow small, mauve, potato-like flowers.

TYPES AND VARIETIES
A few varieties are available, offering a choice of size and colour.
EASTER EGG AND OVA Novelty varieties with many small, white fruits.
LONG PURPLE Medium sized, elongated fruits.
MONEYMAKER F_1 Elongated, purple-black fruits. Early and prolific.
SLICE RITE F_1 Large, almost black fruits weighing up to 450 g (1 lb) each.

CULTIVATION
Aubergines are best grown in a greenhouse like tomatoes. Raise seed under glass in March at not lower than 20°C (68°F).

Eventually move the plants into 20 cm or 23 cm (8 in or 9 in) pots, or into growing bags. Alternatively, plant them in well-drained and manured soil in the border, 60 cm (24 in) apart each way.

For large fruits, pinch out the growing point when 30 cm (12 in) tall and limit each plant to 5 or 6 fruits, or fewer. They will need supporting.

Mist plants with water frequently to discourage red spider mite, and water a little and often, applying a liquid tomato feed regularly once the fruits start to develop.

Cut the fruits from the stem with secateurs when they are fully grown and while the skin is still shiny and smooth. Overripe fruits have a dull skin and are bitter. Aubergines may be kept for a few days in the salad drawer of a refrigerator, but keep them apart from tomatoes and apples, which will cause the aubergines to overripen.

PESTS AND DISEASES
Red spider mite and aphids are likely to be found on aubergines; also whitefly in greenhouse crops. They may suffer from grey mould and damping-off diseases.

Beans, Broad
Vicia faba
Leguminosae

Broad beans are easy to grow, needing little attention other than providing support for the plants – most varieties reach 1-1.4 m (3-4½ ft) tall. The white-and-black flowers have a heavy sweet scent and develop into long green pods, with a 'furry' lining, that are filled with white or green beans.

TYPES AND VARIETIES
There are two types of broad bean: Longpods and Windsors. Longpods are the hardier, early to mature and high yielding, having 8-10 kidney-shaped beans in pods up to 40 cm (16 in) long. Windsor varieties – considered to have better flavour – are generally later to mature, with shorter and broader pods containing 4-7 flat, circular beans in each.

● *Longpods*
AQUADULCE CLAUDIA Reliable longpod variety for sowing in autumn or early spring, growing to 1.3 m (4½ ft). Good flavour.
EXPRESS An early maturing and prolific longpod, good flavour. For early sowing.
IMPERIAL GREEN LONGPOD Tall growing, extra long pods with large green seeds of fine flavour, good for freezing.
RELON Tall, vigorous, late. Has very long pods with green seeds of fine flavour, good for freezing.
THE SUTTON Sturdy longpod dwarf variety, 30 cm (12 in) tall. It can be sown in autumn and grown under cloches, or in the open February-July.
● *Windsors*
JUBILEE HYSOR Late Windsor variety, pods

packed with 6 or more large white beans.
RED EPICURE Red flowers followed by green pods with red seeds. Unique flavour.

CULTIVATION
Autumn-sown broad beans require a light soil that will drain well over the winter; spring-sown crops may be grown in heavier clay soils. Certain varieties only, such as Aquadulce Claudia or The Sutton, can be sown in warmer areas in November. Do not add fertiliser to these crops until spring, to avoid soft growth. In colder areas, sowing can start in the early spring, under protection in February, or in the open in March. Sow again at monthly intervals to give a succession of supplies.

Broad beans, especially low-growing varieties, can be grown in blocks or double rows, with seed sown 7.5 cm (3 in) deep, 23 cm (9 in) apart each way, and 60 cm (2 ft) between each pair of double rows. For tall varieties, it is easier to support single rows, 45 cm (18 in) apart, with the seeds 12 cm (4¾ in) apart. Once the plants are growing, support them with string around the rows. Keep the beans well watered once flowering. When they are in full flower and the first pods are swelling, pinch out the tops of the growing shoots to promote growth of the seeds and to discourage blackfly.

HARVESTING AND STORAGE
Harvesting begins in late May and June, depending on sowing time. Pods can be picked very young for cooking whole. Otherwise pick when the beans can be seen swelling inside the pods. When shelled the beans should be tender and the scar where the bean was attached to the pod white or green, not black. Old beans are tough and have poor flavour. Once picked, use as soon as possible, or keep the beans unshelled in a cool place for a few days only.

PESTS AND DISEASES
Black bean aphid is the main problem, especially on later sown crops. Chocolate spot disease may also occur.

Beans,
French or Dwarf
Phaseolus vulgaris
Leguminosae

Most types of french beans are dwarf and bushy in habit, but climbing types (pole beans) are grown on canes or strings like runner beans. French bean pods may be round like a pencil – the slenderest types are called 'filet' or fine beans – or flattened like a runner bean. The colour is usually green, but yellow and purple varieties are also available. The young pods of french beans freeze well, and can be cooked whole or sliced. Older pods are shelled and the fresh green beans (flageolets) are cooked. The beans may also be left to mature fully on the plant and then dried for later use (haricots).

733

TYPES AND VARIETIES

French beans are half-hardy annuals and in a hot summer will be more successful than the other beans or peas. Most types are dwarf, bushy plants which mature earlier than the climbers. Climbing beans give heavier crops than dwarf varieties and need supporting in the same way as runner beans.

● *Dwarf french beans*

ARAMIS Fine filet-type pods, 13-15 cm (5¼-6 in) long and stringless. Good flavour.

MONT D'OR (GOLDEN BUTTER) Yellow, waxy pods, stringless and flat, black seeds within. Good flavour. Upright or semi-climbing habit.

PURPLE QUEEN Dark purple pods easy to see when harvesting. They have excellent flavour and turn dark green on cooking.

TENDERGREEN Heavy crops of stringless, medium length round pods 15-17 cm (6-6¾ in). Recommended for freezing.

THE PRINCE Good crops of long, slender, flat pods, dark green.

● *Climbing french beans*

BLUE LAKE Tender, round, green stringless pods if harvested for fresh beans. Or leave to mature for haricots.

HUNTER Straight, flat pods, 25 cm (10 in) or more. Stringless. Crop well over a long period.

CULTIVATION

The cultivation of french beans is largely the same as for runner beans, except that dwarf varieties can be grown in tubs or growing bags, or entirely under glass or cloches, sowing in April for an early crop. Outdoor sowings can begin in May, but be prepared to sow again if seedlings are caught by frost. Sow again in June – and in July if cloches are available to cover the crop when the nights grow cool in late summer.

Sow dwarf beans in blocks 23 cm (9 in) apart each way for the highest yields, or in rows 45 cm (18 in) apart at 10 cm (4 in) centres for easier picking. Support climbing beans as for runner beans. They may not grow as tall and a closer spacing may be used, rows 45 cm (18 in) apart, the poles or strings 10 cm (4 in) apart within the row.

HARVESTING

Begin picking as soon as the first pods develop – about 7-8 weeks after sowing. Pick young for fresh beans, before they can be seen swelling within the pod. For flageolet beans, allow the seeds to develop on the plant, and pick, shell and cook the beans green. For haricots, leave the pods on the plant until yellow, then harvest the whole plant and hang up to dry. Shell the beans and dry fully before storing in jars.

PESTS AND DISEASES

Slugs, black bean aphid, bean seed fly and red spider mite are all potential pests. Grey mould disease is a possible problem. Brown spots on leaves indicate halo blight. Burn diseased plants and spray the others with copper compound before the first pods develop.

Beans, Runner
Phaseolus coccineus
Leguminosae

The plants are tender climbing perennials that are grown as annuals, because they are cut down by the first frost of autumn. Runner beans were originally grown for their flowers alone, hence their alternative name, scarlet runners.

TYPES AND VARIETIES

Most runner bean varieties have red flowers, a few have white or white and red flowers. Plant breeders have aimed to produce stringless beans. Some dwarf varieties which do not need supports are also available; other varieties can be grown as dwarf plants by 'pinching out' the growing point.

● *Stringless runner beans*

DESIREE White flowers, pods 25 cm (10 in) or more. Good yields.

PICKWICK Dwarf and bushy; short stringless pods. Red flowers.

POLESTAR Red flowers; early and heavy crop of smooth, fleshy pods 25-30 cm (10-12 in) long.

● *Traditional varieties*

ACHIEVEMENT Long, straight beans, for table or exhibition. Freeze well.

ENORMA Very good crop of long, smooth beans 35-38 cm (14-15 in) long. Popular with exhibitors.

KELVEDON MARVEL First to crop, prolific. Can be grown as a pinched crop, in the open or under cloches. Beans 20-25 cm (8-10 in) long.

CULTIVATION

For soil preparation, see Broad beans.

Runner beans are climbing plants and need rigid support for all but dwarf or pinched crops. A double line of canes or poles is ideal if there is space. In a small garden use a wigwam or maypole structure. Netting attached to a south-facing fence is suitable, provided there is easy access for picking later.

Erect the support structure before sowing or planting. For a double row, push a pair of 2.4 m (8 ft) canes firmly into the ground 60 cm (2 ft) apart and tie them together at the top. Place the other pairs at 30 cm (12 in) intervals, and fix a horizontal cane across the tops to give rigidity.

As the plants start to grow, twist the shoots gently anticlockwise around the supports; thereafter they will find their own way. Nip out the top shoot when it reaches the top of the supports. For wigwams (four or five poles tied together) or maypoles (one central pole with strings coming from it), aim for one support at each corner of a square 60×60 cm (2×2 ft).

Runner beans must not be put out until all danger of frost is passed – towards the end of May, depending on the area. Seed can be sown indoors for transplanting, or sown outside, 3 seeds to the inside of each

TWO WAYS TO SUPPORT RUNNER BEANS

WIGWAM

DOUBLE ROW OF CANES

support 5 cm (2 in) deep. Water in transplants. Once the plants are in flower and beans are developing, water freely.

Runner beans can be grown without supports by using dwarf varieties, growing 30 cm (12 in) high, or by pinching out the growing tips of standard varieties.

HARVESTING AND STORAGE

Begin picking beans as soon as the first ones reach a reasonable length and before they can be seen swelling and the pods become tough and stringy – the younger they are, the better. Well-grown plants will crop from late July up to the first frosts.

PESTS AND DISEASES

Slugs, black bean aphid, bean seed fly and red spider mite are all potential pests. Grey mould is a possible disease. Brown spots on leaves indicate halo blight; burn diseased plants and spray the others with copper compound before the first pods develop.

Beetroot
Beta vulgaris
Chenopodiaceae

Beetroots are biennial plants grown as annuals. They thrive in most garden soils and, if space is limited, are not out of place in a flowerbed. The upright growth – up to 25 cm (10 in) high – of deep red stems and glossy green leaves is most attractive. The roots are usually deep red, but pink, yellow and white varieties are also available.

TYPES AND VARIETIES

Most beetroots are the familiar globe shape but longer cylindrical varieties are also available, particularly useful for slicing and good for storing for winter use. Beetroot 'seed' is a dried fruit containing several true seeds. Breeders have produced monogerm varieties which have only one seed per fruit, reducing the need for thinning. These all have 'mono' in the variety name.

BOLTARDY Bolt resistant, medium-sized globe variety for sowing from March to July. Good texture, colour and flavour.

BURPEES GOLDEN Golden-rooted variety with distinctive, succulent flavour. Bolt resistant and stores well. Sow March–July.

CHELTENHAM MONO Long-rooted mono-germ variety. Stores well, bolt resistant.

DETROIT 2 LITTLE BALL Baby beet with small, round, deep red roots, ideal for bottling, pickling and freezing. Good for late sowing in July.

FORONO Medium-length cylindrical variety with good colour and flavour. Sow from May onwards. Stores well.

MONOGRAM Globe-shaped monogerm variety. Rich, deep red colour with smooth skin and good flavour. Vigorous and uniform. Sow March–July.

CULTIVATION

Beetroot for exhibition is best grown in deep, well-drained, sandy soil which has been manured the previous autumn, but a satisfactory crop can be grown in a sunny position in most garden soils. Excessively acid soils will need to be limed.

Soak the seed in warm water for an hour before sowing to aid germination. Sow thinly along the row or in groups of 2 or 3 seeds at intervals along the row, about 2 cm (¾ in) deep. The spacing will depend upon how large you wish the beets to grow – for most uses, space globe varieties in rows 18 cm (7 in) apart and at intervals of 10 cm (4 in). For larger maincrop beets, sow rows at 30 cm (12 in) apart, thinning to 7.5-10 cm (3-4 in) in the rows.

Start sowing outdoors in March when the soil begins to warm up. Continue until July, sowing at 3-4 weekly intervals to give a continuous supply. Earlier sowing can be made under cloches in late February or under glass in cellular trays for planting out. The main crop is sown in May and June when any variety can be used. For spring sowings, and late ones in July, use bolt-resistant varieties only – these are less likely to run to seed before being ready to use. Beetroot can be harvested from about 12 weeks after sowing. It should be kept weed-free and watered gently in dry periods.

HARVESTING AND STORAGE

Globe beetroot can be pulled out of the soil when it is between the size of a golf ball and a cricket ball – roots left in the ground too long become woody. After lifting, twist off the leaves so that 5 cm (2 in) of stalk remains. Cylindrical varieties need to be lifted carefully with a fork. For storing in the autumn, shake the soil off roots and place them in almost dry peat or sand in a cool, frost-free place where they will keep through to the following March. Late globe beetroot, sown in July and ready in October, can be left in the ground in milder areas and covered with straw or leaf-mould.

PESTS AND DISEASES

Beetroot is largely trouble free, but may be attacked by black fly. Damping off may affect seedlings, and mineral deficiencies in the soil will show up in the leaves.

Brassicas
Brassica species
Cruciferae

Many of the vegetables which are called brassicas – broccoli, brussels sprouts, cabbage and cauliflower – are closely related. All are rich in vitamins and minerals, provide dietary fibre and form a major part of the produce grown in vegetable gardens and allotments. They share many cultural requirements and pest and disease problems.

SOILS FOR BRASSICA CROPS

A major problem with growing brassicas of all types (including turnip, swede and kohlrabi) is a soil-borne fungal disease called club root, which can cause huge swellings to grow on the roots, preventing them from functioning properly. To avoid this developing, do not grow brassicas in the same ground more often than once in three years, and add lime to acid soil to bring it up to a pH of 6.5-7.5.

Brassicas grow best in well-drained, fertile soil that has been manured for the previous year's crop. Shallow and sandy soils are not generally suitable.

CULTIVATION OF LEAFY BRASSICA CROPS

Leafy brassicas are usually grown by sowing in a seedbed first and then transplanting to the permanent site. This means the seedbed area can be specially prepared for sowing, leaving the main site free for another crop – legumes (peas and beans) are ideal, as they leave good levels of nitrogen in the soil for brassicas to follow.

Sow thinly in drills 15 cm (6 in) apart and up to 2.5 cm (1 in) deep. Transplant when the seedlings are about 10-15 cm (4-6 in) tall and with 3 or 4 true leaves, using only the strongest and healthiest plants. Ensure that the plants are firm in the ground after planting, and then water in.

Measures will need to be taken against cabbage root fly. Fit a disc of carpet or thick plastic, 7.5 cm (3 in) across, around the base of the plants when they are transplanted.

A general fertiliser or liquid feed can be applied in the growing season to promote growth, especially in the quicker-growing crops, such as summer cauliflower and calabrese (broccoli). Nitrogen should not be applied in autumn to overwintering crops, such as spring cabbage, brussels sprouts and winter cauliflower; fertilise these in spring.

PESTS AND DISEASES OF BRASSICA CROPS

All brassicas are prone to attack by cabbage root fly and cabbage whitefly caterpillars. Aphids, flea beetle, whitefly, pigeons and slugs and snails may be a problem. Club root and downy mildew are the main diseases.

TIMETABLE FOR GROWING BRASSICAS				
VARIETY	SOWING	PLANTING OUT	SPACING	HARVEST
Broccoli Calabrese	Feb–Apr	Apr–July	45×20 cm (18×8 in)	June–Nov
Sprouting	May	June–July	60×75 cm (24×30 in)	Feb–Mar
Brussels sprouts	Feb–Apr	Apr–May	60×75 cm (24×30 in)	Sep–Mar
Cabbage Spring greens	Aug	Sep	30 × 10 cm (12×4 in)	Mar–May
Spring hearts	Aug	Sep	30×30 cm (12×12 in)	Apr–May
Early summer	Feb Under glass	Apr	40×30 cm (16×12 in)	June–July
Summer	Mar–Apr	May–June	40×30 cm (16×12 in)	July–Sep
Autumn/ winter	Mar–May	Apr–July	60×40 cm (24×16 in)	September onwards
Cauliflower Summer	Oct–Feb Under glass	Feb–May	60×45 cm (24×18 in)	June–Aug
Autumn/ winter	Mar–June	May–July	60×60 cm (24×24 in)	September onwards
Mini	Mar–May in situ		15×15 cm (6×6 in)	July onwards

Broccoli

Brassica oleracea Cymosa Group

Broccoli is particularly rich in vitamins A, B and C. It falls into two groups – calabrese and sprouting broccoli. Calabrese is fast-growing, maturing in summer and autumn with a large, dense, central head of flower buds on a single stem. Once this central head has been harvested, most varieties will produce smaller secondary heads. Sprouting broccoli is an extremely hardy vegetable producing several spears of purple or creamy yellow flower buds in early spring. These provide a welcome crop at a time of year when little else is available and can be grown in cold areas and heavy soils where many other vegetables would fail.

For details of cultivation, see Brassicas.

TYPES AND VARIETIES

A good choice of varieties is available to suit a range of garden conditions and to crop between February and November.

● *Calabrese*

CORVET F_1 Mid season variety with big, round, grey-green heads, good for freezing. Good crop of sideshoots. Suitable for growing in northern areas.

GREEN COMET F_1 Tight, deep green central heads, 15-18 cm (6-7 in) across, followed by small secondary spears. Early.

MERCEDES F_1 Early variety with dark, medium-sized heads on short plants. Reliable.

SHOGUN F_1 Late variety with good-quality heads, 15 cm (6 in) across, followed by secondary spears. It will grow in a range of soil types.

TRIXIE F_1 Clubroot resistant, compact plants. Deep rounded heads followed by several secondary spears.

ROMANESCO (Italian broccoli) Unique variety with pyramid-shaped head made up of many tightly packed pointed spears, yellow-green in colour. May also be listed as 'green cauliflower'. Harvest in October-November.

● *Sprouting broccoli*

PURPLE SPROUTING Comes in early and late strains. Masses of small purple spears, packed with flavour and vitamins, throughout spring. Colour turns to dark green on cooking. Very hardy.

WHITE SPROUTING Similar to purple, but with white spears and more delicate flavour; early and late strains available.

Brussels sprouts

Brassica oleracea Gemmifera Group
Cruciferae

Brussels sprouts are hardy biennial plants which mature during autumn and winter. The sprouts should be harvested as required while still tightly closed, starting at the bottom of the stem and working upwards.

A selection of varieties will give a long cropping period, with the tops used as greens after the sprouts have been picked.

For details of cultivation, see Brassicas.

TYPES AND VARIETIES

Plant breeders have developed many new hybrid varieties of sprouts, which produce high yields of good-quality, tight button sprouts on each plant, good for freezing. The following selection is listed in order of their maturity.

OLIVER High yields of pale sprouts; very early. September-October.

PEER GYNT Early crops on compact plants. September onwards.

ROGER Tall plants, giving high yields of large sprouts. November onwards.

RAMPART Mid season; tall plants giving firm sprouts which hold well on the plant. Late November onwards.

FORTRESS Late hardy variety, compact with firm, dark green sprouts. January-March.

Cabbages

Brassica oleracea var. *capitata*
Cruciferae

Cabbages come in a wide range of types and varieties and with careful planning, they can be available throughout the year.

For details of cultivation, see Brassicas.

TYPES AND VARIETIES

The cabbage plant is a biennial which is cultivated as an annual. The varieties that follow are grouped according to the time of harvesting.

● *Spring cabbage*

Sow in August in a row closely spaced – 10 cm (4 in) apart – for fresh greens – or use thinnings for greens and leave others to develop a heart later in the season.

▲ A cut in the stump produces a crop of greens.

Cut a deep cross into the stumps and leave them to grow a second crop of greens.

DURHAM EARLY Dark green leaves for greens; medium-sized conical heart. April-May.

DUNCAN F_1 Compact and early. A dark green, pointed-heart cabbage, ideal for spring. Or sow in spring for use in summer and autumn.

PIXIE Early and compact variety for close spacing. Small, solid, pointed hearts.

SPRING HERO F_1 Large, round hearts in May and June.

● *Summer cabbage*

Solid, round or pointed heads, for cutting between June and September. For the earliest crops, raise young plants under glass and then transplant them. Some varieties 'stand well' – they may be left in the ground for a while once they are ready for harvesting, without deteriorating.

In order of maturity:

HISPI F_1 Large, pointed hearts, dark green; early.

SPITFIRE F_1 A dark green cabbage with pointed head, ready in July from an outdoor sowing.

DERBY DAY Small round heads, or use as greens. June-July.

STONEHEAD F_1 The heads are small, solid, heavy and round. The variety stands well. August-September.

MINICOLE F_1 Small, solid, oval heads, which will stand for up to three months. May be grown at close spacing, 25×25 cm (10 × 10 in). August-September.

RUBY BALL F_1 Solid red cabbage with good flavour. Ready in August, will stand through to winter.

● *Autumn and winter cabbages*

A selection of different types can be grown for use in autumn and winter, either from stored crops or direct from the garden.

CELTIC F_1 Blue-green leaves and dense winter-white type heart, but more frost hardy. November-January.

HOLLAND WINTER WHITE EXTRA LATE Dense heads of white cabbage for cooking, salads or coleslaw. Plant in June, cut in October-November before severe frosts and store until required.

JANUARY KING HARDY LATE STOCK 3 Blue-green leaves, medium-sized firm hearts tinged with red. Very hardy. Plant in June; ready October-November and standing well into the winter.

SAVOY KING F_1 Early savoy variety with green, crinkled leaves and solid hearts with good flavour. Plant early July, harvest September-October.

TUNDRA F_1 Savoy cross with green leaves and white heart, good for cooking or salads. Very hardy. December-February.

WIVOY F_1 Late savoy variety with small heads, ready in December and standing through to March.

Carrots

Daucus carota ssp. *sativa*
Umbelliferae

Carrots are hardy vegetables and can be grown for harvesting throughout the year. They are biennial plants which are grown as annuals. As they are quick to mature, they can be grown in the space between other plants in a mixed bed, or as part of a crop rotation system.

CARROTS: VARIETIES AND TIMING

TYPE/VARIETY	DESCRIPTION	SOWING	HARVEST
Amsterdam Forcing Amsterdam Forcing –Amstel, Amsterdam Forcing –Sweetheart	Small to medium, succulent roots. Early	Jan-Apr under cloches	June-Sep
Nantes Nantes-Express, Nantes-Tiptop, Tamino F$_1$	Medium, cylindrical stump roots. Early	Jan-Apr under cloches	July-Sep
Paris Market Parmex, Rondo	Round. Early	Late Apr-May	July-Sep
Chantenay Chantenay Red Cored, Chantenay Red Cored Supreme, Chantenay Royal	Short, stump-rooted. Maincrop	Late Apr-early May	Oct-Nov
Berlicum Berlicum 2 Berjo Camberley	Large roots. Late maincrop	Mid May	Dec
Autumn King Autumn King, Autumn King-Vita Longa	Large roots. Late maincrop	Mid May	Dec

CULTIVATION

Carrots may follow a 'hungry' crop, such as leafy brassicas, in a crop rotation plan since their need for nitrogen is low. Also, fresh manure in the soil will make the roots fork. Ideally, the soil should be deep, well cultivated with good drainage and free of stones. Shorter wedge varieties can be used for shallower soils.

Choose a sunny or lightly shaded spot for growing carrots. The use of cloches or plastic mulches early in the season and successional sowing times can make carrots available throughout the year. Remove cloches or covers in April.

The soil must not be allowed to dry out and then watered heavily; this can result in the roots splitting. Keep the soil just moist.

The seeds can be sown in shallow drills, with rows 15cm (6in) apart and thinned to a spacing of 8-10cm (3¼-4in). A closer spacing will give a greater number of smaller carrots. Later thinnings can be used as young carrots.

HARVESTING AND STORAGE

Young carrots can be pulled as soon as they are large enough for eating. Small roots of Amsterdam Forcing may be frozen whole and larger roots sliced and frozen. Maincrop roots for keeping through the winter can be left in the ground, with a layer of soil or straw as protection against frost, and lifted as required. Otherwise, lift them in autumn. Loosen them carefully with a fork and shake off the soil, but do not wash the carrots. Remove any damaged roots – either use them immediately or destroy them – and cut the foliage to leave 2cm (¾in) of stalk. Place the carrots separately in a box of sand or dry peat, store them in a cool building and use them through to March.

PESTS AND DISEASES

Carrot fly is a major problem. Aphids can weaken the plants and also bring disease. Sclerotina rot and violet root rot can spoil the plants in the ground or in storage.

Cauliflowers
Brassica oleracea Botrytis Group
Cruciferae

Cauliflowers are available from the garden during three seasons of the year and come in various colours – white, green and purple. Mini-cauliflowers with heads of only 10cm (4in) across are useful where space is limited.

For details of cultivation, see Brassicas.

TYPES AND VARIETIES

Summer cauliflowers grow quickly and generally have smaller heads than later, more slow-growing types. Winter cauliflowers are vulnerable to frosts and can only be grown in frost-free areas.

• *Summer varieties*

DOK ELGON Deep, well-protected heads. Harvest August-September.

DOMINANT More tolerant of drier conditions. May also be used for mini-cauliflowers. Harvest late June-July.

GARANT Mini-cauliflower, quick growing for successional sowing, making heads in summer.

MONTANO F$_1$ Matures about 12 weeks after transplanting. Knobbly, white curds. Harvest in June.

PLANA F$_1$ Vigorous growth, deep heavy heads. Harvest in August.

VIOLET QUEEN F$_1$ Deep purple heads, up to 20cm (8in), cooking to green. Attractive in salads. Harvest August-September.

• *Autumn and winter*

BARRIER REEF Australian-bred variety with vigorous growth protecting large white heads. Harvest in October.

PURPLE CAPE Red-purple curds, cooking green. Matures February-March.

WALCHEREN WINTER SELECTIONS Hardy Dutch-bred selections with firm, white heads. One type is Armado April which matures in April. Another variety, Maystar, matures in May.

CULTIVATION

Cauliflowers are the most difficult of the brassica crops to grow, and they need careful feeding, watering and pest control to be successful.

Mini-cauliflowers may be sown where they are to grow and can be harvested after only a few weeks. All other cauliflowers are usually transplanted after the seeds have been sown and raised in coldframes or in a sheltered seedbed outdoors. A good supply of water to the plants is needed throughout the season.

Summer crops may need protection from the sun by snapping some of the outer leaves to shade the curd – the cauliflower itself.

Crops which are to be grown through the winter need to be planted in a position which is well drained and sheltered from the frost.

Cauliflowers are harvested when the curds are well developed, but before they begin to open out and divide.

Celery
Apium graveolens
Umbelliferae

Celery is a biennial plant, growing 30-60cm (1-2ft) tall. Traditional varieties, which have to be planted in a trench to encourage long white stems, can be difficult to grow. But modern self-blanching and green-stemmed varieties are much easier. Whichever type is grown, celery is still a crop needing good, well-manured soil and frequent watering and feeding. It is also susceptible to pests.

TYPES AND VARIETIES

There are two types of celery. Trench celery is grown in rows in a trench and earthed up to make the stems tall and pale. Self-blanching and green-stemmed varieties are grown in square blocks.

CELEBRITY Self-blanching. Long sticks, crisp, early and vigorous.

GOLDEN SELF-BLANCHING Dwarf variety with crisp, creamy stalks of fine flavour; yellow foliage.

HOPKINS FENLANDER – Hardy trench variety grown for its flavour. Has pale green stems if not earthed up.

LATHOM SELF-BLANCHING Compact plants with crisp stems of good flavour. Resistant to bolting.

VICTORIA F_1 A pale, green-stemmed variety with an excellent flavour. Grow it as self-blanching.

CULTIVATION

Celery needs a sunny site and good, well-manured soil. Seed is sown under glass in March or April and hardened off for planting out in May or June. A check to growth, such as planting out too soon or dryness at the roots, may induce bolting – running to seed – before being ready to eat.

Self-blanching and green-stemmed varieties are not hardy, unlike trench varieties, and must not be planted out until the danger of frost has passed. Seedlings may be

▲ Plant self-blanching types in blocks.

transplanted into a coldframe – with lights removed – from late May onwards, 23 cm (9 in) apart or planted out in square blocks, preferably with straw placed around the edges of the block. The plants will shield each other within the block and encourage creamy yellow or pale green stems, depending on the variety.

For trenching celery, plant out in May or June, either in a single row in a 38 cm (15 in) wide trench, or in two rows 30 cm (12 in) apart. When the plants are 30 cm (12 in) high – about early August – pile earth up around the stalks to blanch them. As the plant grows, keep earthing up to the bottom of the leaves.

Celery must always have a plentiful supply of water – dryness around the roots can lead to stringy growth, splitting along the stems or bolting. Feeding with a liquid or nitrogenous fertiliser is also required throughout the season.

HARVESTING AND STORAGE

Harvest with a knife from August onwards, replacing the straw around the edge of the block. The stems will keep for a short time in the salad section of the refrigerator.

Self-blanching varieties must be lifted before the first frosts; trench-grown types can be left in the ground well into the winter, depending on the variety.

PESTS AND DISEASES

Celery can be prone to attack by celery leaf miner and celery leaf spot. It is also attractive to slugs and snails.

Courgettes see Marrows and Courgettes

Cucumbers and Gherkins
Cucumis sativus
Cucurbitaceae

Two types of cucumber are available: those for growing under glass (in a greenhouse or coldframe), sometimes known as frame cucumbers; and those for growing outdoors, called ridge cucumbers, which include gherkins for pickling. Apple varieties with small, round, yellow fruits which are tasty and juicy can also be found. Outdoor varieties are the easiest to grow in most gardens where there is shelter from the wind and a sunny spot. They are also less prone to pests and diseases than those grown under glass, which are more demanding in the conditions and attention they require.

CULTIVATION

Cucumber seeds require a temperature of 21-25°C (70-75°F) to germinate. Seed which has been 'chitted' – placed on a wet kitchen towel for one or two days before sowing – will be more successful.

Growing in a greenhouse

Sow seeds singly in pots or cellular trays in late February for planting in a heated greenhouse in late April to early May. Sow in late April for planting in an unheated greenhouse in late May. Transplant the seedlings carefully, into large pots of proprietary compost 60 cm (2 ft) apart, or two plants to a growing bag. Cordon cucumbers are traditionally grown by training the main stem up a stake and pinching out the growing point when it reaches the ridge of the roof.

▲ Sideshoots from the main stem are cut off two leaves beyond a young fruit.

The sideshoots are then tied to horizontal wires, 30 cm (12 in) apart, and cut off two leaves beyond a developing fruit or when about 60 cm (2 ft) long.

All-female varieties can be grown more simply by gently winding a string tied to the base of the stem and to the roof around the main stem. Sideshoots are removed altogether because all the fruit forms on the main stem.

Ordinary varieties, and occasionally all-female varieties, will produce male flowers which have only a stalk behind the flower

CUCUMBERS: VARIETIES AND TIMING

VARIETY	WHERE GROWN	NOTES
Burpless Tasty Green F_1	Outdoors	Slender, smooth skin. Easy to digest. Pick at 23 cm (9 in)
Bush Champion F_1	Outdoors	Compact bush habit. Resistant to cucumber mosaic virus
Conda F_1	Outdoors	Gherkin, heavy crop. Pickle or eat fresh
Crystal Apple	Outdoors	Round, pale fruits. Good flavour, quick growing
Femspot F_1	Heated greenhouse	All-female, disease-resistant
Petita F_1	Greenhouse	Mini-cucumbers 20 cm (8 in). All-female
Pepinex 69 F_1	Greenhouse	Large fruits. All-female
Telegraph Improved	Greenhouse	Long, straight, dark green fruits

and no tiny cucumber. They should be pinched out as they appear.

Cucumbers need to be kept well watered and fed regularly with a liquid fertiliser. Keep the humidity high by wetting the floor, and cool on hot days by shading.

Growing outdoors

Growing cucumbers outdoors is simpler than under glass, although the season is shorter. Grow them in large pots of proprietary compost, or in growing bags, in a sheltered, sunny spot. Or grow them in a garden bed. They can be left to scramble over the ground or trained on wires or netting, as in a greenhouse.

Seed can be raised indoors in late April for planting out in early June, or else sown directly into the compost in late May or early June. Cucumbers grown in garden soil need a high humus content, so prepare planting holes 45 cm (18 in) apart enriched with manure or garden compost.

Pinch out the growing point after six or seven leaves have developed on both the main shoot and on sideshoots that have not developed fruits. Leave sideshoots with flowers unpinched. Keep the plants well watered and feed once the cucumbers start to form. Do not pinch out male flowers on outdoor cucumbers as fertilisation is necessary for the fruits to form.

HARVESTING

Cut cucumbers and gherkins from the plant when young for best flavour. Do not allow fruits to mature fully on the plant and turn yellow; this will stop the plant flowering.

PESTS AND DISEASES

Red spider mite and whitefly are likely to be found on greenhouse crops, and slugs and snails will attack outdoors. Aphids may bring cucumber mosaic virus. Many soil-borne diseases can be avoided by using proprietary compost or growing bags.

Gherkins see Cucumbers and Gherkins

Leeks
Allium porrum
Alliaceae

The versatile leek is the easiest member of the onion family to grow. Late varieties are very hardy and will succeed further north than many other crops.

Most garden soils are suitable and pest and disease problems are generally less than with other onion crops. The leek is a biennial plant which is grown as an annual for its long shank of tightly wrapped leaves. Leeks can grow as tall as 45 cm (18 in), depending on variety.

Sometimes only the white shank is used in the kitchen after the coarsest outer leaves have been removed, but both white and green parts can be chopped for use in soups and casseroles. Young thinnings may be used as baby vegetables or 'mini-leeks' – used raw like salad onions or lightly cooked for a delicate flavour. Leeks are one of the most useful of winter vegetables.

TYPES AND VARIETIES

Leeks are classified according to when they are ready for harvest. A wide range of varieties is available, with many seed merchants offering their own selections.

● *Early season*

(Ready in late summer and early autumn)

KING RICHARD Very early. Long, narrow shank with mild flavour; good for mini-leeks and exhibition. Not winter hardy.

LYON PRIZETAKER Long, thick, white shanks popular with exhibitors and cooks. For harvesting throughout autumn.

SWISS GIANT-ALBINSTAR Long and slender white shanks, good for exhibition. Autumn and early winter.

● *Mid-season maincrop*

(Harvest from October to early spring)

AUTUMN MAMMOTH 2-ARGENTA and AUTUMN MAMMOTH-GOLIATH Thick, heavy stems with mild flavour. Long harvest period.

MUSSELBURGH Hardy, reliable and popular; short and thick.

● *Late season*

(Harvest from New Year until spring)

GIANT WINTER 3 AND WINTRA Long stems, January-March.

LONGBOW Long shank, topped with dark green foliage. Harvest through winter to spring.

CULTIVATION

Leeks will grow in most garden soils that have been cultivated and manured and have reasonable drainage. Seed can be sown where the leeks are to grow or in a seedbed for transplanting when the permanent bed is available. Leeks need a long season to mature, but once ready they will remain in good condition for a long time.

Sow leeks outdoors in early spring. Put the seed thinly in shallow drills, in rows 30 cm (12 in) apart. Thin the seedlings to 15 cm (6 in) apart.

If transplanting, lift when 15-20 cm (6-8 in) tall, trim the ends of the leaves and roots and transplant into holes made with a dibber 15-20 cm (6-8 in) deep at the same spacing as for sown crops. Drop the plant into the hole so that the roots reach the soil

▲ Trim the leaves and roots of young leeks.

at the bottom and water in without pushing back the soil.

For a very early crop – summer and early autumn – sow an early variety under glass in January-February and transplant in April. For a spring crop, sow a late variety in June and transplant in July.

Once established, leeks should be watered only in long dry periods and kept weed free. They can be grown on the flat or gradually earthed up by drawing soil around the plants as they grow, to gain a longer length of blanched stem.

For mini-leeks grow a long-stemmed variety such as King Richard, only 1 cm (½ in) apart.

HARVESTING AND STORAGE

Leeks may be used young or left in the ground to mature. Once ready, they will stand for a long time. Lift them carefully with a fork. The hardier varieties may be left in the ground throughout the winter.

PESTS AND DISEASES

Leeks are less susceptible to pests and diseases than other members of the onion family, but may suffer from leek rust, stem and bulb eelworm, onion fly and white rot.

Lettuces
Lactuca sativa
Compositae

Lettuces can be grown in almost any garden. For a few plants in the summer, a packet of mixed seed can be sown in short rows every 2-3 weeks between other plants in the flower border or in tubs.

For a spring crop in cold areas, sow a hardy variety in mid October under cloches and cut them in April. In milder areas, sow outdoors in late August-early September, thin in spring and cut in May.

For summer-autumn crops, sow outdoors from late March to July for harvesting from June to October.

For an early winter crop, sow outdoors in early August and protect with cloches from late September.

TYPES AND VARIETIES

There are four main types of lettuce – butterhead, crisphead, cos and loose-leaf. Butterhead are cabbage-shaped hearting lettuces growing to about 30 cm (12 in) across, with soft round leaves. Crispheads have crinkly, crunchy leaves and tight hearts, and are sometimes sold in the shops as 'Iceberg'. Cos are taller, more upright – reaching up to 25 cm (10 in) high – and have crisp, well-flavoured leaves. Loose-leaf types have crinkly, curly leaves that can be cut as needed, leaving the stump to grow again.

● *Butterhead*

Spacing: outdoors – 30×30-35 cm (12×12-14 in); under glass – 23×23 cm (9×9 in) apart.

ALL THE YEAR ROUND Hardy; sow spring, summer and autumn. Slow to bolt.

AVONDEFIANCE For summer sowing, resistant to mildew and root aphid.

BUTTERCRUNCH (Sometimes listed as Crisphead) Sweet, dark green, compact, long standing. Sow spring and summer.

MAY KING Hardy. Sow spring and summer outdoors; in autumn sow either uncovered or under cold glass or cloche.

MUSETTE Summer and autumn crop. Good disease resistance. Sow late March to early August.

TOM THUMB Sow Mar-May 15×15cm (6×6in) apart. Very compact. Good for small areas, tubs, window boxes.

● *Crisphead*

Spacing: 30×30-35cm (12×12-14in) in the open; 23×23cm (9×9in) under glass.

AVONCRISP Good for summer sowings. Resistant to mildew and root aphid.

GREAT LAKES 659 For spring sowing. Large and spreading. Slow to bolt. Keeps well.

KELLY'S Crisp, bright green leaves. Sow November-January in cold greenhouse or frame.

LAKELAND Reliable, mildew and root-aphid resistant. For use in spring, summer and autumn. Sow late March–early August.

SALADIN Solid iceberg-type head, crisp and sweet. Dark green outer leaves. Stands well. Sow mid February until late July.

WARPATH Sow spring and summer at 23×23cm (9×9in) spacing. Compact heads of good flavour.

WEBB'S WONDERFUL Large, solid, crisp heads; dark green crumpled leaves. Long standing. Sow late March to early August.

● *Cos type*

Spacing: 30×30-35cm (12×12-14in) apart.

LITTLE GEM Small growing, tight hearts, good flavour. Sow 15×15cm (6×6in), spring to autumn.

LOBJOITS GREEN COS Large, tall and upright. Dark green, crisp, sweet leaves. Sow spring and autumn outside.

VALDOR Sow August-September outdoors or under glass. Firm heads in early spring.

VALMAINE Large and crisp. For loose-leaf use or for hearting. Mildew resistance. Sow summer and autumn.

WINTER DENSITY Hardy for autumn sowing outdoors, or spring to summer. Small growing; dense, crisp hearts with good flavour.

● *Loose-leaf*

Spacing: 30×30cm (12×12in). Loose-leaf varieties can also be grown close together and harvested as separate leaves. Sow early spring to summer.

LOLLO BIONDA Pale green, very indented leaves.

LOLLO ROSSA Pretty, crisp, frilly, red-tinged leaves.

RED SALAD BOWL Very attractive, oak-shaped leaves tinged with red.

SALAD BOWL Green oak-leaf lettuce. Rarely bolts.

CULTIVATION AND HARVESTING

Lettuces need an open site with a well-draining and humus-rich soil. Acid soils are

LETTUCES: GETTING THE TIMING RIGHT		
WHEN TO SOW	WHERE TO SOW	WHEN TO HARVEST
Early Feb-Mar	Sow under glass; plant out under cloches	Mid May-June
Late Mar-July	Outdoors	June-Oct
Early Aug	Outdoors. Cover with cloches in late September	Nov-Dec
Aug-Sep	Outdoors in mild areas	May
Sep-Oct	Heated glass, 7°C (45°F)	Jan-Mar
Mid Oct	Outdoors, under cloches	Apr

not suitable – a pH of 6.5-7.5 is required. Slight shading is possible for summer varieties; but avoid cold, wet and exposed sites for winter crops.

As the time from sowing to harvest is short at the height of the season, lettuces can be sown in between rows of slower plants, such as parsnips, or in a spare corner of the flowerbed. The attractive loose-leaf varieties, for instance, can be used as edging plants or grown in tubs.

Lettuces are best sown very thinly in shallow drills where they are to grow. If raising seed to transplant, use pots or peat blocks and ensure the plants are well watered before and after planting. For summer crops, sow outdoors in short rows every 2-3 weeks to give a continual supply that does not all mature at once. For best results, sow at the time of year recommended on the packet.

The seedlings of hearted lettuces must be thinned before they become crowded.

Loose-leaf varieties may be grown close together or at 30cm (12in) spacings. Cut the leaves as required or else cut each plant at the base after 6 weeks and leave the stump to regrow.

Cos varieties can also be grown this way for a continual supply of fresh leaves. Summer lettuce must be kept well watered

▲ Loose-leaf types can be cut and left to regrow.

especially in hot, dry periods to prevent the plants bolting (running to seed before being ready to eat).

For hearted lettuce, pull up as soon as the heart is formed. Left longer, a flower stalk will grow and the plant will become bitter and unusable. Once lifted, use immediately or store for a few days in the refrigerator in a polythene bag.

PESTS AND DISEASES

Birds and slugs are troublesome. Root aphid and cutworm attack roots and stems at ground level, especially during summer. Greenfly can make the leaves unusable and transmit viruses. Damping off is a problem with seedlings. Downy mildew and grey mould are worse in cold, wet conditions.

Lesser known salad crops

CORN SALAD Also known as lamb's lettuce, corn salad is a hardy annual forming a rosette of small, flat leaves with a flavour between that of lettuce and dandelion. It is most usefully sown in August and September as a winter crop. Thin to 10cm (4in) apart. Keep well watered in dry periods and free of weeds. Harvest like spinach.

ROCKET Salad rocket is a hardy annual which forms a rosette of deeply lobed leaves with a sharp spicy flavour. Older leaves may be cooked like spinach. Sow in succession from early spring outdoors and again in early autumn in mild areas; otherwise sow under glass in September for a winter seedling crop. Pick the leaves when about 5-8cm (2-3¼in) long, and allow the stump to regrow.

CHINESE LETTUCE Chinese stem lettuce (also known as Celtuce) grows on a stem up to 30cm (12in) high. Cultivate it like lettuce.

Marrows and Courgettes

Cucurbita pepo
Cucurbitaceae

Marrows and courgettes (marrow fruits cut young) are tender annuals originating in the Americas and easy to grow in a border or growing bags on a sunny patio. Courgettes

Pumpkins and squashes

Unusual types of marrow, pumpkins and squash are grown in the same way as marrows. The types for use during the summer mostly have soft skins, like courgettes, and can be treated the same way; those for use during winter have hard skins and can be successfully stored. Edible gourds may be listed in catalogues as squash.

can be cut from each plant throughout the summer; indeed, cutting is important to encourage new fruits to form. Courgettes is the French name, zucchini the Italian.

The plants are quick growing with large indented, slightly prickly leaves and stems and large edible yellow flowers. A bush variety will grow to about 1 m (3 ft) across while trailing types can reach several metres long. Two or three plants are enough to supply a family with courgettes all summer.

TYPES AND VARIETIES

Varieties sold as courgettes are strains of bush marrow that will produce a succession of small fruits, as long as they are harvested regularly. All will produce larger fruits as well if left to develop.

ALL GREEN BUSH An all-rounder. A heavy crop of green courgettes or marrows.

AMBASSADOR F_1 Bush type with long fruiting season.

EARLY GEM (STORR'S GREEN F_1) Early bush variety with bright green fruits; marrows or courgettes.

GOLD RUSH F_1 Compact bush type with golden yellow fruits, best for courgettes.

LONG GREEN TRAILING Variety for the larger garden. Has distinctive dark green fruits with pale green stripes. Long Green Bush also available.

TIGER CROSS F_1 – Attractive striped fruits for marrows or courgettes. Resistant to cucumber mosaic virus.

CULTIVATION

Marrows are a tender crop and need a sunny site – and crops will be heavier during a hot summer. Plants grown in a border will do best in humus-rich soil with good drainage. Prepare planting holes 30 cm (12 in) wide, with garden compost or manure dug in.

Trailing varieties can be grown on strong supports or along the ground; bush varieties are more compact.

If cloches are available, seed can be sown indoors in mid April, two to a pot or cellular tray, growing on the stronger seedling for 5-6 weeks until it has three or four true leaves. Chitting will improve germination – place the seed on moist kitchen paper in a warm place for a day or two before sowing. Plant the seedlings out at a spacing of 1 m (3 ft) apart for bush varieties or 1.5 m (5 ft) for trailing types. Growing bags are particularly suitable for marrows and courgettes – two plants to a bag.

Where no protection from frost is avail-

able, sowing must be delayed until early or mid May. Seeds can be sown directly in the planting position in a growing bag or in pots for transplanting.

Young plants will need protection from slugs and snails. Once established, they grow quickly and thrive in sunshine, but mulch them to conserve moisture. The plants must be kept well watered but do not require feeding until the fruits begin to form. A liquid tomato fertiliser is suitable.

Deep yellow male and female flowers appear, the female having a small, unformed fruit behind it. They will be pollinated by insects. Cut the fruits throughout the season

▲ Flowers may be male (left) or female (right).

to keep the plants flowering. Courgettes should be cut when 10-15 cm (4-6 in) long; marrows will have the best flavour if cut when 20-25 cm (8-10 in) long.

HARVESTING AND STORAGE

Harvest courgettes and marrows by cutting the stalk behind the fruits, taking care not to cut leaves or flowers. Courgettes should be used within a few days, or frozen. Marrows will keep longer in a cool but frost-free place. If they are allowed to mature on the plant and are brought in before the frosts, they can be stored up to Christmas.

PESTS AND DISEASES

Slugs and snails can destroy young plants and spoil the fruits. Cucumber mosaic virus causes stunted, twisted growth with a yellow mottling on leaves and fruits.

Onions and Shallots

Allium cepa
Alliaceae

Onions can be grown easily if the soil is fertile and the drainage is good, although some pests and diseases may be a problem. Shallots are also easy to grow and have extremely good keeping qualities.

TYPES AND VARIETIES

Onions are biennials grown as annuals. They can be grown from seed or from 'sets' – small bulbs from the previous year. Growing from sets is quicker, easier and reliable, but more expensive.

● *Spring-sown bulb onions*

Grown from seed sown in spring, and harvested in September-October.

AILSA CRAIG Exhibitors' favourite. Large, good colour and flavour.

ALBION F_1 Large, white-skinned globes.

BEDFORDSHIRE CHAMPION Large, brown skin.

BRUNSWICK Red skin, mild flavour. Good for salads.

HYGRO F_1 High quality, mild, yellow-skinned and round.

RED BARON Dark red skin, strong flavour.

RIJNSBURGER Several strains available, firm, good quality.

● *Autumn sown bulb onions*

The onions are grown from seed sown in autumn and are overwintered for harvest the following June-July. They generally do not store for as long as spring-sown bulbs.

In order of maturity: 'Express Yellow F_1'; 'Buffalo F_1'; 'Imai Yellow'; 'Senshyu Semi Globe Yellow'.

● *Bulb onions grown from sets*

Only a few varieties are available as sets, but they will give a reliable crop of good-quality bulbs which will store well. Sets are useful where the growing season is shorter. Some sets are sold after heat treatment to reduce the chance of bolting. Examples are 'Centurion F_1', 'Sturon', 'Stuttgart Giant', 'Turbo'. A few varieties often grown from seed may also be offered as sets.

● *Shallots*

Shallots are perennial onions with distinctive flavour, usually sold as sets. They can be used fresh in salads, in cooking or for pickling. They store well.

ATLANTIC Early and high yielding. Crisp and crunchy.

CREATION F_1 New hybrid grown from seed.

HATIVE DE NIORT Large, brown skinned. Exhibitors' choice.

PIKANT Strong flavoured. Bolt resistant.

● *Pickling and mini-onions*

A few varieties are sold specifically for pickling or as mini-onions. Use fresh as salad onions or pickle in vinegar.

BARLETTA White skins for pickling or mini-onions.

GIANT ZITTAU Brown skinned. Grow at close spacing for pickling.

PARIS SILVERSKIN Tiny, white cocktail onions. Quick growing. Will succeed in poor soils.

PURPLETTE Multipurpose, red-skinned onion. Grow as mini-onions for salad or pickling, or grow for bulb onions.

● *Salad and bunching onions*

Salad onions come in two types – the familiar spring onions, which are pulled as the bulb starts to swell, and Japanese bunching onions, which grow long and straight. Japanese types may be earthed up for a longer blanched length and can be left in the ground for use as required. Use both for salads or oriental cooking.

HIKARI For harvest late summer. Not winter hardy.

ISHIKURA Long straight white stems.

NORTH HOLLAND BLOODRED-REDMATE Red, crisp and mild. Can also be grown to maturity for bulb onions.

WHITE LISBON Familiar spring onion variety. Mild flavoured and quick growing.

WHITE LISBON WINTER HARDY Very hardy. First to harvest from an autumn sowing.

• Welsh onions

Welsh onions grow in large clumps and are very hardy, remaining green all year. The hollow leaves up to 45-60 cm (18-24 in) tall can be cut and used like chives, although they have a stronger flavour. Alternatively, divide the plants and use them as salad onions, raw or in oriental dishes. Sow in spring and thin until clumps are 30×23 cm (12×9 in) apart. Divide every 2-3 years and replant the outer sections.

CULTIVATION

Onions need a sunny position in fertile and cultivated ground with good drainage. Manure should be dug in the previous autumn and a firm, fine seedbed prepared if using seed. Add lime if necessary. Sow seed thinly in shallow drills; germination may be slow.

▲ Sow onion seeds thinly in a sunny bed.

Onions should be grown as part of a rotation system wherever possible to reduce the build-up of soil-borne diseases.

The main crop of bulb onions is har-vested in early autumn, and most varieties will store well into the winter. The spacing given will provide a good crop of medium-sized onions; use a wider spacing for larger ones. For earlier crops, raise seed under glass in January and transplant in April, or sow under cloches.

Bulb onions need to be kept weed free and watered only in dry periods. In late summer, the foliage turns yellow and falls over. Ensure that the tops of the bulbs are exposed and leave them in the ground for a fortnight to ripen.

▲ Leave the bulbs exposed to ripen.

For autumn-sown bulb onions, look at the back of the seed packet for the precise sowing time for your area of the country. Thin the seedlings in early spring and apply a top dressing of general fertiliser.

Sets should be planted so that the tops are just at ground level. Plant shallot sets in a drill 15 cm (6 in) apart in rows 20 cm (8 in) apart, so that only the tips protrude – in both cases push them back into the ground if they are lifted by birds or frost.

Sow shallots from seed as for spring-sown bulb onions, with seedlings at 5 cm (2 in) centres. Pickling onions should be left unthinned to encourage a crop of small bulbs. Salad onions can be obtained from the thinnings of other types, or from succes-sional sowings from spring through to late summer. Sow them in close rows or broad-cast thinly.

Harvesting can begin 6-8 weeks after sowing. Cloches will make the first crops available sooner from sowings made in August or spring.

HARVESTING

Bulb onions need to be dried fully before storage. Lift with a fork and dry them on the surface in good weather, or under cover. Store only sound bulbs; use any imperfect or large-necked bulbs first. Store in trays, nets, old tights or in onion ropes in a cool, dry place. Salad onions may be lifted as needed, at 1-2 cm (up to 1 in) across for bulbing types. Japanese varieties may be harvested when pencil thick or left until the size of small leeks.

PESTS AND DISEASES

Bulb onions are the type that are most sus-ceptible to pests and diseases, but other onion crops may be affected as well. Onion fly and stem and bulb eelworm are common pests; downy mildew and white rot may also occur.

Growing garlic

A hardy perennial of the onion family, garlic needs a long growing season, so should be planted either in late autumn or early spring.

▲ Plant cloves in late autumn or early spring.

Plant single cloves 15 cm (6 in) apart each way with only the tips protruding. Lift in July-August and dry thoroughly. Garlic can be stored for several months.

Parsnips
Pastinacea sativa
Umbelliferae

Parsnips can be slow to germinate but from then on they are easy crops to grow. They are biennials grown as annuals. They thrive in most garden soils which can offer a sunny or lightly shaded site. The choice of canker-resistant varieties and use of crop rotation will help to avoid disease.

ONIONS: GETTING THE TIMING AND SPACING RIGHT

VARIETY	SOWING	SPACING	HARVEST
Bulb onions (spring sown)	Feb-Apr	23-30×4 cm (9-12×1½ in)	Sep-Oct
Bulb onions (autumn sown)	Aug	23-30×4 cm (9-12×1½ in)	June-July
Bulb onion sets	Plant in Mar-Apr	25×5 cm (10×2 in)	Aug
Shallots	Plant in mid Feb/mid Mar	20×15 cm (8×6 in)	July
Pickling onions	Apr	30×1 cm (12×⅜ in)	July-Aug
Salad onions (spring sown)	Feb-June	10×2.5 cm (4×1 in)	June-Nov
Salad onions (autumn sown)	Aug-Sep	10×2.5 cm (4×1 in)	Apr-June

TYPES AND VARIETIES

Varieties can be selected for their flavour and according to their length – choose shorter varieties for shallower soils and canker resistance.

AVONRESISTER Small, bulbous-shaped roots with good canker resistance. Creamy, sweet flesh.

COBHAM IMPROVED MARROW Medium-sized, wedge-shaped, white roots of fine flavour. Good resistance to canker.

GLADIATOR F₁ A high-yielding, high-quality, sweet-flavoured variety with good canker resistance. Wedge-shaped.

LANCER A bayonet-shaped variety with excellent flavour and canker resistance.

TENDER AND TRUE Long, smooth, white, fleshy roots of very good flavour. Good for the kitchen or exhibition. High canker resistance.

WHITE GEM Early maturing, large, wedge-shaped roots with smooth skin and white flesh of excellent flavour. Good canker resistance.

CULTIVATION

The best results will be obtained in deep, cultivated sandy loam soil, with good drainage. Parsnips can be grown in a sunny position or light shade. Lime very acid soils. Parsnips should ideally follow a well-manured crop in a rotation system; fresh manure can cause the roots to fork.

Sow the seeds from mid February to April in shallow drills 40 cm (16 in) apart, and thin to 15 cm (6 in) apart. Or sow 2 or 3 seeds to a station and thin to the strongest seedling.

Germination takes up to 28 days. Put a few radish seeds in with the parsnips to come up early and show where the row is. Water during dry spells. Quicker crops, such as lettuce and radish, can be sown between rows while the parsnips develop.

HARVESTING AND STORAGE

Parsnips can be lifted with a fork once the leaves have died down. Parsnips are very hardy and can be left in the ground until needed; indeed, frost is said to improve the flavour by turning the starch in the roots to sugar. Some may be lifted in autumn for use when the ground is too hard for harvesting – keep these cool in sand or damp peat.

PESTS AND DISEASES

Parsnips may be attacked by carrot fly, celery leaf miner and sometimes aphids. Parsnip canker can be avoided by the choice of resistant varieties, by using a crop rotation system, by liming and by using good general cultural practice.

Peas

Pisum sativum
Leguminosae

Young peas picked straight from the vine are among the sweetest tastes of summer, superior to anything that can be bought in the shops. Once peas have been picked, their eating quality deteriorates rapidly.

TYPES AND VARIETIES

• *Round-seeded*

Hardy varieties of pea that can be sown in the open – or under protection in late autumn or early spring for an early crop.

• *Wrinkle-seeded*

Less hardy varieties that cannot be sown until the soil warms up in the spring. They are sweeter than round-seeded types. There are three groups of wrinkle-seeded peas – first earlies which can be picked 11-12 weeks after sowing, second earlies after 13-14 weeks, and maincrop after 15-18 weeks. A single sowing of different types will give a short succession of crop, and a series of sowings will give the longest season. Mildew-resistant varieties are recommended for mid summer sowings.

Leafless peas are new wrinkle-seeded varieties with more clinging tendrils than leaves, able to cling to supports without being tied. The pods grow on the top of the plants away from slugs and are easy to pick.

• *Petis pois*

Sweet dwarf varieties of garden peas that are picked when they are young and tender.

• *Mangetout*

The pods and seeds are eaten whole, and are generally the easiest to grow. There are two types – flat podded, with tiny undeveloped seeds (also called sugar peas or snow peas); and snap peas, with full, fleshy pods which snap if broken. When fully mature, snap peas may be used whole or podded like garden peas.

• *Asparagus pea*

A half-hardy bushy plant unrelated to the pea. It grows 15-30 cm (6-12 in) high and up to 60 cm (2 ft) across. It has red flowers which develop into green-winged pods, best harvested when 2.5 cm (1 in) long. The pods have the flavour of asparagus and are cooked like mangetout.

CULTIVATION

Mangetout varieties are the easiest to grow. To sow peas, use a hoe or spade to draw out a flat drill 15 cm (6 in) wide and 5 cm (2 in) deep. Space the seeds 5-8 cm (2-3¼ in) apart each way along the drill – losses can be expected in overwintered sowings. Make the next drill 60 cm (2 ft) away, or as far away as the expected height of the plants. Cover the seed and protect from birds.

▲ Pea plants can be supported by twigs or nets.

Support is necessary for all but the leafless kinds – use twiggy sticks stuck in the ground or a line of plastic netting held up on canes.

Crops will be disappointing on poor or wet soils, and in hot, dry summers.

Asparagus peas need a warm, sunny site in light, fertile soil. Sow in May at 20 cm (8 in) intervals and 40 cm (16 in) between rows and water well; in colder areas sow under glass and plant out in June. A second sowing will give a longer cropping period. Pick regularly during August.

PEAS: VARIETIES AND TIMING			
VARIETY	TYPE	SOWING	HARVEST
Feltham First Douce Provence Meteor	Round-seeded hardy	Oct-Nov or Jan-Mar	May-June
Early Onward Kelvedon Wonder Little Marvel Hurst Beagle	Round, or first early wrinkled	Mar	June-July
Hurst Green Shaft Onward Cavalier Senator Leafless vars.	Second early and maincrop wrinkled	Mar-June	June-Sep
Kelvedon Wonder Cavalier Senator	Mildew-resistant varieties for mid summer sowing	June-July	Sep-Oct
Wavereux Oregon Sugar Pod Sugar Snap	Petis pois and mangetout	Mar-June	July-Sep

HARVESTING AND STORAGE

First earlies can be picked 11-12 weeks after sowing; second earlies after 13-14 weeks; maincrop after 15-16 weeks. For the most succulent peas and mangetout, begin picking as soon as the first pods are ready, and use or freeze immediately. Peas may also be dried, by leaving them on the plant until fully mature and hanging the whole plant in a shed at the end of the season.

PESTS AND DISEASES

Peas must be protected from birds, slugs and possibly mice. Pea moth larvae and thrips may be troublesome in mid summer.

Peppers, Sweet and Hot
Capsicum annuum
Solanaceae

Sweet peppers (also known as capsicums) are hollow with the seeds held on a central core inside the thick fleshy skins. They are green ripening to red, sometimes to white, yellow or deep purple. The flesh is crunchy and juicy; fully ripe fruits are the sweetest. Hot peppers (cayenne and chilli) have much smaller, pointed fruits, 2.5-5 cm (1-2 in) long or more, depending on variety.

TYPES AND VARIETIES

• *Sweet peppers*
ARIANNE F$_1$ Thick-walled variety ripening to orange. Compact plants.

CANAPE F$_1$ High yielding and early. May be grown outdoors.

GYPSY F$_1$ Early, light green, tapered fruits, ripening to deep red. Good yields under glass. Resistant to tobacco mosaic virus.

LUTEUS F$_1$ Quick growing, large, thick-walled fruits, green, turning to a mild, sweet yellow. Resistant to tobacco mosaic virus.

NEW ACE F$_1$ Reliable and early to crop. Green fruits, turning to red, thin walled, square shape. Best grown under glass.

REDSKIN F$_1$ Compact plants around 38 cm (15 in) tall, ideal for containers outside or even a large windowsill. Early fruiting, green to red.

SLIM PIM F$_1$ Japanese type, 10 cm (4 in) slim fruits, green to red, for cooking whole in oriental dishes.

Seed companies offer mixed colours.

• *Hot peppers*
APACHE F$_1$ Compact plants bearing good crop of medium-hot chillis. Green to red.

CHILLI SERRANO Prolific variety with small, very hot fruits. Green to red.

HUNGARIAN WAX Tapered fruits 10 cm (4 in) long, sweet in flavour when picked young, maturing to hot. Green, ripening through yellow and orange to red.

CULTIVATION

Both sweet and hot peppers are best grown in a greenhouse or under polythene. Sweet peppers may also be grown outdoors in a sheltered and sunny spot; and compact varieties can be raised on a warm windowsill.

Sow seed under heated glass in March and pot seedlings on in stages. Plant in 20 or 23 cm (8 or 9 in) pots, or growing bags, or in the greenhouse soil 45 cm (18 in) apart.

If growing sweet peppers outdoors, plant out in May under cloches or June in the open. Support will be needed.

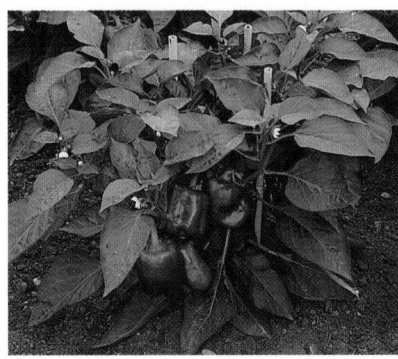

▲ Outdoor plants need support with stakes.

Keep plants moist. Once the fruits have started to form, feed regularly with liquid tomato fertiliser. Mist with water to discourage red spider mite. High temperatures may induce flowers to drop in sweet peppers, but will improve flavour in hot types.

The fruits of both sweet and hot peppers may be used at any time between green and red (colour depending on variety) once grown to full size. For fullest flavour allow them to mature on the plant. Pick while the skin is smooth and shiny. They keep in the refrigerator for up to two weeks. Peppers freeze well and hot types may also be dried.

PESTS AND DISEASES

Peppers are susceptible to red spider mite, aphids and whitefly. Blossom end rot may also be a problem.

Potatoes
Solanum tuberosum
Solanaceae

Potatoes are easy to grow, tolerant of most soils and can also be grown successfully in large pots or tubs. Some diseases can be a problem and potatoes are not frost-hardy.

Potatoes consist of three groups – first earlies, second earlies and maincrop. Maincrop are the 'old' potatoes that are stored and used through winter. In most gardens it is impracticable to grow enough for all your needs, but an early variety is worth growing for its flavour. The plants grow about 60 cm (2 ft) high and wide.

Potatoes are members of the nightshade family, and all green parts – shoots, tubers exposed to the light which turn green, and any green tomato-like fruits which form – are poisonous.

TYPES AND VARIETIES

A wide range of varieties is available. Some are less susceptible to disease than others. A few of the freely available varieties are as follows:

• *First earlies*
ARRAN PILOT Heavy cropper with resistance to scab and drought. White skin and flesh of good flavour.

MARIS BARD Very early with heavy yield. White skin and creamy flesh.

PENTLAND JAVELIN Very white, waxy flesh. Resistant to eelworm and scab.

• *Second earlies*
ESTIMA A heavy crop of white-skinned tubers with yellow flesh. Cooks and keeps well. Resistant to blight, slugs and drought.

NADINE A new variety with exhibition looks, white skin and cream flesh. Stays moist and firm on cooking. Resistant to eelworm.

WILJA Dutch-bred variety with light yellow skin and flesh. High yielding and resistant to blight.

• *Maincrop*
CARA High yield of pink tubers, good for baking. Resistant to blight and eelworm.

DESIREE High yield of red-skinned tubers with yellow flesh, good for chips or baking. Succeeds in most soil types and in drought.

MARIS PIPER High yields of white-skinned tubers with cream flesh, especially good for baking or chips. Eelworm resistant.

CULTIVATION

Potatoes are susceptible to soil pests and virus diseases, so ensure that these problems do not build up in the garden. Potatoes should be grown in a different part of the garden each year in as long a rotation as possible. Only 'seed' potatoes which are certified as being virus free should be used for planting. Early varieties require 'chitting' – keeping the seed in a well-lit, frost-free place so that the eyes can develop into short shoots before planting out.

A first early crop can be grown in warmer areas of the country; second earlies and maincrops can be grown everywhere, avoiding frost pockets or heavy shade. The soil should be fertile but most soil types are suitable. The seed tubers should be planted in furrows 7.5-15 cm (3-6 in) deep and then covered with soil.

As shoots reach 23 cm (9 in), loosen the soil between rows and pull it up around the leaves to ensure that tubers are not exposed to light – a process called earthing up.

▲ Draw soil around plants to cover the tubers.

TYPE	PLANTING DISTANCE	HARVEST
First earlies Arran Pilot Maris Bard Pentland Javelin	End March 30×60 cm (12×24 in)	June–July When flowers fully open
Second earlies Estima Nadine Wilja	First half of April 30×60 cm (12 × 24 in)	July–Aug When flowers fully open
Maincrop Cara Desiree Maris Piper	Second half of April 38×75 cm (15×30 in)	Sept–Oct When top growth dies down

POTATOES: GETTING THE TIMING RIGHT

▲ When harvesting, lift all tubers from soil.

Water regularly once the tubers begin to form. You can lift a plant gently with a fork to see them.

HARVESTING AND STORAGE

Potatoes should be lifted carefully with a fork to limit damage. Leave them to dry on the surface for a few hours. All the tubers must be removed from the soil to prevent disease being carried over to next year. Store healthy potatoes in the dark, in an airy, frost-free place. Maincrop tubers will store for several months if allowed to mature and provided the skins do not come off when rubbed with the fingers.

PESTS AND DISEASES

Aphids may carry virus disease. Potato cyst eelworm, slugs and wireworms may cause damage. Potato blight can ruin crops.

Pumpkins and Squashes see
Marrows and Courgettes

Radishes
Raphanus sativus
Cruciferae

Radishes are quick and easy to grow and are an ideal crop for small areas. As well as the familiar red roots, there are two other main types – white Japanese mooli varieties and winter radishes, such as Black Spanish Round which grows to around 450 g (1 lb) in weight. Small salad varieties have leaves 13 cm (5¼ in) high but the larger types may reach 60 cm (24 in) high with a spread of 45 cm (18 in). All are grown as annuals.

TYPES AND VARIETIES

• *Summer salad varieties*

Varieties may be red, red and white, or all white – and either globe-shaped or cylindrical. Sow January–February under cloches, March to mid summer outdoors, at fortnightly intervals for a continual supply. Space the plants 2.5 cm (1 in) apart, in rows 15 cm (6 in) apart.

CHERRY BELLE Round scarlet roots with crisp white flesh, especially good for early sowings.

FRENCH BREAKFAST Cylindrical red roots with white tip. Mild, sweet and crisp when harvested young.

LONG WHITE ICICLE Use when 7–15 cm (3–6 in) long. Has an excellent flavour; crisp and mild.

SCARLET GLOBE A quick-maturing variety for sowing from January to August. Has a pungent taste.

• *Japanese radish – Mooli*

White-skinned, up to 30 cm (12 in) long. Use fresh or cooked. Sow 5–10 cm (2–4 in) apart in rows 15 cm (6 in) apart.

APRIL CROSS F₁ For spring or late summer sowing. Stays in good condition in the ground, slow to bolt.

MINO EARLY A crisp, tender and mild variety. Sow June–September for use in autumn–winter.

MINOWASE SUMMER F₁ Sow in summer. Harvest from when roots are 15 cm (6 in). Late to bolt.

• *Winter radishes*

Sow late July and August. Thin to 15 cm (6 in) apart, in rows 23 cm (9 in) apart. Harvest after 10–12 weeks.

BLACK SPANISH ROUND Black skin, crisp white flesh of good flavour. Hardy.

CHINA ROSE Deep pink skin, white flesh, 12 cm (4¾ in) long.

MANTANGHONG F₁ Tennis-ball-sized Chinese radish. Light green skin and magenta flesh. For salads or stir fries.

CULTIVATION

Radishes are easy to grow. Choose a sunny site, except for summer sowings which do better in slight shade. Larger varieties need an open, stone-free soil. Ground which has been manured for a previous crop is ideal.

▲ Harvest summer radishes when young.

Radishes are quick to germinate – the small salad varieties requiring very little space – and are ready in only 3–6 weeks. Sow in shallow drills 1 cm (⅜ in) deep, very thinly – or broadcast them – and rake over lightly. Thin if necessary as soon as the seedlings emerge. Water when dry to keep the plants growing quickly.

Winter radish is sown in July and August and is ready for use after 10–12 weeks.

HARVESTING AND STORAGE

Summer radish is at its best when grown quickly and used young. If left too long, roots become strong flavoured and woody. Japanese varieties can be used when about 15 cm (6 in) long, or left in the ground longer if wanted for cooking.

Once pulled, use summer radish as soon as possible. In mild areas, winter radishes can be left in the ground until required, with a covering of soil or straw to protect them from frost. In colder areas, lift in October and store in a cool, frost-free place.

PESTS AND DISEASES

Radishes are largely untroubled by disease but may need protection from birds, slugs, flea beetle and cabbage root fly.

Spinach
Spinacia oleracea
Chenopodiaceae

Spinach, a hardy and quick-growing annual, is grown as a cut-and-come-again crop. The young leaves are picked as required and used in salads or cooked – young, raw spinach leaves have the flavour of pea pods. Successional sowings can make spinach available throughout the year.

TYPES AND VARIETIES

Spinach is usually divided into winter and summer varieties, but many newer strains can be used in either season.

BROAD-LEAVED PRICKLY Very hardy winter variety with prickly coated seeds.

745

RED OR PINK FLOWERS

TRUMPET OR BELL SHAPED

Crinodendron hookerianum
Daphne species

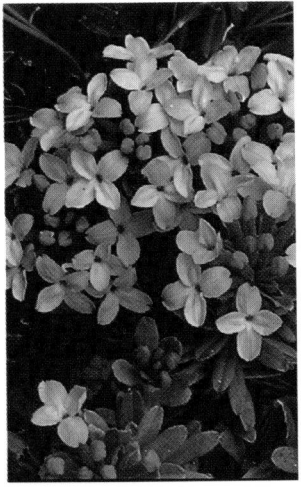

▲ *Daphne cneorum*

Embothrium coccineum
  & cultivars
Enkianthus species & cultivars
Lonicera tatarica 'Arnold's Red'
Malus species & cultivars
x *Phylliopsis* species & cultivars
Rhododendron species
  & cultivars
Ribes sanguineum & cultivars
Ribes speciosum
Syringa reflexa
Vaccinium species

BOWL OR PLATE SHAPED

Camellia x *williamsii*

▲ *Camellia* x *williamsii*

Chaenomeles x *superba* 'Knap
  Hill Scarlet'
Cornus florida 'Cherokee Chief'
Crataegus x *lavallei* 'Carrierei'
Cydonia oblonga & cultivars

Magnolia species & cultivars
Malus species & cultivars
Prunus species & cultivars
Rhododendron species
  & cultivars
Rubus spectabilis
Sorbus cashmiriana

POMPOM SHAPED

Crataegus laevigata 'Paul's
  Scarlet'

▲ *Crataegus laevigata* 'Paul's Scarlet'

PEA-LIKE

Caragana arborescens 'Lorbergii'
Cercis canadensis 'Forest Pansy'
Cercis siliquastrum
Indigofera heterantha
Robinia hispida

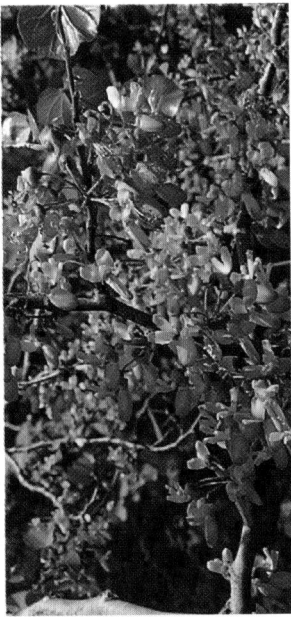

▲ *Cercis siliquastrum*

FLOWERS IN SMALL, TIGHT CLUSTERS

Parrotia persica & cultivars

▲ *Parrotia persica*

ORANGE FLOWERS

TRUMPET OR BELL SHAPED

Rhododendron cinnabarinum
  'Conroy'
Rhododendron cultivars

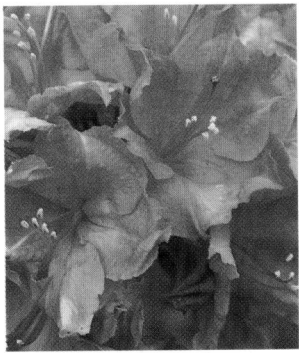

▲ *Rhododendron* 'Fireball'

YELLOW FLOWERS

TRUMPET OR BELL SHAPED

Corokia buddlejoides
Enkianthus chinensis
Forsythia species & cultivars

▲ *Forsythia viridissima* 'Bronxensis'

Lonicera involucrata
Mahonia species & cultivars
Rhamnus catharticus
Rhododendron species
  & cultivars
Ribes americanum
Ribes odoratum
Stachyurus praecox

BOWL OR PLATE SHAPED, BORNE SINGLY

Halimium lasianthum
  & cultivars

▲ *Halimium lasianthum* ssp. *formosum*

Helianthemum lunulatum
Hypericum aegypticum
Kerria species & cultivars
Magnolia 'Elizabeth'
Rosa 'Canary Bird'
Rosa ecae
Rosa 'Helen Knight'

BOWL OR PLATE SHAPED, BORNE IN GROUPS

Cornus mas

▲ *Cornus mas*

Corokia x *virgata*
Corylopsis species & cultivars
Euonymus europaeus 'Red
  Cascade'
Lindera species
Paeonia delavayi var. *ludlowii*
Rhamnus frangula
Rhododendron wardii
Sassafras albidum
Stephanandra incisa

POMPOM SHAPED

Acacia species
Aurinia saxatilis & cultivars
Azara lanceolata
Azara petiolaris
Buxus sempervirens & cultivars

▲ *Buxus sempervirens* 'Latifolia'

DAISY-LIKE

Euryops acraeus

▲ *Euryops acraeus*

PEA-LIKE

Caragana arborescens
  & cultivars
Coronilla valentina

▎▲ *Coronilla valentina*

Cytisus species & cultivars
Genista species & cultivars
Sophora species & cultivars

▲ *Cytisus* × *praecox* 'Warminster'

PURPLE OR VIOLET FLOWERS

TRUMPET OR BELL SHAPED

Clematis addisonii
Lonicera rupicola var. *syringantha*
Paulownia tomentosa
Penstemon davidsonii
Rhododendron species
  & cultivars

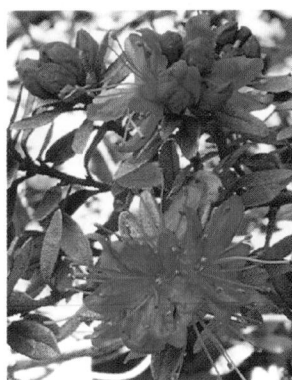

▲ *Rhododendron polycladum* Scintillans Group

Ribes divaricatum
Syringa species & cultivars
Thymus caespititius

▲ *Syringa vulgaris* 'Charles Joly'

BOWL OR PLATE SHAPED

Akebia species
Brunfelsia pauciflora
  & cultivars
Hebe 'Caledonia'

▲ *Hebe* 'Caledonia'

Hebe 'Wingletye'
Magnolia liliiflora 'Nigra'
Magnolia × *soulangeana* 'Picture'
Malus species & cultivars

GREEN FLOWERS

BOWL OR PLATE SHAPED

Aucuba japonica & cultivars
Azara microphylla
Daphne pontica

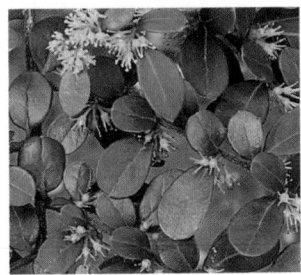

▲ *Azara microphylla*

TREES AND SHRUBS WITH CATKINS

Alnus species & cultivars
Betula species & cultivars
Carpinus betulus & cultivars
Corylopsis species
Corylus species & cultivars

▲ *Corylus avellana*

▲ *Garrya elliptica*

Garrya elliptica
Ostrya species
Myrica gale
Salix species & cultivars

TREES AND SHRUBS WITH COLOURFUL NEW FOLIAGE

Acer species & cultivars
Aesculus indica & cultivars
Aesculus × *neglecta*
  'Erythroblastos'
Alnus × *spaethii*
Catalpa × *erubescens* 'Purpurea'
Corylopsis sinensis var. *sinensis*
  'Spring Purple'
Fagus sylvatica 'Zlatia'
Gymnocladus dioica
Gleditsia triacanthos 'Sunburst'
Osmanthus heterophyllus 'Goshiki'
Osmanthus yunnanensis
Picea orientalis 'Aurea'
Pieris species & cultivars
Tilia mongolica

▲ *Picea orientalis* 'Aurea'

▲ *Pieris formosa* var. *forestii* 'Wakehurst' ▎

BLUE FLOWERS

TRUMPET OR BELL SHAPED, FLOWERS BORNE IN GROUPS

Buddleja alternifolia
Buddleja davidii cultivars

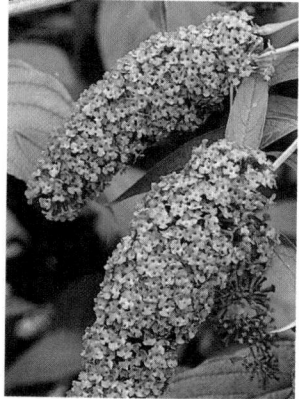

▲ *Buddleja davidii* 'Nanho Blue'

Buddleja lindleyana
Calluna vulgaris 'Spring Torch'
Calluna vulgaris 'Winter Chocolate'
Cestrum elegans
Lavandula species & cultivars
Penstemon species
Rhododendron ponticum
Syringa × *persica*
Teucrium fruticans
Thymus species

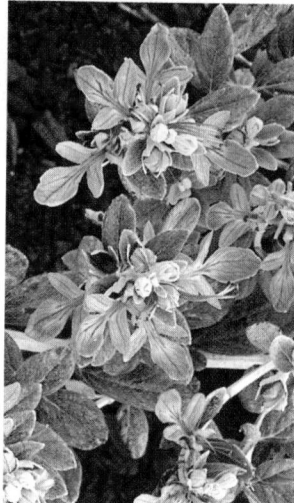

▲ *Teucrium fruticans*

BOWL OR PLATE SHAPED

Hebe cupressoides & cultivars
Hebe 'Mrs Winder'
Hebe pimeleoides 'Quicksilver'
Hydrangea 'Blue Deckle'
Hydrangea involucrata
Hydrangea macrophylla & cultivars
Hydrangea serrata & cultivars

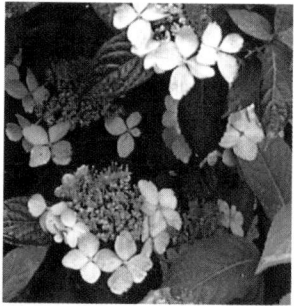

▲ *Hydrangea serrata* 'Bluebird'

PURPLE FLOWERS

TRUMPET OR BELL SHAPED, FLOWERS BORNE SINGLY

Clematis addisonii
Clematis simsii
Lavatera arborea 'Variegata'
Lavatera maritima

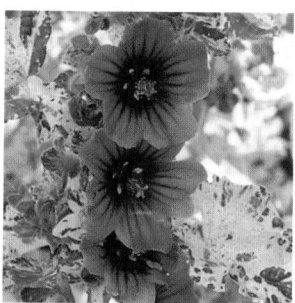

▲ *Lavatera arborea* 'Variegata'

BOWL OR PLATE SHAPED, FLOWERS BORNE SINGLY

Cistus × *pulverulentus* & cultivars
Paeonia delavayi
Rubus thibetanus

▲ *Cistus* × *pulverulentus* 'Sunset'

BOWL OR PLATE SHAPED, FLOWERS BORNE IN GROUPS

Deutzia compacta 'Lavender Time'
Fuchsia 'Mantilla'
Hebe 'Caledonia'
Hebe × *franciscana* 'Blue Gem'

Hebe × *franciscana* 'Variegata'
Hebe 'Wingletye'
Hebe 'Youngii'

▲ *Hebe franciscana* 'Variegata'

Hydrangea aspera & cultivars
Lantana montevidensis
Pittosporum crassifolium
Rubus cockburnianus
Solanum laciniatum

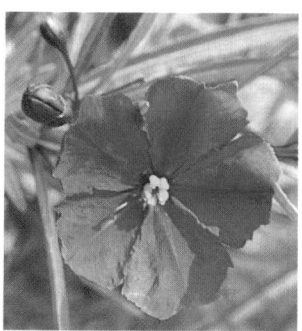

▲ *Solanum laciniatum*

POMPOM SHAPED

Hydrangea species & cultivars
Melaleuca gibbosa
Rosa cultivars

▲ *Hydrangea macrophylla*

PEA-LIKE

+ *Laburnocytisus adamii*
Ononis repens

CLIMBING AND RAMBLING PLANTS

WHITE OR CREAM FLOWERS

TRUMPET OR BELL SHAPED

Billardiera longiflora
Clematis macropetala 'Snowbird'
Codonopsis convolvulacea 'Alba'
Jasminum species & cultivars
Lonicera caprifolium
Lonicera etrusca 'Superba'
Lonicera japonica 'Halliana'

▲ *Lonicera japonica* 'Halliana'

Lonicera japonica 'Hall's Prolific'
Lonicera periclymenum 'Graham Thomas'

BOWL OR PLATE SHAPED

Clematis species & cultivars
Hydrangea anomala ssp. *petiolaris*
Hydrangea serratifolia
Rosa cultivars
Schizophragma hydrangeoides
Schizophragma integrifolium
Trachelospermum asiaticum
Trachelospermum jasminoides

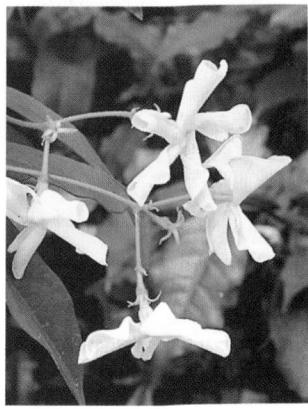

▲ *Trachelospermum jasminoides*

PEA-LIKE

Lathyrus odoratus & cultivars
Lathyrus sativus
Wisteria venusta

▲ *Wisteria venusta*

WHITE & RED FLOWERS

TRUMPET OR BELL SHAPED

Lonicera etrusca 'Donald Waterer'

▲ *Lonicera etrusca* 'Donald Waterer'

RED OR PINK FLOWERS

TRUMPET OR BELL SHAPED

Clematis 'Duchess of Albany'
Clematis 'Gravetye Beauty'
Clematis macropetala 'Markham's Pink'
Clerodendrum splendens
Lonicera × americana
Lonicera × brownii 'Dropmore Scarlet'
Lonicera giraldii
Lonicera periclymenum 'Belgica'

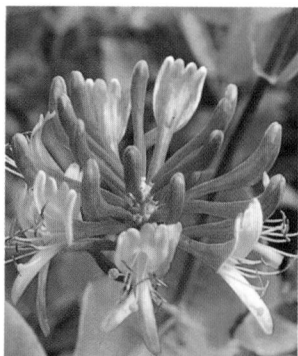

▲ *Lonicera × heckrottii*

Lonicera × heckrottii
Rhodochiton atrosanguineus
Tropaeolum species

BOWL OR PLATE SHAPED

Clematis species & cultivars
Jasminum × stephanense
Passiflora × exoniensis
Passiflora sanguinolenta
Rosa cultivars
Rubus henryi
Rubus odoratus

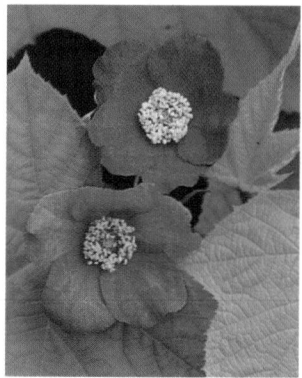

▲ *Rubus odoratus*

Schisandra rubrifolia
Tropaeolum species

POMPOM SHAPED

Rosa cultivars

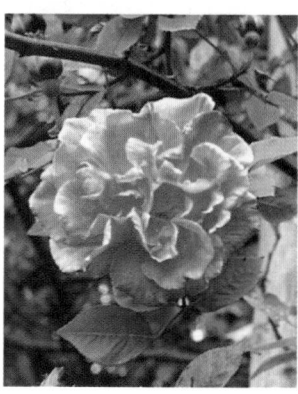

▲ *Rosa* 'Zepherine Drouhin'

PEA-LIKE

Lathyrus grandiflorus
Lathyrus latifolius
Lathyrus odoratus & cultivars

▲ *Lathyrus latifolius*

ORANGE FLOWERS

TRUMPET OR BELL SHAPED

Campsis grandiflora
Campsis radicans
Eccremocarpus scaber
Lonicera etrusca 'Superba'

▲ *Lonicera etrusca* 'Superba'

Lonicera sempervirens
Thunbergia alata

▼ *Lonicera sempervirens*

POMPOM SHAPED

Rosa 'Mrs Sam McGredy, Climbing'
Rosa 'Orange Sunblaze, Climbing'

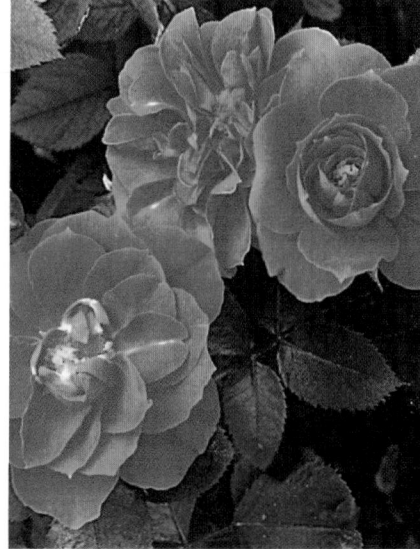

▲ *Rosa* 'Orange Sunblaze, Climbing'

DAISY-LIKE

Mutisia decurrens

▲ *Mutisia decurrens*

DAISY-LIKE

Brachyglottis compacta
Brachyglottis monroi
Brachyglottis 'Sunshine'

▲ *Brachyglottis* 'Sunshine'

Euryops acraeus
Helichrysum italicum
Helichrysum splendidum

PEA-LIKE

Colutea arborescens
Lupinus arboreus
Piptanthus nepalensis

▼ *Lupinus arboreus*

BLUE FLOWERS

TRUMPET OR BELL SHAPED

Buddleja davidii 'Nanho Blue'
Buddleja 'Lochinch'
Caryopteris × *clandonensis*
& cultivars

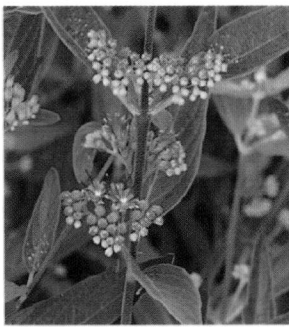

▲ *Caryopteris* × *clandonensis*
'Heavenly Blue'

Hibiscus syriacus & cultivars
Lavandula angustifolia
'Munstead'
Rosmarinus officinalis

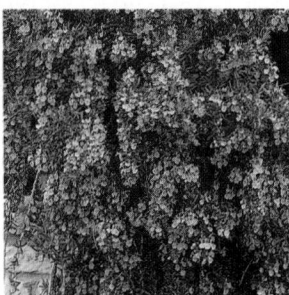

▲ *Rosmarinus officinalis*

BOWL OR PLATE SHAPED

Hebe cupressoides & cultivars
Hebe 'Mrs Winder'
Hydrangea species & cultivars

▼ *Hydrangea serrata*

PURPLE FLOWERS

TRUMPET OR BELL SHAPED

Buddleja species
Calluna vulgaris cultivars
Caryopteris × *clandonensis*
'Ferndown'
Cestrum elegans
Clematis addisonii
Fuchsia 'Mantilla'
Lantana montevidensis
Lavandula species & cultivars
Phlomis purpurea
Teucrium fruticans
Thymus species & cultivars
Vitex agnus-castus

▲ *Vitex agnus-castus*

BOWL OR PLATE SHAPED

Cistus × *pulverulentus*
Hebe species & cultivars
Hydrangea aspera & cultivars

▼ *Hydrangea aspera* Villosa Group

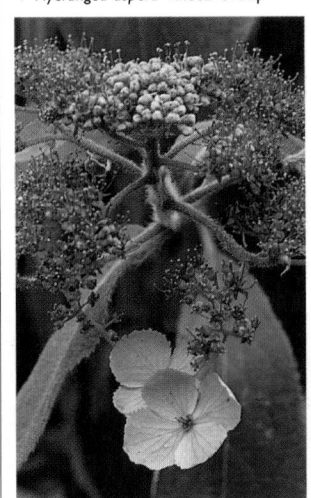

TREES AND SHRUBS WITH WINGED SEEDPODS

Acer species & cultivars
Fraxinus angustifolia 'Raywood'
Fraxinus excelsior 'Westhof's
Glorie'
Fraxinus ornus

▲ *Fraxinus ornus*

TREES AND SHRUBS WITH COLOURFUL FRUIT, BERRIES AND SEEDPODS

SMALLER THAN PEA-SIZE

Azara microphylla & cultivars
Berberis species & cultivars
Daphne species & cultivars
Lonicera nitida 'Baggesen's Gold'
Lonicera pileata
Osmanthus decorus
Ribes sanguineum & cultivars

▼ *Ribes sanguineum*

PEA-SIZE, RED OR PINK

Aucuba japonica & cultivars
Crataegus laevigata 'Paul's
  Scarlet'
Crataegus laevigata 'Plena'
Crataegus monogyna
  & cultivars
Daphne acutiloba
Lindera species
Lonicera species
Malus hupehensis

▲ *Malus hupehensis*

▲ *Malus × moerlandsii 'Liset'*

Malus × moerlandsii 'Liset'
Photinia villosa
Prunus pumila var. depressa
Skimmia japonica reevesiana
Viburnum species & cultivars

PEA-SIZE, YELLOW

Azara dentata
Celastrus species
Daphne cneorum
Malus floribunda
Malus × hartwigii 'Katherine'
Pyracantha 'Soleil d'Or'

▼ *Pyracantha 'Soleil d'Or'*

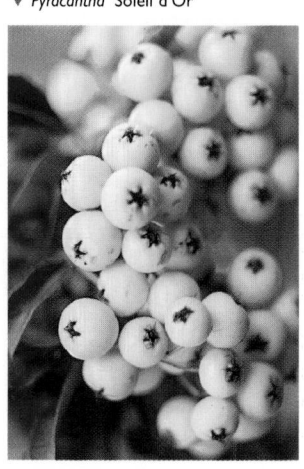

PEA-SIZE, BLUE/PURPLE/
VIOLET/BLACK

Amelanchier species
Azara petiolaris
Azara serrata
Berberis candidula
Lindera obtusiloba
Lonicera species & cultivars

▲ *Lonicera henryi*

Phillyrea latifolia
Prunus laurocerasus & cultivars
Prunus padus & cultivars
Prunus spinosa
Prunus × yedoensis & cultivars
Ribes species & cultivars
Rosa × harrisonii
Sambucus nigra

CHERRY-SIZE, BLUE/
PURPLE/VIOLET/BLACK

Amelanchier laevis
Azara lanceolata
Morus nigra
Osmanthus species
Prunus avium 'Plena'
Prunus × cistena
Prunus virginiana 'Shubert'
Rubus cockburnianus
Rubus thibetanus

▼ *Morus nigra*

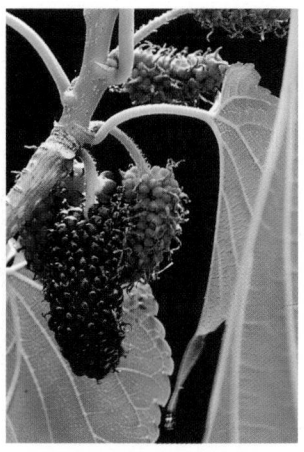

CHERRY-SIZE, BROWN

Illicium anisatum
Illicium floridanum
Lindera praecox
Platanus × hispanica

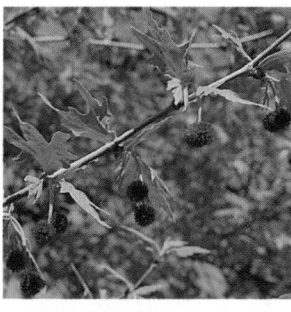

▲ *Platanus orientalis*

Platanus orientalis
Rosa xanthina 'Canary Bird'

CHERRY-SIZE, GREEN

Alnus glutinosa & cultivars

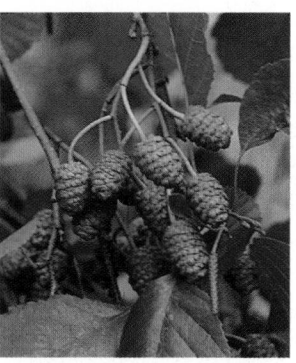

▲ *Alnus glutinosa*

Alnus incana & cultivars
Betula costata
Betula 'Jermyns'
Betula pendula & cultivars

CHERRY-SIZE, ORANGE

Crataegus × lavallei 'Carrierei'

▼ *Crataegus × lavallei 'Carrierei'*

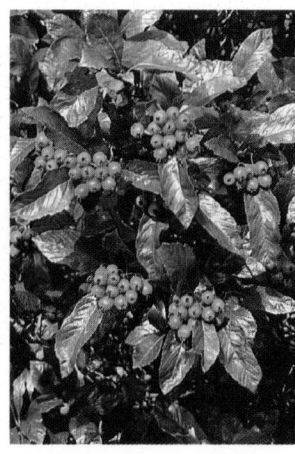

Malus × purpurea 'Neville
  Copeman'

▲ *Malus × purpurea 'Neville Copeman'*

Rosa fedtschenkoana
Rosa sericea ssp. omeinensis f.
  pteracantha
Rubus spectabilis

CHERRY-SIZE, RED

Daphne retusa
Malus species & cultivars

▲ *Malus 'Evereste'*

Morus alba
Prunus species & cultivars
Rosa × alba 'Alba Semiplena'
Rosa 'Fru Dagmar Hastrup'
Rosa 'Geranium'
Rosa 'Maiden's Blush'
Rosa rugosa cultivars
Rosa xanthina hugonis
Rubus species

CHERRY-SIZE, YELLOW

Malus × robusta 'Yellow
  Siberian'
Prunus tenella & cultivars
Rubus biflorus

▼ *Malus × robusta 'Yellow Siberian'*

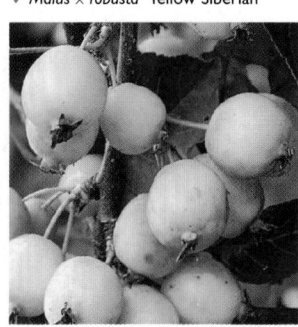

779

CHERRY-SIZE, WHITE

Cornus alba 'Sibirica'
Gaultheria species & cultivars
Sorbus cashmeriana
Symphoricarpos albus & cultivars

▲ *Symphoricarpos albus*

MORE THAN CHERRY-SIZE, BROWN

Aesculus × *carnea*
Alnus cordata

▲ *Alnus cordata*

MORE THAN CHERRY-SIZE, GREEN

Aesculus indica & cultivars
Aesculus × *neglecta*
  'Erythroblastos'
Aesculus parviflora
Aesculus pavia
Alnus glutinosa & cultivars
Pyrus nivalis
Pyrus salicifolia 'Pendula'

▼ *Pyrus salicifolia* 'Pendula'

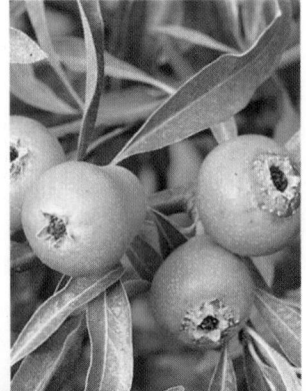

MORE THAN CHERRY-SIZE, RED

Arbutus species
Cornus kousa
Malus species & cultivars

▲ *Malus* 'Veitch's Scarlet'

MORE THAN CHERRY-SIZE, YELLOW

Malus × *zumi* 'Golden Hornet'
Poncirus trifoliata
Prunus mume & cultivars

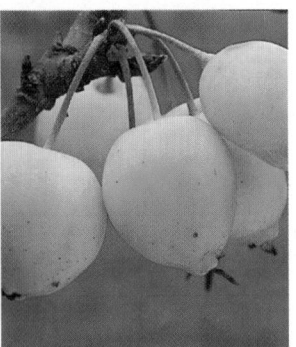

▲ *Malus* × *zumi* 'Golden Hornet'

CLIMBING AND RAMBLING PLANTS

WHITE OR CREAM FLOWERS

TRUMPET OR BELL SHAPED

Clematis campaniflora
Codonopsis convolvulacea 'Alba'
Jasminum officinale
Thunbergia alata & cultivars

▼ *Jasminum officinale*

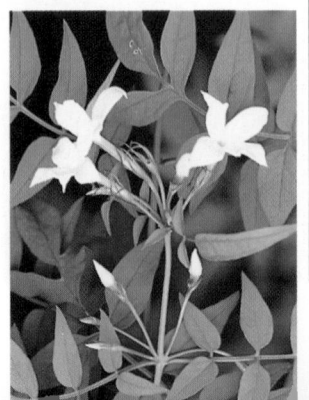

BOWL OR PLATE SHAPED

Clematis fargesii
Clematis – Early Large-
  Flowered Group (second
  flowering)
Clematis – Late Large-
  Flowered Group

▲ *Clematis* 'John Huxtable'

Clematis × *triternata*
  'Rubromarginata'
Clematis – Viticella Group
Jasminum azoricum
Trachelospermum species

HYDRANGEA-LIKE FLOWERS

Hydrangea anomala ssp.
  petiolaris

▲ *Hydrangea anomala* ssp. *petiolaris*

Hydrangea serratifolia
Schizophragma
  hydrangeoides
Schizophragma integrifolium

▼ *Schizophragma integrifolium*

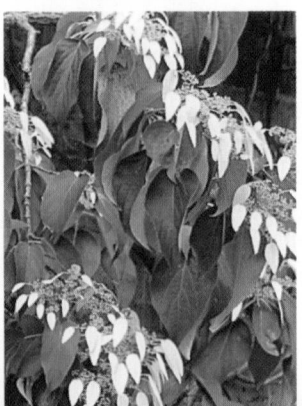

WHITE-AND-BLUE FLOWERS

TRUMPET OR BELL SHAPED

Ipomoea tricolor 'Flying Saucers'
Ipomoea tricolor 'Heavenly Blue'

▲ *Ipomoea tricolor* 'Heavenly Blue'

RED OR PINK FLOWERS

TRUMPET OR BELL SHAPED

Clematis 'Comtesse de
  Bouchaud'
Clematis 'Duchess of Albany'
Clematis 'Gravetye Beauty'

▲ *Clematis* 'Gravetye Beauty'

BOWL OR PLATE SHAPED

Clematis 'Edward Prichard'
Clematis – Early Large-
  Flowered Group (second
  flowering)
Clematis – Late Large-
  Flowered Group
Clematis – Viticella Group
Clerodendrum splendens
Jasminum × *stephanense*
Passiflora × *exoniensis*
Rubus henryi
Tropaeolum speciosum
Tropaeolum tuberosum

▲ *Clematis* 'Rouge Cardinale'

ORANGE FLOWERS

TRUMPET OR BELL SHAPED

Campsis grandiflora
Campsis radicans
Eccremocarpus scaber
Thunbergia alata & cultivars

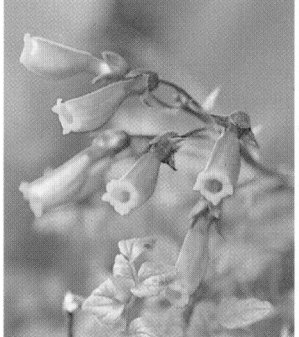

▲ Eccremocarpus scaber

DAISY-LIKE

Mutisia decurrens

▲ Mutisia decurrens

YELLOW FLOWERS

TRUMPET OR BELL SHAPED

Campsis radicans f. flava
Clematis 'Aureolin'
Clematis 'Bill Mackenzie'
Clematis 'Burford'
Clematis 'Corry'
Clematis 'Helios'

▼ Clematis 'Helios'

Clematis rehderiana
Clematis tangutica
Thunbergia alata 'Susie Hybrids'

BOWL OR PLATE SHAPED

Clematis akebioides
Clematis 'Gravetye'

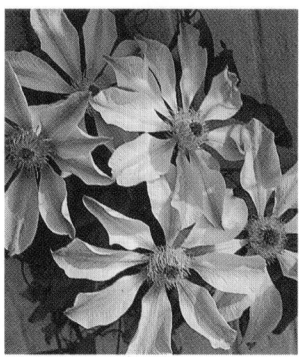

▲ Clematis 'Moonlight'

Clematis ladakhiana
Clematis 'Moonlight'
Clematis petriei
Clematis 'Wada's Primrose'
Smilax china
Smilax discotis
Tropaeolum majus & cultivars

FAN SHAPED

Tropaeolum peregrinum

▲ Tropaeolum peregrinum

BLUE FLOWERS

TRUMPET OR BELL SHAPED

Clematis 'Arabella'
Codonopsis clematidea

▼ Codonopsis clematidea

Codonopsis convolvulacea
Codonopsis forrestii
Convolvulus tricolor
  & cultivars
Ipomoea indica
Ipomoea nil

BOWL OR PLATE SHAPED

Clematis – Early Large-
  Flowered Group (second
  flowering)
Clematis – Late Large-
  Flowered Group

▲ Solanum crispum

Clematis – Viticella Group
Solanum crispum

PURPLE FLOWERS

TRUMPET OR BELL SHAPED

Clematis 'Arabella'
Clematis 'Etoile Violette'
Clematis 'Petit Faucon'
Ipomoea indica
Ipomoea purpurea

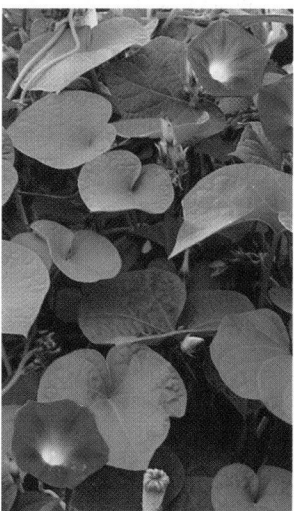

▲ Ipomoea purpurea

BOWL OR PLATE SHAPED

Clematis patens
Clematis – Early Large-
  Flowered Group (second
  flowering)
Clematis – Late Large-
  Flowered Group
Clematis – Viticella Group
Clematis 'Vyvyan Pennell'
Passiflora × caeruleoracemosa

▲ Clematis 'Vyvyan Pennell'

▲ Passiflora × caeruleoracemosa

PEA-LIKE

Lathyrus odoratus
Vicia species

▲ Lathyrus odoratus

SOFT-STEMMED PLANTS

WHITE OR CREAM FLOWERS

TRUMPET OR BELL SHAPED, ON PLANTS LESS THAN 30 CM (12 IN) TALL

Cymbalaria muralis 'Nana Alba'
Gypsophila species & cultivars
Liriope spicata 'Alba'
Lobelia erinus & cultivars
Nemesia caerulea 'Innocence'
Petunia × hybrida cultivars
Prunella grandiflora cultivars

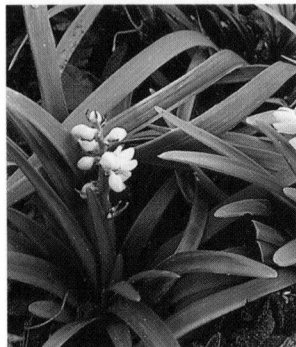

▲ Liriope spicata 'Alba'

TRUMPET OR BELL SHAPED, ON PLANTS 30 CM–1 M (1–3 FT) TALL

Agapanthus species & cultivars
Antirrhinum majus cultivars
Gypsophila species & cultivars
Hibiscus moscheutus
  'Disco Belle Mixed'
Hibiscus trionum
Hosta species & cultivars
Limonium sinuatum
Lobelia siphilitica 'Alba'
Malope trifida 'White Queen'
Mentha longifolia & cultivars
Nepeta species & cultivars
Nicotiana alata
Nicotiana × sanderae & cultivars
Penstemon digitalis

▼ Hibiscus trionum

TRUMPET OR BELL SHAPED, ON PLANTS MORE THAN 1 M (3 FT) TALL

Acanthus mollis
Acanthus spinosus
Crinum × powellii 'Album'
Hemerocallis cultivars
Hibiscus manihot & cultivars
Hibiscus moscheutus
Lilium species & cultivars
Nicotiana species & cultivars

▲ Nicotiana sylvestris

BOWL OR PLATE SHAPED, ON PLANTS LESS THAN 30 CM (12 IN) TALL WITH OVAL-SHAPED LEAVES

Begonia semperflorens
  & cultivars
Houttuynia cordata & cultivars
Lychnis species & cultivars
Pratia species
Rhodohypoxis cultivars

▲ Houttuynia cordata

BOWL OR PLATE SHAPED, ON PLANTS LESS THAN 30 CM (12 IN) TALL WITH LONG, NARROW LEAVES

Dianthus species & cultivars
Libertia pulchella
Sisyrinchium 'Pole Star'

▼ Dianthus 'Dewdrop'

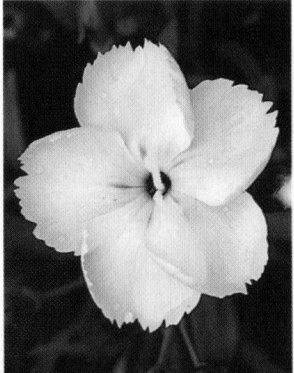

BOWL OR PLATE SHAPED, ON PLANTS LESS THAN 30 CM (12 IN) TALL WITH FEATHER-LIKE OR LOBED LEAVES

Oenothera acaulis
Pelargonium species & cultivars
Potentilla alba
Thalictrum kiusianum

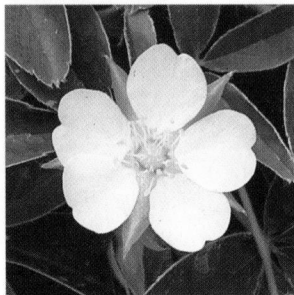

▲ Potentilla alba

BOWL OR PLATE SHAPED, ON PLANTS LESS THAN 30 CM (12 IN) TALL WITH SUCCULENT LEAVES

Sedum species & cultivars

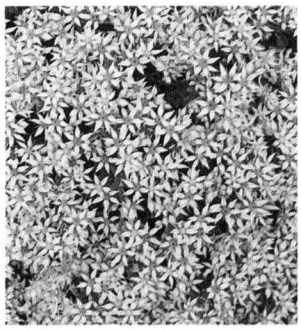

▲ Sedum forsterianum

BOWL OR PLATE SHAPED, ON PLANTS 30 CM–1 M (1–3 FT) TALL WITH OVAL-SHAPED LEAVES

Begonia grandis ssp. evansiana
  'Alba'
Begonia × tuberhybrida cultivars

▼ Begonia × tuberhybrida 'Non-Stop'

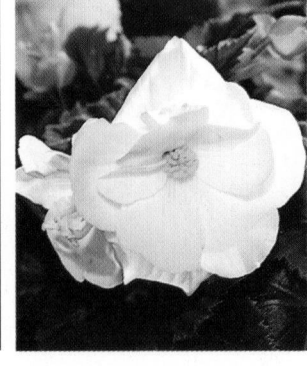

Lychnis species & cultivars
Polemonium caeruleum
  var. album
Saponaria officinalis 'Alba Plena'

BOWL OR PLATE SHAPED, ON PLANTS 30 CM–1 M (1–3 FT) TALL WITH LONG, NARROW LEAVES

Allium carinatum ssp. pulchellum
  f. album
Libertia species
Schizostylis coccinea var. alba
Xerophyllum tenax

▲ Schizostylis coccinea var. alba

BOWL OR PLATE SHAPED, ON PLANTS 30 CM–1 M (1–3 FT) TALL WITH FEATHER-LIKE OR LOBED LEAVES

Anemone vitifolia
Astrantia major ssp. involucrata
  'Shaggy'

▲ Astrantia major ssp. involucrata
'Shaggy'

Delphinium grandiflorum
Malva moschata var. alba
Nigella species
Oenothera speciosa
Papaver orientale 'Perry's White'
Pelargonium species & cultivars
Thalictrum tuberosum

BOWL OR PLATE SHAPED, ON PLANTS MORE THAN 1 M (3 FT) TALL

Anemone × hybrida & cultivars
Clematis recta 'Purpurea'
Liatris spicata 'Alba'
Papaver somniferum
  'White Cloud'
Romneya coulteri
Selinum wallichianum
Yucca species & cultivars

▲ Romneya coulteri

POMPOM SHAPED

Achillea ptarmica
  The Pearl Group
Artemisia schmidtiana
  & cultivars
Callistephus chinensis cultivars
Dahlia 'Hillcrest Albino'
Dahlia 'Kenora Challenger'
Dahlia 'My Love'
Dahlia 'Omo'
Dahlia 'Small World'
Dendranthema
  species & cultivars
Dianthus cultivars

▼ Dahlia 'Hillcrest Albino'

DAISY-LIKE ON PLANTS LESS THAN 30 CM (12 IN) TALL

Achillea species & cultivars
Aster species
Gazania 'Cream Beauty'
Tanacetum species
Zinnia species & cultivars

▲ Achillea clavennae

DAISY-LIKE ON PLANTS 30 CM –1 M (1-3 FT) TALL

Achillea species & cultivars
Argyranthemum species
Aster species
Echinacea purpurea
  'White Lustre'
Erigeron cultivars
Osteospermum 'Silver Sparkler'
Stokesia laevis
Tanacetum species

▲ Osteospermum 'Silver Sparkler'

DAISY-LIKE ON PLANTS MORE THAN 1 M (3 FT) TALL

Achillea species & cultivars
Aster species & cultivars
Dahlia merckii 'Alba'
Eupatorium species
Senecio smithii

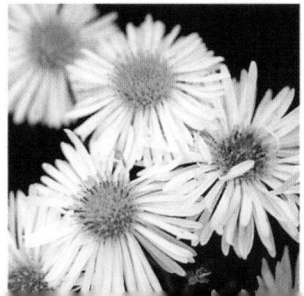
▼ Aster novae-angliae 'Herbstschnee'

ARUM-LIKE

Arisaema candidissimum
Calla palustris

▲ Arisaema candidissimum

FLOWERS IN FEATHERY PLUMES

Artemisia lactiflora
Aruncus species & cultivars
Astilbe species & cultivars
Astilboides tabularis
Filipendula purpurea f. alba
Filipendula ulmaria

▲ Aruncus dioicus

BOTTLEBRUSH SHAPED

Sanguisorba albiflora

▼ Sanguisorba albiflora

FLOWERS IN DENSE, FLATTENED CLUSTERS

Achillea millefolium
Lychnis chalcedonica 'Alba'

▲ Achillea millefolium

WHITE FLOWERS WITH PURPLE SPOTS

TRUMPET OR BELL SHAPED, ON PLANTS 30 CM–1 M (1-3 FT) TALL

Tricyrtis hirta
Tricyrtis macropoda

▲ Tricyrtis hirta

RED OR PINK FLOWERS

TRUMPET OR BELL SHAPED, ON PLANTS LESS THAN 30 CM (12 IN) TALL

Lobelia erinus 'Rosamund'
Nemesia denticulata
Nicotiana × sanderae

continued on next page

▼ Nicotiana × sanderae

783

Origanum species & cultivars
Petunia × *hybrida* cultivars
Silene schafta

TRUMPET OR BELL SHAPED, ON PLANTS 30 CM–1 M (1–3 FT) TALL WITH OVAL-SHAPED LEAVES

Antirrhinum majus cultivars
Clematis integrifolia cultivars
Diascia species & cultivars
Hibiscus moscheutus 'Disco Belle Mixed'
Lobelia species & cultivars
Origanum × *hybridum*
Origanum majorana
Penstemon species & cultivars
Platycodon grandiflorus cultivars
Prunella grandiflora
Salpiglossis sinuata & cultivars
Salvia greggii

▲ *Salpiglossis sinuata* 'Splash'

TRUMPET OR BELL SHAPED, ON PLANTS 30 CM–1 M (1–3 FT) TALL WITH LONG, SLENDER LEAVES

Amaryllis belladonna
Anigozanthos flavidus red
Crocosmia cultivars
Hemerocallis cultivars
Lilium species & cultivars
Nerine bowdenii & cultivars
Tritonia disticha ssp. *rubrolucens*

▼ *Amaryllis belladonna*

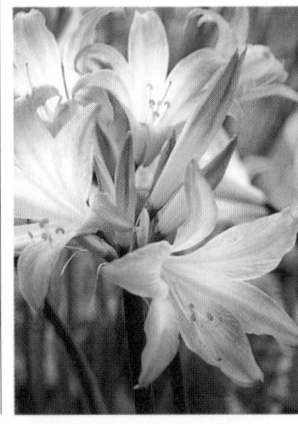

TRUMPET OR BELL SHAPED, ON PLANTS 30 CM–1 M (1–3 FT) TALL WITH FEATHER-LIKE OR LOBED LEAVES

Ipomopsis aggregata
Lavatera trimestris & cultivars
Limonium sinuatum
Malope trifida & cultivars

▲ *Lavatera trimestris* 'Silver Cup'

TRUMPET OR BELL SHAPED, ON PLANTS MORE THAN 1 M (3 FT) TALL

Canna cultivars
Crinum × *powellii*
Crocosmia 'Lucifer'
Hibiscus moscheutus
Ipomoea coccinea
Ipomopsis rubra
Lavatera species & cultivars
Lilium martagon
Lilium Pink Perfection Group
Lilium speciosum var. *rubrum*
Lobelia 'Pink Flamingo'
Physostegia virginiana
Salvia species

▼ *Lilium* Pink Perfection Group

BOWL OR PLATE SHAPED, ON PLANTS LESS THAN 30 CM (12 IN) TALL

Begonia semperflorens & cultivars
Dianthus erinaceus
Dianthus petraeus
Dianthus superbus
Geranium sanguineum var. *striatum*
Lobularia maritima 'Wonderland'
Lychnis alpina 'Rosea'
Lychnis flos-cuculi 'Nana'

▲ *Lychnis flos-cuculi* 'Nana'

Malvastrum lateritum
Oenothera speciosa 'Rosea'
Oxalis triangularis
Pelargonium species & cultivars
Portulaca grandiflora & cultivars
Rhodohypoxis species & cultivars
Silene keiskei
Verbena × *hybrida* cultivars

BOWL OR PLATE SHAPED, ON PLANTS 30 CM–1 M (1–3 FT) TALL WITH OVAL-SHAPED LEAVES

Alonsoa warscewiczii
Begonia grandis ssp. *evansiana*

▼ *Begonia* × *tuberhybrida*

Begonia × *tuberhybrida* cultivars
Catharanthus roseus
Impatiens species & cultivars
Lychnis species & cultivars
Nomocharis species
Saponaria officinalis
Tradescantia cultivars

BOWL OR PLATE SHAPED, ON PLANTS 30 CM–1 M (1–3 FT) TALL WITH LONG, NARROW LEAVES

Hemerocallis cultivars
Nomocharis species

▲ *Hemerocallis* 'Luxury Lace'

BOWL OR PLATE SHAPED, ON PLANTS 30 CM–1 M (1–3 FT) TALL WITH FEATHER-LIKE OR LOBED LEAVES

Anemone hupehensis & cultivars
Anemone tomentosa
Astrantia species & cultivars
Dianthus caryophyllus & cultivars
Glaucium corniculatum
Ipomopsis aggregata
Papaver species & cultivars
Pelargonium species & cultivars
Potentilla atrosanguinea

▼ *Potentilla atrosanguinea*

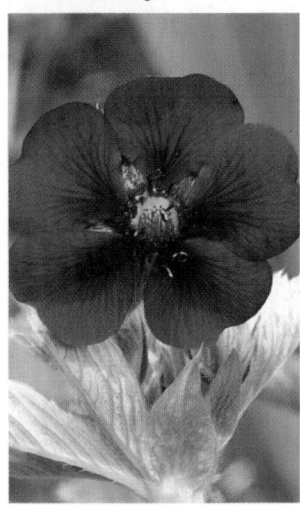

BOWL OR PLATE SHAPED, ON PLANTS MORE THAN 1 M (3 FT) TALL

Anemone × hybrida & cultivars
Butomus umbellatus
Delphinium cardinale

▲ Delphinium cardinale

Eremurus robustus
Ipomopsis rubra
Malva moschata
Papaver somniferum
  'Pink Chiffon'

POMPOM SHAPED

Dahlia cultivars

▲ Dahlia 'Ellen Houston'

DAISY-LIKE

Cosmos atrosanguineus

▼ Cosmos atrosanguineus

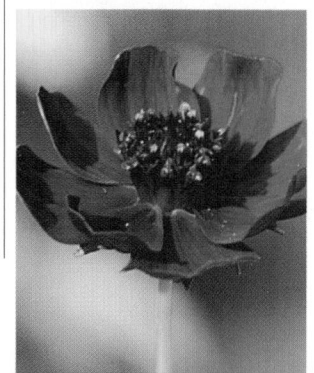

Cosmos bipinnatus & cultivars
Crepis incana
Dahlia coccinea
Dahlia 'Bishop of Llandaff'
Eupatorium species & cultivars
Gazania 'Christopher'
Helipterum 'Goliath'
Lampranthus species
Osteospermum 'Hopleys'
Osteospermum 'Langtrees'
Osteospermum 'Pink Whirls'
Zinnia 'Chippendale'

PEA-LIKE

Clianthus species
Lathyrus latifolius 'Red Pearl'
Lotus bertholetti
Lupinus cultivars

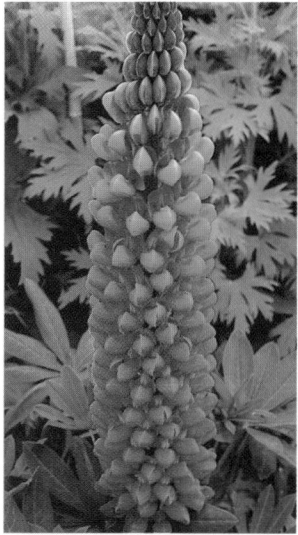

▲ Lupinus 'Chelsea Pensioner'

FLOWERS IN FEATHERY PLUMES

Astilbe species & cultivars
Filipendula camtschatica
Filipendula purpurea
Filipendula rubra & cultivars

▼ Filipendula rubra

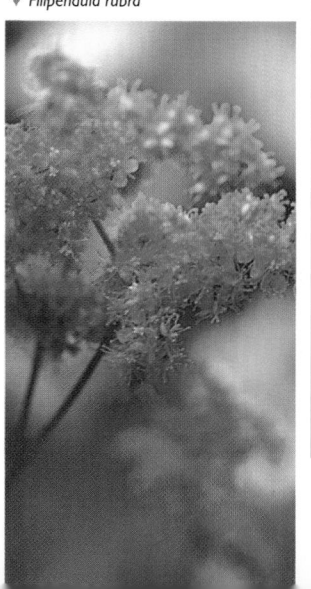

Filipendula ulmaria 'Rosea'
Sanguisorba obtusa

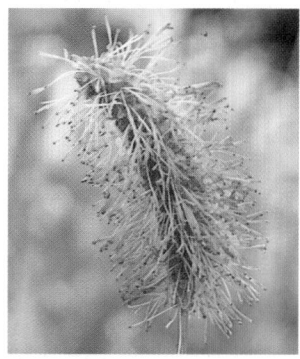

▲ Sanguisorba obtusa

THISTLE-LIKE

Silybum marianum

▲ Silybum marianum

FLOWERS IN DENSE, FLATTENED CLUSTERS

Achillea 'Apfelblüte'
Achillea 'Fanal'
Achillea 'Lachsschönheit'
Achillea millefolium
  'Cerise Queen'
Lychnis chalcedonica & cultivars

▼ Achillea 'Fanal'

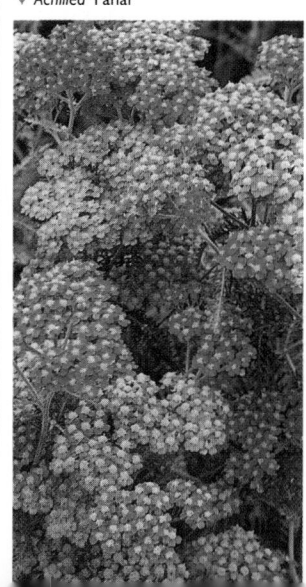

RED-AND-WHITE FLOWERS

POMPOM SHAPED

Dahlia 'Barbary Snowball'
Dahlia 'Kyoto'
Dahlia 'Wootton Cupid'

▲ Dahlia 'Wootton Cupid'

RED-AND-YELLOW FLOWERS

TRUMPET OR BELL SHAPED

Abutilon megapotamicum

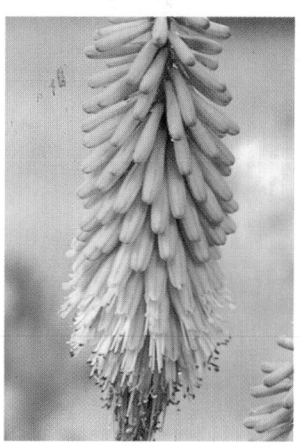

▲ Kniphofia uvaria

Kniphofia species & cultivars
Lobelia laxiflora

▼ Lobelia laxiflora

785

PINK, PURPLE AND YELLOW FLOWERS

BOWL OR PLATE SHAPED, ON PLANTS 30 CM–1 M (1–3 FT) TALL

Schizanthus pinnatus

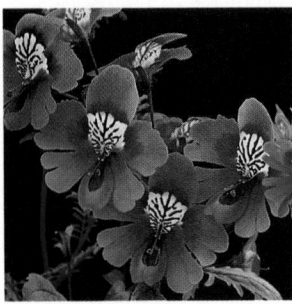

▲ *Schizanthus pinnatus*

ORANGE FLOWERS

TRUMPET OR BELL SHAPED

Crocosmia cultivars
Hemerocallis cultivars
Lilium species & cultivars
Salpiglossis sinuata & cultivars

▲ *Hemerocallis* 'Hornby Castle'

BOWL OR PLATE SHAPED

Begonia sutherlandii
Begonia × *tuberhybrida* cultivars
Geum cultivars
Impatiens walleriana
Malvastrum lateritium
Papaver species & cultivars
Pelargonium cultivars
Portulaca grandiflora & cultivars

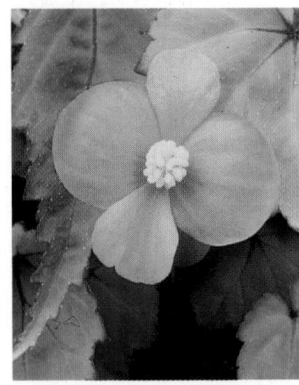

▲ *Begonia sutherlandii*

POMPOM SHAPED

Dahlia cultivars
Dendranthema cultivars
Tagetes species & cultivars

▲ *Dahlia* 'David Howard'

DAISY-LIKE

Cosmos sulphureus
Gazania rigens
Gazania 'Sundance'
Lampranthus aurantiacus

▲ *Lampranthus aurantiacus*

Lampranthus brownii
Ligularia dentata 'Desdemona'
Sanvitalia procumbens cultivars
Tagetes species & cultivars
Ursinia anthemoides
Zinnia cultivars

YELLOW FLOWERS

TRUMPET OR BELL SHAPED, ON PLANTS LESS THAN 30 CM (12 IN) TALL

Allium flavum
Epilobium glabellum 'Sulphureum'
Mimulus moschatus
Penstemon confertus
Petunia × *hybrida* cultivars
Teucrium polium

▼ *Penstemon confertus*

TRUMPET OR BELL SHAPED, ON PLANTS 30 CM–1 M (1–3 FT) TALL

Anigozanthos flavidus 'yellow'
Antirrhinum majus cultivars
Cautleya spicata

▲ *Cautleya spicata*

Crocosmia 'Canary Bird'
Crocosmia 'Citronella'
Hemerocallis 'Stella de Oro'
Hibiscus trionum & cultivars
Limonium sinuatum
Linaria dalmatica
Linaria vulgaris
Monarda punctata
Nicotiana × *sanderae*
Penstemon pinifolius 'Mersea Yellow'
Polemonium pauciflorum
Salpiglossis sinuata & cultivars
Sisyrinchium striatum
Tricyrtis species

TRUMPET OR BELL SHAPED, ON PLANTS MORE THAN 1 M (3 FT) TALL

Canna cultivars
Clematis aethusifolia
Lilium Citronella Group
Lilium 'Limelight'
Monarda punctata
Teucrium polium

▲ *Lilium* Citronella Group

BOWL OR PLATE SHAPED, ON PLANTS LESS THAN 30 CM (12 IN) TALL

Azorella trifurcata & cultivars
Oenothera species & cultivars
Papaver miyabeanum

▲ *Oenothera macrocarpa*

Polemonium species
Portulaca grandiflora & cultivars
Portulaca oleracea
Potentilla species & cultivars
Sedum species & cultivars
Trollius acaulis
Trollius pumilus

BOWL OR PLATE SHAPED, ON PLANTS 30 CM–1 M (1–3 FT) TALL

Begonia × *tuberhybrida* cultivars
Chelidonium majus & cultivars
Eremurus stenophyllus ssp. *stenophyllus*
Eschscholtzia species
Glaucium flavum
Oenothera species & cultivars
Papaver species
Polemonium species
Potentilla species

▲ *Glaucium flavum*

BOWL OR PLATE SHAPED, ON PLANTS MORE THAN 1M (3FT) TALL

Verbascum species & cultivars

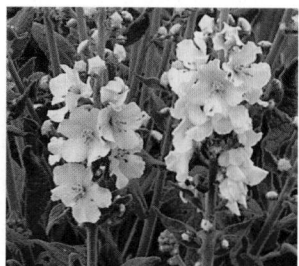

▲ *Verbascum 'Gainsborough'*

POMPOM SHAPED

Artemisia species
Dahlia cultivars
Dendranthema cultivars
Tagetes species & cultivars

▲ *Dahlia 'Hamari Gold'*

DAISY-LIKE, ON PLANTS LESS THAN 30CM (12IN) TALL

Achillea × lewisii
Anthemis tinctoria & cultivars
Asteriscus maritimus
Chamaemelum nobile
Gazania cultivars
Sanvitalia procumbens
Tagetes species & cultivars

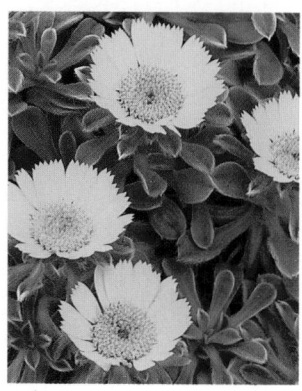

▲ *Asteriscus maritimus*

DAISY-LIKE, ON PLANTS 30CM-1M (1-3FT) TALL

Achillea species & cultivars
Anthemis species & cultivars
Argyranthemum maderense
Buphthalmum salicifolium
Helichrysum bracteatum
Lindheimera texana
Matricaria recutita
Osteospermum 'Buttermilk'
Rudbeckia fulgida & cultivars

▲ *Rudbeckia fulgida* var. *deamii*

Solidago species & cultivars
× *Solidaster luteus*
Ursinia species

DAISY-LIKE, ON PLANTS MORE THAN 1M (3FT) TALL

Helianthus species & cultivars
Inula species
Ligularia species & cultivars
Rudbeckia species & cultivars
Telekia speciosa

▲ *Telekia speciosa*

PEA-LIKE

Lupinus species & cultivars
Scutellaria prostrata
Thermopsis lupinoides
Thermopsis montana

▼ *Thermopsis lupinoides*

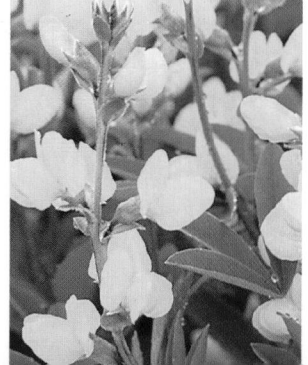

FLOWERS IN DENSE, FLATTENED CLUSTERS

Achillea 'Coronation Gold'
Achillea filipendulina 'Gold Plate'
Achillea 'Hoffnung'
Achillea × lewisii 'King Edward'
Achillea 'Moonshine'
Achillea 'Taygetea'

▲ *Achillea 'Coronation Gold'*

SLIPPER SHAPED

Calceolaria integrifolia & cultivars

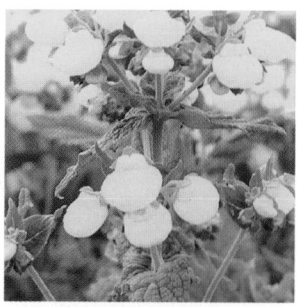

▲ *Calceolaria integrifolia 'Sunshine'*

YELLOW OR RED FLOWERS SPOTTED CRIMSON OR BROWN

BOWL OR PLATE SHAPED

Tigridia pavonia & cultivars

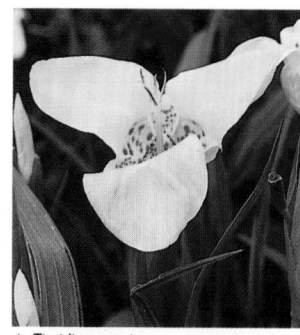

▲ *Tigridia pavonia*

GREEN FLOWERS

TRUMPET OR BELL SHAPED

Ballota 'All Hallows Green'
Epipactis gigantea

▲ *Ballota 'All Hallows Green'*

Eucomis bicolor
Galtonia princeps
Galtonia viridiflora
Heuchera cylindrica 'Greenfinch'
Nicotiana langsdorffii
Nicotiana × sanderae cultivars

▲ *Nicotiana × sanderae 'Lime Green'*

BOWL OR PLATE SHAPED

Molucella laevis

▲ *Molucella laevis*

FLOWERS IN LONG, DROOPING TASSELS

Amaranthus caudatus 'Viridis'

▼ *Amaranthus caudatus 'Viridis'*

BLUE FLOWERS

TRUMPET OR BELL SHAPED, ON PLANTS LESS THAN 30 CM (12 IN) TALL

Codonopsis ovata
Corydalis cashmeriana
Limonium species & cultivars
Lobelia erinus & cultivars
Lobelia tenuior & cultivars
Petunia × hybrida cultivars
Phacelia sericea
Prunella grandiflora

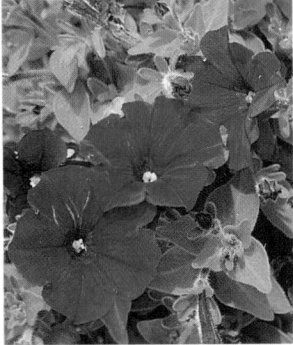

▲ Petunia 'Fantasy Blue'

TRUMPET OR BELL SHAPED, ON PLANTS MORE THAN 30 CM (12 IN) TALL

Agapanthus species & cultivars
Clematis integrifolia cultivars
Echium plantagineum
 'Blue Bedder'
Gentiana species & cultivars
Gilia species
Limonium species & cultivars
Nepeta species & cultivars
Penstemon cultivars
Penstemon glaber
Penstemon strictus
Phacelia tanacetifolia
Platycodon grandiflorus
 & cultivars
Salvia species & cultivars

▼ Platycodon grandiflorus

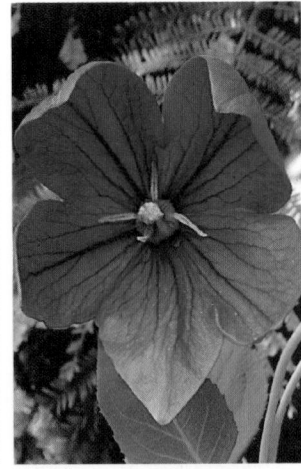

BOWL OR PLATE SHAPED, ON PLANTS LESS THAN 30 CM (12 IN) TALL

Myosotis scorpioides 'Mermaid'
Nemophila menziesii
Polemonium boreale
Verbena × hybrida 'Imagination'

▲ Myosotis scorpioides 'Mermaid'

BOWL OR PLATE SHAPED, ON PLANTS 30 CM-1 M (1-3 FT) TALL

Delphinium grandiflorum
Linum species
Lobelia species & cultivars
Malva sylvestris
 'Cottenham Blue'
Matthiola longipetala
Nemesia versicolor
Nigella species & cultivars

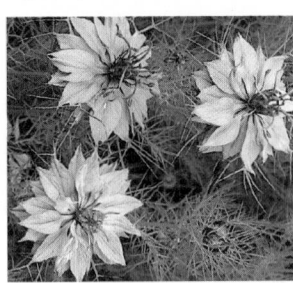

▲ Nigella damascena 'Persian Jewels'

Phacelia sericea ssp. ciliosa
Phacelia tanacetifolia
Polemonium species
Tradescantia virginiana
 'Zwanenburg Blue'

DAISY-LIKE

Aster species & cultivars
Dahlia merckii
Osteospermum 'Whirligig'
Stokesia laevis & cultivars

▼ Stokesia laevis 'Blue Star'

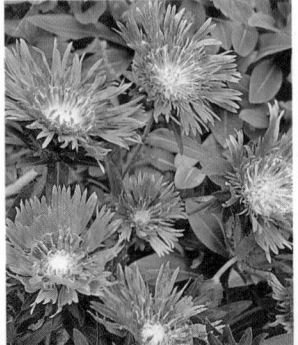

POMPOM SHAPED

Ageratum houstonianum
Gilia capitata

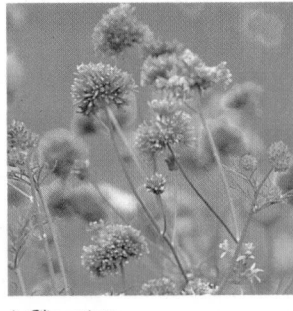

▲ Gilia capitata

HOOD OR HELMET SHAPED

Aconitum carmichaelii
Aconitum napellus

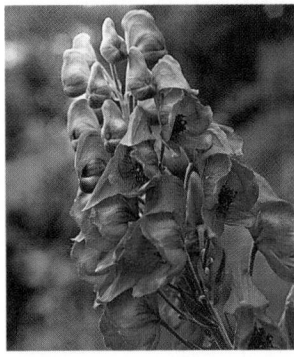

▲ Aconitum carmichaelii Wilsonii Group

FAN SHAPED

Scaevola aemula

▲ Scaevola aemula

THISTLE-LIKE

Eryngium species

▼ Eryngium × tripartitum

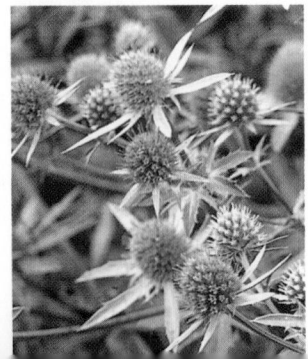

BLUE AND WHITE FLOWERS

TRUMPET OR BELL SHAPED

Ipomoea cultivars
Lobelia erinus
Nemesia strumosa 'K.L.M.'

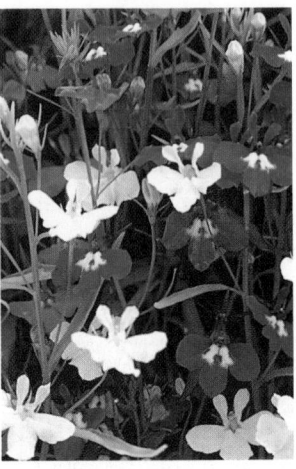

▲ Lobelia erinus (mixed)

PURPLE FLOWERS

TRUMPET OR BELL SHAPED, ON PLANTS LESS THAN 30 CM (12 IN) TALL

Campanula poscharskyana
Clintonia andrewsiana
Cyananthus lobatus
Cymbalaria hepaticifolia
Hemerocallis cultivars
Liriope spicata
Lobelia erinus cultivars
Mentha × gracilis & cultivars
Penstemon cultivars
Salpiglossis sinuata & cultivars
Teucrium species
Thymus species & cultivars

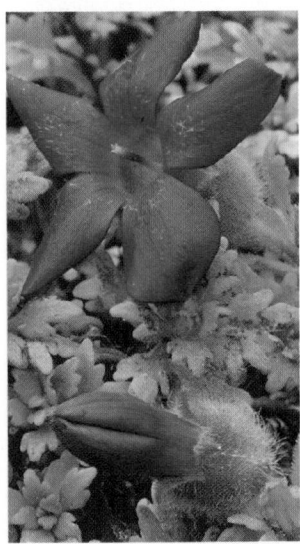

▲ Cyananthus lobatus

TRUMPET OR BELL SHAPED, ON PLANTS 30 CM–1 M (1–3 FT) TALL WITH OVAL-SHAPED LEAVES

Ballota nigra
  'Archer's Variegated'
Clematis integrifolia 'Tapestry'
Cuphea hyssopifolia
Echium vulgare
Hosta species & cultivars
Lobelia cultivars
Lychnis flos-cuculi
Mentha longifolia & cultivars
Origanum vulgare
Penstemon species & cultivars

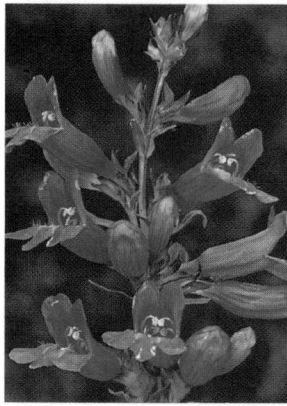

▲ *Penstemon* 'Catherine de la Mare'

Salvia species & cultivars
Tulbaghia violacea

TRUMPET OR BELL SHAPED, ON PLANTS MORE THAN 1 M (3 FT) TALL

Lilium martagon var. *cattaniae*
Nicandra physalodes
Salvia przewalskii
Strobilanthes atropurpureus
Verbena hastata

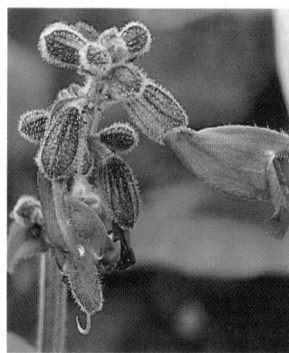

▲ *Salvia przewalskii*

BOWL OR PLATE SHAPED, ON PLANTS LESS THAN 30 CM (12 IN) TALL

Allium senescens
Dianthus cultivars
Erodium glandulosum

▲ *Erodium manescaui*

Erodium manescaui
Lobularia maritima
  'Violet Queen'
Lychnis species & cultivars
Nemesia species & cultivars
Oxalis species & cultivars
Pelargonium species & cultivars
Sedum species & cultivars
Thalictrum species
Verbena × *hybrida*
  'Tapien Purple'
Viola odorata
Viola pedata

BOWL OR PLATE SHAPED, ON PLANTS 30 CM–1 M (1–3 FT) TALL

Allium species
Anemone hupehensis & cultivars
Delphinium grandiflorum
Epilobium fleischeri
Impatiens balsamina & cultivars
Lychnis viscaria
Malva sylvestris
Pelargonium species & cultivars
Potentilla nepalensis
Thalictrum diffusiflorum
Tradescantia virginiana
  'Purple Dome'
Tulbaghia violacea

▼ *Tulbaghia violacea*

POMPOM SHAPED

Dahlia cultivars
Echinops species & cultivars
Liatris spicata & cultivars
Thalictrum aquilegifolium
  & cultivars

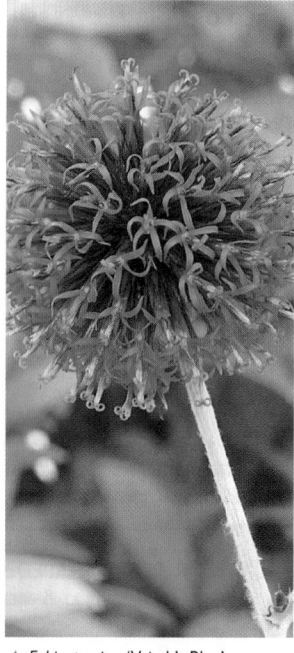

▲ *Echinops ritro* 'Veitch's Blue'

DAISY-LIKE

Aster amellus 'Framfieldii'
Aster × *frikartii* 'Flora's Delight'
Centaurea cineraria
Dahlia merckii
Eupatorium purpureum
Lampranthus species & cultivars
Osteospermum jucundum
Stokesia laevis
Zinnia elegans

▼ *Lampranthus blandus*

PEA-LIKE

Hedysarum coronarium
Lupinus species & cultivars
Polygala myrtifolia

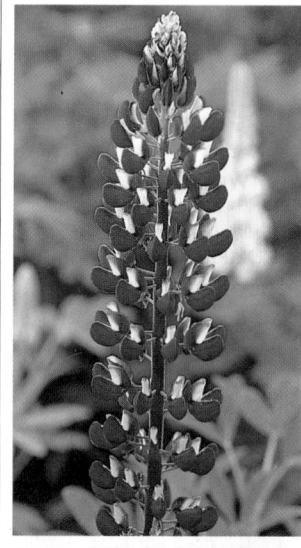

▲ *Lupinus* Band of Nobles Series

HOOD OR HELMET SHAPED

Aconitum carmichaelii

▲ *Aconitum carmichaelii*

THISTLE-LIKE

Cynara cardunculus

▼ *Cynara cardunculus*

YELLOW FLOWERS

BOWL OR PLATE SHAPED
Clematis tibetana ssp. *vernayi*

▲ *Clematis tibetana* ssp. *vernayi*

BLUE FLOWERS

BOWL OR PLATE SHAPED
Clematis 'Ascotiensis'
Clematis 'Lady Betty Balfour'

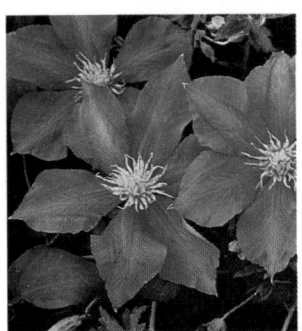

▲ *Clematis* 'Ascotiensis'

PURPLE FLOWERS

TRUMPET OR BELL SHAPED
Clematis 'Etoile Rose'
Clematis 'Etoile Violette'
Passiflora amethystina

▲ *Clematis* 'Etoile Violette'

BOWL OR PLATE SHAPED
Clematis 'Blue Belle'
Clematis × *eriostemon*
  'Hendersonii'

Clematis 'Polish Spirit'
Clematis 'Prince Charles'
Clematis 'Royal Velours'
Clematis viticella

▲ *Clematis* 'Prince Charles'

SOFT-STEMMED PLANTS

WHITE OR CREAM FLOWERS

TRUMPET OR BELL SHAPED
Colchicum autumnale f. *album*
Colchicum speciosum 'Album'
Crocus boryi
Gentiana sino-ornata 'Alba'
Hibiscus species & cultivars
Kniphofia species & cultivars
Leucojum autumnale
Lilium formosanum

▲ *Colchicum autumnale* f. *album*

BOWL OR PLATE SHAPED
Anemone vitifolia
Liriope cultivars
Lobularia maritima cultivars
Schizostylis coccinea var. *alba*
Sedum species & cultivars

▼ *Schizostylis coccinea* var. *alba*

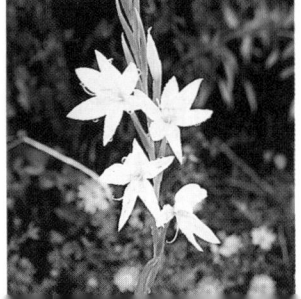

DAISY-LIKE
Aster species & cultivars
Dahlia merkii 'Alba'
Dendranthema species
Echinacea purpurea 'White
  Lustre'
Eupatorium altissimum
Eupatorium perfoliatum
Tanacetum balsamita

▲ *Aster* 'Albanian'

CYCLAMEN FLOWERS
Cyclamen hederifolium 'Album'

◄ *Cyclamen hederifolium* 'Album'

WHITE FLOWERS WITH PURPLE OR BROWN SPOTS

BOWL OR PLATE SHAPED
Tricyrtis species

▲ *Tricyrtis formosana*

RED OR PINK FLOWERS

TRUMPET OR BELL SHAPED
Colchicum species & cultivars
Diascia vigilis
Hibiscus moscheutus & cultivars
Origanum species & cultivars

▲ *Silene schafta* 'Shell Pink'

Physostegia virginiana
Salvia confertiflora
Salvia fulgens
Salvia involucrata
Silene schafta & cultivars
Teucrium chamaedrys

BOWL OR PLATE SHAPED
Alonsoa warscewiczii
Anemone tomentosa
Lobularia maritima
  'Wonderland Rose'
Persicaria campanulata
Persicaria vacciniifolia
Schizostylis coccinea
Sedum species & cultivars
Verbena × *hybrida* cultivars

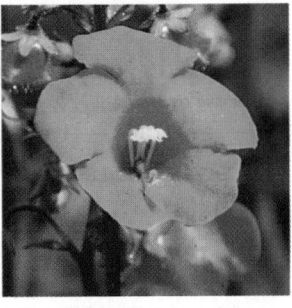

▲ *Alonsoa warscewiczii*

DAISY-LIKE
Aster cultivars
Dahlia coccinea
Dahlia 'Bishop of Llandaff'
Senecio pulcher

▲ *Dahlia* 'Bishop of Llandaff'

CYCLAMEN FLOWERS
Cyclamen species

▼ *Cyclamen cilicium*

FLOWERS IN FEATHERY PLUMES
Astilbe cultivars

▲ *Astilbe* 'Jo Ophorst'

PINK, PURPLE AND YELLOW FLOWERS

BOWL OR PLATE SHAPED
Schizanthus pinnatus

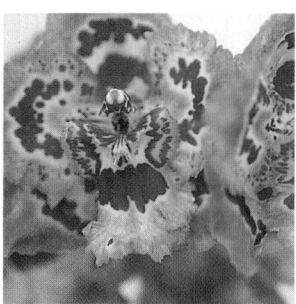

▲ *Schizanthus pinnatus*

ORANGE FLOWERS

TRUMPET OR BELL SHAPED
Hedychium coccineum 'Tara'

▲ *Hedychium coccineum* 'Tara'

BOWL OR PLATE SHAPED
Malvastrum lateritium

▼ *Malvastrum lateritium*

DAISY-LIKE
Lampranthus aurantiacus
Lampranthus brownii
Zinnia haageana

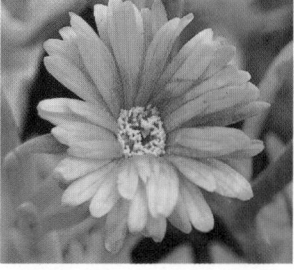

▲ *Lampranthus aurantiacus*

YELLOW FLOWERS

TRUMPET OR BELL SHAPED

▲ *Epilobium glabellum* 'Sulphureum'

Epilobium glabellum
  'Sulphureum'
Hibiscus manihot
Hibiscus trionum & cultivars
Monarda punctata
Sternbergia lutea
Tricyrtis macrantha ssp.
  macranthopsis
Tricyrtis ohsumiensis

BOWL OR PLATE SHAPED
Oxalis purpurea 'Ken Aslet'

▲ *Oxalis purpurea* 'Ken Aslet'

DAISY-LIKE
Bidens ferulifolia 'Sunshine'
Rudbeckia fulgida var. *deamii*

▲ *Rudbeckia fulgida* var. *deamii*

Rudbeckia maxima
X *Solidaster luteus*

BLUE FLOWERS

TRUMPET OR BELL SHAPED
Crocus pulchellus
Cyananthus lobatus
Gentiana asclepiadea
Gentiana × *macaulayi* cultivars
Gentiana sino-ornata
  & cultivars
Salvia patens
Salvia uliginosa

▲ *Salvia uliginosa*

DAISY-LIKE
Aster species & cultivars

▲ *Aster novi-belgii* 'Audrey'

PURPLE FLOWERS

TRUMPET OR BELL SHAPED
Colchicum 'Lilac Wonder'
Crocus banaticus

▲ *Crocus medius*

Crocus medius
Cyananthus microphyllus
Origanum vulgare
Salvia buchananii
Strobilanthes atropurpureus

BOWL OR PLATE SHAPED
Epilobium fleischeri
Liriope species & cultivars
Oxalis oregana
Sedum cauticola & cultivars
Sedum telephium
Verbena × *hybrida* 'Tapien
  Purple'

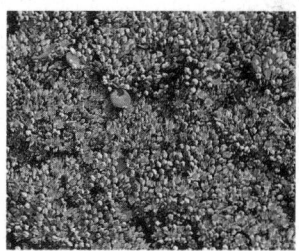

▲ *Sedum cauticola* 'Bertram Anderson'

DAISY-LIKE
Aster species & cultivars
Dahlia merckii
Senecio pulcher
Zinnia elegans

▲ *Aster novi-belgii* 'Remembrance'

IRIS-LIKE
Iris unguicularis & cultivars
Roscoea auriculata
Roscoea purpurea

▼ *Roscoea purpurea*

WINTER

In the darkest days of the year winter-flowering shrubs,
cyclamens and the earliest irises bring interest to the garden

TREES AND SHRUBS

WHITE OR CREAM FLOWERS

TRUMPET OR BELL SHAPED

Buddleja asiatica
Daphne mezereum f. *alba*
Elaeagnus × *ebbingei*
 & cultivars
Lonicera fragrantissima
Lonicera × *purpusii* & cultivars
Lonicera standishii
Pieris japonica
Rhododendron 'Nobleanum
 Album'
Rhododendron mucronulatum
 'Winter Brightness'
Viburnum farreri

▲ *Pieris japonica*

BOWL OR PLATE SHAPED

Crataegus monogyna 'Biflora'
Prunus incisa 'Praecox'
Prunus × *subhirtella* 'Autumnalis'
Viburnum tinus

▲ *Prunus* × *subhirtella* 'Autumnalis'

TASSEL-LIKE

Sarcococca confusa
Sarcococca ruscifolia

▼ *Sarcococca confusa*

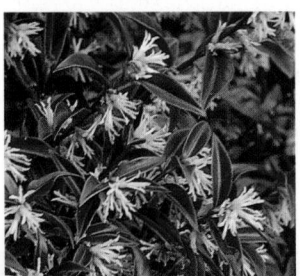

RED OR PINK FLOWERS

TRUMPET OR BELL SHAPED

Daphne mezereum var. *rubra*
Erica species & cultivars
Rhododendron 'Nobleanum'
Rhododendron sutchuenense
Salvia oppositiflora

▲ *Erica carnea* 'Challenger'

BOWL OR PLATE SHAPED

Prunus × *subhirtella* 'Autumnalis
 Rosea'
Viburnum × *bodnantense*

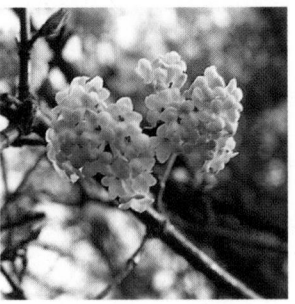

▲ *Viburnum* × *bodnantense* 'Deben'

FLOWERS SIMILAR TO HONEYSUCKLE

Grevillea rosmarinifolia

▼ *Grevillea rosmarinifolia*

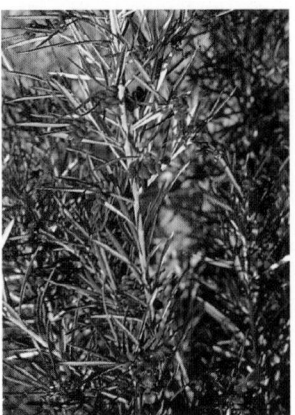

TASSEL-LIKE

Hamamelis × *intermedia*
 & cultivars
Sarcococca hookeriana var.
 digyna
Sarcococca hookeriana var.
 humilis

▲ *Sarcococca hookeriana* var. *digyna*

YELLOW FLOWERS

TRUMPET OR BELL SHAPED

Mahonia species & cultivars

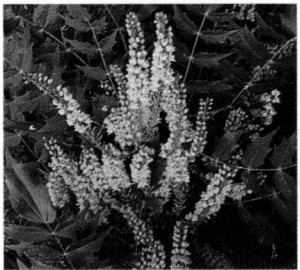

▲ *Mahonia* × *media* 'Charity'

BOWL OR PLATE SHAPED

Chimonanthus praecox
 'Grandiflorus'
Chimonanthus praecox 'Luteus'
Cornus mas

▼ *Chimonanthus praecox* 'Grandiflorus'

POMPOM SHAPED

Acacia dealbata

▲ *Acacia dealbata*

TASSEL-LIKE

Hamamelis japonica
Hamamelis mollis
Hamamelis vernalis

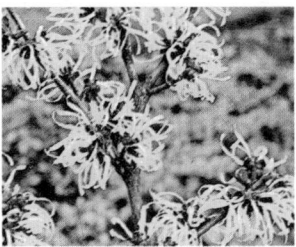

▲ *Hamamelis mollis* 'Pallida'

YELLOW-GREEN FLOWERS

TRUMPET OR BELL SHAPED

Daphne laureola

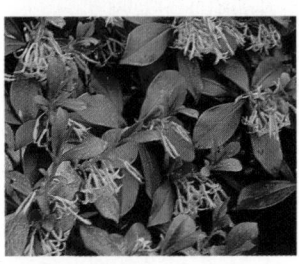

▲ *Daphne laureola*

PURPLE FLOWERS

BOWL OR PLATE SHAPED

Rhododendron dauricum
 'Midwinter'

▼ *Rhododendron dauricum* 'Midwinter'

TREES AND SHRUBS WITH CATKINS

Betula species & cultivars
Corylus species & cultivars
Garrya elliptica & cultivars
Populus tremula
Salix aegyptiaca

▲ Garrya elliptica

CLIMBING PLANTS

YELLOW FLOWERS

BOWL OR PLATE SHAPED
Jasminum nudiflorum

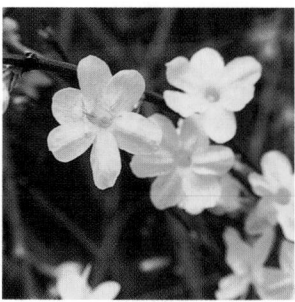

▲ Jasminum nudiflorum

SOFT-STEMMED PLANTS

WHITE OR CREAM FLOWERS

TRUMPET OR BELL SHAPED
Galanthus cultivars
Crocus species & cultivars
Salvia leucantha

▼ Crocus chrysanthus 'Cream Beauty'

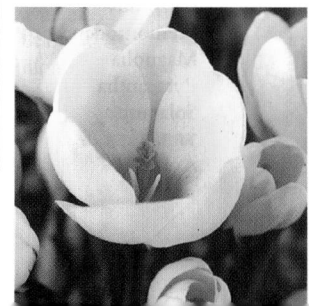

BOWL OR PLATE SHAPED

Helleborus niger & cultivars
Helleborus orientalis & cultivars
Hepatica nobilis white form
Ranunculus calandrinioides

▲ Helleborus niger 'Sunset'

CYCLAMEN FLOWERS

Cyclamen coum & cultivars
Cyclamen hederifolium album

▲ Cyclamen hederifolium album

IRIS FLOWERS

Iris 'Natascha'
Iris unguicularis 'Alba'

▲ Iris 'Natascha'

RED OR PINK FLOWERS

BOWL OR PLATE SHAPED
Helleborus orientalis pink form
Helleborus × sternii 'Boughton Beauty'

▼ Helleborus orientalis pink form

CYCLAMEN FLOWERS

Cyclamen species & cultivars

▲ Cyclamen libanoticum

YELLOW FLOWERS

TRUMPET OR BELL SHAPED
Crocus ancyrensis
Crocus chrysanthus & cultivars
Narcissus species & cultivars

▲ Crocus 'Goldilocks'

BOWL OR PLATE SHAPED
Hacquetia epipactis
Helleborus orientalis Kochii Group

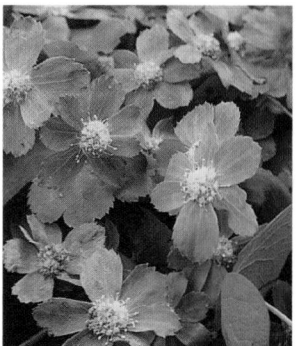

▲ Hacquetia epipactis

IRIS FLOWERS

Iris danfordiae

▼ Iris danfordiae

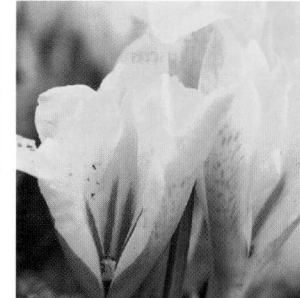

GREEN FLOWERS

BOWL OR PLATE SHAPED
Helleborus species & cultivars

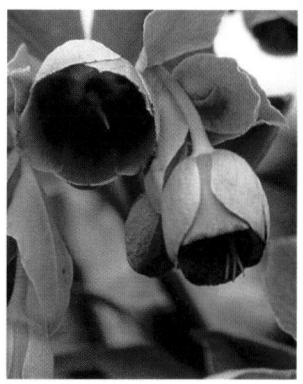

▲ Helleborus foetidus

PURPLE FLOWERS

BOWL OR PLATE SHAPED
Helleborus orientalis cultivars
Helleborus purpurascens
Helleborus torquatus
Hepatica americana

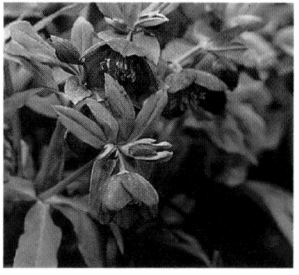

▲ Helleborus purpurascens

IRIS FLOWERS

Iris 'George'
Iris 'Pauline'
Iris unguicularis & cultivars

▼ Iris unguicularis

795

Prunus x subhirtella 'Autumnalis'

Mahon...

Narcissus Scilla Iris reticulata Helleboru... orient...

• WINTER-FLOWERING PLANTS •

BULBS
Anemone
Chionodoxa
Crocus
Cyclamen
Eranthis
Galanthus
Iris
Leucojum vernum
Narcissus
Scilla

CLIMBERS
Clematis
Jasminum

PERENNIALS
Bergenia
Helleborus
Hepatica
Iris
Pulmonaria
Viola

SHRUBS
Camellia
Chimonanthus
Cornus
Daphne
Erica
Garrya

Hamamelis
Lonicera
Mahonia
Rhododendron
  'Christmas cheer'
R. moupinense
Sarcococca
Viburnum

TREES
Corylus
Hamamelis
Parrotia
Prunus × subhirtella
  'Autumnalis'

• PLANTS WITH GREY OR SILVER FOLIAGE •

Rosa glauca

Verbascum

Festuca glauca

Santolina Anthemis Dianthus

E = Evergreen

ANNUALS AND BIENNIALS
Eschscholzia
Papaver
Salvia
Senecio

BULBS
Allium
Cyclamen

GRASSES
Cortaderia
Festuca

PERENNIALS
Achillea
Anaphalis (E)
Androsace
Anthemis (E)
Arctotis (E)
Argyranthemum
Centaurea
Cerastium

Cynara
Dianthus (E)
Eryngium
Euphorbia
Helichrysum (E)
Leontopodium
Lychnis
Nepeta
Onopordum
Perovskia
Pulsatilla
Salvia
Saxifraga (E)
Sedum (E)
Sempervivum (E)
Senecio
Stachys
Tanacetum
Verbascum

SHRUBS
Artemisia (E)
Ballota (E)
Brachyglottis (E)

Buddleja
Calluna (E)
Convolvulus (E)
Hebe (E)
Helianthemum (E)
Hippophae (E)
Lavendula (E)
Phlomis (E)
Rosa glauca
Ruta (E)
Salix
Salvia
Santolina (E)

TREES
Cedrus (E)
Chamaecyparis (E)
Cupressus (E)
Eucalyptus (E)
Juniperus (E)
Picea (E)
Populus
Pyrus
Salix

• PLANTS FOR CUT FLOWERS •

★ = Suitable for
drying

ANNUALS AND PERENNIALS
Anthemis
Antirrhinum
Calendula
Callistephus
Catananche
Clarkia
Coreopsis
Cosmos
Dahlia
Delphinium
Dianthus
Digitalis
Gaillardia
Gomphrena
Gypsophila
Helianthus
Helichrysum
Iberis
Lathyrus
Matthiola
Moluccella★
Nigella★
Reseda★
Silene
Verbascum
Verbena
Zinnia

BULBS
Allium
Crocosmia
Freesia
Gladiolus
Iris

Lilium
Narcissus
Nerine
Ornithogalum
Sparaxis
Tulipa
Zantedeschia

GRASSES
Briza
Cortaderia
Lagurus
Pennisetum
Stipa

PERENNIALS
Achillea★
Agapanthus
Alstroemeria
Anaphalis
Anemone
Antirrhinum
Aquilegia
Aster
Astilbe★
Catananche★
Centaurea★
Coreopsis
Dahlia
Delphinium
Dendranthema
Dianthus
Digitalis
Doronicum
Echinops★

Erigeron
Eryngium★
Erysium
Euphorbia
Gaillardia
Geum
Gypsophila
Helenium
Helianthus
Helichrysum★
Heuchera★
Iberis
Iris
Liatrus
Limonium★
Lupinus
Lychnis
Monarda
Paeonia
Phlox
Physostegia
Rudbeckia
Scabiosa
Schizostylis
Silene
Solidago★
Tanacetum
Trollius
Valeriana
Verbascum
Verbena

SHRUBS
Camellia
Forsythia
Philadelphus
Rosa
Syringa

TREES
Acacia

Philadelphus

Cosmos

Moluccella

Nigella Reseda Iris Matthiola
  Delphinium

Digitalis Phlox

How to grow and increase your plants

The health of plants in a garden depends on the condition of the soil, together with proper feeding and appropriate pruning. Healthy plants can then be propagated to increase your stock

Manures, mulches and fertilisers

The addition of organic material helps to create a well-balanced soil and increase its fertility. Organic materials are those derived from animal matter or plant debris. Generally, materials regarded as manures are those having an organic origin, such as dung, garden compost and leaf-mould, which break down into humus. They must be well rotted.

Mulches are materials applied to the surface of soil in order to enrich it, suppress annual weeds and help to keep the soil warm and moist. Well-rotted organic material used as a mulch, rather than being dug into the soil, breaks down more slowly and reduces the speed of nutrients being leached.

Fertilisers provide little or no humus, but have concentrated salts – for example, superphosphate of lime, sulphate of ammonia and sulphate of potash – which supplement the soil's own nutrients.

TYPES OF FERTILISER

Both artificial and organic fertilisers supplement the three principal nutrients that are essential to the growth of healthy plants – nitrogen, phosphorus and potassium. These chemicals can be bought separately or combined in a general-purpose fertiliser. Growmore, for example, consists of equal amounts of nitrogen, phosphorus and potassium, in the form of sulphate of ammonia, superphosphate of lime and sulphate of potash.

Nitrogen produces growth. Too much of it creates lush, leafy soft growth; too little results in small yellow leaves and lack of vigour. Phosphorus is important to seedlings and in the formation of seeds. Too little turns leaves dull purple and slows down growth; too much causes premature ripening. Potassium enhances flower colour; it also improves resistance to pests and diseases and hardens the tissues. Other nutrients, called trace elements, are also necessary for healthy growth, but in tiny quantities. They are present in a number of fertiliser formulations, including those based on seaweed. Trace-element deficiencies can often be remedied with a foliar feed (see below). Slow-release formulas, such as Osmacote and Vitex Q4, also contain trace elements, and are ideal on permanent plantings.

As well as being sold as powder, pellets or granules (for slow release), fertilisers are available in liquid form which can be applied to the roots of a plant for rapid absorption. Alternatively, they are sold as foliar feeds, applied with a watering can and rapidly absorbed through the leaves. Liquid fertilisers are available as a balanced feed for general purposes, or as mixtures for specific plants, such as roses, tomatoes and carnations.

Fertilisers must be applied according to the manufacturer's instruction or the result may be counterproductive. Always wear gloves when handling fertilisers in dry form.

HOW TO MAKE A COMPOST HEAP

The decomposed remains of garden waste and kitchen peelings, combined with a limited amount of shredded paper, coffee grounds and tea bags, provide a useful soil improver and source of humus. If quantities are small, they need to be mixed with other organic material brought in from elsewhere, such as straw and animal manure. Do not put fallen leaves on a compost heap; they take longer to decompose so rot them down separately in a wire-mesh bin to make leaf-mould.

To make a heap that rots quickly, use only soft material. Grass cuttings can be used if they are well mixed with other material. Never use cooked food, diseased plants, weeds carrying seeds, or the roots of perennial weeds such as couch grass, oxalis or bindweed. Woody material, such as prunings, need to be shredded before being added to the heap.

Build a container (preferably two) of slats and posts plus a lid, or buy ready-made ones.

• FIVE STEPS TO GOOD COMPOST •

1 The compost heap should be at least 1 m (3 ft) square and about 1 m high, but if possible make it larger. The bigger the heap the hotter and more efficient the result. Start with a 15 cm (6 in) layer of woody stems and prunings to allow air to penetrate the heap.

2 Mix together enough soft vegetable material to form a layer 15 cm (6 in) deep.

A layer of animal manure can be placed on top of the vegetable matter to aid decomposition.

If possible, build up the heap in 15 cm (6 in) layers. If you have no manure, add to each layer a proprietary compost starter or other source of nitrogen such as sulphate of ammonia or dried blood.

3 To keep in the heat produced by decomposition, cover the heap with perforated plastic sheeting, topped by an old carpet, or by the compost-bin lid. The covering will also prevent the heap from drying out or becoming too wet.

4 The heap should not need watering. If it becomes soggy, mix in dry material, such as straw; if it seems too dry, add soft leafy material or grass mowings. Turn the heap twice to aerate it.

5 When the heap becomes dark and crumbly – in three to six months, but longer in winter – it can be forked into the soil or spread round plants as a mulch, but first make sure the soil is moist.

The uses of foliar feeding

Foliar feeds enter a plant's sap stream slightly quicker than fertiliser applied to the soil, but by only a day or two. However, foliar feeding is useful for giving a boost to plants growing in containers, as the leaves will absorb nutrients even though the roots are restricted.

Foliar feeds are often used to apply trace elements, such as iron for plants that are growing on alkaline soil, or to rectify other mineral deficiencies.

To make a foliar feed, mix a normal-strength solution of liquid fertiliser, following the instructions on the packet. Spray it on the plants – the finer the droplets the more readily they are absorbed.

Organic manures and fertilisers

MATERIAL	CHARACTERISTICS	SOURCE	APPLICATION
BARK (COMPOSTED)	Bark increases the soil's humus content, protects roots, suppresses weeds and retains moisture. It also increases the acidity of the soil. Softwood bark is more acidic and contains fewer nutrients than hardwood bark.	Garden centres and mail-order companies. Use only commercially bagged supplies which have been detoxified. Avoid cheap bulk supplies.	Surface mulch and soil-texture improver. Use with a nitrogen-rich fertiliser. As a surface mulch, spread it 5 cm (2 in) thick. As a soil conditioner dig in 4–8 kg per m² (7–14 lb per sq yd).
BONEMEAL	Has 20–25% phosphorus and 3–6% nitrogen. A good slow-release fertiliser.	Garden centres and mail-order companies, in bags.	Good for use in autumn and winter. Use 140–200 g per m² (4–6 oz per sq yd). To apply as a liquid manure, add to water, stir well and apply at once.
COIR/ COCONUT FIBRE	Good moisture-holding capacity but tends to dry out quickly on the surface. Little nutrient value.	Garden centres and by mail order.	Use as an alternative to peat when making up composts for potting and propagation. For ecological reasons coir is not recommended for large-scale use as a soil conditioner or mulch.
DRIED BLOOD	Has about 12% nitrogen content. One of the fastest-acting fertilisers. Good for spring and summer.	Sold in bags at garden centres and by mail order.	Before sowing or planting in spring or summer and to plants in growth. Apply 35–100 g per m² (1–3 oz per sq yd). It is not fully soluble but it can be used as a liquid manure if stirred well and applied at once at a rate of 15–30 g per 4.5 litres (½–1 oz per gallon) of water.
FARMYARD MANURE	Well-balanced plant food, containing nitrogen, phosphorus and potassium. Avoid on acid soils. Horse manure is richer, dryer and more open-textured than pig or cattle manure. When mixed with straw and rotted, it is a soil improver, source of organic matter and protective, weed-suppressing mulch.	Farms, stables (when it is often mixed with straw) and garden centres. Quality varies according to the animals' diet and how manure is stored. Ideally, buy it fresh from a farm and add it to the compost heap to rot. Proprietary brands are an acceptable substitute, but are concentrated and expensive.	Use decayed or composted manure as a top dressing – either neat or mixed with an equal measure of soil. Apply it only in spring or summer – one wheelbarrowful of well-rotted manure to each 10 m² (12 sq yd) per year.
FISH, BLOOD AND BONE	About 3% nitrogen and 8% phosphorus.	Garden centres and by mail order.	In late winter or early spring, use as a general-purpose soil dressing before putting plants in a bed or sowing seeds. Apply 140 g per m² (4 oz per sq yd).
GARDEN COMPOST	Soil improver and source of organic matter. As a mulch, it retains moisture and protects roots from frost. Dug in, it improves soil texture.	See facing page.	Spread it 5 cm (2 in) thick as a mulch. To improve the soil dig in generously, as with farmyard manure.
GREEN MANURE	Organic material rich in nitrogen, such as mustard, rape and clover. Dug in it improves soil fertility; as a mulch it retains moisture and protects roots from frost. Use it to supplement manure or fertiliser. Also grow it as a winter ground cover to prevent nutrients from being washed through the soil.	Sow your own where it is to be used, following the instructions on the seed packet.	Sow in autumn. Cut down to ground when 20 cm (8 in) high, and dig into the soil two days later while still green. As a mulch, cut and lay it 5 cm (2 in) thick over the soil.
HOOF AND HORN MEAL	Contains 12–14% nitrogen. Coarse-ground meal is slower acting than fine-ground.	Garden centres and by mail order, but expensive.	Apply in spring and summer at 90 g per m² (2½ oz per sq yd).

MATERIAL	CHARACTERISTICS	SOURCE	APPLICATION
LEAF-MOULD	A nutritious mulch, but needs anchoring with sand, bark or netting. Also good as a soil-texture improver. Compost separately from other organic material for at least a year.	Garden centres or homemade.	Use leaf-mould with a nitrogen-rich fertiliser, which will help to break it down. As a mulch spread a layer 2.5 cm (1 in) thick. As a soil improver, dig in 2.5 kg per m² (5 lb per sq yd).
MUSHROOM COMPOST	Has nitrogen, phosphorus and potassium, according to nature of compost. Good improver of soil texture. Contains lime, so do not use it on alkaline soil or on lime-hating plants.	Garden centres or mushroom growers.	As a surface mulch at any time. Or dig in up to 11 kg per m² (20 lb per sq yd). Good way of raising pH if the soil is acid.
PEAT	Peat has little value as plant food, but for several decades has been a valuable ingredient in composts used for propagation. It can also be used to bulk up soil-based compost when it is used in large containers or small raised beds. Difficult to re-wet once it has dried out.	Garden centres and by mail order.	To make your own compost for raising cuttings, mix 50% peat with 50% horticultural sand (measured by volume). Large-scale use of peat is not recommended because its extraction destroys unique wildlife habitats. Alternatives include coir and composted bark.
SEAWEED MEAL	Contains about 2% nitrogen, 2% phosphorus, and is rich in trace elements. Acts as a soil conditioner and encourages plant growth. Particularly useful on poor soil.	Garden centres and by mail order.	Use in autumn as a general-purpose fertiliser/soil conditioner, or three months before planting, at 140 g per m² (4 oz per sq yd).
WOOD ASH	An alkaline material and good source of potassium. Amount of potassium varies between 15% and 4%. Keep it dry to prevent nutrients from being washed out, or add it to the compost heap.	Bonfires or wood-burning stoves.	Use wood ash to reduce acidity of soil. May be used at any time of the year. Apply up to 140 g per m² (4 oz per sq yd). As a liquid 15 g per 4.5 litres (½ oz per gallon) of water.

Inorganic fertilisers

MATERIAL	CHARACTERISTICS	SOURCE	APPLICATION
PHOSPHATE OF POTASH	Roughly 50% phosphorus, 35% potassium. Soluble fertiliser and highly concentrated. Good liquid fertiliser during growth.	Garden centres but expensive.	At any time of year. As a liquid fertiliser use up to 15 g per 4.5 litres (½ oz per gallon) of water. Or dig in 140 g per m² (4 oz per sq yd).
ROCK PHOSPHATE	Contains about 3% nitrogen and 20% phosphorus. It is a slow-acting fertiliser which is used as an alternative to bone meal.	Garden centres.	Use in the same way as bone meal. Apply in autumn or winter – either before planting or raked into the soil as a top dressing – at 120 g per m² (3½ oz per sq yd).
SULPHATE OF AMMONIA	Contains 20% nitrogen and is used in many compound fertilisers. Fairly rapid action. Good on limy soils but increases the acidity of acid soils. Must be stored in a dry place.	Garden centres.	Use in spring or early summer. Never mix it with lime as ammonia gas will be released, wasting nitrogen. Apply up to 75 g per m² (2 oz per sq yd) of soil. As a liquid manure, use 15 g per 4.5 litres (½ oz per gallon) of water.
SULPHATE OF MAGNESIUM (EPSOM SALTS)	Has 10% magnesium, is soluble and quick-acting, so best used as a foliar feed. Less a fertiliser than a supplement of magnesium.	Garden centres.	Use in spring and summer. Apply up to 75 g per m² (2 oz per sq yd). As a liquid spray use 15 g per 4.5 litres (½ oz per gallon) of water.
SULPHATE OF POTASH	Contains 48% potassium. Holds well in the soil.	Garden centres.	Use at any time of the year. Apply up to 140 g per m² (4 oz per sq yd). As a liquid, use 15 g per 4.5 litres (½ oz per gallon) of water.
SUPERPHOS-PHATE OF LIME	Contains 12-18% phosphoric acid. Quick-acting, reasonably soluble fertiliser. Despite its name, it will not increase soil alkalinity as the lime is a form of gypsum.	Garden centres.	Use alone or mixed with other fertilisers in spring or early summer. Apply up to 140 g per m² (4 oz per sq yd). As a liquid, mix 30 g per 4.5 litres (1 oz per gallon) of water.

Gardening the organic way

Organic gardening is gardening with the wider environment in mind. It relies on natural methods to control pests and to build up the fertility of the soil. Organic gardening recycles farm and garden wastes rather than disposing of them in ways that would pollute the environment

ENRICHING THE SOIL

The starting point for effective organic gardening is to create soil that holds moisture but drains well and encourages extensive root growth. It will provide plants with a balanced, slow-release diet to promote steady growth. The plants will then be less prone to attack by pests and diseases than chemically fed plants.

The ground should be cultivated as little as possible. Don't walk on the soil when it is wet, and keep it covered with growing plants or a mulch wherever possible.

SOIL IMPROVERS To improve the soil, use garden compost and leaf-mould – made by recycling kitchen and garden waste – augmented with brought-in ingredients such as animal manure and extra autumn leaves. Do not use manures derived from intensive farming systems because of the higher levels of food additives, antibiotics and other chemicals.

Garden compost, well-rotted manure, mushroom compost, hay, seaweed, cocoa shells and grass cuttings are all rich in nutrients. Use them only during the spring or summer. If they are applied when plants are not actively growing, their goodness will be leached from the soil and wasted.

Low-nutrient materials, such as straw, leaf-mould, composted bark and prunings chopped up in a shredder, may be applied at any time of the year and in any quantity.

If possible, use one wheelbarrow load of well-rotted farmyard manure or two barrow loads of garden compost to each $10\,m^2$ (12 sq yd) of ground each year.

Organic soil improvers can be used either as a surface mulch or mixed with the top 15 cm (6 in) layer of soil. A mulch acts as an insulating layer and should be applied to warm, wet soil only.

Unrotted soil improvers, such as hay, straw, seaweed and grass cuttings, can be composted first or added straight to the garden. If they are not composted, use them as a mulch.

GREEN MANURES Plants grown specifically to benefit the soil's fertility and structure are called green manures. They may be dug into the soil or cut and used as a mulch, and are especially useful in the vegetable garden. Grazing rye, for example, can be grown in winter as a soil cover to prevent plant nutrients being washed out. It also improves the structure of the soil and prevents weeds. Other plants used as green manures are clover, *Phacelia tanacetifolia*, mustard, fenugreek and winter tares. All can be bought as seeds.

SLOW-RELEASE FERTILISERS AND MINERAL SUPPLEMENTS Fertilisers of natural origin – plant, animal and rock – release their nutrients slowly. They can be used to adjust a major deficiency, or where compost and other materials are not available in sufficient quantities. They include hoof and horn, fish blood and bone meal, rock phosphate, dolomite limestone (to raise alkalinity), vinash (a by-product of the wine industry), seaweed meal, calcified seaweed, crab shells, gypsum and sulphur.

MAKING ORGANIC LIQUID MANURE

In organic gardening the aim is to feed the soil, which feeds the plants. Although liquid feeds do not strictly comply with this aim because they supply the plant more or less directly, their use can be essential when plants are grown in pots, tubs and other containers. And you can make your own.

NETTLE LIQUID Soak 1 kg of nettle tops in 10 litres of water (2 lb to 2 gallons) for two weeks. Strain the mixture and use one part of the nettle liquid in ten parts of water. Be prepared – this is a smelly process.

▲ Soak nettles in water for two weeks to make liquid manure.

COMFREY LIQUID Find a bucket or barrel with a small hole in the bottom and stuff it with comfrey (*Symphytum*) leaves. Place a container beneath the hole to catch the black liquid which will seep out as the leaves decay – after about two weeks. Dilute this 10 to 20 times with water before using.

CONTROLLING PESTS AND DISEASES

A great deal of pest control occurs naturally – ladybirds eating greenfly, beetles eating weevils, frogs eating slugs, and so on. And there are many things that can be done to encourage these gardener's allies (see page 32). Plants are

PREVENTATIVE METHODS OF PLANT PROTECTION

Barriers, traps and scaring devices are available to protect plants from pests, and from the diseases that they can introduce.

NETTING

Netting is used to exclude birds, rabbits, cats and other large pests. Fleece and other fine-mesh crop covers can be used to keep out smaller pests, such as greenfly, cabbage caterpillars, cabbage and carrot root fly, flea beetles and weevils. Lightweight covers can be laid directly over plants, or supported on canes or wire hoops.

PLASTIC BOTTLES

Cut the bottom off plastic bottles and stand them over young plants to protect them from slugs, snails and other pests. The larger the bottle the more growing space for the plant, but take care not to trap a slug inside. The bottles also act as cloches, protecting plants against the weather.

STICKY TRAPS AND BARRIERS

Cards covered with a non-drying glue, available from garden centres, can trap greenhouse pests, including whitefly. Protect fruit trees and shrubs from climbing pests, such as winter moth and ants, with grease bands or with fruit-tree grease applied to the trunks. Apply the bands above any supporting stakes or to the stakes as well.

PHEROMONE-BAITED TRAPS

Use traps baited with synthetic pheromones (female sex hormones) to catch codling moths and plum moths. The male moths are lured away from the females which remain unfertilised, and so the population is reduced.

capable of withstanding low concentrations of pests, which provide useful feeding grounds for the pests' predators.

HELPING PLANTS TO HELP THEMSELVES

Choosing the right plant for the right place is essential. A sun-loving plant will not thrive in shade; roses will always be more prone to powdery mildew in dry soils – especially in a small dry bed against a house; and hostas will be eaten by slugs in moist conditions.

Buy plants that look healthy and are not pot-bound. When buying fruit trees and bushes, choose plants that are certified as being virus-free. Consider planting resistant varieties if you know that a problem is likely to occur, and when transplanting, choose sturdy plants that will grow quickly.

THE IMPORTANCE OF TIMING

Avoid sowing too early, before the soil has warmed up. Slow-growing seedlings are much more likely to succumb to pests or diseases.

In the greenhouse, a heated bench is an effective remedy against 'damping off' early in the season. Outdoors, if an early start is required, soil can be warmed with cloches or a sheet of clear plastic for a couple of weeks before planting. And cloches can be left on after planting until the weather improves.

By carefully sowing at the right time, and avoiding periods when plants are particularly at risk, some pests and diseases, such as pea moth, pea mildew and potato-cyst eelworms, can be avoided (see 'Directory of Pests', p.824).

CROP ROTATION

Vegetable growers rotate crops every year, only returning to the original site after three or four years. Perennials, shrubs and trees are not suitable for regular rotation, but the same principles apply. Never replace a rose with another rose, for example. Likewise, new fruit trees and bushes are best planted in a fresh position where the same type of fruit has not been grown for several years.

DEALING WITH AN ATTACK

When a problem arises, first identify the cause (see 'Pests' p.824 and 'Diseases and Disorders' p.838). Fruitless hours can be wasted trying to eliminate a pest when, for example, the cause may be a disease, mineral deficiency or virus.

BIOLOGICAL CONTROL

The section 'Allies in the Gardener's World' (p.32) illustrates the wide range of creatures that are on the gardener's side, helping to keep pests and diseases under control.

A major drawback is that they are not always present in large enough numbers when you want them. One solution is to purchase suitable creatures in quantity to release when a particular pest occurs.

Predators and parasites that are commercially produced – and are usually known as biological control agents – are available from some garden centres and mail-order catalogues. They can be used to deal with a range of pests occurring in both the greenhouse and the open garden, including glasshouse whitefly, red spider mite, mealy bug, aphids, vine weevil and slugs.

HAND PICKING

An effective way of dealing with a small outbreak of pests or diseases is to pick, squash or cut out the problem area. Regular 'health' checks can prevent problems getting out of hand.

SPRAYING

In an organic garden try to avoid the use of any pesticide sprays. If spraying is essential, use a non-persistent pesticide such as derris, pyrethrum, insecticidal soap or sulphur. Follow the instructions on the label, and treat only those plants that are infected.

▲ If a plant is badly infested, spray with insecticidal soap.

CONTROLLING WEEDS

Organic gardeners control weeds by digging, hoeing, mulching and hand weeding; there are no organic weed-killers. In some cases, weeds can be useful. For example, clover in a lawn extracts nitrogen from the air and feeds the grass. Other weeds provide food and shelter for garden allies.

USING A MULCH

Since weeds cannot grow in the dark, covering the soil with a mulch will inhibit or prevent their growth. The ultimate effect, however, will depend on how much light the mulch keeps out.

LIVING MULCHES

Close-growing plants help to keep the soil free of weeds as they compete with them for light and space.

BIODEGRADABLE MULCHES

Organic material that gradually decays in the soil is more appropriate in a 'green' garden than sheets of black polythene. The choice of material depends on the appearance you want to achieve. Bark chips, for exam-

▲ Bark chips make an attractive mulch in an organic garden.

ple, may be more pleasing to the eye than grass cuttings in an ornamental border.

For the effective control of weeds, use a minimum 10cm (4in) layer of mulch. A thinner layer may be used over a skin of cardboard, newspaper or a synthetic membrane. The following are all effective mulches: leaf-mould, shredded prunings, cocoa shells, straw, hay, wood chips (from garden centres), bark chips and grass cuttings.

Planting new perennials, shrubs and trees

Whether a new plant comes in a container or with bare roots, the correct planting technique is essential if it is to get off to a rapid and healthy start.

ESTABLISHING A NEW • CONTAINER-GROWN PLANT •

Container-grown shrubs are sold in plastic pots of compost. They can be planted at any time of the year, but if you plant them in summer make sure to keep the soil moist until the autumn.

1 Remove all weeds from the bed, and dig over the soil to a spade's depth. Then firm the soil with your feet.

2 Dig a hole as deep as, and slightly wider than, the plant's container. The surface of the compost in the container should be level with the surrounding soil.

3 Break up the soil at the bottom of the hole with a fork and incorporate some organic material. Separately, mix some soil with more of the organic material.

4 Water the plant thoroughly. Then remove the container and check the extent of the root system (right). If the roots are wound around the outside of the rootball, gently tease out some of the outer roots so they will establish more quickly in the surrounding soil.

5 Holding the plant by the stem, and with one hand supporting the ball of soil, place it in the hole (left). Fill the hole to the top with the planting mixture and tread it down firmly. Top up with more of the mixture, tread down again and water thoroughly. Finally mulch the soil around the plant.

PLANTING BARE-ROOT TREES
• AND SHRUBS •

Bare-rooted trees and shrubs are ordered from a nursery in advance and delivered between November and March. They should be planted as soon as possible after delivery, but not when the ground is frozen.

1 Prepare the planting hole in advance so that the tree or shrub can be planted without delay. Make the hole large enough for the roots to be spread out completely. Fork over the base of the hole and incorporate some organic matter such as garden compost.

2 Before planting the tree or shrub, soak the roots in water for two hours and trim off any broken or damaged roots.

3 Hold the plant in the hole so that the mark on the stem indicating the old soil level matches ground level (left). Fill in with a mixture of soil and organic material. Gently shake the plant up and down so that soil settles around the roots. Firm the soil with your fingers to eliminate any air.

4 Check the finished planting level; it should coincide with the soil mark on the stem. Finally, firm the soil with your heel. Water thoroughly and mulch the soil around the plant, leaving a gap of 10cm (4in) around the base of the stem.

PLANTING A CLIMBING SHRUB
• AGAINST A WALL OR FENCE •

Climbers of borderline hardiness need a warm and sheltered spot, facing south or west. North and east-facing borders receive less sunshine and are exposed to the coldest winds. East-facing borders tend to be very dry because they are sheltered from the rain-bearing winds, which mostly come from the west.

1 The soil at the foot of a wall or fence is usually dry, so before planting dig in plenty of organic matter, such as garden compost, and give it a soaking. Make sure the soil is kept moist in future. Plant a climber 30cm (12in) away from the fence so it benefits from rain.

2 Ivy, Virginia creeper and climbing hydrangea fasten themselves to a fence and need no assistance once they have become established, but most other climbers need support throughout their lives. Put up trellis, horizontal wires or rigid plastic netting with a mesh size of 10-15cm (4-6in). Fix it on battens 2.5cm (1in) away from the wall. Fasten shoots with string or a wire plant ring.

HOW TO TRANSPLANT
• ESTABLISHED SHRUBS •

Shrubs – either deciduous or evergreen – can be moved to a new part of the garden in autumn or spring, but not when the soil is frozen or waterlogged. Small, young shrubs transplant most easily.

1 Dig a trench around the shrub – beneath the outer edge of the canopy. Then dig under and lever it out. Crumble away loose soil to lighten the plant and limit the size of its new hole. Slip a tarpaulin or strong plastic sheet under the shrub and get someone to help you to move it. Trim off any diseased or damaged roots.

2 Dig the planting hole as deep as, and wider than, the rootball. Mix two parts of soil from the hole with one part of well-rotted compost, manure or composted bark. Hold the plant in place so that the top of the rootball is flush with the new ground level, and fill in around the plant with the prepared soil mixture.

3 Tread the soil down firmly and top up with more of the planting mixture. Water the soil thoroughly and apply a feed.

STAKING A YOUNG
• TREE •

Until a young tree has established a root system – which takes from two to three years – it is vulnerable to wind damage and unable to support its own weight. Stout wooden stakes impregnated with preservative, and various ties for restraining trees to the stakes, can be bought from most garden centres.

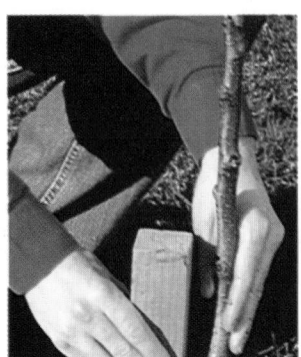

1 Drive the stake in 60 cm (2 ft) before planting, so that the roots do not get damaged.

2 The top of the stake should reach about one-third of the way up the trunk.

3 After planting the tree, secure it as close as possible to the top of the stake in order to reduce the danger of rubbing. Use a plastic strap-and-buckle that has a rubber buffer. Loop the strap around the tree and thread it through the buffer. Pull the strap tight, then buckle it around the stake.

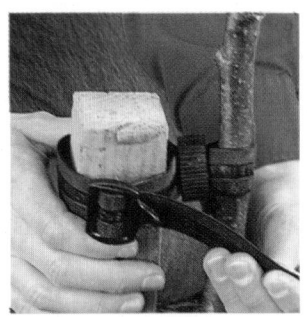

4 Check the tie at least twice a year, loosening or tightening as necessary so as not to chafe or strangle the trunk. The tree should be independent of the stake after three years.

Giving support to perennials and annuals

TWIGGY FRAMEWORK Most tall perennials and annuals need supporting during the growing season. Twiggy branches pruned from your own trees make good supports, and they will soon become invisible as the plants grow. Push each branch into the soil between the plants. Bend the tops over and interlock them to form a framework that the plants will grow through.

SUPPORT BY TWIGS

BAMBOO CANES AND STRING A cheap but time-consuming method is to use canes and garden string, fillis or raffia – not wire or nylon cord, which will cut into the plant stems. Place three or four canes in the soil around a plant, and link them at two or three levels – not above the plant – with the string. Add new layers of string as the plants grow taller.

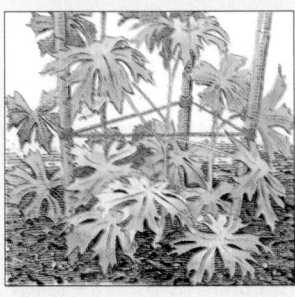

CANE-AND-STRING FRAME

HEAVY CANES OR NETTING Thick-stemmed plants can be tied to canes. As the plant grows, the canes may need to be replaced with thicker, longer ones. Nylon netting or chicken wire stretched horizontally between wooden stakes can make an effective support for plants in an herbaceous border.

PURPOSE-MADE SYSTEMS Many plant-support systems are available from garden centres. Some consist of interlocking metal stakes which can be linked together to create miniature scaffolding; others have adjustable ring supports through which the plants grow. They vary in cost and finish, and are reusable for several years.

METAL 'SCAFFOLDING'

Four ways of staking a tree

SHORT VERTICAL STAKE
A short stake allows the upper part of a tree to move in the wind, strengthening the trunk as it develops. The tie is made a third of the way up the trunk – usually about 50 cm (20 in) high on a normal tree. Loosen the tie once or twice a year as the tree grows.

SHORT DIAGONAL STAKE
As the stake is placed on an angle, the bottom end is well away from the tree's roots. So this is a good way of staking a container-grown tree. The stake should lean into the prevailing wind, and the tie should still be 50 cm (20 in) high.

TWO STAKES AND A CROSSBAR
Two stakes are used to give greater support in an exposed situation. The tree is tied to the centre of a crossbar 50 cm (20 in) from the ground. This sturdy frame is suitable for a fairly large tree. As with all methods, remove the stakes after three or four years.

GUY-ROPE STAKING
To hold large trees while they establish themselves, three stakes can be driven into the ground at an angle, with guy ropes attached to the trunk. Proprietary systems can be bought which include guy ropes with rubber anti-friction tubes.

Planting and caring for bulbs and corms

Most bulbs perform best in a sunny position, but cyclamens, endymions, erythroniums and eranthis (winter aconites) grow well in shade. Crocus, galanthus (snowdrops) and eranthis thrive under trees and shrubs. Gladioli, amaryllis, nerines and sparaxis are sensitive to cold and are best planted at the foot of a south-facing wall where they will get plenty of sun and protection from cold wind. Plant spring-flowering bulbs between September and November. Plant summer-flowering bulbs in March – or April/May for the less-hardy types. Plant autumn-flowering bulbs in July/August.

• PREPARING THE SOIL •

1 Several days before planting, dig the ground and remove weeds and stones. Good drainage is essential so add gravel to heavy soil.

2 Mix plenty of well-rotted garden compost, leaf-mould or composted bark into the soil – a bucketful to the square metre – and leave it to settle for a few days.

3 A slow-release fertiliser such as bone meal or seaweed meal, can also be added, but is not essential.

• PUTTING IN THE BULBS •

1 Using a narrow trowel, or a bulb planter (shown below), dig holes about twice as deep as the bulbs. In clay or loam soil, put a little sharp sand or grit in the bottom of the hole. Insert each bulb point upwards. Gently press and twist the bulb so that it makes firm contact with the earth. Then cover it with the excavated soil.

If new bedding plants or herbaceous perennials are to be planted at the same time, put them in before the bulbs.

2 Mark and label the position of each group of bulbs so that you do not disturb them before the shoots appear.

PLANTING BULBS AMONG MAT-FORMING PLANTS
Loosen the surface slightly with a hand fork, then use a blunt dibber to make holes for the bulbs. Under plants that have only a single root, such as *Gypsophila repens*, roll the matted stems to one side and plant the bulbs with a narrow trowel.

• LIFTING AND STORING BULBS •

Bulbs may need to be lifted to survive the winter, or to make room for other plants, or because they are too congested.

Ideally, spring-flowering bulbs, including hyacinths, narcissi and tulips, should not be touched until the foliage has died down. Then they can be split up and replanted straight away. But the demands on space for summer bedding plants may mean that the bulbs need to be moved to another position where they can die down naturally.

1 With a garden fork, ease the bulbs from the ground, complete with the leaves, stems and soil. Then crumble off the soil without damaging the skins. Throw away any bulbs that are pulpy or rotting, and move the remaining ones to a spare bed in an area of the garden that is lightly shaded.

2 Dig a trench 30 cm (12 in) deep and wide. Lay a length of fine-mesh wire netting or plastic netting along the bottom of the trench so that it protrudes a little at each end.

3 Place the bulbs along the netting – almost but not quite touching each other – with at least half their stems and leaves clear of the trench. Fill in the trench to cover the bulbs and water them in. This will allow the bulbs to build up their reserves to produce flowers the following growing season.

When the leaves and stems have shrivelled, pull the netting at each end of the trench to lift the bulbs clear. Lay them in deep trays of moist compost or coir, with the leaves uncovered, and leave them in a lightly shaded place to finish drying out. When the leaves have withered completely, clean off the dead leaves, roots and shrivelled skins. Use any bulblets attached to the mother bulb for propagation, or discard them. Place the bulbs in shallow boxes, in single layers and uncovered, and store them in a cool dry place until replanting time.

• LIFTING AND STORING CORMS IN WINTER •

In areas where the weather is mild, gladioli, ixias and sparaxis corms may be left in the ground throughout the year. Elsewhere, when the leaves begin to brown in October, the corms should be lifted.

1 Carefully lift the corms with a fork. Cut off the top stems and leaves to within about 2.5 cm (1 in) of the corm. Place the corms in trays and leave uncovered for seven to ten days in a cool airy shed to dry.

2 Break away old shrivelled corms and put aside any small cormlets for increasing stock. Remove the tough outer skins from the large corms and burn any that appear to have lesions or that are rotting.

Dust the corms with pirimiphos-methyl to control thrips. To prevent dry rot and gladiolus scab, dust with sulphur or dip in a solution of carbendazim. Store in trays in a cool but frost-free place until spring.

Forcing bulbs for indoor display

In early autumn, plant bulbs in pots of compost – or if the container has no drainage hole, use bulb fibre. Daffodils, tulips and crocuses can be planted alternately in two layers, but keep hyacinths in a single layer. Moisten the compost, wrap the bowl in newspaper and put it in the dark in a shed. After six or eight weeks check for growth. Then move the container into a light, cool room. When buds are visible, put the container on display.

Pruning Shrubs and Climbers

Pruning is a way of controlling a plant's growth. It may encourage its vigour, alter its size and shape, or improve its flowers and foliage. Not all shrubs need annual pruning; many need only occasional tidying up

Six main methods of pruning

Pruning tools

Three types of tool will cope with all normal pruning needs for shrubs and small trees.

ANVIL SECATEURS

BYPASS SECATEURS

• Secateurs (either anvil or bypass types) are used for pruning most shrubs and evergreen hedging plants.

LONG–HANDLED LOPPERS

• A pair of long-handled loppers are needed for cutting thick shoots and branchlets on shrubs and small trees.

PRUNING SAW

• A pruning saw is necessary for cutting off large branches.

Keep all your pruning tools clean and sharp so that they work efficiently. To avoid the danger of spreading diseases, it is advisble to clean secateurs with a garden sterilant after use.

• METHOD 1 •

Shrubs which flower on previous year's wood

Some shrubs produce their flowers on shoots that developed the previous year. They can be pruned immediately after they finish flowering. This encourages fewer but larger flowers and keeps the shrub's growth within bounds.

WHEN TO PRUNE
Just as soon as the flowers have died down.

HOW TO PRUNE

▲ Pruning *Buddleja alternifolia* after flowering.

Cut back each shoot that has borne flowers to two or three shoots or buds from its junction with the main stem. This will reduce the shrub to its main framework. The new shoots that then grow in the coming months will produce flowers the following season.

WHICH SHRUBS TO PRUNE
Buddleja alternifolia, Cytisus (all species except *C.* 'Porlock'), *Deutzia, Kerria, Mahonia aquifolium* (when it is used as ground cover), *Prunus glandulosa, P. triloba, Rubus, Spiraea* 'Arguta', *Weigela.*

• METHOD 2 •

Shrubs which flower on the new shoots

Some shrubs flower on the new shoots that grow each year. They can be pruned in the spring as the shoots start to grow. The method of pruning is used to restrict a shrub's size or to encourage larger but fewer flowers.

WHEN TO PRUNE
In early spring, when the severe weather is over and new shoots are beginning to grow.

HOW TO PRUNE
Cut back last year's flowered shoots to two or three buds or green shoots before the old shoots meet a main branch. Unless you need to remove a branch altogether, avoid cutting back into the older wood because new shoots might not grow. After pruning, mulch with a 5 cm (2 in) layer of rotted manure or garden compost, and feed with a general fertiliser at 75 g per m^2 (2 oz per sq yd).

WHICH SHRUBS TO PRUNE
Buddleja davidii, Caryopteris, Ceanothus (deciduous types), *Ceratostigma, Colutea, Cytisus* 'Porlock', *Fuchsia, Indigofera, Lippia, Passiflora, Santolina, Solanum crispum, Spartium, Spiraea japonica* 'Bullata', *S. × bumalda, S. douglasii, S. japonica, S. salicifolia, Tamarix ramosissima.*

▼ Pruning a caryopteris in spring.

• METHOD 3 •

Clearing out old growth from the centre

Some shrubs, including the common forsythia and *Hydrangea macrophylla* and its cultivars, are improved by having some of the oldest growth taken out low down on the bush every year. The technique is used to reduce overcrowding and allow sunlight to penetrate into the centre of the shrub.

WHEN TO PRUNE
Spring.

HOW TO PRUNE

▲ Pruning a Forsythia shrub in spring.

Cut out the oldest stems almost to the ground. These are rough-looking and have sub-laterals as well as laterals. Two-year-old stems – which have laterals only – may be removed if you wish.

WHICH SHRUBS TO PRUNE
Hydrangea macrophylla, and overgrown specimens of *Berberis, Clethra, Corylopsis, Cotoneaster, Forsythia, Genista, Kolkwitzia, Potentilla, Ribes sanguineum, Symphoricarpos.*

• METHOD 4 •

Cutting out dead and straggly growth

Most shrubs at some time become straggly or damaged, or a branch may have died. This is the technique to use for a general tidying up.
WHEN TO PRUNE
At any time of the year, as required.

How to make a pruning cut

Cut the stem just above an outward-facing shoot or bud, slanting the secateurs in the same direction as the shoot or bud. Avoid leaving a stump of the stem above the cut – it will be vulnerable to die-back or disease.

▲ Outward-facing shoot.

▲ Opposite shoots.

On a plant where the shoots or buds appear opposite each other, cut straight across the stem, just above them.

HOW TO PRUNE
Cut out diseased shoots to clean, healthy wood about 12.5 cm (5 in) below the diseased area. Cut back any dead or damaged branches to a healthy shoot or bud, facing outwards, near the ground. Any particularly weak shoots can be cut right back to the main branch. Prune straggly or unsightly branches by half, to a strong shoot or bud facing outwards. Do not remove well-shaped, healthy wood, as you will only remove buds that will produce flowers later.

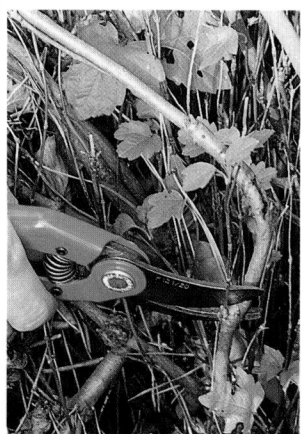

▲ Removing a damaged stem of *Viburnum opulus*.

WHICH SHRUBS TO PRUNE
Just a few of the most popular shrubs that can be pruned this way are *Camellia, Cistus, Daphne, Euonymus, Hebe, Potentilla* and *Viburnum*.

• METHOD 5 •

Rejuvenating large overgrown evergreens

Evergreens do not usually need routine pruning, apart from cutting out damaged stems or untidy growth. However, after several years they can become overgrown or bare at the base, and may then be given a very hard pruning. But, they will not flower the following year.
WHEN TO PRUNE
Early spring.
HOW TO PRUNE
Begin by using long-handled loppers to remove the top growth. Then, using a saw, cut off all the main branches down almost to ground level.

Mulch the ground around the shrub with well-rotted

▲ Cutting back an old specimen of *Pieris japonica*.

manure or garden compost, and apply a general-purpose fertiliser at the rate of 75 g per m² (2 oz per sq yd).
WHICH SHRUBS TO PRUNE
Aucuba (spotted laurel), *Olearia* (daisy bush), *Pernettya, Philadelphus* (mock orange), *Pieris, Prunus laurocerasus* and *P. lusitanica* (cherry laurels).

• METHOD 6 •

Restricting the size of climbing plants

Most climbing plants can be left unpruned until they have overrun their space. Then they may be pruned when the flowers have faded. For the pruning of *Clematis* and *Wisteria*, see the individual genus entries.
WHEN TO PRUNE
For flowering climbers, prune after the flowers have faded. For non-flowering climbers, prune in spring or summer.
HOW TO PRUNE
Cut back self-clinging climbers, such as ivy, as far as necessary on the wall. Detach others from their supports first. Then prune all lateral growths, leaving the main stems, which can be shortened. Remove any very old stems, but keep younger ones that are growing from ground level or low down on the plant.

Finally, retie the remaining stems to the supports, spacing them evenly. Flowering climbers should bear blooms again the following year.
WHICH SHRUBS TO PRUNE
Actinidia, Campsis, Fallopia baldschuanica (Russian vine) *Hedera* (ivy), *Hydrangea anomala* ssp. *petiolaris* (climbing hydrangea),

Preventing reversion

Shrubs with variegated foliage may develop shoots with all-green foliage. These will grow more vigorously than the variegated shoots and will eventually take over the plant. Cut them out completely as soon as you notice them, right back to variegated growth.

All-gold or all-cream shoots may also appear and should be removed, although they tend to grow less vigorously than the variegated shoots.

Variegated shrubs which can show reversion include cultivars of *Elaeagnus, Euonymus* and *Ilex* (holly).

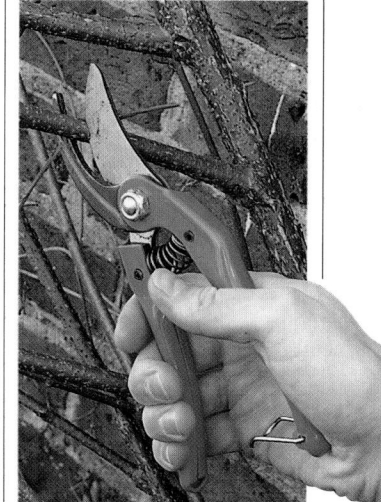

▲ Cutting back *Actinidia kolomikta* after flowering.

Lonicera japonica and *L. periclymenum* (honeysuckles), *Parthenocissus* (Virginia creeper), *Vitis* (grape vine).

How to Propagate Plants

You can multiply the plants in your garden at almost no cost by sowing seed or by taking pieces from your existing stock and growing them into young plants

Growing plants from seed

Raising seedlings under cover

Plants which cannot survive in the open during frosty weather, such as half-hardy annuals, are first sown in containers under cover – either in a greenhouse or indoors. The technique can also be used to bring on early blooms or crops. Sow the seeds between February and early April. You can buy them from a garden centre or collect them from your own plants. Use plastic containers, as they are strong and easy to clean. Small seed trays or 13 cm (5 in) pots are usually most suitable. Scrub containers that have been used before in warm soapy water.

• SOWING THE SEEDS •

1 Fill the container with slightly moist seed compost. When sowing very fine seeds, first sprinkle a little fine-sieved compost on the surface. Using the bottom of another pot, gently firm down the compost.

2 Sow seeds thinly and evenly. For easier control, fold the open flap to form a spout and carefully tap them out of the packet. Fine seed can be distributed more evenly if first mixed with a little silver sand.

3 Cover the seeds with a thin layer of sifted compost or vermiculite – a layer of about the seeds' own depth is enough. Some seeds should be left uncovered – very fine ones, such as begonias, lobelias and calceolarias, and those that need light to germinate, such as sinningias, streptocarpus and saintpaulias.

4 Identify the contents with a plastic label. Stand the container in water to half its depth until the compost is wet.

5 Ideally, put the container in a heated frame or propagator at a temperature of 12-18°C (54-64°F).
Alternatively, cover the container with a polythene bag and fold it underneath. Stand the container in a warm shady place, such as a shaded windowsill. For extra warmth put it in an airing cupboard, but check daily for germination and then immediately move it into the light.

6 Once the seeds have germinated, turn the bag inside out each day to prevent drips. When growth is established, take off the cover and move the container into good light, but not direct sun.

• PRICKING OUT •

1 Seedlings are ready to be pricked out' when the first true leaves appear above the seed leaves. Fill a standard seed tray – about 33×20 cm (13×8 in) – with moist potting compost and mark out plant holes about 4 cm (1½in) apart with a pointed stick or pencil.

2 Gently prise up a small clump of seedlings, complete with the compost clinging to the roots. Hold a seedling by a seed leaf – not the stem, which is easily damaged – and gently tease it from the other seedlings with the stick.

3 Lower the seedling into a hole and gently firm the soil down around it so that it will not yield if gently tugged. When the tray is full, label it and water the seedlings with a fine-rosed can.

4 Put the trays in a greenhouse or coldframe, or on a shaded windowsill. Three days later, move them to a sunnier, but lightly shaded, position. Keep the compost moist.

The danger of damping off

Seedlings planted too closely or overwatered may contract damping-off disease which causes rot at soil level. Remove and destroy dead seedlings or leaves and spray the rest with copper fungicide or Cheshunt compound. Next time, give your seedlings more space, and always use fresh compost and clean containers.

DAMPING OFF

Hardening off half-hardy annuals

In early May, or April in mild areas, move the seedlings of half-hardy annuals to an unshaded coldframe, cloche or polythene tunnel. For the first few days open the frame or raise the sides of the tunnel slightly. Gradually increase ventilation until – by mid May at the earliest (the end of May in northern England and frosty areas) – the coverings are completely open. Delay opening fully if the weather is cold, wet or windy. Close all openings at night until the danger of frost has passed.

PUT SEEDLINGS IN A COLDFRAME

GRADUALLY INCREASE VENTILATION

Growing seedlings outdoors

An outdoor seedbed needs careful preparation if the plants are to germinate successfully. It must be firm, moist and consist of a fine tilth. Dig heavy soil in autumn or winter to allow it to settle before the frost arrives. Light, sandy soils can be left until spring. There is no need to add organic matter; if the soil is poor, rake in a balanced fertiliser.

Hardy annuals are usually sown in March and April, but some can be sown in autumn to give the young plants a quick start in spring. Seed packets advise on the best times for sowing. Perennials are treated in the same way as hardy annuals, but if you collect seeds from your own plants sow them as soon as possible. The viability of seed decreases with time, so sow old seed more thickly than fresh. Discard any seed that is more than two years old.

Pelleted seeds, coated with clay or other material, are easier to handle but need to be kept moist until the seedlings appear. Primed, also called pregerminated, seed is available for plants that need high germination temperatures.

• PREPARING THE SEEDBED •

1 In warm weather, when the soil is dry enough to walk on without sticking to your boots, hoe or lightly fork it over to a depth of 7.5 cm (3 in). When the soil has dried out, tread it down firmly to break up lumps, then rake the surface to create a fine tilth (the particles should be small and evenly sized).

2 Prepare rows in the soil for sowing – running from north to south if possible so that the seedlings will receive the greatest amount of sunshine when they germinate. Space the rows according to the advice on the seed packet. Use the edge of a draw hoe to make shallow 'drills' about 1.5 cm (½ in) deep.

• SOWING THE SEED •

If the weather is dry, water the seedbed the day before sowing – not after sowing. Sow thinly to simplify thinning later. Or sow pinches of seeds at regular intervals according to the advice on the packet.

1 Mix very small seeds with fine sand to help to distribute them evenly. To control the seeds, dribble them from your hand between the folds in the skin.

2 To close the drills, use the back of a rake to pull the raised earth back over the seeds – working along the length of the rows, not across them.

3 Tamp soil down gently with the back of the rake. Be careful not to bury the seeds too deeply or to press the soil down too hard. As a rule of thumb, cover seeds with soil to about twice their size. Sow some surplus seeds at the end of rows to fill gaps later.

• THINNING OUT THE SEEDLINGS •

Seedlings are ready to be thinned out when they have two or three 'true leaves', above the first pair of 'seed leaves'. If the weather is particularly dry, thin in the evening and water the bed afterwards.

1 Lift the unwanted seedlings from the soil with one hand while holding down the soil around nearby seedlings with the other. Remove weak or malformed seedlings first.

2 Thin the rest so they are spaced at half the distance required. Do not leave discarded seedlings on the ground; they will attract pests, so put them on the compost heap.

3 When the leaves of adjacent plants touch, remove alternate seedlings to leave the row at the full spacing. Fill any gaps with the surplus seedlings that were sown at the end of the rows.

Growing new plants from cuttings

Cuttings can be taken from most parts of a plant, but the techniques vary according to the time of year. Different plants respond better to different methods. Take cuttings only from healthy, well-established plants. In general, the younger and softer the material, the faster it will root.

WHICH TECHNIQUE TO USE, AND WHEN

ROOT CUTTINGS
During late autumn or winter, pieces of root are removed and replanted. The method is suitable for perennials and shrubs that have fleshy roots, including bergenias, romneyas and oriental poppies. Do not take root cuttings from grafted plants; only the rootstock will grow.

LEAF CUTTINGS
Some houseplants are commonly propagated from leaf cuttings, which can be taken at any time of the year. There are three methods.
Leaf petiole A healthy leaf is taken from the parent plant and the stem (petiole) is inserted into compost. Suitable for peperomias and saintpaulias.
Leaf section A leaf is cut into pieces, each containing a portion of the main vein. The pieces are pushed vertically into the soil or laid across it. Suitable for sansevieria and streptocarpus.

▲ Hypericum growing from softwood cuttings.

Basal cuttings are taken of soft new growth from herbaceous perennials, just as it emerges from the soil. The technique is used for plants which become hollow-stemmed later in the season, such as dahlias, delphiniums and dendranthemas (chrysanthemums).
Softwood cuttings are taken in spring. The entire cutting consists of soft growth with no woodiness. Suitable for fuchsias and hydrangeas.
Greenwood cuttings are taken in early summer when the bottom end of the cutting is just beginning to ripen. Greenwood cuttings are slightly slower to root than softwood cuttings, but are less prone to wilt. Suitable for dendranthemas and pelargoniums (geraniums).
Semi-ripe cuttings are taken in July or August when most of the stem is fresh and green but the bottom end is turning ripe and brown. Suitable for forsythias, philadelphus and weigelas.
Ripewood cuttings are usually used for evergreens. The cuttings are taken in late summer or early autumn and left in a coldframe to root. Suitable for aucuba, escallonia and hebe.
Hardwood cuttings are taken in autumn – usually from deciduous shrubs – after the leaves have fallen and the stems have become woody. This is an easy method of propagation but the cuttings take the longest time to root.

▲ Plantlets from peperomia leaf-petiole cuttings.

Leaf slashing The underside of a leaf is slit across the main veins and the whole leaf laid flat on compost. New plants emerge from the slits. Most commonly used on rex-type begonias.

STEM CUTTINGS
Six types of cutting can be taken from a stem or shoot of a plant. The type of cutting that is used depends on the time of year and the state of development of the stem.

• ROOT CUTTINGS FOR PERENNIALS •

Herbaceous perennials are often propagated by division (see p. 820), but root cuttings are an excellent alternative.

1 During autumn or winter, lift the plant, wash off the soil and remove a root. Then replant the parent plant.

2 Cut thick or fleshy roots, as found on dicentras, oriental poppies and romneyas, into pieces 5-7.5 cm (2-3 in) long. Trim off any excess fibrous roots. Cut the upper end – nearest the plant – straight across and cut the lower end at a slant. This is in order to distinguish the top from the bottom when you put the cutting in the compost. Cut thin-rooted plants, such as phlox and verbascums, into 5 cm (2 in) pieces.

3 Fill a large pot with equal parts of peat and horticultural sand. For thick cuttings, make planting holes 5 cm (2 in) apart, and about 5-7.5 cm (2-3 in) deep. Insert each cutting, slanted end down, until the flat top is flush with the surface of the compost. Cover with 5 mm (1/4 in) of sand. Leave the pot of cuttings in a closed coldframe during winter.

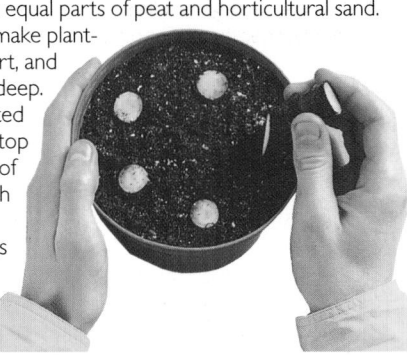

With thin cuttings, lay them flat on the surface of a seed tray filled with cuttings compost and cover with a layer of compost. Leave them in a closed coldframe throughout winter.

4 Pot the rooted cuttings individually in spring, when they have developed three or four pairs of leaves and also some roots which develop after the leaves. Up to this point water sparingly, if at all. Put each one in an 8 cm (3 in) pot of John Innes No.1 compost or a soilless equivalent and return them to the coldframe. Stand them outdoors through the summer, and plant them in their flowering positions in autumn.

LEAF-PETIOLE CUTTINGS FOR • SOME HOUSEPLANTS •

The easiest way of producing new plants from leaves is with leaf-petiole cuttings. The method is used for saintpaulias and peperomias. Clean equipment and fresh compost are essential as the cuttings are susceptible to rotting and disease. Cuttings can be taken at any time, as long as the leaves are new and fully developed, but they root faster in summer.

▶ Saintpaulia and peperomia plants.

1 Use a craft knife or garden knife to slice through a leaf stalk about 5 cm (2 in) from the leaf itself. Fill a seed tray with an equal mix of peat and perlite, or cuttings compost for African violets, and firm the surface until the compost is within 1 cm (3/8 in) of the rim.

2 Use a dibber or pencil to make a shallow hole in the compost. Insert the leaf at an angle so that it is almost lying flat in the compost but is firmly held by it. Press the compost down around the stalk. When all cuttings are planted, water them carefully with a fine spray.

3 Put the cuttings in a lightly shaded, bottom-heated propagator at a temperature of about 20°C (68°F).

4 As new plantlets start to appear, usually within five or six weeks, feed them with a liquid houseplant fertiliser. When they are large enough to be handled, put them into individual pots to harden off in a greenhouse or on a windowsill.

LEAF CUTTINGS FOR
• MOTHER-IN-LAW'S TONGUE •

1 During spring or summer, use a craft knife or garden knife to cut a healthy and fully expanded leaf from the plant, close to the crown. Cut the leaf at right angles to the midrib into a series of 2.5 cm (1 in) long sections. This is easiest to do on a hard, clean surface.

2 Fill a 13 cm (5 in) pot with moist cuttings compost. Press the leaf sections into the compost for half their depth, with the end nearest the leaf tip uppermost. Firm the compost and spray with water. Cover the pot with a polythene bag or put it in a heated propagator. Keep the cuttings out of direct sunlight in a constant temperature of 20°C (68°F).

3 In about six weeks, when the sections start to produce plantlets (left), remove the cover. Pot the plantlets singly in 8 cm (3 in) pots of John Innes No.1 compost or in a soilless potting compost.

LEAF SLASHING FOR
• LARGE-LEAVED BEGONIAS •

A single leaf, provided it is large enough, can be used to produce several new plants – a method commonly used for large-leaved begonias such as *Begonia masoniana* and *B. rex*.

1 At any time between June and September, select a mature healthy leaf that is fully expanded and cut it about 2.5 cm (1 in) from the base with a sharp knife. Make a series of fine cuts, about 2 cm (3/4 in) long, on the underside of the leaf across the major veins. This is easiest on a hard, clean surface.

2 Fill a seed tray with moist John Innes No.1 compost or cuttings compost. Lay the leaf, cut side down, on the compost and secure it with a few pebbles or wire staples. Cover with polythene. Keep the tray where it will receive light – but not direct sunlight – with a temperature of 20°C (68°F).

3 Little plantlets will start to sprout from the cuts in the veins within three or four weeks. Remove the polythene cover and leave the young plants to grow on in a warm and shady position for another two or three weeks.

4 Carefully separate the rooted cuttings and pot them individually in 8 cm (3 in) pots of potting compost.

• BASAL CUTTINGS FOR PERENNIALS •

As well as being propagated by division, many clump-forming perennials, such as dendranthemas (chrysanthemums), delphiniums and lupins, can be propagated from young basal shoots.

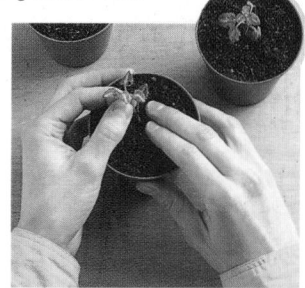

1 In spring, when the young shoots which appear at the base of the plant are about 10 cm (4 in) long, cut them off at crown level or just below.

2 Plant them individually in 8 cm (3 in) pots, filled with cuttings compost or equal parts of horticultural sand and peat and put them in a coldframe.

3 Keep the cuttings well watered by spraying from overhead, and keep the frame closed. About six weeks later, pot the cuttings singly in 8 cm (3 in) pots of John Innes No.1 compost or soilless potting compost. Keep them in the coldframe until frosts have finished. Plant them in their flowering positions in autumn.

Using rooting compound on cuttings

Stem cuttings can be dipped in a rooting hormone to increase the speed with which they take root. The compounds are available as powder, gel or liquid. Buy the right type for the cuttings you are taking, and follow the instructions given on the packet.

Treat only the cut base of the stem and any other wounded area that has been made to encourage rooting. Tap off any excess.

Most healthy plants will root if taken at the right time, so rooting hormones are not essential. For example, cuttings of impatiens (busy lizzie), *Tradescantia zebrina*, hedera (ivy), pelargonium and salix (willow) all root quickly without artificial help.

• SOFTWOOD CUTTINGS FOR PERENNIALS •

Softwood cuttings are immature, soft shoot tips in the first flush of growth, taken in April or May. The method is commonly used for hardy herbaceous perennials and greenhouse plants, as well as fuchsias and hydrangeas. Cuttings will root best in a warm propagating case with heating cables in the bottom.

Softwood cuttings wilt quickly; get all the materials ready before taking the cuttings so that they can be inserted into the compost immediately. Take the cuttings in the morning and put them straight into a polythene bag.

1 Softwood cuttings should be young and non-flowering, just firm but not hard, and about 7.5 cm (3 in) long. Remove a shoot that has four or five pairs of leaves.

▶ This young spring shoot of a fuchsia is ideal material for a softwood cutting.

2 Using a craft knife or garden knife, slice the bottom off the shoot, just below the lowest pair of leaves. Without damaging the stem, pull off the bottom two pairs of leaves. Then dip the base of the cutting in hormone rooting powder – preferably one that contains a fungicide.

3 Fill a 13 cm (5 in) pot with cuttings compost to just below the rim. Alternatively, use a mixture of equal parts (by volume) of peat and horticultural sand. The pot will take up to ten cuttings around the edge, according to their size. Using a pointed stick or a pencil, make holes in the compost about a third the length of the cuttings.

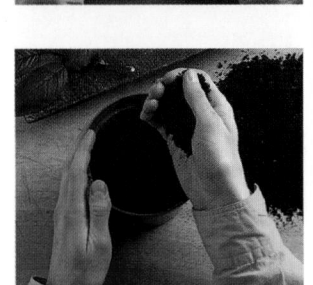

4 Insert each cutting in a hole and press it in place. Water them in, using a fungicidal solution to prevent rot. Keep the cuttings in a propagator (preferably with bottom heat), covered and shaded.

5 When the cuttings have rooted – after about a month – pot them individually in 8 cm (3 in) pots of potting compost. Keep them watered and shaded until they have become established. Plant them in their flowering positions the following spring.

GREENWOOD CUTTINGS FOR • SHRUBS AND SUB-SHRUBS •

Greenwood cuttings are taken from the soft tip of a stem when spring growth has started to slow – about the beginning of June. The lower stem is firm but not hard. The technique is used for ericas, lantanas, pelargoniums and dendranthemas (chrysanthemums).

1 Take the cuttings early in the morning and put them in a plastic bag – if they start to dry out they may not root.

2 Use a craft knife or garden knife to trim the cuttings to about 7.5-10 cm (3-4 in) long. Cut the leaves from the lower half of the cutting. Dip the cut end in a hormone rooting powder of softwood strength, preferably containing a fungicide.

3 Almost fill a 13 cm (5 in) pot with cuttings compost. Make small holes in the compost around the edge of the pot, and insert the cuttings up to the leaves. Then firm them in.

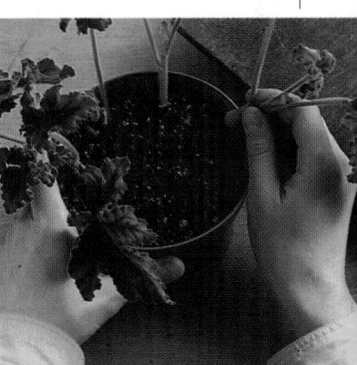

4 Put the pot in a covered propagating case, preferably with bottom heat, or beneath a polythene tent to prevent dehydration. Ensure the cuttings have plenty of light, but shade them from direct sunlight.

5 Repot the young plants individually in 8 cm (3 in) pots of potting compost. Plant them in their flowering positions the following spring.

6 After five to eight weeks the cuttings should have rooted and they can be gradually hardened off by increasing the ventilation.

• SEMI-RIPE CUTTINGS FOR SHRUBS •

Many shrubs root well from semi-ripe material taken from mid July to the end of August – earlier in very hot summers. Some examples are actinidia, choisya, lavandula, philadelphus and weigela.

Semi-ripe cuttings need to be rooted in warm conditions in a cold-frame or propagating case. Bottom heat helps, but is not essential.

1 The cuttings are taken from the current year's growth – the tips of the shoots are soft but the lower stem is firm. Remove 15-20 cm (6-8 in) long, non-flowering sideshoots with leaves growing on them. Take off the leaves from the lower part of the shoot and sever it just below a leaf joint. Cut off the soft tip above a leaf to leave a cutting 5-10 cm (2-4 in) long.

2 Use an 8 cm (3 in) pot for up to five cuttings, a 13 cm (5 in) pot for from five to ten. Almost fill with cuttings compost. Dip the base of the cutting in a hormone rooting agent. Make holes in the compost around the edge of the pot, but make sure the leaves will not touch. Insert each cutting to a third of its length and firm the compost. Water well, preferably using a fungicidal solution.

3 To prevent the cuttings drying out, a humid atmosphere is essential. Fit a plastic bag over the pot, supported by two hoops of galvanised wire. Water the cuttings and put them in a draught-free, warm and shaded place such as a coldframe or propagator. Rooting is faster with bottom heat.

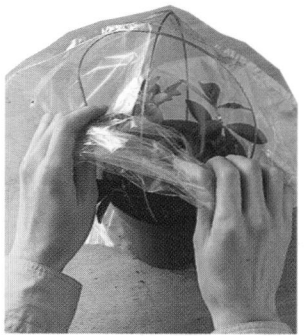

4 Once the cuttings have rooted, harden them off by making a few holes in the plastic bag to let air in. Slit the bag a week later, and a week after that remove the cover completely.

5 Remove the rooted cuttings and carefully separate them with a plant label or pencil. Then pot each young plant in an 8 cm (3 in) pot of potting compost. Water them in, and do not allow the compost to dry out.

Keep the pots under cover and harden off in spring when the young plants can be planted out or transferred to larger pots.

Taking heeled cuttings

Some semi-ripe cuttings will root more strongly if they are removed from the shrub with a heel-like sliver of the previous year's wood attached. This heel helps roots to form because it surrounds the base of the new growth, an area rich in the plant's growth hormones. Cut off a main shoot that has several sideshoots – preferably without flowers. Pull off a sideshoot, or make a slanting cut into the main stem below the junction with the sideshoot; then cut in the opposite direction to remove the shoot.

• RIPEWOOD CUTTINGS FOR EVERGREENS •

Evergreen shrubs are often propagated from ripewood cuttings which are taken in late summer or early autumn. The cuttings are planted in a coldframe or heated propagator and left over winter. Aucuba, escallonia and hebe can be reproduced in this way.

1 Take heel cuttings (see box, above) in late summer from a stem of the current season's growth. Trim the leaves off the bottom third and pinch out the tip.

With plants that are difficult to root – such as daphne and eleagnus – cut a 2.5 cm (1 in) long shallow vertical groove in the stem. Dip the cut end in a rooting hormone powder of ripewood strength and cover the groove with the powder.

2 Dig the soil in a coldframe thoroughly and add a mixture of peat and sand. Plant each cutting up to its leaves. Be sure that the leaves of adjacent cuttings are not touching or they may rot. Close the lid securely and keep the plants shaded. Remove the shading as the days grow shorter. In cold weather, cover the frame with insulation – such as old carpet, blanket or newspapers.

3 Grow the shrubs on for another year in individual pots. Then plant them out in spring.

Helping evergreens to stay moist

Cuttings of evergreen shrubs and trees may dry out as they lose moisture through their leaves. And this will cause them to fail. To prevent evaporation, you can put the cuttings in a cold-frame and spray them with an antidesiccant spray. such as a Christmas-tree spray. But best of all, if you have a greenhouse, install a mist propagating unit which maintains the moisture level automatically.

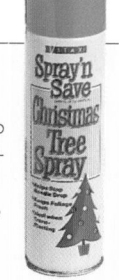

HARDWOOD CUTTINGS FOR • TREES AND SHRUBS •

The easiest way of growing new deciduous shrubs or trees is to take hardwood cuttings in late autumn or early winter – ideally in October or early November. After the cuttings have been planted, little attention is needed for the next 12 months when the new young plants are moved to their permanent positions. Before taking the cuttings, choose a patch of soil sheltered from north and east winds, and dig it thoroughly – if the soil is clay dig in horticultural sand or grit and organic matter to help drainage.

1 Choose a shoot that has just completed its first season's growth. Use a sharp knife or secateurs to cut it from the plant close to the main stem. Trim the cutting just below a bud at the base and just above a bud at the top so that it is about 25 cm (10 in) long.

2 To encourage the cutting to root, remove a thin sliver of bark near the base on one or both sides, using a sharp knife. Lightly dip the base and the wounded strips into hormone rooting compound.

3 Make a narrow V-shaped trench in the prepared soil by pushing in a spade to its full depth and pulling it forwards. Spread horticultural sand 2.5 cm (1 in) deep in the bottom of the trench and stand the cuttings on it, 10 cm (4 in) apart, so that half or two-thirds of each cutting is below ground. Fill the trench with soil and tread it firm.

4 In early spring tread the soil firm if it has been lifted by frost. Keep the area free of weeds, and water during dry spells throughout spring and summer. Some plants, including populus, salix, cornus and ribes, will be ready to be moved to their permanent sites, or potted up, the following autumn. But if little growth has been made, leave the cuttings for another year.

Increasing perennials by division

The easiest way of propagating herbaceous perennials is by division, which involves lifting a plant from the soil and separating it into two or more pieces. Each piece when replanted will grow as an identical plant to the parent. Division is not only used to increase the number of plants, but also to perpetuate existing stocks which are beginning to deteriorate or become overcrowded.

Division is done between October and April, but not when the soil is frozen or sticky. Perennials that flower early in the year are best divided in autumn.

• FIBROUS-ROOTED PLANTS •

Fibrous-rooted perennials, such as heleniums, phlox and Michaelmas daisies (*Aster novi-belgii*), need to be pulled apart into separate pieces. Young ones can often be separated by hand, but old, overgrown plants can be difficult to divide because the roots and crowns form a solid mass. Two garden forks make the job easier.

 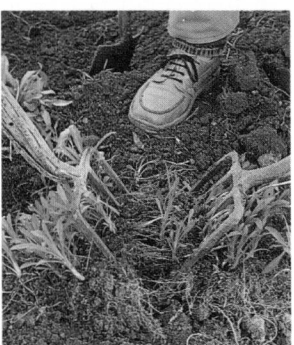

1 Once the plant has been lifted, force the prongs of two garden forks into the clump, back to back. Separate the clump by first pushing the handles of the forks together.

2 Then pull them wide apart. Repeat until you have two halves, then separate the halves. Alternatively, cut the clump into pieces with an old knife or a sharpened spade.

3 Cut away and discard the central woody part of each piece. Then divide the remainder into pieces, each containing about six buds or shoots. Discard unhealthy growth and plant the divisions in their flowering positions. Water well in dry weather.

• RHIZOMATOUS-ROOTED PLANTS •

Plants that grow from rhizomes, which lie just below the surface, are easily lifted – ideally in early spring when new growth buds are sprouting. Examples of rhizomatous plants are bergenias, monardas, physalis and polygonatums.

1 Lift the rootstock with a garden fork and prise off the soil to reveal the main rhizome and the younger stems coming from it. If necessary, wash the clump under a tap or in a bucket of water. Choose side growths about 7.5 cm (3 in) long which have healthy roots and two or three vigorous growth buds. Cut them off with a knife.

2 Discard the old rhizome and trim the cut pieces to just below a cluster of fine healthy roots, removing any dead material. Plant the cut pieces, with the root cluster downwards, at about the same depth as the original plant. Fill in the soil and press it firmly into place around the new plant.

• FLESHY AND TUBEROUS ROOTS •

Some herbaceous perennials grow from tubers, which are thickened, fleshy rootstocks or crowns.

The small tubers of liatris and spring-flowering anemones can be easily pulled apart by hand (see left).

However, the large, fleshy roots of hemerocallis and peonies have to be cut into pieces with a knife, as follows.

1 Lift a clump of plants – in autumn for peonies – and carefully clean off the soil. Wash them in a bucket of water, if necessary. This will reveal growth buds, as with these hemerocallis tubers (right).

2 Divide the rootstock into several pieces, cutting through the crown from the top downwards. Then plant them immediately in their flowering positions. A piece with only one bud will take longer to establish itself than a section of three or four tubers and buds.

Peonies, which often resent disturbance, may take a season or longer to recover.

Dividing bearded irises

Lift the plants and cut off the younger rhizomes from around the edge of the clump. Each portion of rhizome should have one or two strong, healthy leaves. Peel off withered leaves and trim the remainder to a fan shape to reduce wind rock. Then plant in the flowering position.

A TRIMMED RHIZOME

Increasing shrubs, climbers and houseplants by layering

Layering is a simple way of inducing the stem of a healthy plant to take root while still attached to the plant. Some trees and shrubs, such as willows and hazels, do this naturally when their stems touch the ground. Layering is a method that can succeed where cuttings fail.

Carnations and pinks are examples of herbaceous plants that respond to layering. Suitable shrubs include magnolia, viburnum, cassiope, corylopsis, heathers and many climbers, including wisteria and clematis. Deciduous plants are best layered in autumn or winter; evergreens in autumn or spring.

• ORDINARY LAYERING •

1 Fork over the soil near the plant – beneath the branch to be layered – and enrich it with well-rotted compost or manure. Lighten heavy soil with horticultural sand.

2 Select a vigorous, young and flexible shoot, like the one on this willow (right) and bend it down to soil level, about 25 cm (10 in) from its tip. Strip the leaves where the shoot touches the soil and snick the underside with a knife, cutting towards the growing tip.

3 Dig a hole 7.5-10 cm (3-4 in) deep beneath the wound and partly-fill it with seed compost or a mixture of peat and horticultural sand. Bend a piece of galvanised wire into a hairpin and peg the wounded stem into the hole. Cover it with compost and water thoroughly. Ensure that the compost never dries out.

4 A year later, check that the shoot has taken root by carefully scraping away the soil. If it has, sever the new plant from the parent with its rootball, and replant in its flowering position. If the roots are not yet established, replace the soil and leave for a few more months.

• SERPENTINE LAYERING •

Climbers with long flexible stems, such as honeysuckle and jasmine, may produce three or four new plants from a single stem.

1 In autumn, choose a trailing shoot that has grown during the current year. Bend it down to the ground and make a small hole. Then wound the shoot by cutting a shallow tongue in the underside (cutting towards the growing tip) or twisting it sharply. Pin the shoot into the hole with bent wire and cover it with seed compost.

2 Leave the next two pairs of leaves above ground and repeat the process along the length of the shoot.

3 Firm the compost and water well. Keep the soil moist until the following autumn, when the young plants that have developed can be severed from the stem and transplanted.

Increasing heathers by 'dropping'

Heaths and heathers can be propagated by a form of layering called 'dropping'. The plant is transplanted into a deeper hole so that the branches are almost buried, with only the tips exposed. Roots develop on the branches, which can then be used as separate plants. The same technique can also be used for dwarf rhododendrons.

In late autumn or spring, dig a bowl-shaped hole deep enough to take the plant with only the tops of the branches above ground. On heavy soil, dig in sand and organic material in the bottom of the hole to improve drainage.

Lift the plant and put it in the hole, spreading the stems in a circle so that only 2.5 cm (1 in) is exposed.

Then fill in the centre with a mixture of soil, sand and organic matter, working it well around each stem.

Keep the soil moist and free of weeds until the following autumn. Then lift the plant, cut off those stems that have developed shoots and plant them out. Discard the parent plant.

• TIP LAYERING •

Blackberries and loganberries will produce roots from the tip of a cane if it touches the ground. This habit can be used to increase your stock of plants, including the ornamental berry *Rubus* 'Benenden'.

1 In summer, bend a new shoot down to the ground and tie it to a bamboo cane. Then bury the tip 12 cm (5 in) deep. Alternatively, tie the shoot down and plant the tip in a pot of seed compost that has been buried in the ground (right). Water the soil and keep it moist. A new plant should develop in the pot within a few weeks.

2 To check that roots are growing on the young plant, scrape away some of the compost (right).

In the autumn, sever the new plant from the parent and move it to its permanent growing position.

• AIR LAYERING •

Branches that are too stiff to bend for normal layering can be 'layered in the air'. The method is used for rubber plants indoors and rhododendrons and magnolias outdoors. It is done from May to July.

1 From the current year's growth, select a branch and strip off the leaves from the middle. Using a sharp knife, make a shallow cut into the stem, slicing upwards, and dust the wound with hormone rooting powder.

2 Wrap a piece of polythene around the stem below the cut to make a tube, and secure it with sticky tape or string. Pack the tube tightly with an equal mixture of moist peat, horticultural sand and sphagnum moss, and secure the top of the tube.

3 Between three and six months later, when the stem has rooted, cut off the stem below the roots at a leaf joint (left) and remove the polythene. Cut off the stump (above) and put the new plant in a 13cm (5in) pot of potting compost. Keep a hardy shrub moist in a closed coldframe for two weeks and then harden off. Plant out in spring.

Growing shrubs from suckers

Some plants produce shoots, or 'suckers', which arise from below ground level next to the plant. To produce a new plant, expose the base of a sucker in autumn or winter to establish that roots have formed. If they have, cut off the sucker close to where it originated from a root or stem of the parent plant and replant in a permanent site.

Increasing your stock of bulbs and corms

Plants that grow from bulbs, such as narcissi and tulips, or corms, such as crocuses and gladioli, can be increased by removing the young bulblets and cormlets (called offsets) that develop on the parent each year.

• GROWING NEW PLANTS FROM OFFSETS •

When the plant has finished flowering and the foliage has faded, dig it up and pull off the offsets. Throw away the smallest. Half-hardy bulbs and corms such as gladioli should be stored in a frost-free place until late the following spring.

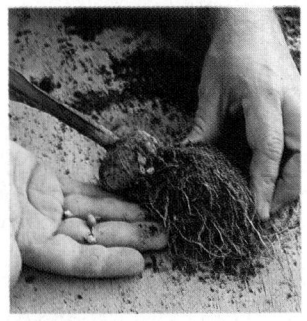

Choose a piece of ground in a sunny or lightly shaded part of the garden that will not be needed for the next two years.

1 Dig out a shallow trench about 12cm (5in) deep for large bulblets or 5cm (2in) deep for cormlets.

2 Put a 1cm (⅜in) layer of horticultural sand or grit in the trench, and plant the offsets twice as far apart as their width.

3 Cover them with another layer of sand about 2.5cm (1in) deep and fill in the trench with soil.

Budding and grafting

Budding and grafting are propagation methods used for plants which are difficult or slow to increase from seed or by other methods. The plant to be increased, known as the scion, is united with a chosen root system, known as the stock, so that the two become a single unit. The result is a plant that has the best of both plants – the vigour of the stock and the flowering or fruiting quality of the scion. Budding and grafting are specialised methods of propagation that are best left to professionals.

T-BUDDING

WHIP-AND-TONGUE GRAFT

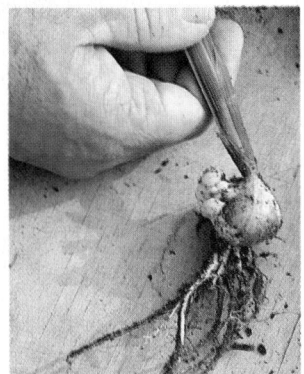

4 When the young plants reach flowering size two or three years later, move them to their final positions.

Trouble-shooting in the garden

*P*ests, diseases and various plant disorders may affect your garden from time to time, but in most cases the trouble can be controlled with good growing techniques and by using chemical sprays only on those plants that are most seriously affected

Directory of Pests

GARDEN CHEMICALS
All garden sprays and powders recommended in these pages are listed under their chemical names. They are sold by various trade names, but the chemical contents are always given on the labels

PROBLEM	PLANTS AT RISK	RECOGNITION	DANGER PERIOD	TREATMENT
ADELGIDS	Many conifers, such as larch, pine, spruce and fir.	Small dark insects, related to aphids, suck the sap of the leaves and stems. They excrete a sticky honeydew on which sooty moulds develop. In early summer, colonies cluster beneath white waxy wool.	April and May.	Spray thoroughly once with malathion from early March through to May, and again about three weeks later.
APHIDS	Most cultivated plants growing in the open, under glass or indoors.	Colonies of small round-bodied insects suck the sap from leaves and distort plant growth. They excrete honeydew on which sooty mould grows, and can also spread viruses. Aphids, which are mostly wingless, may be black, green, pink, red, yellow or variously coloured.	Spring and early summer in the open, but any time of the year under glass or indoors.	Outdoors or in a greenhouse, spray thoroughly with systemic insecticide such as heptenophos, or with non-systemic insecticides such as malathion, pirimicarb, fenitrothion or derris. Inside the house, use derris only. See also WATER LILY APHIDS. **Organic advice** Encourage predators – ladybirds, bluetits, hoverflies, beetles (p. 32).

APPLE BLOSSOM WEEVILS See WEEVILS

APPLE CAPSIDS See CAPSID BUGS

PROBLEM	PLANTS AT RISK	RECOGNITION	DANGER PERIOD	TREATMENT
APPLE SAWFLIES	Apples and plums.	Small ant-like flies lay their eggs in the blossom. The newly hatched caterpillars burrow through to the cores of the young fruit which either fall prematurely or develop scars as they grow.	May and June.	Spray thoroughly at weekly intervals when the petals start to fall, using malathion, pirimiphos-methyl or fenitrothion. **Organic advice** If the level of attack warrants it, spray with derris liquid – usually at petal-fall.
ASPARAGUS BEETLES	Asparagus.	Yellow-and-black beetles and their humpbacked larvae feed on the foliage and shoots. A severe infestation of the beetles can strip plants.	May and early June.	Spray with derris or malathion as soon as damage is seen. **Organic advice** Pick off and destroy beetles as they are seen. Clean up plant debris at all times, but especially in late autumn to prevent overwintering.
BEAN SEED FLIES	Beans, peas, sweetcorn and other vegetable crops.	Seedlings fail to emerge. Small maggots eat germinating seeds and the stems of young seedlings.	Seed-sowing time and as seedlings emerge.	Apply pirimiphos-methyl dust to the seed drill before sowing, and dust along the drill when the seedlings emerge. **Organic advice** Raise plants indoors or cover newly sown seed with horticultural fleece or polythene to encourage quick growth.

PROBLEM	PLANTS AT RISK	RECOGNITION	DANGER PERIOD	TREATMENT
BIRDS	Plums, pears, gooseberries, flowering cherries and forsythia damaged by bullfinches; ripening apples and pears by blackbirds and tits; many plants attacked by sparrows; brassica seedlings and fruit by wood pigeons.	Flower buds, ripening fruit and seedlings eaten.	November to May.	Cover plants with netting. Use bird scarers such as black cotton or string stretched between canes above plants, strips of foil hung from lines or canes, and small windmills, preferably with a rattle device. Change the scarer at least once a week.

BLACKCURRANT GALL MITES See GALL MITES

BLACKFLIES See APHIDS

BOX SUCKERS	Box shrubs and trees.	The tips of leaves curve inwards and form tight clusters. Caused by tiny yellowish or green nymphs which suck the sap.	Spring.	Control the nymphs by spraying in spring with a systemic insecticide, such as heptenophos & permethrin. Kill the adults in mid summer with malathion spray. Cut out damaged shoots and destroy them before April.
BRYOBIA MITES	Apples, gooseberries, ivies.	The leaves develop a light freckling on the upper surface, and later turn bronze and wither. Unlike red spider mites, bryobia mites feed on the top of the leaf and do not produce silk webbing.	March onwards throughout the growing season.	Spray with heptenophos & permethrin, fenitrothion or malathion during the growing season. In winter, spray thoroughly with tar-oil wash to destroy the overwintering eggs.

BULB EELWORMS See STEM AND BULB EELWORMS

BULB MITES	Bulbs of narcissi, hyacinths, tulips, lilies, gladioli, dahlias and freesias.	Small, pearl-white mites invade damaged tissue of the bulbs, whether the damage is caused by other pests, a disease or by garden tools.	Depends on the time of the damage.	Take control measures against the primary problem.
BULB SCALE MITES	Narcissi and hippeastrums.	The foliage of narcissi becomes slightly distorted. Cutting the bulb in half reveals brown marks. On hippeastrums, the leaves are malformed and stained with russet-brown scars.	January to April on narcissi, especially if forced; any time on hippe-astrums under glass.	Destroy badly affected plants – no chemical is really effective although powdered sulphur may relieve the symptoms. Maintain good hygiene in a greenhouse, and do not handle healthy bulbs after diseased ones. Expose dormant bulbs to frost for several nights before planting.
CABBAGE ROOT FLIES	Recently transplanted brassicas, especially cabbages, cauliflowers and brussels sprouts. Radishes, turnips, swedes and wallflowers.	Outer leaves wilt and develop a purple/blue/red tinge. Young plants wilt and are easily pulled out of the ground. Established plants may survive but give a smaller yield. Small white maggots feed on the roots.	April to August.	Protect transplants with pirimiphos-methyl dust in the soil, or water with spray-strength pirimiphos-methyl when established. **Organic advice** Protect transplants with a 13 cm (5 in) square of rubbery carpet underlay, slit to the centre. Place it on the soil around the stem. Cover crop with horticultural fleece.

PROBLEM	PLANTS AT RISK	RECOGNITION	DANGER PERIOD	TREATMENT
CABBAGE WHITEFLIES	Cabbages, brussels sprouts and other brassicas.	Leaves may be sticky and covered with sooty mould. Clouds of small white flies rise up when plants are disturbed.	Growing season.	Spray the underside of the leaves regularly with malathion, pirimiphos-methyl or pyrethrum, or a systemic spray such as heptenophos & permethrin. Do not spray within a week of harvest. Remove and burn infected plants after harvest. **Organic advice** Pick off leaves infested with young whitefly scales (usually the lower leaves). Spray with insecticidal soap, preferably on a cold day when the whiteflies are less active.
CAPSID BUGS	Apples, beans, currants, buddleja, dahlias, forsythias, hydrangeas and many other plants.	Tattered holes appear in younger leaves as adult bugs and nymphs feed on the sap. Flower buds and shoots may be killed or deformed. On apples, raised brown patches occur on buds, fruit and leaves.	April to August.	Bugs have usually left before symptoms are seen. Spray plants with heptenophos, permethrin, fenitrothion or malathion in spring, summer and early autumn. In winter, clear up all garden debris.
CARNATION FLIES (Carnation leaf miner)	Carnations and pinks.	Maggots tunnel into the leaves and stems causing infected shoots to wilt and die.	Through-out the year.	Not easily eradicated. Spray with heptenophos, permethrin or malathion as soon as the mines appear on the foliage in September.
CARROT FLIES	Carrots, parsnips, parsley and celery.	Reddening of foliage and sometimes stunted growth. Roots riddled with tunnels made by fly maggots.	June to October.	In areas where the pest is prevalent, sow thinly in May. Protect plants by watering the soil with a spray-strength solution of pirimiphos-methyl. Alternatively, dust rows with pirimiphos-methyl when sowing. Grow carrots under very fine netting or horticultural fleece. Early or late sowings will avoid the worst periods of attack. If possible, grow the crop in a windy spot. Intercrop with onions – four rows of onions for every row of carrots.
CATERPILLARS	Many different species.	Foliage with irregularly shaped edges and holes. Caterpillars present.	From March onwards in the open but any time under glass.	Crush small outbreaks by hand, including eggs. Spray large infestations with fenitrothion, malathion, permethrin, heptenophos & permethrin, or derris as soon as the buds open. Wrap a grease band around trees in mid autumn to trap wingless female moths. See also TORTRIX CATERPILLARS. **Organic advice** Encourage wasps and birds. A biological control in spray form, *Bacillius thuringiensis,* can be used outside and under glass.
CATS	Seedlings in newly cultivated soil.	Holes dug in fresh soil. Seedlings scattered.	Any time.	Spray soil with cat repellent.

PROBLEM	PLANTS AT RISK	RECOGNITION	DANGER PERIOD	TREATMENT
CELERY LEAF MINERS (Celery flies)	Celery, carrots and parsnips.	Brown blotches on foliage caused by small white maggots tunnelling through the leaves, which shrivel and die. Severe outbreaks can destroy plants.	From May to autumn.	Spray plants with heptenophos & permethrin or malathion when symptoms are first seen, or cut off and burn affected leaflets. **Organic advice** Pick off infected leaves, or squash the larvae within them. If the pest is a regular problem, grow celery under fine netting or horticultural fleece.
CHAFER BEETLES	Many annuals and perennials, tubers and stems of fruit and vegetables.	Top growth wilts and dies as the fat, white, C-shaped larvae, 4 cm (1½ in) long, with three pairs of legs and a brown head, eat the roots.	May/June.	Before planting, treat the soil with pirimiphos-methyl dust, or work it in around the roots of existing plants. **Organic advice** Mainly a problem of newly cultivated land. Numbers are quickly reduced by cultivation and weed control.
CHERRY BLACKFLIES	Flowering and fruiting cherries.	Young leaves curl and twist as black aphids feed on them. Sticky honeydew and sooty mould often present.	May to July.	Immediately after flowering, spray with a systemic insecticide, such as heptenophos & permethrin. In late December/early January treat with a tar-oil winter wash. **Organic advice** Encourage the aphids' natural enemies – ladybirds, spiders, earwigs, hoverflies, ground beetles, parasitic wasps and bluetits (p. 32).
CHRYSANTHEMUM EELWORMS (Leaf and bud eelworms)	Primarily dendranthemas (chrysanthemums), but also callistephus, calceolarias, peonies and other ornamentals.	Buds damaged, blooms distorted and stems scarred. Caused by microscopic worms. Severe infestation can kill plants.	July to September.	There is no safe treatment for chrysanthemum eelworms. Dig up and burn all infected plants.
CHRYSANTHEMUM LEAF MINERS	Mainly dendranthemas (chrysanthemums), but also cinerarias and other pot plants.	White meandering tracks left by maggots tunnelling inside the leaves.	Any time under glass; late spring or summer outdoors.	Immediately symptoms are seen spray with heptenophos & permethrin or pirimiphos-methyl. Repeat fortnightly if infestation is severe. If only a few leaves affected, pick and destroy them. Eliminate sow thistle and groundsel to prevent overwintering.
CHRYSANTHEMUM STOOL MINERS	Dendranthemas (chrysanthemums).	The growth of shoots is inhibited by maggots – light yellow in colour – which tunnel into the stools of the plant and cause damage to the roots.	September to May.	Dust stools with pirimiphos-methyl. After lifting stools to take cuttings, water them with a spray-strength solution of fenitrothion.

PROBLEM	PLANTS AT RISK	RECOGNITION	DANGER PERIOD	TREATMENT
CODLING MOTHS	Mainly apples but also pears.	Entry tunnels through the eye end of fruit where caterpillars eat their way to the core. Damage is rarely noticed until the fruit is cut open.	June to August.	Spray in mid June with fenitrothion, permethrin, heptenophos & permethrin, or malathion, and repeat three weeks later to kill young caterpillars before they enter the fruit. **Organic advice** Encourage bluetits into the garden, especially in winter; they are very effective predators of codling moths. Hang pheromone traps in the trees from late spring to late summer.

CRANE-FLY LARVAE See LEATHERJACKETS

PROBLEM	PLANTS AT RISK	RECOGNITION	DANGER PERIOD	TREATMENT
CUTWORMS	Lettuces, other vegetables and young ornamental annuals.	Stems often eaten at soil level by fat green or grey-brown caterpillars which curl up into a C shape when picked up.	Dry spells from early spring to late summer.	Eliminate weeds, which attract cutworms. Protect plants at sowing time by working a little pirimiphos-methyl dust into the soil. **Organic advice** Fork over soil in winter to expose the pests to predators, particularly blackbirds. Protect young plants with collars made from toilet rolls, cans or drainpipe. Push the collar into the soil around the plant. At the first sign of damage, search in the soil and destroy any caterpillars.
EARWIGS	Dendranthemas (chrysanthemums), clematis, dahlias and other ornamentals.	Petals and leaves left tattered by feeding insects.	May to October.	Spray or dust with pirimiphos-methyl or malathion. Trap earwigs in rolls of corrugated cardboard, old sacking or flowerpots filled with straw, and then destroy them. **Organic advice** Control earwigs only if they are causing harm. They eat greenfly and are valuable pest controllers in their own right.

EELWORMS
• See also CHRYSANTHEMUM EELWORMS, POTATO-CYST EELWORMS, STEM AND BULB EELWORMS

PROBLEM	PLANTS AT RISK	RECOGNITION	DANGER PERIOD	TREATMENT
	Many herbaceous plants, vegetable crops and strawberries.	Deformed and discoloured leaves or flowers caused by microscopic worms tunnelling through plant tissue. They multiply at alarming speed.	Growing season.	None. Destroy all infested plants. Remove all weeds, especially over winter. Remove all plant debris in autumn. Do not plant soft bulbs.
FLEA BEETLES	Cabbages, radishes, turnips, wallflowers and related plants. Young seedlings are particularly at risk, especially in dry weather.	Young leaves pitted with minute holes by tiny shiny black beetles which jump when disturbed.	Sunny spells in April and May or when soil is dry.	Dust vulnerable seedlings with pirimiphos-methyl. Good garden hygiene will help to reduce the risk of attack. **Organic advice** Encourage quick early growth of plants. Water regularly in hot, dry weather. Grow highly susceptible plants under fine net or horticultural fleece.
FROGHOPPERS	Dendranthemas, lavenders, roses, solidagos, perennial asters and many other plants.	Frothy masses of cuckoo spit on stems and leaves. Small sap-feeding insects are concealed beneath the froth.	May to July.	Spray forcefully with malathion or heptenophos & permethrin. **Organic advice** Damage is seldom severe enough to warrant control. Spray with a strong jet of water to dislodge the creatures.

PROBLEM	PLANTS AT RISK	RECOGNITION	DANGER PERIOD	TREATMENT
FRUIT-TREE RED SPIDER MITES	Apples, plums, pears, damsons, cotoneasters, hawthorns, sorbus.	Leaves turn bronze and wither. In a bad attack, they fall off in July. The mites are invisible to the naked eye. Tiny red spiders that run over leaves are called brick spiders and do no harm.	April to September.	Spray with tar-oil wash to kill overwintering eggs, or spray immediately after flowering with heptenophos & permethrin, fenitrothion or malathion. **Organic advice** Mulch trees, and water in dry weather. Predators usually keep the pest under control. If attack is severe, spray with derris or insecticidal soap.
GALL MIDGES	Many cultivated species.	Disfiguring galls on stems, leaves and flowers caused by tiny red, white or yellow maggots.	Late winter, early spring.	Remove and burn infected buds in early spring. When the first flowers open, spray with carbendazim and again after about three weeks.
GALL MITES	Many deciduous trees, including elm, lime, maple and sycamore. Also blackcurrants.	Small galls on the leaves' upper surface are caused by mites feeding. The galls are harmless to trees. On blackcurrants the buds are greatly enlarged, and the mites transmit reversion virus.	Spring. From February and March on blackcurrants.	None for trees but remove and burn affected buds on blackcurrants in early March. When the first flowers open, spray with lime sulphur and repeat about three weeks later. Use carbendazim on sulphur-shy varieties.
GALL WASPS	Oaks, and some species of roses and willows.	Solitary or numerous outbreaks of galls – similar to peas, cherries, silk buttons and spangles – grow out of leaves. Caused by tiny wasps living in plant tissues.	May to October.	Remove and destroy the galls if possible; however, damage to the plant is rarely serious, so gall wasps are not a real cause for concern.

GLADIOLUS THRIPS See THRIPS

GLASSHOUSE LEAFHOPPERS See LEAFHOPPERS

PROBLEM	PLANTS AT RISK	RECOGNITION	DANGER PERIOD	TREATMENT
GLASSHOUSE RED SPIDER MITES	Mainly plants in a greenhouse, but also peaches, nectarines, vines, fuchsias, impatiens and primulas. Strawberries and runner beans can be affected outdoors in a hot, dry season.	Fine, light mottling of the leaves, and later a bronze discoloration. Fine cobwebbing over the plant indicates a severe attack; throw the plant away.	Any time under glass; soft fruits from June to September.	Spray with heptenophos & permethrin, pirimiphos-methyl or insecticidal soap. **Organic advice** Keep plants growing strongly. Do not allow them to dry out or become pot bound. Keep atmosphere moist. Introduce *Phytoseiulus persimilis,* a predatory mite. In autumn remove debris from the greenhouse and scrub down the fittings with hot soapy water.
GLASSHOUSE WHITEFLIES	In a greenhouse: tomatoes, cucumbers, fuchsias, abutilons, dendranthemas (chrysanthemums). In the house: pelargoniums and coleus.	Whiteflies often seen on underside of leaves, which become soiled with honeydew and sooty mould.	All year.	In a greenhouse, spray regularly with malathion, heptenophos & permethrin or permethrin. Fumigate with pirimiphos-methyl smokes. In the house, use derris. **Organic advice** Gently suck up the flies with a vacuum cleaner. Hang up sticky traps. Introduce *Encarsia formosa,* a parasitic wasp, as soon as the first pests are seen. Spray with insecticidal soap.

GOLDEN NEMATODE See POTATO-CYST EELWORMS

PROBLEM	PLANTS AT RISK	RECOGNITION	DANGER PERIOD	TREATMENT
GOOSEBERRY SAWFLIES	Gooseberries.	Leaf tissue stripped down to skeleton of veins by green, black-spotted caterpillars.	April to August.	Spray early in May, or when symptoms first appear, with fenitrothion, malathion, pyrethrins or derris. **Organic advice** Frequently inspect the underside of the leaves at the centre of the bush, and pick off sawfly eggs and caterpillars. Cordons or espaliers are easier to treat.
GREENFLIES See APHIDS				
HOLLY LEAF MINERS	Holly.	White blotches on the leaves caused by maggots tunnelling through them. The leaves may fall from young trees.	Late May to July.	Spray regularly with heptenophos & permethrin, following manufacturer's instructions.
LEAF AND BUD EELWORMS See CHRYSANTHEMUM EELWORMS				
LEAF-CURLING APHIDS	Apples, damsons, pears, peaches and plums.	Immature leaves pucker and curl as aphids feed on plant tissue.	Mid spring to mid summer.	Spray with a systemic insecticide such as heptenophos & permethrin before the trees blossom and again, if necessary, after blossom appears. Also spray with tar-oil wash in winter. **Organic advice** See APHIDS.
LEAF EELWORMS	Particularly troublesome in greenhouses with begonias, coleus, gloxinias, ferns and other foliage plants. Outdoors: mint, strawberries and other soft fruit.	Brown or black blotches between leaf veins, and distortion of buds and young growth, caused by tiny pests.	Winter.	No cure; severely infested plants should be burnt. Maintain good hygiene and grow plants in dry conditions.
LEAFHOPPERS • See also RHODODENDRON LEAFHOPPERS	Roses, pelargoniums, primulas and others, both under glass and in the open.	Coarse white flecks on leaves and – often on the underside – the cast-off skins of the insects.	April to October, but any time under glass.	Spray with fenitrothion, malathion or heptenophos & permethrin, repeating if necessary at fortnightly intervals.
LEAF MINERS See CELERY LEAF MINERS, CHRYSANTHEMUM LEAF MINERS, HOLLY LEAF MINERS, LILAC LEAF MINERS				
LEAF-ROLLING ROSE SAWFLIES	Bush and climbing roses.	Leaves become tightly rolled up along their length. The sawflies are unlikely to damage the plant.	May, June and July.	Pick off and burn affected leaves. Alternatively, spray every fortnight in May with heptenophos & permethrin, fenitrothion or liquid derris. **Organic advice** Clear away mulches in autumn and lightly fork over the soil to expose the pupae to predators.

PROBLEM	PLANTS AT RISK	RECOGNITION	DANGER PERIOD	TREATMENT
LEATHERJACKETS (Crane-fly larvae)	Brassicas, other vegetables and various ornamental plants. Young plants and lawns are particularly susceptible.	Plants turn yellow, wilt and sometimes die as the roots are attacked by fat, grey-brown, legless grubs. Large numbers of grubs on a lawn will cause yellow patches in dry spells.	April to June.	Incorporate pirimiphos-methyl dust in the soil around established plants. **Organic advice** Fork over infested soil thoroughly and frequently to expose pests to birds. On lawns, water the grass well then cover it with sacking or thick cardboard overnight. The leatherjackets will come to the surface and can be swept up or left for the birds. On cultivated land, put grass mowings under the cover, leave for two days, then uncover.
LILAC LEAF MINERS	Lilac *(Syringa)* and privet *(Ligustrum).*	The caterpillars of a species of moth burrow into lilac leaves. They also cause leaf-mine blotches on privet leaves.	June onwards.	Spray large infestations with malathion, pirimiphos-methyl or heptenophos & permethrin. On small outbreaks pick off and burn affected leaves.
LILY BEETLES	Lilies, fritillaria, nomocharis and polygonatum.	Scarlet beetles with black heads and legs feed on the leaves and other aerial parts of plants. Primarily found in parts of Surrey and adjoining counties.	May onwards.	Spray with malathion, fenitrothion, permethrin, or heptenophos & permethrin. **Organic advice** Check plants frequently in spring and remove any beetles. Spray plants with derris.
MEALY BUGS	Many greenhouse and houseplants, especially succulents, hippeastrums, vines, camellias, citrus, coleus and orchids.	Patches on leaves and stems of tiny sap-eating pink insects, covered with tufts of woolly or mealy white wax.	Any time.	Spray with systemic insecticide such as heptenophos & permethrin or with non-systemic insecticides such as malathion. **Organic advice** Introduce the biological control agent *Cryptolaemus montrouzieri* – a beetle which eats mealy bugs.
MICE AND VOLES	Bulbs and corms, including crocus, lily, narcissus and tulip, in open ground or in storage. Peas and beans at sowing time.	Damage and droppings.	Any time between autumn and spring, especially with bulbs recently planted where the soil is still soft.	Before planting, dust bulbs and corms with a proprietary animal repellent. Rodent traps should be covered to avoid endangering birds and pets. In storerooms lay bait containing coumatetralyl or difenacoum.
MILLIPEDES	Root vegetables, bulbs, tubers and corms.	Grey-black worm-like insects, similar to centipedes but slower in movement and with more legs, feed inside the rootstock of plants.	Late summer to autumn.	Improve garden hygiene and dig deeply. Protect seeds, bulbs and corms with pirimiphos-methyl dust.

PROBLEM	PLANTS AT RISK	RECOGNITION	DANGER PERIOD	TREATMENT
MUSTARD BEETLES	Mustard, watercress, cabbages, swedes and turnips.	Stems and leaves attacked by metallic-blue beetle and brown-yellow larvae.	May to August.	Dust or spray with malathion, but not on watercress, to avoid killing fish. Raise the water level of watercress beds to drown beetles and larvae. **Organic advice** See FLEA BEETLES.
NARCISSUS FLIES	Amaryllis, narcissi and snowdrops.	Softening and rotting of bulbs as grubs burrow into them, particularly in dry soil. Affected bulbs fail to flower, just producing narrow grass-like leaves.	Late spring to early summer. Bulbs planted in sunny sites are more vulnerable than those planted in shade.	Lift and burn affected bulbs and any grubs still in the soil. Apply pirimiphos-methyl dust to the soil before or soon after planting. **Organic advice** As foliage dies down, holes are left in the soil which allow narcissus flies to lay eggs near the bulbs. Rake soil into the holes. Alternatively, cover bulbs with horticultural fleece as the leaves die.
OAK-APPLE GALL See GALL WASPS				
ONION FLIES	Young plants of onions, shallots and leeks.	Adult flies lay eggs on the leaves from which white maggots hatch to tunnel into the plant tissues. The leaves yellow and wither, and the stems and bulbs rot. Small white maggots are found in roots and bulbs.	Most damage occurs in June/July, but plants can be attacked at other times in the growing season.	Burn infested plants and dig over the ground to expose insects' dormant pupae to the winter cold and to birds. Treat the soil with pirimiphos-methyl before sowing or planting.
PEA AND BEAN WEEVILS	Young garden peas and beans; older plants are unaffected.	Leaf edges are scalloped where eaten by the small beetle-like insects and their larvae.	March to July.	Apply pirimiphos-methyl dust or fenitrothion spray as soon as the symptoms appear. **Organic advice** Spray with derris dust.
PEA MOTHS	Garden peas.	Small maggot-like caterpillars of a moth feed on the peas inside the ripening pods.	May to August.	Spray when flowers first open, and again two weeks later, with fenitrothion or permethrin. Alternatively, grow early-maturing varieties of peas. **Organic advice** Sow peas early (February) or late (May) so that they are not in flower in June/July.
PEAR-LEAF BLISTER MITES	Pears, sorbus, cotoneasters and other related trees.	Clusters of dark brown pustules on the upper surface of the leaves where mites burrow into plant tissue. Young shoots may also be damaged.	April to August.	Pick off and burn infested leaves. If the attack is severe, spray at the end of March with lime-sulphur (available from some garden centres) or with fenitrothion. A difficult pest to eliminate.

PROBLEM	PLANTS AT RISK	RECOGNITION	DANGER PERIOD	TREATMENT
PEAR MIDGES	Pears.	Young fruits swell rapidly, then fail to develop. Black cavities contain small yellowish white larvae. Affected fruit falls in May/June.	April to May.	Spray with fenitrothion just before the blossoms open. **Organic advice** Pick off affected fruitlets when first seen and burn them. Fork over the soil under the trees in summer and remove old leaves or fruit in autumn.
PEA THRIPS See THRIPS				
PLUM SAWFLIES See APPLE SAWFLIES				
POPLAR BEETLES	Poplar trees.	The leaves are shredded to a skeleton of veins by beetles and their larvae.	May to September.	Spray young trees with malathion when symptoms are first seen or in early spring. Repeat if necessary.
POTATO-CYST EELWORMS (Golden nematode, Yellow potato-cyst eelworms)	Potatoes and tomatoes.	Plants grow poorly. If infection is severe, they may wilt and die. Roots reveal tiny white, yellow or brown cysts which can only be seen through a magnifying glass.	May to August.	Dig up and burn affected plants and avoid planting potatoes or tomatoes on the same site for five years. **Organic advice** Build up the organic level in the soil by applying leaf-mould, compost or well-rotted manure. Grow early potatoes which may crop before eelworm levels build up. Choose varieties that are resistant to eelworm.
RABBITS	Many plants, particularly lettuces.	Chewed or damaged plants. On young trees, bark can be stripped just above soil level.	Growing season.	Protect plants with high wire-mesh fencing, buried 30 cm (12 in) below soil level to prevent burrowing.
RASPBERRY BEETLES	Raspberries, loganberries and blackberries.	The tiny larvae of the raspberry beetle feed on the ripening fruit.	June to August.	Spray thoroughly with fenitrothion, derris or malathion as soon as flowering ceases. **Organic advice** In autumn lightly fork over the soil around raspberries. Remove any mulch and replace it with fresh material in spring.
RASPBERRY CANE MIDGES See GALL MIDGES				
REDCURRANT BLISTER APHIDS	Red, white and black currants.	Irregular red or green blisters raised on leaves. Aphids may be seen underneath leaves, but symptoms will persist after the pests have flown.	May and June.	Spray in January with tar-oil wash to kill overwintering eggs. Repeat a fortnight later and again immediately after leaf-fall. Rake up any leaves from under plants and destroy them. **Organic advice** Encourage natural predators of aphids (p. 32).
RED SPIDER MITES See FRUIT-TREE RED SPIDER MITES, GLASSHOUSE RED SPIDER MITES				

PROBLEM	PLANTS AT RISK	RECOGNITION	DANGER PERIOD	TREATMENT
RHODODENDRON LACEBUGS	Young and adult rhododendrons.	Fine mottling on the upper surface of leaves, with a rusty-brown or chocolate spotting on the underside.	May and June.	Cut out and burn infested branches in May. Spray in late May with fenitrothion or permethrin, and again in mid June. **Organic advice** Don't grow rhododendrons in exposed, dry or sunny sites. Some species and hybrids are less vulnerable than others; grow them if the pest is known to be a problem.
RHODODENDRON LEAFHOPPERS	Rhododendrons.	Dark green insects with red stripes lay their eggs in the flower buds. Leafhoppers are harmless but leave entry sites for rhododendron bud blast (p. 854).	Late July to October.	Spray with heptenophos & permethrin or fenitrothion two or three times in August and September.
ROOT APHIDS AND ROOT MEALY BUGS	Cacti and succulents, primulas and other pot plants, lettuces and some outdoor ornamentals.	Colonies of white, wax-covered aphids or mealy bugs infest the roots of plants. Growth is checked, and the plants may turn yellow and wilt.	Outdoors: late summer and autumn. Under glass: any time.	Water the affected plant roots with a spray-strength solution of pirimiphos-methyl. **Organic advice** Grow resistant varieties of lettuce. Mealy bugs are worse in dry conditions, so keep the soil or compost moist.
ROOT-KNOT EELWORMS	Cucumbers and tomatoes under glass, as well as other greenhouse and pot plants. Also some outdoor plants.	Roots develop lumpy galls where eelworms are present which check and affect growth.	Any time.	No chemical cure. Burn infested plants and wash contaminated pots in garden disinfectant.

ROOT MEALY BUGS See ROOT APHIDS AND ROOT MEALY BUGS

SAWFLIES See APPLE (AND PLUM) SAWFLIES, GOOSEBERRY SAWFLIES, SOLOMON'S-SEAL SAWFLIES.

PROBLEM	PLANTS AT RISK	RECOGNITION	DANGER PERIOD	TREATMENT
SCALE INSECTS	Particularly troublesome on greenhouse and houseplants, but also ornamental shrubs, trees and fruit grown outside.	Brown, yellow or white scales – flat or oval – mainly on the underside of leaves and clustered alongside the veins and on the stems.	Late spring or early summer outdoors, but at any time of the year when under glass.	Spray with pirimiphos-methyl, heptenophos & permethrin, or malathion three times at two-week intervals. **Organic advice** A parasitic wasp, *Metaphycus helvolus,* can be bought for use in a greenhouse. Alternatively, gently remove scales by hand or with a soft toothbrush, or spray with insecticidal soap.
SLUGS AND SNAILS	Many garden plants, including their roots, tubers, bulbs and corms.	Irregularly shaped holes eaten in bulbs, roots, stems, leaves and flowers. Slime trails reveal their active presence. Slugs and snails usually feed at night, hiding by day.	Warm and humid weather in spring and autumn.	Remove decaying plant material and scatter metaldehyde or methiocarb pellets, or a slug killer based on aluminium-sulphate. **Organic advice** Avoid heavy dressings of manure or mulch around young plants. Never transplant seedlings into cold wet soil. Protect young plants with individual cloches made from plastic water bottles. Encourage predators (p. 32).

PROBLEM	PLANTS AT RISK	RECOGNITION	DANGER PERIOD	TREATMENT
SOLOMON'S-SEAL SAWFLIES	Solomon's seal and other polygonatums.	Grey-blue larvae with black heads strip the foliage.	Summer.	Spray with heptenophos & permethrin or malathion when the larvae are first seen. **Organic advice** Pick off the larvae when they begin to appear in late spring.
SPANGLE GALL See GALL WASPS				
SQUIRRELS	Many shrubs and trees, including ripe fruits. Also bulbs and corms.	Bark stripped from trees, fruits damaged and bulbs and corms dug up.	Between autumn and spring, particularly where gardens adjoin woodland.	Dust bulbs and corms with proprietary rodent repellent before planting. Protect valuable crops with a covering of netting.
STEM AND BULB EELWORMS	Daffodils, tulips, hyacinths, onions, phlox and many other plants.	Leaves become swollen and distorted; bulbs crack and rot; plants die.	Dormant bulbs in late summer and autumn; growing plants usually in spring.	Destroy affected plants and avoid replanting in the same soil for at least three years. Maintain good hygiene in the garden.
STRAWBERRY BEETLES	Strawberries.	Glossy-black ground beetles, 2 cm (¾ in) long eat pieces of the fruit as it ripens, causing damage similar to that made by birds. The pest may be found under the plants.	Early summer.	Remove any debris and garden litter, remove weeds and maintain good hygiene. Use methiocarb slug pellets to kill the pest, but follow the harvest-interval details on the packaging. **Organic advice** In winter, remove debris and litter.
STRAWBERRY EELWORMS See LEAF EELWORMS				
SUCKING INSECTS • See also BOX SUCKERS	Apples and pears.	Plants fouled by sap-sucking insects, leaving sticky excretions which together distort young growth. Also infest blossom trusses causing symptoms similar to frost damage.	April to July.	Spray fruit trees with heptenophos & permethrin, or malathion soon after petal-fall. As an alternative for apple trees, apply a winter spray of tar oil.
SWIFT MOTHS	Carrots, parsnips and various herbaceous perennials.	The caterpillars of the swift moth are dirty-white with brown heads. They live in the soil and feed on roots, tubers, corms and rhizomes, and may eat up into the stems.	During the growing season.	Protect susceptible plants by incorporating pirimiphos-methyl dust in the soil. **Organic advice** Usually a problem only on newly cleared land. Thorough winter digging will expose caterpillars and kill them. Good weed control and regular cultivation reduce the risk.

PROBLEM	PLANTS AT RISK	RECOGNITION	DANGER PERIOD	TREATMENT
TARSONEMID MITES	Begonias, dahlias, fuchsias, gerberas, pot cyclamens, ferns and other greenhouse plants. Outdoors, similar mites attack strawberries and Michaelmas daisies (*Aster*).	Tiny mites feed on the concealed parts of plants causing leaf distortion and discoloration. The mites may also infest the flowers, which then do not open properly.	Any time of the year under glass.	There is no effective chemical control, but the symptoms may be relieved with the application of powdered sulphur. Maintain good hygiene in the greenhouse at all times.
THRIPS	Roses, carnations, privets, gladioli and some other species. Also peas and onions.	Fine silvery flecks on infected petals and foliage are caused by tiny thrips. Severe infestation can discolour and kill the flowers.	Early summer to early autumn, particularly in hot, dry weather.	Treat corms before storage – and again before planting – with pirimiphos-methyl dust. If symptoms appear, spray the plants with malathion or heptenophos & permethrin. **Organic advice** Keep the plants growing strongly by giving them good conditions. Do not let the soil dry out.
TORTRIX CATERPILLARS	Shrubs, trees and herbaceous perennials especially dendranthemas (chrysanthemums), heleniums and perennial phlox. Various greenhouse and house plants are also at risk.	Leaves and stems are drawn together by silken webs which are spun by the caterpillars to create protective coverings while they feed.	May and June outdoors; any time under glass.	Remove and destroy the caterpillars by hand. Alternatively, spray the plants with fenitrothion or derris.
VINE WEEVILS	Many, especially those grown in containers. Cyclamen, primulas and begonias are particularly susceptible.	Plants wilt and collapse suddenly. Fat, white, brown-headed larvae are found in the soil around the roots. Adult weevils eat notches out of the leaves. Most damage is done under glass.	Most of the year.	Spray heavily with pirimiphos-methyl. **Organic advice** Check the compost of newly bought plants. Protect pots and greenhouse staging with a band of non-drying glue, which can be bought at some garden centres. Adult vine weevils cannot fly; they must walk up the side of pots. Use a parasitic nematode *Heterorhabditis megedis*.

VOLES See MICE AND VOLES

PROBLEM	PLANTS AT RISK	RECOGNITION	DANGER PERIOD	TREATMENT
WASPS	The ripening fruits of apples, pears and plums.	The wasps enlarge the damage already caused to fruit by birds.	Late summer to early autumn.	Trace the nest and spray an anti-wasp insecticide at the entrance at dusk, when most of the wasps will be inside. **Organic advice** Wasps are excellent natural predators, controlling caterpillars and other pests. They should only be killed if really necessary.

PROBLEM	PLANTS AT RISK	RECOGNITION	DANGER PERIOD	TREATMENT
WATER LILY APHIDS	Water lilies (*Nymphea* and *Nuphar*) and pondside plants.	Colonies of aphids disfigure the leaves and stems and discolour the flowers.	Growing season.	Spray plants frequently with a strong jet of water to dislodge the aphids; fish will eat them. Alternatively, submerge the foliage with sacking or weighted netting for several hours.
WATER LILY BEETLES	Water lilies, especially *Nuphar*.	Holes are eaten in the upper surface of the leaves by the brown adult beetles and their dark brown or black larvae. The flowers may also be eaten.	Early to late summer.	Spray plants regularly with a strong jet of water to dislodge the beetles and larvae; fish will then eat them. Alternatively, submerge the foliage with sacking or weighted netting for several hours.
WEEVILS • See also VINE WEEVILS	Various species of cultivated plants.	Adult weevils are small or medium-sized, usually dark coloured and with a long snout; larvae are white legless grubs with a discernible head. Both feed on roots, tubers, corms, stems, leaves, flowers and fruit, but damage is seldom severe.	Late spring, early summer.	Dust or spray foliage, soil or potting composts with pirimiphos-methyl.

WHITEFLIES See CABBAGE WHITEFLIES, GLASSHOUSE WHITEFLIES

PROBLEM	PLANTS AT RISK	RECOGNITION	DANGER PERIOD	TREATMENT
WIREWORMS	Potatoes, lettuces, tomatoes and dendranthemas (chrysanthemums).	Yellow-brown larvae live in the soil to feed on the roots of potato tubers, and also on the stems of other plants.	The early years of newly cultivated land.	Use pirimiphos-methyl dust when planting. Reduce the colonies of wireworms by frequent cultivation of the soil.
WOOLLY APHIDS	Apple trees and related ornamental trees and shrubs, including crab apples, cotoneasters and pyracanthas.	Tufts of waxy white wool on trunks, branches and twigs produced by aphids. Galls can also occur and may split, allowing diseases to enter the plant.	April to September.	Immediately wool appears, spray with a high volume of malathion or heptenophos & permethrin. In winter, spray trees with tar-oil wash. A difficult pest to control. **Organic advice** Encourage natural aphid predators (p. 32). Cut out severely galled branches. Spray with insecticidal soap under high pressure.

YELLOW POTATO-CYST EELWORMS See POTATO-CYST EELWORMS

Directory of Diseases and Disorders

PROBLEM	PLANTS AT RISK	RECOGNITION	DANGER PERIOD	TREATMENT
ANTHRACNOSE OF BEANS	Dwarf and climbing french beans and sometimes runner beans.	Sunken, dark brown patches occur on pods, and brown spots appear on the leaves. They are caused by fungus.	Growing season, particularly during cool wet weather.	Destroy all diseased plants and grow fresh plants from new seeds in a new position. Do not save seed from plants that may have the disease. If a serious outbreak reappears, spray before flowering with carbendazim or mancozeb.
ANTHRACNOSE OF CUCUMBERS	Cucumbers, melons and vegetable marrows grown under glass.	Leaves often very pale with transparent spots which become dry and brown in the centre.	Growing season.	Burn all infected leaves. Spray or dust with sulphur during the growing season. Reduce humidity in the greenhouse and provide adequate ventilation. At the end of the season disinfect with cresylic acid or other sterilant.
ANTHRACNOSE OF TREES	Weeping willows and London planes.	Leaves curl, become discoloured and fall prematurely. Severe outbreaks can denude trees by August, followed by die-back.	Spring or during mild wet summers.	Cut out infected shoots and burn, together with any fallen leaves. As leaves unfold spray small trees with copper fungicide, such as Bordeaux mixture, and repeat twice during the summer.
APPLE CANKER See CANKER				
APPLE SCAB	Only trees of the genus *Malus*.	Small blister-like pimples on young shoots and fallen leaves. The blisters later burst the bark and form ring-like cracks or scabs.	Growing season, but particularly after a wet May.	Cut out and burn diseased shoots in winter. Spray regularly, following the maker's instructions, with myclobutanil or carbendazim (except on sulphur-shy varieties). **Organic advice** Pick up fallen apple leaves in autumn, or run a mower over them. Worms will take the pieces into the soil, burying the spores. Grow resistant varieties.
APRICOT DIE-BACK	Apricots.	Branches exude large amounts of gum, and die. Often caused by fungi entering the branches through a wound.	Through-out the year.	Cut out and burn all the dead wood. Avoid pruning in winter. If appropriate, improve cultural conditions, as the disease can be caused by malnutrition of the plant.
ARABIS MOSAIC VIRUS	Herbaceous, bulbous and woody plants; fruit crops such as strawberries; vegetables such as celery and lettuce.	Mottling of the leaves and plant distortion caused by a virus in the soil and transmitted by a type of eelworm.	Growing season.	No chemical control – destroy diseased plants. Avoid growing plants susceptible to infection. Remove plant debris in autumn.

PROBLEM	PLANTS AT RISK	RECOGNITION	DANGER PERIOD	TREATMENT
ARMILLARIA See HONEY FUNGUS				
ASH CANKER See CANKER				
ASTER WILT	Primarily asters of the *novi-belgii* species.	The leaves turn yellow and wilt, then die. The disease is caused by a microscopic fungus that inhabits the rootstock, transmitting a poison through the sap.	Growing season.	Destroy infected plants and – since the disease is soil-borne – propagate from healthy stock on a fresh site.
AZALEA GALL	Small-leaved rhododendrons, including pot-grown *R. simsii* and Kurume azaleas.	Leaves and flowers are replaced by red or pale green fleshy galls, which later produce a white floury coating of fungus spore. The disease is spread by air or by insect-borne spores which enter the plant tissue.	Growing season.	Remove and burn the galls before they turn white and produce fresh spores. In the greenhouse control spore-bearing insects, such as aphids. Spray severe attacks before the leaves curl, using Bordeaux mixture or other copper fungicide.
BACTERIAL CANKER	Primarily plums (particularly 'Victoria'), but also peaches, damsons and cherries, as well as ornamental prunus.	In late spring, small brown spots appear on leaves. The spots later drop out to give a 'shot hole' appearance. Elongated lesions exude amber-coloured gum on dying shoots.	Autumn and winter, although symptoms do not appear until the following year.	Cut out and burn all infected areas. Spray foliage with Bordeaux mixture in mid August, mid September and mid October. Prune during summer. **Organic advice** Take care not to wound trees when staking, tying up or strimming.
BARK SPLITTING	Many species, including fruit trees.	The tree's bark splits and fissures open up.	Any time.	Cut out dead wood and remove loose bark to reveal a clean wound. Feed, mulch and water the tree properly and the wound should heal naturally.
BASAL ROT	Crocuses, narcissi and onions.	Bulbs usually do not grow in spring, and the roots start to rot. If a corm or bulb is sliced downwards, it shows dark strands spreading from the chocolate-brown rot at the base, up through the inner scales.	Any time, including storage of narcissi bulbs.	Destroy rotten corms and bulbs. **Organic advice** Grow resistant varieties of the bulbs.
BASAL (or fusarium) ROT OF LILIES	Lilies.	Growth either fails to appear above ground or is yellow and weak. Bulbs quickly rot and disintegrate.	Any time.	Examine bulbs carefully before planting. Burn affected bulbs. Do not plant new lily bulbs in the same bed for several years.

PROBLEM	PLANTS AT RISK	RECOGNITION	DANGER PERIOD	TREATMENT
BEECH BARK DISEASE	Young and mature beech trees.	Insect feeding holes in the bark create wounds through which fungus enters. Wounds weep at first, followed by yellowing of foliage and red-black bumps on the bark. Branches die back and the tree eventually dies.	Late spring.	In the early stages, insect attacks can be prevented by using a tar-oil wash in winter or spraying with malathion during the growing season.
BIRCH POLYPORE	Birch trees.	Die-back caused by grey-brown horseshoe-shaped bracket fungus, up to 15 cm (6 in) across. The fungus attacks dead wood and rapidly spreads decay.	Any time.	Cut out and destroy dead wood. Mulch trees regularly with well-decayed manure.
BITTER PIT	Apples.	Sunken brown spots develop beneath the skin of the fruit and throughout the flesh.	Particularly in hot dry summers with acute water shortages. Not apparent until harvesting or in storage.	Feed, mulch and prevent the soil from drying out. In mid June spray with calcium nitrate – 8 rounded tablespoons to 23 litres (5 gallons) of water – and repeat three times at three-weekly intervals. **Organic advice** Avoid high applications of nitrogen-rich manures.
BLACKLEG	Pelargoniums and potatoes.	Affected tissues become soft, the leaves turn yellow and the cutting or plant dies – the result of a black rot developing at the base of the stem. The rot is caused by fungi or bacteria.	Soon after pelargonium cuttings are taken. In June for potatoes. A problem on cold wet soil.	Destroy severely affected plants. No treatment for potatoes other than to plant healthy seed tubers and to choose less susceptible varieties. Protect pelargoniums with sterilised compost. Maintain strict greenhouse hygiene and water carefully with mains water.
BLACK SPOT See ROSE BLACK SPOT				
BLIGHT	Tomatoes and potatoes.	In damp conditions, leaves develop yellow-brown blotches and a white furry coating underneath. They turn brown and rot. On tomato fruits, a dry brown rot develops which may not be obvious till after picking. Potatoes may rot in store.	Any time between May and August.	Spray every 10-14 days, particularly in a wet season, with mancozeb or carbendazim. Spray potatoes before the leaves touch other plants, and tomatoes when the first fruits set. **Organic advice** Grow resistant potatoes. Earthing up or mulching helps. As symptoms spread, cut off all foliage, and wait three weeks before harvesting.
BLINDNESS	Narcissi and tulips, especially those grown in containers.	Shoots fail to develop flower buds – or those which do turn brown and wither – due to waterlogged or excessively dry roots.	Hot summers.	The cause may be waterlogged or very dry roots, or BASAL ROT. Blindness can also be caused by shallow planting. If so, allow container plants to die down, then store the bulbs in a well-lit cool shed over summer and replant at the correct depth in autumn.
BLOSSOM END ROT	Tomatoes, peppers and aubergines.	Circular brown or black patch at the blossom end of the fruit, which gradually enlarges to penetrate the flesh. Caused by a calcium shortage and dehydration.	As fruit develops.	Prevent the soil from drying out and maintain even growth. This disease is particularly a problem with plants that are grown in pots or growing bags, where they may need to be watered several times a day.

PROBLEM	PLANTS AT RISK	RECOGNITION	DANGER PERIOD	TREATMENT
BLOTCHY RIPENING • See also GREENBACK	Tomatoes.	Hard green or yellow patches on the fruit, most often on lower trusses.	Growing season.	The problem may occur if plants have poor soil, are growing too fast under poor light, or are overwatered or too dry. A high temperature can also be a factor. Take appropriate action. A potash feed may help. Grow resistant varieties such as 'Alicante', 'Eurocross', 'Grenadier' and 'Shirley'.
BLUE MOULD	Stored vegetables, corms and bulbs.	Blue or blue-green spores of fungus, encouraged by a moist atmosphere, appear on plant material.	Any time.	Ensure dry and cool conditions and that all plant material is healthy when stored. Dust bulbs – not vegetables – with carbendazim before storing.
BOOTLACE FUNGUS See HONEY FUNGUS				
BORON DEFICIENCY	Beetroots, swedes and celery.	Edible roots turn brown inside; celery stalks develop brown cracks.	May to August.	Mix 30 g (1 oz) of borax with 10 litres (2 gallons) of water and spread it over 10 m² (12 sq yd) of soil.
BOTRYTIS See GREY MOULD				
BRACKET FUNGUS	All trees, especially alder, ash, beech, oak, poplar and – particularly vulnerable – birch.	Fungi, up to 30 cm (12 in) across, sprout from trunks and branches of trees. The spores spread through dead or damaged tissues and may cause die-back.	July to October, but fungi may appear months after infection.	Bracket fungus can be a symptom of many different diseases. Seek professional advice.
BROWN CORE	Primulas.	Plants wilt and can easily be lifted due to the roots rotting back from the tips.	Growing season.	The disease only affects plants that are set too deeply in the soil or are overcrowded. Burn affected plants and avoid growing primulas on the infected site for several years.
BROWN ROT	All tree fruit.	Concentrically ringed browny white fungus appears on fruits originally injured by insects and birds.	Summer, and in store.	Destroy infected fruit and cut out dead shoots. Spray fruit with carbendazim before picking to protect in storage. Do not store diseased or damaged fruit. **Organic advice** At end of season remove remaining fruit from the tree. Remove and destroy all plant debris.
BUD BLAST See RHODODENDRON BUD BLAST				
BUD-DROP	Camellias, sweet peas, wisterias and many houseplants.	Buds drop before flowering.	Growing season.	Nothing can save falling buds. Prevent bud-drop by mulching with organic matter. Water well in dry periods – for camellias particularly June-September. Bud-drop is caused by a shortage of water, sometimes in autumn when you may not think of watering.

PROBLEM	PLANTS AT RISK	RECOGNITION	DANGER PERIOD	TREATMENT
CALLISTEPHUS WILT • See also FUSARIUM WILT	Callistephus.	Blackened stems with white or pink fungus outgrowths. Prevalent on wet, badly drained soils.	Growing season.	Remove and burn infected plants. Improve drainage by adding coarse grit to soil or installing a drainage system.
CANE BLIGHT	Raspberries.	Leaves on fruiting canes wilt and wither in summer, and canes may snap in the wind. The canes have dark patches at ground level and the bark splits or cracks.	Growing season.	Cut out all diseased canes to below soil level and burn. Disinfect knife immediately. Spray new canes with Bordeaux mixture. Handle canes with care to prevent damage. Do not transplant infected canes to a new site. **Organic advice** Tie in canes well to prevent wind-rock, which can cause damage that is then a source of entry for the disease.
CANE SPOT	Raspberries, loganberries and hybrid berries.	Round purple spots which later form cankers on canes, spots with a whitish centre on leaves and misshapen fruits – the result of bacterial infection.	May to October.	Cut out and burn badly infected canes. Spray with carbendazim fortnightly from bud-burst to petal-fall.
CANKER • See also BACTERIAL CANKER, PARSNIP CANKER, STEM CANKER	Many trees and shrubs, including apple, ash and poplar.	Brown, cracked and sunken patches appear on the bark. Slime oozes from the area. Encirclement of a shoot or trunk causes die-back.	Any time.	Cut out and burn infected areas and small branches. Spray with Bordeaux mixture or copper fungicide, following the instructions on the label. If a tree is badly affected, destroy it. **Organic advice** Do not grow apple trees on wet, badly drained soil. *Populus nigra* is resistant to canker.
CARNATION RINGSPOT	Two carnation species – *Dianthus barbatus* and *D. caryophyllus.*	Circular grey spots develop on foliage, stems and occasionally on the flowers. Foliage may shrivel under damp conditions. Grey fungus may appear in the centre of the spots.	Growing season.	Remove diseased leaves and spray at regular intervals with Bordeaux mixture, following the instructions on the label.
CARNATION STEM-ROT AND DIE-BACK	All species.	Rotting caused by soil-borne fungus which enters the stems through wounds.	During wet periods and on poorly drained soil.	Spray stock plants with carbendazim. Use only sterilised composts for potting.
CELERY HEART ROT	Celery.	When celery is lifted the centres have a wet, slimy brown rot, often extending up the stalk. Bacteria are believed to enter through wounds caused by slugs, or severe frost injury.	Growing season.	Ensure good cultivation on well-drained soil and use a balanced fertiliser. Choose a fresh site for new celery to avoid a build-up of bacteria in the soil. Control slugs and give winter protection in cold districts. Carry out crop rotation.

PROBLEM	PLANTS AT RISK	RECOGNITION	DANGER PERIOD	TREATMENT
CELERY LEAF SPOT	Celery and celeriac – mature plants and seedlings.	Small brown spots on leaves and stems develop to become black fruiting bodies of fungus.	Wet weather.	Spray seedlings and plants with Bordeaux mixture or mancozeb, repeating at weekly intervals if necessary. Feed established plants with high-potash fertiliser to avoid soft growth. **Organic advice** Clear up all crop debris. Do not overuse nitrogen-rich feeds. Destroy any infected plants at the end of the season.
CHLOROSIS (Mineral)	Many plants, especially hydrangeas, peaches, ceanothus, raspberries and acid-loving plants, such as camellias and rhododendrons, on alkaline soil.	Leaves lose their rich green colour to become pale yellow or white.	Growing season.	Dig peat, pulverised bark or crushed bracken into the soil and use only fertilisers sold as lime-free. For iron deficiency (the commonest form of chlorosis) use a chelated-iron compound.
CHLOROSIS (Viral)	Vast range of garden plants.	The foliage turns yellow, either across the whole leaf, on the margins or just on the veins. The yellowing may occur in patterns of lines or rings.	Growing season.	Control aphids (see p. 824) which spread infection. Destroy badly infected plants, and buy virus-free plants where they exist.
CHOCOLATE SPOT	Broad beans.	Beans, foliage and sometimes the stems become covered with chocolate-coloured spots caused by a fungal disease. The whole plant may die.	June or July, or after severe winter frosts. Over-wintered crops are most at risk in a wet spring.	Spray with Bordeaux mixture or carbendazim as foliage appears. Encourage strong growth by liming the soil if necessary, using a potash fertiliser, ensuring good drainage and sowing seeds thinly. **Organic advice** Don't sow autumn or early spring crops on wet soils. Don't sow or plant too close together.
CHRYSANTHEMUM VIRUS DISEASES	Most varieties of dendranthema (chrysanthemum), both plants grown outdoors and those under glass.	Distorted blooms, break-up or greening of the flower colour, leaf mottling or stunted growth – the result of viruses transmitted by pests, including aphids.	Growing season.	Destroy all the affected plants. Prevent further infection by thoroughly washing your hands in hot soapy water and sterilising any equipment that has been used in tri-sodium orthophosphate.
CLEMATIS WILT	Clematis, especially large-flowered varieties.	Upper parts of shoot wilt, with young leaves wilting first and leaf stalks blackening where they join the blade. Caused by fungus.	Early spring and through the growing season.	Cut wilted shoots back to below soil level. Drench shoots with carbendazim when first damage is seen and again in spring. **Organic advice** Plant new clematis 15 cm (6 in) deeper than their level in the pot. Avoid wounding stems when planting, and tie stems to their support in the growing season to prevent damage. Clear up all diseased material and burn it.
CLUB ROOT	Brassicas, wallflowers, stocks, turnips and radishes.	Leaves of brassicas wilt and turn red, purple or yellow; roots become swollen and distorted. Plants wilt on hot days, but may recover if watered.	Throughout the growing season.	Once soil is infected, little can be done. Prevent the disease by liming the soil in winter to keep pH at 7-7.5. On badly drained soil make raised beds. Never bring in plants that may have the disease; raise your own from seed in sterilised compost. Kale, winter broccoli and spring cabbage grow better in infected soil than other brassicas. There are a few resistant types.

PROBLEM	PLANTS AT RISK	RECOGNITION	DANGER PERIOD	TREATMENT
COLLAR ROT	Plants grown in greenhouses.	Plants collapse at or just above soil level due to organisms rotting the tissue.	Any time.	Remove all dead and decaying tissues, and dust with Bordeaux powder. Repot plants in a lighter, sterilised compost and water carefully.
COMMON SCAB	Potatoes, beetroots, radishes, swedes and turnips.	Ragged-edged scabs develop on potato tubers due to organisms related to bacteria. The scabs do not render the potatoes inedible, but they should be removed before the potatoes are cooked.	Growing season.	Burn peelings or severely infected tubers. Avoid liming the soil before sowing or planting; instead, add humus – such as green manure – and maintain even growth by keeping the soil moist and by mulching. Grow resistant varieties, such as 'Arran Pilot', 'King Edward' and 'Pentland Crown'. Put a layer of grass mowings in the bottom of the trench when planting.
CORAL SPOT	Many trees and shrubs, including acers, maples, magnolias and redcurrants.	Rashes of pink or coral-red spots on dead twigs. Coral spot is a fungus that can kill trees or shrubs if it is able to enter living shoots. Affected plants may recently have been transplanted or suffered from drought or waterlogging.	Any time in plants under stress.	Cut out and burn all dead wood and prune 10-15 cm (4-6 in) below the diseased area. **Organic advice** Identify and rectify any cultural problems. Avoid injury to bark which would allow the disease to enter.
CORE ROT	Freesia and gladiolus corms.	Rotting spreads from the centre outwards, as the corm becomes spongy and turns brown or black.	During storage.	Burn infected corms. After lifting corms, dust them with sulphur or soak them in carbendazim, and store them in a dry atmosphere at 7-10°C (45-50°F).
CORKY SCAB OF CACTI	Cacti, especially epiphyllums and opuntias.	Sunken patches of irregular rusty or corky scabs.	Growing season.	Destroy badly affected plants and improve cultural conditions.
CORTICIUM See RED THREAD				
COX SPOT	'Cox's Orange Pippins' and (less so) some other apple varieties.	Small, round tan-coloured spots on leaves due to an unknown PHYSIOLOGICAL DISORDER	Usually after drought.	Try watering during dry spells and mulching the trees.
CRACKING	All types of root vegetables, especially carrots and parsnips. Also apples, pears, plums, gages and tomatoes.	Roots split lengthways; no symptoms appear above soil level. Fruit skins split to expose inner flesh.	Growing season – dry periods followed by heavy rain.	Avoid irregular growth by mulching heavily and maintaining even watering to prevent the soil from drying out.

PROBLEM	PLANTS AT RISK	RECOGNITION	DANGER PERIOD	TREATMENT
CRINKLE	Strawberries.	Yellow spots appear on the leaves, the centre of which may become red or purple. When these spots multiply and turn brown and the leaves pucker, the outbreak is severe. The cause is an aphid-borne virus which stunts growth.	Growing season.	Burn diseased plants and protect remainder by controlling aphids.
CROWN GALL	Many species, including soft and tree fruit, vegetables, shrubs and herbaceous perennials.	Hard or soft galls, sometimes in a chain along a root or shoot and often occurring in wet soil, are the result of bacteria entering through wounds.	Growing season.	Destroy infected plants and provide suitable drainage to prevent soil from becoming waterlogged. Avoid damage when planting and during cultivation.
CROWN ROT OF RHUBARB	Rhubarb.	Leaves become spindly and discoloured and die early. The main bud rots, followed by the whole of the crown, due to bacterial disease. Most common in wet soil.	Growing season.	Dig up and burn entire plant and never plant rhubarb on the same site again.
CUCUMBER MOSAIC VIRUS	Cucumbers and many other plants.	Leaves and fruit become mottled and puckered, and growth is stunted. Caused by an aphid-borne virus.	Growing season.	Burn affected plants immediately and control aphids. If the disease is a regular problem, grow resistant varieties.
DAMPING-OFF	Seedlings sown under glass in crowded and wet conditions.	Seedlings rot at ground level, topple over and die – killed by a parasitic fungus.	From seed-sowing to emergence of third pair of true leaves.	Remove and destroy dead seedlings. Water seed boxes with copper or Cheshunt compound. To prevent future trouble, sow thinly, use a sterilised seed compost, water carefully and ensure good ventilation. Always use clean containers, and never use rainwater from a butt unless the butt is cleaned regularly.
DIANTHUS LEAF SPOT	*Dianthus barbatus, D. caryophyllus* and occasionally *D. chinensis.*	Leaves develop circular or oval spots with tiny black spores, surrounded by a purple border, or small, round purple spots which gradually increase and coalesce. Infected leaves wither and die off at the tips. Caused by several fungi.	During damp periods of the growing season.	Remove infected leaves and spray plants with Bordeaux mixture or carbendazim.
DIE-BACK	Mainly fruit trees and shrubs.	Shoots die back from the tips, often killing larger branches. Foliage turns brown or yellow and withers. Damage may be due to frost, fungal infection or PHYSIOLOGICAL DISORDERS.	Any time.	Cut out all infected areas back to healthy wood and burn the cuttings. Treat identifiable disease appropriately; if unidentifiable, improve cultural conditions.

PROBLEM	PLANTS AT RISK	RECOGNITION	DANGER PERIOD	TREATMENT
DOWNY MILDEW	Brassica seedlings, marrows, courgettes and onions.	Plants develop a grey or whitish furry covering on the underside of the leaves, with blotches of yellow on the upper side, the result of being overcrowded, poorly watered and inadequately ventilated. Onion bulbs may rot in store.	During growing season, and on onions in store.	Thin out plants and spray with carbendazim or mancozeb (wait 14 days before eating). **Organic advice** Rotate future crops. Grow resistant varieties where available. Always sow seeds in fresh sterilised compost, and improve ventilation when raising plants under glass.
DROPSY See OEDEMA				
DRY ROT	Potatoes and some other tubers; also crocuses, freesias and gladioli.	Exposed growth turns yellow-brown and then collapses as leaf sheaths rot. Tubers (or corms) develop small dark lesions which enlarge and merge as the tubers shrivel and die. The cause is a soil-borne fungus.	From January onwards and during storage.	Destroy all infected tubers or corms as soon as the first symptoms appear. Before storing or replanting healthy ones, dust them with sulphur or dip them in a solution of carbendazim. Store them in a dry, cool, frostproof place. Plant tubers or corms in a fresh site each year.
FAIRY RINGS	Lawns.	Inner and outer rings of lush, dark green grass appear in the lawn, with brown or dead turf between them. In summer and autumn – especially during wet weather – small brown-capped toadstools flourish between the rings.	Any time.	Remove diseased turf to a depth of 30 cm (12 in) and water the soil with a solution of carbendazim. Alternatively, fork over the area to a depth of 8 cm (3 in) and water with carbendazim solution. **Organic advice** Improving the growing conditions might help, together with applications of sulphate of iron.
FIRE BLIGHT	Cotoneasters, hawthorns, sorbus species, apples, pears and other related ornamentals.	Flowers turn black, leaves turn brown and wither. Golden or white slime may exude from the stems. The symptoms can appear suddenly, giving the plant the appearance of having been scorched by fire.	Flowering time.	Remove and destroy the diseased shoots when the symptoms are identified, cutting back beyond the damage by at least 30 cm (12 in). If the whole plant shows symptoms, dig it up and remove it. Plant a resistant variety, such as *Sorbus intermedia*, *Malus × moerlandsii* 'Liset' or *Pyrus calleryana* 'Bradford'.
FOOT ROT	Tomatoes, bedding plants, sweet peas, peas and beans.	Stem bases turn black and rot, and the roots usually die due to various fungi.	Growing season.	Rotate vegetable and bedding plants, and always use sterile compost for pot plants. Water bedding plants in seed boxes with Cheshunt compound when they are put in their planting holes. If necessary, repeat at weekly intervals.
FROST DAMAGE	Young leaves and shoots on most species of flowering plants, shrubs and trees.	Cracking of tree trunks, blackening and shrivelling of leaves, and blackened flower centres and buds.	Mid winter and spring.	Cut out frostbitten shoots to prevent entry of fungi. Protect plants from further damage by covering them with paper, straw or sacking. Harden off tender plants before planting out.
FRUIT-DROP	All tree fruit.	Fruits drop prematurely while still immature.	Flowering time and just after.	Ensure that suitable pollinators are in the garden, and feed, mulch and water the tree. In cold seasons, fruit-drop is due to poor pollination and nothing can be done.

PROBLEM	PLANTS AT RISK	RECOGNITION	DANGER PERIOD	TREATMENT
FUSARIUM WILT • See also CALLISTEPHUS WILT	Carnations, dianthus species, dwarf and runner beans, garden peas and sweet peas.	Leaves become discoloured and plants wilt due to several species of fungus. Stems may also become discoloured.	Growing season.	Remove and burn the infected plants. Sterilise the soil or grow susceptible plants on a fresh site each year. Propagate carnations and dianthus species from healthy plants only. Drench with carbendazim, according to the instructions on the label.
GLADIOLUS DRY ROT See DRY ROT				
GLADIOLUS SCAB	Gladioli.	Reddish specks appear on the leaves, which enlarge and darken. Leaf tips shrivel. Craters develop at the base of the corms with raised rims and glossy coating. Yellow spots on the corms exude gum.	Scab strikes in summer but may not reveal itself until corms are lifted and stored.	As for DRY ROT.
GLADIOLUS YELLOWS	Gladioli.	Yellow stripes appear on the leaves, which gradually turn completely yellow and then die back. The flower stems may be crooked and greener than normal.	During the growing season, but the disease develops in storage.	Burn the infected plants immediately symptoms appear. Grow gladioli corms on a fresh site each year, and avoid nitrogen-rich fertilisers and manures.
GOOSEBERRY MILDEW (AMERICAN)	Gooseberries.	White mealy powder, caused by a fungal disease, covers leaves, shoots and fruits which later turn brown. Shoots may become distorted. The fruits are small and tasteless.	April onwards.	Remove diseased shoots and burn them immediately. Spray with carbendazim or bupirimate & triforine. **Organic advice** A problem when soil is dry and the weather is humid. Mulch plants and keep them well pruned to allow air to circulate. Grow resistant varieties. Do not overfeed with nitrogen-rich fertilisers.
GOOSEBERRY MILDEW (EUROPEAN)	Gooseberries, blackcurrants and occasionally redcurrants.	A light, powdery white covering develops on the upper leaf surface and sometimes on the underside and berries. Widespread on old bushes, but not as damaging as American gooseberry mildew.	Late April on gooseberries; late May to September on currants.	As for GOOSEBERRY MILDEW (AMERICAN).
GREENBACK • See also BLOTCHY RIPENING	Tomatoes.	As fruit starts to ripen, a ring (partial or complete) of hard leathery tissue is left around the stalk end. This area does not turn red – see PHYSIOLOGICAL DISORDERS.	As fruit develops.	The major cause is thought to be exposure to heat, so even fruits shaded from the sun in a greenhouse can succumb. In hot weather, ventilate the greenhouse and provide shade. Maintain even growth by ensuring that the soil does not dry out. Alternatively, grow resistant varieties.
GREY BULB ROT	Tulips, hyacinths and other bulbous plants.	Young shoots do not appear in spring. A dry grey rot at the neck of the bulbs gradually spreads to develop clusters of black fungi, and then the bulbs disintegrate.	Soon after planting.	Remove and burn all debris from infected plants; replace surrounding soil with sterilised compost. Dust bulbs and corms with carbendazim before planting. Preferably avoid planting bulbs in infected areas for several years.

PROBLEM	PLANTS AT RISK	RECOGNITION	DANGER PERIOD	TREATMENT
GREY MOULD (Botrytis)	Many types, both outdoors and under glass.	A grey velvety mould, caused by a fungal disease, forms on leaves, flowers and soft fruits. The disease is encouraged by damp, overcrowded conditions and poor ventilation in a greenhouse.	Growing season. Worst in winter for lettuces.	If possible destroy infected plants. Pick off dying flowers and buds. Spray herbaceous plants with carbendazim. Destroy diseased bulbs; dust healthy ones with carbendazim. Cut out infected areas on trees or shrubs. Spray soft fruit with carbendazim when flowers appear, and until just before fruits ripen. Under glass, spray with carbendazim or propiconazole as symptoms appear.
GUMMING	Cherries and other prunus species.	Gum, exuding on the surface of branches and trunks, gradually hardens – the result of unsuitable soil conditions or malnutrition.	Any time, but at its worst in summer.	Gumming should stop with good feeding, mulching and watering. Gum may have to be removed in order to cut out dead wood beneath. Do this in October.
GUMMOSIS OF CUCUMBER	Cucumbers, melons, vegetable marrows and courgettes that are grown in a greenhouse or coldframe.	Small grey sunken spots exude sticky liquid. This develops into a velvety dark green mould, and the fruits crack. The symptoms sometimes appear on the leaves and stems as brownish patches.	Inadequate ventilation and heat under cool damp conditions.	Burn all diseased fruits. Disinfect greenhouse or coldframe with phenolic compound or a garden disinfectant before planting another crop.
HARD ROT	Chiefly gladiolus corms, but also the corms of crocus and freesia.	Sharply defined tiny brown spots on leaves which develop infectious fungi in diseased tissue; black-brown sunken spots on corms. More common in the south of Britain than the north.	Fungus spreads fast in wet weather in poor soils. Symptoms may appear in storage.	Destroy all diseased bulbs and corms, and burn the foliage at the end of the season as the disease may overwinter on dead plant debris. Dip healthy corms in a solution of carbendazim before storing.
HEATHER DIE-BACK	Calluna and erica.	The foliage develops a greyish tinge, then wilts, turns brown and dies.	Throughout the growing season in badly drained soil.	No cure. Dig up and burn infected plants. Keep remaining plants healthy by applying an acid-formulation fertiliser in April, and mulching with leaf-mould, shredded bark or woodchips. Improve drainage.
HONEY FUNGUS (Bootlace fungus)	Most trees and shrubs. Common among rotting tree stumps, some herbaceous perennials and some bulbs.	Toadstools at soil level at the base of the trunk. White fan-shaped growths of fungus occur beneath the bark of roots and at soil level. Black 'bootlace' threads on diseased roots spread infection.	Autumn.	Destroy dead or dying plants and as many roots as possible. Sterilise the soil with a phenolic compound such as Armillatox. The 'bootlaces' do not necessarily mean disaster. Many species of the fungus are not invasive.
HORMONE WEEDKILLER DAMAGE	All types, but tomatoes and vines particularly susceptible.	Leaves become narrow, often yellow, fan-shaped and frequently cupped.	Growing season.	Plants usually recover without treatment. To avoid future damage, do not use weedkiller spray on a windy or hot day, or use weedkiller equipment for any other jobs. Mowings from a freshly treated lawn can be put on a compost heap, provided they are not spread on the garden for at least six months and are well decomposed.

PROBLEM	PLANTS AT RISK	RECOGNITION	DANGER PERIOD	TREATMENT
INK DISEASE	Bulbous irises, lachenalias, tritonias and crocosmias.	As the young leaves show through the ground, they have yellow streaks which become black blotches. If the leaves develop, they may turn red and wither. Diseased bulbs have black crusty patches on their outer scales.	Wet season.	Remove and burn all infected bulbs.
INTERNAL RUST SPOT	Potatoes.	Brown spots and blotches in the flesh of potato tubers, possibly due to dry soil.	Growing season.	Incorporate plenty of well-rotted manure or compost into the soil before planting, and water regularly.
IRIS MOSAIC VIRUS	Bulbous and bearded irises.	Yellow streaks and spots occur on young leaves. Plants may be stunted. The flowers often show darker streaks on the normal ground colour.	Growing season.	Destroy all infected plants. Control aphids which spread the virus (see p. 824).
LEAF MOULD	Tomatoes that are being grown under glass. Rare on outdoor plants.	Purple-brown mould on the underside of leaves, with yellow blotches on the upper side. The plant's growth is checked and fruit develops poorly.	Summer. Sometimes as early as April, but not usually until June.	Improve the cultural conditions and maintain a maximum temperature in the greenhouse of 21°C (70°F) with good ventilation. Do not let high temperature coincide with high humidity. Remove and destroy lower foliage if it shows signs of attack. Check the disease by spraying with carbendazim or copper fungicide. Grow resistant varieties.
LEAF ROT	Dianthus species, including garden pinks.	Leaves and stems develop white or brownish water-soaked spots with dark margins, or grey spots. Flower buds may also be affected.	Growing season.	Remove and burn all diseased tissues and spray plant with Bordeaux mixture.
LEAF SPOT	Blackcurrants and gooseberries, celery and spinach, plus a wide range of ornamental plants.	The leaves and stems develop round or oval brown spots – sometimes with a black pinpoint – and the leaves then fall prematurely.	Late spring onwards.	Remove and burn all diseased leaves. Spray plants with mancozeb, carbendazim or Bordeaux mixture, following the instructions on the label.
LEAFY GALL	Many species, but in particular sweet peas, dahlias, pelargoniums, chrysanthemums, carnations, gladioli and strawberries.	Abortive shoots, often flattened with thickened distorted leaves, develop at soil level due to bacterial infection.	During propagation and the growing season.	Remove and burn all infected plants. Wash tools in tri-sodium orthophosphate and wash your hands after handling infected material. When replanting, choose a non-susceptible plant. Always grow susceptible plants in clean containers and sterilised compost.

PROBLEM	PLANTS AT RISK	RECOGNITION	DANGER PERIOD	TREATMENT
LEEK RUST	Leeks.	Shoots become twisted or malformed and covered with an orange powder.	Summer and early autumn, or in spring on over-wintered crops.	If rust attacks late varieties of leeks, spray with mancozeb. **Organic advice** On leeks, symptoms often disappear when autumn arrives, so no treatment is necessary. Leek rust is more likely where potash is low, nitrogen is high and drainage is poor.

LETTUCE VIRUS DISEASES See ARABIS MOSAIC VIRUS, CUCUMBER MOSAIC VIRUS

LICHENS	Grass, trees and shrubs.	Grass: overlapping leaf structures which grow horizontally in the turf – deep green-black when moist, and grey-green or brown when dry. Trees and shrubs: thin crusts of grey or orange tissue, or leafy-looking plants, growing on the bark.	Grass: at any time; trees and shrubs: harmless.	Grass: rake out the growths and treat affected areas with dichlorophen. Drain if possible and spike the surface. Brush in lime-free sand, top-dress and feed. Trees and shrubs: lichen on these are harmless and should be left. Encourage vigorous growth of the host by feeding in spring and summer.
LILAC BLIGHT	Syringas.	Brown angular spots develop on the leaves, followed by young shoots turning black and withering.	Spring.	Cut the infected shoots back to healthy buds and spray with Bordeaux mixture. Spray again the following spring when the leaves start to appear.
LILY DISEASE	Lilies – particularly *Lilium candidum*.	Leaves develop small red-brown oval-shaped, water-saturated spots of fungus which spread rapidly. In humid conditions, leaves may turn brown, flowers rot and stems collapse.	Wet seasons.	Cut off and burn infected growths. When new leaves appear in spring, spray all plants with carbendazim or Bordeaux mixture. Repeat at fortnightly intervals until flowering begins and, during a wet season, again after flowering. Destroy all infected material at the end of the season, as the fungus can overwinter in the soil.

LIME-INDUCED CHLOROSIS See CHLOROSIS

MAGNESIUM DEFICIENCY	All types of plants, particularly tomatoes and apples.	Leaves turn yellow (sometimes orange-brown) between the veins, giving a marbled effect; they then fall prematurely. Symptoms appear first on older leaves. In light, acid, sandy soil the problem is worse in a wet season as magnesium is easily leached.	During the growing season, or following the use of a high-potash fertiliser.	Spray the plants with a solution of magnesium sulphate – 8 tablespoons to 11 litres (2½ gallons) of water – plus a few drops of liquid detergent. **Organic advice** If lime is needed, use dolomitic (magnesian) limestone.
MANGANESE DEFICIENCY	Many species.	Yellowing occurs between the veins of older leaves. Dead patches may appear among the yellow areas. The disorder occurs mainly in poorly drained sandy soil, highly organic soil and wet areas of low acidity.	Growing season.	Spray the plants with a solution of manganese sulphate – 2 tablespoons to 11 litres (2½ gallons) of water plus a few drops of liquid detergent – or apply chelated or fritted compounds.

MILDEW See DOWNY MILDEW, GOOSEBERRY MILDEW (AMERICAN), GOOSEBERRY MILDEW (EUROPEAN), POWDERY MILDEW

PROBLEM	PLANTS AT RISK	RECOGNITION	DANGER PERIOD	TREATMENT
MINERAL DEFICIENCIES See BORON DEFICIENCY, CHLOROSIS (Mineral), MAGNESIUM DEFICIENCY, MANGANESE DEFICIENCY, NITROGEN DEFICIENCY, POTASSIUM DEFICIENCY, WHIPTAIL				

MINT RUST

	Mint.	Thickened and distorted shoots bear orange-coloured fungal spores.	Symptoms appear in spring; affected plants are permanently diseased.	Cut out and burn affected shoots, and spray the soil with propiconazole. Burn off withered top growth of the mint bed in autumn or early winter.

MOSAIC VIRUS See ARABIS MOSAIC VIRUS, CUCUMBER MOSAIC VIRUS, IRIS MOSAIC VIRUS

MOULD See BLUE MOULD, GREY MOULD, LEAF MOULD, SNOW MOULD, SOOTY MOULD

NARCISSUS FIRE

	Narcissi – particularly in the West Country.	Rotting flowerheads caused by fungal disease, together with GREY MOULD spreading to the leaves.	Wet seasons.	Burn infected leaves to stop fungus overwintering. Remove plants showing infection in spring. Spray remainder when 2.5 cm (1 in) high with bupirimate & triforine, or thiram. Repeat at 10 day intervals until the flower buds emerge from the leaf sheaths.

NECK ROT

	Onions.	A grey velvety mould develops near the neck of stored onions causing them to rot rapidly.	Growing season, but symptoms do not appear until storage.	Destroy diseased onions as they appear. Store only those onions which are well ripened and hard in a dry, airy place. Use a 3 or 4 year rotation system. Do not overfeed with nitrogen-rich manures or fertilisers as large bulbs are more prone to neck rot than smaller ones.

NITROGEN DEFICIENCY

	All types, but most commonly fruit trees and vegetables.	The young leaves turn pale yellow-green, and later develop yellow, red or purple tints. The plants are small, stunted and lack vigour.	Growing season.	Use nitrogenous fertiliser such as blood, fish and bone or sulphate of ammonia in spring. Improve soil structure and fertility generally. For a quick result, water with a liquid feed or apply a nitrogen-rich foliar feed. A temporary deficiency can arise in cold weather, but it will disapper as the soil warms up.

OEDEMA (Dropsy)

	Many species, but frequently on succulents, semi-succulents, camellias and ivy-leaved pelargoniums.	Small bumps on the leaves are caused by too much water inside the plant. This can be due to a saturated soil or to a wet atmosphere. Leaves sometimes fall off.	Any time.	Reduce watering. Increase greenhouse ventilation to reduce humidity. The infected leaves will not recover but they should be left; they will help the plant to lose its excess water.

ONION NECK ROT See NECK ROT

PANSY SICKNESS

	Violas.	Roots and stems are attacked by soil-borne organisms causing plants to collapse.	Growing season.	Remove and destroy diseased plants and their roots. Water seedlings and established plants with Cheshunt compound, repeating at weekly intervals if necessary. Choose a new site every year.

PROBLEM	PLANTS AT RISK	RECOGNITION	DANGER PERIOD	TREATMENT
PARSNIP CANKER	Parsnips.	Reddish brown cankers may form on the shoulder of a root, with the leaves developing small black spots with green halos. The disease is caused by fungus.	June onwards.	Avoid disease by sowing seeds early in deep loamy soil, enriched with balanced fertiliser, and lime if needed. Improve drainage and rotate crops. Control carrot fly (see p. 826). If trouble persists, grow resistant varieties. **Organic advice** Small roots, produced by growing parsnips at a spacing of 7.5-10 cm (3-4 in), are less prone to canker. Earthing up may help.
PEACH LEAF CURL	Almonds, apricots, nectarines, peaches and related ornamental prunus species.	Leaves develop large red blisters, turn white, then brown and finally fall prematurely due to fungus.	Before bud-burst.	Remove and burn infected leaves. Spray with mancozeb or Bordeaux mixture in January/early February. Repeat a fortnight later and just before leaf-fall. **Organic advice** Wall-trained trees can be protected from rain with a small roof of polythene. It should be in place before bud-burst, and may be removed once all foliage is expanded. The sides should be left open.
PEAR SCAB	Pears.	Leaves and fruit form dark brown velvety blotches, and the fruit becomes distorted. The symptoms are caused by a fungus disease that overwinters on fallen leaves and also on the tree, so young shoots in spring may be blistered and cracked.	Growing season, but most severe after a wet May.	See APPLE SCAB.
PEONY WILT (Peony blight)	Peonies.	GREY MOULD forms on the stems at soil level, causing them to collapse. It then spreads to form brown blotches on the leaves of neighbouring plants.	Growing season.	Cut out all affected shoots to below soil level, and burn them. Dust the crowns of the plants with dry Bordeaux powder. Spray with carbendazim or mancozeb soon after the leaves appear.
PETUNIA WILT	Petunias, zinnias, salpiglossis and other bedding plants.	Plants wilt, often as they are about to flower, and the base of the stems may become discoloured.	Growing season.	Burn all diseased plants. Rotate bedding plants so that vulnerable types are grown on a fresh site each year.
PHYTOPHTHORA ROOT ROT	Trees and shrubs. Most common on Lawson cypress, rhododendrons and azaleas, beech, heathers, limes, apples, prunus and yews.	Small, sparse yellow foliage, with partial die-back often up one side of the plant. The whole plant may die. Sometimes only recognised when new growth fails to appear in spring.	Warm wet periods.	None. Only obtain plants from a reputable nursery. Avoid waterlogging or poorly drained soil. Never transplant from an infected area onto clean soil.

PROBLEM	PLANTS AT RISK	RECOGNITION	DANGER PERIOD	TREATMENT

• PHYSIOLOGICAL DISORDERS •

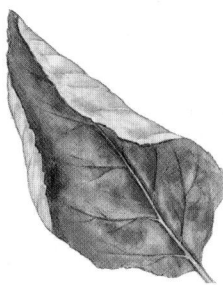

Healthy plants depend on a combination of essentials – water, mineral salts, air, temperature and light. If any of these essentials is lacking or the balance is wrong, the result may produce a physiological disorder.

Correct watering must be available at each stage of a plant's growth. Too much, too little or sporadic watering can create problems from which a plant may never recover.

Mineral salts should be present in the soil in the correct quantities and form. Some plants need more or less nutrients than others, according to the nature of the soil, the growing conditions and the care they are given. Symptoms of plant problems often indicate MINERAL DEFICIENCIES.

An atmosphere that is too humid can lead to the growth of fungal diseases, while one that is too dry may cause poor growth and induce flower buds to drop. Fluctuating temperatures which are either too high or too low can cause similar problems, while a lack of light leads to thin, weak and colourless plants, with the flowering reduced or non-existent.

Physiological disorders can usually be rectified by careful cultivation – feeding, mulching, watering, drainage and correct spacing.

POTASSIUM DEFICIENCY

| | Plants in clay, chalky soil or peat, particularly those that need extra potash – potatoes, beans, tomatoes, apples, pears, currants. | Stunted growth and reduced leaf size. The leaves turn a dull blue-green, and turn brown at the tips or margins, or curl downwards. Shoots, and sometimes whole branches, die back. Fruit are sparse, small, highly coloured. | Any time. | For fruit, apply sulphate of potash every March at 100-140 g per m² (3-4 oz per sq yd). To improve flowering or berrying on trees and shrubs, apply sulphate of potash at 18g per m² (½ oz per sq yd) in early spring or late summer. |

POTATO BLACKLEG See BLACKLEG

POTATO BLIGHT See BLIGHT

POWDERY SCAB

| | Potatoes. | Raised round scabs which subsequently burst to release a powdery mass of spores. Tubers may be deformed by a soil-inhabiting fungus and have an earthy taste. | In heavy soils, during cool damp weather through the growing season. | Destroy diseased tubers. Avoid planting potatoes on the same site for several years. Improve drainage and grow resistant varieties. |

POWDERY MILDEW

| | A wide range of plants including strawberries, roses and apples. | A white mildew, caused by a fungus, appears on leaves, shoots and flowers, and weakens the plant. Warm dry weather encourages the disease. | Growing season. | Remove and burn infected growth. Water well and mulch with garden compost, leaf-mould or well-rotted manure. Avoid overuse of nitrogenous fertiliser. Spray with dinocap or triforine, following the instructions on the label. Sulphur can be applied as a dust. Buy resistant varieties of rose, apple and strawberry plants. |

PYRACANTHA SCAB

| | Pyracanthas. | Leaves and berries acquire a thick, felt-like, olive-brown or black coating – a fungal disease resembling soot – and scabby lesions form on the shoots. Leaves may drop early and berries become disfigured and shrivelled. | During wet periods. | Cut out and burn all diseased shoots. Spray with carbendazim at fortnightly intervals as soon as the disease is seen. **Organic advice** Don't grow pyracanthas in damp places. Grow resistant varieties. |

RASPBERRY VIRUS

| | Raspberries. | Leaves develop yellow blotches and become distorted. Canes are stunted and the crop is poor. | Growing season. | Dig up and burn all affected plants. Plant new canes on a fresh site and control aphids, which spread the virus disease. Only buy raspberry canes which are certified free from virus. |

PROBLEM	PLANTS AT RISK	RECOGNITION	DANGER PERIOD	TREATMENT
RAY BLIGHT	Dendranthemas in the greenhouse.	Dark, water-soaked spots or blotches on petals cause flowers to rot.	Spreads rapidly in humid conditions when the temperature reaches 16°C (61°F).	Reduce humidity and remove all infected plants. Sterilise or change the soil.
RED THREAD (Corticium)	Grass.	Dead patches of turf with outbreaks of red fungus.	Autumn, after rain.	Spray with dichlorophen and, if necessary, alternate treatment with carbendazim, according to manufacturer's instructions. Aerate the soil and apply a nitrogenous fertiliser in spring.
REVERSION	Blackcurrants.	Flower buds are hairless and a bright magenta instead of the normal dull grey. Despite vigorous shoots, the leaves are also smaller and have fewer lobes than normal. The disease is caused by a virus.	Early summer.	Control the gall mites which spread the virus (see p. 829). Destroy badly diseased bushes and replace with plants which are certified as free of virus disease.
RHIZOME ROT	Rhizomatous irises.	Leaf fan collapses at soil level due to the soft, yellow and evil-smelling rot at its growing point.	Any time, but mostly in wet weather.	Destroy badly infected plants. On less severe outbreaks, cut out the rotting parts and dust the wounds with Bordeaux mixture.
RHODODENDRON BUD BLAST	Evergreen rhododendron species and hybrids.	Buds turn grey or brown. In spring, black, bristle-like structures appear on the infected buds, bearing a pinhead of fungus spores which are transmitted by rhododendron leafhoppers.	Between October and December.	Control the rhododendron leafhoppers (see p. 834). Destroy all affected buds and spray with Bordeaux mixture just before flowering and at monthly intervals.
ROSE BLACK SPOT	Roses.	Leaves develop sooty irregular spots on both surfaces which, when severe, can lead to yellowing and leaf-fall. Caused by a fungal disease.	Growing season.	Spray with carbendazim, myclobutanil or mancozeb in February and then at two-weekly intervals. **Organic advice** Grow resistant varieties. Do not overfeed with nitrogen-rich fertilisers. Remove dead leaves from the soil in autumn. In spring, cut out infected shoots before bud-burst, remove old leaves and apply mulch.
RUSSETING	Apples, pears and other fruits.	Roughening of the skin – a natural characteristic, but sometimes a symptom of disease, such as powdery mildew, frost damage, or chemical damage.	Any time.	Control mildew, use chemicals carefully and ensure good cultivation. See FROST DAMAGE and POWDERY MILDEW.

PROBLEM	PLANTS AT RISK	RECOGNITION	DANGER PERIOD	TREATMENT
RUST • See also LEEK RUST, MINT RUST, WHITE RUST	Many decorative plants, including rose bushes, fuchsias and hollyhocks.	Shoots become malformed and covered with orange-coloured fungal spores.	Growing season.	Remove all the affected stems. Spray plants with myclobutanil or mancozeb at the first sign of an attack, following the instructions on the label.
SALIX WATERMARK	Willows – most common on *Salix alba* varieties.	Leaves turn red and wilt, then die but remain on the tree. Infection can be confirmed by cutting through an affected branch. A watery reddish brown or brown-black stain will be found on the wood.	Growing season.	Remove and burn all infected plants. Sterilise tools that have been used with tri-sodium orthophosphate.
SCAB See APPLE SCAB, COMMON SCAB, CORKY SCAB OF CACTI, GLADIOLUS SCAB, PEAR SCAB, POWDERY SCAB, PYRACANTHA SCAB				
SCALD	Plums, apples and soft fruit – particularly tomatoes and grapes under glass.	Plums have red sunken patches; apples have discoloured patches on the skin encircled by a halo; tomatoes have creamy white wrinkled patches; grapes have discoloured patches.	Long hot summers.	Remove affected fruits – even if the flesh beneath is undamaged – before GREY MOULD develops. Damp down the greenhouse early in the day so that any moisture on the fruit dries out before the sun is too strong. Shade greenhouse crops during bright periods.
SCLEROTINIA DISEASE	Herbaceous perennials, bulbs, corms, tubers – including stored root crops, especially carrots and parsnips.	Plants may wilt suddenly, develop yellow basal leaves and collapse where the disease entered. Diseased tissue has a white fluffy mass containing large black fungal growth. The roots eventually soften and decay.	During growing season and when crops are in store.	Burn all diseased plants to prevent risk of the infection spreading. **Organic advice** Use a minimum 4 year rotation. Control weeds in the garden, on which the disease may overwinter.
SCORCHING (Scorch)	Most types of greenhouse and indoor plants, plus acers and beeches.	Affected leaves develop pale brown spots or become papery, either due to cold drying winds or – often when in a greenhouse – scorching by the sun.	Spring for trees and shrubs; summer for greenhouse and indoor plants.	Shade the greenhouse or remove vulnerable plants, especially if the panes are damaged. Ensure that plants are adequately watered, but avoid wetting the leaves during bright warm periods. Water indoor plants from the base to avoid wetting the leaves.
SEEDLING BLIGHT	Zinnias.	Leaves develop red-brown spots with grey centres; the stems develop brown canker-like areas; and the seedlings collapse and die – all due to a fungal disease.	While the plant is small.	Once the symptoms have appeared, the affected plants must be burnt. Protect seedlings in boxes with a copper-containing fungicidal spray.
SHOTHOLE	Cherries, plums, peaches and ornamental prunus species.	Leaves develop brown patches which become irregularly shaped holes, either due to leaf-spotting fungi or BACTERIAL CANKER.	Growing season.	Feed trees annually. Mulch and water well in spring, and give small trees a foliar feed. If symptoms appear next season, spray with carbendazim during summer, and at leaf-fall.

PROBLEM	PLANTS AT RISK	RECOGNITION	DANGER PERIOD	TREATMENT
SILVER LEAF	Peaches, plums, cherries and other prunus species; apples, pears and lilacs; and other trees and shrubs.	Some leaves become silvered and later turn brown, while infected branches die back. A flat purple fungus develops on dead wood.	September to May.	Cut a branch, at least 2.5 cm (1 in) thick, and moisten the wound. If it is diseased a brown or purple stain will appear. Cut out the affected branches to a point 15 cm (6 in) below the fungus. Sterilise tools with tri-sodium orthophosphate. Prune plums and cherries only in June-August. Try biological control with trichoderma pellets.
SMOULDER	Narcissi.	Leaves develop grey velvety mould and rot, and bulbs decay – the result of a fungal disease. More severe in a cold, wet season.	Foliage symptoms in the spring; bulbs during storage.	Destroy infected bulbs and store remainder in a cool, dry place. Remove and burn affected plants during the growing season as soon as symptoms are seen. Spray the rest with mancozeb at 10 day intervals.
SMUTS	Herbaceous perennials, bulbs, corms, tubers, onions, sweetcorn.	Blister-like swellings form on leaves and stalks, then burst to discharge masses of sooty spores. Caused by a fungal disease. Looks similar to SOOTY MOULD.	Long hot summers.	Burn diseased plants and plant new ones on a different site. Protect healthy plants by spraying with Bordeaux mixture or bupirimate & triforine. Disinfect coldframes or greenhouse.
SNOW MOULD	Grass.	Most obvious after a snow thaw or during moist weather when patches of turf turn brown and die, and are covered with a white, cotton-like growth of fungus.	Any time, but most severe in October.	Treat as for RED THREAD. After August, apply an autumn lawn fertiliser only, which is low in nitrogen but high in phosphate and potash.
SOFT ROT	Root vegetables and stored roots.	A bacterial disease which reduces plants to a soft, slimy and foul-smelling rot. The disease enters the plant through damaged tissues.	Any time.	Destroy infected plants and vegetables. Improve your cultural methods and storage conditions.
SOOTY MOULD	Very wide range of plants, both outdoors and under glass.	Dark brown or black sooty fungus appears on the top side of the leaves. It is always associated with sap-feeding insects such as aphids, adelgids, scale insects, whiteflies and mealy bugs.	Throughout the year.	Wipe off the mould with a damp cloth, then apply a systemic insecticide, such as heptenophos & permethrin, to control the pest that is feeding on the plant.
SPLITTING See CRACKING				
SPUR BLIGHT	Raspberries and loganberries.	Canes develop purple to silver blotches, spotted with black, caused by a fungal disease. The spores spread the disease to healthy plants.	Spring and summer.	After fruiting, cut out and destroy infected canes. When new canes are a few centimetres high, spray with carbendozim or bupirimate & triforine, and repeat 3 or 4 times at fortnightly intervals.

PROBLEM	PLANTS AT RISK	RECOGNITION	DANGER PERIOD	TREATMENT
STEM CANKER	Conifers.	The red fruiting bodies of a fungal disease appear on dead bark. The fungus enters through wounds caused by frost, damage or injury to cause DIE-BACK of shoots.	After frost.	Cut out all infected shoots right back to healthy wood.
STEM ROT	Tomatoes, godetias, lobelias and carnations, each of which is affected by a different disease.	Rotting of stems – but no obvious fungal growth – is visible on the affected areas.	Growing season.	Where possible, cut out and burn all diseased tissue, and spray plants with carbendazim. Alternatively, destroy diseased plants.
STONY PIT VIRUS	Old pear trees.	Fruit pitted and deformed, with patches of dead, stony cells in the flesh making it inedible. The virus appears first on one branch and then over the years spreads throughout the whole tree until all the fruit is affected.	Any time.	Cut down and burn diseased trees.
STRAWBERRY VIRUS DISEASES	Strawberries.	Virus diseases that are spread by aphids are ARABIS MOSAIC VIRUS and CRINKLE.	Any time.	Control the aphids (see p. 824). Destroy all diseased plants and replenish the stock with certified virus-free plants.
TAR SPOT	Acers, especially sycamores.	Fruiting bodies of fungi appear as yellow patches on the upper surface of leaves, developing into large black blotches, or red-brown to yellowish blotches.	When the tree is in leaf.	Burn diseased leaves as they fall. Spray small trees in spring, when the leaves unfold, with copper-containing fungicide or bupirimate & triforine. **Organic advice** The effect of the disease is mainly on appearance. No treatment is needed other than for cosmetic reasons.
TOBACCO MOSAIC VIRUS	Primarily tomatoes, but also some cacti, orchids and herbaceous species.	Various strains produce varied symptoms – dark and light green mottling on the leaves; bright yellow spots and patches on leaves and fruit stalks; and fruits blotched with brown.	Growing season.	None. Burn all diseased plants and their roots, including debris in the soil. Eradicate greenhouse pests. Sow only tomato seeds that are certified to be free of virus infection.
TOMATO SPOTTED WILT VIRUS	Tomatoes under glass, houseplants and herbaceous species outdoors.	A mosaic or mottling of the foliage, which may be distorted, due to a virus transmitted by thrips.	Growing season.	Destroy all infected plants and control thrips (see p. 836).

PROBLEM	PLANTS AT RISK	RECOGNITION	DANGER PERIOD	TREATMENT

TOMATO VIRUS DISEASES See ARABIS MOSAIC VIRUS, CUCUMBER MOSAIC VIRUS, TOBACCO MOSAIC VIRUS, TOMATO SPOTTED WILT VIRUS

PROBLEM	PLANTS AT RISK	RECOGNITION	DANGER PERIOD	TREATMENT
TREE RUST	Mainly birch, plum, poplar and willow.	Masses of brown, orange or yellow spores, caused by fungi developing on the underside of leaves and stems. Serious outbreaks can kill plants.	Summer.	Destroy severely infected plants. Remove affected leaves on mild outbreaks and spray with propiconazole, bupirimate & triforine, or mancozeb when symptoms are first seen. Encourage vigorous growth by good cultural treatment.
TULIP FIRE	Tulips.	Small brown spots on the petals, which later become covered in GREY MOULD. Caused by a fungal disease. Bulbs rot and bear small black fungal growths.	Flowering time – particularly in cold wet weather; bulbs shortly before or after planting.	Destroy all diseased plants and rotting or fungus-bearing bulbs. If possible, choose a fresh site each year, especially after the disease has appeared. Spray with carbendazim or mancozeb when leaves are about 5 cm (2 in) high and repeat at 10 day intervals until flowering.
VERTICILLIUM WILT	Cotinus, rhus and acer, tomatoes and carnations in greenhouses, Michaelmas daisies.	The leaves of one or two shoots wilt, and affected branches eventually die back. The disease is caused by a soil-borne fungus entering wounds. On tomatoes all leaves wilt, but recover overnight.	Growing season.	On trees and shrubs cut back affected branches to living tissue. If trouble recurs, lift and burn the plant. Destroy diseased greenhouse plants, and sterilise the greenhouse at the end of the season. Take tip cuttings of diseased Michaelmas daisies, and burn old plants. Carbendazim gives some control.
VIOLET ROOT ROT	Primarily carrots, parsnips and asparagus, but also some ornamentals and fruit crops.	Leaves turn yellow and die as purple-violet threads of fungus attack the roots.	Growing season.	Lift and burn diseased plants. Isolate the infected area by sinking pieces of rigid polythene or corrugated iron 30 cm (12 in) deep for the rest of the life of the bed. Avoid growing vulnerable plants there for several years. **Organic advice** Avoid planting crops in wet, acid soils.

• VIRUS DISEASES •

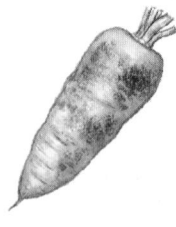

Viruses are microscopic particles, capable of causing disease in living cells, and can enter plant tissues only through wounds.

Viruses may be transmitted to other plants through the air, soil, fungi, seeds, vegetative grafting, propagation and by handling. Most viruses, however, are spread by insects, such as aphids, eelworms, leafhoppers, mites, thrips and whiteflies. Symptoms of a virus disease vary. There may be colour variation in the leaves, stems, flowers and tubers, or there may be plant distortion, wilting, stunted growth and tissue decay.

A plant may suffer from one or many viruses, with a different combination of viruses producing a number of different symptoms.

There is no chemical treatment for virus-infected plants, and any that are severely diseased should be destroyed. Use only healthy plants for propagation and where possible buy only new stock certified as being free of viruses. Good garden hygiene and the control of the insects that carry the viruses both help to prevent virus diseases from entering the garden.

PROBLEM	PLANTS AT RISK	RECOGNITION	DANGER PERIOD	TREATMENT
WART DISEASE	Potatoes.	Developing tubers produce large warty outgrowths, and subsequently disintegrate, due to a soil-borne fungus.	Growing season.	This is a Notifiable Disease and must be reported to the local plant health inspector or the Ministry of Agriculture, Fisheries and Food. All new potato varieties are immune to the disease, but some older ones are not. All diseased potatoes must be destroyed.

PROBLEM	PLANTS AT RISK	RECOGNITION	DANGER PERIOD	TREATMENT
WHIPTAIL	Broccoli and cauliflowers.	Leaves become distorted — ruffled, thin and strap-like — due to a lack of molybdenum.	During the growing period in acid soils.	Water with a solution of molybdate — 1 rounded tablespoon in 9 litres (2 gallons) of water for every 8 m² (10 sq yd) of soil. **Organic advice** As molybdenum is not available to plants on acid soils, lime the soil, if necessary, to bring pH to 6.5.
WHITE BLISTER	Brassicas and related ornamental plants, including honesty (lunaria).	Leaves and stems develop white glistening pustules filled with powdery spores. The disease is caused by a fungus. Severely affected foliage may be very distorted.	Growing season.	Remove and burn all diseased leaves and stems from the plant.
WHITE ROT	Mainly salad onions, and occasionally leeks, shallots and garlic.	Bulbs develop a white fungus at their base and rot.	Growing season.	Burn the affected plants. Grow onions on a new site each year — once the disease has struck, the soil remains contaminated for up to 20 years. No chemical treatment is available to amateur gardeners.
WHITE RUST	Chrysanthemums (dendranthemas).	The upper leaf surface develops yellow to pale green spots. The underside has buff or white spots. The spots may turn brown and die in the centre.	Growing season.	Cut off the infected parts of the plant and destroy them. Spray the remainder of the plant with a fungicide such as Tumbleblite to kill off any incipient infection.
WINTER KILLING	Mainly wallflowers.	Sideshoots either die back or the plant dies. Caused by FROST DAMAGE and GREY MOULD.	Late winter to late spring.	Set out plants early so that they are fully established before winter and carry out good cultivation.
WIRE STEM	Brassicas and other seedlings.	The base of the stems turns brown and shrinks, and easily breaks. Seedlings die or become stunted, both due to a fungal disease.	During early growth.	Destroy diseased plants. Raise seedlings in sterilised compost.
WITCHES BROOMS	Prunus species and birches.	Clusters of erect shoots, growing abnormally from a single point, on infected branches. The condition is caused by a fungal disease.	Throughout the life of the tree.	Cut off the affected branch to a point 15 cm (6 in) below the broom.

Glossary

Technical terms have been avoided wherever possible
in this book, but sometimes they are unavoidable.
The following definitions will make them clear

a

ALPINE
Strictly speaking, any plant that is native to mountainous regions, growing between the tree line and permanent snow line. 'Alpine' is also loosely applied to any small plant suitable for growing in a rock garden.

ALPINE HOUSE
A greenhouse that has continuous ventilation along the eaves, vents at bench level and, ideally, a door at each end. No heat is necessary; however, as alpine plants dislike cold wet conditions, some growers maintain their alpine houses at 1°C (34°F).

ANNUAL
A plant that completes its life cycle in a single growing season – from seed to flowering, to setting seed and dying.

b

BASAL LEAVES
Leaves arising directly from the crown of a plant or on a very short stem.

BIENNIAL
A plant which takes two seasons to complete its life cycle – for example, the foxglove. In year one it forms leaves; in year two it forms flowers and seeds, then dies.

BRACT
A modified leaf which is sometimes brightly coloured and conspicuous to attract pollinating insects, such as the scarlet bracts of poinsettia (*Euphorbia pulcherrima*).

BULB FRAME
A coldframe in which bulbs in pots can be plunged in sand, soil or gravel for winter to protect them from frost. A bulb frame can be used instead of an alpine house.

c

CAPSULE
The dry or nearly dry fruit containing loose seeds. When the capsule is ripe the seeds may be shaken out by the action of the wind or passing animals, or it may split, forcibly ejecting the seeds.

CATKIN see FLOWER FORMATIONS, p. 861

CHITTING
Sprouting tubers, particularly potatoes and dahlias, before planting. Also applied to seeds germinated before sowing.

CHLOROSIS
The loss or insufficiency of chlorophyll – the green pigment in the cells of leaves and young stems. The lack of chlorophyll causes the leaves to appear bleached or yellowish. Chlorosis is usually due to mineral deficiency, but viruses may be a cause.

CLOCHE
Sheets of clear glass, rigid plastic or plastic film that are used for raising early crops in open ground, and for protecting plants from bad weather – alpines, for example.

CLONE
A group of identical plants raised from a single parent plant by cuttings or division rather than by seed.

COMPOST
A mixture of loam, sand, peat, leaf-mould or other materials used for growing plants in containers. The term also refers to organic material obtained by stacking plant remains such as vegetable trimmings, straw and grass mowings until they decompose.

COMPOUND
Leaves, flowers or fruits having two or more similar units.

CONIFER
Tree or shrub, usually evergreen and having linear or needle-like leaves, and which usually bears its seeds in cones.

COPPICING
The cutting back of trees and shrubs close to the ground, often annually, to produce vigorous young shoots. In gardens it is usually done for decorative purposes – to encourage brightly coloured stems or the formation of large leaves.

CORM
The underground storage organ of some plants, including crocuses and gladioli. Similar to a bulb, it consists of a swollen stem with a bud at the top which produces shoots and a new corm.

COROLLA see FLOWER

CORONA
The trumpet or cup-like flower part of such genera as *Narcissus* and *Hymenocallis*.

CORYMB see FLOWER FORMATIONS, p. 861

COTYLEDON
The first leaf or pair of leaves to appear when a seed germinates. They are also called seed leaves because they are formed within the seed. In some cases, such as the broad bean, the seed leaves remain underground – the first shoot to appear bears the true leaves. Seed leaves frequently differ in shape from true or adult leaves.

CROWN
The part of an herbaceous perennial at soil level from which roots and shoots grow.

CULTIVAR
Cultivated variety: a variant of a plant produced in cultivation as opposed to one that occurs in the wild (see also GENUS).

CUTTINGS see p. 816

CYME see FLOWER FORMATIONS, p. 861

d

DAMPING DOWN
Watering the floor and benches of a greenhouse to create a humid atmosphere.

DEADHEADING
Nipping off dead or faded flowerheads from a plant to prevent seeding and to encourage new flowers. Roses and many bedding plants need regular deadheading.

DICOTYLEDON
All flowering plants are botanically classified into two main groups by the number of cotyledons (seed leaves) present in the seed at maturity. Monocotyledons have one seed leaf, dicotyledons have two.

DIOECIOUS
Plants having male and female flowers on separate plants, such as willow and holly.

DISC
The flattened or domed centre of a daisy flower, composed of tiny tubular florets.

DOT PLANT
An isolated or specimen plant – usually tall – in a formal flowerbed, selected to emphasise contrast in height, colour and texture.

DRILL
A straight, usually narrow, furrow in which seeds are sown outdoors.

e

EPIPHYTE
A plant, such as an orchid or bromeliad, which has adapted to living above the soil, adhering to tree branches or rocks.

ERICACEOUS
A term used for plants that grow best in acid soil, such as ericas (heather). Also used to refer to lime-free compost used for growing ericaceous plants.

ETIOLATED
Growth which has become long, thin and pallid because of lack of light or as a result of blanching – as in forcing rhubarb.

EYE
Immature growth bud, such as the eyes of potato or dahlia tubers. The term is also used to describe the centre of a flower if it is different in colour from the petals.

f

F₁ HYBRID
Seeds obtained by crossing two pure bred closely related varieties which have been inbred for several generations. The plants produced tend to have an increased level of vigour and uniformity.

FASTIGIATE
Erect habit of growth developed by some trees and shrubs, such as Lombardy poplars.

FEATHERED
Lateral shoots on the main stem of a young tree. They are left on the tree until the trunk is fully established – about a year or two – when they must be removed.

FERTILISERS see p.804

FLORET
A small individual flower which is part of a large head or cluster.

FLOWER
The part of a plant concerned with sexual reproduction. The essential parts are the female ovaries (or carpels), which eventually bear the seeds, and the anthers which produce pollen, the male sex cells. The carpels and anthers are usually surrounded

PARTS OF A FLOWER

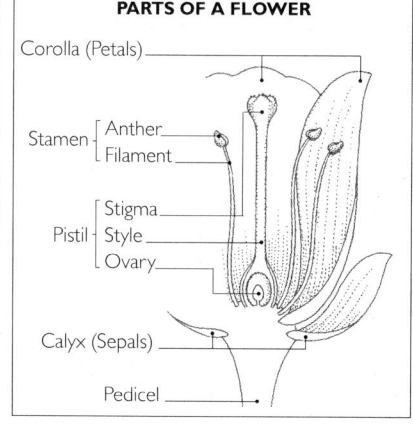

by an inner ring of coloured leaves, known as petals, and an outer ring of protecting sepals, usually green. There are, however, a great many variations to this basic pattern. The great majority of plants bear flowers with both male and female organs (monoecious), but others have single-sex flowers on separate plants (dioecious).

Petals and sepals are usually clearly differentiated in shape, size and colour, but sometimes – with the tulip, for example, they are similar. Petals and sepals may be separate, as in buttercups, or fused, as in primroses or convolvulus. They may both be absent, as in hazel or poplar, or the petals may be missing (pachysandra and parrotia).

FRUITING BODY
The reproductive organ of a fungus, such as a mushroom or toadstool. Also the pin-head-like growth on bread mould.

FUMIGATE
A system of destroying pests and diseases in a greenhouse or coldframe with poisonous fumes. Canisters or pellets are ignited to produce a dense smoke.

g

GENUS (plural: genera)
The category in botanical classification below family. A genus is a group of closely related plants known as species. All the species of beech trees, for example, are grouped under the genus *Fagus*. Related genera are grouped in turn into a family, in this case Fagaceae. The common beech is identified by a genus and a species name, *Fagus sylvatica*. A natural variety is identified by a third name in italics, such as *Fagus sylvatica* var. *heterophylla*, and a cultivated variety (or cultivar) by quotation marks, as *Fagus sylvatica* 'Dawyck'. A cross (or hybrid) between two species is identified by a multiplication sign: for example, the hybrid willow *Salix* × *rubens*.

GERMINATION
The initial stage of a plant's development from a seed. Germination periods vary: given the right conditions of temperature, moisture, light and oxygen, it may occur within days or take many weeks or months.

GLABROUS
Smooth or bare – used to describe a part of a plant that is hairless.

GLAUCOUS
Describing the grey-blue colour of some plants, or the grey or white waxy bloom on them. An example is the white bloom on the leaves of some brassicas, particularly cabbages, and succulents such as sedums.

GRAFTING
Propagating plants by joining a stem or bud of one plant to the root of another so they unite to form a new individual. It is widely used in cultivating fruit trees and roses.

h

HABIT
The characteristic shape and growth form of a plant.

HALF-HARDY
Frost-tender species of plants that can only be grown in the open reliably during summer – for example, canna and French and African marigolds. See also TENDER.

HALF-STANDARD
A tree or shrub, usually with a single stem growing 75 cm–1.2 m (2½–4 ft) high before the head branches.

HARDENING OFF
The gradual acclimatisation of tender and half-hardy plants, grown under heated glass or other forms of protection, to outside conditions. Plants are usually placed in a coldframe in late spring, with air gradually admitted until the lights of the frame are left off entirely.

FLOWER FORMATIONS

Catkin

Corymb

Cyme

Panicle

Spike

Umbel

Plume

Whorl

Raceme

HARDY

Plants which survive frosts in the open, year by year, anywhere in Great Britain.

HERBACEOUS

Any plant that does not form a persistent woody stem. Botanically, the term applies to annuals, biennials and perennials – but by common usage is chiefly associated with perennials which die down in autumn and reappear the following spring.

HOSE-IN-HOSE

An abnormal floral mutation in which flowers appear to grow in pairs, one arising from the centre of another. Primrose and polyanthus are examples.

HUMUS

The dark brown residue from the final breakdown of dead vegetable matter. The term is often used to describe partly decayed matter that is brown and crumbly, such as well-made compost or leaf-mould.

HYBRID

The result of crossing two distinct varieties or, occasionally, genera. Hybrids may either show a blending of characteristics from each parent or favour one more than the other.

i

INCISED

The margins of a leaf, stipule or bract that is deeply and sharply toothed or lobed.

INFLORESCENCE

The arrangement of flowers on a stem, often referred to as a flowerhead.

INORGANIC

A chemical compound or fertiliser that does not contain carbon. The term is applied to synthetically produced fertilisers, although some naturally occurring plant nutrients have inorganic origins, as, for example, the mineral fertiliser rock phosphate.

j

JOINT see NODE

JUVENILE

Plants which have a distinct early phase, when either the habit, leaf shape or some other characteristic differs from those of the adult. Eucalyptus trees commonly bear juvenile and adult leaves.

l

LATERAL

A stem or shoot that branches off from a bud in the leaf axil of a larger stem.

LEADER

The main stem (or stems) of a tree or shrub that extends the existing branch system.

LEAF see box, below

LEAF-MOULD

Partially decayed dead leaves which have broken down to a brown, flaky condition resembling peat. Oak and beech leaves are the most suitable materials.

LIME

Calcium, a chemical used in horticulture, particularly to neutralise acid soils.

LOAM

A reasonably fertile soil that is neither wet and sticky, nor dry and sandy. It is moisture-retentive and contains a blend of clay, silt, sand and humus, and is rich in minerals.

LOBE

Descriptive of leaves, stipules, bracts or petals that are cleft into separate areas that are still united by part of the surface.

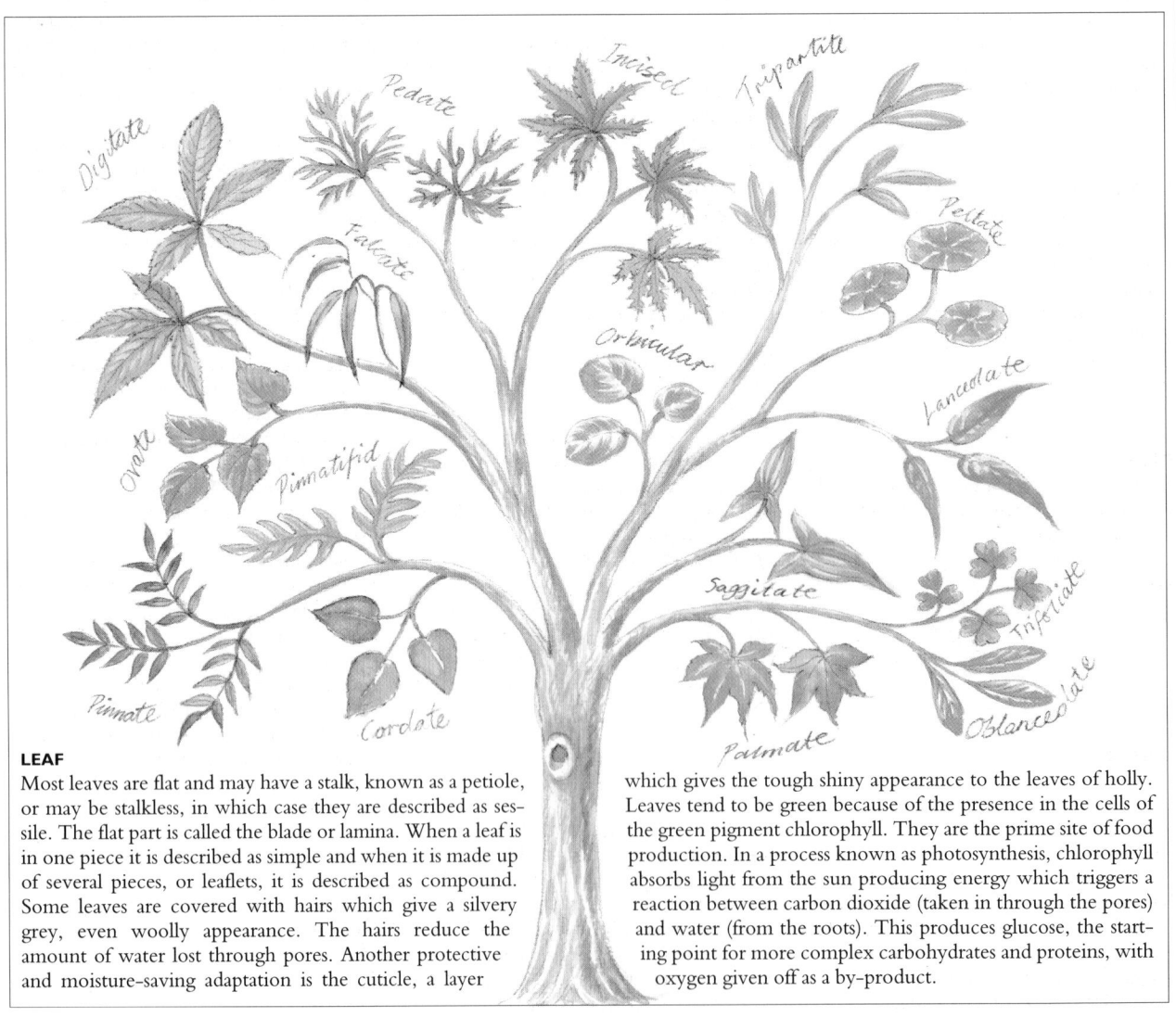

LEAF

Most leaves are flat and may have a stalk, known as a petiole, or may be stalkless, in which case they are described as sessile. The flat part is called the blade or lamina. When a leaf is in one piece it is described as simple and when it is made up of several pieces, or leaflets, it is described as compound. Some leaves are covered with hairs which give a silvery grey, even woolly appearance. The hairs reduce the amount of water lost through pores. Another protective and moisture-saving adaptation is the cuticle, a layer which gives the tough shiny appearance to the leaves of holly. Leaves tend to be green because of the presence in the cells of the green pigment chlorophyll. They are the prime site of food production. In a process known as photosynthesis, chlorophyll absorbs light from the sun producing energy which triggers a reaction between carbon dioxide (taken in through the pores) and water (from the roots). This produces glucose, the starting point for more complex carbohydrates and proteins, with oxygen given off as a by-product.

m

MAIDEN
A nursery term for a young grafted tree in the process of being trained. Applied particularly to one-year-old fruit trees.

MANURE see p.804

MONOCARPIC
A plant which dies after flowering and seeding. Annuals and biennials are true monocarpic plants, but the term is also applied to perennial plants which grow for a number of years before flowering and then dying.

MONOCOTYLEDON
A group of flowering plants that have only one seed leaf in each mature seed. See also COTYLEDON and DICOTYLEDON.

MONOECIOUS
A plant that bears bisexual flowers or separate male and female flowers on the same plant; for example, corylus (hazel) and juglans (walnut).

MULCH
A layer of organic matter, such as decayed manure, leaf-mould, garden compost, straw or composted bark, which is spread on the soil around plants. A mulch conserves moisture in the soil, adds nutrients and suppresses weeds. The term is also used for inorganic material including gravel and black polythene sheeting.

n

NATURALISING
Growing plants, particularly bulbs, in simulated natural environments, such as grass or woodland conditions.

NODE
A stem joint, which is sometimes slightly swollen, from where young leaves and side-shoots arise.

o

OFFSET
A young plant that arises naturally on the parent, as with many sorts of bulbs, or on short lateral stems, as with semper-vivum (right).

OPPOSITE
The arrangement of leaves in alternate opposite pairs, as on ligustrum and syringa. See also LEAF.

ORGANIC
Any chemical compound containing carbon. The term is applied to substances derived from the decay of living organisms, such as garden compost. It is also applied to a style of gardening that rejects the use of synthetic chemicals and products.

p

PANICLE see FLOWER FORMATIONS

PEDICEL
The stalk of an individual flower – applied particularly to branched flowers.

PEDUNCLE
The stem that supports a flowerhead.

PERENNIAL
Any plant that lives for three or more years; usually applied to a non-woody plant.

PERIANTH
A term used when sepals and petals are indistinguishable from each other. The combined sepals and petals of a tulip or hyacinth flower are known as the perianth.

PERLITE
Lightweight expanded volcanic rock in granular form, used in place of sand or grit to open up or lighten composts used for potting or cuttings.

PETAL see FLOWER FORMATIONS, p.861

PETIOLE
The stalk that attaches a leaf to the stem.

pH see p.803

PINCHING OUT see STOPPING

PISTIL see PARTS OF A FLOWER, p.861

PLUNGE
To set a pot or any other plant container up to the rim in the soil, or in a special bed of ashes, peat, grit or sand.

POLLARD
A tree cut back to the main trunk and maintained in a bushy state by regular pruning at intervals of between one and a few years.

POLLEN
The male cells of a plant contained in the anthers or pollen sacs.

POLLINATION
The transference of pollen grains onto the stigma of a flower. This may occur naturally by gravity, wind or insects, or can be done artificially by hand.

PRICKING OUT
The first planting out of seedlings or small-rooted cuttings. The resulting plantlets are later moved into larger pots, pans or trays, or set out into a nursery bed or into their growing position.

PROPAGATION see p.814

PROVENANCE
The place where seed originated in the wild. Knowing the provenance will have a bearing on the conditions under which the progeny will thrive in cultivation.

r

RACEME see FLOWER FORMATIONS, p.861

RADICAL
Usually used to describe the basal leaves of biennials or perennials. The leaves arise at the base of the plant or near to soil level.

RAY FLORET
Small flower with long strap-shaped petals. Typical of the daisy family where a ring of ray florets surrounds the central boss of disc florets to form the flowerhead.

REMONTANT
Flowering at intervals throughout the growing season, as in repeat-flowering roses.

RESTING PERIOD
The period when a plant is either dormant or making little or no extension growth.

RHIZOME
A horizontal, creeping underground stem, which acts as a storage organ.

ROOTSTOCK
A propagation term for a plant upon which another is grafted. The term also applies to the crown and root system of herbaceous perennials and suckering shrubs.

ROSETTE
Ring of leaves that all arise at more or less the same point on the stem, often basal.

RUNNER Prostrate stems, such as those produced by strawberry plants, which root at the nodes to form new plantlets.

s

SAND PLUNGE see PLUNGE

SCION
A shoot, part of a shoot, or bud of one plant that is joined to a rootstock of another as a propagation technique. Scions and rootstocks are the means of propagating fruit trees by grafting, and roses by budding.

SCREE
A heap or a slope of rocky detritus eroded from mountainsides or cliffs. Since some types of plants require these conditions in a garden, a scree bed can be created by mixing coarse gravel or stone chippings with soil.

SELECTION
A particular variation of an existing variety or species that is selected for its desirable characteristics. It is always raised from seed. Also incorrectly referred to as a 'strain'.

SELF-COLOURED
A flower having a single uniform colour.

SELF-FERTILE
A plant, particularly a fruit tree, that does not need pollen from another plant to set seed and produce fruit.

SELF-STERILE
Fruit trees, especially sweet cherries, that need pollen from another plant to set fruit.

SEPAL see FLOWER

SERIES
A selection or colour mixture of a plant variety (usually an annual, bedding plant or vegetable variety) raised from seed. A particular named series or mixture raised by two or more seedsmen may vary slightly.

SERRATED
The sharply cut indentations in the margin of a leaf – like the teeth of a saw.

SESSILE
Stalkless – a leaf or flower that arises straight from the stem.

SHRUB
A branched perennial plant with persistent woody stems.

SPADIX
A fleshy flower spike with small flowers embedded in shallow pits. It is primarily found in members of the Araceae, or aroid family, such as anthurium and zantedeschia, where it is surrounded and protected by a white or coloured bract called a spathe. In some cases, the spadix terminates in a naked club or spindle-shaped organ which may heat up, giving off a fetid smell that attracts pollinating insects.

SPATHE
A modified leaf or large bract, sometimes coloured, which surrounds the flower spike (spadix) in members of the Araceae, or aroid family.

SPECIES
A unit of classification applied to an individual, or a group of closely allied plants, within a genus. Species have unique characters, which consistently breed true to type from seed. The type species refers to the original plant collected and described.

SPECIMEN PLANT
Any plant, but usually a tree or shrub, which is grown where it can be viewed from all angles, as when planted in a lawn.

SPHAGNUM (MOSS)
The generic name for bog mosses. They have unique water-holding, aerating and cleansing properties, and are frequently used as a growing medium for orchids.

SPIKE see FLOWER FORMATIONS, p. 861

SPIT
The depth to which soil is dug with a spade or a fork – about 25–30 cm (10–12 in).

SPORE
A minute dust-like body composed of a single cell, by which lower plants – such as ferns, fungi and mosses – reproduce. A spore gives rise to an intermediate generation upon which the sex organs appear and which eventually produce plantlets.

SPUR
1: A short lateral branchlet of a tree – particularly on apple and pear trees – which bears flower buds.
2: A tubular outgrowth of a sepal or petal that produces nectar.

STAMEN see FLOWER

STAMINODE
A non-functional, rudimentary male reproductive organ, sometimes similar to a narrow petal, as in pulsatillas.

STERILE
Plants that rarely or never set seed. Many double-flowered varieties are sterile, as the reproductive organs have become petals.

STIPULE
One of the pair of leaf-like outgrowths at the base of a leaf-stalk, for example, as in rose and potentilla.

STOLON
A stem which, on contact with moist soil, roots at the tip and forms a new plant – for example, the cane of a blackberry. The term is sometimes incorrectly used to mean RUNNER.

STOOL
Often describing a tree or shrub which is maintained as a clump of young stems by annual pruning close to ground level. Stooling is carried out to provide young growth for propagation purposes, or to maintain a foliage effect, such as the juvenile state of some eucalyptus. Also called 'coppicing'. The term also applies to crowns and rootstock of some herbaceous plants – dendranthema (chrysanthemum), for example.

STOPPING
Removing or pinching out the growing point of a stem, either to promote a branching habit or to induce flower buds.

STRAIN see SELECTION

STRATIFICATION
A method of breaking the dormancy of seeds born in fleshy fruits of many hardy plants. The seeds are exposed to a period of low temperature prior to sowing.

SUB-ALPINE
A plant native to mountain regions just below the alpine zone.

SUB-SHRUB
A low-growing shrub, or one with soft stems and a woody base, such as argyranthemums and many pelargoniums.

SUCCULENT
Plants with thick fleshy leaves or stems adapted to life under arid conditions. Cacti, with leafless stems swollen with water storage tissue, are examples.

SUCKER
A shoot which arises from below ground, usually from the roots of a plant.

SYNONYM
An alternative name for a plant. Sometimes a plant has been named by more than one botanist or has been reclassified in the light of further knowledge. In such cases, the oldest or most taxonomically accurate name takes priority.

t

TAP ROOT
The main anchoring root of a plant, particularly applied to trees.

TENDER
A term to describe any plant vulnerable to frost damage. See also HALF-HARDY.

TENDRIL
A modified stem or leaf that twines around supports, enabling certain plants, such as sweet peas, grapes, hops and passionflowers, to climb.

TEPAL
A term used to describe petals and sepals where they are indistinguishable, as in lilies and tulips.

TERNATE
In groups of three. Trillium has leaves and floral organs in groups of three, and laburnum leaves have three leaflets.

TERRESTRIAL
Used in reference to plants, such as some bromeliads and orchids which are primarily epiphytic, that have become adapted to living in the soil.

TESSELLATED
A term that describes petals which have a distinct chequered pattern of a contrasting shade or colour – as, for example, *Fritillaria meleagris*.

TOOTHED
Teeth-like indentations, usually along the margins of leaves, also described as dentate. See also SERRATED.

TRUSS
A popular term used to describe a cluster of flowers or fruits.

TUBER
A thickened fleshy root, as on a dahlia, or an underground stem, such as a potato, which serves as a storage organ, and as a means of surviving periods of cold or drought.

TUFA
Soft limestone which, because of its ability to absorb and retain moisture, is often used in rock gardens or troughs, where small alpine plants are able to grow on it.

TUFT
Bristly, sometimes mat-like, habit of growth, found particularly in alpine plants.

u

UNDERPLANT
To surround and interplant larger plants with smaller ones.

UNDULATE
Leaf, sepal or petal margins that are waved or crimped.

v

VARIEGATED
Leaves – and sometimes petals – that are marked, spotted or otherwise decoratively patterned with a contrasting colour, most commonly cream or gold.

VEGETATIVE
Propagation by cuttings, division, layering or grafting, as distinct from propagation with seeds.

w

WEEPING
Applied to a tree or shrub of pendulous habit, either natural, as in some species of salix, or artificially induced, as in weeping standard roses.

WHORL see FLOWER FORMATIONS, p. 861

Acknowledgments

Production credits

BOOK PRODUCTION MANAGER
Chris Reynolds

ASSISTANT BOOK PRODUCTION MANAGER
Tony Ashe

ASSISTANT BOOK PRODUCTION CONTROLLER
Dean Russell

PRE-PRESS PRODUCTION MANAGER
Martin Hendrick

PRE-PRESS SUPPORT
Jim Lindsay, Howard Reynolds, Tony Rilett

Picture Credits

Below is a list of the images used in *New Encyclopedia of Garden Plants & Flowers* supplied by photograph libraries and specialist sources. Some abbreviations have been used: GPL = The Garden Picture Library, HSC = The Harry Smith Collection and PHPL = Photos Horticultural Picture Library. B = Bottom. T = Top. C = Centre. L = Left. R = Right. Where given, the names of gardens and designers are shown in brackets.

21 BR PHPL. 27 BC HSC. 28 BL GPL/John Glover. 32 CL PHPL, BL GPL/Geoff Dann. 32-33 B GPL/Steven Wooster. 33 TR GPL/Alan Bedding. 38 BR GPL/Mel Watson. 43 C GPL/Christopher Fairweather. 47 C PHPL. 51 BL GPL/Jerry Pavia, BC GPL/Clive Boursnell. 53 BR GPL/John Glover. 55 C PHPL. 61 GPL/Densey Clyne. 76 C GPL/Morley Read, BL John Glover, BR David Crampton, Drysdale Garden Exotics, Fordingbridge. 77 TL PHPL/MJK, C PHPL, BL GPL/Brigitte Thomas, BC PHPL. 78 CR GPL/Brian Carter (Trebah Gardens, Cornwall), BR Beckett Picture Library. 79 TL HSC, TR David Crampton, Drysdale Garden Exotics, Fordingbridge, C BC PHPL, BL Beckett Picture Library, BR David Crampton, Drysdale Garden Exotics, Fordingbridge. 84 BL Jerry Harpur/RHS Garden Wisley. 84-85 T John Glover, B Photon Photo Library. 85 TR John Glover (Nash's Garden, Shrops), BR GPL/Howard Rice (Clare College, Cambs). 86 TL Jerry Harpur/CG Carey-Parker, BL Clive Nichols (Designer: Jill Billington). 86-87 T Jerry Harpur/Peter Ottaway, B Clive Nichols/Graham Strong. 87 BL Clive Nichols (Keukenhof Gardens, Holland). 92 TC PHPL. 96 BR GPL/Marianne Majerus. 100 TR GPL/John Glover. 104 CR GPL/Chris Burrows. 106 TC T.M. Hewitt, Holly Gate Nursery, Ashington, BL Eric Crichton. 109 TR BR HSC, C CL Beckett Picture Library, BL T.M. Hewitt, Holly Gate Nursery, Ashington. 110 TC Pat Brindley, BL Plant Portraits Worldwide. 113 TC HSC. 125 TR John Glover. 150 TR HSC. 162 BL GPL/Howard Rice, BR Eric Crichton. 162-3 T John Glover. 163 T Eric Crichton, B John Glover. 164 BR (inset) Ardea, London/Bob Gibbons, BR NHPA/David Woodfall. 165 BL PHPL. 166 CR BR HSC. 181 CR GPL/Howard Rice. 182 C GPL/JS Sira, BC GPL/John Glover. 189 TC GPL/John Glover. 192 BL HSC. 207 TL GPL/Juliette Wade. 210 ('Heide') GPL/Chris Burrows, BR GPL/John Glover. 211 ('Yellow Heide') GPL/Chris Burrows. 224 TL GPL/Brigitte Thomas. 226 BL PHPL. 227 TR Beckett Picture Library. 238 TR BL PHPL. 262 BL Clive Nichols (Spinner Nursery, Hampshire). 263 TL GPL/Howard Rice, TC Beckett Picture Library. 264 TR PHPL. 265 CL Andrew Lawson, BR Clive Nichols (Designer: J. Billington). 267 BR HSC. 269 CL, 271 BL, 280 BR PHPL. 286 TC GPL/Kathy Charlton, BC PHPL. 289 TC GPL/Henk Dijkman. 292 CL GPL/Neil Holmes.

294 TR GPL/Neil Holmes, CL GPL/Brian Carter, BL GPL/Paul Windsor. 295 T B GPL/John Glover. 299 TL GPL/Howard Rice. 300 TR GPL/David Russell, BL Sheila & Oliver Mathews, BR PHPL. 301 CL GPL/David Askham, C (*Hordeum*) Andrew Lawson, BR HSC, BR Eric Crichton. 302 TL Andrew Lawson, BR A-Z Botanical Collection. 303 CR GPL/Sunniva Harte, BR Jonathan Buckley. 306 TR GPL/Jerry Pavia, CL GPL/Ron Sutherland, BL GPL/JS Sira. 306-7 B Eric Crichton, T GPL/John Miller. 310 TR Holt Studios Ltd/Bob Gibbons, CL GPL/Neil Holmes, BL John Glover. 310-11 Eric Crichton. 311 T B John Glover. 318 CL Sheila & Oliver Mathews, BL Clive Nichols (Stourton House, Wiltshire). 318-19 T GPL/Didier Willery, B GPL/Densey Clyne. 319 TR Clive Nichols (Designer: Jill Billington). 330 BR Jerry Harpur. 337 C HSC. 341 BR Biofotos/Heather Angel. 342 C GPL/Lamontagne, B GPL/Lynne Brotchie. 342-3 T Eric Crichton, B GPL/Steven Wooster. 343 T GPL/JS Sira, B Eric Crichton. 344 T GPL/Zara McCalmont, B Elizabeth Whiting/Dennis Stone. 345 T Arcaid/Richard Bryant (Designer: David Falla), B Eric Crichton. 346 CR PHPL. 347 CL HSC. 353 TR GPL/Chris Burrows, C GPL/David Russell. 362 L Beckett Picture Library. 363 BR HSC. 374 BL PHPL. 377 BL GPL/Sunniva Harte. 382 BL GPL/David Russell. 383 TL GPL/John Glover. 386 BC PHPL. 387 CL John Sutton. 390-1 T Jerry Harpur (Designer: Christopher Masson), B John Glover (Nash's Garden, Shrops). 391 TR Holt Studios Ltd/Nigel Cattlin, CR Eric Crichton. 392 BR HSC. 393 BR PHPL. 398-9 Sheila & Oliver Mathews. 403 TL GPL/Howard Rice. 408 BR NHPA/Anthony Bannister. 410 BR PHPL. 414 R Beckett Picture Library. 419 TR PHPL. 420 T GPL/John Glover. 424 TL GPL/Howard Rice. 428 T PHPL. 429 C Bruce Coleman Ltd/Eckart Pott, BR PHPL. 430 PHPL. 431 L GPL/Jerry Pavia. 433 TL Beckett Picture Library, BC GPL/Howard Rice, BR Ardea, London/John Mason. 434 C Eric Crichton. 439 BC GPL/Howard Rice. 444 TL PHPL. 451 BL GPL/Howard Rice, BL (*Nemophila menziesii*) GPL/Marijke Heuff. 452 BC GPL/Philippe Bonduel. 454 L NHPA, C PHPL. 455 TL, 460 CL, 461 L, 463 TC, C PHPL. 464 TR PHPL. 465 TC HSC, C John Glover, BR Eric Crichton. 466 TL CL Eric Crichton, CR PHPL, BR HSC. 467 BL Beckett Picture Library, TR John Glover, C PHPL, BL Ardea, London/Ian Beames, BR PHPL. 491 CR, 494 L, 495 TC, 496 BR PHPL. 497 C HSC. 504 CR PHPL. 511 L Plant Portraits Worldwide, C HSC. 520 TR Eric Crichton. 540 BR Plant Portraits Worldwide. 552 L PHPL. 552-3 GPL/Lamontagne. 555 BL GPL/Lamontagne. 558 TC GPL/Brian Carter, CR GPL/David Askham. 559 BR GPL/Christopher Fairweather. 560 BR GPL/Michael Howes. 561 TC GPL/Lamontagne, BC GPL/Christopher Fairweather. 562 TL GPL/Brian Carter. 565 TL GPL/Christopher Fairweather, TC GPL/John Glover, BC GPL/Brian Carter. 566 TL GPL/Brian Carter, CL GPL/John Glover, BL GPL/Clive Boursnell. 572 BL Eric Crichton. 572-3 T Eric Crichton, B John Glover. 573 T Jerry Harpur (Home Farm, Royle), B Eric Crichton. 575, 580 B, 583 TL BR, 585 BR, 586 CR, 587 BL Michael Gibson. 589 BR David Austin Roses Limited. 590 TC David Austin Roses Limited, TR BL BR Michael Gibson. 591 L BR David Austin Roses Limited. 600 Michael Gibson. 606 L PHPL. 614 BC GPL/John Glover. 619 BL, 627 BC PHPL. 630 C GPL/Kathy Charlton. 632 BC PHPL. 636 L HSC. 638 TR Beckett Picture Library. 641 R GPL/Rex Butcher. 646 T GPL/Howard Rice. 651 R PHPL. 659 TR GPL/Philippe Bonduel. 667 TR CR PHPL. 670 T Eric Crichton, CL GPL/John Glover,

BL GPL/Gary Rogers. 670-1 B GPL/Jerry Pavia. 671 T GPL/David Secombe. 673 BR GPL/Lamontagne. 676 CL Jerry Harpur (Eastgrove Cottage), BL Sheila & Oliver Mathews. 677 TC Jerry Harpur (Iden Croft), CR Jonathan Buckley. 678 Eric Crichton. 678-9 T Jonathan Buckley, B John Glover (The Anchorage, Kent). 682 BL PHPL/MJK. 684 L GPL/Rex Butcher, TR PHPL/ACM. 685 TL TR GPL/Brian Carter. 686 BL GPL/Howard Rice. 688 TC HSC. 690 TL PHPL, TC Plant Portraits Worldwide. 693 BR HSC. 694 BL GPL/John Glover, BC GPL/Brian Carter, BR GPL/Didier Willery. 695 GPL/John Glover. 702 BL GPL/Brian Carter. 704 BR PHPL. 706 B Jerry Harpur (Designer: Chris Grey-Wilson). 706-7 T PHPL, B GPL/JS Sira. 707 T Jonathan Buckley, B GPL/Ron Sutherland. 708 BL PHPL. 709 TL C PHPL, TC GPL/John Glover. 710 CL GPL/Marijke Heuff, B GPL/Steven Wooster. 710-11 HSC. 711 T Andrew Lawson, B GPL/Gary Rogers. 712 GPL/Lynne Brotchie. 712-13 Clive Nichols. 713 Andrew Lawson. 714 BL, 717 GPL/John Glover. 718 TR GPL/JS Sira. 726, 727 HSC. 728 GPL/Jane Legate. 729 GPL/Michael Howes. 731 HSC. 733 PHPL. 738 HSC. 745 L GPL/Mel Watson. 746 R HSC. 751 TR PHPL. 753 BL GPL/Neil Holmes. 754 CR GPL/Howard Rice, BR GPL/JS Sira. 756 TC(R) BC(L) GPL/Howard Rice. 757 TR GPL/Brian Carter, C(L) GPL/John Glover, CR PHPL, BC(R) Andrew Lawson, BR GPL/JS Sira. 758 TC(R) GPL/Morley Read. 759 TL HSC. 760 TC(R) GPL/Brigitte Thomas, C Beckett Picture Library. 761 BL GPL/Brigitte Thomas. 762 TL GPL/Jerry Pavia. 763 CL Andrew Lawson, C(R) PHPL. 764 TL PHPL. 765 CL PHPL, CR HSC. 766 TL PHPL, C GPL/John Glover. 768 CR Andrew Lawson, BL HSC. 769 C GPL/Jerry Pavia. 770 C(R) HSC. 772 CL GPL/Neil Holmes C(L) GPL/Howard Rice, BL PHPL, BR HSC. 774 BC(L) HSC. 776 TC(R) GPL/Brian Carter. 778 TR PHPL, C(L) GPL/John Glover, BR PHPL. 779 TC(L) PHPL, TC(R) HSC, BC(L) GPL/Michel Viard. 780 TC(L) HSC, TR GPL/John Glover, CL A-Z Botanical Collection/Maurice Nimmo. 781 TC(L) CL HSC, C Clive Nichols, BL GPL/Howard Rice. 782 C(R) HSC, BL PHPL, BC(R) A-Z Botanical Collection/Dan Sams. 783 TC(L) PHPL, TR GPL/Marijke Heuff, C GPL/John Glover, BC(R) GPL/Brian Carter. 784 TL A-Z Botanical Collection/Mike Danson, TC(L) GPL/Joanne Pavia. 785 TR GPL/Chris Burrows, BC(R) PHPL, BR GPL/John Glover. 786 TL GPL/David Russell, CL HSC. 787 TC(R) Clive Nichols, CR(lower) GPL/Chris Burrows, BL GPL/Rex Butcher, BR PHPL. 788 TR PHPL, (*Scaevola*) BC(L) HSC. 789 CR A-Z Botanical Collection. 790 TC(L) CR BL John Glover, C(L) HSC. 792 TL HSC, BL Clive Nichols. 793 A-Z Botanical Collection, TR A-Z Botanical Collection/Margaret Higginson, CL(upper) A-Z Botanical Collection/Andy Williams, CL(lower) BL HSC, C(L) Beckett Picture Library, BC(R) PHPL. 794 CL CR Clive Nichols, BL BR John Glover, BC PHPL. 795 TC(L) BC(L) John Glover, (*Iris* 'Natascha') PHPL. 805 (all) Cranfield University Soil Survey and Land Research Centre. 811 T B, 820 TL TC PHPL. 821 TL CL Eric Crichton, CR BR PHPL. 822 TL TC C CL C HSC, CR BR Eric Crichton. 840 CL John Glover.

ORIGINATION: Opus Graphics Ltd and Rodney Howe Ltd, London, England
PAPER: Townsend Hook Ltd, Snodland, England
PRINTING: Maury Imprimeur SA, Malesherbes, France
BINDING: Reluires Brun SA, Malesherbes, France